VOLUME TWO

HANDBOOK OF
HEALTH ECONOMICS

INTRODUCTION TO THE SERIES

The aim of the *Handbooks in Economics* series is to produce Handbooks for various branches of economics, each of which is a definitive source, reference, and teaching supplement for use by professional researchers and advanced graduate students. Each Handbook provides self-contained surveys of the current state of a branch of economics in the form of chapters prepared by leading specialists on various aspects of this branch of economics. These surveys summarize not only received results but also newer developments, from recent journal articles and discussion papers. Some original material is also included, but the main goal is to provide comprehensive and accessible surveys. The Handbooks are intended to provide not only useful reference volumes for professional collections but also possible supplementary readings for advanced courses for graduate students in economics.

KENNETH J. ARROW and MICHAEL D. INTRILIGATOR

VOLUME TWO

HANDBOOK OF
HEALTH ECONOMICS

Edited by

MARK V. PAULY
THOMAS G. McGUIRE
PEDRO P. BARROS

ELSEVIER

Amsterdam • Boston • Heidelberg • London • New York • Oxford
Paris • San Diego • San Francisco • Singapore • Sydney • Tokyo
North Holland is an imprint of Elsevier

North Holland is an imprint of Elsevier
The Boulevard, Langford Lane, Kidlington, Oxford OX5 1GB, UK
225 Wyman Street, Waltham, MA 02451, USA

First edition 2012

Notice

No responsibility is assumed by the publisher for any injury and/or damage to persons
or property as a matter of products liability, negligence or otherwise, or from any use or
operation of any methods, products, instructions or ideas contained in the material herein.
Because of rapid advances in the medical sciences, in particular, independent verification
of diagnoses and drug dosages should be made

British Library Cataloguing-in-Publication Data
A catalogue record for this book is available from the British Library

Library of Congress Cataloging-in-Publication Data
A catalog record for this book is availabe from the Library of Congress

ISBN: 978-0-444-53592-4

For information on all North Holland publications
visit our web site at books.elsevier.com

Printed and bound by CPI Group (UK) Ltd, Croydon, CR0 4YY
Transferred to Digital Print 2012

CONTENTS

11. Health Care Spending Risk, Health Insurance, and Payment to Health Plans 691
Friedrich Breyer, M. Kate Bundorf, Mark V. Pauly

12. Markets for Pharmaceutical Products   **763**

Fiona Scott Morton, Margaret Kyle

13. Intellectual Property, Information Technology, Biomedical Research, and Marketing of Patented Products   **825**

Dana Goldman, Darius Lakdawalla

14. Medical Workforce 873

Sean Nicholson, Carol Propper

PREFACE

INTRODUCTION

The increased public policy interest in all countries in improving population health while at the same time slowing the escalation of medical care spending has motivated substantial growth in empirical and theoretical research in health economics since the publication more than a decade ago of Volume 1 of the *Handbook of Health Economics*. Some areas of research have grown from small beginnings to significant bodies of work, and other areas already active have grown to maturity, while still others have opened up new directions of research and of thinking.

These developments made it opportune to compile a second volume of the Handbook. We consulted with leaders of the profession, explored the patterns of publication and research that have emerged over the years, and tried out various specifications of different topics, approaches, and authors. The final selection, we are pleased to say, was one that seemed to satisfy all of our advisors and was accepted without delay by the authors we had targeted for each topic. The editors are extremely grateful to the chapter authors for their willingness to undertake what was substantial work, for the greater benefit of the profession.

WHAT WERE WE LOOKING FOR?

In addition to updating and greater comprehensiveness in the two handbook volumes taken together, we had two other distinctive goals for this volume which we think have been realized. Historically, health economics in the US has focused on problems associated with the operation of voluntary markets (and even the market aspects of government insurance) whereas research in Europe and elsewhere has been more concerned with the needs of planning and the desire for equity in the health and health insurance system. We thought that this distinction was blurring as a result of expansion of public insurance in the United States and the addition of more market-like arrangements to dominant government plans elsewhere in the world. To that end we chose joint US and European authorship for several chapters, and we think these pairings did result in more integrated treatments of many of the subjects.

Methods in health economics have evolved over the past ten years, reflecting developments in economic theory and econometrics generally. Non-maximizing (behavioral) theories have become more common in economics, and standards for identifying causal relationships have been elevated generally. Health economics is a natural area for applications of these new ideas and approaches, and we think that can be seen in many of the chapters. General economists may benefit from seeing how these broader methods and concerns have been adapted and further developed in the emerging health economics literature.

WHAT'S NEW?

While there are novel contributions in all of the chapters in the Handbook, the parts targeted for inclusion that had not been treated in depth in Volume 1 include the chapters on health in development and the determinants of health. We recruited authors to write on cost growth and on geographic variation in spending levels, two topics for research and policy that have emerged since Volume 1. In view of the importance of normative analytic methods such as cost effectiveness and comparative effectiveness analysis applied to medical technologies, we include two chapters, one on methods and the other on their policy uses. These two chapters also bring together the discussions occurring on both sides of the Atlantic Ocean. We expanded the focus in a number of areas that have seen substantial development in recent years. Insurance, both as an object of public and private choice and as an institution challenged by variation in risk, is dealt with in depth. While there is relatively little that is novel in hospital payment, the broader issues of physician payment and payment of physician—hospital combinations is included. In view of the renewed interest in markets with choices in many countries and the challenges posed to that model in the United States, we have included an extensive discussion of what is known about competition (across providers and insurers) and its regulation. Equity issues have always ranked high in health economics, and a discussion of the conceptual framework for its analysis is warranted.

DIFFERENCES IN APPROACHES

There are a number of valid ways to approach a handbook topic. In all cases the authors need to put some framework in place to organize their review of work. Probably the most straightforward approach is to identify several themes or controversies in the literature at the start of the period, and then provide a running commentary on how views about those subjects changed and controversies were either resolved or accentuated. Most of the chapters take this approach, which combines considerable descriptive material with a narrative of recent research findings. Chapters by Chernew and Newhouse, Garber and Sculpher, Dranove, Scott-Morton and Kyle, Nicholson and Propper, and Goldman and Lakdawalla are in this set. Another approach proposes a contrarian hypothesis or new thematic approach, and uses that to distinguish the conventional wisdom from what the authors regard as a more correct and correctly nuanced view. Here chapters by Cutler, Chandra and Song, Skinner, Breyer, Bundorf and Pauly, and Fleurbaey and Schokkaert break new ground. Still a third approach is to develop an inclusive framework *de novo*, and fit analyses into that framework. Kremer and Glennerster, McGuire, Barros and Siciliani, and Meltzer and Smith took this approach. Finally, authors sometimes wish to propose a new or validated "big picture" strategy that combines all of these elements to produce a treatise on the field. All chapters do some of this kind of combination, but it is most pronounced in the comprehensive chapters by Cawley and Ruhm and by Gaynor and Town.

HOW TO USE VOLUME 2

We suspect readers will find it helpful to use this book in several ways. The most common is likely to be as a first step in becoming familiar with an area in health economics. Authors have put considerable effort into covering everything that matters for the current state of discourse in an area. Another would be a mirror image: someone highly familiar with an area will learn something new by seeing how a leading scholar in a research area puts the pieces together; both the reader's agreement and surprise will be productive. Finally, the book is a source document for a very wide range of specific topics and issues in health economics, so dipping in, finding the right paragraphs, and getting up to date will be something we think many scholars will choose to do. Along the way we expect they will be tempted to read what comes before and what follows, to get that crucial understanding of the broader context that generates specific findings. None of the chapters here should be regarded as a replacement for the impressive set of essays in the earlier Culyer–Newhouse effort. The chapters in this volume were conceived to stand on their own, to complement and not just be direct updates of previous chapters in Volume 1.

There is a potentially deeper purpose here. Many articles submitted to journals often get the reaction "we already knew that story even though we cannot give a specific prior citation." This is because scholars fill in the gaps between what is published with intuition about the missing parts, transferring findings about behavior and evidence from one setting to others which are close but not identical. Our reaction in reading these chapters is that, taken as a whole, they convey that sense of how respected and experienced scholars think things generally happen, as well as a vibrant sense of which settings are those in which current research does not provide very good evidence at all on what is going on—or at least does not provide evidence that makes intuitive sense. We hope that this meta-purpose of the Handbook is one readers will find fulfilled.

Mark V. Pauly
Thomas G. McGuire
Pedro P. Barros

LIST OF CONTRIBUTORS

ACKNOWLEDGEMENTS

Two authors' conferences, in Boston, October 2010, and in Lisbon, November 2010, jump-started the writing and gave authors a chance to air their ideas and get feedback from other authors and additional attendees. We thank our three institutions, University of Pennsylvania, Harvard Medical School, and Nova School of Business and Economics, for their generous financial support of these meetings. We also thank Kathleen Paoni from Elsevier for shepherding the product from start to finish and for her wise counsel on the process.

CHAPTER ONE

Health Care Spending Growth

Michael E. Chernew and Joseph P. Newhouse

Contents

Abstract

This chapter provides a conceptual and empirical examination of health care spending growth (as opposed to the level of health care spending). Given that an equilibrium spending level exists, spending growth requires some variable to change. A one-time change in such a variable (or a one-time policy intervention) will generate a new equilibrium spending level, though the length of the transition period will depend on switching costs and information lags. After the new equilibrium is established, spending growth will cease. Yet we observe persistent spending growth. This implies at least one continually changing variable and the variable most commonly identified as continually changing is medical technology, broadly defined. We review theoretical models related to spending growth, including some that treat technology as exogenous and others that treat technology as endogenous. We then review the empirical literature related to spending growth and medical technology.

Keywords: spending growth; inflation

JEL Code: I19 (Health, Other)

Handbook of Health Economics, Volume 2
ISSN: 1574-0064, DOI: 10.1016/B978-0-444-53592-4.00001-3

1. INTRODUCTION

This chapter provides a conceptual and empirical examination of spending growth.

The benefits associated with rising health care spending are undoubtedly crucial for societal well-being. Nonetheless, policy makers across the globe are increasingly concerned with the growing burden that such spending places on the private sector and public coffers. Even countries with a low share of GDP currently devoted to health care will eventually be overwhelmed by health care spending growth if such spending rises faster than income for a prolonged period—as in fact it has historically. Although we focus on the American context, many if not most of the issues related to spending growth are similar in all countries.

1.1. Spending Growth in the US

For decades, high health care spending growth (relative to income growth) has been a feature of health care systems in all developed countries. In the United States, which devotes a larger share of GDP to health care than any other country (17.6 percent in 2009), inflation adjusted per capita health expenditures have increased from approximately $809 in 1960 to $7,375 in 2009 (Figure 1.1), an average annual growth rate of approximately 4.7 percent (Centers for Medicare & Medicaid Services, 2011b).

While spending growth in the US has varied over time, it has consistently exceeded income growth (Table 1.1). The share of each decade's income growth devoted to health care has ranged from 5 to 42 percent. On average, the annual gap between real per capita health spending growth and real per capita GDP growth in the US from 1970 to 2009 has been about 2.2 percentage points (Centers for Medicare & Medicaid Services, 2011b). Recent projections suggest that total health care spending will consume 19.6 percent of the US GDP by 2019 (Sisko et al., 2010). Even if the gap between income and health spending growth shrinks to 1 percentage point, about 40 percent of the growth in GDP between 2010 and 2050 will be devoted to increased health care spending, compared with about 20 percent during the 1980s and 1990s (Chernew et al., 2009a). The 2011 CMS Trustees Report forecasts that under current law Medicare alone will represent 5.6 percent of GDP by 2035 and 6.3 percent by 2080 (Centers for Medicare & Medicaid Services, 2011a). In a more realistic alternative scenario, which takes into account likely changes in current law, CMS estimates Medicare will represent 5.9 percent of GDP by 2030 and 10.4 percent by 2080 (Centers for Medicare & Medicaid Services and Department of Health and Human Services, 2010). In 2009 Medicare accounted for 20 percent of US health care spending.

Although the increased spending on health care has brought health benefits, financing that growth has generated substantial concern among private and public payers as well as many other stakeholders (Cutler, 2004; Ford et al., 2007; Hall and

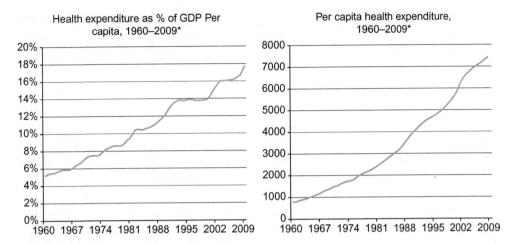

Figure 1.1 Growth of US health care spending.
* 2005 dollars.
Source: Spending and population data obtained from Centers for Medicare & Medicaid Services National Health Expenditures Data (2011) and Newhouse (1992), Table 1. GDP and inflation data from the Bureau of Economic Analysis, National Economic Accounts (2011).

Table 1.1 Percentage of the Increase in Real Per Capita Income Devoted to Health Care, 1960–2009*

	1940– 1950	1950– 1960	1960– 1970	1970– 1980	1980– 1990	1990– 2000	2000– 2009
Average annual growth in per capita health expenditures	4.0%	3.6%	5.6%	4.2%	4.9%	3.0%	3.2%
Average annual growth in per capita GDP	3.1%	1.5%	2.7%	2.0%	2.0%	2.1%	0.5%
Excess growth in health expenditures	0.9	2.1	2.9	2.2	1.4	0.9	2.7
Share of per capita income growth devoted to health care	5.3%	5.5%	12.9%	16.5%	25.5%	18.7%	91.5%

*2005 dollars.
Source: Spending and population data obtained from Centers for Medicare & Medicaid Services National Health Expenditures Data (2011) and Newhouse (1992).

Jones, 2007). For example, the growing share of public budgets allocated to health care has serious consequences for fiscal policy. Peter Orszag, the former Director of the Office of Management and Budget and Congressional Budget Office (CBO), has testified before Congress that the United States' long-term fiscal balance will be determined primarily by the future rate of health care spending growth (Congressional Budget Office, 2007). Analysis in 2007 by the CBO suggested that financing even a

1 percentage point gap between income and health spending growth without cutting other public programs would require an increase in taxes of more than 70 percent by 2050, which, if financed entirely by proportionately raising all individual income tax rates, would bring the highest marginal tax rate to 60 percent and have broad adverse economic ramifications (Congressional Budget Office and Orszag, 2007).

High and rising health care costs also threaten the viability of private and public institutions providing health insurance. Historically, in the US the gap between growth in health care spending and income has been associated with a decline in insurance coverage for the non-elderly (Kronick and Gilmer, 1999; Chernew et al., 2005a and b). This reflects the inability of employers to shift increases in health care spending to wages for lower paid employees and the failure of public coverage to offset declines in private coverage.

The Patient Protection and Affordable Care Act of 2010 includes mandates to purchase insurance and subsidies to assist some households in doing so. This will likely dampen the relationship between spending growth and the deterioration of coverage, assuming the subsidies keep pace with future increases in health care spending (on both the extensive and intensive margins). Of course, the subsidies are financed through taxes, so the costs of maintaining widespread coverage, which are ultimately financed by households and individuals in their role as taxpayers, will rise if health care spending continues to rise. If, alternatively, this escalating spending growth in the non-elderly population is not accompanied by increased subsidies, the financial burden on individuals will rise, either directly through higher premiums and cost sharing at the point of service or indirectly through lower wages and pension benefits that their employers will be willing to pay. Moreover, without rising subsidies compliance with a coverage mandate will fall with more rapid spending growth.

1.2. Spending Growth in Other Countries

Spending growth is not a uniquely American problem. The past century has seen rapid and steady growth in health care spending in most modern industrial democracies, irrespective of how health care is financed and organized. Real per capita annual growth in health care spending in national currency units from 1970 to 2008 and the excess over GDP growth is given in Table 1.2.

Importantly, the results of comparisons of health care spending growth are sensitive to the years of data in consideration as well as the unit of measurement. During 1970–2008 the real per capita annual spending growth in the United States was only slightly (0.3 percentage points) above the average of these countries and the US ranked 14 out of 21 OECD countries. In later years, however, the United States has moved up in this list. From 1980 to 2007 the United States growth rate (3.9 percent) was greater than all but three OECD countries (Spain, Ireland, and Portugal) and the average was 3.2 percent (Organization for Economic Co-Operation and Development (OECD), 2009).

Table 1.2 Health Care and GDP Growth Rate

	Real Per Capita Growth Rate, in Health Care Spending, 1970–2008	Excess Growth Over Per Capita GDP, 1970–2008
Denmark	2.4%	**1.6%**
Sweden	2.6%	**1.9%**
Switzerland	2.8%	**2.7%**
New Zealand	2.9%	**1.1%**
Canada	3.0%	**0.6%**
Netherlands	3.0%	**1.0%**
Germany	3.0%	**1.9%**
Australia	3.3%	**1.4%**
Finland	3.6%	**1.5%**
Greece	3.7%	**1.7%**
France	3.8%	**1.3%**
Japan	3.8%	**1.6%**
United Kingdom	3.8%	**1.0%**
United States	4.1%	**1.7%**
Austria	4.2%	**1.7%**
Iceland	4.4%	**3.9%**
Norway	4.5%	**2.4%**
Spain	4.8%	**0.8%**
Belgium	4.9%	**1.8%**
Ireland	5.3%	**1.7%**
Portugal	6.4%	**2.1%**

Data for Australia, Denmark, and Netherlands are from 1971 to 2007. Data for Greece and Japan from 1970 to 2007. Data for Portugal from 1970 to 2006.

2. SPENDING GROWTH VS. SPENDING LEVEL

At time t the level of spending, S_t, is by definition the product of a vector of unit prices, P_t, and the associated quantities, Q_t. This accounting identity holds no matter how prices and quantities are determined. We begin with the elemental observation that prices and quantities in health care are determined by the interaction among patients, providers, payers, and government. Furthermore, we regard the interaction as leading to prices and quantities being in equilibrium at time t. We mean "equilibrium" in the conventional economic sense, defined broadly to include political as well as private sector actors: parties are following behavioral rules given the circumstances they face, and, given the variables they consider exogenous, they are content not to change their behavior.[1] We are not claiming any welfare properties for

---

[1] The behavioral rules need not be rational, fully informed, or even "maximizing" in order to result in an equilibrium in health care.

the resulting equilibrium (i.e. we do not claim it to be efficient or fair). The key point is simply that an equilibrium exists. As a result, health care quantities and prices, and thus spending, will not change if exogenous factors, such as population composition, do not change.

In other words, given an equilibrium at time t, spending growth requires some variable that causes the equilibrium spending level to change. A one-time change in such a variable will, under standard assumptions, generate a new equilibrium, though the length of the transition period will depend on switching costs and information lags. After the new equilibrium is established, spending growth would cease. Yet we observe persistent spending growth. This implies at least one continually changing variable (or an implausibly long transition period that robs the meaning of equilibrium of any practical significance). As discussed below, the changing variable that the literature has focused on is often identified as "technology." Continual introduction of technology could generate persistent spending growth, although it leaves open the question of the degree to which economic conditions affect the continual change in technology; i.e. the degree to which technological change is endogenous.

A key distinction is between the level of spending and the rate of spending growth. A variable that changes the equilibrium but does not continually change will generally not affect long-run spending growth; rather it will simply generate a new equilibrium. As a result, variables that are correlated with the level of spending (i.e. the equilibrium at a point in time) are not necessarily related to the rate of spending growth. For example, an area's proportion of primary care physicians is strongly negatively correlated with its level of spending at a point in time (Starfield et al., 2005; Sepulveda et al., 2008), but not correlated with an area's rate of spending growth (Chernew et al., 2009b).

More generally, the empirical literature suggests the rate of spending growth in a market is not systematically related to the level of spending in the market. Although a large body of research documents geographic variation in use and spending levels with little visible variation in quality (McClellan et al., 1994; Guadagnoli et al., 1995; Pilote et al., 1995; Wennberg et al., 1996; Skinner and Fisher, 1997; Tu et al., 1997; Wennberg et al., 2002; Fisher et al., 2003a and b; Baicker and Chandra, 2004; Weinstein et al., 2006; Bynum et al., 2010; Gottlieb et al., 2010; Song et al., 2010), Chernew et al. (2010) find no relationship between the level of Medicare spending in 1992 and spending growth from 1992 to 2006. In fact, the correlation (ρ) between spending growth from 1992 to 1999 and spending growth from 2000 to 2006 is weakly negative (-0.12), consistent with regression to the mean. To illustrate this point, they point out that some initially low Medicare spending areas such as Salt Lake City and Rochester MN had among the highest spending growth rates from 1992 to 2006 (4.3 and 3.8 percent, respectively, compared with an average annual national growth rate of 3.2 percent) (Chernew et al., 2010).

3. TECHNOLOGY AND SPENDING GROWTH

The evidence suggests that over long periods of time a primary determinant of spending growth is the development, adoption, and diffusion of new medical technology, though the definition of technology is often ambiguous and its introduction is not independent of market conditions. All health care services, from the simplest to the most sophisticated, represent the application of some "technology" to a health care problem. Equating the change in the use of medical services to the change in use of technology, however, obscures the essence of the relationship between medical technology and spending growth because the growth in the use of medical services is affected by many factors. The changes in utilization driven by advances in medical technology should be considered distinct from those driven by other factors, such as changes in the incidence or prevalence of disease or the incentives and structures surrounding the provision of care.

We define new medical technology as new products, procedures or practice styles related to new knowledge about disease or diagnostic or treatment technologies that alter the mix of medical goods and services that are used. New technology is thus characterized by different types of innovation. One type is innovation that results in a new product (e.g. a new pharmaceutical) or equipment that allows a new service to be provided (e.g. an advanced membrane for dialysis). Another type is new knowledge that results in a new application of existing products. For example, the discovery that ulcers were related to a bacterium led to prescribing antibiotics rather than surgery for peptic ulcer disease. The discovery that tighter control of blood sugar and cholesterol improved outcomes led to more aggressive treatment of those risk factors. A third type of innovation, process innovation, is new knowledge that leads to lower production cost of existing products.

New knowledge often results from learning-by-doing. Repeated use of a procedure or drug or device teaches practitioners how to perform existing procedures better and/or less expensively. Such learning, however, also drops the clinical threshold for intervention and thus enables procedures to be performed on clinically riskier patients. For example, Fuchs finds growth rates of various procedures in the elderly Medicare population grow steadily with age (Fuchs, 1999). This observation is consistent with a greater proportion of frail patients in older cohorts who were presumptively excluded based on their clinical risk in earlier periods, but became suitable candidates for intervention as the technique was refined.

Product, knowledge, and process innovation generally alter the cost, price, effectiveness, or side effects of care. Specifically, process innovation is generally thought to lower cost of care (and thus likely lowers the price). The relationship between product and knowledge innovation and cost and price is ambiguous. Innovations influence demand (and thus use) of the services directly affected by the innovation as well as demand for (and thus use of) related services. Assuming that the innovation leads to lower cost (and thus price) and that the price elasticity of demand for health care products is less than 1 as the data suggest, process innovation should lead to a fall in spending (Manning et al., 1987; Newhouse, 1993a). The persistent growth in spending across all developed countries, however, implies that in medicine product and knowledge innovation have been cost increasing and have dominated process innovation.

Moreover, the impact of introducing new medical technologies on spending growth extends beyond that implied by the price and use of the innovative services themselves to how their introduction influences the entire process of producing health care. New technology may cause the use of some services to rise and the use of others to fall. Because we conceptualize new technology as related to changes in knowledge and information in addition to new products or services, and because the role of "prices" in health care is more complex than in standard consumer theory, we define substitute and complement in a non-standard fashion to relate to quantities used rather than prices.

Specifically, we define complementary services as those whose use increases with use of a new technology (or the new knowledge). For example, consider an improvement in diagnostic imaging that provides higher quality images, improving surgical outcomes. The better outcomes may increase the likelihood that individuals elect surgery. The spending due to the innovation includes not only the spending on the new imaging procedure, but also the spending associated with the increased likelihood of surgery. In this case imaging and surgery are complementary technologies. The use of complementary services may increase the costs associated with use of new innovations by as much as 50 percent (Lee, 1992).

Often an innovation creates complementarity by improving health outcomes and thus making treatment more attractive. In turn, this pulls people into an expensive treatment path whereas without the innovation they would have managed their symptoms inexpensively or even outside of the health care system altogether. For example, surgical advances in the early 1990s reduced the mortality and morbidity of cholecystectomy and led to a 60 percent increase in its use in some delivery systems, a classic case of a changing threshold for medical intervention (Legorreta et al., 1993; Chernew et al., 1997). Prior to the innovation, many asymptomatic or mildly symptomatic individuals may not have been treated because the risk and morbidity associated with treatment exceeded that associated with the disease. Moreover, expenditures grew not only because the number of cholecystectomies increased but also because office visits and diagnostic testing associated with the procedure increased.

Another type of complementarity arises when innovations extend life expectancy because survivors will generally consume additional health care services over their now longer life. These incremental services, although commonly beneficial, and even potentially cost effective, will usually raise health care expenditures. For example, one study suggests that the rising incidence of end-stage renal disease is, in part, attributable to innovations in treating coronary artery disease because heart disease patients are at risk of developing renal disease (Port, 1995). Another suggests the decrease in cardiovascular mortality has masked improvements in cancer mortality because patients who would have once died from cardiovascular disease were also at elevated risk for cancer and died from that instead (Honore and Lleras-Muney, 2006).

Conversely, we define substitute services to be services whose quantity falls because of the introduction of the new technology. The savings associated with reducing these services offset the costs associated with the innovative technologies and complementary services. In many cases, an innovation supplants an established service. For example, one might consider laparoscopic techniques to substitute for the traditional open procedures. Similarly, in some cases coronary angioplasty may substitute for more invasive coronary artery graft bypass surgery. The net cost (or savings) of the new technology depends on the magnitude of any quantity changes and the relative costs of the two services.

If the innovation improves health outcomes, substitution away from medical services that would have been consumed later also may occur. It is hoped that this type of substitution would accompany most preventive services and many other innovations that yield a long-run reduction in morbidity. For example, pharmaceuticals that reduce serum cholesterol may reduce expenditures if they enable sufficient substitution away from treatment for coronary artery disease that otherwise would have occurred had cholesterol levels remained high. Yet existing evidence suggests that the savings associated with reduced use of health care downstream are generally not sufficient to offset the cost of most preventive services so that preventive services as a whole tend to increase overall spending in the course of a lifetime (Fendrick et al., 1996; Cohen et al., 2008). The logic operates in both directions. A recent evaluation of cost-sharing among Medicare beneficiaries with supplemental insurance found that an increase in co-payments for office visits and prescription drugs reduced the use of those (preventive) services, but was associated with an increase in hospitalization (Chandra et al., 2010). The increased expenditure on hospitalizations, however, offset only around 20 percent of the savings gained from the reduced use of office visits and drugs. An important caveat to this result is that the sickest patients saw a much larger offset (over 170 percent), indicating that targeting specific high-risk and high-expenditure groups might result in (probably one-time) cost savings. (Of course, even when the offset does not negate the savings, the reduction in the use of office visits and drugs may have caused adverse changes in health whose value exceeded the monetary savings from the increased cost sharing.)

Most health care innovation will generate changes in both complementary and substitute services. What matters for overall spending growth is how use patterns change on balance. The pattern of changes in use depends on the responsiveness of the demand for all services with respect to the innovation and the relative costs of the services.

4. MODELS OF SPENDING GROWTH

Whether spending growth reflects steady-state growth or simply movement from one equilibrium to another, models of spending growth must emphasize variables that change over time. Empirical evidence suggests a prominent role for medical innovation in driving health care steady-state spending growth, so most economic models of long-run health care spending growth emphasize technology. Some models take technical progress as exogenous, asking how equilibrium changes in different environments as new technology is introduced. Others focus on the process of the technical innovation and how it is affected by institutional details of the health care system such as income, insurance, and other environmental factors that affect the incentives for innovation.

These models of spending growth differ from the more common models designed for comparative statics analysis of the impact of changes in payment policies on spending at a point in time because they emphasize changes in steady-state spending growth as opposed to emphasizing one-time shifts in spending due to the change. For example, models of technology-driven spending growth focus on changes in the Production Possibility Frontier (PPF) associated with new technology as opposed to shifts along the frontier or even movements from an inefficient point in the interior of the PPF to a point closer to or on the PPF.

4.1. Models with Exogenous Technology

4.1.1. Managed Care and Spending Growth

Baumgardner developed a model that compares the welfare implications of exogenous technical change for individuals with fee-for-service (FFS) coverage (with a coinsurance rate) and consumers enrolled in an HMO (Baumgardner, 1991). The key feature of his model is that care is rationed by some combination of a technical boundary reflecting the limits of medical knowledge and capabilities and price parameters set by the insurance plan. Specifically, an FFS insurance plan can set a coinsurance rate, which provides an incentive to limit the amount of care, while an HMO can set condition-specific limits on the amount of care patients can consume (in effect, price versus command-and-control rationing mechanisms). At any point in time there are unobserved illness shocks of varying severity, and both types of insurance plans must pick their parameters that ration care (coinsurance rates for FFS and managerial boundaries for HMOs) taking account of the variance of the shocks. Technical progress that extends the boundary of possible care will not affect the welfare in the HMO because the HMO can adjust the managerial boundary to compensate. Spending may still rise, but only to the extent that HMOs find it in their interest to extend the managerial boundary. Thus, in Baumgardner's managed care environment, health plans control the rate of spending growth (up to a maximum rate determined by the rate of innovation). In other words, even though technological progress is exogenous, spending growth is endogenously determined by the actions of the managed care plans. (Baumgardner does not consider the potential liability the HMO may incur under American law from failing to meet the prevailing standard of care.)

In contrast to the managed care environment, an FFS environment may be less effective at controlling the impact of technical change that increases the boundary of possible care because the coinsurance rate might not rise enough in equilibrium to fully offset the effects of new technology. Technical progress could thus reduce welfare. It is uncertain whether spending growth over the long run would be higher in an FFS environment. Even though HMOs may be better positioned to make selective use of boundary-increasing technologies and could have a lower level of costs because of that, the impact of HMOs on cost *growth* is indeterminate because the percentage rate of growth depends on the differences in baseline costs. For example, even if HMOs reduce the dollar increase in spending, they may have the same rate of spending growth as FFS plans in equilibrium due to a lower baseline level of spending. In addition to concerns about liability, any comparison of spending and spending growth across insurance types must also recognize that they compete with one another for enrollees.

The foregoing considered boundary-changing technological change. Some technical change, however, could reduce the non-pecuniary costs of care, for example by reducing side effects. Such change will also affect welfare differently for patients in FFS plans as opposed to those in HMO plans. In this case, however, FFS plans can offset a change in non-pecuniary costs by adjusting the coinsurance rate and thus control moral hazard for patients not limited by the technical boundary, allowing them to limit spending growth when faced with this type of technical progress. In contrast, HMO plans (in the model) do not have that tool and thus have a harder time controlling spending growth driven by this type of innovation. In this model one would expect technical change that reduces non-pecuniary costs to generate more spending growth in the managed care setting.

In reality, however, HMO plans can and do use cost sharing as well as managerial limits and through coverage denials or limits. Thus, in theory, HMO plans could limit spending growth and avoid the welfare loss associated with changes in technology that reduce the non-pecuniary costs of treatment (Pauly and Ramsey, 1999). Similarly, FFS plans may decline to cover certain technologies or adopt managed care techniques that mimic HMO managerial limits on the technical boundary of care. However, FFS plans may have more difficulty than HMOs in targeting such limits.

4.1.2. Income Effects and Spending Growth

McGuire (unpublished) models demand for health care to investigate the extent to which income effects will dampen the rate of spending growth in the presence of exogenous technological change. Technology is assumed to change the parameters of a consumer's maximization problem both by enhancing the value of medical care and by affecting the costs of production. McGuire assumes that because parts of medical care are a service industry, subject to Baumol's cost disease (Baumol, 1967), that value-enhancing change comes at increased cost. Technological change thus shifts up both the cost curve and the demand curve. The ultimate impact on quantity (and thus spending) depends on the magnitude of these two shifts and the demand elasticity.

Ultimately the demand curve constrains spending. For any given shift in value and unit cost, greater demand elasticity reduces the equilibrium quantity and thus spending. The demand elasticity depends on the substitutability of medical care and non-medical care services, and, crucially, an income effect. A larger income effect increases the demand elasticity and yields slower spending growth for any technology-induced shift in unit costs or value. As health care becomes a greater share of a consumer's budget, the Slutsky equation term of budget share times the income elasticity likely rises and thus the impact of technology on spending growth slows as the share of income devoted to health care rises.

In the model the magnitude of the income effects are not influenced by whether care is paid for at the site of service or via a premium. However, a number of policy variables affect the term in income elasticity. Specifically, if care is subsidized, either via reduced premium or reduced cost sharing, the income effect, and thus the spending dampening effect of the demand curve, is diminished. This is specifically relevant for Medicare and other public programs where taxpayers subsidize beneficiaries. In the extreme case, where both premiums and cost sharing are fully subsidized, there will be no income effect (or cost-sharing effect because of the subsidies) other than from any increase in taxes. In this case the rate of technology-induced spending growth will be determined by the rate of value-enhancing medical innovation (provided the necessary tax financing is forthcoming from those paying taxes). Only the demand-side lever of reduced subsidies, which inherently cause hardship for some, controls spending growth among Medicare beneficiaries. In the absence of such cost sharing, other supply-side constraints would be needed. Of course, there may be an offsetting income effect from the taxpayers who fund the subsidy, but in public programs the recipients of the subsidies are typically not the relevant taxpayers—and the opposing income effects of the beneficiaries and taxpayers need not exactly offset. Ultimately, the extent to which income effects constrain overall spending growth depend on the magnitude of the income effects across taxpayers and beneficiaries.

4.2. Models of Endogenous Technology

Weisbrod sketched a model that connects technical progress, health care payment systems, quality of care, and health care spending (Weisbrod, 1991). A portion of technical advance may be reasonably regarded as exogenous to the health care system, reflecting advances in knowledge stemming from government funded research or spillovers from other industries. For example, certain clinical advances required the sequencing of the human genome while others, including many advances in imaging, required the development of computing power. Similarly, advances in optics also have enabled advances in medical imaging. While the rate of such advances is certainly influenced by macro-economic variables that affect federal research support and by non-health care research, they are plausibly exogenous to the health care system.

Nonetheless, to some extent technological progress in health care is endogenous, influenced by the parameters of demand for health care. Greater demand generates greater returns for innovation and thus more innovation, specifically more cost-increasing innovation. Thus, is it not surprising that on balance the technical advances that are observed tend to increase spending, either because the technologies have higher unit prices than current services or because they induce greater utilization, or both. Higher prices may reflect higher production cost, rents from market power per-haps stemming from patents, or errors in setting administered prices, especially failure to adjust such prices downward as productivity improves from learning-by-doing.

In Weisbrod's model higher mean spending tends to generate higher absolute vari-ance in spending. Depending on utility function parameters that determine risk aver-sion, the demand for insurance may also increase, further increasing demand for care (Phelps, 1976; Herring, 2005).[2] The increased demand generates greater incentives for firms to conduct research and development (R&D), increasing the pace of techni-cal progress in medicine. Moreover, the form of insurance influences the nature of incentives for R&D. Traditional insurance, which shields patients from most of the cost of care at the margin and which passively reimburses on a disaggregated, fee-for-service basis, gives greater encouragement to quality and cost-increasing technologies.

Goddeeris formalized the connection between insurance and the incentives for technological advance (Goddeeris, 1984a). In his model, profit-maximizing firms develop medical technologies but are assumed to choose a maximum "effort" to put towards each potential technology. By giving each technology a "chance-of-success" function, Goddeeris compares firm behavior in the absence of insurance with behav-ior in a world with insurance. Insurance increases the consumption of health services by subsidizing medical care at the margin. This increase in demand is especially important for expensive medical services that might otherwise not be adopted. By increasing the chance an expensive service is adopted, insurance tends to bias firms to develop innovations that increase medical expenditures.

Changes in health care reimbursement, such as bundling payment (i.e. paying a fixed fee for a broad set of services associated with an episode of care or a period of time such as capitation), may alter the incentives for technology development or the nature of

---

[2] Because health insurance typically subsidizes the marginal dollar, demand will rise relative to the uninsured state. Even if insurance were to reimburse in a lump sum fashion, demand would increase in the sick state (relative to no insurance) because of the income transfer to that state.

technology development. Similarly, insurance schemes that subsidize the marginal dollar less heavily will alter the incentives for technology development.[3] For example, in the Medicare Part D drug insurance program, the use of coinsurance of 25–33 percent for expensive drugs and biologics rather than co-payments, which are used for most oral drugs (i.e. pills), alters the incentives to develop such drugs (Berndt et al., 2011).

Goddeeris also addressed the welfare effects of technical progress in the presence of insurance (Goddeeris, 1984b). His model focused on the interaction between insurance and technological advances. In the absence of insurance, technological advances that reduce the consumer's or purchaser's utility, i.e. those whose price exceeds their benefit, would never be adopted. However, insurance that subsidizes the marginal dollar shields the consumer from the full price, allowing innovative firms, which will have at least temporary market power, to charge more than they would without insurance. In effect, insurance transfers the cost of health care services from the point of service to the point of insurance purchase. At the point of service, individuals treat the premium cost as sunk and make decisions without regard to the full price of the technology. (The model does not consider the demand for insurance.) This encourages innovation and implies that some technology not adopted in the absence of insurance will be adopted. In this model it is possible for technological innovation to reduce utility at the population level by expanding the population who demand the service. Some technologies benefit a subset of the population disproportionately, but insurance could increase demand to a larger population who value the service less than its cost, potentially causing an overall decrease in welfare. A similar result is found by Garber et al. (Garber et al., 2006).

Although Goddeeris focuses on the welfare-reducing effects of insurance, i.e. an inefficiently high rate of innovation, insurance can increase welfare because of income effects and risk aversion (DeMeza, 1983; Goddeeris, 1984b). An example of a case in which welfare-increasing income effects are important is an expensive treatment for a rare disease. Assume the value of the treatment is sufficiently high that individuals would be willing to purchase actuarially fair insurance that would pay off if they acquired the rare disease, but that an uninsured consumer would not purchase the treatment because of the expense. In an extreme case the cost of the treatment might exceed the individual's lifetime income and assets. If this were the case for many individuals and there were substantial fixed costs to bring the good to market, the treatment would likely not be on the market in a world with no insurance even if many individuals would be willing to pay the expected cost ex ante. Hence, in some cases welfare could increase due to the impact of insurance on available technology, even ignoring the insurance value of mitigating risk.

---

[3] In a fee-for-service context new procedures require a new billing code, which may introduce some delay in implementing any new advance. In a more aggregated reimbursement scheme such as capitation, lags in updating reimbursement to account for the new technology may also similarly introduce delay.

The conceptual framework of spending growth reflecting successive equilibria that change due to a continually changing variable is crucial for empirical analyses. Specifically, by assuming that the health care system is in equilibrium at any point in time, spending growth—and by implication a change in the equilibrium spending—must then be due to changes in the factors affecting prices and quantities.

At any point in time, exogenous factors include demographics, X_t (e.g. age, gender, and income), information or knowledge, I_t, and available technology, T_t. Some variables, such as regulations, R_t, are exogenous to some actors (e.g. individual patients and providers), but not to the system because the government is an actor. Moreover, even though we treat technology as exogenous at a point in time, over time technology responds to market conditions.

We define P_t^* and Q_t^* as the equilibrium prices and quantities that give rise to spending S_t^*. Analogously, S_{t+1}^* is defined as equilibrium spending at $t+1$. Equilibrium spending growth is then simply $\frac{S_{t+1}^* - S_t^*}{S_t^*}$.

As pointed out above, the relationship between any variable and the *level* of equilibrium spending (S_t^* or S_{t+1}^*) likely differs from the relationship between that variable and spending *growth*. Specifically, $S_{t+1}^* - S_t^*$ is a function of the change in the variables and the change in the coefficients that relate those variables to spending. If the value of any given variable does not change, it may not affect spending growth even if it affects the level of spending unless the coefficient of that variable (which measures its impact on the level of spending) changes.

In this formulation there are only two periods. If, in $t+1$ whatever changed ceases to change and all else is constant, we will remain at S_{t+1} since we have assumed S_{t+1} is an equilibrium. If, however, what caused a change between t and $t+1$ is a variable such as income that continues to change, further growth will ensue. We emphasize this seemingly obvious point because many policy interventions result in one-time savings rather than changes in the growth rate, and the lay public dialog often confuses the two. We illustrate this graphically with Figure 1.2, which relates spending to time. The level of spending refers to the height of the curve and the trajectory relates to its slope. A shock that lowers the curve at time t will slow spending growth between $t-1$ and $t+1$ but does not necessarily alter the steady-state trajectory of spending. For example, if $\ln(S_t) = \alpha + \beta^* t$, a one-time reduction in α affects spending, but not steady-state spending growth.

The next section of this chapter considers empirical studies, and as a transition to that section, we conclude this section with some general remarks about moving from a theoretical model of spending growth to empirical work. Medical technology, which many American writers have emphasized as an influence on medical spending, is not readily measured by econometricians.[4]

---

[4] Although there is a consensus among American health economists that technology is an important determinant of growth, a similar consensus does not exist among British health economists (Fuchs, 1996; Newhouse, 1998). Perhaps this perception stems from the differences in the two countries' financing institutions.

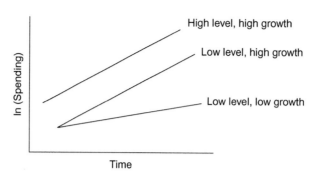

Figure 1.2 Alternative spending paths.

The inability to measure technology and its resulting omission in empirical models of spending growth has important econometric implications, since its effect is picked up by the vector of included variables and can alter their coefficients. For example, an unchanging level of a system trait such as provider competition may affect spending growth, if more competitive markets have different spending growth than less competitive markets. This could be the case because the degree of competition may affect the ability or willingness of providers to limit access to new services relative to old services or may depend on whether the technology is invasive or non-invasive. If the new technology driving spending is imaging, for example, the degree of competition may affect the degree to which some physicians limit the use of imaging. Physicians may limit other, more invasive services differently. The extent to which the relationship between competition and the use of services changes over time depends on the nature of the change in technology (and demand for it) as well as the cost of controlling its use (which may vary with the nature of technology). For this reason, the parameters in a spending model, β, are likely to change over time so it will be often best to use a specification that allows the coefficient, β_t to change over time.

This reasoning is embodied in the following model in which S_t is a function of available technology at time t, which is unmeasured, a vector of observed covariates, and parameters, β, that relate the covariates to spending. Changes in unmeasured factors such as technology may cause the observed relationship between covariates and spending to change over time. Thus the coefficients, β, are subscripted to reflect the possibility they may change as technology (or other unobserved factors) change over time. A specific framework captures the notion that there is a general, technology-driven component of spending, $S(T(t))$, as well as other factors (X_t) that modify spending according to a function θ:

$$S_t = S(T(t))\theta(X_t, \beta_t) \tag{1.1}$$

We assume $\partial S/\partial T > 0$ and $\partial T/\partial t > 0$ to capture the contribution of new technology to spending growth, which we assume in this model to be independent of system factors (though, as we see below, we recognize that there are feedback effects of system variables on technology development). At any point in time available technology is constant, and the covariates, including system factors such as provider traits, influence how it is used and determine the resulting spending. For example, provider competition is captured in the X vector and its corresponding parameter is related to the impact of competition on spending at a point in time. If technology were measured, its interaction with competition could be captured by an interaction term between competition and technology. Yet technology is unmeasured. However, the effect can still be captured by including an interaction term between competition and time. The coefficient on the interaction term can be interpreted as measuring the extent to which competition affects technology diffusion. A similar interpretation could be given to the coefficient on competition (or other system traits) in a first differenced model.

Simple forms of S and θ can illustrate the inherent interaction between technology and system variables (Chernew et al., 2005a). If we specify $S(T(t))$ as $\exp(\alpha_0 + \alpha_1 t)$, we capture the general trend that we attribute to technology. If we specify $\theta(X_t, \beta_t)$ as $\exp(\beta_0 X_t + \beta_1 t X_t)$, the β_0 parameters measure the extent to which each covariate modifies spending at any point in time and the β_1 parameters allow the impact of any X on spending to change over time and therefore affect spending growth. Thus, $\ln(S_t) = \alpha_0 + \alpha_1 t + \beta_0 X_t + \beta_1 t X_t$. This formulation allows for spending growth even when the Xs are held constant and all that changes is technology. Other functional forms are of course possible, but this one illustrates that spending growth may differ in systems with different Xs or different βs, even if the Xs do not change or if they change by similar amounts. Of course, spending will grow with change in the Xs, but in this model the steady-state trajectory of spending holding the Xs constant will be captured by the α_1 and β_1 parameters.

5. EMPIRICAL EVIDENCE

5.1. Causes of Spending Growth[5]

Studies that examine the causes of health care spending growth typically rely on one of two approaches. The *residual* method recognizes that continually changing variables are needed to generate steady-state spending growth. They measure important variables that continually change and relate those variables to spending growth. Specifically they measure time-varying factors such as general inflation, population aging, the spread of insurance, and rising income. The residual method studies

---

[5] This section draws on and updates Chernew et al. (1998). Literature published after 1998 was found by running queries in the EconLit and PubMED databases as well as by linking relevant citations found in these publications. The terms *spending*, *cost*, *expenditure*, *growth*, and *rate* were submitted and relevant titles and keywords flagged.

generally attribute the rest of spending growth to technology (Table 1.3).[6] This method was pioneered by Solow for the entire economy over 50 years ago (Solow, 1957). Schwartz (1987) was probably the first to apply this approach to the growth of health care spending and, like Solow for the aggregate economy, concluded that technological change was the prime determinant of health care spending growth (Schwartz, 1987). Newhouse (1992, 1993b), who controlled for more non-technological factors and examined a longer time period than Schwartz, came to a similar conclusion (Newhouse, 1992, 1993b).

Newhouse had earlier carried out work that estimated a model of medical care unit price inflation to test among three alternative models of spending in the health care sector: (1) spending growth is caused by an ever increasing demand curve attributable to rising health insurance coverage and rising income; (2) spending growth stems from increases in costs due to the development and diffusion of medical technology induced by high levels of insurance coverage; and (3) spending growth stems from rising inefficiency in the health care market (Newhouse, 1988). Although the evidence he amassed did not clearly reject any of these models, it generally supported the premise of the second model, which emphasized technical change from associated high *levels* of coverage as the dominant explanations of increasing unit prices.[7] This explanation is consistent with the notion that at higher levels of coverage, more of the steady stream of possible innovations will be taken to market, although both unit price and the size of the market determine returns to the innovator.

Several other studies report results consistent with the finding that technology is a primary determinant of spending growth. For example, Bundorf, Royalty, and Baker decompose spending growth into a price component and a quantity component for private claims between 2001 and 2006 (Bundorf et al., 2009). They find that all of the spending growth in outpatient services and around three-fourths of the spending growth in pharmaceuticals can be attributable to increases in quantity rather than increases in price. Frogner evaluated the impact of growth in the average health care wage on growth in spending across the United States, Australia, and Canada between 1970 and 2005 and found wages were not a significant contributor (Frogner, 2010). While this does not speak directly to the role of technology, it suggests an alternative explanation, rising wages, is not a major contributor to spending growth.

---

[6] Some residual studies, such as Newhouse (1993a or b), recognize that other unobserved factors besides technology may be in the residual, but "technology" broadly defined is often considered the most prominent component of the residual.

[7] Baumol (1967) had emphasized lagging medical sector productivity as a reason for rising relative unit prices; rising unit prices together with inelastic demand in his model accounted for rising spending. Newhouse, however, argued that although this explanation may apply in certain parts of medical care such as chronic long-term care, lagging productivity did not seem plausible in a sector with so much technological change and that spending in those parts of medical care in which lagging productivity might be plausible were not growing as a share of spending after accounting for demographics.

A central issue with the studies using the residual method is how factors that may encourage technology development are treated. In particular, as Weisbrod, Goddeeris, and the above discussion indicate, greater insurance skews the development of new technology and biases it toward product innovation, which empirically appears to have been cost increasing, rather than toward process innovation, which is cost decreasing (Goddeeris, 1984a and b; Weisbrod, 1991). Thus, the portion of spending growth attributable to technology depends in part on how insurance is treated in the residual approach. And as already pointed out, like more generous insurance, higher incomes will also make more innovations profitable to introduce, so that income growth will also induce technological change.

Newhouse's 1992 work used results on the insurance elasticity of spending from the RAND Health Insurance Experiment to account for the effects of the spread of insurance (Newhouse, 1992, 1993b). This elasticity estimated from the RAND Experiment, however, held technology constant and thus did not capture any effect of induced technological change from improved insurance.

From 1950 to 1990, Finkelstein estimates that the spread of health insurance may account for approximately half of the six-fold increase in real per capita health care Medicare spending (Finkelstein, 2007). Her estimate is identified by variation in the proportion of American elderly who had health insurance prior to Medicare, and in particular from the substantially lower percentage in the South. Because Medicare at that time reimbursed its share of hospital cost (roughly a third for the average hospital), it is possible that Medicare simply allowed a one-time adjustment in the South to desired capital stock, and that this is much of the effect Finkelstein has estimated. This, of course, is not a change in the steady-state growth rate.[8]

Income elasticity is a somewhat problematic variable in the residual studies because estimated income elasticities in the literature vary substantially depending on the level of aggregation. Estimates of income elasticities using the household as the unit of observation and exploiting cross-sectional variation in income find relatively low values of 0.1−0.2, although one estimate is markedly higher (Newhouse, 1993a; Acemoglu et al., 2009). These cross-section estimates, of course, hold technology constant. In contrast, estimates generated with longitudinal data or at a national level (which allow technology to vary) typically find higher income elasticities often exceeding 1.0 (Gerdtham and Jonsson, 2000). In his 1992 paper Newhouse used various estimates of the income elasticity to try to bound the effect of income growth.

---

[8] This argument also points up that how insurance reimburses providers, i.e. how it sets supply prices, matters; if the Medicare Prospective Payment System had been in effect in 1966, Finkelstein may have observed a very different demand elasticity. (The demand elasticities estimated from the RAND Experiment, however, are based on supply prices that are analytically similar to those Medicare used at the outset, so Finkelstein's comparison with RAND is apt.) See also the discussion of Smith et al., below.

Other work tries to allocate some of the spending that would otherwise be attributed to technology to insurance because insurance induces medical innovation. The most recent effort along these lines (as of the writing of this chapter) is by Smith et al. (Smith et al., 2009). Smith and her collaborators used the OECD panel data across 23 countries from 1960 to 2006, regressing per capita spending on per capita GDP, a measure of insurance coverage, and demographic variables, with country and year fixed effects. A novel feature of this analysis was interpreting the year fixed effects as measuring the effects of technological change that is common across countries. This interpretation allowed Smith et al. to estimate an interaction between income growth and technical change, but they were unable to estimate an insurance—technology interaction with any precision, in part because of difficulties in measuring theoretically appropriate measures of insurance across countries, including levels and methods of reimbursement. Overall, Smith et al. attribute between 29 and 43 percent of the increase in health spending to growth in income and another 27 percent to an interaction between technical change and income. They attribute between 0 and 26 percent to a pure technology residual, depending on assumptions about income elasticities and medical productivity. In short, Smith et al. attribute a larger part of the cost growth to income than does the earlier work.

Other studies try to capture forces that drive technological progress, instead of simply assigning the residual to a technology bucket. For example, Peden and Freeland examined the role of insurance coverage and research and development in influencing technology development and thus spending growth (Newhouse, 1981, 1988; Peden and Freeland, 1995). They estimated that about 70 percent of health care spending growth since 1960 was attributable to the development and diffusion of new medical technology, much of which they believed was induced by insurance coverage and non-commercial medical research spending. These studies are included in Table 1.3 along with the residual studies because, like the residual studies, they do not attempt to measure technology directly.

In contrast to the residual approach, the *affirmative* approach attempts to assess the extent to which specific technologies have contributed to rising expenditures, often focusing on the treatment of specific diseases (Table 1.4). By identifying specific diseases or technologies, the affirmative approach provides a more direct, clinically meaningful understanding of the role that technology has played in health care spending growth. The inherent shortcoming of the affirmative approach is that it is for practical purposes impossible to capture all of the potential cost ramifications of even one new technology, let alone encompass the totality of all medical innovations.

Using the affirmative approach, Scitovsky (1985) and Scitovsky and McCall (1976) analyzed the costs of treating a variety of illnesses during three different periods to determine the magnitude of, and reasons for, changes in the costs associated with treating these ailments (Scitovsky and McCall, 1976; Scitovsky, 1985). Holding prices constant, they concluded that between 1951 and 1964, increased spending to treat

Table 1.3 Medical Technology and Spending Growth, Residual and Related Studies

Study	Study Period	Method	Findings
(Newhouse, 1992, 1993b)	Varied	Residual approach, reviewing non-technology cause of spending growth	"The principal cause of increased costs appears to be the increased capabilities of medicine."
(Schwartz, 1987)	1977–1984	Residual approach, reviewing non-technology cause of spending growth	Medical innovation and diffusion is the primary, controllable factor contributing to the underlying, upward trend in health care expenditures.
(Peden and Freeland, 1998)	1960–1993	Regression analysis using the level of insurance coverage and non-commercial research spending as proxies for technology	70% of spending growth is attributable to medical technology (much of which was induced by insurance coverage).
(Newhouse, 1981, Varied, 1988)		Regression analysis examining the change in prices as a function of the level of, and changes in, insurance coverage and gross national product (GNP)	The most important explanation of medical price inflation is that high levels of insurance coverage induced high rates of new product development and use.
(Cutler, 1995)	1940–1990	Residual approach	Technology accounts for 49% of the growth in real health care spending per capita from 1940 to 1990.
(Smith et al., 2009)	1960–2007	Residual approach (update to Newhouse's 1992 paper, with some modifications to model)	Attribute 27 to 48% of growth to spending on new technologies.
(Bundorf et al., 2009)	2001–2006	Decompose spending growth into increases in price and increases in quantity	Attributed 100% of growth in outpatient services and 72% of growth in pharmaceuticals to increases in quantity.
(Frogner, 2010)	1970–2005	Evaluate impact of growth in average health care wage on growth in spending in the US, Australia, and Canada	Growth in wages is not a significant driver of spending growth.
(Finkelstein, 2007)	1950–1990	Estimated impact of expanded health insurance on spending growth	Spread of insurance accounts for ~50% of the growth in Medicare spending.

Table 1.4 Medical Technology and Spending Growth, Affirmative Studies

Study	Study Period	Method	Findings
(Scitovsky, 1985)	1971—1981	Examined changes in treatment patterns for common illnesses at the Palo Alto Medical Clinic	Big ticket new technologies were responsible for spending growth.
(Scitovsky and McCall, 1976)	1951—1971	Examined changes in treatment patterns for common illnesses at the Palo Alto Medical Clinic	Little ticket items were responsible for spending growth.
(Showstack et al., 1982)	1972—1977	Examined changes in treatment patterns for patients hospitalized at the UCSF hospital for 1 of 10 diagnoses	Increased use was largely attributable to the use of new technologies.
(Holahan et al., 1990)	1983—1985	Used two-stage least squares regression analysis to examine changes in Medicare expenditures per enrollee in different specialties	Spending growth was greatest in specialties likely to have experienced the greatest rate of technical innovation.
(Cutler and McClellan, 1996)	1984—1991	Examined hospital adoption of, and patient receipt of, coronary revascularization technologies	The expansion of invasive cardiac surgeries accounts for almost all of the growth in treatment costs for heart attacks.
(Bradley and Kominski, 1992)	1984—1987	Decomposed Medicare inpatient costs per case into input price inflation, changes in costs with diagnostic related groups (DRGs), and changes in case mix across DRGs	Technology-related factors accounted for at least 35% of the real increase in costs per case.
(Katz et al., 1997)	1987—1992	Examined spending growth across different clinical categories	Spending growth was greatest in service categories considered more technologically expensive.

(Continued)

Table 1.4 (Continued)

Study	Study Period	Method	Findings
(Okunade and Murthy, 2002)	1960–1997	Used total research and development spending and health research and development spending as a proxy for technological change	"Technological change is a major escalator of health care expenditure and confirm a significant and stable long-run relationship among per capita real health care expenditure, per capita real income and broad-based R&D expenditures."
(Di Matteo, 2005)	1975–2000	Used time as a partial proxy for technological change	Technological change accounts for approximately two-thirds of the increases in real per capita health expenditures in US and Canada from 1975 to 2000.
(Mas and Seinfeld, 2008)	1982–1995	Hospitals' acquisition of technology (as a proxy for spending growth)	Increases in HMO market share reduce the adoption of technologies that are new and already at the steady-state level, thus lowering the ultimate level of technology and leading to ultimate long-term reductions in medical spending growth.

most of the diseases they studied was related to the increased use of "little ticket" technologies (i.e. technologies with a relatively low unit price) such as lab tests and X-rays. They did not attempt to identify specific changes in knowledge that led to these changes in use patterns.

A similar analysis of experience between 1964 and 1971 revealed that the little ticket technologies continued to account for observed cost increases, with one important exception: the cost of treating acute myocardial infarction (heart attack) rose

33 percent, largely because of the introduction of intensive care units, a clear advance in medical science.

In the period from 1971 through 1981 Scitovsky found substantial cost increases for only seven of the 16 diseases she examined, but in most of these cases the increase arose from specific medical innovations that she identified (Scitovsky, 1985). For example, in childbirth the cost-increasing technology was the increase in the cesarean section rate. In breast cancer the cost-increasing technologies included the diffusion of radiation therapy in the earlier periods and the introduction of combination therapies including chemotherapy in the later period. In treatment of heart attacks the prime cost-increasing technologies were the introduction of intracoronary streptokinase infusion and coronary bypass surgery.

Showstack, Schroeder, and Matsumoto also studied the treatment of specific illnesses to delineate the causes of spending growth (Showstack et al., 1982). They compared inpatient resource use for 10 diagnoses over a shorter period of time than Scitovsky did—1972 to 1977. They reported that technologies that were commonly available in 1972 were used similarly in 1977, but several new technologies, such as ultrasound, nuclear medicine, and fetal monitoring, were used much more frequently in 1977. This pattern suggests that, in aggregate, the new technologies were additive rather than substitutive.

Cutler and McClellan, using Medicare claims from 1984 to 1991, reported a 4 percent annual increase in the average real reimbursement for treating elderly heart attack patients (Cutler and McClellan, 1996). They attributed the majority of this increase to the diffusion of new technologies for performing invasive revascularization procedures. Over the study period, cardiac catheterization rates rose from 11 to 41 percent of heart attack patients. Bypass rates rose from 5 to 13 percent, and angioplasty rates from 1 to 12 percent.

The affirmative approach employed by Scitovsky, Scitovsky, and McCall, and Showstack, Schroeder, and Matsumoto measures changes in costs per case (Scitovsky and McCall, 1976; Showstack et al., 1982; Scitovsky, 1985). They capture use of complementary and substitutive technology only during the episode of care. Thus, this method of selecting patients diagnosed with specific diseases underestimates the fiscal impact of technological change if methods complementary with the technology expand or if the number of individuals diagnosed with the specific disease expands (and conversely with respect to substitutive technology).

Showstack et al. reported evidence consistent with underestimation, noting that the changing mix of patients treated over time suggested that indications for treatment had expanded (Showstack et al., 1982). This point is exemplified further in studies of specific procedures or diseases including cholecystectomy (as referred to above) (Legorreta et al., 1993; Steiner et al., 1994), prostate cancer (Lu-Yao et al., 1993), and heart attacks (Cutler and McClellan, 1996). As Legoretta et al. demonstrated, even when a new procedure is less expensive than potential substitute services on a per-case basis, its introduction may increase aggregate expenditures (Legorreta et al., 1993). The cost increase may occur in situations when a diagnostic test or treatment becomes less expensive to the patient or less clinically risky, perhaps from learning-by-doing, leading many people who would not have used the technology previously to use it.

Because the affirmative approach focuses on individual technologies or diseases, it inherently suffers from an inability to assess the aggregate impact of all technological change on spending growth. It also does not account for potential effects on the incidence of other diseases if survival is affected; e.g. if anti-hypertensives lowered the incidence of fatal cardiovascular disease, the incidence of other diseases would subsequently rise. Nor does it, at least as implemented in the above studies, account for the endogeneity of technology. Moreover, the evidence indicates that the impact of technology varies by disease, making it risky to generalize about the effect of technology on spending. Weisbrod (1991) notes that in certain cases, technological change clearly lowers costs, particularly when it prevents a disease. The oft cited example of this type of innovation is the Salk—Sabin polio vaccine, which is inexpensive itself and has almost completely eliminated the high costs of treating polio; a similar example from an earlier era is smallpox vaccine. These examples, however, are a half century or more old, and it is difficult to think of other innovations that substantially lowered total treatment costs. Perhaps the HPV vaccine will be similar. But, as noted above, even in these cases it is not clear that health care spending over the life cycle was lowered.

Several studies provide evidence linking the conclusion most authors have drawn from the residual approach—that technology, vaguely defined, is responsible for health care spending growth—to that of the affirmative approach—that in specific clinical areas emerging technologies have been responsible for health care spending growth. Bradley and Kominski (1992) used various criteria based on observed changes in cost and use to identify technology-related changes in expenditures. They did not examine specific technologies. Their findings indicated that technical change was the single largest cause of the increase in the inflation-adjusted cost per inpatient case and much of the remaining increase might also be attributable to medical innovations.

Two studies examined overall growth in physician expenditures during the late 1980s and early 1990s (Holahan et al., 1990; Katz et al., 1997). Although they did not examine any specific diseases or medical technologies, they disaggregated the growth of expenditures by physician type or service type. In both cases they concluded that spending growth was greatest in areas where technological innovation was high, such as cardiology or orthopedic surgery. Hence, when one combines this evidence with that from the residual approach and affirmative approach, medical technology, as modulated by market conditions, appears, on balance, to be a prime driver of health care spending growth. For this reason, the long-run impact on spending growth of changed reimbursement arrangements, changed cost sharing, and direct interventions in the clinical process will depend on the extent to which such changes alter the rate of adoption and diffusion of medical technology.

5.2. Spending Growth by Insurance Type[9]

Models such as Baumgardner's suggest that managed care may slow technology adoption and spending growth. Though the evidence is out of date and today's HMOs differ considerably from those of 30 years ago with respect to network composition and management techniques, direct comparisons between FFS and HMO systems generally suggest similar spending growth across systems, but there are some exceptions which suggest slower growth in HMOs (Table 1.5). See also Glied (2000).

The similarity of spending growth between these two types of insurance may reflect common increases in input costs, or, as alluded to above, tort law, or in markets with a dominant HMO a pricing strategy to peg premiums to those charged in the FFS sector. (Prior to the 1990s staff and group model HMOs were often unique to local markets and so competed only against fee-for-service arrangements.) Ginsburg and Pickreign (1996, 1997) presented head-to-head estimates of growth in employer

Table 1.5 Managed Care and Spending Growth

Study	Observation Period	Type of Managed Care	Managed Care Spending Growth/ FFS Spending Growth
(Luft, 1980)	1962/1963–1970/1971	HMO	95.8%
(Newhouse et al., 1985)	1976–1981	HMO	98.9%
(Ginsburg and Pickreign, 1996)	1991–1995 (Hay Huggins data)	HMO	96.0%
	1991–1995 (KPMG data)		80.4%
(Ginsburg and Pickreign, 1997)	1992–1996	HMO	76.7%
		PPO	88.4%
		POS	83.7%

Source: Chernew et al. (1998).

---

[9] This section is adapted from Chernew et al. (1998).

premiums from 1992 to 1996. They reported that HMO premiums increased at a lower annual rate (3.3 percent) than conventional (indemnity) (4.3 percent), PPO (3.8 percent), and POS (3.6 percent) plan premiums during this four-year period. Premium growth, however, is not the same as spending growth, since cost sharing and covered benefits can and very likely did change differentially between the two systems.

In contrast, at the market level, evidence generally indicates that spending growth is slower in markets with more managed care (largely defined as HMOs) (Table 1.6). Many of the studies in this literature focus only on hospital expenses or revenues, however. For example, Robinson (1991) and Robinson and Casalino (1996) measured changes in hospital expenses in California, adjusting for input price differences, finding as much as a 44 percent slower rate of hospital care spending growth in markets with high HMO penetration relative to markets with low HMO penetration.[10] Robinson and Luft (1988) compared hospital spending growth rates between 1982 and 1986 in California, a state with high managed care penetration, with those in four regulated states (New York, New Jersey, Maryland, Massachusetts) and with those in all other states. They did not explicitly adjust for managed care penetration. Both regulation and managed care reduced spending growth, but the results were mixed regarding which approach had the larger effect.

Gaskin and Hadley (1997) use a national sample to examine changes in hospital costs as a function of market-wide HMO penetration. They found hospital spending growth to be inversely related to HMO penetration, estimating that from 1992 to 1993 health care spending growth in a market with 40 percent HMO penetration would be 3.4 percentage points lower than in markets with a 5 percent HMO penetration. HMO penetration, however, is endogenous, so one should not infer causality.

A series of studies by Zwanziger, Melnick, and colleagues examined hospital cost and revenue growth over time in California before and after 1982 (Melnick and Zwanziger, 1988; Zwanziger and Melnick, 1988; Melnick et al., 1989a and b; Zwanziger et al., 1994a and b). 1982 was significant because California passed legislation that encouraged selective contracting by health plans with providers in that year.[11] Although they did not examine the impact of managed care on spending growth directly, they examined a period of rising selective contracting in California and managed care grew substantially during the 1980s after the 1982 legislation passed. Preferred Provider Organization (PPO) penetration in the non-Medicare market in California rose from 1 percent in 1983 to 50 percent by 1987 and HMO

---

[10] HMO penetration is generally low enough so a single HMO does not have a monopsony.

[11] Selective contracting means that insurers could charge patients higher out-of-pocket prices if they used providers that did not give the insurer lower supply prices.

Table 1.6 Managed Care and Spending Growth, Market-level Studies

Study	Study Period	Main Unit of Observation	Primary Findings
(Robinson, 1991)	1982—1988	Hospitals in California	An increase of 10 percentage points in HMO penetration results in a 9.4% reduction in the rate of increase in cost per admission.
(Robinson and Casalino, 1996)	1983—1993	Hospitals in California	Spending growth per admission was 44% lower in markets with high HMO penetration compared with markets with low HMO penetration, largely because of reductions in the volume and mix of services.
(Robinson and Luft, 1988)	1982—1986	Hospitals	All payer rate regulation reduced cost between 6.3 and 16.3%. California's market-oriented strategy reduced costs by 10.1%.
(Gaskin and Hadley, 1997)	1985—1993	Hospitals	Spending growth in hospitals in areas with high rates of HMO penetration was slower than in areas with low HMO penetration (8.3% vs. 11.2%).
(Melnick et al., 1989a and b)	1980—1987	Hospitals in California	Hospital revenue growth in competitive markets was similar to that in non-competitive markets prior to selective contracting, but lower after selective contracting.
(Zwanziger et al., 1994a)	1982—1988	Hospitals in California	Hospitals in the most competitive markets had a 17% lower increase in inflation-adjusted expenses relative to hospitals in the least competitive markets. These reductions in expense growth were not concentrated in particular cost or revenue centers.

(Continued)

Table 1.6 (Continued)

Study	Study Period	Main Unit of Observation	Primary Findings
(Zwanziger et al., 1994b)	1975–1990	Hospitals in California	Prior to selective contracting, costs in highly competitive areas were 17% higher than those in less competitive markets. By 1990, after selective contracting, the gap narrowed to 4%.
(Melnick and Zwanziger, 1995)	1980–1991	Statewide and national data on hospital, physician, and pharmaceutical expenditures	Inflation-adjusted expenditures in California for hospital, physician, and pharmaceuticals grew by 27, 58, and 41%, respectively, over the study period. Comparable national figures were 54, 82, and 65%.
(Zwanziger and Melnick, 1988)	1980–1995	Hospitals in California	The introduction of selective contracting reduced the magnitude of the positive relationship between hospital competition and hospital costs.
(Melnick and Zwanziger, 1988)	1980–1985	Hospitals in California	Between 1983 and 1985 inflation-adjusted inpatient costs in highly competitive markets decreased by 11.3% compared with a less than 1% increase in less competitive markets.
(Melnick et al., 1989a and b)	1977–1986	Hospitals	Hospital expenses as a percentage of per capita income fell in California between 1982 and 1986. Most of the decline, and most of the divergence in the trend between California and the United States, is attributable to the 1982–1983 period. California and the United States had similar trends from 1984 through 1986.
(Wickizer and Feldstein, 1995)	1985–1992	Insured employee groups	A 25% increase in market-level HMO penetration would result in a 16% decline in premium growth.

(Continued)

Table 1.6 (Continued)

Study	Study Period	Main Unit of Observation	Primary Findings
(Hill, and Wolfe, 1997)	1981–1994	Health plans offered to state employees in Madison, Wisconsin	Lower premium growth occurred in the first two years following a rapid transition for managed care and the rate of increase returned to national trends.
(Cutler and Sheiner, 1998)	1988–1993, 1980–1993	Physician, prescription, and drug expenditures	Between 1988 and 1993, every 10 percentage point increase in average HMO penetration resulted in a 0.5% reduction in hospital spending growth and a 0.4% reduction in overall spending growth. From 1980 to 1993, increases in physician and prescription drug spending growth mostly offset the reduction in hospital spending growth.

Source: Chernew et al. (1998).

penetration rose from 17 percent in 1980 to 26 percent in 1987 (Melnick et al., 1989a and b).

The central findings from these studies were that hospital cost and revenue growth slowed markedly following the introduction of selective contracting and that the effects were stronger in more competitive markets. This latter result supports the interpretation that attributes the changes in cost trends to the spread of managed care and specifically the increase in demand elasticities that providers faced as a result of managed care plans' networks. Because selective contracting affected a wide spectrum of managed care plans, the definition of managed care in these studies is broader than that employed by the earlier studies that focused on HMOs, especially staff and group model HMOs. The earlier studies, in fact, tended to emphasize effects of organization of the delivery system, especially integration of care, rather than price competition. (And, as noted above, the early HMOs often did not compete on premium with fee-for-service providers.) Also many of the studies examine relatively short time periods, so at least a portion of the difference they measure could be a once-and-for-all change in the level of spending, for example a possible reduction in rents in provider markets.

The studies that focus on the experience of hospitals also do not measure expenditures from the health system's perspective for two reasons. First, from the health system's perspective, expenditures by payers, including the patient, are the relevant variable as opposed to costs incurred by the providers. However, if HMOs decrease the margin between price and cost for health care services, as suggested by other studies, the effects on system expenditures would be even greater than those reported. Second, these studies obviously do not capture expenditures on non-hospital-based health care services, an important, and growing, component of overall spending.

Several studies, however, used a broader perspective to measure the impact of managed care on costs and reached similar conclusions. Melnick and Zwanziger (1995) compared growth in expenditures on hospitals, physicians, and pharmaceuticals in a state with high managed care penetration, California, with that in the nation as a whole and also with that in several states with low managed care penetration that relied on regulation to control health care costs. Their study period was considerably longer than that of Robinson and Luft, extending from 1980 to 1991 (Robinson and Luft, 1988). They reported that the lower growth in hospital expenditures in California was accompanied by lower growth in physician and pharmaceutical spending categories, but that the reductions in spending growth for these services were less than the reductions in hospital spending growth.

Cutler and Sheiner (1998) employed a similarly broad approach, exploring the relationship between cross-state average HMO penetration and total physician, prescription drug, and hospital spending growth. They estimated that every 10 percentage point increase in average HMO penetration from 1988 to 1993 resulted in a 0.5 percent reduction in hospital spending growth, but also an increase in spending growth for physician services which partially offset the reduction in hospital spending growth, leading to a 0.4 percent reduction in overall spending growth. They found an even stronger offset from 1980 to 1993, with increases in physician and prescription drug spending growth mostly offsetting the reduction in hospital spending growth.

Using data from employment groups between 1985 and 1992, Wickizer and Feldstein (1995) estimated the impact of market-level HMO penetration on premium growth. Employing multivariate regression, they reported that a 25 percent increase in HMO market share reduced inflation-adjusted premium growth by 16 percent.

The one exception to the set of findings from market comparison studies is based on an analysis of state employees in Madison, Wisconsin, after the state encouraged enrollment in HMOs (Hill and Wolfe, 1997). Despite examining only one employer in the market, the size of this employer relative to the market suggests that this work is best included with the market comparison studies. The results indicated that premium growth rates (for all types of coverage) fell for the first two years following the

transition to managed care but then returned to a trend similar to the national experience. The findings from Madison are significant because the transition to managed
care was very rapid. Prior to the state initiative only 8 percent of state employees were
enrolled in HMOs. Two years later, the enrollment rate in HMOs was 85 percent, a
much greater penetration rate than that observed in the other market comparison
studies. As noted below, this finding is consistent with the US cost trends in the
1990s, which showed a marked slowing of growth in mid-decade, followed by a
resumption of growth at roughly the historical rate, suggesting that much of the effect
of the increase in managed care was a once-and-for-all reduction in the level of
spending, though some of the rapid increase could be a one-time reversion to a higher
level. This illustrates the difficulty in disentangling multiple shifts in the level of
spending from changes in the underlying steady-state trajectory.

The studies by Robinson (1991) and Ginsburg and Pickreign (1996) bridge the
gap between the studies that follow the horse race approach comparing growth rates
under two types of payment regimes and those that are based on market comparisons.
Robinson (1991) related spending growth at the hospital level to both market-level
HMO penetration and the share of HMO patients in the hospital. The market-level
HMO penetration influenced spending growth, but spending growth was not related
to the share of hospital patients in an HMO.

Ginsburg and Pickreign's (1996) work is basically a horse race study and as
such found similar rates of spending growth in different systems using data from
Hay/Huggins' surveys of employers. However, their work found a general reduction in the rate of spending growth over time as managed care penetration grew,
suggesting a potential market-level effect of HMO penetration.

In most studies the estimated reduction in health care spending growth was insufficient to bring that growth in line with the general rate of inflation. Melnick and
Zwanziger (1995) reported a 3 percent per capita annual increase in health care spending above the rate of inflation in California (a market with high managed care penetration). Cutler and McClellan (1996) reported a similar rise in inflation-adjusted
expenditures for treatment of heart attacks. Ginsburg and Pickreign (1996) and
Robinson and Casalino (1996) also reported a real increase in health care expenditures
in markets with high HMO penetration.

Moreover, the magnitude of spending growth in the most comprehensive of these
studies (those including more than just hospital expenses) suggests that the increases in
expenditures not only exceed the inflation rate but have also outpaced growth in the
gross domestic product (GDP), even in markets with high managed care penetration.
For example, the 2.2 percent per capita annual real expenditure growth reported by
Melnick and Zwanziger (1995) compares with a national growth in real per capita
GDP of 1.9 percent from 1980 to 1991 (Bureau of Economic Analysis, 2011).

These studies may underestimate the underlying trend in health care spending growth because they incorporate savings from reductions in inefficiencies and movement toward competitive pricing that are one-time savings. In particular, the slowdown in the growth of total health care spending in the mid-1990s is widely attributed to managed care. Although the attribution may be correct, the spread of managed care most likely led to a more price competitive provider market, thereby lowering unit prices. There is little support in simple time trends of US health care spending that managed care much affected the steady-state spending growth. Indeed, spending growth relative to GDP growth accelerated in the first decade of the 21st century (Table 1.1). Moreover, the pressure on prices from HMOs generated consolidation of providers in some markets, suggesting further price reductions would be difficult to achieve.

Wickizer and Feldstein (1995) report an inflation-adjusted growth rate of 5.5 percent per year for premiums in markets with high HMO penetration. This is well above per capita GDP growth during the study period, although some of the growth may have been attributable to less healthy patients enrolling as enrollment grew. In the Hill and Wolfe study of state employees in Wisconsin, however, HMO penetration by 1985 was 85 percent (Hill and Wolfe, 1997), and they nonetheless reported nominal premium growth of 8.2 percent between 1985 and 1989 and 12.6 percent between 1989 and 1993. Nominal growth in per capita Wisconsin state product during the years 1985 to 1992 was less than 5 percent per year. Collectively, these studies suggest that the success of managed care, although potentially an improvement over the traditional indemnity FFS system with respect to spending growth, is not enough to stabilize or reduce the share of GDP devoted to health care. We caution, however, that much technological innovation is valuable, so that stabilizing the level of spending at current levels is almost certainly not a desirable goal (Hall and Jones, 2007). Still, as we have emphasized, spending growth cannot continue to exceed GDP growth indefinitely.

In sum, the findings of the studies of market-wide impacts of managed care penetration support the conclusion that, when analyzed as head-to-head comparison, HMO expenditure growth matches that in other systems; yet, at the market level, higher HMO penetration reduces spending growth. Hence, if HMO penetration does lower spending growth, it appears to do so for non-HMOs as well. This suggests a spillover effect across systems, a finding supported by other studies (Baker, 1997; Baker and Shankarkumar, 1998; Chernew et al., 2008).

What might account for a spillover between HMO penetration and costs in less-managed delivery systems? Several possibilities exist. First, physicians and hospitals may tend to treat all patients similarly, or at least all commercially insured patients similarly. Hence, some HMO-induced changes in practice patterns, such as reductions in length of hospital stay, may spill over into FFS or weakly managed systems. In fact,

Robinson and Casalino (1996) estimate that almost two-thirds of the reduction in spending growth attributable to HMO penetration resulted from reductions in admissions and length of stay, behaviors that may be influenced by changes in practice style related to the HMO penetration (Baker, 1997; Baker and Shankarkumar, 1998; Chernew et al., 2008).

Second, as HMO penetration grows, FFS or weakly managed plans may be able to extract some of the same price concessions that more strongly managed plans realize. Perhaps the mechanism by which this occurs is through cost reductions that affect inputs common to all payers. Yet, realization of substantial reductions in prices will require FFS or weakly managed plans to negotiate strongly with providers, perhaps more strongly than their organizational form will permit. The existence of this type of spillover would imply that price concessions achieved by managed care plans do not result in a shifting of costs to other payers.

Finally, the spillover may exist because managed care plans, particularly HMOs, cause a change in the health care infrastructure (i.e. the resources available to deliver care). Considerable evidence suggests that HMO penetration does influence infrastructure (Chernew, 1995; Robinson and Casalino, 1996; Hill and Wolfe, 1997). The work of Robinson and Casalino (1996) suggests that this accounts for a relatively small part of the reduction in spending growth, but work by Cutler and McClellan reviewed in more detail below attributes the HMO effect largely to HMO-induced infrastructure changes (Cutler and McClellan, 1996). Evidence of the impact of the introduction of Medicare is consistent with an infrastructure effect. Finkelstein estimates that the introduction of Medicare was associated with a 37 percent increase in hospital expenditures, due to both higher spending at existing hospitals and new hospital entry, suggesting that the introduction of Medicare was associated with fixed cost investments that likely spilled over to all payers in the market. Nonetheless, given the growth of health care spending relative to GDP in the 2000s, it is a fair question whether the spillovers are quantitatively important.

5.3. Spending Growth by Disease/Health Status

Spending growth is not uniform across diseases. For example, Frank and Glied (2006) find that the growth in overall health expenditure outpaced the growth of mental health expenditure almost two-fold from 1971 to 2001. Similarly, Thorpe et al. (2004b) report that between 1987 and 2000 spending per treated case for cerebrovascular disease rose about 20 percent, while cost per treated cancer rose about 40 percent and cost per treated case of heart disease rose almost 70 percent. Thorpe et al. (2004b) decompose spending growth into three parts: population growth, an increase in disease prevalence, and an increase in spending per case. Population growth accounts for between a fifth and two-fifths of the growth in spending for the top 15 (of 259) conditions. In some conditions the increase in spending is due predominantly to an increase in treated prevalence, 60 percent in the case of cerebrovascular disease. In other diseases such as heart disease, rising spending is largely due to a rise in cost per treated case (69 percent).

In a similar analysis of Medicare beneficiaries, Thorpe and Howard (2006) report that Medicare spending growth is dominated by those with five or more medical conditions. Yet much of this growth is due to a rise in the prevalence of beneficiaries with five or more conditions, which rose from 31 percent in 1987 to over 50 percent in 2002. Moreover, the self-reported health status of beneficiaries with five or more treated conditions appears to have improved dramatically; whereas 33 percent reported they were in excellent health in 1987, 60 percent did so in 2002. This may reflect better treatment of their conditions, but it likely also reflects increased propensity to diagnose and treat different conditions, suggesting the health status of the incrementally treated patients is better, driving up the average health status in the more heavily treated group.

The increase in treated prevalence is consistent with the explanation that technology drives spending growth because introduction of new medications over the period encourages treatment. Moreover, new knowledge about the value of treatment also increases the likelihood of being treated. For example, in 1997 the Joint National Committee on Prevention, Detection, Evaluation and Treatment of High Blood Pressure expanded its treatment recommendation of hypertension to include a subset of patients with systolic blood pressure of 140 mm Hg or more from the previous level of 160 mm Hg or more (National Heart, Lung and Blood Institute, 1997).

Some evidence suggests that the rise in obesity has driven spending growth (Thorpe et al., 2004a). Yet this largely reflects an increase in cost in diseases associated with obesity as opposed to the effects of a simple shift in distribution of the population across disease categories. For example, from 1987 to 2001 nominal per capita spending for the obese rose 3.6 percent per year compared with 2.3 percent per year among those with normal weight. This likely reflects new technologies (including drugs) developed for treating obesity-associated diseases. If one holds spending by weight category constant at 1987 levels and simply reweights spending by the 2001 weight distribution, one finds that spending growth due solely to the change in weight distribution was less than 1 percent per year over the entire period 1987–2001.

Finally, although the evidence suggests that the majority of spending at a point in time is concentrated among beneficiaries with poor health status, especially those who require hospital inpatient services, who have multiple chronic conditions, or who are in the last year of life, the relationship between disease burden and spending *growth* is not concentrated among the sickest. Analyses of the distribution of spending in different years suggest the proportion of spending attributed to low health status/high cost beneficiaries has in fact decreased over time. For example, the costliest 5 percent of beneficiaries accounted for 54 percent of total spending in 1975, but only 43 percent of total spending in 2002. These findings suggest treatment intensity (and spending) has increased more rapidly for patients with less disease burden (Medicare Payment Advisory Commission, 2009). This conclusion is also supported by Chernew et al., who report that spending among Medicare beneficiaries rose more rapidly for those with less disability (Chernew et al., 2005a).

6. VALUE OF SPENDING GROWTH

Because technology has been identified as a primary driver of long-run spending growth, it is reasonable to expect that we would receive clinical benefits associated with the higher spending. As alluded to in the introduction, empirical evidence supports this view. For example, Cutler et al. (2006) use life expectancy data from 1960 to 2000 to assess costs per year of life gained assuming, based on the literature, that 50 percent of gains were due to medical care. They find that the average cost per year of life gained during this period was $19,900 at birth, $31,600 at 15 years of age, $53,700 at 45 years of age, and $84,700 at 65 years of age, with costs growing faster than life expectancy for the latter group. With the exception of spending on the elderly, they conclude that the spending growth between 1960 and 2000 has provided reasonable value. Using a model that divides consumption into the categories of health and non-health, Hall and Jones (2007) conclude that the growth in health spending is a rational response to the growth of income per person.

Other studies have examined the relationship between spending growth and value for specific populations of patients. Cutler and Meara (2000) evaluated the benefits of increased spending for low-birth weight infants from 1950 to 1990, during which time there was a $40,000 increase in per birth spending. They concluded that this spending growth was very valuable, estimating a rate of return for care of low-birth-weight infants of over 500 percent. Cutler and McClellan (2001) reported on a series of studies that compared the costs and benefits of medical technologies for specific diseases/patient groups, namely heart attacks, low-birth-weight babies, depression, cataracts, and breast cancer. Assuming that a year of life is worth $100,000, they concluded that for all conditions analyzed with the exception of breast cancer, the added benefits of technology exceeded the costs of treatment. In the case of breast cancer, they concluded that the added benefits roughly equaled the costs. Eggleston et al. (2009, 2011), who studied several cohorts of diabetic Mayo Clinic employees, found real costs per patient went up over 4 percent per year between 1999 and 2009, but that the gains in averted premature mortality from improved control of risk factors somewhat outweighed the increased spending. Skinner et al. (2006) compared Medicare costs with survival gains for acute myocardial infarction (AMI) from 1986 to 2002. Although they concluded that the added spending on AMI was valuable (a $10,000 increase in the costs of treating heart attack was associated with a one-year increase in life expectancy), they noted that survival gains have stagnated since 1996. In addition to aggregate trends, they also examined the relationship within regions. They found a negative correlation between growth in spending for AMI treatment and survival gains across hospital referral regions, suggesting high-spending regions may provide unnecessary and wasteful care. In addition, a more recent report assessing the marginal returns for seven common diagnoses between 2000 and 2004 found that additional dollars purchase inconsistent value (Rothberg et al., 2010). From these studies one could conclude that on average increased health care spending is likely valuable, but at the margin higher spending is not.

7. CONCLUSION

One of the more remarkable transformations of developed economies over the past several decades has been the striking rise in the share of GDP devoted to health care. Clearly some, perhaps much, of this increased spending has been worthwhile. A commonly cited number is the increase in life expectancy, over 10 percent in the United States since 1970, about half of which has been attributed to medical advances (Ford et al., 2007). But much medical care has little to do with life expectancy and much more to do with quality of life (e.g. hip and knee replacements, cataract surgery). Although it seems clear that the United States has a large amount of inefficiencies in its delivery system at any point in time (Garber and Skinner, 2008), it is far less clear that the proportion of inefficiency has grown over time. It is an exaggeration, but probably not a large one, to say that over the past few decades commercially insured and most Medicare patients, who account for the bulk of health care spending in the United States, commonly received any medical advance that promised more than a *de minimis* benefit for them.

Although historical data do not indicate any persistent slowing in health care spending growth (Newhouse, 1992; Congressional Budget Office and Orszag, 2007), the rate of health care spending growth cannot exceed income growth indefinitely. If we can achieve efficiencies in the short run or if we are willing to devote more resources to health care, we can forestall the need to address the underlying question of technology-driven spending growth, perhaps for many years. But eventually we will need to develop a financing system that is sustainable in the long run. Such a system will inherently alter the process by which new innovation moves into medical practice.

It is unclear what this future financing system will or should look like; that is, what mix of regulatory and market forces will or should be used to slow spending growth. The answer will depend in part on the impact of different strategies on spending growth and their ability to preserve as much access to the most beneficial medical innovations as possible. The preferred strategy will also likely depend on preferences for different distributional outcomes regarding access to care and new innovations across all of society and hence may well differ in different countries. Much of the health economics literature has concentrated on the effect of various instruments and policy interventions on the level of spending. Assessing the impact of instruments and interventions on the steady-state rate of spending growth is thus a prime topic for future research.

REFERENCES

Acemoglu, D., Finkelstein, A., & Notowidigdo, M. J. (2009). Income and health spending: Evidence from oil price shocks. NBER Working Paper w14744.

Baicker, K. & Chandra, A. (2004). Medicare spending, the physician workforce, and beneficiaries' quality of care. *Health Affairs*, January–June (Web Exclusives): W4–184-197.

Baker, L. C. (1997). The effect of HMOs on fee-for-service health care expenditures: Evidence from medicare. *Journal of Health Economics*, *16*(1), 453–481.

Baker, L. C. & Shankarkumar, S. (1998). Managed care and health care expenditures: Evidence from Medicare, 1990–1994. *Forum for Health Economics & Policy*, 1 (Frontiers in Health Policy Research): Article 5.

Baumgardner, J. R. (1991). The interaction between forms of insurance contract and types of technical change in medical care. *RAND Journal of Economics*, *22*(1), 36–53.

Baumol, W. J. (1967). Macroeconomics of unbalanced growth: The anatomy of urban crisis. *American Economic Review*, *57*(3), 415–426.

Berndt, E. R., McGuire, T. G., & Newhouse, J. P. (2011). A primer on the economics of prescription pharmaceutical pricing in health insurance markets. NBER Working Paper 16879.

Bradley, T. B. & Kominski, G. F. (1992). Contributions of case mix and intensity change to hospital cost increases. *Health Care Financial Review*, *14*(2), 151–163.

Bundorf, M. K., Royalty, A., & Baker, L. C. (2009). Health care cost growth among the privately insured. *Health Affairs*, *28*(5), 1294–1304.

Bureau of Economic Analysis (2011). National economic accounts: Current-dollar and "real" gross domestic product. Retrieved February 9, 2011, from < http://www.bea.gov/national/index. htm#gdp/ > .

Bynum, J., Song, Y., & Fisher, E. (2010). Variation in prostate-specific antigen screening in men aged 80 and older in fee-for-service Medicare. *Journal of the American Geriatric Society*, *58*(4), 674–680.

Centers for Medicare & Medicaid Services (2011a). 2011 Annual Report of the Boards of Trustees of the Federal Hospital Insurance and Federal Supplementary Medical Insurance Trust Funds. Retrieved June 3, 2011, from < https://www.cms.gov/ReportsTrustFunds/downloads/tr2011.pdf/ > .

Centers for Medicare & Medicaid Services (2011b). National Health Expenditure Data. Retrieved April 25, 2010, from < http://www1.cms.gov/NationalHealthExpendData/07_NHEA_Related_Studies. asp#TopOfPagedownloads/tables.pdf/ > .

Centers for Medicare & Medicaid Services and Department of Health and Human Services (2010). Projected Medicare Expenditures under an Illustrative Scenario with Alternative Payment Updates to Medicare Providers. Retrieved October, 2010, from < http://www.cms.gov/ActuarialStudies/ Downloads/2010TRAlternativeScenario.pdf/ > .

Chandra, A., Gruber, J., & McKnight, R. (2010). Patient cost-sharing and hospitalization offsets in the elderly. *American Economic Review, 100*(1), 193–213.

Chernew, M. E. (1995). The impact of non-IPA HMOs on the number of hospitals and capacity. *Inquiry, 32*(2), 143–154.

Chernew, M. E., Cutler, D. M., & Kennan, P. S. (2005b). Increasing health insurance costs and the decline in insurance coverage. *Health Services Research, 40*(4), 1021–1039.

Chernew, M. E., DeCicca, P., & Robert, T. (2008). Managed care and medical expenditures of Medicare beneficiaries. *Journal of Health Economics, 27*(6), 1451–1461.

Chernew, M. E., Fendrick, A. M., & Hirth, R. A. (1997). Managed care and medical technology: Implications for cost growth. *Health Affairs, 16*(2), 196–206.

Chernew, M. E., Goldman, D. P., Pan, F., & Shang, B. (2005a). Disability and health care spending among Medicare beneficiaries. *Health Affairs, 24, Suppl. 2*, W5R242–52.

Chernew, M. E., Hirth, R. A., & Cutler, D. M. (2009a). Increased spending on health care: Long-term implications for the nation. *Health Affairs, 28*(5), 1253–1255.

Chernew, M. E., Hirth, R. A., Sonnad, A. A., Ermann, R., & Fendrick, A. M. (1998). Managed care, medical technology, and health care cost growth: A review of the evidence. *Medical Care Research and Review, 55*(3), 259–288.

Chernew, M. E., Sabik, L., Chandra, A., & Newhouse, J. P. (2009b). Would having more primary care doctors cut health spending growth? *Health Affairs, 28*(5), 1327–1335.

Chernew, M. E., Sabik, L., Chandra, A., & Newhouse, J. P. (2010). Ensuring the fiscal sustainability of health care reform. *New England Journal of Medicine, 362*(1), 1–3.

Cohen, J. T., Neumann, P. J., & Weinstein, M. C. (2008). Does preventive care save money? Health economics and the presidential candidates. *The New England Journal of Medicine, 358*(7), 661–663.

Congressional Budget Office (2007). Testimony: Statement of Peter R. Orszag before the Committee on the Budget. *Health Care and the Budget: Issues and Challenges for Reform.*

Congressional Budget Office & Orszag, P. R. (2007). Financing projected spending in the long run. Retrieved October 12, 2010, from < http://www.cbo.gov/ftpdocs/82xx/doc8295/07–09-Financing_Spending.pdf/ > .

Cutler, D. M. (1995). Technology, Health Costs, and NIH. National Institutes of Health Roundtable on the Economics of Biomedical Research.

Cutler, D. M. (2004). *Your money or your life: Strong medicine for America's health care system.* New York, NY: Oxford University Press.

Cutler, D. M. & McClellan, M. (1996). The determinants of technological change in heart attack treatment. NBER Working Paper 5751.

Cutler, D. M. & McClellan, M. (2001). Is technological change in medicine worth it? *Health Affairs, 20*(5), 11–29.

Cutler, D. M. & Meara, E. (2000). The technology of birth: Is it worth it? *Forum for Health Economics & Policy* 3 (Frontiers in Health Policy Research): Article 3.

Cutler, D. M. & Sheiner, L. (1998). Demographics and medical care spending: Standard and non-standard effects. NBER Working Paper 6866.

Cutler, D. M., Rosen, A. B., & Vijan, S. (2006). The value of medical spending in the United States, 1960–2000. *The New England Journal of Medicine, 355*(9), 920–927.

DeMeza, D. (1983). Health insurance and the demand for medical care. *Journal of Health Economics, 21*(1), 47–54.

Di Matteo, L. (2005). The macro determinants of health expenditure in the United States and Canada: Assessing the impact of income, age distribution and time. *Health Policy, 71*(1), 23–42.

Eggleston, K. N., Shah, N. D., Smith, S., Berndt, E. R., & Newhouse, J. P. (2011). Quality adjustment for healthcare spending on chronic disease: Evidence from diabetes treatment, 1999–2009. *American Economic Review, 101*(2), 206–211.

Eggleston, K. N., Shah, N. D., Smith, S. A., Wagie, A. E., Williams, A. R., Grossman, J. H., et al. (2009). Assessing the productivity of diabetes treatment, 1997–2005. *Annals of Internal Medicine, 151*(6), 386–393.

Fendrick, A. M., Chernew, M. E., Hirth, R., & Menonq, D. (1996). Understanding the behavioral response to medical innovation. *American Journal of Managed Care, 2*(7), 793–799.

Finkelstein, A. (2007). The aggregate effects of health insurance: Evidence from the introduction of Medicare. *Quarterly Journal of Economics, 122*(2), 1–37.

Fisher, E. S., Wennberg, D. E., Stukel, T. A., Gottlieb, D. J., Lucas, F. L., & Pinder, E. L. (2003a). The implications of regional variations in Medicare spending. Part 1: The content, quality, and accessibility of care. *Annals of Internal Medicine, 138,* 273–287.

Fisher, E. S., Wennberg, D. E., Stukel, T. A., Gottlieb, D. J., Lucas, F. L., & Pinder, E. L. (2003b). The implications of regional variations in Medicare spending. Part 2: Health outcomes and satisfaction with care. *Annals of Internal Medicine, 138,* 288–298.

Ford, E. S., Ajani, U. A., Croft, J. B., Critchley, J. A., Labarthe, D. R., Kottke, T. E., et al. (2007). Explaining the decrease in U.S. deaths from coronary disease, 1980–2000. *New England Journal of Medicine, 356*(23), 2388–2398.

Frank, R.G. & Glied, S. (2006). Changes in mental health financing since 1971: Implications for policy makers and patients. *Health Affairs, 25*(3), 601–613.

Frogner, B. K. (2010). The missing technology: An international comparison of human capital investment in healthcare. *Applied Health Economics and Health Policy, 8*(6), 361–371.

Fuchs, V. R. (1996). Economics, values, and health care reform. *American Economic Review, 86*(1), 1–24.

Fuchs, V. R. (1999). Health care for the elderly: How much? Who will pay for it? *Health Affairs, 18*(1), 11–21.

Garber, A. M. & Skinner, J. (2008). Is American health care uniquely inefficient? *Journal of Economic Perspectives, 22*(4), 27–50.

Garber, A. M., Jones, C. I., & Romer, P. (2006). Insurance and incentives for medical innovation. *Forum for Health Economics & Policy, 9*(2) (Article 4).

Gaskin, D. J. & Hadley, J. (1997). The impact of HMO penetration on the rate of hospital cost inflation, 1985–1993. *Inquiry, 34*(3), 205–216.

Gerdtham, U. G. & Jonsson, B. (2000). International comparisons of health expenditure: Theory, data and econometric analysis. In A. J. Culyer & J. P. Newhouse (Eds.), *Handbook of health economics.* Amsterdam: North-Holland/Elsevier.

Ginsburg, P. B. & Pickreign, J. D. (1997). Tracking health care costs: An update. *Health Affairs, 16*(4), 151–155.

Ginsburg, P. B. & Pickreign, J. D. (1996). Tracking health care costs. *Health Affairs, 15*(3), 140–149.

Glied, S. A. (2000). Managed care. In A. J. Culyer & J. P. Newhouse (Eds.), *Handbook of health economics.* Amsterdam: North-Holland.

Goddeeris, J. H. (1984a). Medical insurance, technological change, and welfare. *Economic Inquiry, 22*(1), 56–57.

Goddeeris, J. H. (1984b). Insurance and incentives for innovation in medical care. *Southern Economic Journal, 51*(2), 530–539.

Gottlieb, D. J., Zhou, W., Song, Y., Andrews, K. G., Skinner, J. S., & Sutherland, J. M. (2010). Prices don't drive regional Medicare spending variations. *Health Affairs, 29*(3), 537–543.

Guadagnoli, E., Hauptman, P. J., Ayanian, J. Z., Pashos, C. L., McNeil, B. J., & Cleary, P. D. (1995). Variation in the use of cardiac procedures after acute myocardial infarction. *New England Journal of Medicine, 333*(9), 573–578.

Hall, R. E. & Jones, C. I. (2007). The value of life and the rise in health spending. *Quarterly Journal of Economics, 122*(1), 39–72.

Herring, B. (2005). The effect of the availability of charity care to the uninsured on the demand for private health insurance. *Journal of Health Economics, 24*(2), 225–252.

Hill, S. C. & Wolfe, B. L. (1997). Testing the HMO competitive strategy: An analysis of its impact on medical resources. *Journal of Health Economics, 16*(3), 261–286.

Holahan, J., Dor, A., & Zuckerman, S. (1990). Understanding the recent growth in Medicare physician expenditures. *JAMA, 263*(12), 1658–1661.

Honore, B. E. & Lleras-Muney, A. (2006). Bounds in competing risks models and the war on cancer. *Econometrica, 74*(6), 1675–1698.

Katz, S. J., Welch, W. P., & Verrilli, D. (1997). The growth of physician services for the elderly in the United States and Canada: 1987—1992. *Medical Care Research and Review, 54*(3), 301—320.

Kronick, R. & Gilmer, T. (1999). Explaining the decline in health insurance coverage, 1979—1995. *Health Affairs, 18*(2), 30—47.

Lee, D. W. (1992). Estimating the effect of new technology on Medicare Part B expenditure and volume growth: Do related procedures matter? *Advances in Health Economics and Health Services Research, 13*, 43—64.

Legorreta, A. P., Silber, J. H., Costantino, G. N., Kobylinski, R. W., & Zatz, S. L. (1993). Increased cholecystectomy rate after the introduction of laparoscopic cholecystectomy. *JAMA, 270*(12), 1429—1432.

Luft, H. S. (1980). Trends in medical care costs. Do HMOs lower the rate of growth? *Medical Care, 18*(1), 1—16.

Lu-Yao, G. L., McLerran, D., Wasson, J., & Wennberg, J. E. (1993). The Prostate Patient Outcomes Research Team. An assessment of radical prostatectomy. *JAMA, 269*(1), 2633—2636.

Manning, W. G., Newhouse, J. P., Duan, N., Keeler, E. B., Leibowitz, A., & Marquis, M. S. (1987). Health insurance and the demand for medical care: Evidence from a randomized experiment. *American Economic Review, 77*(3), 251—277.

Mas, N. & Seinfeld, J. (2008). Is managed care restraining the adoption of technology by hospitals? *Journal of Health Economics, 27*(4), 1026—1045.

McClellan, M., McNeil, B. J., & Newhouse, J. P. (1994). Does more intensive treatment of acute myocardial infarction reduce mortality? *JAMA, 272*(11), 859—866.

Medicare Payment Advisory Commission (2009). Reforming the health care delivery system. Statement of Glenn M. Hackbarth before the Committee on Energy and Commerce, US House of Representatives. Retrieved October, 2010, from < http://energycommerce.house.gov/Press_111/20090310/testimony_hackbarth.pdf/ > .

Melnick, G. A. & Zwanziger, J. (1988). Hospital behavior under competition and cost-containment policies. The California experience, 1980 to 1985. *JAMA, 260*(18), 2669—2675.

Melnick, G. A. & Zwanziger, J. (1995). State health care expenditures under competition and regulation, 1980 through 1991. *American Journal of Public Health, 85*(10), 1391—1396.

Melnick, G. A. Zwanziger, J., & Bradley, T. (1989a). Competition and cost containment in California: 1980—1987. *Health Affairs, 8*(2), 129—136.

Melnick, G. A., Zwanziger, J., & Verity-Guerra, A. (1989b). The growth and effects of hospital selective contracting. *Health Care Management Review, 14*(3), 57—64.

National Heart, Lung, and Blood Institute (1997). The sixth report of the Joint National Committee on prevention, detection, evaluation and treatment of high blood pressure. *Archives of Internal Medicine, 157*(21), 2413—2446.

Newhouse, J. P. (1981). The erosion of the medical marketplace. In R. Scheffler (Ed.), *Advances in health economics and health services research* (Vol. 2). Westport, CT: JAI Press.

Newhouse, J. P. (1988). Has the erosion of the medical marketplace ended? *Journal of Health Politics Policy and Law, 13*(2), 263—268.

Newhouse, J. P. (1992). Medical care costs: How much welfare loss? *Journal of Economic Perspectives, 6*(3), 3—21.

Newhouse, J. P. (1993a). *Free for all? Lessons from the RAND health insurance experiment.* Cambridge, MA: Harvard University Press.

Newhouse, J. P. (1993b). An iconoclastic view of health cost containment. *Health Affairs, 12*(Suppl), 152—171.

Newhouse, J. P. (1998). UK and US health economics: Two disciplines separated by a common language? *Health Economics, 7*(Suppl. 1), S79—S92.

Newhouse, J. P., Schwartz, W. B., Williams, A. P., & Witsberger, C. (1985). Are fee-for-service costs increasing faster than HMO costs? *Medical Care, 23*(8), 960—966.

Okunade, A. A. & Murthy, V. N. R. (2002). Technology as a "major driver" of health care costs: A cointegration analysis of the Newhouse conjecture. *Journal of Health Economics, 21*(1), 147—159.

Organization for Economic Co-Operation and Development (OECD) (2009). Health Data 2009—comparing health statistics across OECD countries. Retrieved October, 2010, from <http://www.oecd.org/document/54/0,3343,en_2649_201185_43220022_1_1_1_1,00.html/>.

Pauly, M. V. & Ramsey, S. D. (1999). Would you like suspenders to go with that belt? An analysis of optimal combinations of cost sharing and managed care. *Journal of Health Economics*, *18*(1), 443–458.

Peden, E. A. & Freeland, M. S. (1995). A historical analysis of medical spending growth, 1960–1993. *Health Affairs*, *14*(2), 235–247.

Peden, E. A. & Freeland, M. S. (1998). Insurance effects on US medical spending. *Health Economics*, 7, 671–687.

Phelps, C. E. (1976). The demand for reimbursement insurance. In R. Rosett (Ed.), *The role of health insurance in the health services sector*. Cambridge, MA: National Bureau of Economic Research.

Pilote, L., Califf, R. M., Sapp, S., Miller, D. P., Mark, D. B., Weaver, W. D., et al. (1995). GUSTO-1 investigators. Regional variation across the United States in the management of acute myocardial infarction. *New England Journal of Medicine*, *9*(333), 565–572.

Port, F. K. (1995). End-stage renal disease: Magnitude of the problem, prognosis of future trends and possible solutions. *Kidney International Supplement*, *50*, S3–S6.

Robinson, J. C. (1991). HMO market penetration and hospital cost inflation in California. *JAMA*, *266*(19), 2719–2723.

Robinson, J. C. & Casalino, L. P. (1996). Vertical integration and organizational networks in health care. *Health Affairs*, *15*(1), 7–22.

Robinson, J. C. & Luft, H. S. (1988). Competition, regulation, and hospital costs, 1982 to 1986. *JAMA*, *260*(18), 2676–2681.

Rothberg, M. B., Cohen, J., Lindenauer, P., Maselli, J., & Auerbach, A. (2010). Little evidence of correlation between growth in health care spending and reduced mortality. *Health Affairs*, *29*(8), 1523–1531.

Schwartz, W. B. (1987). The inevitable failure of current cost-containment strategies. *JAMA*, *257*(2), 220–224.

Scitovsky, A. A. (1985). Changes in the costs of treatment of selected illnesses, 1971–1981. *Medical Care*, *23*(12), 1345–1357.

Scitovsky, A. A. & McCall, N. (1976). *Changes in treatment costs for selected illnesses, 1951–1964–1971*. Washington, DC: US Department of Health Education and Welfare, National Center for Health Services Research.

Sepulveda, M.-J., Bodenheimer, T., & Grundy, P. (2008). Primary care: Can it solve employers' health care dilemma? *Health Affairs*, *27*(1), 151–158.

Showstack, J. A., Schroeder, S. A., & Matsumoto, M. (1982). Changes in the use of medical technologies, 1972–1977—a study of 10 inpatient diagnoses. *New England Journal of Medicine*, *306*(12), 706–712.

Sisko, A. M., Truffer, C. J., Keehan, S. P., Poisal, J. A., Clemens, M. K., & Madison, A. J. (2010). National health spending projections: The estimated impact of reform through 2019. *Health Affairs*, *29*(10), 1–9.

Skinner, J. S. & Fisher, E. S. (1997). Regional disparities in Medicare expenditures: An opportunity for reform. *National Tax Journal*, *50*, 413–425.

Skinner, J. S., Staiger, D. O., & Fisher, E. S. (2006). Is technological change in medicine always worth it? The case of acute myocardial infarction. *Health Affairs*, *25*(2), w34–w47.

Smith, S. D., Newhouse, J. P., & Freeland, M. S. (2009). Income, insurance, and technology: Why does health spending outpace economic growth? *Health Affairs*, *28*(5), 1276–1284.

Solow, R. M. (1957). Technical change and the aggregate production function. *Review of Economics and Statistics*, *39*(3), 312–320.

Song, Y, Skinner, J., Bynum, J., Sutherland, J., Wennberg, J. E., & Fisher, E. S. (2010). Regional variations in diagnostic practices. *New England Journal of Medicine*, *363*(1), 45–53.

Starfield, B., Shi, L., & Macinko, J. (2005). Contribution of primary care to health systems and health. *Milbank Quarterly*, *83*(3), 457–502.

Steiner, C. A., Bass, E. B., Talamini, M. A., Pitt, H. A., & Steinberg, E. P. (1994). Surgical rates and operative mortality for open and laparoscopic cholecystectomy in Maryland. *New England Journal of Medicine, 330*(6), 403–408.

Thorpe, K. E. & Howard, D. H. (2006). The rise in spending among Medicare beneficiaries: The role of chronic disease prevalence and changes in treatment intensity. *Health Affairs, 25,* w378–w388.

Thorpe, K. E., Florence, C. S., & Joski, P. (2004b). Which medical conditions account for the rise in health care spending? *Health Affairs, W4,* 437–445.

Thorpe, K. E., Florence, C. S., Howard, D. H., & Joski, P. (2004a). The impact of obesity on rising medical spending. *Health Affairs, 23*(Suppl.), Web Exclusives (W4-480-6).

Tu, J. V., Pashos, C. L., Naylor, C. D., Chen, E., Normand, S. L., Newhouse, J. P., et al. (1997). Use of cardiac procedures and outcomes in elderly patients with myocardial infarction in the United States and Canada. *New England Journal of Medicine, 336*(21), 1500–1505.

Weinstein, J. N., Lurie, J. D., Olson, P. R., Bronner, K. K., & Fisher, E. S. (2006). United States' trends and regional variation in lumbar surgery: 1992–2003. *Health Service Research Journal, 31*(23), 2707–2714.

Weisbrod, B. A. (1991). The health care quadrilemma: An essay on technological change, insurance, quality of care, and cost containment. *Journal of Economic Literature, 29*(3), 523–552.

Wennberg, J. E., Fisher, E. S., & Skinner, J. S. (2002). Geography and the debate over Medicare reform. *Health Affairs, 21*(Suppl.) (Web Exclusive): W96–W114.

Wennberg, J. E., Kellett, M. A., Dickens, J. D., Malenka, D. J., Keilson, L. M., & Keller, R. B. (1996). The association between local diagnostic testing intensity and invasive cardiac procedures. *JAMA, 275*(15), 1161–1164.

Wickizer, T. M. & Feldstein, P. J. (1995). The impact of HMO competition on private health insurance premiums, 1985–1992. *Inquiry, 32*(3), 241–251.

Zwanziger, J. & Melnick, G. A. (1988). The effects of hospital competition and the Medicare PPS program on hospital cost behavior in California. *Journal of Health Economics, 7*(4), 301–320.

Zwanziger, J., Melnick, G. A., & Bamezai, A. (1994a). Costs and price competition in California hospitals, 1980–1990. *Health Affairs, 13*(4), 118–126.

Zwanziger, J., Melnick, G. A., Mann, J., & Simonson, L. (1994b). How hospitals practice cost containment with selective contracting and the Medicare Prospective Payment System. *Medical Care, 32*(11), 1153–1162.

CHAPTER TWO

Causes and Consequences of Regional Variations in Health Care[1]

Jonathan Skinner

Department of Economics, Dartmouth College, Hanover, NH, USA

Contents

Abstract

There are widespread differences in health care spending and utilization across regions of the US as well as in other countries. Are these variations caused by demand-side factors such as patient preferences, health status, income, or access? Or are they caused by supply-side factors such as provider financial incentives, beliefs, ability, or practice norms? In this chapter, I first consider regional health care differences in the context of a simple demand and supply model, and then focus on the empirical evidence documenting causes of variations. While demand factors are important—health in

[1] This chapter was written for the *Handbook of Health Economics* (Vol. 2). My greatest debt is to John E. Wennberg for introducing me to the study of regional variations. I am also grateful to Handbook authors Elliott Fisher, Joseph Newhouse, Douglas Staiger, Amitabh Chandra, and especially Mark Pauly for insightful comments, and to the National Institute on Aging (PO1 AG19783) for financial support.

Handbook of Health Economics, Volume 2
ISSN: 1574-0064, DOI: 10.1016/B978-0-444-53592-4.00002-5

particular—there remains strong evidence for supply-driven differences in utilization. I then consider evidence on the causal impact of spending on outcomes, and conclude that it is less important how much money is spent, and far more important *how* the money is spent—whether for highly effective treatments such as beta blockers or anti-retroviral treatments for AIDS patients, or ineffective treatments such as feeding tubes for advanced dementia patients.

Keywords: health economics; health care productivity; spatial models; regional variations; small-area analysis

JEL Codes: I100; I110; I120; I180; R120

1. INTRODUCTION

A recently published Atlas documented dramatic differences in the utilization of an important health input. Relative to the rates observed in the Boston area, utilization was 74 percent higher in New Haven and more than 200 percent higher in San Francisco.[2] One might explain differences in utilization by variations in income, health status, or prices, yet these factors do not appear to explain away the wide variations we observe. So why have these patterns—in per capita consumption of *meat and poultry*, ranging from 31 pounds in the Boston region to 113 pounds per capita in the San Francisco region—not received more attention from health experts or health economists?

In this chapter, I attempt to distinguish between the admittedly puzzling geographic variation in meat and poultry consumption and geographic variation in health care utilization. There are certainly many reasons why regional variations in utilization can be justified by underlying health status, preferences and income, or productivity differences among providers—surgical rates should be higher in regions where surgeons get better results (Chandra and Staiger, 2007). But there are also reasons why such variations might not be efficient. We know that specific components of the health care industry, such as the widespread use of insurance with modest co-payments, leads to the twin problems of moral hazard and adverse selection. And beginning with Arrow (1963), economists have argued that many of the unique features and institutions associated with medical care—ranging from not-for-profit ownership to licensure of providers to the structure of insurance—are best understood as the result of "uncertainty in the incidence of disease and in the efficacy of treatment" (Arrow, 1963, p. 941).

---

[2] http://maps.ers.usda.gov/FoodAtlas/

Health care is not the only sector of the economy with these characteristics—car repair, home construction, and management consultancies exhibit uncertainty about the efficacy of the fix, even if they are not typically insured to the same degree. While regional variations surely exist in the quality and cost of automotive repairs, it is less likely that the government would propose accountable car repair organizations, for example.

Regional variations in health care are different, for at least two reasons. First, assuming that the variation we observe is "unwarranted" in the sense that it cannot be explained by legitimate causes such as health status, the magnitude of variation is so large that the potential gain from erasing such inefficiencies—3 percent of GDP or more in the United States—is worth pursuing. And second, these inefficiencies are unlikely to be shaken out by normal competitive forces, given the patchwork of providers, consumers, and third-party payers each of which faces inadequate incentives to improve quality or lower costs (Fuchs and Milstein, 2011).

Following on the earlier survey by Charles Phelps in the Handbook (Phelps, 2000), this review considers five general questions in reflecting on the economics of regional variations in health care. First, what are the *theoretical* causes of such differences? Traditionally, the presence of regional variation in medical care utilization has been viewed through the lens of "supplier-induced demand," the idea that regional variations can be explained by the utility-maximizing behavior of health care providers responding to a fee-for-service environment and relative scarcity (or abundance) of providers (McGuire, 2011). The problem arises when individual physicians in two seemingly similar regions—with identical insurance mechanisms and similar patients—end up providing much different quantities of health care. That is, standard supplier-induced demand models may argue that physicians do more for their patients than is optimal, but does not typically explain why physicians in McAllen, TX, do so much more for their Medicare patients than those in El Paso (Gawande, 2009). To address these issues, I adopt a model based on Chandra and Skinner (2011) and Wennberg et al. (2002) to parse out both supply and demand factors that might be expected to explain regional variation in specific types of treatment, ranging from highly effective care that clearly saves lives at minimal cost (such as beta blockers for heart attack patients) to very expensive treatment without known benefits for patients (like proton beam therapy for prostate cancer).

Second, I use this basic framework to consider the empirical evidence on *causes* of geographic variation in health care utilization and expenditures. This is the key section to assess the evidence on whether supply-side variations really do exist. If all of the regional variation in observed utilization rates can be explained by other factors such as patient preferences, relative prices, income, and health, then the puzzle of regional variations is not even a puzzle any more. I focus in this chapter largely on

US regional variations, but document also a growing literature reflecting international variations both within and across countries.[3]

Third, what are the *consequences* of higher health care spending? Does more spending yield better outcomes—or is how the money spent more important for health? A key focus of this section is to understand how geography might be used as a statistical instrument in health economics to help estimate whether greater intensity of care is associated with better health outcomes. Starting with the early work by Glover (1938) and Wennberg and Gittelsohn (1973), and continuing through the more formal analysis using instrumental variables, there has been a long-standing tradition of using geography as an instrument to make inferences about the health care "production function"(Fisher et al., 2003b; McClellan et al., 1994). Some studies have suggested a negative association between spending and outcomes, while others have found a positive association, but what is most striking is how much variability there is in outcomes across providers or regions, and how poorly such variability is associated with factor inputs.

Fourth, what are the policy implications of observing variations in health care utilization? If there are enormous variations in the productivity of concrete, a seven–digit SIC code output with readily apparent quality measures (Syverson, 2004), is it any surprise that there are even greater disparities in the productivity of health care across regions or hospitals where outputs are difficult to measure and rarely made public? The sometimes slow diffusion of valuable and highly efficient medical innovations, as in Phelps (2000), has strong parallels with the slow diffusion of knowledge observed across countries (Eaton and Kortum, 1999; Skinner and Staiger, 2009), yet the practical challenges of how to "fix" such slow diffusion rates across regions (or countries) are still being debated.

Finally, while there are regional variations in health care utilization, there are also strong gradients across the US in health (Kulkarni et al., 2011), and the two appear only incidentally correlated (Fuchs, 1998). Explaining variations in health is perhaps even more important, and suggests a greater focus on factors other than medical care that may have a more direct impact on health, such as regional variation in the per capita consumption of beef and poultry.

2. AN ECONOMIC MODEL OF REGIONAL VARIATIONS IN HEALTH CARE

Economic models typically include a demand and supply side, and so I adopt a simple model from Chandra and Skinner (2011) to characterize each side of the market.

[3] For a useful bibliography of such studies, see WIC (2011).

2.1. The Demand Side

The demand side, based on Hall and Jones (2007) and Murphy and Topel (2006), is a simplified two-period model of consumption and leisure where the individual's perceived quality of life, $s(x)$, is in turn influenced by medical spending x:

$$V = U(C_1) + \frac{s(x)U(C_2)}{1+\delta} \qquad (2.1)$$

where C_i is consumption in period i, δ is the discount rate, and x measures health care inputs.

Assume the expected survival or quality of life function is concave, so that $s'(x) \geq 0$, $s'' < 0$. The Grossman model includes a variety of different approaches that individuals may improve their health "stock" but in this simplified model the demand for health is expressed solely through the demand for x (Grossman, 1972). Utility is maximized subject to the budget constraint:

$$Y_1 + \frac{Y_2}{1+r} - P = C_1 + px + \frac{C_2}{1+r} \qquad (2.2)$$

where Y_i is income or transfer payments in period i, p the consumer price of health care, P the premium (or tax) paid for insurance, and r is the interest rate. Assume that x is measured in units of what one dollar in real resources will purchase, meaning that the true or social cost (q) per unit of x is normalized to one, but where the patient pays p. (Thus if the coinsurance rate is 20 percent, $p = 0.2$.) This demand-side model is straightforward, even if the assumptions implicit in this model can sometimes be at odds with the empirical evidence.[4]

Maximizing the utility function (2.1) subject to (2.2), and rearranging yields the optimality condition:

$$\Psi = \frac{U(C_2)}{(1+\delta)\frac{\partial U}{\partial C_1}} = \frac{p}{s'(x)} \qquad (2.3)$$

Let Ψ be individual demand for an extra quality-adjusted year of survival, which could in theory vary across regions for a variety of reasons: higher income, for example, implies a lower marginal utility of first-period consumption and hence a much higher demand for health care. Differences in the curvature of the utility function

---

[4] For example, because demand is a function of the inverse of the marginal utility of first-period consumption, when the Arrow–Pratt risk aversion parameter is 3 (or the intertemporal elasticity of substitution is 1/3), doubling consumption increases demand and leads to 2^3 times the demand for health care (Murphy and Topel, 2006). As Hall and Jones explain, the marginal utility of a third flat-screen TV falls rapidly relative to the demand for the ultimate luxury good—health (Hall and Jones, 2007). Yet we do not typically observe such large income elasticities at a point in time.

(and hence risk aversion) and the time preference rate can further affect the trade-off between current consumption and future health.

2.2. The Supply Side

I assume that physicians seek to maximize the perceived value of health for their patient, given by $\Psi s(x)$, subject to financial considerations, resource capacity, ethical judgment, and patient demand (Chandra and Skinner, 2011). While there are dishonest physicians that belie this assumption, it is at least consistent with the majority of physician behavior. In this simple model, physicians act as price takers, but may still face a wide array of different prices paid by private insurance, Medicare, and Medicaid, for the identical procedure. This model therefore misses the complexity of markets in which hospital groups and physicians jointly determine quantity, quality, and price (Pauly, 1980).

Physicians also care about the income they make. For simplicity, let income be represented by $R + \pi x$, where R is the physician's salary and π measures the net revenue arising from the procedure (or more generally, the vector of different procedures) x. Note that the price paid by the patient, p, could be quite different from the profitability of the procedure, π, and that when the provider is paid less than marginal cost, then $\pi > 0$, but when the procedure is profitable, $\pi < 0$.

Thus the health care provider is assumed to maximize the sum $\Psi s(x) + \Omega(R + \pi x)$, where Ω is a function that captures the trade-off between the physician's desire to improve the value of patient survival and her own income. But the provider may still be constrained by factors such as capacity constraints (a lack of available hospital beds, so that $x \leq X$, where X is the local hospital bed supply) or ethical judgment (the treatment is not worth the social cost or the patient is not better off as a consequence when $s'(x)$ is small or even negative and out-of-pocket expenses are high); these additional restrictions are reflected in a portmanteau constraint μ.[5] In this simplified case, the optimality condition for the provider can be written as

$$\Psi s'(x) = -\omega\pi + \mu \equiv \lambda \tag{2.4}$$

where ω is the derivative of Ω with respect to x, or the marginal value of an extra dollar of income, and the combination of constraints is summarized by the shadow price λ. For example, if financial incentives to do more (that is, $-\omega\pi < 0$) are in turn offset by ethical standards to "do no harm" to patients ($\mu = \omega\pi$), so that $\lambda = 0$, then physicians seeking to do the best for their patients would drive $s'(x)$ to zero.

Consider Figure 2.1, showing both $\Psi s'(x)$ and λ.[6] Note also the key assumption that patients are sorted in order from most appropriate to least appropriate for

---

[5] See Chandra and Skinner (2011) for a complete derivation of the model.
[6] Note that λ could vary with x; for simplicity it is held constant.

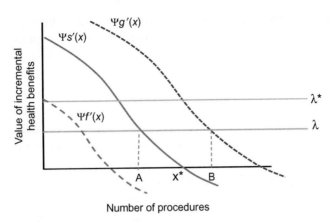

Figure 2.1 Marginal productivity of health outcomes, for different production functions and constraints.

treatment, thus describing a downward sloping $\Psi s'(x)$ curve (Baicker et al., 2006). The equilibrium occurs where, as in equation (2.4), $\Psi s'(x) = \lambda$, or at point A in Figure 2.1. In most health care systems λ will generally not be equal to the social cost of an additional unit of x, equal to one; typically capacity constraints would lead to $\lambda > 1$, and the existence of insurance (and hence $p < 1$) would push λ below 1; either condition leads to static inefficiency.

How can this model be used to explain regional variations? Consider two general classes of variations across regions. The first is that all physicians and hospitals are subject to the same $s(x)$ production function, but that regional variation in utilization occurs because of movements along the $s'(x)$ curve because of variations in λ to (say) $\lambda\star$ as in Figure 2.1. Examples of such movements would include:

(a) Marginal financial incentives (variations in π) arising from differences across regions in reimbursement rates and prices for procedures—more of an issue perhaps for Medicaid and private insurance than for Medicare, where prices are fixed, albeit with rough adjustments for differences in cost of living and other factors (IOM, 2011). More generally, physicians may differ across regions with regard to their sensitivity towards financial incentives, as summarized by the marginal utility of income ω. For example, Gawande (2009), in trying to explain why Medicare spending was so much higher in McAllen, Texas, compared to El Paso, emphasized the more "entrepreneurial" characteristics of physicians in McAllen—that is, an increased sensitivity to profitable activities, or a larger ω.

(b) Capacity or ethical constraints that reflect quasi-fixed factors in the region (showing up as μ), for example the density of catheterization laboratories, specialists, hospital and ICU beds, and diagnostic imaging facilities (for example, an MRI down the hall from the physician's office). This is the mechanism that, as we discuss below, underlies the idea of "supply-sensitive" or Category III care, that the shadow price of the extra bed-day is so low because there are empty beds.[7] These differences in quasi-fixed capacity may in turn arise from historical accidents; in contrast to New Haven, for example, there were a larger number of religious groups establishing hospitals in Boston (Wennberg, 2010).

(c) Patient price or access. If most patients are uninsured and facing full dollar cost, or if they tend to be wary of surgical procedures, then the physician is assumed to account for their higher costs and avoid marginally valuable treatments. Conversely, if it takes a long time for patients to get to the clinic or hospital, or they face high implicit costs of doing so, then x will be lower (and $s'(x)$ higher).

(d) Malpractice risk, which changes the implicit costs or benefits of performing the procedure. In some cases, "defensive medicine" can work to reduce λ and increase utilization: the CT scan to provide cover for sending a patient home from the emergency room or the PSA test to avoid lawsuits in the event that the patient is later diagnosed with prostate cancer (King and Moulton, 2006). In other cases, malpractice concerns may increase the implicit costs if by performing the procedure the physician puts herself at greater risk of a lawsuit (Baicker et al., 2007; Currie and MacLeod, 2008).

Recall that all these variations in capacity, financial incentives, and so forth would lead to different points along the same production function. Thus if all regions were on the same production function $s(x)$, the cross-sectional association across regions between spending and outcomes should trace out the production function and hence the marginal "value" of health care spending. If regions also differ with regard to their production function $s(x)$, as is argued below, then these cross-regional comparisons will no longer trace out $s(x)$ over ranges of x, but some combination of both variation in the production function and variation in λ. As I argue below, this creates difficulties in interpreting regression coefficients seeking to answer the question "is more better?"

A second approach to explaining geographic variations arises by allowing the production function to differ across regions or physicians. Most obviously, this will occur because of differences in health status; Lafayette, LA, has more underlying disease burden than Hawaii, so we might expect the physician production function in Lafayette to look more like $f(x)$ than $s(x)$ in Figure 2.1—there is most likely no amount of health care spending that will make Lafayette as healthy as Hawaii. As well, one would expect that for any given x, $f'(x) > s'(x)$.

A more interesting reason for variations in the production function—shifted from $s(x)$ to $g(x)$ in Figure 2.1—is that physicians may have adopted more effective

---

[7] This also begs the question of why a particular region might have so much capacity to begin with; capacity can best be described as predetermined rather than exogenous. One study did find evidence that hospital beds are less likely to move than people; thus regions subject to out-migration tend to have the greatest supply of beds (Clayton et al., 2009).

innovations with small costs, such as checklists for surgeries or beta blockers for heart attacks, thus enhancing the productivity of a given level of inputs x (de Vries et al., 2010; Skinner and Staiger, 2009). Similarly, physicians may also be more skilled at a specific procedure for people with similar health status. For example, in one study of heart attack patients, patients experienced better outcomes from cardiac interventions in regions with higher rates of surgery, consistent with a Roy model of labor market sorting (Chandra and Staiger, 2007). Other explanations for such differences rely also on systematically different organizational structures of practices (de Jong, 2008).

Physicians may also be overly optimistic (as in $g'(x)$ in Figure 2.1) or pessimistic ($f'(x)$) about their ability in performing procedures, or more generally about the marginal effectiveness of specific treatments. For example, arthroscopic surgery to treat osteoarthritis of the knee was a common procedure in the early 2000s, with 650,000 performed annually at a cost of about $5,000 each. In this procedure, surgeons enter the joint area with tiny instruments, and clean out the joint while removing loose particles. In 2002, a randomized study of this procedure was conducted, with "sham" surgery performed on the control group (Moseley et al., 2002). No benefit was found relative to the control group, suggesting that, prior to the study's publication, the perceived surgical production function was to the right of the true production function in Figure 2.1.

Alternatively, physicians may not understand that in treating a patient for a specific disease, their prescription drug may interact with others already prescribed by other providers (Zhang et al., 2010b), reflecting the problem that networks become increasingly complex with more specialists involved (Becker and Murphy, 1992). In either case, one can end up with different regions operating on different production functions, with vastly different approaches to treatments, even though patients may not be aware that they are receiving more or less intensive care (Fowler et al., 2008).

What about the interaction between supply and demand? After all, every one of the 650,000 patients annually undergoing arthroscopic knee surgery (prior to 2002) agreed to the procedure, which even in the absence of out-of-pocket costs involved pain and lost time for recovery. Presumably the patient formed beliefs of her marginal benefit in part based on the physician's expertise, and so the perceived demand for the procedure would depend on physician advice. This is not "supplier-induced demand" *per se*; after all, it is the physician's job to convey expert information about the incremental benefits of the procedure to the patient. But given the spectrum of opinions held by physicians across regions (Sirovich et al., 2005), it should not be surprising if variations in physician opinions are mirrored by variations in patient beliefs across regions.

Less well understood is why patients sometimes appear to hold a more optimistic view of the marginal benefits of treatment than even their physician. For example, the COURAGE trials for patients with stable angina showed that stents, wire-mesh cylindrical devices inserted in narrowing cardiac arteries to improve blood flow, provided no

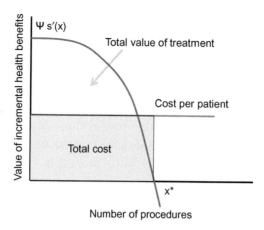

Figure 2.2 Benefits (area under the curve) and costs of effective (category i) innovation. *Source: Chandra and Skinner (2011).*

survival or heart-attack benefit to their patients, although it did reduce pain and improve functioning modestly for several years (Boden et al., 2007). In a matched survey of patients and physicians, physicians in one teaching hospital understood this evidence from the COURAGE trial. By contrast, their patients believed, falsely, in the protective effects of a stent against early death and heart attacks (Rothberg et al., 2010b).

Another way in which the traditional demand model falls short is where patients are observed to use too little of high-value drugs such as anti-hypertensives, suggesting an absurdly low value placed on their own life (Chandra et al., 2010). Indeed, even when the monetary price is zero or even negative (Volpp et al., 2008), utilization of effective treatments is below what it should be, raising questions of whether behavioral models of demand are better descriptions of behavior. Still, it seems unlikely that such anomalies in behavior should explain *regional* variations in demand.

In considering the empirical evidence, I will attempt to distinguish between the λ-based variation, which may reflect both supply- and demand-side factors, and variations in actual or perceived production functions (or marginal productivity measures), as has been found in other non-health care industries (Syverson, 2011).

2.3. A Typology of Health Care Services

I follow Wennberg et al. (2002) and Chandra and Skinner (2011) in considering three broad categories of health care inputs. The first is for highly effective treatments such as antibiotics for infections, beta blockers for heart attack patients, or a splint for a broken bone. These effective (or Category I) treatments are either productive across a wide swath of individuals, but very low cost—for example, aspirin for heart attack patients—or are highly productive and expensive for a well-defined group of patients. For example, in Figure 2.2 the graph showing the marginal value of anti-retroviral

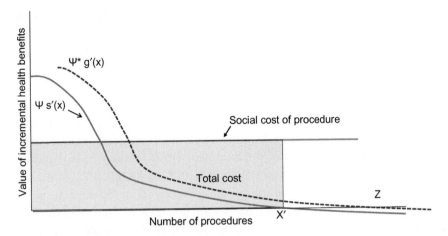

Figure 2.3 Benefits (area under the curve) and costs of category ii innovation. *Source: Fisher and Skinner (2010).*

treatments for HIV and AIDS patients. These are clearly beneficial (albeit very expensive) for those with the disease. But even when $s'(x)$ is driven to zero—that is, physicians do not worry about the high price but only give the drug to patients who would benefit—there is still little margin for overuse, because the side-effects are sufficiently serious to preclude widespread usage. Thus net value, or the area under the curve minus the cost (shown as the shaded rectangle in Figure 2.2), is still very large (Chandra and Skinner, 2011).

A second category of treatments exhibits considerable heterogeneity in benefits across different types of patients. One example is stents, where benefits are well established for patients who have very recently experienced a heart attack (Hartwell et al., 2005). These patients are shown on the left side in Figure 2.3, where benefits $\Psi s'(x)$ are considerably above social costs. But there is also a larger group of patients with more modest benefits. For example, the use of stents for the treatment of stable angina (compared to optimal medical management), as noted above, yields no improvement in mortality, no reduction in subsequent heart attacks, and a modest improvement in functioning over the next several years (Weintraub et al., 2008). Similarly, back surgery is effective for spinal stenosis, a type of back pain involving compression of the spinal cord or of nerves emanating from the spinal cord (Weinstein et al., 2008). But much less is known about its value for patients without any organic cause for the back pain, comprising the majority of those suffering from back problems, as shown by the flat region of the marginal benefit curve in Figure 2.3, where benefits are below social cost. And given the shape of $s'(x)$ as drawn in Figure 2.3, the overall benefits (the area under the curve to the left of X') are not much greater than the overall costs, given by the rectangle to the left of X' (Chandra and Skinner, 2011).

Figure 2.3 also shows that small changes in the marginal benefit curve could have a strong impact on demand when the incremental medical value of the treatment is small, at least relative to other options. For example, preferences could play an important role in tonsillectomy rates, or choosing between mastectomy (removal of the breast) and lumpectomy followed by radiation therapy for the treatment of breast cancer, given that the two options yield similar long-term prognosis. These preferences would affect the perceived value of the treatment ($g'(x)$ versus $s'(x)$ in Figure 2.3) or differences in income or demand more generally ($\Psi\star$ versus Ψ) all could exert a large influence on overall unconstrained utilization (Z versus X' in Figure 2.3), particularly at a point where out-of-pocket costs are low or non-existent and physicians are well compensated for providing the treatment. To the extent that patient preferences, physician skills, or capacity constraints for these procedures might differ across regions, we might expect to find large differences in utilization rates across otherwise similar patients.

"Supply sensitive" or Category III variations are types of treatments where the evidence either points to very small or zero effects, such as arthroscopy of the knee, or where the benefits are simply not known. For example, there are a variety of treatments for prostate cancer, with wide variations in costs but no clear evidence of superiority for one type of treatment over another (Leonhardt, 2009). Category III treatments also reflect the importance of available resources such as intensive care unit (ICU) beds, hospital beds, specialists, and other "system"-level parameters, but where there's really no evidence on what is the right rate of ICU admissions among chronically ill patients. As noted above, capacity is reflected by variations in λ, but to the extent that capacity is in turn determined by the perceived value of specific procedures (e.g. $g(x)$ versus $s(x)$), then capacity constraints become endogenous across regions. Given the close association between overall Medicare expenditures and Category III utilization rates (e.g. Wennberg et al., 2002), these types of utilization are likely to play a large role in explaining overall spending differences across regions.

The next section provides a selected tour of the geographic variations literature in light of this model, although the question addressed at each stage is: What is the *regional* factor (and not simply idiosyncratic characteristics of physicians or patients) that might be expected to explain geographic variation in expenditures? In other words, it is not enough to find that (for example) physician practice varies dramatically across individual physicians even after controlling for health status of the patient (Phelps, 2000), since random variations among physicians would tend to cancel out when averaged over very large numbers of physicians in New York or Los Angeles. More interesting is what causes characteristics of patients and providers to be correlated systematically *within* regions.

3. EMPIRICAL EVIDENCE ON GEOGRAPHIC VARIATIONS IN EXPENDITURES AND UTILIZATION

By necessity, much of the evidence from the United States uses Medicare claims data for the over-65 population, which is the closest insurance program to universal health care in the US. Given that standard economic variables such as co-payment rates and deductibles are the same across regions in the Medicare program, Medicare utilization should in theory exhibit less variation than for the under-65 population where characteristics of insurance plans—particularly Medicaid benefits—vary broadly across the country. And while patterns from Medicare spending do not always generalize to the under-65 population, the elderly do consume a disproportionate fraction of health care spending, and growth in the Medicare program represents considerable financial risk for the future stability of US government finances.

3.1. Units of Measurement and Spatial Correlations

In the early 1990s, the Dartmouth group sought to characterize regional markets in preparation for what was supposed to have been Clinton-era health care reform. They used 1992/93 discharge data from the Medicare population to determine "catchment areas" for local hospitals, or "hospital service areas" (HSAs). There were 3,436 HSAs, which in turn were combined to create 306 "hospital referral regions" (HRRs) required to have at least one tertiary hospital providing cardiovascular and neurosurgical services. As in the 1973 Wennberg and Gittelsohn study, utilization was determined by residence (in this case zip code), and not by where the treatment was actually received. Thus treatments received in Minneapolis by a resident of Davenport, Iowa, would be assigned to the Davenport HRR, and not to Minneapolis. The 306 HRRs did not generally follow county or state boundaries, but instead reflected the actual migration patterns of Medicare patients, sometimes by following interstate highway routes. These definitions have not been changed since the original Dartmouth Atlas, published in 1996 (Wennberg and Cooper, 1996), which makes temporal comparisons straightforward, as the zip code-based crosswalks have been modified over time to preserve the same geographical boundaries. The temporal stability, however, means that regions may no longer be as sharply defined given secular changes in hospital market catchment areas.

Some studies have used state-level data, with the idea that some part of regional variations may be explained by differences in state policies such as nursing home bedhold policies or Medicaid payments (Intrator et al., 2007). However, there is considerable variation within states, particularly large ones such as California, Texas, Florida, or New York. Another approach is to use county-level data, which provides a much larger sample of counties and the ability to match with other county data, for example from the Center for Disease Control's Behavioral Risk Factor Surveillance System (BRFSS) data on health and health behaviors. Still, county boundaries may be imperfect aggregations of where people actually seek their care, particularly in rural areas with small counties that do not have their own hospital.

An alternative is to create cohorts based on relative distance to specific hospitals, such as a 10-mile circumference, or based on relative distance to specific types of hospitals. For example, McClellan et al. (1994) considered heart attack patients living relatively near to, or far from, a hospital with a catheterization laboratory used to provide surgical treatment. Thus patient zip code was an instrument to predict whether the individual received surgical intervention for their heart attack, with the implicit assumption that unobservable health status was similar across zip codes.

Another approach is to avoid the use of zip codes altogether, but instead to create "physician—hospital networks" or cohorts of individual patients based on where they tend to seek care. For example, several studies created such networks using Medicare claims data by first assigning patients to the primary care physician who sees them the most, and then by assigning the physician to the hospital to which they are most loyal (Bynum et al., 2007; Fisher et al., 2007). That is, the Princeton-Plainsboro physician—hospital network comprises patients who see the set of physicians who in turn are most likely to admit to Princeton-Plainsboro, even if the patient has never been admitted to that (or any) hospital.[8] While these groups are no longer based on zip codes, they do provide measures of costs and quality at a potentially relevant decision-making unit, particularly for integrated delivery systems.

One key disadvantage of the Medicare claims data is the presence of Medicare-sponsored managed care plans (Medicare Advantage). These are capitated plans by which Medicare pays a fixed amount (adjusted by risk factors) to insurance companies to provide coverage for their enrollees. As such, claims data are unavailable for this group, yet in some regions of the country, roughly 40 percent are enrolled in Medicare managed care. While there are concerns that the population in these plans are systematically healthier than in the fee-for-service plans (Brown et al., 2011), there is less evidence that selection issues have introduced bias in estimated measures for the fee-for-service population, particularly when risk adjusters are specific to that same population.[9]

Finally, a methodological shortcoming for most of this literature, particularly in section 4, is the lack of accounting for spatial autocorrelation across regions. For

---

[8] Nearly every Medicare enrollee sees at least one doctor annually, meaning that few enrollees are unassigned. These networks are very similar to the structure of patient populations in "accountable care organizations" under the 2010 health care reform legislation in the US.

[9] One might be concerned that regions with rapid growth in Medicare Advantage would also experience above-average growth in per-capita fee-for-service expenditures as healthier patients risk-select into Medicare Advantage. However, unpublished data suggest that the change in Medicare Advantage enrollment across HRRs does not have much predictive power in explaining growth in fee-for-service spending, as one might expect.

example, when researchers run a regression with 306 HRRs, they implicitly assume independence; that the error term in the regression for Boston tells us nothing about the error term for Worcester. But as Ricketts and colleagues have shown, this assumption is demonstrably false (Ricketts and Holmes, 2007). Often, although not always, adjusting for spatial autocorrelation leads to wider confidence intervals; thus studies without such adjustments (including most of the Dartmouth studies) who find either negative or positive influences of spending on outcomes could be falsely rejecting the null of no effect.

3.2. Health Care Expenditures

Differences in expenditures across regions provides a first look at variations, as well as highlighting the magnitude of spending differences, at least in the Medicare claims data. Table 2.1 shows a select group of regions along with a set of measures corresponding to overall expenditures in Columns 1 and 2. Column 1 shows average per-capita Medicare expenditures adjusted for age, sex, and race for 2007. There are remarkable differences in expenditures across regions, from $6,196 in Grand Junction, CO, to $16,316 in Miami, FL, with a coefficient of variation equal to 0.18.[10] Indeed, Miami is something of an outlier, having been at the top of the list for expenditures per capita in every year since the Atlas began collecting data in 1992. The difference in Medicare expenditures across regions is considerably larger in present value terms; for Grand Junction versus Miami, the net difference in expected lifetime payout approaches $100,000 assuming a 3 percent growth rate in real expenditures and a 3 percent discount rate. Thus Medicare redistributes substantial amounts of money across regions—particularly as a fraction of a typical elderly person's lifetime wealth and income—even after controlling for income and taxes paid (Feenberg and Skinner, 2000).

3.2.1. Adjusting for Prices

One objection to comparing expenditures across regions is that Medicare pays more per procedure in high-cost cities than in low-cost rural areas. When Medicare pays its providers, it adjusts payments in several ways: (1) cost-of-living (using slightly different approaches for hospital payments versus physician payments), (2) the disproportionate-share program (DSH) which provides additional reimbursements for hospitals serving low-income patients, and (3) providing additional reimbursements (per DRG) to compensate for training medical and surgical residents. Following the earlier work by the Medicare Payment Advisory Commission (MedPAC, 2009), Gottlieb et al. removed these price differences by applying common national prices per diagnostic-related

---

[10] The coefficient of variation reported in Table 2.1 is the ratio of the standard deviation to the mean, weighted by the overall Medicare population in each region.

Table 2.1 Regional Variation in Utilization and Health: Selected Measures

Column/HRR	1	2	3	4	5	6	7	8	9
Year	2007 Medicare Expenditures	2007 Medicare Expenditures (price adjusted)	2007 Mortality Rates (per 1,000)	2005 Hip Fractures (per 1,000)	1994/95 β Blocker Use (%) ideal pts	2007 Back Surgery (per 1,000)	2003 PSA Tests Age 80+ (%)	2007 End-of-Life ICU Days	2001–05 Last 2 yrs MD Visits
Grand Junction, CO	6,196	6,283	4.58	7.47		5.9	9.0	1.4	38
Huntington, WV	8,634	9,269	6.38	8.73	46	2.8	12.0	2.0	59
New York, NY	12,190	9,691	4.37	6.30	61	2.0	27.0	4.0	88
Rochester, NY	6,613	6,923	5.50	6.99	82	3.4	5.3	2.1	45
Chicago, IL	10,369	9,782	4.70	6.70	36	2.5	13.7	7.4	81
San Francisco, CA	8,498	6,881	4.25	5.45	65	3.1	13.4	4.6	64
Los Angeles, CA	10,973	9,685	4.42	6.24	44	4.0	24.8	8.0	109
Seattle, WA	7,126	6,718	4.68	6.27	52	5.3	13.4	2.9	45
McAllen, TX	14,890	15,026	4.59	6.30	5	3.3	24.9	8.0	100
Miami, FL	16,316	15,971	4.96	7.27	52	2.5	30.4	10.7	106
Bend, OR	6,520	6,457	4.67	7.72	50	7.4	8.4	1.6	38
US average	8,571	8,571	5.04	7.34	51	4.5	19.0	3.9	61
Coefficient of variation	0.18	0.16	0.09	0.14	0.27	0.31	0.35	0.43	0.32
Correlation coefficient*	0.87	1.00	0.37	0.33	-0.24	-0.12	0.36	0.62	0.68

*With price adjusted per capita Medicare spending.
Sources noted in text.

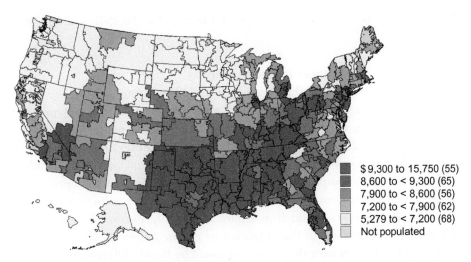

■	$ 9,300 to 15,750 (55)
■	8,600 to < 9,300 (65)
■	7,900 to < 8,600 (56)
▨	7,200 to < 7,900 (62)
☐	5,279 to < 7,200 (68)
▧	Not populated

Figure 2.4 Price-adjusted per capita medicare expenditures 2007. *Dartmouth atlas of healthcare.*

group (DRG) weight for inpatient care, and resource-value unit (RVU) for outpatient care (Gottlieb et al., 2010). For other categories where quantity units were less apparent, such as outpatient care, they applied a wage-index adjustment.

These price-adjusted measures are shown in Table 2.1, Column 2.[11] Price adjustment had little impact on the two major outliers: McAllen, TX, and Miami. And not surprisingly, larger cities like San Francisco experienced a much larger drop in reported spending; it now becomes one of the lower-cost regions. On net, the population-weighted standard deviation in per capita expenditures declined modestly from $1,510 to $1,318; the correlation coefficient between the two measures is 0.87.

Price adjustment has perhaps the largest impact on expenditures for New York City (Manhattan), where per capita spending falls from $12,190 (unadjusted) to $9,691 (adjusted). The shift reflects not solely the wage index, but also the importance of graduate medical education subsidies for the large population of residents training in New York hospitals. Once adjusted for these differences in expenditures, however, they are only 13 percent above the national average. Table 2.1 and Figure 2.4 also illustrate the wide variation in overall expenditures even within states; Rochester, NY, on a price-adjusted basis, spends $6,923 per patient compared to $9,691 in New York City, and average spending in San Francisco is similarly nearly one-third below that in Los Angeles ($6,881 versus $9,685). The Pacific Northwest also tends to experience

[11] The price adjustment is normalized to the mean value of Medicare spending, $8,571 in 2007.

lower spending levels, with Seattle ($6,178) and Bend, OR ($6,457), among the lowest in the country.

3.2.2. Adjusting for Differences in Health Status

An immediate concern with these comparisons of spending is that the standard age–sex–race adjustment fails to adjust for health status. Bend, OR, may experience low levels of spending, but this may in turn reflect a healthier population who maintain exercise and healthy diets after retirement. In the context of the model, regions with poorer health status will experience greater incremental value of health care spending, such as $g'(x)$ compared to $s'(x)$ in Figure 2.1, leading to appropriate spending differences across regions (for the same λ) given different production functions of health, as shown by points A and B in Figure 2.1. Ideally, one would want to adjust for differences across regions in illness burden to ask the question of whether there is any regional variation left over that is not explained by health differences.

The most straightforward approach to risk adjustment is to consider mortality—a reliably measured marker of illness, particularly since simply being in one's last year of life predicts elevated spending. Huntington, West Virginia, is distinguished by one of the highest age–sex–race-adjusted Medicare mortality rates in the US: 6.32 percent compared to a US average of 5.12 percent, as shown in Table 2.1, Column 3.[12] Yet overall expenditures in Huntington, WV, are just 8 percent above average ($9,269). It may be that the larger share of lower-income households in Huntington experience worse access to care—fewer physicians in rural areas surrounding Huntington, for example. However, income *per* se (independent of health status) does not appear to explain regional variations in overall expenditures (Zuckerman et al., 2010), although other factors, such as rural location and local poverty, could have a larger impact on the supply of health care providers.

Note that mortality rates in the highest-expenditure regions, McAllen (4.47 percent) and Miami (5.12 percent), are below the national average. One could interpret this correlation in two ways. One is that these regions are in fact healthier than average, making their high level of health care spending all the more remarkable.[13] But a different interpretation reverses the causation: high spending in Miami and McAllen leads to better health and hence lower mortality rates. Strictly speaking, one cannot distinguish between these two hypotheses without estimating the causal effects of spending, discussed in section 4 below.

---

[12] These mortality estimates, from 2007, are for all Medicare enrollees, and not just those in the fee-for-service population.

[13] Recall that residence is determined by the zip code from the Medicare denominator file corresponding to the billing address. For snowbirds who travel back and forth between (say) McAllen and Rochester, NY, the billing address could be in either locale, but health care expenditures would be a weighted average of health care received in the two regions. Thus retirees would attenuate regional differences; McAllen's spending would be lower and Rochester's higher because of this assignment rule.

An alternative health risk factor is the rate of hospital admissions for hip fractures. Nearly every elderly person with a hip fracture is admitted to the hospital, and nearly every doctor agrees on the clinical criteria for hip fractures. Furthermore, hip fractures are largely determined by bone density, arising from early-life nutritional habits rather than current environment or health care services (Lauderdale et al., 1998). Huntington, WV, also experiences an elevated rate of hip fractures (8.73 per thousand), higher than the US average (7.34). Miami (7.27) and McAllen (6.30) are lower than average, with San Francisco among the lowest in the country (5.45). As discussed in section 6, variations in *health* are large (the coefficient of variation for hip fractures is 0.14), and not highly correlated with spending; the correlation coefficient between hip fracture rates and price-adjusted expenditures is 0.33.

Yet hip fracture captures only one dimension of underlying health status. The Medicare Current Beneficiary Survey (MCBS) includes self-reported health and disease prevalence (e.g. smoking, diabetes, obesity). Several studies have used the MCBS to show that at the micro level, variations in health status can explain at least some of the observed differences in expenditures across regions (Sutherland et al., 2009; Zuckerman et al., 2010). Zuckerman et al., for example, found that the gap between the highest and lowest spending quintiles shrank from about 52 percent without any price or illness adjustment to 33 percent after adjustment for patient reported illnesses such as diabetes, smoking, weight, and whether their doctor has told them they have any new diseases. On the one hand, these adjustments could understate true disease burden because of unobservable factors orthogonal to observed risk factors.[14] On the other hand, patients were asked what their physicians had recently told them, leading to a potential reverse causation: the more contact one has with the health care system, the more likely a diagnosis (Song et al., 2010).

A different approach is to use the risk-adjustment measures in the Medicare administrative file to elicit underlying health status (MedPAC, 2011). The advantage of this approach is the vast size of the database, and the ability to adjust every Medicare enrollee for risk factors. The Hierarchical Condition Coding (HCC) counts the number of different diagnoses that patients have received over the course of a year, and weight them for severity, with some diagnoses closely related to whether the patient had a specific procedure. Because the risk adjustment comes directly from the billing data (unlike the MCBS, which asks patients questions), it is even more likely to result in the "up-diagnosis" bias. For example, one study compared Medicare enrollees who moved to a high-intensity region with those moving to a low-intensity region (Song et al., 2010). Despite the sample being similar at baseline, those moving

---

[14] Recall that observed health factors will reflect the correlated component of unmeasured health factors; it is only the component of the unmeasured health factors that is orthogonal to observables that will cause trouble in interpreting results.

to a higher-intensity region experienced as much as 19 percent higher diagnosis rates.[15]

The problem of determining "true" risk adjustment is not simply an issue for measuring regional variations, but is a more general challenge when trying to compensate health care systems (or "accountable care organizations") for treating sicker patients and for rewarding better risk-adjusted outcomes. The incentives become stronger to up-diagnose when institutions are paid on the basis of risk-adjusted costs and rewarded for above-average risk-adjusted outcomes.

A third approach is to use cohort measures of utilization, whether "backward-looking" cohorts that begin at (e.g.) the date of death and work backwards, or "forward-looking" cohorts that begin at the time of the heart attack or hip fracture.[16] The idea behind these measures is that people with a heart attack, or in their last six months of life, are more similarly ill whether in Huntington, WV, or Bend, OR. This may not hold, however—the decedent in Huntington may have had a host of complications that make her more expensive to treat. A hybrid approach considers cohorts, but performs additional risk adjustment, for example by only considering end-of-life cohorts with serious chronic illnesses, as in Wennberg (2008).

3.2.3. Adjusting for Income

Another possibility is that income explains differences across regions in expenditures, for example by shifting the marginal benefit curve $\Psi_S'(x)$. (Recall that Ψ, the marginal dollar value of a life-year, is highly income elastic.) It is not entirely clear what would be the normative implications of a finding that high-income households are heavier users of Medicare—is it "warranted" or "unwarranted" variation given that Medicare is a publicly funded program? Certainly at the individual level, elderly people with lower education and income account for more Medicare expenditures in a given year (Battacharya and Lakdawalla, 2006; McClellan and Skinner, 2006; Sutherland et al., 2009), but these gradients conflate both income effects and health effects. Still, there is no evidence that individual income differences across regions explain more than a minor fraction of overall variation in regional Medicare expenditures for the US, particularly after controlling for health status (Sutherland et al., 2009; Zuckerman et al., 2010). On the other hand, strong positive associations between aggregate income

---

[15] Some papers used HRR-level or metropolitan region-level health and ethnicity characteristics to risk-adjust Medicare expenditures (Cutler and Scheiner, 1999; Rettenmaier and Saving, 2010; Skinner et al., 2005). The advantage of such variables is that they are typically well measured and include the kind of information one needs for unbiased risk adjustment, such as smoking rates. The disadvantage is these aggregated measures are more prone to the "ecological fallacy" problem. For example, the variable measuring percent Hispanic is highly significant and positive in HRR-level regressions. Yet at the individual level, there is no impact of Hispanic origin on spending. The discrepancy is explained by the large population of Hispanics in Miami, McAllen, and Los Angeles, regions where spending rates are also high (for both Hispanics and non-Hispanics).

[16] The "backward" and "forward" terminology is from Ong et al. (2009).

(and hence tax revenue) and health care spending are more the norm across states in the US Medicaid program, and in countries such as Italy (Mangano, 2010).

This section has demonstrated that there are sharp differences in both per capita expenditures across regions, with some of these differences attributed to prices being higher in urban areas, and differences across the country in health status—West Virginia and Louisiana have a larger burden of disease than Oregon and should be expected to spend more. While price adjustments are straightforward, adjusting for health is more difficult, and represents a balancing act between under- and overadjustment. Still, there is considerable residual variation in expenditures that cannot be explained away by these factors.

3.2.4. Regional Variation in Non-Medicare Expenditures

Earlier work from California has shown a strong correlation between utilization for the over-65 Medicare population, those covered by Medicare Advantage plans, and the under-65 population (Baker et al., 2008). Similarly, a recent study comparing Medicare utilization and private health insurance among larger employers who self-insure showed a correlation of about 0.6 between these private insurance individuals and Medicare utilization (Chernew et al., 2010b).

But there are other results that suggest much greater differences in the behavior of the under-65 and the Medicare markets. For example, Chernew et al. find a surprising *negative* correlation between under-65 expenditures (or prices times quantity) and Medicare spending. Nor was the wide gap in Medicare spending between McAllen and El Paso, TX, replicated in the under-65 Blue-Cross Blue-Shield population (Franzini et al., 2010), suggesting that private insurance may have more leverage in restricting high utilization rates (Philipson et al., 2010).

Transacted prices for health care are known to vary tremendously across regions and hospitals depending on market structure and concentration on the side of providers such as hospitals and physician groups, and payers such as insurance companies or large employers (Gaynor and Town, 2011). So the variability at a point in time in prices in the under-65 population may bear little relation to the cost per procedure (or cost per patient) in the over-65 population where prices are largely fixed.[17] Hospitals might be shifting costs from the Medicare market to the private market and vice versa, although a recent paper suggests that when hospitals feel pressure to constrain their costs they are able to do so (Stensland et al., 2010). Understanding this interaction between private insurance markets and Medicare is a topic for further research.

---

[17] Complicating things further, there is evidence that this association is changing over time; at the state level, the correlation between non-Medicare and Medicare spending declined from nearly 0.6 in 1991 to roughly −0.15 in 2004 (Rettenmaier and Saving, 2010).

One consistent finding is the lack of correlation between state-level Medicaid and Medicare spending (Cooper, 2009; Rettenmaier and Saving, 2010). This suggests that states with less generous Medicaid programs are shifting costs to federally supported Medicare. Because Medicare is a fixed-price mechanism, the only way to increase Medicare income is by providing more intensive care to the relatively well-compensated Medicare patients, a classic "supply-driven" response in which physicians do more (by working further down the appropriateness curve) for their Medicare patients, leading to a lower λ and hence more utilization.

Expenditures provide a good measure of the opportunity cost of health care spending, particularly when aggregated over large populations of Medicare enrollees. But expenditures are simply averages of different types of health care, some of which is highly valuable in improving health (Category I) and others much less so (Category III). It is therefore useful to consider geographic variation in the three categories of treatments separately.

3.3. Effective Care (Category I)

The 1999 Cardiovascular Atlas provided an early national perspective on regional variations in Category I treatments that are both highly cost effective and have clear clinical benefits (Wennberg and Birkmeyer, 1999). It drew on the Cooperative Cardiovascular Project (CCP), a comprehensive survey of more than 200,000 heart attack patients in 1994/95 over the age of 65 with detailed chart review data. One example of effective Category I care is the use of β blockers for the treatment of heart attack patients. These help to block β-adrenergic receptors, thereby reducing the demands on the heart. In 1985, one study summarized the consensus knowledge: "Long-term beta blockage for perhaps a year or so following discharge after an MI is now of proven value, and for many such patients mortality reductions of about 25% can be achieved" (Yusuf et al., 1985).

At the time of the CCP survey, beta blockage, while inexpensive and off-patent, was widely variable across the country. As shown in Table 2.1, rates of β blocker use at discharge for ideal heart attack patients—that is, people for whom there was no contraindication for taking β blockers—ranged from 5 percent (McAllen, TX) and 13 percent (St. Josephs, MI) to 82 percent (Rochester, NY) and 91 percent (Dearborn, MI). The "right rate" for every region is something close to 100 percent, hence there is no need to risk adjust for differences in health.

There are two puzzling features of these patterns. The first is why overall adoption of β blockers was so low—even by 2000/2001, just two-thirds of ideal heart attack patients were being treated with beta blockers in the median state (Jencks et al., 2003). In part, it is because doctors gain little credit from doing a much better job (Phelps, 2000); patients rarely realize that they are being treated with effective care for their heart attack. But it is also a reticence to use new technologies in the absence of institutional "opinion leaders" supporting the adoption of new technologies (Bradley et al., 2005). During the 2000s, β blocker use became a standard measure of quality, reported on Medicare's "Hospital Compare" website,[18] so that by now, few hospitals report use rates below 95 percent. In general, efficient care diffuses to near-universal use, although the diffusion process may be remarkably slow (Berwick, 2003).

A more difficult puzzle is why some regions adopted so much more quickly than others; why should Rochester, NY (82 percent), and San Francisco (65 percent) be so much higher than Los Angeles (44 percent) and Chicago (36 percent)? One might understand that "opinion leaders" might differ with regard to their views of β blockers, but it is more difficult to think of why opinion leaders favoring β blockers would tend to be concentrated in Rochester, NY, rather than in Chicago. Certainly price-adjusted spending is not associated with the more rapid diffusion of β blockage ($\rho = -0.24$) (Table 2.1). Nor is per capita income, thus casting doubt on a demand-side explanation in which higher-income regions hire higher-quality physicians.[19] However, β blockage at the state level *is* associated with the adoption of other efficient technologies such as tractors in the 1920s and hybrid corn in the 1930s and 1940s, which in turn are linked by higher degrees of social capital, an index of education, civic participation, and trust (Skinner and Staiger, 2007). These correlations do not solve the puzzle of course, but do point to persistent differences across regions in the adoption of new technology, something that is also found for country-level adoption of new technologies (Comin and Hobijn, 2004).

These Category I treatments may have an outsized impact on health outcomes, but they are not likely to play a large role in explaining variations across regions in expenditures. I next turn to surgical and other preference-sensitive procedures with a greater impact on spending.

3.4. Preference-sensitive Treatments with Heterogeneous Benefits (Category II)

The first scientific study of regional variations arose in a 1938 article by J. Alison Glover on tonsillectomy rates. He calculated population-based rates for children ranging across England from 0.4 percent in Wood Green to 5.8 percent in Stoke or Peterborough (Glover, 1938). The classic study by Wennberg and Gittelsohn, using comprehensive health-level data across small communities in Vermont during the late

---

[18] See http://www.hospitalcompare.hhs.gov/. Since there is no longer much variation in β blocker use, some have dropped it as a marker for quality.

[19] It seems unlikely that these variations could be explained by patient demand at the individual level; it is not clear why supine heart attack patients in Rochester, NY, should know so much more about β blockers—and be insistent on demanding such treatments—than those in Chicago. One anecdotal story relayed to me was that the chief cardiologist in one hospital (in the early 2000s) responded to requests to raise β blockers by saying "Why would you ever use β blockers for someone who just had a heart attack?"

1960s, also found community-level "surgical signatures" in tonsillectomy rates, ranging from 13 to 151 per 10,000 people (Wennberg and Gittelsohn, 1973). In these
small areas, a single school physician could have a disproportionate impact on surgical
rates, depending on his beliefs about the efficacy of the procedure.

Why so much variation in tonsillectomy rates in the 1930s and 1960s, and why
does it appear to persist into the 2000s (Suleman et al., 2010)? One reason could be a
vacuum of professional guidelines on appropriateness for surgery. A 1937 textbook
included a long laundry list of symptoms for which tonsillectomies were deemed
appropriate, including "Any interference with respiration, day or night" (Burton,
2008). Nor had guidelines improved by the 1970s, where a qualitative study of
Scottish physicians found quite different decision rules to decide who got surgery.
One physician paid particular attention to inflammation near the tonsil as a "reliable"
sign, while another ignored such inflammation but instead focused on cervical lymph
nodes in the neck. Other physicians focused on physical diagnosis, while still others
relied on medical history[20] (Bloor et al., 1978a and b).

Physicians may adopt a rule-of-thumb—recommend surgery for a certain percentage or number of recently seen patients. For example, a 1934 study by the American
Child Health Association in New York was designed to measure the overall fraction
of children deemed appropriate for tonsillectomy. John Wennberg described the surprising results of the study:

> The research design required random sampling of 1000 school children. Upon examina-
> tion, 60% were found to have already undergone tonsillectomy. The remaining 40% were
> examined by the school physicians, who selected 45% in need of an operation. To make
> sure that no one in need of a tonsillectomy was left out, the Association arranged for the
> children not selected for tonsillectomy to be re-examined by another group of physicians.
> Perhaps to everyone's surprise, the second wave of physicians recommended that 40% of
> these have the operation. Still not content that unmet need had been adequately
> detected, the Association then arranged yet a third examination of the twice-rejected chil-
> dren by another group of physicians. On the third try, the physicians produced recom-
> mendations for the operation on 44% of the children. By the end of the three-
> examination process, only 65 children of the original 1000 had not been recommended
> for tonsillectomy. (Wennberg, 2008, p. 26)

This finding is supportive of a rule-of-thumb decision process, but it doesn't
explain why there might be different rules of thumb across the country. Clearly, if just
a few pediatricians have the responsibility for diagnosing tonsillectomy in a given
region, idiosyncratic beliefs could translate into regional variations. Alternatively, a
common rule of thumb could interact with exogenous factors outside the health care
system. Gruber and Owings (1996) find that in areas where fertility rates fell the
most, Cesarean section rates rose the most, a result consistent with one in which

---

[20] See Wennberg (2010) for a further discussion of these studies.

obstetricians do about the same number of Cesarean sections every year (see also Wennberg, 2010). Alternatively, one might expect to observe network effects, in which junior physicians adopt the practice style of more senior ones in the region. However, one study of Cesarean section rates in Florida found surprisingly little evidence of such spillover effects—even within practices there was a remarkably large variation in rates of Cesareans (Epstein and Nicholson, 2009).

Another key factor in affecting utilization is demand. As noted earlier in Figure 2.3, relatively small differences in demand could generate large variation in utilization, particularly where there is a vacuum of scientific evidence. Dr. R.P. Garrow, commenting upon Glover's 1938 study, noted that some of the "strange facts" regarding the unusually high rates of tonsillectomy among high-income households could be explained by "maternal anxiety" (p. 1236). Aside from the physician's disdain for such anxiety, this could either signal a pure income effect, or could also reflect a (perhaps mistaken) belief among higher income parents that tonsillectomies were the best approach to reducing discomfort for their children. Even now, most parents of children seeking tonsillectomies have "made up their mind what they want to have done beforehand" (p. 24) (Burton, 2008).

But one cannot explain the 10-fold variation across regions solely by the income elasticity of demand, time preference rates, or even possible differences in prices. Instead, the variation is likely a combination of factors: parents willing to give a "low-risk" procedure a try, coupled with a trusted family physician who is enthusiastic about the procedure, and who might not have entirely understood the risks of an adverse event; the underlying mortality rate in the 1930s was more than 0.1 percent.[21]

Back surgery is another example of Category II treatment, as discussed in section 2.3. Table 2.1 shows the variation in back surgery rates across regions in the US Medicare population. While the coefficient of variation is large (0.31), patterns of surgery are more idiosyncratic, with Bend, OR, exhibiting rates of 7.4 per thousand compared to low-rate regions such as New York (2.0) or Miami (2.4). Overall the correlation between price-adjusted spending and back surgery rates is −0.12. In other words, high rates of back surgery are slightly more likely in regions with overall lower Medicare expenditures. These rates are also higher in western states, and while one might conjecture that such residents are more likely to be engaged in outdoor activities, one might equally conjecture more back problems for industrial states with large blue-collar populations. Another example of regional variations, prescription drug spending (Medicare Part D), showed a similar lack of association with overall Medicare spending (Zhang et al., 2010a).

---

[21] Glover (1938) reported roughly 85 deaths per year during 1931–35, slightly more than 0.1 percent of the average of overall procedures during this period.

One explanation for these variations in Category II procedures is that some physicians and hospitals are simply better at providing specific services. For example, Chandra and Staiger estimated a Roy model of surgical treatments for heart attack patients, and found that in regions with high rates of surgical interventions, the marginal value of such interventions was considerably higher than in the low-rate areas ($g(x)$ instead of $s(x)$ in Figure 2.1) (Chandra and Staiger, 2007). They also found in regions with these high-quality surgeons or interventional cardiologists that overall survival rates were no better because of poorer-quality medical management, as reflected in the lower use of β blockers in high-surgery regions.

Similarly, Wennberg (2010) has observed that surgeons tend to specialize in a specific procedure within their field in which (presumably) they are most skilled and comfortable. This leads to a trade-off: Patients benefit from surgical specialization if they happen to be appropriate for the surgeon's favored procedure, but they could also be worse off if that procedure is not quite right for them. Physicians prescribing antipsychotics also tend to specialize in one specific treatment, particularly those with low volumes of patients or nearing retirement (Levine Taub et al., 2011).

Another example of preference-sensitive or Category II treatment is PSA testing. These simple blood tests detect early evidence of prostate cancer development in men, but there is considerable controversy about the value of such tests. First, there is a very long lag time between an elevated PSA test and the point at which prostate cancer adversely affects health. And second, many types of prostate cancer are benign—more than half of men over age 80 have evidence of prostate cancer, even when they die of something else. While there is evidence of small but significant benefits of PSA screening on survival for men under age 65 (Bill-Axelson et al., 2011), the treatments carry risks of incontinence and loss of sexual functioning. Thus preferences—quality versus quantity of life—should have an impact on decisions to be screened for prostate cancer, particularly if they vary widely across regions in the US.

More puzzling is the presence of variations for PSA testing where there really is no good evidence of benefits: for men over age 80. Studies show no benefit of either screening or treatment (versus watchful waiting) for men over age 65 (Bill-Axelson et al., 2011; Esserman et al., 2009). Indeed, the US Preventive Services Task Force recommended *against* the use of PSA screening for men over age 75 (US Preventive Services Task Force, 2008). Yet there was considerable variation across regions in 2003 rates of PSA testing for men over age 80, ranging from 2.2 percent in Burlington, VT, and 5.3 percent in Rochester, NY, to 27 percent in New York City, 30 percent in Miami, and 37 percent in Sun City, AZ[22] (Bynum et al., 2010). Rates

---

[22] The coefficient of variation was 0.35. The data used in the Bynum study predate the formal recommendation by the US Preventive Services Task Force; the previous guidelines had cautioned the use of PSA tests for men with life expectancies of less than 10 years. More recent unpublished data, however, suggest little downward trend.

of PSA testing for men over age 80 were positively associated with higher overall expenditure rates ($p = 0.36$).

How much of these variations are the consequence of movements along a per-ceived production function (because of changes in λ, as in Figure 2.1), and how much are the consequence of different production functions ($s'(x)$ versus $g'(x)$)? Like tonsillectomies, the variation is likely the consequence of both supply—physicians who follow a rule-of-thumb in checking the PSA testing box on the blood test form—but also of demand, in which 80-year-old men have grown accustomed to get-ting their "all clear" test results for prostate cancer while younger, and cannot imagine why they would not continue while older. (One physician explained to me that she did not have the 20 minutes to explain to these older men that they did not need the test any more.) Still, the fact that rates vary more than 10-fold between Burlington, VT, and Sun City, AZ, suggests a multiplier or network model, whether in patient demand (men want what their friends get) or physician supply (following community norms reduces the risk of a malpractice suit.)

What about geographic variation for these Category II procedures in other coun-tries? An earlier study found evidence of variations in health care utilization in England, Wales, and Canada that on a proportional basis were similar to those observed in the US, even if the non-US countries generally experienced lower overall rates (McPherson et al., 1981). More recently, variations have been found for hip replacements in Finland (Makela et al., 2010), antibiotic prescriptions in France (Mousques et al., 2010), and the treatment of bladder cancer and antibiotic use in the Netherlands (Goossens-Laan et al., 2010; Westert et al., 2010).

Two comprehensive studies of variations in the British National Health Service (NHS) also found considerable variability in Category II treatments such as stents and hip replacements (Appleby et al., 2011; National Health Service, 2010). As the Kings Fund study showed, the extent of variation for the entire population (that is, not spe-cific to just the over-65s) in percutaneous coronary interventions (most of which are stents) exhibited nearly 10-fold variation across regions, with a coefficient of variation equal to 0.39. That such variations are observed even in a national health system with salaried physicians suggest that it is not simply the presence of a fee-for-service Medicare system, or income-maximizing physicians in a supplier-induced demand model, that generates variations in Category II or preference-sensitive conditions.

3.5. Supply-sensitive (Category III) Treatments with Unknown or Marginal Benefits

In 1965, Martin Feldstein published a study of regional variation in hospital capacity across England, and found notable variations in beds per thousand, ranging from 4.61 in Sheffield to 6.79 in Liverpool (Feldstein, 1965). Hospital utilization is a Category III treatment because—at least for levels typically observed in developed economies—the incremental health value of greater hospital capacity is either small or zero (Fisher et al., 1994), or simply unknown.[23] These variations in hospital use did not appear to be explained by differences in health, nor did Feldstein observe the standard response to organizational scarcity, such as greater occupancy rates in regions with fewer beds, or shorter length-of-stay.

One potential explanation suggested by Feldstein for variations in hospital capacity is that building decisions were made decades ago, and hospital beds are less likely to migrate than individuals. Thus even after adjusting for disease burden, past changes in population predict current per capita bed capacity (Clayton et al., 2009). This idea was also expressed in "Roemer's law": building a hospital bed changes the informal medical rules-of-thumb for which conditions (and which severity levels) merit hospital admissions (Wennberg, 2010).

These hospital variations were also found in the Wennberg and Gittelsohn study of small Vermont communities, where rates ranged between 122 and 197 days per thousand (Wennberg and Gittelsohn, 1973). They also found a strong association between physician supply and utilization of physician services, the analogue of Feldstein's finding that hospital bed scarcity was not associated with more intensive use of each bed.

To see the variability in Category III or supply-sensitive care across the sample regions in Table 2.1, I consider two measures of end-of-life care among the chronically ill: ICU days in the last six months (2007) and physician visits in the last two years (2001–05), shown in Columns 8 and 9 of Table 2.1.[24] One might be concerned with end-of-life measures, since the treatment intensity of the region may affect the composition of the end-of-life sample: heroic efforts would save someone in a more intensive region who might otherwise be a decedent in some other region (Bach, 2010). Thus the highest cost (and successfully treated) patients would be missing from the sample of decedents in high-intensity hospitals and regions, leading to lower spending measures for higher-cost regions and conversely. Thus, estimates of end-of-life spending in theory could understate or overstate true variation, but in practice these measures are very strongly correlated with forward-looking cohorts of spending (Ong et al., 2009; Skinner et al., 2010). It is also important to note that end-of-life spending should not necessarily be interpreted as futile—physicians *ex ante* do not typically know which patients will survive—but instead as a signature of spending intensity for all chronically ill patients, some of whom die.[25]

---

[23] The story is quite different in emerging economies where the availability of high-quality hospital facilities is very limited.

[24] The latter end-of-life measure was limited to (and risk adjusted for) those diagnosed with serious illnesses (such as COPD, dementia, cancer, or multiple diagnoses) and who also died.

[25] An alternative approach is to use forward-looking cohorts, such as people who had heart attacks or hip fractures, although forward-looking and backward-looking measures are highly correlated (Skinner et al., 2010). In one study the correlation coefficient between the two types of measures was 0.95, although the rank ordering shifted for several of the intermediate-cost hospitals (Ong et al., 2009).

Rates of ICU days in the last six months varied widely, from 1.4 days per decedent in Grand Junction, CO, to 10.7 days in Miami; the coefficient of variation is 0.43. Similarly, physician visits ranged from an average of 38 in Grand Junction and Bend, OR, to 106 in Miami and 109 in Los Angeles.[26] These end-of-life measures are also strongly correlated with overall price-adjusted Medicare expenditures; correlation coefficients are 0.65 and 0.68, respectively (Wennberg et al., 2002).

Category III variations are also found in other countries (WIC, 2011). For example, wide variations in rates of asthma hospitalization found across regions in Canada were explained less by the frequency of emergency-room visits and more by the probability of subsequent admission to hospital (Lougheed et al., 2006). Similarly, variations for asthma hospitalizations were also variable both within and between Scandinavian countries (Kocevar et al., 2004).

One way to view these patterns of geographic variations comes from the theory of reasoned action, an approach developed by psychologists Ajzen and Fishbein (1980). In their model, individual behavior can be broken down into two parts: goals or objectives (e.g. health-seeking behavior is motivated by the desire to live more disease-free years), and beliefs about how to attain those goals. Presumably, patients and their physicians share the same broad goals: better functioning and longer lifespan. But different local health care systems may have quite different perceived approaches to attaining those goals. One study surveyed physicians across the United States and presented each with vignettes about a specific patient, and then asked the physicians how they would treat the patient (Sirovich et al., 2008). For questions where the scientific basis for treatment was clear and well established, there was very little variation in responses across regions. However, when the vignettes asked about scenarios where there was no clear right or wrong answer, there was considerably more variation across regions in how the physicians indicated they would proceed.

For example, at the UCLA hospital, where end-of-life utilization rates are among the highest in the country, the chief executive officer declared that "If you come to this hospital, we are not going to let you die." The hallmark of UCLA-style intensive care is not giving up on what might appear to be hopeless patients, with examples of both success and failure (Abelson, 2009). By contrast, end-of-life patients in low-cost Grand Junction, CO, experience a different philosophy that appears to reflect different beliefs about how to provide "best quality" care:

> Thanks to the area's single nonprofit hospice, which also offers palliative care, physicians are educated about initiating discussions with elderly patients about advance directives, and the public is informed about end-of-life choices. As a result, Grand Junction's population spends 40% fewer days in the hospital during the last 6 months of life and 74% more

---

[26] Physician visit measures do not include visits by medical residents, who cannot bill Medicare directly for their services. Thus true measures of physician visits are likely understated.

days in hospice than the national averages, and 50% fewer deaths than average occur in the hospital. (Bodenheimer and West, 2010)

Perhaps it is not surprising that academic medical centers position themselves to provide more intensive care, given their relative strengths. But too little is known about the overall impact of these different approaches to treating chronic illness. While Barnato et al. (2010) found slightly higher six-month survival rates in hospitals using more intensive end-of-life care, another study at a major medical center showed worse outcomes (survival and quality of life) arising from regular care versus early palliative care for metastatic lung cancer (Temel et al., 2010).

Given the lack of strong clinical evidence favoring one approach over another, patient preferences should play a role. Some will want everything possible done for them, while others would prefer the Grand Junction model, particularly if they were being asked to pay out-of-pocket for the difference between UCLA-style care and Grand Junction-style care.[27] It seems likely, however, that regional practice norms trump patient preferences, whether in high-intensity or low-intensity regions, a result that was found in the SUPPORT study[28] (Pritchard et al., 1998).

There are several other examples of Category III treatments where the clinical value is zero or most likely even negative. For example, the use of feeding tubes for patients with advanced dementia (such as Alzheimer's disease) represents a considerable burden for confused patients but with no better longevity (Finucane et al., 1999). One study found regional end-of-life care expenditures to be strongly predictive of its use (Teno et al., 2010). Yet there was considerable variation even within regions and teaching hospitals.[29] Other examples of variation in Category III treatments include inappropriate combinations for prescription drugs, where the lack of coordination in prescriptions leads to serious health risks (Zhang et al., 2010b), and the use of two CT scans on the same day, exposing patients to extra radiation with no clinical benefit (Bogdanich and McGinty, 2011).

Why do regions differ so much with regard to these Category III treatment rates? As noted above, Atul Gawande documented higher spending rates in McAllen, TX (as shown in Table 2.1), with the most pronounced entrepreneurial efforts focused on home health care, where physicians would often form a business affiliation with a home care agency (Gawande, 2009). As a consequence, price-adjusted spending for home health services per

[27] More complicated still is when family members also have strong preferences regarding treatment options.

[28] Another set of studies examined patient preferences for health care (e.g. if your doctor said you probably do not need an X-ray, would you still want one?) at the individual level for Medicare enrollees. While there was considerable variation in preferences across individuals, there was little difference in the fraction of patients wanting more care across regions—in other words, preferences did not appear to explain differences across regions in utilization (Anthony, et al., 2009; Barnato, et al., 2007).

[29] Cedar-Sinai and UCLA hospitals in Los Angeles are both very high-cost hospitals, as measured by end-of-life treatments, yet the use of feeding tubes for advanced dementia patients was zero at UCLA, in contrast to Cedar-Sinai, whose rate was more than double the national average (Teno et al., 2010).

Medicare enrollee was \$3,496 in the McAllen HRR, or about seven times the national average of \$496 and 13 times per enrollee spending in Grand Junction.

Why McAllen? In 1992, McAllen and El Paso were nearly identical with regard to Medicare spending, but by the 2000s they had sharply diverged. One anecdotal story from a physician recruiter suggested that it was far more difficult to recruit physicians to work in McAllen than in El Paso, requiring larger bonus payments to attract physicians there. The selection process would therefore lead to a population of physicians who were unusually motivated to respond to incentives. In sum, high-cost regions may be high for at least two reasons. The first is a larger perceived or actual productivity of health care ($g'(x)$ versus $s'(x)$ in Figure 2.1). The second is an entrepreneurial environment (one that could even verge on fraud) leading to a low or even negative λ (as in Figure 2.1).[30] The former explanation can hold under any health care system, fee-for-service or not. The latter model is better suited for explaining "outlier" spending measures in fee-for-service-based insurance programs for regions such as Miami and McAllen.

4. ESTIMATING THE CONSEQUENCES OF REGIONAL VARIATION: GEOGRAPHY AS AN INSTRUMENT

To this point, I have focused solely on whether geographic variations in utilization and expenditures exist, and if so what are the causes of such variations. This section considers the consequences of greater health care intensity, a topic on which there is a growing literature, with often seemingly contradictory results—sometimes positive coefficients, sometimes negative, other times zero.

To make sense of the often disparate results, consider a stylized model of aggregate health care outcomes, where the aggregation is across individuals in a specific region.[31] These individuals may have a given disease (like a heart attack), or the study may aggregate across all diseases. Let survival or functioning (or both—in the sense of quality-adjusted or disability-adjusted life years) be written S_j for region j, where

$$S_j = X_j\beta + m_{1j}\gamma_1 + m_{2j}\gamma_2 + m_{2j}\gamma_2 + \varepsilon_j \qquad (2.5)$$

The variables m_i are the dollar-equivalent input quantities for each of the three treatment categories discussed in section 2 above, while the vector X measures health-related

---

[30] Miami appears to be a "hot spot" for fraud, as evidenced by one newspaper story about Dr. Christopher Wayne, the "Rock Doc," who billed Medicare \$1.2 million in 2008, mostly for physical therapy (Schoofs and Tamman, 2010). But fraud alone is unlikely to explain why Miami is such an outlier, since such behavior is also pervasive in New York, Los Angeles, and Detroit (Schoofs et al., 2011).

[31] I ignore here the considerable challenge of determining the "correct" spatial unit of analysis (Fotheringham and Wong, 1991).

risk adjusters, β the vector of coefficients, and ε is the error term. The key coefficients are γ_i , or the average marginal productivity of input i, with an assumed ranking of $\gamma_1 > \gamma_2 > \gamma_3$ reflecting the assumption above that, on average, Category I inputs are more cost effective than Category II, and Category II more cost effective than Category III.

Aggregate per-enrollee expenditures $M_j^\star$ are given by

$$M_j^* = P_j[m_{1j} + m_{2j} + m_{3j}] \tag{2.6}$$

where the aggregate price P_j reflects the differential price indices for reimbursements across regions. Thus, price-adjusted spending m_j is defined implicitly by

$$m_j = m_{1j} + m_{2j} + m_{3j} \tag{2.7}$$

Now that a set of outcome and spending variables has been defined, one can turn next to the variety of studies seeking to ask the question of "Is more better?" There are two general categories of such studies: The first considers specific inputs and thus can be viewed as capturing an estimate of a specific γ_i. Another set of papers considers a broader classification of aggregate spending, and in some cases uses an estimate of one type of spending, such as m_3, as an instrument for other inputs in the production function.

As an example of the first type of study, Glover's original 1938 paper considered a natural experiment in which Hornsey Borough declined suddenly from 186 tonsillectomies per 1,000 in 1928 to just 12 in 1929, and remained low thereafter owing to the "courageous" efforts of the local doctor. The outcome measure, otitis media (an inflammation of the inner ear), continued a secular decline during this period, and so Glover therefore concluded that the fall in tonsillectomy rates carried no risks to children (Glover, 1938). The estimated marginal impact of tonsillectomies on otitis media (γ_2) was therefore zero.

Amber Barnato and colleagues in turn estimated the association between greater intensity of care (higher utilization) and 30-day and six-month survival in Pennsylvania hospitals (Barnato et al., 2010). Because so little is known about the incremental effectiveness of the intensity of hospital treatments, this study corresponds to an estimate of γ_3 for Category III treatments.[32] The key feature of this study is that they were able to measure specific components of treatment: ICU use, mechanical ventilation, hemodialysis, tracheostomy and feeding tubes. On average, they found survival benefits of more intensive care: a roughly $14,000 increase in per capita expenditures for these treatments translated into a 1.5 percent improvement in the chance of surviving an extra six months, with unclear evidence of persistence beyond six months. The largest benefits were seen at the lowest level of spending, where the

---

[32] See Fisher and Skinner (2010) for further discussion of this and other studies.

hospitals may have lacked a fully staffed ICU facility. For this case, γ_3 was estimated to be positive, albeit with poor cost effectiveness.[33]

Another example of using geography to estimate specific treatment effectiveness comes from the classic study by McClellan et al., who used differential distance to a catheterization laboratory to study the effectiveness of surgical interventions for heart attack patients (McClellan et al., 1994). Their results suggest modest cost–effectiveness of surgical interventions; a different study showed such beneficial results persisting over long periods of time (Cutler, 2007). One potential limitation of these studies, recognized by the authors, is that hospitals with catheterization laboratories may also provide higher quality care along other dimensions—that is, the observable Category II measure could be correlated positively (or negatively) with other dimensions of care.[34]

One study compared state-level Medicare expenditures with state-level process quality measures like beta blocker use after heart attacks, or flu shots (Baicker and Chandra, 2004). They found a negative association between overall expenditures and effective (or Category I) care for the Medicare population.[35] The advantage of this study is its simplicity; process measures of care did not require risk adjustment since heart attack patients in Louisiana should be as likely to receive β blockers at discharge as those in New Hampshire, especially if they are sicker. This study has sometimes been interpreted as showing that "more is not better," but it tells us little about the marginal effectiveness of specific treatments (γ). Instead, it tells us about the partial correlation coefficient $r_{1M\star}$ between unadjusted spending $M\star$ (as in equation (2.6)) and effective care m_1. Thus effective or Category I care is not necessarily positively associated with higher levels of Category II or III care. (This can also be seen in Table 2.1 by the negative association between spending and β blocker use.) Another paper used more recent quality data from Medicare's Hospital Compare program at the hospital level to find negative or zero correlations between reported quality and end-of-life spending (Yasaitis et al., 2009).

Other studies have used end-of-life and other types of measures as an instrument for overall expenditures. For example, a two-part study in the *Annals of Internal Medicine* examined patients who were hospitalized with one of three different conditions: heart attack, hip fracture, and colon cancer (Fisher et al., 2003a and b). First, they divided regions into five equally sized quintiles based on average end-of-life spending in the region. In other words, the "look-back" end-of-life measures were

---

[33] Another approach is to consider supply measures of specific inputs such as specialists; one study found positive but rapidly diminishing returns (in terms of infant mortality) to an increased supply of neonatologists (Goodman et al., 2002).

[34] Also see Xian et al., who find beneficial effects of stroke centers on health outcomes of stroke patients (Xian et al., 2011).

[35] This correlation is specific to Medicare quality measures and Medicare expenditures, but may not extend to non-Medicare data (Cooper, 2009).

used to assign regions to quintiles; Los Angeles was a high-cost region (for end-of-life care) and so anyone with a heart attack, hip fracture, or colon cancer in Los Angeles was assigned to that quintile.

They then "looked forward" to see what happened to each of the three risk-adjusted cohorts of patients, starting on the day the patient was hospitalized for heart attack, hip fracture, or colon surgery.[36] Patients treated in regions where utilization (and spending) were higher received about 60 percent more care over the first year after their initial hospitalization. But in general, there was no pattern showing better risk-adjusted outcomes when compared with those treated in regions where utilization was lower—of the 42 separate hypothesis tests in the paper, 23 showed significantly worse outcomes in high-spending regions, 14 showed no significant effects, and five showed significant positive effects.[37]

In the context of the model above, the expected value of the reduced-form coefficient arising from this type of regression, where a Category III measure is used as an instrument, is given by the following:

$$E\{\hat{\gamma}\} = \gamma_3 + r_{13}\gamma_1 + r_{23}\gamma_2 \qquad (2.8)$$

That is, without including the other categories of treatment on the right-hand side, the estimated coefficient implicitly captures the primary estimate γ_3, but also the estimates of average marginal effects for Category I and II treatments, multiplied by the partial regression coefficient of these different components on m_3. For example, suppose that γ_1 is large and positive (by assumption), but that Category I effective treatments are negatively correlated with Category III supply-sensitive care for these specific cohorts. Even if γ_3 is positive, when $r_{13} < 0$, the estimated *association* between m_3 and risk-adjusted outcomes could be negative or zero. Or conversely, if the coefficient γ_3 is zero or even negative, a positive association between Category III spending and effective Category I care—as has been found in cancer treatments (Landrum et al., 2008)—could still yield a positive estimated coefficient when end-of-life spending is used as an instrument. In other words, it is not whether "more spending is better" but instead how the money is spent—is it for home health care yielding no health benefits at the margin (McKnight, 2006), or primary angioplasty for heart attack patients?

A number of other studies have since been published with end-of-life measures using either the reduced form approach in the Fisher et al. studies, or an explicit instrumental variables approach (Skinner et al., 2005). As noted above, the use of end-of-life care as an instrument could bias against finding that more spending is

---

[36] They also considered data from the Medicare Current Beneficiary Survey and the Cooperative Cardiovascular Project, which included chart data and thus provided the highest quality risk adjustment.

[37] Adjusting for spatial clustering (which was not done in these studies) most likely would have moved several of the negative and positive results into the insignificant bin.

associated with better outcomes—as this is the component of spending *least* likely to yield health benefits—but a more recent set of studies has found positive associations between end-of-life spending and health outcomes. These have differed from the earlier studies by including different disease categories, using two years of "start-up" data to collect comorbidities (and where respondents must remain alive to be included in the cohort), or by focusing on in-hospital mortality for all age groups (Hadley et al., 2011; Ong et al., 2009; Romley et al., 2011; Silber et al., 2010).

Still others have attempted to develop a natural experiment by focusing on tourists who got sick and were admitted to hospital in Florida (Doyle, 2010). In this case, greater intensity of care for acutely ill tourists was found to yield real benefits. For non-tourists, however, more intensive care was not associated with better outcomes; this is either consistent with heterogeneity in benefits (tourists benefit most from intensive care) or a positive correlation between high spending areas and unobservable poor health of residents.[38] More generally, the wide range of estimates could be explained by heterogeneity across diseases and treatment strategies in the correlations r_{ij}.

One way to address this problem is to enter inputs for Category I, II, or III treatments directly, and thereby attempt to estimate separate γ coefficients rather than some weighted average of the underlying coefficients. One study using hospital-level data found a faintly negative association between overall risk-adjusted and price-adjusted spending and risk-adjusted one-year survival for heart attack patients in the Medicare program. This can be explained in party by a slightly negative association between Category I and total spending measures (Skinner and Staiger, 2009). However, when hospital-specific Category I treatments were included in the regression (aspirin, β blocker, and primary reperfusion such as angioplasty or clot-busting drugs), along with total expenditures $(m_2 + m_3)$ on the right-hand side of the equation, both coefficients became positive—with γ_1, the effect of Category I treatments, dominating the (positive, but diminishing) impact of spending.

Figure 2.5 captures their results graphically; the empty dots represent hospitals with rapid adoption of Category I treatments, while the full dots are those with slow adoption. The functions $s(x)$ and $f(x)$ measure the conventional "production function" association between spending more and outcomes. Thus knowing the simple correlation between spending and survival in Figure 2.5, which as drawn could be either positive or negative, tells us little about the deeper parameters of the model.[39]

Other studies have found similar patterns, including one comprehensive study of mortality rates for Medicare beneficiaries undergoing major vascular, orthopedic, and

---

[38] Other more recent studies found negative or zero associations between spending, whether in levels (Glance et al., 2004), or in growth rates (Rothberg et al., 2010a).

[39] Another approach is to consider Category I and III treatments in the context of a difference-in-difference model, as in Skinner et al. (2006).

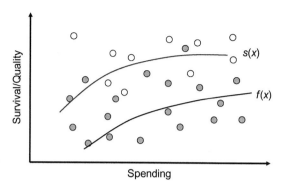

Figure 2.5 Hypothetical spending and outcome measures.

general surgical procedures at US acute care hospitals (Silber et al., 2010). The primary results were that when end-of-life hospital resource use in the region is higher, 30-day surgical mortality rates and the relative risk of failure to rescue (having a complication and dying) were lower. In other words, hospitals spending more on Category III treatments also experienced better Category II outcomes for their surgical patients.

These results are also consistent with the pattern pictured in Figure 2.5, in finding that a $10,000 increase in end-of-life expenditures, while substantially improving survival in the first 30 or 90 days, is more modest in the longer term, leading to just a 0.12 percent increase in the probability of surviving one year post-surgery (Fisher and Skinner, 2010). And like Figure 2.5, the individual-specific variations in hospital productivity are very large in magnitude relative to the treatment effects or slope of the production function.[40]

These findings are also consistent with other evidence on productivity. For example, the finding that total factor productivity differences explain much of the variation in GDP per capita across countries is by now well established, as is the finding that some countries (like some health care systems) are consistently ahead in innovation (Comin and Hobijn, 2004). Similarly, the lack of correlation between the level of regional health care spending and growth in such spending (Chernew et al., 2010a) is also consistent with the macroeconomics literature on the weak convergence properties of country-level per capita GDP. As noted above, productivity differences across hospitals are consistent with similar variation across firms in the concrete industry

---

[40] Focusing on the 30-day mortality rates, the standard deviation for the "across hospital variation" was 0.19396, while the (linear) coefficient on end-of-life spending was 0.06584 (in units of 10,000 dollars). Thus increasing end-of-life spending by $10,000 was roughly equivalent to a 1/3 standard deviation increase in the random effect parameter (or a movement from the 50th to the 63rd percentile). See also Kaestner and Silber (2010) for additional evidence on 30-day outcomes across a variety of conditions. I am grateful to the authors for sharing these estimates from their model.

(Syverson, 2004). The lesson of the concrete industry, however, is important: we do not necessarily think that creating a government-financed Concrete Innovation Center (CIC) would necessarily improve productivity in that sector. What then are the policy levers in health care that might improve efficiency by addressing regional variations in health care?

5. INEFFICIENCY AND THE POLICY IMPLICATIONS OF REGIONAL VARIATIONS

There are a variety of approaches to estimating the overall degree of inefficiency in the US health care system. One approach that focuses on benchmarking low-cost communities yields estimates of efficiency costs of 15–25 percent, with 30 percent an upper limit; these assume that the benchmark regions are perfectly efficient, which is overly optimistic—Bend, OR, is a low-cost region despite its high rates of back surgery.[41] A McKinsey Report estimates that the US wastes $650 billion (or 30 percent of total spending on health) relative to health care systems in other developed countries (McKinsey, 2008), while Thomson Reuters estimates 33 percent waste (Kelly, 2009). However, these estimates ignore the potential loss in health outcomes arising from the underuse of efficient treatment—the vertical variation in Figure 2.5, not just the horizontal variation. Accounting for such differences would lead to substantially higher levels of inefficiency relative to overall expenditures.

But how much of that 20 or 30 percent waste is really extractable through public policies? For some treatments where procedure rates are either too low or too high, simply publishing and circulating region- or hospital-specific measures can help to reduce inefficiency. Following the dissemination of area tonsillectomy rates from Wennberg and Gittelsohn's 1973 study, rates dropped from 60 to 10 percent in Morrisville, VT, one previously high-utilization community (Wennberg, 2010). The adoption of β blocker use as a publicly reported quality measure has increased its diffusion to near-universal use among appropriate patients. In general, the reporting of quality measures has been found to affect patient demand, but public reporting can lead to perverse outcomes if providers "game" the measures (Dranove, 2011). For example, one study found higher rates of cardiac bypass surgery as surgeons sought healthier patients to improve their quality measures (Dranove et al., 2003). Public reporting of Category III treatments might also affect patient demand if there were clear risks associated with high rates, for example receiving two CT scans on the same day (Bogdanich and McGinty, 2011). But given the very low cost-sharing in most

---

[41] For example, see Fisher et al. (2003a and b), Skinner et al. (2005), Sutherland et al. (2009).

health care systems, fewer patients would be scared away from hospitals simply because of their very high rates of overall spending.

Another approach to reducing unwarranted variation for preference-sensitive treatments is the use of decision aids for patients to make informed choices. These typically involve DVDs that present both probabilities and magnitudes of benefit and side-effects, as well as patient interviews describing why they did or did not choose the treatment. Whether utilization rates rise or fall (and typically they fall), this approach leads to greater efficiency with regard to matching patient preferences to treatment strategies (Barry, 2002; O'Connor, et al., 2004). As well, making decision aids the standard for informed choice has potential to reduce the likelihood of malpractice cases (King and Moulton, 2006).

None of these proposed reforms are likely to have much impact on regional differences in big-ticket Category III expenditures. One approach to addressing such variation is simply to reduce reimbursement rates in high (health-adjusted) spending areas. Certainly there is evidence that current adjustments for prices do not always reflect actual costs of doing business (IOM, 2011). But adjusting prices is a very blunt instrument, does less to improve productivity, and could in fact lead to worse outcomes (Dranove, 2011). One largely unexplored approach is to use quantity regulation to reduce regional variation, for example by buying back older MRIs in regions with high rates of imaging, or stricter enforcement of "Certificate of Need" programs.

The 2010 health care reform legislation in the United States hoped to capture some cost savings from regional variations by implementing nationwide "accountable care organizations" (ACOs) that can in theory hold down cost growth while maintaining or improving quality. The ACO was designed to reduce costs by instituting a system of shared saving in which holding growth rates below a benchmark yields bonus payments from Medicare, but exceeding a different benchmark triggers penalties.[42] The theory behind these reforms is that the physician—hospital network (as in section 3.1 above) is the appropriate decision-making unit; the providers know better than regulators what types of Category III expenditures can be cut or how care can be reorganized to maintain quality but reduce cost. But should ACOs be expected to reduce regional variations in expenditures?

In theory, ACOs could generate the greatest savings in the highest-cost regions, which should attenuate regional variations. As well, built into the legislation is an updating rule that further encourages convergence, since percentage growth rate benchmarks are defined relative to the national average, and not to the region. Thus an update of 4 percent of the national average would be translated to a dollar amount applied consistently to all regions, leading to a much smaller proportional update in Miami compared to Grand Junction.

---

[42] New ACOs can avoid penalties for the first few years.

A different approach to health care reform comes from "premium support" plans in which enrollees receive a voucher with a preset amount, used as credit towards the purchase of a private insurance policy. Most notably, such an approach was proposed by Representative Paul Ryan in 2011, but a variety of other voucher plans, albeit with more generous premium support and greater regulatory control, have been proposed in the past (Emanuel and Fuchs, 2005).

Voucher plans could represent a very direct way to attenuate regional variations in spending. They would most likely provide different dollar amounts depending on health status, but the key unknown is to what extent they would accommodate existing regional variation not caused by health differences. Would Congress really allow residents of Miami to receive vouchers worth twice as much as those in Grand Junction? Conversely, if vouchers adjust only for individual health status and price differences, how would the consequent precipitous decline in the regional variation in federal Medicare expenditures affect the organization (and quality) of care in Miami (Brownlee and Schultz, 2011)?

As noted in section 3.1, risk adjustment for populations with different health status is particularly challenging whether in ACOs or for risk-adjusted vouchers. Tying the payment level (and performance or outcome measures) to the average level of illness among plan enrollees will create financial incentives for "gaming" the system, whether by diagnosing more disease or by avoiding the higher cost patient's conditional on their risk-adjustment score (Brown et al., 2011b). In sum, it is too early to tell how successfully new policies will pare away at regional variation, but improved risk adjustment and better ways of measuring health system performance and quality are all necessary (if not sufficient) steps.

6. REGIONAL VARIATIONS IN HEALTH OUTCOMES

One limitation of this study has been the emphasis on regional variations in health care utilization rather than regional variations in health. It is important to note that there are also clear geographic patterns in health. One study documented variations in life expectancy across counties in the United States that varied by as much as 15 years, for example (Kulkarni et al., 2011). And Figure 2.6 shows death rates from heart disease for people over age 35, based on Centers for Disease Control (CDC) data, by US county. The magnitude of regional variation in heart disease is larger than for many health care services, ranging from less than two deaths to over seven deaths per 1,000, with strong patterns of spatial correlation particularly in the South. Nor do these rates appear to be highly correlated spatially with actual Medicare expenditures (Figure 2.4). While there is a growing literature devoted to measuring and

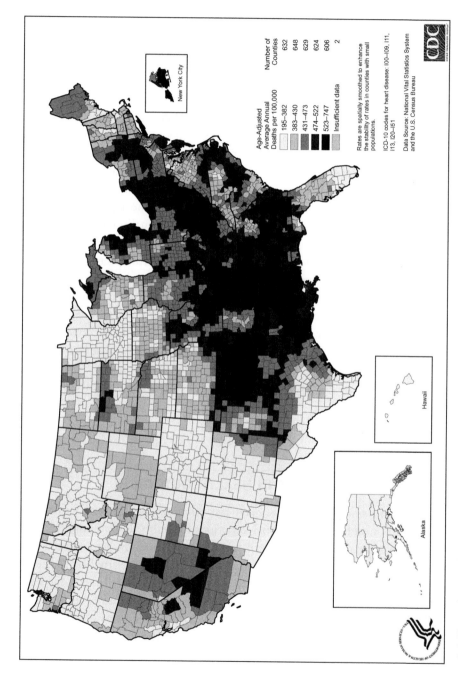

Figure 2.6 Heart disease death rates 2000–2006, adults age 35+, by county. *Source: http://www.cdc.gov/dhdsp/maps/national_maps/hd_all. htm*

understanding the geography of health and health care (Cromley and McLafferty, 2002), we do not know as much about how geographical patterns of health care expenditures and quality affect geographical patterns of health outcomes. For example, how much do the low process quality measures in Louisiana and Mississippi contribute to the higher disease burden and mortality in those states?

It is reasonable to view regional variations in meat and poultry consumption, attendance at yoga and spinning classes, or smoking and drinking, rather than regional variation in health care utilization, as the important causal factors explaining regional variation in health. This was a point made early on by Victor Fuchs; despite similar levels of health care spending in Utah and Nevada, there is much less disease in Utah (Figure 2.6), most likely the consequence of a higher fraction of Mormons in Utah who eschew smoking and drinking (Fuchs, 1998).

It is less clear how efforts to improve health by changing lifestyles and behavior should account for geographical variation. If the government chooses to tax soda, for example (Brownell et al., 2009), should rates of taxation or enforcement depend on one's state of residence? As well, taxes on poor health habits are typically borne by the individuals, and not financed through massive transfer programs such as Medicare and Medicaid, so both the efficiency and equity issues are not so closely tied into one's zip code of residence. Still, the remarkable geographic patterns of poor health are highly suggestive of network factors not yet entirely well understood (Christakis and Fowler, 2007).

7. DISCUSSION AND CONCLUSION

The regional variations literature reviewed typically appears in the health services research literature and is not always visible to the practicing health economist. Not that there's anything wrong with that, but the insights of this literature can often be used to shed light on the efficiency of health care markets, as well as providing new approaches to causality and risk adjustment. Taken as a whole, the literature points to a number of factors leading to "warranted" variation in health care expenditures, but there remains persistent and sometimes large differences in both rates of utilization and quality of care that are not explained by prices, illness, or income, or other factors. Nor are aggregate utilization rates systematically associated with health outcomes; it appears to depend more on how the money is spent than on the total amount spent.

But there is also much that is not well understood about regional variations. Most of the evidence thus far identifies regional variation as a residual, and not something that can be predicted beforehand, for example being able to foresee in 1992 that

McAllen would have grown so much more rapidly than El Paso. One can speculate that the level and growth of spending is a function of entrepreneurial capacity, market competition, the relative generosity of private firms and insurance companies, and patient preferences, but at this point we do not yet have a unified theory of regional variation that would allow us to *predict* the future evolution of health care costs and quality diffusion.

I return to the original question of why should variations in health care be viewed any differently from variations in the consumption of meat and poultry? There are two key differences. The first is that the geographic variations are being financed largely by third parties, and so the costs of regional variations in Category III treatments are borne not by the patients receiving such treatments, but by workers experiencing stagnating wages owing to health insurance premium hikes, or taxpayers facing higher statutory rates (and tax distortions) to maintain growth in Medicare spending (Baicker and Skinner, 2011). By contrast, most of the cost arising from over-consumption of marbled beef is borne by the individual (and her family) through a reduction in life expectancy. And second, existing regional variations in health care utilization are symptomatic of an enormous lack of knowledge about what works and what does not in health care—something that is less of a concern for poultry consumption.

This chapter has also highlighted some of the key difficulties in better understanding the interplay between and among supply and demand in health care markets. There are complex networks of primary care physicians who refer to specialists, who in turn recommend procedures to patients who have often done their research on the internet, leading to challenges in allocating how much of the regional the variation arises from patient demand, physician beliefs, financial incentives, or capacity constraints (Bederman et al., 2011). While unraveling this complex structure presents modeling and empirical challenges, the remarkable differences in regional practice styles and outcomes provides a fertile ground to identify, measure, and one hopes reduce the vast degree of inefficiency in health care worldwide.

REFERENCES

Abelson, R. (2009). Months to live: Weighing medical costs of end-of-life care. *The New York Times* (December 29).

Ajzen, I. & Fishbein, M. (1980). *Understanding attitudes and predicting social behavior.* Englewood Cliffs, NJ: Prentice-Hall.

Anthony, D. L., Herndon, M. B., Gallagher, P. M., Barnato, A. E., Bynum, J. P., et al. (2009). How much do patients' preferences contribute to resource use? *Health Affairs (Millwood), 28*(3, May–June), 864–873.

Appleby, J., Raleigh, V., Frosini, F., Bevan, G., Gao, H., et al. (2011). *Variations in health care: The good, the bad and the inexplicable.* London: The Kings Fund.

Arrow, K. J. (1963). Uncertainty and the welfare economics of medical care. *American Economic Review, 53*, 941–973.

Bach, P. B. (2010). A map to bad policy—hospital efficiency measures in the Dartmouth Atlas. *New England Journal of Medicine, 362*(7, February 18), 569—573 (discussion 574).

Baicker, K. & Chandra, A. (2004, April 7). Medicare spending, the physician workforce, and beneficiaries' quality of care. *Health Affairs (Millwood)*.

Baicker, K. & Skinner, J. (2011). Health care spending growth and the future of U.S. tax rates. National Bureau of Economic Research Working Paper Series, 16772.

Baicker, K. Buckles, K. S., & Chandra, A. (2006). Geographic variation in the appropriate use of cesarean delivery. *Health Affairs, 25*(5), w355—w367.

Baicker, K., Fisher, E. S., & Chandra, A. (2007). Malpractice liability costs and the practice of medicine in the medicare program. *Health Affairs (Millwood), 26*(3, May—June), 841—852.

Baker, L. C., Fisher, E. S., & Wennberg, J. E. (2008). Variations in hospital resource use for Medicare and privately insured populations in California. *Health Affairs (Millwood), 27*(2, March—April), w123—w134.

Barnato, A. E, Herndon, M. B., Anthony, D. L., Gallagher, P., Skinner, J. S., et al. (2007). Are regional variations in end-of-life care intensity explained by patient preferences? A study of the US Medicare population. *Medical Care, 45*(5), 386—393.

Barnato, A. E., Chang, C. C., Farrell, M. H., Lave, J. R., Roberts, M. S., et al. (2010). Is survival better at hospitals with higher "end-of-life" treatment intensity? *Medical Care, 48*(2, February), 125—132.

Barry, M. J. (2002). Health decision aids to facilitate shared decision making in office practice. *Annals of Internal Medicine, 136*(2, January 15), 127—135.

Battacharya, J. & Lakdawalla, D. (2006). Does Medicare benefit the poor? New answers to an old question. *Journal of Public Economics, 90*(1—2), 277—294.

Becker, G. & Murphy, K. (1992). The division of labor, coordination costs, and knowledge. *Quarterly Journal of Economics, 107*(4), 1137—1160.

Bederman, S. S., Coyte, P. C., Kreder, H. J., Mahomed, N. N., McIsaac, W. J., et al. (2011). Who's in the driver's seat? The influence of patient and physician enthusiasm on regional variation in degenerative lumbar spinal surgery: A population-based study. *Spine (Philadelphia, Pa 1976), 36*(6, March 15), 481—489.

Berwick, D. M. (2003). Disseminating innovations in health care. *JAMA, 289*(15, April 16), 1969—1975.

Bill-Axelson, A., Holmberg, L., Ruutu, M., Garmo, H., Stark, J. R., et al. (2011). Radical prostatectomy versus watchful waiting in early prostate cancer. *New England Journal of Medicine, 364*(18, May 5), 1708—1717.

Bloor, M. J., Venters, G. A., & Samphier, M. L. (1978a). Geographical variation in the incidence of operations on the tonsils and adenoids. An epidemiological and sociological investigation (part 2). *Journal of Laryngology & Otology, 92*(10, October), 883—895.

Bloor, M. J., Venters, G. A., & Samphier, M. L. (1978b). Geographical variation in the incidence of operations on the tonsils and adenoids. An epidemiological and sociological investigation. Part I. *Journal of Laryngology & Otology, 92*(9, September), 791—801.

Boden, W. E., O'Rourke, R. A., Teo, K. K., Hartigan, P. M., Maron, D. J., et al. (2007). Optimal medical therapy with or without PCI for stable coronary disease. *New England Journal of Medicine, 356*(15), 1503—1516.

Bodenheimer, T. & West, D. (2010). Low-cost lessons from Grand Junction, Colorado. *New England Journal of Medicine, 363*(15, October 7), 1391—1393.

Bogdanich, W. & McGinty, J. C. (2011). Medicare claims show overuse for CT scanning. *The New York Times*, June 17.

Bradley, E. H., Herrin, J., Mattera, J. A., Holmboe, E. S., Wang, Y., Frederick, P., et al. (2005). Quality improvement efforts and hospital performance: Rates of beta-blocker prescription after acute myocardial infarction. *Medical Care, 43*(3), 282—292.

Brown, J., Duggan, M., Kuziemko, I., & Woolston, W. (2011). How does risk selection respond to risk adjustment? Evidence from the Medicare Advantage program. National Bureau of Economic Research Working Paper Series, 16977.

Brownell, K. D., Farley, T., Willett, W. C., Popkin, B. M., Chaloupka, F. J., et al. (2009). The public health and economic benefits of taxing sugar-sweetened beverages. *New England Journal of Medicine, 361*(16, October 15), 1599—1605.

Brownlee, S. & Schultz, E. (2011). *Paul Ryan's unintended consequences*. Kaiser Health News.

Burton, M. J. (2008). Commentary: Tonsillectomy—then and now. *International Journal of Epidemiology, 37*(1, February), 23–25.

Bynum, J. P. W., Bernal-Delgado, E., Gottlieb, D., & Fisher, E. (2007). Assigning ambulatory patients and their physicians to hospitals: A method for obtaining population-based provider performance measurements. *Health Service Research, 42*(1).

Bynum, J. Song, Y., & Fisher, E. (2010). Variation in prostate-specific antigen screening in men aged 80 and older in fee-for-service Medicare. *Journal of the American Geriatric Society, 58*(4, April), 674–680.

Chandra, A., & Skinner, J. (2011). Productivity growth and expenditure growth in U.S. health care. *Journal of Economic Literature* (forthcoming, January).

Chandra, A. & Staiger, D. O. (2007). Productivity spillovers in healthcare: Evidence from the treatment of heart attacks. *Journal of Political Economy, 115*, 103–140.

Chandra, A., Gruber, J., & McKnight, R. (2010). Patient cost-sharing and hospitalization offsets in the elderly. *American Economic Review, 100*(1), 193–213.

Chernew, M. E., Sabik, L., Chandra, A., & Newhouse, J. P. (2010a). Ensuring the fiscal sustainability of health care reform. *New England Journal of Medicine, 362*(1, January 7), 1–3.

Chernew, M. E., Sabik, L. M., Chandra, A., Gibson, T. B., & Newhouse, J. P. (2010b). Geographic correlation between large-firm commercial spending and Medicare spending. *American Journal of Management Care, 16*(2, February), 131–138.

Christakis, N. A. & Fowler, J. H. (2007). The spread of obesity in a large social network over 32 years. *New England Journal of Medicine, 357*(4, July 26), 370–379.

Clayton, L. L., Kreiman, C., & Skinner, J. (2009). *Why is there regional variation in hospital bed capacity?* Hanover, NH: Dartmouth Medical School.

Comin, D. & Hobijn, B. (2004). Cross country technology adoption: Making the theories face the facts. *Journal of Monetary Economics, 51*, 39–83.

Cooper, R. A. (2009). States with more health care spending have better-quality health care: Lessons about Medicare. *Health Affairs (Millwood), 28*(1, January–February), w103–w115.

Cromley, E. K. & McLafferty, S. (2002). *GIS and public health*. New York: Guilford Press.

Currie, J. & MacLeod, W. B. (2008). First do no harm? Tort reform and birth outcomes. *Quarterly Journal of Economics, 123*(2), 795–830.

Cutler, D. & Scheiner, L. (1999). The geography of Medicare. *American Economic Review, Papers and Proceedings, 89*(2), 228–233.

Cutler, D. M. (2007). The lifetime costs and benefits of medical technology. *Journal of Health Economics, 26*(6), 1081–1100.

De Jong, J. D. (2008). *Explaining medical practice variation: Social organization and institutional mechanism*. Utrecht, The Netherlands: Nivel.

De Vries, E. N., Prins, H. A., Crolla, R. M., den Outer, A. J., van Andel, G., et al. (2010). Effect of a comprehensive surgical safety system on patient outcomes. *New England Journal of Medicine, 20*(November 11), 1928–1937.

Doyle, J. (2010). Returns to local-area healthcare spending: Using shocks to patients far from home. MIT Sloan School of Management Working Paper.

Dranove, D. (2011). Reporting on and paying health care providers. In T. McGuire, M. Pauly & P. P. Baros (Eds.), *Handbook of health economics*. Amsterdam: Elsevier.

Dranove, D., Kessler, D., McClellan, M., & Satterthwaite, M. (2003). Is more information better? The effects of health reports on health care providers. *Journal of Political Economy, 111*(3, June), 555–558.

Eaton, J. & Kortum, S. (1999). International technology diffusion: Theory and measurement. *International Economic Review, 40*(3, August), 537–570.

Emanuel, E. J. & Fuchs, V. R. (2005). Health care vouchers—a proposal for universal coverage. *New England Journal of Medicine, 352*(12, March 24), 1255–1260.

Epstein, A. J. & Nicholson, S. (2009). The formation and evolution of physician treatment styles: An application to cesarean sections. *Journal of Health Economics, 28*(6, December), 1126–1140.

Esserman, L., Shieh, Y., & Thompson, I. (2009). Rethinking screening for breast cancer and prostate cancer. *JAMA, 302*(15, October 21), 1685–1692.

Feenberg, D. & Skinner, J. (2000). Federal Medicare transfers across states: Winners and losers. *National Tax Journal, 53*, 713−732.

Feldstein, M. S. (1965). Hospital bed scarcity: An analysis of the effects of inter-regional differences. *Economica, 32*(128, November), 393−409.

Finucane, T. E., Christmas, C., & Travis, K. (1999). Tube feeding in patients with advanced dementia: A review of the evidence. *JAMA, 282*(14, October 13), 1365−1370.

Fisher, E. & Skinner, J. (2010). Comment on Silber et al.: Aggressive treatment styles and surgical outcomes. *Health Service Research, 45*(6, Pt 2), 1908−1911.

Fisher, E. S., Staiger, D. O., Bynum, J. P., & Gottlieb, D. J. (2007). Creating accountable care organizations: The extended hospital medical staff. *Health Affairs (Millwood), 26*(1, January−February), w44−w57.

Fisher, E. S., Wennberg, D. E., Stukel, T. A., Gottlieb, D. J., Lucas, F. L., et al. (2003a). The implications of regional variations in Medicare spending. Part 1: The content, quality, and accessibility of care. *Annals of Internal Medicine, 138*(4, February 18), 273−287.

Fisher, E. S., Wennberg, D. E., Stukel, T. A., Gottlieb, D. J., Lucas, F. L., et al. (2003b). The implications of regional variations in Medicare spending. Part 2: Health outcomes and satisfaction with care. *Annals of Internal Medicine, 138*(4, February 18), 288−298.

Fisher, E. S., Wennberg, J. E., Stukel, T. A., & Sharp, S. M. (1994). Hospital readmission rates for cohorts of Medicare beneficiaries in Boston and New Haven. *New England Journal of Medicine, 331*(15, October 13), 989−995.

Fotheringham, A. S. & Wong, D. W. S. (1991). The modifiable areal unit problem in multivariate statistical-analysis. *Environment and Planning A, 23*(7, July), 1025−1044.

Fowler, F. J., Jr., Gallagher, P. M., Anthony, D. L., Larsen, K., & Skinner, J. S. (2008). Relationship between regional per capita Medicare expenditures and patient perceptions of quality of care. *JAMA, 299*(20, May 28), 2406−2412.

Franzini, L., Mikhail, O. I., & Skinner, J. S. (2010). McAllen and El Paso revisited: Medicare variations not always reflected in the under-sixty-five population. *Health Affairs (Millwood), 29*(12, December), 2302−2309.

Fuchs, V. (1998). *Who shall live? Health, economics, and social choice.* World Scientific.

Fuchs, V. R. & Milstein, A. (2011). The $640 billion question—why does cost-effective care diffuse so slowly? *New England Journal of Medicine, 364*(21, May 26), 1985−1987.

Gawande, A. (2009). The cost conundrum. *New Yorker* (June).

Gaynor, M. & Town, R. J. (2011). Competition in health care markets. In T. McGuire, M. Pauly, & P. P. Baros (Eds.), *Handbook of heatlh economics.* Amsterdam: Elsevier (Chapter 9).

Glance, L. G., Osler, T. M., Dick, A., & Mukamel, D. (2004). The relation between trauma center outcome and volume in the national trauma databank. *Journal of Trauma, 56*(3, March), 682−690.

Glover, J. A. (1938). The incidence of tonsillectomy in school children. *Proceedings of the Royal Society of Medicine, 31*, 1219−1236.

Goodman, D. C., Fisher, E. S., Little, G. A., Stukel, T. A., Chang, C. H., et al. (2002). The relation between the availability of neonatal intensive care and neonatal mortality. *New England Journal of Medicine, 346*(20, May 16), 1538−1544.

Goossens-Laan, C. A., Visser, O., Wouters, M. W., Jansen-Landheer, M. L., Coebergh, J. W., et al. (2010). Variations in treatment policies and outcome for bladder cancer in the Netherlands. *European Journal of Surgical Oncology, 36*(Suppl. 1, September), S100−S107.

Gottlieb, D. J., Zhou, W., Song, Y., Andrews, K. G., Skinner, J. S., et al. (2010). Prices don't drive regional Medicare spending variations. *Health Affairs (Millwood), 29*(3, March−April), 537−543.

Grossman, M. (1972). On the concept of health capital and the demand for health. *Journal of Political Economy, 80*(2, March/April), 223−255.

Gruber, J. & Owings, M. (1996). Physician financial incentives and Cesarean section delivery. *RAND Journal of Economics, 27*(1), 99−123.

Hadley, J., Waidmann, T., Zuckerman, S., & Berenson, R. A. (2011). Medical spending and the health of the elderly. *Health Service Research* (May 24).

Hall, R. & Jones, C. I. (2007). The value of life and the rise in health spending. *Journal of Political Economy, 122*(1), 39−72.

Hartwell, D., Colquitt, J., Loveman, E., Clegg, A. J., Brodin, H., et al. (2005). Clinical effectiveness and cost-effectiveness of immediate angioplasty for acute myocardial infarction: Systematic review and economic evaluation. *Health Technology Assessment, 9*(17, May), 1–99, iii–iv.

Intrator, O., Grabowski, D. C., Zinn, J., Schleinitz, M., Feng, Z., et al. (2007). Hospitalization of nursing home residents: The effects of states' Medicaid payment and bed-hold policies. *Health Service Research, 42*(4, August), 1651–1671.

IOM (2011). *Geographic adjustment in Medicare payment: phase 1: Improving accuracy.* Washington, DC: Institute of Medicine.

Jencks, S. F., Huff, E. D., & Cuerdon, T. (2003). Change in the quality of care delivered to Medicare beneficiaries, 1998–1999 to 2000–2001. *JAMA, 289*(3), 305–312.

Kaestner, R. & Silber, J. H. (2010). Evidence on the efficacy of inpatient spending on Medicare patients. *Milbank Quarterly, 88*(4), 560–594.

Kelly, R. (2009). *Where can $700 billion in waste be cut annually from the U.S. healthcare system?* Thomson Reuters.

King, J. S. & Moulton, B. W. (2006). Rethinking informed consent: The case for shared medical decision-making. *American Journal of Law and Medicine, 32*(4), 429–501.

Kocevar, V. S., Bisgaard, H., Jonsson, L., Valovirta, E., Kristensen, F., et al. (2004). Variations in pediatric asthma hospitalization rates and costs between and within Nordic countries. *Chest, 125*(5, May), 1680–1684.

Kulkarni, S. C., Levin-Rector, A., Ezzati, M., & Murray, C. J. (2011). Falling behind: Life expectancy in US counties from 2000 to 2007 in an international context. *Population Health Metrics, 9*(1, June 15), 16.

Landrum, M. B., Meara, E. R., Chandra, A., Guadagnoli, E., & Keating, N. L. (2008). Is spending more always wasteful? The appropriateness of care and outcomes among colorectal cancer patients. *Health Affairs (Millwood), 27*(1, January–February), 159–168.

Lauderdale, D. S., Thisted, R. A., & Goldberg, J. (1998). Is geographic variation in hip fracture rates related to current or former region of residence? *Epidemiology (Cambridge, Mass.), 9*(5), 574–577.

Leonhardt, D. (2009). In health reform, a cancer offers an acid test. *The New York Times*, July 7.

Levine Taub, A. A., Kolotilin, A., Gibbons, R. S. & Berndt, E. (2011). The diversity of concentrated prescribing behavior: An application to antipsychotics. NBER Working Paper 16823.

Lougheed, M. D., Garvey, N., Chapman, K. R., Cicutto, L., Dales, R., et al. (2006). The Ontario asthma regional variation study: Emergency department visit rates and the relation to hospitalization rates. *Chest, 129*(4), 909–917.

Makela, K. T., Peltola, M., Hakkinen, U., & Remes, V. (2010). Geographical variation in incidence of primary total hip arthroplasty: A population-based analysis of 34,642 replacements. *Archives of Orthoptic Trauma Surgery, 130*(5, May), 633–639.

Mangano, A. (2010). An analysis of the regional differences in health care utilization in Italy. *Health Place, 16*(2, March), 301–308.

McClellan, M. & Skinner, J. (2006). The incidence of Medicare. *Journal of Public Economics, 90*(1–2, 2006/1), 257–276.

McClellan, M., McNeil, B. J., & Newhouse, J. P. (1994). Does more intensive treatment of actue myocardian infarction in the elderly reduce mortality? Analysis using instrumental variables. *Journal of the American Medical Association, 272*, 859–866.

McGuire, T. C. (2011). Physician agency and payment for primary medical care. In S. Glied & P. C. Smith (Eds.), *The Oxford handbook of health economics.* Oxford University Press.

McKinsey (2008). *Accounting for the cost of us health care: A new look at why Americans spend more.* McKinsey Global Institute.

McKnight, R. (2006). Home health care reimbursement, long-term care utilization, and health outcomes. *Journal of Public Economics, 90*(1–2, January), 293–323.

McPherson, K., Strong, P. M., Epstein, A., & Jones, L. (1981). Regional variations in the use of common surgical procedures: Within and between England and Wales, Canada, and the United States. *Social Science & Medicine. Part A: Medical Sociology, 15*(3, Part 1, May), 273–288.

MedPAC (2009). *Measuring regional variation in service use.* Medicare Payment Advisory Commission.

MedPAC (2011). *Regional variation in Medicare service use.* Washington, DC: Medicare Payment Advisory Commission.

Moseley, J. B., O'Malley, K., Petersen, N. J., Menke, T. J., Brody, B. A., et al. (2002). A controlled trial of arthroscopic surgery for osteoarthritis of the knee. *New England Journal of Medicine, 347*(2, July 11), 81–88.

Mousques, J., Renaud, T., & Scemama, O. (2010). Is the "practice style" hypothesis relevant for general practitioners? An analysis of antibiotics prescription for acute rhinopharyngitis. *Social Science & Medicine, 70*(8, April), 1176–1184.

Murphy, K. M. & Topel, R. H. (2006). The value of health and longevity. *Journal of Political Economy, 114*(5), 871–904.

National Health Service (2010). *The NHS atlas of variation in healthcare.* < http://www.rightcare.nhs.uk/atlas/qipp_nhsAtlas-LOW_261110c.pdf/ > (November).

O'Connor, A. M., Llewellyn-Thomas, H. A., & Flood, A. B. (2004). Modifying unwarranted variations in health care: Shared decision making using patient decision aids. *Health Affairs* Suppl. Web Exclusive, VAR63–VAR72.

Ong, M. K., Mangione, C. M., Romano, P. S., Zhou, Q., Auerbach, A. D., et al. (2009). Looking forward, looking back: Assessing variations in hospital resource use and outcomes for elderly patients with heart failure. *Circulation: Cardiovascular Quality and Outcomes, 2*(6, November), 548–557.

Pauly, M. (1980). *Doctors and their workshops: Economic models of physician behavior.* Chicago: University of Chicago Press.

Phelps, C. E. (2000). Information diffusion and best practice adoption. In A. J. Culyer & J. P. Newhouse (Eds.), *Handbook of health economics.* Elsevier Science.

Philipson, T. J., Seabury, S. A., Lockwood, L. M., Goldman, D. P., & Lakdawalla, D. N. (2010). Geographic variation in health care: The role of private markets. *Brookings Papers on Economic Activity, 2010*(1, Spring), 325–355.

Pritchard, R. S., Fisher, E. S., Teno, J. M., et al. (1998). Influence of patient preferences and local health system characteristics on the place of death. Support investigators. Study to understand prognoses and preferences for risks and outcomes of treatment. *Journal of the American Geriatrics Society, 46,* 1242–1250.

Rettenmaier, A. J. & Saving, T. R. (2010). *Exploring state level measures of health care spending.* College Station, TX: Private Enterprise Research Center, Texas A&M University.

Ricketts, T. C. & Holmes, G. M. (2007). Mortality and physician supply: Does region hold the key to the paradox? *Health Service Research, 42*(6 Pt 1, December), 2233–2251 (discussion 2294–2323).

Romley, J. A., Jena, A. B., & Goldman, D. P. (2011). Hospital spending and inpatient mortality: Evidence from California: An observational study. *Annals of Internal Medicine, 154*(3, February 1), 160–167.

Rothberg, M. B., Cohen, J., Lindenauer, P., Maselli, J., & Auerbach, A. (2010a). Little evidence of correlation between growth in health care spending and reduced mortality. *Health Affairs (Millwood), 29*(8, August), 1523–1531.

Rothberg, M. B., Sivalingam, S. K., Ashraf, J., Visintainer, P., Joelson, J., et al. (2010b). Patients' and cardiologists' perceptions of the benefits of percutaneous coronary intervention for stable coronary disease. *Annals of Internal Medicine, 153*(5, September 7), 307–313.

Schoofs, M. & Tamman, M. (2010). Confidentiality cloaks Medicare abuse. *Wall Street Journal,* December 22. < http://online.wsj.com/article/SB10001424052748704457604576011382824069032.html/ >.

Schoofs, M., Tamman, M., & Kendall, B. (2011). Medicare-fraud crackdown corrals 114. *Wall Street Journal,* February 18. < http://www.tilrc.org/assests/news/0211news/0211fed18.html/ >.

Silber, J. H., Kaestner, R., Even-Shoshan, O., Wang, Y., & Bressler, L. J. (2010). Aggressive treatment style and surgical outcomes. *Health Service Research, 45*(6 Pt 2, December), 1872–1892.

Sirovich, B., Gallagher, P. M., Wennberg, D. E., & Fisher, E. S. (2008). Discretionary decision making by primary care physicians and the cost of U.S. health care. *Health Affairs (Millwood), 27*(3, May–June), 813–823.

Sirovich, B. E., Gottlieb, D. J., Welch, H. G., & Fisher, E. S. (2005). Variation in the tendency of primary care physicians to intervene. *Archives of Internal Medicine, 165*(19, October 24), 2252–2256.

Skinner, J. & Staiger, D. (2009). Technology diffusion and productivity growth in health care. Working Paper Series (National Bureau of Economic Research, Cambridge MA), 14865.

Skinner, J. & Staiger, D. O. (2007). Technological diffusion from hybrid corn to beta blockers. In E. Berndt & C. M. Hulten (Eds.), *Hard-to-measure goods and services: Essays in honor of Zvi Griliches*. Chicago: University of Chicago Press and NBER.

Skinner, J., Fisher, E. S., & Wennberg, J. E. (2005). The efficiency of Medicare. In D. A. Wise (Ed.), *Analyses in the economics of aging*. Chicago: University of Chicago Press.

Skinner, J., Staiger, D., & Fisher, E. S. (2010). Looking back, moving forward. *New England Journal of Medicine, 362*(7, February 18), 569−574 (discussion 574).

Skinner, J. S., Staiger, D. O., & Fisher, E. S. (2006). Is technological change in medicine always worth it? The case of acute myocardial infarction. *Health Aff airs (Millwood), 25*(2, March−April), w34−w47.

Song, Y., Skinner, J., Bymum, J., Sutherland, J., Wennberg, J. E., et al. (2010). Regional variations in diagnostic practices. *New England Journal of Medicine, 363*(1, July 1), 45−53.

Stensland, J., Gaumer, Z. R., & Miller, M. E. (2010). Private-payer profits can induce negative Medicare margins. *Health Affairs (Millwood)*, March 18.

Suleman, M., Clark, M. P., Goldacre, M., & Burton, M. (2010). Exploring the variation in paediatric tonsillectomy rates between English regions: A 5-year NHS and independent sector data analysis. *Clinical Otolaryngology, 35*(2, April), 111−117.

Sutherland, J. M., Fisher, E. S., & Skinner, J. S. (2009). Getting past denial—the high cost of health care in the United States. *New England Journal of Medicine, 361*(13, September 24), 1227−1230.

Syverson, C. (2004). Market structure and productivity: A concrete example. *Journal of Political Economy*, December.

Syverson, C. (2011). What determines productivity? *Journal of Economic Literature, 44*(2, June), 326−365.

Temel, J. S., Greer, J. A., Muzikansky, A., Gallagher, E. R., Admane, S., et al. (2010). Early palliative care for patients with metastatic non-small-cell lung cancer. *New England Journal of Medicine, 363*(8), 733−742.

Teno, J. M., Mitchell, S. L., Gozalo, P. L., Dosa, D., Hsu, A., et al. (2010). Hospital characteristics associated with feeding tube placement in nursing home residents with advanced cognitive impairment. *JAMA, 303*(6, February 10), 544−550.

US Preventive Services Task Force (2008). Screening for prostate cancer: U.S. preventive services task force recommendation statement. *Annals of Internal Medicine, 149*(3, August 5), 185−191.

Volpp, K. G., Loewenstein, G., Troxel, A. B., Doshi, J., Price, M., et al. (2008). A test of financial incentives to improve warfarin adherence. *BMC Health Service Research, 8*, 272.

Weinstein, J. N., Tosteson, T. D., Lurie, J. D., Tosteson, A. N., Blood, E., et al. (2008). Surgical versus non-surgical therapy for lumbar spinal stenosis. *New England Journal of Medicine, 358*(8, February 21), 794−810.

Weintraub, W. S., Spertus, J. A., Kolm, P., Maron, D. J., Zhang, Z., et al. (2008). Effect of PCI on quality of life in patients with stable coronary disease. *New England Journal of Medicine, 359*(7, August 14), 677−687.

Wennberg, D. E., & Birkmeyer, J. D. (1999). *The Dartmouth Atlas of cardiovascular health care*. Chicago: AHA Press.

Wennberg, J. (2008). Commentary: A debt of gratitude to J. Alison Glover. *International Journal of Epidemiology, 37*(1, February), 26−29.

Wennberg, J. & Gittelsohn, A. (1973). Small area variations in health care delivery. *Science, 182*(117, December 14), 1102−1118.

Wennberg, J. E. (2010). *Tracking medicine: A researcher's quest to understanding health care*. New York: Oxford University Press.

Wennberg, J. E., & Cooper, M. M. (Eds.) (1996). *The Dartmouth Atlas of health care* Chicago, IL: American Hospital Publishing, Inc.

Wennberg, J. E., Fisher, E. S., & Skinner, J. S. (2002). Geography and the debate over Medicare reform. *Health Affairs*, Web (www.healthaffairs.org), February 13, W96−W114.

Westert, G. P., van den Berg, M. J., Zwakhals, S. L. N., de Jong, J. D., & Verkleij, H. (Eds.) (2010). *Dutch health care performance report 2010*. Dutch Ministry of Health.

WIC (2011). *Bibliography on international small-area health care variation studies*. Wennberg International Collaborative.

Xian, Y., Holloway, R. G., Chan, P. S., Noyes, K., Shah, M. N., et al. (2011). Association between stroke center hospitalization for acute ischemic stroke and mortality. *JAMA, 305*(4, January 26), 373–380.

Yasaitis, L., Fisher, E. S., Skinner, J. S., & Chandra, A. (2009). Hospital quality and intensity of spending: Is there an association? *Health Affairs (Millwood), 28*(4, July–August), w566–w572.

Yusuf, S., Peto, R., Lewis, J., Collins, R., & Sleight, P. (1985). Beta blockade during and after myocardial infarction: An overview of the randomized trials. *Progress in Cardiovascular Diseases, 27*(5, March–April), 335–371.

Zhang, Y., Baicker, K., & Newhouse, J. P. (2010a). Geographic variation in Medicare drug spending. *New England Journal of Medicine, 363*(5, July 29), 405–409.

Zhang, Y., Baicker, K., & Newhouse, J. P. (2010b). Geographic variation in the quality of prescribing. *New England Journal of Medicine, 363*(21, November 18), 1985–1988.

Zuckerman, S., Waidmann, T., Berenson, R., & Hadley, J. (2010). Clarifying sources of geographic differences in Medicare spending. *New England Journal of Medicine, 363*(1), 54–62.

CHAPTER THREE

The Economics of Risky Health Behaviors[1]

John Cawley* and Christopher J. Ruhm**

*Department of Policy Analysis and Management and Department of Economics, Cornell University, Ithaca, NY, USA
**Frank Batten School of Leadership and Public Policy, University of Virginia, Charlottesville, VA, USA

Contents

[1] We thank the editors of this Handbook, Pedro Pita Barros, Tom McGuire, and Mark Pauly, for their feedback and helpful guidance. We also thank the other authors in this volume for their valuable feedback and comments at the Authors' Conference, and we are grateful to Abigail Friedman for transcribing the comments at that conference.

Abstract

Risky health behaviors such as smoking, drinking alcohol, drug use, unprotected sex, and poor diets and sedentary lifestyles (leading to obesity) are a major source of preventable deaths. This chapter overviews the theoretical frameworks for, and empirical evidence on, the economics of risky health behaviors. It describes traditional economic approaches emphasizing utility maximization that, under certain assumptions, result in Pareto-optimal outcomes and a limited role for policy interventions. It also details non-traditional models (e.g. involving hyperbolic time discounting or bounded rationality) that even without market imperfections can result in suboptimal outcomes for which government intervention has greater potential to increase social welfare. The chapter summarizes the literature on the consequences of risky health behaviors for economic outcomes such as medical care costs, educational attainment, employment, wages, and crime. It also reviews the research on policies and strategies with the potential to modify risky health behaviors, such as taxes or subsidies, cash incentives, restrictions on purchase and use, providing information, and restricting advertising. The chapter concludes with suggestions for future research.

Keywords: health behaviors; alcohol; tobacco; smoking; drugs; obesity; diet; food; physical activity; public health; public policy; taxation; subsidies; addiction; externalities; advertising; information; behavioral economics; neuroeconomics; human capital; education; prices; sex; income; time preference; peers; bounded rationality; medical costs; employment; wages; crime; hyperbolic discounting

JEL Codes: I1; I18; I20; D01; D03; H2; D1; D6; D87

1. INTRODUCTION

Health has many determinants, including market goods and services such as medical care, investments of time, and environmental conditions such as air pollution, sanitation and water purity. However, in industrialized countries where morbidity and mortality are primarily related to chronic rather than infectious diseases, health behaviors are particularly important. Such health behaviors are the subject of this chapter and can be broadly construed as any action, or deliberate inaction, by an individual that affects his or her own health or the health of others. This chapter focuses on the specific behaviors—like smoking, drinking, diet, and physical activity—that have strong direct effects on own health. The empirical evidence cited in this chapter is primarily drawn from high-income countries, particularly the United States, so the analysis is particularly relevant for industrialized nations. Previous Handbook chapters have provided detailed discussions of individual health habits such as smoking (Chaloupka and Warner, 2000), alcohol consumption (Cook and Moore, 2000), and prevention (Kenkel, 2000). For the most part, we neither repeat nor update those discussions.[2] Instead, we provide a broad overview of theoretical frameworks and empirical evidence on the economics of health behaviors. In doing so, we examine traditional economics approaches emphasizing utility maximization that, under certain assumptions (e.g. perfect information and no externalities), result in Pareto optimal outcomes and at most a limited role for policy interventions. We also describe a variety of factors (e.g. market imperfections and hyperbolic time discounting) that can result in Pareto suboptimal outcomes in which government intervention has the potential to increase social welfare.

1.1. The Importance of Health Behaviors

An influential study by McGinnis and Foege (1993) estimated that approximately half of the 2.1 million deaths occurring in the United States in 1990 resulted from external modifiable risk factors. Their findings, summarized in the first column of Table 3.1, suggest that health behaviors play a major role. Tobacco use was responsible for almost a fifth of mortality in that year and the combined influence of smoking, diet, physical activity, and alcohol consumption accounted for 38 percent of deaths. Unsafe sexual behaviors, driving and illicit drug use accounted for another 3 percent of deaths. An update to this study (Mokdad et al., 2004, 2005), shown in the second column of Table 3.1, indicated that the situation was relatively similar in 2000, when 36 percent of deaths were related to smoking, diet, physical activity, and alcohol

---

[2] For more recent, but also generally more selective, reviews of the literature on alcohol consumption, and obesity, see: Cook and Moore (2002), and Cawley (2010).

Table 3.1 US Deaths Related to Modifiable Risk Factors, 1990 and 2000

Cause of Death	1990	2000
Tobacco	400,000 (19%)	435,000 (18%)
Poor diet/physical inactivity	300,000 (14%)	365,000 (15%)
Alcohol consumption	100,000 (5%)	85,000 (4%)
Microbial agents	90,000 (4%)	75,000 (3%)
Toxic agents	60,000 (3%)	55,000 (2%)
Motor vehicles	25,000 (1%)	43,000 (2%)
Fire arms	35,000 (2%)	29,000 (1%)
Sexual behavior	30,000 (1%)	20,000 (1%)
Illicit drug use	20,000 (1%)	17,000 (1%)
All modifiable risks	1,060,000 (50%)	1,159,000 (48%)

Note. Sources: 1990—McGinnis and Foege (1993); 2000—Mokdad et al. (2004, 2005). The estimate of deaths due to poor diet and physical inactivity was revised downward from 400,000 in Mokdad et al. (2004) to 365,000 in Mokdad et al. (2005). All other figures in the Year 2000 column are from Mokdad et al. (2004).

Table 3.2 US Deaths Related to Modifiable Risk Factors, 2005

Cause of Death	2005
Tobacco smoking	467,000
High blood pressure	395,000
Overweight—obesity (high BMI)	216,000
Physical inactivity	191,000
High blood glucose	190,000
High LDL cholesterol	113,000
High dietary salt (sodium)	102,000
Low dietary omega-3 fatty acids	84,000
High dietary trans fatty acids	82,000
Alcohol use	64,000
Low intake of fruits and vegetables	58,000
Low dietary polyunsaturated fatty acids	15,000

Note. Source: Danaei et al. (2009).

consumption and an additional 3 percent of deaths were attributable to unsafe sex, driving, or drug use.

The results of more recent research, examining a different set of risk factors for US mortality in 2005, are shown in Table 3.2 (Danaei et al., 2009). Whereas McGinnis and Foege (1993) and Mokdad et al. (2004, 2005) examine the composite risk factor of poor diet and physical inactivity, Danaei et al. (2009) separately break out the effects of: high BMI (to which they attribute 216,000 annual deaths), physical inactivity (191,000 deaths), high blood glucose (190,000 deaths), high LDL cholesterol (113,000 deaths), high dietary salt (102,000 deaths), low dietary omega-3 fatty acids (84,000 deaths), high dietary trans fatty acids (82,000 deaths), low intake of fruits and vegetables (58,000 deaths), and low dietary polyunsaturated fatty acids (15,000).

Table 3.3 Leading Causes of Death and Disability-Adjusted Life-Years (DALYs) in High Income Countries

Risk Factor	% of Deaths	% of DALYs
Tobacco use	17.9	10.7
High blood pressure	16.8	6.1
Overweight and obesity	8.4	6.5
Physical inactivity	7.7	4.1
High blood glucose	7.0	4.9
High cholesterol	5.8	3.4
Low fruit and vegetable intake	2.5	1.3
Urban outdoor air pollution	2.5	
Alcohol use	1.6	6.7
Occupational risks	1.1	1.5
Illicit drugs		2.1

Note. Source: World Health Organization (2009), Tables 1 and 2. Table shows top ten risk factors contributing to deaths or DALYs for countries with 2004 per capita incomes exceeding $10,066. A blank entry implies that the specified risk factor is not in the top ten. A given death or DALY may be attributed to multiple risk factors and the risk factors may interact with each other (e.g. obesity may cause high blood pressure).

All of these estimates should be interpreted with considerable caution because the sources of most deaths are multifactorial, making it quite difficult to ascertain the independent effect of specific determinants, and because of the difficulty of fully adjusting for potential confounding variables.[3] This uncertainty notwithstanding, modifiable behaviors represent an important determinant of premature death. In addition, mortality is only part of the negative consequences of poor health habits; morbidity must also be considered. For example, obesity is associated with high rates of arthritis, which is chronic and disabling but rarely deadly, and Type II diabetes, which can lead to medical complications such as blindness and amputation of toes or feet (Dixon, 2010). Smoking is similarly linked to a myriad of quality-of-life reducing health problems such as lung cancer, emphysema, and chronic obstructive pulmonary disease (US DHHS, 1990).

The World Health Organization (WHO) has recently examined how modifiable risk factors are related to both mortality and morbidity, as measured by disability-adjusted life years (DALYs) (World Health Organization, 2009). The results for high-income countries (those with 2004 per capita incomes in excess of $10,065), which are summarized in Table 3.3, differ from those presented in Tables 3.1 and 3.2 in that there is no attempt to identify a single (primary) cause of death or disability, nor to account for interactions between them (e.g. smoking may be a cause of hypertension). As a result, many of the risk factors may reflect a combination of health behaviors and medical treatments.

---

[3] For example, Flegal et al. (2005) calculate that the number of excess deaths associated with clinical weight classifications (relative to the normal weight category of $18.5 \leq BMI < 25$) were 112,000 for obesity ($BMI \geq 30$), negative 86,000 for overweight ($25 \leq BMI < 30$), and 34,000 for underweight ($BMI \leq 18$), which is difficult to reconcile with the Mokdad et al. (2005) estimate that 365,000 deaths are due to poor diet and physical inactivity.

The estimates from the WHO, shown in Table 3.3, rate smoking as the most damaging health behavior, responsible for 18 percent of deaths and 11 percent of DALYs. Excess body weight is third on the list, responsible for 8 percent of deaths and 7 percent of DALYs, and physical inactivity is fourth, responsible for 8 percent of deaths and 4 percent of DALYs. The second, fifth, and sixth ranked risk factors—high blood pressure, blood glucose, and cholesterol—are all affected by health behaviors such as smoking, physical inactivity, and diet. Indeed, only two of the risk factors listed—outdoor air pollution and occupational risks—are unrelated to individual health behaviors.

The WHO analysis underscores the importance of individual health behaviors in modern industrialized economies. This is in contrast to poorer nations, where infectious diseases and environmental risks play a greater role. For example, in countries with 2004 per capita incomes of $825 or less, the top ten risks of death included child underweight, unsafe water/sanitation/hygiene, and indoor smoke from solid fuels (ranked first, fourth, and sixth), all of which are a direct consequence of poverty (poverty could, in turn, affect behaviors). Low incomes are also important for suboptimal breastfeeding (ranked ninth) and limiting the availability of medical treatments that might offset the consequences of unsafe sex, which is the third ranked mortality risk. Tobacco use and physical inactivity play a smaller role in poorer countries—each is involved in around 4 percent of deaths and is ranked as the seventh and eighth risk factors.[4]

1.2. Trends in Health Behaviors

Figures 3.1 and 3.2 depict trends in a variety of health behaviors in the United States, based on information from a variety of sources (detailed in the figure notes).[5] Figure 3.1 illustrates alcohol consumption per capita, the prevalence of current smoking among adults, illicit drug use during the past year by high school seniors, daily calorie intake (separately for males and females), and obesity prevalence.[6] The results are mixed, with a trend toward healthier behaviors on some dimensions but not others. Most importantly, smoking prevalence fell by almost half among adults between 1974 and 2007 (from 37 to 20 percent), while obesity more than doubled (rising from

[4] The risks associated with DALYs appear to be even more directly related to poverty. Child underweight, unsafe water/sanitation/hygiene, unsafe sex, suboptimal breastfeeding, and indoor smoke from solid fuels are the top five risks, with vitamin A and zinc deficiencies ranking sixth and tenth. Rounding out the list are high blood pressure, alcohol use, and high blood glucose (ranked seventh through ninth). Smoking, overweight/obesity, physical inactivity, and illicit drug use are notably absent from this list.

[5] Some databases provide information on health behaviors for a broader set of countries (although completeness and comparability of the data sometimes present challenges. For instance, the *OECD Health Data* (www.oecd.org/health/healthdata) indicates food, alcohol, and tobacco consumption, and rates of overweight and obesity, for most OECD countries. Data on these behaviors, as well as on physical activity, oral health and health risks such as blood pressure, cholesterol, and diabetes, can be obtained from the World Health Organization's *WHO Global Infobase* (https://apps.who.int/infobase/).

[6] Data are unavailable in some years for many of these outcomes, with linear interpolation used to impute these missing values. Unless otherwise noted, obesity is defined throughout as a body mass index (BMI, calculated as weight in kilograms divided by height in meters squared) of 30 or higher.

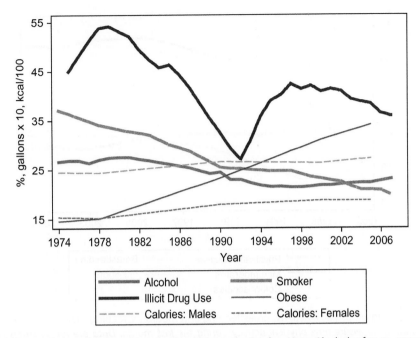

Figure 3.1 Trends in substance use, obesity and energy intake. *Note: Alcohol refers to apparent per capita ethanol consumption (tenths of gallons) for persons aged ≥14 years (source: www.niaaa.nih. gov/Resources/DatabaseResources/QuickFacts/AlcoholSales/consum01.htm). Smoker is the percent of adults who are current smokers (source: National Health Interview Survey, www.cdc.gov/tobacco/ data_statistics/tables/trends/cig_smoking/index.htm). Illicit drug use indicates use in last year by 12th graders (source: Johnston et al., 2009). Obesity refers to persons aged ≥ 20 years with a body mass index ≥ 30 (source: NCHS, 2010). Calories are average daily energy intake (kcal/100) for persons aged ≥20 years (source: NCHS, 2010). Linear interpolation is used to fill in periods with missing data. The y-axis indicates the percent of the relevant population smoking or who are obese; number of gallons of alcohol consumption × 1/10, and kcal consumed × 1/100.*

15 percent in the early 1970s to 34 percent in 2003–2006). The increase in obesity was fueled by an increase in average daily calorie consumption (12 percent rise for males and 23 percent rise for females). Alcohol consumption per capita declined 20 percent between 1974 and 1997 but has increased modestly (by around 8 percent) since then. The effects of this change are ambiguous because light drinking may yield some health benefits (Gaziano et al., 1993; Thun et al., 1997). However, during 1997–2007 there was either no change or an increase in binge and heavy drinking (National Center for Health Statistics, 2010), which are likely to negatively affect health.[7] Finally, illicit drug use (among high school seniors) shows no clear time trend: it fell

---

[7] There is no evidence of reductions in heavy drinking (more than 14 drinks per week for males and 7 drinks per week for females) or binge drinking (5 or more drinks on a single occasion).

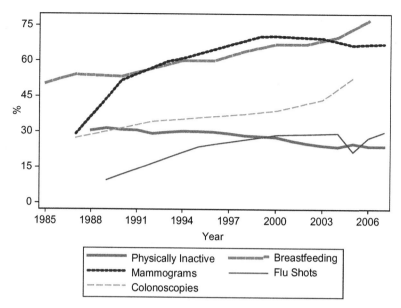

Figure 3.2 Trends in physical activity, breastfeeding and medical screening. *Note: Inactive adults are those reporting no leisure-time physical activity during the last month. Data are for 36 states (source: www.cdc.gov/nccdphp/dnpa/physical/stats/leisure_time.htm). Breastfeeding indicates infants ever breastfed (source: NCHS, 2010; McDowell et al., 2006). Mammograms refer to women aged ≥40 years receiving mammograms in last 2 years. Flu shots refers to percent of adults receiving influenza vaccination in the last 12 months (source: NCHS, 2010). Colonoscopy indicates the percentage of persons aged ≥50 years who have ever had a colonoscopy or sigmoidoscopy (source: http://progressreport.cancer. gov/doc_detail.asp?pid = 0&did = 0&chid = 72&coid = 718&mid = #trends). Linear interpolation is used to fill in periods with missing data.*

sharply from a peak of 54 percent in 1979 to a trough of 27 percent in 1992, before rising rapidly to 42 percent in 1997, after which it declined modestly.[8]

Figure 3.2 depicts trends in health behaviors such as physical inactivity (no leisure-time physical activity during the last month), medical screening tests (mammograms and colorectal endoscopy), vaccinations (flu shots), and breastfeeding. Obviously, these represent only a subset of possible health behaviors that could be considered and their inclusion is illustrative rather than exhaustive. Consistent data on these behaviors is available for a shorter period of time (with the exception of breastfeeding) than those presented in the previous figure; however, they tend to suggest that healthy behaviors are becoming increasingly common over time. Thus, mammography and colonoscopies have both become more widely used over time, as has influenza vaccination and the fraction of

---

[8] Illicit drugs include: marijuana, LSD, other hallucinogens, cocaine, heroin, other narcotics, amphetamines, barbiturates, or tranquilizers not under a doctor's orders.

infants that are breastfed.[9] There also appears to have been an increase in physical activity, although most adults do not meet recommended levels (Troiano et al., 2008).

Overall, changes in health behaviors since the 1970s (particularly the rapid decline in smoking) have mostly operated in the direction of improving overall health (Cutler et al., 2009); however, many of these beneficial trends ended or slowed by the early or mid-1990s. Moreover, the main exception to this pattern—the rapid and continuing growth in obesity—has important negative consequences. As always, it is difficult to extrapolate from the past to predict the future. Cutler et al. (2009) suggest that mortality risks will increase during the first two decades of the 21st century due to increases in obesity,[10] and Olshansky et al. (2005) raise the possibility that its rise may lead to reductions in life expectancy.[11]

1.3. Differences in Health Behaviors across Population Subgroups

Health-related behaviors differ, sometimes substantially, across population subgroups. Table 3.4 summarizes disparities in health behaviors like smoking, obesity, drinking, physical inactivity, two types of medical screening testing (mammograms and colorectal exams), sexually transmitted disease, and the use of sun protection. The estimates are based on 2008 data from the National Health Interview Survey (NHIS).[12] The subsamples examined are stratified by sex, race/ethnicity, age, education and annual family income; within those categories the averages and prevalences reported are unconditional. Because many of these factors may be correlated (i.e. better educated persons tend to be in families with higher incomes), the disparities observed should not be interpreted as causal. Table 3.5 displays probit estimates of the corresponding predicted subgroup differences after including controls for demographic characteristics.

The two tables reveal fairly similar patterns. Females are more likely than males to engage in certain healthy behaviors (they are less likely to smoke or binge drink, and are more likely to use sunscreen) but are less likely than males to engage in other healthy behaviors (they are less likely to engage in physical activity and are more likely to have sexually transmitted diseases (STDs), although the STD disparity may be due to biological differences in susceptibility rather than differences in behaviors).

Blacks and Hispanics are less likely than non-Hispanic whites to smoke or drink heavily, but are more likely to be obese and physically inactive. Minorities less commonly receive colorectal screening and Hispanic women are less likely to obtain mammograms

---

[9] The results for breastfeeding are part of a longer-term secular increase. For instance, 30 percent of infants were breastfed (for at least some period of time) in 1974 as compared to 53 percent in 1990 and 77 percent in 2006.

[10] Their estimates of mortality risk are not strictly limited to changes in health behaviors. In particular, they allow for direct effects of education and of blood pressure and cholesterol; the former influences health behaviors, while the latter are affected by them.

[11] However, Flegal et al. (2007) find that most types of mortality risk from obesity have been falling over time.

[12] See http://www.cdc.gov/nchs/nhis.htm for information on the NHIS.

Table 3.4 Percent of Group with Specified Health Behavior or Risk Factor, 2008

Group	Smoker	Obese	Heavy Drinker	Binge Drinker	Physically Inactive	Mammogram	Colorectal Screening	STD	Sunscreen
Full sample	20.6	27.4	5.5	22.7	38.2	57.8	42.3	3.0	16.9
Sex									
Male	23.1	27.0	6.2	31.9	36.0	—	43.1	2.0	9.7
Female	18.3	27.8	4.9	14.2	40.3	57.8	41.6	3.9	23.7
Race/ethnicity									
White (non-Hispanic)	22.0	26.2	6.5	25.1	35.2	59.8	45.8	2.6	19.6
Black (non-Hispanic)	21.3	36.1	3.4	14.3	47.4	59.0	37.6	4.9	5.9
Hispanic	15.8	31.3	3.9	21.7	46.9	47.1	25.2	3.4	13.0
Age (years)									
18–34	23.4	22.3	6.4	34.8	31.6	—	—	4.2	15.0
35–54	23.8	30.6	6.1	24.5	36.4	56.5	24.0	1.7	18.8
55–74	16.8	32.5	4.5	10.8	43.9	75.7	59.0	—	18.0
Education									
<High school graduate	27.5	33.3	4.9	15.7	61.9	47.4	31.9	2.3	8.3
High school graduate/GED	27.1	33.5	5.6	20.2	48.9	58.2	40.7	2.7	13.9
Some college	22.7	30.6	5.1	22.8	35.1	58.6	44.6	2.8	18.8
College graduate	8.9	21.4	5.0	22.2	22.0	62.4	48.2	2.7	25.8
Family income									
<$35,000	27.6	29.2	6.0	21.1	50.1	49.9	39.3	4.5	10.9
$35,000–$74,999	21.4	30.4	5.5	23.0	38.6	57.8	42.4	3.0	16.0
≥$75,000	14.4	24.2	5.9	26.6	24.7	64.5	44.2	2.0	23.3

Note: Data refer to adults from the 2008 National Health Interview Survey and are weighted so as to be nationally representative. The results for education subgroups refer to individuals aged 25 and older. "Smoker" indicates current smoking and "obese" refers to having a body mass index of 30 or higher. "Heavy" drinkers refer to males (females) averaging > 14 (>7) drinks per week during the last year and "binge" drinking refers to persons consuming 5 or more drinks during a single day at least once in the last year. Persons are considered "physically inactive" if they engaged in vigorous or moderate physical activity or strength training less than once per week. "Mammograms" indicates had a mammogram in the past two years for females aged 30 and higher. "Colorectal screening" indicates ever in lifetime had such screening for persons 40 and older. "STDs" indicate sexually transmitted diseases other than HIV/AIDS during the last five years for 18–49-year-olds. "Sunscreen" indicates always use sunscreen when outside on warm sunny days for more than one hour.

Table 3.5 Conditional correlations with Health Behaviors, 2008

Characteristic	Smoker	Obese	Heavy Drinker	Binge Drinker	Physically Inactive	Mammo-gram	Colorectal Screening	STD	Sun-screen
Female	-0.055 (0.004)	0.021 (0.006)	-0.017 (0.002)	-0.176 (0.004)	0.024 (0.006)	—	-0.011 (0.007)	0.017 (0.004)	0.134 (0.006)
Black (non-Hispanic)	-0.054 (0.006)	0.121 (0.009)	-0.023 (0.003)	-0.085 (0.005)	0.075 (0.008)	0.066 (0.010)	-0.014 (0.010)	0.017 (0.006)	-0.113 (0.004)
Hispanic	-0.125 (0.005)	0.041 (0.009)	-0.025 (0.003)	-0.051 (0.006)	0.062 (0.008)	0.033 (0.011)	-0.100 (0.011)	-0.001 (0.005)	-0.015 (0.006)
Age: 25–34	0.362 (0.014)	0.128 (0.013)	0.069 (0.012)	0.457 (0.017)	-0.162 (0.010)	-0.519 (0.009)	—	0.024 (0.003)	0.039 (0.010)
Age: 35–54	0.309 (0.013)	0.159 (0.012)	0.061 (0.010)	0.295 (0.017)	-0.110 (0.010)	-0.100 (0.012)	-0.382 (0.009)	—	0.042 (0.009)
Age: 55–74	0.235 (0.014)	0.185 (0.012)	0.044 (0.009)	0.169 (0.017)	-0.050 (0.010)	0.098 (0.012)	-0.036 (0.010)	—	0.044 (0.010)
High school graduate/GED	-0.017 (0.007)	-0.001 (0.009)	-0.001 (0.004)	0.021 (0.008)	-0.068 (0.008)	0.076 (0.011)	0.074 (0.011)	0.010 (0.007)	0.055 (0.010)
Some college	-0.046 (0.006)	-0.012 (0.009)	0.001 (0.005)	0.030 (0.009)	-0.162 (0.007)	0.102 (0.011)	0.124 (0.011)	0.015 (0.008)	0.101 (0.010)
College graduate	-0.139 (0.004)	-0.087 (0.008)	-0.009 (0.004)	-0.003 (0.008)	-0.223 (0.007)	0.126 (0.012)	0.153 (0.012)	0.020 (0.009)	0.160 (0.012)
Income: $35,000–$74,999	-0.062 (0.005)	0.005 (0.007)	-0.002 (0.003)	0.009 (0.006)	-0.073 (0.006)	0.087 (0.009)	0.062 (0.009)	-0.011 (0.003)	0.040 (0.006)
Income: ≥ $75,000	-0.105 (0.004)	-0.040 (0.007)	-0.002 (0.004)	0.028 (0.007)	-0.143 (0.007)	0.132 (0.010)	0.087 (0.010)	-0.019 (0.003)	0.076 (0.008)
Baseline	0.207	0.296	0.051	0.197	0.405	0.564	0.424	0.032	0.169

Note: The table shows average predicted marginal effects from probit models that control for the specified covariates. Standard errors are in parentheses. Data refer to adults aged 25 and higher from the 2008 National Health Interview Survey. See Table 3.4 for definitions of the dependent variables. The reference group is non-Hispanic white male high school dropouts aged 75 or higher, with family incomes less than $35,000. "Baseline" estimates indicate average predicted values for the full sample, with covariates evaluated at their actual values.

but most of these differences are associated with correlated factors (like education and income) rather than race/ethnicity itself. Smoking and problem drinking tend to decrease with age, while obesity, physical inactivity, and medical screening tend to rise.

By far the strongest results are that higher socioeconomic status (SES), as proxied by educational attainment or family income, is generally correlated with healthier behaviors. For example, compared to high school dropouts, college graduates were 13.9 percentage points less likely to smoke, 8.7 percentage points less likely to be obese, 0.9 percentage points less likely to drink heavily, and 22.3 percentage points less likely to be physically inactive. In addition, they are 12.6 percentage points more likely to receive mammograms, 15.3 percentage points more likely to receive colorectal screening, and 16.0 percentage points more likely to use sunscreen when outside on warm sunny days. The only exception is that the highly educated were 2 percentage points more likely to have had an STD during the last five years. Income also appears to be associated with healthy behaviors, independent of education. Compared to persons with family incomes below \$35,000, those with family incomes of at least \$75,000 had relatively low rates of smoking, obesity, physical inactivity, and STDs; they also have a high prevalence of medical screening and sunscreen use. The exception to this pattern is that high family income is associated with modestly greater rates of binge drinking.

Previous evidence of healthier behaviors by more advantaged individuals was obtained in the two influential "Whitehall studies" of British civil servants (Marmot et al., 1978, 1991), which documented a strong positive relationship between occupational status, healthy behaviors, and life expectancy.[13] In these, and in many subsequent examinations, drinking is an exception, as it was in the NHIS data discussed above. For example, Adler et al. (1994) provide evidence of a negative association between SES (usually proxied by income or education) and smoking or physical inactivity but a positive correlation of SES with alcohol consumption. Cutler and Lleras-Muney (2010) show that education is positively associated with healthier behavior as regards to smoking, diet and obesity, health knowledge, household safety, medical testing, screening and vaccinations, and the control of high blood pressure and diabetes. Conversely, the highly educated were more likely to have ever used marijuana (but had smoked it less frequently within the last year) and had more often engaged in light (but not heavy) drinking.

Differences in health behaviors are one possible explanation for why socioeconomic status is positively related to health status and life expectancy. Interestingly, the original Whitehall studies, and much research that has followed (e.g. Lynch et al., 1996; Lantz et al., 2001), suggests that behaviors explain only a small fraction of the better health and longer life expectancy experienced by high individuals with high socioeconomic

---

[13] See Marmot and Wilkinson (2006) for an in-depth discussion of these issues.

status. However, using data from the British Health and Lifestyle Survey, Contoyannis and Jones (2004) and Balia and Jones (2008) potentially resolve this contradiction, showing that accounting for endogeneity in behavioral choices increases the estimated effect of behaviors on health outcomes and reduces the size of the residual SES effects. This occurs because persons with worse latent health tend to adopt healthier behaviors (e.g. someone who is diagnosed with cancer may quit smoking), introducing a negative bias into the predicted effects of health-enhancing behaviors.

Over time, SES-related gradients have widened for most, but not all, health behaviors. Probably most dramatic is the change for tobacco use, where a large gap has emerged over the last four decades because of larger reductions in smoking for more advantaged adults. Kanjilal et al. (2006) present evidence from the National Health and Nutrition Examination Surveys (NHANES) showing that the gap in current smoking between persons with more versus less than a high school education was 11.6 percentage points (33.5 vs. 45.1 percent) in 1971–1974 but had almost doubled to 21.5 points (17.1 vs. 38.6 percent) in 1999–2002; during the same period the smoking differential between the highest and lowest poverty-income-ratio (PIR) quartiles rose from 10.5 (33.5 vs. 44.0 percent) to 23.5 (13.9 vs. 37.4 percent) percentage points. Kenkel (2007) finds that the gap in smoking rates between those with and without a college degree grew from 2 percentage points in 1954 to 15 points in 1999. A substantial portion of the recent differential occurs because the highly educated tobacco users are much more likely than their less educated counterparts to quit smoking. For instance, in 2008, the quit ratio—defined as the percentage of persons who had ever smoked (more than 100 cigarettes) but who were *not* current tobacco users—was 45.7 percent for adults (aged 25 and over) without a high school diploma, compared to 80.7 percent of those with a graduate degree (Dube et al., 2009).

In contrast, most of the available evidence suggests that SES-related differentials in obesity have narrowed over time, as body weight has increased for all groups but at a somewhat faster rate for those with high education or income. Zhang and Wang (2004) find that between 1971–1974 and 1999–2000 the prevalence of obesity rose 16.2 percentage points (from 7.4 to 23.6 percent) for college educated men (aged 20 to 60) and 14.7 percentage points (from 12.0 to 26.7 percent) for those with less than a high school education. Over the same period the education gradient narrowed even more for women: the prevalence of obesity increased 22.6 percentage points (from 7.3 to 29.9 percent) for college educated women versus 12.9 percentage points (from 24.9 to 37.8 percent) for women with less than a high school education. The results of Chang and Lauderdale (2005) are also suggestive of a weakening in the negative relationship between income and obesity between 1971–1974 and 1999–2002, to the extent that income and obesity are now positively correlated for non-Hispanic black males. Among low SES individuals, the prevalence of obesity was already quite high in the early 1970s and so has grown relatively little over time, raising the possibility that differentials in *severe obesity* might have continued to widen over time. However, Cutler et al. (2010) find that the combined prevalence of Class 2 obesity (BMI between 35.0 and 39.9) and Class 3 obesity (BMI of 40 or higher) rose between 1971–1974 and 1999–2004 by the same amount for adults with and without college educations: by 8 percentage points for males and 11 percentage points for females in both education groups.

There is weaker evidence on the behaviors that determine body weight: diet and physical activity. Popkin et al. (1996) find improvements in dietary quality between 1965 and 1989–1991, with larger gains for highly educated persons (who had worse diets at the beginning of the period but similar quality diets at the end of it). Casagrande et al. (2007) find that the consumption of fruits and vegetables changed little between 1988–1994 and 1999–2002, with possibly higher levels and slight increases observed for high SES individuals. Conversely, Kant and Graubard (2007) show that income and education-related differentials in the consumption of healthy foods declined between 1971–1975 and 1999–2002, largely due to a decrease among advantaged individuals. All of these findings should be considered preliminary and are not informative about net energy intake, which is of primary interest when one is concerned about obesity.

There is even less evidence on whether and how energy expenditure has changed over time across groups. Simpson et al. (2003) find that the prevalence of walking rose between 1987 and 2000 but without clear differences across education. On the other hand, Brownson et al. (2005) document modest increases in the probability of achieving recommended levels of physical activity for persons with 16 or more years of education but decreases for those with fewer than 12 years of schooling. However, they emphasize that this includes only leisure-time physical activities, and so does not provide information on other sources of energy expenditure (e.g. the strenuousness of work), which has declined over time, quite possibly differentially across groups.[14]

1.4. Health Economics Research on Health Behaviors

The introduction to Volume 1A of the *Handbook of Health Economics* (Culyer and Newhouse, 2000) includes an organizational chart of the field of health economics. Six of the eight categories of research relate to the health care sector and there is no explicit category for economics research on health behaviors; this is presumably included under the vague residual grouping of "what influences health, other than

---

[14] There have also been important changes in a variety of medical conditions—like hypertension, high blood pressure, and diabetes mellitus—that are determined by an interaction of health behaviors and medical care. Better control of blood pressure and cholesterol, particularly when combined with reductions in smoking, represent significant improvements in cardiovascular risk factors. These health risks have declined over the last three decades of the 20th century for virtually all groups but without clear differences across education or income categories (Kanjilal et al., 2006; Cutler et al., 2010). Conversely, diabetes diagnoses have increased dramatically over time, particularly for those with less education or low incomes (Kanjilal et al., 2006).

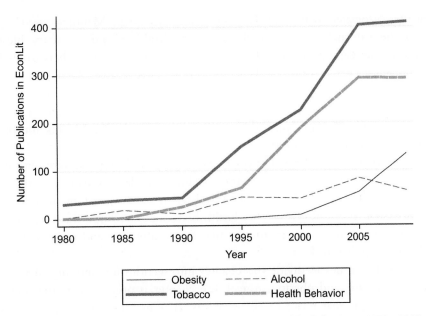

Figure 3.3 Number of economics publications examining health behaviors, 1980–2009. *Notes: Figure is based on year-specific searches of EconLit, a database of journal articles, dissertations, and working papers in economics. Obesity indicates the number of publications with the keyword "overweight" or "obesity." Alcohol indicates the number of publications with the keyword "alcohol" or "drinking." Tobacco indicates the number of publications with the keyword "tobacco," "cigarettes," or "smoking." Health behavior indicates the number of publications with the keyword "health behavior."*

health care?" (see Cawley and Kenkel, 2008). However, 50 percent of US health economists surveyed in 2005 reported studying "the behavior of individuals," which makes this as popular as any sub-specialty of health economics (Morrisey and Cawley, 2008), and economics research on health behaviors has increased considerably in the past three decades.[15] Figure 3.3 depicts the trend in the number of economics publications concerning various health behaviors identified in EconLit, the database of journal articles, dissertations, and working papers in economics. Between 1980 and 2009, the annual number of economics publications on obesity increased from 0 to 135, the number on alcohol rose from 2 to 99, those on tobacco or smoking grew from 31 to 410, and the number on health behaviors generally increased from 2 to 292.[16] These trends are likely due to many factors, including greater awareness of the

[15] While it seems likely that most of the health economists stating that they research "the behavior of individuals" study health behaviors, it is possible that some are referring to non-health behaviors.

[16] The annual number of publications in health care economics also rose substantially, but less than the increase in health behaviors research. For example, the annual number of publications in EconLit with the keyword "hospital" rose from 30 in 1980 to 235 in 2009, and the number with the keyword "medical care" rose from 5 in 1980 to 61 in 2009.

externalities associated with unhealthy behaviors (see, e.g., Manning et al.'s (1991) study on the external costs of smoking, heavy drinking, and sedentary lifestyles), growth in the availability of large secondary datasets allowing researchers to track and model unhealthy behaviors (e.g. the Behavioral Risk Factor Surveillance System (BRFSS) began in 1984 and the Youth Risk Behavior Surveillance System (YRBSS) started in 1991), and rising interest in government action to internalize the negative externalities associated with some health behaviors (e.g. the Federal tax increases on tobacco enacted during the 1990s).

The importance of health behaviors in explaining morbidity and mortality in economically developed countries, increasing richness of data available to study these behaviors, and the policy relevance of the related research questions, makes us optimistic about the future of research on health behaviors. We hope this chapter will be useful to the researchers contributing to that future literature and of broader interest to students and policy makers.

We have chosen not to divide this chapter into sections for smoking, alcohol consumption, drug use, and obesity; instead, the chapter is organized by the underlying economic concepts that relate to all behaviors. It is our hope that this organization will enable researchers to see common patterns and important differences across the various health behaviors, and bring researchers of specific health behaviors out of their separate silos to learn from the synergistic research on other health behaviors.

Interested readers are also referred to the previous Handbook chapters on smoking (Chaloupka and Warner, 2000), alcohol consumption (Cook and Moore, 2000), and prevention (Kenkel, 2000), the chapter on health behaviors among young people in the *Elgar Companion to Health Economics* (Kenkel, 2006), and that on health behaviors and addictions in the *Oxford Handbook of Health Economics* (Kenkel and Sindelar, 2011).

2. THE TRADITIONAL ECONOMIC APPROACH TO STUDYING HEALTH BEHAVIORS

2.1. Model of Health Capital

The foundation for much economics research on health behaviors is Michael Grossman's model of health capital (Grossman, 1972, 2000), which has been detailed in a previous volume in this series (Grossman, 2000).[17] Basic aspects of the model are that people receive an endowment of health capital at birth, which depreciates with

---

[17] Related empirical work is often inspired more by the intuition of this model than strict adherence to its theoretical features.

age but can be raised through investments; death occurs when the health stock falls below a minimum level. Health has both consumption and investment aspects, as it enters the utility function directly and determines the amount of healthy time available for market and non-market activities. People produce health by combining market goods and services with time, consistent with Becker's model of household production (Becker, 1976). For example, an individual might produce health by buying a treadmill and running shoes and spending time running on the treadmill.

Individuals allocate time and money to maximize the present discounted value of lifetime utility. Indirectly, length of life is a choice in the original model which contains no uncertainty. Specifically, the timing of death results from conscious decisions regarding health investments made with full knowledge of their implications for longevity.[18] Assuming that health has only investment aspects (i.e. it does not enter the utility function directly and is only valuable for producing healthy days), optimal health capital is characterized by an equality of the supply of health capital (i.e. the opportunity cost of health capital) and the demand for health capital (i.e. the marginal monetary return on health investments).

Application of the health capital model to health behaviors such as sleep and exercise is straightforward (see Kenkel, 2000): people invest in such behaviors until, at the margin, the return on investments in health equals the opportunity cost of health capital. However, the model also applies to unhealthy behaviors, which can be interpreted as negative investments in health. When the individual has solved the constrained maximization problem, the optimal participation in unhealthy behaviors will be characterized by an equality of the marginal costs of the unhealthy behavior (both the monetary cost of purchasing market goods like cigarettes and alcohol and the non-pecuniary cost of reduced health and shorter lifespan) and the marginal benefits (such as the instantaneous pleasure derived from consumption).

2.2. Education and Health Behaviors

A literature review by Grossman and Kaestner (1997) concluded that education is the most important correlate of good health for both individuals and groups; in particular, health is more strongly correlated with schooling than with occupation or income. In the model of health capital (Grossman, 1972), schooling may improve health by enhancing allocative efficiency (participation in healthier behaviors) or productive efficiency (obtaining more health from the same set of inputs). Cutler and Lleras-Muney (2010) provide an overview of the differences in health behavior by education, noting that in a parsimonious model estimated using the National Health Interview Survey data, an additional year of education is associated with a 3.0 percentage point lower

---

[18] However, at high ages, the depreciation rate of health capital may become so large that the individual is unable to afford sufficient investment flows to stay alive.

probability of being a current smoker, 1.4 percentage point lower probability of being obese, a 1.8 percentage point lower probability of being a heavy drinker, and a 0.1 percentage point lower probability of using marijuana in the past month.

Economists have used a variety of identification strategies to measure the causal effect of education on health behaviors. Focusing on the studies that used instruments that are both powerful and plausibly exogenous, the results are mixed. Three studies find evidence of a causal effect of education on smoking. Currie and Moretti (2003) instrument for a woman's education using college openings in her county of residence and find that education reduces the probability of smoking. De Walque (2007b) and Grimard and Parent (2007) exploit college attendance as a draft avoidance strategy during the Vietnam war and both find that college education reduces the probability of smoking by males.

Other studies are unable to reject the null hypothesis of no causal effect of education on health behaviors. Reinhold and Jurges (2009) examine the exogenous variation in education due to the abolition of school fees in Germany and conclude that there is no evidence that education causes reductions in smoking or obesity. Clark and Royer (2010) exploit two changes to British compulsory schooling laws that compelled a large percentage of the student population to stay in school longer. This exogenous variation in education had no detectable effect on smoking, drinking, diet, or exercise.

Other studies find mixed results. For example, Kenkel et al. (2006) exploit education policies (e.g. number of courses required to graduate from high school) as instruments and find that high school completion significantly reduces the probability of current smoking by adult men (but not women), but has no effect on overweight or obesity for either men or women.

2.3. Habit and Addiction

Marshall (1920) may have been the first work in which an economist addressed the phenomenon of habit or addiction; it contains the observation that "...the more good music a man hears, the stronger his taste for it is likely to become..." (Marshall, 1920, p. 94; Stigler and Becker, 1977). In this sense, the individual's utility function includes not just the current consumption of music C but also the stock of past consumption of music S.

In general, there are three characteristics of addiction. *Reinforcement* implies that the marginal utility of current consumption rises with the stock of past consumption ($U_{CS} > 0$). This is called adjacent complementarity because consumption of the good in adjacent time periods is complementary.[19] *Tolerance* implies that the stock of past

[19] Ryder and Heal (1973) also describe the possibility of distant complementarity, which they illustrate with the following example: "a person with distant complementarity who expects to receive a heavy supper would tend to eat a substantial breakfast and a light lunch. A person with adjacent complementarity would tend to eat a light breakfast and a substantial lunch in the same circumstances" (p. 5).

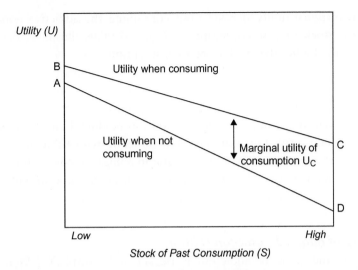

Figure 3.4 Graphical representation of characteristics of addiction. *Notes: Adapted from Rachlin (1997).*

consumption lowers utility $(U_S < 0)$. This assumes that the addiction is harmful; one can also have a beneficial addiction (like exercise) in which the stock of past consumption raises utility $(U_S > 0)$. Finally, *withdrawal* implies that there is a positive marginal utility of current consumption $(U_C > 0)$.[20]

These characteristics of addiction are depicted in Figure 3.4, which is adapted from Rachlin (1997). The vertical axis is utility (U) and the horizontal axis is the stock of past consumption of the habitual or addictive good (S). The lower line AD shows the utility associated with each possible level of the stock of past consumption, conditional on not currently consuming the addictive good. The upper line BC shows the utility associated with each possible level of the stock of past consumption, conditional on currently consuming the addictive product. The graph illustrates withdrawal, as at every stock of past consumption, consuming the addictive good provides higher utility than abstaining: $U_C > 0$. The graph also illustrates tolerance. It depicts a harmful addiction because the stock of past consumption lowers utility: $U_S < 0$. For example, the first time an individual consumes the addictive substance, he has a stock of past consumption of zero, so he is at point B. After the individual has been a heavy user for sufficiently long to have the maximum stock of past consumption, when he consumes he is at point C, which is not only far below the utility he enjoyed during his first use of the addictive substance, it is also below the utility A that he enjoyed when he was still abstinent. Finally, the graph illustrates reinforcement, as the

---

[20] More complicated (but realistic) models of withdrawal include a kink in the marginal utility function at or near levels of recent previous use, as detailed below.

instantaneous marginal utility derived from consuming the addictive good is greater the higher the stock of past consumption: $U_{CS} > 0$. This illustrates that quitting a habit is harder the higher the stock of past consumption.

Houthakker and Taylor (1970) make the important empirical distinction between habitual (or addictive) goods, for which the stock of past consumption positively affects current use, and durable goods, for which prior consumption is negatively correlated with current use. They note that a good can be durable in the short term and habitual in the long term. For example, even someone who habitually overeats will, in the short term, experience satiation (resulting in a negative correlation in consumption in nearby time periods) but over the longer term, consumption will be positively correlated and thus food is habitual over longer periods of time.

2.3.1. Theory of Rational Addiction (TORA)

A landmark in the study of addiction is Becker and Murphy's (1988) Theory of Rational Addiction (TORA). In this model, addiction is optimal in the sense that it involves forward-looking utility maximization with stable preferences.[21] Previously, models of habit formation or addiction assumed that consumers were naïve: they realized that current consumption of the addictive good depended on its past consumption, but did not take into account the impact of current consumption on future consumption (Pollak, 1975).[22] An appealing aspect of the TORA is that it allows consumers to be sophisticated regarding the intertemporal dynamics of consumption and utility.

The TORA assumes that instantaneous utility depends on current consumption of the addictive good, the stock of past consumption of the addictive good, and current consumption of all other goods. Individuals allocate income to addictive goods and all other goods, taking into account the future consequences of their actions, including tolerance and reinforcement.[23] In the TORA, a person for whom a good is highly addictive (i.e. for whom the good has high adjacent complementarity) might knowingly consume enough to become an addict, because he calculates that by doing so he maximizes the present discounted value of utility. Becker and Murphy describe the model as applicable to a wide spectrum of behaviors, including harmful addictions such as smoking, drinking, gambling, using cocaine or heroin, and overeating, as well as beneficial addictions such as religiosity and jogging.

Formally, the consumer maximizes the present discounted value of lifetime utility by allocating her budget to consumption of an addictive good C and all other (non-addictive) goods Y. Current utility depends not just on instantaneous consumption of

---

[21] This does not mean that addicts will necessarily be glad to be addicted, a point to which we return below.

[22] For an example of a model of myopic habit formation, see Houthakker and Taylor (1970).

[23] A parsimonious rational addiction model expresses the adverse future consequences of substance use as a higher level of addictive stock, which causes disutility, but one could also incorporate into the model other adverse future consequences, such as probability of marital strife, criminal victimization, or arrest.

C and Y but also on the stock of past consumption of C, which is denoted S. (The stock of past consumption of all other (non–addictive) goods does not enter the utility function.) The lifetime utility function is:

$$U(0) = \int_0^T e^{-\sigma t} U[Y(t), C(t), S(t)]dt.$$

where σ is a constant rate of time preference. Reinforcement implies that $U_{CS} > 0$: a higher level of the addictive stock raises the marginal utility of consuming the addictive good. Tolerance implies that $U_S < 0$ for harmful addictions and that $U_S > 0$ for beneficial addictions.

The stock of past consumption S changes over time according to:

$$\dot{S}(t) = S(t) - S(t-1) = C(t) - \delta S(t) - h[D(t)],$$

where C is consumption of the addictive good in period t, δ is the exogenous depreciation rate in the addictive stock, and $D(t)$ represents expenditures on endogenous depreciation or appreciation of the stock. Consumers also face a lifetime budget constraint.

The TORA yields several important implications regarding the responsiveness of consumption to price. First, in almost any model of addiction, consumption at a point in time is related not only to current prices but also to past prices, because the latter determine the current addictive stock. Second, in models where agents exhibit foresight (like TORA but not myopic addiction), current consumption is also related to anticipated future prices because future prices will affect desired future consumption, which is a complement with the future level of the addictive stock; this in turn is affected by current consumption. Third, a future price change will have a greater impact on current demand the sooner it is anticipated, because individuals will then react to it earlier. Fourth, permanent price changes affect demand more than temporary ones, because forward-looking persons anticipate and make decisions based on future dynamics in prices. Fifth, the price elasticity of demand for the addictive good will be greater in the long run than in the short run, and that difference will rise with the level of addictiveness.

Finally, an arguably counter-intuitive implication is that the more addictive the good, the greater the long-run price elasticity of demand (see equation (18) and the related discussion in Becker and Murphy, 1988). The first reason that higher price leads to a reduction in quantity demanded is the usual reason that applies to all goods: the law of demand states that when price rises, the quantity demanded falls. However, for addictive goods there is a second reason that higher price leads to a reduction in quantity demanded: adjacent complementarity. Specifically, a rise in price that is expected to persist implies less consumption in the future, so it becomes optimal to hold a lower quantity of addictive stock, which is achieved by reducing consumption today. The more addictive the good, the greater the adjacent complementarity, and the greater the extent to which current consumption falls in response to an expected reduction in future consumption. This prediction—that all else equals addiction implies a greater price elasticity—is in stark contrast to early models of addiction that hypothesized that addicts were irrational and therefore unresponsive to incentives (see Cawley, 2008).

2.3.2. Empirical Tests of Rational Addiction

Most papers testing the TORA use the empirical model developed by Chaloupka (1991) that represents a simplified version of the Becker and Murphy (1988) framework. The utility function is assumed to be quadratic, which yields linear first-order conditions and, with additional assumptions, the demand function:

$$C_t = \beta_0 + \beta_1 P_t + \beta_2 P_{t-1} + \beta_3 P_{t+1} + \beta_4 C_{t-1} + \beta_5 C_{t+1} + \varepsilon, \tag{3.1}$$

where P are prices and C are consumption levels of the addictive good in different time periods.[24] If omitted determinants of demand are autocorrelated then lags and leads of consumption will be correlated with the residual of current consumption, and OLS estimates of (3.1) will yield biased estimates of β_4 and β_5. A common strategy for dealing with this problem is to instrument for lagged and future consumption using further lags and leads of prices, under the assumption that any effect on current consumption of prices before $(t-1)$ or after $(t+1)$ must operate through their effects on consumption in $(t-1)$ or $(t+1)$ (Becker et al., 1994; Chaloupka, 1991).

The signs of the coefficients in (3.1) are used to test for addiction and forward-looking behavior. Table 3.6 lists predictions about the signs of the key coefficients implied by alternative hypotheses. Regardless of whether the good is addictive, consumption is always negatively correlated with contemporaneous price, because of the law of demand. The key test for addiction is whether past consumption raises current consumption; this is informative about adjacent complementarity. The key test for whether addiction is farsighted is whether current and future consumption are positively correlated—a rational (forward-looking) addict considers future events when choosing current consumption.

Table 3.6 also shows the possibly surprising prediction of the TORA that past and future prices are positively correlated with current consumption, after controlling for past and future consumption (see the discussion in Chaloupka (1991) concerning equations (3.2) and (3.3)).[25] Because the model already controls for past and future

---

[24] An interesting feature of this regression model is that the estimated coefficients on past and future prices, and past and future consumption, can be used to calculate the rate of time discount (σ) because $\beta_3 = \beta_2/(1 + \sigma)$ and $\beta_5 = \beta_4/(1 + \sigma)$.

[25] Gruber and Köszegi (2001) point out that, in many other applications, a positive correlation between future prices and current consumption is interpreted as a failed specification test of the model, not as evidence of forward-looking behavior.

Table 3.6 Testing Models of Addiction

Predicted Sign of Coefficient On:	Non-addictive	Myopic Addiction	Rational Addiction
$P(t)$	−	−	−
$P(t-1)$	0	+	+
$C(t-1)$	0	+	+
$P(t+1)$	0	0	+
$C(t+1)$	0	0	+

Note: Applies to coefficients from the Chaloupka (1991) empirical model of rational addiction.

consumption, for past (or future) prices to be higher holding constant past (or future) consumption, some unobserved correlate of demand must have changed. It is assumed that the change in unobservables persists today, implying higher demand today.[26]

Empirical tests of rational addiction have been conducted for: tobacco (Becker et al., 1991; Chaloupka, 1991), alcohol (Waters and Sloan, 1995), cocaine (Grossman and Chaloupka, 1998), and obesity (Cawley, 1999). Comprehensive reviews are available in Grossman (1993), Chaloupka (1996), Chaloupka and Warner (2000), and Cook and Moore (2000).

There are several challenges beyond those already mentioned to estimating empirical models of rational addiction. First, data on consumption of addictive goods may contain significant reporting error, (see, e.g., Brener et al., 2003). Individuals may fear prosecution if they report consumption of illegal substances, and stigma may lead to underreporting their use, even if legal.[27] Also, heavy consumers of some addictive products may be unable to accurately recall their consumption. Moreover, sales data provide a noisy measure of consumption because some purchases may be shared with others, stored until later, wasted, or transported across borders. In future research, biomarkers (e.g. levels of nicotine, alcohol, or drugs in the blood) could serve as more objective measures of consumption but, to provide statistical power, would need to be collected (ideally repeatedly) for large numbers of people.[28]

A second empirical challenge is that prices are generally measured with error. This is especially true for illegal drugs, but it can be remarkably challenging to determine prices faced by consumers even for cigarettes or alcohol because there are many varieties and brands (which may vary in quality), and because purchases may occur in a different state with a lower tax rate, on Native American reservations with no excise

---

[26] In the Chaloupka (1991) model, the long-run price elasticity of demand, defined as movement from one steady state of addictive consumption to another, is: $\varepsilon = (\partial C\star/\partial P)\,(P/C\star) = (\beta_1 + \beta_2 + \beta_3)/(1 - \beta_4 - \beta_5) \cdot (P/C\star)$.

[27] This may be especially true in certain subpopulations. For instance, pregnant women may be more likely to underreport smoking or drinking than the general population.

[28] In an early use of biomarkers to study health behaviors, Farrell and Fuchs (1982) used carbon monoxide in expired air samples and thiocyanate in blood samples to confirm the accuracy of self-reports of smoking in the Stanford Heart Disease Prevention Program data.

taxes, or over the internet. Even when prices are accurate, consumers act based on anticipated future prices that the econometrician does not observe.

Finally, some papers estimate variants of the rational addiction model using aggregate data, but these are unconvincing as there is no reason to believe that adjacent complementarity at the individual level should be detectable in aggregate data (Ferguson, 2000). Auld and Grootendorst's (2004) falsification test finds evidence of rational addiction, using conventional estimation techniques, for annual national aggregate quantities of milk, eggs, and oranges for Canada between 1961 and 2000. Moreover, their estimates suggest that milk is more addictive than cigarettes. They show that rational addiction can generally not be distinguished from serial correlation when one uses aggregate time-series data and that the discount rates implied in such situations are unreliable.[29]

2.3.3. Less-tested Implications of TORA

Under the TORA, greater adjacent complementarity implies a higher likelihood of unstable steady states. Becker and Murphy (1988) observe that, for many addictive goods, the distribution of consumption is bimodal. For example, few people consume small quantities of crystal meth or crack cocaine year after year; people tend to quickly converge to either a steady state with high consumption (addiction) or one with zero consumption (abstinence). Becker and Murphy suggest that exogenous shocks such as job loss or divorce could nudge a person out of the abstinence steady state, resulting in a rapid transition to the addicted steady state. Conversely, a shock such as a bad drug experience or "bottoming out" could lead an addict to quit "cold turkey" and eventually end up abstaining from use.[30]

In contrast to the large number of studies using empirical models of rational addiction to calculate price elasticities of demand, we know of no empirical work examining unstable steady states or the possibility that shocks drive a person from abstinence to addiction or vice versa. This may be due to a lack of large longitudinal datasets that include both accurate data on addictive consumption and credibly exogenous shocks for a substantial number of respondents. Moreover, the shocks leading to movement between steady states may be idiosyncratically person-specific and therefore difficult to identify in secondary data.

Consumption of addictive goods is sometimes characterized by cyclicality; for example, binging and purging with food, repeatedly quitting drinking but then falling

---

[29] As an alternative, Gruber and Köszegi (2001) examine responses to increases in future cigarette taxes that have been enacted but not yet implemented. They find that cigarette sales rise but consumption falls, suggesting that consumers are both stock-piling (to avoid the higher future prices) and reducing smoking (to reduce the future addictive stock), both consistent with forward-looking behavior.

[30] Becker and Murphy argue that, when addiction is strong, the only effective way to quit is to go "cold turkey" because any consumption is likely to lead the consumer back to the addicted steady state.

off the wagon, or cold turkey cessation of drugs followed by subsequent use. The original Becker and Murphy (1988) model, and the elaboration on it by Dockner and Feichtinger (1993), permit such cycles of addictive behavior by incorporating a second addictive stock into the utility function. Whereas the original addictive stock exhibits adjacent complementarity, the second stock exhibits adjacent substitutability (i.e. higher values of the stock lower the marginal utility of consumption). The first stock is assumed to have a high rate of depreciation (i.e. it is very sensitive to recent consumption) while the second stock depreciates more slowly (i.e. it is less sensitive to recent consumption). Suppose, for example, that an individual who has previously always abstained from the addictive good (so that both stocks are zero) begins to use the substance. The first addictive stock, which has a high depreciation rate (making it sensitive to recent events), increases rapidly, and the adjacent complementarity of the stock promotes greater future consumption. However, as the individual continues to consume in period after period, the second addictive stock (which has a low depreciation rate) increases. Eventually the effect of the second stock (characterized by adjacent substitutability) overwhelms the effect of the first stock (characterized by adjacent complementarity), and consumption begins to fall. The stock with adjacent complementarity depreciates quickly, and that with adjacent substitutability more slowly, so consumption remains relatively low even as both stocks depreciate. At some point, both stocks have fallen back to zero and the cycle may begin anew.

We are unaware of studies that have empirically tested the two-stock model of rational addiction. One reason may be that it is hard to measure or even define the two stocks (and little effort has been made in the theoretical literature to do so). It might be possible to define the stock with adjacent complementarity as "addiction" and that with adjacent substitutability as "bad health" but there is no clear justification for doing so and these concepts are difficult to measure. Other models that emphasize adjustment costs of deviating from recent levels of consumption (e.g. Dragone, 2009) may prove easier to estimate and test.

2.3.4. Rational Addiction with Learning and Uncertainty

A potential criticism of the TORA is that it predicts that addicts should be satisfied with their consumption patterns or, at least, view them as preferable to alternative states of the world in which they consume less of the addictive product and have a lower addictive stock. In an important extension, Orphanides and Zervos (1995) point out that this need not hold once the assumption of perfect foresight is relaxed. Specifically, inexperienced individuals are assumed to be uncertain about the harm of consuming the addictive good, with learning occurring over time. Persons with high addictive tendencies or excessive initial optimism (about the probability of avoiding addiction) will most frequently end up being addicts and will regret their addiction once it occurs.

Orphanides and Zervos (1995) assume there are two types of individual: "non-addicts," for whom $\theta = 0$, and "potential addicts," for whom $\theta = 1$. Individuals do not initially know to which group they belong but at time t assign a subjective probability, $P(t)$, to the likelihood that they are non-addicts. Utility at time t is:

$$U(Y(t), C(t)) + \theta\eta(t)\nu(C(t), S(t)),$$

where $U(.)$ represents the immediate reward from consuming the non-addictive good (Y) and the addictive product (C), ν is the detrimental addictive side-effect of past consumption, S is the stock of addictive capital, and η is a dichotomous variable indicating whether a harmful addiction has occurred, with $\Pr(\eta = 1)$ increasing in S. Individuals maximize discounted expected lifetime utility:

$$\max E\left\{ \sum_{t=0}^{\infty} \delta^t [U(Y(t), C(t)) + \theta\eta(t)\nu(C(t), S(t))] \right\},$$

subject to a budget constraint and the equation of motion of the stock of addictive capital. δ is the discount factor.

The key distinction between this and the standard TORA model is the uncertainty in the last term: individuals do not initially know their type θ or the exact point at which addiction occurs. The subjective probability of being a non-addict $(\theta = 0)$ is initially set at $P(0)$ and changes based on a Bayesian updating rule. If $\theta\eta(t) > 0$ then the consumer updates his beliefs so $P(t+1) = 0$. In other words, harm from consuming the potentially addictive good reveals to the individual that he cannot be a non-addict. Conversely, if $\theta\eta(t) = 0$, the consumer updates his beliefs so $P(t+1) > P(t)$, because consuming the addictive good without harm makes it more likely that he is a non-addict.

As in the standard model of rational addiction, the particularly interesting cases involve multiple steady states, and Orphanides and Zervos focus on the situation with two equilibria for potential addicts: one a low level of consumption capital, S_1, where harm does not occur, and the other a high and harmful level of addictive consumption, S_2.[31] The likelihood that potential addicts end up at the higher steady state primarily depends on the baseline probability $P(0)$, with individuals who are overoptimistic (i.e. have too large a value of $P(0)$) at greatest risk of becoming addicted. By construction, all addicts regret their decision, *ex post*.[32] The initial value of the crucial subjective probability, $P(0)$, is determined outside the model but the potential importance of peer

---

[31] Non-addicts consume an amount of the potentially addictive good that results in a stock intermediate between S_1 and S_2.

[32] Wang (2007) extends upon the framework of Orphanides and Zervos in three ways. His model is solved in continuous rather than discrete time. There is uncertainty about the ability to stop using the addictive product, as well as in the probability of becoming an addict—thus quitting behavior (including unsuccessful quit attempts) is the focus of this model. Finally, all individuals are potential addicts, but with initially unknown heterogeneity in the threshold for addiction.

influences, unwarranted optimism, and misinformation are emphasized. All of these determinants yield policy implications that are potentially quite different than those from the original TORA model (e.g. government policies might influence values of P (0)) and none have received detailed empirical examinations.

2.4. Price Elasticities of Health Behaviors

There are enormous research literatures estimating the price elasticity of demand for habitual or addictive substances. There are comprehensive reviews of this literature available for tobacco products (Chaloupka and Warner, 2000; Gallet and List, 2003), alcohol (Cook and Moore, 2000; Wagenaar et al., 2009), and food (Andreyeva et al., 2010). Grossman (2005) summarizes the empirical evidence on the importance of price as a determinant of the demand for cigarettes, alcohol, and illicit drugs. In this section we will cite the consensus estimates reported in the reviews and meta-analyses, and single out for special mention some studies that utilize exceptionally rich data or especially insightful methods. However, we caution that these studies vary in terms of data utilized and models estimated, so for specifics readers should refer to the original studies as well as the comprehensive literature reviews cited above.

Early studies estimated price elasticities of demand using aggregate data on sales and state taxes, and as a result were limited by multicollinearity, the discrepancy between sales and consumption, smuggling and cross-border shopping, and an inability to estimate elasticities separately for important subgroups such as youths or to measure the price elasticity of initiation or cessation. In response to these limitations, and thanks to the arrival of richer data, more recent studies have used longitudinal individual-level data on consumption. However, challenges persist in accurately measuring price, which may vary even within small geographic areas, and at any location vary by brand and quantity purchased. Common data sources for prices are: for tobacco the Tax Burden on Tobacco (Orzechowski and Walker, 2009), for alcohol and food the American Chamber of Commerce Researchers Association (or ACCRA) Cost of Living Index, and for illicit drugs the System to Retrieve Information from Drug Evidence (STRIDE).

Cigarettes are the addictive substance for which the most price elasticities of demand have been estimated. The *Handbook of Health Economics* chapter on smoking concludes that the price elasticity estimates for overall cigarette demand mostly fall within the range of -0.3 to -0.5 (Chaloupka and Warner, 2000). More recently, Gallet and List (2003) located 523 published estimates of the price elasticity of demand for cigarettes, the mean of which is -0.48, with a large standard deviation (0.43) and ranging from -3.12 to 1.41. They find that the median estimate of the price elasticity of demand for cigarettes is larger for the long run (-0.44, $N = 155$) than the short run (-0.40, $N = 368$), and larger for men (-0.50, $N = 24$) than women (-0.34,

$N = 15$). Aggregation of the data matters; the 87 studies using individual–level data found a smaller median price elasticity (−0.39) than the 101 studies using data at the level of the state or province (−0.60). See Table 3.7 for the median price elasticities of demand for cigarettes for different samples. The meta-analysis by Gallet and List (2003) finds that cigarette price elasticities are not affected by many aspects of the empirical model (e.g. whether accounting for rational addiction or estimating a double hurdle model, whether data are time series or cross-sectional, or whether data are from before or after the release of the 1964 Surgeon General's report on smoking); they conclude that estimation methods have little impact on estimates of the price elasticity of demand for cigarettes.

Some studies separately estimate the impact of price on smoking at the extensive margin. The consensus price elasticity of smoking participation is around −0.5 (Gilleskie and Strumpf, 2005; Grossman, 2005). Gilleskie and Strumpf (2005) show that higher cigarette prices lead to particularly large decreases in the probability of initiation by non-smokers. Conversely, in their preferred estimates, DeCicca et al. (2002) find no impact of cigarette taxes on smoking initiation by youths (both genders pooled) and, estimating models separately by gender, Cawley et al. (2004) estimate that smoking initiation by boys, but not girls, is sensitive to cigarette price.

The next largest relevant literature on price elasticities concerns food. Andreyeva et al. (2010) locate 160 studies that calculate the price elasticity of demand for major food categories. They find that the mean price elasticity of demand for food away from home is −0.81 ($N = 13$), for soft drinks is −0.79 ($N = 14$), for fats and oils is −0.48 ($N = 13$), and for sweets and sugars is −0.34 ($N = 13$). Consumption of high-nutrient, less energy dense foods is also sensitive to price; the mean price elasticity of demand for fruit is −0.70 ($N = 20$) and that for vegetables is −0.58 ($N = 20$). The few studies that calculated price elasticities of demand for food separately by income

Table 3.7 Estimates of Price Elasticity of Demand for Cigarettes

Category	Variable	Median Price Elasticity	Number of Estimates
Elasticity estimate	Short run	−0.40	368
	Long run	−0.44	155
Aggregation	Country	−0.40	335
	State/province	−0.60	101
	Individual	−0.39	87
Gender	Men	−0.50	24
	Women	−0.34	15
Age	Adult	−0.32	17
	Young adult	−0.76	22
	Teen	−1.43	8

Source: Gallet and List (2003), Table 2, column 1.

group found essentially no difference between the price sensitivity of low-income consumers and the population as a whole (Andreyeva et al., 2010). See Table 3.8 for mean price elasticities of demand for various food categories.

There are also a large number of studies estimating the price elasticity of demand for alcohol. Wagenaar et al. (2009) located 112 such studies containing a total of 1,003 estimates of price elasticity. The simple means of these price elasticities are −0.51 for alcohol as a whole ($N = 91$), −0.46 for beer ($N = 105$), −0.69 for wine ($N = 93$), and −0.80 for spirits ($N = 103$), and −0.28 for heavy drinking ($N = 10$). They conclude that there is "overwhelming" evidence that higher prices decrease consumption of alcohol (Wagenaar et al., 2009, p. 187). See Table 3.9A for price elasticities of demand for alcohol for different types of alcohol.

Gallet (2007) conducts a meta-analysis of 132 studies of the price elasticity of demand for alcohol. Across 1,172 published estimates, the median price elasticity is −0.535. The median price elasticity of demand for alcohol is larger in the long run (−0.816, $N = 148$) than in the short run (−0.518, $N = 1,024$). The one study located by Gallet (2007) that estimated the price elasticity of demand for alcohol separately by gender found that price elasticity is larger for women (−0.750) than men (−0.509). See Table 3.9B for price elasticities of demand for alcohol for different samples.

Table 3.8 Estimates of Price Elasticity of Demand for Food

Food Category	Mean Price Elasticity of Demand	Number of Estimates
Food away from home	−0.81	13
Soft drinks	−0.79	14
Fats/oils	−0.48	13
Sweets/sugars	−0.34	13
Fruit	−0.70	20
Vegetables	−0.58	20

Source: Andreyeva et al. (2010), Table 1.

Table 3.9A Estimates of Price Elasticity of Demand for Alcohol

Consumption	Mean Price Elasticity of Demand	Number of Estimates
All alcohol consumption	−0.51	91
Beer	−0.46	105
Wine	−0.69	93
Distilled spirits	−0.80	103
Heavy alcohol use	−0.28	10

Source: Wagenaar et al. (2009).

Table 3.9B Estimates of Price Elasticity of Demand for Alcohol

Category	Variable	Median Price Elasticity	Number of Estimates
Elasticity estimate	Short run	−0.518	1024
	Long run	−0.816	148
Aggregation	Country	−0.490	699
	State/province	−0.671	375
	Individual	−0.640	87
Gender	Men	−0.509	1
	Women	−0.750	1
Age	Adult	−0.556	22
	Young adult	−0.386	13
	Teen	1.167	1

Source: Gallet (2007), Table 2, column 1.

Table 3.10 Estimates of Price Elasticity of Demand for Various Illicit Drugs

Addictive Good	Estimate of Price Elasticity of Participation	Estimate of Price Elasticity of Demand Conditional on Use	Source
Marijuana	−0.3		Pacula et al. (2001)
Cocaine	−1.0	−0.3 to −0.4	Chaloupka et al. (1999)
Heroin	−0.89		Saffer and Chaloupka (1999)

Some studies estimate the price elasticity of demand for alcohol at the extensive margin. For example, Manning et al. (1995) calculate that a 10 percent increase in the price of alcohol decreases by 5.5 percent the probability that an individual is a current drinker.

A much smaller literature examines the price elasticity of demand for illicit drugs, generally focusing on the extensive margin of use; this literature confirms that even drug use is sensitive to price. Pacula et al. (2001) find that a 10 percent increase in the price of marijuana decreases its use at the extensive margin among high school seniors by 3 percent. Even the use of hard drugs is price sensitive. A permanent 10 percent increase in the price of cocaine is estimated to reduce the probability of its use by approximately 10 percent and to reduce by 3 to 4 percent the number of times cocaine users take the drug (Grossman and Chaloupka, 1998; Chaloupka et al., 1999). The price elasticity of heroin participation is −0.89, and is similar across race and gender groups (Saffer and Chaloupka, 1999). See Table 3.10 for price elasticities of demand for various illicit drugs.

Others have estimated price elasticities of demand for opium based on historic data from East Asia. Van Ours (1995) examines the opium market in the Dutch East Indies for 1923−1938 and estimates that the short-term and long-term price elasticity of demand were about −0.7 and −1.0. Liu et al. (1999) use data from the opium market in Taiwan for 1914–1942 and calculate that the short- and long-run elasticities of demand were −0.48 and −1.38.

An important question is whether price sensitivity varies by intensity of use; i.e. when prices rise, is the reduction in consumption limited to casual users, or do heavy users decrease their consumption as well? The answer varies by substance. For alcohol, there is strong consistent evidence that the heaviest drinkers are the least sensitive to price. Manning et al. (1995) find that the price elasticity of demand for alcohol is U-shaped across drinking intensity; demand is relatively inelastic (−0.55) at the fifth percentile of drinkers, price elastic (−1.19) for the median drinker, and essentially zero at the 95th percentile. Likewise, Wagenaar et al. (2009), in their review of the literature, find a mean price elasticity of heavy drinking of −0.28 ($N = 10$), which is only a third of the overall price elasticity of alcohol consumption of −0.91 ($N = 91$). Similarly, Cook and Moore (2001) estimate that a one-dollar increase in the beer excise tax would reduce the prevalence of youth alcohol use by two percentage points, but would have no effect on binge consumption (Cook and Moore, 2001). In models estimated separately by gender, Markowitz and Grossman (2000) find that heavy drinking is elastic to the price of beer for women, but not men.

In contrast to alcohol, when it comes to food the heaviest consumers may be the most price sensitive. Auld and Powell (2009) estimate quantile regressions, which indicate that food prices have small effects on most of the population but have larger effects on youths above the 80th or so quantile of the distribution of BMI; e.g. the effect of fast food prices at the 90th or 95th quantile are three to five times higher than estimates for the entire population. Evidence is more mixed for smoking; price is a greater deterrent to heavy smoking (11 + cigarettes per day) than lighter smoking (6–10 cigarettes per day), but demand is relatively price elastic at both amounts (Gilleskie and Strumpf, 2005).

Another important question is whether youths are more or less price sensitive than adults, and the results are mixed. Gallet and List (2003), in their review of the literature, find that price elasticities of demand for cigarettes are larger for teens (−1.43, $N = 8$) and young adults (−0.76, $N = 22$) than for adults (−0.32, $N = 17$). However, more recent studies using richer data suggest that price has less impact on the smoking initiation of youths than that of adults (DeCicca et al., 2002, 2008a and b). When panel data are treated as repeated cross-sections, this research obtains estimates similar to those obtained in previous cross-sectional studies; e.g. the estimated price elasticity of teen smoking participation is around −0.7. However, when the longitudinal nature of the data is exploited by examining the smoking initiation decisions of non-smoking youths, cigarette taxes are found to have little impact on the probability of smoking initiation.

Table 3.11 Estimates of Income Elasticity of Demand for Cigarettes

Category	Variable	Median Income Elasticity	Number of Estimates
Elasticity estimate	Short run	0.28	295
	Long run	0.39	80
Aggregation	Country	0.33	341
	State/province	0.30	24
	Individual	0.06	10
Gender	Men	0.27	11
	Women	1.23	8
Age	Adult	0.06	6
	Young adult	0.05	1
	Teen	—	0

Source: Gallet and List (2003), Table 2, column 2.

For alcohol, the literature review by Gallet (2007) found a mean price elasticity of demand that was lower for young adults (-0.386, $N = 13$) than for adults (-0.556, $N = 22$). Saffer and Chaloupka (1999) find that the price elasticity of demand for cocaine and heroin is similar across age groups (Saffer and Chaloupka, 1999).

Another important question is whether the health behaviors of pregnant women are sensitive to price. Two studies (Colman, Grossman, and Joyce, 2003; Gruber and Köszegi, 2001) find that a 10 percent increase in cigarette prices is estimated to cause 10 percent of women to stop smoking during pregnancy. An important direction for future research is to better understand how price elasticities of demand vary across unhealthy behaviors, types of consumers (especially youths and pregnant women) and amounts of use.

2.5. Income and Health Behaviors

Income could either increase or decrease unhealthy behaviors. Income could lead to a rise in unhealthy behaviors if cigarettes, alcohol, drugs, and food are normal goods. However, good health and appearance may also be normal goods, leading one to invest more time and money in the production of health as income rises (Philipson and Posner, 1999).

Hundreds of published studies have calculated the income elasticity of smoking and drinking. Gallet and List (2003) located 375 published estimates of the income elasticity of cigarette smoking, the mean of which is 0.42, with a standard deviation equal to 0.49 and ranging from -0.80 to 3.03. They find that the median estimate of the income elasticity of demand for cigarettes is greater in the long run (0.39, $N = 80$) than in the short run (0.28, $N = 295$), and is greater for women (1.23, $N = 8$) than men (0.27, $N = 11$). Aggregation of the data matters; the 10 studies using individual data found a median income elasticity of 0.06, whereas the 24 studies using

Table 3.12 Estimates of Income Elasticity of Demand for Alcohol

Category	Variable	Median Income Elasticity	Number of Estimates
Elasticity estimate	Short run	0.676	901
	Long run	0.860	113
Aggregation	Country	0.768	581
	State/province	0.572	359
	Individual	0.213	74
Gender	Men	0.193	2
	Women	0.120	11
Age	Adult	0.267	30
	Young adult	0.328	4
	Teen	−0.001	2

Source: Gallet (2007), Table 2, column 2.

data at the level of state or province found a median income elasticity of 0.30. See Table 3.11 for estimates of the income elasticity of smoking for various samples.

Gallet (2007) documents 1,014 published estimates of the income elasticity of demand for alcohol, for which the median estimate is 0.69. As found for the price and income elasticities of demand for smoking, the income elasticity of demand for alcohol is sensitive to the aggregation of the data, with studies based on individual data finding a smaller median elasticity than those based on data at the state or province level. See Table 3.12 for estimates of the income elasticity of alcohol consumption for various samples.

In order to measure the causal effect of income on health behaviors, researchers have exploited a variety of natural experiments. A few papers have been able to use lottery winnings as an exogenous source of variation in income. Lindahl (2005) finds that higher lottery winnings reduce the probability of being overweight, but Apouey and Clark (2010) find that lottery winnings lead to an increase in smoking and social drinking. Other research uses variation in government income transfer policies as a source of exogenous variation. Cawley et al. (2010) find no detectable impact of income on weight or obesity, using as a natural experiment the Social Security notch that endowed certain cohorts of retirees with higher benefits. Schmeiser (2009) exploits variation across states in the generosity of the Earned Income Tax Credit (EITC) and is unable to reject the null hypothesis of no effect of income on weight for men. His results for women indicate that an additional $1,000 per year is associated with a gain of between 0.84 and 1.80 pounds. In a randomly assigned conditional cash transfer program in Mexico, a doubling of cash transfers to a household was associated with significantly higher BMI and prevalence of obesity among adults (Fernald et al., 2008a) but significantly lower BMI for age and prevalence of overweight among children (Fernald et al., 2008b).

2.6. The Role of Advertising

Economists have long debated how advertising affects consumer welfare. One possibility is that it provides valuable information about product attributes, quality, price, and lowers search costs. Alternatively, advertising may change consumer preferences or differentiate products in superficial ways, allowing higher prices to be charged. Joseph Stiglitz states flatly, "Most advertising is not informative. The typical Marlboro ad, with a cowboy smoking a cigarette, or a Virginia Slims ad, or a Budweiser Beer ad conveys no credible information concerning the nature of the product being sold, the price at which the product is sold, or where the product may be obtained" (Stiglitz, 1989, p. 842).

Advertising may allow oligopolists to differentiate their products, reduce cross-price elasticities of demand and thereby avoid price competition. This was the strategy of US cigarette manufacturers in the early 1920s, when producers tacitly colluded to keep prices high, and competed only on the basis of advertising, creating substantial barriers to the entry of potential new rivals (Adams, 1952).

The net effect of advertising may partly depend on the characteristics of a good. Advertisements for "search goods"—whose qualities are well known to consumers—may focus on price and availability, whereas those for "experience goods"—whose qualities can only be determined upon consumption—may include relatively little factual information on price or product characteristics (Carlton and Perloff, 2000).[33] This may be even truer for credence goods, whose qualities are difficult to evaluate, even after consumption. For example, a smoker may buy low-tar cigarettes under the assumption that they are less harmful, but whether that is true will not be clear even after the cigarettes are smoked. Deceptive advertising is particularly advantageous to firms selling experience or credence goods.[34]

Adding complexity is that advertising may be a complement to consumption of the advertised good, enhancing welfare even if it does not provide specific useful information about product characteristics or price (Becker and Murphy, 1993). However, Stiglitz (1989) expresses reservations about this possibility.

It is unclear to what extent unhealthy behaviors involve search, experience, or credence goods. Brands of cigarettes, alcohol, and food that one has not yet tried are experience goods. For many such goods, each unit of a specific brand is homogeneous, so after having tried the product once it becomes a search good. However, some product attributes may not be known even after consumption (e.g. the long-run

---

[33] For example, antidepressants are experience goods because they have idiosyncratic effects (regarding efficacy and side-effects) that are only revealed (to the patient and physician) after being used for an extended period of time.

[34] For example, all of the 58 advertisements (run during the first half of 1965) found to be deceptive by the Federal Trade Commission concerned experience, rather than search, qualities (Nelson, 1974).

health consequences of use), so there are certain ways in which these are credence goods.

Another ambiguity is whether advertising is cooperative (expanding the market by convincing new people to begin consuming the good) or competitive (increasing the advertised brand's share of a fixed market by stealing users from rival firms) or both. Limited empirical evidence suggests that advertising of soft drinks is competitive (Gasmi et al., 1992) while cigarette advertising is cooperative (Roberts and Samuelson, 1988).

Researchers examining how advertising influences unhealthy behaviors face several challenges, beyond those already mentioned. It is hard to measure an individual's exposure to advertising, or to find data that include both exposure to advertising and consumption of the advertised good. Perhaps most importantly, it is difficult to exploit exogenous variations in advertising in order to identify its impact on consumption. As pointed out by Avery et al. (2007, p. 449): "The relationship between advertising and consumption is literally a textbook example of simultaneous equations...Are consumers responding to the advertising or are advertisers responding to the consuming?"

Comprehensive literature reviews of the effect of advertising on tobacco consumption indicate that the evidence is mixed as to whether advertising increases use or has no detectable effect. Blecher (2008) identifies 18 studies that find no significant effect of advertising on smoking, and 17 analyses that uncover a significant positive impact. Saffer and Chaloupka (2000) classify studies of advertising and cigarette consumption according to whether the data are time series or cross-sectional. Among the time-series studies, nine find no effect of advertising and six find a small positive effect. All three cross-sectional studies examined indicate a positive effect of advertising.

Two meta-analyses of advertising elasticities of demand for cigarettes and alcohol find that use is less sensitive to advertising than to prices or income. Gallet and List (2003) located 137 published estimates of the advertising elasticity of cigarette smoking, the mean of which is 0.10, with a standard deviation equal to 0.13 and ranging from −0.10 to 069. Gallet (2007) located 132 studies containing 322 estimated advertising elasticities of alcohol consumption, of which the median estimate is 0.029.

Chou et al. (2008) merge data from the 1979 and 1997 National Longitudinal Surveys of Youth (NLSY79 and NLSY97) with information on weekly hours of television advertisements for fast food restaurants by designated market area (DMA) and year. They estimate that if youths were exposed to an additional half hour of fast food advertising per week, the probability of being overweight would rise by 2.2 percentage points (15 percent) for boys aged 3−11 years, 1.6 percentage points (or 12 percent) for girls aged 3−11 years, 2.5 percentage points (17 percent) for boys aged 12−18 years, and 0.6 percentage points (4 percent) for girls aged 12−18 years. This research is limited by a lack of information about fast food consumption (the outcome examined is BMI). Moreover, the child's exposure to advertising is estimated using the number of hours that the child reports watching television and the ads aired in that DMA; the researchers do not know how many and which fast food commercials each child saw. Moreover, advertising in the DMA may be endogenous; fast food restaurants likely target advertising to areas whose residents are expected to have a high demand for fast food. Controlling for DMA fixed effects accounts for time-invariant differences in demand but there remains potentially endogenous variation in demand over time within DMAs.

Saffer and Dave (2006) pursue a similar strategy, merging individual-level data from the Monitoring the Future and NLSY97 with market-level data on alcohol advertising in television, newspapers, radio, and outdoor media. They examine the 75 largest DMAs in the US and find that advertising is positively, although modestly, correlated with the probability of alcohol use and binge drinking. They acknowledge that the results may be biased if advertising expenditures are a function of factors affecting demand for alcohol. This study also suffers the limitation of not being able to accurately estimate exposure to ads within DMAs.

Virtually all previous studies examining the impact of advertising on health behaviors are limited by the likelihood that advertising exposure is endogenous, e.g. through targeting of ads to consumers likely to demand the products. A recent review of the literature examining the impact of cigarette marketing on smoking criticizes this work for failing to address the endogeneity of marketing exposure and concludes that the findings "fall far short of those required to establish well-founded causal relationships" (Heckman et al., 2008, p. 43). The study that best estimates the effects of advertising exposure, while addressing the endogeneity of exposure, is Avery et al. (2007). Using the Simmons National Consumer Survey, the authors merge data on the number of advertisements for smoking cessation products in the specific magazine issues read by the respondent. To control for the selective targeting of ads, the authors control alternately for categories of magazines read (so variation in advertising exposure comes from, for example, reading *Time* instead of *Newsweek*) and for magazine fixed effects, thus exploiting variation over time in the number of ads in each magazine. The authors consistently find that exposure to magazine advertisements for smoking cessation products raises quit attempts, with weaker evidence of increases in successful quitting.[35]

2.7. Time Preference and Health Behaviors

The rate of time preference refers to an individual's willingness to exchange utility today for utility later: it is the marginal rate of substitution between current and future

---

[35] As a falsification test, they check whether future advertisements for smoking cessation products (in the same magazines the respondent currently reads) affect the current probability of quitting, and find that they do not.

utility (Becker and Mulligan, 1997). Suppose that an individual seeks to maximize the present discounted value of lifetime utility:

$$U = \sum_{t=1}^{T} \delta^t(U(C_t)) \quad \text{for } \delta = \frac{1}{1+\sigma},$$

where $U(C_t)$ is utility in period t. A higher rate of time preference σ indicates that the person is less patient (to a greater extent prefers utility today to utility tomorrow). The discount factor δ has the opposite correlation: a smaller discount factor implies less patience (future utility receives a weight closer to zero) and a higher discount factor implies greater patience (a higher weight for utility in later periods).

Victor Fuchs (1982) was one of the first economists to examine the relationship between rate of time preference and health behaviors, motivated by the large literature documenting a positive correlation between education and health. Fuchs (1982) argues that the correlation of education with good health could reflect differences in rate of time preference. Patient individuals are more likely to forego current utility in exchange for long-run benefits; this is likely to result in healthier behaviors (e.g. more exercising) and higher education, even if schooling has no causal effect on health. Fuchs finds that a more patient rate of time preference (elicited from questions about willingness to exchange a certain amount of money today for a larger amount in the future) is associated with greater schooling and usually also with healthier behaviors, although the point estimates are often small and not always statistically significant.

Time preference is notoriously difficult to measure. Most of the empirical literature attempting to do so uses one of two approaches. The first is to infer a discount factor from Euler equations of consumption (e.g. Lawrance, 1991) or wealth (e.g. Samwick, 1998) in different periods. A limitation of this approach is that identification of the rate of time preference is dependent on strong assumptions about functional form (Lawrance, 1991; Zhang and Rashad, 2008). A second common method is to survey respondents using hypothetical scenarios regarding willingness to exchange money today for (more) money in the future (e.g. Fuchs, 1982; Farrell and Fuchs, 1982). This approach is limited because people may not provide accurate answers to hypothetical scenarios and responses to such questions may instead measure expectations about interest rates, rates of return on investments, or attitudes toward risk, rather than discount factors.

A fundamental challenge for all methods of calculating the discount rate is that rates of time preference may vary across types of consumption. For example, an individual may be happy to save rather than spend money, but eager to defer physical pain rather than to experience it immediately. Moreover, the marginal rate of substitution for consumption in two particular periods may change over time or across the life-cycle.[36] These issues will be discussed in detail in section 3.

---

[36] See Frederick et al. (2002) for a general discussion of these issues.

Becker and Mulligan (1997) model time preference as endogenous. They point out that there is an incentive to reduce the rate of time discount because doing so raises the present discounted value of lifetime utility. They, along with Fuchs (1982), hypothesize that schooling may provide a method of decreasing one's rate of time discount and that this provides a possible mechanism through which education improves health. Becker and Mulligan (1997) further suggest that precommitment mechanisms (such as "Christmas clubs" that enforce saving) may be investments in learning patience. Parents may invest in reducing their children's discount rates, so that the youth will be more willing to make investments that involve short-term costs but long-term gain, which can yield benefits for health, human capital, and wealth. In the addiction model of Orphanides and Zervos (1998), discussed above, consumption of addictive substances raises the rate of time preference (reduces patience) but individuals are aware of this and account for it when making consumption decisions.

Farrell and Fuchs (1982) find that among white, non-Hispanic adults with between 12 and 18 years of schooling, in the Stanford Heart Disease Prevention Program, the negative correlation between eventual completed schooling and smoking is as strong at age 17 (when all were in the same grade, and differences in education had not yet arisen) as at age 24 (when they differed in attained education). Based on this, Farrell and Fuchs (1982) reject the hypothesis that years of schooling reduce smoking and conclude that omitted variables explain the observed correlation. They are unable to test which omitted variables are responsible, but hypothesize that one is rate of time discount.

Several recent papers demonstrate a correlation between body mass index (BMI) or obesity and proxies for rate of time preference such as savings rates (Komlos et al., 2004; Smith et al., 2005) or willingness to delay financial rewards or other gratification (Borghans and Golsteyn, 2006; Ikeda et al., 2010). Conversely, Chapman et al. (2001) find weak or no association between health behaviors (influenza vaccination, adherence to medication for high blood pressure, adherence to medication for high cholesterol) and time preference assessed using hypothetical scenarios. Khwaja et al. (2007) show that smokers and non-smokers have similar rates of time discount when the latter is proxied by willingness to undergo a colonoscopy and conclude that variation in discounting is not a major explanation for differences in smoking behavior.

Cutler and Glaeser (2005) argue that if discount rate heterogeneity explains variations in health behaviors, we should observe high within-person correlations across health behaviors—e.g. alcohol consumption should be higher among smokers than non-smokers. They test this using data for individuals 45 and older from the 1990 National Health Interview Survey on: current smoking, consumption of three or more alcoholic beverages per day, obesity, use of recommended hypertension medication, and (for women) receiving mammograms in the past three years. They find that the correlations across health behaviors are "surprisingly low" (p. 238), most below

10 percent, with the highest (alcohol and smoking) at 16 percent. They obtain similarly weak correlations using data from the Behavioral Risk Factor Surveillance System on smoking, drinking, obesity, seatbelt use, flu shots in the past year, and cancer screening. Changes over time in health behaviors (smoking, heavy drinking, being overweight, and physical inactivity) are also weakly correlated (in the Health and Retirement Study). While these results are consistent with the hypothesis that time preference is not a major determinant of health behaviors, other explanations are that these behaviors are primarily substitutes (rather than complements), and myopia about future consequences leads people to become addicted to certain unhealthy behaviors but not others.

3. ALTERNATIVE APPROACHES TO STUDYING HEALTH BEHAVIORS

3.1. Peer Effects

In the basic model of health capital, individuals make decisions in isolation from each other. Manski (2000) notes, however, that there are three channels through which individuals may affect each other. The first is through constraints on shared resources. For example, there may be only so many treadmills at the gym, or so many roster spots on the school sports team, and as a result one individual's decision to exercise or play sports can prevent another from doing the same. Second, individuals may influence each other's behavior through expectations. For example, teenagers may update beliefs about the marginal benefits and costs of risky behaviors by discussing their sexual experiences or observing each other's drug use. Third, individuals may directly affect each other's preferences.

This third mechanism is the focus of Leibenstein (1950). He emphasizes the role of "bandwagon" effects (deriving utility from consuming the same goods and services as peers), which makes the demand curve more elastic because, when price falls, demand increases both directly (because of lower prices) and indirectly (because others are more likely to be using the good). Conversely, "snob" effects work in the opposite direction. When something becomes common, people may not want to consume as much of it (perhaps because it no longer signals exclusivity). Snob effects make the demand curve less elastic because the increased consumption associated with a price decrease makes the good less desirable to consume. Bandwagon and snob effects imply that the market demand curve is not simply the horizontal summation of all individual demand curves in the market and that peer interactions matter in ways not captured by simple economic models.

For many addictive goods, consumers may strike a balance between bandwagon and snob effects. For example, teenagers may wish to rebel against the majority (consistent with a snob effect), but probably not in an utterly unique way that leaves them isolated from everyone else, so they choose to emulate a small subset of peers, consistent with a limited bandwagon effect.

A rapidly growing empirical literature has investigated peer effects in health behaviors. Manski (2000) notes three possible explanations for the correlation of behaviors within groups: (1) *endogenous interactions*, where behavior of the group affects behavior of the individual; (2) *contextual interactions*, where exogenous characteristics of group members (such as age or family background) affect behavior of the individual; and (3) *correlated effects*, a non-social effect in which the group behaves similarly because they have similar characteristics or environment. For example, smoking may be correlated within youth peer groups for any or all of these reasons. There may be endogenous interactions such as peer smoking increasing own tobacco consumption because smoking is a bandwagon activity. There may be contextual interactions if teens who hang out with older kids tend to have smoking peers (because the peers are older), and having older friends (whether smokers or not) is associated with more frequent initiation of smoking. Finally, there may be correlated effects in the sense that low-income youth tend to hang out together, and low income is associated with smoking initiation.

The source of correlated group behaviors has important implications for public policy. For example, smoking cessation programs targeted to individual teens may have spillover effects to peers if there are endogenous interactions, but not if there are only contextual interactions or correlated effects.

Manski (1993, 2000) emphasizes the difficulty in empirically distinguishing between these effects because of the "reflection problem": the observed correlation between an individual and his peers is a composite of both the impact of peers on the individual and of the individual on the peers. Researchers have sought to overcome the reflection problem by: assuming a specific length of lag between mean group behaviors and those of the individual, modeling individual behavior as a specific non-linear function of group behavior (i.e. assuming that individuals are responsive to some feature of the group distribution of behavior other than the mean), or using instrumental variables approaches that exploit exogenous variation in either the behavior of group members or the membership of the peer group. Even if endogenous interactions can be proven, Manski (2000) argues that such a finding is only useful if one can demonstrate that the mechanism is preferences (e.g. the stigma of drug consumption falls when its use rises), expectations (e.g. youths learn how pleasurable drugs can be by seeing others enjoy them), or constraints (e.g. search costs for drugs are reduced when friends buy and use them).

The nature and variety of empirical investigations on peer effects can usefully be illustrated by focusing on studies of obesity, which have received considerable attention, particularly in response to a study of data on adults from the Framingham Heart Study that concluded obesity spreads within social networks (Christakis and Fowler, 2007). That study does not exploit any exogenous variation in either peer group membership or in the behavior of peers; instead it attempts to control for correlated effects by controlling for lags of both respondent obesity and peer obesity in a model that regresses respondent contemporaneous obesity on peer contemporaneous obesity status. Key findings are that the chances of becoming obese rose by 57, 40 and 37 percent, respectively, if the respondent had a friend, sibling, or spouse who became obese. These findings could reflect selection (friends and spouses choosing each other based on future weight or weight trajectories), correlated effects due to shared environments (such as local food prices and availability, or availability of exercise opportunities), or true endogenous interactions (i.e. causal peer effects). Christakis and Fowler (2007) and Fowler and Christakis (2008) argue that there is likely to be a true peer effect because the estimated effects are stronger for pairs who both list each other as friends than pairs in which one but not both individuals claim friendship. They also find that geographic proximity of peers does not matter—the authors interpret this second result as ruling out a common environment effect. However, even for true endogenous interactions, one might expect proximity to be important if the size of the peer effect depends on the frequency of interactions with the peer.

Cohen-Cole and Fletcher (2008a) investigate the sensitivity of the findings in Christakis and Fowler (2007) using a different dataset (the National Longitudinal Survey of Adolescent Health or Add Health) and age group.[37] When using the same regression model, they largely replicate the findings of Christakis and Fowler; however, when controls for school-specific time trends (as a proxy for the environment) were included, the peer correlations fall more than 30 percent, suggesting the importance of omitted group-level characteristics.[38] In addition, they conduct falsification tests, using the Add Health data, showing that Christakis and Fowler's (2007) regression model generates apparent network effects for outcomes for which true peer effects are unlikely (e.g. acne, height, and headaches) and that these disappear after controlling for environmental confounders.[39] They conclude that the method used by Christakis and Fowler (2007) is not sufficiently specific to separate true network effects from spurious correlations due to insufficient controls for the local environment.

---

[37] Add Health is a nationally representative sample of 7—12th graders first interviewed in 1994—95.

[38] However, Fowler and Christakis (2008) interpret this work as supporting their own, pointing out that their original estimates are within the 95 percent confidence intervals of Cohen-Cole and Fletcher (2008a).

[39] Falsification tests apply the empirical methods to outcomes for which the hypothesized relationships should *not* exist. Large or statiscally significant associations suggest problems with the empirical strategy. In a classic falsification test, Dranove and Wehner (1994) used a standard method of testing for demand inducement for medical care in a situation where it should not hold: pregnancies. Their finding that obstetricians/gynecologists appear to increase the number of pregnant women suggests shortcomings of the standard test.

Identifying the correct peer group is a challenge. "However severe the reflection problem may be when group composition is known, the problem becomes insurmountable when group composition is unknown" (Manski, 2000, p. 129). Moreover, peer groups may vary across outcomes; for example, a teenage boy might experience bandwagon effects for physical fitness from his sports teammates, for risky sexual activity from his classmates, and for alcohol from his older brother. In practice, researchers examining health behaviors have examined a variety of peer groups, almost always driven by their opportunistic availability in secondary data, including: class-mates (Lundborg, 2006; Argys and Rees, 2008), friends (Christakis and Fowler, 2007; Cohen-Cole and Fletcher, 2008b), siblings (Christakis and Fowler, 2007), spouses (Christakis and Fowler, 2007), neighbors (Christakis and Fowler, 2007; Case and Katz, 1991), and college roommates (Yakusheva, 2010; Duncan et al., 2005).[40]

The method of instrumental variables can be applied to estimate peer effects by utilizing exogenous variations in peer behavior. For example, Trogdon et al. (2008) and Renna et al. (2008) instrument for the weight of a peer using the obesity status of the peer's parents. The validity of these instruments is questionable, however, because friendships could also be selected on the basis of obesity status, with obese youths rela-tively likely to have obese parents. This strategy may also suffer from a second-order case of the reflection problem—friend's parents' weight may be affected by friend's weight which in turn may be affected by the respondent's weight.

A second strategy for identifying causal peer effects is to instrument for peer behav-ior using exogenous variation in peer group membership; this has most frequently con-cerned classmates or roommates. For instance, Argys and Rees (2008) use birth date relative to the cutoff for starting kindergarten to generate exogenous variation in the age of the youth relative to classmates; they find that females with older peers are more likely to use substances (marijuana, alcohol, tobacco) but find few peer effects for boys. Lundborg (2006) assumes that while schools may be chosen by parents, the specific classroom within a grade is randomly assigned; utilizing across-classroom differences in peer behavior by controlling for school and grade fixed effects, he finds effects of class-mates on binge drinking, smoking, and use of illicit drugs. Duncan et al. (2005) use randomized roommate assignment and find that boys who binge drank in high school consume more alcohol in college if their roommate binge drank in high school. No such peer effects were found for boys who did not binge drink in high school, or for

---

[40] Other relevant peer groups may include an online community or adolescents seen on television. In Christakis and Fowler (2007), "friends" were those that respondents listed as being able to get in touch with them in case they had moved and the surveyors were unable to find their new address or phone number. These might be friends or merely those most likely to know their whereabouts. Add Health asked respondents to list their five closest male and five closest female friends. This survey also contains information on a large number of students in the same schools, allowing researchers to use classmates as another peer group. In both the Framingham and Add Health data, one is able to explore the importance of symmetry: do two respondents list each other as friends, or does one person list the other as a friend but it is not reciprocated?

girls, or for marijuana use or sexual behavior for either boys or girls. Yakusheva et al. (2009) also exploit random roommate assignment and find that female college students gained less weight during freshman year when their roommate was heavier. Carrell et al. (2010) exploit random assignment of United States Air Force Academy cadets to squadrons (of approximately 30) with whom cadets live, eat, study, and compete in intramural sports. They find substantial peer effects; e.g. that the effect on the respondent's current fitness of friends' high school fitness is nearly 40 percent as strong as the effect of the respondent's own high school fitness. These peer effects are caused primarily by friends who are the least fit; this may be due to the sample consisting of unusually fit individuals who may not have much room for improvement.

In the Moving to Opportunity experiment, adults receiving a waiver to move to a higher-income neighborhood were 5 percentage points less likely to be obese than similar persons not receiving a waiver (Kling et al., 2007); this intent-to-treat estimate is consistent with those moving to more advantaged neighborhoods adopting a new set of peers with healthier habits. An alternative explanation is that the design of, and amenities in, the new neighborhoods better facilitate healthy eating and physical activity.

Another general empirical challenge in the peer effects literature is correctly modeling which aspects of the distribution of behavior in the peer group are relevant. Most analyses model individual behavior as a function of the central (especially average) tendencies of the peer group, but the presence or absence of extreme actions could be more important. High outliers ("bad apples") and low outliers ("straight arrows") might be especially influential on behavior. For example, the probability that a female college student develops an eating disorder might be influenced by the number of sorority sisters who are underweight, rather than average body weight of sorority members.

3.2. Information Constraints

Individuals may lack the information needed to accurately assess the costs and benefits associated with various health behaviors. One important question is whether individuals understand how health behaviors alter the risks of morbidity and mortality. If individuals underestimate the risks associated with unhealthy behaviors, government intervention to either directly provide the missing information or require disclosure of information by producers could be warranted. Kenkel (1991) provides evidence that health knowledge is related to smoking, drinking, and exercise in the expected directions, but that even some highly knowledgeable persons have poor health habits.

A large economics literature has examined consumer awareness of, and sensitivity to, information on the health consequences of smoking. Smoking is especially informative because its risks are well understood and have been widely publicized since the

1964 Surgeon General's report (US Department of Health, Education and Human Welfare, 1964).

A landmark study by Viscusi (1990) found that adults were much more likely to *overestimate* than to *underestimate* the extent to which smoking raises the risk of lung cancer. Specifically, he estimated that the true lifetime risk of lung cancer for smokers was between 5 and 10 percent but respondents to a national telephone survey estimated that the risk was 43 percent. Assuming the true risk was 10 percent, approximately 90 percent of the sample overestimated the risk, with 51 percent thinking it exceeded 50 percent. Smokers had lower risk estimates than non-smokers but still overstated the true risk fairly dramatically—the average stated subjective risk was 37 percent; 86 percent estimated greater than a 10 percent lifetime risk for smokers and 42 percent put the odds above 50 percent. These risks are overestimated even if respondents' answers were based on all of the risks of smoking (e.g. including those from heart disease, strokes, and emphysema).

Analyses of data from the Health and Retirement Survey (HRS) reach a starkly different conclusion. Schoenbaum (1997) finds that 50—62-year-old heavy smokers had expectations of living to age 75 that were almost twice as high as actuarial predictions. Khwaja et al. (2007), using the same data, find that, for the sample as a whole, subjective beliefs about survival were similar overall to the objective data but that current smokers were overly optimistic about survival while those who had never smoked were relatively pessimistic.[41] Smith et al. (2001) estimate that heavy smokers are more optimistic about their self-assessed longevity than their smoking behavior would warrant.[42]

One explanation for the difference in the aforementioned findings is that individuals may suffer from optimism bias; i.e. they may have accurate knowledge of population risks but still underestimate their personal risk. Viscusi's (1990) question "Among 100 cigarette smokers, how many do you think will get lung cancer because they smoke?" may measure knowledge of risks to the general population, whereas the HRS data analyzed by Schoenbaum (1997) and Khwaja et al. (2007) contained respondents beliefs that they personally would live to age 75.

Supporting this possibility, Smith et al. (2001) show that smokers and non-smokers in the HRS respond to health information differently: smokers dramatically reduce their subjective life expectancies when confronted with smoking-related health shocks but decrease their subjective life expectancies less than non-smokers in response to

---

[41] Objective survival probabilities were based on actual mortality within the HRS sample, rather than on life tables. Khwaja et al. (2009) find that 50—70-year-olds relatively accurately predict their probability of survival to age 75 regardless of their smoking status.

[42] Similarly, in an interesting analysis of secondary life insurance markets (viatical settlements) for individuals with HIV/AIDS, Bhattacharya et al. (2009) provide evidence that relatively healthy individuals understate their remaining life expectancy while those who are relatively unhealthy overstate it.

non-smoking-related health shocks. The authors conclude that smokers may not personalize the risks of tobacco use unless there is clear evidence that it is negatively affecting their own health. If true, this implies that general information (such as that required by labeling laws) may have only a limited effect on behavior until individuals incur a health shock related to the unhealthy behavior.

3.3. Time-inconsistent Preferences and Hyperbolic Discounting

Models of intertemporal choice have typically been based on the exponential discounting model of Samuelson (1937); e.g. the Samuelson framework is the basis for the optimization problem in the rational addiction model discussed above. A key feature is that the discount rate between any two periods t and $t+1$ is a constant (d), implying that the discount rate between periods t and $t+n$ is d^n, for all n. Such behavior is often referred to as "time consistent" because the marginal rate of substitution for consumption in any two periods remains constant over time.

Exponential discounting quickly became standard in models of intertemporal decisions because it provides a straightforward method of extending single-period utility maximization into a multi-period context, not because it accurately depicts the way that such decisions are actually made. To the contrary, as discussed below, individuals often have "time-inconsistent" preferences, e.g. discount rates are higher for intertemporal trade-offs that occur in the near future than for longer time horizons. This is called "hyperbolic" discounting (Ainslie, 1991).[43]

A key implication of hyperbolic discounting is "present-biased" preferences; the trade-off between utility in the current versus the next period is greater than that for any two adjacent periods in the future. Hyperbolic discounting results in time-inconsistent behavior. For example, assume a person is willing to trade one "util" of happiness in period n in the future for two utils received in period $n+1$. With exponential discounting and stable preferences, a person who is willing to make that trade when periods n and $n+1$ are in the distant future will also be willing to make that trade when it actually is period n. However, with hyperbolic discounting, there may be a preference reversal; the person might be willing to trade one util in period n for two utils in period $n+1$ while those periods are in the distant future, but when it actually is period n the individual might suddenly decide that more than two utils would be needed in the next period to compensate them for giving up a util immediately. Consider an individual who is choosing on Monday how much ice cream to eat on Friday. An exponential discounter will carry out on Friday the plans made on Monday (assuming no changes in income, prices, or other relevant variables) because preferences are time consistent. However, a hyperbolic discounter may plan on Monday to skip ice cream on Friday, but when Friday comes she may experience a preference reversal, suddenly being unwilling to

[43] This idea was first formalized by Strotz (1955–1956).

deny herself the current utility from consuming the ice cream. Thus, time-inconsistent preferences lead to self-control problems and future plans to engage in healthy behavior are consistently undone by (abnormally) high present discount rates.

Time-inconsistent preferences can affect many health behaviors. Plans made the night before to exercise in the morning will not be realized when the alarm clock goes off, intentions to consume alcohol in moderation will be undone as the immediate plea-sures of having "just one more drink" are repeatedly acted upon, and so forth. Individuals who are naïve about their time-inconsistent preferences may be endlessly optimistic about their ability to improve future health behaviors. Those who are more sophisticated may seek precommitments that compel their future self to adhere to healthy behaviors. For instance, they may avoid bringing home ice cream, knowing that doing so will result in overeating. Or they may plan to run with a friend, aware that this will make it harder for them to skip the workout. Each of these tactics is designed to ensure that binding decisions are made when the marginal rate of substitution between two future periods is relatively low, rather than later, when the marginal rate of substitution will change in such a way that incentivizes immediate gratification.[44]

By far the most common way that economists have modeled hyperbolic discount-ing is using the quasi-hyperbolic (or $\beta-\delta$) framework developed by Laibson (1997), based on the functional form first used by Phelps and Pollak (1968) in their study of optimal intergenerational savings. Specifically, the utility function is characterized by:

$$U_t = u(C_t) + \beta \sum_{n=1}^{T-n} \delta^t \, u(C_{t+n}), \qquad (3.3)$$

where $u(\cdot)$ is utility in the specified period, C is a composite consumption good, T is the time horizon over which utility is measured (known with certainty), with $\beta \leq 1$ and $\delta \leq 1$. The key implication is that the discount factor for consumption between period t and $t+1$ is $\beta\delta$, whereas that between any two future periods, $t+j$ and $t+j+1$ (for $j > 0$) is δ. If $\beta = 1$ this reduces to exponential discounting. However, if $\beta < 1$, the discount factor is lower (and the discount rate higher) for immediate than future consumption trade-offs. This results in time-inconsistent preferences and self-control problems similar (but not identical) to those in more general forms of hyper-bolic discounting and that can be relatively easily incorporated into standard economic models of intertemporal choice.

Substantial research suggests that hyperbolic discounting explains many real-world decisions more accurately than standard exponential discounting. For example, Thaler

---

[44] Sophistication is a double-edged sword. O'Donoghue and Rabin (1999) point out that sophisticated hyperbolic discounters are more likely than naïve hyperbolic discounters to develop precommitment strategies but may also more frequently "preoperate"—realizing that they are unlikely to be able to stick to their plan, they abandon it earlier. For example, a sophisticated hyperbolic discounter may realize that she is unlikely to be able to stick to her diet and may cease even trying, whereas a naïve hyperbolic discounter may naïvely start diet after diet.

(1981) found that the future payments required to make individuals indifferent between receiving a prize now versus later yielded implied (per period) discount rates that declined dramatically as the length of time increased, consistent with hyperbolic discounting.[45] Angeletos et al. (2001), and the references contained therein, indicate that a wide variety of time preference experiments show that decision makers are more impatient in the short run than the long run. Frederick et al. (2002) examine a large number of empirical studies and find that discount factors increase (discount rates decrease) as the time horizon of the study increases but that this relationship disappears when studies covering less than one year are eliminated. Such results are consistent with hyperbolic discounting.[46]

Gruber and Köszegi (2001) incorporate time-inconsistent preferences in a model of smoking and distinguish between sophisticated and naïve agents, where the former understand that their preferences are time inconsistent but the latter do not. A key prediction is that future price increases reduce current consumption (in models that do not also control for future consumption). Because this is generally the key test for rational addiction, standard econometric tests (focusing on responses to future changes) cannot distinguish between the TORA and similar frameworks with time-inconsistent preferences.[47] Cutler et al. (2003) also use an informal model with hyperbolic discounting to consider (but not formally test) how time-inconsistent preferences affect eating decisions and obesity, and the resulting consequences for social welfare.[48]

3.4. Cognitive Limitations and Bounded Rationality

Hyperbolic discounting does not change the utility maximization assumptions standard in economic models, only the method of discounting. However, it is possible that individuals cannot (or for whatever reason, do not) maximize utility when faced with highly complex problems. Such limitations are the basis of the models of bounded rationality and "satisficing" developed by Herbert Simon (1984) and applied by economists to many decision processes (e.g. see Thaler and Sunstein, 2009), including those related to health behaviors.

For instance, in Suranovic et al.'s (1999) modified rational addiction framework, an individual decides how much to smoke (S) at age t by maximizing:

$$U_t(S) = B_t(S) + L_t(S) + C_t(S), \qquad (3.4)$$

---

[45] Discount rates also declined with the size of the prize and losses were discounted differently from gains.

[46] There is also clear evidence that animals discount hyperbolically (e.g. see Berns et al., 2007).

[47] Differential responses to price changes occurring at two or more future periods could theoretically be used to test for the existence and amount of time inconsistency; however, the data requirements to perform this exercise are severe.

[48] Their model emphasizes the secular decline in time spent on food preparation.

where B is the current benefit of smoking, L is the fully discounted future loss from smoking, and C is the adjustment cost to changing tobacco use from recent levels. The key assumptions are that most utility losses occur at or near the end of life (and so are discounted heavily at young ages) and that adjustment costs are zero for smoking at or above recent levels but positive for lower amounts of use.[49] The model is forward looking, in that future health costs are accounted for, but myopic in that the consequences of current smoking on future adjustment costs are not considered. It allows for several realistic consequences that are either difficult to explain or require strong assumptions using models with fully rational addiction. For instance, gradual rather than "cold turkey" withdrawal may occur if addiction is "weak" (i.e. if adjustment costs for deviating from past history rise at an increasing rate), and quitting may become more likely late in life, because the number of periods until losses are incurred decreases so that these are discounted less heavily. Importantly, by failing to fully account for the consequences of current smoking on future quitting costs, individuals may enter a consumption "trap," strengthening the potential case for policy intervention.

Akerlof (1991) provides a sophisticated analysis in which bounded rationality leads to choices that separately are close to utility maximizing but, in combination, can result in large errors. Key aspects of his formulation are that decision makers are slightly biased toward present rather than future utility (as described above) in ways that they are either unaware of or do not fully account for. The result is that they avoid large mistakes at any single point in time but may make small errors that accumulate across periods.

Procrastination is an example of such behaviors. Individuals may intend to start an exercise program or stop smoking at a date in the near future but time inconsistency repeatedly prevents these intentions from being realized. Akerlof's analysis also emphasizes the role of peer influences in encouraging these decision errors, particularly in situations, as with gangs or cults, where the social milieu may be constructed to encourage initially small but cumulatively large changes in behaviors.

In Rubinstein's (2003) model of bounded rationality, agents simplify choices by applying "similarity relations." Specifically, when considering uncertain and multidimensional outcomes, individuals do not fully account for dimensions of the choices that are "similar" but instead focus on those characteristics that are dissimilar. Consider lotteries of the form (X, p), in which a payout X is won with probability p and a payout of zero is won with probability $1 - p$. Rubinstein argues that, faced with the choice between ($3,000, 0.25$) and ($4,000, 0.2$), the difference in the size of the prize will be the decisive factor because the probabilities (0.20 and 0.25) will be interpreted as "similar" (and thus the difference will be ignored) whereas the prize amounts ($3,000 versus

---

[49] By contrast, Dragone (2009) has developed a fully rational model of eating in which there are costs to any changes (either positive or negative) in food consumption. Under specified assumptions, overshooting will cause individuals to oscillate between gaining and losing weight, before eventually converging on the steady state.

$4,000) will be interpreted as dissimilar.[50] He argues that this model explains some observed time-inconsistent behavior better than hyperbolic discounting. Specifically, he argues that individuals may perceive "10 years from now" and "11 years from now" to be similar, but perceive "today" and "a year from now" as dissimilar.

Education is likely to be correlated with cognitive ability (which is measured with error, if at all), possibly explaining some of the strong positive relationship between schooling and healthy behaviors noted in section 1 of this chapter. Education might also influence behaviors in other ways (e.g. by being correlated with or causally affecting discount rates, health knowledge, or access to high-quality medical care) but an emerging body of research suggests that differences in cognition partly explain variations in health behaviors.

Cutler and Lleras-Muney (2010) conclude that about 30 percent of the average education gradient in a wide variety of health behaviors in the United States and Great Britain is related to disparities in cognitive ability, with high-level processing being more important than measures of memory. Interestingly, cognitive ability is more important at later ages than earlier in life, suggesting that cognitive skills are learned (and helping to rule out explanations based on factors that are confounded with education and cognitive skill levels at a point in time). Similarly, using Australian data, Antsey et al. (2009) find that cognitive skill (proxied by verbal ability and processing speed) is correlated with vitamin and mineral supplement use, high rates of physical activity and light/moderate alcohol use, and reduced smoking.[51]

Chen and Lange (2008) and Lange (2010) examine how education is related to breast, colorectal, and cervical cancer screening, with particular attention paid to differences between objective versus subjective cancer risk. A key result is that subjective risks of highly educated individuals more accurately reflect objective risks than do those of counterparts with less schooling, and that differences in subjective risks are more closely linked to the relevant screening decisions. These education differences do not appear to occur because of a positive correlation between schooling and income or the quality of medical care but could reflect the more scientific world-view of those with more schooling. One overall conclusion is that the highly educated are better at processing information related to medical risks and the behaviors required to ameliorate them (although it is not clear that schooling causes these differences).

De Walque (2007a) demonstrates that a series of HIV/AIDS prevention campaigns in Uganda during the late 1980s and early 1990s resulted in larger reductions in the incidence of HIV infection for highly educated young men and (particularly) women than for their counterparts with less schooling, with increased condom use playing a key role. Although alternative explanations cannot be completely ruled out, the

---

[50] Conversely, when choosing between ($3,000, 1) and ($4,000, 0.8) both the prize amounts and probabilities are dissimilar so that other criteria (like maximizing expected payouts) will be used.

[51] This study does not identify the direction of causation.

greater ability of highly educated persons to process the information provided in these campaigns may represent a significant source of these schooling-related differences.[52]

Rosenzweig and Schultz (1989) show that education increases the ability of couples to successfully use complicated contraceptive methods (rhythm or withdrawal) but with no corresponding differences for simpler methods (e.g. the pill or IUD). Contraceptive effectiveness also increased with schooling following unplanned pregnancies. Both results suggest that increased cognitive ability favorably influences behaviors, particularly when information is limited or idiosyncratic.

Goldman and Smith (2002) show that education increases the probability that individuals with HIV or diabetes adhere to the complicated medical regimes developed to treat these diseases and that this superior health management is linked to better outcomes.[53] Although this evidence refers to disease management, the same mechanisms seem likely to operate for health behaviors; for example, many of the measures of adherence (particularly for diabetes) are behavioral in nature.[54] They further show that the education differential in adherence to diabetes treatment largely disappears after controlling for scores on the Wechsler Adult Intelligence test (measuring high-level abstract reasoning), further indicating the key role of cognitive skills.[55]

3.5. Non-traditional Models

The models described above deviate from standard economic models of constrained maximization by adding constraints related to information or cognitive processing or by incorporating time-inconsistent preferences. However, attention has increasingly been paid, particularly in the areas of behavioral economics and neuroeconomics, to decision processes that differ more fundamentally from those traditionally used in economics. Kahneman (1994) distinguishes between "decision utility" and "experience utility." The key distinction is that individuals, when attempting to optimize based on decision utility, may incorrectly forecast the hedonic experiences (realized well-being) of different decisions (experience utility) and these errors may be systematic.

---

[52] Similarly, De Walque (2007b) and Grimard and Parent (2007) find that education has a negative causal effect on smoking—using IV procedures exploiting college attendance as a strategy to avoid the Vietnam war—but they are not able to say whether the effect of schooling reflects increased cognitive processing abilities or other factors, such as education-related decreases in discount rates, improvements in access to information, or wage increases.

[53] Maitra (2010) confirms that the highly educated have better diabetes treatment adherence but raises questions about the extent to which this explains better self-reported health.

[54] For instance, Goldman and Smith (2002) show that highly educated diabetics self-monitored their blood glucose and self-tested their blood or urine more frequently than their counterparts with less schooling.

[55] Less educated persons also have higher rates of undiagnosed diabetes, controlling for health insurance coverage (Smith, 2007), which is suggestive of a behavioral response although it could also reflect differences in access to care. Lleras-Muney and Lichtenberg (2005) show that educated individuals tend to use more recently developed drugs, particularly in cases where learning is required (e.g. when drugs are repeatedly purchased to treat a medical condition), and that these effects are unlikely to result from differences in insurance or access to medical care.

Kahneman and Thaler (2006) offer the example of someone grocery shopping while hungry: she may buy overly large quantities of food because her current hunger leads her to overestimate the experience utility of eating in the future.

A possible reason for systematic errors is that decisions are influenced by immediate emotional experiences, called "visceral factors" by Loewenstein (2000), such as anger, fear, thirst, hunger, or sexual desire. Loewenstein argues that such factors have been traditionally discounted by economists because they fluctuate rapidly (although often in highly predictable ways) and because their impact is underestimated during "cool states" when individuals are not under their influence. In "hot" states, where visceral factors are operative, individuals "who otherwise display 'normal' decision-making behavior...behave in ways that give the appearance of extreme discounting of the future" (p. 430).[56] In Laibson's (2001) cue theory of consumption, repeated pairing of a cue and a consumption good eventually creates complementarity between the cue and consumption of the good (i.e. the presence of the cue raises the marginal utility of consumption). He gives examples such as the smell of baking cookies and the sound of ice falling into a whiskey tumbler. Thus, cues can generate cravings in addicts and can be used in marketing to increase the consumption of food or alcohol. In contrast to the TORA, this model predicts high-frequency variations in craving and marginal utility, which can lead to seemingly random patterns of consumption. (Although Laibson notes that "cue effects can be captured using minor variants" of the TORA; see p. 82.) An important implication of the cue theory is that sophisticated consumers will actively engage in strategic cue management, which is consistent with the philosophy of, for example, Alcoholics Anonymous that its members must avoid people and locations (and, of course, the sight or smell of alcohol) that could be cues that would lead to cravings and falling off the wagon. This theory also implies that there are negative externalities associated with cues, with consequent implications for policy to ensure that the production of cues does not exceed the level that would maximize social welfare.

A number of economists have used models of "multiple selves" to characterize decision-making processes. Thaler and Shefrin (1981) postulate that consumer behavior represents an internal battle between a farsighted "planner," who values utility received in the distant future, and a myopic "doer," who prefers immediate gratification. The doer controls decisions but can be constrained by the farsighted planner through expenditures of (costly) willpower, (costly) precommitment devices restricting the choices available to or the trade-offs faced by the doer, or other techniques for achieving self-control (e.g. rules, mental accounting, and framing). Similarly,

---

[56] For example, Lerner and Keltner (2001) provide evidence that anger (but interestingly not fear) is associated with more risk-taking choices. Ariely and Loewenstein (2006) find that the willingness to engage in unsafe sex or in morally questionable behavior to obtain sexual gratification is higher for sexually aroused than non-aroused persons and that individuals poorly predict how sexual arousal will influence their behavior.

Fudenberg and Levine (2006) view decision problems as a game between a long-run patient self and a series of short-run impulsive selves. The long-run actor may again choose self-control actions influencing the utility function of the myopic self, even though short-run costs must be incurred to reduce the future cost of self-control. Brocas and Carrillo (2008) use a principal—agent approach in which the individual is split into a myopic but informed system (the agent) and a forward-looking but uninformed system (the principal) who maximizes the expected utility of all of the agents. Because the principal lacks complete information, she will optimally delegate certain choices to the agents but not others. For instance, the principal will offer the agent pairs of positively correlated labor supply-consumption choices that limit the consumption of "tempting" goods" but otherwise leave the agent free to make consumption decisions. This, for example, may take the form of strict prohibition on the consumption of addictive products, while allowing complete freedom in the use of those that are non-addictive.[57]

3.5.1. Brain Structure and Decision Making

Many of the models just discussed link decision making to the structure of the brain. In Thaler and Shefrin (1981), decisions of the "planner" primarily reside in the prefrontal cortex, while those of the "doer" occur in the more primitive limbic system (described below). Fudenberg and Levine (2006) similarly appeal to evidence that short-term impulsive behavior and long-term planned behavior occur in different parts of the brain. Brocas and Carrillo (2008) explicitly appeal to neuroscience evidence of multiple brain systems that split individual decision making into two processes.

The following elements of brain anatomy provide insight into these characterizations.[58]

- The human brain evolved by *adding* new capabilities rather than *replacing* those previously existing. The brain stem and cerebellum, which developed first, control autonomic functions such as heartbeat and breathing. Surrounding this is the limbic system (the amygdala, thalamus, hypothalamus, and hippocampus), which coordinates sensory inputs to generate subjective feelings and drives states like anger, pleasure, and aggression. The neocortex, which came last, consists of the occipital, parietal, temporal and frontal lobes (that deal with sensory processing), and the prefrontal cortex which is the locus of abstract thinking, conceptualization, and planning.
- The limbic system responds to cues and stimuli without accounting for the long-term consequences of current actions, whereas the deliberative system, located in the neocortex, involves higher cognitive processes that do consider long-term consequences. The limbic and deliberative systems operate in parallel to yield

---

[57] In a somewhat related model of "temptation utility," Gul and Pesendorfer (2001) show that individuals may choose to limit the available choice set so as to avoid needing to exercise costly self-control.

[58] This discussion draws heavily on Ruhm (2010), which in turn is based on material in MacLean (1990), Massey (2002), Bernheim and Rangel (2004), Loewenstein and O'Donoghue (2004), and Camerer et al. (2005).

differences in perception and memory, so that emotional feelings exist independently of rational assessments. We argue that many decisions about health behaviors involve an interaction of rational calculations with processes based on emotions, chemical responses, and feelings.

- The limbic system often acts upon external stimuli *before* deliberative processes take place in the neocortex. The number of neural connections running from the limbic system to the cortex also far exceeds those in the reverse direction, suggesting that emotional impulses frequently overwhelm cognitive processes.

Bernheim and Rangel (2004) draw on this neuroscience evidence in developing their model of cue-triggered decision processes. Specifically, they assume the brain contains a hedonic forecasting mechanism that learns from experience. However, the consumption of addictive substances interferes with this normal learning process by acting directly on the limbic system. Over time this system will be activated upon the presentation of the cues and the individual will enter a "hot" mode in which rational utility-maximization processes are bypassed. When the individual is in a "cold" mode, he makes decisions rationally with recognition of future consequences but in hot modes these cognitive processes do not operate.[59] The sophisticated decision maker is aware of this and rationally chooses a lifestyle that reduces the possibility of being cued into hot modes.

This model differs from the TORA in a number of ways. Most importantly, consumption of the addictive good is frequently viewed to be a mistake because stochastic shocks (i.e. encountering cues that trigger hot modes) cause decisions to diverge from rationality.[60] Cue-triggered addiction can also account for behaviors such as intentional use followed by half-hearted and later concerted attempts at abstention, or intentional recidivism.

One could alternatively model behavior as the result of multiple simultaneously operating brain systems, without an extreme division into hot and cold modes. For example, in Loewenstein and O'Donoghue (2004), decisions reflect the interaction between the cognitively sophisticated deliberative system (located in the prefrontal cortex) and a rapidly responding affective system (occurring in more primitive brain structures).[61] The affective system primarily controls behavior but the deliberative system exerts influence through the use of costly cognitive effort or willpower.[62] Exposure to (potentially learned) cues and stimuli can trigger affective system

---

[59] Metcalfe and Mischel (1999) provide an earlier and less formal treatment of the hot and cool states of decision-making.

[60] Addiction also does not necessarily require adjacent complementarity in this model.

[61] Similar decision processes are modeled in the psychological literature without explicit linkages to brain function. For example, in cognitive-experiential self-theory, information is processed by "experiential" and "rational" systems that operate in parallel and are interactive: the experiential system is automatic, preconscious, rapid, and non-verbal; the rational system is analytic, deliberative, slow and affect-free (Epstein, 2003).

[62] Thaler and Sunstein (2009) refer to these as the "automatic" and "reflective" systems.

responses but, in contrast to "hot/cold" models, the deliberative system almost always exerts at least some influence. The standard model of rational choice corresponds to the special case in which the deliberative system is in full control (i.e. exerting cognitive effort is costless) and hot states occur when the affective system is in full control (i.e. exerting cognitive effort has infinite cost).

This model provides insight into a variety of behaviors. First, individuals may simultaneously do one thing while wishing they were actually doing another (e.g. "I should not be eating this donut"). Second, actions may frequently be influenced by transitory emotional states that result from affective system stimuli. Third, hyperbolic discounting and preference reversals occur naturally because future planning reflects deliberative processes but immediate decisions are strongly influenced by the affective system. Fourth, discount rates may vary across types of consumption (because affective system responses will be more important for some types than others) and situations (depending on how strongly the affective system has been triggered and how much willpower has been depleted). Fifth, the model can explain phenomena such as loss aversion (if the affective system weights losses more heavily than gains) and non-linear probability weighting (individuals may consistently overestimate the probability of unlikely events and underestimate the probability of likely events) that are difficult to reconcile with standard utility maximization.

Ruhm (2010) has developed and applied a variant of Loewenstein and O'Donoghue's model in his examination of overeating and obesity. In his model, food consumption is influenced by the affective and deliberative systems and overeating has become more common over time partly because of lower food prices (as in traditional economic models) and partially because of the greater sophistication of "food engineering" whereby food products are increasingly designed to appeal to the affective system.

3.5.2. Behaviors Difficult to Explain using Traditional Models

Many aspects of generally observed behavior are difficult to reconcile with the traditional economic models in which decision makers are fully rational.[63] For example, Bernheim and Rangel (2004) point out that addicts typically describe their substance use to be a mistake even, in some instances, while they are in the act of taking the drug.

The data also suggest that the use of a single discount rate—whether exponential or hyperbolic—is unlikely to adequately describe many aspects of decision making. For instance, Frederick et al. (2002) summarize a large body of evidence indicating that: gains are discounted more than losses (loss aversion); small amounts are discounted more than large amounts; improving sequences are preferred to worsening sequences; and discount rates differ dramatically across situations and types of

---

[63] Although this section focuses on non-rational behavior, the consequences will, in practice, often be difficult to distinguish from non-exponential (e.g. hyperbolic) discounting. Either can cause, for example, self-control problems.

consumption.[64] Many discounting "anomalies" can be explained if decision making is based on multiple brain systems. Evidence that such brain modularity is important has been obtained from patients with brain damage. For example, persons with deficient limbic system function are less able to engage in gradual learning or to acquire conditioned responses to emotional stimuli, while individuals with damage to their prefrontal cortex exhibit impaired decision making, with a particular inability to act on long-term goals (see Loewenstein and O'Donoghue, 2004; Camerer et al., 2005; or Brocas and Carrillo, 2008 for useful discussions of this literature). Some neuroscience evidence obtained from magnetic resonance imaging (MRI) supports the possibility that multiple-system models of decision making arise directly from the structure of the brain (e.g. McClure et al., 2004); however, there remains ambiguity about these MRI results (e.g. see Glimcher et al., 2007).

The empirical data also suggest that the deliberative system exerts less power when cognitive processing resources are limited (when self-control is depleted) than when it is not. For example, Shiv and Fedorikhin (1999) describe an experiment in which subjects are asked to memorize either a two-digit or a seven-digit number and were then asked to choose a snack: either chocolate cake or fruit salad. Those who were asked to memorize a seven-digit number were more likely than those asked to memorize a two-digit number to request the chocolate cake (this was particularly true for those with high self-rated measures of consumer impulsivity), which the authors interpret as evidence that greater cognitive processing demands increase the likelihood that choices are driven by lower-order affective reactions rather than by higher-order processes like thinking or reasoning. More recently, Vohs et al. (2008) have shown that the cognitive effort involved in making choices reduces self-control among a variety of dimensions.[65]

The frequent use of precommitment or other self-control devices is cited as evidence of time-inconsistent preferences of which agents have at least some awareness. For example, Gruber and Köszegi (2001) highlight the use of socially managed incentives to reduce smoking, such as announcing a New Year's resolution to quit smoking to create embarrassment for oneself if one resumes smoking. Ruhm (2010) emphasizes the increasing frequency of bariatric surgery, which can be viewed as an extremely strong precommitment strategy. The drug Antabuse is another market-generated precommitment device: by taking it in the morning an alcoholic can ensure that if he consumes alcohol later in the day he will be made ill by the interaction of the drug

---

[64] Consistent with this, Cutler and Glaeser (2005) show that within-person correlations across health behaviors are quite low both at a point in time and when looking at behavioral changes across time. This variation results in part from genetic factors but behavior-specific situational influences are also important.

[65] They examine how making choices among consumer goods or college course options were related to physical stamina, persistence, procrastination, and the ability to perform cognitive calculations. In each case, the group required to make choices experienced greater reductions in self-control or cognitive processing ability.

with the alcohol. A key distinction is that rational addicts may pay for technologies that help them quit or weaken their addiction but they should not be willing to pay to limit their future choices. Conversely, under alternative models, agents frequently make choices they will subsequently regret and so, under some circumstances, may choose to voluntarily constrain their future options.

Experimental and non-experimental evidence suggests that individuals recognize their time-inconsistent preferences and act strategically to at least partially overcome them. Using data from three health clubs, Della Vigna and Malmendier (2006) compare the behavior of members to non-members, where the latter are allowed to use the clubs by paying for each visit. They find that members have higher per visit average costs and overestimate their future attendance. Those with monthly memberships are more likely, than annual members, to stay enrolled beyond one year (despite paying a higher fee for the flexibility to quit each month) and their attendance declines over time, in contrast to the increases observed for annual members. The researchers believe that overconfidence about future self-control provides the most likely explanation for these results.

Considerable ingenuity is required to distinguish between rational and non-rational use of addictive products. Most previous "tests" of the TORA identify forward-looking behavior without distinguishing between complete or partial foresight, or between time-consistent preferences and self-control problems. Gruber and Köszegi (2001) emphasize that both the TORA and models of hyperbolic discounting imply responsiveness of current consumption to anticipated future price changes and the authors show that forward-looking behavior by smokers need not indicate rational behavior.[66]

Because such direct tests are difficult to obtain, researchers have begun to use indirect evidence to distinguish between the two classes of models. Using data from the United States and Canada, Gruber and Mullainathan (2005) find that the happiness of smokers is increased when taxes are raised, consistent with sophisticated awareness of time-inconsistent preferences but probably not with rational addiction (because that model implies that higher prices reduce utility). Similarly, Kan's (2007) IV estimates suggest that Taiwanese smokers who intend to quit are relatively supportive of smoking bans or cigarette tax increases. This is interpreted as evidence of a demand for self-control devices that are predicted with time-inconsistent preferences and forward-looking behavior.[67] Ruhm (2010) tests a variety of predictions of a two-system model

---

[66] Specifically, they find that announced future tobacco taxes have a positive effect on current cigarette *sales*, a result that suggests forward-looking behavior as consumers stock up prior to price hikes in order to save money. However, current *consumption* (not sales) appears to decline in response to future tax increases, as predicted by both TORA and less than fully rational models in which consumers have some foresight.

[67] However, the appropriateness of the instruments (awareness of the health risks of smoking and weight loss attempts) is questionable as quit attempts may increase the disutility of second-hand smoke, prompting support for these measures.

of overeating and obesity, with food engineering, against a standard model with full rationality. Among the most important predictions are that the frequency of eating mistakes—as evidenced by weight loss attempts—and of the consumption of engineered foods (that are high in fat and salt) will have increased over time, particularly for heavy individuals, and that actual weight will have increased over time without an accompanying rise in desired weight. All of these predictions are borne out using data for adults in the US.

3.6. Short-term Effects

The discussion on health behaviors to this point has emphasized long-term factors and influences. (For example, education is anticipated to have lasting effects on decisions.) However, health behaviors are also influenced by short-term factors, including some that are poorly explained by many standard models. We discuss two examples below.

3.6.1. Full Wallets Hypothesis

According to the permanent income hypothesis (PIH), short-term changes in income should have little influence on consumption decisions because spending is based on "permanent" rather than current income (Hall, 1978). However, liquidity constrained individuals may not be able to smooth consumption as the PIH model predicts; moreover, decision makers with time-inconsistent preferences, or operating using the nontraditional models described above, may not even try to smooth consumption. The empirical evidence indicates that violations of PIH are common and that even very short-term changes in income affect a variety of types of consumption, including many health behaviors. This is sometimes referred to as the "full wallets" hypothesis.

Stephens (2003) showed that for persons receiving a major portion (at least 70 percent) of their income from Social Security, expenditures on "instantaneous consumption goods" (expenditures on food away from home and entertainment) increase by 33 percent on the day Social Security checks are received and by 35 percent on the next day, relative to average spending. The interpretation is that consumers have "full wallets" immediately after receiving their checks, which results in higher spending because consumers are liquidity constrained at other times of the month.[68] A similar responsiveness to the receipt of pay checks has been observed in the United Kingdom (Stephens, 2006) and to the receipt of food stamp benefits in the United States (Wilde and Ranney, 2000).[69]

---

[68] Such behavior could occur without liquidity constraints if retailers discount prices at the beginning of the month (when Social Security checks are received). Instead, Hastings and Washington (2010) show that food prices decline slightly over the month (by about 3 percent between the first and fourth weeks of the month) and that almost all of the change in food expenditures is due to variation in the quantities of food purchased.

[69] Energy intake also falls at the end of the "food stamp month" for those who shop infrequently.

Shapiro (2005) expands on this last result, showing that caloric intake declines 10 to 15 percent over the food stamp month. This is interpreted as evidence for quasi-hyperbolic discounting because, under exponential discounting, an annual discount rate of 146 percent would be needed to explain these results.[70] Mastrobuoni and Weinberg (2009) find even greater evidence of declining within-month food consumption for persons receiving 80 percent or more of their income from Social Security and who have little or no savings: annual discount factors are 0.08 for these persons, compared to flat consumption profiles for recipients with savings. The probability of consuming less than the recommended daily calories also increases dramatically toward the end of the benefit month for the former group but not for the latter.

The potential food insufficiency described above could have deleterious health consequences for at least some individuals. However, most detrimental consequences of short-term changes in income appear to work in the opposite direction (i.e. "full" wallets are more harmful than "empty" wallets). Riddell and Riddell (2006) show that intravenous drug users are much more likely to be admitted to Vancouver hospitals with overdoses in the two days after welfare checks are received than at other times of the month.[71] Dobkin and Puller (2007) obtain similar results for drug-related admissions, particularly for cocaine overdoses, among California recipients of Supplemental Security Income (SSI) or Disability Income (DI). Interestingly, they do not find a corresponding "pay check" effect, suggesting that the consequences across population segments may be heterogeneous.[72]

Such spikes in drug use due to full wallets have severe negative health consequences. Riddell and Riddell (2006) show that the death rates of SSI beneficiaries increase 22 percent on the day of benefit receipt—generally the first of the month. Mortality also increases at the beginning of the month for other reasons. Phillips et al. (1999) find that the overall US death rate rises by 0.9 percent in the first week of the month due to large increases in mortality from substance abuse (13.8 percent) but also because of increases in mortality due to homicide, suicide, other external causes, motor vehicle accidents, and liver disease with mention of alcohol (6.5, 5.3, 4.6, 2.8 and 2.6 percent, respectively).[73] They also uncover evidence of smaller (less than 1.0 percent) but still significant first-of-the month effects for deaths due to respiratory or circulatory disorders, neoplasms, and liver disease without mention of alcohol.

---

[70] Evidence is also provided that the implied discount rates increase dramatically (0.24 percentage points per day) over the food stamp month.

[71] These effects may be reinforced by cue-driven behavior (as in the models of Laibson, 2001 or Bernheim and Rangel, 2004 discussed above) because the majority of drug users in Vancouver live in close proximity of each other.

[72] Also, the SSI/DI impact on alcohol-related hospital admissions is smaller than that for other drugs—possibly because acute health problems are less common for alcohol.

[73] They point out that alcohol or substance abuse seems likely to play an indirect role in many deaths from some of the other sources (e.g. homicide and suicide).

Using data from the 1973–2005 Multiple Cause of Death Files, Evans and Moore (forthcoming) confirm that mortality increases by 0.9 percent in the first week of the month, relative to the preceding week. This is due in part to a 3.0 percent rise in deaths due to substance abuse (versus a 0.8 percent increase in other fatalities) but because substance abuse deaths are relatively rare, the absolute within-month fluctuations in mortality are much greater for deaths from non-substance-related causes.[74] They also show that first-of-the-month increases in various types of consumption (e.g. food and non-food items, lottery tickets, movie box office receipts, as well as foot traffic at malls, retail and apparel establishments) are greatest for the groups most likely to be liquidity constrained (the less educated, government transfer payment recipients, low-income households), and that within-month variation in mortality declines with education. Their overall conclusion is that deaths rise at the beginning of the month because many inherently risky activities increase when liquidity constrained consumers have full wallets.

3.6.2. Macroeconomic Fluctuations and Health Behavior

Many aspects of health-related behaviors exhibit a counter-cyclical variation. Evidence that mortality is procyclical dates back more than 80 years (Ogburn and Thomas, 1922; Thomas, 1927) but it is only in the last 15 years that these patterns, and the mechanisms for them, have begun to be understood. A major empirical innovation has been the use of data containing multiple geographic locations observed at several points in time, allowing the use of panel data methods, in particular the inclusion of location-specific fixed effects and general time effects.[75]

In a series of papers, Ruhm has provided evidence that, when economic conditions (typically proxied by unemployment rates) weaken, heavy drinking and drunk-driving, smoking, obesity, and physical inactivity decrease and diets improve (Ruhm, 1995, 2000, 2005a; Ruhm and Black, 2002). Two potential mechanisms for these effects have been highlighted. First, income reductions during bad economic times appear to reduce some types of unhealthy consumption (e.g. drinking), as in the discussion of full wallet effects above. Second, some healthy behaviors (e.g. exercise) are time intensive and work hours are generally procyclical.

Other research examining these health behaviors, using similar techniques, generally also finds that behaviors become healthier in bad times. Evidence that alcohol sales and driving problems decline during a weak macroeconomy has been provided by Evans and Graham (1988), Ettner (1997), and Freeman (1999), among others; Dee (2001) uncovered a drop in alcohol use and heavy consumption, but also an increase

---

[74] They estimate that there are 647 extra deaths from substance abuse during the first week of the month, compared with 3,636 additional fatalities from other sources.

[75] Ruhm (2008) provides a detailed discussion of these issues, and a review of the related empirical literature.

in binge drinking.[76] Gruber and Frakes (2006) verify the decline in smoking and Courtemanche (2009) shows that shorter work hours decrease obesity because they are associated with increases in exercise and reduced consumption of fast food and prepared processed foods. Xu and Kaestner (2010) use an instrumental variables approach to show that the lower work hours occurring during economic downturns cut smoking and increase exercise while Edwards (2008) indicates that having more non-work time increases sleeping, socializing, and time spent caring for the elderly. On the other hand, Charles and DeCicca (2008) find that obesity and BMI rise for men with low *ex ante* probabilities of employment.[77]

Interestingly, better health during economic downturns occurs even though screening tests (mammograms, pap smears, and colorectal exams) are less often received (Ruhm, 2000) and doctor visits and hospital episodes decrease (Ruhm, 2003; Xu and Kaestner, 2010). However, there are exceptions. Dehejia and Lleras-Muney (2004) find that pregnant women obtain earlier and more extensive prenatal care when the economy is weak and Ruhm (2007) shows a similar increase in sophisticated treatments for heart disease (e.g. coronary bypass and angioplasty) among senior citizens.

The macroeconomic variations in health behaviors provide one reason why mortality is procyclical. Research using the empirical methods just discussed generally predicts that a 1 percentage point increase in unemployment reduces total mortality by 0.3 to 0.5 percent, with a similar decline in deaths from coronary heart disease and much larger decreases in deaths from external causes (particularly traffic accidents); conversely, cancer mortality changes little because such fatalities are unlikely to respond to short-term changes in behaviors.[78]

It is not obvious whether these behavioral changes represent rational or non-rational responses to changing incentives. On the one hand, individuals will optimally substitute labor supply from periods when wages are low to those when they are high, implying that it may be optimal to devote less time to health-enhancing behaviors when the economy is robust, even if doing so increases the risk of death. On the other hand, Evans and Moore (2009) show that the causes of death with high macro-economic fluctuations are the same ones that exhibit large within-month variations, presumably due to full wallets effects that are inconsistent with intertemporal optimization.

---

[76] However, Arkes (2007) finds that drinking and drug use by teenagers is counter-cyclical.

[77] More complete discussions of this literature, including evidence for countries outside the United States, are provided by Ruhm (2006) or Ruhm (2008).

[78] For more detailed reviews of previous research examining how macroeconomic conditions influence mortality, see Ruhm (2005b, 2006, 2008).

4. ECONOMIC CONSEQUENCES OF HEALTH BEHAVIORS

We next discuss the challenges to identifying the causal impact of health behaviors and summarize the substantial body of research examining such consequences for a variety of outcomes including: medical care costs, education, employment, wages, and crime.

4.1. Reasons to (and not to) Conduct Cost of Behavior Studies

Cost of Illness (COI) studies calculate the difference in medical costs between those with and without a specific medical condition, controlling for observable characteristics. Such analyses can be conducted not just for diseases like cancer and diabetes but also for health behaviors such as alcoholism, smoking, drug abuse, and a sedentary lifestyle; we refer to these as Cost of Behavior (COB) studies.

Costs can be divided into direct payments for medical care and indirect costs for which no payments are made—such as productivity losses due to job absenteeism or premature death. Public health advocates use COB studies to lobby for greater expenditures to improve health behaviors. However, such arguments are often circular. For example, some health behaviors have substantial medical resources devoted to them, and thus a high COB, but that does not necessarily justify still greater spending (see, e.g., Shiell et al., 1987). Because medical expenses arise from the decision to treat the outcomes of unhealthy behaviors, a simplistic (but not necessarily desirable) way to reduce these costs is simply to refuse to treat such consequences. Another limitation is that COB studies tend not to consider marginal effects (of expanding or reducing the scale of interventions) but instead assume that unhealthy behaviors can be completely eradicated (Shiell et al., 1987).[79] Given these shortcomings, it is sometimes argued that health economists should devote their efforts not to COI or COB studies but instead to studying the cost effectiveness of specific interventions designed to change health behaviors (e.g. Roux and Donaldson, 2004).

There are, nevertheless, several situations where COB studies may be of interest. First, they indicate the amount of medical resources currently devoted to treatment—e.g. how much does the US spend treating alcoholism? Second, they enhance our understanding of disparities across gender, race, or income. Third, they provide help in calculating external costs, which may justify government intervention (Zohrabian and Philipson, 2010; Baumol, 1972). Fourth, they represent one input into cost-effectiveness analyses of candidate interventions, by providing estimates of the value of avoided unhealthy behaviors.

---

[79] Still another potential difficulty is in distinguishing between annual and lifetime costs. For example, Fang and Gavazza (2007) provide evidence that greater investments in medical care prior to age 65 are associated with reduced medical expenditures after that age, along with commensurate reductions in total lifetime spending.

4.2. Challenges to Identifying the Consequences of Health Behaviors

It is critically important to accurately estimate the causal effects of health behaviors on outcomes (e.g. medical care costs and wages). However, it is frequently the case that only correlations are estimated, which provide limited information because they reflect three factors: (1) the causal impact of unhealthy behaviors on outcomes; (2) the impact of poor outcomes on unhealthy behaviors (*reverse causation*); and (3) the influence of omitted variables that affect both unhealthy behaviors and poor outcomes (*confounding*).

In order to estimate the causal effect of unhealthy behavior on an outcome of interest, the most convincing research design would randomly assign large numbers of otherwise similar individuals into treatment and control groups, with the treatment group then compelled to engage in unhealthy behaviors. Comparing differences in outcomes between the treatment and control groups would then generate a consistent estimate of the impact of unhealthy behaviors. Fortunately for subjects, and unfortunately for researchers, such randomized experiments are neither ethical nor feasible. As an alternative, economists frequently seek out "natural experiments" that exploit exogenous variation in health behaviors; i.e. not the result of reverse causation (e.g. poor labor market outcomes causing unhealthy behaviors) or confounding (e.g. differences in risk aversion or rate of time preference).

Such natural experiments are often exploited using the method of instrumental variables (IV). However, the instruments (i.e. the natural experiments) must be both powerful and valid.[80] In terms of power, a rule of thumb is that the F statistic for the null hypothesis that the coefficients on the instruments are jointly equal to zero, in the first stage of two-stage least squares, should be 10 or higher (Stock et al., 2002). There is no simple convincing test of instrument validity (see, e.g., French and Popovici, 2011). With multiple instruments, over-identification tests can be conducted.[81] However, such over-identification tests are only reliable when the instruments are both powerful and valid (French and Popovici, 2011; Wooldridge, 2002).[82] As a result, McCloskey (1998) argues that instruments are ultimately accepted (or rejected) based on rhetoric— the author must make a convincing logical argument for their validity. French and Popovici (2011) observe that IV studies of the consequences of health behaviors conducted during the 1990s often used intuitive or

---

[80] Angrist and Krueger (2001) and Angrist and Pischke (2009) summarize theoretical and practical difficulties associated with using instrumental variables to identify causal effects; Auld (2006) and Auld and Grootendorst (2011) examine these challenges in the context of health behaviors.

[81] For instance, the two-stage least squares residuals can be regressed on all exogenous variables (the instruments and other regressors); the F statistic testing the hypothesis that the coefficients on the instruments are jointly equal to zero is then computed.

[82] More generally, the requirements of power and validity interact in that the bias resulting from an invalid instrument is greater the weaker it is. With sufficiently weak instruments, bias may be larger in IV than OLS estimates and the "cure can be worse than the disease" (Bound et al., 1995).

theoretic arguments in favor of instrument validity, whereas those published in the 2000s papers relied more heavily on statistical evidence.

French and Popovici (2011) summarize 60 studies, published between 1990 and 2009, that use IV methods to measure the impact of using alcohol, illicit drugs, and tobacco on a variety of economic outcomes. They note that economists have used the following variables as instruments for risky behaviors: family history of risky behaviors, religiosity, and state policies affecting access and taxes. However, they note that these instruments are now more widely regarded as potentially invalid because of unobserved heterogeneity and policy endogeneity.

Prices of, or taxes on, addictive substances may be valid instruments for their consumption, but power may be lacking. Other, more recently used instruments for risky behaviors are described in subsequent sections. As in many fields of economics, the search for powerful and valid instruments is ongoing in this literature.

In considering the impacts of health behaviors, it is important to note that some behaviors (like smoking) are never health enhancing. In contrast, increased calorie consumption can reduce the risk of mortality if one is underweight (Flegal et al., 2005, 2007) and moderate consumption of alcohol may improve cardiovascular health (Cook, 2007). Such non-linear effects of consumption represent an additional challenge for empirical work measuring the consequences of healthy behaviors.

4.3. Impacts on Medical Care Costs

Relatively few studies have used econometric techniques to measure the *causal* effect of health behaviors on medical care utilization or costs.[83] In contrast, many investigations have, in the tradition of COI studies, estimated the correlation between behaviors and medical costs. For instance, Dorothy P. Rice, one of the pioneers of COI studies, quickly moved from estimating the direct costs of conditions such as cancer and AIDS to estimating the direct costs of health behaviors such as smoking, alcohol abuse, and drug abuse.

Many studies have examined the medical care costs of smoking; Sloan et al. (2004) identifies at least 165 published between the 1960s and 2002. For example, Rice et al. (1986) calculated that $14.4 billion was spent in the US in 1980 treating smoking-related illness. In an unusually detailed and careful analysis, Sloan et al. (2004) calculate that smoking at age 24 is associated with $3,757 higher lifetime medical expenditures for women and $2,617 greater expenditures for men (in year 2000 dollars).

Rice et al. (1991) estimated that the direct medical care costs of alcohol abuse were $6.8 billion and those related to drug abuse were $2.1 billion in 1985. Cook (2007) reviews COB studies of alcohol abuse, the most recent of which (Harwood,

---

[83] Other methods, such as propensity score matching, could be used to estimate the causal effect of risky health behaviors on medical care costs, but to our knowledge have not yet been used for this purpose.

2000) calculates that the medical consequences of alcohol abuse (including fetal alcohol syndrome) totaled $19 billion in 1998. The Office of National Drug Control Policy calculates that $15.8 billion was spent on medical treatments and prevention of drug abuse in 2002 (Office of National Drug Control Policy, 2004). French et al. (2000) compared self-reported health service utilization among drug users and non-users and calculate that chronic drug users and injecting drug users generated $1,000 per year in excess health services utilization relative to non-drug users. Finkelstein et al. (2009) analyze data from the Medical Expenditure Panel Survey (MEPS) and calculate that, in 2006, obese people (i.e. those with a body mass index of 30 or higher) had medical spending that was $1,429 (in 2008 dollars) or 41.5 percent higher than that for healthy-weight people (those with a body mass index of 18.5 to 25). They calculate, across all payers, $85.7 billion (in 2008 dollars) was spent treating obesity in 2006, which represents 9.1 percent of all medical spending that year. To reiterate, each of these studies estimates the correlation of health behaviors with medical care costs, not the causal effect.

A smaller number of studies use IV methods to estimate the causal effect of health behaviors on medical care utilization and costs. McGeary and French (2000) use access to drug markets, neighborhood sightings of intoxicated individuals, and drug sales as instruments for chronic drug use.[84] They estimate that chronic drug use raises the probability of an emergency room visit by 30 percent for females and 36 percent for males. Balsa et al. (2008) examines how alcohol consumption affects health care utilization, instrumenting for alcohol consumption using state alcohol and drug policies and other state characteristics (including, curiously, average precipitation). They are unable to reject the exogeneity of alcohol consumption and thus prefer their non-IV estimates which show that moderate drinking decreases the likelihood of emergency room visits for both sexes and hospitalizations for women but not men. Cawley and Meyerhoefer (2010) estimate the impact of obesity on medical care costs, using obesity status of a biological child to instrument for weight of the parents. Obesity is found to raise annual medical care costs by $2,741 (in 2005 dollars), which is more than four times as large as the corresponding OLS estimate ($676). They hypothesize that OLS results suffer attenuation bias due to measurement error in self-reported weight.

An important direction for future research is to obtain more comprehensive and reliable estimates of the causal effects on medical costs of health behaviors.

4.4. Impacts on Education

The effects of alcohol consumption on educational outcomes have been frequently studied (see the meta-analysis by Lye and Hirschberg, 2010). For instance, the IV

---

[84] The validity of these instruments is questionable if they are correlated with unobserved socioeconomic status.

estimates of Renna (2007) suggest that binge drinking decreases the probability of graduating high school (by age 19) by as much as 5.2 percent for women and 14.5 percent for men.[85] Using state policies as instruments for drinking, Chatterji (2006a) finds that high school alcohol use has little effect on educational attainment. Cook and Moore (1993) instrument for alcohol consumption using cross-state variation in minimum legal drinking age and conclude that high school seniors who are frequent drinkers (or frequently drunk) eventually complete 2.2 fewer years of college. Dee and Evans (2003) disagree with using across-state variation in such laws out of concern for unobserved heterogeneity across states. Instead, they estimate two-sample IV models in which teen drinking is instrumented using within-state variation in minimum legal drinking ages, and they conclude that teen drinking has no detectable effect on high school completion, college entrance, or college persistence. Koch and Ribar (2001) instrument for age of first alcohol use with sibling age of alcohol initiation, and conclude that delaying the start of drinking has small effects on educational attainment—a one-year delay in onset is predicted to raise completed education by roughly one-tenth of a year. On the whole, these findings suggest that heavy alcohol consumption by youths decreases educational attainment, but that moderate use may not have a detectable effect.

IV methods have been less commonly used to estimate the impact of drug use on educational outcomes. Chatterji (2006b) uses state drug policies and middle school characteristics as instruments for drug use during high school but uncovers no evidence of significant effects on educational attainment. This may be due in part to weak instruments.

Two recent investigations—Fletcher and Lehrer (2009) and Ding et al. (2009)—use genetic markers associated with brain chemistry to instrument for obesity and other health conditions when examining how the former is related to educational outcomes. However, this requires the unattractive identifying assumption that genes that affect brain chemistry do not affect educational attainment, except through obesity and other regressors; in fact, the specific genes used as instruments in these papers have been linked to many other conditions that could also affect education, such as alcoholism, schizophrenia, aggression, and violence (see Cawley et al., 2011). Notwithstanding this caveat, Fletcher and Lehrer uncover little evidence that being overweight during adolescence influences completed years of schooling; however, Ding et al. conclude that obesity lowers grade point average (GPA) by 0.45 (roughly one standard deviation).

Sabia (2007), when using parental obesity status to instrument the weight of the respondent, finds that a 50 to 60 pound (approximately two standard deviation) weight increase reduces the GPA of white females by 8 to 10 percentile points (e.g.

---

[85] For women, binge drinking is instrumented using state alcohol taxes and state minimum legal drinking ages. Those variables do not strongly predict binge drinking by men, so religiosity and whether a parent was a problem drinker are instead used for men. However, these are of questionable validity as they may directly affect education.

from the median to around the 40th percentile) with little evidence of effects on the GPA of white males or non-whites.

4.5. Impacts on Employment

The most frequently studied consequences of health behaviors are labor market impacts such as a lower probability of employment or lower wages. For example, a large literature examines how alcohol consumption affects employment. Mullahy and Sindelar (1996) instrument for problem drinking using state beer and cigarette taxes, and per capita ethanol sales. Their estimates suggest that problem drinking is associated with statistically insignificant reductions in the probability of employment. Using the same data and similar specifications but allowing for non-linear effects, Terza (2002) finds that the reduction in employment associated with problem drinking is statistically significant. In contrast, instrumenting for problem drinking using indicator variables for whether county of residence is wet or dry, Feng et al. (2001) uncover a positive and significant association between problem drinking and male employment, and an insignificant association for females. Using Finnish data and a large number of instruments, Johansson et al. (2007) conclude that alcohol dependency lowers the probability of employment by 50 percent for men and 40 percent for women.[86]

Negative effects of drug use on employment have also been fairly widely documented. For instance, DeSimone (2002) instruments drug use with the regional price of cocaine and state decriminalization of marijuana, and concludes that marijuana and cocaine use lower employment probabilities by 15–17 and 23–32 percent, respectively. Similarly, French et al. (2001) find that chronic drug use lowers employment probabilities by 9 percentage points for both sexes but that light or casual use has no detectable effect. MacDonald and Pudney (2000) estimate a joint model of occupational attainment, unemployment, and drug use using data of British young adults; they find that past hard drug use and current drug use are both associated with a higher probability of current unemployment.

Studies of the impact of obesity on employment obtain mixed results. Cawley (2000) uses weight of a biological child as an instrument for the weight of the mother and finds no significant impact of weight on female employment. Morris (2007) uses the local area prevalence of obesity as an instrument and concludes that obesity reduces the employment of both males and females. Norton and Han (2008) estimate the effect of obesity on employment, instrumenting for obesity using a similar set of genetic markers related to brain chemistry as were used by Fletcher and Lehrer (2009) to study the impact of obesity on educational outcomes. Using this IV method, Norton and Han (2008) find no effect of lagged obesity on the employment of either men or women. Rooth (2009) conducted an audit study in which fictitious job

---

[86] The instruments include parental alcohol or mental health problems, religiosity, and respondent diabetes or asthma.

applications were submitted for real job openings. Applications sent with a photo of an obese male (female) were 6 (8) percentage points less likely to receive a job interview than non-obese counterparts.

4.6. Impacts on Income, Earnings, and Wages

Cook (2007) notes that alcohol consumption is generally positively correlated with earnings; he refers to this as the "drinker's bonus" but suspects it is the result of reverse causality or confounding. However, a number of high-quality studies suggest that the effect may be causal. Auld (2005) examines how drinking and smoking affect income, assuming that religiosity and alcohol/tobacco prices affect smoking/drinking but not income directly. His estimates suggest that moderate alcohol consumption raises income by 10 percent and heavy drinking raises it by 2 percent (relative to abstaining), while smoking reduces income by 24 percent. Van Ours (2004) instruments for drinking and smoking using dichotomous indicators of initiation before age 16 and concludes that alcohol use raises men's wages by 10 percent while smoking reduces them by the same amount; neither drinking nor smoking affects female earnings.

Early studies of the NLSY that addressed the endogeneity of drug use found mixed results, including finding positive effects of drug use on wages for at least some groups and/or specifications (e.g. Kaestner, 1991; Register and Williams, 1992; Kaestner 1994). Using data of male workers residing in Amsterdam, and with an identification strategy based on the discrete factor method, van Ours (2007) estimates that marijuana use lowers wages by around 10 percent but that cocaine use has no wage effect.[87]

The large recent literature estimating how weight affects wages generally finds an obesity earnings penalty for women (especially white females), with less consistent results for men, including sometimes a wage premium associated with being overweight (e.g. Cawley, 2004; McLean and Moon, 1980).[88] Using weight of a biological sibling as an instrument, Cawley (2004) estimates that a two standard deviation (roughly 65 pound) increase in weight is associated with 18 percent lower wages for white females; however, the OLS estimates, which Hausman tests imply are preferable, are only half as large. Using parental BMI as an instrument in a non-parametric model, Kline and Tobias (2008) uncover obesity wage penalties for British men and women. Conversely, using as instruments for obesity the genes related to brain chemistry mentioned above, Norton and Han (2008) fail to detect an obesity wage penalty for young adults of either sex. Gregory and Ruhm (2011) employ flexible functional forms to show that the wages of women begin to decline after a BMI of around 23. Since this is well within the "healthy" weight range, they speculate that this may

---

[87] Parental cannabis use and the presence of children are used as instruments. The absence of an effect of cocaine use on wages may be due to lack of statistical power.

[88] McLean and Moon hypothesize that among mature men, large size may signal power and accomplishment; they label this the "portly banker" effect.

reflect returns to "beauty" (Hamermesh and Biddle, 1994) rather than obesity *per se*. They also find that male wages decline at higher levels of BMI. European studies using weight of relatives as instruments also find obesity wage penalties for women but less so for males (e.g. Lundborg et al., 2007; Brunello and d'Hombres, 2007; Atella et al., 2008; Greve, 2008), although the effects of obesity vary across nations.[89]

4.7. Impacts on Crime

Substance use may lead to criminal activity, for instance by increasing aggression or lowering inhibitions; see the discussion of "hot" states in section 3. Related research spans the literatures in health economics and the economics of crime, and can generally be divided into studies directly relating substance use to crime and those evaluating how substance abuse policies or sin taxes (rather than substance use itself) are associated with criminal behavior.

French and Maclean (2006) instrument underage drinking by young adults with parental drinking problems and state beer taxes. They find that, among males (females), consuming 12 or more alcoholic drinks in the past year is associated with a 30.9 (2.8) percentage point increase in the probability of vandalizing property, a 28.9 (19.8) percentage point increase in the probability of stealing, and a 50.1 (57.2) percentage point increase in the probability of committing any illegal act.

Other studies use indirect measures of substance use. Fryer et al. (2005) find that an index of cocaine prevalence (based on the factors of arrests, emergency room visits, drug busts, and newspaper stories involving cocaine) predicts higher homicide rates among black youths. Grogger and Willis (2000) estimate that the introduction of crack cocaine into a city (based on FBI crime reports) raised urban crime rates by roughly 10 percent.

Taxes that raise the monetary cost of alcohol or drugs, and policies that increase the time cost of acquiring alcohol or drugs, are generally associated with decreases in crime. Carpenter and Dobkin's (2010) comprehensive review of research on alcohol regulation concludes that higher alcohol taxes and age-based restrictions on alcohol availability reduce crime. Markowitz (2005) finds little evidence that increases in drug or alcohol prices reduce violent victimizations but higher beer taxes do appear to reduce alcohol-related assaults.[90] Carpenter (2005, 2007) shows that zero tolerance drunk-driving laws for minors reduced male nuisance crimes such as vandalism, public drunkenness, and disorderly conduct by 1−2 percent but have no effect on violent crime. Biderman et al.'s (2009) difference-in-differences estimates indicate that homicides were reduced by 10 percent when Sao Paulo Metropolitan Area municipalities adopted laws mandating closing hours for bars and restaurants to restrict alcohol

---

[89] Brunello and d'Hombres find that BMI lowers earnings more in Southern than Northern Europe; Lundborg et al. (2007) find particularly large obesity wage penalties in Central Europe.

[90] The data set utilized, the National Crime Victimization Survey, provides information about whether alcohol and drugs were involved in an incident.

consumption. Dobkin and Nicosia (2009) find that after the US shut down two plants producing more than half of the precursors to production of methamphetamines, felony arrests for methamphetamines fell by half, but there were no significant reductions in property or violent crime. Weatherburn et al. (2002) find that the heroin "drought" in Australia was accompanied by a sharp increase in robberies and breaking and entering offenses, but these quickly declined.

A general methodological concern is that local crime rates are sometimes used as an instrument for drug and alcohol use (e.g. see the review in French and Popovici, 2011), whereas some of the research described here concludes that crime is a consequence of such use.

5. STRATEGIES FOR MODIFYING HEALTH BEHAVIORS

The first fundamental theorem of welfare economics states that perfectly functioning free markets are Pareto efficient and that government intervention cannot increase social welfare (see, e.g., Mas-Colell et al., 1995). However, there frequently exist failures in markets for addictive substances or other goods involving unhealthy behaviors. The traditional economic approach is for government intervention to fix these market failures. For example, in the case of a negative externality in consumption A. C. Pigou advocates a tax on consumption equal to the amount of the externality, thus internalizing costs of the externality to the decision maker and resulting in socially optimal levels of consumption (see, e.g., Baumol, 1972). Another example is that, if consumers lack relevant information, the government can require that manufacturers provide the missing information, leading to socially optimal decisions.

The economic approach differs from the public health perspective. For example, the economic perspective is that the socially optimal levels of unhealthy behaviors are characterized by marginal social benefits equaling marginal social costs, whereas the public health perspective seems to be that the socially optimal prevalence of smoking and obesity is zero. The public health perspective is generally supportive of government action to reduce unhealthy behaviors, whether or not there are market failures. Interestingly, recent work emphasizing time-inconsistent or other non-optimizing economic behavior may partially reconcile differences between these two approaches, suggesting situations where government involvement may raise social welfare even in the absence of market failures.

5.1. Taxes and Subsidies

5.1.1. Economic Rationale for Taxation

Unhealthy behaviors such as smoking, excessive drinking, and obesity impose substantial external costs. As discussed, Pigovian taxes—which are set equal to the external cost—can correct these distortions and result in socially optimal levels of consumption by agents who equalize marginal social benefit with marginal social cost.

Measuring the external costs of unhealthy behaviors will always be difficult because randomized controlled trials are unethical and researchers must rely on observational data, with the result that confounding factors (e.g. rate of time preference, cognitive ability, or mental health) may bias estimates and lead to an overstatement of external costs. On the other hand, causal effects may be understated if the economically disadvantaged are both more likely to engage in unhealthy behaviors and have less access to medical care. One promising direction for future research is to find and exploit natural experiments in which behaviors vary but other determinants of medical costs do not.

Manning et al.'s (1991) comprehensive study of participants in the RAND Health Insurance Experiment examined both the costs (e.g. medical costs, sick leave, early retirement, disability benefits, and lost wage tax revenue) and the "benefits" (e.g. lower payments from retirement pensions and long-term care insurance) associated with smoking, drinking alcohol, and a sedentary lifestyle. They conclude that lifetime external costs (in 1986 dollars) amount to $1,000 per smoker, $19,000 per heavy drinker, and $1,650 per sedentary person. Put another way, the external costs amount to 15 cents per pack of cigarettes smoked, 54 cents per excess drink, and 24 cents for each mile not walked.

Sloan et al. (2004) provide an even more comprehensive investigation of the external costs associated with smoking that considers: disability life-years, lifecycle earnings, Social Security and Medicare benefits, as well as spouse morbidity, disability, and mortality. They estimate that the lifetime external cost of smoking (net of cigarette taxes paid) is $3,829 (in 2000 dollars) for a female 24-year-old smoker and $8,001 for a corresponding 24-year-old male; the latter amounts to $1.44 per pack of cigarettes.

Obesity imposes external costs through both public and private health insurance. In 2008, obesity-related illness cost taxpayers $19.7 billion through Medicare and $8 billion through Medicaid, while private health insurance plans paid $49 billion in 2008 to treat obesity-related illnesses (Finkelstein et al., 2009). Using the method of instrumental variables in which respondent weight is instrumented using the weight of a biological child, Cawley and Meyerhoefer (forthcoming) estimate that the causal impact of obesity on medical care costs for Medicaid recipients is $3,674 (2005 dollars), of which $3,521 is paid by Medicaid; however, given the relatively small sample, these estimates are not statistically significant.

If consumers have time-inconsistent preferences, the optimal tax should include not only external costs but also the internal costs that consumers impose on themselves. Using such reasoning, Gruber and Köszegi (2001) estimate that cigarette taxes should be raised by an additional dollar per pack, while Sloan et al. (2004) obtain dramatically higher ($32.78/pack) estimates of the internal costs of smoking. Consistent with this, Gruber and Mullainathan (2005) report that smokers in the US and Canada are happier in jurisdictions (states or provinces) with higher cigarettes taxes, as might occur with time-inconsistent preferences—because the government is helping them to smoke less, which they would prefer but otherwise could not do on their own.

To internalize the externalities associated with smoking it is clear that cigarettes should be taxed. However, for other unhealthy behaviors the ideal tax policy is less obvious. For instance, moderate drinking may yield medical benefits, as discussed above, implying that higher alcohol taxes could have negative effects on health for moderate consumers. The situation is even more complex for obesity.[91] The most direct application of the Pigovian logic would be to tax body fat; for example, charging the obese a higher premium for their public and private health insurance. For example, section 2705 of the 2010 Patient Protection and Affordable Care Act (PPACA) allows employers to provide premium discounts, rebates, or rewards of up to 30 percent of employee-only insurance premiums (up to 50 percent with approval from the Secretary of Health and Human Services) if they participate in qualifying wellness programs, such as those to promote healthy weight. A decision instead to tax the behaviors, goods, or services that contribute to obesity leads to the different problem of determining the ideal scope and structure of such taxes. For example, tax policy is hindered by the impossibility of dividing foods into those that are "bad" (promote obesity) or "good" (prevent obesity). Recently, some public health researchers have called for taxes on full-calorie soft drinks (e.g. Brownell et al., 2009; Brownell and Frieden, 2009). However, the approach of taxing or subsidizing specific foods raises many questions. For example: should fruit juices that are high in calories also be taxed? Does the answer depend on the vitamin content of the juice? Should diet soft drinks that are low in calories be subsidized? Or should diet soft drinks be taxed because they may promote the habit of consuming sweets or may be complements with other energy-dense foods (Brownell et al., 2009)? Obesity is the result of energy imbalance; specifically, more calories consumed than burned or excreted. Thus, obesity can equally well be attributed to insufficient physical activity as to excessive caloric intake. Does this imply that taxes should be increased on complements to sedentary behaviors, such as televisions, video games, or internet access?

Optimal taxation becomes still more complicated when allowing for cognitive limitations, bounded rationality or other sources of decision errors. For instance, Bernheim and Rangel (2004) point out that many unhealthy behaviors represent mistakes (which have a stochastic component), implying that higher taxes may unfairly penalize people whose genetic endowment predisposed them to drug addiction or

---

[91] For a discussion of the issues surrounding taxes on energy-dense foods to promote healthy eating, see Cawley (forthcoming).

other undesirable outcomes. On the other hand, such individuals may most desire government policies as precommitment devices (Gruber and Mullainathan, 2005).

In contrast to the complexities of taxing unhealthy behaviors, the economic argument for eliminating *subsidies* that promote unhealthy behaviors seems quite strong. For example, current US agricultural policies expand the availability and reduce the cost of "program" crops—like soybeans and corn—that have become major inputs into processed energy-dense food products (Wallinga et al., 2009; Cawley and Kirwan, 2011). Removing such subsidies would raise the relative prices of such foods, with the desirable effect of reducing body weight, although, depending on the elasticity of consumption to the price of agricultural commodities, this effect may be small (Cawley and Kirwan, 2011).

5.1.2. Concerns about Regressivity of Taxes

Vertical equity suggests that those with greater ability to pay should be taxed more heavily than those with less ability to pay (Rosen, 2002). Because those of low socio-economic status tend to be more likely to engage in many unhealthy behaviors including tobacco use, physical inactivity, and poor diet (see, e.g., Pampel et al., 2010, and Cutler and Lleras-Muney, 2010), Pigovian taxes on products like cigarettes and energy-dense foods will tend to be regressive. Thus there may be a trade-off between the two socially desirable goals of vertical equity and population health. In principle, this trade-off can be avoided by pairing the excise tax with a means-tested income transfer, with the combined effect of allowing the substitution effect of the price change to affect behavior while eliminating the income effect of the price change that would lower utility (see, e.g., Perloff, 2008). In practice this may be difficult to implement. Moreover, it is important to note that taxes imposed on behaviors disproportionately engaged in by the poor will not automatically be regressive, because elasticity of demand for the taxed product may decline with income. However, this also raises the question of whether an attempt should be made to design taxes to focus on those whose (unhealthy) behaviors are most price elastic.

5.1.3. Extent to which Tax is Passed through to Retail Price

In perfectly competitive markets, the pass-through of a tax to retail prices is $\frac{S}{S-D}$, where S and D are the price elasticities of supply and demand (see, e.g., Perloff, 2008). Thus, the pass-through of a tax is bounded by zero and one. However, with imperfectly competitive markets, taxes may be "overshifted" such that prices can rise by more than the amount of the tax (Besley and Rosen, 1999). The logic is that manufacturers may use the tax hike as an opportunity to raise prices, although this begs the question of why the apparently collusive oligopolists were not previously maximizing profits. One possibility is that concerns about fairness constrain profit seeking (Kahneman et al., 1986). For instance, price increases with no apparent justification may cause an outcry among consumers that cuts sales and profits; tax increases then provide manufacturers with an excuse to raise prices.

Studies confirm that tax pass-through rates sometimes exceed 100 percent. For sales tax rates ranging from 0 to 8.25 percent, the tax pass-through rate has been estimated to be 100 percent for fast food hamburgers and over 100 percent for Coca-Cola (Besley and Rosen, 1999). Chaloupka and Warner (2000) review evidence that the pass-through exceeds 100 percent for cigarettes, while Young and Bielinska-Kwapisz (2002) and Kenkel (2005) found pass-through of greater than 100 percent when alcohol taxes were increased.

5.1.4. Cross-border Shopping, Smuggling, and Excise Tax Evasion

When excise taxes are higher in one jurisdiction than another, there is an incentive for organized or casual cross-border shopping (more pejoratively called "smuggling"). Beatty et al. (2009) present evidence suggesting that differentials across international borders in rates of alcohol and tobacco taxation result in economically important amounts of cross-border shopping and tax avoidance behavior. Chaloupka and Warner (2000) conclude that a large proportion of cigarette sales in states with low cigarette taxes represent smuggling to higher-tax states and describe how cross-border shopping between the US and Canada has varied with differences in their tobacco taxes. Tosun and Skidmore (2007) show that when West Virginia raised its food sales tax from 0 to 6 percent in 1990, food sales in border counties fell by 8 percent, as consumers increasingly made purchases in neighboring states that taxed food at a lower rate or exempted it from sales taxation altogether.

The extent of these effects will generally vary depending on how close customers are to jurisdictional borders. For example, most Texas residents will find cross-border shopping to be uneconomical because of the time and travel costs involved. Conversely, the District of Columbia is so small that it is relatively easy and cheap for residents to shop across the border. Thus, it is estimated that food demand in DC is highly elastic to local taxes, with each 1 percentage point increase in the food sales in the District of Columbia, relative to neighboring states, reducing food purchases in the District by 7 percent (Fisher, 1980).

The implication of this literature is that individual cities and states whose citizens live close to state borders may find that excise taxes reduce domestic sales but have little impact on consumption. If states do not take into account the impact of their lower excise taxes on the health behaviors of residents of neighboring states, there may be a "race to the bottom" in which states jockey to have excise taxes slightly lower than their neighbors in order to increase tax revenue. Excise taxes set at the national level would prevent the race to the bottom, but at the cost of preventing states from tailoring such tax policy to their circumstances.

5.1.5. Effect of Taxes on Unhealthy Behaviors

Section 2 provides detailed information on price elasticities of demand for unhealthy behaviors. The estimates presented there confirm that consumption of even addictive goods is responsive to price, which implies that tax policy can be used to reduce the prevalence of unhealthy behaviors.

Other research explicitly examines the effects of taxes in particular (rather than variation in prices from other sources) on health behaviors. For instance, an analysis of almost 30 years of state-level data found that a 1 percent increase in beer taxes is associated with a 1.0 percent decrease in youth drinking (Carpenter et al., 2007). Others estimate that a one-dollar increase in the beer excise tax would reduce the prevalence of youth alcohol use by two percentage points, but with no effect on binge consumption (Cook and Moore, 2001). Forster and Jones (2001) use duration analysis to study the decisions to initiate and quit smoking; they estimate that a 5 percent increase in the cigarette tax would reduce by 2 to 3.5 percent the total number of years spent smoking. The 1998 Master Settlement Agreement between cigarette manufacturers and the State Attorneys general immediately increased cigarette prices by 43.5 cents per pack (nearly 20 percent) and raised prices further during the next two years. This reduced smoking rates by 13 percent for youths and 5 percent among adults (Sloan et al., 2004) but smoking by pregnant women fell by less than 3 percent (Levy and Meara, 2006).

Recent research suggests that food taxes may not have much impact on caloric intake or obesity. For example, existing soft drink taxes have no detectable effect on child weight (Fletcher, Frisvold and Tefft, 2010). This may be due to the fact that existing taxes on soft drinks are quite small—they average 2.7 percent of soft drink prices (Fletcher et al., 2010). Larger taxes have been proposed and might have bigger impacts on consumer behavior, but convincing evidence of this has not yet been obtained. For instance, Chouinard et al. (2007) estimate that even a 10 percent *ad valorem* tax on fat in dairy products (milk, cream, cheese, butter, ice cream, and yogurt) would reduce average fat consumption by less than a percentage point. Based on their review of the literature, Powell and Chaloupka (2009) conclude that small taxes and subsidies are not likely to significantly reduce obesity or BMI, but non-trivial price hikes might have a measurable effect.

Consumers may respond strategically to tax increases. For example, smokers respond to higher cigarette prices by switching to cigarettes that are higher in tar and nicotine per cigarette (Farrelly et al., 2004). In addition, smokers respond to increases in cigarette taxes by extracting more nicotine per cigarette (Adda and Cornaglia, 2006). For most age groups, this compensating behavior is so large that the average daily tar intake is unaffected by cigarette taxes, with one study documenting *increases* in tar and nicotine consumption for 18–24-year-olds (Evans and Farrelly, 1998).

More generally, consumer responsiveness may depend on the salience of the tax (Chetty et al., 2009). For instance, taxes that are added at the register may have less effect on purchases than those that are included in product list prices and thus are seen when consumers make decisions of what to buy. These issues are particularly relevant for efforts to impose Pigovian taxes designed to produce socially optimal levels of consumption.

Another empirical challenge is that variation across jurisdictions in taxes may be correlated with variation across jurisdictions in voter sentiments regarding unhealthy behaviors (DeCicca et al., 2002). For example, cigarette taxes are low in Kentucky but high in California. This may partly occur because Kentucky is a major tobacco-growing state, and California is not; it may also reflect differences across states in preferences about health.

Failure to control for policy endogeneity may bias coefficient estimates of the impact of taxes on health behaviors. For example, DeCicca et al. (2008b) measure state anti-smoking sentiment using data from the Tobacco Use Supplements of the Current Population Survey, which ask respondents their opinions on anti-smoking policies such as clean indoor air laws and restrictions on tobacco promotion and advertising. They then show that controlling for state anti-smoking sentiment leads to a reduction in the estimated price elasticity of demand for cigarettes and that the failure to do so leads to overestimates of the price responsiveness of youth smoking.

5.1.6. Effect of Taxes on Outcomes Subsequent to Consumption

A large literature estimates the effect of alcohol taxes on outcomes subsequent to consumption. (Parallel literatures are less complete for smoking or eating because those behaviors are not contributors to crime, and a related literature does not exist for drugs because illicit drugs are not taxed.) Many of the studies on the effects of alcohol taxes estimate reduced-form models using state-level data, so the results need to be interpreted with caution, given concerns about policy endogeneity, modest within-state variation in taxes, and omitted variables.

Alcohol taxes (most commonly beer taxes) are negatively correlated with physical child abuse committed by women but not men (Markowitz and Grossman, 2000), child homicides (Sen, 2006), teen abortions (Sen, 2003), gonorrhea and syphilis (Chesson et al., 2000), work days lost due to industrial injuries (Ohsfeldt and Morrisey, 1997) and male but not female suicides (Markowitz et al., 2003). Pacula (1998) shows that beer and marijuana are complements, with the result that higher beer taxes reduce marijuana use.

The effects of alcohol taxes on motor vehicle fatalities have been widely studied with most research suggesting a strong negative association (e.g. Cook, 1981; Chaloupka et al., 1993; Ruhm, 1996; Young and Bielinska-Kwapsiz, 2006). Some (but likely not all) of this inverse relationship is probably spurious or reflects policy endogeneity (Dee, 1999; Mast et al., 1999; Young and Likens, 2000). Cook and Moore (1993) show that higher alcohol taxes are associated with increased educational attainment but Dave and Kaestner (2002) find little association between alcohol taxes and labor market outcomes. Cook et al. (2005) estimate that a permanent reduction of 1 percent in alcohol consumption (whether through taxes or another policy) would have a negligible effect on the death rate of those aged 35–69 years but Cook and Tauchen (1982) show that higher alcohol taxes reduce cirrhosis mortality, presumably due to decreases in heavy drinking.

5.2. Cash Incentives for Healthy Behaviors

The TORA predicts that individuals engage in unhealthy behaviors when the discounted lifetime benefits exceed the discounted lifetime costs. However, other models emphasize the likelihood of mistakes. In these cases (and even with rational addiction if there is *ex ante* uncertainty about outcomes) agents will often attempt to change their unhealthy behavior but fail to do so. Indeed, this is why Orphanides and Zervos (1995) and Bernheim and Rangel (2004), among others, suggest that harm reduction policies such as subsidized rehabilitation may be desirable.

One possible way to "help people help themselves" is to provide financial incentives for reductions in drinking, drug use, weight, or food consumption, or for increases in physical activity.[92] Such incentives are potentially useful for several reasons. First, the benefits of behavior change may otherwise not be salient, because their magnitude is not known with any degree of certainty. Second, the benefits of behavior change may not be immediate. (In contrast, the *costs* of behavior change, such as withdrawal, usually are immediate.) For this reason, the effectiveness of rewards generally declines the further in the future they occur (Ainslie, 1975). Third, time-inconsistent preferences may result in preference reversals and an inability to adhere to plans for more healthful behavior.

Offering immediate cash rewards for behavior change may help to solve these problems. Interestingly, even small incentives may be effective if they are salient and provided in exchange for clearly defined short-term objectives. Even small rewards may be effective because people tend not to compare payoffs to their income or wealth but instead "bracket" them—i.e. consider them in isolation (Read et al., 1999; Kahneman and Tversky, 1979). Financial rewards can also be structured to create precommitment devices, helping to reduce problems created by time-inconsistent

---

[92] Financial incentives can also be used to encourage patients to receive screening tests, show up for appointments or adhere to recommended regimes for taking prescription medications. In the review by Giuffrida and Torgerson (1997), 10 of 11 studies found that financial incentives improve patient compliance on these outcomes.

preferences. For example, recovering addicts might post a bond that is automatically forfeited if they relapse.

Contingency management offers incentives for addicts to remain abstinent by providing them with vouchers that can be exchanged for market goods in exchange for negative results on drug tests (Higgins et al., 2002).[93] This program was originally devised for cocaine addicts but has since been applied to the treatment of addiction to alcohol, marijuana, nicotine, and opiates. A meta-analysis of voucher-based reinforcement therapy found overwhelming evidence of increased abstinence; the vouchers raised compliance by an average of 30 percent, with larger effect sizes for rewards that were more valuable or were delivered immediately (Lussier et al., 2006). However, contingency management appears to be more effective at treating use of opiates and cocaine than tobacco (Prendergast et al., 2006). A striking feature of these programs is the relatively high success rates obtained for small vouchers—as little as $2.50 for a single negative test for cocaine (Higgins et al., 2002) or a $137 average payment over a three-month period (Petty and Martin, 2002).

The results for weight loss efforts are more mixed. Cawley and Price (2011) find that worksite programs offering modest cash rewards for specific reductions in weight (e.g. $30 per quarter for a 10 percent weight reduction) were not successful—the treatment group lost slightly less weight over a 12-month period than the control group—although modest improvements were obtained when the treatment group posted substantial ($110) bonds that were only refunded upon successful achievement of year-end weight loss goals.[94] Similarly, Finkelstein et al. (2007) present evidence of modest weight loss at three months but no difference at six months for financial rewards ranging from $7 to $14 per percentage point of weight reduction (after six months), and Butsch et al. (2007) fail to detect significant effects at 12 weeks for a treatment group offered a $150 refund of their enrollment fee if they lost 6 percent of their initial weight.

Burger and Lynham (2010) examine data from the British bookmaker William Hill of 51 people who placed bets that they would be able to lose a specific number of pounds (verified by a physician) over a period of time. Weight loss averaged 78 pounds (from a starting mean of 263 pounds) over an average of 243 days. However, despite payoffs averaging $2,332, roughly 80 percent of bettors failed to meet their weight loss goals. This is an interesting example of the private market offering precommitment mechanisms for time-inconsistent consumers and it is possible that many individuals considered themselves better off for having participated because they lost weight, even if they "lost" their bet.

---

[93] Vouchers are awarded instead of cash because recovering addicts might be tempted to spend cash on drugs.

[94] However, attrition was extremely high in this study, 51.2 percent after one quarter and 76.4 percent after one year.

Giné et al. (2010) implemented a voluntary precommitment program for smoking cessation whereby smokers deposited funds for six months and had these deposits returned to them if they tested negative for nicotine use, with the funds forfeited to charity for positive urine tests. Those who participated were three percentage points more likely than a control group to have quit smoking at six months, and this effect persisted at 12 months.

The success of such interventions may often be highly dependent on the precise structure of incentives. For example, Volpp et al. (2008) uncovered substantial short-run weight loss (at 16 weeks) for a program in which participants successfully meeting weight loss goals were entered into a lottery with a one-in-five chance of receiving a small ($10) reward and a one-in-one hundred probability of obtaining a large ($100) reward. The short-term weight loss was dramatic (weight reductions averaging 16 pounds), but the longer-term effects (at seven months) were less so. Similarly, Volpp et al. (2006) found that modest financial incentives combined with enrollment in a smoking cessation program substantially reduced tobacco use in the short term (at 30 and 75 days), but not in the longer run (at six months). On the other hand, in a follow-up intervention, Volpp et al. (2009) found evidence of decreased smoking even at 18 months, possibly because the incentives were of relatively large size and dependent on longer-term behavioral changes.[95]

5.3. Restrictions on Purchase or Use

A variety of policies have been implemented with the goal of directly restricting availability or raising the time costs for using unhealthy products. A large literature has examined the impacts of state minimum legal drinking ages (MLDA), which make it more difficult for teens to acquire alcohol. Wagenaar and Toomey (2002) conducted an in-depth review of research conducted between 1960 and 2000, covering periods of both falling (during the 1970s) and then rising (during the 1980s) drinking ages. They concluded that the evidence persuasively indicates an inverse relationship between the MLDA and youth alcohol consumption, traffic crashes, and other social problems (like suicides, homicides, and vandalism). However, they also find that the evidence is insufficient to say whether the effects vary across subpopulations, such as for college students. More recent analyses confirm these effects. For instance, Cook and Moore (2001) find that youths who are younger than the minimum purchase age for alcohol in their state are 5.5 percentage points less likely to drink in the past 30 days and are 2.5 percentage points less likely to binge drink. A recent analysis of almost 30 years of state-level data concluded that increases in the MLDA during the

---

[95] Individuals were paid $250 for not smoking three or six months after program completion and an additional $400 if still abstinent at nine or 12 months. However, reflecting the difficulty of making permanent behavioral changes, only 9.4 percent of the treatment group abstained from smoking at nine or 12 months (compared to 3.6 percent of the controls).

1970s and 1980s reduced drinking participation and heavy drinking by 4 percent among high school seniors (Carpenter et al., 2007). However, minimum purchase ages may have the unintended consequence of leading youths to switch from alcohol to drugs: DiNardo and Lemieux (2001) estimate that raising the state MLDA from 18 to 21 increases the prevalence of youth marijuana consumption by 2.4 percentage points.

Laws barring youth possession, use, and/or purchase of tobacco also deter smoking participation by teens but with little evidence of changes at the intensive margin for adolescent and young adult smokers (Tauras, Markowitz, and Cawley, 2005).

A large body of research suggests that restrictions on smoking in public places and private workplaces (e.g. clean indoor air laws) reduce the prevalence of tobacco use (see Chaloupka and Warner, 2000, for an extensive review). Some evidence (see Picone, Sloan, and Trogdon, 2004) suggests that bans on smoking in public places also reduce alcohol consumption by women (but not men), which for women is consistent with complementarity between smoking and drinking. Bitler et al. (2010) show that the impact of clean indoor air laws varies by industry, with larger reductions in smoking among bartenders than for those employed in other industries (e.g. schools, restaurants, and government).

Most related studies are unable to examine the extent to which smoking was displaced from public places to private places such as homes, or the related issue of whether such laws affect the exposure of non-smokers to environmental tobacco smoke (ETS) in public places or private homes. Two investigations of these issues yield somewhat conflicting results. Adda and Cornaglia (2010) suggest that smoking bans in the US displaced smoking from public to private places, with the net result of increased exposure to ETS by non-smokers, particularly those sharing a household with smokers. However, Carpenter et al. (2011) find that Canadian bans on public smoking led to large reductions in ETS exposure in public places for both smokers and non-smokers, and that these laws did not significantly affect ETS exposure in homes. However, they do estimate that non-smokers' exposure to ETS increased at building entrances. Neither Adda and Cornaglia (2010) nor Carpenter et al. (2011) find a significant impact of smoking bans on the probability of smoking.

A potential limitation of all of this research is that estimates may be biased by policy endogeneity. Gallet et al. (2006) find that the adoption of clean indoor air laws is correlated with state characteristics such as political affiliation, urban population, per capita income, and tobacco production.

A dramatic policy enacted to restrict the consumption of an addictive substance was Prohibition, which outlawed the sale and purchase (but not use) of alcohol in the United States from 1919 to 1933. Individual-level data on alcohol consumption do not exist for this era, but the impact of Prohibition on heavy alcohol consumption has been estimated using deaths from cirrhosis of the liver or alcoholism (Miron and

Zwiebel, 1991) and police records regarding arrests for drunkenness (Dills et al., 2005). Both proxy measures suggest that alcohol consumption initially fell sharply, to around 30 percent of the previous level, immediately after the enactment of Prohibition, before rebounding over the next several years to between 60 and 70 percent of its prior level (Miron and Zwiebel, 1991). These proxy measures also suggest that, after the repeal of Prohibition, heavy drinking initially declined but returned to the pre-Prohibition level after a decade.

Drug legalization may be analogous to the repeal of Prohibition. Miron (2003) estimates that the black market prices of cocaine are 2 to 4 times higher than they would be if the drug was legal and that heroin prices are 6 to 19 times as high. Legalization would therefore decrease prices substantially, resulting in higher consumption (see section 2 of this chapter for estimates of the price elasticity of demand for illicit drugs).

Consumption of illicit drugs is deterred not only by higher prices but also by the legal penalties for purchase and possession. For example, fines for possession and the probability of arrest decrease marijuana use among young adults (Farrelly et al., 2001). However, doubling the fines for marijuana possession would reduce the probability of use by youths by less than 1 percent, while decriminalization would increase it by 4 to 5 percent (Chaloupka et al., 1999; Saffer and Chaloupka, 1999). On the other hand, doubling of the fines for cocaine possession would reduce corresponding use by roughly 4 percent (Chaloupka et al., 1999).

Some studies have examined the impact of increased drug law enforcement on drug price, purity, and consumption. For example, Weatherburn et al. (2002) investigate the Australian heroin "drought," in 2000, that partly resulted from increased law enforcement. Using a survey of 165 heroin users in that country's largest heroin market, they found that the drought raised prices and lowered purity of heroin, reduced consumption and rates of overdose, but that the associated health benefits were partially offset by increased use of other drugs, most commonly cocaine. Dobkin and Nicosia (2009) examine the impact of the US government's decision in 1995 to shut down two suppliers providing more than half of the precursors used to produce methamphetamine. Focusing on California, the authors find that the supply of methamphetamine was halved, purity declined from 90 to 20 percent, and the price tripled. Use of the drug among arrestees declined 55 percent, and related hospital admissions fell 50 percent. However, the impact was largely temporary, with the price restored to its original level within four months and other outcomes returned to their original levels within 18 months (suggesting that meth producers were able to find substitute ingredients). In contrast to Weatherburn et al. (2002), Dobkin and Nicosia (2009) find little evidence of substitution away from the newly expensive drug and towards other drugs.

An empirical challenge to measuring the causal effect of policies on health behaviors is that the policies are endogenous, and are more likely to be adopted in states where voter sentiment is against such unhealthy behaviors. For example, Cawley and Liu (2008) find that state laws to prevent or reduce childhood obesity (such as mandatory physical education for school-aged children) are more likely to be enacted in states with large gaps between the desired and actual weight of adults. Carpenter et al. (2007) find that alcohol consumption fell just as much 1–2 years before as 1–2 years after a rise in the minimum legal drinking age; they interpret this as evidence that increases in the minimum legal drinking age are endogenous responses to high levels of teen drinking (they find no evidence that zero tolerance underage drunk-driving laws are endogenously adopted).

For this reason, simple estimates of the impact of policies on health behaviors may suffer from omitted variables bias. Ruhm (1996) uses state fixed effects to control for differences across states in (e.g.) unobserved social attitudes against drinking and finds that omitted variables strongly affect parameter estimates for policies designed to deter drunk driving (but do not much affect the estimates for alcohol taxes).

5.4. Providing Information

Information is generally a public good, and as a result is underprovided by private markets (see, e.g., Perloff, 2008). When consumers have incomplete information, free markets may fail to maximize social welfare (Mas-Colell et al., 1995), providing an efficiency rationale for the government either to deliver the missing information or to require suppliers to do so. Orphanides and Zervos (1995) discuss how information, education, or counter-advertisement efforts may be desirable, even with perfect rationality, to reduce *ex ante* errors in subjective probabilities—particularly because individuals tend to underestimate their own probabilities of becoming addicts, in part because they overstate rates of substance use by peers. Information that reduces the divergence between subjective and objective risk assessments may therefore improve *ex post* utility.

Consumers sometimes respond strongly to the provision of new information. A dramatic example is the release of the first Surgeon General's report on smoking and health in 1964, which was followed by an immediate 5 percent decrease in smoking; other research indicates that both warning labels on cigarette packs and paid anti-smoking advertisements significantly cut tobacco use (Chaloupka and Warner, 2000). However, the reductions were larger for more highly educated individuals (Grossman, 2000), perhaps reflecting differences in cognitive ability. Information about adverse health consequences can also decrease the use of other addictive goods. For instance, perceived risk of harm from regular use is negatively correlated with the probability of smoking marijuana in the past year (Pacula et al., 2001).

These findings are not limited to addictive products. In an experiment in Kenya, teenagers in randomly selected schools were provided information that the HIV infection was more common among adult males than teenage boys. This information led to a 61 percent reduction in the impregnation of teenage girls by adult males, as girls substituted away from unprotected sex with older men toward condom-utilizing sex with teenage boys (Dupas, 2011). Information campaigns to prevent HIV/AIDS in Africa have the largest impact for better educated persons (De Walque, 2007a).

Consumers also respond to nutritional information. The Nutrition Labeling and Education Act (NLEA) required manufacturers of packaged foods to provide information about their products in the form of the Nutrition Facts panel. One study concludes that this increased the consumption of iron and fiber, without affecting consumption of total or saturated fat or cholesterol (Variyam, 2008). However, other research suggests that the Nutrition Facts panel led more consumers to choose low-fat options (Mathios, 2000) and that the NLEA lowered obesity among white females by 2.4 percentage points (Variyam and Cawley, 2006). Notably, competition between food manufacturers did not result in this information being voluntarily provided prior to the government mandate (Mathios, 2000). Between 1975 and 1985, government campaigns to encourage lower consumption of fats successfully reduced the fat intake of US women. Even larger decreases were observed after 1985, when food companies received permission to make health claims about their products (Ippolito and Mathios, 1995). Most discussion of policies to counter externalities involves an increased role for government, but this is an example of how in certain instances decreasing regulation can reduce market failures, improve efficiency, and enhance social welfare.

One recent policy innovation, implemented in New York City in 2008 and as part of the US health care reform bill in 2010, requires calorie labeling on menus and menu boards in restaurant chains. Elbel et al. (2009) found that the New York City labeling law raised the percentage of customers who reported seeing calorie labels at four major fast-food chains (relative to controls in Newark, NJ, which does not have a labeling law); however, calories, saturated fat, sodium, or sugar in the food actually purchased did not change. On the other hand, Bollinger et al. (2011) found that the New York City law reduced calories per transaction at Starbucks by 6 percent (15 calories), almost entirely due to decreases in calories from food (rather than beverages).[96] Wisdom et al. (2010) summarize the experimental data showing that customers provided calorie information at a fast-food restaurant ordered meals with around 60 fewer calories than those not receiving the information.

---

[96] They utilize rich data on every transaction at Starbucks stores in New York City and the control cities Boston and Philadelphia (with no calorie posting), from January 1, 2008 until February 28, 2009—before and after the law's April 1, 2008 implementation. Most of the reduction in calories was due to consumers buying fewer food items, rather than substituting to lower calorie foods.

5.5. Advertising Restrictions

A common public health response to a high prevalence of unhealthy behaviors involving legal substances such as tobacco, alcohol, or energy-dense foods is to ban or regulate advertisements for these products, or to call for voluntary limits on advertising by manufacturers. (For a description of the history of US regulation of cigarette advertising, see Nelson, 2006.)

Saffer and Chaloupka (2000) examine the impact of various bans on cigarette advertising in 22 OECD countries during the period 1970—1992. They conclude that comprehensive bans (i.e. bans on such ads on television, radio, print, outdoors, movies, sponsorship and at point of purchase) can reduce tobacco consumption but that more limited restrictions have little or no effect. However, the results of later research are more ambiguous. Blecher (2008) extends the approach of Saffer and Chaloupka (2000) to 30 developing countries over the period 1990—2005 and finds that both comprehensive and limited policies to restrict tobacco advertising reduce smoking. Nelson (2003) examines data for 20 OECD countries over the period 1970—1995 and concludes that Saffer and Chaloupka's (2000) results are not robust to the use of stationary data in the form of consumption growth rates, or to controlling for other policies (such as warning labels), or analyzing different time periods; Nelson (2003) concludes that advertising bans, whether comprehensive or limited, do not affect cigarette consumption, which is also the conclusion of meta-analysis of nine studies examining the US government's 1971 ban on television broadcast advertising of cigarettes (Nelson, 2006).

While television advertisements of cigarettes have been illegal in the US since 1971, television advertisements of liquor were kept off the airways by a voluntary agreement among manufacturers until November 1996, when the liquor industry's national trade organization agreed to lift the self-imposed ban (see Frank, 2008).

Nelson (2010) examines the relationship between advertising bans and alcohol consumptions in 17 OECD countries between 1975 and 2000. He criticizes earlier studies for failing to control for the stringency of other alcohol policies, speculating that this may have led to omitted variables bias in estimates of the impact of the advertising bans. In his preferred models, Nelson (2010) detects no impact of alcohol advertising bans on the demand for alcohol.

Recently, researchers have begun to estimate the possible impact of regulation of advertisements for energy-dense foods. Using data from the NLSY79 and NLSY97, Chou et al. (2008) estimate that a ban on fast-food television advertisements would reduce the prevalence of overweight among 3—11-year-olds by 18 percent and the fraction of overweight adolescents (12—18-year-olds) by 14 percent. Eliminating the tax deductibility of TV advertising for fast-food companies (which the authors state would raise the price of advertising by 54 percent) is estimated to decrease the share of overweight children by 7 percent and of overweight adolescents by 5 percent. However, these estimates do not account for targeting of advertising towards heavier youths.

5.6. Defaults and Choice Architecture

Behavioral economists emphasize that individuals frequently make systematic mistakes, raising the possibility that social welfare can be improved by changing the default options to account for factors such as procrastination, lack of self-control, and status quo bias. A key component of these interventions, sometimes referred to as "libertarian" or "asymmetric" paternalism (Loewenstein et al., 2007; Thaler and Sunstein, 2009), is that few limitations are placed on the available choice set but small cognitive costs are charged for individuals to select options that are perceived by planners to represent *ex post* mistakes. A risk of this strategy is that planners may underestimate the knowledge and sophistication of consumers, and may needlessly distort decision making, lowering social welfare.

There are many potential applications of behavioral economics to unhealthy behaviors; to date, it has been applied most to food consumption. Examples of proposed policy changes include moving energy-dense items to less convenient locations in school cafeterias, making water rather than soft drinks the default beverage option for fast-food meals; and making food choices several hours before the meal will be eaten (Just, 2006; Loewenstein et al., 2007).

While such policies hold considerable promise, empirical analyses of them have just begun to be conducted and it will be some time before we have high-quality evaluations of these interventions. To provide one example, Wisdom et al. (2010) find that making lower-calorie sandwiches more salient, by listing them first on the menu, had no effect on total calories consumed because, although these sandwiches were more often ordered, the calorie savings were compensated for by increased consumption of other products. However, a "stronger" intervention, in which individuals had to unseal an envelope with additional menu choices, to purchase more caloric items, did reduce total energy intake.

6. FUTURE DIRECTIONS

Economic research on health behaviors has reached the stage of "early adolescence." At the beginning of this chapter, we documented the remarkable increase over the past two decades in economics journal articles devoted to risky health behaviors. During the "infancy" period, economists demonstrated to skeptical health professionals and policy makers that economic factors really do play a role in determining health behaviors like drinking and smoking. Much of this research was documented at length in dedicated chapters in volume 1B of this Handbook (Chaloupka and Warner, 2000; Cook and Moore, 2000; Kenkel, 2000). The early effort was highly successful in convincing public health researchers and practitioners that health behaviors are responsive to prices and other incentives. As a result, taxes are now routinely used by state and federal governments in their attempts to reduce smoking and alcohol consumption and are receiving considerable attention in current efforts to reduce obesity.

The "toddler" years were dominated by theoretical development and empirical testing of the model of rational addiction. This work has also been extremely influential, particularly among economists, for most of whom the TORA is often the default model for examining health behaviors. This framework has many attractive features, including emphasizing the role of prices and forward-looking behavior, an appreciation of the distinction between long-run and short-run elasticities, and for demonstrating that even seemingly undesirable outcomes can be consistent with fully rational decision making. With additional assumptions it can explain many interesting phenomena like quitting "cold turkey," cycles of binging and purging, and entry into addiction following adverse life events.

That said, the assumptions required for the TORA—including perfect foresight, complete optimization, and time-consistent preferences—may be violated for many health behaviors. During the "childhood" of research in this area, economists began to incorporate such considerations into their models of health behavior. Thaler and Sunstein (2009) note that health economists have begun to examine the actual behavior of homo sapiens rather than the stylized behavior of "homo economicus." We anticipate that such work will continue during the coming decade or two, the period of "adolescence" in the economic analysis of health behaviors, and we are optimistic that this work will yield important theoretical and empirical advances that lead to improvements in public health policy that enhance social welfare.

This discussion does not imply that there is nothing more to be gained from the traditional theoretical and empirical models. To the contrary, we expect that the majority of economic analyses on health behaviors in the near future will be based on such models, in part because most current health economists have familiarity and expertise with them but also because standard utility maximization is simple, powerful, and will continue to yield important insights. We therefore conclude this chapter by providing a brief overview of what we see as promising areas for future study, first focusing on traditional economic models of health behavior and then moving to less standard frameworks.

6.1. Future Research using Traditional Economic Models

Policy endogeneity represents an important challenge for efforts to estimate the causal impact of policies on health behaviors. Many previous studies take state taxes and substance use policies to be exogenous, but the median voter theorem implies that states with strong voter sentiment against unhealthy behaviors will enact policies designed to discourage them (e.g. DeCicca et al., 2008; Cawley and Liu, 2008) and policies may be enacted in response to high levels of substance use (see, e.g., Carpenter et al., 2007). While there is growing appreciation of the problem of policy endogeneity, there is mixed evidence of the extent to which it biases estimates (see, e.g., Carpenter et al., 2007 and Ruhm, 1996), making this an important area for additional research.

Future empirical investigations will certainly benefit from new data collection, but also from better use of existing data. For instance, there is increased awareness in obesity research that body mass index is a noisy measure of fatness. Recently, economics studies have begun to use alternative measures of fatness, such as percent body fat and waist circumference (see, e.g. Burkhauser and Cawley, 2008; Johansson et al., 2009; Wada and Tekin, 2010), but economists are limited by the available data; for instance, many secondary data sets include self-reported weight and height but not more accurate measures of fatness. Biomarkers are also becoming more available in data used by economists, suggesting that such research will become more common in the future.[97] For example, Adda and Cornaglia (2006) examine the concentration of cotinine, a metabolite of nicotine, in bodily fluids and find that smokers compensate for tax hikes by extracting more nicotine from each cigarette smoked. In subsequent work, Adda and Cornaglia (2010) use data on cotinine concentration to determine whether taxes and public smoking bans affect exposure to environmental tobacco smoke. For an in-depth discussion of the uses and limitations of biomarkers in social science data, see volume 55 (2009), issue 2 of *Biodemography and Social Biology.*

More in-depth analysis will be facilitated by richer data. For example, recent research on smoking (Loomis et al., 2006), drinking (Bray et al., 2009), and food purchases (Zhang et al., 2008) documents purchases by individual consumers using scanner data from retail establishments, rather than relying on aggregate sales data or recall in consumer surveys. Similarly, heart rate monitors, pedometers, and accelerometers are being used to measure physical activity (e.g. see Berlin et al., 2006), although each has limitations when applied to general populations (Sirard and Pate, 2001).

However, data limitations continue to pose obstacles for many potentially interesting analyses. For example, it is hard to survey the severely drug addicted because they may not have a permanent residence or phone; as a result, even large social science data sets may not provide statistical power for an analysis of heavy drug users. Another example is that data on food consumption tends to be collected over brief periods (e.g. using 24-hour dietary recalls) in repeated cross-sections; longitudinal data would better

---

[97] For information on biomarkers in US population-based data see: http://biomarkers.uchicago.edu/studiescollectingbiomarkers.htm.

allow for more in-depth study of the dynamics of eating and weight changes. Information on mental health, and its determinants, is generally not as good as that for physical health and large secondary data sets rarely provide reliable information on job and non-job sources of stress. The field would also benefit from better theoretical definitions of peer and reference groups, and data corresponding to these categorizations.

Perhaps most importantly, most of the empirical evidence summarized in this chapter focuses on a limited set of health behaviors—particularly smoking, drinking, substance use, and obesity. This reflects a relative paucity of research on other outcomes, although some research has been conducted on behaviors like risky sexual activity and prostitution (Oettinger, 1999; Levine, 2001; Gertler et al., 2005), immunizations (Philipson, 1996; Mullahy, 1999), and seatbelt or motorcycle helmet use (Carpenter and Stehr, 2008; Dee, 2009).[98] Future analyses of a wider array of health behaviors are likely to be highly informative.

6.2. Future Research using Non-traditional Models

This chapter highlights the promise of emerging non-traditional models that marry strengths of the standard rational economic framework with an understanding of biological considerations, and which incorporate insights from behavioral economics and neuroeconomics. From a modeling perspective, the most important development to date has been the use of quasi-hyperbolic discounting, which provides a straightforward method of incorporating time-inconsistent preferences into otherwise conventional frameworks. However, this is just one way of capturing such behavior, and it does not account for other aspects of observed decision making, such as the apparent heterogeneity of discount rates across types of purchases or alternative mental states. We anticipate that there will be active research over the coming decades aimed at more realistic modeling decision making related to health behaviors. Several areas of study seem particularly promising.

Increased attention is being paid to the role of genetic determinants of health, motivated in part by the mapping of the human genome and the inclusion of genetic markers on datasets that are frequently used by economists (e.g. the National Longitudinal Survey of Adolescent Health). To date, most economics research in this area has used genetic markers as instrumental variables when examining how specific behaviors or health conditions affect outcomes such as educational attainment and school performance (Ding et al., 2009; Fletcher and Lehrer, 2009) or labor market outcomes like employment or wages (Norton and Han, 2008).[99] Thoughtful use of genetic markers in health economics will require awareness of the following issues

---

[98] Chapters on prevention (Kenkel, 2000) and infectious diseases (Philipson, 2000) in volumes 1A and 1B of this Handbook cover some of these issues in greater detail.

[99] Goldman et al. (2005) provide a detailed discussion of how genetics influence addictive behaviors but do not integrate this into an economic model.

(see, e.g., Conley, 2009 and Cawley et al., 2011). First, behaviors are often influenced by multiple genes (they are polygenic) in ways that are difficult to quantify. Second, behavior is often the result of complicated interactions between genes and environment. Finally, genes tend to affect multiple health behaviors and conditions, implying that genes may be invalid instruments in many contexts.

The emerging field of neuroeconomics also offers promise, some of which may have begun to be realized through the use of brain scans undertaken while individuals engage in the decision making related to health and other behavioral outcomes (e.g. McClure et al., 2004; Glimcher et al., 2007; Hare et al., 2009). However, it is not yet clear to what extent brain structure is a dominant determinant of economic behavior nor, even if it is, whether current methods of examination provide useful information. Thus, it is difficult to refute Rubinstein's (2008, p. 493) conclusion that brain studies, while "fascinating," have not yet yielded fundamental insights that change economics.

Additional interdisciplinary work with biomedical researchers is almost certainly desirable, in part because health behaviors are influenced by the system in which medical care is provided. For example, evidence suggests that physician counseling raises the likelihood that sedentary individuals increase physical activity (Calfas et al., 1996) and that tobacco users stop smoking (Stead et al., 2008) but many patients, particularly ethnic minorities, do not receive such advice from their doctors (US Department of Health and Human Services, 2009). A second reason is that while economists are especially well trained in addressing potential design problems in randomized experiments—such as attrition or substitution bias, heterogeneous treatment effects, or treatment contamination—they generally lack a corresponding understanding of biological or medical aspects of the interventions.

Finally, insights from other social sciences—particularly psychology and sociology—are likely to provide rich additions to traditional economic models. Indeed, some of the most exciting recent economic research on health behaviors has incorporated factors such as peer groups, social capital and relative status, all of which originally arose from other social science disciplines. In addition, many stylized facts that are central to behavioral economics were first identified by psychologists. One of the great strengths of economics is its ability to incorporate useful theories and findings from other disciplines while retaining a central role for incentives, trade-offs and constrained optimization. Continuation of this process is likely to allow exciting progress to be made in understanding the determinants of health behaviors and in developing public policies and interventions that can enhance social welfare.

REFERENCES

Adams, W. (1952). Price policies in the cigarette industry by William H. Nicholls [book review]. *American Economic Review, 42*(3), 461–463.
Adda, J. & Cornaglia, F. (2006). Taxes, cigarette consumption and smoking intensity. *American Economic Review, 96*(4) (September), 1013–1028.

Adda, J. & Cornaglia, F. (2010). The effect of bans and taxes on passive smoking. *American Economic Journal: Applied Economics, 2*(1), 1–32.

Adler, N. E., Boyce, T., Chesney, M. A., Cohen, S., Folkman, S., Kahn, R. L., et al. (1994). Socioeconomic status and health: The challenge of the gradient. *American Psychologist, 49*(1) (January), 15–24.

Ainslie, G. (1975). Specious reward: A behavioral theory of impulsiveness and impulse control. *Psychological Bulletin, 82*(4), 463–496.

Ainslie, G. (1991). Derivation of "rational" economic behavior from hyperbolic discount curves. *American Economic Review, 81*(2), 334–340.

Akerlof, G. (1991). Procrastination and obedience. *American Economic Review, 81*(2) (May), 1–19.

Andreyeva, T., Long, M. W., & Brownell, K. D. (2010). The impact of food prices on consumption: A systematic review of research on the price elasticity of demand for food. *American Journal of Public Health, 100*(2), 216–222.

Angeletos, G.-M., Laibson, D., Repetto, A., Tobacman, J., & Weinberg, S. (2001). The hyperbolic consumption model: Calibration, simulation, and empirical evaluation. *Journal of Economic Perspectives, 15*(3) (Summer), 47–68.

Angrist, J. D. & Krueger, A. B. (2001). Instrumental variables and the search for identification: From supply and demand to natural experiments. *Journal of Economic Perspectives, 15,* 69–85.

Angrist, J. D. & Pischke, J. (2009). *Mostly harmless econometrics: An empiricist's companion.* Princeton, NJ: Princeton University Press.

Antsey, K. J., Low, L.-F., Christensen, H., & Sachdev, P. (2009). Levels of cognitive performance as a correlate and predictor of health behaviors that protect against cognitive decline late in life: The path through life study. *Intelligence, 37*(6) (November–December), 600–606.

Apouey, B. H. & Clark, A. (2010). *Winning big but feeling no better? The effects of lottery prizes on physical and mental health.* IZA Discussion Paper No. 4730.

Argys, L. M. & Rees, D. I. (2008). Searching for peer group effects: A test of the contagion hypothesis. *Review of Economics and Statistics, 90*(3), 442–458.

Ariely, D. & Loewenstein, G. (2006). The heat of the moment: The effect of sexual arousal on sexual decision making. *Journal of Behavioral Decision Making, 19*(2) (April), 87–98.

Arkes, J. (2007). Does the economy affect teenage substance use? *Health Economics, 16*(1) (January), 19–36.

Atella, V., Pace, N., & Vuri, D. (2008). Are employers discriminating with respect to weight? European evidence using quantile regression. *Economics and Human Biology, 6,* 305–329.

Auld, M. C. (2005). Smoking, drinking, and income. *Journal of Human Resources, 15,* 504–518.

Auld, M. C. (2006). Using observational data to identify the causal effects of health-related behaviour. In A. M. Jones (Ed.), *The Elgar companion to health economics.* New York: Edward Elgar.

Auld, M. C. & Grootendorst, P. (2004). An empirical analysis of milk addiction. *Journal of Health Economics, 23,* 11117–111133.

Auld, M. C. & Grootendorst, P. (2011). Challenges for causal inference in obesity research. In J. Cawley (Ed.), *Handbook of the social science of obesity.* New York: Oxford University Press.

Auld, M. C. & Powell, L. M. (2009). Economics of food energy density and adolescent body weight. *Economica, 76,* 719–740.

Avery, R., Kenkel, D., Lillard, D., & Mathios, A. (2007). Private profits and public health: Does advertising smoking cessation products encourage smokers to quit? *Journal of Political Economy, 115*(3), 447–481.

Balia, S. & Jones, A. M. (2008). Mortality, lifestyle and socio-economic status. *Journal of Health Economics, 27*(1) (January), 1–26.

Balsa, A. I., Homer, J. F., Fleming, M., & French, M. T. (2008). Alcohol consumption and health among elders. *The Gerontologist, 48,* 622–636.

Baumol, W. J. (1972). On taxation and the control of externalities. *American Economic Review, 62*(3), 307–322.

Beatty, T. K. M., Larsen, E. R., & Sommervoll, D. E. (2009). Driven to drink: Sin taxes near a border. *Journal of Health Economics, 28*(6), 1175–1184.

Becker, G. & Murphy, K. (1988). A theory of rational addiction. *Journal of Political Economy, 96*(4), 675–700.

Becker, G. S. (1976). *The economic approach to human behavior.* Chicago, IL: University of Chicago Press.

Becker, G. S. & Mulligan, C. B. (1997). The endogenous determination of time preference. *Quarterly Journal of Economics, 112*(3), 729–758.

Becker, G. S. & Murphy, K. M. (1993). A simple theory of advertising as a good or bad. *Quarterly Journal of Economics, 108,* 941–964.

Becker, G. S., Grossman, M., & Murphy, K. M. (1994). An empirical analysis of cigarette addiction. *American Economic Review, 84*(3), 396–418.

Berlin, J. E., Storti, K. L., & Brach, J. S. (2006). Using activity monitors to measure physical acticvity in free-living conditions. *Physical Therapy, 86*(8) (August), 1137–1145.

Bernheim, B. D. & Rangel, A. (2004). Addiction and cue-triggered decision processes. *American Economic Review, 94*(5) (December), 1558–1590.

Berns, G. S., Laibson, D., & Loewenstein, G. (2007). Intertemporal choice—toward an integrative framework. *Trends in Cognitive Science, 11*(11) (November), 482–488.

Bhattacharya, J., Goldman, D., & Sood, N. (2009). Market evidence of misperceived mortality risk. *Journal of Economic Behavior and Organization, 72*(1) (October), 451–462.

Biderman, C., De Mello, J. M. P., & Schneider, A. (2009). Dry laws and homicides: Evidence from the Sao Paulo metropolitan area. *The Economic Journal, 120,* 157–182.

Bitler, M. P., Carpenter, C., & Zavodny, M. (2010). Effects of venue-specific state clean indoor air laws on smoking-related outcomes. *Health Economics, 19*(12), 1425–1440.

Blecher, E. (2008). The impact of tobacco advertising bans on consumption in developing countries. *Journal of Health Economics, 27,* 930–942.

Bollinger, B., Leslie, P., & Sorensen, A. (2011). Calorie posting in chain restaurants. *American Economic Journal: Economic Policy, 3,* 91–128.

Bound, J., Jaeger, D., & Baker, R. (1995). Problems with instrumental variables estimation when the correlation between the instruments and the endogenous explanatory variable is weak. *Journal of the American Statistical Association, 90*(430), 443–450.

Bray, J. W., Loomis, B. R., & Engelen, M. (2009). You save money when you buy in bulk: Does volume-based pricing cause people to buy more beer. *Health Economics, 18*(5) (May), 607–618.

Brener, N. D., Billy, J. O. G., & Grady, W. R. (2003). Assessment of factors affecting the validity of self-reported health-risk behavior among adolescents: Evidence from the scientific literature. *Journal of Adolescent Health, 33,* 436–457.

Brocas, I. & Carrillo, J. D. (2008). The brain as a hierarchical organization. *American Economic Review, 98*(4) (September), 1312–1346.

Brownell, K. D. & Frieden, T. R. (2009). Ounces of prevention—the public policy case for taxes on sugared beverages. *New England Journal of Medicine, 360*(18), 1805–1808.

Brownell, K. D., Farley, T., Willett, W. C., Popkin, B. M., Chaloupka, F. J., Thompson, J. W., et al. (2009). The public health and economic benefits of taxing sugar-sweetened beverages. *New England Journal of Medicine, 361,* 1599–1605.

Brownson, R. C., Boehmer, T. K., & Luke, D. A. (2005). Declining rates of physical activity in the United States: What are the contributors? *Annual Review of Public Health, 26*(April), 421–443.

Brunello, G. & d'Hombres, B. (2007). Does body weight affect wages? Evidence from Europe. *Economics & Human Biology, 5,* 1–19.

Burger, N. & Lynham, J. (2010). Betting on weight loss…and losing: Personal gambles as commitment mechanisms. *Applied Economics Letters, 17*(12), 1161–1166.

Burkhauser, R. V. & Cawley, J. (2008). Beyond BMI: The value of more accurate measures of obesity in social science research. *Journal of Health Economics, 27*(2) (March), 519–529.

Butsch, W. S., Ard, J. D., Allison, D. B., Patki, A., Henson, C. S., Rueger, M. M., et al. (2007). Effects of a reimbursement incentive on enrollment in a weight control program. *Obesity, 15*(11), 2733–2738.

Calfas, K. J., Long, B. J., Sallis, J. F., Wooten, W. J., Pratt, M., & Patrick, K. (1996). A controlled trial of physician counseling to promote the adoption of physical activity. *Preventive Medicine, 25*(3) (May), 225–233.

Camerer, C., Loewenstein, G., & Prelec, D. (2005). Neuroeconomics: How neuroscience can inform economics. *Journal of Economic Literature, 43*(1) (March), 9−64.

Carlton, D. W. & Perloff, J. M. (2000). *Modern industrial organization* (3rd ed.). Reading, MA: Addison-Wesley Longman.

Carpenter, C. (2005). Heavy alcohol use and the commission of nuisance crime: Evidence from underage drunk driving laws. *American Economic Review Papers and Proceedings, 95*(2), 267−272.

Carpenter, C. (2007). Heavy alcohol use and crime: Evidence from underage drunk driving laws. *Journal of Law and Economics, 50*(3), 539−557.

Carpenter, C. & Dobkin, C. (2010). Alcohol regulation and crime. NBER Working Paper No. 15828.

Carpenter, C., Postolek, S., & Warman, C. (2011). Public-place smoking laws and exposure to environmental tobacco smoke (ETS). Paper presented at the 2011 Annual Meeting on the Economics of Risky Behaviors at IZA in Bonn, Germany.

Carpenter, C. S. & Stehr, M. (2008). The effects of mandatory seatbelt laws on seatbelt use, motor vehicle fatalities, and crash-related injuries among youths. *Journal of Health Economics, 27*(3) (May), 642−662.

Carpenter, C. S., Kloska, D. D., O'Malley, P., & Johnston, L. (2007). Alcohol control policies and youth alcohol consumption: Evidence from 28 years of monitoring the future. *B.E. Journal of Economic Analysis and Policy, 7*(1—Topics), Article 25.

Carrell, S.E., Hoekstra, M., & West, J.E. (2010). Is poor fitness contagious? Evidence from randomly assigned friends. National Bureau of Economic Research Working Paper No. 16518, November.

Casagrande, S. S., Wang, Y., Anderson, C., & Gary, T. L. (2007). Have Americans increased their fruit and vegetable intake? The trends between 1988 and 2002. *American Journal of Preventive Medicine, 32* (4) (April), 257−263.

Case, A.C. & Katz, L.F. (1991). The company you keep: The effects of family and neighborhood on disadvantaged youth. NBER Working Paper 3705.

Cawley, J. (1999). *Rational addiction, the consumption of calories, and body weight.* Ph. D. dissertation, Department of Economics, University of Chicago.

Cawley, J. (2000). Body weight and women's labor market outcomes. NBER Working Paper #7841.

Cawley, J. (2004). The impact of obesity on wages. *Journal of Human Resources, 39*(2), 451−474.

Cawley, J. (2008). Reefer Madness, Frank the Tank or Pretty Woman: To what extent do addictive behaviors respond to incentives? In F. Sloan, & H. Kasper (Eds.), *Incentives and choice in health and health care.* Cambridge, MA: MIT PressChapter 7.

Cawley, J. (2010). The economics of childhood obesity. *Health Affairs, 29*(3), 364−371.

Cawley, J. (forthcoming). Taxes on energy dense foods to improve nutrition and prevent obesity. In K. D. Brownell & M. S. Gold (Eds.), *Handbook of food and addiction.* New York: Oxford University Press.

Cawley, J. & Kenkel, D. S. (2008). Introduction. In Cawley & Kenkel (Eds.), *The economics of health behaviours* (Vol. 1−3). Northampton, MA: Edward Elgar.

Cawley, J. & Kirwan, B. (2011). Agricultural policy and childhood obesity. In J. Cawley (Ed.), *Handbook of the social science of obesity.* New York: Oxford University Press.

Cawley, J. & Liu, F. (2008). Correlates of state legislative action to prevent childhood obesity. *Obesity, 16* (1), 162−167.

Cawley, J. & Meyerhoefer, C. (forthcoming). The medical care costs of obesity: An instrumental variables approach. NBER Working Paper #16467.

Cawley, J. & Price, J. A. (2011). Outcomes in a program that offers financial rewards for weight loss. In M. Grossman & N. Mocan (Eds.), *Economic aspects of obesity.* Chicago IL: NBER and University of Chicago Press.

Cawley, J., Han, E., & Norton, E.C. (2011). The validity of genes related to neurotransmitters as instrumental variables. *Health Economics, 20*(8), 884−888.

Cawley, J., Markowitz, S., & Tauras, J. (2004). Lighting up and slimming down: The effects of body weight and cigarette prices on adolescent smoking initiation. *Journal of Health Economics, 23*(2), 293−311.

Cawley, J., Moran, J., & Simon, K. (2010). The impact of income on the weight of elderly Americans. *Health Economics, 19*(8), 979−993.

Chaloupka, F. (1991). Rational addictive behavior and cigarette smoking. *Journal of Political Economy, 99* (4) (August), 722–742.

Chaloupka, F. (1996). A review of economic models of habitual and addictive behavior and their empirical applications to cigarette smoking. In L. Green & J. H. Kagel (Eds.), *Advances in behavioral economics, Vol. 3, Substance use and abused.* Norwood, NJ: Ablex Publishing.

Chaloupka, F. J. & Warner, K. E. (2000). The economics of smoking. In A. J. Culyer & J. P. Newhouse (Eds.), *Handbook of health economics* (Vol. 1, pp. 1539–1628). New York: Elsevier.

Chaloupka, F. J., Grossman, M., & Tauras, J. A. (1999). The demand for cocaine and marijuana by youth. In F. J. Chaloupka, M. Grossman, W. K. Bickel, & H. Saffer (Eds.), *The economic analysis of substance use and abuse* (pp. 133–156). Cambridge, MA: National Bureau of Economic Research.

Chaloupka, F. J., Saffer, H., & Grossman, M. (1993). Alcohol control policies and motor vehicle fatalities. *Journal of Legal Studies, 22*(1) (January), 161–186.

Chang, V. & Lauderdale, D. S. (2005). Income disparities in body mass index in the United States, 1971–2002. *Archives of Internal Medicine, 165*(18) (October 10), 2122–2128.

Chapman, G. B., Brewer, N. T., Coups, E. J., Brownlee, S., Leventhal, H., & Leventhal, E. A. (2001). Value for the future and preventive health behavior. *Journal of Experimental Psychology—Applied, 7,* 235–250.

Charles, K. & DeCicca, P. (2008). Labor market fluctuations and health: Is there a connection and for whom? *Journal of Health Economics, 27*(6) (December), 1532–1550.

Chatterji, P. (2006a). Does alcohol use during high-school affect educational attainment? Evidence from the National Education Longitudinal Study. *Economics of Education Review, 25,* 482–497.

Chatterji, P. (2006b). Illicit drug use and educational attainment. *Health Economics, 15,* 489–511.

Chen, K. & Lange, F. (2008). Education, information and improved health: Evidence from cancer screening. IZA Discussion Paper No. 3548, June.

Chesson, H., Harrison, P., & Kassler, W. J. (2000). Sex under the influence: The effect of alcohol policy on sexually transmitted disease rates in the United States. *Journal of Law and Economics, 43*(1), 215–238.

Chetty, R., Looney, A., & Kroft, K. (2009). Salience and taxation: Theory and evidence. *American Economic Review, 99*(4), 1145–1177.

Chou, S.-Y., Rashad, I., & Grossman, M. (2008). Fast-food restaurant advertising on television and its influence on childhood obesity. *Journal of the Law of Economics, 51,* 599–618.

Chouinard, H. H., Davis, D. E., LaFrance, J. T., & Perloff, J. M. (2007). Fat taxes: Big money for small change. *Forum for Health Economics & Policy, 10*(2), Article 2.

Christakis, N. & Fowler, J. (2007). The spread of obesity in a large social network over 32 years. *New England Journal of Medicine, 357,* 370–379.

Clark, D. and Royer, H. (2010). The effect of education on adult health and mortality: Evidence from Britain. NBER Working Paper #16013.

Cohen-Cole, E. & Fletcher, J. M. (2008a). Is obesity contagious? Social networks vs. environmental factors in the obesity epidemic. *Journal of Health Economics, 27*(5), 1382–1387.

Cohen-Cole, E. & Fletcher, J. M. (2008b). Are all health outcomes "contagious"? Detecting implausible social network effects in acne, height, and headaches. *British Medical Journal, 3337,* a2533.

Conley, D. (2009). The promise and challenges of incorporating genetic data into longitudinal social science surveys and research. *Biodemography and Social Biology, 55*(2), 238–251.

Contoyannis, P. & Jones, A. M. (2004). Socio-economic status, health and lifestyle. *Journal of Health Economics, 23*(5) (September), 965–995.

Cook, P. J. (1981). The effect of liquor taxes on drinking, cirrhosis and auto fatalities. In M. H. Moore & D. R. Gerstein (Eds.), *Alcohol and public policy: Beyond the shadow of prohibition* (pp. 375–437). Washington, DC: National Academy Press.

Cook, P. J. (2007). *Paying the tab: The economics of alcohol policy.* Princeton, NJ: Princeton University Press.

Cook, P. J. & Moore, M. J. (1993). Drinking and schooling. *Journal of Health Economics, 12*(4), 411–429.

Cook, P. J. & Moore, M. J. (2000). Alcohol. In A. J. Culyer & J. P. Newhouse (Eds.), *Handbook of health economics* (Vol. 1, pp. 1629–1674). New York: Elsevier.

Cook, P. J. & Moore, M. J. (2001). Environment and persistence in youthful drinking patterns. In J. Gruber (Ed.), *Risky behavior among youths: An economic analysis* (pp. 375–437). Chicago: University of Chicago Press.

Cook, P. J. & Tauchen, G. (1982). The effect of liquor taxes on heavy drinking. *Bell Journal of Economics, 13*(2) (Autumn), 379–390.

Cook, P. J, Michael, J., & Moore, M. J. (2002). The economics of alcohol abuse and alcohol-control policies. *Health Affairs, 21*(2), 120–133.

Cook, P. J., Ostermann, J., & Sloan, F. A. (2005). The net effect of an alcohol tax increase on death rates in middle age. *American Economic Review, 95*(2), 278–281.

Courtemanche, C. (2009). Longer hours and larger waistlines? The relationship between work hours and obesity. *Forum of Health Economics and Policy, 12* (2—Obesity) (Article 2).

Culyer, A. J. & Newhouse, J. P. (2000). The state and scope of health economics. In A. J. Culyer & J. P. Newhouse (Eds.), *Handbook of health economics* (Vol. 1A, pp. 1–8). New York: Elsevier.

Currie, J. & Moretti, E. (2003). Mother education and the intergenerational transmission of human capital: Evidence from college openings and longitudinal data. *Quarterly Journal of Economics, 118*(4), 1495–1532.

Cutler, D. M. & Glaeser, E. (2005). What explains differences in smoking, drinking, and other health-related behaviors. *American Economic Review, 95*(2), 238–242.

Cutler, D. M. & Lleras-Muney, A. (2010). Understanding differences in health behaviors by education. *Journal of Health Economics, 29*(1) (January), 1–28.

Cutler, D. M., Glaeser, E. L., & Rosen, A. B. (2009). Is the US population behaving healthier. In J. R. Brown, J. B. Liebman, & D. A. Wise (Eds.), *Social security policy in a changing environment* (pp. 423–441). Chicago: University of Chicago Press.

Cutler, D. M., Glaeser, E. L., & Shapiro, J. M. (2003). Why have Americans become more obese? *Journal of Economic Perspectives, 17*(3) (Summer), 93–118.

Danaei, G., Ding, E. L., Mozaffarian, D., Taylor, B., Rehm, J., et al. (2009). The preventable causes of death in the United States: Comparative risk assessment of dietary, lifestyle, and metabolic risk factors. *PLoS Med, 6*(4), e1000058. doi:10.1371/journal.pmed.1000058.

Dave, D. & Kaestner, R. (2002). Alcohol taxes and labor market outcomes. *Journal of Health Economics, 21*(3), 357–371.

DeCicca, P., Kenkel, D., & Mathios, A. (2002). Putting out the fires: Will higher taxes reduce the onset of youth smoking? *Journal of Political Economy, 110*(1), 144–169.

DeCicca, P., Kenkel, D., & Mathios, A. (2008a). Cigarette taxes and the transition from youth to adult smoking: Smoking initiation, cessation, and participation. *Journal of Health Economics, 27*(4), 904–917.

DeCicca, P., Kenkel, D., Mathios, A., Shin, Y.-J., & Lim, J.-Y. (2008b). Youth smoking, cigarette prices, and anti-smoking sentiment. *Health Economics, 17*(6), 733–749.

Dee, T. S. (1999). State alcohol policies, teen drinking and traffic fatalities. *Journal of Public Economics, 72* (2), 289–315.

Dee, T. S. (2001). Alcohol abuse and economic conditions: Evidence from repeated cross-sections of individual-level data. *Health Economics, 10*(3) (March), 257–270.

Dee, T. S. (2009). Motorcycle helmets and traffic safety. *Journal of Health Economics, 28*(2) (March), 398–412.

Dee, T. S. & Evans, W. N. (2003). Teen drinking and educational attainment: Evidence from two-sample instrumental variables estimates. *Journal of Labor Economics, 21*, 178–209.

Dehejia, R. & Lleras-Muney, A. (2004). Booms, busts, and babies' health. *Quarterly Journal of Economics, 119*(3) (August), 1091–1130.

Della Vigna, S. & Malmendier, U. (2006). Paying not to go to the gym. *American Economic Review, 96*(3) (June), 674–719.

DeSimone, J. (2002). Illegal drug use and employment. *Journal of Labor Economics, 20*, 952–977.

De Walque, D. (2007a). How does the impact of an HIV/AIDS information campaign vary with educational attainment? Evidence from Uganda. *Journal of Development Economics, 84*(2) (November), 686–714.

De Walque, D. (2007b). Does education affect smoking behaviors? Evidence using the Vietnam draft as an instrument for college education. *Journal of Health Economics, 27*(5) (September), 877–895.

Dills, A. K., Jacobson, M., & Miron, J. A. (2005). The effect of alcohol prohibition on alcohol consumption: Evidence from drunkenness arrests. *Economics Letters, 86*(2005), 279–284.

DiNardo, J. & Lemieux, T. (2001). Alcohol, marijuana, and American youth: The unintended consequences of government regulation. *Journal of Health Economics, 20*, 991–1010.

Ding, W., Lehrer, S. F., Rosenquist, J. N., & Audrain-McGovern, J. (2009). The impact of poor health on academic performance: New evidence using genetic markers. *Journal of Health Economics, 28*, 578–597.

Dixon, J. B. (2010). The effect of obesity on health outcomes. *Molecular and Cellular Endocrinology, 316*, 104–108.

Dobkin, C. & Nicosia, N. (2009). The war on drugs: Methamphetamine, public health, and crime. *American Economic Review, 99*(1), 324–349.

Dobkin, C. & Puller, S. (2007). The effects of government transfers on monthly cycles in drug abuse, hospitalization and mortality. *Journal of Public Economics, 91*(11–12) (December), 2137–2157.

Dockner, E. J. & Feichtinger, G. (1993). Cyclical consumption patterns and rational addiction. *American Economic Review, 83*(1) (March), 256–263.

Dragone, D. (2009). A rational addiction model of binges, diets and obesity. *Journal of Health Economics, 28*(4) (July), 799–804.

Dranove, D. & Wehner, P. (1994). Physician-induced demand for childbirths. *Journal of Health Economics, 13*, 61–73.

Dube, S. R., Asman, K., Malarcher, A., & Carbollo, R. (2009). Cigarette smoking among adults and trends in smoking cessation—United States, 2008. *Morbidity and Mortality Weekly Report, 58*(44) (November 13), 1227–1232.

Duncan, G. J., Boisjoly, J., Kremer, M., Levy, D. M., & Eccles, J. (2005). Peer effects in drug use and sex among college students. *Journal of Abnormal Child Psychology, 33*(3), 375–385.

Dupas, P. (2011). Do teenagers respond to HIV risk information? Evidence from a field experiment in Kenya. *American Economic Journal: Applied Economics, 3*(1), 1–34.

Edwards, R. (2008). *American time use over the business cycle.* Mimeo, Queens College (August).

Elbel, B., Kersh, R., Brescoll, V. L., & Dixon, L. B. (2009). Calorie labeling and food choices: A first look at the effects on low-income people in New York City. *Health Affairs, 28*(6), w1110–w1121.

Ettner, S. L. (1997). Measuring the human cost of a weak economy: Does unemployment lead to alcohol abuse? *Social Science and Medicine, 44*(2) (January), 251–260.

Evans, W. & Graham, J. D. (1988). Traffic safety and the business cycle. *Alcohol, Drugs, and Driving, 4*(1) (January–March), 31–38.

Evans, W. N. & Farrelly, M. C. (1998). The compensating behavior of smokers: Taxes, tar, and nicotine. *Rand Journal of Economics, 29*(3), 578–595.

Evans, W. N. & Moore, T. J. (Forthcoming). Liquidity, activity and mortality. *Review of Economics and Statistics.*

Fang, H. & Gavazza, A. (2007). Dynamic inefficiencies in an employment-based health insurance system: Theory and evidence. National Bureau of Economic Research Working Paper No. 13371, September.

Farrell, P. & Fuchs, V. R. (1982). Schooling and health: The cigarette connection. *Journal of Health Economics, 1*, 217–230.

Farrelly, M. C., Bray, J. W., Zarkin, G. A., & Wendling, B. W. (2001). The joint demand for cigarettes and marijuana: Evidence from the National Household Surveys on Drug Abuse. *Journal of Health Economics, 20*(1), 51–68.

Farrelly, M. C., Nimsch, C. T., Hyland, A., & Cummings, M. (2004). The effects of higher cigarette prices on tar and nicotine consumption in a cohort of adult smokers. *Health Economics, 13*, 49–58.

Feng, W., Zhou, W., Butler, J. S., Booth, B. M., & French, M. T. (2001). The impact of problem drinking on employment. *Health Economics, 10*, 509–521.

Ferguson, B. (2000). Interpreting the rational addiction model. *Health Economics, 9*(7), 587–598.

Fernald, L. C. H., Gertler, P. J., & Hou, X. (2008a). Cash component of conditional cash transfer program is associated with higher body mass index and blood pressure in adults. *Journal of Nutrition*, *138*, 2250–2257.

Fernald, L. C. H., Gertler, P. J., & Neufeld, L. M. (2008b). Role of cash in conditional cash transfer programmes for child health, growth, and development: An analysis of Mexico's Oportunidades. *Lancet*, *371*, 828–837.

Finkelstein, E. A., Linnan, L. A., Tate, D. F., & Birken, B. E. (2007). A pilot study testing the effect of different levels of financial incentives on weight loss among overweight employees. *Journal of Occupational and Environmental Medicine*, *49*(9), 981–989.

Finkelstein, E. A., Trogdon, J. G., Cohen, J. W., & Dietz, W. (2009). Annual medical spending attributable to obesity: Payer- and service-specific estimates. *Health Affairs,* Web Exclusive, July 27.

Fisher, R. C. (1980). Local sales taxes: Tax rate differentials, sales loss, and revenue estimation. *Public Finance Quarterly*, *8*(2), 171–188.

Flegal, K. M., Graubard, B. I., Williamson, D. F., & Gail, M. H. (2005). Excess deaths associated with underweight, overweight, and obesity. *JAMA*, *293*(15) (April 20), 1861–1867.

Flegal, K. M., Graubard, B. I., Williamson, D. F., & Gail, M. H. (2007). Cause-specific excess deaths associated with underweight, overweight, and obesity. *JAMA*, *298*(17), 2028–2037.

Fletcher, J. M. & Lehrer, S. F. (2009). The effects of adolescent health on educational outcomes: Causal evidence using genetic lotteries between siblings. *Forum for Health Economics & Policy*, *12*(2) (Article 8).

Fletcher, J. M., Frisvold, D., & Tefft, N. (2010). Can soft drink taxes reduce population weight? *Contemporary Economic Policy*, *28*(1), 23–35.

Forster, M. & Jones, A. M. (2001). The role of tobacco taxes in starting and quitting smoking: Duration analysis of British data. *Journal of the Royal Statistical Society*, *164*(Part 3), 517–547.

Fowler, J. H. & Christakis, N. A. (2008). Estimating peer effects on health in social networks: A response to Cohen-Cole and Fletcher; and Trogdon, Nonnemaker, and Pais. *Journal of Health Economics*, *27*, 1400–1405.

Frank, M. W. (2008). Media substitution in advertising: A spirited case study. *International Journal of Industrial Organization*, *26*, 308–326.

Frederick, S., Loewenstein, G., & O'Donoghue, T. (2002). Time discounting and time preference: A critical review. *Journal of Economic Literature*, *40*(2) (June), 351–401.

Freeman, D. G. (1999). A note on "economic conditions and alcohol problems". *Journal of Health Economics*, *18*(5) (October), 661–670.

French, M. T. & Maclean, J. C. (2006). Underage alcohol use, delinquency, and criminal activity. *Health Economics*, *15*, 1261–1281.

French, M. T. & Popovici, I. (2011). That instrument is lousy! In search of agreement when using instrumental variables estimation in substance use research. *Health Economics*, *20*, 127–146.

French, M. T., McGeary, K. A., Chitwood, D. D., & McCoy, C. B. (2000). Chronic illicit drug use, health services utilization, and the cost of medical care. *Social Science and Medicine*, *50*, 1703–1713.

French, M. T., Roebuck, M. C., & Alexandre, P. K. (2001). Illicit drug use, employment, and labor force participation. *Southern Economic Journal*, *68*, 349–368.

Fryer Jr., R. G., Heaton, P. S., Levitt, S. D. & Murphy, K. M. (2005). Measuring the impact of crack cocaine. NBER Working Paper #11318.

Fuchs, V. R. (1982). Time preference and health: An exploratory study. In V. R. Fuchs (Ed.), *Economic Aspects of Health* (pp. 93–120). University of Chicago Press for the NBER.

Fudenberg, D. & Levine, D. K. (2006). A dual-self model of impulse control. *American Economic Review*, *96*(5) (December), 1449–1476.

Gallet, C. & List, J. A. (2003). Cigarette demand: A meta-analysis of elasticities. *Health Economics*, *12*, 821–835.

Gallet, C. A. (2007). The demand for alcohol: A meta-analysis of elasticities. *Australian Journal of Agricultural and Resource Economics*, *51*, 121–135.

Gallet, C. A., Hoover, G. A., & Lee, J. (2006). Putting out fires: An examination of the determinants of state clean indoor-air laws. *Southern Economic Journal*, *73*(1), 112–124.

Gasmi, F., Laffont, J. J., & Vuong, Q. (1992). Econometric analysis of collusive behavior in a soft drink market. *Journal of Economics & Management Strategy, 1*(2), 277–311.

Gaziano, J. M., Buring, J. E., Breslow, J. L., Goldhaber, S. Z., Rosner, B., VanDenburgh, M., et al. (1993). Moderate alcohol intake, increased levels of high-density lipoprotein and its subfractions, and decreased risk of myocardial infarction. *New England Journal of Medicine, 329*(25) (September 16), 1829–1834.

Gertler, P., Shah, M., & Bertozzi, S. M. (2005). Risky business: The market for unprotected commercial sex. *Journal of Political Economy, 113*(3) (June), 518–550.

Gilleskie, D. & Strumpf, K. (2005). The behavioral dynamics of youth smoking. *Journal of Human Resources, 40*(4), 822–866.

Giné, X., Karlan, D., & Zinman, J. (2010). Put your money where your butt is: A commitment contract for smoking cessation. *American Economic Journal: Applied Economics, 2*, 213–235.

Giuffrida, A. & Torgerson, D. J. (1997). Should we pay the patient? Review of financial incentives to enhance patient compliance. *British Medical Journal, 315*, 703–707.

Glimcher, P. W., Kable, J., & Kenway, L. (2007). Neuroeconomic studies of impulsivity: Now or just as soon as possible. *American Economic Review, 97*(2) (May), 142–147.

Goldman, D., Oroszi, G., & Ducci, F. (2005). The genetics of addictions: Uncovering the genes. *Nature Reviews Genetics, 67*(6) (July), 521–532.

Goldman, D. P. & Smith, J. P. (2002). Can patient self-management help explain the SES health gradient. *Proceedings of the National Academy of Sciences, 99*(16) (August 6), 10929–10934.

Gregory, C. A. & Ruhm, C. J. (2011). Where does the wage penalty bite. In M. Grossman & N. Mojan (Eds.), *Economic aspects of obesity.* University of Chicago Press.

Greve, J. (2008). Obesity and labor market outcomes in Denmark. *Economics and Human Biology, 6*, 350–362.

Grimard, F. & Parent, D. (2007). Education and smoking: Were Vietnam war draft avoiders also more likely to avoid smoking? *Journal of Health Economics, 27*(5) (September), 896–926.

Grogger, J. & Willis, M. (2000). The emergence of crack cocaine and the rise in urban crime rates. *Review of Economics and Statistics, 82*(4), 519–529.

Grossman, M. (1972). On the concept of health capital and the demand for health. *Journal of Political Economy, 80*(2), 223–249.

Grossman, M. (1993). the economic analysis of addictive behavior. In M. E. Hilton & G. Bloss (Eds.), *Economics and the prevention of alcohol-related problems.* Rockville, MD: US Department of Health and Human Services.

Grossman, M. (2000). The human capital model. In A. J. Culyer & J. P. Newhouse (Eds.), *Handbook of health economics* (Vol. 1A). New York: Elsevier.

Grossman, M. (2005). Individual behaviours and substance use: The role of price. *Advances in Health Economics and Health Services Research, 16*, 15–39.

Grossman, M. & Chaloupka, F. J. (1998). The demand for cocaine by young adults: A rational addiction approach. *Journal of Health Economics, 17*(4), 427–474.

Grossman, M. & Kaestner, R. (1997). Effects of education on health. In J. R. Behrman & N. Stacey (Eds.), *The social benefits of education.* Ann Arbor, MI: University of Michigan Press.

Gruber, J. & Frakes, M. (2006). Does falling smoking lead to rising obesity? *Journal of Health Economics, 25*(2) (March), 183–197.

Gruber, J. & Köszegi, B. (2001). Is addiction "rational"? Theory and evidence. *Quarterly Journal of Economics, 116*(4) (November), 1261–1303.

Gruber, J. & Mullainathan, S. (2005). Do cigarette taxes make smokers happier? *Advances in Economic Analysis and Policy, 5*(1) (Article 4).

Gul, F. & Pesendorfer, W. (2001). Temptation and self-control. *Econometrica, 69*(6) (November), 1403–1435.

Hall, R. E. (1978). Stochastic implications of the lifecycle–permanent income hypothesis: Theory and evidence. *Journal of Political Economy, 86*(6) (December), 971–987.

Hamermesh, D. S. & Biddle, J. E. (1994). Beauty and the labor market. *American Economic Review, 84*(5), 1174–1194.

Hare, T. A., Camerer, C. F., & Rangel, A. (2009). Self-control in decision-making involves modulation of the vmPFC valuation system. *Science, 324* (May 1), 646–648.

Harwood, H. (2000). *Updating estimates of the economic costs of alcohol abuse in the United States: Estimates, update methods, and data.* National Institute on Alcohol Abuse and Alcoholism.

Hastings, J. & Washington, E. (2010). The first of the month effect: Consumer behavior and store responses. *American Economic Journal: Economic Policy, 2*(2) (May), 142–162.

Heckman, J. J., Flyer, F., & Loughlin, C. P. (2008). An assessment of causal inference in smoking initiation research and a framework for future research. *Economic Inquiry, 46*(1), 37–44.

Higgins, S. T., Alessi, S. M., & Dantona, R. L. (2002). Voucher-based incentives: A substance abuse treatment innovation. *Addictive Behaviors, 27,* 887–910.

Houthakker, H. S. & Taylor, L. D. (1970). *Consumer demand in the united states: Analyses and projections.* Cambridge, MA: Harvard University Press.

Ikeda, S., Kang, M.-I., & Ohtake, F. (2010). Hyperbolic discounting, the sign effect, and the body mass index. *Journal of Health Economics, 29,* 268–284.

Ippolito, P. M. & Mathios, A. D. (1995). Information and advertising: The case of fat consumption in the United States. *American Economic Review, 85*(2), 91–95.

Johansson, E., Alho, H., Kiiskinen, U., & Poikolainen, K. (2007). The association of alcohol dependency with employment probability: Evidence from the population survey "Health 2000 in Finland". *Health Economics, 16,* 739–754.

Johnston, L. D., O'Malley, P. M., Bachman, J. G., & Schulenberg, J. E. (2009). *Teen marijuana use tilts up, while some drugs decline in use.* Ann Arbor, MI: University of Michigan News Service. Retrieved from www.monitoringthefuture.org, 4/19/2010.

Just, D. R. (2006). Behavioral economics, food assistance, and obesity. *Agricultural and Resource Economics Review, 35*(2) (October), 209–220.

Kaestner, R. (1991). The effect of illicit drug use on the wages of young adults. *Journal of Labor Economics, 9*(4), 381–412.

Kaestner, R. (1994). New estimates of the effect of marijuana and cocaine use on wages. *Industrial and Labor Relations Review, 47*(3), 454–470.

Kahneman, D. (1994). New challenges to the rationality assumption. *Journal of Institutional and Theoretical Economics, 150*(1), 18–36.

Kahneman, D. & Thaler, R. H. (2006). Anomalies: Utility maximization and experienced utility. *Journal of Economic Perspectives, 20*(1), 221–234.

Kahneman, D. & Tversky, A. (1979). Prospect theory: An analysis of decision under risk. *Econometrica, 47*(2), 263–292.

Kahneman, D., Knetsch, J. L., & Thaler, R. (1986). Fairness as a constraint on profit seeking: Entitlements in the market. *American Economic Review, 76*(4), 728–741.

Kan, K. (2007). Cigarette smoking and self-control. *Journal of Health Economics, 26*(1) (January), 61–81.

Kanjilal, S., Gregg, E. W., Cheng, Y. J., Zhang, P., Nelson, D. E., Mensah, G., et al. (2006). Socioeconomic status and trends in disparities in 4 major risk factors for cardiovascular disease among US adults. *Archives of Internal Medicine, 166*(21) (November 27), 2348–2355.

Kant, A. & Graubard, B. (2007). Secular trends in the association of socio-economic position with self-reported dietary attributes and biomarkers in the US population: National Health and Nutrition Examination Survey (NHANES) 1971–1975 to NHANES 1999–2002. *Public Health Nutrition, 10* (2) (February), 158–167.

Kenkel, D., Lillard, D., & Mathios, A. (2006). The roles of high school completion and GED receipt in smoking and obesity. *Journal of Labor Economics, 24*(3), 635–660.

Kenkel, D. S. (1991). Health behavior, health knowledge and schooling. *Journal of Political Economy, 99*(2) (April), 287–305.

Kenkel, D. S. (2000). Prevention. In A. J. Culyer & J. P. Newhouse (Eds.), *Handbook of health economics* (Vol. 1, pp. 1675–1720). New York: Elsevier.

Kenkel, D. S. (2005). Are alcohol tax hikes fully passed through to prices? Evidence from Alaska. *American Economic Review, 95*(2), 273–277.

Kenkel, D. S. (2006). Health behaviours among young people. In A. M. Jones (Ed.), *The Elgar companion to health economics*. Northampton, MA: Edward Elgar, Chapter 6.

Kenkel, D. S. (2007). *The evolution of the schooling-smoking gradient*. Mimeo, Cornell University (March).

Kenkel, D. S. & Sindelar, J. (2011). Economics of health behaviors and addictions: Contemporary issues and policy. In S. Glied, (ed.), *Oxford handbook of health economics*. New York, NY: Oxford University Press.

Khwaja, A., Silverman, D., Sloan, F., & Wang, Y. (2009). Are mature smokers misinformed. *Journal of Health Economics*, *28*(2) (March), 385−397.

Khwaja, A., Sloan, F., & Chung, S. (2007). The relationship between individual expectations and behaviors: Mortality expectations and smoking decisions. *Journal of Risk and Uncertainty*, *35*(2) (October), 179−201.

Kline, B. & Tobias, J. L. (2008). The wages of BMI: Bayesian analysis of a skewed treatment-response model with nonparametric endogeneity. *Journal of Applied Econometrics*, *23*, 767−793.

Kling, J. R., Liebman, J. B., & Katz, L. F. (2007). Experimental analysis of neighborhood effects. *Econometrica*, *75*(1), 83−119.

Koch, S. F. & Ribar, D. C. (2001). A siblings analysis of the effects of alcohol consumption onset on educational attainment. *Contemporary Economic Policy*, *19*(2), 162−174.

Komlos, J., Smith, P. K., & Bogin, B. (2004). Obesity and the rate of time preference: Is there a connection? *Journal of Biosocial Science*, *36*, 209−219.

Laibson, D. (1997). Golden eggs and hyperbolic discounting. *Quarterly Journal of Economics*, *112*(5), 443−477.

Laibson, D. (2001). A cue-theory of consumption. *Quarterly Journal of Economics*, *116*(1) (February), 81−119.

Lange, F. (2010). *Does education help with complex health decisions: Evidence from cancer screening*. Mimeo, Yale University.

Lantz, P. M., Lynch, J. W., House, J. S., Lepkowski, J. M., Mero, R. P., Musick, M. A., et al. (2001). Socioeconomic disparities in health change in a longitudinal study of US adults: The role of health-risk behaviors. *Social Science and Medicine*, *53*(1) (July), 29−40.

Lawrance, E. (1991). Poverty and the rate of time preference: Evidence from panel data. *Journal of Political Economy*, *99*(1), 54−77.

Leibenstein, H. (1950). Bandwagon, snob, and Veblen effects in the theory of consumers' demand. *Quarterly Journal of Economics*, *64*(2), 183−207.

Lerner, J. S. & Keltner, D. (2001). Fear, anger, and risk. *Journal of Personality and Social Psychology*, *81*(1) (July), 146−159.

Levine, P. B. (2001). The sexual activity and birth-control use of American teenagers. In J. Gruber (Ed.), *Risky behavior among youths* (pp. 167−217). Chicago: The University of Chicago Press.

Levy, D. E. & Meara, E. (2006). The effect of the 1998 Master Settlement Agreement on prenatal smoking. *Journal of Health Economics*, *25*, 276−294.

Lindahl, M. (2005). Estimating the effect of income on health and mortality using lottery prizes as an exogenous source of variation in income. *Journal of Human Resources*, *40*(1), 144−168.

Liu, J.-L., Liu, J.-T., Hammitt, J. K., & Chou, S.-Y. (1999). The price elasticity of opium in Taiwan, 1914−1942. *Journal of Health Economics*, *18*, 795−810.

Lleras-Muney, A. & Lichtenberg, F. (2005). The effect of education on medical technology adoption: Are the more educated more likely to use new drugs? *Annales d'Economie et Statistique*, *79/80*, July−December.

Loewenstein, G. (2000). Emotions in economic theory and economic behavior. *American Economic Review*, *90*(2), 426−432.

Loewenstein, G.F. & O'Donoghue, T. (2004). Animal spirits: Affective and deliberative processes in economic behavior. Working Paper 04-14, Center for Analytic Economics, Cornell University.

Loewenstein, G., Brennan, T., & Volpp, K. G. (2007). Asymmetric paternalism to improve health behaviors. *JAMA*, *298*(20), 2415−2417.

Loomis, B. R., Farrelly, M. C., Nonnemaker, J. M., & Mann, N. H. (2006). Point of purchase cigarette promotions before and after the mast settlement agreement: Exploring retail scanner data. *Tobacco Control*, *15*(2) (April), 140−142.

Lundborg, P. (2006). Having the wrong friends? Peer effects in adolescent substance use. *Journal of Health Economics, 25*(2), 214−233.

Lundborg, P., Bolin, K., Hojgard, S., & Lindgren, B. (2007). Obesity and occupational attainment among the 50+ of Europe. In K. Bolin & J. Cawley (Eds.), *Advances in health and health services research, Vol. 17: The economics of obesity.* New York: Elsevier.

Lussier, J. P., Heil, S. H., Mongeon, J. A., et al. (2006). A meta-analysis of voucher-based reinforcement therapy for substance use disorders. *Addiction, 101*, 192−203.

Lye, J. & Hirschberg, J. (2010). Alcohol consumption and human capital: A retrospective study of the literature. *Journal of Economic Surveys, 24*, 309−338.

Lynch, J. W., Kaplan, G. A., Cohen, R. D., Tuomilehto, J., & Salonen, J. T. (1996). Do cardiovascular risk factors explain the relation between socioeconomic status, risk of all-cause mortality, cardiovascular mortality and acute myocardial infarction. *American Journal of Epidemiology, 144*(10) (November 15), 934−942.

MacDonald, Z. & Pudney, S. (2000). The wages of sin? Illegal drug use and the labour market. *Labour, 14*(4), 657−674.

MacLean, P. D. (1990). *The triune brain in evolution: Role in paleocerebral functions.* New York: Plenum.

Maitra, S. (2010). Can patient self-management help explain the SES Health Gradient? Goldman and Smith's "Can Patient Self-Management Help Explain the SES Health Gradient?" (2002) Revisited. *Social Science and Medicine, 70*(6) (March), 802−810.

Manning, W. G., Blumberg, L., & Moulton, L. H. (1995). The demand for alcohol: The differential response to price. *Journal of Health Economics, 14*(2), 123−148.

Manning, W. G., Keeler, E. B., Newhouse, J. P., Sloss, E. M., & Wasserman, J. (1991). *The costs of poor health habits.* Cambridge, MA: Harvard University Press.

Manski, C. F. (1993). Identification of endogenous social effects: The reflection problem. *Review of Economic Studies, 60*(3), 531−542.

Manski, C. F. (2000). Economic analysis of social interactions. *Journal of Economic Perspectives, 14*(3), 115−136.

Markowitz, S. (2005). Alcohol, drugs and violent crime. *International Review of Law and Economics, 25*(1), 20−44.

Markowitz, S. & Grossman, M. (2000). The effects of beer taxes on physical child abuse. *Journal of Health Economics, 19*(2), 271−282.

Markowitz, S., Chatterji, P., & Kaestner, R. (2003). Estimating the impact of alcohol policies on youth suicides. *Journal of Mental Health Policy and Economics, 6*(1), 37−46.

Marmot, M. & Wilkinson, R. G. (2006). *Social determinants of health* (2nd ed.). Oxford: Oxford University Press.

Marmot, M. G., Davey Smith, G., Stansfeld, S., Patel, C., North, F., Head, J., et al. (1991). Health inequalities among British civil servants: The Whitehall II study. *The Lancet, 337*(8754) (June 8), 1387−1393.

Marmot, M. G., Rose, G., Shipley, M., & Hamilton, P. J. S. (1978). Employment grade and coronary heart disease in British civil servants. *Journal of Epidemiology and Community Health, 32*(4) (December), 244−249.

Marshall, A. (1920). *Principles of economics* (8th ed). London.

Mas-Colell, A., Whinston, M. D., & Green, J. R. (1995). *Microeconomic theory.* New York: Oxford University Press.

Massey, D. S. (2002). A brief history of human society: The origin and role of emotion in social life. *American Sociological Review, 67*(1) (February), 1−29.

Mast, B. D., Benson, B. L., & Rasmussen, D. (1999). Beer taxation and alcohol-related fatalities. *Southern Economic Journal, 66*(20) (October), 214−249.

Mastrobuoni, G. & Weinberg, M. (2009). Heterogeneity in intra-monthly consumption patterns, self-control and savings at retirement. *American Economic Journal: Economic Policy, 1*(2) (August), 163−189.

Mathios, A. (2000). The impact of mandatory disclosure laws on product choices: An analysis of the salad dressing market. *Journal of Law and Economics, 43*(2), 651−677.

McCloskey, D. N. (1998). *The rhetoric of economics* (2nd ed.). University of Wisconsin Press.

McClure, S. M., Laibson, D. I., Loewenstein, G., & Cohen, J. D. (2004). separate neural systems value immediate and delayed monetary rewards. *Science, 306* (October 15), 503−507.

McDowell, M. A., Wang, C.-Y., & Kennedy-Stephenson, J. (2006). *Breastfeeding in the United States: Findings from the National Health and Nutrition Examination Surveys 1999−2006.* Hyattsville, MD: National Center for Health Statistics.

McGeary, K. A. & French, M. T. (2000). Illicit drug use and emergency room utilization. *Health Services Research, 35,* 153−169.

McGinnis, J. M. & Foege, W. H. (1993). Actual causes of death in the United States. *JAMA, 270*(18) (November 10), 2207−2212.

McLean, R. A. & Moon, M. (1980). Health, obesity, and earnings. *American Journal of Public Health, 70* (9), 1006−1009.

Metcalfe, J. & Mischel, W. (1999). A hot/cool system analysis of delay of gratification: Dynamics of will-power. *Psychological Review, 106*(1), 3−19.

Miron, J. A. (2003). Do prohibitions raise prices? Evidence from the markets for cocaine and heroin. *Review of Economics and Statistics, 85*(3), 522−530.

Miron, J. A. & Zwiebel, J. (1991). Alcohol consumption during Prohibition. *American Economic Review, 81*(2), 242−247.

Mokdad, A. H., Marks, J. S., Stroup, D. F., & Gerberding, J. L. (2004). Actual causes of death in the United States, 2000. *JAMA, 291*(10) (March 10), 1238−1245.

Mokdad, A. H., Marks, J. S., Stroup, D. F., & Gerberding, J. L. (2005). Correction: Actual causes of death in the United States, 2000. *JAMA, 293*(3), 293.

Morris, S. (2007). The impact of obesity on employment. *Labour Economics, 14,* 413−433.

Morrisey, M. A. & Cawley, J. (2008). U.S. health economists: Who we are and what we do. *Health Economics, 17*(4), 535−543.

Mullahy, J. (1999). It will only hurt for a second? Microeconomic determinants of who gets flu shots. *Health Economics, 8*(1) (February), 9−24.

Mullahy, J. & Sindelar, J. (1996). Employment, unemployment, and problem drinking. *Journal of Health Economics, 15,* 409−434.

National Center for Health Statistics (2010). *Health United States, 2009: With special feature on medical technology.* Hyattsville, MD: National Center for Health Statistics.

Nelson, J. P. (2003). Cigarette demand, structural change, and advertising bans: International evidence, 1970−1995. *Contributions to Economic Analysis & Policy, 2*(1) (Article 10).

Nelson, J. P. (2006). Cigarette advertising regulation: A meta-analysis. *International Review of Law and Economics, 26,* 195−226.

Nelson, J. P. (2010). Alcohol advertising bans, consumption and control policies in seventeen OECD countries, 1975−2000. *Applied Economics, 42*(7), 803−823.

Nelson, P. (1974). Advertising as information. *Journal of Political Economy, 81,* 729−754.

Norton, E. C. & Han, E. (2008). Genetic information, obesity, and labor market outcomes. *Health Economics, 17*(9) (September), 1089−1104.

O'Donoghue, T. & Rabin, M. (1999). Doing it now or later. *American Economic Review, 89*(1) (March), 103−124.

Oettinger, G. S. (1999). The effects of sex education on teen sexual activity and teen pregnancy. *Journal of Political Economy, 107*(3) (June), 606−635.

Office of National Drug Control Policy (2004). *The economic costs of drug abuse in the United States, 1992−2002.* Washington, DC: Executive Office of the President (Publication No. 207303).

Ogburn, W. F. & Thomas, D. S. (1922). The influence of the business cycle on certain social conditions. *Journal of the American Statistical Association, 18*(139) (September), 324−340.

Olshansky, S. J., Passaro, D. J., Hershow, R. C., Layden, J., Carnes, B. A., Brody, J., et al. (2005). A potential decline in life expectancy in the United States in the 21st century. *New England Journal of Medicine, 352*(11) (March 17), 1138−1145.

Orphanides, A. & Zervos, D. (1995). Rational addiction with learning and regret. *Journal of Political Economy, 103*(4) (August), 739−758.

Orphanides, A. & Zervos, D. (1998). Myopia and addictive behaviors. *The Economic Journal, 108*(446) (January), 75–91.

Orzechowski, W. & Walker, R. C. (2009). *The tax burden on tobacco.* Historical Compilation 1999, vol. 44. Arlington, VA.

Pacula, R. L. (1998). Does increasing the beer tax reduce marijuana consumption? *Journal of Health Economics, 17*(5), 557–585.

Pacula, R. L., Grossman, M., Chaloupka, F. J., O'Malley, P. M., & Farrelly, M. C. (2001). Marijuana and youth. In J. Gruber (Ed.), *Risky behavior among youths: An economic analysis* (pp. 271–326). Chicago: University of Chicago Press.

Pampel, F. C., Krueger, P. M., & Denney, J. T. (2010). Socioeconomic disparities in health behaviors. *Annual Review of Sociology, 36*, 347–370.

Perloff, J. M. (2008). *Microeconomics.* New York: Addison Wesley.

Petty, N. M. & Martin, B. (2002). Low-cost contingency management for treating cocaine- and opiod-abusing metadone patients. *Journal of Consulting and Clinical Psychology, 70*(2), 398–405.

Phelps, E. S. & Pollak, R. A. (1968). On second-best national saving and game-equilibrium growth. *Review of Economic Studies, 35*(2) (April), 185–199.

Philipson, T. (1996). Private vaccination and public health: An empirical examination. *Journal of Human Resources, 31*(3) (Summer), 611–630.

Philipson, T. (2000). Economic epidemiology and infectious diseases. In A. J. Culyer & J. P. Newhouse (Eds.), *Handbook of health economics* (Vol. 1, pp. 1539–1628). New York: Elsevier.

Philipson, T. & Posner, R. A. (1999). The long-run growth in obesity as a function of technological change. NBER Working Paper 7423.

Phillips, D. P., Christenfeld, N., & Ryan, N. M. (1999). An increase in the number of deaths in the United States in the first week of the month: An association with substance abuse and other causes of death. *New England Journal of Medicine, 341*(2) (July 8), 93–98.

Pollak, R. A. (1975). The intertemporal cost of living index. *Annals of Economic and Social Measurement, 4*, 179–195.

Popkin, B. M., Sieg-Riz, A. M., & Haines, P. S. (1996). A comparison of dietary trends among racial and socioeconomic groups in the United States. *New England Journal of Medicine, 335*(10) (September 5), 716–720.

Powell, L. M. & Chaloupka, F. J. (2009). Food prices and obesity: Evidence and policy implications for taxes and subsidies. *Milbank Quarterly, 87*(1), 229–257.

Prendergast, M., Podus, D., Finney, J., Greenwell, L., & Roll, J. (2006). Contingency management for treatment of substance use disorders: A meta-analysis. *Addiction, 101*(11), 1546–1560.

Rachlin, H. (1997). Four teleological theories of addiction. *Psychonomic Bulletin and Review, 4*(4), 462–473.

Read, D., Loewenstein, G., & Rabin, M. (1999). Choice bracketing. *Journal of Risk and Uncertainty, 19* (1–3), 171–197.

Register, C. A. & Williams, D. R. (1992). Labor market effects of marijuana and cocaine use among young men. *Industrial and Labor Relations Review, 45*(3), 435–448.

Reinhold, S. & Jurges, H. (2009). Secondary school fees and the causal effect of schooling on health behavior. *Health Economics, 19*(8), 994–1001.

Renna, F. (2007). The economic cost of teen drinking: Late graduation and lowered earnings. *Health Economics, 16*, 407–419.

Renna, F., Grafova, I. B., & Thakur, N. (2008). The effect of friends on adolescent body weight. *Economics and Human Biology, 6*, 377–387.

Rice, D. P., Hodgson, T. A., Sinsheimer, P., Browner, W., & Kopstein, A. N. (1986). The economic costs of the health effects of smoking, 1984. *Milbank Quarterly, 64*(4), 489–547.

Rice, D. P., Kelman, S., & Miller, L. S. (1991). Estimates of economic costs of alcohol and drug abuse and mental illness, 1985 and 1988. *Public Health Reports, 106*(3), 280–292.

Riddell, C. & Riddell, R. (2006). Welfare checks, drug consumption, and health: Evidence from Vancouver injection drug users. *Journal of Human Resources, 41*(1) (Winter), 138–161.

Roberts, M. J. & Samuelson, L. (1988). An empirical analysis of dynamic nonprice competition in an oligopolistic industry. *RAND Journal of Economics, 19*, 200–220.

Rooth, D.-O. (2009). Obesity, attractiveness, and differential treatment in hiring: A field experiment. *Journal of Human Resources, 44*(3), 710–735.

Rosen, H. S. (2002). *Public finance* (6th ed.). New York: McGraw Hill.

Rosenzweig, M. R. & Schultz, T. P. (1989). Schooling, information and nonmarket productivity: Contraceptive use and its effectiveness. *International Economic Review, 30*(2) (May), 457–477.

Roux, L. & Donaldson, C. (2004). Economics and obesity: Costing the problem or evaluating solutions? *Obesity Research, 12*(2), 173–179.

Rubinstein, A. (2003). Economics and psychology"? The case of hyperbolic discounting. *International Economic Review, 44*(4) (November), 1207–1216.

Rubinstein, A. (2008). Comments on neuroeconomics. *Economics and Philosophy, 24*(3) (November), 485–494.

Ruhm, C. J. (1995). Economic conditions and alcohol problems. *Journal of Health Economics, 14*(5) (December), 583–603.

Ruhm, C. J. (1996). Alcohol policies and highway vehicle fatalities. *Journal of Health Economics, 15*(4) (August), 435–454.

Ruhm, C. J. (2000). Are recessions good for your health? *Quarterly Journal of Economics, 115*(2) (May), 617–650.

Ruhm, C. J. (2003). Good times make you sick. *Journal of Health Economics, 22*(4) (July), 637–658.

Ruhm, C. J. (2005a). Healthy living in hard times. *Journal of Health Economics, 24*(2) (March), 341–363.

Ruhm, C. J. (2005b). Mortality increases during economic upturns. *International Journal of Epidemiology, 34*(6) (December), 1206–1211.

Ruhm, C. J. (2006). Macroeconomic conditions, health and mortality. In A. M. Jones (Ed.), *Elgar companion to health economics* (pp. 5–16). Cheltenham, UK: Edward Elgar Publishing.

Ruhm, C. J. (2007). A healthy economy can break your heart. *Demography, 44*(4) (November), 829–848.

Ruhm, C. J. (2008). Macroeconomic conditions, health and government policy. In R. F. Schoeni, J. S. House, G. A. Kaplan, & H. Pollack (Eds.), *Making Americans healthier: Social and economic policy as health policy: Rethinking America's approach to improving health* (pp. 173–200). New York: Russell Sage Foundation.

Ruhm, C. J. (2010). *Understanding overeating and obesity.* Mimeo, University of North Carolina at Greensboro, April.

Ruhm, C. J. & Black, W. E. (2002). Does drinking really decrease in bad times? *Journal of Health Economics, 21*(4) (July), 659–678.

Ryder, H. E., Jr. & Heal, G. M. (1973). Optimal growth with intertemporally dependent preferences. *The Review of Economic Studies, 40*(1), 1–31.

Sabia, J. J. (2007). The effect of body weight on adolescent academic performance. *Southern Economic Journal, 73*(4), 871–900.

Saffer, H. & Chaloupka, F. (2000). The effect of tobacco advertising bans on tobacco consumption. *Journal of Health Economics, 19*, 1117–1137.

Saffer, H. & Chaloupka, F. J. (1999). Demographic differentials in the demand for alcohol and drugs. In F. J. Chaloupka, M. Grossman, W. K. Bickel, & H. Saffer (Eds.), *The economic analysis of substance use and abuse* (pp. 133–156). Cambridge, MA: National Bureau of Economic Research.

Saffer, H. & Dave, D. (2006). Alcohol advertising and alcohol consumption by adolescents. *Health Economics, 15*, 617–637.

Samuelson, P. (1937). A note on the measurement of utility. *Review of Economic Studies, 4*(2) (February), 155–161.

Samwick, A. (1998). Discount rate heterogeneity and social security reform. *Journal of Development Economics, 57*, 117–146.

Schmeiser, M. D. (2009). Expanding wallets and waistlines: The impact of family income on the BMI of women and men eligible for the earned income tax credit. *Health Economics, 18*, 1277–1294.

Schoenbaum, M. (1997). Do smokers understand the mortality effects of smoking? Evidence from the Health and Retirement Survey. *American Journal of Public Health, 87*(5) (May), 755–759.

Sen, B. (2003). Can beer taxes affect teen pregnancy? Evidence based on teen abortion rates and birth rates. *Southern Economic Journal, 70*(2), 328–343.

Sen, B. (2006). The relationship between beer taxes, other alcohol policies, and child homicide deaths. *B.E. Journal of Economic Analysis and Policy: Topics in Economic Analysis and Policy, 6*(1), 1–17.

Shapiro, J. M. (2005). Is there a daily discount rate? Evidence from the food stamp nutrition cycle. *Journal of Public Economics, 89*(2) (February), 303–325.

Shiell, A., Gerard, K., & Donaldson, C. (1987). Cost of illness studies: An aid to decision-making? *Health Policy, 8*, 317–323.

Shiv, B. & Fedorikhin, A. (1999). Heart and mind in conflict: The interplay of affect and cognition in consumer decision making. *Journal of Consumer Research, 26*(3) (December), 278–292.

Simon, H. A. (1984). *Models of bounded rationality*, Volume 1. Cambridge, MA: MIT Press.

Simpson, M. E., Serdula, M., Galuska, D. A., Gillespie, C., Donehoo, R., Macera, C., et al. (2003). Walking trends among U.S. adults: The behavioral risk factor surveillance system, 1987–2000. *American Journal of Preventive Medicine, 25*(2) (August), 95–100.

Sirard, J. R. & Pate, R. R. (2001). Physical activity assessments in children and adolescents. *Sports Medicine, 31*(6), 439–454.

Sloan, F. A. & Trogdon, J. G. (2004). The impact of the master settlement agreement on cigarette consumption. *Journal of Policy Analysis and Management, 23*(4), 843–855.

Sloan, F. A., Ostermann, J., Conover, C., Taylor, D. H., Jr., & Picone, G. (2004). *The price of smoking*. Cambridge, MA: MIT Press.

Smith, J. P. (2007). Nature and causes of trends in male diabetes prevalence, undiagnosed diabetes, and the socioeconomic status health gradient. *Proceedings of the National Academy of Sciences, 104*(33) (August 14), 13225–13231.

Smith, P. K., Bogin, B., & Bishai, D. (2005). Are time preference and body mass index associated? Evidence from the National longitudinal survey of youth. *Economics and Human Biology, 3*, 259–270.

Smith, V. K., Taylor, D. H., Jr., Sloan, F. A., Reed Johnson, F., & Desvousges, W. H. (2001). Do smokers respond to health shocks? *Review of Economics and Statistics, 83*(4) (November), 675–687.

Stead, L. F., Bergson, G., & Lancaster, T. (2008). Physician advice for smoking cessation (review). *Cochrane Database Systematic Review, 2*(April 16) (Article No. CD000165).

Stephens, M. (2003). "3rd of the month": Do social security recipients smooth consumption between checks. *American Economic Review, 93*(1) (March), 406–422.

Stephens, M. (2006). Paycheque receipt and the timing of consumption. *Economic Journal, 116*(513) (July), 680–701.

Stigler, G. J. & Becker, G. S. (1977). De gustibus non est disputandum. *American Economic Review, 67*(2), 76–90.

Stiglitz, J. E. (1989). Imperfect information in the product market. In R. Schmalensee & R. D. Willig (Eds.), *The handbook of industrial organization*. New York: Elsevier. Chapter 13.

Stock, J. H., Wright, J. H., & Yogo, M. (2002). A survey of weak instruments and weak identification in generalized method of moments. *Journal of Business and Economic Statistics, 20*(4), 518–529.

Strotz, R. H. (1955–1956). Myopia and inconsistency in dynamic utility maximization. *Review of Economic Studies, 23*(3), 165–180.

Suranovic, S. M., Goldfarb, R. S., & Leonard, T. C. (1999). An economic theory of cigarette addiction. *Journal of Health Economics, 18*(1) (January), 1–29.

Tauras, J., Markowitz, S., & Cawley, J. (2005). Tobacco control policies and youth smoking: Evidence from a new era. *Advances in Health Economics and Health Services Research, 16*.

Terza, J. V. (2002). Alcohol abuse and employment: A second look. *Journal of Applied Econometrics, 17*, 393–404.

Thaler, R. (1981). Some empirical evidence on dynamic inconsistency. *Economic Letters, 8*(3), 201–207.

Thaler, R. H. & Shefrin, H. M. (1981). An economic theory of self-control. *Journal of Political Economy, 89*(2), 392–406.

Thaler, R. H. & Sunstein, C. R. (2009). *Nudge*. New York: Penguin Books.

Thomas, D. S. (1927). *Social aspects of the business cycle*. New York: Alfred A. Knopf.

Thun, M. J., Peto, R., Lopez, A. D., Monaco, J. H., Henley, S. J., Heath, C. W., Jr., et al. (1997). Alcohol consumption and mortality among middle-aged and elderly U.S. adults. *New England Journal of Medicine, 337*(24) (December 11), 1705–1714.

Tosun, M. S. & Skidmore, M. L. (2007). Cross-border shopping and the sales tax: An examination of food purchases in West Virginia. *B.E. Journal of Economic Analysis & Policy: Topics, 7*(1), Article 63.

Trogdon, J. G., Nonnemaker, J., & Pais, J. (2008). Peer effects in adolescent overweight. *Journal of Health Economics, 27*, 1388–1399.

Troiano, R. P., Berrigan, D., Dodd, K. W., Masse, L. C., Tilert, T., & McDowell, M. (2008). Physical activity in the United States measured by accelerometer. *Medicine & Science in Sports & Exercise, 40*(1), 181–188.

US Department of Health, Education and Human Welfare (1964). *Smoking and health: Report of the Advisory Committee to the Surgeon General of the Public Health Service.* Washington, DC: US Government Printing Office.

US Department of Health and Human Services (1990). The health benefits of smoking cessation: A report of the surgeon general. Atlanta, GA: US Dept. of Health and Human Services, Public Health Service, Centers for Disease Control, Center for Chronic Disease Prevention and Health Promotion, Office on Smoking and Health.

US Department of Health and Human Services (2009). *National healthcare disparities report* (March). Rockville, MD: AHRQ Publication No. 10-0004.

Van Ours, J. C. (1995). The price elasticity of hard drugs: The case of opium in the Dutch East Indies, 1923–1938. *Journal of Political Economy, 103*(2), 261–279.

Van Ours, J. C. (2004). A pint a day raises a man's pay; but smoking blows that gain away. *Journal of Health Economics, 23*, 863–886.

Van Ours, J. C. (2007). The effects of cannabis use on wages of prime-age males. *Oxford Bulletin of Economics and Statistics, 69*(5), 619–634.

Variyam, J. N. (2008). Do nutrition labels improve dietary outcomes? *Health Economics, 17*, 695–708.

Variyam, J. N. & Cawley, J. (2006). Nutrition labels and obesity. NBER Working Paper #11956.

Viscusi, W. K. (1990). Do smokers underestimate risks? *Journal of Political Economy, 98*(6) (December), 1253–1269.

Vohs, K., Baumeister, R. F., Schmeichel, B. J., Twenge, J. M., Nelson, N. M., & Tice, D. M. (2008). Making choices impairs subsequent self-control: A limited-resource account of decision making, self-regulation, and active initiative. *Journal of Personality and Social Psychology, 94*(5) (May), 883–898.

Volpp, K. G., Gurmankin Levy, A., Asch, D. A., Berlin, J. A., Murphy, J. J., Gomez, A., et al. (2006). A randomized trial of financial incentives for smoking cessation. *Cancer Epidemiology, Biomarkers and Prevention, 15*(1) (January), 12–18.

Volpp, K. G., John, L. K., Troxel, A. B., et al. (2008). Financial incentive based approaches for weight loss: A randomized trial. *Journal of the American Medical Association, 300*(22), 2631–2637.

Volpp, K. G., Troxel, A. B., Pauly, M. V., Glick, H. A., Puig, A., Asch, D. A., et al. (2009). A randomized, controlled trial of financial incentives for smoking cessation. *New England Journal of Medicine, 360*(7) (February 12), 699–709.

Wada, R. & Tekin, E. (2010). Body composition and wages. *Economics and Human Biology, 8*(2), 242–254.

Wagenaar, A. C. & Toomey, T. L. (2002). Effects of minimum drinking age laws: Review and analysis of the literature from 1960 to 2000. *Journal of Studies on Alcohol Supplement No. 14, 63*(2) (March), 206–225.

Wagenaar, A. C., Salois, M. J., & Komro, K. A. (2009). Effects of beverage alcohol price and tax levels on drinking: A meta-analysis of 1003 estimates from 112 studies. *Addiction, 104*, 179–190.

Wallinga, D., Schoonover, H., & Muller, M. (2009). Considering the contribution of US agricultural policy to the obesity epidemic: Overview and implications. *Journal of Hunger and Nutrition, 4*(1) (January), 3–19.

Wang, R. (2007). The optimal consumption and quitting of harmful addictive goods. *B.E. Journal of Economic Analysis and Policy, 7*(1) (*Contributions*: Article 15).

Waters, T. M. & Sloan, F. A. (1995). Why do people drink? Tests of the rational addiction model. *Applied Economics*, *27*, 727–736.

Weatherburn, D., Jones, C., Freeman, K., & Makkai, T. (2002). Supply control and harm reduction: Lessons from the Australian heroin "drought." *Addiction*, *98*, 83–91.

Wilde, P. E. & Ranney, C. K. (2000). The monthly food stamp cycle: Shopping frequency and food intake decisions in an endogenous switching regression framework. *American Journal of Agricultural Economics*, *82*(1) (February), 200–213.

Wisdom, J., Downs, J. S., & Lowenstein, G. (2010). Promoting health choices: Information versus convenience. *American Economic Journal: Applied Economics*, *2*(2) (April), 164–178.

Wooldridge, J. M. (2002). *Econometric analysis of cross section and panel data*. Cambridge, MA: MIT Press.

World Health Organization (2009). *Global health risks: Mortality and burden of disease attributable to selected major risks*. Geneva: WHO Press.

Xu, X. and Kaestner, R. (2010). The business cycle and health behaviors. National Bureau of Economic Research Working Paper No. 15737, February.

Yakusheva, O., Kapinos, K. & Weiss, M. (2009). The Freshman 15: Evidence of peer effects and environmental influences from a natural experiment. Working Paper, Marquette University.

Young, D. J. & Likens, T. W. (2000). Alcohol regulation and auto fatalities. *International Review of Law and Economics*, *20*(1) (March), 107–126.

Zhang, F., Huang, C. L., & Lin, B.-H. (2008). Modeling fresh organic produce consumption with scanner data: A generalized double-hurdle model approach. *Agribusiness*, *24*(4) (October), 510–522.

Zhang, Q. & Wang, Y. (2004). Trends in the association between obesity and socioeconomic status in U. S. adults: 1971 to 2000. *Obesity Research*, *12*(10) (October), 1622–1632.

Zhang, L. & Rashad, I. (2008). Obesity and time preference: The health consequences of discounting the future. *Journal of Biosocial Science*, *40*, 97–113.

Zohrabian, A. & Philipson, T. J. (2010). External costs of risky health behaviors associated with leading actual causes of death in the U.S.: A review of the evidence and implications for future research. *International Journal of Environmental Research Public Health*, *7*, 2460–2472.

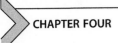

CHAPTER FOUR

Improving Health in Developing Countries: Evidence from Randomized Evaluations[1]

Michael Kremer* and Rachel Glennerster**
*Harvard University, Center for Global Development, USA
**Abdul Latif Jameel Poverty Action Lab, MIT, USA

Contents

[1] We are grateful to Jacobus de Hoop, Ludovica Gazze, Martin Rotemberg, Mahvish Shaukat, and Anna Yalouris for excellent research assistance. This chapter draws on Ahuja et al. (2010); Holla and Kremer (2009); Glennerster et al. (2009); and Bates et al. (2011).

Handbook of Health Economics, Volume 2
ISSN: 1574-0064, DOI: 10.1016/B978-0-444-53592-4.00004-9

Abstract

We summarize evidence from the growing body of randomized evaluations on health in developing countries from the perspective of the human capital investment model, cost-effectiveness analysis, and behavioral economics. Many cost-effective methods of infectious disease prevention have limited uptake. Contributing factors include externalities from infectious disease prevention, public goods problems, liquidity constraints, and behavioral factors, such as present bias and limited attention. Across a variety of contexts, consumer use of cost-effective products for prevention and non-acute care is highly sensitive to price and convenience. Health education has a mixed record, often working in combination with incentives and functioning through increasing salience rather than delivering information. The quality of health services in many developing countries is very poor, with weak incentives for public sector health workers. Reforms that strengthen incentives show promise but institutional details matter. Programs based on this more nuanced understanding of health decision making can save millions of lives.

Key words: health; developing countries; randomized experiments; program evaluation

JEL code: C93; D03; I15; O12

1. INTRODUCTION

The development of modern medical and public health technologies, such as vaccines, antibiotics, and anti-malarials, has allowed for huge progress against infectious disease, and has made historically unprecedented levels of health possible even at low income levels. Life expectancy in countries with per capita income of under $1,000 is 57 years (WHO, 2010b), a decade longer than it was in the US in 1900, when per capita income was over $5,000 (in current dollars).

Whereas historical improvements in health in today's rich countries came largely from rising incomes, better nutrition, improved sanitation, and cleaner water (Fogel, 2002; Cutler and Miller, 2005), analyses of worldwide health trends in the 20th century suggest that most improvements resulted from technological advances rather than income growth. Preston (1975) estimates that income growth accounted for only 10–25 percent of the increase in worldwide life expectancy between the 1930s and the 1960s, and suggests that technological advances were a key factor driving the improvement. Subsequent research—for example, Jamison et al. (2001)—also suggests a key role for technological advances.

Largely as a result of the development and diffusion of low-cost, easy to implement public health technologies for control of infectious disease, the likelihood of a child in a low-income country dying before reaching age five almost halved, falling from 233 per 1,000 live births in 1970 to 118 per 1,000 births in 2009 (World Bank, 2011). Life expectancy rose 27 percent, from 45 to 57 years, over that period.

Yet infectious and parasitic diseases continue to account for one-third of the disease burden in low-income countries, and over half of Africa's disease burden—compared to less than 3 percent of the burden of disease in high-income countries (WHO, 2008).

This is in large part because the spread of low-cost technologies for prevention of infectious disease remains incomplete. The excess burden of disease in developing countries could be substantially reduced by higher take-up of a range of low-cost public health products that do not require individual diagnosis, such as mosquito nets, vaccinations, chlorine treatment of drinking water, deworming, and male circumcision (which reduces the rate of HIV transmission). These approaches are the low hanging fruit of global health, easily meeting the cost-effectiveness thresholds used for developing countries in the health cost-effectiveness literature, thresholds that are themselves a tiny fraction of those used in developed countries.

Increasingly, however, as economies and health budgets grow, the burden of disease in today's poor and middle-income countries will become more similar to that in richer countries. Further improving health will require diagnosis, and thus will require effectively motivating health providers. Unfortunately, health systems in developing countries are often highly dysfunctional, with public providers facing very weak incentives and many private providers facing distorted incentives.

In this chapter, we review evidence on these issues from the new wave of randomized evaluations in development economics that began in 1995 with a series of evaluations in western Kenya (Kremer, 2003). Like earlier randomized evaluations, such as the major evaluation of consumer responsiveness to different copayments and deductibles in the US in the 1970s (Manning et al., 1987), these are designed to allow isolation of the causal impact from potential confounding variables. There is considerable evidence that non-experimental estimates often differ from experimental ones (LaLonde, 1986). Unlike the earlier, very large, studies, which typically focused on a single program or issue, the new wave often involves academics working iteratively with NGOs and other implementers, allowing examination of multiple approaches to addressing an issue in a common setting. This enables researchers to tease out the relative importance of different factors and allows comparisons of the cost effectiveness of different approaches. Moreover, by forcing researchers to engage with realities on the ground, it allows the discovery of new factors influencing behavior beyond those suggested by existing models. As studies accumulate, we are increasingly learning not just about the impact of specific programs, but uncovering underlying determinants of behavior. This in turn is allowing the development of new approaches to health challenges.

Much of the recent literature focuses on understanding the reasons for apparently suboptimal take-up of public health measures against infectious disease. There is evidence of multiple market failures in public health that lead to under-provision of these goods in the absence of public action: externalities from prevention of infectious disease transmission, public goods such as water infrastructure, credit constraints that prevent investment, and lack of information among health consumers. Failures to invest in some highly effective child health interventions could be interpreted as reflecting contracting difficulties within the family.

Beyond these market failures, there is evidence that behavioral factors further reduce consumption below the level that would be chosen by rational investors in human capital in the face of these market distortions. Much of this evidence comes from studies of the impact of pricing that, if not necessarily delivering sharp rejections of models of rational health human capital investment individually, collectively seem to point to a role for time-inconsistent preferences and limited attention in explaining health behavior. Across a variety of settings, many people who use public health technologies for prevention or non-acute care at a zero price will not use them at even a small positive price. Convenience has a big impact on take-up. Households which could benefit more from particular health technologies often are not willing to pay more for them. Small incentives can have seemingly disproportionate effects. Consumers exhibit demand for commitment. While some responses to health education and peer behavior are consistent with a model of Bayesian learning, others seem more consistent with the importance of salience.

Policy approaches based on these insights, such as free (or negatively priced), convenient, and salient provision, seem to hold promise for encouraging take-up of cost-effective public health goods that are aimed at prevention or non-acute care of infectious disease and that do not require diagnosis. Improved take-up of these products in turn holds the promise of substantially low-cost improvements in health.

Many of the market failures and behavioral factors that lead to suboptimal investment in preventive health measures against infectious disease do not necessarily apply to the majority of curative care services. These services often require skilled personnel for diagnosis, but incentive systems for public health workers are weak enough that some question the utility of public health facilities in improving health (Das and Hammer, 2004, 2007; Das et al., 2008). Many therefore turn to private providers, but weak regulatory systems mean these are often untrained and have distorted incentives.

Earlier, non-randomized, work suggests that consumers bear considerable risk due to health shocks. Despite this, demand for unsubsidized insurance seems low.

While it is too early to draw firm conclusions, there is evidence that stronger incentives for providers, for example through competitive contracts to provide health care in an area, and empowerment of local communities can improve provision. Yet there is also evidence that reform will be politically difficult to implement.

As noted, this chapter focuses on randomized evaluations addressing issues of health economics (rather than medical trials of whether a technology works). We pay particular attention to the poorest countries where health challenges are particularly acute and returns to health investment can be very high. Although we draw on non-randomized research that describes the state of health and health systems in the developing world, as this is essential background to understanding the challenges that the policies and programs evaluated are seeking to address, and we do provide some signposts to key papers and literature reviews, we do not attempt to cover the large non-randomized literature on health.

Readers who want to know more about the global burden of disease or the cost effectiveness of different health technologies can refer to WHO (2008), Deaton (2003), Jamison et al. (2006), and Rao et al. (2006). For more information on the complex relationship between health and population policies we refer the reader to Schultz (2009). Readers interested in traditional care in developing countries may refer to Debas et al. (2006), while those interested in global health R&D, pharmaceutical markets, or intellectual property rights may refer to Goldberg (2010), Kremer (2002), and to Kremer and Glennerster (2004). Readers interested in health care financing may refer to Hsiao (2007) and Dunlop and Martins (1995) for reviews. Major reviews on the impact of health in the larger process of economic development and growth include Strauss and Thomas (1998, 2007), López-Casasnovas et al. (2005), Glewwe and Miguel (2007), Currie (2009), Spence and Lewis (2009), Bleakley (2010a), Eide and Showalter (2011), and Dupas (2011b).

This chapter is about health in developing countries, and the health context and institutions differ with country income levels. Nonetheless, it is worth noting that many of the issues we discuss reflect general issues in health economics. In particular, the insights of behavioral economics are proving relevant for understanding health behavior in both developed and developing countries contexts (see Frank, 2004 for a review of behavioral economics implications on health care that apply to developed countries).

This chapter is organized as follows. Section 2 briefly discusses two conceptual frameworks that the rest of the chapter draws on: a model of rational investment in health, human capital, and cost-effectiveness analysis. Section 3 presents evidence on the importance of externalities and public goods issues that the human capital model of health investment suggests will lead to under-provision of public health goods in the absence of subsidies. Section 4 examines the impact of pricing and convenience on take-up of cost-effective technologies for prevention and non-acute care of infectious disease. Section 5 discusses the impact of conditional cash transfers and smaller-scale incentives to encourage take-up. Section 6 examines evidence on the price sensitivity of demand for acute care and general health services. Section 7 analyzes the impact of liquidity constraints on health behavior. In section 8, we argue that behavioral models of present bias and limited attention may be useful in explaining why small prices or convenience barriers can dramatically reduce take-up of cost-effective approaches to prevention and non-acute care. Section 9 examines health education. Section 10 examines peer influences on health behavior. We argue that while some of the findings on health education and peer effects are potentially driven by learning, others likely reflect salience and social norms.

Having discussed determinants of household demand for health, we turn our attention to supply. Section 11 briefly reviews the descriptive literature on health delivery systems in poor countries, noting both the weak incentives and high absence rates common among public sector health workers and the presence of many untrained, low-quality private providers (Banerjee et al., 2004a and b; Chaudhury et al., 2006; Das and Hammer, 2007). Section 12 summarizes evidence on the effectiveness of alternative reform approaches that seek to improve incentives of suppliers, including contracting out health services, payment for performance, and strengthening the knowledge and bargaining power of consumers through community mobilization and participation.

Section 13 provides background on the impact of health on non-health outcomes, and on the impact of addressing other economic variables on health.

2. CONCEPTUAL FRAMEWORK FOR HOUSEHOLD DECISION MAKING

In this handbook chapter, we will draw both on a model of rational investment in health as human capital investment and on cost-effectiveness analysis.

2.1. Health as Human Capital Investment

The revealed preference interpretation of human capital theory (Grossman, 2000) suggests that consumers will invest in health if the expected discounted private benefit, including the utility benefit, exceeds the cost, both in financial and in utility terms. Under this approach, one could interpret decisions not to use a condom or chlorinate water, for example, as reflecting disutility from prevention activities, high discount rates (due either to time preference or to high expected mortality rates), or low valuation of life.

Suppose that in every period, individuals have an endowment w_t that they can spend on a consumption good (denoted c_t), prevention, or drug treatment.[2] People who do not undertake a prevention measure (vaccination, for example) have an episode of illness with an independent probability π each period. If sick, individual i receives a disutility x_i. This varies across the population with distribution g. For example, children and women pregnant with their first child are much more likely to die of malaria than most adults. Moreover, the disease reduces people's endowment of time by z.

A vaccine permanently lowers the probability of getting sick to $\pi^V < \pi$ at a price p^V. Getting vaccinated causes a one-time disutility of $m_i \sim f$, which is uncorrelated with the disutility from getting sick. A drug to treat the disease can be purchased at a price p^D and works with probability $1 - \pi^D$. The utility function at time t can thus be expressed by:

$$V_t = U_t(c, h, m) + \beta \sum_{s=t+1}^{\infty} \delta^s E_t[U_s(c, h, m)], \tag{4.1}$$

given a utility function

$$U_t(c, h, m) = u(c_t) - x_i * 1(h_t) - m_i(P). \tag{4.2}$$

$1(P)$ is the indicator function for whether the individual buys the prevention good at time t, and $1(h_t)$ is an indicator function of health status of the individual ($h = 1$ if sick, $h = 0$ if healthy).

By allowing for both a β and a δ term we allow for hyperbolic discounting but for now we will focus on the case in which $\beta = 1$ so people are exponential discounters. Assume also that people can borrow and save at the constant world interest rate $1 - \delta$.

Diminishing marginal utility implies that people will want to smooth consumption over time and to buy insurance against the cost of treatment to smooth consumption across states of the world. Consider the case of a perfectly competitive insurance market with perfect monitoring. In this case, the decentralized competitive equilibrium will be the equivalent of the social planner problem.

Given that all people are perfectly insured, there will be a constant consumption level that is supported in equilibrium, denoted c^*, and the marginal utility from consumption at that level is $u'(c^*)$.[3]

---

[2] Think of w_t as the individual's endowment of productive time times their wage rate.

[3] We approximate marginal utility from consumption as constant around this level. This approximation simplifies the expressions below and does not change the key qualitative results. A full solution would need to take into account that the marginal utility of consumption will be slightly different depending on whether people spend money on vaccination or not, but as vaccines are a trivial share of world GDP, this seems innocuous.

Solving the social planner's problem, people should take a treatment if they are sick if the marginal utility cost of the treatment is smaller than the marginal benefit of the treatment, the time and non-pecuniary costs of being sick:

$$u'(c^*)p^D \leq (1 - \pi^D)[u'(c^*)z + x_i]. \tag{4.3}$$

For simplicity, assume this condition is satisfied for the entire population. (Note that if people differed in the risk of infection, there could be an adverse selection problem, but we abstract from that here.)

It is efficient to invest in prevention if the marginal consumption and non-pecuniary costs of vaccination are less than the discounted sum of the benefits from the reduced probability of getting sick. These benefits consist of the cost of treatment plus the loss of time endowment and the non-pecuniary costs of actually being sick if the treatment does not work. Algebraically, this is equivalent to:

$$u'(c^*)p^v + m_i \leq \frac{\delta}{1 - \delta}(\pi - \pi^v)\left[\pi^D(x_i + u'(c)z_\square) + u'(c^*)p^D\right]. \tag{4.4}$$

For an insurance contract to implement this, prevention would have to be monitorable. If there is no way to monitor vaccine use, there may be a moral hazard problem, because, over a range of parameter values, while it would be socially efficient for people to take the vaccine, they may not do so since they incur the full disutility from vaccinating but do not incur the full costs of getting sick, since it is borne in part by the insurance company. This may lead to suboptimal provision of insurance.

The model suggests that insurance providers (including governments in the case of social insurance) may wish to subsidize the cost of prevention or even mandate prevention since they bear part of the cost of disease.

While we focused on the case in which $\beta = 1$, it is worth noting that there is substantial evidence of people behaving according to a quasi-hyperbolic discounting model with $\beta < 1$ (Laibson, 1997). Under hyperbolic discounting, people are present biased, i.e. discount at a higher rate between the present and the immediate future than between two future time periods (Ainslie, 1975, 1992; Loewenstein and Prelec, 1992). This implies that even a small cost in the short run can have a big effect on consumers' behavior. If people are aware that they are present biased (sophisticated) then they may want to commit their future selves to save (Strotz, 1956; Pollack, 1968). In this context, they might want to commit to vaccinate or to treat a chronic disease. (Note that a cure for a chronic disease looks very much like prevention in this model—a one-time upfront cost produces an ongoing stream of benefits.)

The model implies people make the same calculation of expected discounted health benefit against cost for treatment and prevention. Most experts on health cost effectiveness argue that much treatment expenditure is on medically unneeded or even harmful procedures (Das and Hammer, 2007), while many cost-effective prevention opportunities go unexploited. In sections 8 and 9, respectively, we discuss the possibility that consumers are subject to behavioral biases in decision making and/or are ill-informed about prevention.

The model implies that health subsidies will generate increased investment in health both by lowering the price of health investment and through an income effect that stimulates consumption of health care by reducing the marginal utility of other consumption. The model also implies that if people decide to vaccinate, they will do it as soon as possible, without postponing. In the absence of financial markets, individuals' treatment and prevention decisions may depend on their endowments in each period, and someone who has a low endowment in a particular period may wait to vaccinate until later. Below we discuss evidence that some people are more likely to purchase prevention technologies if they are given more time to pay. This can be taken as evidence of credit constraints.

The human capital model is theoretically consistent with a wide variety of patterns through which demand could respond to price, since the distribution of disutility from prevention creates an arbitrary number of free parameters. Note, however, that there is nothing special about a price of zero in this model. For example, a finding of low demand for deworming medicine at a small positive price would indicate that many people had strong disutility from consuming the medicine (assuming health benefits are high). Large disutility costs would need to be invoked to offset the large benefits. Only in a knife-edge case would a large proportion of the population be switched into use by a switch from a low to a zero price. The odds that this would occur for multiple products in multiple settings are particularly low.[4]

The case in which $\beta \ll 1$ (people are present biased) would make the benefits of vaccination small, and hence would imply that small changes in price could have a large impact without invoking large disutility costs that exactly offset large health benefits. As discussed below, the data suggest many people take up health prevention products at zero price, but not at small positive prices.

The model implies that the elasticity of demand for prevention with respect to price will not be a constant, and in fact suggests that elasticities are probably not the most useful way to measure price responsiveness. Any formulation with constant elasticity would imply that as price goes to zero, demand becomes infinite. Demand here is capped at one dose of prevention per household.

We have implicitly assumed a unitary household model. Another implication of the model is that if the prevention good protects all members of the household, such as water treatment, and if some individuals have higher benefits from prevention, such as children who are more vulnerable to diarrhea than adults, then those households

---

[4] High exponential discount rates could also generate this, but would not be consistent with the fact that many people in the studies cited below own land and invest in education, both of which generate only modest returns.

that have a higher share of these vulnerable individuals should value prevention more. It is straightforward to consider several extensions. In the presence of positive epidemiological externalities from vaccination, in any interior solution in which only a portion of the population becomes vaccinated, the level of vaccination will be too low in the absence of subsidies.[5] Since the marginal non-user is close to indifferent to vaccination if there are positive externalities subsidies financed out of taxation can be welfare improving. Section 3 examines externalities.

Above we have taken prices for the vaccine and drug as given. If vaccines and drugs are competitively produced then this assumption is innocuous. However, if production involves paying fixed costs and then some low marginal cost for each additional unit, producers may have market power. Research and development and certain types of health infrastructure (e.g. water and sanitation infrastructure) will have this property. In general, unless the producer can perfectly price discriminate, the monopolist will price above marginal production cost. There will be a static deadweight loss since some consumers who would use the vaccine at marginal cost will not use it at equilibrium prices. Moreover, incentives to invest in developing the vaccine or building the water infrastructure will be suboptimal because the monopolist will capture only a fraction of the consumer surplus. (Kremer and Snyder (2006) examine differences in the ability of vaccine and drug producers to appropriate consumer surplus.)

2.2. Cost-effectiveness Analysis

In many societies, governments and policymakers believe that it is normatively desirable to improve average population health as much as possible within the budget that has been allocated to health. Under cost-effectiveness analysis, expenditure on one health measure is considered more desirable than another when the cost of achieving a particular outcome (such as averting an infant death) with this measure is lower. In some variants of this approach, systems such as Disability Adjusted Life Years (DALYs) or Quality Adjusted Life Years (QALYs) are used to put morbidity and mortality on a common scale, as well as to compare deaths at different ages.[6] (In contrast, the revealed preference version of the human capital approach takes satisfying people's preferences as the normative objective.) In this chapter we will examine health issues from both points of view.

Many different cutoff points have been used in the literature to define what health expenditures are cost effective for governments and donors in poor countries. These range from $100 per DALY used by some in the 1980s, to $150 per DALY suggested by the WHO in the 1990s, to more recent calls to use per capita GDP as a threshold

---

[5] While this proposition is straightforward, actually solving for equilibrium in these models is more complicated because prevalence and health behavior are simultaneously determined (Geoffard and Philipson, 1997; Kremer et al., 2008; Kremer, 1996).

[6] The assumptions underlying such systems are debatable. See Lewin et al. (2008) and Walker and Fox-Rushb (2000).

(which would imply around $400 per DALY saved for even the poorest countries). Programs that cost $50,000 or even $100,000 per DALY are often considered cost effective in developed countries.

The uncertainties, conceptual and empirical, in estimating costs per DALY or QALY suggest that such estimates should be interpreted as giving a rough sense of priorities rather than a precise ranking. Moreover, the actual cost effectiveness of a program will vary considerably depending on local circumstances, such as population density and disease prevalence.

Below we provide some background on technologies which: are highly cost effective under even the most conservative standard for cost effectiveness, with costs per DALY averted under $100; have incomplete coverage; and have been the subject of randomized evaluations in health economics and are thus discussed later in this chapter.

One million people die every year from malaria (WHO, 2010a). Insecticide-Treated Nets (ITNs) have been estimated to reduce all-cause child mortality by up to 38 percent in areas where malaria is endemic (D'Alessandro et al., 1995), and have an estimated cost per DALY saved of less than $50.[7] It was estimated that only 19 percent of children in areas where malaria is endemic in Africa were protected by ITNs in 2007 (Noor et al., 2009), although coverage rates for ITNs have increased sharply in past years as a result of concentrated policy action.

Roughly two million children die each year from water-borne diseases. Point-of-use chlorination of drinking water reduces reported incidence of diarrhea, and under certain assumptions has an estimated cost of $53 per DALY saved (J-PAL, 2010),[8] but less than 10 percent of households in sub-Saharan Africa use point-of-use chlorination.

Coverage rates for childhood immunization are much higher than the other technologies discussed here. Nevertheless, at least 27 million children do not receive the basic package of immunizations each year, despite vaccination being one of the most cost-effective health products known (with an estimated cost of $13 per DALY saved), and 2—3 million people die yearly from vaccine-preventable diseases (WHO, 2008; UNICEF, 2008).

Simple deworming drugs can rid children and adults of intestinal parasites that cause lethargy and anemia, and cost only pennies per dose. Deworming is estimated to cost $5 per DALY saved, and to lead to gains between 21 and 29 percent in

---

[7] These estimates take into account the benefits to others in the community of hanging an insecticide-treated net. Wiseman et al. (2003) estimate that cost per DALY rises to $65 excluding the positive externality to the rest of the (uncovered) community, society as a whole. Note that if consumers are free to save and borrow, and if prevention works indefinitely, they will either purchase prevention as early as possible or not at all.

[8] J-PAL's estimates are based on the assumption that the treatment-on-treated effect of chlorine on diarrhea is 37 percent and that reductions in diarrhea mortality and morbidity are proportional to reductions in reported diarrhea.

earnings for those who work for wages later in life (Baird et al., 2011a). Yet, despite these benefits, of the 400 million children estimated to be infected with these parasites worldwide, only 10 percent are being treated (WHO, 2006).

While these examples suggest that many cost-effective prevention technologies against infectious disease are not being used, as discussed in later sections, there is reason to believe that much treatment of acute conditions has a higher cost per DALY or is medically ineffective altogether.

3. EXTERNALITIES AND PUBLIC GOODS

The human capital model suggests that in the absence of subsidies, health investment will be suboptimal if (1) treatment or prevention creates positive externalities by reducing transmission of disease, or (2) infrastructure investment is a public good, so that once, for example, water infrastructure is in place, it can be accessed at a marginal cost less than the average cost.

Section 3.1 examines non-excludable externalities, focusing on the case of deworming, and section 3.2 examines the case of excludable public goods, focusing on water infrastructure.

3.1. Non-excludable Public Goods

Intestinal helminthes, or worms, including hookworm, roundworm, whipworm, and schistosomiasis, are spread through contact with contaminated soil and water. Because worms can be treated relatively simply and cheaply, but diagnosis is expensive, the WHO recommends yearly treatment for all schoolchildren in schools where more than half of the children are believed to be infected or where any child passes blood in their urine as a result of schistosomiasis. (Schools are a particularly convenient way to target children and school-age children have high worm loads and are considered to be a major source of infection.) Treatment kills worms that are already in a person's body, reducing the chance that they will deposit eggs into the environment.

Miguel and Kremer (2004) estimate the direct and externality impact of deworming. They argue that studies of the impact of disease control that are randomized at the individual level may yield biased estimates of treatment effects, because the treatment may affect the comparison group.

They examine an NGO program which provided school-based mass treatment with inexpensive deworming drugs (Albendazole and Praziquantel) and health education. The order in which treatment was phased in to 75 primary schools was determined by counting off on a list which schools were grouped geographically and then alphabetically within geographical locations. In the first treatment group, 92 percent

Table 4.1 Externalities and Public Goods

Technology	Researchers	Country	Program Tested	Results
3.1. Non-excludable Externalities				
Deworming treatment	Miguel and Kremer (2004)	Kenya	Mass school-based deworming treatment provided to students free of charge. Education component stressed the importance of worm-prevention behaviors.	Deworming reduced student absenteeism by 25% in treatment schools and had substantial health benefits. 25 percentage point reduction in moderate/heavy infections. Significant externalities: Untreated students in treatment schools have 12 percentage points less heavy worm infections. Untreated children in nearby schools also had lower infections. No impact of health education on behavior.
Deworming treatment (long-run follow-up)	Baird et al. (2011a)	Kenya	Follow-up study to Miguel and Kremer (2004) tracks long-run outcomes of children dewormed in 1998.	Deworming treatment leads to average consumption increase of 0.1 meals per day and 12% more hours worked. Among those with wage employment, earnings are 21–29% higher and one-third fewer days are lost to illness.
Deworming treatment (long-run externalities)	Ozier (2010)	Kenya	Investigates whether primary school deworming had long-run impacts on younger siblings who were not dewormed.	Younger children who were not directly treated gained 0.5cm in height, had 6 percentage points reduction in stunting, and improved cognitive outcomes.

(Continued)

Table 4.1 (Continued)

Technology	Researchers	Country	Program Tested	Results
Insecticide-treated nets (spatial analysis)	Hawley et al. (2003)	Kenya	Spatial analyses of the effect of net use on nearby households both with and without nets.	With 50% of households sleeping under net, households within 300 meters have equivalent protection to those with nets.
3.2. Excludable Public Goods				
Water source improvement	Kremer et al. (2011b)	Kenya	To protect water from ground contamination, natural springs were encased in concrete with pipe to bring water to surface.	Spring protection reduces fecal contamination by two-thirds at the water source, 25% reduction in child diarrhea. Combining a structural model with estimated valuations based on willingness to walk suggests that private ownership of springs would lead to substantial underinvestment and static distortions.

Note: Shaded rows represent non-randomized studies.

of pupils had at least one worm infection prior to treatment and 37 percent had a moderate-to-heavy infection. Distances between schools were tracked so that spillovers between schools could be estimated.

After one year, the group of schools treated first (Group 1) experienced substantial health benefits relative to comparison schools, which only received the treatments later after the second and third phase-ins (Groups 2 and 3). The share of children with moderate to heavy infections caused by hookworms, roundworms, and schistosomiasis was significantly lower: 27 percent in Group 1 versus 52 percent in the comparison groups 2 and 3. Pupils in Group 1 also displayed better height-for-age measurements and less self-reported illness.

There was also evidence of treatment externalities. Controlling for the total density of school children within three and within six kilometers, infection rates were lower if more of these pupils were in Group 1 schools. The presence of each additional thousand pupils attending Group 1 schools located within three kilometers of a school is associated with 26 percentage points fewer moderate-to-heavy infections. Going further away, each additional thousand pupils attending a Group 1 school located between three and six kilometers away is associated with 14 percentage points fewer moderate-to-heavy infections. Moreover, the rate of moderate-to-heavy infections after the first year of the program was 12 percentage points lower among Group 1 pupils who did not receive deworming treatment in year one (about 22 percent of the treatment school pupils did not receive treatment) than among students in Group 2 schools who did not receive treatment in the second year of the program (their schools' first year of the program).[9]

In addition to these health benefits, the program substantially increased school participation, which was measured by four unannounced visits per year. Deworming reduced the baseline absence rate of 30 percent by 7 percentage points (or one-quarter) in treatment schools, a gain in attendance that reflects both the direct effect of deworming and any within-school externalities.[10] Positive cross-school externalities were also observed in school attendance. Including the cross-school externalities, deworming increased schooling by 0.14 years per pupil treated. Therefore, taking into account these externalities, each $3.50 spent on deworming is estimated to generate an additional year of school participation. As Figure 4.1 demonstrates, this makes school-based deworming one of the most cost-effective ways of improving school attendance, although welfare judgments should obviously be based on a range of factors beyond the impact on schooling. See Dhaliwal et al. (2011).

---

[9] The potential for selection bias precludes any comparison between students in Group 1 who did not receive treatment in the first year and all of Group 2 students in the first year of the program (when Group 2 schools still had not received any treatment) because the children who chose not to receive treatment may be systematically different in terms of observed and unobserved health or education-related behaviors from children who chose to receive treatment (most of the Group 2 students in the second year of the program).

[10] Bleakley and Lin (2007) find an effect of a similar magnitude in their non-randomized study of hookworm eradication in the US South in the early 20th century.

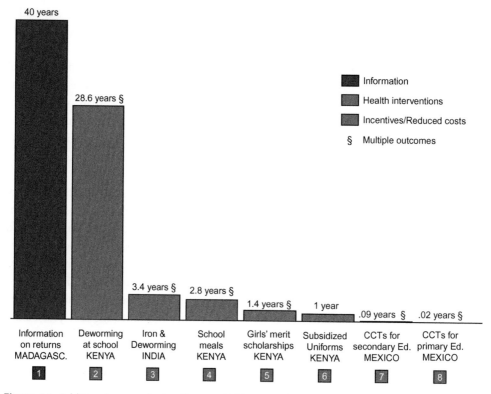

Figure 4.1 Additional years of schooling per $100 spent. *Source: www.povertyactionlab.org*

Baird et al. (2011a) examine the long-term consequences of deworming, estimating that treatment leads to an increase in consumption of about 0.1 meals per day on average and that hours worked increase by 12 percent. Among those with positive hours, work days lost to illness fall by a third. For those with wage employment, earnings are 21 to 29 percent higher in the treatment group. A large share of the earnings gains are explained by sectoral shifts, for instance through a doubling of manufacturing employment and a drop in casual labor. Both education and health gains are plausible channels. If better health improves the capacity to work longer hours, as in the original formulation of health capital in Grossman (2000), who argues that it is precisely this increase in "non-sick" time that distinguishes health investments from other types of human capital investment, then gains in work hours could be considered as part of a welfare gain, which would imply very high returns to deworming.

Long-run externality benefits are not estimated precisely. Almost all estimated effects are positive, and some, such as that on the number of meals consumed the previous day, are significant. Point estimates suggest that just the externality benefit of deworming would be sufficient to justify fully subsidizing treatment.

Ozier (2010) estimates the long-run spillover effects of deworming on younger children who were not directly treated. These children are at ages where developmental effects are likely to be more important. He estimates that the program led to an additional 0.5 cm in height, a 6-percentage-point reduction in stunting, and substantial cognitive gains. Most of these effects are likely to occur within households where they could potentially be internalized.

Positive externalities are likely to be found more generally in treatment or prevention of infectious diseases. Insecticide-treated nets kill mosquitoes, thus providing some protection to neighbors. The medical evidence is unclear, but a reasonable hypothesis is that at low levels of coverage, there is substantial private benefit from hanging an insecticide-treated net, but that at high levels of coverage, the benefit is primarily an externality. Hawley et al. (2003) find that if more than 50 percent of households within a 300-meter radius had long-lasting insecticide-treated nets hung, the remaining households had equivalent protection to those that had nets. Similar studies have not been undertaken to test the extent of externalities for some of the other technologies discussed here, such as water treatment. It is plausible to think that externalities would be important here, however, because of the risk of passing diarrhea on to other members of the community. This is an important gap in the literature where further research would be useful.

Kremer et al. (2008) argue that in a simple model of infectious disease, the benefits of vaccination or other prevention efforts are primarily captured by the user at high levels of prevalence, but are primarily externality benefits at low levels of prevalence. Not all health externalities, however, are positive. The use of partial courses of antibiotics increases the risk of drug resistance. The resulting negative externality creates a potential rationale for taxation or regulation.

3.2. Excludable Public Goods

Some health goods, such as water infrastructure, are public goods in the sense that the marginal cost of serving additional customers is low once the infrastructure is in place, although the good or service is nonetheless excludable. Such goods are natural monopolies. If an infrastructure supplier could perfectly price discriminate, exactly extracting consumer surplus from consumers, there would be no static losses from market power. Firms would have appropriate incentives to invest if and only if total consumer surplus from the infrastructure were greater than the cost of provision. However, if the supplier cannot perfectly price discriminate, there will be static deadweight losses and insufficient investment incentives. Depending on parameter values, society may be better off regulating prices to reduce static inefficiencies, even if this limits dynamic incentives to install infrastructure.

Kremer et al. (2011b) examine the case of spring protection, a water infrastructure technology. In the study area, many people collect water from naturally occurring springs, which can be contaminated with fecal matter from runoff from surrounding fields or by contact with people's hands when they collect water. Springs can be protected by adding a pipe to bring the spring water to the surface and surrounding the spring with a simple concrete base. Since water from these springs otherwise trickles away, the marginal cost of the water is zero, and a price of zero creates static efficiency. Social norms, as in many parts of the world, make it difficult for landowners to charge neighbors for collecting drinking water. However, a zero price provides landowners with very little incentive to invest in improving the quality of their source, for example through spring protection.

The authors evaluate a program which protected a random subsample of springs. They estimate that protecting springs reduced fecal contamination as measured by the presence of *E. coli* bacteria by two-thirds in water at the source, and by 25 percent for water stored at home. (The difference is likely due in large part to recontamination in transport and storage within the household (Wright et al., 2004).) Mothers reported about 25 percent less child diarrhea in the treatment group. Children under three years old are the most affected by the program, and in the medium run (three years after the program) shows increases in Body Mass Index (BMI).

After estimating the impact of spring protection on health, Kremer et al. (2011b) use a travel cost model and information on households' choices of whether to walk further to collect water from protected springs to estimate their willingness to pay for spring protection. Under some additional assumptions, including the maintained assumption of a model of health behavior as rational human capital investment, they can estimate willingness to pay for reductions in diarrhea and the value of a statistical life. They find that revealed preference measures of valuation are much lower than stated preference measures, and estimate very low willingness to pay for child survival under a human capital model. These estimates are consistent with the Hall and Jones (2007) model, which suggests an income elasticity greater than one for the value of life. (As discussed below, an alternative interpretation is that the maintained assumptions of the rational human capital model are a poor guide to behavior in this situation.)

A final section of the spring protection paper combines the estimates of willingness to pay with a structural model to estimate the impact of alternative policies and property right systems on water investment and welfare. The authors compute the pattern of spring protection that would be chosen either by a "revealed-preference social planner" seeking to maximize welfare as indicated by the revealed preference of households or by a "health planner" willing to spend $125 per DALY (roughly five times the estimated households' average revealed valuation). The "health planner" would protect many more springs.

The local social norms preventing spring owners from charging neighbors for household water achieves static efficiency because the marginal cost of collecting spring water is zero since water flows out of the ground without a pump, user congestion is minimal, and unused water simply flows away. But, as noted above, these norms are at odds with dynamic efficiency because at zero price landowners will not invest in spring protection. Private property rights allow spring owners to charge for access to spring water, providing an incentive to invest in protection, but also introduce a static distortion in water source choice as households choose water sources that would be less preferred based on walking time and water contamination, the factors that are statically efficient for them to consider.

The authors find that at current income levels, the existing system of common property rights delivers higher welfare than a private property rights system, since landowners would protect only 5 percent of springs even under private property rights. However, at higher levels of income, private property rights could stimulate sufficient investment in spring protection to outweigh the static costs associated with giving landowners local market power over water resources.

For realistic values of the deadweight loss of taxation, from the perspective of either the "revealed preference social planner" or the "health social planner," public financing of springs together with free provision of water generates higher welfare than either common property without government investment in spring protection or pure private property. A voucher system in which spring owners who protect springs receive payments based on the number of users could potentially do a reasonably good job of approximating the social planner solution. Although the authors do not model this explicitly, such a system would also provide landowners with incentives to maintain water sources.

A huge problem with water infrastructure is maintenance. For a discussion of the high rates of poor maintenance and the impact of ethnic diversity on maintenance of water infrastructure, see Miguel and Gugerty (2005). Leino (2011) finds that increasing women's participation did not impact maintenance outcomes or quality, although Chattopadhay and Duflo (2004) and Duflo and Topalova (2003) find that villages randomly selected to have leadership positions reserved for women invest more in water and have higher quality drinking water. Kremer et al. (2011c) discuss the impact of various approaches to community management of local water infrastructure.

4. THE IMPACT OF PRICE AND CONVENIENCE ON PREVENTION BEHAVIOR AGAINST INFECTIOUS DISEASE

In this section we review evidence on the impact of price and convenience on demand for health goods. We first outline the effects of price and convenience on overall demand for the prevention and non-acute treatment of infectious disease. We then examine the evidence on whether prices help target these health investments to those who would benefit most. Across disparate products and contexts, small prices deter many from investing in prevention and prices do not effectively target those with the greatest health needs. In the following sections, we discuss the impact of conditional cash transfers and of smaller incentive payments and the evidence on the impact of pricing on demand for general health care and for treatment (section 5), and discuss their implications for models for health as human capital investment. We then discuss the extent to which liquidity constraints (section 7), behavioral factors (section 8), and lack of information (section 9) are plausible contributors to low demand.

Under the human capital investment model with heterogeneous agents, those with greater health benefits from a product will, ceteris paribus, be more willing to pay for it (unless benefits are highly negatively correlated with disutility from prevention activities). Partly based on this rationale, in the 1980s there was a strong push from organizations, such as the World Bank and the International Monetary Fund, to charge fees in order to prevent wastage and improve targeting of products on those who need them. The push was supported by evidence from surveys suggesting that the poor were willing to spend money on health.[11]

Opponents of fees were and are concerned that fees reduce the take-up of highly cost-effective products and impede the poor's access to health care.[12] They point out that even when government policies theoretically exempt the poor in practice, this type of price differentiation is often not well enforced.[13]

---

[11] Some of the original advocates of charging fees, including Akin, Birdsall, and de Feranti (1987), suggest that fees should be charged on certain types of services that are not price sensitive and the resulting savings could then be focused on subsidizing programs with positive externalities which might otherwise be under-consumed (such as prevention against infectious diseases).

[12] See Russell (1996) for a model of ability to pay and opportunity costs, as well as a review of common household responses to payment difficulties, ranging from borrowing to more serious "distress sales" of productive assets (e.g. land), delays to treatment and, ultimately, abandonment of treatment.

[13] A study in Sierra Leone, for example, found no distinction between the fees paid for medical care by age of the child even though children under five were exempt from fees (IRCBP, 2007). The same study found that roughly half of families had to pay to get their child immunized even though vaccinations were officially free.

Table 4.2 Impact of Price and Convenience on Prevention Behavior against Infectious Disease

Technology	Researchers	Country	Program Tested	Results
4.1. Pricing and Demand for Preventive and Non-acute Care				
Deworming treatment (cost-sharing)	Kremer and Miguel (2007)	Kenya	Free treatment vs. small fee for deworming treatment.	Free treatment increased take-up from 18% to 75%.
Insecticide-treated nets (prenatal clinics)	Cohen and Dupas (2010)	Kenya	Insecticide-treated nets provided for free or at highly subsidized prices to pregnant women visiting prenatal clinics.	Take-up falls by 60 percentage points when the price increases from zero to $0.60. Charging does not reduce product wastage on those who will not use it, nor target the product to women who need it more. 60% of nets in use in follow-up visits.
Water chlorination	Ashraf et al. (2010a)	Zambia	Bottles of water disinfectant sold door-to-door at varying prices. Additional discount offered once households agreed to buy at initial offer price.	Take-up fell by over 30 percentage points when prices increased from $0.09 to $0.25.
Water chlorination	Kremer et al. (2011a)	Kenya	Suite of randomized experiments test take-up of individually packaged chlorine at free or subsidized prices. Local promoters encourage chlorine use.	Majority of households chlorinate water when provided for free. Take-up is less than 10% at market price and only slightly higher with a 50% discount.

(Continued)

Table 4.2 (Continued)

Technology	Researchers	Country	Program Tested	Results
Water chlorination	Dupas et al. (2010)	Kenya	Mothers bringing their children to vaccination clinics provided with 12-month supply of coupons for dilute chlorine.	Among those offered a 50% discount, less than 15% had detectable chlorine in their water, compared to 40% for those given free supply.
Hand-washing soap	Spears (2010)	India	Handwashing soap sold at varied discounted prices, with highest price still a significant discount. Random group asked questions designed to require thinking about the value of money.	Take-up of soap falls from 84% to 30% as price increases from 3 to 15 rupees. Asking questions about value of money made individuals slightly less sensitive to price.

4.2. Distance, Convenience, and Take-up

Technology	Researchers	Country	Program Tested	Results
HIV testing	Thornton (2008)	Malawi	Free door-to-door HIV testing offered with distance to center to pick up test results randomized. Vouchers for different cash values redeemable upon obtaining results also randomly provided.	Living over 1.5 km from test center reduced result pick-up by 6%.
Water source improvement	Kremer et al. (2011b)	Kenya	To protect water from ground contamination, subset of natural springs were encased in concrete with pipe to bring water to surface. Water source choice measured.	Individuals are only willing to walk 3.5 minutes further to collect water from a protected spring.

	Citation	Country	Description	Findings
Iron-fortified flour	Banerjee et al. (2010a)	India	Iron-fortified premix to combat anemia given to local millers to add to households' flour.	Take-up of the program rose initially, but then declined. Take-up decline was particularly severe for households whose closest miller was not fortifying.
Incentives for immunization	Banerjee et al. (2010b)	India	Regular immunization camps held in villages. In subsample of communities, parents offered 1 kg of lentils per visit and set of metal plates upon completion of a child's full immunization.	Relatively small incentives were sufficient to induce people to travel up to 5 kilometers to get their children immunized.
4.3. Pricing and Targeting				
Deworming treatment (cost-sharing)	Kremer and Miguel (2007)	Kenya	Free treatment *vs.* small fee for deworming treatment.	Charging did not target treatment to sicker students. Children were less likely to take deworming medicine if they knew people in schools where deworming had been introduced.
Insecticide-treated nets (prenatal clinics)	Cohen and Dupas (2010)	Kenya	Insecticide-treated nets provided for free or at highly subsidized prices to pregnant women visiting prenatal clinics.	Take-up falls by 60 percentage points when the price increases from zero to $0.60. Charging does not reduce product wastage on those who will not use it, nor target the product to women who need it more.

(Continued)

Table 4.2 (Continued)

Technology	Researchers	Country	Program Tested	Results
Water chlorination	Ashraf et al. (2010a)	Zambia	Bottles of water disinfectant sold door-to-door at varying prices. Additional discount offered once households agreed to buy at initial offer price.	Families with at-risk children are not willing to pay a higher price. Households who are more likely to use the product are more likely to pay more.
Water chlorination	Kremer et al. (2011a)	Kenya	Suite of randomized experiments test take-up of individually packaged chlorine at free or subsidized prices. Local promoters encourage chlorine use.	Those with young children no more likely to pay for chlorine.
Water source improvement	Kremer et al. (2011b)	Kenya	To protect water from ground contamination, natural springs were encased in concrete with pipe to bring water to surface.	Those with young children no more willing to walk to collected protected water.
Insecticide-treated nets (cash or nets)	Hoffmann et al. (2009)	Uganda	Households given either free nets or enough money to purchase one.	Households with at-risk children are willing to pay less for nets, but are no less likely to sell nets received for free.

Note: Shaded rows represent non-randomized studies.

4.1. Evidence on Pricing and Demand for Preventive and Non-acute Care

Nine randomized studies in four countries have examined the impact of fees on demand for a range of cost-effective health products (often for the prevention of communicable disease). In all cases, the price at which a health product was offered was randomized—in some cases at the individual level, in others at the clinic or school level.

As discussed above, treating children for parasitic worms is highly cost effective, improving children's health, reducing school absence, and improving adult living standards. International Child Support (ICS) generally requires cost sharing for all its programs but tried free distribution in a subset of schools. Kremer and Miguel (2007) compare take-up of deworming in schools where deworming was free and in schools where families had to share part of the cost. Costs varied between $0.40 and $1.30 per family depending on whether the area had just geohelminths or also schistosomiasis, and thus required more expensive drugs. In schools where distribution was free, take-up was 75 percent.[14] In contrast, take-up in communities with the user fee was just 18 percent. This would only be consistent with the simple model in section 2 if, for many people, the disutility from taking the medicine just offset the benefits of deworming when the medicine is free, but not when it cost $0.40.

Because the same price was charged to each family regardless of how many children they had in school, it was possible to test whether families with more children, who faced a lower price per child, were more willing to pay the (smaller) fee. There was no difference in take-up rates by size of family, suggesting that even a very small fee was sufficient to deter users. Because the fees reduced demand so dramatically, they raised very little revenue. Charging, however, dramatically increased the administrative costs per pupil because the fixed costs of visiting the school to deliver drugs were amortized over fewer pupils. As a result, charging fees would allow only about a 5 percent increase in coverage given a fixed budget. Taking the costs to the families into account as well as the program costs, the user fees made the program much less cost effective.

Although deworming creates positive externalities, the private benefits of deworming are still substantial. Deworming kills worms already in the body, which are not affected by whether others consume medicine and can remain in the body for a year or more. The finding of such large benefits from an average of 2.4 years of deworming suggests that the additional worm-free time obtained by killing worms already in the body provides substantial benefits. Estimated benefits to

---

[14] Very few people actively refused treatment. However, parents had to give permission for children to be treated and some did not do this.

children in schools with deworming who did not take pills are smaller than those for children who took the pills, suggesting that there are important private benefits from treatment.

Every year, an estimated 900,000 people in sub-Saharan Africa die from malaria, with pregnant women and children under five the most vulnerable. Provision of insecticide-treated nets reduces overall child mortality by up to 38 percent in regions of Africa where malaria is the leading cause of death among children under five (D'Alessandro et al., 1995) and reduces severe maternal anemia during pregnancy (which is associated with premature childbirth and low birth weight) by up to 47 percent (Ter Kuile et al., 2003). These are Intention to Treat (ITT) estimates.[15] ITNs cost from $5 to $7 per net, and can provide protection for up to five years (WHO, 2010a). Nets also provide some protection to others living in the community by killing infected mosquitoes.

Cohen and Dupas (2010) worked with TAMTAM Africa and the Kenya Ministry of Health to test how demand for ITNs responded to price. TAMTAM provided nets to 16 randomly chosen prenatal clinics for pregnant women attending the clinic at a subsidized rate ranging from zero (free distribution) to $0.60. Since nets cost about $6.00, even the highest price corresponds to a 90 percent discount. Demand for nets was highly sensitive to price. Take-up drops by 60 percentage points (ITT) when the price increases from zero to $0.60, a price still $0.15 below the price at which nets were typically sold to pregnant women in Kenya at the time.

Thirteen percent of deaths of children under the age of five in South-East Asia and 18 percent in Africa are due to diarrhea (WHO, 2010b). Multiple randomized trials have found that chlorination of drinking water reduces reported diarrhea, with a meta-analysis finding an average ITT reduction of 29 percent (Arnold and Colford, 2007). Dilute chlorine solution is extraordinarily cheap, costing well under 1/100th of a US cent per liter of water treated, and meeting even the toughest cost-effectiveness tests (Ahuja et al., 2010). Yet less than 10 percent of households in sub-Saharan Africa use point-of-use water chlorination (Stockman et al., 2007).

Studies in Zambia and Kenya both find price sensitivity of demand to exist. Ashraf et al. (2010a) worked with the Society for Family Health and Population Services International to test how take-up of point-of-use chlorine changed with price in Zambia. Clorin, an inexpensive chlorine bleach solution used to kill pathogens in drinking water, is a popular product in Zambia to reduce the incidence of water-borne illnesses. Bottles of Clorin, sufficient to disinfect up to 1,000 liters of water, were sold during (one time only) house-to-house visits at prices varying from $0.06 to $0.16 (300 Kw to 800 Kw). If the respondent agreed to buy at the initial offer

---

[15] Intention to Treat estimates compare outcomes among all people assigned to the treatment group to those among all people assigned to a comparison group. The Treatment on Treated (TOT) estimate measures the impact on the people who were actually treated.

price, they were offered an additional discount, such that final prices ranged from 0 to 700 Kw. Take-up of Clorin fell as price rose; 80 percent of respondents bought Clorin at 300 Kw ($0.06) and only 50 percent bought it at 800 Kw ($0.17).

Kremer et al. (2011a) found that less than 10 percent of households in their Kenyan study area chlorinated their water. When the product was provided for free, the majority of households were found to be chlorinating their water. When households were provided with coupons that entitled them to purchase chlorine at half the normal retail price of approximately $0.30 for a month's supply, take-up was only slightly higher than when households had to pay full price.

Given the particularly high burden of diarrhea on young children, one approach that could target the product would be to distribute chlorine solution to mothers of young children. Dupas et al. (2010) report on the impact of providing coupons for dilute chlorine solution, either a one-year supply of chlorine or a 50 percent discount on one month's supply of chlorine, to mothers who bring children to vaccination clinics. Enough coupons were provided to cover water supplies for the 12 months until children reach approximately age two. Mothers were told how and where to redeem coupons and urged to treat water for their children. At an unannounced follow-up visit three to four months later almost 40 percent of those who were given a year's supply either directly or through coupons redeemable at local shops had chlorine in their water. In contrast, among those who were offered a 50 percent discount on immediate purchase of a month's supply of chlorine, less than 15 percent had detectable chlorine in their water. Another group of mothers, given just one month's free supply, had a usage rate of just over 20 percent at follow-up. As discussed below, the rate of coupon redemption fell over time.

Recent meta-analyses by Curtis and Cairncross (2003) and WHO (2002) have found that frequent hand-washing with soap can reduce the risk of diarrhea by an average of 42 to 47 percent. Spears (2010) tested how demand for soap varied by price in India. Individuals were offered soap at prices ranging from 3 rupees to 15 rupees. Take-up of the soap was on average 84 percent at the price of 3 rupees and 30 percent at 15 rupees (ITT). The low take-up at the higher price is despite the fact that 15 rupees represents a significant discount to the price at which soap could be purchased in the area (depending on the exact location the discount to the market price ranged from 42 to 33 percent). Note that while soap does have important health impacts and the high sensitivity of demand to price for soap is similar to other health prevention products, the policy implications from this finding are not as straightforward as from other studies because of the high likelihood that highly subsidized soap might be used for non-health purposes.

Figure 4.2 (J-PAL, 2010) shows the findings from these studies on pricing in one graph, showing take-up percentages at different prices (in US dollars). Figure 4.2 illustrates the striking similarity in the slope of the demand curve for these different health

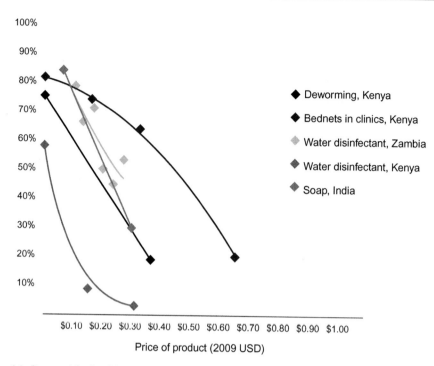

Figure 4.2 Demand for health care products based on price. *Source: www.povertyactionlab.org*

products and in different countries. From the standpoint of the human capital model, it seems odd that such a large mass of the population all experience the cutoff point between costs and benefits at very similar prices for such a large range of goods which have very different benefits. Yet the slope of the demand curve is almost as steep for soap and deworming drugs as it is for mosquito nets, even though these are very different products which operate over very different time horizons and have very different market prices. In the case of ITNs, for example, the fee represents only a small fraction of the market price.

All the studies discussed above test the price responsiveness of demand for specific, highly cost-effective technologies for prevention or treatment of chronic disease. As discussed in section 2, under the human capital model there is nothing special about a price of zero. While it is possible to generate a large change in demand for small price changes around zero, it would require that a large number of people were at a knife-edge decision point between the costs and benefits of a technology precisely at this price. It is very unlikely that this knife-edge point was at an almost identical point for so many different people and technologies. A more plausible explanation for these results is that people exhibit present bias as discussed in section 8.1.

4.2. Distance, Convenience, and Take-up

Under a model with fully functioning markets, time is valued at the marginal wage rate and distance traveled to purchase or receive health care would have an impact on take-up similar to that of a user fee. Thus if take-up declines with price we would expect to see take-up decline with distance at an equivalent rate. If working brings more disutility than time travel, as typically assumed in transportation economics, the effective wage rate might be lower for travel time. Under a human capital model, take-up should not decline over time (unless people learned that the technology was not as effective as they thought). Nor should take-up become more sensitive to distance over time. Finally, in a world of both liquidity constraints and lumpy income earning opportunities (in which people cannot translate every marginal hour of time into additional income), people may be more liquidity constrained than they are time constrained. This would suggest that take-up would fall less steeply with distance than with the equivalent price.

A number of studies have either directly or indirectly tested the sensitivity of take-up of cost-effective health investments to distance, although not all explicitly randomized the location of the provider of health or health prevention program. Most have found that take-up is sensitive to distance. According to the metrics of a cost-effectiveness analysis, people appear to be underinvesting in prevention in terms of time as well as in money.

Every year millions of people receive HIV testing and counseling. Where instant tests are not available, as many as 66 percent of individuals tested fail to pick up their test results (Thornton, 2008). There are many potential reasons—including the psychological cost of learning one is HIV positive. But a study by Rebecca Thornton (2008) in Malawi suggests that price and distance may explain much of the observed behavior. As part of a larger study on HIV prevalence, health workers went door to door offering free testing for HIV (and sexually transmitted infections or STIs). Swabs (and for STIs, urine) were collected and processed at testing sites. Individuals were encouraged to pick up the results of their tests at the centers. The location of these Voluntary Counseling and Treatment (VCT) centers was determined randomly, creating random variation in the distance individuals had to travel to receive their results. Living over 1.5 kilometers from the VCT center reduced attendance by 6 percent. Compared to the potential psychological cost of knowing one's HIV status, a 1.5 kilometer walk does not seem like very much. As with the pricing results, it would be surprising if the balance between benefits and costs fell for most people at exactly the point where a small distance would make the difference between the two. In comparison, the same study reports that take-up fell by 9.1 percentage points as the incentive to pick up the test fell by $1. Comparing the responsiveness of price and distance suggests that an additional kilometer is valued $0.274. In other words, assuming an individual can walk at least four kilometers in an hour, the implied wage rate per hour of walking is more than the average daily wage ($1). The finding that convenience has such a big effect relative to cash is surprising.

As discussed earlier, Kremer et al. (2011b) evaluated a program in rural Kenya that improved the quality of drinking water from natural springs by adding a pipe to bring the spring water to the surface and surrounding the spring with a simple concrete base. The authors find that people are willing to switch water sources and walk further to obtain the water from protected springs. However, they are not willing to walk that much farther. On average, people were only willing to walk 3.5 minutes further (additional round-trip time cost) to collect water from an improved source. Under certain additional assumptions, this implies a willingness to pay per year of life saved of about $23.68 (the value of averting one DALY). This could be interpreted either as indicating that people put a low value on a statistical life (in particular the life of young children) or that behavioral factors such as present bias or limited attention are at play, which would make it conceptually difficult to estimate a consistent measure of willingness to pay for a statistical life.

A program run by Seva Mandir in India and evaluated by Banerjee et al. (2010a) provided iron-fortified premix to local millers (chaki) in rural Rajasthan. At a village meeting the community was told about the high prevalence of anemia in the area and that they could go to certain millers in the community who would, if they signed up to the program, add a small amount of iron when milling their flour. Take-up of the program rose initially and then fell off sharply—a pattern that is not uncommon for health promotion campaigns. While take-up was high, individuals reported feeling stronger and healthier. The falloff in take-up was particularly steep for those whose closest miller was not fortifying and for those more than 1.5 kilometers away from a fortifying miller.

In contrast, another program in the same area, also run by Seva Mandir, demonstrated that relatively small incentives were sufficient to induce people to travel up to 5 kilometers to get their children immunized (Banerjee et al., 2010b). If the explanation for the high drop-off with distance is that the cost of time is very high, then we would not expect to see large positive responses to small incentives. We discuss this result and others demonstrating the power of incentives in promoting positive health behaviors in section 5 below.

To the extent that convenience is important, and that individuals are not good at going out of their way to invest in prevention, biofortified crops offer a promising way to promote health without having to rely on consumers regularly taking supplements or on the public health infrastructure to deliver such supplements. A number of crops are being modified to have higher vitamin A content, for example. A randomized evaluation of the distribution of biofortified sweet potatoes, for example, found that it substantially increased intake of vitamin A (Hotz et al., 2010).

4.3. Pricing and Targeting

One prediction of the human capital model is that, ceteris paribus, those with the most health benefit from a product should be willing to pay more for it. This implies that charging a small fee could help target a subsidized health product to those for whom it would have the biggest health impact. On the other hand, those who could gain most from a health product may be particularly poor and least able to pay a fee, in which case charging might reduce the effective targeting of a product. A number of the studies discussed above examine the impact of prices on targeting.

In general, there is little evidence that those with higher health benefits are more willing to pay, contrary to the predictions of the model in section 2. Kremer and Miguel (2007) find no evidence that parents of children with a high parasitic worm load are more likely to pay for deworming treatment. As discussed above, malaria in pregnant women can result in anemia with potentially negative impacts on a woman's health and the health of her child. But Cohen and Dupas (2010) find that anemic women are not more likely to purchase a mosquito net than women who are not anemic. Ashraf et al. (2010a) and Kremer et al. (2011a) find that families with young children (who are most likely to die from diarrhea) are not more likely to pay a higher price for chlorine. Kremer et al. (2011b) find households with more children under five are not more likely to walk to further but protected springs, although travel costs may also be higher for women in households with young children. As discussed in section 7, Hoffmann et al. (2009), studying mosquito nets in Uganda, also find no evidence to support the idea that charging helps target resources.

5. INCENTIVES

This section reviews the growing body of evidence on providing people with external incentives to encourage usage of health and education programs. Conditional Cash Transfer (CCT) programs, pioneered in Mexico, are now implemented in dozens of countries around the world. Smaller incentives have also shown to be effective in promoting health-seeking behavior, including by Banerjee et al. (2010b) incentivizing immunization with bags of lentils. Section 5.1 goes through the evidence on CCTs, and section 5.2 discusses smaller, non-monetary incentives.

5.1. Conditional Cash Transfer Programs

The human capital model suggests that conditional cash transfers could affect health through an income effect and through the conditionality. Higher incomes can allow households to increase spending on health nutrition, water, and sanitation. Many

Table 4.3 Incentives

Technology	Researchers	Country	Program Tested	Results
5.1. Conditional Cash Transfer Programs				
Conditional cash .transfer (PROGRESA)	Gertler and Boyce (2001), Gertler (2004), Schultz (2004)	Mexico	Cash transfers provided conditional on households' take-up of certain health care services and educational programs.	Visits to clinics increased by 18.2%, and children under 3 yrs were 22.3% less likely to be reported ill. On average school enrollment increased by 0.66 yrs.
Conditional cash transfer	Fiszbein and Schady (2009)	Multiple	Review of health impacts of CCTs drawing on multiple studies.	Mixed results, some papers find health effects, others do not.
Conditional cash transfer (ZCTP)	Baird et al. (2010), Baird et al. (2011c)	Malawi	Girls randomly offered unconditional cash transfer (UCT) or cash transfer conditional on attending school (CCT).	CCT more effective at reducing dropout rate than UCT. UCT significantly reduced teenage pregnancy and marriage rates compared to CCT, due to impact of transfer on these outcomes among girls who dropped out of school.
HIV education, free uniforms	Dupas (2011a)	Kenya	Evaluation of combining subsidized access to school (free uniforms) and providing pupils with information on risky sexual behavior and HIV.	Within 3 yrs, girls given free uniforms were 3.2 percentage points less likely to have dropped out and 2.6 percentage points less likely to have had a pregnancy. Bundling free uniforms with HIV information leads to a lower STI risk, but HIV curriculum by itself has no impact on STI rates or on early pregnancy.

5.2. Small Incentive Programs

HIV testing	Thornton (2008)	Malawi	Free door-to-door HIV testing offered with distance to center to pick up test results randomized. Vouchers for different cash values redeemable upon obtaining results also randomly provided.	Receiving any cash value voucher doubled likelihood of picking up test results.
Incentives for immunization	Banerjee et al. (2010b)	India	Regular immunization camps held in villages. In subsample of communities, parents offered 1 kg of lentils per visit and set of metal plates upon completion of a child's full immunization.	39% of children 1–3 yrs fully immunized in communities served by incentive camp, compared to 18% in communities with regular camps and 6% in communities with no camps.
Conditional cash transfer (ZCTP)	Baird et al. (2011c)	Malawi	Girls randomly offered unconditional cash transfer (UCT) or cash transfer conditional on attending school (CCT).	Smallest payment under CCT is as effective in reducing dropout as average effect under CCT.

Note: Shaded rows represent non-randomized studies.

programs tie transfers to regular health checkups for children and immunization. Other channels are not captured by the model discussed above. Many programs tie transfers to enrollment or attendance at school, creating a potential channel on health through schooling. Higher, more secure, income could reduce stress. There have been many randomized studies of these programs, some of the more recent of which attempt to sort out channels of impact. Here we provide a brief overview of the evidence of health impacts.

Mexico's Programa de Educacion, Salud y Alimentacion (PROGRESA) provided incentives for school attendance and take-up of health care services. It was implemented in 1998 in rural Central and South Mexico. The program disbursed cash transfers that amounted to an average of about one-third of household income for the beneficiary households if they participated in certain health and nutrition-related activities, such as prenatal care, immunization, nutritional monitoring and supplementation, and educational programs about health and nutrition.

The designers of the program structured its phase-in so as to allow for a rigorous evaluation. From administrative and census data, they identified approximately 500 rural areas that were considered to be the poorest and the least likely to experience economic growth, and randomly allocated the program to two-thirds of these areas for the first two years. The remaining third were phased into the program by the third year.

PROGRESA led to changes in health-seeking behavior and improved child health outcomes. Public health clinics in treatment areas received two or more visits per day (an 18 percent increase) as a result of the program (Gertler and Boyce, 2001). PROGRESA beneficiaries comprised only about one-third of the number of families in a clinic's service area, so if all of the increase can be attributed to beneficiaries, then visits in the treatment group increased by 60 percent.

Children under the age of three who received the conditional cash transfers were 22.3 percent less likely to be reported as ill in the previous four weeks than children in the comparison group (ITT). Children young enough to be exposed to the program for 24 months were 39.5 percent less likely to be reported ill, which suggests that the program generated cumulative health benefits. They were also around 1 centimeter taller and 25.5 percent less likely to display hemoglobin levels indicative of anemia (Gertler, 2004). The program also improved education outcomes, on average increasing school enrollment by 0.66 years (Schultz, 2004).

Based in part on the evidence of program impact provided by the randomized evaluation, the Mexican government expanded the program to cover poor rural and urban households in the rest of Mexico, and nearly 30 other countries have established similar conditional cash transfer programs (The Brookings Institution, 2006).[16] By 2006, five million families, or one-quarter of Mexico's population, were participating

---

[16] See Parker et al. (2006) for an evaluation of the urban Oportunidades program.

in the program, now called *Oportunidades* (WHO, 2006). Similar programs established in other countries include Brazil (*Bolsa Escola*, now *Bolsa Familia*), Ecuador (*Bono de Desarrollo Humano—BDH*), Honduras (*Programa de Asignacion Familiar—PRAF*), and Nicaragua (*Red de Proteccion Social—RPS*).

A number of these later conditional cash transfer programs were also subject to randomized or quasi-experimental evaluations. Fiszbein and Schady (2009) discuss and summarize these evaluations.[17] They argue that the PROGRESA impact on child height and hemoglobin could not always be replicated in other settings. While some studies find a substantial impact of cash transfers on these outcomes, other studies find no effects or even negative effects of conditional cash transfers. The impact of conditional cash transfers on child health as reported by mothers is also mixed (impacts on school participation are more consistent across studies).

The review by Fiszbein and Schady (2009) does not include a series of recent papers on a randomized evaluation of cash transfers to girls in Malawi which seeks to tease out channels of impact of CCTs by randomizing whether transfers were conditional or unconditional (Baird et al., 2010, 2011b and c).[18] A recent non-randomized paper not contained in these reviews (de Brauw and Peterman, 2011) on a CCT in El Salvador finds positive impacts on health outcomes at birth, but no effect on health-seeking behavior, either pre- or post-natal.

The Malawi results suggest that conditional cash transfers (CCTs) are more effective in increasing schooling rates than unconditional cash transfers (UCTs). However, unconditional cash transfers are (in their context) more effective in reducing teenage pregnancy. CCTs and UTCs could reduce sexual activity through several mechanisms: schooling conditionality can boost school attendance, which has been found elsewhere to reduce marriage and sexual activity; and the income effect of the transfer could delay marriage, increase schooling, and/or reduce the need to engage in transactional sex with "sugar daddies." The results suggest that the CCT mainly impacts sexual activity indirectly through increased schooling while the unconditional transfer works almost entirely through the direct channels (there was little to no impact on schooling). Overall, the UCT reduced teenage marriage from 18 percent in the control to 10 percent. The overall impact of the CCT on marriage was not significantly different from zero (although the coefficient was negative). However, looking just at the subgroup of girls who had dropped out of school at the baseline (i.e. the group where the schooling effect is most intense) there is an impact on marriage and sexual activity. Within this group the CCT led to a drop in marriage of 11 percentage points and a drop in pregnancy rates of 5 percentage points. The authors conclude that

---

[17] See also Parker et al. (2007) for a review of the literature on conditional cash transfers.

[18] The amount of transfer was also randomized as was the proportion of the transfer given to the girl vs. the parent. The amount received by parents was randomized at the community level, while the transfers for the girls were randomized within community.

whether CCTs or UCTs are more effective in delaying marriage and pregnancy depends on the size of their impacts on schooling and the links between schooling, income, and marriage and pregnancy decisions in a particular context.

Baird et al. (2011b) show that receiving unconditional transfers reduces the rate at which adolescent girls report symptoms associated with mild mental disorders on a health questionnaire by 38 percent.[19] The beneficial effect on health, however, disappears as soon as the transfer's flow stops. Moreover the improvement among those receiving conditional transfers is much lower—just 17 percent, albeit still statistically significant. The authors find that the higher the transfer to the parents conditional on the girls' attendance, the lower the gains on mental health (suggesting that too much riding on conditionality can induce stress). Interestingly, there is no gain in mental health for the girls who are out of school at the start of the program, even though many of them return to school as a result of the program. One potential explanation discussed by the authors is that returning to school may be stressful (dropouts who return to school report sleeping less and having less leisure time).

The result that incentives tied to participation in education can have positive health impacts—including postponing risky sexual behavior—is found in other studies such as Duflo et al. (2011), which examines the impact of providing free school uniforms to girls. These results on school participation and health are discussed in section 9.

5.2. Small Incentive Programs

Incentives would change investment in health under a human capital model and under several behavioral models. Conditional cash transfers were designed under the assumption that parents weigh the costs and benefits of sending children to school or taking them to the clinic. Transfer amounts were designed to offset the income that could be generated from child labor. Since they were intended to reduce poverty, transferring substantial sums to the poor was an objective in itself. A number of studies have tested the effect of small incentives on take-up health products and services.

Above, we discussed the results from Thornton (2008) on how take-up of HIV test results varies with distance to the VCT center in Malawi. The paper also examines the sensitivity of consumer demand for test results in response to small incentives. Under the program, nurses went door to door offering free HIV testing as well as randomly assigned vouchers, valued at between zero and three dollars, redeemable upon obtaining their results at the VCT center. On average, respondents who received any cash value voucher were twice as likely to go to the VCT center to obtain their HIV test results as individuals receiving no incentive. While the average incentive was

---

[19] The follow-up rate in the control group is 37 percent among baseline schoolgirls and 45 percent among baseline dropouts. The measure used is a standard set of questions used to screen for potential mental disorders.

worth a day's wage, even the smallest amount (worth roughly one-tenth of a day's wage) resulted in large attendance gains. Compared to the magnitude of the costs and benefits of knowing one's HIV status (i.e. the stigma of being positive, the benefits of receiving treatment), these incentives are tiny. The magnitude of the impact of changes in behavior is more compatible with a procrastination model of behavior (i.e. rather than influencing the decision of whether to pick up one's result, the incentive offsets the costs associated with picking up the result today).

Banerjee et al. (2010b) find a similarly strong response to small incentives. Seva Mandir, an NGO operating in rural Rajasthan, introduced a program to help increase the immunization rate—which at baseline was just 3 percent of the under fives population. In some (randomly selected) communities, immunization camps were held regularly (to address the problem of health worker absenteeism, discussed in section 11). In a subsample of these communities, incentives were offered to households who brought their children to be immunized. The incentives consisted of 1 kg of lentils for every visit and a set of metal plates when the full schedule of immunization had been completed. Full immunization rates reached 39 percent in communities served by incentive camps, compared to 6 percent in control communities, and 18 percent in communities with regular camps but no incentive. Interestingly, regular camps were sufficient to increase the percentage of children receiving at least one shot to levels comparable with those in the incentive camps (78 and 74 percent, respectively). Incentives, however, were particularly effective at encouraging families to stay the course and reach full immunization (five shots plus the oral polio vaccine). The rate for non-incentive camps was not significantly different from the rate in control communities, suggesting that the incentive was particularly effective in getting families to undertake the inconvenience of attending the camps. Immunization rates were also higher in hamlets nearby immunization camps, suggesting that people were willing to walk to benefit from the incentive. Hamlets within a few kilometers had immunization rates three times as high as in control communities.

Finally, in the CCT program in Malawi discussed in section 5.1 (Baird et al., 2011c), in which the magnitude of the transfer was varied randomly, the smallest transfers had an effect that was statistically indistinguishable from the average transfer.

6. CONSUMER BEHAVIOR, ACUTE TREATMENT, AND INSURANCE

The standard human capital model discussed in section 2 suggests that consumers' decisions on treatment should reflect similar cost-effectiveness thresholds as their decisions on prevention. It also suggests consumers should accept actuarially fair insurance against health shocks, although moral hazard and adverse selection could potentially limit the scope for these markets.

Models of present bias might suggest that cost-effectiveness thresholds for prevention and for treatment of chronic conditions would exceed those for acute care. Under these models, one might see high levels of price sensitivity of demand for prevention and treatment of chronic conditions, but much lower price sensitivity for acute care. Such models might also suggest that many people might not buy a contract that would require expenditure now for benefits that would take place over the next year.

Before turning to evidence from randomized evaluations on acute care or general health insurance, either private insurance or government-sponsored social insurance, it is worth providing some background on private health in the developing world.

The poor often spend considerable sums on health care and bear considerable risk from health shocks. For example, in Bangladesh, China, India, Nepal, and Vietnam, surveys suggest that out-of-pocket payments for health care comprise more than a quarter of household resources net of food costs in at least 10 percent of all households (van Doorslaer et al., 2006a and b). Spending is highly skewed in most studies, with a small proportion of the population accounting for a large share of total spending at any moment. While the data are not broken down into acute vs. preventive spending, it is unlikely that these households are spending these sums on the type of cheap prevention products discussed above.

Non-experimental work suggests that health shocks have longer-term impacts by reducing earnings, increasing health costs, and depressing non-health consumption (Gertler and Gruber, 2002 for Indonesia, and Wagstaff and van Doorslaer, 2003, Wagstaff, 2007 for Vietnam). Households are typically only partly able to insure themselves against these financial risks. Over (2009) estimates that even in South Asia, where HIV infection rates are much lower than in southern and eastern Africa, HIV could increase poverty rates by 3 percent because of the costs of treatment and lost earnings.

6.1. Consumer Behavior and Acute Treatment

Consumers often lack information on the impact of health care on health, and it seems likely that much of their expenditure on health care does not effectively contribute to improved health (as we discuss more in the section on health supply below). However, there may be other areas of underspending on acute conditions.

The evidence on the effect of reducing the price of clinic visits on health is limited and what we have is mixed. There is at least one example that appears to suggest that general health fees led to suboptimal investment in health, but the mechanisms through which this worked are unclear and, as discussed below, in other cases, social insurance programs that reduce costs of health treatment did not increase utilization or improve health status. We discuss these results in the next subsection.

Table 4.4 Consumer Behavior, Acute Treatment, and Insurance

Technology	Researchers	Country	Program Tested	Results
6.1. Consumer Behavior and Acute Treatment				
Clinic fees	Dow et al. (2003)	Indonesia	Exogenous increase in the price of public health care services, based on government randomly allowing certain districts to charge fees at clinics. Prices in treatment areas rose on average by 145% and by 25% in control areas.	Self-reported general health improved where fees were introduced; however, more objective measures were worse with fees and ability to perform simple daily tasks declined.
Antimalarial treatment	Cohen et al. (2011)	Kenya	Consumers are offered vouchers of exogenously different sizes for subsidized antimalarials to be redeemed at the closest drug shop.	Increasing the price of an antimalarial treatment course for young children from $0.30 to $1.5 does not reduce share of households buying treatment (about 32%). Demand falls at much higher prices (4% of households buy treatment at $3).
6.2. Insurance				
Health insurance (RS6BY)	Rajasekhar et al. (2011)	India	RSBY program provided highly subsidized health insurance coverage for in-patient care for people below the poverty line.	2 yrs after program launch, 68% of eligible people are enrolled and by 6 months after enrollment, 0.4% of enrolled households had utilized the card to obtain treatment.

(Continued)

Table 4.4 (Continued)

Technology	Researchers	Country	Program Tested	Results
Insurance (informal workers)	Thornton et al. (2010)	Nicaragua	Voluntary health insurance scheme made available to informal sector workers, using microfinance institutions as delivery agents.	Initial take-up was only 20%. Less than 10% of the vendors who initially enrolled in the insurance scheme were still enrolled one year later.
Health insurance (Seguro Popular)	King et al. (2009)	Mexico	Evaluation of Seguro Popular, a program to deliver health insurance, regular and preventive medical care, medicines, and health facilities to uninsured individuals.	In first 10 months, program reduced catastrophic health expenditures for households by 23%. No effect on medication spending, health outcomes, or health care utilization.
Insurance (CRHIE)	Cretin et al. (2006)	China	Government pilot insurance program randomly assigned different coinsurance rates for outpatient and inpatient visits.	Introducing health insurance increases expenditure on health. Results suggest that outpatient expenditures may be more sensitive to price than inpatient.

Note: Shaded rows represent non-randomized studies.

In Indonesia, the government was faced with sharply rising health care costs from free health services and (working with researchers) decided to test what would happen if districts were allowed to charge user fees at local clinics (Dow et al., 2003). Five treatment and six control districts were chosen at random (from a potentially eligible pool). Prices rose on average by 145 percent in treatment areas and 25 percent in control areas (although there was heterogeneity across treatment districts in price increases). The researchers tracked self-reported and objectively measured health outcomes as well as labor force participation. After two years, they found that self-reported general health improved in districts where fees were introduced. However, self-reported symptoms did not improve with fees, and the ability to perform simple daily tasks (a measure that mainly picks up changes among those with worse health) was worse in the treatment group (significant only for men). The authors argue that their evidence is consistent with reporting bias in self-reported health—more contact with medical professionals may make people less aware of health problems and less likely to report them. Indeed, the authors even find labor force impacts, with lower participation rates for women and lower wages for men where fees were charged. The effects are large in magnitude (7.3 percent lower labor force participation for women and 15 percent lower wages among men), but very imprecisely estimated (because so few districts were included). Unfortunately the authors do not provide much information on the potential mechanisms through which the effects might work—in particular whether fees led to fewer visits to clinics, reduced use of drugs for long-term treatment, or reduced prevention visits. As the study only looked at outcomes for adults, and the effects were concentrated on adults in their 40s, it is unlikely that cutting back on prevention was a large part of the story.[20] Taking the point estimates of the effects at face value, the evidence seems to suggest fees for the general health care system may prevent efficient health investment. A study in Mexico, discussed below, however, did not find evidence of changes in utilization with insurance that offset prices.

A more recent study (Cohen et al., 2011) looks at price sensitivity for antimalarial treatment. In this study consumers are offered vouchers for subsidized antimalarials to be redeemed at the closest drug shop. Increasing the price of an antimalarial treatment course for young children by 250 percent, from $0.30 to $1.5, does not reduce the share of households buying the treatment (about 32 percent). Demand does fall at much higher prices (only 4 percent of households buy the treatment at $3).

This area seems one that is ripe for further research, given its importance and the limitations of existing studies.

---

[20] Most of the major prevention products, such as vaccinations, insecticide-treated nets, and clean water, are particularly important for young children.

6.2. Insurance

The model discussed in section 2 implies that consumers will seek insurance to smooth the cost of treatment and lost wages from illness. Health insurance may also protect households from having to reduce other productive investments, for example in children's education, in response to shocks.

As discussed in more detail below, insurance programs can also be set up to cover only qualified providers and to set standards for quality of care, which may be important if consumers do not have sufficient information to distinguish between good and bad health investments or good and bad health suppliers.

Health insurance, however, is not without its problems. A large literature on developed country health systems examines incentive problems with insurance systems (Zweifel and Manning, 2000). Patients and providers may have incentives to consume more health care or to devote less effort to prevention than if they faced the full marginal cost. Insurance providers undertake various sorts of monitoring to prevent this. Especially when there is competition among multiple providers, providers may have incentives to cherry pick or cream skim healthy customers in ways that shift costs from the provider onto other parts of society. For a discussion of these and other aspects of social health insurance as a health financing instrument we refer the reader to Wagstaff (2010).

Take-up and utilization of health insurance in the developing world has typically been low.[21] Standard models would suggest that moral hazard, adverse selection, and high administrative costs of providing insurance to the poor could limit the amount insurance providers are willing to supply, and increase costs for consumers. However, take-up of even highly subsidized insurance seems low, which poses a puzzle for the human capital model in section 2, which suggests that people would purchase actuarially fair insurance. For example, when SKS, the Indian microfinance organization, experimented with adding mandatory health insurance to their credit programs, demand fell for micro-credit (Banerjee et al., 2011). The Indian government's Rashtriya Swasthya Bima Yojna (RSBY) program provides highly subsidized coverage for inpatient care for people below the poverty line. Consumers pay only an Rs 30 ($0.67) registration fee while the government provides a per-person subsidy of up to Rs 750 ($16.50). Rajasekhar et al. (2011) found that in Karnataka, two years after the launch of the program, only 68 percent of the eligible people were enrolled.

Low utilization rates are another puzzle. By six months after enrolment, only 0.4 percent of enrolled households had utilized the card to obtain treatment. Since many poor households presumably had a stock of health problems requiring inpatient care, these utilization figures seem low. The authors argue that incomplete take-up and low

---

[21] Take-up for many types of insurance is low. See, for example, Giné et al. (2008) on rainfall insurance in India.

utilization are partly due to poor program implementation. Insurance companies may have had inadequate incentives to encourage utilization under the program.

Thornton et al. (2010) found that only 20 percent of eligible vendors took up a voluntary health insurance scheme for informal sector workers in Nicaragua, and less than 10 percent of these were still enrolled one year later. Although enrollment resulted in lower out-of-pocket expenditures, insurance did not significantly increase health care utilization, and the quality of care obtained does not appear to have improved for individuals who entered the insurance scheme.

A major randomized evaluation of the introduction of social health insurance has been recently completed in Mexico (King et al., 2009) while health insurance studies are ongoing in Nigeria and India.

Seguro Popular was launched in 2003 to provide government-funded health insurance to 50 million Mexicans, with the objective of increasing health care utilization and reducing catastrophic health expenditures. The study design sought to effectively speed up introduction of Seguro Popular by a year in randomly selected treatment clusters by instituting a campaign to notify those who were automatically enrolled of the existence of the program, encourage eligible families who were not automatically signed up to do so, and support clinics to prepare for the program. Treatment clusters did see higher affiliation with the program (44 vs. 7 percent). The program was successful in reducing catastrophic payments—cases in which households spent more than 30 percent of their post-subsistence income on health fell from 8.4 to 6.5 percent. There was no increase in utilization of outpatient, hospitalization, or preventive care, although the 10-month period of study (before the program was rolled out everywhere) was rather short. There was no significant effect on self-reported health after controlling for baseline levels (ITT).

In China, in the 1990s, the government undertook a pilot insurance program which randomly assigned different coinsurance rates to test the extent to which insurance increased utilization and costs (Cretin et al., 2006) very much along the model of the health insurance experiments carried out in the US (Manning et al., 1987).[22] Different communities were offered plans with different coinsurance rates for outpatient and inpatient visits (premiums were set based on predicted usage and costs and varied in a non-experimental way between sites). In total, 25 communities were included in the experiment and the main outcome was expenditure on health. Coinsurance rates were changed after one year. So, for example, a village that faced a coinsurance of 70 percent for outpatient care and 40 percent for inpatient care in the first year would face rates of 40 percent for outpatient and 70 percent for inpatient care the next year. While this switching of rates between years allows the authors to factor out fixed community effects, it does raise concerns about whether households

---

[22] Both the China and US studies were undertaken by RAND.

reacted differently to changes in coinsurance rates than they might to levels of rates. The study was not able to look at long-term effects on health outcomes. The authors report that introducing health insurance increases expenditure on health. The coefficient on treatment for inpatient expenditure is lower than for outpatient expenditure (suggesting that outpatient expenditures might be more sensitive to price) but the estimates (especially for inpatient care) are so noisy that it is impossible to rule out that the effects are the same. Unfortunately, as the study was primarily designed to estimate whether insurance would increase costs and whether health insurance would be affordable for the government, it did not examine whether the increased expenditures that came from insurance improved health or increased utilization of cost-effective health care.[23]

Better evidence is needed on the sensitivity of demand for clinic visits in general and acute care in particular. Some of the studies in this section suggest that demand (at least for clinic visits) may be sensitive to price. In other cases there seems to be less price sensitivity. In general, the health impact of reducing costs at clinics will depend not only on the price sensitivity of demand for clinic visits, but also on the impact of clinic visits on health. There are considerable concerns about the quality of health care provided at outpatient clinics in the developing world, as discussed in section 11 below.

7. LIQUIDITY CONSTRAINTS AND CONSUMER BEHAVIOR

The evidence reviewed in the preceding sections suggests several puzzles from the point of view of a model of rational human capital investment by consumers facing complete markets. Those who should value health services more do not seem to be willing to pay more, there are sharp changes in demand around zero prices, and demand for insurance products is low even when they are actuarially profitable to purchase. In the next few sections we examine whether liquidity constraints, behavioral factors, and lack of information could explain some of these puzzles.

If consumers face liquidity constraints they may be unable to invest in cost-effective health technologies. Three studies shed light on the issue of liquidity constraints by providing people with more time to raise the funds they need to purchase a technology (Dupas, 2009); by providing cash to people before offering them the chance to purchase a technology (Hoffman et al., 2009); and by allowing people to purchase nets through microfinance loans (Tarozzi et al., 2011).

---

[23] Non-experimental evidence suggests that China's new cooperative medical system, a voluntary subsidized health insurance scheme introduced in 2003, increased health care utilization but did not reduce the costs of treatment (Yip and Hsiao, 2009).

Table 4.5 Liquidity Constraints and Consumer Behavior

Technology	Researchers	Country	Program Tested	Results
Insecticide-treated nets (vouchers)	Dupas (2009)	Kenya	Households randomly assigned to receive a voucher for a free or discounted net, which they could redeem within 3 months.	Demand for nets in this study falls less steeply with price when households were given more time to raise the funds compared to other studies. Marketing strategies tried did not increase take-up.
Insecticide-treated nets (cash or nets)	Hoffmann et al. (2009)	Uganda	Households given either free nets or enough money to purchase one.	Demand curve is less steep than in other studies when immediate liquidity constraints are relieved.
Insecticide-treated nets (credit)	Tarozzi et al. (2011)	India	Microfinance clients randomly offered nets for free or at full price with option of 1 yr credit contract at 20% interest.	52% of households purchased at least one net on credit, while nearly all households accepted the free net.
Savings device (ROSCAs)	Dupas and Robinson (2011)	Kenya	Evaluation of Rotating Saving and Credit Associations. Participants offered a metal Safe Box, a Locked Box, a Health Pot or a personal Health Savings Account.	Large demand for the savings device. In the following 12 months, the Safe Box increased investment in preventative health by 67% and the Health Pot by 128%. Health Savings Account and Lock Box had no effect on investment.
Microfinance	Banerjee et al. (2010c)	India	Evaluation of the introduction of microcredit in a new market.	Health expenditures (including both medical treatment and hygene products such as soap) do not increase in the first 18 months of access to microfinance.
Microfinance	Karlan and Zinman (2010)	Philippines	Randomizing access to credit for marginally creditworthy applicants.	No evidence that access to credit increases the likelihood of having health insurance.

Note: Shaded rows represent non-randomized studies.

In Dupas (2009), individuals were given vouchers to purchase nets at a discount in local stores. Unlike in the Cohen and Dupas (2010) study where pregnant women were required to make on-the-spot purchases, in this study, households were given three months to redeem their vouchers. Figure 4.3 shows how the three-month demand curve is much less steep than the demand curve estimated in Cohen and Dupas. The author suggests this is evidence of the role of liquidity constraints in explaining the steep demand curve for nets.

In Uganda, Hoffman et al. (2009) offered consumers the chance to purchase a net at different prices after they have been given cash, relieving their immediate liquidity constraint. The result is a less steep demand curve, suggesting that liquidity constraints matter (or that subjects feel some obligation to buy something from someone who has just given them some money, as we discuss below). But while the curve is less steep than in other experiments, it is still very steep and 51 percent of consumers still do not purchase the net at a price of $7.63.

In a randomized evaluation in rural Orissa, India, some microfinance clients were offered insecticide-treated nets for free, while others could buy them at full price with the option of a one-year credit contract at 20 percent interest. After having two days to think about the offer, 52 percent of households purchased at least one net on credit. In the free group, 96 percent of households received a net (Tarozzi et al.,

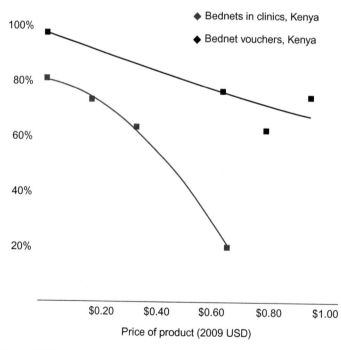

Figure 4.3 Price sensitivity declines with more time to purchase. *Source: www.povertyactionlab.org*

2011). While the microfinance clients in this study represent a different population than that of the other studies discussed in this chapter, demand fell much less steeply with price when credit was available for the bed net. This provides some evidence for the role of liquidity constraints (although it would be useful to compare the demand curve with cash and loans to get a more precise impact of the role of microfinance on take-up). It is worth noting that the behavior exhibited here is also consistent with a model of present bias in which loan repayments are sufficiently in the future that they do not factor much into the decision of whether to take or purchase an ITN.

One concern with some of the studies cited above is that it may be difficult to distinguish the liquidity constraint hypothesis from experimenter demand effects and the fact that the experiment focuses attention on health investments. As discussed below, merely interviewing people about health seems to affect decisions about health.

It is also worth noting that most of the consumers in these studies hold some kinds of assets—including land and animals. Furthermore, some of the purchases, such as dilute chlorine, can be made in small quantities at very low absolute cost (50 cents or less) and the need for them is predictable, making it unlikely that households literally could not have the money to pay for health products. The question remains why they do not save to finance purchase of products for prevention of disease. Dupas and Robinson (2011) find that saving devices targeted to health can lead people to invest more in health, as discussed in section 8 below. This, as well as the Tarozzi et al. (2011) results discussed above, suggests that while credit constraints play a likely role in demand for health products, other factors, such as mental accounts, may also be important.

Randomized studies on the impact of microcredit generally have not found an increase in health expenditure. Banerjee et al. (2010c) randomly select slums in India to open an MFI branch, and study the impact of increased credit availability on households' expenditure. Health expenditure, which includes expenditure for both medical and cleaning products (soap), does not increase in areas where the new MFI branches are opened. Analogously Karlan and Zinman (2010) find no evidence that access to credit increases the likelihood of having health insurance. In their study, they randomize the lender's approval decision for marginally creditworthy applicants in Manila.

8. BEHAVIORAL MODELS AND HEALTH

Externalities and liquidity constraints both contribute to underinvestment in health, but other factors also seem to be at play. Consumers still underinvest in prevention and non–acute treatment (such as deworming) even when taking into account only private returns to health investments. People seem surprisingly sensitive to small upfront costs. In this section and the next we discuss evidence on several behavioral models, arguing that there is evidence that present bias and limited attention play an important role in health behavior. There is less evidence for two behavioral mechanisms that might militate against price subsidies, sunk cost fallacies and price anchoring.

8.1. Present Bias

Health experts often feel that people are more willing to spend on treatment than prevention, holding cost effectiveness constant.

Models of present bias or hyperbolic discounting generate such behavior. As described in section 2, under hyperbolic discounting, people discount at a higher rate between today and tomorrow than between future time periods. A hyperbolic discounter may prefer $10 today to $11 tomorrow but prefer $11 a year and a day from now to $10 a year from now. If people place a large weight on immediate needs, then their valuation of future health benefits from prevention will be low, and even in the absence of substantial disutility from prevention, small fees could prevent take-up.

If people are aware that they are present biased, then they may want to commit their future selves to save (Strotz, 1956; Pollak, 1968), including through health commitment contracts. A commitment contract ties a consumer to future behavior. In the absence of present bias, such a contract would never be optimal as a consumer would always prefer to keep their options open to be able to adjust to new information or circumstances. However, if an individual is sophisticated about being present biased, they know they may be tempted to underinvest in their health at a future point and may be willing to lock themselves into "better" behavior now, even if such a commitment comes at a cost.

Addictive behavior seems like a prototypical case in which many people would like to commit to change their behavior. Giné et al. (2010) randomized the offer of a savings account to smokers. By accepting, people agree to take a urine test after six months, to verify that they have quit smoking. If they pass, their money is returned; otherwise, their money is forfeited to charity. Take-up was 11 percent of smokers, and smokers offered the saving device were 3 percentage points more likely to pass the test than the control group. This effect persisted in surprise tests at 12 months, indicating that the commitment device produced lasting smoking cessation. The fact that consumers were willing to pay to commit their future selves is strong evidence of present bias.

In section 7 we discussed the possibility that the high observed responsiveness of take-up of health prevention products to price reflects liquidity constraints. Yet as mentioned many households in these studies own assets with modest rates of return, such as land, which seems at odds with the findings that liquidity constraints are important. A model with present bias can help explain these seemingly contradictory

Table 4.6 Behavioral Models and Health

Technology	Researchers	Country	Program Tested	Results
8.1. Present Bias				
Savings device (ROSCAs)	Dupas and Robinson (2011)	Kenya	Rotating Saving and Credit Associations. Members offered a metal Safe Box, a Locked Box, a Health Pot or a personal Health Savings Account.	Large demand for commitment savings devices. In the following 12 months, the Safe Box increased investment in preventative health by 67% and the Health Pot by 128%.
Commitment device	Giné et al. (2010)	Philippines	Savings account offered to smokers. Money from account returned conditional on passing a urine test after 6 months to verify that they have quit smoking.	Take-up was 11% of smokers, and smokers offered the saving device were 3 percentage points more likely to pass the test.
Insecticide-treated nets (credit)	Tarozzi et al. (2011)	India	Microfinance clients randomly offered nets for free or at full price with option of 1 yr credit contract at 20% interest. Option to pay in advance for net re-treatments.	About half of households opt to purchase the commitment product that locks them in to re-treatment of their nets.
8.2. Deliberation Costs and Limited Attention				
Hand-washing soap	Spears (2010)	India	Hand-washing soap sold at varied discounted prices, with highest price still a significant discount. Random group asked questions designed to require thinking about the value of money.	Asking questions about value of money made individuals slightly less sensitive to price.

(Continued)

Table 4.6 (Continued)

Technology	Researchers	Country	Program Tested	Results
8.3. Pricing and Use: Testing the Sunk Cost Fallacy Hypothesis				
Insecticide-treated nets (prenatal clinics)	Cohen and Dupas (2010)	Kenya	Insecticide-treated nets provided for free or at highly subsidized prices to pregnant women visiting prenatal clinics.	Those who get nets for free are just as likely to be using them as those that pay for them.
Insecticide-treated nets (cash or nets)	Hoffmann et al. (2009)	Uganda	Households given either free nets or enough money to purchase one.	Those who get nets for free are just as likely to be using them as those that pay for them.
Water chlorination	Ashraf et al. (2010a)	Zambia	Bottles of water disinfectant sold door-to-door at varying prices. Additional discount offered once households agreed to buy at initial offer price.	The act of paying more for chlorine did not make people more likely to use it.
8.4. Endowment Effect for Health Technologies				
Insecticide-treated nets (cash or nets)	Hoffmann et al. (2009)	Uganda	Households given either free nets or enough money to purchase one.	Being given a net increases valuation of the net.

8.5. Learning vs. Price Anchoring: Long-term Implications of Free Delivery

Insecticide-treated nets (follow-up)	Dupas (2010)	Kenya	Households from Dupas (2009) that had been offered vouchers for free or discounted nets were offered chance to purchase subsidized nets 1 year later.	Households given the first net for free were 6.2 percentage points more likely to purchase a second one at a uniform price than those who paid a positive price on the first occasion. Peers of people given free nets are also more likely to buy nets later.
Water chlorination	Kremer et al. (2011a)	Kenya	Suite of randomized experiments test take-up of individually packaged chlorine at free or subsidized prices. Local promoters encourage chlorine use.	People given a free 1-month supply were more likely to be using chlorine after supply ran out.

Note: Shaded rows represent non-randomized studies.

findings. Under a model, in which some assets are liquid and some are not (Laibson, 1997), hyperbolic discounters will spend down liquid assets but will hold on to illiquid assets. The illiquid asset serves as a commitment device because people cannot immediately turn them into temptation goods. Dupas and Robinson (2011) find support for this model in Kenya in a program that offers various commitment devices, sometimes labeled for health savings (such as a metal "Safe Box" or a personal health savings account). Expenditure on health increases when people save using these commitment devices.

Tarozzi et al. (2011) investigate demand for a commitment device for preventive health whereby households pay in advance to re-treat their ITNs (a practice that increases protection) at six and 12 months. Some households received nets (and re-treatment) for free; others could choose either to purchase only the nets and eventually re-treat them at six and 12 months and pay for re-treatment at the time of re-treatment, or to buy a bundle including a net and two re-treatment sessions. With the second contract, the household purchased not only the ITN but also a sequence of two re-treatments. About half of the households in the group chose the bundle contract involving commitment to re-treat.

The studies described here provide considerable support for a present bias model. Present bias and other behavioral models present a challenge for conventional economic welfare analysis as it is unclear how to compare the welfare of alternative approaches when preferences are inconsistent over time. An important topic for future work therefore is thinking through welfare economics in a world of present bias. The authors found that free provision led to the highest take-up but that offering credit, or credit combined with commitment, can boost take-up. (Note that the authors did not find health effects from nets in their study.)

From a health cost-effectiveness standpoint, the finding that many consumers are present biased suggests that making cost-effective health prevention technologies free and convenient may be a cost-effective way to improve health.

8.2. Deliberation Costs and Limited Attention

Spears (2010) suggests another potential explanation of the high price sensitivity of health products. Determining how much value to place on a product and therefore whether to purchase it at a given price or not takes time and effort. When the calculation involves contemplating the likelihood of disease and death, the psychological costs of going through this calculation may be even higher. Even very small amounts of time or effort needed to think through whether a product is worth a certain price may be sufficient to deter people from making a purchase decision. If the product is free, the calculation becomes much simpler—there are no costs, only benefits, so it is clearly the right decision to take the good.

Spears designed a randomized trial to test this idea in Kutch, India. A randomly selected treatment group was asked questions designed to require thinking about the value of money while at the same time avoiding informing or prompting people to think about the benefits of soap specifically. Subsequently this group was offered soap at either 3 rupees (close to free) or 15 rupees. The control group was simply given the chance to purchase soap at a randomly determined price (3 or 15 rupees). The treatment group was somewhat less sensitive to price in their decisions of whether to purchase soap than the control group (an elasticity of demand with respect to price of −0.5 compared to −0.7). While the direction of the effect supports the thesis that decision costs are important, the magnitude of the effect is relatively small.

The finding that take-up is high immediately after a promotion campaign and then falls over time, for example after dilute chlorine solution was distributed to mothers in Kenya (Kremer et al., 2011a), or fortified flour is introduced in India (Banerjee et al., 2010a), or information on contamination of water in Kenya (Luoto, 2009), seems consistent with a model of limited attention.[24]

As discussed in section 9.2, there is evidence that sometimes education works by increasing salience, an important implication of limited attention models. Understanding the role of deliberation costs and limited attention is an important topic for further work.

8.3. Pricing and Use: Testing the Sunk Cost Fallacy Hypothesis

While models of present bias and deliberation costs suggest that making products free will boost their use, other behavioral models could generate the opposite prediction. A theory of psychological commitment (or sunk cost fallacy) would suggest that charging a small fee could help ensure that products that require some effort to use are actually used. This argument has been taken up by the emerging social entrepreneurship movement who frequently claim that "people don't value what they get for free." Easterly (2006) makes a similar claim, arguing that if mosquito nets are given away for free they will not be valued or used for the intended purpose. The social entrepreneurship movement in health also argues that charging helps solve the incentive problems of suppliers to cater to the needs of the poor, an issue we will return to in the section on supply.

For some products, such as deworming in the context of a school-based program, there is no step between take-up and use. A child who turns up for a mass deworming program is given a pill by the teacher who watches them swallow it. For nets and chlorination, however, taking the product home is not sufficient to achieve the desired health impact. Dilute chlorine needs to be added to drinking water and

---

[24] Dupas (2010), among others, finds this pattern.

mosquito nets need to be hung. Some behavioral theories (such as the theory of psychological commitment or the sunk cost fallacy) suggest that charging a small fee could help individuals take the steps needed to use a product appropriately. The act of paying for a good may cause people to rationalize their purchase by using the good.

Before discussing the evidence on this issue, it is worth distinguishing the sunk cost fallacy from other factors that could generate correlations between payment and use. Individuals who have a high valuation of a product may be both more likely to pay for a product and more likely to use it once they have it. In this case, a user fee could help screen out those who are not likely to use the product, but it would not encourage use. Under the sunk cost fallacy, the same person is more likely to use a product they pay for than one they have not paid for because the very act of paying changes their attitude to or valuation of the good.

Three studies tested the link between price and use. The literature on usage of mosquito nets has found large variation in the percentage of nets delivered through different mechanisms that are found to be in use during follow-up visits (see, for example, Maxwell et al., 2006; Guyatt and Ochola, 2003). In both of the net studies discussed in this section that varied prices, enumerators visited households who had either received or bought nets to see whether the nets had been hung up or, if they had not, were still in the house. Cohen and Dupas (2010) find on average that 60 percent of nets in Kenya were in use during visits made to households shortly after purchase/delivery, with no difference across different price groups. A follow-up in the same area in another study found 69 percent of those who received the nets for free and 70 percent of those who paid a positive price had nets confirmed in use by a fieldworker who visited the house after one year (as reported in Bates et al., 2011). In the Hoffman et al. (2009) study, 87 percent of free nets and 89 percent of nets which were paid for were in use after three weeks. Among those not using the net, the most common reasons given for not using it were waiting for the birth of the child or waiting for another net (typically untreated with insecticide) to wear out. There was no difference in usage rates between those who had received their nets for free and those who had purchased their nets. In other words, there is no evidence for either a screening effect or a psychological/sunk cost fallacy effect.

Ashraf et al. (2010a) randomize both the price at which households are offered chlorine and a discount that the households receive once they have decided to buy the chlorine (i.e. once the screening effect has already screened out those with low demand). In practical terms, once a household agreed to buy at a given price between $0.06 and $0.16 (300–800 Kw), the household was provided with an envelope that contained a discount voucher that could take the values between $0.02 and the value they were willing to pay. Thus, some households who had agreed to pay some price for the chlorine ended up getting it for free. Ashraf et al. find no evidence that the size of the voucher impacts the likelihood of use. In other words, there was no evidence of a psychological/sunk cost fallacy effect. The act of paying more for the chlorine did not make people more likely to use it.

Households that were willing to pay more for chlorine were more likely to have chlorine in their water on a follow-up visit. The authors suggest one possible reason for the screening effect is that there may be alternative (non-health) uses for the chlorine and that those with a lower willingness to pay for the chlorine may be more likely to use the chlorine for these other, non-health-related, purposes (e.g. cleaning). But it seems odd that many people would have purchased the product for this purpose, because the water treatment product is a considerably more expensive source of chlorine than bleach. If households bought the chlorine to try it, or if they stored the product for a diarrhea outbreak or gave it away to neighbors, then the effects the authors discuss would not appreciably reduce the cost effectiveness of programs to subsidize chlorine for water treatment since few people would continue to buy the product and not use it on a long-term basis. It also seems possible that experimenter demand led some people to buy the product who subsequently did not use it. Widespread long-term use of the product for non-health purposes would raise the cost of subsidizing water treatment. However, there is not much evidence that this has been a major factor in actual programs and if it turned out to be an issue, it could potentially be controlled by strategies such as a chlorine dispenser that releases only a few drops of the solution, sufficient to treat one container of water, at a time.[25]

8.4. Endowment Effects

Hoffmann et al. (2009) tested whether receiving a net for free changes how people valued the product. In half of the sample, individuals were given cash and offered the chance to buy a net, with random variation in the price at which they were offered nets for sale. In the other half of the sample, they were given a net for free and then offered the chance to resell the net to the provider at a range of prices that varied at random. The median price at which those who were given a net for free were willing to sell their net ($7.16) was higher than the median price at which those given cash were willing to buy nets ($5.94). Seventy-three percent of the respondents who had received free nets were unwilling to accept the maximum price of $7.63 in exchange for even one of their nets. This price represents 3.1 percent of annual per capita non-health consumption and 6.9 percent of annual per capita cash expenditures. In other words, being given a net appears to raise people's valuation of a net—a phenomenon referred to by psychologists as the endowment effect. The endowment effect reduces the likelihood that products given out for free will be onsold.

[25] The dispenser delivers the appropriate dose of chlorine, and the required agitation and wait time for chlorine-treated water are at least partially accomplished automatically during the walk home from the source.

8.5. Learning vs. Price Anchoring: Long-term Implications of Free Delivery

A concern often expressed in the policy community over free delivery of health products is that once funding for free distribution runs out and prices have to rise again, people will be unwilling to pay for a product they used to get for free. This could arise due to a behavioral "price anchoring" effect.[26] On the other hand, offering a product for free could boost long-run demand by building habits of use or by allowing people to learn the benefits of the good, which could stimulate later demand if previously people underestimated the benefits. Two studies suggest that if a price anchoring effect exists, it is outweighed by other factors.

Dupas (2010) randomly offered individuals the opportunity to purchase nets at different prices (ranging from zero to $3.80 (250 Ksh)). A year later, the program returned to the same individuals and offered them the chance to buy a net at $2.30 (150 Ksh). Dupas finds that those who were given the first net for free were 6.2 percentage points more likely to purchase a second net at the uniform price than those who paid a positive price on the first occasion.[27] This is true even though those who were previously offered the nets for free are more likely to already own a net. Indeed, Dupas suggests that because they own a net they have learned the value of the nets and so are more willing to buy them.

Kremer et al. (2011a) find a similar result for water treatment products. People given a one-month supply of chlorine solution were more likely to be using chlorine to treat their water long after their free supply runs out.

9. INFORMATION AND HEALTH EDUCATION

This section discusses evidence on the impact of health education. A plausible theory for the observed low demand by consumers for the highly effective health approaches discussed in section 4 is that consumers do not know their benefits. Especially in the case of health prevention measures—where the benefits are only imperfectly correlated with behavior, and come many months or years after the prevention program takes place—it can be hard to estimate the benefits of these programs. If people underestimate the health benefits of certain behavior, then one natural response is to provide information on the benefits to consumers. While one

---

[26] Price anchoring occurs when the decision maker takes into account a good's reference price (Koszegi and Rabin, 2006).

[27] This is an effect of the treatment on the treated, rather than an intention-to-treat, estimate.

possible channel through which health education could affect behavior is information, other channels may also be important. For example, in limited attention models, consumers may respond to the salience of a health threat. They may also respond to social norms.

If people are rational processors of information, then health education messages that only convey information that is already known to the subject will have no impact on behavior. Moreover, under a rational model, people might start out with overly optimistic initial beliefs about a technology and might learn over time that it is harder to use or less effective than they initially believed, so rational models are consistent with findings that in some contexts people will be less likely to use a technology if more of their social contacts have been exposed to it. In contrast, models in which some people merely wish to conform to what their neighbors are doing suggest that generating more adoption among social contacts should always increase adoption.

Some of the evidence on the impact of health education is consistent with the hypothesis that people have imperfect information and that they are optimally processing new information provided to them in a Bayesian sense. In other cases, effects seem more likely to be driven by salience.

Section 9.1 discusses general health education, section 9.2 discusses complementarities between education and pricing, and section 9.3 discusses cases in which consumers are provided information that is specific to them, such as information on whether their water is contaminated or whether they have malaria or HIV.

9.1. General Education

Below we discuss three health education programs, one highly successful in influencing behavior, one with moderate impact, and one with no impact.

The Kenya Ministry of Education, Science, and Technology, the National AIDS Council of Kenya, and International Child Support Africa (an NGO) piloted several cross-cutting programs aimed at reducing risky sexual behavior among adolescents in Kenya's Western Province. Some were designed to improve knowledge and awareness about HIV as a form of prevention and are discussed here. Another attempted to reduce risky sexual behavior through the indirect means of reducing the cost of school.

Dupas (2011a) discusses an HIV/AIDS education program for Kenyan schools that provided basic statistics about the infection rates of men and women by age—showing that older men are much more likely to be infected than younger men and that young women are more likely to be infected than young men. The program also included a video about the dangers of schoolgirls having relationships with older men. It was delivered by visiting NGO workers, and was extremely cheap and effective in terms

Table 4.7 Information and Health Education

Technology	Researchers	Country	Program Tested	Results
9.1. General Education				
HIV education (relative risk information)	Dupas (2011a)	Kenya	Sugar Daddy Awareness Campaign provided adolescents with information about variation in HIV prevalence by age, with the aim of reducing cross-generational sex.	Information reduced adolescent girls childbearing with older partners by 65% without affecting childbearing with same-age partners.
Malaria education	Rhee et al. (2005)	Mali	Evaluation of malaria education program on net use.	Education increased individuals treating their nets with insecticide by 15 percentage points.
Education on worm prevention	Miguel and Kremer (2004)	Kenya	Education component stressed the importance of worm-prevention behaviors, focusing on washing hands, wearing shoes, and not swimming in infected waters.	No impact of health education on behavior.
9.2. Complementarities between Education and Pricing				
HIV education (teacher training, free uniforms)	Duflo et al. (2006)	Kenya	Teacher Training Program provided in-service training for primary school teachers to enhance delivery of the national HIV/AIDS education curriculum. Furthermore, it provided free uniform as a way to reduce the cost of staying in school.	Teacher training had a clear impact on teaching time dedicated to HIV/AIDS and some impact on knowledge and attitudes of students, but did not reduce teenage childbearing (proxy for risky sex). Teen mothers more likely to marry. Provision of uniforms reduced dropout rates by 15% and incidence

				of teen childbearing by 10%. Information on HIV rates by age reduced childbearing with older men by 65%.
HIV education, free uniforms	Duflo et al. (2011a)	Kenya	Evaluation of combining subsidized access to school (free uniforms) and providing pupils with information on risky sexual behavior and HIV.	Bundling free uniforms with HIV information leads to a lower STI risk, but HIV curriculum by itself has no impact on STI rates or on early pregnancy.
Health information (water quality)	Ashraf et al. (2011)	Zambia	Households offered water treatment product randomly given more information about its effectiveness.	Information increased effectiveness of price subsidies from 3.4% to 5.4%, although the difference is significant only at the 10% level.
Insecticide-treated nets (vouchers)	Dupas (2009)	Kenya	Households randomly assigned to receive a voucher for a free or discounted net, which they could redeem within 3 months. Framing of marketing messages varied.	No impact of "health" or "financial" framing on sensitivity of demand to price.

9.3. Information on Individual and Local Risk Factors

Health information (water quality)	Jalan and Somanathan (2008)	India	Households randomly assigned to receive information on whether or not their drinking water tested positive for fecal contamination.	Among households not purifying water initially, information increased reported water purification by 11 percentage points and increased water purification expenditures by about $7. No

(Continued)

Table 4.7 (Continued)

Technology	Researchers	Country	Program Tested	Results
				effect for households informed that their water was not contaminated.
Health information (water quality)	Luoto (2009)	Kenya	Randomized study on sharing information on water fecal contamination with households in context in which treatment products were provided for free.	Water treatment increases by 8–13 percentage points (between 12% and 23% of baseline usage rates). Contrast-framed messages have bigger impact on behavior change than positive framed alone.
Health information (arsenic)	Madajewicz et al. (2007)	Bangladesh	Households provided with coarse information on whether their water source was contaminated with arsenic.	Households told their water exceeded safe threshold for arsenic levels are 37 percentage points more likely to switch water sources.
Health information (arsenic)	Bennear et al. (2011)	Bangladesh	All households told the concentration of arsenic in all of the wells in their village and the nationally-dictated threshold for safety. Random subsample given additional information that they should always try to go to the well with the minimum amount of arsenic.	Telling people that their well is contaminated leads to switching water sources, but providing information about the continuous effects of arsenic makes those close to the threshold (insignificantly) more likely to switch, and those far from the threshold (significantly) less likely.
HIV testing	Thornton (2008)	Malawi	Free door-to-door HIV testing offered with distance to center to pick up test results randomized. Vouchers for different cash values redeemable upon obtaining results also randomly provided.	Individuals who learned their HIV-positive status bought 3 times as many subsidized condoms, but no effect on learning HIV-negative status.

HIV testing	Delavande and Kohler (2009)	Malawi	Experimental results from Thornton (2008) combined with survey eliciting subjective expectations on HIV infection likelihood two years after the program.	Providing HIV-positive individuals with knowledge about their HIV status results in safer sexual behavior.
HIV testing (behavior change)	Gong (2010)	Tanzania, Kenya	Offers of HIV testing randomly assigned.	Individuals surprised by an HIV-positive test are more likely to contract an STI (indicating riskier behavior). Individuals surprised by an HIV-negative test are less likely to contract an STI (safer sexual behavior).
Malaria diagnostic test	Cohen et al. (2011)	Kenya	Subsidized Artemisinin Combination Therapies (ACTs) offered along with vouchers for subsidized Rapid Diagnostic Tests (RDTs) for malaria.	32% of ACT takers actually do not have malaria. Subsidies are effective in raising take-up for RDTs. Negative RDTs reduce demand for ACTs, but many still purchase.

Note: Shaded rows represent non-randomized studies.

of changing behavior, and therefore averting pregnancies. The information led girls to avoid unprotected cross-generational partnerships and reduced childbearing with older partners by 65 percent, without affecting childbearing with same-age partners. Most girls had previously believed that older men were less likely to be infected than boys their own age, so the results could plausibly be interpreted as consistent with an information transmission model of health education (Figure 4.4).

Rhee et al. (2005) analyze the impact of a malaria education program on ITN use. At an at-cost price of 200 CAF ($0.46), 48 percent of individuals who received the education treated at least one of their nets with insecticide, compared to 33 percent of those in the control group.

On the other hand, Miguel and Kremer (2004) can detect no behavioral impact of a health education program designed to teach students how to reduce worm infection. The deworming campaign discussed above was accompanied by a health education effort that cost as much money as drug distribution. Key messages included the importance of wearing shoes, keeping hands clean, and avoiding swimming in fresh water. Following the program, there was no difference between the comparison and treatment group in hand cleanliness, ownership of shoes, or reported swimming in fresh water. One interpretation is that the schoolchildren did not attach high importance to avoiding worms, could not afford shoes, already knew they were supposed to keep their hands clean, and found it costly to avoid fishing in the lake.

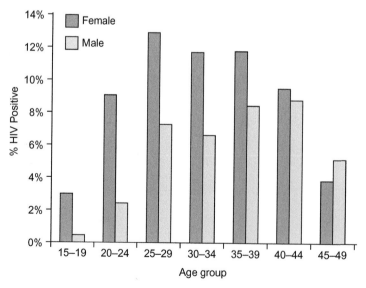

Figure 4.4 Infection rates of HIV by age and gender in Kenya. *Source: J-PAL (2007).*

9.2. Complementarities between Education and Subsidies

The interaction between health education and pricing is explored by Ashraf et al. (2011), who find that price subsidies increase the probability that a household buys the product by 3.4% relative to the control group, and providing consumers with specific information about how an unfamiliar water-cleaning product in addition to the price subsidy increases the probability that the household buys the product by another 2 percent, a marginally significant difference (the p-value on the interaction term is 0.055). Information on its own has no significant effect.

Duflo et al. (2011a) similarly find complementarities between health education and subsidies (see also Duflo et al., 2006). They evaluate the impact of training teachers in the Kenyan government's HIV/AIDs education curriculum, which stresses abstinence and faithfulness as ways to prevent infection, the impact of providing free school uniforms to lower the cost of education, which raises the cost of early pregnancy, since girls who become pregnant are de facto unable to continue in school, and the impact of combining the two programs. The HIV/AIDS education program had a clear impact on teaching time focused on HIV/AIDS and some impact on the knowledge and attitudes of students, but it had no impact on STI rates or on early pregnancy. However, it encouraged girls who were pregnant to get married, since the number of unwed teenage pregnancies was reduced by 1.4 percentage points (or about 10 percent).

Girls in schools where free uniforms were provided were 3.2 percentage points (17 percent) less likely to have dropped out and 13.4 percent less likely to become pregnant, on a base of 16 percent of girls in the comparison group becoming pregnant. Girls were also 2.6 percentage points (20 percent) less likely to be married. After two more years, girls in uniform schools were still less likely to have started childbearing (4.4 percentage points). Much like the teacher training intervention, free uniforms had no impact on STI risk.

There is a strong interaction between information and the incentives to stay eligible for school, since bundling the education subsidy with the delivery of the HIV information leads to a lower STI risk for girls (girls were 2.1 percentage points less likely to have contracted Herpes Simplex Virus of type 2). The authors argue the results are consistent with a model in which girls choose whether to have casual or committed relationships, and teenage pregnancy may be a desired outcome for girls who cannot continue their education.

Dupas (2009) looks at pricing and at messages focusing on morbidity and mortality related to malaria or on the financial gains from being healthy. Neither of the marketing strategies, which did not add information about the product, affected take-up, which was influenced only by the actual price of the net, and there were no significant interactions.

9.3. Information on Individual and Local Risk Factors

Several studies examine the effect of providing consumers with information not just on general health risks, but rather on their own health risk or status, for example by providing information on microbiological or arsenic contamination levels in their water or on people's HIV status. This tailored information is more expensive to provide because it requires large-scale testing. Under a human capital model this information would change behavior (such as water treatment) differently depending on whether the individual finds they are more or less exposed to contamination than they had previously believed (which in a well-informed population would be in line with average population levels).

Under a limited attention model, individual level information may change behavior even if it does not lead to an updating of an individual's risk perception because individual information may be more salient than general information. Knowing that one has fecal matter in one's drinking water may focus attention.

In the presence of externalities, how people respond to individual (or general) information will also depend on their level of altruism and self-interest. For example, a self-interested person who finds out they are HIV positive may have less reason to take prevention measures while an altruistic person would have more reason to take prevention measures.

Several papers suggest that health education on microbial contamination of water can sometimes change behavior, but that the effects of information are small relative to the impact of reducing the price of treatment. Moreover, the studies suggest that people may not be responding as Bayesian decision makers, rationally processing information. Rather, other factors, such as the salience of water contamination, may be at play, consistent with models of limited attention.[28]

Jalan and Somanathan (2008) randomly assign households in their urban Indian sample to receive information on whether or not their drinking water had tested positive for fecal contamination. About 42 percent of the study population purified (meaning filtered, boiled, purchased bottled water or, more rarely, chemically treated) their water at baseline. Among households not purifying their water initially, the provided information led to an 11 percentage point increase in reported water purification as measured eight weeks after information provision. It also increased reported water purification expenditures by about $7. People who received information that their water was contaminated were more likely to purify, but those who received

---

[28] Interestingly, in a non-randomized paper, Field et al. (2011) find large changes in behavior in response to information about arsenic contamination even though the study finds that moving away from arsenic contaminated sources sharply increases death rates of young children (as water has to be brought from further away, is stored for longer, and thus is more likely to be contaminated). One interpretation is that arsenic contamination is more salient than fecal contamination. Another explanation is that households put a much higher weight on adult health (adults are vulnerable to arsenic poisoning) than child health (children are more vulnerable to fecal contamination).

information that their water was not contaminated were not less likely to treat. The asymmetric response to testing suggests that the channel through which information campaigns work may be salience rather than Bayesian learning. Some Bayesian learners would probably respond to information that their water is safer or cleaner than they thought by reducing expenditure on purification. One could imagine some initial distribution of priors that would rationalize the results within a Bayesian framework, but this would be a knife-edge case, with many more households holding priors that led them to just not purify water than holding priors that just lead them to purify water.

Luoto (2009) examines the effect of providing individual information on fecal contamination in rural Kenya in a context in which water treatment products are provided for free. The study explicitly tests a number of behavioral models against the human capital model. Overall she finds sharing information on fecal contamination increases water treatment by 8–13 percentage points (or between 12 and 23 percent of baseline usage rates). This result would only be consistent with the human capital model if the general priors in the population substantially underestimated the average risk prior to receiving the information and that providing individual-level information increased the perceptions of risk on average in the population. While Luoto finds different perceptions of risk at different times, she finds that virtually all households believed their water needed treatment just before the individual-level information was provided, and that there was no difference in average perceived levels of contamination between those who had received individual information and those who had not. This supports the view that individual information is working through salience.

Luoto introduced randomized variation in how the information was provided. Some households received positive framing—pictures of smiling healthy children who received treated water—while others received contrast framing (first, they receive a picture of crying children who were sick because their water was not treated, followed by the same picture from positive framing of smiling/healthy children who had treated water). Those who received the contrast framing were more likely to treat their water (while the coefficient on contrast framing is not significant in all specifications, it is always positive and economically important).

Luoto also finds that people use the water treatment technologies more just after they have received the information and compliance tails off over time. One potential explanation is that people regard the information as most reliable just after the test has been conducted (although in this case, those who found their water was clean should start using the technology more over time as their clean result became less reliable). A more plausible explanation is that recent messages are more salient.

Luoto finds some evidence that verbal commitments to use water purification technologies increase use, a finding that is inconsistent with a human capital story. While the power on the commitment effect and the contrast framing on their own is weak (with not every specification significant), when the two interventions are combined, the effect is large and consistently significant.

Finally, the study finds no additional impact from sharing information on water contamination in the household once source water information has been shared.

Further evidence consistent with the idea that information processing may not be fully rational is provided by Madajewicz et al. (2007) and Tarozzi et al. (2009), who study how people respond to information about water quality in an area of Bangladesh where wells are frequently contaminated with arsenic. Madajewicz et al. (2007) evaluate the effectiveness of providing coarse information about well safety to a random sample of households about whether their water source has arsenic concentrations above a threshold level. Households that are informed their water exceeds this threshold are 37 percentage points more likely to switch sources than control households within one year. These households increase their walking time about four minutes, on average, in response to the information.

Bennear et al. (2011) perform an evaluation in Bangladesh where all of the wells in the study area had previously been labeled with a metal plate displaying the arsenic concentration level and a clear picture indicating whether the water had been deemed safe for drinking (under 50 parts per billion). A random subsample received additional information explaining that whatever the level of arsenic in the current water source, it is better to drink water from the well with the lowest level of arsenic. If households are Bayesian decision makers, this finer information should lead to improved outcomes. Households far from any uncontaminated well, for instance, might switch from a well that is highly contaminated to a well with a lower contamination level. In practice, however, receiving additional information decreases the impact the arsenic level has on the probability of switching to a new source of drinking water compared to receiving the simple information about the national safety threshold. For households using moderately unsafe wells (contamination of 50–100 ppb), the additional information increased switching rates by 52 percent (35 vs. 23 percent), although these results are not statistically significant. However, for users of wells with higher arsenic concentrations, the effect of the additional information is to decrease switching by 38 percent (29 vs. 47 percent, a significant difference), which drives the average results, and the authors have some evidence that some of this result may because the extra information may lead people to believe it less.

Another set of studies examines the impact of providing individuals with information on their HIV status. As discussed above, Thornton (2008) examined how random variations in distance to Voluntary Counseling and Testing Centers and the size of the incentive to collect HIV test results changed the probability of people finding out their HIV status in Malawi. This generates random variation in whether people knew their HIV status. Thornton measures how this affects willingness to purchase subsidized condoms during household visits two months later. (Subjects were provided cash prior to being offered the opportunity to purchase condoms.) She finds that sexually active, HIV-positive individuals respond to learning their status by purchasing three times as many subsidized condoms as sexually active, HIV-positive patients who did not learn their status. However, the absolute magnitude of the effect is small, as on average the HIV-positive patients purchased only two additional condoms. There was no significant effect of learning HIV-negative status on the purchase of condoms.

Delavande and Kohler (2009) examine follow-up survey data on individuals who participated in the Thornton (2008) study. They find that testing had unexpected results on subjective expectations of infection. Of those who were told they were positive in 2004, 45 percent reported they had "no likelihood" of being infected in 2006. Using the encouragement to collect their test results as an instrument for whether individuals knew their status shows that those who learned they were negative were more likely to think they were positive than those who did not learn their status. The authors do find evidence that testing changed self-reported behavior. In particular, those that found they were positive reported 0.4 fewer sexual partners in the last 12 months. The only objective outcome indicator, however, is pregnancies, which also declined for unmarried participants who learned they were HIV positive. It is important to take data on the self-reported sexual behavior with a grain of salt, especially given the results from Gong (2010) discussed below. The study also suffers from attrition between waves, with those who were HIV positive having higher attrition rates. However, the findings of changes in pregnancy rates despite only weak changes in subjective probabilities as a result of testing suggests that information processing may be quite complicated. Finally, this study does not distinguish behavior change according to whether testing updated or confirmed individuals' initial assumptions about their status.

Using data from a study by Coates et al. (2000) that randomly assigns offers of HIV testing in Nairobi and Dar Es Salaam, Gong (2010) examines the effects of testing, taking into account people's beliefs about their HIV status prior to testing.[29] He also benefits from having objective, rather than self-reported, measures of sexual behavior. In contrast to the other studies discussed in this section, Gong finds strong evidence of an asymmetric response to individual information depending on whether the information was or was not aligned with initial priors. In this study, risky sexual behavior is proxied using gonorrhea and chlamydia infections contracted during the six months after testing. Both treatment and comparison groups were surveyed for their initial beliefs about the likelihood that they were positive and the general likelihood of contracting HIV. The author finds that individuals surprised by an HIV-positive

[29] For a non-randomized study assessing the impact of learning HIV status on the likelihood of getting appropriate treatment, see Goldstein et al. (2008).

test (i.e. those who stated they had a low probability of being infected but in fact were positive) are over five times more likely to contract an STI compared to a similar untested control group—suggesting that self-interest dominates altruism in this context. This result confirms the importance of using objective measures of sexual activity as self-reported activity among this group declines. Individuals surprised by an HIV-negative test are 73 percent less likely to contract an STI relative to a similar untested control group. As predicted by a human capital model, when HIV tests agree with a person's belief regarding their HIV status there is no change in sexual behavior.

On average, HIV testing has no impact on contracting an STI as the effects in the two groups cancel each other out. However, epidemiologically, an increase in risky sexual activity by HIV-positive individuals and a reduction in risky activity by HIV-negative people are likely to lead to an increase in infections. Gong uses the estimates derived from his estimation to simulate the overall impact on HIV infections—finding that HIV infections increase by 25 percent when people are tested compared to when they are unaware of their status. These estimates do not account for reductions in disease transmission if testing allows treatment, however.

All the studies we have examined in this section so far deal with disease prevention. However, information is also relevant for treatment decisions. Malaria has been subject to a cycle of introduction of new therapies and evolution of drug resistance, leading to the need for new therapies. In many regions, malaria is resistant to the cheapest drugs. Artemisinin Combination Therapies (ACTs) are more expensive, but address the issue of drug resistance. Cohen et al. (2011) report that in their Kenyan study region, most of the individuals who go to drugstores to buy ACTs are self-medicating, and 64 percent of ACT takers age 9 and over (and 32 percent overall) do not have malaria. In a randomized experiment, Cohen et al. (2011) offer subsidized ACTs along with vouchers for subsidized rapid diagnostic tests (RDTs) for malaria. Subsidies raise take-up for ACTs and rapid diagnostic tests: when offered a voucher for subsidized rapid diagnostic tests, more than 80 percent of households who visit the drug shop choose to get the patient tested prior to ACT purchase. Among those who went to a pharmacy to purchase ACTs but then tested negative for malaria, 60 percent purchased ACTs anyway, compared to 100 percent of those who did not learn their status. While the information changed behavior sharply it raises the question of why anyone continued to purchase the ACT once the result showed they were negative. Interestingly, the more educated the female household head, the more likely they were to purchase the ACT even when they tested negative for malaria (Cohen et al., 2011).[30] The authors point out that the technology is relatively new and the older technology of lab tests has a high rate of false negatives

---

[30] Non-randomized studies in the US, and some in developing countries, have found in other contexts that more educated people have higher take-up of new or more complicated health technologies. See, for example, Rosenzweig and Schultz (1983), Cutler and Lleras-Muney (2010), Thomas et al. (1991) and DeWalque (2007).

so that treatment following a negative result is standard and even recommended practice using the older technology.

The evidence summarized in this section suggests that health education campaigns may indeed affect behavior in certain circumstances. At least in some cases, health education and subsidies seem to be complements in changing behavior. There are examples (in particular Gong, 2010) where the behavior change is as predicted in a human capital model and many other cases where the evidence suggests health education changes behavior through other channels. Understanding these channels is an important topic for future work.

10. SOCIAL INFLUENCES ON HEALTH BEHAVIOR

This section discusses a number of cases in which health behavior is influenced by peers. We first discuss some cases that are consistent with a model of rational social learning. We then discuss evidence that being surveyed affects behavior, consistent with the idea that salience or social norms play an important role. Finally, we discuss evidence on programs that try to promote changes in social norms.

Kremer and Miguel (2007) find that additional social links to early treatment schools reduce the probability that children take deworming drugs. Negative social effects on take-up are especially large empirically for families with more schooling. They interpret this as learning, arguing that the educated start out with particularly favorable beliefs about the technology but then rapidly revise their beliefs downwards as they acquire more information.

Dupas (2010) finds that people given free nets are more likely to buy nets later and that their peers are also more likely to buy nets. Both sets of results are consistent with the hypothesis that people learn over time about the private costs and benefits of using technologies, and that this information is less favorable than people expected for deworming and more favorable for insecticide-treated nets.

Oster and Thornton (2009) randomize the provision of menstrual cups in Chitwan, a district in south-western Nepal, and measure how the technology spreads. Usage is significantly higher for individuals with more treatment friends. In early months after distribution this difference is as high as 25 percentage points per treatment friend, whereas later on this effect loses significance, suggesting that peers are important in learning how to use the cups.

Zwane et al. (2011) find that health behavior can be influenced by surveying, based on examination of a diarrhea survey and two general surveys. As part of a study of spring protection mothers were interviewed about child diarrhea. People were asked if they chlorinated their water, and if they reported affirmatively, their water

Table 4.8 Social Influences on Health Behavior

Technology	Researchers	Country	Program Tested	Results
Deworming treatment	Kremer and Miguel (2007)	Kenya	Free treatment vs. small fee for deworming treatment.	Children were less likely to take deworming medicine if they knew people in schools where deworming had already been introduced.
Insecticide-treated nets (follow-up)	Dupas (2010)	Kenya	Households from Dupas (2009) that had been offered vouchers for free or discounted nets were offered the chance to purchase subsidized nets 1 year later.	Peers of people given free nets are more likely to buy nets later.
Menstrual cups	Oster and Thornton (2009)	Nepal	Randomized evaluation of menstrual cups take-up among girls and their mothers.	3 months after distribution, one additional friend in the treatment group increases usage by 12 percentage points.
Surveying	Zwane et al. (2011)	Kenya, Philippines	Mothers interviewed about child diarrhea biweekly or every six months. People were asked if they chlorinated their water, and if they reported affirmatively, their water was tested. In other areas, people given a general household survey.	Health behavior can be influenced by surveying. People who are interviewed biweekly about diarrhea report much lower rates of diarrhea than those who were interviewed less frequently. General household surveys increase uptake of health insurance.
Water chlorination	Kremer et al. (2011a)	Kenya	Suite of randomized experiments test take-up of individually packaged chlorine at free or subsidized prices.	No estimated social effect in adoption of chlorine packaged for household use, but evidence of sustained social effects on use of public chlorine dispensers.

Water treatment (chlorine dispenser)	Kremer et al. (2011a)	Kenya	Provision of free dilute chlorine via dispenser system located at water source, coupled with community-based promoter with short-term payment to encourage use.	Dispenser system makes water treatment salient and public. By 3–6 months the majority of households were using chlorine, and effects continued after 30 months, long after payments to the promoter had ceased.
Sanitation	Pattanayak et al. (2009)	India	Randomized sanitation campaign that provides subsidies to the poor to construct a pit latrine, education on sanitation, and "shaming exercise" to trigger a collective emotional response.	A combination of shaming and education (even without the provision of subsidies) had a pronounced effect on latrine ownership.
Safe driving	Habyarimana and Jack (2009)	Kenya	Signs encouraging passengers of minibuses to ask drivers to drive safely were randomly placed across a sample of minibuses.	Program led to a 50% reduction in the overall number of insurance claims as well as the number of claims involving injury or death.

Note: Shaded rows represent non-randomized studies.

was tested. There was no education message. People who were interviewed biweekly about diarrhea reported much lower rates of diarrhea than those who were interviewed every six months for a two-year period. The effects seem to go beyond simple reporting bias and suggest that being surveyed can affect behavior. Rates of chlorine use were higher in the group that was frequently surveyed. Moreover, the frequency of surveying influenced the estimates of the impact of spring protection, suggesting that it may be better to employ survey techniques that involve surveying many households infrequently rather than few households frequently.

Two general surveys in the Philippines were found to increase later uptake of hospitalization insurance and general health insurance, respectively. Take-up data were administrative, not survey based, suggesting the results cannot be explained by reporting bias. The authors interpret the survey effect as due to changes in the salience of potential health shocks relative to more immediate needs.

Some health education programs explicitly try to change social norms. Pattanayak et al. (2009) evaluate a cluster randomized sanitation campaign in India. The campaign provides subsidies to the poor to construct a pit latrine, provides education on sanitation, and seeks to trigger a change in social norms around sanitation practices. The authors find that even without the provision of subsidies the other elements of the program had a pronounced effect on latrine ownership. It is difficult to know if these changes would be present without the social component of the program, but it seems plausible.

Traffic accidents in developing countries are responsible for over 1 million deaths annually (comparable to the mortality burden of malaria). Habyarimana and Jack (2009) investigate the impact of signs in minibuses in Kenya encouraging passengers to ask drivers to drive safely. The signs provided no additional information to passengers that they did not already know. Instead they sought to make it more socially acceptable to speak up against dangerous driving.

The signs were randomly placed across a sample of minibuses. The program led to a dramatic reduction in the overall number of insurance claims as well as the number of claims involving injury or death—both were down by at least 50 percent. A very simple program thus appears to have effectively tackled an important collective action problem, empowering passengers to take action.

Kremer et al. (2011a) argue that changing the characteristics of a technology can change the scope for social effects. They present evidence that water treatment behavior is potentially open to peer effects, noting the impact of a local promoter on chlorine use, as well as the impact of surveys discussed above. The distribution of free chlorine packaged for household use promoted conversations about the product as well as about drinking water more generally, and peer exposure led to more *reported* chlorination. However, there was no evidence peers affected use of chlorine as measured using chlorine tests. Excess variance tests also provide no evidence of peer effects for a product packaged for household use. In contrast, when chlorine is distributed in a public dispenser at a point of water collection, excess variance tests suggest an important social component of the adoption decision. Whereas use of the household product tails off over time following other approaches to chlorine promotion, the majority of people with access to a public dispenser continue to use it 30 months after installation.

11. HEALTH CARE SUPPLY IN THE DEVELOPING WORLD: BACKGROUND

Total health expenditure in low-income countries is 5 percent of GDP, of which 60 percent is spent privately. This compares to global health expenditure which is 10 percent of GDP, with 60 percent of this being publically financed (World Bank, 2011). In addition to having fewer resources, health care systems in the developing world tend to generate weaker incentives for providers. In many poor countries, public providers are frequently absent, often provide poor service, and regularly charge unofficial fees. In consequence, at least in some countries, the poor often turn to fee-for-service care from private providers. Private providers have stronger incentives, but their incentives are frequently misdirected due to asymmetric information between patients and providers and the existence of health externalities; for instance, many of these providers have little or no formal medical training.

The health sector in developing countries is often polarized between the extremes of pure public sector delivery and fee-for-service provision from the private sector, unmediated by insurance companies. Private health insurance or government-supported social insurance is typically restricted to those in the formal sector, a fraction of the population in most developing countries. This raises questions of how incentives can be strengthened for public-sector health workers and how to address the problems associated with fee-for-service provision. Another issue is industrial organization in health, including interactions between public and private providers and the potential role of intermediary institutions such as insurance companies and health purchasers within the public sector. This section discusses the difficulties faced by both the public and private health sectors in developing countries, while section 12 examines evidence on efforts to reform health delivery systems in developing countries.

11.1. Public Health Care

Many developing countries have a high absence rate of medical personnel. A survey covering Bangladesh, Ecuador, India, Indonesia, Peru, and Uganda found an overall absence rate of 35 percent among health workers (Chaudhury et al., 2006). The rate tended to be higher in poorer countries. Higher-ranking providers, such as physicians, are more likely to be absent than lower-ranking health care providers. Providers in small facilities are more likely to be absent than their counterparts in larger facilities.

A survey of 100 villages in Udaipur district in Rajasthan, India, which sampled the same primary health care centers on repeated occasions, found that there was no predictable pattern to absences—nurses were as likely to be absent on a Wednesday as on a Monday, making it harder for patients to work around nurses' absence (Banerjee et al., 2004a).[31]

When medical personnel are present, the poor quality of care provided by physicians is another major problem. A series of papers uses vignettes to evaluate the competence and knowledge of physicians in developing countries (see, for instance, Das and Hammer, 2004, 2007; Das and Gertler, 2007; Das et al., 2008). Vignettes compare the examination and treatment that physicians say they would provide to a hypothetical patient to the examination and treatment that should be provided according to official protocols or committees of experts. This line of research indicates that even rudimentary examinations are often not conducted when patients present symptoms of common but severe diseases such as diarrhea, malaria, and tuberculosis. To give an example, health care providers in Delhi, India, indicate that they carry out only 18 percent of the necessary procedures for children with diarrhea (Das and Hammer, 2007).

On top of this lack of knowledge of basic procedures, there is a gap between what health care providers know they should do and what they do in practice. Direct clinical comparisons, for instance, show that the actual examination and treatment provided often falls short of the examination and treatment physicians say they would provide in the hypothetical vignettes. Together, the lack of knowledge of basic procedures and the fact that physicians only conduct part of the procedures they deem necessary often result in very limited interaction between physicians and patients. During 130 hours of observations in two north Indian hospitals, researchers found that physicians spent an average of 3.8 minutes per patient, asked an average of 3.2 questions, and prescribed on average 2.63 medications (Das and Hammer, 2007). And a study of 450 consultations in Tanzania found that in only 29 percent of cases did the doctor discuss with the patient activities they should adopt or avoid to improve their health. When nurses were asked to give the patient drugs, they only checked to see if the patient knew how or when to take the drug in 32 percent of the cases (Leonard, 2003).

Limited provider effort per patient does not seem to be merely a consequence of heavy caseloads. While in some cases caseloads are high, particularly at higher-level facilities, such as district hospitals, many primary health care centers face low

---

[31] The authors verified that nurses were not absent because they were taking care of patients at their homestead.

Table 4.9 Health Professional Absence (%), 2006

Bangladesh	35%
India	40%
Indonesia	40%
Peru	25%
Uganda	27%
Unweighted Average	35%

Source: Chaudhury et al. (2006)

utilization. Recall that conditional cash transfers in Mexico increased the number of patient visits by two per day and that this constituted an 18 percent increase. Among 159 clinicians in 126 health facilities in rural Tanzania et al. (2010) did not detect an association between caseload and effort per patient (as measured by the number of relevant history-taking questions asked and physical examinations performed). Instead, Mæstad et al. (2010) conclude that the health care providers in their study sample are not overworked and have ample idle time.

Even if the staff is present *and* makes the correct diagnosis, essential drugs and supplies may not be available to treat the patient. In a representative survey of clinics in Sierra Leone, only 37 percent of clinics had all 11 drugs considered essential by the Ministry of Health in stock during a random visit (IRCBP, 2007). Thirty percent of clinics had none of the drugs in stock.

In general, a high proportion of the health care budget in poor countries is spent on salaries of health care workers, leaving little room for drugs and supplies—potentially because of a ratchet effect in which staff positions are increased in good times, but drugs and supplies are much easier to cut than staff when funding falls. Limited supplies of drugs may also reflect inefficient and corrupt purchasing and distribution systems (see, for example, Di Tella and Schargrodksy, 2001).

Patients often have to pay either for their consultation or for drugs or both—even when the official government policy is that they should receive the service for free. In rural Rajasthan, the average visit to a public provider costs Rs 110 (about $2.50), more than double the average daily wage in the area (Rs 53, $1.17) even though the public service is meant to be free (Banerjee et al., 2004b). In Sierra Leone, 46 percent of those immunizing a child in 2007 and 65 percent of those in 2008 reported having to pay for the immunization, even though immunizations are meant to be free (IRCBP, 2010).[32]

---

[32] Part of the fee is for the immunization card and part was for the immunization itself, but the card is a requirement for having a child immunized.

One reason the quality of public provision is so poor is that medical staff face few incentives to make it better. They tend not to be fined or fired for failing to show up or for charging unofficial fees, and there are rarely systems of quality review. Many health workers may prefer urban postings, where, for example, their children have better educational opportunities. In some countries, many health workers are not paid on time or in full.[33] Low utilization and provider absence may be mutually reinforcing.

11.2. Private Health Care

Perhaps in part because of the weaknesses of public systems, even the poor in most developing countries are frequent users of private, fee-for-service health care. The World Bank estimates that in 2009 public health expenditures in Latin America, sub-Saharan Africa, and South Asia, respectively, represented only 52, 44, and 33 percent of total health expenditures.[34] A compilation of data covering 40 developing countries estimated that 55 percent of physicians work in the private sector (Hanson and Berman, 1998).

If lack of incentives is one reason that the public system is so bad, then private providers, who have an incentive to show up and keep their clients happy, might seem to be the answer. However, a recent review by Berendes et al. (2011) suggests that, although private sector health workers in developing countries indeed typically provide more personalized and client-centered service and longer average consultation times, ultimate differences in the quality of care offered by the public and the private sector are minimal. Accordingly, Leonard et al. (2007) show that, while doctors running a single-provider private practice are more responsive to patients, they do not provide higher quality health care.

While private providers working on a fee-for-service basis face stronger incentives, these incentives are often not aligned with the needs of patients due to asymmetric information between patients and providers. Patients are often unable to tell good treatment from bad—a recognized problem even in countries with strong regulatory systems and much higher levels of education, where patients are better informed about what constitutes good medical care. In many developing countries, people often see untrained or barely trained private fee-for-service providers (Banerjee et al., 2004b).

Health care providers often give treatments which do not improve, and may worsen, long-term health, but which may make patients feel better in the short run. Phadke (1998) categorized more than 50 percent of all drugs prescribed in India as

---

[33] In Sierra Leone, over half of clinics are more than five miles from the nearest road, most of the staff are not paid on time, and 44 percent report not being paid at all (IRCBP, 2007). One of the reasons given by health staff for charging fees in Sierra Leone was to cover the salaries of staff that had not been paid.

[34] Source: World Bank's World Development Indicators, http://data.worldbank.org. Accessed on May 23, 2011.

"unnecessary or contra-indicated." A survey of eight countries across Africa found that 25 to 96 percent of outpatient visits resulted in an injection, and in five of the surveyed countries, 70 to 99 percent of the injections were judged unnecessary. In Pakistan, the typical person is estimated to receive 8.5 injections per year (Simonsen et al., 1999).

This inappropriate care is not only wasteful; it can be harmful. Unnecessary injections can lead to infection of the injection site, HIV, and hepatitis B and C. Steroid shots (which make patients feel better in the short run and thus can lead to repeat business for providers) can have long-term negative consequences for the individual patient. The common overuse of antibiotics is contributing to drug resistance.

These issues affect both the public and private sector but private providers have stronger incentives to prescribe treatments that make patients feel that something is being done and that makes them feel better in the short run even if it is not good for them in the long run. A survey in rural Rajasthan by Banerjee et al. (2004b) found that private providers were much more likely to give injections and drips (68 percent and 12 percent of all visits, respectively) compared to public providers in the same area (32 percent and 6 percent, respectively).

Providers in a fee-for-service health care system also have no incentive to take into account the consequences of treatment on others in the community whether they are negative (as with antibiotics) or positive (as they are for immunizations). Many of the most cost-effective health approaches are preventive ones, which many people are reluctant to pay for, and which as a result tend to be underprovided by providers responding to market incentives.

Private fee-for-service provision leaves households bearing financial risk from serious illness. Gertler and Gruber (2002) estimate that 35 percent of the costs of serious illness are not insured by other sources available to households. They also find that the more severe the illness, the less households are able to insure. They estimate that households are able to fully insure the economic costs of illnesses that do not affect physical functioning, 71 percent of the costs resulting from illnesses that moderately limit an individual's ability to function physically, but only 38 percent of the costs from illnesses that severely limit physical functioning.

12. HEALTH CARE DELIVERY AND SYSTEM REFORM

Given the level of dysfunction documented above, the need for health system reform is clear. This section discusses four programs that were subject to randomized evaluations, a failed program aimed at decreasing the absence of nurses in India and three successful programs: contracting of management of health delivery to non-governmental organizations in Cambodia, a program to increase accountability of local medical staff to communities in Uganda, and conditional and unconditional grants to communities to improve health in Indonesia, as well as a non-randomized evaluation of a successful incentive program in Rwanda. A large literature examines alternative health service delivery arrangements (including task shifting to lay health workers). See Lewin et al. (2008) for a review of the reviews on this literature. For a discussion of the lessons for developing countries from health system reforms in developed (Asian) countries we refer the reader to Wagstaff (2007).

12.1. Paying for Provider Presence in India and Rwanda

While most contracts for health providers already include sanctions for persistent absenteeism, it is rarely tracked or enforced. In the Udaipur district in Rajasthan, India (population of over 2.5 million), a sample of local clinics in rural areas was found to be closed 56 percent of the time and in 45 percent of cases the nurse could not be found anywhere in the village (Banerjee et al., 2004b). Since nurse absence was unpredictable, coverage of basic services was below that seen in much poorer areas; only 3 percent of under five-year-old children were fully immunized.

In 2005, Seva Mandir, a local NGO, began discussion with government officials to pilot a monitoring program for nurses in local health clinics (Banerjee et al., 2008a) aimed at increasing the regularity and predictability of the attendance of Auxiliary Nurse Midwives (ANMs) in rural subcenters serving 135 villages in Udaipur. Seva Mandir was asked to undertake the monitoring of ANMs on certain days. To help ensure that subcenters were open, additional ANMs were hired for some subcenters while other nurses were told they should always be in the center on Mondays regardless of whatever other responsibilities they had. Presence was monitored with time/date stamping machines and with absence records, along with exempt day records (for field visits approved by supervisors), that were sent to each nurse's supervisor to be checked. The supervisor would then take the appropriate action, potentially including penalties.

ANM attendance improved sharply at the beginning of the program, when the government threatened pay deductions (it is unclear if any deductions were ever carried out). In the first six months, treatment ANMs were about 15 percentage points more likely to be present than comparison ANMs.

However, over time the nurses and administration figured out ways to undermine the system. In particular nurses intentionally broke the time clocks, forcing personal supervision, which was more costly and less frequent. Furthermore, nurses requested and received an increased number of exempt days for field activities which were

Table 4.10 Health Care Delivery and System Reform

Technology	Researchers	Country	Program Tested	Results
12.1. Paying for Provider Presence in India and Rwanda				
Health care quality (incentives for attendance)	Banerjee et al. (2008a)	India	Incentives program to improve nurse attendance at rural subcenters. Nurses required to sign in at time/date-stamping machines. Punitive pay incentives accompanied monitoring.	Nurse attendance improved initially when nurses thought government would deduct pay, but after the 6 months, local health administration began to undermine the incentive structure. Ultimately there was no improvement in nurse attendance.
Health care quality (paying for performance)	Basinga et al. (2010)	Rwanda	Evaluation of national program that provides financial incentives for providers to increase quality of prenatal, institutional delivery, and child preventive care.	Findings suggest financial performance incentives can improve both the use of and the quality of health services, with differential impacts depending on the size of the incentives and the ability of the staff to respond to the incentives.
12.2. Contracting for Health in Post-conflict Cambodia				
Health care reform (Cambodia)	Bhushan et al. (2006)	Cambodia	Management of government health services contracted out to NGOs in districts randomly made eligible for contracting. Contracts specified targets for maternal and child health service improvement.	Targeted outcomes improved by about 1 standard deviation, representing 42% increase in children under 5 receiving vitamin A supplements, and 36% increase in prenatal care coverage. Health center management was also better, absence rates decreased, and

(Continued)

Table 4.10 (Continued)

Technology	Researchers	Country	Program Tested	Results
				availability of supplies increased.
12.3. Paying for Results at the Community Level				
Health care quality (incentives)	Olken et al. (2011)	Indonesia	Evaluation of providing incentives to improve service delivery through block grants to communities. Performance bonuses paid based on maternal and child health indicators.	Several key health metrics improved, such as regular weight checks for children and iron tablets for pregnant women. Malnutrition was reduced by 2.2 percentage points. About 50–75% of overall health benefits of the program can be attributed to the performance incentives.
12.4. Community Mobilization, Accountability, and Reform				
Community monitoring	Bjorkman and Svensson (2009)	Uganda	Evaluation of program to encourage greater community monitoring and involvement in health services to increase provider effort and make them more accountable to local communities.	Project was successful in improving community participation, provider effort, and health. Provider absenteeism was reduced by 14%, vaccination rates increased by 46% and twice as many children received vitamin A supplements.
Community monitoring	Banerjee et al. (2008b)		Interventions to encourage beneficiaries' participation: providing information; training community members.	No effect was found on community effort, provider effort, or education outcomes.

Note: Shaded rows represent non-randomized studies.

almost impossible to verify. By 16 months after the program started, there was no difference between the absence rates in the treatment and control groups.

The authors conclude that nurses, like other public service providers, are responsive to incentives when properly administered. However, ensuring that nurses come to work was a low priority for the health administration. In this case, an incentive system can be quickly undermined from the inside if supervisors are given any discretion over how and whether incentives are applied.

More favorable results from incentivizing providers were found in a study in Rwanda (Basinga et al., 2010). Although the study was originally intended to be randomized, due to a change in district boundaries it became impossible to maintain the randomized assignment for identification. Clinics were evaluated on the basis of existing quarterly visits and a review of medical records for difficult-to-forge activities such as deliveries. They were rewarded at the clinic level for each patient treated during the day, with different incentives for different treatments (ranging from $0.09 for a first prenatal care visit to $4.59 for a delivery). The authors estimate improvements in quality and utilization, with a larger impact on services with higher incentives and for services that are more in the control of the provider and depend less on patients' decisions. There are several possible reasons why the effort to incentivize providers was apparently more successful in Rwanda. This could reflect differences in the nature of the Rwandan and Indian state or it could be that incentives work better at the facility level than at the provider level.

12.2. Contracting for Health in Post-conflict Cambodia

Cambodia's health system was in very poor shape in the late 1990s: only 50 doctors had survived the Khmer Rouge, and the public system relied on new doctors with low salaries and little training who often supplemented their salaries by moonlighting in the private sector. There was substantial private spending on health, but much of the care provided was inappropriate.

As part of a massive expansion of public health facilities that had started a few years earlier, Cambodia experimented in 1999 with contracting out the management of health care on a district-by-district basis to non-governmental organizations.[35]

The approach offers the potential to strengthen the weak incentives associated with public provision while avoiding some of the distortions associated with the private sector. Contracts were issued at the district level rather than for individual providers to allow for risk sharing from health shocks without the adverse-selection

---

[35] Two types of contracting were tested in Cambodia: contracting in and contracting out. Contracting-out districts had more flexibility over pay and staff appointments (although they started with previous government staff) and were responsible for their own procurement of drugs and supplies. Contracting-in districts relied on government personnel and procurement. However, some of these distinctions were blurred in practice and due to the small sample size it was not possible to pick up many differences between contracting-in and contracting-out districts.

problems associated with individual insurance. Finally, the program allowed for bench-mark competition between providers, which would not be possible if a single contract had been given to a group to manage the entire national system.

Twelve districts were chosen to participate in the experiment and were then randomly assigned to one of two different types of contracting groups, or to a comparison group in which the government continued to directly operate health care facilities.[36] As part of the contracting program, which would cover about 11 percent of the population, prospective bidders were directed to target eight outcomes: child-hood immunization, administration of vitamin A to children, antenatal care for pregnant women, child delivery by a trained professional, delivery in a health facility, the knowledge and use of birth control, and use of public facilities when seeking curative care. Since many of these services were preventive and could result in externalities, it is likely that they would be under-supplied by fee-for-service arrangements. Contractors were required to provide a Minimum Package of Activities (MPA) at the clinics. Performance was measured against this MPA, and contractors were informed that poor performance could lead to sanctions and non-renewal of the contract.

During the study of the Cambodian contracting experiment, the country as a whole experienced huge improvements in health (Bhushan et al., 2006). Nevertheless, the evaluators of the program were able to identify large, positive impacts on health in the contracting districts because they could compare results to those in non-contracted districts. Using baseline and post-intervention survey data, they found that targeted outcomes increased by about one standard deviation. This improvement represented an increase of 42 percent in the number of children under five receiving nutritional supplements of vitamin A, and an increase in prenatal care coverage of 36 percent in contracted districts compared to non-contracted districts. In addition, health center management was better, absence rates decreased, services were more likely to be available 24 hours per day, and the number of supervisory visits and the availability of supplies increased. Measures of management quality also improved.

A concern with basing contracts on a few indicators is that attention may be paid to only these indicators and other aspects of performance not explicitly mentioned in the contract may fall in quality. The study found no evidence of this. There were no large effects on non-targeted indicators—either positive or negative.

The population responded to these improvements in the quality of public provision. Visits to government facilities increased, while visits to drug sellers and traditional healers decreased, and consequently private health spending decreased. While

---

[36] Sixteen proposals were submitted by ten different bidders for the eight districts. However, contracting was not executed in three of the districts because the bids submitted were not acceptable. When evaluating the program, the authors used intention-to-treat analysis—in other words, they analyzed districts according to the groups into which they had originally been randomized. The estimated effect size was then scaled up, according to treatment on the treated methodology, to adjust for the fact that not all the treatment districts had been treated.

the government spent more on the contracted districts, this increase in expenditure was roughly offset by a decrease in private spending on health, so that overall expenditure in contracted and non-contracted districts was roughly the same.

While the contracting experiment in Cambodia produced exciting results, it was a radical reform that was made politically more palatable because the entire health system was in need of reconstruction. It is also worth noting that the effectiveness of a contracting system will depend on the quality of procedures for awarding contracts and monitoring outcomes.

Similar results were found in Rwanda (Basinga et al., 2010). Clinics were evaluated on the basis of quarterly visits which were already happening and a review of medical records for difficult-to-forge activities such as deliveries. They were rewarded at the clinic level for each patient treated during the day, with different incentives for different treatments (ranging from $0.09 for a first prenatal care visit to $4.59 for a delivery). They find a larger impact on services with higher incentives and for services that are more in the control of the provider and depend less on patients' decisions, and do not look for spillovers for non-prenatal services.

12.3. Paying for Results at the Community Level

An Indonesian program examined the effectiveness of paying block grants to communities to fund health and education services and tying the size of subsequent grant to results at a community level. The idea was to provide funds for communities to use to improve health services as they saw fit, and create incentives to ensure proper implementation. The performance bonuses were based on eight maternal and child health indicators similar to those used in conditional cash transfer programs, and to those used in the Cambodia experiment discussed above: pre- and postnatal care; deliveries by trained midwives; iron tablets for pregnant mothers and vitamin A for young children; immunizations; regular weight checks for children under five years old; regular weight gain; and enrollment and attendance at primary and junior secondary schools. The performance bonus was based on each village's performance relative to other villages in the same subdistrict.

The Indonesian government randomly allocated subdistricts to receive the program with incentives, to a comparable program that lacked financial performance incentives but was otherwise identical, or to a control group. By comparing the program with the performance incentives to the program without such incentives, the evaluators were able to isolate the impact of the performance incentives per se (Olken et al., 2011). The program covered over 2,000 treatment villages with over 1.8 million target beneficiaries.

Overall, the program improved several of the key health process metrics, such as regular weight checks for children and iron tablets for pregnant women, and by the end of the second year of the program, the program had reduced malnutrition (defined as being 2 standard deviations or more below average in weight-for-age) by 2.2 percentage points, about 9.6 percent of the baseline level. Overall, the authors' preliminary calculations suggest that about 50–75 percent of the overall health benefits of the program can be attributed to the performance incentives. While the overall impacts of the program were modest, in areas off of the main island of Java where baseline levels of health and education service delivery were much lower, both the program as a whole and the additional impact of the performance incentives were substantially more effective, with impacts more than double in magnitude. Notably, the performance incentives were effective only for the health side of the program—while by the second year the program had begun to show small but statistically measurable impacts on school enrollment, there were no differences in impacts on education between the incentivized and non-incentivized versions of the program.

12.4. Community Mobilization, Accountability, and Reform

A recent focus of reform efforts has been to make service providers more accountable to the local population rather than to the central bureaucracy. This approach was advocated in the World Development Report "Making Services Work for the Poor" (World Bank, 2004). There has been relatively little work on this issue in health, although more is now under way. If we look at the results from health and education the results are mixed—suggesting that this approach can work but the details of the program and the institutional context matter.

In Uganda, there is a formal link between local dispensaries (much larger units than the small local clinics covered in the Indian reform) and communities through Health Unit Management Committees (HUMCs). These committees bring together dispensary staff and locally elected community representatives. HUMCs are responsible for monitoring drugs and the finances of dispensaries, can warn staff about inappropriate behavior, and recommend staff be transferred—although they have no direct power over staff. When Bjorkman and Svensson (2009) did a careful examination of these HUMCs at the start of their study they found that many of them were non-operational or ineffective.

The authors report the results of a randomized evaluation designed to encourage greater community monitoring and involvement in health services as a way to increase provider effort and make them more accountable to local communities. Viewing lack of information as a key constraint for effective community monitoring, the project undertook a detailed baseline of health service quality, including absence rates for providers. Local non-governmental organizations active on health issues held two rounds of community engagement sessions—jointly with the HUMCs—where the information for that facility was presented to staff and the community and action plans developed to improve service quality.

The project was extremely successful in achieving community participation, increasing provider work effort, and improving health. A third of HUMCs in treatment areas were either dissolved and newly elected, or received new members. An average of six local council meetings was held during 2005 in treatment communities, most of which discussed health. Seventy percent of treatment clinics had some form of community monitoring system (such as suggestion boxes) visible during a subsequent survey and more data on free services were available. Provider absenteeism was 14 percent lower in treatment facilities. BCG vaccination rates among newborns were up by 46 percent and twice as many children as prior to the program received vitamin A supplements.

Like in Cambodia, utilization of public facilities increased and visits to traditional healers went down. These improvements in service quality and usage translated into better health—with fewer underweight children and an under-five mortality rate of 95 in treatment communities vs. 147 in control.

Another study attempted to test whether community accountability is effective in improving health in Uttar Pradesh in India through a randomized trial. The authors report positive results. Randomization, however, was carried on at the district level. Because of the likelihood of correlated shocks within a district the study did not have much statistical power to distinguish the impact of the treatment (Pandey et al., 2007).

The dramatic success of the program in Uganda should be taken alongside the finding from the same study that the community monitoring institutions in place before the new program started (and operated in the comparison clinics throughout the study) were not active. The evidence on community monitoring and accountability therefore is that it can work but that the institutional details matter. This echoes the experience from the education sector (Glewwe and Kremer, 2006; Duflo et al. 2011b). For example, a very similar program to that described by Bjorkman and Svensson was tried in Uttar Pradesh in India in the education sector and failed to increase community monitoring, reduce provider absence, or improve outcomes (Banerjee et al., 2008a). That study similarly found that at the start of the program the official government system of community oversight was entirely non-functional. For a detailed discussion of the advantages and disadvantages of alternative ways to structure community accountability models of service delivery reform see Banerjee et al. (2008a). We are some way away from being able to provide clear policy guidance on whether and how to structure community monitoring and accountability in the health sector. The program that was most effective (evaluated by Bjorkman and Svensson) was quite intensive and expensive. Studies that look at cheaper and more scalable versions of community monitoring are currently under way.

13. INTERACTIONS BETWEEN HEALTH AND BROADER SOCIO-ECONOMIC VARIABLES

This review focuses on the health and public health systems. However, before concluding, we briefly discuss the impact that factors outside the health system can have on health and the impact of health on other socio-economic outcomes. While we continue to focus on results of randomized evaluations, in this section we also try to discuss some observational evidence, since most of the evidence is non-experimental.

13.1. Impact of Economic and Social Factors on Health

Health is affected by many factors outside the formal health sector, from nutrition and pollution to social factors, such as education or women's empowerment. There are major literatures on some of these factors, in particular nutrition and fertility. These literatures include important contributions from economics as well as public health researchers and demographers. We cannot cover these substantial literatures here but in this section we briefly discuss three aspects of the social and environmental determinants of health where economists have been active, where we are unaware of other recent reviews, and where randomized evaluations are being used. First, we look at the evidence on how education impacts health—in particular sexual health. Next, we examine the evidence on women's empowerment or bargaining position and health. Finally, we discuss an important area where randomized evaluations are starting to have more of a role, namely air pollution.

13.1.1. Women's Bargaining Position and Health

It has long been postulated in the policy community that improving the position of women in society could lead to improvements in health. This hypothesis comes from cross-country and within-country correlations between women's education and other measures of women's empowerment and health outcomes, particularly for children. Still, omitted variable bias is a major concern for interpreting correlations from observational data (see Lloyd et al., 2005), and recent randomized evaluations are shedding more light on the issue.

A series of papers examining the impact of providing more political power to women in India show that villages randomly selected to have leadership positions reserved for women invest more in water and the quality of the drinking water is better (Chattopadhyay and Duflo, 2004; Duflo and Topalova, 2003). In contrast, Leino (2011) finds no improvements in water provision when women are given more control over grants to communities to improve water in Kenya. One difference between these studies is that in India women could change the allocation of resources from other (mainly non-health) priorities to water whereas in Kenya all the funds were allocated to water and increasing women's power could only work through improving the efficiency with which the funds were used.

Receipt of cash transfers by women has been found to be associated with improved health outcomes. Duflo (2003) evaluates the impact of the large South-African social pensions program on the anthropometric status of children residing with a pensioner. This study is non-experimental, but exploits both the age at which people become eligible for the pension program and the time children have been exposed to the program to obtain causal estimates. Duflo (2003) finds that pensions received by women are associated with improved anthropometric status of girls (but not of boys). Pensions received by men do not affect the anthropometric status of either boys or girls.

Friedman et al. (2011) find that a merit-scholarship program for girls in Kenya increased girls' education. The authors argue that the increased human capital (test scores are found to improve in treatment schools by 0.196 standard deviations) leads to girls' empowerment and awareness and this is reflected in fewer arranged marriages, as members in the treatment group were 4 percentage points (more than 50 percent) less likely to be in an arranged marriage. The program also reduces girls' willingness to accept domestic violence: on a zero to one scale, treatment leads to a 0.067 reduction in respondents' support for the claim that "Men can beat their wives and children if they misbehave" as opposed to the statement that "No one has the right to use physical violence against anyone else," a reduction of roughly one-quarter on average support of 0.25 in the control group.

Attanasio and Lechene (2010) observe that the PROGRESA cash transfers resulted in increased nutritional intake and argue that this is because these transfers were given to women (while PROGRESA is randomized the identification of the role of women is not based on randomization because all the transfers in PROGRESA went to women). Access to microfinance for women (which may or may not increase bargaining power of women but does increase access to resources), on the other hand, is not associated with increased expenditure on health (Banerjee et al., 2010c).

Economic opportunities for women appear to increase investment in the health of girls by families. Jensen (2010) evaluates the impact of an intervention that sent recruiters from the "business process outsourcing" industry (which covers a range of back office services such as call center work) to randomly selected villages around Delhi, India. In these villages, the recruiters organized information and recruitment meetings. These meetings were only open to women. Jensen (2010) argues that the intervention increased the actual and perceived economic opportunities for older girls and shows that the intervention led to greater investment in education and nutrition of young girls, with an increase in body mass index for young girls but not for boys.

Table 4.11 Interactions between Health and Broader Socio-economic Variables

Technology	Researchers	Country	Program Tested	Results
Merit scholarships	Friedman et al. (2011)	Kenya	Merit-based scholarship awarded to 6th grade girls who scored in the top 15% on tests administered by the Kenyan government.	Girls in treatment schools are more than 50% less likely to be in an arranged marriage 4–5 yrs after the scholarship competition. Program also reduces girls' willingness to accept domestic violence.
13.1.1. Women's Bargaining Position and Health				
Female participation (reservations)	Chattopadhyay and Duflo (2003); Duflo and Topalova (2003)	India	Series of evaluations on the impact of reserving leadership positions for women on policy decisions.	Villages randomly selected to have leadership positions reserved for women invest more in water and the quality of the drinking water is better.
Female participation (user committees)	Leino (2011)	Kenya	Communities randomly selected to receive encouragement to increase female participation on their user committees responsible for maintaining newly improved water sources.	Increasing women's participation did not impact maintenance outcomes or maintenance quality.
Contraceptive use	Ashraf et al. (2010b)	Zambia	Women received vouchers for appointments with a family planning nurse, with guaranteed access to choice of modern contraceptive method. Women given vouchers either alone, or in the presence of their husband.	Women given the vouchers jointly with their husbands saw no decrease in unwanted pregnancies, while women given the vouchers in private saw a 57% decrease in unwanted pregnancies.
Conditional cash transfer (pension)	Duflo (2003)	South Africa	Evaluation of the impact of a large South-African social pensions program on the anthropometric status of children residing with a pensioner.	Pensions received by women are associated with improved anthropometric status of girls (but not of boys). Pensions received by men do not affect the anthropometric status of either boys or girls.

Conditional cash transfer (PROGRESA)	Attanasio and Lechene (2010)	Mexico	Cash transfers provided conditional on households' take up of certain health care services and educational programs.	Cash transfers resulted in increased nutritional intake; authors argue that this is because these transfers were given to women.
Microfinance	Banerjee et al. (2010c)	India	Evaluation of the introduction of microcredit in a new market.	Access to microfinance for women (which does increase access to resources) does not appear to affect female decision-making, health, or education. Health expenditure does not increase.
Recruiting services	Jensen (2010)	India	Provision of 3 years of recruiting services to help young women in villages get jobs in the business process outsourcing industry.	Increase in the actual and perceived economic opportunities for older girls and greater investment in education and nutrition of young girls, increase in BMI.
Gender imbalance	Qian (2008)	China	Exploits reforms in the second half of the 20th century in China to identify the relationship between adult female income and the survival rates of girls.	Increasing female income compared to male income by 10% of average rural income increases the fraction of surviving girls by 1 percentage point. Educational attainment increases both for boys and girls.

(Continued)

Table 4.11 (Continued)

Technology	Researchers	Country	Program Tested	Results
Television	Jensen and Oster (2009)	China	Evaluation of the impact of cable television to rural India on women's empowerment.	The introduction of cable television is associated with an increase in women's autonomy. For instance, it leads to a 3.7% decrease in the likelihood of pregnancy, and a 10% decrease in the number of situations where respondents consider it acceptable for a husband to beat his wife.
Television	Chong and La Ferrara (2009)	Brazil	Evaluation of the impact of soap operas on divorce rates.	The diffusion of soap operas, with their example of autonomous women, corresponds to an increase in separation and divorce rates of about 1/10 of a standard deviation (as well as 1/10 of the mean), and a decrease in fertility by 0.029 live births per household.

13.1.2. Environment, Health, and Pollution

Temperature	Burgess et al. (2010)	India	Examination of the effects of weather shocks on health.	A one standard deviation increase in the number of higher temperature days in rural areas during the growing season is associated with a 9% increase in mortality.

Indoor air pollution	Pitt et al. (2010)	Bangladesh, India	Exploit extended family structures to investigate the impact of indoor air pollution from cooking stoves on respiratory health.	Women who are responsible for cooking and who use biomass to do so are more likely to have respiratory health problems, as are children under 5, most likely because they are close to their mother when she is cooking.
Indoor air pollution	Duflo et al. (2008)	India	Distribution of improved cooking stoves to households to reduce indoor air pollution.	Cleaner cooking stoves can improve health outcomes, but take-up and maintenance of stoves is problematic.
Outdoor air pollution	Jayachandran (2009)	Indonesia	Examination of the impact of air pollution from large-scale wildfires on fetal, infant, and child mortality.	Impact of wild fires on early life mortality is estimated to be 15,600 additional deaths.

Note: Shaded rows represent non-randomized studies.

In the early 1990s Sen (1990, 1992) warned that 100 million women were missing, in particular in China and India. There has been substantial debate about the causes of these sex imbalances, but there is now strong evidence that sex-selective abortion is a major cause of the skewed sex ratio (see among others Junhong, 2001; Oster, 2005; Das Gupta, 2005, 2008; Oster, 2006; Lin and Luoh, 2007; Oster et al., 2008; Ebenstein, 2010). Jayachandran and Kuziemko (2009) argue that Indian girls are weaned from breast milk earlier than boys because their parents want to have another child and that this accounts for some of the differential outcomes between girls and boys in India.

Qian (2008) exploits economic reforms that differentially affected male and female income in different regions in the second half of the 20th century in China to identify the relationship between adult female income and the survival rates of girls. She estimates that increasing adult female income relative to adult male income by 10 percent of the average rural household income increases the fraction of surviving girls by one percentage point. In addition, such increases in relative female income increase the educational attainment of both boys and girls.

Two (non-randomized) studies look at the fertility impact of the media on social norms, women's role, and fertility. Using panel data, Jensen and Oster (2009) examine the effect of the introduction of cable television on women's status in rural India. The introduction of cable television is associated with a 0.16 decrease in the number of situations in which it is considered acceptable for a man to beat his wife (relative to a base of 1.61). Adding cable is associated with a 12 percentage point decrease in the reported preference to have the next child be a boy. Getting cable leads to approximately a 3.7 percentage point decrease in the likelihood of pregnancy.

Chong and La Ferrara (2009) study the effect of soap opera availability on divorce rates in Brazil. The diffusion of soap operas, with their example of autonomous women, corresponds to a significant decrease in fertility by about 0.029 live births per household during the study period (from a mean of 2.66), larger than the predicted effect of increasing the household head's education by one year. They also find an increase in separation and divorce rates of about one-tenth of a standard deviation (as well as one-tenth of the mean), the same effect as an increase of almost one-half year in women's education, in a context where the mean of women's years of education over the period is 3.2 years.

There is evidence that household bargaining affects demand for health and family planning services in particular. Women are more likely to use contraception and have fewer unwanted pregnancies if they are offered contraception without their husbands present, while couples are more likely to buy insecticide-treated nets if they are offered to the couple together.

Ashraf et al. (2010) provide women in Zambia access to free and convenient long-term contraceptive methods. Women who were given the vouchers to access the contraception jointly with their husbands saw no decrease in unwanted pregnancies. Women who were given the vouchers in private, without the knowledge of their husbands, saw a 57 percent fall in unwanted pregnancies. Dupas (2009) examines that household bargaining affects demand for insecticide-treated nets. Women were not more likely to buy nets than men, but handing out vouchers for nets in the presence of both household heads increases take-up by about 7 percentage points compared to targeting either of them alone. Nevertheless, the authors argue that this effect is relatively small, especially in comparison with the price effect: a similar increase of 7 percentage points in take-up can be achieved with an 18 percent ($0.27) decrease in price from the current price at which nets are subsidized on the retail market by PSI (100 Ksh or $1.50).

13.1.2. Environment, Health, and Pollution

Pollution is a major cause of poor health in developing countries. Regulatory standards and enforcement are much weaker than in developed countries and levels of particulate matter are often many times the levels considered unacceptable in rich countries.

In addition to the industrial and vehicular sources of air pollution that are common in developed countries, indoor air pollution from the use of biomass and coal as a source of household energy is a major cause of mortality in poor countries, causing an estimated 1.6 million deaths every year (WHO, 2005a). Pitt et al. (2010) exploit extended family structures in Bangladesh and India to investigate the impact of indoor air pollution on respiratory health. They argue that women who are responsible for cooking and who use biomass to do so are more likely to exhibit respiratory symptoms. Young children (under five) raised by these women are also more likely to exhibit poorer respiratory health, most likely because they are close to their mother when she is cooking. The effect of respiratory health problems incurred at an early age appears to persist among children five to nine years old.

Improved cooking stoves can improve health outcomes (Duflo et al., 2008) but take-up and maintenance of these stoves is problematic. Finding ways to address this problem or to allow people to use other technologies such as gas canisters at lower income levels could have a major health impact.

Jayachandran (2009) uses (non-random) variation in exposure to major forest fires in Indonesia in 1997 to estimate the impact of air pollution on early life mortality, finding an estimated 15,600 additional deaths due to the fires. She finds a much higher burden on those with lower economic status and discusses a number of possible reasons why the poor were so much more vulnerable to air pollution than the rest of the population. This work is similar in approach to that done in the US on air pollution and health, such as Chay and Greenstone (2003).

Global warming also affects health. Burgess et al. (2010) find that a one standard deviation increase in days above 32 degrees centigrade in rural areas of India during the growing season leads to higher prices and lower yields for farmers, and therefore less income and consumption. They also find it leads to a 9 percent higher crude death rate.

13.2. The Impact of Health on Other Economic Variables

As mentioned in the introduction, existing reviews of the literature on the impact of health on other variables include Strauss and Thomas (1998, 2007), López-Casasnovas et al. (2005); Glewwe and Miguel (2007); Currie (2009); Spence and Lewis (2009); Bleakley (2010a); and Eide and Showalter (forthcoming). The relationship between health and economic outcomes has been studied using micro-data, theory and simulations, and cross-country evidence. We briefly mention key papers in each literature. The vast majority of the studies here are not randomized, although many have robust identification strategies.

Studies using micro-data have produced convincing evidence regarding the impact of particular health risks and health conditions on a variety of outcome variables, including education and income. A series of influential studies have shown large long-run economic impacts of in utero or child health and nutrition shocks resulting from natural experiments, including the worldwide influenza epidemic of 1918 (Almond, 2006), war-induced famine in Zimbabwe (Alderman et al., 2006), the Great Famine in China (Meng and Qian, 2009), and economic shocks driven by rainfall variation in Indonesia (Maccini and Yang, 2009). The INCAP experiment which provided nutritional supplements to children in Guatemala (described in Hoddinott et al., 2008; Maluccio et al., 2009; and Behrman et al., 2009) was found to have large impacts on wages, cognitive skills and intergenerational effects. However, the sample size was extremely small (two treatment and two comparison villages) and attrition was very high, suggesting more work is needed in this area.

Studies in less developed countries that attempt to address the issue of long-run impacts of child health include those that deal with iodine deficiency in utero (Xue-Yi et al., 1994; Pharoah and Connolly, 1991; Field et al., 2009); the impact of breast-feeding on cognitive development (Reynolds, 2001); prenatal exposure to Ramadan (Almond and Muzumder, 2008); early childhood malaria prophylaxis (Jukes et al., 2006); and early childhood under-nutrition (Mendez and Adair, 1999; Glewwe et al., 2001), among many others. Though these studies are generally non-experimental (Jukes et al., 2006 is an exception), taken together they provide considerable evidence that adult cognitive performance may be affected by nutrition in the womb and early childhood. Related work on the long-run benefits of child health, nutrition investments and low birth weight in the US and other developed countries include Currie and Thomas (1995), Garces et al. (2002), Conley and Bennett (2000), and Sorensen et al. (1997).

There is also microeconomic evidence on the relationship between anti-retroviral treatment (ARVs) and labor supply. Habyarimana et al. (2010) examine the impact of free ARVs in Botswana on absence rates in an African firm, concluding that increases in workers' productivity are too small to make it privately profitable for the firm to provide ARVs to HIV-positive employees. Thirumurthy et al. (2008) use longitudinal survey data from western Kenya to estimate that ARVs leads to a 20 percent increase in patients' likelihood of participating in the labor force and a 35 percent increase in weekly hours worked.

Recent reviews discuss the potential impact of health on education (Bleakley, 2010a; Glewwe and Miguel, 2007; Eide and Showalter, forthcoming). Several of the studies on this topic are randomized, including studies on iron supplementation and deworming in India (Bobonis et al., 2006), deworming in Kenya (Miguel and Kremer, 2004), and provision of eye-glasses in China (Glewwe et al., 2010). Other noteworthy micro-empirical contributions on nutrition, health, and productivity include Schultz (2005), Alderman (2007), and Thomas et al. (2006). Most of these studies find that health has important implications for education. A randomized study by Oster and Thornton (forthcoming), however, find that a technology that helps girls manage blood flow more effectively during menstruation does not lead to more education despite popular perceptions that this is a major barrier to education.

Most of this research investigates how child health affects education. However, there is also a strand of literature that examines whether improvements in life expectancy for *adults* could be an important driver of increased investment in education, as it potentially increases the return to such investments. Two recent microeconomic papers provide evidence on this channel. Jayachandran and Lleras-Muney (2009) estimate that reductions in maternal mortality in Sri Lanka increased literacy by 0.7 percentage points (2 percent) and years of education by 0.11 years (3 percent). Fortson (2011), exploiting regional HIV prevalence rates in 15 sub-Saharan countries, also provides evidence consistent with the hypothesis that longevity matters for investments in education. Bleakley (2010a), however, argues that the microeconomic estimates are likely to be upper bounds, as adult health changes can also affect schooling through other channels, and that in developed countries increased longevity was accompanied by a decrease in hours worked.

Overall, the microeconomic studies suggest that some health investments, such as iodine supplementation, deworming, or malaria control, have extremely high rates of return due to their impact on education and income, even setting aside the direct welfare benefits of improved health (Miguel and Kremer, 2004; Bleakley, 2007; Bleakley, 2009a; Field et al., 2009; Lucas, 2010; Bleakley, 2010b; Cutler et al., 2010; Baird et al., 2011a).

Even though rates of return to investment in health seem to be high, microeconomic evidence does not suggest that the direct effect of improved health is likely to create transformative macroeconomic consequences. Using microeconomic estimates of the effect of health on individual outcomes to construct estimates of the impact of health on GDP per capita, Weil (2007) estimates that eliminating health differences among countries would reduce the variance of log GDP per worker by 9.9 percent, and reduce the ratio of GDP per worker at the 90th percentile to GDP per worker at the 10th percentile from 20.5 to 17.9.[37] The impact of eliminating any single disease, such as malaria, let alone that of plausible reductions in disease burden from feasible health programs would be much smaller.

Note that microeconomic studies of the impact of health on income may miss certain general equilibrium or disease externality effects.[38] Disease externalities will typically have to be considered to get valid welfare measures, but to the extent they are local, they can potentially be measured with micro-data (Miguel and Kremer, 2004). General equilibrium effects, for example on capital accumulation, are harder to measure with micro-data, but may not be relevant for welfare if society was initially optimizing given health (Bleakley, 2010a).

A sense of the range of hypothesized general equilibrium effects is provided by the literature simulating the impact of HIV/AIDS. Some argue that the decrease in life expectancy will reduce incentives to save and to invest in education, further decreasing physical and human capital (Dixon et al., 2001; Ferreira and Pessoa, 2003; Corrigan et al., 2005; Bell et al., 2006). Using an overlapping generations model Bell et al. (2006) forecast that the HIV/AIDS epidemic could bring the South African economy to a complete collapse within three generations if nothing is done to combat it. Similarly, Ferreira and Pessoa (2003) simulate that schooling would decrease by a half due to the lower incentives to invest in human capital. This, in turn, would lead to a decline in savings and capital investments, leading to a 25 percent decline in output per capita. On the other hand, Young (2005) argues that widespread community infection will lower fertility and increase human capital investment by increasing the scarcity of labor and the value of women's time, leading to large increases in income per capita.

Another strand of the literature uses cross-country regressions to estimate the impact of health on economic outcomes, presumably capturing general equilibrium effects. Gallup and Sachs (2001), for instance, use cross-country growth regressions to

---

[37] See also Shastry and Weil (2003) and Ashraf et al. (2009).
[38] See also Bleakley (2010a).

argue that countries with intensive malaria grew 1.3 percent less per year and that a 10 percent reduction in malaria was correlated with 0.3 percent higher growth. A major concern with any cross-country regression of this kind is the potential for omitted variable bias, as countries that are prone to malaria tend to have many other characteristics that might impede growth.

More recent macro-papers have attempted to deal with the problem of omitted variable bias while still capturing general equilibrium effects, by using instrumental variable approaches to better identify the impact of health shocks. While it is too early to draw firm conclusions, this literature tends not to find impacts of health on aggregate growth in income per capita that are anywhere near those of Gallup and Sachs.

Acemoglu and Johnson (2007) argue that the wave of international health innovations that began in the 1940s led to an increase in population in areas with high pre-intervention disease burden. They do not find a significant increase in GDP. As a result, they estimate that the effect of the international epidemiological transition on GDP per capita was negative. Aghion et al. (2009), on the other hand, argue that in cross-country regressions, per capita GDP growth is significantly affected by both the initial level and the accumulation of life expectancy, and that convergence in life expectancy across countries explains the lack of causal link found by Acemoglu and Johnson (2007). Bleakley (2009b) points out that health improvements that primarily affect mortality may not generate this type of Malthusian effect and may be more likely to increase per capita income. The Malthusian effects which Acemoglu and Johnson (2007) find may or may not be operative in contemporary contexts.

Ahuja et al. (2006), using the male circumcision rate in various African countries to instrument for HIV prevalence, find no measurable impact of AIDS on economic growth or savings. However, standard errors are large and the paper does find weak evidence that AIDS has led to a decline in fertility, a slowdown in education gains, as measured by youth literacy, and a rise in poverty, as measured by malnutrition.

The impact of malaria has been studied extensively. Bleakley (2010b) studies the effect of malaria eradication campaigns on income and education in Brazil, Colombia, Mexico, and the United States. Using malaria mortality rates and an ecology index to identify pre-eradication disease prevalence, Bleakley finds that childhood exposure to malaria lowers labor productivity and leads to lower adult income. Results for years of schooling are mixed. (Bleakley points out that improvements in child health have theoretically ambiguous effects on education, depending on their relative impact on productivity in school and in work.) Lucas (2010) finds that malaria eradication in Paraguay and Sri Lanka in the 1940s to the 1960s led to increases in female education and literacy rates. Cutler et al. (2010) use the national malaria eradication program in India in the 1950s as a quasi-experiment and exploit geographic variation in malaria prevalence prior to the eradication campaign. Difference-in-differences estimates show no gains in literacy or primary school completion, but modest relative increases in income (proxied by per capita household expenditure) for prime-age men. Two other studies use weather conditions to instrument for malaria exposure in the United States and examine the effects on long-run health and economic outcomes. Hong (2007) finds that malarial risk leads to adverse long-run health outcomes, lower labor force participation, and lower wealth. Barreca (2009) finds that in utero and postnatal malaria exposure leads to lower educational attainment.

It is important not to lose sight of the fact that health directly affects welfare and that these affects are likely to have very large impacts on overall measures of welfare across countries. Jones and Klenow (2011) construct a measure of welfare that includes mortality, consumption, inequality, and leisure. While income grew at a rate of only 3 percent annually between 1980 and 2000, the broader measure of welfare including life expectancy grew at a 4 percent annual rate. Becker et al. (2005) compute a "full" income measure that takes into account the value of life expectancy gains experienced by 49 countries between 1965 and 1995. They find evidence of convergence in welfare levels. Countries starting with lower income tended to grow more in terms of "full" income than countries starting with higher income (which is not true for GDP growth). The average growth rate of "full" income is about 140 percent for developed countries, compared to 192 percent for developing countries.

In sum, there is considerable microeconomic evidence that health has very important effects on non-health outcomes and that certain investments in health are highly productive, yielding benefits that greatly exceed their costs. However, there is limited evidence for the idea that health investments could eliminate much of the difference across countries in GDP per capita, or allow countries to escape a poverty trap. In our view, the primary reason to invest in health is its direct impact on human welfare. In specific areas where there is direct evidence that health has an impact on other variables, it is appropriate to consider these impacts as well in evaluating the cost effectiveness of health investments.

14. CONCLUSION

Over the last 15 years development economists have conducted randomized evaluations of many specific approaches to improve health in developing countries. While each individual study tests specific health questions or sets of questions in specific contexts, it is now possible to draw more general conclusions about how humans behave, both as consumers of health care and as suppliers as part of health delivery systems. Here we first summarize some of the lessons for policy and then discuss some lessons for research and potential directions for future work.

14.1. Policy Implications

Both the analytic frameworks discussed in section 2, the human capital investment model and cost-effectiveness analysis, can contribute to analysis of which health services should be subsidized and to the design of appropriate regulatory policy.

The human capital model suggests that in the absence of subsidies, consumers will underinvest in measures against infectious disease that create externality benefits for others and that the market will undersupply even excludable public goods, such as water and sanitation infrastructure. In the cases where these effects have been measured, they seem quantitatively important, although more work is needed on this issue.

Several studies suggest that financial market imperfections are important in health. Insurance markets are highly imperfect, with consumers bearing considerable financial risk due to health shocks and liquidity constraints limiting investment in health human capital.

The finding that households with young children who are more vulnerable to diarrhea and malaria are no more willing to pay for prevention is a puzzle under the model. One possible interpretation is that household decision making puts little weight on child health.

Several studies suggest that present bias leads consumers to underinvest in prevention and treatment of chronic conditions relative to acute care. Limited attention also seems to affect health behavior, with consumers responding more to health education programs in the short run than the long run, for example.

All this suggests private decision making in health may lead to inefficient outcomes and points to a potential role for government. Cost-effectiveness analysis can then be a useful tool in prioritizing government spending.

While multiple market failures make private solutions suboptimal, government health systems are often highly dysfunctional, with many health workers absent and corruption common. In light of this it is worth distinguishing between different types of cases in thinking about policy.

The easiest case is that of cost-effective products for the prevention and non-acute care of infectious disease that do not require individual diagnosis and cannot easily be diverted to other uses, or where diversion can be controlled.[39] This includes, for example, immunization, mosquito nets, and water treatment. In this case, many of the studies suggest free distribution has important advantages over partial subsidies. Even small fees typically deter many consumers from using highly cost-effective technologies and they do not raise much revenue. Fees do not seem to target products to those who most need them or induce consumers to utilize health prevention products. Endowment effects may make consumers less likely to on-sell products they were

---

[39] Some prevention products (such as soap) have common, alternative, non-health uses.

given for free than might be expected under standard economic assumptions. In many cases, it may make sense to go beyond free distribution and provide targeted incentives. Incentives can induce large increases in take-up even when they are much smaller than those in conditional cash transfer programs. (These larger transfer programs, however, may be desirable as an efficient form of redistribution to the poor, and they have important effects on education.)

Beyond price, the evidence also suggests other factors are important for take-up. Convenience has a large effect in multiple studies—people are unwilling to walk very far to pick up HIV tests, get clean water, or get fortified flour. There is growing evidence that salience is important, consistent with models of limited attention, and that health behavior is subject to peer effects.

The evidence therefore suggests that it may be desirable to make preventive approaches against infectious disease free, convenient, and salient, and to do so in a way that facilitates social interaction and the development of social norms. Increasingly, researchers are not only evaluating existing programs, but also helping design new approaches to address health challenges. In some cases products can be delivered most conveniently to users by going beyond the formal health system. Schools, for example, create a venue where it is possible to reach large numbers of people quickly, conveniently, and cheaply. Schools are more widely dispersed than clinics in many countries, absenteeism rates of teachers tend to be lower than those for health workers, and children gather together at school in any case, so it is much easier to reach children through schools than by waiting for them to come into clinics. School-based mass deworming has reached millions of children and this approach could potentially be used for other health needs, for example screening children for visual impairment (Glewwe et al., 2010). Two examples illustrate the potential health gains from designing programs based on the findings summarized in this chapter.

Kremer et al. (2011a) developed and tested provision of dilute chlorine via a point-of-collection system, including a dilute chlorine dispenser placed at the water source; a local promoter, with temporary payment, to encourage its use; and free provision of a supply of chlorine solution packed in bulk. The system makes it convenient for users to treat water when they collect, provides a daily salient visual reminder to households to treat their water, and increases the potential for learning, norm formation, and social network effects by making the dispenser public.

The majority of households with access to the dispenser continued to treat their water 30 months later, well after the end of the six-month period for which the promoter was paid. This bulk supply dramatically reduces delivery costs relative to the retail approach that requires packaging chlorine in small bottles, making estimated long-term costs at scale as low as $20–30 per DALY saved.[40]

---

[40] See also Dhaliwal and Tulloch (2009).

Another example is a program in India that simultaneously addressed problems on the consumer and health worker side (discussed in more detail in section 5.2). Through careful monitoring and linking provider pay to attendance, the program was able to ensure highly reliable and predictable vaccination camps. These were combined with small incentives to help overcome present bias and encourage parents to complete the full course of vaccinations for their children. Together this led to a more than six-fold increase in the rate at which children were fully immunized in Rajasthan.

There is scope for more work to determine how best to distribute free products for prevention and treatment of infectious disease that do not require diagnosis, using what we have learnt about consumer behavior in this area.

The harder case is finding ways to improve general health services and strengthen incentives for health care workers. Reforms of the public system have been highly successful (including in Indonesia, Uganda, and Cambodia) using a variety of approaches: incentives for local government, community empowerment, and contracting out of health facility management. However, reform may be difficult to implement politically, as the experience of India with nurses, discussed in section 12.1, suggests.

14.2. Directions for Future Research

A review of the literature suggests directions for future research both methodologically and in terms of substantive areas.

Methodologically, the new approach of conducting multiple, iterative randomized evaluations to test alternative approaches to a problem is now well established. On the consumer side at least, certain consistent patterns of behavior have emerged across studies and countries, and across different health technologies. Randomized evaluations have also been used to shed light not just on the impact of particular programs, but on underlying mechanisms.

What directions are important for the future?

Following programs over longer time periods is important for both policy and for understanding human behavior. For example, understanding the longer-run impact of health education programs is important for gauging their cost effectiveness as well as for understanding the mechanisms influencing health behavior.

Some randomized evaluations examine policies that could potentially be easily scaled up; others involve techniques more akin to laboratory experiments; and still others involve a combination of the two. While laboratory-style experiments are a valuable tool, and offer the potential to isolate issues of theoretical interest, a downside is that actions in these artificial situations may differ from those in more natural contexts. Familiarity with the context may be important to reduce the risk of misinterpreting behavior in these contexts.

Randomized evaluations can be combined with structural models. For example, Kremer et al. (2011b) use a randomized evaluation to estimate the impact of a particular program, but also to estimate the parameters of a structural model which can then be used to make out-of-sample predictions and simulate the impact of a range of policy alternatives that themselves could not be examined through randomized evaluations.

One important issue for future work is survey effects and experimenter demand effects. Zwane et al. (2011) suggest that the mere act of surveying people can change their behavior, consistent with models of limited attention. Finding ways to limit these effects seems important.

Substantively, one area of importance for policy is understanding how to implement free distribution. Many governments have announced free primary education or free health care for pregnant women and children, but unofficial fees have remained in place (IRCBP, 2008). How can governments translate a policy of free provision of certain goods and services into practice? Corruption is common in health centers and hospitals (Guyatt et al., 2002; Di Tella and Schargrodsky, 2002; Vian, 2008). Even in the absence of corruption, it may be difficult to motivate health workers if they are not paid by users. In the social entrepreneurship model, staff are motivated by earning a living from the sale of products, and in the public system, nurses may be motivated to come to work by the informal fees they charge. Fees are often a source of income that clinic staff use to fix infrastructure or replace supplies that are out of stock. Research is needed on whether these delivery system issues get worse if fees are abolished and whether alternative systems can be put in place.

While there is now strong evidence on the impact of pricing of products for prevention and non-acute treatment of infectious disease, more research is needed on the impact of fees for clinic visits and acute care for a range of health conditions that do require individual diagnosis. As countries grow economically and undergo the health and demographic transition, these issues will loom ever larger. While the burden of disease in poor countries currently has a huge role for infectious and parasitic disease, in the future it is expected to become much smaller (WHO, 2008).

The economic issues involved when the disease burden changes are likely to be quite different. Disease externalities will become less relevant. Present bias would not necessarily lead to underinvestment in acute treatment as the cost of acute illness is incurred immediately.

Present-bias and limited-attention issues may increasingly be around problems of obesity, tobacco, alcohol, and compliance with medication for chronic conditions, as in much of the developed world. Understanding the role of social norms around these issues will be important.

Social insurance will be a key issue as incomes grow and the burden of disease evolves. The trade-off between optimal risk sharing and moral hazard considerations might suggest social insurance provision for certain defined inpatient procedures but not outpatient care, as in India's RSBY program. On the other hand, given the low utilization of many rural primary health clinics, the marginal cost of seeing additional patients may be low, and these clinics may be an important entry point, suggesting a rationale for including them in social insurance programs.

There are substantial questions about the health value of much health care delivered in developing countries, suggesting potential complementarity between reform measures that raise the quality of care and measures to reduce the cost of care with covered providers in either the public or private sector.

While many evaluations have shed light on consumer behavior it will increasingly be important to compare different health care delivery and financing systems. Understanding more about when and how health workers and systems can be made more accountable is an important area for further research, as results in this area may be dependent on the details of the political and institutional context.

There are many other areas where more research is needed. We know relatively little about human capital in the health sector: Where is the biggest return to an additional dollar of investment in health care training? How can community health workers best be selected, trained, and managed? Should we be training more traditional birth attendants (or will this simply dissuade women from delivering in clinics) or more doctors (or will they simply emigrate to rich countries, e.g. Clemens and Pettersson, 2006; Bhargava and Docquier, 2008)? We need to know how best to regulate the private and non-government sector in health, which ranges from highly effective to dangerous quacks. We need to understand how to deal with the growing issue of chronic diseases and mental health in very resource constrained environments.

The industrial organization of health care, including interactions among private and public-sector health facilities, is an important area for future work.

Interactions between patients and providers in the presence of asymmetric information is another important area. Existing theory and non-experimental work suggest that there is underprovision of diagnostic tests and overprovision of treatments that produce short-run improvements for the patient, such as glucose drips or steroids; that signal provider effort, such as injections and medicine; that address self-limiting conditions (Das and Hammer, 2004); and that generate negative externalities, such as antibiotics. Understanding how to address these issues is important for policy.

Advances in information and communication technology raise interesting questions around mental health, monitoring of providers, and even international trade in medical services.

Regulatory policy is another important area for further research. As discussed by Dupas (2011b), governments in developed countries routinely use regulatory policy and mandates to encourage public health measures such as vaccination. Historically, colonial and post-independence governments in much of the developing world mandated public health measures, for example requiring households to construct latrines or eliminate stagnant water where mosquitoes can breed. The community-led total sanitation movement can be interpreted in this context, since in practice some programs rely on incentivizing local officials.

Regulation of private providers is an important issue given the large role of private providers in health care in much of the developing world, the limited enforcement of regulations on pharmaceutical sales, and the prevalence in some countries of untrained providers. The balance between efforts to train untrained providers and the effort to restrict the provision of medical care and the sale of pharmaceuticals to those who are qualified to do so will be an important issue for the future.

Issues of political economy, personnel economics within the health system, and corruption in health are critical, albeit difficult to study.

The returns to work on health in developing countries are substantial. The health care systems of developing countries are so far away from the production possibility frontier that it is possible to find areas of improvement that can make very substantial differences to the health of many. Tens of millions of lives have already been impacted by the scale-up of approaches that have been found to be effective by research discussed in this chapter. There is scope for millions more to benefit from further improving our understanding of how best to improve health in the developing world.

REFERENCES

Acemoglu, D. & Johnson, S. (2007). Disease and development: The effect of life. *Journal of Political Economy, 115*(6), 925–985.

Aghion, P., Howitt, P., & Murtin, F. (2009). The relationship between health and growth: When Lucas meets Nelson-Phelps. Working Paper.

Ahuja, A., Kremer, M., & Zwane, A. P. (2010). Providing safe water: Evidence from randomized evaluations. *Annual Reviews of Resource Economics, 2*, 237–256.

Ahuja, A., Wendell, B., & Werker, E. (2006). Male circumcision and AIDS: The macroeconomic impact of a health crisis. Harvard Business School Working Paper 07-025.

Ainslie, G. W. (1975). Specious reward: A behavioral theory of impulsiveness and impulsive control. *Psychological Bulletin, 82*, 463–496.

Ainslie, G. W. (1992). *Picoeconomics*. Cambridge: Cambridge University Press.

Akin, J., Birdsall, N., & Ferranti, D. (1987). *Financing health services in developing countries: An agenda for reform*. Washington, DC: World Bank.

Alderman, H. (2007). Improving nutrition through community growth promotion: Longitudinal study of nutrition and early child development program in Uganda. *World Development, 35*(8), 1376–1389.

Alderman, H., Hoddinott, J., & Kinsey, B. (2006). Long term consequences of early childhood malnutrition. *Oxford Economic Papers, 58*(3), 450–474.

Almond, D. (2006). Is the 1918 influenza pandemic over? Long-term effects of in-utero influenza exposure in the post-1940 U.S. population. *Journal of Political Economy, 114*(4), 672–712.

Almond, D. & Mazumder, B. (2008). Health capital and the prenatal environment: The effect of maternal fasting during pregnancy. NBER Working Paper.

Arnold, B. & Colford, J. (2007). Treating water with chlorine at point-of-use to improve water quality and reduce child diarrhea in developing countries: A systematic review and meta-analysis. *American Journal of Tropical Medicine and Hygiene, 76*(2), 354–364.

Ashraf N., Berry, J., & Shapiro, J. (2010a). Can higher prices stimulate product use? Evidence from a field experiment in Zambia. *American Economic Review.* (in press).

Ashraf, N., Field, E., & Lee, J. (2010b). Household bargaining and excess fertility: An experimental study in Zambia, Working Paper, available online at < http://www.povertyactionlab.org/publication/household-bargaining-and-excess-fertility-experimental-study-zambia >.

Ashraf, N., Jack, B. K., & Kamenica, E. (2011). *Information and subsidies: Complements or substitutes?* Cambridge, MA: Harvard University.

Ashraf, Q., Lester, A., & Weil, D. (2009). When does improving health raise GDP? *NBER Macroeconomics Annual 2008.* University of Chicago Press.

Attanasio, O. & Lechene, V. (2010). Efficient responses to targeted cash transfers. Available at < http://www.homepages.ucl.ac.uk/ ~ uctpjrt/ >.

Baird, S., Chirwa, E., McIntosh, C., & Özler, B. (2010). The short-term impacts of a schooling conditional cash transfer program on the sexual behavior of young women. *Health Economics* (forthcoming).

Baird, S., Hicks, J.H., Kremer, M. & Miguel, E. (2011a). Worms at work: Long-run impacts of child health gains. Working Paper.

Baird, S., Hoop, J., & Özler, B. (2011b). Income shocks and adolescent mental health. Working Paper.

Baird, S., McIntosh, C., & Özler, B. (2011c). Cash or condition? Evidence from a randomized cash transfer program. *Quarterly Journal of Economics, 126*(4), (forthcoming).

Banerjee, A., Banerji, R., Duflo, E., Glennerster, R., & Khemani, S. (2008b). Pitfalls of participatory programs: Evidence from a randomized evaluation in education in India. Working Paper.

Banerjee, A., Deaton, A., & Duflo, E. (2004a). Health, health care, and economic development. *American Economic Review, 94*(2), 326–330.

Banerjee, A., Deaton, A., & Duflo, E. (2004b). Health care delivery in rural Rajasthan. Poverty Action Lab working paper No. 4. Available at < http://www.povertyactionlab.org/publication/health-care-delivery-rural-rajasthan >.

Banerjee, A., Duflo, E., & Glennerster, R. (2008a). Putting a Band-Aid on a corpse: Incentives for nurses in the Indian Public Health Care System. *European Economic Association, 6*(2–3), 487–500.

Banerjee, A., Duflo, E., & Glennerster, R. (2010a). Is decentralized iron fortification a feasible option to fight anemia among the poorest? In D. A. Wise (Ed.), *Explorations in the economics of aging.* University of Chicago Press.

Banerjee, A., Duflo, E., Glennerster, R., & Kinnan, C. (2010c). The miracle of microfinance? Available online at < http://www.povertyactionlab.org/publication/miracle-microfinance-evidence-randomized-evaluation >.

Banerjee, A., Duflo, E., Glennerster, R., & Kothari, D. (2010b). Improving immunization coverage in rural India: A clustered randomized controlled evaluation of immunization campaigns with and without incentives. *British Medical Journal,* 340:C2220.

Banerjee, A., Duflo, E., & Hornbeck, R. (2011). Impacts of health insurance in rural India: Evidence from randomized insurance requirements for microfinance clients. Work in Progress.

Barreca, A. (2009). *The long-term economic impact of in utero and postnatal exposure to malaria.* Tulane University mimeo.

Basinga, P., Gertler, P. J., Binagwabo, A., Soucat, A. L. B., Sturdy, J. R., & Vermeersch, C. M. J. (2010). Paying primary health care centers for performance in Rwanda. World Bank Policy Research Working Paper 5190.

Bates, M.A., Glennerster, R., & Gumede, K. (2011). The price is wrong: user fees, access and sustainability. Available online at < http://www.povertyactionlab.org/publication/the-price-is-wrong >.

Becker, G. S., Philipson, T. J., & Soares, R. R. (2005). The quantity and quality of life and the evolution of world inequality. *American Economic Review, 95*(1), 277–291.

Behrman, J. R., Murphy, A., Quisumbing, A. R., & Yount, K. (2009). Are returns to mothers' human capital realized in the next generation? The impact of mothers' intellectual human capital and long-run nutritional status on children's human capital in Guatemala. IFPRI discussion paper, available online at < http://www.ifpri.org/sites/default/files/publications/ifpridp00850.pdf/ >.

Bell, C., Devarajan, S., & Gersbach, H. (2006). The long-run economic costs of AIDS: A model with an application to South Africa. *World Bank Economic Review, 20*(1), 55–89.

Bennear, L. S., Tarozzi, A., Pfaff, A., Soumya, H. B., Ahmed, K. M., & van Green, A. (2011). Bright lines, risk beliefs, and risk avoidance: Evidence from a randomized experiment in Bangladesh. Working Paper.

Berendes, S., Heywood, P., Oliver, S., & Garner, P. (2011). Quality of private and public ambulatory health care in low and middle income countries: Systematic review of comparative studies. *PLoS Med, 8*, 4.

Bhushan, I., Bloom, E., Clingingsmith, D., Hong, R., King, E., Kremer, M., et al. *Contracting for health: Evidence from Cambodia*. Working Paper Harvard University.

Björkman, M. & Svensson, J. (2009). Power to the people: Evidence from a randomized field experiment on community-based monitoring in Uganda. *Quarterly Journal of Economics, 124*(2), 735–769.

Bleakley, H. (2007). Disease and development: Evidence from hookworm eradication in the American south. *Quarterly Journal of Economics, 122*(1), 73–117.

Bleakley, H. (2009a). Economic effects of childhood exposure to tropical disease. *American Economic Review, 99*(2), 218–223.

Bleakley, H. (2009b). Comment on "When Does Improving Health Raise GDP?" NBER chapters. In *NBER macroeconomics annual 2008*, Volume 23, pp. 205–220.

Bleakley, H. (2010a). Health, human capital, and development. *Annual Review of Economics, 2*, 283–310.

Bleakley, H. (2010b). Malaria eradication in the Americas: A retrospective analysis of childhood exposure. *American Economic Journal: Applied, 2*(2), 1–45. Working Paper, CEDE/Los Andes.

Bleakley, H. & Lin, J. (2007). Thick-market effects and churning in the labor market: Evidence from U.S. cities. Working Papers 07-23, Federal Reserve Bank of Philadelphia.

Brauw, A. De & Peterman, A. (2011). Can conditional cash transfers improve maternal health and birth outcomes? Evidence from El Salvador's *Comunidades Solidarias Rurales*. International Food Policy Research Institute. Working Paper.

Burgess, R., Deschenes, O., Donaldson, D., & Greenstone, M. (2010). Weather and death in India. Unpublished Manuscript.

Chattopadhyay, R. & Duflo, E. (2004). Women as policy makers: Evidence from a randomized policy experiment in India. *Econometrica, 72*(5), 1409–1443.

Chaudhury, N., Hammer, J., Kremer, M., Muralidharan, K., & Halsey Rogers, F. (2006). Missing in action: Teacher and health worker absence in developing countries. *Journal of Economic Perspectives, 20*(1), 91–116.

Chay, K. Y. & Greenstone, M. (2003). The impact of air pollution on infant mortality: Evidence from geographic variation in pollution shocks induced by a recession. *Quarterly Journal of Economics, 118*(3), 1121–1167.

Chong, A. & La Ferrara, E. (2009). Television and divorce: Evidence from Brazilian novelas. *Journal of the European Economic Association P&P, 7*(2–3), 458–468.

Coates, T. (2000). The Voluntary HIV-1 Counseling and Testing Efficacy Study Group. Efficacy of voluntary HIV-1 counselling and testing in individuals and couples in Kenya, Tanzania, and Trinidad: A randomised trial. *Lancet, 356*, 103–112.

Cohen, J. & Dupas, P. (2010). Free distribution or cost-sharing? Evidence from a malaria prevention experiment. *Quarterly Journal of Economics* (in press).

Cohen, J., Dupas, P. & Schaner, S. (2011). Prices, diagnostic tests and the demand for malaria treatment: Evidence from a randomized trial. Unpublished Manuscript.

Conley, D. & Bennett, N. G. (2000). Is biology destiny? Birth weight and life chances. *American Sociological Review, 65*(3), 458–467.

Corrigan, P., Glomm, G., & Mendez, F. (2005). AIDS crisis and growth. *Journal of Development Economics,* 77(1), 107–124.

Cretin, S., Williams, A., & Sine, J. (2006). China rural health insurance experiment. RAND Working Paper.

Currie, J. (2009). Healthy, wealthy, and wise: Socioeconomic status, poor health in childhood, and human capital development. *Journal of Economic Literature, 47*(1), 87–122.

Currie, J., & Thomas, D. (1995). *Nature vs. nurture? The Bell curve and children's cognitive achievement.* RAND—Labor and Population Program.

Curtis, V. & Cairncross, S. (2003). Effect of washing hands with soap on diarrhea risk in the community: A systematic review. *Lancet Infectious Diseases, 3*(5), 275–281.

Cutler, D., & Miller, G. (2005). The role of public health improvements in health advances: The 20th century United States. *Demography, 42*(1), 1–22.

Cutler, D., Fung, W., Kremer, M., Singhal, M., & Vogl, T. (2010). Early-life malaria exposure and adult outcomes: Evidence from malaria eradication in India. *American Economic Journal: Applied Economics, 2*(2), 72–94.

D'Alessandro, U. D., Olaleye, B. O., McGuire, W., Langerock, P., Bennett, S., Aikins, M., et al. (1995). Mortality and morbidity from Malaria in Gambian children after introduction of an impregnated bednet programme. *The Lancet, 345,* 479–483.

Das Gupta, M. (2005). Explaining Asia's "Missing Women": A New Look at the Data. *Population and Development Review, 31*(3), 529–535.

Das Gupta, M. (2008). Can biological factors like Hepatitis B explain the bulk of gender imbalance in China? A review of the evidence. *World Bank Research Observer, 23*(2), 201–217.

Das, J. & Gertler, P. J. (2007). Variations in practice quality in five low-income countries: A conceptual overview. *Health Affairs (Milwood), 26*(3), 296–309.

Das, J. & Hammer, J. (2004). Strained mercy: The quality of medical care in Delhi. *Policy Research Working Paper Series* 3228, World Bank.

Das, J. & Hammer, J. (2007). Money for nothing: The dire straits of medical practice in Delhi, India. *Journal of Development Economics, 83*(1), 1–36.

Das, J., Hammer, J. & Leonard, K. (2008). The quality of medical advice in low-income countries. *Policy Research Working Paper Series* 4501, World Bank.

Deaton, A. (2003). Health, inequality, and economic development. *Journal of Economic Literature, 41*(1), 113–158.

Debas, H. T., Laxminarayan, R., & Straus, S. E. (2006). Complementary and alternative medicine. In *Disease control priorities in developing countries* (2nd ed.), pp. 1.281–1.292. New York: Oxford University Press.

Delavande, A. & Kohler, H. P. (2009). The impact of HIV testing on subjective expectations and risky behavior in Malawi. Working Paper.

Dhaliwal, I. & Tulloch, C. (2009). Cost-effectiveness of interventions to prevent child diarrhea. Abdul Latif Jameel Poverty Action Lab. Available online.

Dhaliwal, I., Duflo, E., Glennerster, R., & Tulloch, C. (2011). Comparative cost-effectiveness to inform policy in developing countries: A general framework with applications for education. Available online at http://www.povertyactionlab.org/publication/cost-effectiveness.

Di Tella, R. & Schargrodsky, E. (2001). The role of wages and auditing during a crackdown on corruption in the city of Buenos Aires. Working Paper.

Di Tella, R. & Schargrodsky, E. (2002). *The role of wages and auditing during a crackdown on corruption in the city of Buenos Aires.* Harvard Business School.

Dixon, S., McDonald, S., & Roberts, J. (2001). AIDS and economic growth in Africa: A panel data analysis. *Journal of International Development, 4,* 411–426.

Dow, W. H., Gertler, P., Schoeni, R. F., Strauss, J., & Thomas, D. (2003). Health care prices, health, and labor outcomes: Experimental evidence. PSC Research Report 03-542.

Duflo, E. (2003). Grandmothers and granddaughters: Old-age pensions and intrahousehold allocation in South Africa. *World Bank Economic Review, 17*(1), 1–25.

Duflo, E. & Topalova, P. (2003). Unappreciated service: Performance, perceptions, and women leaders in India. Natural Field Experiments 0037, the Field Experiments Website.

Duflo, E., Dupas, P., & Kremer, M. (2011a). Education, HIV and early fertility: Experimental evidence from Kenya. Unpublished Manuscript.

Duflo, E., Dupas, P., & Kremer, M. (2011b). School governance, pupil-teacher ratios, and teacher incentives: Evidence from Kenyan primary schools. Working Paper.

Duflo, E., Dupas, P., Kremer, M., & Sinei, S. (2006). Education and HIV/AIDS prevention: Evidence from a randomized evaluation in Western Kenya. World Bank Policy Research Paper 4024.

Duflo, E., Greenstone, M., and Hanna, R. (2008). Indoor air pollution, health and economic well-being. Working Paper.

Dunlop, D. W., & Martins, J. M. (1995). *An international assessment of health care financing: Lessons for developing countries.* World Bank, Washington, DC.

Dupas, P. (2009). What matters (and what does not) in households decision to invest in malaria prevention? *American Economic Review, 99*(2), 224–230.

Dupas, P. (2010). *Short-run subsidies and long-run adoption of new health products: Evidence from a field experiment.* UCLA.

Dupas, P. (2011a). Do teenagers respond to HIV risk information? Evidence from a field experiment in Kenya. *American Economic Journal: Applied Economics, 3*(1), 1–36.

Dupas, P. (2011b). Health behavior in developing countries. Prepared for the *Annual Review of Economics,* vol. 3.

Dupas, P. & Robinson, J. (2011). *Why don't the poor save more? Evidence from health savings experiments.* Mimeo, UCLA.

Dupas, P., Hoffmann, V., Kremer, M., & Zwane, A. (2010). Short-term subsidies, lasting adoption? Habit formation in chlorine use. Working Paper.

Easterly, W. (2006). *The white man's burden: Why the West's efforts to aid the rest have done so much ill and so little good.* Penguin Press.

Ebenstein, A. (2010). The "missing girls" of China and the unintended consequences of the one child policy. *Journal of Human Resources, 45*(1), 87–115.

Eide, E. R. & Showalter, M. H. (2011). Estimating the relation between health and education: What do we know and what do we need to know? *Economics of Education Review, 30*(5), 778–791.

Ferreira, P. C., & Pessoa, S.D. (2003). The long-run economic impact of AIDS. Working Paper.

Field, E., Glennerster, R., & Hussam, R. (2011). Throwing the baby out with the drinking water: Unintended consequences of arsenic mitigation efforts in Bangladesh. Working Paper. Available at < http://www.povertyactionlab.org/publication/throwing-baby-out-drinking-water-unintended-consequences-arsenic-mitigation-efforts-bangladesh >.

Field, E., Robles, O., & Torero, M. (2009). Iodine deficiency and schooling attainment in Tanzania. *American Economic Journal: Applied Economics, 1*(4), 140–169.

Fiszbein, A. & Schady, N. (2009). *Conditional cash transfers: Reducing present and future poverty.* World Bank Publications.

Fogel, R. W. (2002). *Nutrition, physiological capital, and economic growth.* Panamerican Health Organization and InterAmerican Development Bank.

Fortson, J. (2011). Mortality risk and human capital investment: The impact of HIV/AIDS in sub-Saharan Africa. *Review of Economics and Statistics, 93*(1), 1–15.

Frank, R.G. (2004). Behavioral economics and health economics. NBER Working Paper.

Friedman, W., Kremer, M., Miguel, E., & Thornton, R. (2011). Education as liberation? NBER Working Paper Series, vol. w16939. Available at < http://www.povertyactionlab.org/publication/education-liberation >.

Gallup, J. L. & Sachs, J. D. (2001). The economic burden of malaria. *American Journal of Tropical Medicine and Hygiene, 64*(1, Supplement), 85–96.

Garces, E., Thomas, D., & Currie, J. (2002). Longer-term effects of head start. *American Economic Review, 92*(4), 999–1012.

Geoffard, P. -Y. & Philipson, T. (1997). Disease eradication: Public vs. private vaccination. *American Economic Review, 87*, 222–230.

Gertler, P. (2004). Do conditional cash transfers improve child health: Evidence from PROGRESA's control randomized experiment. *American Economic Review, 94*(2), 336—341.

Gertler, P. & Boyce, S. (2001). *An experiment in incentive-based welfare: The impact of PROGRESA on health in Mexico.* Berkeley: Mimeo, University of California.

Gertler, P. & Gruber, J. (2002). Insuring consumption against illness. *American Economics Review, 92*(1), 51—70.

Giné, X., Karlan, D., & Zinman, J. (2010). Put your money where your butt is: A commitment contract for smoking cessation. *American Economic Journal, 2*(4), 213—235.

Giné, X., Townsend, R., & Vickery, J. (2008). Patterns of rainfall insurance participation in rural India. *World Bank Economic Review, 22*(3), 539—566.

Glennerster, R., Gumede, K., & Sears, D. (2009). Fighting poverty: What works? issue 2: Absenteeism: Showing up is the first step. Available online at < http://www.povertyactionlab.org/publication/absentteeism-showing-first-step > .

Glewwe, P., Park, A., & Zhao, M. (2010). The impact of eyeglasses on academic performance of primary school students: Evidence from a randomized trial in rural China. Working paper.

Glewwe, P. & Kremer, M. (2006). Schools, teachers, and education outcomes in developing countries. In E. A. Hanushek & F. Welch (Eds.), *Handbook on the economics of education* (vol. 2). Amsterdam and London: North-Holland.

Glewwe, P., Koch, S., & Nguyen, B. L. (2001). Child nutrition and economic growth in Vietnam in the 1990s. 2001 Annual meeting, American Agricultural Economics Association.

Goldberg, P. K. (2010). Alfred Marshall lecture intellectual property rights protection in developing countries: The case of pharmaceuticals. *Journal of the European Economic Association, 8*(2—3), 326—353.

Goldstein, M., Zivin, J. G., Habyarimana, J., Pop-Eleches, C., & Thirumurthyk, H. (2008). Health worker absence, HIV testing and behavioral change: Evidence from Western Kenya. Working Paper. Available online at < http://www.rand.org/content/dam/rand/www/external/labor/seminars/adp/pdfs/2008_thirumurthy.pdf/ > .

Gong, E. (2010). *HIV testing & risky behavior: The effect of being surprised by your HIV status.* Berkeley: University of California.

Grossman, M. (2000). The human capital model. In A. J. Culyer & J. P. Newhouse (Eds.), *Handbook of health economics,* edition 1 (vol. 1, pp. 347—408).

Guyatt, H. L. & Ochola, S. A. (2003). Use of bednets given free to pregnant women in Kenya. *Lancet, 362*(9395), 1549—1550.

Guyatt, H. L., Gotink, M. H., & Ochola, S. A. (2002). Free bednets to pregnant women through antenatal clinics in Kenya: A cheap, simple and equitable approach to delivery. *Tropical Medicine and International Health* 409—420.

Habyarimana, J. & Jack, W. (2009). *Heckle and chide: Results of a randomized road safety intervention in Kenya.* Center for Global Development Working Paper 169.

Habyarimana, J., Mbakile, B., & Pop-Eleches, C. (2010). The impact of HIV/AIDS and ARV treatment on worker absenteeism: Implications for African firms. *Journal of Human Resources, 45*(4), 809.

Hall, R. E. & Jones, C. I. (2007). The value of life and the rise in health spending. *Quarterly Journal of Economics, 122*(1), 39—72.

Hanson, K. & Berman, P. (1998). Private health care provision in developing countries: A preliminary analysis of levels and composition. *Health and Policy Planning, 13*(3), 195—211.

Hawley, W. A., Phillips-Howard, P. A., ter Kuile, F. O., Terlouw, D. J., Vulule, J. M., & Ombok, M., et al. (2003). Community-wide effects of permethrin-treated bed nets on child mortality and malaria morbidity in Western Kenya. *American Journal of Tropical Medicine and Hygiene, 68*(4 Suppl.), 121—127.

Hoddinott, J., Maluccio, J., Behrman, J., Flores, R., & Martorell, R. (2008). Effect of a nutrition intervention during early childhood on economic productivity in Guatemalan adults. *The Lancet, 371*(961), 411—416.

Hoffmann, V., Barrett, C. B., & Just, D. R. (2009). Do free goods stick to poor households? Experimental evidence on insecticide treated bednets. *World Development, 37*, 607—617.

Holla, A. & Kremer, M. (2009). *Pricing and access: Lessons from randomized evaluations in education and health.* Paper prepared for the Brookings Institution.

Hong, S. C. (2007). *A longitudinal analysis of the burden of malaria on health and economic productivity: The American case.* University of Chicago mimeo.

Hotz, C., Gilligan, D., de Brauw, A., Loechl, C., Arimond, M., Abdelrhaman, L., et al. (2010). A large-scale intervention to introduce beta-carotene rich orange sweet potato was effective in increasing vitamin A intakes among children and women in rural Uganda and Mozambique. Available at < http://biofortconf.ifpri.info/resources/ >.

Hsiao, W. C. (2007). Cost pressures: Why is a systemic view of health financing necessary? *Health Affairs, 26,* 4950–4961.

IRCBP (2007). *Primary health care In Sierra Leone: Clinic resources and perceptions of policy after one year of decentralization.* IRCBP Evaluations Unit.

IRCBP (2008). *Report on the IRCBP 2007 national public services survey: public services, governance, dispute resolution and social.* IRCBP Evaluations Unit.

IRCBP (2010). *Report on the IRCBP 2008 National public services survey: Public services, governance, and social dynamics.* IRCB Evaluations Unit.

Jalan, J. & Somanathan, E. (2008). The importance of being informed: Experimental evidence on demand for environmental quality. *Journal of Development Economics, 87,* 14–28.

Jamison, D. T., Breman, J. G., Measham, A. R., Alleyne, G., Claeson, M., Evans, D. B., Jha, P., Mills, A., & Musgrove, P. (Eds.) (2006). *Disease control priorities in developing countries* New York: Oxford University Press and World Bank.

Jamison, D.T., Sandbu, M., & Wang, J. (2001). Cross-country variation in mortality decline, 1962–87: The role of country-specific technical progress. Commission on Macroeconomics and Health Working Paper.

Jayachandran, S. (2009). Air quality and early-life mortality: Evidence from Indonesia's wildfires. *Journal of Human Resources, 44*(4), 916–995.

Jayachandran, S. & Kuziemko, I. (2009). Why do mothers breastfeed girls less than boys? Evidence and implications for child health in India. NBER Working Paper 15041.

Jayachandran, S. & Lleras-Muney, A. (2009). Life expectancy and human capital investments: Evidence from maternal mortality declines. *Quarterly Journal of Economics, 124*(1), 349–397.

Jensen, R. & Oster, E. (2009). The power of TV: Cable television and women's status in India. *Quarterly Journal of Economics, 124*(3), 1057–1094.

Jensen, R.T. (2010). Economic opportunities and gender differences in human capital: Experimental evidence for India. NBER Working Paper.

Jones, C. I. & Klenow, P. J. (2011). Beyond GDP? Welfare across countries and time. Working Paper. Available online at < http://www.stanford.edu/~chadj/rawls300.pdf/ >.

J-PAL (2007). J-PAL Policy Briefcase No. 3: Cheap and effective ways to change adolescents' sexual behavior. Available online at < http://www.povertyactionlab.org/publication/cheap-and-effective-ways-change-adolescents039-sexual-behavior >.

J-PAL (2010). Cost-effectiveness methodology. Available online at < www.povertyactionlab.org/ >.

Jukes, M. C. H., Pinder, M., Grigorenko, E. L., Smith, H. B., Walraven, G., & Bariau, E. M. (2006). Long-term impact of malaria chemoprophylaxis on cognitive abilities and educational attainment: Follow-up of a controlled trial. *Plos Clinical Trials, 1,* 4.

Junhong, C. (2001). Prenatal sex determination and sex-selective abortion in rural central China. *Population and Development Review, 27*(2), 259–281.

Karlan, D. & Zinman, J. (2010). *Expanding microenterprise credit access: Using randomized supply decisions to estimate the impacts in Manila.* Mimeo, Dartmouth and Yale.

King, G., Imai, L., Moore, N., Ravishankar, V., & Téllez-Rojo, A. (2009). Public policy for the poor? A randomised assessment of the Mexican Universal Health Insurance Programme. *The Lancet, 373*(9673), 1447–1454.

Koszegi, B. & Rabin, M. (2006). A model of reference-dependent preferences. *Quarterly Journal of Economics, 121*(4), 1133–1166.

Kremer, M. (1996). Integrating behavioral choice into epidemiological models of the AIDS epidemic. *Quarterly Journal of Economics, 111*(2), 549–573.

Kremer, M. (2002). Pharmaceuticals and the developing world. *Journal of Economic Perspectives, 16*(4), 67–90.

Kremer, M. (2003). Randomized evaluations of educational programs in developing countries: Some lessons. *American Economic Review, 93*(2), 102–106.

Kremer, M. & Glennerster, R. (2004). *Strong medicine.* Princeton University Press.

Kremer, M. & Miguel, E. (2007). The illusion of sustainability. *Quarterly Journal of Economics, 112*(3), 1007–1065.

Kremer, M. & Snyder, C. (2006). Why is there no AIDS vaccine? Working Paper.

Kremer, M., Leino, J., Miguel, E., & Zwane, A. (2011c). Managing rural water infrastructure in Kenya. Working Paper.

Kremer, M., Miguel, E., Leino, J., & Zwane, A. (2011b). Spring cleaning: Rural water impacts, valuation and property rights institutions. *Quarterly Journal of Economics, 126*(1), 145–205.

Kremer, M., Miguel, E., Mullainathan, S., Null, C., & Zwane, A. (2011a). Social engineering: Evidence from a suite of take-up experiments in Kenya. Working Paper.

Kremer, M., Snyder, C, & Williams, H. (2008). Which diseases generate the largest epidemiological externalities? Working Paper.

Laibson, D. (1997). Golden eggs and hyperbolic discounting. *Quarterly Journal of Economics, 62*(May), 443–477.

LaLonde, R. (1986). Evaluating the econometric evaluations of training programs with experimental data. *American Economic Review, 76,* 604–620.

Leino, J. (2011). Ladies first? Gender and the community management of water infrastructure in Kenya. CID Graduate Student and Research Fellow Working Paper.

Leonard, K., Masatu, M., & Vialou, A. (2007). Getting doctors to do their best: The roles of ability and motivation in health care quality. *Journal of Human Resources, 42*(3), 682–700.

Leonard, K. L. (2003). African traditional healers and outcome-contingent contracts in health care. *Journal of Development Economics, 71*(1), 1–22.

Levy, S. (2006). *Progress against poverty: Sustaining Mexico's progresa-oportunidades program.* Washington, DC: Brookings Institution Press.

Lewin, S., Lavis, J. N., Oxman, A. D., Bastías, G., Chopra, M., Ciapponi, A., et al. (2008). Supporting the delivery of cost-effective interventions in primary health-care systems in low-income and middle-income countries: An overview of systematic reviews. *Lancet, 372*(9642), 928–939.

Lin, M. & Luoh, M. (2007). Can Hepatitis B mothers account for the number of missing women? Evidence from three million newborns in Taiwan. *American Economic Review, 98*(5), 2259–2273.

Lloyd, C. B., Behrman, J., Stromquist, N. P., & Cohen, B. (Eds.) (2005). *The changing transitions to adulthood in developing countries: Selected studies.* Washington, DC: National Academies Press.

Loewenstein, G. & Prelec, D. (1992). Anomalies in intertemporal choice: Evidence and an interpretation. *Quarterly Journal of Economics, 57*(2), 573–598.

López-Casasnovas, G., Rivera, B., & Currais, L. (2005). *Health and economic growth: Findings and policy implications.* Cambridge, MA: MIT Press.

Lucas, A. (2010). Malaria eradication and educational attainment: Evidence from Paraguay and Sri Lanka. *American Economic Journal: Applied Economics, 2*(2), 46–71.

Luoto, J. (2009). Information and persuasion: Achieving safe water behavior in Kenya. Working Paper.

Maccini, S. & Yang, D. (2009). Under the weather: Health, schooling, and economic consequences of early-life rainfall. *American Economic Review, 99*(3), 1006–1026.

Madajewicz, M., Pfaff, A., van Geen, A., Graziano, J., Hussein, I., Momotaj, H., et al. (2007). Can information alone change behavior? Response to arsenic contamination of groundwater in Bangladesh. *Journal of Development Economics, 84,* 731–754.

Mæstad, O., Torsvik, G., & Aakvik, A. (2010). Overworked? On the relationship between workload and health worker performance. *Journal of Health Economics, 29*(5), 686–698.

Maluccio, J. A., Hoddinott, J., Behrman, J. R., Martorell, R., Quisumbing, A. R., & Stein, A. D. (2009). The impact of improving nutrition during early childhood on education among Guatemalan adults. *Economic Journal, 119*(537), 734–763.

Manning, W. G., Newhouse, J. P., Duan, N., Keeler, E., Benjamin, B., Lebowitz, A., et al. (1987). Health insurance and the demand for medical care: Evidence from a randomized experiment. *American Economic Review, 77*(3), 251–277.

Maxwell, C. A., Rwegoshora, R. T., Magesa, S. M., & Curtis, C. F. (2006). Comparison of coverage with insecticide-treated nets in a Tanzanian town and villages where nets and insecticide are either marketed or provided free of charge. *Malaria Journal, 5,* 44.

Mendez, M. A. & Adair, L. S. (1999). Severity and timing of stunting in the first two years of life affect performance on cognitive tests in late childhood. *Journal of Nutrition, 129,* 1555–1562.

Meng X. & Qian, N. (2009). The long term consequences of famine on survivors: Evidence from a unique natural experiment using China's Great Famine. NBER Working Papers.

Miguel, E. & Gugerty, M. K. (2005). Ethnic diversity, social sanctions, and public goods in Kenya. *Journal of Public Economics, 89*(11–12), 2325–2368.

Miguel, E., & Kremer, M. (2004). Worms: Identifying impacts on education and health in the presence of treatment externalities. *Econometrica, 72*(1), 159–217.

Noor, A., Mutheu, J., Tatem, A., Hay, S., & Snow, R. (2009). Insecticide treated net coverage: Africa mapping progress in 2000–07. *Lancet, 373*(9657), 58–67.

Olken, B., Onishi, J. & Wong, S. (2011). Should aid reward performance? Evidence from a field experiment on health and education in Indonesia. Working Paper.

Oster, E. (2005). Hepatitis B and the case of the missing women. *Journal of Political Economy, 113*(6), 1163–1216.

Oster, E. (2006). On explaining Asia's "missing women": Comment on Das Gupta. *Population and Development Review, 32*(2), 323–327.

Oster, E. & Thornton, R. (2009). *Determinants of technology adoption: Private value and peer effects in menstrual cup take-up. Forthcoming. Journal of the European Economic Association.*

Oster, E. & Thornton, R. (forthcoming). Menstruation, sanitary products and school attendance: Evidence from a randomized evaluation. *American Economic Journal: Applied Economics.*

Oster, E., Chen, G., Yu, X., & Lin, W. (2008). Hepatitis B does not explain male-biased sex ratios in China. NBER Working Paper 13971.

Over, M. (2009). AIDS treatment in South Asia: Equity and efficiency arguments for shouldering the fiscal burden when prevalence rates are low. Working Papers 161, Center for Global Development.

Ozier, O. (2010). Exploiting externalities to estimate the long-term benefits of early childhood deworming. Unpublished Working Paper, U.C. Berkeley.

Pandey, P., Sehgal, A. R., Riboud, M., Levine, D., & Goyal, M. (2007). Informing resource-poor populations and the delivery of entitled health and social services in rural India: A cluster randomized controlled trial. *Journal of the American Medical Association, 298*(16), 1867–1875.

Pattanayak, S. K., Yang, J. C., Dickinson, K. L., Poulos, C., Patil, S. R., Mallick, R. K., et al. (2009). Shame or subsidy revisited: Social mobilization for sanitation in Orissa, India. *Bulletin of the World Health Organization, 87*(8), 580–587.

Phadke, A. (1998). *Drug supply and use: Towards a rational policy in India.* Sage Publications.

Pharoah, P. O. & Connolly, K. J. (1991). Effects of maternal iodine supplementation during pregnancy. *Archives of Disease in Childhood, 66*(1), 145–147.

Pitt, M. M., Rosenzweig, M., & Hassan, N. (2010). Short- and long-term health effects of burning biomass in the home in low-income countries. Working Paper. Available at < http://www.pstc. brown.edu/~mp/papers/iapchild7.pdf/ >.

Pollak, R. A. (1968). Consistent planning. *Review of Economic Studies, 35*(102), 201.

Preston, S. H. (1975). The changing relation between mortality and level of economic development. *Population Studies, 2,* 231–248.

Qian, N. (2008). Missing women and the price of tea in China: The effect of sex-specific earnings on sex imbalance. *Quarterly Journal of Economics, 123,* 3.

Rajasekhar, D., Berg, E., Ghatak, M., Manjula, R., & Roy, S. (2011). Implementing health insurance for the poor: The rollout of RSBY in Karnataka, India. *Economic and Political Weekly of India, XLVI*(20), 56—63.

Rao, C., Lopez, A., & Hemed, Y. (2006). Causes of death. In R. Feachem & D. Jamison (Eds.), *Disease and mortality in sub-Saharan Africa.* Washington, DC: World Bank Publications.

Reynolds, A. (2001). Breastfeeding and brain development. *Pediatric Clinics of North America, 48*(1), 159—171.

Rhee, M., Sissoko, M., Perry, S., McFarland, W., Parsonnet, J., & Doumbo, O. (2005). Use of insecticide-treated nets (ITNs) following a malaria education intervention in Piron, Mali: A control trial with systematic allocation of households. *Malaria Journal, 4,* 35.

Rosenzweig, M. R. & Schultz, T. P. (1983). Estimating a household production function: Heterogeneity, the demand for health inputs, and their effects on birth weight. *Journal of Political Economy, 91*(5), 723—746.

Russell, S. (1996). Ability to pay for health care: Concepts and evidence. *Health Policy and Planning, 11,* 219—237.

Schultz, T. P. (2004). School subsidies for the poor: Evaluating a Mexican strategy for reducing poverty. *Journal of Development Economics, 74*(1), 199—250.

Schultz, T. P. (2005). Productive benefits of health: Evidence from low-income countries. Yale Economic Growth Center Discussion Paper #903.

Sen, A. (1990). More than 100 million women are missing. *New York Review of Books, 37*(20), December 20, 1990.

Sen, A. (1992). Missing women. *British Medical Journal, 304*(March), 587—588.

Shastry, G. K. & Weil, D. (2003). How much of cross-country income variation is explained by health. *Journal of the European Economic Association, 1*(2—3), 387—396.

Simonsen, L., Kane, A., Lloyd, J., Zaffran, M., & Kane, M. (1999). Unsafe injections in the developing world and transmission of blood-borne pathogens: A review. *Bulletin of the World Health Organization, 77*(10), 789—800.

Sorensen, H., Sabroe, S., Olsen, J., Rothman, K., Gillman, M., & Fischer, P. (1997). Birth weight and cognitive function in young adult life: Historical cohort study. *British Medical Journal, 315,* 401—403.

Spears, D. (2010). *Bounded rationality as deliberation costs: Social marketing uses Lifebouy...and it still stinks.* Princeton University.

Spence, M. & Lewis, M. (Eds.) (2009). *Health and growth commission on growth and development.*

Stockman, L. J., Fischer, T. K., Deming, M., Ngwira, B., Bowie, C., Cunliffe, N., et al. (2007). Point-of-use water treatment and use among mothers in Malawi. *Emerging Infectious Diseases, 13,* 7.

Strauss, J. & Thomas, D. (1998). Health, nutrition, and economic development. *Journal of Economic Literature, XXXVI,* 766—817.

Strauss, J. & Thomas, D. (2007). *Health over the life course.* UC Los Angeles: California Center for Population Research.

Strotz, R. H. (1956). Myopia and inconsistency in dynamic utility maximization. *Review of Economic Studies, 23*(3), 165—180 (1955—1956).

Tarozzi, A., Mahajan, A., Blackburn, B., Kopf, D., Krishnan, L., & Yoong, J. (2011). Micro-loans, insecticide-treated bednets and malaria: Evidence from a randomized controlled trial in Orissa (India). Working Paper. Available at < http://econ.duke.edu/ ∼ taroz/TarozziEtAl2011RCT.pdf/ >.

Ter Kuile, F. O., Terlouw, D. J., Phillips-Howard, P. A., Hawley, W. A., Friedman, J. F., Kariuki, S. K., et al. (2003). Reduction of malaria during pregnancy by peremethrin-treated bed nets in an area of intense perennial malaria transmission in Western Kenya. *American Journal of Tropical Medicine and Hygiene, 68* (Suppl. 4), 50—60.

Thirumurthy, H., Zivin, J. G., & Goldstein, M. (2008). The economic impact of AIDS treatment: Labor supply in Western Kenya. *Journal of Human Resources, 43*(3), 511—552.

Thomas, D., Frankenberg, E., Friedman, J., Habicht, J. P., Hakimi, M., Ingwersen, N., et al. (2006). Causal effect of health on labor market outcomes: Experimental evidence. Working Paper at the California Center for Population Research, UCLA.

Thornton, R. (2008). The demand for, and impact of, learning HIV status. *American Economic Review, 98* (5), 1829–1863.

Thornton, R., Hatt, L., Field, E., Islam, M., Solís, F., & González Moncada, M. A. (2010). Social security health insurance for the informal sector in Nicaragua: A randomized evaluation. *Health Economics, 19*(S1), 181–206.

UNICEF (2008). *Handbook on water quality.* New York, NY, USA.

Van Doorslaer, E., O'Donnell, O., Rannan-Eliya, R. P., Somanathan, A., Adhikari, S. R., Garg, C. C., et al. (2006a). Effect of payments for health care on poverty estimates in 11 countries in Asia: An analysis of household survey data. *Lancet, 368*, 1357–1364.

Van Doorslaer, E., O'Donnell, O., Rannan-Eliya, R. P., Somanathan, A., Adhikari, S. R., Garg, C. C., et al. (2006b). Catastrophic payments for health care in Asia. *Health Economics, 16*, 1159–1184.

Vian, T. (2008). Review of corruption in the health sector: Theory, methods and interventions. *Health Policy and Planning, 23*(2), 83–83-94.

Wagstaff, A. (2007). The economic consequences of health shocks: Evidence from Vietnam. *Journal of Health Economics, 26*, 82–100.

Wagstaff, A. (2010). Social health insurance reexamined. *Health Economics, 19*, 503–517.

Wagstaff, A. & van Doorslaer, E. (2003). Catastrophe and impoverishment in paying for health care: With applications to Vietnam 1993–1998. *Health Economics, 12*(11), 921–933.

Walker, D., & Fox-Rushby, J. (2000). Economic evaluation of parasitic diseases: A critique of the internal and external validity of published studies. *Tropical Medicine & International Health, 5*, 237–249.

Weil, D. (2007). Accounting for the effect of health on economic growth. *Quarterly Journal of Economics, 122*(3), 1265–1306.

Wiseman, V., Hawley, W. A., ter Kuile, F. O., Phillipa-Howard, P. A., Vulule, J. M., Nahle, B. L., et al. (2003). The cost-effectiveness of permethrin-treated bed nets in an area of intense malaria transmission in Western Kenya. *American Journal of Tropical Medicine and Hygiene, 68*(Suppl. 4), 161–167.

World Bank (2004). *World development report 2004: Making services work for the poor.* Washington, DC: World Bank Publications.

World Bank (2009). *Conditional cash transfers: Reducing present and future poverty.* Washington, DC: World Bank Publications.

World Bank (2011). *World DataBank.* http://databank.worlbank.org/dpp/home.do/ >, Accessed 05.11.2011.

World Health Organization (2002). *The world health report 2002: Reducing risks promoting healthy life.* Geneva: WHO.

World Health Organization (2005a). Indoor air pollution and health. Fact Sheet 292. Available at < http://www.who.int/mediacentre/factsheets/fs292/en/ >.

World Health Organization (2006). *Country health system fact sheet 2006, Benin.* Geneva: WHO.

World Health Organization (2008). *The global burden of disease, 2004 update.* Geneva: WHO.

World Health Organization (2010a). 10 facts on malaria. < http://www.who.int/features/factfiles/malaria/en/index.html/ >.

World Health Organization (2010b). World health statistics. Available online at < http://www.who.int/whosis/whostat/EN_WHS10_Full.pdf/ >.

Wright, J., Gundry, S., & Conroy, R. (2004). Household drinking water in developing countries: A systematic review of microbiological contamination between source and point-of-use. *Tropical Medicine and International Health, 9*(1), 106–117.

Xue-Yi, I., Xin-Min, J., Kareem, A., Zhi-Hong, D., Rakeman, M. A., & Zhang Ming, L. (1994). Irrigation of water as a method of supplying iodine to a severely iodine-deficient population in Xinjiang, China. *The Lancet, 334*, 107–110.

Yip, W. & Hsiao, W. C. (2009). Non-evidence-based policy: How effective is China's new cooperative medical scheme in reducing medical impoverishment? *Social Science and Medicine, 68*(2), 201–209.

Young, A. (2005). The gift of the dying: The tragedy of AIDS and the welfare of future African generations. *Quarterly Journal of Economics, 120*(2), 423–466.

Zwane, A., Zinman, J., van Dusen, E., Pariente, W., Null, C., Miguel, E., et al. (2011). Being surveyed can change later behavior and related parameter estimates. *Proceedings of the National Academy of Sciences, 108*(5), 1821−1826.

Zweifel, P. & Manning, W. G. (2000). Moral hazard and consumer incentives in health care. In A. J. Culyer & J. P. Newhouse (Eds.), *Handbook of health economics* (Vol. 1, pp. 409−459). Boston: North Holland. (Chapter 8).

CHAPTER FIVE

Demand for Health Insurance[1]

Thomas G. McGuire
Harvard Medical School, Boston, MA, USA

Contents

[1] Research on this chapter was partially supported by NIA P01 AG032952, The Role of Private Plans in Medicare, and NIMH R01 MH094290. I am grateful to Martin Anderson, Sebastian Bauhoff, Pedro Pita Barros, Emily Corcoran, Jacob Glazer, Mark Pauly, Anna Sinaiko, and Jacob Wallace for many helpful comments.

317

Abstract

This chapter reviews topics related to the demand for health insurance, including the question of how choice of health insurance should be structured for consumers. After the first section summarizes some of the institutional features of health insurance in high- and middle-income countries, a second section synthesizes the normative and empirical literature on demand-side cost sharing in health insurance, integrating new developments in multiple goods, consumer errors in valuing health care and "offset effects" with the traditional risk protection-appropriate incentives trade-off. The practice of selective contracting on the supply side is an alternative to demand-side cost sharing. A third section proposes a theory of selective contracting and relates this supply-side policy to the question of optimal demand-side cost sharing. We observe two distinct approaches to structuring choice of health insurance in the US, private employers who severely limit choice, and public payers' (and individual insurance markets') market-determined choices. A fourth section reviews the pluses and minuses of these alternatives, and discusses the implications for structuring health insurance markets in the US.

Keywords: adverse selection; HMOs; insurance; managed care; moral hazard; selective contracting; demand for health; demand for health care; health care costs

JEL Code: I10.

1. INTRODUCTION AND OVERVIEW: HEALTH SYSTEMS WITH CHOICE OF HEALTH INSURANCE

The organization and supply of health insurance varies greatly across and within countries, putting consumers in very different circumstances in terms of choice and demand for health insurance. In countries with well-financed universal public insurance (e.g. France, UK) insurance choice is not an issue. In other countries, consumers choose from among many (Germany, Switzerland) or a few (Israel, Netherlands) regulated plans with minor variations in premiums and coverage. In these countries, competition among plans and effective choice are major components of national health policy. In some countries with publicly provided health care (Columbia, Russia), a private market offers insurance upgrades for the high-end consumer, and the main problems for policy are coordinating private and public financing and the inequities of a two-tiered system.

Variation within the US rivals across-country variation in the rest of the world. A typical 64-year-old worker in America has little or no choice of insurance (50 percent of workers have no choice at all). Just one year later, upon turning 65, the same worker faces more choices in health insurance than anyone anywhere: scores of private health plans and traditional Medicare covering basic services, private supplemental plans to go along with traditional Medicare, and scores of private plans offering coverage for prescription drugs. Most Medicare beneficiaries choose traditional Medicare for coverage of hospital and physician services (Parts A and B), a private supplemental policy to fill in Medicare cost sharing (Medigap), and a private drug plan offered through and subsidized by Medicare (Part D)—paying three premiums for three separate health insurance plans. A major set of policy questions in the US, brought to the fore by the Affordable Care Act (ACA) and health care reform, center around structuring choice of health insurance.[2] Is our worker-Medicare beneficiary more effectively served by an employer (or other intermediary) narrowing the set of choices she might take to two or three, or by the open market in which many plans can enter, offering diverse coverages and setting premiums?

Health insurance is also priced differently across and within countries.[3] In countries following some form of the "managed competition" model, demand prices are set to zero (Israel), regulated within small bounds (Germany), or are determined in a market by an equilibrium premium above the subsidized voucher-like public payment (Switzerland). For the largest group of buyers in the US, workers at medium and large

---

[2] The Patient Protection and Affordable Care Act of 2010 (P.L. 111–148).

[3] My comments here and in this chapter are concerned with demand-side prices for health insurance. Practices around setting supply prices also differ across and within countries. Paying plans to contend with variation in cost risk is primarily covered in Breyer, Bundorf and Pauly (2011, this Handbook).

firms, demand prices for insurance are set administratively by the employer as part of employee benefits, not by the health plans. Demand prices in the public Medicare and Medicaid programs in the US are set by regulation. Pricing in the private plans that offer insurance as an alternative or supplement to traditional Medicare is also subject to regulation. Health care reform in the US creates new individual/family private health insurance markets, called "Exchanges," where plans will set premiums meant to cover plan costs but subject to regulation of what can be used as a basis for premium differences.

In terms of what is covered in health insurance plans, differences among countries and across institutional settings within countries seem less. Basic hospital and office-based care is covered nearly everywhere. Demand-side cost sharing remains a primary means of cost control in many health plans, and an important concern for policy in times like the present when the magnitude and growth of health care costs are major social issues. Most plans give the patient choice of many physicians and facilities. The imperatives of medical technology and the basic function of health insurance—to pay for care at the time of illness—together seem to have impelled some commonality in the form of health insurance among payers.

These preliminary comments call attention to the three principal topics of this chapter. The first is a longstanding issue in the economics of health insurance—the design of optimal health insurance and the trade-off between the dual goals of health insurance, financial risk protection and encouraging efficient care. From its initial focus on demand-side cost sharing for a single medical service, the literature on this topic has branched out to consider efficient (second-best) cost sharing with multiple goods, "offset effects," and corrections for consumer mistakes about the value of health care, among other issues. The objective of section 2 is to integrate this literature within a single theoretical framework.

The second topic relates supply-side health plan policies to demand-side cost sharing. Provider contracting is an integral part of modern managed health care plans.[4] Some aspects of the relationship between supply- and demand-side cost sharing are well known and these will be mentioned briefly. Section 3 develops a less-appreciated aspect of the relationship, how demand-side cost affects a plan's leverage with providers. Health plan provider contracts are "negotiated" because the plan is not a price-taker in the market for provider services.[5] In other words, plans cannot take provider prices as "given"; nor can the plan (or patients) choose the mix of quality and quantity of services they desire at a given set of prices.[6] For this reason, a plan can benefit

---

[4] Dranove (2011, this Handbook) covers the general literature on provider payment.

[5] A price taker on the demand or supply side faces a given price and can choose to demand or supply any quantity desired without affecting the price. Consumers and producers in competitive markets are price takers. In a standard monopoly market, consumers are price takers, though the monopoly firm is not.

[6] Chandra, Culter and Song (2011, this Handbook), address the topic of how treatments are decided, going well beyond standard models of demand-determination.

by bargaining power in relation to sellers. As we will show, lower demand-side cost sharing enhances the plan's bargaining position—this then is another factor feeding into the question of how demand-side cost sharing should be set.

The third topic returns to the predicament of the 64-year-old worker/65-year-old retiree. Was her employer doing her a disservice by limiting her choices? This question serves to organize some older and newer strands of the literature in structuring markets and choices for health insurance. Older strands include selection, adverse and otherwise, and economies of joint purchasing; new strands include consumer difficulty in decision making and studies of the value of choice. We related this literature to the design of state health insurance "exchanges" as part of ACA.

Although sections 2—4 are organized around normative topics in the economics of health insurance, the relevant empirical literature is reviewed as we go.

One chapter cannot do justice to the vast literature on the economics of health insurance. Fortunately, excellent reviews allow some limits on what is covered here. Cutler and Zeckhauser's "The Anatomy of Health Insurance" in the *Handbook of Health Economics* Volume 1 remains relevant to present-day research and policy, and will be referred to frequently in what follows. Their coverage of classic models of moral hazard and adverse selection need not be repeated, and their review of the empirical literature up through the late 1990s remains the most comprehensive available. The Breyer, Bundorf and Pauly chapter (2011, this Handbook) on risk, health care cost variation and health plan payment complements the current chapter. Other reviews, particularly of the empirical literature on demand response to health insurance and factors determining the choice in health insurance will be noted as we go along.[7]

The remainder of this section contains some institutional background on health insurance in the US, high- and middle-income countries. Health insurance, particularly public insurance, plays some role in financing care in low-income countries as well, but is less about risk spreading and more about providing access to care (see Kremer and Glennerster, 2011, this Handbook).

1.1. United States

Health insurance in the US traces back to Baylor University Hospital responding to unpaid bills of school teachers by creating a prepayment plan (Austin and Hungerford, 2009). Other hospitals, first in Texas, later in California, New Jersey and elsewhere, created similar plans, securing payment for themselves while, as a byproduct, protecting consumers from financial risk of illness. Early health insurance served providers' interests in another way as well. Associations of hospitals formed state- and

---

[7] Recent excellent reviews include Bundorf and Royalty (2011), Einav and Finkelstein (2011), Baicker and Goldman (2011), Gruber (2008), Gruber and Levy (2009), Morrisey (2008), Swartz (2010), and Zweifel et al. (2009).

substate-level Blue Cross Plans which forestalled competition among "delivery systems" by combining all hospitals within the same plan. The American Hospital Association required Blue Cross Plans to operate in exclusive territories so they would not compete against one another (Starr, 1983).

Prior to World War II, fewer than 10 percent of the US population had any form of private health insurance, which then consisted primarily of hospital-sponsored Blue Cross Plans, some physician-sponsored Blue Shield plans, and in some areas, nascent prepaid group practices (Morrisey, 2008, chapter 1). Wage-price controls imposed by the National War Labor Board diverted demand for labor to fringe benefits, forging the link between employment and health insurance that is such an important institutional feature in the US. In 1954, a rewrite of the tax code formalized the exemption of employer contributions to workers' health insurance premiums from federal income taxation, expanding the market for Blue Cross Blue Shield plans as well as the commercial insurers better set up to serve multistate employers. Commercial insurers introduced competition to Blue Cross Plans and, by pricing according to experience of employer-customers, undermined the system of community rating sustained by Blue Cross (Austin and Hungerford, 2009). Today, the distinction between Blue Cross (and Blue Shield) Plans and commercial insurers is largely historical. Blue Cross Plans can be either for-profit or non-profit. States have repealed many (but not all) of the tax benefits for non-profit Blue Plans, and commercial insurers have merged with or acquired Blue Plans. For example, Wellpoint, the second largest insurer by enrollment in 2008, is composed of former Blue Plans from 14 states.[8]

In response to concerns about the viability of private pension plans, in 1974 Congress passed the Employee Retirement Income Security Act (ERISA) placing employer self-funded (self-insured) health insurance plans under federal regulation, and exempting them from state health insurance regulation, such as reserve requirements, mandated coverages, and premium taxes. As Morrisey (2008, pp. 13–14) points out, ERISA fundamentally altered the health insurance market by creating a role for the insurer as a "claims administrator," adjudicating claims, contracting with providers, managing care, but not bearing risk. As long as the plan stayed away from the "insurance" function, the employer's plan fell outside of state regulation. Employers large enough to bear the health insurance risk could in effect "make" rather than "buy" the traditional insurance business of risk pooling.

1.1.1. Financial Risk

Rapidly rising total health care costs in the US have not, until recently at least, translated into increased exposure to financial risk for the average consumer. Deepening of

---

[8] California, Colorado, Connecticut, Georgia, Indiana, Kentucky, Maine, Missouri, Nevada, New Hampshire, New York, Ohio, Virginia, and Wisconsin (Austin and Hungerford, 2009).

health insurance coverage has offset cost trends. In 1960, when health care spending was 5 percent of Gross Domestic Product (GDP), spending was mostly private (68 percent), and most of this private spending (69 percent) was out of pocket (OOP) (Gruber and Levy, 2009). By 2007, health care spending was 17 percent of GDP and private spending had fallen to less than half (47 percent). According to Baicker and Goldman (2011), OOP share fell to less than 20 percent by 2010. However, real OOP spending per capita actually doubled between 1960 and 2010 due to the rise in health care costs. By 2010, the average person was spending $900 OOP per year (in $2009) on health care. With the falling share of OOP, the growth in health care costs has been largely picked up by higher taxes for public programs and premiums for private health insurance (Gruber and Levy, 2009).

Gruber and Levy (2009) point to three ways in which private health insurance has provided more protection against financial risk over time. First is the shift from reliance on demand-side cost sharing to control costs in private health insurance contracts to supply-side mechanisms and managed care, a trend identified earlier by Cutler and Zeckhauser (hereafter CZ (2000)). Second, state and federal continuation-of-coverage regulations led to fewer coverage gaps for working families. And third, state and federal mandated benefit expansions, such as parity regulations for mental health coverage, reduced OOP obligations. Increasing the cost of employer-based health insurance through regulation may have led to lower rates of offering coverage, particularly by small employers (Simon, 2005). Public insurance expansions have also made a difference in risk protection, particularly Medicaid expansions for low income for children.

"Charity care"—free or subsidized care offered by health care providers—also contributes to financial protection, but the amounts are modest. Gruber and Levy (2009) figure that uncompensated care to the uninsured or uncollected bills from those with insurance has been stable at about 5 percent of hospital revenues since 1980. Unlike hospitals which have an obligation to treat medical emergencies regardless of the patient's payer status, physicians are under no obligation to provide free care. Gruber and Rodriguez (2007) find that physicians' small amount of free care is counterbalanced in aggregate by the higher prices doctors charge to patients without insurance but who can pay.

Bankruptcies are one clear indicator of the financial impact of illness. Some research shows that households that file for bankruptcy have high health care costs (Himmelstein et al., 2005), but the causal connection in these studies has been questioned (Dranove and Millenson, 2006). Cook et al. (2010) use data from the Health and Retirement Study (HRS) to measure the effect of a new serious illness on assets of near elderly households with pre-illness assets in the range of $1,000 to $200,000. A household with assets of $20,000 pre-illness would have about the same level of assets two years later if they either did not experience a heath shock, or they were insured. If uninsured, the household's assets would drop to about $10,000, half of the previous value. The financial shock of illness could of course extend to consumption or friends/family as well as to a household's asset position.

Various social insurance mechanisms provide at least some financial protection to the uninsured. Herring (2005) estimates that the low-income uninsured (those with income less than 300 percent of the federal poverty line) pay only for one-third of the care they receive. Higher-income uninsured pay for about half of the care they receive.

The fundamental purpose of health insurance is to reduce the risk associated with health care spending, risk interpreted as some measure of the variation of health costs faced by an individual or household. In any year, health care spending is very skewed. Swartz (2010, p. 9) reports data from 2007 that the top 1 percent of spenders account for 23 percent of total spending and the top 5 percent of spenders for half of all spending. Year-to-year health care costs are correlated on the order of about 0.1, leaving room for a great deal of unpredictability of spending in aggregate. Variation in spending is usually assessed empirically by calculating measures of variance for individuals and households with similar characteristics. Gruber and Levy (2009) conduct a series of calculations establishing that the health care risk households are exposed to has changed little since 1980. In 1980, the non-elderly household at the median spent 2.0 percent of its income on premiums and out-of-pocket costs, with a standard deviation (square root of the variance) of 6.0 percent.[9] By 2007, premiums had taken the share to 2.6 percent but the standard deviation remained at about 6 percent.[10] This measure of risk overstates the risk for a particular household since the standard deviation is figured across all households as opposed to households "like us."[11] The elderly spend about 10 percent of their budgets on premiums and health care costs (including long-term care). This has been drifting up slowly over time. Although Medicare includes considerable demand-side cost sharing, the standard deviation of elderly spending is only about the median spending, 10 percent, due in part to the supplemental coverage available to many beneficiaries.

1.1.2. Health Insurance Contracts

Employer-based health insurance covers about half of the US population. The Kaiser Family Foundation/Health Research & Education Trust (2010) is a comprehensive annual survey of employer health benefits, for a representative sample of US employers. Several salient features of employer-based insurance are worth noting:

---

[9] Gruber and Levy (2009) use data from the Consumer Expenditure Survey Interview Component of the March, CPS.

[10] Findings were similar for subgroups of the population.

[11] By figuring the standard deviation across all households, the measure includes, for example, the risk of becoming uninsured. For many households this risk is negligible.

- Almost all (99 percent) of large employers (200+) offer health insurance as a benefit, but among smaller firms only 68 percent offer coverage. Overall, 59 percent of workers in any firm (whether or not the firm offers coverage) receive health benefits through work.[12]
- Choice is not common. Forty-eight percent of workers have no choice of plan type, and another 35 percent have choice among only two plan types.
- The type of plan offered changed rapidly in the decade up to 2000, and changed considerably in the most recent decade as well. Conventional plans (see Table 5.1 for definitions of major plan types) fell from 73 percent of covered workers in 1988 to 8 percent in 2000, and virtually disappeared by 2010. See Figure 5.1. Plans with more limited networks, the HMOs and POS plans, lost share between 2000 and 2010, shares picked up by PPO plans and the newer HDHP/SO forms.[13]
- Employees pay a substantial share of their health care costs through premiums and cost sharing at the time of use. Table 5.2 depicts coverage in typical conventional, HMO, PPO, and a high-deductible plan for 2010.

1.1.3. Buyers and Sellers in the Market for Health Insurance

The demand side of health insurance in the US is a complex mix of public and private purchasers. The 48 million elderly (65+) are covered by Medicare. Traditional Medicare (TM) is a form of socialized health insurance, similar to the national health insurance plans covering all age groups in Germany, Israel, and other countries where the supply of health care remains private. TM, financed by the payroll tax and general revenues, consists of compulsory coverage for hospital care (Part A) and highly subsidized elective coverage for physician services (Part B), chosen by almost all beneficiaries. Parts A and B have deductibles and coinsurance that beneficiaries may cover by supplemental coverage from former employers or purchase individually. Including Medicaid eligibles, such supplemental coverage is held by the majority of beneficiaries (McGuire et al., 2011).

In 1985, the new Medicare Part C authorized payment of a risk-adjusted premium to private health plans, required to provide at least the basic Medicare benefits and meet other regulations. Part C, currently referred to as Medicare Advantage, is an attempt to modernize Medicare, and create options for beneficiaries while saving Medicare money through management and contracting methods applied in private health insurance markets. Medicare payment levels have vacillated leading to boom and bust in plan participation and beneficiary enrollment. Payment levels are currently high enough to induce supply in most of the country. Partly due to selection of

---

[12] Some employees turn down coverage through their employer; not all employees are eligible for coverage (e.g. part-time employees).

[13] See, for a parallel presentation, Baicker and Goldman (2011).

Table 5.1 Major Types of Health Plans

Plan type	Description
Conventional or Fee-for-Service (FFS) Plan	Conventional health plans reimburse all covered medical services—each service is paid for separately. The plan may have a deductible, and it usually requires co-payments or coinsurance. Patients (with their physician) can choose when and how much medical care to receive, and patients' choice of provider is not restricted by the plan.
Health Maintenance Organization (HMO)	HMOs provide comprehensive health care coverage through a network of physicians and hospitals. Usually HMOs require low cost sharing (i.e. office visit co-payments), with no deductible or coinsurance. Patients select a primary care physician, and HMOs require authorization from that physician for patients to see a (within network) specialist physician. Generally there is no coverage for care received from providers outside the plan's network. Providers are usually paid by capitation.
Point-of-Service (POS)	POS plans provide a comprehensive health care benefit through a network of physicians and hospitals (akin to an HMO benefit), but also provide some coverage for care received from out-of-network providers. Out-of-network care requires greater cost sharing (i.e. partial coinsurance). POS plans may allow self-referral to specialist physicians.
Preferred Provider Organization (PPO)	PPO plans provide comprehensive health care coverage where patients can choose whether to see providers from within the plan's network of providers and pay lower cost sharing (i.e. office visit co-payments), or to see a provider outside the plan's network and pay higher cost sharing (i.e. partial coinsurance). PPO plans may or may not require a deductible. PPO plans do not require authorization from a primary care physician for visits with a specialist.
High-Deductible Health Plan (HDHP)	An HMO, PPO, POS, or conventional plan that has a "high" annual deductible, usually a minimum of $1,000 for individuals and $2,000 for families. Often these plans are provided along with a financial account, called a Health Reimbursement Account (HRA) or a Health Savings Account (HSA), that can be used to pay for health care services.

Sources: Kaiser Family Foundation /HRET Annual Survey (2010).

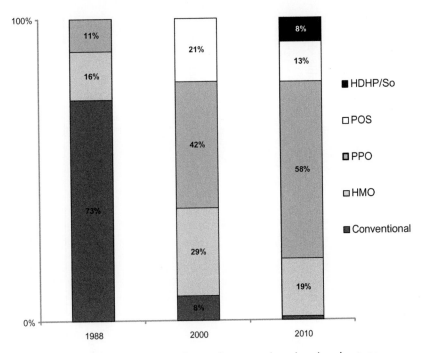

Figure 5.1 Distribution of health plan enrollment for covered workers by plan type.

healthier beneficiaries into Medicare Advantage plans, Medicare has not found a way to set plan payment and beneficiary premiums to save Medicare program funds (McGuire et al., 2011).[14]

The Medicare Modernization Act of 2003 established Part D of Medicare, a voluntary outpatient prescription drug benefit which went into effect on January 1, 2006 (KFF, November, 2009). Drugs were the largest uninsured category of expenditures in TM, and as Duggan et al. (2008, p. 69) put it, Part D "represents the largest expansion of an entitlement program [in the US] since the start of Medicare itself." Beneficiaries are directly responsible for only about 25 percent of the premium of Part D coverage, making it a highly attractive deal.[15] By 2009, 59 percent of the 45.2 million Medicare beneficiaries were in a Part D plan (either a stand-alone plan or as part of a Medicare Advantage plan), and only 10 percent of beneficiaries lacked any drug coverage.

---

[14] This is in spite of the fact that the HMO-type plans, in which most beneficiaries enroll, provide health insurance at lower cost than TM.

[15] The subsidy does not apply at the margin, however, transmitting costs of more generous coverage into premiums. The market for Part D coverage favors plans that cover only some of the available drugs and that require considerable beneficiary cost sharing.

Table 5.2 Typical Health Plans Offered by a Private Employer for Individual Coverage

Type of Plan	Conventional Plan	HMO	PPO	High-deductible Health Plan[*]
Monthly premium[**]	$550	$350	$425	$375
Deductible	$250	$0	$0	$1,000
Primary care office visit	$15/visit	$15/visit	$15/visit	$15/visit
Specialist office visit (in-network)	$15/visit	Requires pre-authorization, then $15/visit	$15/visit	Subject to deductible, then $15/visit
Specialist office visit (out-of-network)	n/a	No coverage	20% coinsurance	Subject to deductible, then 20% coinsurance
Inpatient (in-network)	Subject to deductible, then covered	Covered	Covered	Subject to deductible, then covered
Inpatient (out-of-network)	n/a	No coverage	20% coinsurance	Subject to deductible, then covered
Emergency room visit	Subject to deductible, then $50/visit	$50/visit	$50/visit	Subject to deductible, then $50/visit
Mental health	Covered	Requires pre-authorization, then covered	Covered (20% coinsurance if out-of-network)	Subject to deductible, then covered (20% coinsurance if out-of-network)

[*] This sample high-deductible plan is modeled after a PPO-like health plan with a high deductible. High-deductible plans can also be like conventional plans or HMOs with a high deductible.

[**] Monthly premium represents the total insurer charged monthly premium. Typically, some portion of this is paid by employees with the remainder paid by their employer.

Table 5.3 US Non-Elderly Population with Selected Sources of Health Insurance 2000 and 2008

	2000	2008
Total[*]	244.8 (100.0%)	262.8 (100.0%)
Employment based	167.5 (68.4%)	160.6 (61.1%)
Own name	84.6 (34.6%)	82.5 (31.4%)
Dependent	82.9 (33.8%)	78.1 (29.7%)
Individually purchased	16.0 (6.5%)	16.7 (6.3%)
Public	38.5 (14.6%)	51.0 (19.4%)
Medicare	5.4 (2.2%)	7.7 (2.9%)
Medicaid	26.2 (10.7%)	39.2 (14.9%)
Military[**]	6.8 (2.8%)	7.8 (3.0%)
No health insurance	38.2 (15.6%)	45.7 (17.4%)

[*]TRICARE/ CHAMPVA.
[**]Some individuals have more than one source of coverage.
Source: Fronstin (2009) using data from March 2000, 2008 supplements to the Current Population Survey.

Sources of health insurance among the non-elderly are more variable. Table 5.3 from Fronstin (2009) summarizes sources of coverage for the 262.8 million under-65 population in the US in 2008. Private, employment-based coverage predominates, accounting for slightly above 60 percent of the non-elderly population, down from a peak of 68.4 percent in 2000. The number of uninsured is up a bit from 2000, to an estimated 17.4 percent of the population, but the main growth has been coverage in public programs, especially Medicaid, the joint state-federal program for the poor and disabled. Health care reform in the US is expected to reduce this number markedly.

Employers offer insurance to full-time workers (and sometimes part-time workers) with some minimum tenure at the firm. Furthermore, employers typically pay most of the cost of health insurance, averaging 84 percent of the cost for single plans and 73 percent for family plans. Take-up of employer-sponsored coverage is around 75 percent, with many of the balance attaining coverage on a family member's plan, leaving only 7 percent of those offered coverage without insurance (Gruber and Washington, 2005).

Employment-based health insurance makes sense for workers for two reasons. First is the tax subsidy. Employees do not pay state or federal income or payroll taxes on the employer contribution to health insurance premiums. Gruber (2008) figures this subsidy to be 35 percent for a low-income worker; obviously, the effective subsidy increases with marginal tax rates. Employee contributions are subsidized too through cafeteria-plan provisions of the federal tax code.[16] Gruber and Levy (2009, p. 29) estimate the tax expenditure associated with these exclusions to be $125 billion in 2006,

---

[16] In the non-group market, the self-employed can deduct 100 percent of their health insurance premiums (Gruber, 2008).

nearly twice the federal tax foregone because of the deductibility of interest on home mortgages.

Second, employers may be able to purchase health insurance more effectively on behalf of a group of workers than the workers could as individuals. Pooling workers reduces risk, and selling and administrative costs are lower for a larger group. Furthermore, by serving as an intermediary in buying health insurance, an employer can select one or a few plans to offer to employees. This not only subverts selection-related inefficiencies in individual health insurance markets, but also can address the prisoner's dilemma feature of moral hazard. Prudent-buying employers can serve as the buying groups proposed by Diamond (1992) as a fundamental solution to inefficiencies in health insurance markets. Advantages and disadvantages of employer procurement methods are reviewed in section 5.

More than anywhere else, the US relies on private, for-profit firms to supply health insurance. Reliance on private supply, instead of a public "single payer" to insure residents, is controversial.[17] Private insurers handle employer-based health insurance and manage care plans in Medicaid, 20 percent of Medicare beneficiaries in Part C Plans, and all drug coverage for beneficiaries in Part D. Private insurers are relied upon in health care reform to supply the plans in the state-level "Exchanges" (Kingsdale and Bertko, 2010). Competition can in principle keep costs down, match products to consumer preferences, and supply useful innovation, and these arguments have been made in support of continued reliance on private supply of health plans (Enthoven, 1978).

Local markets for health insurance appear to be highly concentrated when assessed by conventional measures. The Department of Justice labels a market to be "highly concentrated" when the Hirschman−Herfindahl Index (HHI) based on the sum of the squares of market shares is 1,800 or above.[18] An American Medical Association study in 2008 of the HMO and PPO market finds 295 of 314 metropolitan statistical areas to have HHIs above 1,800.[19] The option to self-insure, exercised by most large employers, broadens competition, and probably leads the AMA numbers to overstate market power of insurers. More problematic is market structure in the private individual health insurance market, which is also highly concentrated (US GAO, 2009).[20] Private health insurance markets are the vehicle relied upon in expanding access to health insurance in US health care reform initiatives. In 2010, seven insurers offered products in the Massachusetts Connector's unsubsidized market, a model for exchanges in national health care reform (McGuire and Sinaiko, 2010).

---

[17] For a sharp critique of private insurers, see Relman (2010).

[18] A market with five firms with 20 percent market share has an HHI of 2,000. As the shares become unequally distributed the HHI rises.

[19] See Austin and Hungerford (2009) for references including web addresses and discussion.

[20] Breyer, Bundorf, and Pauly (2011, this Handbook) discuss the performance of individual health insurance markets.

Early evidence on pricing and profitability was inconclusive about the exercise of market power in health insurance pricing (Gaynor and Haas-Wilson, 1999), partly due to the difficulty of assessing price in relation to cost in health insurance contracts. Large employers buy health insurance with the aid of brokers from benefits consulting companies. Negotiations work out details of plan design and premium payments which are specific to the plan—employer match. Plans negiotiate different premiums for the same plan for different employers, and employers when they do offer choice pay different premiums to health plans even for similar coverage.[21] Monopoly-driven markups are hard to see in this context. Making use of an innovative research design, Dafny (2010) studied employer premium payments for full-risk health insurance to see if a measure of lagged employer profitability was associated with premium increases, the theory being that in a context in which bargaining between the employer and plan determines premiums, a plan might extract a higher payment from a more profitable employer. Profit shocks led to higher premiums, especially in markets with more concentrated supply. She found that a 10 percentage point increase in profits led employers to pay about 0.3 percent more in premiums (Dafny, 2010, p. 1411).

1.2. High-income Countries

Countries in the Organization for Economic Cooperation and Development (OECD) and the European Union rely on varying combinations of public and private institutions to collect contributions, pool risk and purchase health care services. The spectrum ranges from national health services in the UK, Poland, and Sweden to competitive markets with multiple insurers in the Netherlands, Germany, and Israel. A stylized distinction between these systems rests on the role of government in financing and health care delivery. In practice, there is a common movement toward competition and incentive-based contracting with regard to insurers (Germany, Switzerland) and providers (fundholding and pay-for-performance initiatives in the UK) within the institutional boundaries of each system. Concerns about equity and adverse selection have prompted redistribution across regions and the use of increasingly sophisticated risk adjustment methodologies (Thomson et al., 2009; van de Ven et al., 2007).

Contributions, often in the form of general or dedicated taxes, are often administratively determined. Switzerland collects individual premiums that may vary by region, age group, and level of the deductible (Squires et al., 2010). Outpatient

---

[21] Glazer and McGuire (2002) report plan-specific premium amounts paid by university employers in the Boston area (this information was publicly available) to document the match-specific prices negotiated in employer health insurance. From the health plan's point of view, the cost of covering a population from a particular employer involves the likely costs of the group, which will be influenced by the other health plans an employer may choose to offer. Often, both the employer and the plan will have some data about past experience of employees in that plan to serve as a basis of negotiation.

providers receive a mix of salary, capitation, and fee-for-service: the UK uses all three elements whereas French physicians are paid fee-for-service. Hospital reimbursements may be through some form of DRG system or global budgets, as in Canada (Squires et al., 2010).

1.2.1. Financial Risk

Across high-income countries, public expenditures represent about 61 percent of total expenditures on health, while private out-of-pocket spending and private prepaid insurance account for approximately 14 and 20 percent, respectively (WHO, 2010; Figure 5.2).[22] Public spending represents more than half of total spending in all OECD countries except Mexico and the USA, and well above 70 percent in half of the countries. Private out-of-pocket health expenditures (including cost-sharing and direct outlays) as share of GDP are low and remarkably similar across countries: in 26 of the 33 OECD countries they were below 2 percent of GDP in 2007.

The degree of financial risk protection is very high in these settings, although there is substantial variation across countries (Xu et al., 2007; Figure 5.3). Similarly, while cost-sharing mechanisms are common they often include provisions to protect households that are poor, chronically ill or otherwise in need. In recent years several countries have introduced small co-payments for office visits, specific procedures or drugs that are primarily designed to manage demand rather than raise revenues (e.g. in Germany and France; Thomson et al., 2009).

1.2.2. Market Structure

1.2.2.1. Sources of Health Insurance

Most OECD countries have near-universal coverage through public programs. Only the USA and Germany have substantial primary coverage through private health insurance (58 and 10 percent, respectively, in 2007; OECD, 2004). See Figure 5.4. However, many countries feature sizeable markets for duplicate, complementary or supplementary private insurance.[23] These arrangements can improve choice, risk protection or coverage but also lead to financial spillovers to public payers and concerns for equity. For instance, in Germany high-income earners can opt out of the public system and obtain primary private coverage that improves waiting times (Lungen et al., 2008). Since the contributions to social insurance are income based whereas private premiums tend to be risk rated, the option of private insurance may lead to adverse selection and negative financial consequences for the public system.

---

[22] About 5 percent of expenditures are due to spending by firms and non-profits.

[23] Complementary insurance may cover costs that are not reimbursable in the public scheme, while supplementary insurance covers additional services (OECD, 2004).

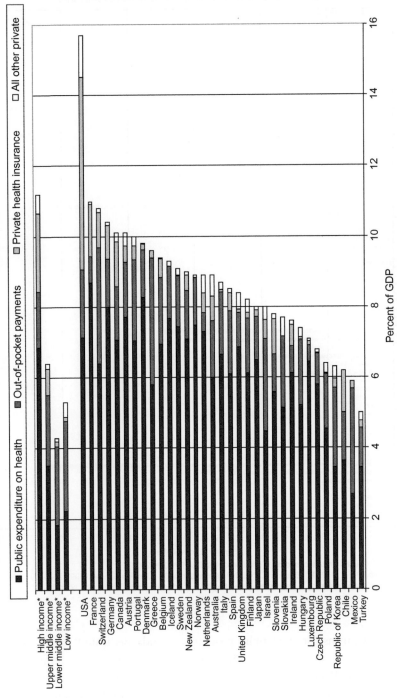

Notes: * Based on World Bank country classification (July 2008). OECD countries ranked by total expenditure as share of GDP. Other private includes expenditures by firms and non-profits; calculated as residual.
Source: World Health Statistics 2010 (WHO, 2010).

Figure 5.2 Expenditure on health as percentage of GDP by source of financing in 2007.

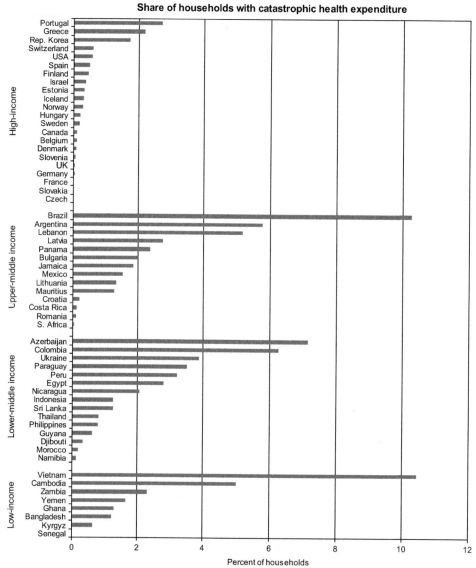

Figure 5.3 Share of households with catastrophic health expenditure.

Financing mechanisms for the public programs include dedicated social insurance contributions (e.g. Germany, France, the Netherlands) or taxation (e.g. Denmark, Italy, Spain, and the United Kingdom; see also Thomson et al., 2009). In many European Union countries, contributions are capped and split between employers and employees.

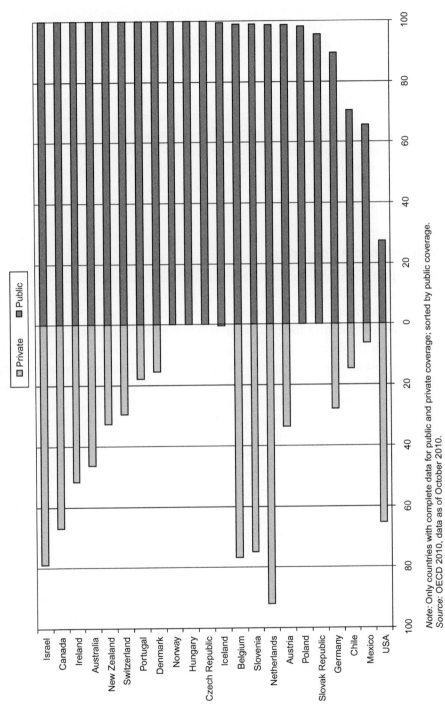

Figure 5.4 Coverage rates of private and public insurance in 2007 (%).

1.2.2.2. Participation

In most EU and OECD countries, participation in the public insurance schemes is mandatory although certain groups may be eligible to opt out or purchase supplemental private insurance. Consumer choice of insurer is an important feature in countries with competitive markets, such as Belgium, Germany, Israel, the Netherlands, and Switzerland (van de Ven et al., 2007). Choice is seen as instrumental to improve efficiency and equity of financial contributions. For instance, historical contributions in Germany varied significantly until the social health insurance introduced competition in 1996, which led to a steep reduction in the number of sickness funds and a convergence of contribution rates (McGuire and Bauhoff, 2007). Across countries the number of choices in these public systems varies significantly, from four insurers in Israel to 275 in Germany in 2006 (van de Ven et al., 2007).

1.3. Middle-income Countries

Insurance programs in middle-income countries have traditionally focused on improving access to care, while quality, costs, and risk protection are emerging policy concerns. The development of public insurance programs is limited by difficulties of raising revenues and demand for private insurance may be concentrated among better-off households (Pauly et al., 2009). Existing large-scale insurance programs tend to build on legacy structures (Eastern Europe; Waters et al., 2008) or leverage existing but fragmented public and private systems (Chile, Thailand) or community insurance schemes (Ghana). Efforts to introduce social health insurance have proliferated since about 2000 (Hsiao et al., 2007). In many middle-income countries, targeted safety-net programs complement a small private insurance market, limiting coverage to selected benefits and groups such as formal sector employees. In line with new concerns about costs and efficiency, strategies like managed competition (Colombia) and gatekeepers (Thailand) are now emerging in these settings.

1.3.1. Financial Risk

The share of public spending in total health spending tends to increase with countries' income, while private out-of-pocket spending is simultaneously displaced by private insurance (Figure 5.5). Similarly, the prevalence of catastrophic health spending is generally negatively correlated with the income level of the country (Xu et al., 2007).[24] The cross-country variations in catastrophic spending are more pronounced in the middle-income group than for high-income countries. Several countries such as Chile, Mexico, and Thailand have recently introduced (subsidized) universal

---

[24] Xu et al. (2007) rely on 116 household surveys between 1990 and 2003. Expenditure is classified as catastrophic if it exceeds 40 percent of a household's non-subsistence spending.

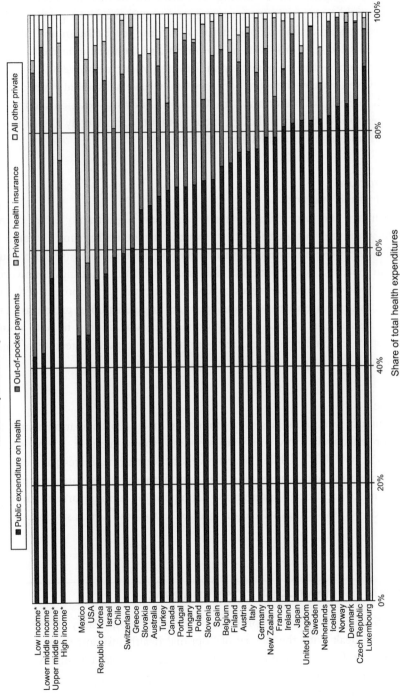

Figure 5.5 Health expenditure by source of health financing in 2007.

insurance, partly by complementing existing structures for formal and public-sector employees. Chile's public insurance program staggers premium and co-payment contributions in four levels according to beneficiaries' income level (Bitran and Munoz, 2010). Means-tested safety-net programs in Colombia and Georgia appear effective at improving risk protection for vulnerable populations (Miller et al., 2009; Bauhoff et al., 2010). However, narrow benefits packages often leave substantial residual risk, for instance with regards to prescription in Georgia. Informal payments remain a common concern in most settings although such payments seem largely absent in the Thai experience (Damrongplasit and Melnick, 2009).

1.3.2. Market Structure
1.3.2.1. Sources of Health Insurance
Social health insurance and targeted programs tend to have significantly larger coverage than private insurance. Although primary private insurance remains a source of coverage for some formal-sector workers, this market is generally small (see also Pauly et al., 2009 on the potential for private insurance markets in these settings). However, countries such as Colombia and Georgia actively facilitate the development of insurance markets by using private carriers to deliver their targeted public programs. The use of regulatory instruments such as risk adjustment remains limited in both countries. Risk pooling based on employment status remains an important feature of middle-income countries that have not introduced health reforms.

1.3.2.2. Participation
Social health insurance programs in several countries include participation mandates that explicitly or effectively only apply to certain groups such as formal-sector employees (Hsiao et al., 2007). Chile's near-universal program mandates payments to the public insurance fund while providing the option to switch to primary private coverage at potentially additional premiums. Competition among private insurers tends to be limited even in settings where the private sector coverage is sizeable.

2. OPTIMAL DEMAND-SIDE COST SHARING

The first papers in health economics—Arrow (1963), Pauly (1968), and Zeckhauser (1970)—dealt with the theory of "optimal health insurance" and considered whether market failures would interfere with private markets supplying this insurance. Against an institutional background of limited private health insurance and practically non-existent public insurance, Arrow called attention to the "missing market" for risk bearing. Why were not risk-averse patients able to purchase policies to shift risk to pools of subscribers? Arrow's answer (p. 945): "...it is impossible to draw up insurance policies which will sufficiently distinguish among risks, particularly since observation of the results will be incapable of distinguishing between avoidable and unavoidable risks, so that incentives to avoid losses are diluted"; in other words, the problem was moral hazard in health insurance design. Later in his "Uncertainty and the Welfare Economics of Medical Care," Arrow made explicit reference to moral hazard.

Arrow explicitly implicated both the physician and the patient in moral hazard in response to insurance coverage.[25] Pauly (1968) and Zeckhauser (1970) followed Arrow and made two contributions. First, they clarified that markets can solve the second-best problem of dealing with moral hazard in health insurance design. Second, both cast the decision about treatment determination as *demand*, setting the development of the theory of health care payment on a path emphasizing the patient—insurer relationship in insurance and de-emphasizing the insurer—provider side of the contract. Pauly, Zeckhauser, and later authors regarded the supply of medical care to be given by a perfectly horizontal marginal cost curve. Patients choose quantity to maximize utility at given prices, that is, act as price takers.[26] No information problems obscure the connection between patient demand and benefits. In retrospect, it is probably fair to say that Arrow was more concerned with the role of the physician in determining treatment than the role of the patient. Certainly, today, the insurer—provider contract in health insurance gets a great deal of attention. Had the first papers linking insurance to treatment decisions focused on the physician rather than the patient, health economics, and maybe even health policy, might have evolved differently.

The divide between demand- and supply-side models of health insurance remains. Papers on insurance and demand tend to view the supply side as competitive and accommodating; papers on supply tend to view patients as passively accepting provider recommendations.[27]

---

[25] Arrow (1963, pp. 961–962): "...The professional relationship between physician and patient limits the normal [did Arrow mean "moral"?] hazard in various forms of medical insurance ...Needless to say, it is a far from perfect check; the physicians themselves are not under any control and it may be convenient for them or pleasing to their patients to prescribe more expensive medication, private nurses, more frequent treatments, and other marginal variations of care."

[26] My "Physician Agency" chapter in *The Handbook of Health Economics*, Vol. 1, stresses that patients are not price takers for health care. In the presence of a downward sloping demand and selling a non-retradable service, profit maximization implies the physician will engage in quantity setting. If the physician has other objectives, she will still take advantage of quantity-setting ability to pursue those (McGuire, 2000).

[27] In this respect, Chandra, Cutler and Song (2011, this Handbook) represent a major departure from writing about treatment determination. For extensive discussion of supply-side models and contracting, see Dranove (2011, this Handbook).

2.1. Optimal Health Insurance Basics with no Moral Hazard

The basics of optimal health insurance results are covered in CZ (2000),[28] drawing on analysis in the Appendix to Arrow (1963). To summarize:

- With actuarially fair insurance and no moral hazard, full insurance is optimal. Actuarially fair insurance means the premium charged is equal to expected payout (no profits, no administrative costs). Health insurance, by allowing the consumer to pay for part of health care costs when healthy, transfers purchasing power from healthy to sick times. If the consumer is risk averse (utility of income is characterized by declining marginal utility of income), this transfer improves expected utility.[29]

- If insurance is sold with some administrative cost, optimal insurance with fixed financial risk is full insurance after a deductible. A deductible is optimal with administrative expenses, since for any actuarial value of a policy (assuming administrative expenses are a function of payout or actuarial value), it is better for the consumer to insure the expenses when disposable income is low rather than high, implying that insurance funds should always be first spent on the highest expense and optimal insurance takes the form of a deductible.

To go beyond these basic statements about optimal health insurance coverage it is necessary to introduce an economic model of utility to capture the trade-off between risk and incentives to use care efficiently.

2.2. Overview of Topics in Optimal Health Insurance[30]

We develop a model of health insurance and health care demand based on an explicit and general utility function for the purpose of pulling together findings on optimal insurance including various extensions.[31] The intention is to provide a unified treatment of the topic of the factors feeding into optimal demand-side cost sharing.

The first feature to consider is moral hazard or demand response, the effect of the presence of health insurance on health care demanded. We move on to integrate additional perspectives on optimal health insurance, such as "offsets" and cross-price elasticities, and consumer misinformation about the value of care. Along the way, we summarize recent (since CZ, 2000) empirical work that bears on the importance of each perspective. The topics to be covered in section 2 are laid out in Table 5.4.

---

[28] For a rigorous and comprehensive treatment, see also Zweifel et al. (2009).

[29] This result is demonstrated in the baseline case below.

[30] For a non-mathematical discussion of these issues, see Baicker and Goldman (2011). For a related comprehensive treatment, see Zweifel et al. (2009).

[31] Other approaches to optimal health insurance are sometimes diagrammatic (e.g. Pauly and Blavin, 2010) or based on approximations of separate expressions for the value of risk reduction and welfare loss due to overconsumption (e.g. Ellis and Manning, 2007). These approaches can be insightful and easy to work with in the case of a particular question but are not useful for integrating the numerous perspectives on optimal health insurance covered here. For other formulations, see Phelps (2010), Manning and Marquis (1996), Zweifel et al. (2009).

Table 5.4 Summary of Results on Optimal Health Insurance

Topic	Main Result	Insurance Market Solves?	Selected Readings	Precursors
Uncertainty, risk aversion	Full insurance	Yes	CZ (2000)	Arrow (1963)
Transactions costs	Full insurance after deductible	Yes	Arrow (1963)	
Demand response to insurance	Coverage inversely related to demand elasticity	Yes	Besley (1988); Manning and Marquis (1996) CZ (2000)	Zeckhauser (1970); Pauly (1968)
Prevention, offsets, cross elasticities	Substitutability implies more coverage; complementarity less	Yes if goods in same plan; no otherwise	Goldman and Philipson (2007) Ellis and Manning (2007)	Pauly and Held (1990)
Consumer mistakes in demand	Subsidize/penalize according to under- or overvaluation by consumers	No, unless consumers (or their agent) anticipate mistakes at time of insurance purchase	Fendrick and Chernew (2006); Pauly and Blavin (2010); Newhouse (2006)	Pigou (1920); Rice (1992); Jack and Sheiner (1997)

As part of the review of each topic, we comment on whether a competitive market for health insurance would lead to the optimal (second-best) form of coverage.

2.3. Optimal Health Insurance: First-best Benchmark

Consumers will be assumed to maximize expected utility. Let

$$EU = pU^s(x, y^s) + (1 - p)U^h(y^h) \tag{5.1}$$

With probability p, the individual is sick and benefits from health care x. When healthy, health care confers no benefit. I assume $U_x^s, U_y^s, U_y^h > 0, U_{xx}^s, U_{yy}^s, U_{yy}^h < 0, U_{yx}^s = 0$. Importantly, the utility from money could differ between the two states. Normally, we would expect the marginal utility of income to be greater when sick as illness may put other demands on income in addition to health care itself.

The price of health care is 1. Insurance takes the form of coinsurance and is actuarially fair. Thus, if the coinsurance is c and the individual consumes x when sick, the fair premium, $\pi = p(1-c)x$. Then, $y^s = I - \pi - cx$ and $y^h = I - \pi$. I here is income.

First-best choice of x and c is attained when the consumer takes account of the effect of choice of c and x on the premium paid.[32] In this case, it is as if the consumer is facing a perfectly competitive health insurance market that prices a policy just right for him, both in terms of the risk of illness, p, and the amount of health care he would consume, x. Obviously, with this pricing, the consumer pays for, and recognizes he pays for, the full cost of health care. The costs of moral hazard in consumption are internalized and coinsurance can be chosen without overconsumption.

Substituting for the premium and the budget constraints in the sick and healthy periods:

$$EU = pU^s(x, I - p(1 - c)x - cx) + (1 - p)U^h(I - p(1 - c)x) \tag{5.2}$$

Take the first-order derivatives with respect to x and c. I do not equate them to zero since boundary conditions on c are relevant to the maximization.

$$BFx : p(U_x^s + U_y^s(- p(1 - c) - c)) + (1 - p)U_y^h(- p(1 - c)) \tag{5.3}$$

$$FBc : pU_y^s x(p - 1) + (1 - p)U_y^h px \tag{5.4}$$

The FBc condition is about transferring income between the sick and the healthy states. As c goes up (with fixed x), income is transferred from the sick to the healthy state. The FBc condition can be rewritten:

$$(1 - p)px(U_y^h - U_y^s) \tag{5.5}$$

---

[32] Setting up the maximization in terms of c and x is done in Goldman and Philipson (2007).

We know from the budget constraints that $y^s < y^h$ for any $c > 0$. (The individual pays the premium in both states and cost sharing only when sick.) The typical case is then that the marginal utility of income is higher in the sick than the healthy state, implying that the FBc is negative for any $c > 0$. From the standpoint of choice of c, this means that c should fall (i.e. the derivative of EU of c when $c > 0$ is negative). When the marginal utility of income is higher in the sick state, c should be driven down to its boundary at $c = 0$. At $c = 0$, $y^s = y^h$. The marginal utilities of income in the two states could be equal in that case,[33] and if so, the FBc condition would be satisfied as an equality at $c > 0$.

The "atypical" case is also possible in which the individual does not want to use choice of coinsurance to fully smooth income between the sick and healthy state. One can imagine some illnesses that interfere with the consumption value of income and decrease the marginal utility of income when sick compared to when healthy.[34] In that case, there might be an interior solution to FBc with $1 > c > 0$. In what follows, we will assume that utility functions are such that in the first best, the individual prefers full insurance.

At $c=0$, the first best, FBx can be rewritten as:

$$\frac{U_x^s}{p(U_y^s) + (1 - p)U_y^h} = 1 \qquad (5.6)$$

The marginal rate of substitution (MRS) between health care and expected value of the marginal utility of income, the left-hand side of (5.6), is set at 1, the price of x.

Some formulations of the optimal insurance present the problem as a purely financial one, in which illness imposes a monetary loss (e.g. Morrisey, 2008). Nyman's work (1999a, 2003, 2008) stresses the role of the consumption value of health care (improvements in health) obtained as insurance transfers purchasing power to the sick state. Approaches dating back to Zeckhauser (1970), with a utility function including health care and money, capture the consumption value of health care in demand for insurance.[35] In this chapter, the consumption value of health care is fully captured as $U^s(x, y^s)$.

---

[33] Utility functions in healthy and sick states would have to take very special forms for the marginal utility of income to depend only on non-health consumption in each state. Such strong assumptions are not needed and not made here. The important point is that the consumer desires to transfer purchasing power to state when non-health consumption is less and ends up being constrained by the boundary condition that $c = 0$.

[34] Finkelstein et al. (2009) argue that this is not the normal case at all, and that the marginal utility of non-health consumption is generally lower when people are ill.

[35] Nyman uses the term "access motive" to buy health insurance to represent the idea that by transferring purchasing power to the sick state, the consumer can buy some types of care that were not previously feasible with his budget. This is the case of buying more due to the income effect of the insurance-facilitated transfer. de Meza (1983) also recognized the role of income effects. Our formulation explicitly allows for income transfer to affect consumption in the sick state and incorporates the consumption value into the calculation for optimal health insurance. There is no need to account for other reasons for insurance with a maximization of expected utility including consumption value. The framework here emphasizes interior solutions where the moral hazard trade-off is part of the second best. Nyman's example of a very expensive fixed price treatment would turn out to be fully insured in the first- and second-best solutions because of the inelastic demand response.

2.4. Demand Response (Moral Hazard) and a Second-best Coverage[36]

Pauly (1968) equated moral hazard, the insurance term, and used more broadly by Arrow, to consumer demand response.[37] His diagrammatic analysis showed that even if a consumer were risk averse, with moral hazard, a consumer might be better off without than with insurance.[38] Zeckhauser (1970) presented a formal analysis of the risk-spreading/ efficiencies in consumption trade-off explicitly incorporating demand response.[39]

The second-best insurance policy maximizes consumer expected utility in the presence of a constraint: when health care is demanded, the consumer disregards the effect of his purchase on the premium he pays for health insurance. Health insurance is sold to groups or classes of individuals. It is generally infeasible for an enrollee to commit to only using a certain amount of health care when sick in exchange for being charged a lower premium. The main reason is that there are too many health states and too many promises to make. Another way to put this is that insurers cannot easily tell the difference between persons that use a lot of health care because they are sicker, and those that use a lot of health care because they demand more for a given level of illness. Members of an insurance pool are trapped in a prisoner's dilemma. My use has a trivial effect on the average premium and it is not rational for me to hold back when I am sick. We all think like this and our premium must be higher to cover the cost of demand induced by insurance.

Finding the second-best policy involves two steps. First, the consumer maximizes utility by choice of health care taking the premium as fixed. By disregarding the cost of health care paid for through the premium, the consumer demands too much health

---

[36] Analysis of the role of demand response in affecting the optimal degree of coverage has been addressed using many approaches. Zeckhauser (1970) was the first explicit analytical treatment. For alternative models that lead to the same finding—higher demand response implies less coverage—see Besley (1988), Ellis and Manning (2007), and Zweifel et al. (2009). We draw here on Goldman and Philipson's (2007) set-up adding explicit mathematical analysis.

[37] "...seeking more medical care with insurance than in its absence is a result not of moral perfidy, but of rational economic behavior" (Pauly, 1968, p. 535).

[38] In response to a question about how came to write the paper, Pauly wrote: "The story is that I had already written a paper on optimal subsidization of education and Jim Buchanan noticed the first announcement of grants from the National Center for Health Services Research (now AHRQ) and suggested applying for money to work on optimal subsidization of medical care and make that my thesis. My original (or unoriginal) thought was that I could just adapt the education piece for medical care but then I noticed, to my great irritation, that subsidizing medical care was effectively health insurance—which prompted me to worry about health insurance and then make a contribution to...administrative costs as a reason for the absence of insurance. Jim Buchanan had written about 'inconsistencies in the UK national health service' pointing out that the government, bound by a budget, was forced to limit access to the care that people demanded at a zero user price, which was a similar idea. Arrow was kind enough to accept my point. I am still rewriting my thesis about public policy but the most useful discovery was something totally unplanned and bothersome at the time" (personal correspondence).

[39] In response to a question of how he came to write this paper, Zeckhauser wrote: "I wrote the paper because I was just running around thinking about risk and incentives issues. This seemed to be a logical way to proceed" (personal correspondence).

care (moral hazard). This becomes the constraint at the second step, finding the policy (coinsurance) that maximizes EU given that the consumer, when sick, pays attention only to c, not the premium, when demanding health care.

When the individual is sick he maximizes $U^s(x, I - \pi - cx)$ disregarding any effect of x on π. Demand for x is described by: $U^s_x - cU^s_y = 0$. Differentiating the demand condition (recalling that $U^s_{yx} = 0$):

$$U^s_{xx}dx - U^s_y dc = 0$$

$$\frac{dx}{dc} = \frac{U^s_y}{U^x_{xx}}$$

Dividing both sides by x we have demand elasticity (dc is a percentage change on a base price of 1) which will figure into the second-best policy:

$$\varepsilon = \frac{dx/x}{dc} = \frac{U^s_y}{U^s_{xx}x} \tag{5.7}$$

Proceeding to the second step to find the second-best health insurance policy we find the c that maximizes EU subject to the constraint describing demand:

$$\text{Max } EU_{x,c} = pU^s(x, I - p(1 - c)x - cx) + (1 - p)U^h(I - p(1 - c)x) - \lambda(U^s_x - cU^s_y), \tag{5.8}$$

where λ is a multiplier on the constraint of demand behavior. The three first-order conditions, which we assume are satisfied as equalities to yield interior solutions, are:

$$SBx : p(U^s_x + U^s_y(-p(1 - c) - c)) + (1 - p)U^h_y(-p(1 - c)) - \lambda U^s_{xx} = 0 \tag{5.9}$$

$$SBc : pU^s_y x(p - 1) + (1 - p)U^h_y px + \lambda U^s_y = 0 \tag{5.10}$$

$$SB\lambda : U^s_x - cU^s_y = 0 \tag{5.11}$$

Using SBc to solve for λ:

$$\lambda = \frac{-px(1 - p)(U^h_y - U^s_y)}{U^s_y} \tag{5.12}$$

Substituting for λ and using $SB\lambda$ to substitute for U^s_x, rewrite SBx:

$$p(cU^s_y + U^s_y(-p(1 - c) - c)) + (1 - p)U^h_y(-p(1 - c)) = U^s_{xx}\frac{-xp(1 - p)(U^h_y - U^s_y)}{U^s_y}$$

Substituting for the definition of demand elasticity, ε, and regrouping:

$$-(1-c)(pU_y^s + (1-p)U_y^h) = \frac{-(1-p)(U_y^h - U_y^s)}{\varepsilon U_y^s}$$

$$(1-c) = \frac{(1-p)(U_y^h - U_y^s)}{\varepsilon U_y^s(pU_y^s + (1-p)U_y^h)} \tag{5.13}$$

The term $(1-c)$ is the degree of coverage. As before, note that $y^s < y^h$ at any positive c. In the typical case in which the marginal utility of income when sick is greater than the marginal utility when healthy, the right-hand side of (5.13) is positive (the elasticity is negative). In other words, c must be less than 1. Some coverage is always optimal. Intuitively, this is because the risk-spreading benefits are due to the income transfer (the xdc at a small change) and difference in the marginal utilities—a first-order effect, whereas the inefficiency created by a small change in c below 1 is proportional to dc^2, a second-order effect.[40]

The key factors influencing the second-best coverage are ε, demand elasticity, and $U_y^h - U_y^s$, the discrepancy in the marginal utility of income between the healthy and sick state. The larger is demand elasticity, the lower is optimal coinsurance. Higher demand response creates larger welfare loss as c is reduced. Figure 5.6 illustrates this well-established and fundamental point. The welfare loss of a reduction of cost sharing from 1 to c is directly proportional to demand response (the base of the welfare triangle). Risk-spreading benefits are in proportion to the original out-of-pocket expense, x_0. These would be the same for the two demands D_1 and D_2, implying that the marginal losses for D_2 would equate to the marginal gains from risk spreading at a higher c than for D_1.

Condition (5.13) also shows the importance of value of the income transfer to sick states with health insurance. The larger the discrepancy between the two marginal utilities of income, the larger the insurance value of the money transfer. Note that even with some demand elasticity, "full" (i.e. $c = 0$) insurance could be optimal if the marginal utility of income when sick is high enough.

Models balancing moral hazard and risk protection have been the basis of calculations of the degree of optimal health insurance, generally leading to the conclusion that cost sharing should be higher than is currently observed in health insurance policies. Manning and Marquis (1989) rely on data from the RAND HIE and estimates of

---

[40] Chernew et al. (2000) analyze an interesting special case in which there are only two possible treatments, one expensive and one cheap, for a given disease. Some people should get the expensive one, but everyone would want the expensive treatment if it were fully covered. The optimal cost sharing as between these two treatments requires the consumer to face the full incremental cost of the more expensive treatment (that way patients sort correctly). To do this while maximizing the risk-spreading value of coverage, the authors propose that the patient gets "cash back" for taking the cheaper treatment—a negative cost sharing—and pays some of the extra cost of the more expensive treatment. By this method, more income can be transferred into the sick state.

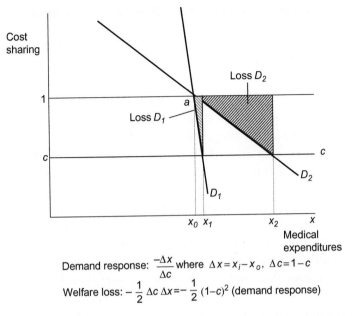

Figure 5.6 Higher demand response creates more inefficiency loss for given coverage.

risk aversion to figure that the optimal health insurance policy has cost sharing around 50 percent (slightly less would not impose much net welfare loss). Phelps (2010), also based on demand response data from the HIE, derives optimal cost sharing of 5 percent for hospital care and 50 percent for physician services.[41]

2.4.1. Empirical Studies of Demand Response since CZ (2000)

CZ (2000) review the early empirical studies estimating price elasticity of demand for medical care conducted in the 1970s.[42] Estimates from these studies ranged from -0.14 up to -1.5, estimates from the higher end of this range implying large effects of cost sharing on quantity demanded. However, as Cutler and Zeckhauser explain, these findings are difficult to interpret because most studies suffer from endogeneity in the rate of health insurance coverage, and because they failed to distinguish between marginal and average coinsurance rates. In response to these methodological shortcomings, the government-sponsored RAND Health Insurance Experiment (HIE) implemented a randomized study design to provide an unbiased estimate of demand

[41] In these papers, utility from income is separable from utility of health care. Assumptions about the degree of risk aversion are used to weigh inefficiency losses against risk protection.

[42] Swartz (2010) contains a comprehensive review of studies since the mid-90s, differentiating results by type of service (e.g. behavioral health), income, and health status.

elasticity for medical care; results from the HIE have set the standard in the literature to date.

The RAND HIE studied demand response among the non-elderly population in a fee-for-service environment, collecting data during the mid-70s. The HIE randomly assigned families to cost-sharing plans (and one prepaid group practice) that differed in initial cost sharing and an out-of-pocket limit.[43] Keeler and Rolph (1988) estimated the overall price elasticity of demand to be around −0.2 to −0.3. Except for evidence of high response for outpatient mental health care, demand responses for other types of services were all estimated to be about the same. There was no evidence of differences in demand response by income, by health status, or, according to whether services were more or less appropriate (Newhouse, 1993). Health care and health care financing have, of course, changed in important ways since 1975. Then, doctors could set their own fees to health insurers. Outside of a few prepaid group practices, there was little managed care. Diagnostic imaging was much less developed, drugs were a small part of health care costs, hospital stays were longer, and there were few surgical procedures that could be done on an outpatient basis. The structure of demand, including demand elasticity for these new products and services, might well deviate from findings in the HIE. Furthermore, the HIE did not include the age 65+ population accounting for almost 40 percent of the health care in the US.[44]

Another important difference is that, whereas in the 1970s cost sharing was applied to all services on a uniform basis, today insurance is likely to charge differential cost sharing by type of service (e.g. an outpatient visit versus an emergency room visit) or for different therapy options (i.e. generic versus different branded pharmaceuticals in a tiered formulary). A set of recent studies have focused on patient response to cost sharing for pharmaceuticals, one of the newer and less settled parts of health insurance coverage. Many of these studies take advantage of natural experiments to analyze demand following introduction of two- and three-tiered formularies, which create price differentials between pharmaceuticals within a therapeutic class. Consumers respond to cost sharing in tiered pharmaceutical formularies in part by switching to lower-tiered (priced) drugs and reducing demand for higher-tiered (priced) drugs.

MarketScan data for 2002 are used in two studies of Medicare retirees receiving drug coverage through their former employer (Gilman and Kautter, 2007, 2008) with estimates of overall demand elasticity in 2008 at around −0.23. Gaynor et al. (2007) use MarketScan data on people with three years' continuous eligibility to study the effect of cost sharing on demand. Using a price index to characterize patient cost sharing, they estimate demand elasticities to be in the −0.5 to −0.8 range. Goldman

---

[43] HIE investigators produce many papers. The main cost-sharing results are in Manning et al. (1987). Newhouse (1993) summarizes results from the entire experiment.

[44] For a concise summary of the RAND HIE, its methods, main results, and continued applicability, see Gruber (2006).

et al. (2007) review the literature on the effect of drug cost sharing, concluding that the price elasticity of demand falls in the range −0.2 to −0.6. Gibson et al. (2005) review 30 studies published from 1974 to early 2005 and conclude that a 10 percent increase in price reduces demand by 1 to 4 percent. Danzon and Pauly (2002) assess the contribution of growth in insurance coverage to the increase in utilization of drugs during the 1990s and settle on an estimate of demand response of −0.3.

Some studies find evidence for demand response without expressing the finding in elasticity terms. Landon et al. (2007) used a quasi-experimental design supplemented by matching on observed covariates to study the move from a single- or two-tier to a three-tier formulary. Total drug spending fell by 5−15 percent. Huskamp et al. (2003) also studied changes in tier placement by two employers who implemented three-tier formularies, comparing switching behavior among patients with tier changes to those among employers who did not alter tiers. Among those using an antihypertensive that was moved to tier 3, 41.6 percent changed to a lower tier drug in the same class with one employer (comparison employer 4.2 percent) and 41.0 percent in another employer (comparison employer 14.9 percent). A follow-up analysis controlling for trends and characteristics of the population confirmed these findings (Huskamp et al., 2005).

Other studies have taken advantage of natural experiments in other dimensions of coverage. To save money, the California Public Employees Retirement System (CalPERS) Board, the third largest purchaser of health insurance in the US, raised co-payments for physician office visits and prescription drugs in a series of moves to its PPO and HMO plans in the early 2000s. Chandra et al. (2010) exploited the staggered introduction of the cost sharing to study demand response in a modern managed care environment for retirees, mostly 65+, and compared their findings to demand response in the HIE. Difference-in-difference estimates from monthly trend data find responses on the low end of the HIE estimates, but excluding months just pre and post the change (not to count any strategic moving forward of utilization to avoid cost sharing), estimated arc elasticities fall to less than −0.1, about half of the HIE estimates.[45]

High-deductible health plans with their theoretical appeal were studied in the RAND HIE, and have since been relabeled as "Consumer Directed Health Plans." The Medicare Modernization Act (2003) created a Health Savings Accounts (HSA) option for employers: a portable spending account financed with pre-tax dollars can offset minimum deductibles set at $1,050 for individuals and $2,100 for families. The portability feature means that the consumer pays for costs up to the deductible. In a large study of the HSA plans from over 700 employers (but from one health insurer), LoSasso et al. (2010) found that the deductible reduced medical spending by about 5 percent, and the services that were affected tended to be the smaller patient-driven

---

[45] This paper also studies the effect of these co-payment changes on hospitalization; results are discussed below under the section related to cross-elasticities of demand.

decisions, such as filling a prescription, rather than the larger more provider-driven decisions like hospital care.[46] Good controls for prior use plus some data on employers who moved employees "involuntarily" support the interpretation that the lower spending is not due to selection, though the authors also found that healthier employees are the ones attracted to the HSA option when given a choice.

Another health plan innovation involving cost sharing is the use of tiered provider networks. In a tiered provider network physicians or hospitals are sorted according to their performance on cost efficiency and quality measures and patients pay higher co-payments for a visit to a provider in a lower performing tier. Two recent studies analyzed patient-level claims data and found some evidence that consumers switched to preferred providers when the price differential between preferred and non-preferred tiers is large. Scanlon et al. (2008) used a difference-in-difference strategy to study consumer response to hospital tiers structured according to whether a hospital has met a set of patient safety standards. The financial incentive for workers to choose one of the preferred hospitals was set at 5 percent coinsurance (an average of approximately $400 in out-of-pocket payments per worker). Comparing two sets of union workers to a control group of salaried, non-union workers this study finds that while workers in one of the unions were more likely to select the preferred hospital for medical visits, workers in a second union and all patients admitted for a surgical diagnosis were no more likely to choose the preferred tier of hospitals. Rosenthal et al. (2009) analyzed patient switching following the narrowing of a PPO physician network that excluded 3 percent (48 out of 1,800) of physicians from the network. While performance data informed the narrowing of the network, plan members were informed only that the affected physicians would no longer be in-network and therefore subject to higher cost sharing. The out-of-pocket cost difference in this setting was a change from a $10 dollar co-payment to 40 percent of allowed charges, with the potential for balance billing. The authors find that 81 percent of patients of affected physicians did not continue to see those physicians following their exclusion from the network, and an additional 7 percent of patients saw their excluded physician only one more time.

Recent studies of the effect of demand-side cost sharing on use among the under-65 population are generally conducted in the context of plans using managed care and provider contracting strategies. Section 3.1 addresses the question of whether "demand response" is moderated in the presence of these supply-side policies.

2.4.2. Competitive Insurance Markets and Second-best Coverage

In the absence of any other barrier to market functioning, competition would force firms to maximize expected utility of consumers at zero profit, solving, in effect, the expected utility maximization laid out above. Competitive health insurance markets would price health insurance at actuarially fair premiums (zero profit), and the

---

[46] For studies with one or a small number of employers see Buntin et al. (2006) and Feldman et al. (2007).

individual choosing from the menu of (π, c) fair policies would choose the optimal policy given the second-best constraint. Moral hazard makes optimal health insurance a second best, but this second best can be achieved by competitive markets, a result appreciated since Zeckhauser (1970).

Gruber (2008) reviews the health insurance market-seeking reasons why the US is characterized by the uninsurance for a large segment of the population, and "overinsurance" for most of the rest. There are clearly a number of mechanisms at work, contributing to one or both of these problems, but the basic pricing story here is a good start to understanding this issue. Basic insurance theory tells us that even in the presence of moral hazard, actuarially fair premiums lead individuals to buy the efficient (second-best) coverage.[47] If insurance is priced too high to some and too low to others, either due to inherent informational limitation or to regulation, the overcharged will underinsure (or forego altogether) and the undercharged will buy too much.

2.5. Multiple Services, Cross-price Elasticity of Demand, Offsets

The natural extension of the analysis of one health care service to more than one service encompasses a number of areas of research on health insurance design. Two covered services can be substitutes or complements. "Offset effects," a term common in the empirical literature, refer to the substitute case, when use of one service "offsets" or reduces use of another. The main insight regarding optimal insurance with multiple services is straightforward: when one service substitutes for another covered service, the increase in demand from insurance generates an efficiency gain from the decreased use of the other covered service. The reason for this is that the other service is itself insured and therefore to a degree "overused." Complementarity works the other way.[48] The under-appreciated subtlety in this result is the role of coverage for the "other" service. Without coverage and overuse, there is no efficiency gain/loss with a change in demand for the other service. The role of coverage emerges in the analysis of multiple services, and has important implications for the way "offset effects" should be measured and interpreted.

With two health care services, we have x_1 and x_2 instead of just x, and we can write expected utility as

$$EU = pU^s(x_1, x_2, y^s) + (1 - p)U^h(y^h). \tag{5.14}$$

---

[47] In other words, given the degree of moral hazard (making the problem one of the second best), individuals will demand the plan consisting of a coinsurance and a fair premium that maximizes their utility.

[48] Goldman and Philipson (2007, p. 427) summarize the intuitive point:

The optimally integrated benefit design differs from the standard single good designs by taking into account cross-price elasticities between the services and goods insured. . . If an insured good [like a new drug] has many other services that are substitutable, then its [optimal] copay will be lower than traditionally argued, as raising its copay will lead to additional use of those other services. If the other services are complementary, the [optimal] copay of the initial good will be higher.

Assume, in addition to assumptions about the first and second derivatives of income on utility from above, $U_1^s, U_2^s > 0$, $U_{11}^s, U_{22}^s < 0$, $U_{y1}^s, U_{y2}^s = 0$. Note that U_{12}^s, the cross term in utility, could take either sign. When $U_{12}^s > 0$, goods 1 and 2 will be complements and a reduction in price of good 1, say by insurance, will increase demand for good 2. When $U_{12}^s < 0$, goods 1 and 2 are substitutes. Assume that coverage for good 2, c_2, is fixed, and the issue is coverage for good 1.

The budget constraints and fair premium expressions now take account of two health goods: $\pi = p[(1 - c_1)x_1 + (1 - c_2)x_2]$, $y^s = I - \pi - c_1 x_1 - c_2 x_2$.

As before, $y^h = I - \pi$, and first-best insurance will feature full coverage for both services. Second-best coverage recognizes that demand behavior when sick ignores the effect of consumption on the premium. Demands for x_1 and x_2 when the individual is sick are found by maximizing $U^s(x_1, x_2, I - \pi - c_1 x_1 - c_2 x_2)$ with respect to choice of x_1 and x_2 assuming the premium is fixed. Demand will thus satisfy the pair of first-order conditions:

$$U_1^s - c_1 U_y^s = 0 \tag{5.15}$$

$$U_2^s - c_2 U_y^s = 0 \tag{5.16}$$

These behaviors then become constraints on second-best coverage.

Maximize EU subject to the two constraints describing demand for x_1 and x_2. To simplify the problem let c_2 be fixed:

$$\text{Max EU}_{x1,x2,c1} = pU^s(x_1, x_2, I - p[(1 - c_1)x_1 + (1 - c_2)x_2] - c_1 x_1 - c_2 x_2)$$
$$+ (1 - p)U^h(1 - p[(1 - c_1)x_1 + (1 - c_2)x_2]) \tag{5.17}$$
$$- \lambda(U_1^s - c_1 U_y^s) - \gamma(U_2^s - c_2 U_y^s)$$

$$SBx_1 : p(U_1^s + U_y^s(-p(1 - c_1) - c_1)) + (1 - p)U_y^h(-p(1 - c_1)) - \lambda U_{11}^s - \gamma U_{21}^s = 0 \tag{5.18}$$

$$SBx_2 : p(U_2^s + U_y^s(-p(1 - c_2) - c_2)) + (1 - p)U_y^h(-p(1 - c_2)) - \lambda U_{12}^s - \gamma U_{22}^s = 0 \tag{5.19}$$

$$SBc_1 : pU_y^s x_1(p - 1) + (1 - p)U_y^h p x_1 + \lambda U_y^s = 0 \tag{5.20}$$

$$SB\lambda : U_1^s - c_1 U_y^s = 0 \tag{5.21}$$

$$SB\gamma : U_2^s - c_2 U_y^s = 0 \tag{5.22}$$

In similar fashion to the case of one health care good, use $SB\lambda$ to substitute for U_1^s in SBx_1, and SBc_1 to substitute for λ:

$$- p(1 - c_1)(pU_y^s + (1 - p)U_y^h) = U_{11}^s \frac{- x_1 p(1 - p)(U_y^h - U_y^s)}{U_y^s} + U_{21}^s \gamma$$

$$(1 - c) = \frac{(1 - p)(U_y^h - U_y^s)}{\varepsilon_1 U_y^s(pU_y^s + (1 - p)U_y^h)} - \frac{\gamma U_{21}^s \gamma}{(pU_y^s + (1 - p)U_y^h)} \qquad (5.23)$$

Presence of a second good can be depicted as modifying the result for one good. The first term on the rhs of (5.23) is the same expression as for one good, where elasticity is redefined as:[49]

$$\varepsilon_1 = \frac{U_y^s}{U_{11}^s x_1} \qquad (5.24)$$

Turning to the second component of (5.23), since γ, the value of the constraint, is positive, as is the expected marginal utility of income, the negative sign in front implies that the second term on the rhs of (5.23) takes the opposite sign of U_{21}^s. When $U_{21}^s < 0$ the goods are substitutes, the new term is positive and $(1 - c_1)$ gets bigger. Thus, c_1 falls and coverage is greater in relation to what it would be considering only own-price elasticity. The opposite case, when $U_{21}^s > 0$ and the goods are complements, implies that the coverage should be less than in consideration of own-price elasticity alone.

Where does coverage for good 2 work into the picture? The shadow value of the constraint on demand behavior, γ, affects the magnitude of the cross effect on optimal coverage for good 1. The shadow value of the constraint can be interpreted as how much EU would increase if we could "relax" the constraint, in other words incrementally reduce consumption of x_2. A reduction in x_2 increases EU because of moral hazard with the consumer paying only $c_2 < 1$. If $c_2 = 1$, and there were no coverage for x_2, x_2 would be chosen optimally, and $\gamma = 0$ (by the envelope theorem). Continuing this point, if x_2 were not covered, the cross term would not matter for optimal insurance for good 1.

Concern about multiple services, substitutability, and complementarity in insurance design is an issue for other *covered* services. Other services, if these are not part of the insurance plan, even if they are health care services, are irrelevant for questions of optimal insurance. For example, suppose coverage for a certain prescription drug for pain offsets use of over-the-counter analgesics. Because these analgesics are not insured, there is no inefficiency associated with their use, and any "offset" in the use of the over-the-counter drugs is irrelevant for insurance design.

With some coverage, the impact of relaxing the demand constraint goes up as c_2 falls. The lower is cost sharing on good 2, the greater is the marginal welfare gain from an incremental reduction in x_2. Thus, we can conclude that the importance of cross-price effects in demand depend on the sign and the degree of substitutability,

---

[49] This is demand elasticity if there were no cross terms in demand. It is not strictly demand elasticity when there are two goods.

the U_{21}^s term, and the degree of coverage of the "other" good—the more coverage, the greater the effect of cross-price on optimal coverage.

2.5.1. Empirical Studies of Cross-elasticities, Offsets and the Welfare Interpretation

Coverage for the "other good" plays a role in the empirical literature studying cross effects in demand. A large literature in health economics and health services research tests for "offset effects," whereby use of one service leads to a reduction in use of another service.[50] The most active area for current research is on the cross effect of coverage for prescription drugs. Drug coverage is relatively new and variable. Furthermore, effective drug treatment for many, particularly chronic illnesses, might reasonably be expected to prevent/offset the need for other forms of care.[51]

Some research on demand for drugs bears on cross-elasticities. Ellison et al. (1997) studied cephalosporins, a class of anti-infectives, using IMS monthly time series data from 1985 to 1991, and found significant elasticities between some therapeutic substitutes. More recently, Ridley (2009) investigated cross-price elasticities for anti-ulcer drugs and drugs to treat migraines using data for 3 million people from a large pharmacy benefit manager in the early 2000s. He found large effects on demand when drugs differ in the co-payment from other drugs in their class.

A particularly interesting case of a cross-elasticity has emerged in statins, used to treat high cholesterol. In June 2006, the second largest-selling statin, Zocor, became available as generic simvastatin. Statin drugs had very high sales. In 2004, Zocor was the fifth largest-selling drug worldwide in terms of dollar sales, and another statin, Lipitor, was the worldwide leader among all drugs from any class at over $12 billion of sales annually. In response to the availability of generic simvastatin, managed care plans moved Lipitor to higher (less favorable) tiers (Aitken et al., 2009, p. W157). One PBM moved Lipitor to tier 3 in January 2006 in anticipation of generic simvastatin, and saw more than 40 percent of patients switch from Lipitor to a lower-tier statin (Cox et al., 2007). Among those with co-payment differences of $21 or more, 80 percent switched.

Such decentralized efforts at substitution aggregated to a major effect on statin sales. As Aitken et al. report, "[a]fter Zocor lost patent protection however, total

---

[50] A related question is insurance coverage for "prevention," health care that affects the probability of illness. On this, see Pauly and Held (1990) and Ellis and Manning (2007). The nature of the conclusions in Ellis and Manning are very similar to those here, including the role of coverage. The argument for coverage for preventive services rests on the presence of coverage for the service for the illness that would be prevented. See their equation (15), page 1139.

[51] When coverage for mental health care was an unsettled element of health insurance, there were many studies of the offset effects of psychotherapy. One of the few studies of offsets of psychotherapy with convincing identification was in the Rand HIE, in which one insurance condition varied the coverage for mental health care to test for cross-elasticities. No evidence was found for an offset effect of better coverage for outpatient mental health care on total expenditures. The HIE also studied and did not find offsets for coverage of outpatient general health care on total health care expenditures (Newhouse, 1993).

monthly Zocor plus generic simvastatin prescriptions boomed...In 2007, the number of prescriptions of Lipitor fell 12 percent, including 26 percent in new starts." [52]

It is typical in this literature to measure the "offset effect" by the effect on *total spending* not just covered or plan spending on the "other service." For example, Shang and Goldman (2007) use Medicare Current Beneficiary Survey (MCBS) data from 1992 to 2000 to show that extra spending, measured by plan plus consumer medical costs, on drugs use induced by Medigap coverage is more than offset by reductions in total health care spending. Hsu et al. (2006) compared medical spending for Medicare beneficiaries with a cap on drug coverage to those without a cap at Kaiser Permanente of Northern California prior to Medicare Part D. Drug spending was 28 percent less in the capped group but other categories of expenditures were higher and total spending for all care was not significantly different between the groups, implying a near dollar-for-dollar offset in total costs. Gaynor et al. (2007) study the effect of increases in co-payments charged for drugs among private employees on total (plan plus consumer) spending. Increases in non-drug spending, largely in outpatient care, offset $0.35 of each dollar saved in drug costs. [53] An exception to the singular focus on total spending is the paper by Chandra et al. (2010), finding that the savings in costs due to higher co-payments for drugs were partly offset by higher spending on hospital services among retired state employees in California. They tracked offsets by payer since a primary (Medicare) and secondary (employer-provided supplemental) shared in offsets unequally. [54] About 20 percent of the cost savings from higher cost sharing for physician services and drugs was "offset" by higher costs of hospitalization overall, with the offset concentrated among those with a chronic illness. Interestingly, as the authors point out, in the CalPERS case, this offset largely takes the form of a negative fiscal externality from the CalPERS supplemental policy (which saves from the elevated co-payments) to Medicare (which pays most of the costs of hospitalization).

---

[52] Aitken et al. (2009, pp. W157–W158). International experience accords with US experience. See McGuire and Bauhoff (2011), op. cit., p. 24.

[53] Other papers use total costs as the measure of offsets. Gibson et al. (2006) measured the effects of lower co-payments for statins (drugs treating high cholesterol) on total medical expenditures, payments from any source, and evidence of an offset. Zhang et al. (2009) found an offset effect in added drug coverage for Medicare Part D. In their group with no prior drug coverage, drug spending went up $41 per person per month with Part D but other medical expenses fell by $33 per month. They computed the offset effect of Medicare Part D on other medical expenditures using total expenditures (plan plus co-payments).

[54] Lichtenberg has conducted a series of studies of the health and medical care cost impacts of newer prescription drugs and found evidence for an offset effect on total health care costs. For a recent paper, see Lichtenberg and Sun (2007). Zhang and Soumerai (2007) question the conclusions of some of Lichtenberg's earlier offset findings. Offset effects of drugs have become so widely accepted that "null effect" papers are published. Duggan (2005) pursued the Lichtenberg line of inquiry for a specific area of treatment and found that newer antipsychotic drugs did not reduce total costs in comparison to older drugs. See also Zhang (2008).

The implicit logic in many papers measuring an offset in terms of total spending on the other service is that if as a result of an increase in coverage of good 1, total medical costs fall, the increase in coverage for good 1 is welfare increasing. In non-technical terms, if a coverage expansion "more than pays for itself" by a reduction in total medical costs, the logic says that the coverage increase is welfare improving. Glazer and McGuire (2010) show that this logic is not correct. If total plan-paid or *covered* costs fall due to offsets, then a coverage expansion is welfare improving; otherwise it may or may not be. As we have argued above, only covered cost changes have welfare implications. It would obviously be incorrect to argue that an "offset effect" matters for uncovered services, and therefore total spending cannot be the welfare-relevant measure of an offset.[55]

2.5.2. Competitive Insurance Markets and Cross-price Effects

Competitive health insurance markets offering a plan covering both goods 1 and 2 would take account of the cross relationship and solve the second-best problem (Goldman and Philipson, 2007). If insurance for the two products were covered under separate insurance contracts, however, the cross effect would not be internalized and coverage decisions could be distorted. For example, suppose better coverage of drugs leads to higher rates of compliance and lower hospital costs, consistent with the findings of Chandra et al. (2010). A Medicare beneficiary in traditional Medicare with Part A and Part B coverage would have no incentive to recognize this offset and pay for a more extensive Part D drug plan with better coverage because the savings from hospital costs go back to Medicare.

Internalizing cross-price effects is one consideration in design of insurance contracts. An integrated plan taking account of cross effects could offer higher expected utility to a consumer than would be offered by two separate insurance products which failed to take account of cross effects. Employer-based health insurance generally includes coverage for drugs in integrated plans. The insurer/employer is in a position to internalize any offset effects. Medicare, by contrast, makes drug coverage available from private plans which, subject to some regulation, set their own benefits and premiums and enjoy no reward for any offset they provide.

2.6. Health Insurance to Correct Consumer Mistakes in Demand for Health Care

The analysis to now of optimal insurance regards the consumer as being equipped with the information necessary to evaluate medical care, and choosing health care in

---

[55] The consumer's budget constraint implies that an increase in spending on one good must be "offset" by spending reductions on another, but this does not, of course, imply that the increase in spending on the good is welfare increasing. Glazer and McGuire (2010) show formally the conditions under which offsets can be interpreted as welfare improving or decreasing.

their best interest so as to maximize expected utility. There is plenty of evidence (see section 2.6.1 below), however, that patients make mistakes in demand for health care, either because they misperceive the risks and other trade-offs involved or they make decisions based on false hope or other irrational bases. What are the implications of consumer mistakes in demand for health care for design of health insurance?

From left to right, a demand curve based on full information and rational choice prioritizes units of health care according to value, ranking by willingness to pay. Cost sharing in health insurance, imposed against this demand, retains high-value and reduces use of low-value services. Rice (1992) called attention to the apparent disconnect between this prediction and the finding in the RAND experiment that "cost sharing was generally just as likely to lower use when care is thought to be highly effective as when it is thought to be only rarely effective" (Lohr et al., 1986, p. S32, quoted in Rice, 1992, pp. 87–88). Rice argued that the real welfare loss from health insurance was the cost of producing ineffective care. Furthermore, he argued that effectiveness, not demand response, should be the central consideration in choice of demand-side cost sharing.

More recently, Chernew, Fendrick and colleagues[56] argue that clinical effectiveness should join moral hazard and risk considerations in design of optimal health insurance, terming the blended approach "value-based insurance design" (VBID): "VBID relaxes the questionable assumption that when faced with cost sharing, consumers will balance cost and clinical value optimally...Because consumers' behavior might not follow standard assumptions, targeted reductions in the level of cost sharing can increase value by reducing underuse..." (Chernew et al., 2007, p. W196).

Pauly and Blavin (2008) were the first, in a diagrammatic analysis, to formally integrate mistakes with the risk/moral hazard trade-off in design of health insurance. Their demand curves are distinct from true marginal benefit curves and illustrate how consumer undervaluation should be associated with more coverage. If health care is "really" more valuable than consumers think it is, the moral hazard cost of a marginal increase in coverage is less, so coverage should be improved. They also call attention to the converse argument: when consumers overvalue care, cost sharing should *increase* in relation to conventionally optimal cost sharing. We usually assume that markets, including health care markets, work better when consumers accurately appreciate the value of what they buy, but Pauly and Blavin point out this is not correct in a VBID context. If patients undervalued care, cost sharing could be reduced to offset this mistake and at the same time provide financial protection. One can see that making undervaluation marginally worse would allow the insurer to decrease cost sharing to just compensate and make the consumer better off (same consumption, lower risk).

---

[56] For a recent statement of the VBID ideas with references, see Chernew and Fendrick (2008).

By the same argument, informing the consumer about the correct value of a medical service, i.e. correcting his mistake, would make him worse off.[57]

Consumer misperception of health benefits can be added to the basic model in this chapter, integrating value-based corrections with conventional moral hazard/risk trade-offs. Demand behavior when health care is chosen to maximize utility was described by $U_x^s - cU_y^s = 0$; suppose instead the consumer misperceives value: $\varphi U_x^s - cU_y^s = 0$, where φ is a parameter capturing the mistake. If $\varphi < 1$, the consumer undervalues medical care; if $\varphi > 1$, he undervalues the care. The second-best health insurance policy maximizes the expected utility, but the behavioral constraint reflects consumers' over- or undervaluation:

$$\varphi U_x^s - cU_y^s = 0 \tag{5.25}$$

Using SBc as before to substitute for λ we now replace U_x^s by $\frac{c}{\varphi} U_y^s$.

Rewriting SBx when consumers may make mistakes:

$$p\left(\frac{c}{\varphi} U_y^s + U_y^s(-p(1-c) - c)\right) + (1-p)U_y^h(-p(1-c)) = U_{xx}^s \frac{-xp(1-p)(U_y^h - U_y^s)}{U_y^s} \tag{5.26}$$

Substituting for the new term and the definition of demand elasticity, ε:

$$\frac{-(cU_y^s - \varphi c U_y^s)}{\varphi} + (1-c)(pU_y^s + (1-p)U_y^h) = \frac{(1-p)(U_y^h - U_y^s)}{\varepsilon U_y^s}$$

$$(1-c) = \frac{(1-p)(U_y^h - U_y^s)}{\varepsilon U_y^s(pU_y^s + (1-p)U_y^h)} + \frac{cU_y^s - \varphi c U_y^s}{\varphi(pU_y^s + (1-p)U_y^h)} \tag{5.27}$$

The sign of the new term, the second one in (5.27), depends on whether φ is greater or less than 1, that is, consumers over- or undervalue health care. When $\varphi < 1$, consumers undervalue care, and the new term will be positive, implying more coverage is efficient (lower c). $\varphi > 1$, consumer overvaluation, implies the opposite, less coverage. Expression (5.27) integrates demand response, risk, and consumer mistakes in a unified expression for optimal coverage.

2.6.1. Evidence for Consumer Misappreciation of Benefits

Literature reviews (e.g. Gibson et al., 2005; Rice and Matsuoka, 2004) conclude that cost sharing leads to cutbacks of health care with positive health effects. These findings

---

[57] This argument is the source of the "blissful ignorance" in the Pauly–Blavin title.

constitute a necessary but not sufficient condition for the VBID argument to have bite. A rational, fully informed consumer paying part of costs would stop using care when it still had a positive marginal benefit. The evidence must go beyond effectiveness to establish that care is effective *and* that consumers undervalue this effectiveness.

"Undervaluation" requires a standard against which to measure patient valuation. The most common approach is to use clinical criteria to identify some services a set of patients certainly should be using and investigate whether cost sharing deters some of this assumed-to-be-worthwhile care. For example, taking medication for hypertension and other chronic illness is something patients ought to do, and by this standard, and if cost sharing interferes with adherence to medication guidelines, there is some case for a VBID correction to lower cost sharing. Chernew et al. (2008c) study a company that decreased co-pays on brand and generic drugs (in comparison to a control company with the same chronic disease management program) used to treat chronic illnesses (such as hypertension), and found patients were less likely to stop taking medication with lower co-payments.[58] Other papers make use of a clinical standard of care, and evaluate whether reducing co-pays moves more patients to comply.[59] So much of health care is of doubtful effectiveness that it seems likely that consumer overvaluation of care is at least as common as undervaluation.[60] If true, systematic incorporation of consumer mistaken valuation of health care would lead to a raising, not lowering, of cost sharing, to discourage patients from seeking care less effective than they believe it to be.

2.6.2. Competitive Insurance Markets and Consumer Mistakes

If consumers apply the same mistaken expected utility function to the demand for health insurance, competitive markets will not deliver the efficient second-best coverage. They will demand coverage for services they regard to be valuable, mistakenly or not, and undervalue coverage for services they undervalue.

It seems possible though that consumers might evaluate health care more "objectively" at the time they choose coverage in comparison to when they face treatment decisions. Prior to having back pain I might prefer a plan with coverage favoring evidence-based treatments, whereas after I am hit with the pain I might want to follow my doctor's recommendations without paying penalties for treatments without a good evidence base. If consumers see the consequences in the premium of "more efficient" cost-sharing designs, they may, at the stage of insurance choice, be receptive

---

[58] Generic co-pays were already low, at $5, and were cut to zero. Brand co-pays were cut in half. Chernew et al. (2008c) did not report brand and generic increases separately.

[59] E.g. Choudhry et al. (2010a) and Maciejewski et al. (2010). For review, see Choudhry et al. (2010b).

[60] Two papers make and assess the case for increasing co-pays for ineffective care, especially in cases where there are alternative treatments of established effectiveness. Robinson (2010) discusses a set of specialty drugs, medical devices, imaging, and surgical procedures he regards to be candidates for higher co-pays. See also Fendrick et al. (2010).

to VBID corrections. Otherwise, mistakes in buying health care would not be corrected by consumer decisions at the time of insurance purchase.

3. SUPPLY-SIDE POLICIES AND DEMAND-SIDE COVERAGE

A health insurance contract consists of more than a set of demand-side prices describing how much the enrollee would have to pay for covered services. With the advent of managed care in the 1970s and 1980s, allocation of resources for care in a plan came to depend also on the providers a patient could choose among, plan-determined resources available to those providers, the rules governing provider decisions, and the financial and organizational incentives facing the providers. Sociologist Friedson (1973), in his influential paper "Prepaid Group Practice and the New 'Demanding Patient'," recognized that the new managed care plans, chiefly staff model Health Maintenance Organizations (HMOs) like Kaiser Permanente in California, put new stresses on the doctor–patient relationship. Low consumer cost sharing paired with limited budgets set up, in economic terms, "excess demand" at the insurance-subsidized price. From the provider's point of view, patients were "demanding" in the commonplace meaning of the term: pushy. Furthermore, doctors, as employees of the plan, felt bound to serve the "difficult patient," in contrast to free-choice private practice where a doctor could tell a patient to take his/her demands elsewhere. When a consumer chooses a health plan, they choose demand-side coverage but also the set of rules the plan uses to ration care and the contracts the plan sets with its participating providers.

Patients' well-publicized frustrations with rationing and lack of choice of provider mirror those of Friedson's physicians. Yet consumer/patients and their agents such as employers demand health plans incorporating managed care in spite of these frustrations for a reason: managed care can mimic the first-best plan with little cost sharing (minimizing financial risk) and limit care to the efficient quantity. In principle, by rationing care, a health plan can fully resolve the moral hazard problem, covering all costs and supplying only the efficient care. Consumers would pay the premium to join such a plan even while recognizing that, when sick, they will demand more care than they are given at the fully insured price.

Dranove (2011, this Handbook) contains a comprehensive treatment of provider contracting. In this chapter I develop two additional aspects of the subject, related to the links between supply-side policies and optimal coverage on the demand side. One link flows from supply side to demand side: managed care and provider contracting take the pressure off cost control, permitting more generous coverage on the demand side. The second link flows from demand side to the supply side: more generous coverage enhances the bargaining power of the plan in relation to suppliers (essentially, the plan has "more to give"), and allows the plan to strike more favorable contract terms. Both of these links imply that the use of supply-side policies should improve coverage on the demand side.

3.1. Supply-side Policies

Demand-side cost sharing refers to the prices consumer/patients pay at the time they use care. Supply-side cost sharing refers to provider payment policies that require providers to, in effect, pay part of the costs of care (at the margin).[61] "Prospective payment" where payment to a provider is based on the classification of a person or episode rather than on the cost of services provided can be regarded as supply-side cost sharing (Ellis and McGuire, 1986). Managed care is a broad term referring to health plan strategies to affect utilization and quality other than demand-side cost sharing. Internal rules for approval based on "medical necessity" are one form of managed care. Construction and contracting with networks of providers is also part of managed care.

Ellis and McGuire (1993) observe that supply-side policies, such as prospective payment, can limit utilization without imposing financial risk on consumers.[62] An argument for the primacy of supply-side cost sharing then follows: "Where possible, use supply-side cost sharing to achieve health care utilization targets, such as a desired cost per episode of inpatient care." This frees demand-side cost sharing to "protect patients against financial risk" (1993, p. 114). Pauly and Ramsey (1999), when evaluating the use of quantity limits (in a model of managed care) in relation to demand-side cost sharing, conclude that at least some quantity limits are part of the optimal health insurance policy.

Concretely, suppose a health plan is contracting with a network of physicians to provide primary care to a group of beneficiaries, and suppose the efficient level of primary for the enrollees is an average of three visits per person per year. One way to hit this target is to pay physicians by a negotiated fee schedule meant to cover average cost per visit (no supply-side cost sharing) and require patients to pay a high enough co-payment to limit *demand* to the average number of visits to three per year. An alternative payment policy would be to pay the physician network with some degree of supply-side cost sharing that limits *supply* to the desired average. This is easiest to imagine (and implement) if the physicians are part of an organization (a group practice, or an "Accountable Care Organization" (ACO)), and the organization receives some payment prospectively and some on the basis of fees. A partly prospective

---

[61] Demand-side cost sharing is also strictly payments required at the margin. Enrollees in a health plan also pay for the balance of costs of care through premiums.
[62] Providers may bear some risk but they have the law of large numbers on their side.

payment, or "mixed" system, would pay something on the basis of patient enrollment with the organization and something on the basis of services provided. Another alternative that would create the same marginal incentives is to pay fees but withhold a share of fee payments that would be paid contingent on hitting utilization targets, as is being done in the context of ACOs.

Accountable Care Organizations (ACOs), created by the Affordable Care Act (ACA), are integrated networks of health care providers serving Medicare. Beneficiaries do not enroll in ACOs, but are attributed to ACOs based on Medicare algorithms using claims. And unlike managed care plans, ACOs cannot restrict beneficiaries to receive care within their network. Payment to ACOs involves a so-called "shared savings" model in an attempt to provide higher-powered payment incentives. The traditional FFS payment system will be modified so that if beneficiary expenditures for patients assigned to the ACO are sufficiently below a benchmark defined by a comparable population in traditional Medicare, the ACO will be paid a bonus that is proportionate to those savings. ACOs may share in gains and losses. This payment model is an example of a "mixed system," partially prospective and partially cost or fee based.

3.1.1. Evidence on the Effects of Supply-side Cost Sharing on Use and Cost

Christianson and Conrad's (2011) recent review documents that providers respond to payment system incentives. After a review of reviews, they summarize as follows: "the relatively large number of published studies that assess the impact of provider financial incentives on medical care utilization and costs have found, with very few exceptions, that providers will take steps to reduce utilization or costs when rewarded to do so" (p. 634). See CZ (2000) for coverage of the earlier literature coming to the same conclusion. The newer literature on effects on quality, including that related to pay-for-performance, is less clear.[63]

Some relevant recent evidence for anticipating cost-related results of ACO financial incentives comes from Massachusetts in response to cost increases from the state-based health reform (Song et al., 2011). In 2009, Blue Cross Blue Shield of Massachusetts (BCBS) implemented a global payment system similar to ACO models; provider groups shared accountability for total health care spending. Participating provider groups included large well-established integrated practices with experience of risk sharing with insurers, to smaller dispersed practices without such experience. Savings in the first year were small, and mainly due to ACOs directing referrals to lower-priced specialists and facilities.

ACOs of the 2010s resemble risk-bearing multispecialty medical group practices of the 1990s that emerged in California and elsewhere. Contracting between these

---

[63] See Dranove (2011, this Handbook).

groups and managed care plans was freely negotiated and evolved over the decade of the 1990s. This older experience with insurer risk contracting with medical groups suggests that the savings could eventually be much larger than seen in the results so far from recent reforms sponsored by public payers.

The leading edge of the managed care boom in the 1990s was California, where the legislature authorized the state Medicaid program (MediCal) and private insurers in the state to selectively contract with hospitals and other providers (Morrisey, 2008, p. 133). Particularly around Los Angeles, a number of large multispecialty group practices had grown up to compete with Kaiser Permanente medical groups. Some of these groups were experimenting with capitation contracts in the late 1980s, and having success, leading other groups to follow suit (Casalino and Robinson, 1997). The medical groups bargained with hospitals over rates and managed hospital care, achieving very significant reductions in hospitals costs. Casalino and Robinson (1997), reporting on case studies of five large medical groups in California, stated:

> Over the past 20 years, these medical groups reduced hospital days per thousand per year to 137 for non-Medicare patients and 900 for Medicare patients—*one-third* of pre-managed care rates. (emphasis added)

In the period between 1990 and 1994 alone, these five groups reduced hospital days per thousand for non-Medicare (commercial) enrollees in five groups; days per thousand fell by 16–40 percent over this four-year period alone.[64] Being paid to bear risk of hospital costs, when those costs could be managed down, was extremely profitable to the medical groups. One large California medical group, Mullikin Medical Center, began entering into "full risk" (including hospital costs) capitation contracts in 1990, and saw its net payments from the hospital portion of the capitation payment go up dramatically relative to its enrollment, from $4.8 million in 1991 to $15.6 million in 1993 (Casalino and Robinson, 1997).

During the boom years of risk contracting, medical groups sought more financial responsibility and risk. According to Casalino and Robinson (1997), "As the [medical] groups became more confident in their ability to manage care, they negotiated to take more and more financial risk—and a larger and larger part of the insurance premium dollar—from HMOs." Medical groups not only sought the risk from insurers, they worked to prevent hospitals from obtaining capitation contracts, seeking to keep risk for hospital services for themselves (Casalino and Robinson, 1997).

Competition among medical groups drove down their payments from plans. According to Bodenheimer (2000), capitation payments to medical groups in 1997–1999 were 20–25 percent lower than what groups were receiving in the early part of the decade. Health insurance premiums fell too. During the second part of the

---

[64] Other research on California over this period substantiates the connection between capitation-based medical groups and the decline in hospital costs. See Robinson (1996).

1990s, premiums paid to MCOs were falling (or falling relative to cost growth) for major buyers of health insurance in California: private employers (Robinson, 1995), individual purchasers (Buntin et al., 2003), the California Public Employees Retirement System (CalPERS, 2004), and the US Office of Personnel Management (OPM, 2004) which purchased on behalf of federal employees. After easy cost reductions were eliminated, profitability of risk contracts for medical groups plummeted, and medical groups retreated from full-risk contracts (Robinson and Casalino, 2001).

On a national level, the spread of managed care and provider contracting transformed health insurance contracts and at least for a time tempered health care cost growth. Between 1988 and 2005, traditional health insurance disappeared in employer-provided health insurance, as the proportion of workers enrolled in managed care plans rose from 27 to 97 percent (Gabel et al., 2005). Health insurance premium growth was falling in the first part of the 1990s, as managed care took hold, and during the middle part of the decade, premiums were *falling in real terms*. Physician incomes were also stagnant in real terms of the entire decade of the 1990s.

3.1.2. Supply-side Policies and Demand Response to Insurance

Managed care and supply-side cost sharing ought to reduce the demand response to health insurance coverage. With supply-side policies, utilization is not exclusively demand determined. If demand runs up against rules or reluctance from suppliers, the moral hazard effect of insurance ought to be dampened.

This dampening appears in models of supply-side cost sharing and managed care. When desired "supply" (of a provider) differs from desired "demand" (of a patient), either a short-side rule about outcomes or a bargaining model implies that equilibrium quantity moves less in response to a change in co-payment (Ellis and McGuire, 1990). In terms of managed care, the literature features two basic approaches. The first views managed care as setting quantities for individuals who may be heterogeneous with respect to severity of illness and demand. For example, Pauly and Ramsey (1999) assumed that in order to control costs, the managed care plan was able to impose uniform-across-severity quantity restrictions on the amount of treatment that was offered. Figure 5.7 illustrates the idea of a quantity limit, q_r, of the kind envisioned by Pauly and Ramsey. At level of cost sharing C_1, the consumer uses q_1. When the coinsurance falls to C_2, the consumer's demand increases to q_2—this would be demand response in an unmanaged plan. Managed care plans rules limit use to q_r. Thus, measured demand response under a managed care plan is thus the difference between q_r and q_1 rather than the larger difference between q_2 and q_1. Since quantity limits in managed care will at least sometimes bind, demand response to demand-side cost sharing should be less in managed care.

The other approach views managed care as rationing services by a "shadow price." For example, Frank et al. (2000) regard the managed care plan as supplying consumers

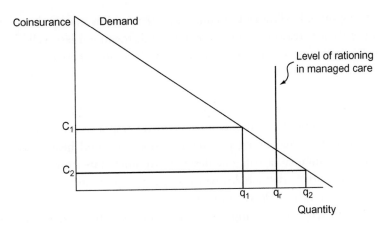

Figure 5.7 The effect of changes in demand-side cost sharing on use in traditional and managed care plans.

all services that are valued above a shadow price (which may differ by type of service), denying care for all uses for which the value was below the shadow price. The shadow price model is supply determined, with coverage and demand in the background.[65] Both approaches imply that, under managed care, observed demand response to out-of-pocket cost will be less elastic than that under indemnity arrangements.

The empirical literature does not uniformly support this clear prediction. Some studies of small co-payment changes within HMO plans find relatively large effects on use. Cherkin et al. (1989) studied Washington state employees' use of office visit care following introduction of a $5 co-pay, and Selby et al. (1996) examined the effect of an emergency room co-pay for Kaiser enrollees for some firms in comparison to enrollees with no co-pay increase. Recent studies with careful identification, for example the Chandra et al. (2010) analysis of public employees in California, found demand responses not very different than the RAND HIE. Gruber (2008), in his review of the effects of insurance, argues for the continuing relevance of the RAND estimates.

The story of demand response in at least some areas of health care is, however, different in managed care. Demand for mental health care, in the RAND HIE and in other earlier studies, was found to be about twice as responsive to cost sharing as other areas of care, a major justification for "discriminatory coverage" (Frank and McGuire, 2000). A number of private and public health plans implemented "parity" or equality in coverage for mental illness within a managed care context and found no or very

---

[65] The assumption in Frank et al. (2000) and subsequent papers using the shadow price is that patients have full coverage and accept any desired supply.

little demand response, leading to the conclusion that within managed care, there was no longer an efficiency reason to cover mental health treatment less well.[66]

Few studies test for a difference in demand response between managed and unmanaged care using similar population and measures. In a pair of papers, Lu, Frank and McGuire (2008, 2009) use data from the Medical Expenditure Panel Survey from 1996 (a high-water mark for managed care, and in a wave of MEPS when linkage to insurance data were possible) and examined demand response for mental health care and for general health care among persons in employer-based health insurance who had no choice of insurance, a data cut designed to ameliorate concerns with adverse selection. In both studies, deductibles had no effect on use, and demand response to co-payments was significantly lower in managed plans.

Consistent with what theory implies, though not with the findings of all empirical studies, managed care plans do contain less demand-side cost sharing than conventional plans, or newer high-deductible health plans (Baicker and Goldman, 2011); see also Table 5.2 above).

3.2. Demand-side Cost Sharing and Selective Contracting

A major function of managed care health plans is contracting with doctors, hospitals, drug and equipment manufactures, and other suppliers of medical care. Traditional Medicare also requires contracts with supplying hospitals and physicians, but "any willing provider" may accept Medicare's terms, and traditional Medicare does not therefore qualify as a managed care plan. The added element in *selective* contracting is exercise of a plan's discretion to limit the suppliers: restricting contracting providers to a subset of the physicians or hospitals in a region, or setting up a drug formulary that excludes certain products.

What is gained by reducing choice of plan enrollees? Limiting choice of provider can accomplish two general goals for a health plan. First, selective contracting can weed out providers who would be poor choices for plan members, for reasons of either quality or cost.[67] Members may be poor judges of quality, and plan coverage shields them from at least some of the effects of higher costs. Second, by promising an enhanced patient flow from network inclusion, a health plan is in a position to negotiate discounts or control over treatment decisions through managed care tactics. In principle, this is a very powerful plan policy. Dranove et al. (1993) were among the first to notice and measure the power of selective contracting, contrasting the new "payer competition" (providers compete for plan contracts) with "patient competition" (providers compete for individual patients). If provider performance is merely

---

[66] Empirical studies of demand response in mental health care are reviewed in Barry et al. (2006).

[67] Plan members in their group self-interest would exclude from the plan's network a provider who was only marginally better in terms of quality but much more expensive.

observable (it need not be contractible), a plan can, for example, specify treatment quantity or quality targets as a condition of contracting (Ma and McGuire, 2002). A provider may accede to a plan's terms in exchange for the extra volume of business associated with participating in the plan's network. As we will see shortly, the plan's ability to promise business is connected to its decision about demand-side cost sharing, creating the link between coverage and the plan's ability to bargain hard with providers.

Selective contracting in health care can be regarded as a two-stage process. The health plan selects providers in a first stage along with the prices patients must pay to use these providers. Then patients/consumers decide who to use in a second stage. Olmstead and Zeckhauser (1999) point out that the plan cannot directly assign patients to providers in stage 2, and the decision rules of patients become a constraint on the payer's maximization process. Olmstead and Zeckhauser (1999) cast the problem as one of "menu setting" where a restaurant has to choose what wines to offer and at what prices, in consideration of how diners will sort themselves among the alternatives.[68] The non-linear programming problem can be set out formally, but an analytical solution is illusive and insights about a solution are hard to come by. Town and Vistnes (2001) contribute a method for assessing a key parameter in network design, the marginal value of adding/dropping a particular provider, taking account of how patients would be redirected as the set of choices change.[69] Deriving easily understood characteristics of the optimal network form remains an elusive goal.

In practice, by playing off one seller against another, an MCO, by threatening to "move market share," can extract favorable prices from a seller (Duggan and Scott Morton, 2010). In this chapter, we tie selective contracting back to plan decisions about coverage and demand-side cost sharing. We show that selective contracting can "work" in this way even when a plan faces a monopoly seller. This serves to highlight the connection between selective contracting and demand-side cost sharing. We then go on to consider the more general case of selective contracting when a plan is buying in an imperfectly competitive market and the plan can "move market share."

3.2.1. Insurance Coverage and Demand Response Convey Market Power to Health Plan Even with Just One Seller

To develop the ideas, consider selective contracting in the case of prescription drugs, a useful application of contracting to discuss for several reasons. Drugs are an increasingly important component of health care and health care spending but insurance coverage for drugs is in flux. Selective contracting for drugs, however, by managed care organizations (MCOs) is nearly universal. The MCO might be an integrated

---

[68] Legend has it that diners tend to go for the second least expensive bottle within a category—the savvy sommelier will set a high markup in this favored spot.

[69] For a related approach, see Capps et al. (2003) who view a network as an issue in "option demand."

health plan or a specialty pharmacy benefit management (PBM) plan managing drug purchasing under contract with the health plan. Branded drugs are sold at large mark-ups over marginal production cost, creating wide ranges for bargaining over price; aggressive selective contracting can yield big price savings. Finally, the "product" is well defined, with no issues of unmeasured or unobserved "quality" or "effort" that play into contracting with physicians and hospitals.

MCOs provide drug benefits in health insurance through formularies. A formulary consists of a list of covered drugs specifying the patient responsibility for each (Huskamp et al., 2009). The typical formulary in the US has two or three "tiers" of coverage (KFF, 2009). Generic drugs reside on Tier 1 with the lowest co-payment (e.g. $5). "Preferred branded drugs" are on Tier 2 with a moderate co-payment (e.g. $15) and "Non-preferred branded drugs" are on Tier 3 with the highest co-payment ($30). Some drugs may not be covered at all. Branded drugs on patent sell at high markups over marginal cost; it is common, however, for MCOs to receive discounts off list price if a branded drug is placed on a favorable tier—this would usually be Tier 2 or 3—on the formulary.[70]

Suppose there is just one drug being considered for coverage at a plan and demand for this drug is independent of all other covered services in the plan. Let x be quantity of the drug considered for formulary coverage by an MCO. The list (monopoly) price of the drug is 1 so that if the drug were not covered, members of the MCO would have to buy the drug at full price and the quantity sold to the enrollees would be $x(1)$. Let m, margin, be the portion of the list price of 1 that represents profit to the manufacturer. Thus, if the drug is not included in the formulary, profit to the manufacturer from selling to members of this health plan would be $\pi(1)=x(1)m$.

Suppose the MCO formulary has just one tier with co-payment c. If the MCO covers the drug, quantity sold would be $x(c) > x(1)$, because of demand response. If the manufacturer offers a discount, d, to the MCO in exchange for inclusion of the drug on its formulary, the manufacturer's profit would be $x(c)(m - d)$. Since $x(c) > x(1)$ there are positive discounts off full price that increase manufacturer profit.

We can think of the drug seller as a monopolist. But note that the MCO has market power too. The only way the manufacturer gets those extra sales, $x(c) - x(1)$, is if the MCO includes the drug on the formulary. The MCO and the manufacturer are thus in a bilateral bargaining situation, in which the added profits the MCO can confer on the manufacturer by subsidizing its product $((x(c) - x(1))m)$ will be divided between the MCO and the manufacturer. The maximum discount the MCO is able to obtain is that which equalizes the profits after coverage to $x(1)m$ is $d^{\max}$:

$$x(1)m = x(c)(m - d^{\max}) \tag{5.28}$$

---

[70] See also Scott Morton and Kyle (2011, this Handbook) for closely related discussion.

We can use (5.28) to solve for d^{max} in relation to the markup (d^{max} must always be less than m for profits to be positive). Rearranging and multiplying by $(1-c)/(1-c)$ to introduce an elasticity form:

$$\frac{d^{\text{max}}}{m} = \frac{x(c)-x(1)}{x(c)} \cdot \frac{1}{1-c} \cdot (1-c) \tag{5.29}$$

Noting that the first two terms are the arc price elasticity of demand for x, which we call ε_x:

$$\frac{d^{\text{max}}}{m} = -\varepsilon_x(1-c) \tag{5.30}$$

Expression (5.30) contains two results of interest. The discount will be larger where demand elasticity is greater in absolute value. The MCO has more to give to the manufacturer when the demand increase with the subsidy is higher. Second, the discount is negatively related to the coinsurance, also because with a lower coinsurance the MCO has more to give. In other words, by subsidizing the drug more, the plan can get a better discount. The outcome of the MCO—manufacturer bargaining depends on factors we will disregard here but are discussed at length in Scott Morton and Kyle (2011, this Handbook). For any given sharing of the joint surplus, a lower c means a higher discount. The power influence the discount adds is another consideration for an insurer, tending to move c downward. Notably, demand elasticity plays the opposite role to that in section 2. Without demand elasticity, there are no discounts to be had.[71]

3.2.2. Selective Contracting with Multiple (Drug) Sellers

Suppose now there are two drugs, x_1 and x_2, which are substitutes in demand, and the MCO is choosing one for its formulary.[72] The non-formulary drug would be available to members on the open market. Firms compete on price to be included in the formulary. We generalize the link, seen in the one-product case above, between the co-payment and bargaining power of the MCO. An example of competing branded drugs (though with more than two alternatives) is the statin drug class used to lower cholesterol and including some of the largest selling branded drugs (Duggan and Scott Morton, 2010).

Suppose that firm 1 manufactures drug 1 and firm 2 manufactures drug 2. For convenience, let marginal production costs be zero. Let the demand functions from patients in the health plan for drugs 1 and 2 be $x_1(p_1,p_2)$ and $x_2(p_1,p_2)$, respectively.

[71] A formulary is an example of a "two-sided market" beginning to be studied in economics (Rysman, 2009). A two-sided market is one in which the pricing on one side is affected by demand, cost, and pricing on the other side of the market. A typical example is credit cards. Health plans with selective contracting share this feature of two-sidedness.

[72] This analysis is adapted from Berndt et al. (2011).

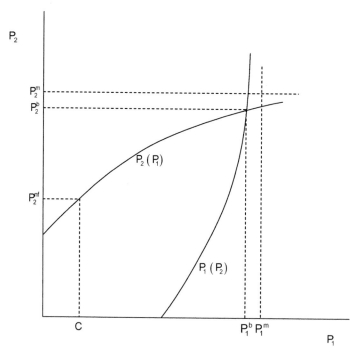

Figure 5.8 Drug formularies reduce procurement prices table.

The goods are substitutes so cross-price terms are positive (e.g. $\partial x_1/\partial p_2 > 0$); own-price effects are of course negative. Furthermore, we assume the products' demand functions are symmetric.

Consider pricing without insurance, assuming Bertrand competition between firms 1 and 2. Firm 1 maximizes profit, $\pi_1 = p_1 x_1(p_1,p_2)$ taking p_2 as given, and firm 2 maximizes $\pi_2 = p_2 x_2(p_1,p_2)$ taking p_1 as given. We can describe the behaviors of the two firms in terms of "reaction functions," and graph them in Figure 5.8. $p_1(p_2)$ describes the best response or reaction function of p_1 to changes in p_2, and $p_2(p_1)$ is similarly the reaction function of p_2 to changes in p_1. Since the goods are substitutes in demand, $p_1'(p_2) > 0$ and $p_2'(p_1) > 0$. A firm would not want to raise its prices without limit, however, in response to a rival's behavior. Suppose the rival firm 2 set a very high price, sufficiently high that firm 1 is in effect a monopolist. In the limit $p_1(\infty) = p_{1m}$ where p_{1m} is the monopoly price of firm 1; similarly for firm 2. Since such a price maximizes a monopolist's profit, the firm would not want to increase its price further. We depict in Figure 5.8 both the monopoly price as well as the Bertrand (or Nash) equilibrium (p_{1b}, p_{2b}), where $p_{1b} = p_1(p_{2b})$ and $p_{2b} = p_2(p_{1b})$. Competition between the substitute products reduces price somewhat below the monopoly price, depending in part on how substitutable the two drugs are.

Now introduce health insurance and a formulary. The formulary takes the form of a reduction in the out-of-pocket price of a covered drug to c (the co-payment), but the insurer stipulates that only one of drugs 1 or 2 will be covered and available at co-payment c. The other drug will not be covered but any enrollee may buy it (with a prescription) at the full market price. In the first stage, the insurer announces that it will choose one drug and will offer that drug to its enrollees for co-payment c. Since demands are symmetric, the MCO will choose the drug whose manufacturer offers the lower procurement price. The other drug will not be covered at all (will be "off-formulary"). Next, in the second stage, firms engage in Bertrand price competition by submitting binding bids simultaneously to the insurer. Finally, the insurer chooses a drug to be on the formulary and patients demand drugs.

The original prices will no longer be an equilibrium. A manufacturer could decrease the price bit to just below p_b, and increase sales and profits by taking all the business from its rival. The new equilibrium will be (p^f, p^{nf}) describing the prices manufacturer 1 must offer to be on the formulary (p^f) and then the equilibrium price manufacturer 2 will charge given it is not on the formulary. With drug 1 on the formulary, quantity sold of the drugs will be $x_1(c, p^{nf})$ and $x_2(c, p^{nf})$, where c is the co-payment patients pay for drug 1.

We can now write the equations determining equilibrium prices:

$$p^{nf} = p_2(c) \tag{5.31}$$

$$p^{nf} x_2(c, p^{nf}) = p^f x_1(c, p^{nf}) \tag{5.32}$$

Equation (5.31) indicates that firm 2's price is on its reaction function (i.e. is profit maximizing). Equation (5.32) is the equilibrium describing equal profit on and off the formulary (recall costs of production are zero). Figure 5.8 shows that the formulary reduces procurement and OOP prices to consumers for both drugs. Clearly, consumers benefit from the formulary, even before taking into account any financial risk protection.[73]

The MCO also chooses c, the co-payment for drugs. This might, concretely, be thought of as corresponding to a choice of Tier 2 or Tier 3 for the branded drug. We can see how the choice of co-payment works through equations (5.31) and (5.32). By lowering c, (5.31) tells us that the reaction of the off-formulary drug will be to lower price. In terms of (5.32), the left-hand side will tend to fall because p^{nf} falls. A bit of ambiguity in the effect is introduced because of the countervailing effects working on x_2. Co-payment for drug 1 falling decreases demand for x_2 but the lower p_{nf} increases it.

[73] I do not formally compare the outcome in this model if the plan were to cover both drugs at c. If the drugs are sufficiently distinct in demand, Bertrand competition will put little downward pressure on procurement price and a one-or-the-other formulary strategy may be inferior to including both drugs. Obviously, the more substitutable the products, the greater the bargaining power of the plan and the less is lost to consumers from limited choice.

The effects of lower c on the right-hand side of (5.32) are, however, more clear. Demand for x_1 will tend to increase from the fall in c which will very likely dominate the effect of the lower price for drug 2. Thus, subject to what looks to be reasonable conditions on the strength of own versus cross terms in demand, decreasing c (offering a more favorable tier to the winning drug) will lead to more vigorous competition between the sellers and lower procurement price.

The optimal co-payment for drugs (standing as services purchased through selective contracting) is lower, all else being equal, because of the effect of a lower co-payment on increasing the bargaining power of the health plan in relation to sellers.[74]

3.2.3. Evidence on Selective Contracting

The paper bearing most directly on the role of formularies is by Duggan and Scott Morton (2010), who studied the path of prices for branded drugs as more drugs were brought under formularies in connection with the introduction of Medicare "Part D," the subsidized drug coverage for Medicare beneficiaries. Drugs used more frequently by the elderly experienced lower price growth in relation to other drugs. The authors interpreted this as being due to the power of MCOs to push prices lower through administration of selective contracting.

Contracting practices of health plans serving state government employees in Massachusetts have been studied in a number of papers. Cutler et al. (2000) found contracting reduced prices for heart attack treatments at hospitals. Ma and McGuire (1998) found quantity reductions when selective contracting was introduced for office-based mental health care providers. More recently, Wu (2009) studied the experience of several MCOs serving state employees and the effects of their contracts for hospital care. Size helps a health plan in bargaining with hospitals over price, but so does the ability to "channel" patients, as estimated by the degree to which the plan moves patients away from a predicted distribution across hospitals in the region.

Experience of contracting in California has also been studied extensively. Melnick et al. (1992) and Melnick and Zwanziger (1988) studied selective contracting for hospitals in California and large metropolitan areas, respectively, and document that MCOs obtain discounts by selective contracting, and more competitive hospital markets allow larger discounts.

---

[74] Selective contracting as in a formulary benefits a payer if there is a markup on the drug and bargaining power can succeed in reducing procurement price. In the case of drugs, this seller market power is due to patents. Even with some buyer market power, the procurement price of drugs will be above marginal social cost of production. In this circumstance, a "two-part" pricing approach to drugs would have value. Goldman et al. (2008) propose that a drug consumer be charged an annual "license" fee and then be able to buy drugs close to marginal cost. A similar idea could work at a higher level. For example, an employer could pay a license fee for all those covered in its plan. At the national level, this corresponds to policy proposals to "buy out" drug and other patents so drugs can be sold closer to marginal cost.

4. STRUCTURING CHOICE OF HEALTH INSURANCE

This section is mainly concerned with structuring the choices of health insurance facing consumers. The major divide in approaches in the US is between an "open" approach where a regulator, e.g. Medicare, or a new state exchange authority, sets rules and allows any qualified health plan to enter, and a "mediated" approach where a public agency or private employer preselects a small number of plans which consumers may then choose among. In this role, private employers also structure the prices consumers face for joining the selected plans. In considering this question we encounter research on the factors influencing the choice of plan, the role of the demand-side premium in affecting sorting, market failures stemming from adverse selection, and the ability of consumers to make rational choices of plan. The issue of structuring choice also opens a window on the question of what policy should be towards the new health insurance markets proposed as part of health care reform in the US.

4.1. "Price" and "Quantity Demanded" of Health Insurance

Study of the relationship between price and quantity in health insurance is challenging for both conceptual and empirical reasons. Simply defining "price" and "quantity" of health insurance is not straightforward. As Phelps (2010, p. 314) points out, the price of health insurance is not the premium paid to the plan, because that premium depends on the extent of coverage as well as how that coverage is "priced." He advocates identifying the actuarial value of a policy (expected payouts) and calling this quantity. The balance of the premium constitutes the "price," perhaps expressed as a percentage of payout, making it the markup or loading fee. Quantity is the part of the premium expected to be paid back to beneficiaries, and the price is the balance, what the beneficiary pays over and above the expected payout. Conceptually, this works well, having the virtue, for example, of correctly predicting that if the premium is actuarially fair, i.e. the price is zero, the risk-averse consumer would demand full insurance.

Putting these concepts into empirical practice is not so easy. Normally, the researcher does not observe expected payout or markup and is not in a position to implement the separation of premium dollars into price and quantity. Expected payout in a plan differs person-by-person according to the expected health care demand: the quantity and therefore price (as premium less expected payout) is individual specific, varies a great deal, and is unobserved. With a fixed total premium, higher expected health care costs imply a larger "quantity" and lower "price" according to the conception above. Since expected health care spending is not well observed or explained well by typically observed covariates, the relationship between price and quantity in health care will not be easy to sort out with individual data on premiums and insurance purchase. For example, Florence and Thorpe (2003) use administrative records from the Federal Employees Health Benefit Program (FEHBP) to study plan choice among employees choosing single coverage. "Price" is full premium. If this premium is partly measuring quantity as well as price, the regression coefficient will be biased upward (towards zero for a negative price effect).[75]

Bundorf and Royalty (2011) review the literature on price and choice of health insurance, with careful attention to the issue of the exogeneity of price effects. The literature is difficult to summarize. Often consumers choose among a small and diverse set of options (insurance/no insurance; a set of plans). Price response is generally observed but comparing across studies is not straightforward. Much of this literature is about choice of type of plan in an employee—benefits context (Cutler and Reber, 1998; Einav et al., 2010; Chernew et al., 2008b; Parente et al., 2004; Royalty and Solomon, 1989). An advantage to studying price response in these settings is that employers can set the premiums paid by workers independently of the premiums charged by plans. An employer may set employee contributions according to factors unrelated to likely health care demands, or different employers in the same market may price the same plans differently. In these cases, cross-sectional variation in plan prices may identify demand response (McGuire, 1981; Dowd and Feldman, 1994—1995). In other cases, employers change employee contributions and likelihood of switching can identify response (Strombom et al., 2002). Choice between private managed care plan and traditional Medicare among elderly Medicare beneficiaries is also frequently studied (Buchmueller, 2006; Atherly et al., 2004; Dowd et al., 2003). Also included are studies of the Federal Employees Health Benefit Plan with its wide array of local HMO and national PPO plans (Florence and Thorpe, 2003; Jin and Sorenson, 2006).

The role of income in demand for health insurance has also been subject to study. Empirically, health insurance is a normal good, although in principle, higher income or wealth could have ambiguous effects on demand for insurance, as the self-insurance option becomes more attractive in ranges in which the marginal utility of income is constant. Early studies using individual income data generally report income elasticities below 1.0 (Goldstein and Pauly, 1976; Phelps, 1973, 1976). Marquis and Long (1995) reported an income elasticity of 0.15 for workers who do not have employment-based insurance. Studies that rely on group-level variation in income tend to yield much larger income elasticities, possibly for reasons similar to why cross-country estimates of income effects on health care are larger than studies that rely on individual-level variation. Keenan et al. (2006) find that low-income individuals are more price sensitive to premiums, suggesting the possibility of

---

[75] For more discussion, see Bundorf and Royalty (2011). The challenges of estimating price response from survey data are confronted in Abraham et al. (2006) who use MEPS data from 1996.

income effects or perhaps an impact of subsidized alternatives available to persons with low income.

4.2. Arguments For and Against Choice in Health Insurance

One of the most active and policy-relevant controversies in the economics of health insurance concerns the efficient way to structure choice for consumers. How much choice is best? How effective are consumers individually and collectively in promoting efficiency through choice? Should the market for health insurance (in US health care reform, for example) be modeled on the individual health insurance market or should it be modeled on employer-based health insurance (where the insurer limits choice to one or a few plans)?

Employers severely limit the choices of health insurance they offer to employees. Employers shop on behalf of theirs workers and decide which plan or plan workers might choose. The Kaiser Family Foundation (2010, pp. 60–61) reports that in 2010, 84 percent of firms offer only one type of plan, and only 2 percent offer more than two types. Large firms are more likely to offer choice. Counting workers, half have no choice of health insurance. Employers not only limit choice, but they intermediate between the premiums health plans charge and what the employee pays to enroll. The employer negotiates payment to the plan. This might be some form of experience rating, a true premium, or a combination (Glazer and McGuire, 2001). Then, the employer decides what premium employees should pay for single and family membership at the selected options. Employers could, but rarely do, provide employee health benefits through a voucher-like policy, fixing a contribution (which could vary by employee) and allowing employees to choose freely among plans offered in a market. Are these limits on choice reducing consumer welfare unnecessarily, or serving the purpose of obtaining good plans at good prices in a market subject to multiple sources of inefficiency? Addressing this question involves a series of considerations in the economics of health insurance.

4.2.1. Individual Purchasing has Higher Transaction Costs

One disadvantage of running health insurance with many individual choices rather than through group purchasing is the higher selling and administration costs of the individual market. The Congressional Budget Office (CBO, 2008) estimates that the loading fee for employers with 1,000+ employees is 7 percent, compared to 30 percent in the individual market. These higher administrative costs would partially offset any consumer benefits from expanded choice.

Table 5.5 keeps track of arguments for and against expanding choice of health insurance options, cast in the context of employer-based health insurance.

Table 5.5 Arguments For and Against Limiting Choice of Health Plan
Do not Limit Choice

Choice promotes competition on cost and quality	Original formulation of arguments for "managed competition" and voucher-support-type mechanisms. Enthoven and Kronick (1989).
Choice lets consumers find plan matching their preferences	Estimating utility function from observed choices and inferring the value of expanded choice through simulations of broader choice sets. Dafny et al. (2010); Bundorf et al. (2011).

Limit Choice

Lower transaction costs	Economies of joint purchasing reduce selling and administrative costs. Lower loading on group plans. CBO (2008).
"Single premium" problem implies inefficient sorting, may be addressed by limiting choice	More choice is not always better with imperfect pricing of premiums. Absence of risk adjustment in premiums paid by enrollees limits and may reverse gains from more choice. Bundorf et al. (2011); Glazer and McGuire (2011)
Adverse selection can be reduced by limiting choice	Eliminating inefficient policies from choice set can improve equilibrium outcomes. Rothschild and Stiglitz (1976).
Selective contracting increases employer bargaining power	Employers can choose plans on the basis of observable characteristics, even if these are not contractible. Bargaining power can counteract plan market power. Glazer and McGuire (2001).
Reduce consumer mistakes	Too many choices can confuse consumers, increasing the number of errors. Frank and Lamiraud (2009); Sinaiko and Hirth (2011); Leibman and Zeckhauser (2008).

4.2.2. Competition and Choice Increase Efficiency of Markets

The primary argument in favor of more choice is that choice improves market functioning and consumer welfare. Expanding options to a rational decision maker (under some assumptions which will be noted later on) leaves the decision maker at least as well off. Standard arguments from economics support the idea that choice (and the competition it engenders) can improve the efficiency of markets for health insurance. Enthoven and Kronick (1989) advocated "managed competition" among plans in which coverage would be regulated in part to deal with selection concerns, and a public or private sponsor would pay a fixed contribution toward the premium of beneficiaries. Plans would then compete over premiums, quality, and supplemental coverage. Managed competition could put a floor on coverage and promote choice and competition above the floor. The idea, as expressed by Pizer et al. (2003), is that "beneficiaries who highly value certain benefits can search for a plan that offers those benefits and pay the marginal premium that corresponds to their choice."

Dafny et al. (2010) recently quantified the value of extra choice by assessing how much better off a set of employees would be if they could choose among any plan offered in a market area instead of only among the plans their employer offered. They find that the median employee with free choice would be willing to accept a 27 percent lower subsidy from the employer.[76] This calculation assumes that individuals can find their way to the plan that is best for them, and in this sense represents a kind of upper bound.

An assumption behind the proposition that "more choice must weakly improve the welfare of the decision maker" is that the decision maker internalizes all benefits and costs of the choice. Economists are familiar with the argument that restricting an insured's choice of covered health *care* options can improve his welfare. This is because when a patient decides about health care, he rationally disregards the effect on the premium paid by the insured group. (Conversely, expanding choice would decrease welfare.) A similar argument comes into play in the choice of health *insurance*. Health insurance premiums are most often not risk rated individually. If they are not, then consumers do not face the cost consequences of their choices. In this context, the proposition that expanding choice weakly increases the welfare of the decision maker does not necessarily hold, a point we take up next.

4.2.3. Consumer Premiums may not Lead to Efficient Sorting

Bundorf et al. (2011) estimate utility and demand for alternative plan offerings with a similar methodology to Dafny et al. They figure that a hypothetical maximum welfare gain from offering additional choice in an employer—benefit context to be on the order of 2–11 percent. Their paper goes on to recognize that the actual pricing of health plans to consumers may limit how much of this hypothetical gain will be realized. The key point they make is that the managed competition approach of allowing a health plan to charge a higher premium for more benefits/higher quality will not, in the presence of consumer heterogeneity, lead to efficient sorting of consumers among plans.

Bundorf et al. illustrate their point by sorting between two health plans. Consider a PPO-type plan with wide choice of provider and integrated delivery system HMO-type plan.[77] Suppose the HMO plan saves money only on the higher-cost (sicker) enrollees. Suppose also in addition to heterogeneity in health cost risk that consumers differ in their taste for choice versus closed provider networks. Efficient

---

[76] The authors discuss the qualifications on this estimate. It may understate the value if a more open market encouraged development of currently unobserved plan options. It may overstate because of assumptions about the match value in random utility models for options not chosen.

[77] The authors have a more formal model. I am elaborating on the presentation in their introduction to make the point without a mathematical model.

sorting of consumers between the plan types would require equal premiums at the HMO and PPO plan for the low-cost enrollees (for whom the cost is the same at both). These consumers could then choose according to their taste for type of management. Efficient sorting of the high-cost enrollees would require a higher premium for the PPO plan. In addition to sorting on taste for management, higher-cost enrollees should see and be able to respond to the lower costs in the HMO plan. In other words, a form of risk-adjusted premium is necessary for efficient sorting.[78]

A "single premium," say when the premium difference between the PPO and HMO plans is equal to the average saving for the low- and high-cost enrollee, will lead to too many low-cost types joining the HMO and too few high-cost types joining the HMO. Recognizing the constraints of uniform premium policies cuts the achievable benefits to about one-quarter of the hypothetical maximum.

Only in artificial cases can a single premium policy achieve efficient sorting between two plan types.[79] The required special feature is that ranking of willingness to pay for option A (say the PPO) is perfectly positively (rank) correlated to cost differences between options A and B. In this case, some single premium (not necessarily the average cost difference) will efficiently sort the group between the plans. Einav and Finkelstein (2011) generalize these simple sorting models between two options, using concepts of willingness to pay and cost differences to study the welfare consequences of pricing and inefficient sorting between plans.

An immediate corollary of this argument is that more choice, with imperfect pricing, does not always improve consumer welfare. We can make this point by an example. Suppose an employer offers two health plans and pays a constant share of plan costs (e.g. 50 percent), requiring employees to pay the balance. The employer now offers a new, much more expensive plan. An employee considering this new choice will see the full difference in benefits between the new plan and the old, but only 50 percent of the difference in the cost. Too many employees will choose the new higher-cost plan and on balance the employee group will be worse off.[80] This is simply a version of the moral hazard problem. A sophisticated pricing strategy in which higher-cost persons face higher incremental prices for the improved coverage is necessary for more options to lead to higher group welfare (Bundorf et al., 2011; Glazer and McGuire, 2011).

---

[78] Glazer and McGuire (2011) make a similar point about the inability of a single premium to implement efficient sorting between a "Gold" and "Silver" health plan. They illustrate this with a simple numerical example and demonstrate it formally within an explicit model of consumer heterogeneity in utility and cost.

[79] See Feldman and Dowd (1982), Ellis and McGuire (1987), and Cutler and Reber (1998) for examples of such models.

[80] This is very clear if we assume that employees through lower wages bear the incidence of employer contribution to health insurance premiums. This analysis neglects tax subsidies, but these would only exacerbate the inefficiency identified.

4.2.4. Inefficiencies from Adverse Selection can be Reduced by Restricting Choice

Adverse selection comes about because consumers choose plans in their best interest, leading plans, in equilibrium, to distort their benefits to attract "good risks." This was demonstrated first by Rothschild and Stiglitz (1976) in the case of coverage against a risky financial event, and by Glazer and McGuire (2000) in the context of managed care health plans offering a mix of services. Cutler et al. (2010) show that adverse selection is alive and well in the Massachusetts individual (and family) market with many choices organized by the state agency responsible for health benefits for state and some local government employees. Health plans have an incentive to "underprovide" benefits that are predictable and predictive in Ellis and McGuire's (2007) terminology, where "predictive" means being correlated with total health care costs (net of any plan payments) on a personal level. Regulation of minimum benefits restricts choice but can lead to improved equilibrium offerings in a market. For example, insurance coverage for mental health care has historically been less than for physical illness, partly because insurers are concerned that better coverage may attract an "adverse selection" of the risks.

An object lesson in the open competition in health insurance markets for coverage for mental health care is the Federal Employees Health Benefit Program (FEHBP). The FEHBP has run a regulated health insurance market, in essence an Exchange, for federal employees (including retirees) and their families since the 1960s. During the early years of the FEHBP, mental health care was covered at parity in national plans, but generous coverage proved unviable with individual choice of coverage. Padgett et al. (1993) found that use of mental health care in the Blue Cross "high option" plan was two to three times higher per person in spite of only slight differences in coverage, pointing to heavy adverse selection as the explanation for the large observed differences in costs. Health plans altered coverage to avoid being the plan favored by likely users. Foote and Jones (1999) document deterioration in coverage throughout the 1980s, in spite of Office of Personnel Management (OPM) resistance to cutbacks. Regulation of the nominal benefits in a plan (e.g. "unlimited visits") cannot prevent plans from "managing" mental health costs aggressively. In 1980, behavioral health services accounted for 7.8 percent of total claims costs; by 1997, this had dropped to 1.9 percent. During this period most private employers were going in the opposite direction, improving coverage for mental health care, and surpassing the coverage offered in the FEHBP. Mandating "parity" in coverage can change the equilibrium offerings, eliminating inefficient plans and causing efficient plans to appear in equilibrium.[81]

---

[81] Coverage for mental health care was less than physical health care also because of evidence for greater demand response. This concern has been ameliorated in managed care plans which rely less on demand-side cost sharing to control use. See Barry et al. (2006) for a review of this evidence and discussion in the context of parity for mental health care.

4.2.5. Selective Contracting Allows an Employer to Choose Plans Effectively and Bargain for Lower Prices

Arguments set out in section 3 above for the advantages of selective contracting for providers also apply to contracting with plans. Employers are in a better position than individual workers to collect and evaluate information on the performance of plans. Consider, for example, a dimension of plan performance such as adequacy of the network offerings in a specialty, say pediatric care. Quality, geographic coverage, and wait time to appointment might be among the relevant criteria. An employee would have only limited experience or what she might be able to learn through her research as a basis for choosing among plans. An employer can collect and evaluate information on network quality centrally and likely make a better choice on behalf of the employee group.

If health plans in a local market have some market power, selective contracting, the ability to decline to offer a plan to a set of employees, puts an employer in a position to bargain for a lower plan premium than employees would be offered in an open market. This point is distinct from the higher loading fee associated with individual purchases due to administrative and selling costs.

4.2.6. How Good are Consumers at Making Choices of Health Insurance?

A special concern about choice stems from consumers choosing ineffectively, and furthermore, that more choices may make matters worse rather than better. A number of recent papers in health economics question how well individual consumers can choose health insurance in their best interest. Leibman and Zeckhauser (2008) lay out the problem in the wider context of research on behavioral economics, and at the close of their paper they flatly conclude (p. 26) that "Health Insurance is too complicated a product for most consumers to purchase intelligently."

A health insurance contract in the US is at least as complicated as a home mortgage, a realm in which millions of households (and investors) made choices they regret. There are so many contingencies associated with health care needs that it is unlikely that many people, at the time they select insurance, are able to conduct an accurate expected utility calculation. Many elderly, for example, are unaware that Medicare does not cover nursing home costs (except as required following a hospital stay). Knowing what is covered is a problem for everyone, not just the elderly. Your teenager has been diagnosed with an eating disorder and the therapist recommends a residential facility out of state. How many people would know if their insurance would pay (and how much)? Your other child chipped a tooth while away at summer camp. Does your insurance cover the dentist in Maine?

Health insurance has some features that have been found to interfere with effective choice. Health insurance involves evaluating small probabilities (which we are poor at evaluating), unpleasant events (which we prefer not to think about), and future consequences (which we may weigh in a time-inconsistent fashion).[82] Consumers in health insurance markets have been accused of having a "status quo" bias by Samuelson and Zeckhauser (1988), meaning that they irrationally stay with what they know rather than switching to a more favorable alternative. Frank and Lamiraud (2009) study switching among very similar plans in the regulated private health insurance market in Switzerland and find consumers there rarely change plans, a result they interpret as confirming the status quo bias. As Handel (2010) points out, more effective utility maximization—i.e. making health plan choice more in one's own best interest—can have adverse consequences for equilibrium and ultimately consumer welfare, due to the forces of adverse selection. In his simulations, reducing subjective switching costs leads to a new equilibrium in which consumers are worse not better off.

Using data from a special survey conducted on behalf of Medicare, Elbel and Schlesinger (2010) find that when choices increase from very few (1−2) to a few (3−4), likelihood of Medicare beneficiaries choosing a Medicare Advantage (MA) plan goes up. A greater number of choices are associated with flat or declining likelihood of choosing an MA plan. McWilliams et al. (2011) report a similar finding with data from the Health and Retirement Survey (HRS). After a point, more choice implies a lower likelihood of choosing MA. Reinforcing the interpretation of these behaviors as due to difficulties beneficiaries have in evaluating so much choice, McWilliams et al. also found that beneficiaries with lower cognitive function were less likely to respond to favorable features of MA plans when making their decisions.

Resistance to change can be rationalized if consumers face high "switching costs," which could be subjective. Handel (2010) finds a powerful status quo bias among employees of a large employer that would take "switching costs" of $1,500 to explain within a rational choice framework.

Sinaiko and Hirth (2011) study a setting in which a "mistake" is clearly defined. Due to an oddity in the way the University of Michigan priced its employee offerings, one of the plans was clearly "dominated" by another, meaning that for any realization of health demand, some employees would unambiguously be better off in one plan than another. Sinaiko and Hirth found that not all employees switched, and furthermore that a small number actively and mistakenly chose the dominated plan when they could have had the better plan. Differences in coverage were relatively small (involving out-of-network options) so the utility and welfare consequences of this set of mistakes were not large.

Medicare Part D, implemented in 2006, is an interesting recent case of creation of an individual health insurance market for Medicare beneficiaries for optional coverage for prescription drugs. Coverage was highly subsidized (at roughly 75 percent) but the

---

[82] Leibman and Zeckhauser (2008) and Frank (2007) both have lively discussions on these points, making many connections to the growing literature questioning the rationality of consumer decision making.

subsidy was capped so beneficiaries paid any incremental premium for benefits beyond the minimum. Medicare regulated the coverage in terms of the drugs covered and the cost sharing, but plans had a good deal of discretion about formulary decisions, the form of cost sharing, and premiums. (See Scott Morton and Kyle, 2011, this Handbook, for more detailed description of Medicare Part D.)

Medicare beneficiaries faced scores of choice of Part D plans. Web-based decision aids offered limited help. There is some evidence that beneficiaries made mistakes. Both McFadden (2006) and Abaluck and Gruber (2011) concluded that the elderly chose plans inferior in terms of expected utility. Assumptions about risk aversion and expected pharmacy utilization were necessary to make these calculations. It was widely believed that insurers priced their plans low in the first year to "buy the business" on the assumption that once in a plan, the elderly would be reluctant to switch and the insurer could raise price later to more than recoup any early losses.

Joyce et al. (2009) yield a more optimistic read of Part D at the market level. After two years, more than 90 percent of the elderly have drug coverage at least as generous as the standard Part D benefit. They judge that most beneficiaries choose plans that suit their health status. Furthermore, premiums for Part D plans came in under forecasts, partly because Part D plans have been very aggressive in encouraging generic substitution. Duggan and Scott Morton (2010) found that branded drugs used more frequently by the elderly experienced lower price increases around the time of implementation of Part D than other drugs. Although insurance surely expanded demand for these drugs, the formulary-selective contracting strategy of the drug plans, by increasing demand elasticity, put downward pressure on price.

There is certainly evidence for consumer mistakes, but this needs to be weighed against the very large and coherent literature on insurance choice consistent with informed and rational choice, including the papers on demand response to price covered by Bundorf and Royalty (2011). The strong tendency of consumers to choose plans that suit their likely future health care needs is the driver of adverse selection—the quantitative importance of this fundamental market failure is driven by the degree to which consumers can predict what they will use (Breyer, Bundorf and Pauly, 2011, this Handbook). Table 9, "Evidence for Adverse Selection in Health Insurance," from Cutler and Zeckhauser (2000) summarizes 30 studies before 2000. Consumers respond to price of health insurance in a way consistent with rationality. A consistent finding in the literature is that older and sicker enrollees with closer ties to their providers are less likely to change plans.

4.2.7. Weighing the Advantages and Disadvantages of Choice—Does Employer-based Health Insurance Constitute a Market Test?

Consumer welfare, perhaps more specifically average expected utility of a group, is the standard for assessing the right structure of choice. Alternatively, we could look to a kind of revealed preference argument and observe that employers, when choosing the form of employee health benefits, with few exceptions do not choose a voucher-type approach and free employees to use the individual health insurance market. Employers almost always use the money they spend on employee health benefits to offer just one or a very few number of choices. Even state and federal governments, in their role as employers, restrict choice of workers (although the range of choice for state and federal workers tends to be larger than private employers).

Employer-based health insurance is expensive, but popular with both employers and workers. Phelps (2010) estimates that in 2010, employers paid an estimated 62.3 percent (or \$520 bn) of the \$835 bn in employer-sponsored health insurance plans.[83] Take-up of health insurance at a firm averages only about 75 percent, but some of the non-takers are covered under a spouse's plan, so that overall only about 7 percent of those offered employer-based insurance end up uninsured (Gruber and Washington, 2005).

Leibman and Zeckhauser argue that employers have the right motives and furthermore are in a good position to serve as agents to structure choice for their workers:

> ...Employers have strong incentives to act as faithful agents for their employees in selecting a very limited number of health insurance options. Effective option selection is a public good; once conducted for one, it is available for all. (Leibman and Zeckhauser, 2008, p. 26)

This argument is not iron-clad because an employer's motive is not to maximize the expected utility of workers; employers seek to maximize profit. Wage costs can be lowered if benefit dollars are devoted to forms of health insurance most valued by workers (this is behind the Leibman–Zeckhauser point). Employers might, however, limit health insurance in order to avoid employees attracted by expensive health insurance. This counterpoint bears on the extent of coverage of health insurance, not directly on why an employer would not offer choice.[84] The durability and popularity of mediated choices of health insurance make the employer model a front-runner for consideration as part of any health care reform.

4.2.8. Structuring Choice in Exchanges as Part of Health Care Reform

The Patient Protection and Affordable Care Act (ACA) aims to largely eliminate the "uninsured" problem in the US. The mechanisms for accomplishing this ambitious goal are Medicaid expansions and mandated coverage, together with subsidies for lower- and middle-income individuals and families. Moreover, states will administer private health insurance markets, referred to as "Exchanges." The Exchanges are modeled loosely on

---

[83] Gruber and Washington (2005) assess the share paid by employees to be less.

[84] Furthermore, if the employer is a monopsonist, it can "mark up" the price on the higher value health insurance option for workers and extract some more worker surplus (Miller, 2005).

the Massachusetts Connector, where regulated health plans are sold through a web-based portal and are subsidized according to enrollee income in an updated version of Enthoven's managed competition. The ACA, however, omits many "details" of how these new insurance markets will operate and be regulated. To mention just one fundamental dimension, the Exchanges could be run by the state, outsourced to a private authority, or left by default to the federal government for operation. Much of the basic economic structure of the Exchanges is thus yet to be determined.

As of January 1, 2014, US citizens and legal residents who are not eligible for employer-sponsored or public coverage are scheduled to be able to purchase health insurance through Exchanges. Exchanges will consolidate and regulate the market for individual insurance. Small businesses will be able to purchase coverage through a separate Exchange, though states have the option of combining the individual and small group Exchanges. Plans offered through the Exchanges will cover a federally defined "essential benefit package," with parity in coverage for mental health care. Premium and cost-sharing subsidies will apply on a sliding scale for individuals and families earning up to 400 percent of the Federal Poverty Level (FPL). Extension of private health insurance through these Exchanges to an estimated 24 million people promises to improve access to care for many low-income individuals, as well as provide financial protection and integrate low-income groups into the mainstream of health care.

In designing the operation of Exchanges, state and federal policy makers face the trade-offs we have identified in terms of the value and pitfalls of choice. By providing information and administrative support for choice of health insurance, Exchanges can effectuate individual preferences and foster competition based on price and quality. On the other hand, the simple idea that choice and competition promote consumer welfare in health insurance cannot be accepted without scrutiny. Competition and choice in private health insurance markets may not lead to an efficient or fair outcome.

Some previous state-level Exchanges have failed (i.e. they have greatly reduced the coverage options offered or have ceased operations entirely), in large part due to adverse selection. In the California Health Insurance Purchasing Cooperative (HIPC) in the 1990s, a voluntary Exchange open to small groups, the risk adjustment methodology excluded mental health experience because, in part, coding for these services was thought to be imprecise and coverage at the time was partial. Adverse selection in the California HIPC sent the more generous PPO plans into a "death spiral."

The Massachusetts Connector, which, as of March 2010, has enrolled 177,000 individuals in health insurance (49 percent of the newly insured in MA since 2006), is the most successful model for a non-group market Exchange (Commonwealth Health Insurance Connector Authority, 2010a). In the unsubsidized portion of the market the Connector supports the development and offering of health insurance categorized into tiers based on the actuarial value of coverage (called gold, silver, bronze, and young adult plans). Legislation restricts carriers to age, residence location, family size, industry, wellness program use, and tobacco use when determining premiums, and requires carriers to merge the small group and non-group markets. Benefits offered by plans within coverage tier have become increasingly standardized (Commonwealth Health Insurance Connector Authority, 2010b). Nevertheless, premiums charged for plans in the same coverage tier and with very similar cost-sharing requirements differ by a factor of 1.5 to 1 in the Boston area, though somewhat less in western Massachusetts. It is unclear whether selection or other factors are responsible for the wide range of premiums in the same market for apparently very similar products. In the Connector's subsidized program, health plans are operated directly by the Connector and are open to uninsured adults who are US citizens/nationals and in families earning less than 300 percent of the FPL.

Even if states do elect to limit choices in an Exchange, Leibman and Zeckhauser (2008) are dubious that a public sector intermediary will do as well as an employer, reasoning that a public agency will be under pressure to offer any qualified plan. State governments and the federal government, in their role as employers, do tend to offer many more choices than private employers.

4.3. Premium Setting and Fairness

As we have seen, risk adjustment of individual premiums is necessary for consumers to sort themselves efficiently among health plan options. In this context, the term "risk adjustment" refers to any factor that is associated with higher costs, including but not limited to health status. Some socio-economic characteristics like income or education may also contribute to health care demand. If higher income groups demand more care, then efficient premium setting would require charging them higher premiums. Risk adjusting premiums by socio-economic characteristics (such as income) or health status (such as prior illnesses) raises considerations of the fairness of financing health care.

In health policy, fairness is about health status (the sick should not pay more than the healthy) as well as ability to pay (the rich should pay more than the poor). The most familiar concept of fairness in health care is the European "solidarity principle" which dictates that individuals in poor health should pay the same for health insurance as those in good health.[85] Principles of solidarity are explicit in policy discussions in Europe. As Stock et al. (2006) explain, the guiding principle of Germany's Social Health Insurance, for example, is solidarity: "Services are rendered according to medical need." Furthermore, "[Financing] implies cross-subsidization from low to high risks, [and] from high-income to low-income earners..."[86] Concern for fairness

---

[85] For a review of the application of solidarity principles in the context of competing health plans, see Van de Ven and Ellis (2000). Sass (1995) is a European philosophical perspective on solidarity. Stone (1993), in a US context, contrasts solidarity principles with ideals of actuarial fairness in the organization and pricing of health insurance.

[86] In a recent interview, the then Minister of Health in Germany, Ulla Schmidt, put it this way: "My over-arching personal goal as Minister of Health has been to preserve for Germany's health system the principle of social solidarity, by which we mean that everyone in Germany should have guaranteed access to state-of-the-art medical care and contribute to the financing of this guarantee on the basis of the household's ability to pay" (Cheng and Reinhardt, 2008, p. 205).

motivates regulation of health insurance premiums in the US as well, prohibiting or limiting discrimination by health status.[87] These strictures limit how well premiums charged to enrollees can match persons with health plans serving their preferences.

Glazer and McGuire (2011) consider how premium and tax policy can lead to an efficient and fair (in a solidarity sense) system of health care financing when heterogeneous consumers are choosing between a "gold" and "silver" plan in an individual market.[88] Heterogeneity in demand comes from health status (which can be taken account of in plan premiums) and other taste factors (e.g. income) which cannot. If income can be taxed based on choice of health plan, efficient and fair sorting is possible; generally, though, there will be a conflict between efficient sorting which requires individuals to face the incremental costs of their choice, and fairness which requires sicker individuals to pay no more than the healthy for health insurance.[89]

5. FINAL COMMENTS

Many would agree with Gruber and Levy (2009, p. 46) that "The real problem facing the health insurance system in the United States is not so much the risk of high spending by individual households as the systematic risk of increasing aggregate spending." Gruber and Levy point out that health care cost growth is like health care costs in a health plan; no individual consumer has much of an incentive to do anything about it because the cost is shared in the premium. We could add to this by saying that the factors affecting growth, technology, practice patterns, expectations of patients, are health care sector-wide. Countries with a single form of health insurance and finance are in a position to account for any effect of policy decisions on health care costs and growth, but in a country like the US, no one payer, with the exception of the federal Medicare program, is in a position to moderate the underlying forces affecting cost growth. This is another reason, in addition to those identified already in

---

[87] Federal non-discrimination policies towards health insurance premiums are described in GAO (2003). Regulations are administered by the IRS, govern ERISA plans, and prohibit discrimination in premiums charged and in premium contributions by employees according to health status. The Kaiser Family Foundation (2009) lists ten states that restrict use of health status in setting premiums in the individual health insurance market (often limiting the differential that can be charged by health status), and eight states that have some form of community rating regulation. This prohibition of discrimination on the basis of health status could also be cast as an efficiency issue: in a socially efficient policy, individuals would be protected from risk of changing health status.

[88] Health insurance Exchanges in health care reform have four metal levels: platinum, gold, silver, and bronze.

[89] "Fairness" can be defined in different ways in the context of an individual market with multiple plan levels. If fairness is only about premiums at the basic (bronze) level, the conflict between fairness and efficiency is minimized by charging everyone the same for the bronze plan. There could still be efficiency problems in sorting among plan levels if incremental premiums are not customized by risk status.

this chapter, that throws design of health insurance plans into the domain of public policy.

Like in health care itself, health insurance is subject to many forms of "market failure." Around the world, financing and insuring against risk of health expenditures is more thoroughly in the public domain, directly or through regulation, than provision of health care. Research on the economics of health insurance is thus highly relevant for social policy as well as bearing on significant research questions in economics.

Most of the research on the economics of health insurance has focused on efficiency, has been predicated on rational actors, and has been concerned with the performance of the health care sector rather than the overall economy. These things are changing. Concern about financing health care fairly is attracting more attention, and the trade-off between what is efficient and what is fair is likely to sharpen as pressures mount to give consumers more economic incentives to choose health insurance and health care with more attention to cost. The influence of behavioral economics is being felt in all areas of microeconomics. Health care and health insurance both involve product features that contribute to "non-rational" choices. How can empirical regularities and insights from behavioral economics be made useful in policy towards health insurance? The growth in health care costs, and the role of health insurance in contributing to that growth, connects health policy to wider issues in public finance and macroeconomics. Choices about financing health care will have intergenerational and other dynamic impacts on the growth path of the entire economy.

Issues raised here are imminent. The US has embarked on an ambitious coverage-expanding set of policies in connection with health care reform. The sustainability of current systems of health care finance are questioned nearly everywhere. Public and private health insurance transmits the forces of cost growth on health care to taxpayers, consumers, employers, and other payers. Health insurance, encompassing both coverage and pricing to patients and rules for including and paying providers, will also be relied upon to carry back to the health care sector society's choices for how to alter decisions about health care.

REFERENCES

Abaluck, J. & Gruber, J. (2011). Choice inconsistencies among the elderly: evidence from plan choice in Medicare Part D. *American Economic Review*: forthcoming.

Abraham, J. M., Vogt, W. B., & Gaynor, M. S. (2006). How do households choose their employer-based health insurance? *Inquiry*, *43*(4), 315–332.

Aitken, M., Berndt, E. R., & Cutler, D. M. (2009). Prescription drug spending trends in the United States: Looking beyond the turning point. *Health Affairs (Millwood)*, *28*(1), w151–w160.

Arrow, K. J. (1963). Uncertainty and the welfare economics of medical care. *American Economic Review*, *53*(5), 941–973.

Atherly, A., Dowd, B., & Feldman, R. (2004). The effect of benefits, premiums, and health risk on health plan choice in the Medicare program. *Health Services Research, 39*(4:1), 847–864.

Atherly, A., Hebert, P. L., & Maciejewski, M. L. (2005). An analysis of disenrollment from Medicare managed care plans by Medicare beneficiaries with diabetes. *Medical Care, 43*(5), 500–506.

Austin, D. A. & Hungerford, T. L. (2009). The market structure of the health insurance industry. Congressional Research Service R40834: November 17.

Baicker, K. & Goldman, D. (2011). Patient cost-sharing and healthcare spending growth. *Journal of Economic Perspectives, 25*(2), 47–68.

Barry, C. L., Frank, R. G., & McGuire, T. G. (2006). The costs of mental health parity: Still an impediment? *Health Affairs (Millwood), 25*(3), 623–634.

Bauhoff, S., Hotchkiss, D. R., & Smith, O. (2010). The impact of medical insurance for the poor in Georgia: a regression discontinuity approach. *Health Economics*: forthcoming.

Berndt, E. R., McGuire, T. G., & Newhouse, J. P. (2011). A primer on the economics of pharmaceutical pricing in health insurance markets NBER Working Paper 16879.

Besley, T. J. (1988). Optimal reimbursement health insurance and the theory of Ramsey taxation. *Journal of Health Economics, 7*(4), 321–336.

Bitran, R. & Munoz, R. (2010). Global marketplace for private health insurance: Strength in numbers. In A. S. Preker, P. Zweifel, & O. Schellekens (Eds.), *Global marketplace for private health insurance: Strength in numbers.* Washington, DC: The World Bank.

Bodenheimer, T. (2000). California's beleaguered physician groups—will they survive? *New England Journal of Medicine, 342*(14), 1064–1068.

Breyer, F., Bundorf, M. K., & Pauly, M. V. (2011). Health care spending risk, health insurance, and payment to health plans. *Handbook of health economics*, Elsevier.

Buchmueller, T. (2006). Price and the health plan choices of retirees. *Journal of Health Economics, 25*(1), 81–101.

Bundorf, M. K. & Royalty, A. B. (2011). Price responsiveness in health plan choice. Working Paper.

Bundorf, M. K., Levin, J. D., & Mahoney, N. (2011). Pricing and welfare in health plan choice. *American Economic Review*: forthcoming.

Buntin, M. B., Damberg, C., Haviland, A., Kapur, K., Lurie, N., McDevitt, R., et al. (2006). Consumer-directed health care: Early evidence about effects on cost and quality. *Health Affairs (Millwood), 25*(6), w516–w530.

Buntin, M. B., Escarce, J. J., Kapur, K., Yegian, J. M., & Marquis, M. S. (2003). Trends and variability in individual insurance products in California. *Health Affairs (Millwood)*, Suppl. Web Exclusives: W3-449–459.

California Public Employees' Retirement System (2004). CalPERS Health Plan Overview. Retrieved August 11, 2010, from < https://www.calpers.ca.gov/index.jsp?bc=/about/benefits-overview/health-benefits.xml/ > .

Capps, C., Dranove, D., & Satterthwaite, M. (2003). Competition and market power in option demand markets. *RAND Journal of Economics, 34*(4), 737–763.

Casalino, L. P. & Robinson, J. C. (1997). The evolution of medical groups and capitation in California. Henry J. Kaiser Foundation and California Health Care Foundation.

Chandra, A., Cutler, D., & Song, Z. (2011). Who ordered that? The economics of treatement choices in medical care. *Handbook of health economics.* Elsevier.

Chandra, A., Gruber, J., & McKnight, R. (2010). Patient cost-sharing, hospitalization offsets, and the design of hospital insurance for the elderly. *American Economic Review, 100*(1), 193–213.

Cheng, T. & Reinhardt, U. E. (2008). Shepherding major health system reforms: A conversation with German Health Minister Ulla Schmidt. *Health Affairs, 27*(3), w204–w213.

Chernew, M. E., & Fendrick, A. M. (2008). Value and increased cost sharing in the American health care system. *Health Services Research, 43*(2), 451–457.

Chernew, M. E., Encinosa, W. E., & Hirth, R. A. (2000). Optimal health insurance: The case of observable, severe illness. *Journal of Health Economics, 19*, 585–609.

Chernew, M. E., Gibson, T. B., Yu-Isenberg, K., Sokol, M. C., Rosen, A. B., & Fendrick, A. M. (2008a). Effects of increased patient cost sharing on socioeconomic disparities in health care. *Journal of General Internal Medicine*, *23*(8), 1131−1136.

Chernew, M. E., Gowrisankaran, G., & Scanlon, D. P. (2008b). Learning and the value of information: Evidence from health plan report cards. NBER Working Paper 8589.

Chernew, M. E., Juster, I. A., Shah, M., Wegh, A., Rosenberg, S., Rosen, A. B., et al. (2010). Evidence that value-based insurance can be effective. *Health Affairs (Millwood)*, *29*(3), 530−536.

Chernew, M. E., Rosen, A. B., & Fendrick, A. M. (2007). Value-based insurance design. *Health Affairs (Millwood)*, *26*(2), w195−w203.

Chernew, M. E., Shah, M. R., Wegh, A., Rosenberg, S. N., Juster, I. A., Rosen, A. B., et al. (2008c). Impact of decreasing copayments on medication adherence within a disease management environment. *Health Affairs (Millwood)*, *27*(1), 103−112.

Choudhry, N., & others (2010a).

Choudhry, N., Rosenthal, M. B., & Milstein, A. (2010). Assessing the evidence for value-based insurance design. *Health Affairs (Millwood)*, *29*(11), 1988−1994.

Christianson, J. B. & Conrad, D. (2011). Provider payment and incentives. In S. A. Glied & P. C. Smith (Eds.), *The Oxford handbook of health economics* (pp. 624−648). Oxford: Oxford University Press.

Commonwealth Health Insurance Connector Authority (2010a). Connector summary report. Commonwealth Health Insurance Connector Authority Boston, MA.

Commonwealth Health Insurance Connector Authority (2010b). Commonwealth care plans by region, from < www.mahealthconnector.org/ >.

Congressional Budget Office (CBO) (2008). *Key issues in analyzing major health insurance proposals, December.*

Cook, K., Dranove, D., & Sfekas, A. (2010). Does major illness cause financial catastrophe? *Health Services Research*, *45*(2), 418−436.

Cox, E., Klukarni, A., & Henderson, R. (2007). Impact of patient and plan design factors on switching to preferred statin therapy. *The Annals of Pharmacotherapy*, *41*(1), 1946−1953.

Cutler, D. M. & Reber, S. J. (1998). Paying for health insurance: The tradeoff between competition and adverse selection. *Quarterly Journal of Economics*, *113*(2), 433−466.

Cutler, D. M. & Zeckhauser, R. (2000). The anatomy of health insurance. In A. J. Culyer & J. P. Newhouse (Eds.), *Handbook of health economics*. Amsterdam: North Holland, Elsevier.

Cutler, D. M., Lincoln, B., & Zeckhauser, R. (2010). Selection stories: Understanding movement across health plans. *Journal of Health Economics*, *29*(6), 821−838.

Cutler, D. M., McClellan, M., & Newhouse, J. P. (2000). How does managed care do it? *RAND Journal of Economics*, *31*(3), 526−548.

Dafny, L. (2010). Are health insurance markets competitive? *American Economic Review*, *100*(4), 1399−1492.

Dafny, L., Ho, K., & Varela, M. (2010). Let them have choice; gains from shifting away from employer-sponsored health insurance and toward an individual exchange. NBER Working Paper 16687.

Damrongplasit, K. & Melnick, G. A. (2009). Early results from Thailand's 30 Baht Health Reform: Something to smile about. *Health Affairs (Millwood)*, *28*(3), w457−w466.

Danzon, P. M. & Pauly, M. V. (2002). Health insurance and the growth in pharmaceutical expenditures. *Journal of Law and Economics*, *45*(1), 587−613.

De Meza, D. (1983). Health insurance and the demand for medical care. *Journal of Health Economics*, *2*, 47−54.

Diamond, P. (1992). Organizing the health insurance market. *Econometrics*, *60*(6), 1233−1254.

Dowd, B. E., & Feldman, R. (1994−1995). Premium elasticities of health plan choice. *Inquiry*, *31*(4), 438−444.

Dowd, B. E., Feldman, R., & Coulam, R. (2003). The effect of health plan characteristics on Medicare+ choice enrollment. *Health Services Research*, *38*(1 Pt 1), 113−135.

Dranove, D. (2011). Health care markets, regulators, and certifiers. *Handbook of health economics*. Elsevier.

Dranove, D. & Millenson, M. L. (2006). Medical bankruptcy: Myth versus fact. *Health Affairs (Millwood)*, *25*(2), w74–w83.

Dranove, D., Shanley, M., & White, W. (1993). Price and concentration in hospital markets: The switch from patient to payer-driven competition. *Journal of Law and Economics*, *36*, 179–204.

Duggan, M. (2005). Do new prescription drugs pay for themselves? The case of second-generation antipsychotics. *Journal of Health Economics*, *24*(1), 1–31.

Duggan, M. & Scott Morton, F. (2010). The effect of Medicare Part D on pharmaceutical prices and utilization. *American Economic Review*, *100*(1), 590–607.

Duggan, M., Healy, P., & Morton, F. S. (2008). Providing prescription drug coverage to the elderly: America's experiment with Medicare Part D. *Journal of Economic Perspectives*, *22*(4), 69–92.

Einav, L., & Finkelstein, A. (2011). Selection in insurance markets: Theory and empirics in pictures. *Journal of Economic Perspectives*, *25*(1), 115–138.

Einav, L. Finkelstein, A., & Cullen, M. R. (2010). Estimating welfare in insurance markets using variation in prices. *Quarterly Journal of Economics*, *125*(3), 877–921.

Elbel, B., & Schlesinger, M. (2010). *How much choice? Nonlinear relationships between the number of plan options and the behavior of Medicare beneficiaries*. Working Paper. Yale University.

Ellis, R. P. & Manning, W. G. (2007). Optimal health insurance for prevention and treatment. *Journal of Health Economics*, *26*(6), 1128–1150.

Ellis, R. P. & McGuire, T. G. (1986). Provider behavior under prospective reimbursement. Cost sharing and supply. *Journal of Health Economics*, *5*(2), 129–151.

Ellis, R. P. & McGuire, T. G. (1987). Setting capitation payments in markets for health services. *Health Care Financing Review*, *8*(4), 55–64.

Ellis, R. P. & McGuire, T. G. (1990). Optimal payment systems for health services. *Journal of Health Economics*, *9*, 375–396.

Ellis, R. P. & McGuire, T. G. (1993). Supply-side and demand-side cost sharing in health care. *Journal of Economic Perspectives*, *7*(4), 135–151.

Ellis, R. P. & McGuire, T. G. (2007). Predictability and predictiveness in health care spending. *Journal of Health Economics*, *26*(1), 25–48.

Ellison, S. F., Cockburn, I., Griliches, Z., & Hausman, J. (1997). Characteristics of demand for pharmaceutical products: An examination of four cephalosporins. *RAND Journal of Economics*, *28*(3), 426–446.

Enthoven, A. C. (1978). Rx for health care economics: Competition, not rigid NHI. *Hospital Progress*, *59*(10), 44–51.

Enthoven, A. C. & Kronick, R. (1989). A consumer-choice health plan for the 1990s. Universal health insurance in a system designed to promote quality and economy (2). *New England Journal of Medicine*, *320*(2), 94–101.

Feldman, R., Parente, S. T., & Christianson, J. B. (2007). Consumer-directed health plans: New evidence on spending and utilization. *Inquiry*, *44*(1), 26–40.

Feldman, R. D. & Dowd, B. E. (1982). Simulation of a health insurance market with adverse selection. *Operations Research*, *30*(6), 1027–1042.

Fendrick, A. M. & Chernew, M. E. (2006). Value-based insurance design: Aligning incentives to bridge the divide between quality improvement and cost containment. *American Journal of Managed Care*, December *12*(Spec no.), SP5–SP10.

Fendrick, A. M., Smith, D. G., & Chernew, M. E. (2010). Applying value-based insurance design to low-value health services. *Health Affairs (Millwood)*, *29*(11), 2017–2021.

Finkelstein, A. N., Luttmer, E., & Notowidigdo, M. J. (2009). What good is wealth without health? The effect of health on the marginal utility of consumption. NBER Working Paper No. 14089.

Florence, C. S. & Thorpe, K. E. (2003). How does the employer contribution for the federal employees health benefits program influence plan selection?. *Health Affairs (Millwood)*, *22*(2), 211–218.

Foote, S. M. & Jones, S. B. (1999). Consumer-choice markets: Lessons from FEHBP mental health coverage. *Health Affairs (Millwood)*, *18*(5), 125–130.

Frank, R. (2007). Behavior economics and health economics. In P. Diamond & H. Vartiainen (Eds.), *Behavioral economics and its applications*. Princeton University Press.

Frank, R. & Lamiraud, K. (2009). Choice, price competition and complexity in markets for health insurance. *Journal of Economic Behavior and Organization*: forthcoming.

Frank, R. G. & McGuire, T. G. (2000). Economics and mental health. In A. J. Culyer & J. P. Newhouse (Eds.), *Handbook of health economics*. North Holland: Elsevier.

Frank, R. G., Glazer, J., & McGuire, T. G. (2000). Measuring adverse selection in managed health care. *Journal of Health Economics*, *19*(6), 829–854.

Friedson, E. (1973). Prepaid group practice and the new demanding patient. *Milbank Memorial Fund Quarterly*, *51*(4), 473–488.

Fronstin, P. (2009). Sources of health insurance and characteristics of the uninsured: Analysis of the March 2009 Current Population Survey. *EBRI Issue Brief*, (334), 1–35.

Gabel, J., Claxton, G., Gil, I., Pickreign, J., Whitmore, H., Finder, B., et al. (2005). Health benefits in 2005: Premium increases slow down, coverage continues to erode. *Health Affairs (Millwood)*, *24*(5), 1273–1280.

Gaynor, M. & Haas-Wilson, D. (1999). Change, consolidation, and competition in health care markets. *Journal of Economic Perspectives*, *13*(1), 141–164.

Gaynor, M., Li, J., & Vogt, W. B. (2007). Substitution, spending offsets, and prescription drug benefit design. *Forum for Health Economics and Policy*, *10*(2), 1–31.

Gibson, T. B., Mark, T. L., McGuigan, K. A., Axelsen, K., & Wang, S. (2006). The effects of prescription drug copayments on statin adherence. *American Journal of Management Care*, *12*(9), 509–517.

Gibson, T. B., Ozminkowski, R. J., & Goetzel, R. Z. (2005). The effects of prescription drug cost sharing: A review of the evidence. *American Journal of Management Care*, *11*(11), 730–740.

Gilman, B. H. & Kautter, J. (2007). Consumer response to dual incentives under multitiered prescription drug formularies. *American Journal of Management Care*, *13*(6 Pt 2), 353–359.

Gilman, B. H. & Kautter, J. (2008). Impact of multitiered copayments on the use and cost of prescription drugs among Medicare beneficiaries. *Health Services Research*, *43*(2), 478–495.

Glazer, J. & McGuire, T. G. (2000). Optimal risk adjustment of health insurance premiums: An application to managed care. *American Economic Review*, *90*(4), 1055–1071.

Glazer, J. & McGuire, T. G. (2001). Private employers don't need formal risk adjustment. *Inquiry*, *38*(3), 260–269.

Glazer, J. & McGuire, T. G. (2002). Setting health plan premiums to ensure efficient quality in health care: Minimum variance optimal risk adjustment. *Journal of Public Economics*, *84*(2), 153–173.

Glazer, J. & McGuire, T. G. (2010). What to count as "offset effects" in health insurance design. *Unpublished* September 14, 2010.

Glazer, J. & McGuire, T. G. (2011). Gold and silver health plans: Accommodating demand heterogeneity in managed competition. *Journal of Health Economics*. Available online: DOI: 10.1016/j.jhealeco.2011.1005.1018.

Goldman, D. P. & Philipson, T. J. (2007). Integrated insurance design in the presence of multiple medical technologies. *The American Economic Review*, *97*(2), 427–432.

Goldman, D. P., Jena, A. B., Philipson, T., & Sun, E. (2008). Drug licenses: A new model for pharmaceutical pricing. *Health Affairs (Millwood)*, *27*(1), 122–129.

Goldman, D. P., Joyce, G. F., & Zheng, Y. (2007). Prescription drug cost sharing: Associations with medication and medical utilization and spending and health. *JAMA*, *298*(1), 61–69.

Goldstein, G. S. & Pauly, M. V. (1976). Group health insurance as a local public good. In R. N. Rosett (Ed.), *The role of health insurance in the health services sector*. New York: National Bureau for Economic Research.

Gruber, J. (2006). The role of consumer copayments for health care: lessons from the RAND Health Insurance Experiment and beyond. Kaiser Family Foundation, October.

Gruber, J. (2008). Covering the uninsured in the United States. *Journal of Economic Literature*, *46*(3), 571–606.

Gruber, J. & Levy, H. (2009). The evolution of medical spending risk. *Journal of Economic Perspectives*, *23*(4), 25–48.

Gruber, J. & Rodriguez, D. (2007). How much uncompensated care do doctors provide? *Journal of Health Economics*, *26*(6), 1151–1169.

Gruber, J. & Washington, E. (2005). Subsidies to employee health insurance premiums and the health insurance market. *Journal of Health Economics, 24*(2), 253–276.

Handel, B. (2010). *Adverse selection and switching costs in health insurance markets: When nudging hurts.* Unpublished Working Paper.

Herring, B. (2005). The effect of the availability of charity care to the uninsured on the demand for private health insurance. *Journal of Health Economics, 24*(2), 225–252.

Himmelstein, D. U., Warren, E., Thorne, D., & Woolhandler, S. (2005). Illness and injury as contributors to bankruptcy. *Health Affairs (Millwood)* Suppl. Web Exclusives: W5-63–W65-73.

Hsiao, W. C., Shaw, R. P., & Fraker, A. (2007). *Social health insurance for developing nations.* Washington, DC: The World Bank.

Hsu, J., Price, M., Huang, J., Brand, R., Fung, V., Hui, R., et al. (2006). Unintended consequences of caps on Medicare drug benefits. *New England Journal of Medicine, 354*(22), 2349–2359.

Huskamp, H. A., et al. (2009).

Huskamp, H. A., Deverka, P. A., Epstein, A. M., Epstein, R. S., McGuigan, K. A., & Frank, R. G. (2003). The effect of incentive-based formularies on prescription-drug utilization and spending. *New England Journal of Medicine, 349*(23), 2224–2232.

Huskamp, H. A., Deverka, P. A., Epstein, A. M., Epstein, R. S., McGuigan, K. A., Muriel, A. C., et al. (2005). Impact of 3-tier formularies on drug treatment of attention-deficit/hyperactivity disorder in children. *Archives of General Psychiatry, 62*(4), 435–441.

Jack, W. & Sheiner, L. (1997). Welfare improving health subsidies. *American Economic Review, 87*(2), 206–221.

Jin, G. Z. & Sorensen, A. T. (2006). Information and consumer choice: The value of publicized health plan ratings. *Journal of Health Economics, 25*(2), 248–275.

Joyce, G. F., Goldman, D. P., Vogt, W. B., Sun, E., & Jena, A. B. (2009). Medicare Part D after 2 years. *American Journal of Management Care, 15*(8), 536–544.

Kaiser Family Foundation and Health Services & Educational Trust (2009). Employer Health Benefits: 2009 Annual Survey, from http://ehbs.kff.org/pdf/2009/7936.pdf.

Kaiser Family Foundation and Health Services & Educational Trust (2010). Employer Health Benefits: 2010 Annual Survey, from http://ehbs.kff.org/pdf/2010/8085.pdf.

Keeler, E. B. & Rolph, J. E. (1988). The demand for episodes of treatment in the Health Insurance Experiment. *Journal of Health Economics, 7*(4), 337–367.

Keenan, P., Cutler, D. M., & Chernew, M. E. (2006). The "graying" of group health insurance. *Health Affairs (Millwood), 25*(6), 1497–1506.

Kingsdale, J. & Bertko, J. (2010). Insurance exchanges under health reform: Six design issues for the states. *Health Affairs (Millwood), 29*(6), 1158–1163.

Kremer, M. & Glennerster, R. (2011). Improving health in developing countries: Evidence from randomized evaluations. *Handbook of health economics.* Elsevier.

Landon, B. E., Rosenthal, M. B., Normand, S. L., Spettell, C., Lessler, A., Underwood, H. R., et al. (2007). Incentive formularies and changes in prescription drug spending. *American Journal of Management Care, 13*(6 Pt 2), 360–369.

Leibman, J. & Zeckhauser, R. (2008). Simple humans, complex insurance, subtle subsidies. NBER Working Paper 14330.

Lichtenberg, F. R. & Sun, S. X. (2007). The impact of Medicare Part D on prescription drug use by the elderly. *Health Affairs (Millwood), 26*(6), 1735–1744.

Lo Sasso, A. T., Shah, M., & Frogner, B. K. (2010). Health savings accounts and health care spending. *Health Services Research, 45*(4), 1041–1060.

Lohr, K. N., Brook, R. H., & Kamber, C. J. (1986). Effect of cost sharing on use of medically effective and less effective care. *Medical Care, 24*(9), S31–S38.

Lu, C., Frank, R., & McGuire, T. G. (2008). Demand response of mental health services to cost sharing under managed care. *Journal of Mental Health Policy and Economics, 11*(3), 113–126.

Lu, C., Frank, R. G., & McGuire, T. G. (2009). Demand response under managed health care. *Contemporary Economic Policy, 27*(1), 1–15.

Lungen, M., Stollenwerk, B., Messner, P., Lauterbach, K. W., & Gerber, A. (2008). Waiting times for elective treatments according to insurance status: A randomized empirical study in Germany. *International Journal of Equity Health*, 7, 1.

Ma, C. A. & McGuire, T. G. (1998). Costs and incentives in a behavioral health carve-out. *Health Affairs (Millwood)*, 17(2), 53−69.

Ma, C. A. & McGuire, T. G. (2002). Network incentives in managed health care. *Journal of Economics & Management Strategy*, 11(1), 1−35.

Ma, C. A. & Riordan, M. H. (2002). Health insurance, moral hazard, and managed care. *Journal of Economics & Management Strategy*, 11, 81−107.

Maciejewski, M. L., Farley, J. F., Parker, J., & Wansink, D. (2010). Copayment reductions generate greater medication adherence in targeted patients. *Health Affairs (Millwood)*, 29(11), 2002−2008.

Manning, W. G., & Marquis, M. S. (1989). Health insurance: Trade-off between risk sharing and moral hazard. Pub. No. R-3729-NCHSR.

Manning, W. G., & Marquis, M. S. (1996). Health insurance: The Tradeoff between risk pooling and moral hazard. *Journal of Health Economics*, 15(5), 609−639.

Manning, W. G., Newhouse, J. P., Duan, N., Keeler, E. B., & Leibowitz, A. (1987). Health insurance and the demand for medical care: Evidence from a randomized experiment. *American Economic Review*, 77(3), 251−277.

Marquis, M. S. & Long, S. H. (1995). Worker demand for health insurance in the non-group market. *Journal of Health Economics*, 14(1), 47−63.

McFadden, D. (2006). Free markets and fettered consumers. *American Economic Review*, 96(1), 5−29.

McGuire, T. G. (1981). Price and membership in a prepaid group medical practice. *Medical Care*, 18(2), 172−183.

McGuire, T. G. (2000). Physician agency. In A. J. Culyer & J. P. Newhouse (Eds.), *Handbook of health economics* (Vol. 1, pp. 461−536). Elsevier.

McGuire, T. G. & Bauhoff, S. (2007). A decade of choice tracking the German national experience with consumer choice of sickness fund. In P. Oberender, & C. Staub (Eds.), *Auf der Suche nach der besseren Lösung* (pp. 145−160). Baden-Baden Nomos Ver Lagsgesellschaft.

McGuire, T. G. & Bauhoff, S. (2011). Adoption of a cost-saving innovation: Germany, UK and simvastatin. In N. Klusen, F. Verheyen, & C. Wagner (Eds.), *England and Germany in Europe—What lessons can we learn from each other?* (pp. 11−26). Baden-Baden, Germany: Nomos Verlag.

McGuire, T. G. & Sinaiko, A. D. (2010). Regulating a health insurance exchange: Implications for individuals with mental illness. *Psychiatric Services*, 61(11), 1074−1080.

McGuire, T. G. Newhouse, J. P., & Sinaiko, A. (2011). An economic history of Medicare Part C. *Milbank Quarterly*, 89(2), 289−332.

McWilliams, J. M., Afendulis, C., Landon, B. E., & McGuire, T. G. (2011). Cognitive functioning and choice between traditional Medicare and Medicare Advantage. *Health Affairs*: forthcoming.

Melnick, G. A. & Zwanziger, J. (1988). Hospital behavior under competition and cost-containment policies. the California experience, 1980 to 1985. *JAMA*, 260(18), 2669−2675.

Melnick, G. A., Zwanziger, J., Bamezai, A., & Pattison, R. (1992). The effects of market structure and bargaining position on hospital prices. *Journal of Health Economics*, 11(3), 217−233.

Miller, G., Pinto, D. M., & Vera-Hernández, M. (2009). High-powered incentives in developing country health insurance: Evidence from Colombia's Régimen Subsidiado. National Bureau of Economic Research Working Paper Series No. 15456.

Miller, N. H. (2005). Pricing health benefits: A cost-minimization approach. *Journal of Health Economics*, 24(5), 931−949.

Morrisey, M. A. (2008). *Health insurance*. Health Administration Press.

Newhouse, J. P. (1993). *Free-for-all: Health insurance, medical costs, and health outcomes: The results of the health insurance experiment*. Cambridge, MA: Harvard University Press.

Newhouse, J. P. (2006). Reconsidering the moral hazard−risk avoidance tradeoff. *Journal of Health Economics*, 25(5), 1005−1014.

Nyman, J. (1999a). The economics of moral hazard revisited. *Journal of Health Economics*, 18(6), 811−823.

Nyman, J. (1999b). The value of health insurance: The access motive. *Journal of Health Economics*, *18*(2), 141–152.

Nyman, J. A. (2003). *The theory of demand for health insurance*. Stanford University Press.

Nyman, J. A. (2008). Health insurance theory: The case of the missing welfare gain. *European Journal of Health Economics*, *9*, 369–380.

Olmstead, T. & Zeckhauser, R. (1999). The menu-setting problem and subsidized prices: Drug formulary illustration. *Journal of Health Economics*, *18*(5), 523–550.

Organization for Economic Cooperation and Development (OECD) (2004). Private health insurance in OECD countries, from http://www.oecd.org/dataoecd/42/6/33820355.pdf.

Padgett, D. K., Patrick, C., Burns, B. J., Schlesinger, H. J., & Cohen, J. (1993). The effect of insurance benefit changes on use of child and adolescent outpatient mental health services. *Medical Care*, *31*(2), 96–110.

Parente, S. T., Feldman, R., & Christianson, J. B. (2004). Employee choice of consumer-driven health insurance in a multiplan, multiproduct setting. *Health Services Research*, *39*(4 Pt 2), 1091–1112.

Pauly, M. (1968). The economics of moral hazard: Comment. *American Economic Review*, *58*, 531–536.

Pauly, M. & Blavin, F. (2008). Moral hazard in insurance, value-based cost sharing, and the benefits of blissful ignorance. *Journal of Health Economics*, *27*(6), 1407–1418.

Pauly, M. V. & Held, P. J. (1990). Benign moral hazard and the cost-effectiveness analysis of insurance coverage. *Journal of Health Economics*, *9*(4), 447–461.

Pauly, M. V. & Ramsey, S. D. (1999). Would you like suspenders to go with that belt? An analysis of optimal combinations of cost sharing and managed care. *Journal of Health Economics*, *18*(4), 443–458.

Pauly, M. V., Blavin, F. E., & Meghan, S. (2009). How private, voluntary health insurance can work in developing countries. *Health Affairs (Millwood)*, *28*(6), 1778–1787.

Phelps, C. E. (1973). The demand for health insurance: A theoretical and empirical investigation. Report R-1054-OEO.

Phelps, C. E. (1976). The demand for reimbursement insurance. In R. Rosett (Ed.), *The role of health insurance in the health services sector*. New York: National Bureau for Economic Research.

Phelps, C. E. (2010). *Health economics* (4th ed.). Addison-Wesley.

Pigou, A. C. (1920). *Economics of welfare*. London, England: Macmillian and Co.

Pizer, S. D., Frakt, A. B., & Feldman, R. (2003). Payment policy and inefficient benefits in the Medicare+Choice program. *International Journal of Health Care Finance and Economics*, *3*(2), 79–93.

Relman, A. S. (2010). Could physicians take the lead in health reform? *Journal of the American Medical Association*, *304*(24), 2740–2741.

Rice, T. (1992). An alternative framework for evaluating, welfare losses in the health care market. *Journal of Health Economics*, *11*(1), 88–92.

Rice, T. & Matsuoka, K. Y. (2004). The impact of cost-sharing on appropriate utilization and health status: A review of the literature on seniors. *Medical Care Research and Review*, *61*(4), 415–452.

Ridley, D. (2009). Payments, promotion, and the purple pill. The Fuqua School of Business, Duke University: Working Paper.

Robinson, J. C. (1995). Health care purchasing and market changes in California. *Health Affairs (Millwood)*, *14*(4), 117–130.

Robinson, J. C. (1996). Decline in hospital utilization and cost inflation under managed care in California. *JAMA*, *276*(13), 1060–1064.

Robinson, J. C. (2010). Applying value-based insurance design to high-cost health services. *Health Affairs (Millwood)*, *29*(11), 2009–2016.

Robinson, J. C. & Casalino, L. P. (2001). Reevaluation of capitation contracting in New York and California. *Health Affairs (Millwood)* Suppl. Web Exclusives: W11–W19.

Rosenthal, M. B., Li, Z., & Milstein, A. (2009). Do patients continue to see physicians who are removed from a PPO network? *American Journal of Management Care*, *15*(10), 713–719.

Rothschild, M. & Stiglitz, J. (1976). Equilibrium in competitive insurance markets: An essay on the economics of imperfect information. *Quarterly Journal of Economics*, *90*(4), 629–649.

Royalty, A. B. & Soloman, N. (1989). Health plan choice: Price elasticities in a managed care setting. *Journal of Human Resources, 34,* 1–41.

Rysman, M. (2009). The economics of two-sided markets. *Journal of Economic Perspectives, 23*(3), 125–143.

Samuelson, W. & Zeckhauser, R. (1988). Status quo bias in decisionmaking. *Journal of Risk and Uncertainty, 1,* 7–59.

Sass, H.-M. (1995). The new triad: Responsibility, solidarity, and subsidiarity. *Journal of Medicine and Philosophy, 20,* 587–594.

Scanlon, D. P., Lindrooth, R., & Christianson, J. B. (2008). Steering patients to safer hospitals? The effect of a tiered hospital network on hospital admission. *Health Services Research, 43*(5 pt II), 1849–1868.

Scott Morton, F. & Kyle, M. (2011). Markets for pharmaceutical products. *Handbook of health economics.* Elsevier.

Selby, J. V., Fireman, B. H., & Swain, B. E. (1996). Effect of a copayment on use of the emergency department in a health maintenance organization. *New England Journal of Medicine, 334*(10), 635–641.

Shang, B. & Goldman, D. P. (2007). *Prescription drug coverage and elderly medicare spending.* NBER Working Paper 13358.

Simon, K. (2005). Adverse selection in health insurance markets: Evidence from state small-group health insurance reforms. *Journal of Public Economics, 89*(9–10), 1865–1877.

Sinaiko, A. D. & Hirth, R. A. (2011). Consumers, health insurance and dominated choices. *Journal of Health Economics, 30*(2), 450–457.

Song, Z., Safran, D., Landon, B. E., He, Y., Ellis, R. P., Mechanic, R., et al. (2011). Effect of the alternative quality contract on health care spending and quality. *New England Journal of Medicine:* forthcoming.

Squires, D., & others (2010). International profiles of health care systems. The Commonwealth Fund. Retrieved April 4, 2010, from http://www.commonwealthfund.org/∼/media/Files/Publications/Fund%20Report/2010/Jun/1417_Squires_Intl_Profiles_622.pdf.

Starr, P. (1983). *The social transformation of American medicine.* Basic Books.

Stock, S., Redaelli, M., & Lauterbach, K. W. (2006). The influence of the labor market on German health care reforms. *Health Affairs (Millwood), 25*(4), 1143–1152.

Stone, D. A. (1993). The struggle for the soul of health insurance. *Journal of Health Politics, Policy and Law, 18*(2), 287–317.

Strombom, B. A., Buchmueller, T. C., & Feldstein, P. J. (2002). Switching costs, price sensitivity and health plan choice. *Journal of Health Economics, 21*(1), 89–116.

Swartz, K. (2010). Cost-sharing: Effects on spending and outcomes; the Synthesis Project Issue 20. Robert Wood Johnson Foundation, from http://www.rwjf.org/files/research/121710.policysynthesis.costsharing.rpt.pdf.

Thomson, S., Foubister, T., & Mossialos, E. (2009). Financing health care in the European Union Challenges and policy responses. European Observatory on Health Systems and Policies. Retrieved April 4, 2010, from http://www.euro.who.int/__data/assets/pdf_file/0009/98307/E92469.pdf.

Town, R. & Vistnes, G. (2001). Hospital competition in HMO networks. *Journal of Health Economics, 20*(5), 733–753.

US Government Accountability Office (GAO) (2003). Private health insurance: Federal and state requirement affecting coverage by small businesses.

US Government Accountability Office (GAO) (2009). Private health insurance: Research on competition in the insurance industry. GAO-09-8645, from http://www.gao.gov/new.items/d09864r.pdf.

US Office of Personnel Management (2004). Health care reform. Retrieved August 11, 2010, from http://www.opm.gov/insure/.

Van de Ven, W. P. M. M. & Ellis, R. P. (2000). Risk adjustment in competitive health plan markets. In A. J. Culyer & J. P. Newhouse (Eds.), *Handbook of health economics.* Amsterdam: Elsevier.

Van de Ven, W. P., Beck, K., Van de Voorde, C., Wasem, J., & Zmora, I. (2007). Risk adjustment and risk selection in Europe: 6 years later. *Health Policy, 83*(2–3), 162–179.

Waters, H. R., Hobart, J., Forrest, C. B., Siemens, K. K., Pittman, P. M., Murthy, A., et al. (2008). Health insurance coverage in Central and Eastern Europe: Trends and challenges. *Health Affairs (Millwood), 27*(2), 478–486.

World Health Organization (WHO) (2010). World Health Statistics. Retrieved July 7, 2010, from http://www.who.int/whosis/whostat/2010/en/index.html.

Wu, V. Y. (2009). Managed care's price bargaining with hospitals. *Journal of Health Economics, 28*(2), 350–360.

Xu, K., Evans, D. B., Carrin, G., Aguilar-Rivera, A. M., Musgrove, P., & Evans, T. (2007). Protecting households from catastrophic health spending. *Health Affairs (Millwood), 26*(4), 972–983.

Zeckhauser, R. (1970). Medical insurance: A case study of the tradeoff between risk spreading and appropriate incentives. *Journal of Economic Theory, 2*, 10–26.

Zhang, Y. (2008). Cost-saving effects of olanzapine as long-term treatment for bipolar disorder. *Journal of Mental Health Policy and Economics, 11*(3), 135–146.

Zhang, Y. & Soumerai, S. B. (2007). Do newer prescription drugs pay for themselves? A reassessment of the evidence. *Health Affairs (Millwood), 26*(3), 880–886.

Zhang, Y., Donohue, J. M., Lave, J. R., O'Donnell, G., & Newhouse, J. P. (2009). The effect of Medicare Part D on drug and medical spending. *New England Journal of Medicine, 361*(1), 52–61.

Zweifel, P., Breyer, F., & Kiffman, M. (2009). *Health economics* (2nd ed.). Oxford University Press.

CHAPTER SIX

Who Ordered That? The Economics of Treatment Choices in Medical Care

Amitabh Chandra, David Cutler, and Zirui Song[1]
Harvard University and NBER, USA

Contents

Abstract

In the United States, two patients with the same medical condition can receive drastically different treatments. In addition, the *same* patient can walk into two physicians' offices and receive equally disparate treatments. This chapter attempts to understand why. It focuses on three areas: the

[1] The authors are grateful to Thomas McGuire for helpful comments. Zirui Song acknowledges support from a National Institute of Aging Pre-doctoral M.D./Ph.D. National Research Service Award (F30-AG039175) and the National Bureau of Economic Research Pre-doctoral Fellowship in Aging and Health Economics (T32-AG000186).

397

patient, the physician, and the clinical situation. Specifically, the chapter surveys patient or demand-side factors such as price, income, and preferences; physician or supply-side factors such as specialization, financial incentives, and professionalism; and situational factors including behavioral influences and systems-level factors that play a role in clinical decision making. This chapter reviews theory and evidence, borrowing heavily from the clinical literature.

Keywords: variations; decision making; demand heterogeneity; preferences; income; supply-side incentives; payment systems; specialization; behavioral economics

JEL Codes: D03; I10; I12; J44; L84

1. INTRODUCTION

There were 3,368 men aged 45–89 diagnosed with localized or regional prostate cancer in Seattle in 2007. Prostate cancer is the second most common cancer among men in the United States and the second leading cause of cancer deaths in men, accounting for about 200,000 diagnoses and 30,000 deaths annually (Howlader et al., 2011; Smith, 2011; Jemal et al., 2009). A large literature exists on the many treatments for prostate cancer. There are also a number of clinical guidelines for treatment choice, including recommendations from the American Urological Association, American Joint Committee on Cancer, and the National Comprehensive Cancer Network (Thompson et al., 2007; National Comprehensive Cancer Network, 2010; AJCC, 2010).

Despite this clinical experience and expansive literature, however, the treatment of these patients is wildly diverse (Wilt et al., 2008). Forty-two percent of the patients in Seattle had their prostate removed, 38 percent had radiation, and others had chemotherapy (many patients received a combination of these treatments). All the while, a substantial number decided not to pursue any aggressive treatment, but instead to monitor the progression of the cancer over time.

How were these treatment choices made? Why are they so diverse? That is the subject of this chapter. We characterize the factors influencing treatment into three categories. The first is standard demand-side factors: price, income, and tastes. In most markets, variation in purchasing decisions is explained by one of these three considerations. Ironically, given the large variation in medical treatments, the roles of price and income in medicine are blunted. Substantial insurance coverage means that prices do not vary significantly across people and income has little role to play in clinical decisions. In the prostate cancer example, most men have Medicare coverage, typically with supplemental insurance, so the cost of any treatment is minimal. Tastes can and do vary, and the different treatments play to these different tastes (Cooperberg et al., 2007; Wei et al., 2002). Prostate removal and radiation therapy can both reduce mortality, but treatment also carries risks to quality of life, such as impotence, urinary incontinence, and disrupted bowel and hormonal function (Bill-Axelson et al., 2005; Hayes et al., 2010; Bolla et al., 1997; Sanda et al., 2008; Litwin et al., 2007; Potosky et al., 2000). Different men care about these outcomes to different degrees.

The supply side is the second factor that may influence treatment decisions. The surgeons at one hospital may be particularly good compared to surgeons at other hospitals, and thus surgical treatment may be preferred to radiation and chemotherapy for men treated at that institution. Even a casual perusal of surgical report cards shows enormous variation in risk-adjusted outcomes across surgeons and institutions. The technology available for treatment may also vary across institutions. The daVinci robotic surgical system is gaining popularity, especially at hospitals that can afford the $1.39 million fixed purchasing cost and $140,000 annual service contract. In 2009, 73,000 men (86 percent of the 85,000 who had prostate cancer surgery) received robot-assisted operations, a dramatic rise from less than 5,000 a decade ago (Kolata, 2010). Through practice or adaptive learning, physicians at different institutions may adopt faith in different guidelines or technologies, steering men along particular courses of therapy.

Finally, situational factors, such as contextual or behavioral influences, may be at work. A particular man may have preferred radiation to surgery, but the urologist on call that day happened to talk the man into surgery. The tragic or salient death of a man during surgery the previous week may lead a primary care physician to refer her next patient in similar condition to a radiation oncologist instead. The lengthy wait for a radiation appointment relative to surgery may lead a patient to choose surgery. These examples illustrate some of the richness and randomness of clinical situations.

At the most basic level, this chapter considers whether the demand side, the supply side, or what we refer to as situational factors is most important in explaining the treatment differences that we observe. Of course, the factors may be more or less appropriate at different levels of aggregation. Demand-side factors may be important in explaining treatment differences between rich and poor regions, but they may be less important within rich or poor regions. Supply-side factors may explain a good share of the differences between one region and another, or even between the United States and other developed nations. For example, prostate cancer guidelines vary within and between countries (Dahm et al., 2008). Situational factors may explain a good deal about why one man gets surgery and another gets radiation, but are likely to be a much smaller part of regional variations in care. Yet they are evident in conceivably every decision to prescribe or receive health care, and understanding them may offer the greatest potential improvements for the productivity of health care spending.

1.1. Overview of Variations in Medical Care

Variation in medical treatments is profound.[2] We noted above the variability in treatment rates for men with localized prostate cancer of the same age and living in the same geographic location. However, variations in utilization extend farther.

Jack Wennberg and colleagues pioneered the study of regional variations in health care in the United States, decades after Glover (1938) first uncovered variations in England and Wales. Wennberg and Gittelsohn (1973) showed that tonsillectomy rates varied significantly across small towns in Vermont. They also showed that treatment patterns were different in Boston, Massachusetts than in New Haven, Connecticut. So-called "small area variations" demonstrate clear differences in demand, supply, or situation across settings (Wennberg and Gittelsohn, 1982; Wennberg et al., 1987). But small area variations are less impressive in some sense. That beliefs about appropriate practice differ across individual physicians and patients is clear. The real issue is whether these differences in beliefs affect care decisions writ large.

In the past decade, there has been enormous emphasis on "large area variations"—differences in medical practice across areas where individual heterogeneity in beliefs is more likely to be averaged out and be a much less important explanation of differences (Fisher et al., 2003a and b; Baicker and Chandra, 2004). We illustrate this in the case of prostate cancer, noted above. There are 17 regions in the *Surveillance, Epidemiology and End Results (SEER)* database over the 2000–2008 time period. We selected all of the cases for local/regional prostate cancer in 2008 and analyzed the treatment that men received. We selected men who were aged 45–89, the bulk of those with prostate cancer. We coded treatment into radical prostatectomy, radiation therapy, or watchful waiting; the SEER data do not indicate if chemotherapy was provided. To control for observable differences across patients, we relate dummy variables for surgery or radiation to age (dummies for the exact year), tumor grade and size, and SEER region. The region dummy variables give the adjusted probability of receiving each treatment in each area.

Figure 6.1 plots the adjusted rate of surgery and radiation in each area. It is clear that treatment proclivities vary enormously by area. In some areas, surgery rates are very high (Seattle being one of them) and in other areas rates of radiation are high (Hawaii is the highest).

Some variation in treatment rates would be expected for natural reasons, such as case mix and patient preferences. However, the variation here is greater than random fluctuations alone would suggest. The Dartmouth Atlas documents such variation along a number of dimensions. Generally, the largest variation is in "supply-sensitive" care or "gray area medicine," in which clinical judgment plays a key role. The use of imaging services and the frequency of specialist office visits are leading examples of

---

[2]For extended discussion of variations, see Skinner (2011, this Handbook).

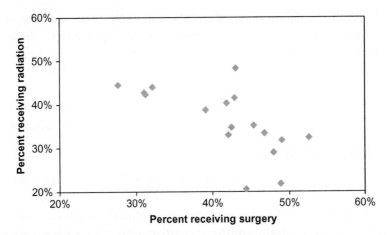

Figure 6.1 Surgery and radiation for prostate cancer in the United States, SEER regions.

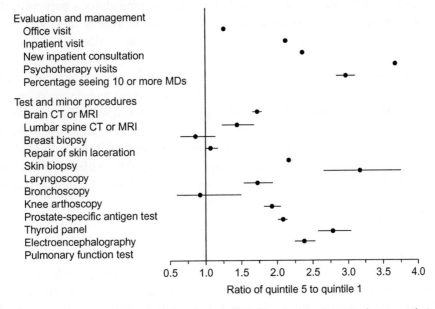

Figure 6.2 Relative rates of utilization for selected clinical services in the united states. relative rate and 95% confidence intervals of specific services provided to cohort members residing in the highest quintile of medicare spending compared with those residing in the lowest quintile for the three chronic disease cohorts combined. (Authors' adaptation of Figure 5 from Fisher, E. S. et al. (2003). *Ann. Intern. Med., 138,* 273—287.)

this type of care. Figure 6.2 shows the rates of utilization for certain services in the highest spending US regions (quintile 5) relative to rates in the lowest spending US regions (quintile 1), demonstrating the extensive variation.

There is significant debate about the drivers of these regional differences. Some researchers argue that variation is accounted for by population disease burden (Zuckerman et al., 2010), but other authors argue that prevalence of diagnoses itself is endogenous across areas (Song et al., 2010; Welch et al., 2011). Most of the literature agrees that patient characteristics and preferences do not explain much of the differences across areas, and that substantial variations in treatment practices remain after controlling for patient characteristics (Anthony et al., 2009; O'Hare et al., 2010; Baicker et al., 2004).

1.2. Gray Area of Medicine

The gray area of medicine, in which economic incentives are likely to have the largest impact, accounts for a significant portion of clinical practice. In many clinical situations, there are no authoritative guidelines or consensus treatment recommendations. In areas of medicine where clinical trials compare alternative treatments, we learn about average benefits. Yet the average benefit tells physicians little about a particular patient's potential marginal benefit. Moreover, average benefits say nothing about a particular physician's own impact on potential marginal benefits, owing to skill or other factors. The result is that when the same patient walks into two physicians' offices, what that patient receives may differ widely. An example of this is the frequency of follow-up for medical care. In regions of the country that spend more on health care, patients are seen back more frequently and are more likely to receive screening tests and discretionary interventions of unproven benefit relative to low-spending regions (Sirovich et al., 2008).

Another example is the use of percutaneous coronary interventions (PCI) for stable coronary disease (chest pain and associated symptoms caused by strenuous activity), where successive trials have found no survival benefit or quality of life benefit over optimal medical therapy (Boden et al., 2007; Weintraub et al., 2008). Yet despite this, some patients will surely benefit from this procedure.

PCI remains one of the most studied procedures in medicine; matters are substantially less clear for things leading up to this intervention. For a person going to the doctor with chest pain, there are over 7,000 cardiology guidelines for individual clinical decisions. Only 11 percent are based on randomized controlled trials, and 48 percent are from expert opinions, case studies, or prior standards of care (Tricoci et al., 2009). For a simple cough, there are over 4,000 infectious disease guidelines, of which 14 percent are based on randomized controlled trials and 55 percent are from opinions or case series (Lee and Vielemeyer, 2011). In addition, many of the guidelines are based on studies excluding people with multiple chronic conditions (often present in the elderly) or based on other non-random samples. Indeed, clinical guidelines in most fields of medicine suffer from poor adherence to methodological standards (Shaneyfelt et al., 1999; Atkins et al., 2004; Dahm et al., 2008).

The gray area of medicine is characterized by at least three attributes. First, as the examples above illustrate, clinical guidance is scarce. Second, the scope of marginal harm is small, as otherwise physicians would learn very quickly to refrain from harmful treatments. Third, benefit is idiosyncratic to the patient. Such elements as pain, nausea, and quality of life enter individual utility functions in idiosyncratic ways. Given this, it is possible for physicians to claim, despite clinical trial evidence, that a particular patient has a particular preference which befits the treatment. In the typology of Chandra and Skinner (forthcoming), these are type II and type III technologies: the former denoting treatments highly effective for some but not for all (e.g. cardiac stents), and the latter referring to treatments with uncertain clinical value (e.g. ICU days among chronically ill patients).

1.3. Demand (Patients) and Supply (Doctors)

The difficulty in understanding treatment choices is not just empirical; it is conceptual as well. What the patient wants to receive (demand) may not be the same as what the physician wants to deliver (supply), and given insurance and price regulation in health care, normal forces of market equilibrium are unlikely to bring these into balance. Consider a simple model of medical treatments based on patient demand and physician assessment of the optimal treatment for the patient (Chandra and Staiger, 2007). We assume a decision is being made between two treatments for a particular disease (where "doing nothing" can be modeled as one of the choices). Denote the treatments $i = \{1,2\}$. Each treatment produces benefits to the patient of $B_i(\sigma)$, where σ is the disease severity. In addition to health, people get utility from non-medical consumption, denoted $Y - P_i$, where P_i is the price the consumer pays for the treatment and Y is income net of any insurance premium. The utility to the patient from each treatment is therefore:

$$\mathbf{U_k}(1) = B_1(\sigma_k) + V(Y_k - P_{k1}) + \theta_{k1} \tag{6.1}$$

$$\mathbf{U_k}(2) = B_2(\sigma_k) + V(Y_k - P_{k2}) + \theta_{k2} \tag{6.2}$$

where k denotes individuals. θ_{k1} and θ_{k2} are person-specific error terms that capture heterogeneity in the benefits of each treatment to that patient—for example, the part due to preferences about side-effects.

1.3.1. Benevolent Physician

In the simplest case, let us assume that physicians are perfect agents for their patients, know everything about benefits, and observe everything about preferences. In this case, there is no additional role for physician utility in the model. The physician chooses treatment 1 over treatment 2 provided $\mathbf{U_k}(1) > \mathbf{U_k}(2)$. This can be expressed in terms of the difference in the two error terms. In particular, treatment 1 will be chosen provided that:

$$\theta_{k1} - \theta_{k2} > [B_2(\sigma_k) - B_1(\sigma_k)] + [V(Y_k - P_{k2}) - V(Y_k - P_{k1})] \tag{6.3}$$

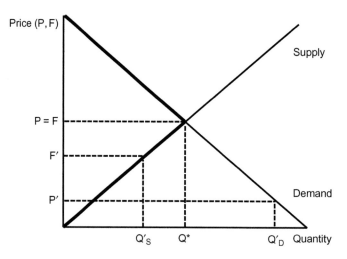

Figure 6.3 Supply and demand in standard market equilibrium. Note: P is the consumer price, F is the physician fee, Q* denotes a standard market equilibrium where P = F, and Q'_D and Q'_S denote quantity demanded and supplied, respectively.

With restrictions on the distributional form of error terms (for example, a normality assumption), this probability can be solved for directly:

$$\begin{aligned}\Pr[\text{treatment } 1] = \Pr\{i = 1\} &= \Pr\{\mathbf{U_k}(1) > \mathbf{U_k}(2)\}\\ &= \Pr\{[B_1(\sigma_k) - B_2(\sigma_k)] + [V(Y_k - P_{k1}) - V(Y_k - P_{k2})] > \theta_{k2} - \theta_{k1}\}\\ &= \Pr\{\Delta B(\sigma_k) + \Delta V(Y_k - P_k) > \Delta\theta_k\}\end{aligned}$$

$$(6.4)$$

Equations (6.1) and (6.2) give a downward sloping demand curve for each treatment as a function of its price, holding the price of the other treatment constant (see below). This demand curve is shown in Figure 6.3. Integrating equation (6.4) over the distribution of severities (σ) in a population produces the market demand curve for treatment 1. Taking $f(\sigma)$ as the distribution of σ in the population, the following must hold in equilibrium:

$$D_1 = \int_{\sigma} \Pr(\Delta B(\sigma_k) + \Delta V(Y_k - P_k) > \Delta\theta_k) f(\sigma) d(\sigma) \qquad (6.5)$$

If providers mistakenly assess idiosyncratic patient preferences, this will result in allocative inefficiency with a potentially large utility loss. The utility loss would be further exacerbated by miscalculations of average benefits and average costs.

1.3.2. Physician as an Imperfect Agent

The supply side is given by physician desires. Modeling physician utility is complex, as we discuss below. Following Ellis and McGuire (1986), we assume that physician utility depends on three components: the benefit to the patient (B_k), the fee the physician earns net of the costs of providing the service (F_i), and other factors (ε_j). These may include the hassles from malpractice (direct malpractice costs would be netted out in F_i), the availability of a particular service in the area or at that particular time, or the guidelines the physician chooses to follow. For simplicity, we assume that utility is linear in these three factors.

$$\mathbf{W_j}(1) = \beta_j B_1(\sigma_k) + V(F_1) + \varepsilon_{j1} \tag{6.6}$$

$$\mathbf{W_j}(2) = \beta_j B_2(\sigma_k) + V(F_2) + \varepsilon_{j2} \tag{6.7}$$

The coefficient β reflects the relative importance of patient health to physicians in comparison to profits; one interpretation is altruism, or professionalism. It may differ across physicians, as denoted by the j subscript. Similarly, ε may differ across physicians because of differing preferences or constraints. In this imperfect agency model, the provider chooses treatment 1 if:

$$\varepsilon_{j1} - \varepsilon_{j2} > \beta_j [B_2(\sigma_k) - B_1(\sigma_k)] + [V(F_2) - V(F_1)] \tag{6.8}$$

Equation (6.8) differs from equation (6.3) in several notable ways that reflect differences in treatment choice between the two models. First, physicians and patients may differ in their person-specific error terms, which would drive differences in treatment choice. Second, the physician coefficient β may be less than 1, in which case the imperfect agent undervalues patient benefit relative to the benevolent physician. In our simple model, we take professionalism to be exogenous, where a fully altruistic physician has $\beta = 1$. As β approaches 0, the relative importance of the physician's own economic motives increases. One consideration that we leave out of this simple model is what happens when β is a function of physician income or reimbursement incentives, $\beta_j = \beta_j(F_i)$. Alternatively, β may depend on the physician's place of training or organizational incentive contracts. Such endogenous versions of β would generate further variation in treatment decisions. Third, physicians may not be reimbursed on a fee-for-service basis, such as in various capitated or other managed care contracts (this could correspond to a negative net margin); moreover, the fee (F_i) need not be equal to the full marginal cost of care faced by the patient (P_{ki}) due to insurance.

Whether fees (F_i) increase or decrease, the amount of care provided is, of course, unknown; there are income and substitution effects. For now, we assume that supply is upward sloping in fees, which our empirical review will demonstrate is generally the case. Figure 6.3 shows an upward sloping supply curve.

In standard markets (markets without insurance and where buyers are perfectly informed), prices adjust so that demand and supply are equal. This is shown by the point Q^* in the figure, where $Q_D = Q_S = Q^*$ and P equals F. In the presence of insurance, however, P' and F' are unequal and thus standard price equilibration cannot take place. For example, patients might face generous cost sharing and so demand $Q'_D > Q^*$. Physicians might not receive a high fee for each service and thus are only willing to supply $Q'_S < Q^*$.

We need to add to the story to describe equilibirum. One possible equilibrium is given by the short-side principle: $Q_E = \min(Q'_D, Q'_S)$. The set of possible equilibria would correspond to the area of demand and supply to the left of Q^*. A second possible view is that physicians are (imperfect) agents for patients and patients implicitly trust their physicians. Thus, $Q_E \approx Q'_S$ provided Q'_S is not too far from Q'_D. Such a model would magnify the role of physician-specific characteristics such as fees, clinical judgment, and beliefs about appropriate care on equilibrium outcomes relative to role of patient preferences and prices.

Further, this model suggests that not all services provided should be interpreted as reflecting demand. That is, one should not necessarily assume that the area of the country where radical prostatectomy rates are 15 percent above the national average (Utah) has patients who are much more likely to believe that radical prostatectomy is the best treatment for localized prostate cancer.

Our goal in the remainder of this chapter is to understand how treatment decisions are actually made. This chapter is not a review in the traditional sense; we do not attempt a definitive summary of all the papers on the determinants of treatment choice—if one could even be conducted. Rather, we selectively summarize the theories and literature that have the most bearing on understanding treatment choices across individuals and areas. Our aim is to provoke, so we shall give our conclusion here: *None of the theories for which there is a lot of evidence can be shown to explain a major part of cross-individual or cross-area variation in treatments.* As a result, we suspect that new theory and empirical work will be needed to address this issue.

The chapter proceeds as follows. Section 2 examines the theory and evidence on the role of demand factors. Section 3 reviews the theory and evidence behind supply factors. Section 4 considers a set of situational factors and systems-level factors that have been shown to influence decision making, but have yet to be incorporated into economic models of treatment choices. Throughout, we focus on how such factors can help to understand treatment decisions.

2. HETEROGENEITY IN DEMAND

2.1. Price and Income Effects: Theory

It is straightforward to show that the demand functions above have a positive income effect and a negative own-price effect. Imagine that treatment 1 is more expensive than treatment 2—for example, treatment 1 might be a stent for stable angina, while treatment 2 might be medical management of the same condition. Recall equation (6.3) for choosing treatment 1 from above, where utility from non-medical consumption is $V(Y - P_i)$, P_i is the price the consumer pays for the treatment, and Y is income net of insurance premiums. Let τ be the right-hand side of equation (6.3). Then $d\tau/dY$ is given by (ignoring the k subscript):

$$d\tau/dY = V'(Y - P_2) - V'(Y - P_1) \tag{6.9}$$

With diminishing marginal utility ($V' > 0$ and $V'' < 0$); given that $P_1 > P_2$, it follows that $V'(Y - P_1) < V'(Y - P_2)$, and therefore $d\tau/dY < 0$. With a lower threshold for τ, the probability that $\theta_1 - \theta_2 > \tau$ increases, and thus higher income patients are more likely to desire treatment 1.

The effect of price on treatment choice is more complex, since one or both prices may change. In general:

$$d\tau = V'(Y - P_1)dP_1 - V'(Y - P_2)dP_2 \tag{6.10}$$

A change in a single price will have an unambiguous effect. For example, an increase in P_1 alone will increase τ (because $V' > 0$) and thus make consumers less likely to desire treatment 1. The opposite is true about an increase in P_2. An equal increase in both P_1 and P_2 has an ambiguous effect on demand for treatment 1, depending on which price is greater. This is akin to an income reduction. In a general setting where one "treatment" option is to do nothing, the consumer may choose to forego care as the price of all treatments increases.

The translation of patient demands into equilibrium outcomes is complex, as noted above. In the classic moral hazard models (Pauly, 1968; Zeckhauser, 1970), this is assumed away. Implicitly in those models, the supply of medical services is competitive: fees equal marginal cost and physicians are willing to supply anything demanded. Without a financial interest in the treatment choice, the physician acts as a perfect agent for the patient and equilibrium outcomes are equal to demand.

2.2. Empirical Evidence on Price and Income Effects

The theory about how prices and income affect treatment decisions makes generally clear predictions. The empirical question asks how large these effects are. There is a lengthy empirical literature on the income and price elasticities for medical care, beginning in the 1960s. The difficulty in estimating demand elasticities in observational data is that moral hazard and adverse selection both imply that better insurance is associated with use of more health care. Moral hazard posits that people exogenously assigned to lower cost sharing plans will use more services. Adverse selection denotes the tendency of people who expect they will use more medical care to choose insurance plans with lower cost sharing. Just observing that low cost sharing in insurance is correlated with high spending does not differentiate between the moral hazard and adverse selection explanations.

The importance of distinguishing moral hazard from adverse selection warranted a randomized experiment. The RAND Health Insurance Experiment (HIE), begun in the 1970s and lasting three to five years, was a controlled trial to empirically examine moral hazard. The HIE randomized approximately 2,750 families into plans with different levels of cost sharing: from essentially no cost sharing to roughly a catastrophic policy (albeit with only a moderate out-of-pocket deductible). Spending was recorded and related to the exogenous plan assignment. There were three important results from the HIE (Manning et al., 1987; Newhouse et al., 1993). First, spending is related to out-of-pocket price; the overall demand elasticity is about -0.2. This effect is statistically significant but modest in magnitude. Second, there is a small income elasticity for care, conditional on being insured; the elasticity is about 0.1. This elasticity is much smaller than the elasticity one gets by looking at area-level spending or cross-country evidence, likely reflecting the endogeneity of medical technology at the national level (Newhouse, 1992). For our purposes, the elasticity holding technology constant is the value of interest. Third, cost sharing affects whether a person gets into the system, but not what happens once a person is in the system. To take an example, cost sharing might influence whether a person with chest pain sees a cardiologist, but not what services the cardiologist performs once care has been initiated. This latter finding contradicts the predictions of the simple demand model, and thus demonstrates that the supply side is important as well.

At this point, the HIE is nearly 30 years old. Because the health care system has changed dramatically—there were few expensive prescription drugs when the HIE was conducted, for example—it is possible that the elasticities uncovered in the HIE are no longer applicable. In fact, research on the demand elasticity for care has continued since the RAND study. Researchers have pursued a variety of natural experiments. For example, some firms increase cost sharing in a year and other firms do not. If one believes these cost-sharing changes are orthogonal to other reasons why people might seek care, comparing patterns of care received between employees of firms that increased cost sharing and employees of firms that did not would allow us to learn about the demand elasticity for care. For example, three recent papers on the role of prices have found "offset" effects, a cross-price elasticity of demand. Chandra et al. (2010) found that while own-price elasticities for physician visits and prescription drug usage in an elderly population were similar to those of the RAND HIE, savings from increased cost sharing were offset by increased costs to Medicare for increased subsequent hospital care. Hsu et al. (2006) also found that savings derived from capping drug benefits were offset by increased spending on hospitalizations and emergency department visits. Similarly, Trivedi et al. (2010) found that increased cost sharing for ambulatory care among Medicare beneficiaries led to increased spending on hospital care. We provide several observations about this literature below; McGuire (2011, this Handbook) discusses it as well.

By and large, the HIE results hold up well. Most of the demand elasticities from these natural experiments are along the lines of the HIE. In some areas, the RAND results have been refined with newer data. In particular, recent studies show that:

- Use of prescription drugs is very price sensitive (Hsu et al., 2006; Huskamp et al., 2003; Joyce et al., 2002). In general, the literature finds elasticities of about −0.2 to −0.6 (Goldman and Joyce, this Handbook).

- People seem to cut back on both necessary and unnecessary care. When cost sharing increases, people use fewer services, but the services foregone are neither uniformly valuable nor wasteful (Buntin et al., 2011; Chandra et al., 2010).

- Higher cost sharing deters recommended preventive and chronic care, which may lead to undesirable "offsets" in greater use and spending on other services, such as hospital care (Trivedi et al., 2010; Chandra et al., 2010; Hsu et al., 2006). The economic theory of offsets is discussed in Goldman and Philipson (2007) and Newhouse (2006).

- There are complementarities across types of care (Buntin et al., 2011). Raising costs for prescription drugs increases hospital costs, and lowering costs for preventive care has only a modest effect on utilization if people need to see their primary care physician before accessing preventive care.

Because the price and income elasticities from the HIE and more recent studies are low, these standard demand factors are unlikely to explain the variation in treatment across individuals or over space. To put it simply: Among insured people with the same condition, cost sharing differs little, yet treatments vary a good deal. Several studies provide direct evidence for this. These studies use micro data to estimate models of medical spending as a function of health status, regional supply characteristics, insurance coverage, and income. They then evaluate the importance of demand factors relative to other characteristics. Typically, this analysis is done with samples of Medicare beneficiaries. This is valuable in part because everyone in the sample has the same base level of coverage, with no quantity or other non-price restrictions on use. Price varies to the extent that people have supplemental insurance, through Medicaid or private insurers.

As noted above, regional variation is extensive in the Medicare population. People living in areas with the highest quintile of spending use, on average, 50 percent more care than people living in areas with the lowest quintile of spending, and it is tempting to believe that area income is an important factor. Sutherland et al. (2009) show that virtually none of these regional differences is accounted for by differences in area income or poverty rates. Health status differences explain about 18 percent of the difference in spending across areas, and the rest is unaccounted for. The lack of a strong income effect is also shown by McClellan and Skinner (2006), who estimate that

Medicare spending is approximately equal across deciles of zip code income. However, there is some disagreement in the literature. In the Health and Retirement Study, for example, Marshall et al. (2010) find that out-of-pocket expenditures vary by wealth, as the richest 20 percent of households spend an average of $18,232 per year, versus $7,173 for the poorest 20 percent of households. These differences were driven by nursing home and home health care.

Zuckerman et al. (2010) estimate a similar model, including supplementary insurance coverage along with income and health status. Supplemental Medicaid coverage is associated with higher spending, while supplemental private insurance coverage is associated with lower spending—in each case perhaps reflecting selection unaccounted for by the health status controls. Still, the combined impact of supplemental insurance on regional differences in spending is small. They estimate that income and supplementary insurance together explain 1 percent of the higher spending in high-cost areas compared to low-cost areas. Thus, while price and income matter for spending, they are unlikely to explain a large part of why spending differs so much across people or areas.

2.3. Preferences

Preferences for different health outcomes (e.g. length vs. quality of life) differ across people. In the case of localized prostate cancer, for example, some men prefer to live with symptom-free cancer under conservative management, while others prefer treatment given its potential associated complications (Stewart et al., 2005). While age and disease severity may explain some of this variation (e.g. selection effects), variation remains (Shappley et al., 2009). Some of the remaining variation is owing to idiosyncratic factors. For example, prostate cancer patients report wildly unstable preferences for different health states that violate basic utility rank order assumptions (Dale et al., 2011). Moreover, preferences conveyed through subjective measures of well-being are subject to a host of psychological influences that often render them unreliable as a tool for comparisons across people (Smith et al., 2006, 2008; Ubel et al., 2005). Similarly, the literature on shared decision-making demonstrates that patients have different preferences, which can lead to different optimal treatments (Barry et al., 1995; Sepucha and Mulley, 2009). One interpretation of this is that preferences for health states vary across people, and the random variation from study to study reflects this. Yet the variation can also be driven by factors outside of the patient's demand. Sommers et al. (2008b) surveyed men who have been diagnosed with localized prostate cancer and are being treated using either surgery or radiation. Preferences for the side-effects of those treatments differ across men, but the care the men received does not correlate highly with those preferences.

The literature has not evaluated, in a general sense, how much patient preferences contribute to treatment differences across individuals or areas. There is some evidence that suggests it is small, however. For example, most patients prefer to die at home, but most actually die in a hospital (Pritchard et al., 1998). Angus et al. (2004) also found that some patients receive more intensive treatment at the end of life than they had preferred, while others received less. At the end of life, when the trade-off between length and quality of life becomes most salient, people actually have particularly strong preferences (e.g. they want their values to be respected, their symptoms to be well controlled, and their time with loved ones maximized) (Steinhauser et al., 2000). Yet intensive treatments are often delivered in place of palliative care. One explanation is poor communication of patient preferences, as patients are transferred to intensive settings and cared for by providers they have never met (Back et al., 2009).

However, another potential explanation is that physicians do not fully take into account patient preferences in clinical decision-making. Evidence suggests that traditional devices for communicating patient preferences to physicians, such as advance directives and orders to forego resuscitation, do not influence end-of-life treatments (Fagerlin and Schneider, 2004; Teno et al., 1997). Pritchard et al. (1998) found that where patients actually die has much more to do with where they live and supply-side factors than with the patient's preferences or demographic and clinical characteristics. In general, patient preferences for primary care and specialty care do not significantly explain regional variations in health care use (Anthony et al., 2009; Baicker et al., 2004; O'Hare et al., 2010).

Overall, our conjecture is that differences in preferences do not explain a large part of treatment variation—not because preferences do not differ, but because they are frequently not accounted for in actual treatment decisions. Indeed, this literature suggests that patients generally prefer less aggressive care than their physicians would recommend. Still, this is an area where more work would be quite valuable.

3. SUPPLY-SIDE DRIVERS OF CLINICAL DECISIONS

Medical care is ultimately provided or supervised by physicians. Understanding the motivation of physicians is critical. Just as the demand-side model simplified physicians to be perfect agents, supply-side models typically simplify patients to be comatose, uninformed, or unable to go elsewhere. In that setting, physicians maximize their utility, unconstrained by patient demands.

A less extreme assumption is that $B_i(\sigma)$ (a term that reflects the benefit to a patient from a particular treatment) in equations (6.6) and (6.7) reflects a constraint that patients cannot be too unhappy with the care received. For example, the threat of a patient leaving for another physician or bringing a lawsuit against the doctor may be increasing in the patient's level of unhappiness with her medical outcome. In this case, even physicians who care only about their own income will implicitly care about the benefits of treatment to the patient. Using equations (6.6) and (6.7), the physician will employ treatment 1 if:

$$W_j(1) > W_j(2) \rightarrow \beta_j(B_1(\sigma_k) - B_2(\sigma_k)) + (V(F_1) - V(F_2)) + (\varepsilon_{j1} - \varepsilon_{j2}) > 0 \quad (6.11)$$

If ε has a stochastic component, this will be a probabilistic expression, as in the optimal decision for the patient. If ε is deterministic, this will yield a definitive cutoff.

In this model, physicians will choose one treatment over another for one of four reasons. First, the benefits to the patient may differ. Second, different physicians may place different weight on patient benefits relative to profits β_j. The extent to which this affects medical practice is determined by physician professionalism and competition in the provider market. Third, the fees (net revenue) associated with the two treatments may induce physicians to provide more of one treatment. Assuming substitution effects dominate income effects, fee increases for treatment 1 will make physicians more likely to prescribe that therapy. Finally, there may be other, non-fee factors that influence care, such as capacity constraints, defensive medicine, or the combination of guidelines and experience.

3.1. Profits versus Patients

There is some evidence about how physicians value patient benefits versus their own net revenue, although the data are limited. Campbell et al. (2007b) surveyed approximately 1,600 physicians about norms and behaviors in professional practice. Ninety-six percent of the physicians agreed with the statement that "Physicians should put the patient's welfare above the physician's financial interests." Actual practices are not this pristine, however. When given the following scenario: "You and your partners have invested in a local imaging facility near your suburban practice. When referring patients for imaging studies, would you: 1. Refer your patients to this facility? 2. Refer your patients to this facility and inform patients of your investment? 3. Refer patients to another facility?" Twenty-four percent of physicians chose scenario 1— they would refer without informing the patients of the financial interest.

Further, there is some suggestion that β_j (professionalism) may vary significantly across areas, and that this may explain a reasonable part of the regional variation in care. In Gawande's (2009) description of care in McAllen and El Paso, Texas, he notes that physicians in McAllen seem to be more entrepreneurial than physicians in El Paso. Stories of dramatic overprovision of certain intensive services, such as angioplasties in Elyria, Ohio, which performs three times more angioplasties than neighboring Cleveland or Provo, Utah, where Medicare beneficiaries receive ten times more shoulder replacements than Syracuse, New York, suggest that professionalism and training play a role (Abelson, 2006; Fisher et al., 2010).

Further, it is plausible that physicians with high or low β_j would choose to work in the same area, or that it might be spread through a community. This discussion may make it seem that there are agglomerations in professionalism—and while there certainly are, there is no reason to believe that this is purely a regional phenomenon. To the extent that physicians with low levels of professionalism are scattered throughout all systems, the scope of improving the overall productivity of health care is large. While professionalism might not be immediately apparent, it partially determines provider income, different referral practices, different decisions about care, and so on. Understanding how professionalism—the extent to which patient well-being is traded off against economic interests—is created and destroyed, and how it affects outcomes, is a high priority for future research efforts.

As mentioned in the previous section, β_j may be a function of other physician incentives. Yet even if β_j were exogenous and equal to 1, implying that the physician cares only about patients' well-being and therefore would always choose the appropriate treatment that maximizes patient benefit (B_i), "appropriateness" can still be difficult to define. In fact, appropriateness may itself be endogenous. An illustrative example is the consensus definition of "an appropriate imaging study" determined by the American College of Cardiology Foundation, American Society of Echocardiography, and related medical societies (2011): "An appropriate imaging study is one in which the expected incremental information, combined with clinical judgment, exceeds the expected negative consequences [risks of the procedure (i.e. radiation or contrast exposure), downstream impact of poor test performance such as delay in diagnosis (false-negatives), or inappropriate diagnosis (false-positives)] by a sufficiently wide margin for a specific indication that the procedure is generally considered acceptable care and a reasonable approach for the indication." Such guidelines leave appropriateness open to interpretation. They also suggest that professionalism, if it is endogenous, may be a function of classic uncertainty (Arrow, 1963). For example, physicians may exhibit greater professionalism when the trade-off between benefits and costs—the width of the "sufficiently wide margin" in the definition above—is clear and salient. In clinical scenarios with less certainty, other incentives that offer certainty in physician gains may trump professionalism. The utility maximizing physician may be more likely to choose the better-reimbursed treatment, for example, when the field of treatment options presents no clear-cut winner *a priori*.

3.2. Payment Systems and Supplier-induced Demand

A substantial literature has examined the impact of payment systems on physician behavior. For recent reviews, see McClellan (2011) and McGuire (2000). The literature is clear that providers respond to payments, and that the response can be very large. These responses need not, of course, be referred to as "supplier-induced demand," which has a very specific meaning whereby the physician increases utilization by changing patients' desired treatments (demand).

The most salient example of the impact of payment systems on supply is the movement from fee-for-service payment to prospective payment. In 1983, the Medicare program moved from a retrospective, fee-for-service payment system for hospital care to the prospective, Diagnostic-Related Group (DRG) payment system. Thus, marginal reimbursement of additional days in the hospital, minor procedures, and tests went from greater than marginal cost to zero. The result was a large reduction in total hospital days (Coulam and Gaumer, 1991): the volume of hospital admissions dropped by 11 percent in the first eight years, while length of stay and total Medicare spending also declined sharply after 1983 (Hodgkin and McGuire, 1994; Ellis and McGuire, 1993).

Some of the inpatient days were substituted to an outpatient setting—beneficiaries who needed rehabilitation after a hip fracture, for example, were often transferred to a skilled nursing facility to receive that care, when it used to be provided in the hospital. For an integrated provider organization, this was beneficial because the skilled nursing facility could bill for rehabilitation services, whereas the hospital could not. In other cases, technology implemented about the time of prospective payment led to a reduction in inpatient days, for example the ability to do cataract surgery on an outpatient basis. Still, some inpatient days were eliminated as hospitals became more efficient. This reduction in inpatient usage was accomplished without significant adverse effects on patient health (Miller and Luft, 1994; Lurie et al., 1994; Cutler, 2004; Berwick, 1996).

Increasing services when fees are high is conceptually similar to reducing services that are underpriced. The literature gives a subset of this increase in services a special name, however: physician-induced demand. Physician-induced demand is defined as a physician providing care that a fully informed patient would not choose for himself. Note that physician-induced demand would not occur in a fully informed market— some degree of information asymmetry (as in Arrow, 1963) or other imperfection is needed to generate care off the demand curve. Similarly, some external constraint is needed to determine when physicians stop providing care, whether that is substantially lower benefits to the patient, fear of being sued, or professional norms. McGuire and Pauly (1991) provide a framework for thinking about induced demand in the context of multiple payers, in which income and substitution effects are important for determining treatment choice.

The literature has explored physician-induced demand in some detail. Early empirical studies tested the physician-induced demand explanation by looking for an "availability" effect: The hypothesis that an increase in the physician–population ratio, which should lead to a decrease in average income, will lead to more services being provided (Fuchs, 1978; Cromwell and Mitchell, 1986; see also Phelps, 1986; Feldman and Sloan, 1988). The general conclusion from these studies is that availability was positively associated with use. The difficulty with these studies is readily apparent, however: supply may be high because demand is high. Distinguishing whether greater equilibrium quantities are provided because supply is high or demand is high is always difficult, and is virtually impossible when prices are not allowed to adjust.

In more recent years, empirical studies have taken two approaches: (1) examining exogenous demand shocks and (2) studying changes in utilization following cuts in physician payment. In each case, the literature has generally hypothesized a backward bending supply curve, along the lines of a target-income model: if physicians' fees are reduced, do physicians provide more care, as a way of supplementing their income. Notable papers in this literature include Rossiter and Wilensky (1984); Dranove and Wehner (1994); Gruber and Owings (1996); Nguyen and Derrick (1997); Yip (1998); Jacobson et al. (2010); and Rice (1983). Yip (1998), for example, finds that following Medicare fee changes for cardiac bypass surgeries in 1988, physicians whose incomes were cut the most responded by performing greater quantities of these surgeries, both in Medicare and privately insured patients. Similarly, following the Medicare Prescription Drug, Improvement, and Modernization Act of 2003 which reduced payments for certain cancer drugs, physicians responded by raising the use of those drugs and substituting towards higher profit drugs (Jacobson et al., 2010). While none of these studies is entirely convincing, the belief in physician-induced demand has played a role in setting Medicare physician payment rates and influenced national policies concerning the physician supply (Reinhardt, 1999).

The role of fee differences in explaining different treatments across patients or areas is unknown. In the case of well-reimbursed patients versus poorly reimbursed patients (either uninsured patients or patients on Medicaid), the effect is clear: many physicians will not even see patients who have Medicaid or no insurance. For patients who are well insured, however, the differences are more difficult to discern. In the Medicare population, for example, fees are similar nationally, yet care differs across patients and regions. We suspect, in this circumstance, that it is not the absolute value of the fee that matters, but rather the relative weight that physicians place upon income versus patient benefits—the β_j term above.

3.3. Physician Specialization and Training

Physician specialty is an example of ε—a factor that may influence treatment separate from patient benefits and fees. It is clear that the specialty of the physician matters for treatment choice. Sommers et al. (2008b) show that when a man with localized prostate cancer sees an oncologist, he is more likely to be treated with chemotherapy, whereas if he sees a surgeon, he is more likely to receive a prostatectomy. Indeed, the physician that a patient sees matters far more for treatment than the patients' preferences (Sirovich et al., 2008). Yet it is also clear that the physician's specialty choice is endogenous. For example, physician wages across specialties vary enormously in the

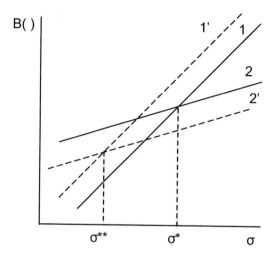

Figure 6.4 Productivity spillovers in the Roy model.

United States, from a mean hourly wage of $132 for neurologic surgery to $50 for primary care (Leigh et al., 2010). A physician-in-training who prefers to provide intensive treatments may specialize in an intensive field, holding constant other factors. Opportunities for specialization in medicine have blossomed in recent years (Cassel and Reuben, 2011).

While it is possible that the effect of physician specialty on utilization reflects physician-induced demand, more benign interpretations are also plausible. For example, it may be that physicians believe what they do is the best course of therapy, because they are trained that their expertise is important and because they experience the success of what they do on successful interventions. They may then translate this into their future recommendations. Alternatively, it may be that specialized physicians who work with uncommon diseases or sicker patients approach each patient as a unique situation and worry more about the marginal benefits specific to that patient, whereas generalists approach patients as part of a population and assign more weight to average benefits (Redelmeier and Tversky, 1990).

Indeed, specialization could matter in another way as well, by changing the true relative benefits of different forms of therapy. Chandra and Staiger (2007) posit increasing returns (positive spillovers) to specialization: in areas that do a lot of one therapy, physicians get better at it and thus render that therapy more optimal over time, even for patients who are less appropriate candidates for that therapy. Figure 6.4 shows an example of this specialization. The two lines denote the benefit from treatment 1 and 2 for patients with different disease severity (σ). Applied to the prostate cancer setting, treatment 1 may denote intensive treatment, which is more appropriate

Who Ordered That? The Economics of Treatment Choices in Medical Care

417

for younger and sicker men, while treatment 2 may represent active surveillance, more appropriate for older and healthier men. Empirical treatment patterns in the United States largely follow these age and severity dichotomies (Shappley et al., 2009). If treatment were allocated with the goal of maximizing patient outcomes, everyone to the left of σ^* would receive treatment 2. If there are benefits to specialization, then the benefit from treatment 1 also depends on the proportion of patients receiving treatment 1, P_1 (analogously, the benefit from treatment 2 depends on 1 minus the fraction of patients receiving treatment 1).

$$\mathbf{U_k}(1) = \alpha_1 P_1 + B_1(\sigma_k) + V(Y_{k1} - P_{k1}) + \theta_{k1} \tag{1'}$$

$$\mathbf{U_k}(2) = \alpha_2(1 - P_1) + B_2(\sigma_k) + V(Y_k - P_{k2}) + \theta_{k2} \tag{2'}$$

The curves 1' and 2' illustrate several implications of this specialization, which produce a new equilibrium, σ^{**}. Patients who are more appropriate for treatment 1 are better off getting it in areas where providers specialize in treatment 1. Patients more appropriate for treatment 2 are worse off in such areas. Any patient who gets treatment 1 in specialized areas would receive a larger benefit relative to getting it in non-specialized areas. Furthermore, the marginal patient receiving treatment 1 in specialized areas will be less appropriate for treatment 1 than the average patient receiving treatment 1.

Chandra and Staiger (2007) argue that this model explains some of the variation in rates and outcomes for heart attacks: areas that do surgery a good deal have better surgical outcomes than areas that are more prone to provide medical management, even given the extent of disease and patient characteristics. The negative and positive spillovers in this model imply that getting better at one type of care necessitates getting worse at the alternative. For example, if physicians have a time budget with which they trade off practicing treatment 1 against practicing treatment 2, and practice matters for outcomes, either choice would produce positive spillovers for the chosen treatment and negative spillovers for the other. In other words, physicians specialize in one skill at the expense of other skills. This simultaneous learning and forgetting of competing treatments may alternatively manifest in a world with selective migration of inputs.

In the clinical literature, a number of studies have uncovered an inverse relationship between procedural volume and adverse outcomes such as mortality, which has been termed the volume–outcome relationship (Birkmeyer et al., 2002; Dudley et al., 2000; van Heek et al., 2005). In this type of learning by doing, the volumes a physician provides of type 1 and type 2 procedures affect patient outcomes (here, N_1 and N_2 are the number of patients receiving each procedure):

$$\mathbf{U_k}(1) = \alpha_1 N_1 + B_1(\sigma_k) + V(Y_k - P_{k1}) + \theta_{k1} \tag{1''}$$

$$\mathbf{U_k}(2) = \alpha_2 N_2 + B_2(\sigma_k) + V(Y_k - P_{k2}) + \theta_{k2} \tag{2''}$$

Chandra and Staiger did not find evidence for this type of specialization in the context of heart attack treatments, but this theory has not been tested rigorously across different types of care, and doing so is a potentially fruitful area of research. Moreover, recent clinical work has suggested that volume may not be as strongly predictive of mortality as previously thought (Finks et al., 2011; Kozower and Stukenborg, 2011). The specialization theory provides a natural explanation for area variation in care, if not individual variation within an area.

Furthermore, independent of specialization, the physician's institution or location of training may matter—another example of ε. Anecdotal evidence in medicine suggests that where providers train heavily influences their treatment styles. The motto for medical training is "see one, do one, teach one." Training programs, including residency and fellowship, place the budding physician under the tutelage of experienced clinicians in a learning process resembling an apprenticeship. A trainee may often encounter the opinion that for the same procedure or the same protocol, one hospital does it one way while another does it another way. Among cardiologists given patient vignettes, whether their colleagues would have ordered a cardiac catheterization in the same situation predicts whether respondents ordered a catheterization (Lucas et al., 2010). Institutional effects owing to training programs undoubtedly fall into the poorly defined black box of within-firm decision-making determinants, which we further note below (section 4.5). There is some evidence on the differential outcomes of patients treated by physicians from highly ranked medical institutions compared to less highly ranked institutions (Doyle et al., 2010). However, evidence from Cesarean sections in Florida shows that while physicians do learn from other physicians, residency programs explain less than 4 percent of the variation in rates of operations (Epstein and Nicholson, 2009). Physicians did not seem to update their prior beliefs, even newly trained physicians, producing a within-area variation that approximately doubled between-area variation.

3.4. Defensive Medicine

Fear of being sued may affect the care that is provided (Lucas et al., 2010). The financial costs of malpractice associated with providing a particular service could be captured in F_i above. But being sued is rarely about the financial cost. Physicians are insured for malpractice expenses, and such expenses are independent of any specific treatment that is provided—though they depend on the specialty of the practice. Rather, the major costs of being sued are the time and energy involved in defending a lawsuit and the psychological costs of having one's professional judgment questioned. These show up in the X_i terms.

Responses to malpractice concerns may involve providing too much care, or too little care. The former is termed defensive medicine; the latter is stinting, or negative defensive medicine. An example of defensive medicine is doing imaging for a routine

Who Ordered That? The Economics of Treatment Choices in Medical Care

419

injury just to be sure that there is nothing seriously wrong. An example of stinting is obstetricians avoiding high-risk women, for fear that the baby will be impaired and they will be blamed. Negative defensive medicine would arise in a malpractice environment where adverse events such as injuries receive compensation even though malpractice had not occurred.

The combined effect of defensive medicine and stinting has been estimated in several studies (Brennan et al., 2004; Localio et al., 1991; Mello et al., 2010). These estimates are not without difficulty: measuring malpractice pressure in an area is difficult, and finding an exogenous measure of that is harder still. Even so, studies have surmounted this problem using area variation in malpractice premiums or other measures of malpractice pressure such as the size of indemnity payments. The results show a surprisingly small net contribution of malpractice concerns to what physicians do. Mello et al. (2010) estimate that medical malpractice and efforts to manage its risks cost the national health care system more than $55 billion a year, about 2.4 percent of annual health care spending. The study summed various components of the medical liability system, including payments made to malpractice plaintiffs; defensive medicine costs; administrative costs, such as lawyer fees; and the costs of lost clinician work time. Defensive medicine costs were the largest segment of total malpractice spending and amounted to approximately $45 billion a year annually. In other work, Baicker et al. (2007) note that malpractice pressure increases the use of imaging procedures but exerts a small overall effect on total spending, perhaps because of the presence of negative defensive medicine.

Almost all of the research quantifying the scope of defensive medicine relies on cross-sectional or panel variation in the relationship between medical spending and malpractice pressure. But this design may understate the amount of defensive medicine if physicians in one state are influenced by the malpractice experience of their friends and colleagues in other states. We have little guidance on how physicians assess the threat of litigation and understanding this channel would be a fruitful area for future work.

4. SITUATIONAL FACTORS

This section is about the error term determining treatment choice. Despite knowing the contributions of income, geography, health status, reimbursement, and other factors in treatment variations, there remains substantial variation in treatment choices. What is the source of this variation? We suspect it may derive from influences specific to the clinical situation in which the treatment determination is made. Such influences would do less to explain regional variation as they are largely orthogonal to geography. In particular, we suspect that physicians and patients follow a number of psychological heuristics, or rules of thumb, which affect clinical decision making in similar ways across regions.

A growing literature in behavioral economics offers a starting point for unpacking these behavioral influences. Frank and Zeckhauser (2007) theorize that physicians deploy heuristics-based ("ready-to-wear") treatments because they minimize a number of behavioral costs relative to patient-specific ("custom-made") treatments. These costs include the cost of patient–doctor communication regarding treatment choices, cognition costs of coming up with custom-made treatments, coordination costs between providers in the increasingly specialized medical profession, and system-level capability or resource costs. Broadly using this framework as a guide, we survey a number of specific behavioral influences below.

4.1. Availability Heuristic

Determining the optimal treatment path among a list of possibilities may require effort and time, which are not costless to the physician. As a result, physicians resort to the *availability heuristic* to make decisions (Groopman, 2007). The availability heuristic refers to the idea that people predict the frequency of an event by the ease with which it comes to mind. Airplane crashes are salient; stomach cancer may be less salient. Thus, people may believe that airplane crashes are a more common cause of death than stomach cancer, even though death from stomach cancer is actually five times more common (Lichtenstein et al., 1978). Since the occurrence of salient events is stochastic, the availability heuristic naturally introduces randomness into treatment choice.

In diagnosis, the availability heuristic suggests that a physician who has just seen a patient with influenza may be more likely to make the diagnosis of influenza for the next patient who walks through the door with a cough, even if this latter patient has a rare lung disease. The reverse may be true if there was a recent case of lung cancer.

Choudhry et al. (2006) found some empirical evidence for this. They showed that physicians who treated a patient with warfarin (a blood thinning drug with the risk of bleeding) and saw that patient experience an adverse bleeding event were 21 percent less likely to prescribe warfarin to other patients for which warfarin is indicated, even 90 days after the adverse bleeding event. The availability heuristic gives the physician a decision-making shortcut that allows the physician to recall and reuse information from the most recent salient cases.

An important note about the availability heuristic is that it is applicable in the absence of easily obtainable information on true risks. Were patients and physicians presented systematic odds about the likelihood of every diagnosis and the appropriate diagnostic tests given those likelihoods, the availability heuristic would be much less operative.

Who Ordered That? The Economics of Treatment Choices in Medical Care

421

4.2. Framing, Choice, and Risk

Framing and choice architecture affect decision making (Thaler and Sunstein, 2008; Botti and Iyengar, 2006; Ubel, 2009). For example, if a physician faces a growing number of treatment choices, all of which are plausible for a patient, the task of choosing one becomes increasingly difficult. In the classic example, supermarket shoppers presented with six different flavors of jelly were able to choose among them, but shoppers presented with 30 brands found the choice too complex and were one-tenth as likely to make a purchase (Iyengar and Lepper, 2000).

Evidence shows that both health care professionals and patients are susceptible to the framing of choice in clinical decisions (Akl et al., 2011; Sommers and Zeckhauser, 2008a; Redelmeier and Tversky, 1990; McNeil et al., 1982). In a systematic review of 35 studies, both providers and patients understood natural frequencies better than probabilities in the presentation of risk (Akl et al., 2011). For example, a 50 percent risk reduction was perceived to be substantially larger than an absolute risk reduction from 2 to 1 percent. Statistics presented as number needed to treat were least persuasive, such as 100 people treated to prevent one case of the disease. Perhaps because of this, there is widespread overly aggressive screening and treatment in prostate cancer (Drazer et al., 2011; Schröder et al., 2009).

Indeed, classic risk aversion may drive decision making for both patients and physicians. Moreover, the magnitude of risk aversion may depend on the clinical scenario, implying that the classic Arrow–Pratt coefficient of risk aversion may not be exogenous at the individual level, but may be a function of the situation. In the simplest example, a clinician's experience dealing with a particular situation may affect risk aversion, as younger physicians often order more procedures than more experienced physicians (Woo et al., 1985). We can also think about how risk aversion would influence the theoretical model set forth in sections 2 and 3. On the physician side, risk aversion can take (at least) two forms. First, physicians may avoid prescribing a treatment that is high risk for the fear of harming the patient (uncertainty in $B_i(\sigma_k)$). Second, physicians may avoid such a treatment for the fear of malpractice litigation (uncertainty in $V(F_i)$). Importantly, such a treatment can be the "do nothing" option, especially in a world in which physicians and patients are loss averse. Depending on the clinical scenario, these two forces may combine to push the physician towards prescribing the state-of-the-art laparoscopic surgery, for example, which lowers blood loss and length of stay. Or these two forces may antagonize each other in cases where low risk for patient benefit $B(\ )$ is high risk for the physician's income $V(\ )$, such as watchful waiting in the case of prostate cancer. On the demand side, patients may similarly be risk averse in the level of uncertainty about $B(\ )$.

In our simple model, increased utilization of certain services may arise when both parties express risk aversion or when either party does. Suppose physicians are fully benevolent ($\beta = 1$), whereby patient preferences dictate the decisions. Suppose also that the patient is risk averse. In this situation, if patients push for the latest and greatest technologies, that is enough to lead to utilization and spending on those treatment options.

4.3. Status Quo and Confirmation Bias

Status quo bias refers to the fact that people tend not to change their behavior unless the incentive to change is strong. In the treatment decision setting, aversion to change can lead to status quo bias. For physicians, changing treatment choices, even the mere process of discussing alternative options with patients, can be very costly (Groopman, 2006). Human beings are also naturally loss averse, so the risk and uncertainty imposed by changing to a new treatment may similarly bias physicians towards familiar paths. For example, physicians may have a favorite drug within a class of equivalent substitutes. The source of this preference may be orthogonal to anything we have considered thus far. Yet the consequence of it is a bias towards this drug.

Patients are also prone to status quo bias, and patients' inertia to change is prevalent outside of the treatment decision. For example, more people stay in their insurance plan from year to year than would be expected to do so, given the value of different policies and the price of those policies. In fact, people often stay in insurance plans dominated in every state of the world, but it is the plan they chose last year (Kahneman et al., 1991).

This status quo bias may be further driven by a self-reinforcing confirmation bias in which prior successes from one treatment induce the provider to continue using that treatment. Confirmation bias describes the idea that people interpret new information in light of their pre-existing biases (Myers and Lamm, 1976; Halpern, 1987). Specialization may be a source of this confirmation bias (Sommers et al., 2008b). A specialist that has experienced success with a particular treatment—for example, radical prostatectomy for patients with localized prostate cancer—will judge that treatment to be effective in a wider range of patients, likely even wider than objective literature would indicate. Whether this judgment is substantiated by any positive spillovers in the learning-by-doing sense, however, is an open question.

4.4. Channel Factors

Channel factors may also play an important role in determining treatment choice. A channel factor is something that affects perceived benefits and costs towards pursuing a particular choice. In a classic example, college seniors given a positive message about tetanus inoculation changed their beliefs about the value of a tetanus inoculation, but few got inoculated. Only when students were also given a map of the campus with the infirmary circled and asked to choose a particular time for inoculation (with no consequence for missing it) did they get inoculated (Bertrand et al., 2004). Channel factors, including a map, a predetermined time, or physical proximity, seem to trump information alone.

There are also unique channel factors in a variety of clinical scenarios. Drug adherence, for example, is a particularly intriguing area. Only about 50 percent of patients adhere to their prescribed drug regimens. Economists often look to the role of cost sharing in determining such variation (Shrank et al., 2010). But even when drugs come with no cost sharing, adherence is not close to 100 percent. One example of a relevant channel factor here is route of medication intake. Consider the drugs Vancomycin and Linezolid, both treatments for methicillin-resistant *Staphylococcus aureus* (an antibiotic-resistant bacterial infection often picked up during hospitalizations). Linezolid is available as an oral medication, facilitating adherence, while Vancomycin is not. While both are equally effective in survival benefit and readmission rates, Linezolid had a lower rate of therapy discontinuation (Caffrey et al., 2010).

4.5. Resource/Capability Factors

To this point, we have modeled the treatment decision as being made by the patient, the individual doctor, or a combination of the two. That may not be right, however. Most providers work in organizations, and the organization itself, or possibly the insurer, may influence the care that is provided. Suppose that the provider is instead a hospital firm that produces medical care. How does the firm internally decide what to produce (or allow) for each type of patient (consumer)? Inside the firm are doctors, each of whom may have his or her own intrinsic views about utilization, and decision-making structure (Snail and Robinson, 1998; Harris, 1977).

The internal decision-making processes of firms have remained largely a black box to economists (Hart and Holmstrom, 2010; Williamson, 2010; Gibbons, 2005; Holmstrom and Roberts, 1998; Gibbons, 1998). Inside the firm, employment contracts, agency contracts, and relational contracts may all affect the production process and treatment choice of the provider. The difficulty of specifying these contracts precisely makes the analysis of treatment choices by health care providers especially difficult—especially given the unique agency and moral hazard complexities in health care. However, there are identifiable components of the provider organization (either the hospital firm or the physician firm) that may influence treatment choice.

Treatment choices may also be influenced by ancillary relationships between the provider and institutions or entities outside of the provider–patient relationship. Pharmaceutical manufacturers and medical device companies spend billions of dollars each year marketing products directly to physicians (see Scott Morton and Kyle, 2011, this Handbook). There are overt conflicts of interests which mechanically influence treatment, where physicians may receive kickbacks for providing a certain drug, although there are federal statutes against such relationships. There are informal relationships where physicians receive fees and vacations in exchange for speaking engagements and informal product endorsements. Then there are psychological influences of reciprocity, where even free samples and free lunch offered by industry sales representatives with no strings attached have been shown to change behavior through intrinsic reciprocity (Fehr and Gächter, 2000).

In 2007, Campbell and colleagues published a national survey of 459 medical school department chairs at 140 institutions, which found that 67 percent of departments and 60 percent of department chairs have relationships with industry. In this study, non-clinical departments were more likely to enter into relationships with industry compared to clinical departments, which the authors attribute to the likely greater degree of licensing and product development activities associated with non-clinical departments. Clinical departments, on the other hand, were far more likely to receive discretionary funding to purchase equipment and support research seminars, graduate medical education, and continuing medical education (Campbell et al., 2007a). A study of patients found that 90 percent of participants in cancer-research trials expressed little worry about financial ties between institutions or researchers and drug companies (Hampson et al., 2006).

Systems-level health care resources matter. Not all resources are available in all settings. Resource-poor settings, for example, rarely have the ability to purchase a state-of-the-art 64-slice CT scanner, whereas an urban academic medical center often can. Consumers in some places may demand more new technology than people in other places, thereby creating a more robust market for technology in places with high demand. Direct-to-consumer advertising from drug or device manufacturers can also induce such a market and catalyze diffusion (Law et al., 2008).

A literature in sociology and management shows that technological innovations diffuse at different rates in different places (Rogers, 1983). The dynamics of diffusion are described by Thomas Schelling among others, who wrote about the tipping point theory (Schelling, 2006). In later work, scholars have expanded upon Schelling's intuition to model and empirically investigate diffusion of innovations (Young, 1998). Differences in adoption are both large and persistent. In a well-documented example, the state-level adoption rate of beta-blockers in the 1980s—a technology to reduce recurrent heart attacks in people who have had a first—was highly correlated with the state-level adoption rate of hybrid corn in the 1950s (Skinner and Staiger, 2005).

Diffusion also has long-run implications for productivity in health care. Skinner and Staiger (2009) find that even small differences in the likelihood of adoption can lead to large differences in productivity across hospitals. Specifically, they find that in the case of heart attack treatments, the speed of diffusion of low-cost technologies such as beta-blockers, aspirin, and primary reperfusion explain the bulk of long-run variations in productivity, overwhelming the impact of traditional factor inputs.

Relative to high-diffusion hospitals, survival rates in low-diffusion hospitals can lag by a decade. Adoption, or uptake, of medical technology can vary for many reasons (Chandra and Skinner, 2011). The structure of provider organizations, the culture of physicians, market power, physician specialization, and the payment system can all affect uptake. Differential adoption is particularly important given the large role that medical technology plays in treatment changes over time (Chernew and Newhouse, 2011, this Handbook).

5. CONCLUSION

The geographic variations literature demonstrates that despite nationally standardized training, physicians in different geographic locations can make markedly different treatment decisions for patients with similar clinical profiles. This was the first evidence to suggest that providers of medical care may not, as a profession, systematically choose the clinically optimal treatment path for patients. Where early literature in health economics mostly focused on the possibility of physician-induced demand—which concerned quantity more so than choice—we attempt to decompose potential explanations for variations in treatment choice.

In general, the literature points to the importance of supply-side incentives over demand-side factors in driving treatment choice. Our views are largely consistent with this paradigm. Yet traditional demand factors such as preferences and patient characteristics are undoubtedly still relevant, and behavioral influences are only beginning to be understood. In the end, one of the ultimate goals of understanding how treatment choices are made is to inform policies that move physician and patient choices towards the social optimum, even as our framework for thinking about treatment choice still rests largely on models of local (i.e. individual) optimum.

The challenges are numerous, owing to the peculiarities of medicine. In this world where the very definition of optimality rests on numerous endogenous determinants, where the supplier who judges relative merits of treatments is the same supplier who directly benefits (or loses) from the decision, and where the appropriateness of patients for any given treatment is, at best, open to interpretation and, at worst, completely unknown, understanding the determinants of treatment choice will be an ever-evolving task.

REFERENCES

Abelson, R. (2006). Heart procedure is off the charts in an Ohio City. *New York Times*, August 18.
Akl, E. A., Oxman, A. D., Herrin, J., Vist, G. E., Terrenato, I., Sperati, F., et al. (2011). Using alternative statistical formats for presenting risks and risk reductions. *Cochrane Database of Systematic Reviews, 3*, CD006776.

American College of Cardiology Foundation, Appropriate Use Criteria Task Force, et al. (2011). Appropriate use criteria for echocardiography. *Journal of the American College of Cardiology, 57*(9), 1126–1166.

American Joint Committee on Cancer (2010). *AJCC cancer staging manual* (7th ed.). New York: Springer, Inc.

Angus, D. C., Barnato, A. E., Linde-Swirble, W. T., et al. (2004). Use of intensive care at the end of life in the United States: An epidemiologic study. *Critical Care Medicine, 32*, 638–643.

Anthony, D. L., Brooke Herndon, M., Gallagher, P. M., Barnato, A. E., Bynum, J. P. W., Gottlieb, D. J., et al. (2009). How much do patients' preferences contribute to resource use? *Health Affairs, 28*(3), 864–873.

Arrow, K. J. (1963). Uncertainty and the welfare economics of medical care. *American Economic Review, 53*, 941–973.

Atkins, D., Best, D., Briss, P. A., Eccles, M., Falck-Ytter, Y., Flottorp, S., et al. (2004). Grading quality of evidence and strength of recommendations. *BMJ, 328*(7454), 1490.

Back, A. L., Young, J. P., McCown, E., et al. (2009). Abandonment at the end of life from patient, caregiver, nurse, and physician perspectives: Loss of continuity and lack of closure. *Archives of Internal Medicine, 169*(5), 474–479.

Baicker, K. & Chandra, A. (2004). Medicare spending, the physician workforce, and beneficiaries' quality of care. *Health Affairs (Millwood),* Suppl. Web Exclusives: W4-184-97.

Baicker, K., Chandra, A., Skinner, J. S., & Wennberg, J. E. (2004). Who you are and where you live: How race and geography affect the treatment of Medicare beneficiaries. *Health Affairs (Millwood),* Suppl. Variation: VAR33–44.

Baicker, K., Fisher, E. S., & Chandra, A. (2007). Malpractice liability costs and the practice of medicine in the Medicare program. *Health Affairs, 26*(3, May–June), 841–852.

Barry, M. J., Fowler, F. J., Jr., Mulley, A. G., Jr., Henderson, J. V., Jr., & Wennberg, J. E. (1995). Patient reactions to a program designed to facilitate patient participation in treatment decisions for benign prostatic hyperplasia. *Medical Care, 33*(8), 771–782.

Bertrand, M., Mullainathan, S., & Shafir, E. (2004). A behavioral-economics view of poverty. *American Economic Review, 94*(2), 419–423.

Berwick, D. M. (1996). Quality of health care. Part 5: Payment by capitation and the quality of care. *New England Journal of Medicine, 335*(16), 1227–1231.

Bill-Axelson, A., Holmberg, L., Ruutu, M., Häggman, M., Andersson, S. O., Bratell, S., et al. (2005). Radical prostatectomy versus watchful waiting in early prostate cancer. *New England Journal of Medicine, 352*(19), 1977–1984.

Birkmeyer, J. D., Siewers, A. E., Finlayson, E. V., et al. (2002). Hospital volume and surgical mortality in the United States. *New England Journal of Medicine, 346*, 1128–1137.

Boden, W. E., O'Rourke, R. A., Teo, K. K., et al. (2007). Optimal medical therapy with or without PCI for stable coronary disease. *New England Journal of Medicine, 356*(15), 1503–1516.

Bolla, M., Gonzalez, D., Warde, P., Dubois, J. B., Mirimanoff, R. O., Storme, G., et al. (1997). Improved survival in patients with locally advanced prostate cancer treated with radiotherapy and goserelin. *New England Journal of Medicine, 337*(5), 295–300.

Botti, S. & Iyengar, S. S. (2006). The dark side of choice: When choice impairs social welfare. *Journal of Public Policy and Marketing, 25*(1), 24–38.

Brennan, T. A., Leape, L. L., Laird, N. M., Hebert, L., Localio, A. R., Lawthers, A. G., et al. (2004). Incidence of adverse events and negligence in hospitalized patients: Results of the Harvard Medical Practice Study I. 1991. *Quality & Safety in Health Care, 13*(2), 145–151.

Buntin, M. B., Haviland, A. M., McDevitt, R., & Sood, N. (2011). Healthcare spending and preventive care in high-deductible and consumer-directed health plans. *American Journal of Management Care, 17*(3), 222–230.

Caffrey, A. R., Quilliam, B. J., & LaPlante, K. L. (2010). Comparative effectiveness of linezolid and vancomycin among a national cohort of patients infected with methicillin-resistant Staphylococcus aureus. *Antimicrobial Agents Chemotherapy, 54*(10), 4394–4400.

Campbell, E. G., Regan, S., Gruen, R. L., Ferris, T. G., Rao, S. R., Cleary, P. D., et al. (2007b). Professionalism in medicine: Results of a national survey of physicians. *Annals of Internal Medicine, 147*(11), 795–802.

Campbell, E. G., Weissman, J. S., Ehringhaus, S., Rao, S. R., Moy, B., Feibelmann, S., et al. (2007a). Institutional academic industry relationships. *JAMA*, *298*(15), 1779–1786.

Cassel, C. K. & Reuben, D. B. (2011). Specialization, subspecialization, and subsubspecialization in internal medicine. *New England Journal of Medicine*, *364*(12), 1169–1173.

Chandra, A. & Skinner, J. S. (2011). Technology growth and expenditure growth in health care. NBER Working Paper 16953.

Chandra, A. & Staiger, D. O. (2007). Productivity spillovers in health care: Evidence from the treatment of heart attacks. *Journal of Political Economy*, *115*(1), 103–140.

Chandra, A., Gruber, J., & McKnight, R. (2010). Patient cost-sharing and hospitalization offsets in the elderly. *American Economic Review*, *100*(1), 193–213.

Choudhry, N. K., Anderson, G. M., Laupacis, A., Ross-Degnan, D., Normand, S. L., & Soumerai, S. B. (2006). Impact of adverse events on prescribing warfarin in patients with atrial fibrillation: Matched pair analysis. *BMJ*, *332*(7534), 141–145.

Cooper, R. A. (2004). Weighing the evidence for expanding physician supply. *Annals of Internal Medicine*, *141*(9), 705–714.

Cooperberg, M. R., Broering, J. M., Kantoff, P. W., & Carroll, P. R. (2007). Contemporary trends in low risk prostate cancer: Risk assessment and treatment. *Journal of Urology*, *178*(3 Pt 2), S14–S19.

Coulam, R. F. & Gaumer, G. L. (1991). Medicare's prospective payment system: A critical appraisal. *Health Care Financing Review*, Annual Supplement, 45–77.

Cromwell, J. & Mitchell, J. B. (1986). Physician-induced demand for surgery. *Journal of Health Economics*, *5*, 293–313.

Cutler, D. M. (2004). *Your money or your life: Strong medicine for America's healthcare system*. Oxford University Press.

Dahm, P., Yeung, L. L., Chang, S. S., & Cookson, M. S. (2008). A critical review of clinical practice guidelines for the management of clinically localized prostate cancer. *Journal of Urology*, *180*(2), 451–459.

Dale, W., Bilir, S. P., Hemmerich, J., Basu, A., Elstein, A., & Meltzer, D. (2011). The prevalence, correlates, and impact of logically inconsistent preferences in utility assessments for joint health states in prostate cancer. *Medical Care*, *49*(1), 59–66.

Doyle, J. J., Jr., Ewer, S. M., & Wagner, T. H. (2010). Returns to physician human capital: Evidence from patients randomized to physician teams. *Journal of Health Economics*, *29*(6), 866–882.

Dranove, D. & Wehner, P. (1994). Physician-induced demand for childbirths. *Journal of Health Economics*, *13*, 61–73.

Drazer, M. W., Huo, D., Schonberg, M. A., Razmaria, A., & Eggener, S. E. (2011). Population-based patterns and predictors of prostate-specific antigen screening among older men in the United States. *Journal of Clinical Oncology*, *29*(13), 1736–1743.

Dudley, R. A., Johansen, K. L., Brand, R., Rennie, D. J., & Milstein, A. (2000). Selective referral to high-volume hospitals: Estimating potentially avoidable deaths. *JAMA*, *283*, 1159–1166.

Ellis, R. P. & McGuire, T. G. (1986). Provider behavior under prospective reimbursement. *Journal of Health Economics*, *5*, 129–151.

Ellis, R. P. & McGuire, T. G. (1993). Supply-side and demand-side cost sharing in health care. *Journal of Economic Perspectives*, *7*(4), 135–151.

Epstein, A. J. & Nicholson, S. (2009). The formation and evolution of physician treatment styles: An application to cesarean sections. *Journal of Health Economics*, *28*(6), 1126–1240.

Fagerlin, A. & Schneider, C. E. (2004). Enough: The failure of the living will. *Hastings Center Report*, 34, 30–42.

Fehr, E. & Gächter, S. (2000). Fairness and retaliation: The economics of reciprocity. *Journal of Economic Perspectives*, *14*(3), 159–181.

Feldman, R. & Sloan, F. (1988). Competition among physicians, revisited. *Journal of Health Politics, Policy and Law*, *13*, 239–261.

Finks, J. F., Osborne, N. H., & Birkmeyer, J. D. (2011). Trends in hospital volume and operative mortality for high-risk surgery. *New England Journal of Medicine*, *364*(22), 2128–2137.

Fisher, E. S., Bell, J., Tomek, I. M., Esty, A. R., & Goodman, D. C. (2010). Trends and regional variation in hip, knee, and shoulder replacement. *The Dartmouth Institute for Health Policy and Clinical Practice*, April 6.

Fisher, E. S., Wennberg, D. E., Stukel, T. A., Gottlieb, D. J., Lucas, F. L., & Pinder, E. L. (2003a). The implications of regional variations in Medicare spending. Part 1: The content, quality, and accessibility of care. *Annals of Internal Medicine, 138*(4), 273–287.

Fisher, E. S., Wennberg, D. E., Stukel, T. A., Gottlieb, D. J., Lucas, F. L., & Pinder, E. L. (2003b). The implications of regional variations in Medicare spending. Part 2: Health outcomes and satisfaction with care. *Annals of Internal Medicine, 138*(4), 288–298.

Frank, R. G. & Zeckhauser, R. J. (2007). Custom-made versus ready-to-wear treatments: Behavioral propensities in physicians' choices. *Journal of Health Economics, 26*(6), 1101–1127.

Fuchs, V. R. (1978). The supply of surgeons and the demand for operations. *Journal of Human Resources, XIII*, 35–56.

Gawande, A. (2009). The cost conundrum: What a Texas town can teach us all about health care. *The New Yorker*, June 1.

Gibbons, R. (1998). Incentives in organizations. *Journal of Economic Perspectives, 12*(4), 115–132.

Gibbons, R. (2005). Four formal(izable) theories of the firm? *Journal of Economic Behavior & Organization, 58*, 200–245.

Glover, J. A. (1938). The incidence of tonsillectomy in children. *Proceeding of the Royal Society of Medicine, 31*, 1219–1236.

Goldman, D. & Philipson, T. J. (2007). Integrated insurance design in the presence of multiple medical technologies. *American Economic Review, 97*(2), 427–432.

Groopman, J. (2007). *How doctors think*. New York: Houghton Mifflin.

Gruber, J. & Owings, M. (1996). Physician financial incentives and Cesarean section delivery. *RAND Journal of Economics, 27*, 99–123.

Halpern, D. F. (1987). *Critical thinking across the curriculum: A brief edition of thought and knowledge*. Lawrence Erlbaum Associates.

Hampson, L. A., Agrawal, M., Joffe, S., Gross, C. P., Verter, J., & Emanuel, E. J. (2006). Patients' views on financial conflicts of interest in cancer research trials. *New England Journal of Medicine, 355*(22), 2330–2337.

Harris, J. E. (1977). The internal organization of hospitals: Some economic implications. *Bell Journal of Economics, 8*(2), 467–482.

Hart, O. & Holmstrom, B. (2010). A theory of firm scope. *Quarterly Journal of Economics, CXXV*(2), 483–513.

Hayes, J. H., Ollendorf, D. A., Pearson, S. D., Barry, M. J., Kantoff, P. W., Stewart, S. T., et al. (2010). Active surveillance compared with initial treatment for men with low-risk prostate cancer: A decision analysis. *JAMA, 304*(21), 2373–2380.

Hodgkin, D. & McGuire, T. G. (1994). Payment levels and hospital response to prospective payment. *Journal of Health Economics, 13*(1), 1–29.

Holmstrom, B. & Roberts, J. (1998). The boundaries of the firm revisited. *Journal of Economic Perspectives, 12*(4), 73–94.

Howlader, N., Noone, A. M., Krapcho, M., Neyman, N., Aminou, R., & Waldron, W. (Eds.) (2011). *SEER cancer statistics review, 1975–2008*. Bethesda, MD: National Cancer Institute.

Hsu, J., Price, M., Huang, J., Brand, R., Fung, V., Hui, R., et al. (2006). Unintended consequences of caps on Medicare drug benefits. *New England Journal of Medicine, 354*(22), 2349–2359.

Huskamp, H. A., Deverka, P. A., Epstein, A. M., Epstein, R. S., McGuigan, K. A., & Frank, R. G. (2003). The effect of incentive-based formularies on prescription-drug utilization and spending. *New England Journal of Medicine, 349*(23), 2224–2232.

Iyengar, S. S. & Lepper, M. R. (2000). When choice is demotivating: Can one desire too much of a good thing? *Journal of Personality and Social Psychology, 79*(6), 995–1006.

Jacobson, M., Earle, C. C., Price, M., & Newhouse, J. P. (2010). How Medicare's payment cuts for cancer chemotherapy drugs changed patterns of treatment. *Health Affairs (Millwood), 29*(7), 1391–1399.

Jemal, A., Siegel, R., Ward, E., Hao, Y., Xu, J., & Thun, M. J. (2009). Cancer statistics, 2009. *CA Cancer Journal for Clinicians, 59*(4), 225–249.

Joyce, G. F., Escarce, J. J., Solomon, M. D., & Goldman, D. P. (2002). Employer drug benefit plans and spending on prescription drugs. *JAMA, 288*(14), 1733–1739.

Kahneman, D., Knetsch, J. L., & Thaler, R. H. (1991). Anomalies: The endowment effect, loss aversion, and status quo bias. *Journal of Economic Perspectives, 5*(1), 193–206.

Kolata, G. (2010). Results unproven, robotic surgery wins converts. *The New York Times*, February 13.

Kozower, B. D. & Stukenborg, G. J. (2011). The relationship between hospital lung cancer resection volume and patient mortality risk: study design: original observational research (population based cohort study). *Annals of Surgery* [Epub ahead of print].

Law, M. R., Majumdar, S. R., & Soumerai, S. B. (2008). Effect of illicit direct to consumer advertising on use of etanercept, mometasone, and tegaserod in Canada: Controlled longitudinal study. *BMJ, 337*, a1055.

Lee, D. H. & Vielemeyer, O. (2011). Analysis of overall level of evidence behind Infectious Diseases Society of America practice guidelines. *Archives of Internal Medicine, 171*(1), 18–22.

Leigh, J. P., Tancredi, D., Jerant, A., & Kravitz, R. L. (2010). Physician wages across specialties: Informing the physician reimbursement debate. *Archives of Internal Medicine, 170*(19), 1728–1734.

Lichtenstein, S., Slovic, P., Fischhoff, B., Layman, M., & Combs, B. (1978). Judged frequency of lethal events. *Journal of Experimental Psychology: Human Learning and Memory, 4*, 551–578.

Litwin, M. S., Gore, J. L., Kwan, L., Brandeis, J. M., Lee, S. P., Withers, H. R., et al. (2007). Quality of life after surgery, external beam irradiation, or brachytherapy for early-stage prostate cancer. *Cancer, 109*(11), 2239–2247.

Localio, A. R., Lawthers, A. G., Brennan, T. A., Laird, N. M., Hebert, L. E., Peterson, L. M., et al. (1991). Relation between malpractice claims and adverse events due to negligence. Results of the Harvard Medical Practice Study III. *New England Journal of Medicine, 325*(4), 245–251.

Lucas, F. L., Sirovich, B. E., Gallagher, P. M., Siewers, A. E., & Wennberg, D. E. (2010). Variation in cardiologists' propensity to test and treat: Is it associated with regional variation in utilization? *Circulation: Cardiovascular Quality and Outcomes, 3*(3), 253–260.

Lurie, N., Christianson, J., Finch, M., & Moscovice, I. (1994). The effects of capitation on health and functional status of the Medicaid elderly: A randomized trial. *Annals of Internal Medicine, 120*, 506–511.

Manning, W. G., Newhouse, J. P., Duan, N., Keeler, E., Leibowitz, A., & Marquis, M. S. (1987). Health insurance and the demand for medical care: Results from a randomized experiment. *American Economic Review, 77*(3, June), 251–277.

Marshall, S., McGarry, K. M., & Skinner, J. S. (2010). The risk of out-of-pocket health care expenditure at end of life. NBER Working Paper No. 16170.

McClellan, M. (2011). Reforming payments to healthcare providers: The key to slowing healthcare cost growth while improving quality? *Journal of Economic Perspectives, 25*(2), 69–92.

McClellan, M. & Skinner, J. (2006). The incidence of Medicare. *Journal of Public Economics, 90*, 257–276.

McGuire, T. G. (2000). Physician agency. In A. J. Culyer & J. P. Newhouse (Eds.), *Handbook of health economics*. Amsterdam: Elsevier (Chapter 9).

McGuire, T. G. & Pauly, M. V. (1991). Physician response to fee changes with multiple payers. *Journal of Health Economics, 10*(4), 385–410.

McNeil, B. J., Pauker, S. G., Sox, H. C., Jr., & Tversky, A. (1982). On the elicitation of preferences for alternative therapies. *New England Journal of Medicine, 306*(21), 1259–1262.

Mello, M. M., Chandra, A., Gawande, A. A., & Studdert, D. M. (2010). National costs of the medical liability system. *Health Affairs (Millwood), 29*(9), 1569–1577.

Miller, R. H. & Luft, H. S. (1994). Managed care plan performance since 1980: A literature analysis. *JAMA, 271*, 1512–1519.

Myers, D. G. & Lamm, H. (1976). The group polarization phenomenon. *Psychological Bulletin, 83*, 602–627.

National Comprehensive Cancer Network (2010). Prostate Cancer: NCCN Guidelines for Patients, version 2010. http://www.nccn.com/images/patient-guidelines/pdf/prostate.pdf. Accessed on June 7, 2011.

Newhouse, J. P. (1992). Medicare care costs: How much welfare loss? *Journal of Economic Perspectives*, *6*(3), 3–21.

Newhouse, J. P. (2006). Reconsidering the moral hazard-risk avoidance tradeoff. *Journal of Health Economics*, *25*(5), 1005–1014.

Newhouse, J. P. & the Insurance Experiment Group (1993). *Free for all? Lessons from the RAND Health Insurance Experiment*. Cambridge, MA: Harvard University Press.

Nguyen, N. X. & Derrick, F. W. (1997). Physician behavioral response to a Medicare price reduction. *Health Services Research*, *32*, 283–298.

O'Hare, A. M., Rodriguez, R. A., Hailpern, S. M., Larson, E. B., & Kurella Tamura, M. (2010). Regional variation in health care intensity and treatment practices for end-stage renal disease in older adults. *JAMA*, *304*(2), 180–186.

Pauly, M. V. (1968). The economics of moral hazard: Comment. *American Economic Review*, *58*(3), 531–537.

Phelps, C. E. (1986). Induced demand: Can we ever know its extent? *Journal of Health Economics*, *5*, 355–365.

Potosky, A. L., Legler, J., Albertsen, P. C., Stanford, J. L., Gilliland, F. D., Hamilton, A. S., et al. (2000). Health outcomes after prostatectomy or radiotherapy for prostate cancer: Results from the Prostate Cancer Outcomes Study. *Journal of the National Cancer Institute*, *92*(19), 1582–1592.

Pritchard, R. S., Fisher, E. S., Teno, J. M., Sharp, S. M., Reding, D. J., Knaus, W. A., et al. (1998). Influence of patient preferences and local health system characteristics on the place of death. SUPPORT Investigators. Study to Understand Prognoses and Preferences for Risks and Outcomes of Treatment. *Journal of the American Geriatric Society*, *46*(10), 1242–1250.

Redelmeier, D. A. & Tversky, A. (1990). Discrepancy between medical decisions for individual patients and for groups. *New England Journal of Medicine*, *322*(16), 1162–1164.

Reinhardt, U. E. (1999). The economist's model of physician behavior. *JAMA*, *281*(5), 462–465.

Rice, T. (1983). The impact of changing Medicare reimbursement rates on physician-induced demand. *Medical Care*, *21*, 803–815.

Rogers, E. M. (1983). *Diffusion of innovations*. New York: Free Press.

Rossiter, L. F. & Wilensky, G. R. (1984). Identification of physician-induced demand. *Journal of Human Resources*, *19*, 231–244.

Sanda, M. G., Dunn, R. L., Michalski, J., Sandler, H. M., Northouse, L., Hembroff, L., et al. (2008). Quality of life and satisfaction with outcome among prostate-cancer survivors. *New England Journal of Medicine*, *358*(12), 1250–1261.

Schelling, T. (2006). *Micromotives and macrobehavior*. W. W. Norton and Co.

Schröder, F. H., Hugosson, J., Roobol, M. J., Tammela, T. L., Ciatto, S., Nelen, V., et al. (2009). Screening and prostate-cancer mortality in a randomized European study. *New England Journal of Medicine*, *360*(13), 1320–1328.

Sepucha, K. & Mulley, A. G., Jr. (2009). A perspective on the patient's role in treatment decisions. *Medical Care Research Review*, *66*(Suppl. 1), 53S–74S.

Shaneyfelt, T. M., Mayo-Smith, M. F., & Rothwangl, J. (1999). Are guidelines following guidelines? The methodological quality of clinical practice guidelines in the peer-reviewed medical literature. *JAMA*, *281*(20), 1900–1905.

Shappley, W. V., 3rd, Kenfield, S. A., Kasperzyk, J. L., Qiu, W., Stampfer, M. J., Sanda, M. G., et al. (2009). Prospective study of determinants and outcomes of deferred treatment or watchful waiting among men with prostate cancer in a nationwide cohort. *Journal of Clinical Oncology*, *27*(30), 4980–4985.

Shrank, W. H., Choudhry, N. K., Fischer, M. A., Avorn, J., Powell, M., Schneeweiss, S., et al. (2010). The epidemiology of prescriptions abandoned at the pharmacy. *Annals of Internal Medicine*, *153*(10), 633–640.

Sirovich, B., Gallagher, P. M., Wennberg, D. E., & Fisher, E. S. (2008). Discretionary decision making by primary care physicians and the cost of U.S. health care. *Health Affairs (Millwood)*, *27*(3), 813–823.

Who Ordered That? The Economics of Treatment Choices in Medical Care

431

Skinner, J. & Staiger, D. (2005). Technology adoption from hybrid corn to beta blockers. NBER Working Paper No. 11251.

Skinner, J. & Staiger, D. (2009). Technology diffusion and productivity growth in health care. NBER Working Paper No. 14865.

Smith, D. M., Brown, S. L., & Ubel, P. A. (2008). Are subjective well-being measures any better than decision utility measures? *Health Economics, Policy & Law, 3*(Pt 1), 85–91.

Smith, D. M., Sherriff, R. L., Damschroder, L., Loewenstein, G., & Ubel, P. A. (2006). Misremembering colostomies? Former patients give lower utility ratings than do current patients. *Health Psychology, 25*(6), 688–695.

Smith, M. R. (2011). Effective treatment for early-stage prostate cancer—possible, necessary, or both? *New England Journal of Medicine, 364*, 1770–1772.

Snail, T. S. & Robinson, J. C. (1998). Organization diversification in the American hospital. *Annual Review of Public Health, 19*, 417–453.

Sommers, B. D. & Zeckhauser, R. (2008a). Probabilities and preferences: What economics can teach doctors and patients making difficult treatment decisions. *Urologic Oncology, 26*(6), 669–673.

Sommers, B. D., Beard, C. J., D'Amico, A. V., Kaplan, I., Richie, J. P., & Zeckhauser, R. J. (2008b). Predictors of patient preferences and treatment choices for localized prostate cancer. *Cancer, 113*(8), 2058–2067.

Song, Y., Skinner, J., Bynum, J., Sutherland, J., Wennberg, J. E., & Fisher, E. S. (2010). Regional variations in diagnostic practices. *New England Journal of Medicine, 363*(1), 45–53.

Steinhauser, K. E., Christakis, N. A., Clipp, E. C., et al. (2000). Factors considered important at the end of life by patients, family, physicians, and other care providers. *JAMA, 284*, 2476–2482.

Stewart, S. T., Lenert, L., Bhatnagar, V., & Kaplan, R. M. (2005). Utilities for prostate cancer health states in men aged 60 and older. *Medical Care, 43*(4), 347–355.

Sutherland, J. M., Fisher, E. S., & Skinner, J. S. (2009). Getting past denial—the high cost of health care in the United States. *New England Journal of Medicine, 361*(13), 1227–1230.

Teno, J. M., Licks, S., Lynn, J., et al. (1997). Do advance directives provide instructions that direct care? *Journal of the American Geriatric Society, 45*, 508–512.

Thaler, R. H. & Sunstein, C. R. (2008). *Nudge.* New Haven, CT: Yale University Press.

Thompson, I., Thrasher, J. B., Aus, G., Burnett, A. L., Canby-Hagino, E. D., Cookson, M. S., et al. (2007). Guideline for the management of clinically localized prostate cancer: 2007 update. *Journal of Urology, 177*(6), 2106.

Tricoci, P., Allen, J. M., Kramer, J. M., Califf, R. M., & Smith, S. C., Jr. (2009). Scientific evidence underlying the ACC/AHA clinical practice guidelines. *JAMA, 301*(8), 831–841.

Trivedi, A. N., Moloo, H., & Mor, V. (2010). Increased ambulatory care copayments and hospitalizations among the elderly. *New England Journal of Medicine, 362*(4), 320–328.

Ubel, P. A. (2009). *Free market madness.* Boston, MA: Harvard Business Press.

Ubel, P. A., Loewenstein, G., Schwarz, N., & Smith, D. (2005). Misimagining the unimaginable: The disability paradox and health care decision making. *Health Psychology, 24*(Suppl. 4), S57–S62.

Van Heek, N. T., Kuhlmann, K. F., Scholten, R. J., de Castro, S. M., Busch, O. R., van Gulik, T. M., et al. (2005). Hospital volume and mortality after pancreatic resection: A systematic review and an evaluation of intervention in the Netherlands. *Annals of Surgery, 242*(6), 781–788.

Wei, J. T., Dunn, R. L., Sandler, H. M., McLaughlin, P. W., Montie, J. E., & Litwin, M. S., et al. (2002). Comprehensive comparison of health-related quality of life after contemporary therapies for localized prostate cancer. *Journal of Clinical Oncology, 20*(2), 557–566.

Weintraub, W. S., Spertus, J. A., & Kolm, P., et al. (2008). Effect of PCI on quality of life in patients with stable coronary disease. *New England Journal of Medicine, 359*(7), 677–687.

Welch, H. G., Sharp, S. M., Gottlieb, D. J., Skinner, J. S., & Wennberg, J. E. (2011). Geographic variation in diagnosis frequency and risk of death among Medicare beneficiaries. *JAMA, 305*(11), 1113–1118.

Wennberg, J., & Gittelsohn, A. (1973). Small area variations in health care delivery. *Science, 182*(117), 1102–1108.

Wennberg, J., & Gittelsohn, A. (1982). Variations in medical care among small areas. *Scientific American, 246*(4), 120–134.

Wennberg, J. E., Freeman, J. L., & Culp, W. J. (1987). Are hospital services rationed in New Haven or over-utilised in Boston? *Lancet, 1*(8543), 1185−1189.

Williamson, O. E. (2010). Transaction cost economics: The natural progression. *American Economic Review, 100,* 673−690.

Wilt, T. J., MacDonald, R., Rutks, I., Shamliyan, T. A., Taylor, B. C., & Kane, R. L. (2008). Systematic review: Comparative effectiveness and harms of treatments for clinically localized prostate cancer. *Annals of Internal Medicine, 148*(6), 435−448.

Woo, B., Woo, B., Cook, E. F., Weisberg, M., & Goldman, L. (1985). Screening procedures in the asymptomatic adult. Comparison of physicians' recommendations, patients' desires, published guidelines, and actual practice. *JAMA, 254*(11), 1480−1484.

Yip, W. (1998). Physician responses to medical fee reductions: Changes in the volume and intensity of supply of Coronary Artery Bypass Graft (CABG) surgeries in the Medicare and private sectors. *Journal of Health Economics, 17,* 675−700.

Young, H. P. (1998). *Individual strategy and social structure: An evolutionary theory of institutions.* Princeton, NJ: Princeton University Press.

Zeckhauser, R. J. (1970). Medical insurance: A case study of the tradeoff between risk spreading and appropriate incentives. *Journal of Economic Theory, 2*(1), 10−26.

Zuckerman, S., Waidmann, T., Berenson, R., & Hadley, J. (2010). Clarifying sources of geographic differences in Medicare spending. *New England Journal of Medicine, 363*(1), 54−62.

CHAPTER SEVEN

Theoretical Issues Relevant to the Economic Evaluation of Health Technologies[1]

David O. Meltzer[*] and Peter C. Smith[**]
[*]University of Chicago, USA
[**]Imperial College, London, UK

Contents

[1] We are grateful for comments from participants at the Handbook's authors' workshop at Harvard University, and from David Epstein at the University of Granada, and Pedro Pita Barros at the Universidade Nova, Lisbon.

Abstract

Medical cost-effectiveness analysis (CEA) is perhaps the most widely applied tool to guide policy decisions concerning the use of health care resources. This chapter first reviews the rationale for and common practice of medical cost-effectiveness analysis. It seeks to place CEA within a conventional microeconomic framework. Methodological controversies in CEA are then discussed within this framework. They include: the decision-making perspective of the analysis; incorporating equity concerns; the treatment of joint costs and benefits; and the treatment of time horizon and discounting.

Keywords: health technology assessment; cost-effectiveness analysis; methodology; medical decision making

JEL Codes: I11; I18

1. INTRODUCTION

Despite the high priority placed on health by both individuals and policy makers, resource constraints are an important concern in health care decision making. Given the extraordinary ability of medical technology to consume resources, and the incentives for excess utilization of health care, approaches that maximize the health benefits derived from health care spending have become increasingly important. Medical cost–effectiveness analysis (CEA) is perhaps the most widely applied tool to guide policy decisions concerning the allocation of health care resources. Globally, CEA has become a central activity for many applied health economists seeking to assess the health and economic effects of alternative medical treatments. Over the more than 30 years during which CEA has developed, its methods have become increasingly codified even as they have become more complex and new methods and controversies have developed (Gold et al., 1996; Drummond et al., 2005).

This chapter reviews the rationale for and common practice of medical cost–effectiveness analysis and discusses how the theoretical foundations of cost–effectiveness analysis inform current practice and methodological controversies in the field. It seeks to place CEA within a conventional microeconomic framework. Methodological controversies in CEA are then discussed within this framework. They include: the decision-making perspective of the analysis; incorporating equity concerns; the treatment of joint costs and benefits; and the treatment of time horizon and discounting.

1.1. The Rationale for Economic Evaluation of Health Technologies

Economic evaluation of health technologies seeks to promote the efficient allocation of health care. Under certain conditions, optimizing behavior by individuals in the context of market exchange can be expected to produce efficient outcomes. For this reason, analysis of models of optimizing behavior by individuals is often used to guide the development of methods for cost-effectiveness analysis that are intended to identify efficient patterns of resource allocation.

The most basic economic model of consumer choice is that of (one period) utility maximization subject to a budget constraint. This model suggests that—subject to numerous simplifying assumptions, including a fixed budget, fixed prices and a single time period—an individual can produce the greatest utility (benefits or effectiveness) with any given level of resources by ranking all forms of consumption according to the ratio of their incremental costs to the incremental utility they will yield, and selecting those with lowest ratios of incremental costs to incremental utility to the point where available resources are exhausted. Beyond this critical margin, the ratio of marginal cost relative to marginal utility is high enough that further consumption of the good reduces the individual's utility by crowding out consumption goods and services with a lower ratio of costs to benefits. Thus, having a ratio of incremental costs to incremental benefit below that critical ratio is a necessary condition for economic efficiency.

1.1.1. Market Failures

The benefits of most health services are targeted at the individuals who receive treatment, and they therefore have many of the characteristics of a conventional consumer good. However, in contrast to competitive markets, most health care in developed countries is financed collectively, through taxation, social health insurance or private health plans. Therefore, unless countervailing measures are put in place, individuals will tend to consume treatment in excess of socially optimal levels, as they do not directly bear the full costs of that treatment at the time of consumption.

This tendency towards overconsumption is exacerbated by the shortage of information held by individuals about the benefits of health services, and their consequent reliance on providers of health care for advice on the use of health services. This can be further complicated by the fact that many health care systems give providers direct or indirect personal incentives to encourage utilization. Thus, whether health care is purchased collectively or by individuals in a conventional marketplace, there is a need to offer purchasers information on the expected benefits offered by health technologies.

These two fundamental sources of inefficiency built into the market for modern health care—a lack of price discipline applied to consumers, and information asymmetry between providers and purchasers—have led policy makers to look for corrective mechanisms. To this end, health economists have advocated the development of measures of cost-effectiveness that seek to replicate the fundamental decision criterion that applies in conventional consumer choice. The intention is that such measures can help both collective and individual purchasers of health care to maximize the total benefit received from any level of spending by ranking treatments by the ratio of incremental costs to incremental effectiveness, and choosing those interventions with the lowest costs relative to benefits. The concept of *incremental* costs and effectiveness reflects the fundamental idea that optimization conditions most hold at the margin. To determine whether a treatment is efficient, it must be compared not only to the alternative of "doing nothing," but to all other possible treatment choices. The goal is to identify whether the additional benefits conferred by a substitute treatment justify their extra costs compared to all other possible interventions.

1.2. Institutional Contexts for CEA

Cost-effectiveness analysis (CEA) has had an impact in a variety of different contexts. The most important of these are informing coverage decisions by public and private payers and providing guidance that may influence providers and patients. As a tool for informing coverage decisions, CEA has had a very important impact in informing health care decision making in many countries. A leading example of embedding the notion of CEA into policy was the establishment in 1999 of the National Institute for Clinical Excellence (NICE)[2] in England, which assesses health technologies and issues guidance for public funding of treatments. Analogous agencies have arisen in many developed countries, including Canada, Germany, and Australia. These countries have adopted similar methodological principles, but vary in the extent to which recommendations are mandatory and other important institutional arrangements.

However, in some countries—most notably the United States—the use of cost-effectiveness analysis to ration care has not been accepted. It is worth noting that this has not prevented CEA from being used to influence resource allocation decisions. Cost-effectiveness analyses have targeted providers and other decision makers to encourage greater use of interventions that are found to be a worthwhile use of resources. For example, the Centers for Disease Control have advocated for preventive interventions, including influenza immunization, Pap Smears, and HIV screening, based on evidence of both effectiveness and cost effectiveness. The development of the concept of comparative effectiveness research (CER) in the US is testimony to the enduring influence of CEA thinking; CER discourages use of interventions that cost more but are not more effective. Further details are discussed in Chapter 8.

Most CEA research is focused on the needs of a decision maker, and therefore requires careful attention to the decision-maker's objectives, and the constraints that apply to the decision. Examples include:
- An individual with limited income seeking to maximize some utility function based on consumption and health (in this case there is no market failure, but CEA serves as a tool to help the individual assess whether their personal benefits are worth the personal costs);

---

[2] Subsequently renamed the National Institute for Health and Clinical Excellence.

- A private health insurer wishing to offer potential customers a package of covered benefits that will maximize profits (i.e. the amount that customers are willing to pay for the coverage (by virtue of the value of health outcomes obtained net of out-of-pocket costs) minus the costs of providing that coverage);
- A social health insurer wishing to maximize the health gain secured from a given health services budget;
- A societal decision maker maximizing a social welfare function (including an argument in population health) subject to finite societal resources and efficiency losses resulting from taxation.

In practice, applications of CEA are often inconsistent in perspective. For example, they may apply a societal objective function, but employ a budget constraint that applies only to a health insurer. Such inconsistencies are relevant to several of the debates that we discuss in this chapter.

2. STANDARD APPROACHES TO METHODOLOGICAL ISSUES IN COST-EFFECTIVENESS ANALYSIS

2.1. Introduction

In introducing the standard approaches to CEA methods, it is important to recognize that CEA emerged as a pragmatic response to a pressing regulatory need for tools to aid decision making about the allocation of health services. Methodologies that were more established at the time, especially cost/benefit analysis (CBA), could have served a similar purpose in principle. Though CBA has formidable information and analytic demands that make its use challenging, it seems likely that those could have been overcome with sustained attention. Nevertheless, the modest informational requirements of CEA compared to CBA made a workable deployment of CEA relatively more feasible. This was especially important given the focus on comparison of technologies, and the need to ensure that researchers in a wide range of settings perform analyses on a consistent basis. Moreover, the reliance of CBA on explicit monetary valuation of health and monetary gains presented large political barriers to adoption. In contrast, the ability of CEA to avoid explicit valuation of changes in health when ranking interventions reduces the political resistance associated with such valuations. The keys to the widespread adoption of CEA may therefore have been its reduced informational requirements and its less explicit reliance on monetary valuations of health.

Early cost-effectiveness researchers therefore recognized that simplicity, feasibility, and minimization of political controversy were essential if CEA was to enjoy widespread adoption and acceptance. The most immediate needs were for methodologies to estimate the numerator and denominator of the cost-effectiveness ratio. It was only once the broad approach was established that researchers began to address the many methodological complexities that arise when seeking to make CEA a logically coherent framework that can be applied across a wide range of circumstances. In an important sense, then, theory followed practice in the development of CEA. As a consequence, the historical practice of CEA is often full of inconsistencies and must be viewed cautiously as methodological guidance. The desire to create comparable and non-biased CEA estimates eventually drove the quest to use theory in order to resolve controversial methodological questions. We defer consideration of these issues to sections 3 and 4, focusing in the following section on the accepted practice of CEA.

2.2. Overview of the CEA Framework

Because the practice of medical cost-effectiveness analysis developed to a large degree in advance of theory, it is probably best understood as a set of core practices that have developed over time that have been informed by, though not always tightly derived from, theory. A pragmatic review of the practice of CEA also serves to provide useful context for the more rigorous examination of the theoretical foundations of CEA in section 3.

The problem that medical cost-effectiveness analysis seeks to solve can be broadly described as choosing health interventions to maximize health or well-being subject to some sort of resource constraint. The conditions for optimization imply that the ratio of incremental costs to incremental benefits should be equal to the marginal value of health (or well-being) across all interventions, often referred to as the acceptance threshold or cost-effectiveness threshold. This applies technically in cases in which an intervention can be continuously varied in intensity of application (e.g. frequency of testing) or target population; when an intervention is discrete in nature, its ratio of costs to benefits will generally sit on one side or another of the value of health, and therefore either be considered cost-effective or not, depending on where it sits relative to that threshold. In general, the cost-effectiveness ratio of an intervention is defined as $(C1-C0)/(E1-E0)$, where C1 and C0 and E1 and E0 are, respectively, the costs and effects of the intervention (1) and the alternative (0). In some cases, the alternative may be some other intervention; in others, it may be no care. Note, therefore, that cost-effectiveness ratios are always incremental, examining the changes in effects and costs with respect to some alternative.

The usual approach to measuring "effects" is to focus primarily on the health gains secured by a treatment. A prime objective of many medical interventions is to enhance life expectancy. However, there was an early recognition that many treatments also had implications for the health-related quality of life. This led to the development of metrics such as the quality-adjusted life year (QALY) and its disability-adjusted

Table 7.1 Cost-effectiveness of Common Medical Interventions

Intervention	Cost/Life Year
Neonatal PKU Screening	<0
Secondary Prevention of Hypercholesterolemia in Men Ages 55—64	2,000
Annual Breast Exam 55—64	14,000—27,001
Treatment of Severe Hypertension	17,000
Annual Breast Exam 65—74	12,000—22,000
Secondary Prevention of Hypercholesterolemia in Men Ages 75—84	25,000
Pap Smear Every 3 Years after 4 Negative Annual Pap Smears	17,000 (ages 20—74)
Annual Breast Exam 40—50	25,000—58,000
One-time Physical Exam for Abdominal Aortic Aneurism	29,000
Moderate Hypertension	34,000
Mammography 55—64 Compared to Breast Examination	28,000—106,000
One-time Ultrasound for Abdominal Aortic Aneurism	42,000
Mammography 65—74 Compared to Breast Examination	45,000—163,000
Mammography 40—50 Compared to Breast Examination	37,000—170,000
Screening Exercise Test in Asymptomatic 40-year-old Males	124,000
Pap Smear Every 2 Years after 3 Negative Annual Pap Smears vs. Every 3 Years	258,000 (ages 20—74)
Physical Exam Every 5 Years for Abdominal Aortic Aneurism	747,000
Ultrasound Every 5 Years for Abdominal Aortic Aneurism	907,000

Source: based on Meltzer (1997), Table 2.

life year (DALY) counterpart. These seek to provide comprehensive measures of health benefit that can facilitate the comparison of the health gains associated with sometimes radically different types of technology that can affect the length and/or quality of life (see section 2.4).

The product of cost-effectiveness analysis is typically a cost-effectiveness ratio (e.g. cost/life year or cost/QALY), which can then be interpreted in comparison to the cost-effectiveness threshold or the cost effectiveness of other interventions. When interventions are not mutually exclusive, the resource allocation decision can be informed by a league table that ranks all interventions from the lowest cost per life year or per QALY to the highest cost per QALY (Table 7.1). A decision maker can then select the interventions with the lowest cost per QALY up to the point where their budget is exhausted, or, if the budget is not fixed, the point at which the additional interventions being considered would have costs that would exceed the level of benefits produced, defined in terms of the cost-effectiveness acceptance threshold. Such thresholds may differ in different policy contexts, but in many cases are tied to statistical estimates of the value of life. These are typically based on individuals' observed willingness to pay to reduce risks to health that are exhibited in other contexts, for example wage differentials required to induce people to accept jobs that present greater risks to health. Estimates for the size of

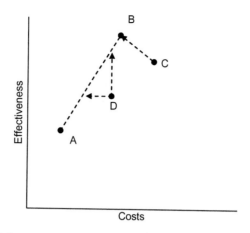

Figure 7.1 Illustration of dominance and extended dominance.

the threshold often range from $50,000 to $200,000 in developed countries, but are generally an order of magnitude lower in lower income countries (Braithwaite et al., 2008; Meltzer, 2006).

When multiple mutually exclusive interventions are considered for a specific condition, it is important to assess the incremental costs and effects of each intervention relative to all other options. The most straightforward way to understand this process is to represent it graphically, as in Figure 7.1, with effectiveness on the y-axis and cost on the x-axis. Some options, such as C, can be eliminated because they are strictly dominated by other options that offer greater benefits at lower costs, e.g. B. Other options, such as D, can be eliminated due to a principle of "extended dominance," which occurs when a linear combination of any two other options (e.g. A and B) dominate that option (as indicated by the fact that points on a line between A and B dominate D). Such points are dominated in the sense that some policies that randomly assigned people to A or B would dominate D. A line drawn from A to B thus defines the set of resource allocation decisions that maximize effectiveness, with the choice among them determined by the amount of resources available.

2.3. Scope of the Analysis (Perspective)

A key issue in most cost-effectiveness studies is the nature of the decision-making "perspective." CEA can be performed from a number of different perspectives, including private, governmental, societal, and multiple perspectives. From a private perspective, CEA can reflect the costs and benefits of a medical intervention to an individual or an organization, such as a health maintenance organization. Such analyses are often useful because they reflect the costs and benefits to these private entities and hence provide insights into their behavior. However, private perspectives may be narrow in failing to reflect the costs and benefits of an intervention for entities other than the decision maker. Furthermore, in many countries the decision maker is effectively a government or some other collective agency. This can lead to the need for a broader perspective, reflecting the costs (and benefits) arising from a medical intervention to a health care system, a governmental budget, or even society as a whole.

Often, collective perspectives applied in cost-effectiveness analyses reflect the perspective of the health care system alone. For example, for a country evaluating a coverage decision for a public insurance program, the effects of an intervention on health care spending might be the only costs considered. However, a broader governmental perspective might consider the effects on other parts of government. For example, the institutionalization of the mentally ill might be understood to have effects on the cost of incarceration. Similarly, improvements in health among older adults might have budgetary impacts if they resulted in decreases in early retirement and resulting increases in tax revenue. Often, however, such effects are rarely considered even in cost-effectiveness analyses done from a governmental perspective.

The limitations of both the private and governmental perspectives have led to increasing interest in the use of a societal perspective for cost-effectiveness analysis. In taking a societal perspective, one seeks to count all costs and benefits of medical interventions regardless of to whom they accrue. In the United States, a very influential report by the US Public Health Service in the 1990s led to the widespread adoption of a societal perspective for cost-effectiveness analysis (Gold et al., 1996). Since that time, a much larger fraction of cost-effectiveness analyses has been conducted from a societal perspective. The societal perspective has the advantage of reflecting a broader set of consequences of an intervention than either the private or governmental perspective. It also has the advantage of corresponding more closely to criteria such as a potential Pareto improvement, i.e. that an intervention has the potential to make at least one person better off without making anyone worse off. This is because persons who benefit from an intervention could potentially compensate persons who are harmed by it and still be better off than without the intervention.

A limitation of a societal perspective is that it ignores the distribution of those effects among various affected parties. This is important because private or governmental perspectives may provide insight into when a given decision maker may fail to have adequate incentives to engage in some intervention even when it provides positive net benefits from a societal perspective. This argues for the value of performing cost-effectiveness analysis from multiple perspectives. This is only infrequently done, however, perhaps because of the complexity of performing an analysis from multiple perspectives and then explaining it within the confines of a specific decision-making forum or a typical publication.

2.4. Measuring Effectiveness in CEA

Fundamental to all CEA is the need to develop some measure of health gain. The most obvious metric is some measure of additional years of life added by the technology under scrutiny. However, this was very quickly acknowledged to be inadequate because it ignores variations in the health-related quality of life arising from treatments. Many treatments—such as pain relief—may have no significant impact on length of life, but offer major improvements in quality of life. Even when treatments do affect life expectancy, the quality of survival can be a material aspect of outcome.

As a result, economists have been central in developing health status measures that enable inferences to be made about the valuation that people attach to different health outcomes (Chapman et al., 2004). A number of different approaches to measuring the trade-off between the length and quality of life have been developed, but the most commonly employed is the quality-adjusted life year (QALY) (Gold et al., 1996). Numerous methodological issues arise in the development of QALYs. How should health-related quality of life be assessed? Whose values should inform the trade-off between dimensions of quality (pain, mobility, etc.), and between length and quality of life? How should future health gains be treated in relation to immediate gains? And how should future QALYs be inferred from limited empirical data? Often, the practice adopted has been to seek to base the QALY on the preferences of a representative individual, offering the potential to secure consistency between evaluations of different treatments. In other cases, the approach has been to directly elicit measures from individuals affected by the health condition or intervention, implicitly or explicitly reflecting a desire to reflect the preferences of individuals who may not be representative of other individuals.

The QALY can be illustrated by means of a health status pathway, as shown in Figure 7.2. This tracks the health status of an individual over time. Health-related quality of life—or health status—$q(t)$ at any time t is measured on a continuous scale from zero to one, with maximum health status at any time t being 1.0, perhaps reflecting the WHO definition of full health as "a state of complete physical, mental and social wellbeing and not merely the absence of disease or infirmity." Conversely, zero can be thought of as death.[3] Future QALYs are represented by the area between the horizontal axis and the pathway.

Such use of a scalar measure presumes that an individual can rank health states ordinally. The QALY literature further assumes that a cardinal scaling of health status $q(\cdot)$ can be chosen to reflect the strength of individual preferences. That is, for all

---

[3] The health status measurement literature does accommodate the possibility that there are states of health "worse than death." This is not considered further here, although the existence of such states does not change our analytic argument, so long as they are given properly scaled negative valuations that permit their aggregation with positive valuations in any QALY calculation.

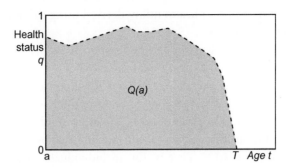

Figure 7.2 A Health status pathway.

values of $0 < q < 1$ the value of q is chosen such that an individual is indifferent between enjoying maximum health status ($=1$) for any period dt, and health status $q < 1$ for a period dt/q. This implies the individual is prepared to trade off perfect health over a period dt for a longer period of survival in imperfect health. It is readily shown that, for any individual set of preferences, such a scaling can be achieved, so long as some undemanding axioms of rationality can be assumed. Quality of life weights are in practice measured using methods such as linear analog scale, standard gamble, or time trade-off that directly assess utilities through various choice questions.

In practice, specific psychometric approaches used to elicit quality of life values may be related in one way or another to these economic underpinnings (Torrance, 1986). In the linear analog approach, respondents are asked to rate their health on a line where the left end is zero and intended to reflect the quality of life in death, and 1 is on the right end and intended to reflect perfect health. This is theoretically justifiable only if quality of life on this scale is viewed as linear, in the sense that, for example, two years with QOL $= 0.5$ are equivalent to 1 year with QOL $= 1$. In the standard gamble, respondents are asked to choose between a given number of years of life in a given limited health state or a gamble in which with some probability (p) they live that number of years of life in full health and with probability ($1 - p$) they die immediately. If p is varied until people are indifferent between the certain outcome and the gamble and people maximize expected utility then $1 * q = p * 1 + (1 - p) * 0$ so $q = p$. Thus, the utility can be estimated by the probability at which respondents are indifferent between these options. Finally, in the time trade-off method, people are asked to choose between T years in some limited quality of life (q) or a shorter life of $t < T$ years in perfect health. Hence, if people maximize the product of the length and quality of life (and we ignore discounting), when people are indifferent between these choices, $qT = 1 * t$, so $q = t/T$ so that quality of life can be estimated as t/T. Quality of life may also be measured indirectly, by using health status questions that have been previously correlated with direct measures of health utility derived using the linear analog, standard gamble, or time trade-off methods.

In practice, measurement of $q(t)$ might be approximated by the use at time t of a generic health status measurement tool, such as the EQ5D, with the scaling chosen according to these established analytic techniques for direct utility elicitation, such as time trade-off methods or standard gambles. The health economics literature is replete with examples of empirical estimation of such valuations (Gold et al., 1996).

For any individual i, health status $q_i(\cdot)$ will usually vary over time, and its integral reflects the notion of the QALY. That is, for an individual i at age a, future QALYs can be measured as

$$Q_i(a) = \int_q^\infty q_i(t)\,\mathrm{d}t$$

Such summation is possible because of the cardinal scaling properties of $q(\cdot)$. Of course, all lifetimes are finite, and in practice the integral will be truncated at death, which occurs at time T. It may be the case that the individual values a given health state enjoyed currently more highly than the identical health state experienced at some time in the future. The QALY calculation is readily amended to accommodate this possibility through the incorporation of a discount term.

When assessing the cost effectiveness of a health care intervention it will usually be necessary to compare the health status pathway following the intervention with some counterfactual. Depending on the nature of the comparison, this counterfactual may be expressed as the receipt either of no treatment, or of an alternative treatment. By way of illustration, Figure 7.3 compares an individual's health status pathway under two alternative health care interventions from age a (Smith and Street, 2011). Intervention A leads to short-term gains in health-related quality of life relative to intervention B. However, A is associated with earlier death, so its advantage is not sustained. The relative advantage of intervention B over A is the difference between the two integrals.

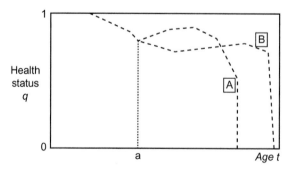

Figure 7.3 Treatment a has only a short-term advantage over B. *Source: Smith and street (2011).*

In general, people will offer different valuations of alternative health states. When seeking to make collective decisions, the issue therefore remains of how to map the heterogeneous preferences of individuals onto a broader set of societal values. Classical welfare economics argues that it is generally not possible to define a social welfare function that can provide a valid basis for decision making that reflects the preferences of individuals (Arrow, 1950). A measure of the benefits of a technology that would be more readily justified on theoretical grounds would be the set of changes in the utility of every individual to which it gives rise, but this does not typically provide a feasible or useful basis for decision making as almost every decision benefits some people and harms others, making societal decision making based on a set of winners and losers from a decision fundamentally a matter of judgment. The challenge of optimal collective decision making may be complicated further if the benefits of treatment extend beyond the individual to family members (Basu and Meltzer, 2005) or to society more generally (in the form of a variety of potential externalities, including concerns of altruism and equity).

2.5. The Measurement of Costs in CEA

The definition of costs to be included in the CEA ratio has been the subject of debate. In principle, CEA should incorporate the true opportunity costs of adopting a particular technology. However, the usual practice is to rely on accounting data, at least as a basis for estimating health services costs. This means that—at best—cost estimates reflect short-run average use of resources, and the current configuration of capital stock and other fixed assets. The limitations of accounting data are well documented. Failure to critically assess their limitations implies that utilization decisions based on cost effectiveness may not have expected implications for cost. For example, the use of average costs implies an assumption of no significant economies or diseconomies of scale; the opportunity cost of ordering an extra MRI when the machine and tech are sitting idle may well be closer to zero than to any standard accounting measure of cost. Similar and probably far more quantitatively important issues arise in considering the costs of pharmaceuticals, which generally are sold at prices far above their marginal costs because there are large fixed costs of producing them but low marginal costs. Thus, much of the price paid for pharmaceuticals would be more appropriately viewed in the short run as a transfer payment from the purchaser to the pharmaceutical company than as an economic cost. It could also be argued that in the long run such transfer payments could be dissipated through R&D, which might not be productive.

The challenges in measuring costs only begin with such issues. Measures of costs in medical CEA have typically focused on direct medical costs, but there is substantial variability in the other types of costs included for a variety of reasons, including both differences in the perspective taken in different cost-effectiveness analyses, and differences in beliefs among investigators as to how to measure costs from various perspectives. In a narrow sense, if one is interested only in the costs to the payer (for example, employer, insurance plan or government), the task is relatively straightforward. Incremental costs can be interpreted as the net financial consequences to the payer of introducing the technology. However, even this apparently simple definition can give rise to quite subtle and methodologically challenging complications, for example if the new technology implies increased short-term costs but gives rise to lower expected costs in the future. We defer until later questions about the inclusion of other types of costs, including medical costs that are not directly related to the intervention in question, and non-medical costs (e.g. consumption). Also, productivity effects that may result from changes in health status or survival are affected by health interventions.

There are numerous unresolved issues in costing methodology, including (1) the best way to attach monetary value to resource use, especially capital assets, (2) the recommended cost perspective of the study, (3) the appropriate measurement and valuation method of informal caregiver time, (4) the measurement and valuation of productivity costs, (5) the cost incurred in added years of life, and (6) the best technique for allocating support center costs to operational units (Mogyorosy and Smith, 2005). Just limiting the definition of costs to direct medical costs presents important challenges. Even the most sophisticated approaches to cost accounting, such as activity-based accounting, are limited in their ability to address certain challenges, such as the treatment of fixed costs and joint costs (Chan, 1993).

Also, the introduction of a new technology often has implications for costs (or savings) well beyond the narrow purview of the payer (Neumann, 2009). For example, it may impose additional costs on the patient or the patient's caregivers (in the form say of additional transport costs). There may be even less direct costs to the household, perhaps in the form of time off work or employment prospects. And even less directly, the new technology may be associated with broader social costs for public services, employers and welfare agencies. The extent to which these should be taken into account remains a matter for debate, and is dependent on the perspective taken and the precise role of the decision maker under consideration. However, it is probably true that the broadening of the perspective for analysis will in general make it more difficult to assure that true comparability is attained when comparing different technologies, because one must assure that a more extensive range of potential costs is assessed. In the extreme, the analyst is driven towards the need to undertake a fuller cost/benefit or even general equilibrium assessment of the proposed innovation. Often there is a trade-off between the comparability of analyses and their ability to ideally reflect increasingly complex measurement issues raised by effort to produce theoretically rigorous analyses.

2.6. Applying CEA

The application of cost-effectiveness analysis requires a process to estimate costs and benefits. Broadly speaking, this can be done either by directly measuring costs and outcomes as part of a randomized trial, or through simulation modeling that combines information on relevant parameters from multiple sources.

2.6.1. CEA Alongside Clinical Trials

The former approach, often called CEA alongside clinical trials, is easier to describe because the relevant outcomes, i.e. costs and QALYs, are directly measured. The challenge in the approach is that the trial must be carried out long enough and with a sufficiently large sample size to allow these effects to be reliably estimated. In practice, this limits the application of cost effectiveness alongside clinical trials to interventions whose effects on costs and outcomes are short term, and hence interventions that do not affect long-term survival. Examples include interventions whose main effects are on quality rather than length of life and are evident rapidly after onset of treatment, such as relief of pain or improvement in functioning, as might come from pain medication, ulcer treatment, or joint replacement.

2.6.2. Mathematical Modeling

The use of mathematical models is therefore the more common approach to practical CEA. These models can be simple, such as the construction of a decision tree for uncertain outcomes that occur in the present, or more complex, such as the construction of Markov models that describe transition across health states over time. The results of these models can be directly calculated or simulated probabilistically. Probabilistic simulation has increasingly been used as computational power has decreased in cost and relevant software packages have become available.

The major advantage of these modeling approaches is that they can allow extrapolation of information outside of clinical trials. This is especially useful when the effects of an intervention are likely to be longer term than is easily followed through randomized trials. Often, a conceptual model of the disease process is used to relate readily measured intermediate outcomes to longer-term outcomes that could not otherwise be measured. Parameters in these models are typically estimated from experimental data from shorter-term clinical trials and observational epidemiological data. Derivation of these parameters may be accomplished through reviews of the literature or re-analysis of available data. Both the models themselves and the data used to estimate them can be very complex, so papers in this area increasingly must document sources and deviations/technical appendixes. Validation of these models can be done by comparing their outputs to known clinical trials or epidemiologic data, or that data can be used directly in estimation. In some cases, these models have even been used to project the outcomes of clinical trials before they are complete (Eddy et al., 2005).

An important limitation of these models is that they often fail to account for behaviors that can have large effects on the outcomes of interventions. Behavior can decrease the effectiveness of interventions if patients fail to comply with treatment well enough to allow them to be effective, for example when a patient prematurely discontinues an antibiotic regimen. Alternatively behavior can increase the effectiveness of an intervention when people discontinue treatment when the intervention is harming them. Similar concerns apply to some extent to traditional efficacy trials, and are reasons for the growing interest in effectiveness trials (Lewis et al., 1995). For modeling approaches to address these concerns, they must develop theoretical and empirical approaches to reflect behavior. In some analyses of intensive therapy for diabetes, modeling self-selection into (and out of) treatment based on patient preferences has first-order effects on the effectiveness and cost-effectiveness of intensive therapy (Meltzer et al., 2002).

3. THEORETICAL FOUNDATIONS OF CEA

Economic evaluation of health technologies is built on disciplinary foundations from within economics, psychology, clinical epidemiology, and operations research. However, welfare economics provides the foundation for most approaches to cost-effectiveness analysis. Such approaches to CEA can be characterized as "welfarist," in the sense that individual utility (or "welfare") characterizes all outcomes and "social welfare" is understood to be a function only of individual utilities (Brouwer et al., 2008). They also conform to the standard distributional principles underlying welfare economics, embodied in the Pareto principle. Furthermore, in principle, individuals should re-optimize planned spending decisions whenever there is an exogenous shock to health or income. This part of a broader set of issues is raised by the fact that CEA typically takes a partial equilibrium approach. When changes are small this may not be much of an issue, but for larger changes, or in the presence of distorting incentives, these issues may be much more complicated to address (Meltzer, 1997).

Welfare maximization approaches provide a conceptually coherent starting point for investigating a rich set of theoretical issues in cost-effectiveness. However, welfarist approaches have been challenged through the development of an "extra-welfarist" critique, which Brouwer et al. (2008) consider has four distinctive characteristics: (1) it permits the use of outcomes other than utility; (2) it permits the use of sources of valuation other than the affected individuals; (3) it permits the weighting of outcomes (whether utility or other) according to principles that need not be preference based; and (4) it permits interpersonal comparisons of well-being in a variety of dimensions, thus enabling movement beyond Paretian economics. The principal practical consequences of adopting the extra-welfarist approach is that it justifies a focus on health alone (rather than utility) as the maximand, and a willingness to countenance interpersonal comparisons of outcome. It then becomes readily applicable to the idea that a social planner might make health coverage decisions on behalf of a specified population. In its simplest form, the planner has a current budget within which current treatment decisions must be made; the objective is to maximize some concept of aggregate population health, and multi-period optimization is not necessary. This perspective is consistent with institutional arrangements in widespread use, in which a collective payer's budget is deployed with the explicit objective only of promoting health. In effect, the decision to organize health care collectively, whether through government action or association in the form of voluntary health insurance, is argued to legitimize the use of a social decision-making rule that need not be tied to concepts in welfare economics.

In this section we set out in broad outline first the conventional welfarist perspective on CEA, and then the application of CEA to collective decision making. We seek to draw out the essence of existing practice, and the main unresolved methodological challenges.

3.1. Individual Utility Maximization and Cost-effectiveness

Weinstein and Zeckhauser (1973) point out that when the quantity of all interventions is continuously variable, utility maximization subject to a budget constraint implies that the quantity of the interventions should be increased to the point at which the ratio of marginal costs to marginal benefits for all interventions should be equal to a constant. When interventions cannot be varied continuously, interventions for which the ratio of marginal costs to marginal benefits is less than this "critical ratio" provide benefits in excess of their costs and are therefore a use of resources that maximizes benefits subject to resource constraints, while interventions whose ratios exceed this threshold do not maximize benefits given resource constraints.

In a stylized form, when all interventions are continuously variable and applied in a single period, the maximization model can be viewed as allocating a total wealth I between medical care M and all other consumption C as follows:

$$\max_{C,M} U(C, M)$$

$$\text{Subject to}$$

$$p_C C + p_M M = I$$

yielding the first-order conditions

$$\frac{\partial U}{\partial M}/p_M = \frac{\partial U}{\partial C}/p_C = 1/\mu$$

where $1/\mu$ is the marginal utility of income, so μ is the income value of an increase in utility.

This can be rewritten in a number of ways, to correspond to alternative but equivalent decision-making formulations. Conventional cost-effectiveness analysis expresses the relationship as a ratio:

$$p_M / \frac{\partial U}{\partial M} = \mu$$

This implies that the amount of any intervention should be varied to the point where the cost-effectiveness ratio equals the threshold level μ. This can be rearranged to yield a criterion consistent with traditional cost/benefit analysis:

$$\mu \frac{\partial U}{\partial M} - p_M = 0$$

This implies that an intervention should be increased to the point where the monetary value of the benefits produced by the intervention net of the costs equals zero. Similarly, the relationship can be expressed in terms of the "net health benefit," implying that the level of an intervention should be set at the point at which the extra utility created a medical intervention net of the utility forgone as a result of its cost equals zero:

$$\frac{\partial U}{\partial M} - \frac{p_M}{\mu} = 0$$

These results assume that the intervention can be continuously varied; below we discuss the case in which the intervention is discrete in nature.

3.1.1. Lifetime Utility Maximization

The above model describes a simple one-period model, but because health can affect survival, it is natural to examine cost effectiveness of medical interventions in a multi-period framework that can reflect the effects of health interventions over a lifetime, including effects on both survival and quality of life over time, as well as related effects on costs.

The uncertainty inherent in survival can be modeled either as the expected utility of a representative individual or a population of individuals. It has been argued (Claxton, 1999; Meltzer, 2001) that assessing the average outcomes and costs is sufficient for decision making if the objective is to maximize expected outcomes net of costs or that risks are small or readily diversifiable. This will not be the case in general when decision makers are risk averse and risks are large. The case of maximizing the expected utility of a representative individual is less complex theoretically than that of maximizing the welfare of a population of individuals and so is a useful framework in which to develop an initial framework for cost effectiveness.

Thus, similar to the framework used in Meltzer (1997) and Garber and Phelps (1997), lifetime utility can be viewed as a discounted sum of the expected utility of health outcomes. Utility in any given period can be viewed as depending on consumption of goods in that period and health in that period $U_t(C_t, H_t)$. While both survival and health conditional on survival could be treated as uncertain, from an expositional perspective it is easier to treat health given survival as deterministic. Let S_t be the probability of surviving to age t. In addition, utility in future periods is assumed to matter less than utility in current periods, following a discounting function β^t where $\beta < 1$. Combining these, the expected lifetime utility of a representative individual is the probability-weighted sum over all potential time periods of the utility at each time S_t $U_t(C_t, H_t)$. Using these principles, similar to Meltzer (1997), it is possible to set out a model for the individual's lifetime consumption of health care, funded from that individual's own income stream. Health expenditure $m_i(t)$ on technology i at time t is chosen so as to maximize lifetime utility as follows:

$$\max_{\{m_i(t)\}_{i=1}^n} EU = \sum_{t=0}^{T} \beta^t S(t) U(t)$$

where

$$U(t) = U(C(t), H(t))$$

$S(t) = S(m(j) : j = 0, 1, \ldots, t-1)$ is probability of survival to period t

$$m(j) = \sum_{i=1}^{n} m_i(j)$$

$H(t) = H(m(j) : j = 0, 1, \ldots, t-1)$ is health status at period t

$$H(0) = H_0$$

With income in period t of $I(t)$, the associated lifetime budget constraint is:

$$\sum_{t=0}^{T} \left(\frac{1}{1+r}\right)^t s(t)\left(C(t) + \sum_{i=1}^{n} m_i(t)\right) = \sum_{t=0}^{T} \left(\frac{1}{1+r}\right)^t S(t) I(t)$$

where

$I(t)$ is income in period t

$C(t)$ is *non-health* consumption in period t

yielding the set of first-order conditions for $m_i(t)$:

$$\frac{\left(\frac{1}{1+r}\right)^t S(t) + \sum_{\tau=t}^{T} \left(\frac{1}{1+r}\right)^\tau \frac{\partial S(\tau)}{\partial m_i(\tau)}\left(C(\tau) + \sum_{i=1}^{n} m_j(\tau) - I(\tau)\right)}{\sum_{\tau=t}^{T} \beta^t \left[\frac{\partial S(\tau)}{\partial m_i(t)} U(\tau) + S(\tau) \frac{\partial U(\tau)}{\partial m_i(t)}\right]} = \frac{1}{\lambda} = \mu$$

where λ is the shadow price of lifetime income. The parameter μ indicates the threshold level that determines the quantity of each treatment, reflecting the opportunity cost of medical care in the form of foregone lifetime consumption opportunities.

These equations provide the theoretical basis for CEA applied to an individual's consumption of health services, in which the benefits of health care to the individual are balanced against the opportunity costs, expressed in the consumption opportunities foregone by the individual. The denominator represents the benefits accruing from the intervention, expressed in terms of the increased duration and quality of life. The numerator represents the expected increased costs associated with the planned use of the intervention at time t; the first term is the discounted expected cost of spending at time t, whereas the second term is the change in expected future costs beyond time t because of the changes in survival to different ages due to that spending, multiplied by net resource use at that age. It is this second term that is the basis for the need to include future costs in cost-effectiveness analysis if they are to be performed from a societal perspective. Though an early analysis by Garber and Phelps suggested such future costs could be neglected without changing the ranking of medical interventions, that result holds only when net resource use (consumption + medical expenditure − earnings) is zero at all ages, which is clearly not the case. In contrast, failing to include future cost will alter the relative cost effectiveness of interventions, with a tendency for the omission of future costs to bias analyses in favor of interventions that extend life, over interventions that improve the quality of life, at least among older persons where net resource use is positive.

3.2. A Mathematical Programming Perspective

The above approach assumes that interventions can be varied continuously, but often treatments may be binary decisions, so that a linear programming approach is appropriate. In such cases, a decision maker's problem can be formulated as a mathematical program in which expected health benefits are maximized subject to a *per capita* budget constraint M (Stinnett and Paltiel, 1995). This has many features in common with the welfare economics perspective outlined above, but makes some important simplifications in line with the extra-welfarist perspective. As above, there is a set of n independent health care problems, and for each problem i there is a single technology available at a known price m_i. In this initial formulation we assume (1) the treatments are independent—there are no interactions between diseases or treatments, (2) citizens are homogeneous and the need for treatment i occurs with equal probability π_i for all people, (3) the incremental health benefits h_i of any treatment are equal for all individuals, (4) the expected cost of each treatment (probability times m_i) is small relative to total expected health care expenditure (there is no "lumpiness" in the health production function), (5) the chosen treatments will be the only source of health care for the insured individuals, and (6) the decision is required for one period only (there are no dynamics to the problem), although of course benefits may accrue over a patient's future life course. The optimization problem for a representative person is then:

$$\text{Maximize } H = \sum_i \lambda_i \pi_i h_i$$
$$\text{Subject to } \sum_i \lambda_i \pi_i m_i \leq M$$
$$\lambda_i \in \{0, 1\}$$

The n variables $\{\lambda_i\}$ are a set of decision variables equal to one if the treatment is made available and zero otherwise. (Alternatively, as above, $\{\lambda_i\}$ can be considered continuous in the range $[0, 1]$, reflecting the *amount* of each treatment to be made available.) The solution of this mathematical program gives rise to the simple decision rule that treatment i is made available ($\lambda_i = 1$) if and only if $m_i/h_i \leq \mu$, where μ is the reciprocal of the Lagrange multiplier for the budget constraint. The ratio m_i/h_i is the treatment's cost-effectiveness ratio, and the value μ is the threshold adopted by the decision maker for accepting treatments.

The CEA decision rule $m_i/h_i \leq \mu$ indicates the "cut-off" or threshold for treatments, based on a ratio of health gains to expenditure, and reflecting the opportunity cost of alternative uses of health care funds. The value of the threshold flows implicitly from the level of the available budget and the scope of available treatments, and in practice a decision maker must adjust the threshold so that the budget limit is not exceeded.[4]

This formulation is readily extended to the case when there is more than one treatment for a health problem, exhibiting different costs and health benefits, as discussed in section 2. Note that in this case the treatments are mutually exclusive—the decision possibilities are only one or the other (or neither). For example, if there are just two alternatives for problem i represented by the pairs $\{h_i^1, m_i^1\}$ and $\{h_i^2, m_i^2\}$, these can be included with the additional constraint that the sum of the associated lambdas $\lambda_i^1 + \lambda_i^2$ must be less than or equal to one.

Note that if the cost-effectiveness ratio for both treatments exceeds the decision maker's threshold μ then neither will be selected. The interesting case arises when treatment 2 offers additional health benefits, but is less cost effective than treatment 1. The question answered by the linear program is then: Is the extra health gain secured by treatment 2 worth the extra expenditure required, relative to treatment 1? This approach to mutually exclusive treatments is readily extended to more than two alternatives. An alternative is dominated if either (1) it is less effective and more costly than another alternative or (2) its incremental cost-effectiveness ratio is less than that of a more effective alternative (this is known as "extended" dominance).

It will sometimes be the case that a new treatment B is not a perfect substitute for an existing treatment A. Rather, it may be a substitute for some but not all patients receiving the existing treatment A. Furthermore, the new treatment B may also be an alternative for "do nothing" for some other patients. This situation is not in principle problematic. It requires separate modeling of each relevant patient group—in this example:

1. Those currently in receipt of treatment A who might benefit from treatment B if it were made available;

---

[4] In principle, the next step would be to make the choice of budget endogenous to the decision-making problem.

2. Those currently in receipt of no treatment who might benefit from treatment B if it were made available;

3. Those currently in receipt of treatment A who would not use treatment B even if it were made available.

Separate incremental CEA can be undertaken for each of these discrete groups of patients.

3.3. Heterogeneity

It is useful to distinguish between heterogeneity that is observable to payers and policy makers compared to that known only to patients. The latter is closely related to the discussion in section 2.6 about the importance of considering the importance of behavior in assessing cost effectiveness. Suppose that the health gain secured from a treatment k differs between individuals. If—having approved a treatment—the decision maker is unable to discriminate among individuals as to who receives the treatment, then the problem remains as before, except that h_k should represent the *expected* health gain among the population that will seek treatment. If a treatment passes the CEA test on this basis, all patients remain entitled to the treatment, even those for whom the potential health gain is low. This situation is common in systems of social health insurance, in which—once a treatment is approved—there are few constraints on who may receive it. These issues are probably critical ones in understanding the full implications of patient heterogeneity for cost effectiveness.

However, the more common focus of the literature on patient heterogeneity focuses on circumstances in which the decision maker is able to enforce discrimination between patients, based on some observable characteristic. In its simplest form, the ability to discriminate between patients results in the creation of a small number of discrete "subgroups," such as (say) smokers and non-smokers. Then the cost effectiveness of the technology under scrutiny can be scrutinized separately for each subgroup, and if only one is below the chosen cost-effectiveness threshold, then the technology is offered to that subgroup only. In effect, the treatment offered to each subgroup is treated as a separate technology, but otherwise the decision problem remains unchanged.

In some circumstances, the observable characteristic may be a continuous metric such as age or body mass index. Suppose, for example, that younger patients can expect to secure a greater health gain from treatment k than their older counterparts. Then it may be feasible to construct a more sensitive decision variable than the simple binary (yes or no) variable λ_k. If the expected health gain is a monotonically decreasing function of age, and that costs remain the same for all ages, the decision variable might take the form ζ_k, the age at which the treatment ceases to be made available.

Of course the treatment is made available to nobody if $\zeta_k = 0$. The mathematical program is then amended to:

$$\text{Maximize } E(H) = \sum_{i \in k} \lambda_i \pi_i h_i + \int_0^{\zeta_k} h_k(v) p_k(v) dv$$

$$\text{Subject to } \sum_{i \neq k} \lambda_i \pi_i m_i + \int_0^{\zeta_k} m_k p_k(v) dv \leq M$$

where $h_k(v)$ is the health gain enjoyed from treatment k at age v and $p_k(v)$ is the incidence of the disease needing treatment at age v. The decision rule then becomes that treatment k is made available to all those aged ζ_k^* or under, where the cut-off age is given by $m_k/h_k(\zeta_k^*) = \mu$. As before, μ is the inverse of the Lagrange multiplier for the budget constraint, the opportunity cost of funds available for health care. By construction, all those younger than the critical age limit will enjoy a cost-effectiveness ratio less than μ. Other treatments are evaluated as before.

This example is highly stylized. It effectively disaggregates the population into different age groups, and considers the differential impact of treatment on those groups. It includes a treatment for a specified age in the insured package only if it is expected to secure cost-effectiveness ratios below the threshold μ, and requires that providers are able to discriminate in offering treatment only to the qualifying population. In practice, the effectiveness of most treatments at different ages is not known with any certainty, and such analysis makes heavy demands on data availability. However, if it is feasible to disaggregate the population into different subgroups with different expected cost effectiveness, according to any observable characteristics that can be verified by providers, an efficiency gain may always be possible if treatment for some groups yields cost-effectiveness ratios below μ while for others it exceeds μ.

A particular class of disaggregation may occur if there are certain measurable indications for treatment of the disease under scrutiny. In this case, if the indication is a predictor of expected health gain, then it could be used by providers as the decision rule for whether the patient may be offered treatment. For example, patients for cataract surgery may be accepted for treatment only if their current visual acuity falls below some predetermined level, indicating that the expected gains from treatment are greater than for those with higher scores. The practical application of subgroup analysis is of course highly circumscribed by data availability. Moreover, decision makers often encounter acute political difficulties when seeking to limit the availability of treatments to subgroups.

3.4. Divisibility

A debate between Johannesson and Weinstein (1993) and Birch and Gafni (1993) highlights the complications that may arise when the simplifying assumptions of divisibility of programs are relaxed. When programs are large and non-divisible (it is infeasible to restrict access to the treatment, if accepted) then—even though its cost-effectiveness is below the threshold—its acceptance in its entirety may lead to a breach of the budget constraint. If partial acceptance of the program is infeasible, integer programming is a solution concept that can then be adopted to maximize health within the budget constraint. This may mean that the accepted treatments are not necessarily those with the lowest cost-effectiveness ratios, but it can ensure that the entire budget is used and no partial programs are adopted. This is necessary because large programs may affect the acceptance threshold, and may also change the ranking of programs if the objective of maximizing health subject to the budget constraint is to be respected.

The integer programming approach towards accommodating "large" indivisible treatment programs entails requiring that all λ_i must take the values only zero or one. This results in a mathematical program, the formulation of which is almost identical to our basic model (Birch and Gafni, 1992). However, its solution is less straightforward whenever there are large treatment programs to consider. Some large programs may be omitted because they preclude inclusion of a larger number of small treatment programs. In aggregate those smaller programs offer better cost-effectiveness than the large program. However, among those included in the package, there may be some selected treatment programs with worse cost effectiveness than that of the omitted large program. The large program is omitted because it "pre-empts" too much of the limited budget.

From an analytic perspective, a simpler approach is to retain the existing model formulation, and to allow the decision variables $\{\lambda_i\}$ to take any value between zero and one. This will retain in the chosen package all treatments with cost-effectiveness ratios less than or equal to μ, but may require that some of the most marginal treatments are made available only partially—that is, a proportion $\lambda_i^* < 1.0$ of some treatments is funded. This outcome of course begs the question as to how the decision maker is expected to implement partial programs. Many methods (such as a lottery) are likely to be socially unacceptable, and there is increasing resistance to long waiting times for treatment. An alternative approach may be to introduce partial charges for the treatment (Smith, 2005).

The practical application of CEA usually considers the incremental cost effectiveness of new technologies in a piecemeal fashion, and does not seek to re-optimize the entire package of benefits every time a new technology emerges. It is usually presumed that the threshold μ is exogenously determined. In principle, however, if a new technology is accepted according to the prevailing threshold, and the aggregate budget M remains unchanged, two important consequences may arise: some existing treatments must be removed from the benefits package in order to make way for the new technology; and the threshold level may change. The treatments removed represent the opportunity cost of the newly accepted treatment. Any change in the threshold reflects the incremental effect of the new treatment on the use of the limited budget. As discussed at the beginning of section 3, such adjustments can sometimes be neglected as long as changes are small and the result of optimizing behavior so that the envelope theorem can be applied.

3.5. Uncertainty

Uncertainty in outcomes of an intervention appears in many forms in CEA. If risks are small or decision makers are not risk averse, then assessing the average outcomes and costs may be sufficient (Claxton, 1999; Meltzer, 2001). This will not be the case in general when decision makers may adopt other strategies to address the existence of uncertainty, such as performing research to uncover new information. When decision makers are risk averse, confidence intervals around measures of costs and effectiveness may aid decision making. It is also possible that uncertainty itself may be reduced through research. In such cases, value of information (VOI) analysis may be the most appropriate perspective as it can provide an estimate of the value of that research relative to costs (see section 3.6).

In considering uncertainty, it is useful to distinguish between the natural stochastic variability inherent in any treatment, the known heterogeneity of patient subgroups and decision uncertainty (Griffin and Claxton, 2011). Decision uncertainty refers to the limited information available for making a decision. Uncertainty can of course often be reduced by collecting further information. However, such activity has direct collection costs, and an indirect cost in terms of delayed adoption of potentially beneficial treatments.

Claxton (1999) sets out a general model for assessing the treatment of uncertainty in decision making, noting that—in the absence of any costs of reversing a faulty decision—analysis of uncertainty is redundant. Decision makers should simply choose treatments on best available evidence (using expected values) and change choices if and when new evidence becomes available. Meltzer (2001) frames this in terms of a societal decision-making problem in which risk-neutrality emerges as a result of the relatively small size of any one technology decision within the context of total spending (Arrow and Lind, 1970; Meltzer, 2001).

If in practice there are large costs associated with reversing decisions, consideration of uncertainty may become more important (Griffin et al., 2010). Using a "real options" approach, Palmer and Smith (2000) show how it is possible to integrate into CEA levels of uncertainty, the costs of reversing a decision, and the opportunity costs of delay. This model implies that—other things being equal—innovations with high levels of uncertainty, large reversal costs and low opportunity costs of delay should be reimbursed at a lower rate than new treatments with the opposite characteristics. However, this approach has to date not been adopted in any systematic way.

In practice, levels of uncertainty have usually been presented to decision makers in a heuristic fashion, to augment the evidence on the expected cost-effectiveness of a treatment. Approaches vary depending on whether the estimates of outcomes come from direct measurement of those outcomes or are developed through decision analytic models. In the former case, the uncertainty in outcomes can be directly characterized from the measured outcomes. In this case, a decision maker can choose to act on the mean values of costs and outcomes, the likely bounds on costs or benefits (e.g. a 95 percent confidence interval) or characterize the likelihood that their ratio meets criteria for cost effectiveness (e.g. a 95 percent cost-effectiveness acceptability curve). When modeling approaches are used, uncertainty in outcomes is generated as the result of uncertainty in the parameters of the model. Commonly adopted approaches to assessing the influence of parameter uncertainty include sensitivity analysis, decision trees and Monte Carlo modeling (probabilistic sensitivity analysis) (Griffin et al., 2010). An important challenge associated with such methods is how to model covariances between parameters, as in general the uncertainties inherent in each parameter will not be independent. Perhaps a more fundamental source of uncertainty is the structure of the model in use. Model structure will often be a matter of judgment, informed by expert opinion, for example on disease progression, particularly when long time scales beyond any available evidence are involved in the calculation of QALYs.

3.6. Value of Information Analysis

Value of information (VOI) analysis is an increasingly popular and influential method to estimate the expected value of research that can reduce the uncertainty about the value of medical interventions. Although VOI has methodological roots in statistical decision theory that dates back to the 1960s (Raiffa and Schlaifer, 1961; Pratt et al., 1965) the theoretical application of VOI to clinical trial design and research prioritization is a relatively recent phenomenon (Claxton and Posnett, 1996; Meltzer, 2001). A fundamental principle of VOI is that information has value only if it has the potential to change decisions. The expected value of information reflects this, and can be represented as $p*E(\text{Gain})$, where p is the probability that research changes the decision as to the preferred alternative and $E(\text{Gain})$ is the expected gain from that change in decision. The gain may be expressed in monetary terms (as in CBA), or in health terms (net health benefit). VOI estimates are generally made on the population level so that the expected benefits of a potential research project net of its costs can be calculated to assess the expected net benefit of possible research projects. In principle, research with a positive net benefit would be worth doing. With a limited research budget, research should be allocated to the projects that offer the greatest population expected benefit per research dollar spent. VOI can also be used to determine optimal study design for specific types of study (e.g. sample size), by comparing alternative study designs to find the one that offers the greatest gain in population health net of research costs (or the one for which additional gains in expected value are just equal to the next best use of research funds if there is a limited research budget).

Estimating VOI requires estimates of the uncertainty in the benefits (or if costs are considered, net benefits) of alternative interventions. This is most often accomplished by building decision-analysis models that reflect the uncertainty in the underlying parameters of the models and simulating these (e.g. by Markov-chain Monte Carlo methods) to generate a probability distribution of net benefits and what the expected gain in benefits would be from a study that reduced uncertainty in one or more of these parameters (Neumann et al., 1999). Often it is difficult to assess how a study might reduce uncertainty in specific parameters or the distribution of net benefits, so VOI methods are used to calculate the expected value of perfect information that eliminates all uncertainty about the actual net benefits of an intervention. This only provides an upper bound on the value of research but has the advantage of being possible to estimate with more limited information. Burden of illness calculations are similar in providing an upper bound with more limited informational requirements. In general, these upper bounds are useful only when they suggest the value of research is small. Meltzer et al. (2011) also describe a set of "minimal modeling" approaches that allow VOI to be estimated directly from outcome measures that are produced from clinical trials when those outcome measures are sufficiently comprehensive to describe decisional uncertainty. Selecting the most practical VOI approaches for specific situations is an area of active research.

4. CONTINUING DEBATES IN CEA

As CEA seeks to evaluate medical interventions in such a way that they can be compared, interventions must be assessed on a similar basis. This requirement has driven the need for simplicity. However, as experience has unfolded, several methodological challenges associated with the rudimentary model of CEA have arisen. Underlying most of the challenges is a concern that a failure to address a methodological weakness may bias comparisons, and offer an inappropriate advantage to one group of patients, or class of treatments, at the expense of others. Given the need for transferability of methodology and simplicity, methodological refinements should only be considered when they make a difference to evaluation results. However, there are several manifest areas of debate. This section discusses several of the most important of these areas of debate.

4.1. Perspective

Most cost-effectiveness analyses focus on the effects of the medical intervention on the individual in question and the economic costs of the intervention. This has given rise to several areas of disagreement. One is whether and how to consider effects on the welfare of other individuals that might be linked altruistically to the individual directly affected. Basu and Meltzer (2005) lay out a framework for considering this issue and provide some empirical evidence consistent with the importance of such linkages in a family context where the utility of spouse is connected. This approach has not yet been widely applied or tested on the literature but may be especially important for interventions that affect the health of individuals closely embedded in families, for example children, spouses, parents. The breadth of such potential areas of importance for this topic suggests it is an area deserving of additional study.

More generally, it is often the case that health treatments have ramifications for societal costs and benefits beyond the health sector. For example, some treatments may have benefits beyond health, such as enabling people to return to productive employment. In contrast, some treatments may impose societal costs beyond the expenditure perspective of the decision maker, for example in the form of private travel costs or time off work to undergo treatment. There is an extensive literature in economics on the "perspective" to be adopted in CEA. The key insight is that this should depend on the specific decision-making context under consideration. However, it is worth noting that a full societal analysis would entail the implementation of cost/benefit analysis. CBA forms the theoretical basis for CEA (Phelps and Mushlin, 1991), and is in effect a generalization of CEA in which the full ramifications of an innovation across the economy are assessed (in monetary terms). However, as discussed in section 2, its implementation is in most circumstances likely to be challenging.

From an extra-welfarist perspective, Claxton et al. (2010) present a generalized model of broader societal costs and benefits to a social decision maker in a single period setting. There is a general social welfare function $W(H,B)$ with arguments H (health benefits) and B (net consumption benefits to society beyond health). Each health treatment i yields health benefits h_i as before, and net benefits beyond the health sector b_i (these can be negative, in the form of net consumption costs to society). The societal optimization problem is then to choose a set of treatments:

$$\text{Maximize} \quad W(H, B) = W\left(\sum_i \lambda_i \pi_i h_i, \sum_i \lambda_i \pi_i b_i\right)$$
$$\text{Subject to} \quad \sum_i \lambda_i \pi_i m_i \leq M$$
$$0 \leq \lambda_i \leq 1$$

where M is the *per capita* health budget constraint.

This yields the societal decision rule:

$$\frac{\partial W}{\partial H}\left(h_i - \frac{m_i}{\mu}\right) + \frac{\partial W}{\partial B}b_i \geq 0$$

which can be rewritten as:

$$\nu\left(h_i - \frac{m_i}{\mu}\right) + b_i \geq 0.$$

where $\nu = (\partial W/\partial H)/(\partial W/\partial B)$ reflects the social value of health consumption.

The first expression captures the net benefits of the treatment to the health sector, as used in our previous model. The second term reflects the net benefits of the treatment to the wider economy. This rule indicates that—from a societal perspective—the conventional (narrow) cost-effectiveness decision rule leads to an underestimate of benefits equal to b_i/ν and should in principle be amended whenever there are non-zero costs or benefits beyond the health sector.

Note in addition that biases will arise if decision makers adopt a hybrid approach, by including some of the societal costs or benefits in their health-related analysis. For example, if broader benefits b_i are added to health benefits in a conventional CEA, then the decision rule used would be:

$$\left(h_i + b_i - \frac{m_i}{\mu}\right) \geq 0$$

with associated bias $\left(\frac{1}{\nu} - 1\right)b_i$, which will be non-zero unless the health budget has been chosen so that $\partial W/\partial H = \partial W/\partial B$. The bias arises because of the failure in setting the budget to take proper account of the societal value attached to health relative to other consumption goods.

The model can be extended to the case where there are interactions with other budget constrained sectors of the economy (such as other public services), by including additional terms reflecting the opportunity cost of health interventions for those services. In principle, the externalities caused by health treatments can be internalized by giving the health decision makers command over the broader societal problem, by extending the ambit of their budget to include other sectors, such as education or criminal justice. Alternatively, appropriate transfers between budgets could be arranged so that the opportunity costs of every service budget are equalized. In practice, pursuit of either solution is likely to be challenging.

Claxton et al. (2010) set out three possible approaches towards the treatment of wider social costs and benefits in the economic appraisal of health technology:

- Ignore the wider costs outside the health sector, the traditional CEA approach.
- Treat any wider costs and benefits as if they fall on the health budget constraint, which—as noted above—is likely to lead to biased assessments.

- Move towards a cost/benefit analysis in which correctly specified shadow prices reflect the opportunity cost of non-market goods.

It is difficult to argue in principle with the desirability of adopting a full societal perspective in the evaluation of health technologies (the third option above). Jönsson (2009) gives ten reasons why the societal perspective is to be preferred, which include comprehensiveness, consistency, absence of bias, interactions with QALY methodology, and openness and accountability. However, in practice society is not usually organized to take health coverage decisions in such a holistic way and it is legitimate to ask whether it is likely ever to be feasible. Even to adopt the second option presented by Claxton et al. (2010), in order to correct for any biases that the narrow budgetary perspective gives rise to, it is necessary to:

- Measure and value all non-health costs and benefits associated with health treatments;
- Correctly specify the social valuation of health gains relative to broader benefits;
- Correctly identify and value the opportunity cost of implications for other public service budgets;
- Ensure that a consistent valuation framework is applied to all the costs and benefits.

Given the challenge of pursuing such ideals, it becomes important to ensure that the application of CEA is internally coherent, that any potential biases are well understood, and that assessment of competing technologies is undertaken on a consistent basis.

4.2. Equity (Distributional) Considerations

Weinstein and Manning (1997) point to some unsettling conclusions arising from the strict application of economic welfare theory to CEA that give rise to profound equity concerns. For example, an individual's cost-effectiveness threshold is an increasing function of income. It can of course be argued that equity concerns should be addressed through income redistribution rather than the health system. However, concerns such as solidarity and fairness have led to the widespread development of collective health care purchasing, in which eligibility to treatments is determined according to clinical need, irrespective of income or other social characteristics.

A principle of utilitarianism underlies the rudimentary cost-effectiveness collective model—the objective is to maximize health gain regardless of who receives those gains. Resources will be directed at those with the greatest capacity to benefit. However, this implies that treatments for those who stand less to gain from treatments (perhaps older people, who have shorter expected lifespans, or chronically sick people, who can never be expected to enjoy perfect health status) will sometimes be deemed less cost effective than those directed at younger, healthier people. Policy makers therefore frequently express a wish to favor certain groups of users (relative to other groups) in the interests of some concept of fairness. For example, many policy makers signal a desire to skew public funding towards disadvantaged people, perhaps because they have lower *ex ante* expectations of long or healthy lives. Williams (1997) conceptualized this thinking as a "fair innings" argument, arguing that resources should be skewed in favor of those who—in the absence of treatment—would be denied a reasonable length or quality of life.

Such concerns require a departure from pure QALY maximization, and imply a need to weight health gains among disadvantaged groups more highly than the rest of the population. There is an extensive literature on how to conceptualize equity concerns, and integrate them into a cost-effectiveness framework (Bleichrodt et al., 2004; Dolan et al., 2005). The problem is often expressed as an equity—efficiency trade-off (Dolan et al., 2005). However, Culyer (2006) argues that this is a "bogus" conflict, and that the more fundamental requirement is to secure a proper understanding of the underlying social welfare function.

From a technical perspective, equity objectives can be readily incorporated into the cost-effectiveness model as follows. Suppose the dimension of disadvantage in the population is indicated by some cardinal measure such as wealth y, with probability density function $\rho(y)$, and that the relative weight to be attached to a person with wealth y is $w(y)$ (a declining function of y). Then, assuming that the need for treatment i is distributed as $p_i(y)$ and health gain from treatment is unrelated to y, the mathematical program becomes:

$$\text{Maximize } W = \sum_i \lambda_i h_i \int_0^\infty w(y)p_i(y)\rho(y)dy$$
$$\text{Subject to } \sum_i \lambda_i m_i \int_0^\infty p_i(y)\rho(y)dy \le M$$
$$\lambda_i \in \{0,1\}$$

Treatment i is selected when $m_i \int_0 p_i(y)\rho(y)dy / h_i \int_0 w(y)p_i(y)\rho(y)dy \le \mu$. This differs from the simple formulation only in the sense that the health benefits are "equity weighted" because the weight given to health benefits declines as wealth increases. The decision rule will therefore in general favor diseases with a higher level of incidence among poor people. Note that it is a trivial matter to amend this model if variations in health gains h_i (or indeed costs m_i) are related to wealth. Note also that there is no implication in this model that only poor people should be offered the treatment. Rather, it signals a desire to favor diseases with relatively high incidence among poor people.

Similar approaches can be envisaged for adjusting CEA calculations along any dimension of equity concern. The major challenges relating to equity and CEA relate not to such technical issues, but rather to how to conceptualize equity concerns, how to quantify their importance, how to secure the data necessary to implement equity weights, and how to integrate into the policy process. From an empirical perspective, there is evidence of concerns with equity relating to attributes such as age and current state of health (Baker et al., 2010). However, the empirical results are largely inconclusive, and subject to methodological challenge. Attempts to address some of the methodological challenges using discrete choice experiments suggest that the case for using differential weights for different population groups has to date not been established (Lancsar et al., 2011).

4.3. Joint Costs/Benefits

Cost-effectiveness analysis must first identify the universe of possible treatments under consideration. Within a specific disease area, there is likely to be a set of *mutually exclusive* treatments (including "do nothing"). After discarding treatments that are eliminated by dominance (or extended dominance, see section 2.2), the choice of the single optimal treatment within a disease area will be guided by the incremental cost-effectiveness ratios of competing treatments and the decision maker's acceptance threshold (Johannesson and Weinstein, 1993). Note that because this decision is based on incremental costs and benefits it is perfectly plausible to consider treatments that are increments of other treatments (perhaps more intensive therapy). In that sense, dependence between mutually exclusive treatments is readily modeled within a CEA framework.

However, a more complex case arises when there is some link between costs or benefits for treatments in different disease areas. Most theoretical CEA models consider various treatments as independent, in the sense that the health benefits secured by the treatment (or its costs) do not vary whatever other treatments are contained in the package of care. This is clearly a demanding requirement that does not always hold. It suggests that the aggregate cost effectiveness of a portfolio of treatments may be a consideration, rather than the cost effectiveness of individual treatments. For example, the incremental costs of a new neonatal screening test may be reduced considerably if there is an existing screening program in place, obviating the costs associated with putting in place an infrastructure for collecting samples.

How interactions between different programs are modeled is usually context specific. Much depends on what is taken to be exogenous to the decision problem. If the problem is simply to examine the incremental cost effectiveness of a single new treatment, then it is likely to be the case that existing cost structures and treatment programs can be taken as given, and the new treatment simply assessed on the basis of its incremental costs and benefits. Unless the new program would lead to the abandonment of existing programs with which it has significant cost or benefit interactions, the analysis merely has to ensure that truly incremental costs and benefits are modeled (including any improvement or diminution of benefits in existing programs). Note, however, that if cost or benefit interactions exist, inclusion of the new treatment may in some circumstances improve the cost-effectiveness ratio of some currently discarded treatments. Care must be taken to consider these changes if appropriate.

If independence does not hold and the intention is to determine the entire contents of the health benefits package, then it becomes necessary to model the costs and benefits of alternative portfolios of treatments. A simple ranking of cost-effectiveness ratios to determine the contents of the package is incorrect. Solution concepts such as mixed integer programming may then be needed (Stinnett and Paltiel, 1995), comparing the cost-effectiveness of alternative portfolios of treatments. Regrettably, such modeling sacrifices the simplicity of the simple ranking of incremental cost-effectiveness ratios, and may have unreasonable informational demands.

Variable returns to scale give rise to similar considerations. For example, if there are significant fixed costs associated with a treatment, which must be charged to the budget, the decision maker should in principle consider those costs when deciding whether to accept the treatment.

4.4. Time Horizon and Discounting

There is general agreement that, in line with conventional economic models, future costs and benefits should be discounted in CEA. However, there has been a continuing debate in the theoretical CEA literature on how such discounting should be undertaken (Gravelle and Smith, 2001; Ades et al., 2006; Gravelle et al., 2007). Early theoretical work generally advocated discounting benefits at the same rate as costs, principally on the grounds of consistency, and policy in countries such as the US is to follow that principle (Keeler and Cretin, 1983; Cropper and Portney, 1990; Lipscomb et al., 1996). However, that position has been challenged in more recent work (Claxton et al., 2011; Nord, 2011). As with most methodological issues arising in CEA, the treatment of discounting depends on the institutional arrangements in place, the objective function, and the precise nature of any budget constraints.

Claxton et al. (2011) set out a general treatment of discounting. The issues involved can be illustrated in a simple two-period model that can be readily generalized. Assume first that the objective is to maximize the present value of current investments in health subject to exogenously constrained health budgets M_0 and M_1 imposed in periods 0 and 1. Under these circumstances, acceptance of a technology in period 0 imposes an opportunity cost in the form of current health foregone. The decision problem is:

$$\text{Maximize } H = \sum_i \lambda_i \pi h_i^0 + 1 \frac{1}{1+r_h} \sum_i \lambda_i \pi_i h_i^1$$

$$\text{Subject to } \sum_i \lambda_i \pi_i m_i^0 \leq M_0$$
$$\sum_i \lambda_i \pi_i m_i^1 \leq M_1$$
$$0 \leq \lambda_i \leq 1$$

where r_h is the discount factor representing the time preference for health benefits. Note that the specification of a future period budget constraint represents a sacrifice of current health benefits, so the period 1 budget constraint must be discounted at the same rate as health benefits, namely $1/(1 + r_h)$.

This gives rise to a decision rule to accept technology i if

$$h_i^0 + \frac{h_i^1}{1 + r_h} \geq \frac{m_i^0}{\mu_0} + \frac{m_i^1}{(1 + r_h)\mu_1}$$

where μ_t indicates the opportunity cost of funds (expressed in health foregone) in period t. This equation effectively indicates the net health benefits of the technology.

The implication of this analysis is that—under these arrangements—it is necessary to use a different discount rate for the costs and benefits unless $\mu_0 = \mu_1$. In general, this will not be the case. For example, if the threshold for the health budget is expected to grow at a rate of g_k, then future costs must be discounted at a rate of approximately $r_h + g_k$ (of course g_k might be negative). Claxton et al. (2011) put forward an analogous argument for differential discount rates when seeking to maximize the consumption value of health under exogenous budget constraints.

When no explicit health budget constraint is applied, the opportunity costs of accepting a treatment fall only on the lost consumption opportunities in each period (rather than on health foregone). Costs can therefore be discounted at a rate that reflects the time preference for consumption r_c. In contrast, benefits must be discounted at a rate that reflects any difference between r_c and the growth rate of the consumption value of health. For example, if incomes are rising and as a result an increasing relative value placed on health gains over time, then a lower discount rate should be applied to health benefits.

In general therefore the treatment of discounting is an unresolved issue that depends on the precise formulation of the decision problem, and the nature of any opportunity cost associated with health treatments. For any multi-period model there will always be a need to consider the time preference for health, and the consumption opportunity costs of the associated treatment. Discounting methodology can have very important implications for many treatments, particular those associated with long-term conditions and disease prevention. No simple general rule can be proposed; what is most important is that the chosen model is consistent with the decision problem under scrutiny.

5. CONCLUDING COMMENTS

The practical application of CEA has had an extraordinary influence worldwide on the assessment of medical technologies, and is a prime example of how economic thinking can inform routine decision making of individuals, organizations, and societies. However, the pragmatic origins of medical CEA have led to certain inconsistencies and biases in the guidance it proffers. Efforts to put in place a coherent theoretical framework for CEA have indicated a number of areas where further work is needed, and where current practice may in some circumstances lead to incorrect conclusions. The principal criterion for new research should be the potential it has to change the health care resource allocation recommendations arising from CEA. With that in mind, we would highlight the following three areas as particularly urgent priorities for further research:

- Development of a coherent framework for handling alternative decision-making perspectives;
- Addressing patient heterogeneity;
- Methods to broaden the practical application of recent insights into the treatment of uncertainty in CEA, and how to prioritize new data requirements.

Throughout the chapter we have highlighted the need to align the CEA with the objectives and constraints confronting the appropriate decision maker. Much of the ambiguity found in the CEA literature can be traced to a need for clarity about how the decision problem is formulated. In practice it is unlikely that the broad conduct of CEA will be challenged by such clarification. However, it will help to resolve important debates that may have a material impact on the guidance of health economists working in this area.

Methodology is an important element of CEA, not only because it helps guide practitioners in their applied work, but also because it can serve to improve the confidence that decision makers have in its recommendations. CEA is increasingly being used to "referee" fundamental debates between governments, insurers, industry, and patient groups. This central role played by CEA in the political economy of health care is a great testimony to the economists who have pioneered its use in an intensely political arena. It is important that the methods remain fit for purpose, and continue to yield the trusted scientific evidence needed for an informed debate.

REFERENCES

Ades, A. E., et al. (2006). Evidence synthesis, parameter correlation and probabilistic sensitivity analysis. *Health Economics, 15*(4), 373−381.

Arrow, K. & Lind, R. (1970). Uncertainty and the evaluation of public investment decisions. *American Economic Review, 16*(3), 364−378.

Arrow, K. J. (1950). A difficulty in the concept of social welfare. *Journal of Political Economy, 58*(4), 328−346.

Baker, R., et al. (2010). Weighting and valuing quality-adjusted life-years using stated preference methods: Preliminary results from the Social Value of a QALY Project. *Health Technology Assessment, 14*(27), 1−162.

Basu, A. & Meltzer, D. (2005). Implications of spillover effects within the family for medical cost-effectiveness analysis. *Journal of Health Economics, 24*(4), 751−773.

Birch, S. & Gafni, A. (1992). Cost-effectiveness analyses: Do current decision rules lead us where we want to be? *Journal of Health Economics, 11*, 279−296.

Birch, S. & Gafni, A. (1993). Changing the problem to fit the solution: Johannesson and Weinstein's (mis)application of economics to real world problems. *Journal of Health Economics, 12,* 469–476.

Bleichrodt, H., et al. (2004). Equity weights in the allocation of health care: The rank-dependent QALY model. *Journal of Health Economics, 23*(1), 157–171.

Braithwaite, R. S., et al. (2008). What does the value of modern medicine say about the $50,000 per quality-adjusted life-year decision rule? *Medical Care, 46*(4), 349–356.

Brouwer, W. B. F., et al. (2008). Welfarism vs. extra-welfarism. *Journal of Health Economics, 27*(2), 325–338.

Chan, Y. (1993). Improving hospital cost accounting with activity-based costing. *Health Care Management Review, 18*(1), 71–77.

Chapman, R. H., et al. (2004). When does quality-adjusting life-years matter in cost-effectiveness analysis? *Health Economics, 13*(5), 429–436.

Claxton, K. (1999). The irrelevance of inference: A decision-making approach to the stochastic evaluation of health care technologies. *Journal of Health Economics, 18*(3), 341–364.

Claxton, K. & Posnett, J. (1996). An economic approach to clinical trial design and research priority-setting. *Health Economics, 5*(6), 513–524.

Claxton, K., Walker, S., Palmer, S., & Sculpher, M. (2010). *Appropriate perspectives for health care decisions.* York: Centre for Health Economics.

Claxton, K., et al. (2011). Discounting and decision making in the economic evaluation of health-care technologies. *Health Economics, 20*(1), 2–15.

Cropper, M. L. & Portney, P. R. (1990). Discounting and the evaluation of lifesaving programs. *Journal of Risk and Uncertainty, 3*(4), 369–379.

Culyer, A. J. (2006). The bogus conflict between efficiency and vertical equity. *Health Economics, 15*(11), 1155–1158.

Dolan, P., et al. (2005). QALY maximisation and people's preferences: A methodological review of the literature. *Health Economics, 14*(2), 197–208.

Drummond, M., et al. *Methods for the economic evaluation of health care programmes* (3rd ed.). Oxford: Oxford University Press.

Eddy, D., et al. (2005). Clinical outcomes and cost-effectiveness of strategies for managing people at high risk for diabetes. *Annals of Internal Medicine, 143,* 251–264.

Garber, A. M. & Phelps, C. E. (1997). Economic foundations of cost-effectiveness analysis. *Journal of Health Economics, 16*(1), 1–31.

Gold, M. (Ed.) (1996). *Cost-effectiveness in health and medicine* Oxford: Oxford University Press.

Gravelle, H. & Smith, D. (2001). Discounting for health effects in cost–benefit and cost-effectiveness analysis. *Health Economics, 10*(7), 587–599.

Gravelle, H., et al. (2007). Discounting in economic evaluations: Stepping forward towards optimal decision rules. *Health Economics, 16*(3), 307–317.

Griffin, S. & Claxton, K. (2011). Analyzing uncertainty in cost-effectiveness for decision-making. In S. Glied & P. Smith (Eds.), *The Oxford handbook of health economics.* Oxford: Oxford University Press.

Griffin, S. C., et al. (2010). Dangerous omissions: The consequences of ignoring decision uncertainty. *Health Economics, 20*(2), 212–224.

Johannesson, M. & Weinstein, M. C. (1993). On the decision rules of cost-effectiveness analysis. *Journal of Health Economics, 12*(4), 459–467.

Jönsson, B. (2009). Ten arguments for a societal perspective in the economic evaluation of medical innovations. *European Journal of Health Economics, 10,* 357–359.

Keeler, E. B. & Cretin, S. (1983). Discounting of life-saving and other nonmonetary effects. *Management Science, 29*(3), 300–306.

Lancsar, E., et al. (2011). Deriving distributional weights for QALYs through discrete choice experiments. *Journal of Health Economics.* In press, Accepted Manuscript.

Lewis, B., et al. (1995). Intention-to-treat analysis and the goals of clinical trials. *Clinical Pharmocology, 57,* 6–15.

Lipscomb, J., et al. (1996). Time preference. In M. Gold, J. Siegel, L. Russell, & M. Weinstein (Eds.), *Cost-effectivness in health and medicine.* Oxford: Oxford University Press.

Meltzer, D. (1997). Accounting for future costs in medical cost-effectiveness analysis. *Journal of Health Economics, 16*(1), 33–64.

Meltzer, D. (2001). Addressing uncertainty in medical cost-effectiveness analysis: Implications of expected utility maximization for methods to perform sensitivity analysis and the use of cost-effectiveness analysis to set priorities for medical research. *Journal of Health Economics, 20*(1), 109–129.

Meltzer, D. (2006). Economic approaches to valuing global health research. In D. Jamison et al. (Eds.), *Disease control priorities in developing countries* (2nd ed.). Oxford: Oxford University Press.

Meltzer, D., et al. (2002). Effects of self-selection on medical cost-effectiveness analysis: Impact in intensive therapy for type 2 diabetes mellitus among the elderly. *Medical Decision Making, 22*(6), 535.

Meltzer, D., et al. (2011). Minimal modeling approaches to value of information analysis for health research. *Medical Decision Making*. Forthcoming.

Mogyorosy, Z. & Smith, P. (2005). The main methodological issues in costing health care services: A literature review. Research Paper RP7. York, Centre for Health Economics.

Neumann, P. (2009). Costing and perspective in published cost-effectiveness analysis. *Medical Care, 47*, S28–S32.

Neumann, P., et al. (1999). Cost-effectiveness of donepezil in the treatment of mild or moderate Alzheimer's disease. *Neurology, 52*(6), 1138.

Nord, E. (2011). Discounting future health benefits: The poverty of consistency arguments. *Health Economics, 20*(1), 16–26.

Palmer, S. & Smith, P. (2000). Incorporating option values into the economic evaluation of health care technologies. *Journal of Health Economics, 19*(5), 755–766.

Phelps, C. E. & Mushlin, A. I. (1991). On the (near) equivalence of cost-effectiveness and cost-benefit analysis. *International Journal of Technology Assesment in Health Care, 7*(1), 12–21.

Pratt, J. W., et al. *Introduction to statistical decision theory.* New York: McGraw-Hill.

Raiffa, H. & Schlaifer, R. (1961). *Applied statistical decision theory.* Harvard Business School, Colonial Press.

Smith, P. (2005). User charges and priority setting in health care: Balancing equity and efficiency. *Journal of Health Economics, 24*, 1018–1029.

Smith, P. & Street, A. (2011). *On the uses of routine patient reported health outcome data.* York: Centre for Health Economics.

Stinnett, A. A. & Paltiel, A. D. (1995). Mathematical programming for the efficient allocation of health care resources. *Journal of Health Economics, 15*, 641–653.

Torrance, G. (1986). Measurement of health state utilities for economic appraisal: A review. *Journal of Health Economics, 5*(1), 1–30.

Weinstein, M. & Zeckhauser, R. (1973). Critical ratios and efficient allocation. *Journal of Public Economics, 2*(2), 145–157.

Weinstein, M. C. & Manning, W. G. (1997). Theoretical issues in cost-effectiveness analysis. *Journal of Health Economics, 16*(1), 121–128.

Williams, A. (1997). Intergenerational equity: An exploration of the 'fair innings' argument. *Health Economics, 6*(2), 117–132.

CHAPTER EIGHT

Cost Effectiveness and Payment Policy

Alan M. Garber* and Mark J. Sculpher**

*117 Encina Commons, Stanford, CA, USA
**Center for Health Economics, University of York, York, UK

Contents

Abstract

Cost-effectiveness analysis is versatile and used widely to assist in health care decision making. This chapter discusses how cost-effectiveness analysis is used at the system or national level, particularly in the domain of coverage and payment policy. We describe its relationship to other techniques, such as cost/benefit analysis, and the theoretical and practical aspects of applying the analytic technique in a decision framework. We then discuss the diverse ways that it is now used in various settings around the world, and the ways that it might be used in the future.

Keywords: cost-effectiveness analysis; cost/benefit analysis; decision making; health policy

JEL Codes: D610; Allocative Efficiency; Cost/Benefit Analysis; I100; Health: General; I120; Health Production; I180; Health: Government Policy; Regulation; Public Health; I190; Health: Other; I110; Analysis of Health Care Markets

Handbook of Health Economics, Volume 2
ISSN: 1574-0064, DOI: 10.1016/B978-0-444-53592-4.00008-6

1. INTRODUCTION

Cost-effectiveness analysis (CEA) has proven to be a versatile tool for assisting in health care decision making. Its origins include disparate intellectual streams; its justification has been based on its approximation to cost/benefit analysis with the attendant grounding in welfare economics (Weinstein and Stason, 1977; Phelps and Mushlin, 1991; Garber and Phelps, 1997), but it is also embraced by those who reject welfare economics as a framework for health care decisions. Thus, particularly in the United Kingdom, claims for its validity have been made on the basis of the "extra-welfarist" perspective (Brouwer et al., 2008). Although the set of techniques known as cost-effectiveness analysis has not been free of controversy, CEA has proven useful in diverse contexts. Anywhere that a determination of the value of a health intervention would be useful is a potential arena for the application of CEA. Its most visible applications fall in the area of health insurance coverage (or health system payment) policy, in which health systems, providers of care, and entities responsible for the distribution of medications decide which health interventions will be made available to patients (Freemantle and Hill, 2004). It has great appeal because it offers a measure of performance that can be applied to diverse interventions and disease states. Furthermore, extensive experience in performing and applying cost-effectiveness analysis gives the technique important advantages over alternative approaches, even those with claims to superior theoretical properties (Gafni and Birch, 1997; Johannesson and Jönsson, 1991; Drummond et al., 2005). It is difficult to imagine how a health care system concerned with improving efficiency, or with obtaining the greatest possible health benefits from fixed resources, can avoid using CEA or another technique that also weighs costs against health benefits.

This chapter discusses the application of CEA to coverage and payment policy, reviewing how it is used in various settings around the world and describing how it might be used in the future.

2. MEASURING THE VALUE OF HEALTH INTERVENTIONS AND HEALTH SYSTEM PERFORMANCE

2.1. The QALY in Cost-effectiveness Analysis

Cost-effectiveness analysis and related techniques are used for a variety of purposes, ranging from assistance in individual decision making to improvements in the overall efficiency of a health care delivery organization or a health system. Indeed, a critical challenge faced by anyone attempting to evaluate overall health system performance is the need to develop an output metric that can be used to inform estimates of productive efficiency. Aggregate characteristics such as population level mortality, hospital days, or days absent from work due to illness or injury are straightforward to measure and commonly available. But not one of these measures is comprehensive. And no measure that omits important aspects of health can serve as the sole basis for assessing health system performance. In the search for comprehensive measures of health outcome, the principal measure used in cost-effectiveness analysis, the quality-adjusted life-year (QALY), has proven to offer an appealing combination of validity and feasibility. That is not to say that QALYs are perfect from a theoretical perspective, nor are they simple to calculate. But they have proven remarkably popular over a long period of time because they have considerable conceptual appeal and, particularly as a contribution of ongoing surveys and other research, they can be calculated in diverse populations. Consequently, despite their imperfections, QALYs remain the best accepted comprehensive measure of health outcome for use in assessing the performance of health systems as well as individual medical interventions (Dolan, 1998; Garrison, 2009).

QALYs are described in Chapter 7. They represent a generalization of life expectancy in which each year of life is adjusted by applying a "utility," or quality weight, whose value ordinarily ranges from 0 (equivalent to death, assumed to be the worst possible state of health) to 1 (best possible health). However, utilities can be and are modified to account for health states considered to be worse than death (i.e. negatively valued). Furthermore, each year of additional life is discounted at a specified interest or discount rate. Although some have questioned the practice of discounting future years of health, failure to do so is generally harder to justify because health, like wealth, is fundamentally tradable over time—i.e. societies can trade today's wealth for health in the future or maintain wealth now and forgo future health (Claxton et al., 2006). More generally, there is nothing inherent in the methods of cost-effectiveness analysis that requires all QALYs to be treated equally, regardless of the identity of the people who gain QALYs and the time in which QALY gains occur. For example, the desire to reduce disparities in health outcomes frequently leads to calls to place greater weight on QALYs accrued by people who have poor health outcomes or are underserved. Furthermore, many political decisions about health care resource allocation either implicitly or explicitly place greater weight on health gains that will occur soon rather than in the distant future. For these reasons, it is important to be clear about the objectives of the analysis and to recognize that in many circumstances it may be desirable to use a complex objective function that allows for flexible counting of QALYs.

DALYs (Murray and Acharya, 1997; Gold et al., 2002) are closely related to QALYs, and HYEs (Healthy Year Equivalents) (Mehrez and Gafni, 1989) represent a generalization of QALYs that allows a more flexible representation of the different values placed on different time patterns of health effects. These methods have

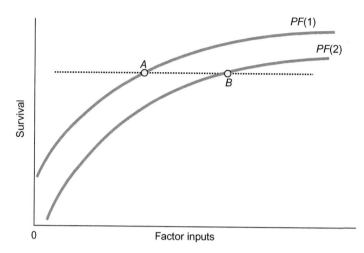

Figure 8.1 Relationship between health expenditures and outcomes for two health systems. reproduced from Garber and Skinner (2008).

important differences, yet they are all variants of the concept of quality-adjusted life expectancy, and from the perspectives of decision makers, the advantages and disadvantages of the methods are similar. It should be noted that few cost-effectiveness analyses have actually measured outcomes in HYEs.

Perhaps the simplest way to portray health system productivity, or productivity at the level of a health care organization, is to display either survival or QALYs achieved as a function of total expenditures (Garber and Skinner, 2008). In Figure 8.1, points A and B represent the combination of expenditures and QALYs at the population level for two different systems. Each point is on a curve representing the production possibility frontier (PF(1) and PF(2)) for the respective system, demonstrating that system A has greater productive efficiency than system B. Although such a display is, in essence, a cost-effectiveness curve at the health system level, it can also be used in the more conventional sense, at the individual level or at the level of a group of homogeneous individuals. Either at the individual or population level, the level of expenditure is set according to a willingness to pay for health outcomes (i.e. demand for health outcomes) or by a societal process that determines budgets or value of the outcomes at the societal level. We return to the question of the relationship between budgets and cost-effectiveness thresholds below.

2.2. Cost Effectiveness versus Cost/Benefit Analysis

A closely related technique for measuring health system performance, and indeed for measuring the welfare consequences of any investment in a public or private program, is cost/benefit analysis. Within economics cost/benefit analysis has long been a favored technique because of its direct grounding in welfare economics; any project or other intervention whose net benefits are positive (i.e. benefits exceed the costs) results in a potential Pareto improvement (Mishan, 1988; Garber, 2000).

The advantages of cost/benefit analysis from the welfare economic perspective are not, in practice, typically sufficient to overcome the considerable skepticism with which cost/benefit analysis is greeted by non-economists. For many, the discomfort stems from the need to explicitly monetize health benefits: in order to apply cost/benefit analysis, both costs and benefits must be expressed in the same monetary units (Garber et al., 1996). The methods used to monetize health benefits are often controversial. This is particularly true for valuations of changes in survival, whether based on contingent valuation or revealed preference approaches. In contingent valuation (Viscusi, 1993; O'Brien et al., 1994), questionnaires are used to elicit trade-offs between income and length (and/or quality) of life, while revealed preference approaches infer the value of life (or of morbidity or time) from economic behavior (Thaler and Rosen, 1976). As a consequence of basing the monetization on demand measures, higher values will be placed on the health of wealthier individuals, as long as the income (or wealth) elasticity of demand for survival and other health outcomes is positive (as it surely is; see Hall and Jones, 2007). In cost-effectiveness analysis, in contrast, only the costs—the numerator of the cost-effectiveness ratio—are expressed in monetary units. Calculating the numerator may require monetization of what are arguably health benefits, for example when the intervention requires significant time input. However, because time costs are usually small compared to the monetary costs of the intervention (with notable exceptions, such as exercise interventions (Hatziandreu et al., 1988)), and because there is no need to value changes in survival, there tend to be fewer objections to this component of CEA than to full-blown CBA.

Although the performance of a cost-effectiveness analysis does not require the *analyst* to place a monetary value on a life-year or a QALY, someone must make a judgment about its value if it is to be used for decision making. That judgment may be implicit, and even unconscious, but it is unavoidable. Indeed, the monetization that occurs in this process and the monetization of health benefits performed as part of cost/benefit analysis differ in form more than substance. Typically it takes the form of setting the cost-effectiveness threshold, or the maximum cost per QALY that is considered an acceptable expense. Alternatively, it may be embedded in the budget allocated to health care. This allows the analyst to claim, with some justification, that he or she is merely reporting the cost effectiveness of the intervention in question, leaving it to policy makers, physicians, or other parties to decide what to do with the numbers.

A reluctance to provide directive conclusions may reflect an admirable humility and a recognition that the analyst can seldom claim authority to speak for the general population. But it also means that the intended user of the findings receives little concrete guidance about whether a particular cost-effectiveness threshold accurately reflects his or her values and desires. Thus many studies merely point out that a number like $50,000 or £30,000, unchanging over time, is generally considered acceptable. In other words, the conversion of life-years or QALYs to monetary units in a CEA is often ad hoc and informal if it is described at all. As CEA becomes more widely used, the need for research to provide estimates of appropriate thresholds to inform policy decisions grows. Depending on the nature of the health system, these would be based on individuals' willingness to trade consumption for health and/or on the threshold implied by an exogenously set budget constraint.

In a cost/benefit analysis, in contrast, the researcher will be required to explain and justify the approach used as part of the analysis itself. Some decision-making authorities specify the cost-effectiveness threshold that they use in decision making—for example, NICE in the UK states its "threshold range is between £20,000 and £30,000 per QALY gained" (NICE, 2008). This allows the researcher to include the relevant threshold directly in the analysis. The adoption of an explicit threshold facilitates the use of the concept of "net monetary benefit" or "net health benefit," which can aid both communication and statistical analysis (Stinnett and Mullahy, 1998). When CEA and CBA are equivalent, it is because the appropriate dollar valuation is placed on QALYs gained by the intervention in question.

However, from a policy-making perspective, a potential drawback of cost-effectiveness analysis is that it is limited to the health domain. Cost/benefit analysis can be used to compare a wide array of interventions, addressing questions such as whether to spend public funds on a bridge, schools, or public health interventions. But cost-effectiveness analysis, since its outcome measure is typically restricted to a measure of health, is best suited for comparisons of alternative health interventions. Of course, comparisons among projects affecting areas as distinct as health and education are more germane for legislators than for most government officials. Many policy decisions are made at the level of specialized agencies, where the alternatives under consideration will typically include different health programs, but not other domains such as education, defense, or transportation. Furthermore, these agencies are often faced with budget constraints that must be respected in the resource allocation decisions. Thus for the governments that apply the technique, the scope is sufficiently large to make cost-effectiveness analysis useful.

3. USE OF COST-EFFECTIVENESS ANALYSIS FOR DECISION MAKING

3.1. CEA in Principle—Decision Rules

The theoretical description of how cost-effectiveness analysis can be used to optimize resource allocation is straightforward and elucidated in textbooks and reviews

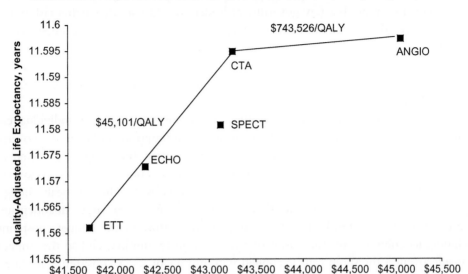

Figure 8.2 Cost-effectiveness of alternative tests for the diagnosis of coronary artery disease among 55-year-old men, using (US) medicare costs. ETT represents the exercise treadmill test, ECHO is stress echocardiography, SPECT is single photon emission computed tomography (nuclear myocardial perfusion study), CTA is coronary CT angiography, and ANGIO is traditional invasive coronary angiography. Here both SPECT and ECHO are eliminated from consideration by extended dominance. Although neither alternative is both more costly and less effective than any other, the cost-effectiveness ratio of going from ETT to ECHO or SPECT, or from ECHO to SPECT, is less than the cost-effectiveness ratio of going from either test to CTA. Consequently, for any cost-effectiveness threshold high enough to lead to the choice of ECHO or SPECT over ETT, CTA would be chosen because the cost-effectiveness ratio of CTA compared to either test is still lower. (Sanders et al., unpublished, 2009.)

(Drummond et al., 2000; Garber, 2000). First, the costs and health outcomes associated with each potential intervention are calculated. Then dominated alternatives are eliminated. Strict dominance occurs when one intervention costs at least as much as an alternative, but produces no greater health benefit. Extended dominance occurs when the cost-effectiveness ratio of an intervention is greater than that of another intervention that produces a greater health benefit (Figure 8.2).

After dominated alternatives are excluded, among the remaining alternatives the interventions that cost more provide greater health benefits. The intervention to be chosen is the one with an acceptable cost-effectiveness ratio that provides the greatest health benefit.

This approach, of course, requires the decision maker to determine an acceptable or threshold cost-effectiveness ratio, as discussed in the preceding section.

How is the threshold set? It might be possible to define a socially acceptable threshold cost-effectiveness ratio, but few government leaders would consider such a task politically attractive. But if the fundamental decision problem is for a government or an individual to maximize health outcomes from a fixed budget, the threshold is determined by the budget constraint. (In technical terms, the cost-effectiveness threshold is the Lagrange multiplier for the budget constraint (Culyer et al., 2007; Garber and Phelps, 1997)).

Inevitably, however, a budget for health is a soft constraint, since an individual can choose to substitute health care for other forms of consumption, and even if a government sets a fixed budget for health care in a single year, the budget can often be adjusted within a single budget period and routinely across budget periods. A government would serve its citizens poorly if, for example, it failed to adjust its health budget in the face of a major public health emergency or any other large, unanticipated change in health care needs. Budget-setting and the nature of the budget constraint, including its enforcement, vary from one jurisdiction to another, and so the implicit cost-effectiveness threshold can be applied with greater or lesser consistency in different settings.

As mentioned above, the UK's NICE is perhaps the best known example of an agency that applies a fixed cost-effectiveness threshold with a high degree of consistency. Even before it made explicit statements about the threshold it applied, its decisions were found to be consistent with a £20,000–30,000/QALY threshold (Devlin and Parkin, 2004). This threshold appears to be roughly related to an overall budget constraint faced by the National Health Service (Devlin and Parkin, 2004; McCabe et al., 2008). Some work has been undertaken to estimate the threshold operating in the NHS in terms of the marginal cost of generating an additional life-year and QALY in particular specialties. For example, the study estimates a cost of a QALY in cancer of £22,332; for circulatory diseases the corresponding figure is £14,909 (Claxton et al., 2008).

In decision making at the individual level, it is readily apparent that the budget for health care is not an invariant number. An individual faces an overall budget constraint. However, the individual's optimization problem is not generally solved by finding an optimal allocation to each broad category of spending followed by a determination of optimal spending subject to category-specific budget constraints. A change in the prices or quantity of any item, or the introduction of a new item, would generally lead to a change in the distribution of resources across categories. Holding everything fixed, this framework can be used to derive the threshold cost-effectiveness ratio, just as in the case of a government agency. But the threshold could shift under a variety of circumstances, such as a change in the price of a non-health good.

3.2. Cost Effectiveness in Practice

Thus theory suggests that it should be straightforward to apply the results of a cost-effectiveness analysis. Practical application, however, can look quite different. In theory, when a new intervention is deemed to be acceptable by a cost-effectiveness criterion, and when there is a fixed budget, interventions with the least favorable cost-effectiveness ratios, all of which have ratios that are greater than those of the intervention in question, are removed first. Thus, if a health authority decides to approve a cancer treatment with a cost-effectiveness ratio of $50,000 per quality-adjusted life-year, it should replace interventions that have the largest cost-effectiveness ratios, such as imaging studies that are costly but performed under circumstances in which they have little effect on health. In this case, expenditures will be held constant and health will improve.

However, if health decision makers cannot selectively cut low-value services, the consequences can be very different. And that has been the claim of some Primary Care Trust directors in the UK. Primary Care Trusts have played the roles of insurers in the National Health Service, paying for the health and medical care of a defined population from a fixed population-based budget (Claxton et al., 2008). They claim that when NICE determines that a new drug meets their criteria, for example having a cost-effectiveness ratio of £30,000/QALY, the PCT is required to cover that cost from its existing budget. In practice, according to some PCT executives, they are unable to reduce selectively the use of costly care that confers little incremental benefit. Instead, they are more likely to engage in across-the-board cuts in expenditures. If the care that is abandoned is, on average, more cost effective than the new drug, coverage of the new drug will be health reducing rather than health enhancing. As this example suggests, the specific details of implementation can determine whether a decision based on cost-effectiveness considerations will in fact improve health outcomes.

Another issue regarding the practical application of CEA in policy making relates to the specification of the maximand. The vast majority of published cost-effectiveness studies use some measure of health gain. Today most are generic health measures, such as QALYs. In principle, such a measure facilitates comparison of health gains and opportunity costs across health systems. However, some studies use measures of effect which are disease specific (e.g. cases detected, asthma attacks avoided). Such analyses are unlikely to assist in the allocation of resources across a health system. In principle, they may have value to support a decision maker with responsibility for only one disease area, where health effects of interventions do not spill out into other areas (e.g. side effects of pharmaceuticals) and where budgets are "ring-fenced" to that disease area. As discussed below, IQWiG in Germany developed methods guidelines which attempt to implement such "disease-specific" decision making, but this has been widely criticized and it is far from clear that these conditions hold for its decisions.

For health systems using cost-effectiveness analysis to inform coverage or reimbursement decisions, health improvement is unlikely to be the only consideration in allocating resources. In other words, although health gain is likely to be a key argument in the decision maker's objective function, it is widely understood not to be the only one. For example, another consideration might be the severity of the patient's health prior to treatment—for instance, should a QALY gain for a patient with mild eczema be considered equivalent to a similar magnitude QALY gain for a patient with advanced cancer? Furthermore, the value of a QALY gain may vary with the magnitude of the effect—the willingness to pay for a large QALY gain may either be less than or greater than proportional to the willingness to pay for a small gain. Thus, if decision makers wish to consider the characteristics of the recipient patient population or the scale of the health effect, the ultimate resource allocation may deviate from the actions suggested by the results of a cost-effectiveness analysis. This is consistent with the view that the purpose of economic evaluation is to inform policy/decision making rather than to determine it, and that policy making is and should be nuanced in the factors it needs to consider.

However, a stream of methodological work has sought to close the gap by incorporating these "additional" factors in economic evaluations. One element of this work has been the attempt to embed social preferences about the distribution of health outcomes across different individuals. This has taken various forms, including the concept of "equity weighting the QALY" to reflect the "deservedness" of the recipient of health gain. In the UK, two large studies were funded to make this concept usable for NICE decision making (Dolan et al., 2008; Baker et al., 2008), although equity weighting has yet to feature in the Institute's methods guidance or decision making. There has also been a broader interest in increasing transparency by making more explicit the factors that decision makers consider important in their decisions. A key aspect of this has been multi-criterion decision analysis (MCDA), in which formal methods are used to identify and score the various factors considered relevant to a decision (e.g. costs, health gain, innovation, severity or "need" of recipient group). MCDA has been used in health care, and there has been pressure to use these methods more widely in resource allocation (Baltussen and Niessen, 2006). For example, pharmaceutical companies have argued that NICE would benefit from the use of MCDA in its decision making to capture factors like a technology's innovative characteristics and maintain transparency. A competing school of thought is that many aspects of decision making cannot be scored and averaged and need to be considered as part of a deliberative approach to decision making (Culyer, 2009). This remains an area of active debate, with several unresolved issues. For example, the claim is often made that the cost-effectiveness threshold should be relaxed (or the QALYs gained should be up-weighted) for innovative products. Implementing such a proposal would require reaching a consensus on an operational definition of "innovative," an obstacle that may be larger than many recognize. And it may pose some uncomfortable questions: Should a government or payer be willing to spend more for a less effective treatment simply because it has, for example, a novel mechanism of action? Is the second drug in a therapeutic class innovative? When does an intervention cease to be innovative? And if there is consensus that innovative products should be rewarded, would a lump-sum payment or other mechanism to pay the innovator prove a more effective reward?

3.3. Application Under Conditions of Uncertainty

Decision making about the value of medical interventions is inevitably characterized by uncertainty arising from diverse sources, including the underlying data used for the analysis. Often health systems make reimbursement and coverage decisions at or shortly after the launch of the product. In the case of new pharmaceuticals, the evidence available at launch largely originates from trials undertaken for purposes of licensing and typically contains little economic data. And frequently the rigorous collection of new clinical data occurs only when approval for a new indication is sought. Information for drugs tends to be far more complete than for other medical technologies (e.g. diagnostics and medical devices), which are regulated less stringently in most countries. Hence the main uncertainty relates, first, to the use of, and outcomes from, the new technology when made available in routine practice; and, second, the implications of its clinical effects for long-term resource use, costs and impact on patients' health outcomes. Estimating a technology's cost effectiveness should, therefore, reflect the uncertainty in available evidence.

In the literature on cost-effectiveness methodology two dominant approaches to quantifying uncertainty have emerged. The first mirrors the methods used in clinical trials and more generally in clinical epidemiology. Studies using this approach report confidence intervals for incremental cost-effectiveness ratios (or confidence intervals for a measure of net monetary benefit, which in turn is calculated by using an explicit cost-effectiveness threshold (Stinnett and Mullahy, 1998)), and investigators estimate appropriate sample sizes for randomized trials to estimate cost effectiveness using standard concepts of power and statistical significance (Glick et al., 2007). The second paradigm has been influenced by Bayesian statistics and statistical decision theory. It has been concerned with concepts such as decision uncertainty—e.g. the use of cost-effectiveness acceptability curves to show the probability that, in deciding to reimburse/cover a new technology due to its apparent cost effectiveness on the basis of current evidence, an incorrect decision is made (O'Hagan and Luce, 2003). This has been taken further to quantify the cost of uncertainty in terms of health system costs or forgone health outcomes and to link this to the value of additional research using concepts such as the expected value of perfect information and, taking into consideration the costs and finite patient samples in research studies, the expected value of sample information (Briggs et al., 2006). In principle, these methods can be used to inform decision makers about the potential value of further research into new technologies, which types of research are of highest value, and the appropriate design of new studies.

This array of methods is now extensively used in published cost-effectiveness studies. Although there is some evidence on the use of value of information methods to inform research funders, such as the Medical Research Council and National Center for Health Research in the UK, and the National Institutes of Health and the Agency for Healthcare Research and Quality in the US, who are at arm's length from the health care system (Claxton and Sculpher, 2006), the influence of these methods on decisions made by health systems is not yet clear. A number of the methods guidelines published by reimbursement agencies around the world have recommended the use of methods like probabilistic sensitivity analysis (Claxton et al., 2005), which can be used to quantify decision uncertainty and value of information. However, analysts and decision-making bodies have had little to say about how formal description of uncertainty can be used to guide such decisions about investments in new knowledge or in clinical and coverage decision making. This is despite the fact that policy options are emerging as a response to evidential uncertainty, including coverage with evidence development and payment for performance schemes.

3.4. Generating Information for Economic Analyses and Policy

Health systems tasked with evaluating health interventions require not only analytic methods but also appropriate data. As noted above, the single greatest barrier to forming an accurate estimate of the value of any health intervention is the lack of comprehensive evidence of effectiveness. That is because measures of effectiveness should include not only the expected health benefits of the health intervention, but anticipated and unanticipated risks, effects on quality of life, and many other aspects of their impact. Furthermore, the time course of all such effects must be measured. Much of the highest quality information about effectiveness has been derived from drug approval processes, but even this information tends to be incomplete. Organizations such as the US Food and Drug Administration (FDA), Japan's Pharmaceuticals and Medical Devices Agency (PMDA), and the European Medicines Agency (EMA) typically demand extensive, highly structured data on efficacy. Measurements are taken and data collected according to the terms of detailed, pre-specified protocols. In other contexts, the information collected has less detail and rigor, and with the exception of administrative data and other large observational databases, fewer observations. The lack of availability of data, of course, reflects the great expense of carrying out large clinical studies, whose costs include the identification and selection of study participants, the development and execution of elaborate study protocols, and monitoring health outcomes (not limited to the principal outcome) throughout the study.

For evidence of evaluation processes in the United States that eschew formal cost-effectiveness analysis, such as Medicare's national coverage decision making under the Medicare Evidence Development and Coverage Advisory Committee and the Blue Cross Blue Shield Association's Technology Evaluation Center, the most common reason for an intervention to fail an effectiveness criterion is lack of adequate evidence, not evidence that convincingly demonstrates that the intervention is ineffective (Garber, 2001).

Consequently, organizations concerned with technology evaluation have sought strategies to improve the quality of evidence (Carlson et al., 2010). One of the most promising approaches that payers or providers of health care can pursue is to agree to pay for or provide services of uncertain value only when the care will be delivered in the context of a structured study. This approach has been termed coverage with evidence development (CED) in the United States, where the centers for Medicare and Medicaid services have taken the lead in such efforts, and Only in Research (OIR) in the UK.

When the alternative is non-coverage, payment or provision conditional on participation in a study creates powerful incentives for patients, physicians, and manufacturers. If the expectation is that the payer or the health care providers would otherwise make the intervention available, providers and manufacturers are unlikely to embrace the limitations that come with a requirement to administer the intervention only in the context of a research effort. One situation in which such approaches may be particularly attractive is when a small device manufacturer does not need a large-scale randomized trial to secure the approval of the relevant regulatory agencies and lacks access to the capital that would be needed to fund a rigorously designed clinical trial. In the United States, under such circumstances the Medicare program and private insurers might well conclude that there is insufficient evidence to support coverage even after the FDA granted permission to market the product. Coverage with evidence development would offer an opportunity for the device to generate revenue while it is being evaluated. For the company, CED is not without risk—after all, the evaluation might show that the device is unsafe or ineffective—but because it has the possibility of success, this mechanism may offer a better path forward than the alternative, which would not result in reimbursement for the device unless and until the company funded an evaluation itself.

The specific forms that the evidence development might take vary. It could include an agreement to participate in one or more formal randomized controlled trials, or alternatively to agree to provide information in a registry, or to participate in another observational study design. Each of these approaches has been used as part of Medicare's implementation of CED (Tunis and Pearson, 2006), in OIR in the UK (Chalkidou et al., 2007, 2008), and in the Ontario technology assessment program (Levin et al., 2007). Such efforts have generated important data. For example, CMS required participation in a randomized trial called NETT (1999) before a patient could be considered for lung volume reduction surgery, a novel approach to treat end-stage emphysema. The trial showed that the surgery did not improve survival overall, though it led to improvements in some measures of respiratory function and other aspects of quality of life (Fishman et al., 2003), and longer-term follow-up suggested that survival might have increased in certain subgroups of patients (Naunheim et al., 2006). Novel data of these kinds can support improved measures of effectiveness, and ultimately of cost effectiveness.

4. APPLICATION TO PAYMENT AND COVERAGE POLICY

One of the features of the policy landscape globally, as it has developed over the last 15 to 20 years, has been the use of formal economic evaluation to establish which interventions and programs are worth allocating resources to. Such methods are most widely used in the context of decisions about new pharmaceutical products. Starting in Australia and Ontario in Canada in the early to mid-1990s, the use of economic evaluation to support decisions about new drugs has spread to many countries in Europe, Asia and Australasia. In the United States, these approaches have been adopted by some state Medicaid programs and, it is often claimed, by private insurers and pharmacy benefits managers. NICE's approach to using economic evaluation as part of guidance on adoption of new technologies (principally pharmaceuticals) has influenced decision-making processes in many other health systems. There are differences between countries; the NICE approach, for example, is more prescriptive about acceptable methods of economic evaluation than otherwise comparable decision-making bodies in other nations (NICE, 2008). This is evidenced in their Reference Case which, following the principle set out by the recommendations of the Cost-Effectiveness Panel for the US Public Health Service in 1996 (Gold et al., 1996), defines NICE's preferred analytical methods. Those making submissions can provide non-Reference Case analyses, as supplements to, but not substitutes for, Reference Case analyses.

Table 8.1 summarizes the NICE Reference Case as set out in the Institute's 2008 methods guidelines (NICE, 2008). Some of the methods designated as "preferred" have proven to be controversial. For example, the cost perspective defines NICE standard interest in costs falling on the NHS alone. Broader costs, such as those borne by patients, as well as productivity losses and costs borne by other parts of the public

Table 8.1 Summary of NICE Reference Case (NICE, 2008). This Shows the Features that NICE Seeks in all Economic Evaluations Which are Submitted Under Its Technology Appraisal Process. This Does Not Preclude the Submission of Additional (Non-Reference Case) Analyses Deemed Relevant

Element of Health Technology Assessment	Reference Case
Defining the decision problem	The scope developed by the Institute
Comparator	Therapies routinely used in the NHS, including technologies regarded as current best practice
Perspective on costs	NHS and PSS
Perspective on outcomes	All health effects on individuals
Type of economic evaluation	Cost-effectiveness analysis
Synthesis of evidence on outcomes	Based on a systematic review
Measure of health effects	QALYs
Source of data for measurement of HRQL	Reported directly by patients and/or carers
Source of preference data for valuation of changes in HRQL	Representative sample of the public
Discount rate	An annual rate of 3.5% on both costs and health effects
Equity weighting	An additional QALY has the same weight regardless of the other characteristics of the individuals receiving the health benefit

Notes: HRQL, health-related quality of life; NHS, National Health Service; PSS, personal social services; QALYs, quality-adjusted life years.

sector, such as schools, are typically absent from NICE evaluations. This has been criticized by manufacturers—for example, in NICE's appraisal of new pharmaceuticals for Alzheimer's disease, the costs associated with unpaid (informal) care of patients by friends and relatives was not considered in the economic evaluation. It should be noted, however, that the health impact on an individual of caring for a sick friend or relative is formally considered by NICE in the denominator of the cost-effectiveness ratio, because all health impacts are considered relevant as part of the effectiveness measure.

NICE is clear about its requirement that health effects be quantified in terms of QALYs. Its recommendations about how QALYs should be measured are detailed. Specifically, for the Reference Case NICE requires that UK public preferences serve as the source of quality of life weights, rather than utilities derived from patients with the conditions in question. There is also a preference (although not defined in the Reference Case) for the use of the EQ5D (Dolan et al., 1996) instrument as a means of describing the health states which are the building blocks of the QALY calculations. There is also a requirement that quality of life weights are elicited using a choice-based method such as the standard gamble or time trade-off. In the case of the EQ5D, the UK values are based on an elicitation exercise using the time trade-off.

The cost-effectiveness literature uses a wider variety of methods, but NICE limits the allowable approaches in order to ensure greater consistency across appraisals. Consistency is particularly important because the new technologies evaluated in the appraisals span diverse clinical areas. The preference for the EQ5D as the measure of health is based on the view that this is the most widely used of such measures, particularly in clinical trials. NICE recognizes that QALYs in general and the EQ5D in particular are not ideally suited to some clinical areas, such as pediatrics and mental health. In these circumstances, NICE requires those making submissions as part of appraisals to demonstrate (rather than to merely assert) that the standard methods for measuring health benefits are inappropriate and the alternative they use is superior.

Table 8.1 also indicates NICE's Reference Case position on equity weighting—namely that no such weighting should be included in submissions. As discussed earlier, this does not mean that the characteristics of the patient populations likely to receive the new technology are ignored. Rather NICE takes a deliberative approach to assessing whether particular characteristics of the recipient group make its members more "deserving" of health gain than the average patient (i.e. their QALY gains merit greater weight than those of other people). This is the case, for example, with patients who have a short life expectancy due to their disease (so-called "end of life decisions") where NICE issued supplementary guidance in 2009 (NICE, 2009). With the characteristics of patients and technologies which qualify for this being carefully defined, the guidance requires the Appraisal Committee to consider whether reasonable up-weighting of health gain for these sorts of patients would be sufficient to bring the technology's incremental cost per QALY gained below the NICE threshold.

The price of a medical technology is obviously a major determinant of its cost effectiveness. In the case of pharmaceuticals in the UK at the date of writing, the NHS does not decide the price it will "reimburse." In this respect, it is unlike many other systems. Rather, the Pharmaceutical Pricing Regulation Scheme (PPRS) allows manufacturers to set prices for their prescription drugs, and the rate of return achieved by manufacturers across products is monitored, with price reductions agreed if rates of return are higher than an agreed level. Within this process, therefore, NICE has no role in recommending prices that might be consistent with a product being cost effective. These arrangements were criticized by the UK Office of Fair Trading (a government agency responsible for protecting consumer interests) (OFT, 2007), which argued for an arrangement called value-based pricing (VBP). In essence VBP would involve a consideration of the cost effectiveness of each prescription drug and the identification of a price which would bring the incremental cost-effectiveness ratio below NICE's threshold. Given that most indications include a range of subgroups for which a given product would be more or less cost effective, the price can effectively determine the revenues from the drug—the manufacturer can agree to a relatively low price and ensure use in a higher proportion of subgroups or a relatively high price and get access to fewer patients (Claxton et al., 2008). Although numerous details would need to be worked out, including whether prices would be permitted to vary for different indications, the current (2011) coalition government has recently published a consultation paper on the key features of the scheme (Department of Health, 2010), and a literature is emerging on the most appropriate specification of the scheme (Claxton et al., 2011).

NICE and SMC in the UK, the Common Drug Review in Canada, PBAC in Australia, Sweden, Netherlands, and Ireland all require manufacturers to submit cost-effectiveness studies using health outcomes as the measure of effect. Even within this paradigm, however, there is variation in factors such as whether QALYs are mandated, preferred or optional; the preferred cost perspective—restricted to the health care/payer budget or including a wider set of costs including those falling on patients, carers and the wider economy; the role of modeling or a reliance on evidence from randomized trials; the support for subgroup analysis rather than average cost effectiveness across a relevant population; the principles of choosing comparators against which to assess the new product; and the type of uncertainty analysis to undertake.

The evolving arrangements in Germany (in the form of IQWiG) are different in key respects (Caro et al., 2010). Although IQWiG recommends cost-effectiveness analysis in its general form, it rejects comparisons across clinical areas and the use of an explicit threshold that applies across specialties and clinical programs. In contrast to nearly all other organizations applying cost-effectiveness analysis, IQWiG does not, generally, support the use of QALYs. IQWiG's approach is to assess the value of a new technology in the context of its specific clinical indication. All relevant comparators within this are selected and incremental cost-effectiveness methods employed (both of these are consistent with other agencies' preferred methods). The main difference is in defining value in this context. Whereas other systems use a generic cost-effectiveness threshold (e.g. in terms of cost per QALY), the definition of which is more or less transparent, IQWiG propose to define a disease/indication-specific threshold which is inferred from previous decisions taken in Germany in that area. The use of a summary measure of outcome is central to the use of cost-effectiveness analysis but, although IQWiQ does not endorse the use of QALYs, it has yet to define its alternative.

IQWiG's proposed approach to economic evaluation has been heavily criticized (Jonsson, 2008; Sculpher and Claxton, 2010; Brouwer and Rutten, 2010). Although the authors of the guidelines describe a series of restrictions placed upon them by German law, the Ministry of Health, and IQWiG itself, are not clear how their proposed methods can inform resource allocation decisions given that costs and effects inevitably extend beyond individual disease areas. Furthermore, there may be implications for dynamic efficiency of using past (pre-IQWiG) decisions in Germany to define "a going rate" (i.e. a cost-effectiveness threshold)—those areas where many new branded drugs have been recently introduced will have high "going rates" and, despite the abundance of new products, offer the largest rewards for new drug developers. Conversely, those clinical areas dominated by generic products where there have been few recent therapeutic developments will have a low "going rate" and will therefore provide little incentive for manufacturers. As yet IQWIG have undertaken few economic evaluations to inform resource allocation decisions. It remains to be seen whether the methods recommended by its panel of experts will actually be used in studies.

The French approach to decision making regarding resource allocation to new medical technologies markedly differs from that of systems using formal cost-effectiveness criteria (de Pouvourville, 2009). Since 2004 HAS (High Health Authority) has advised the sickness funds and government, *inter alia*, about drug reimbursement. A prominent role in determining this guidance resides in the Transparency Commission (TC) which has a series of tasks within the process. The first is to determine the importance of a new drug based on the Service Medical Rendu (SMR) which classifies the product on one of four levels: important, moderate, low and insufficient. Depending on the SMR, the level of reimbursement is set. No formal cost-effectiveness analysis informs this decision, which is primarily based on generally defined clinical criteria including prevalence, severity, and unmet need. The second TC role is to define the size of the relevant patient population—this frames a discussion about the price and volumes for the product. Although this deals with overtly economic considerations, cost-effectiveness analysis is not mandatory; on the contrary, it seems to have little role. The third role of the TC is to undertake a relative effectiveness assessment to define the best use of a new product relative to existing interventions. This uses a five-level grading system to indicate importance compared to existing therapies and this feeds directly into price setting: for example, the manufacturers of products given the top three grades have greater (but not complete) freedom in setting their prices than those with lower grades. Again, these fundamentally economic decisions are not informed by explicit cost-effectiveness analysis but appear driven by largely clinical considerations.

Recently, a new development in France has been seen to offer a greater role for economic analysis. Since 2007, the Commission for Economic and Public Health Evaluation covers all health care and feeds information into HAS on a range of issues broadly relating to efficiency. However, this role seems to relate mostly to the implementation of new technologies in the health system rather than decisions about whether they should be reimbursed and, if so, at what price.

Thus there are pronounced differences between the larger countries in the use of economic analysis generally, and cost-effectiveness analysis in particular, to inform decisions about medical technologies. As published methods guidelines make clear, there is considerable variation in the ways that different countries use economic evaluation. For example, Table 8.2 shows the differences between jurisdictions in how they

Table 8.2 International Variation between International Methods Guidelines—the Selection of Comparators. Each term in the table relates to how a particular guideline has described its preferred choice of comparator(s) against which to assess the costs and benefits of a new technology. Based on data presented in Tarn and Smith (2004)

Expressed Preference Regarding Choice of Comparator(s)	Number of Jurisdictions
Most commonly used	8
Existing, most effective or minimum practice	2
Existing or most effective	1
Justify	1
Existing and no treatment	2
Most common, least costly, no treatment	1
Most common, least costly, no treatment, most effective	2
Most common, least costly, most effective	1
Most likely to be displaced	1
Most efficient, most effective, do nothing	2
All relevant comparators	2
Most effective and no treatment	1
Not clear/specific	3

Reproduced from Sculpher and Drummond (2006).

define their preferred approach to identifying relevant comparators to the technology of interest (as of 2004, when the data were collected). Although the general principle defined in the methods literature would be to select all relevant comparators, many countries appear to define a single comparator based on a range of criteria. This type of variation is reflected in a number of other methods areas, including the preferred approach to sensitivity analysis (Sculpher and Drummond, 2006).

This international variation in the requirements for economic evaluation between jurisdictions is a source of concern to the manufacturers of new technologies, in particular to pharmaceutical companies, because it often forces them to tailor different analyses of the same product to different decision-making bodies across the world. This has raised interest in the possibility of increased harmonization between countries in their methodological requirements, mirroring the interaction between some of the pharmaceutical licensing authorities internationally. This is most likely to happen in Europe, where discussions already take place between the agencies using economic evaluation to inform decisions in the larger markets, and where there is considerable collaboration between those organizations which undertake and commission health technology assessment through EUnetHTA—the European Network for Health Technology Assessment (Kristensen et al., 2009). There may be scope for harmonization in terms of the evidence used in economic evaluations—for example, commissioning and sharing single systematic reviews of the clinical evidence used in analyses or economic models to extrapolate over longer-term time horizons. However, even this is likely to be limited by strong differences of opinion between agencies regarding what constitutes legitimate evidence to inform decisions. There seems very little chance of harmonization at the decision-making end, not least because of the differences between countries in the resources they have available to fund health care and in the priorities they set for those interventions and programs deserving access to collective funding.

Despite variation in the specific methods employed, cost effectiveness is now widely used in developed countries to inform the selection of new pharmaceuticals for coverage/reimbursement. There has also been an increase in the number of middle income countries which are using these methods, in particular in Central and South America and in South-East Asia. Apart from pharmaceuticals, there are few examples of economic evaluation being regularly and formally used to support decisions. In the UK, NICE routinely uses economic evaluation as part of its clinical guidelines and appraisal of medical devices, diagnostics and public health programs. Other decision-making bodies around the world also use formal economic analysis to support decisions about non-pharmaceutical medical technologies (for example, the Medical Device Evaluation Committee in Australia). However, NICE is a centralized body and most resource allocation decisions are made at a local level, where the use of economic evaluation is much more limited.

Notably absent from this discussion is the United States, where economic evaluation is not as widely applied. With rare exceptions, in the United States private health insurers and government funders of care avoid explicit use of cost-effectiveness analysis to determine coverage or to decide which medical or health services to provide. Safety and effectiveness, but not cost, are considered in formal coverage decision making (Carlson et al., 2010; Garber, 2004). Similarly, the Food and Drug Administration considers safety and efficacy, not cost, in issuing regulatory approvals for drugs and medical devices. The Federal government made major commitments to improving the evidence base for health care by supporting comparative effectiveness research (CER) in both the American Recovery and Reinvestment Act of 2009 (the stimulus bill) and the 2010 health reform law, the Patient Protection and Affordable Care Act (ACA). ACA defines CER as "research evaluating and comparing health outcomes and the clinical effectiveness, risks, and benefits of 2 or more medical treatments, services, and items" (Patient Protection and Affordable Care Act (HR 3590), Subtitle D, Section 6301). Despite this support for evaluative research akin to economic evaluation techniques, the debate leading up to the passage of these laws as well as the language of the laws made it clear that these techniques remain controversial in the United States. For example, even supporters of federally sponsored CER objected to the inclusion of costs in the research (Wilensky, 2008). As a result the law contains explicit limitations on the way that Federal programs can apply cost-effectiveness analysis, including a prohibition on the use of a cost per QALY threshold by the Medicare program:

> The Patient-Centered Outcomes Research Institute [the organization responsible for coordinating comparative effectiveness research]...shall not develop or employ a dollars-per-quality adjusted life year (or similar measure that discounts the value of a life because of an individual's disability) as a threshold to establish what type of health care is cost effective or recommended. The Secretary shall not utilize such an adjusted life year (or such a similar measure) as a threshold to determine coverage, reimbursement, or incentive programs under title XVIII [including Medicare, the universal health insurance program for the elderly and disabled].
>
> **(From Section 1182 of the Patient Protection and Affordable Care Act of 2010)**

Both this language and the political debates leading up to the passage of the law suggest that there is little likelihood that in the near-term public insurers in the United States will formally consider costs and cost-effectiveness analysis, akin to the ways that the British National Health Service incorporates the results of NICE appraisals. This reluctance to embrace cost-effectiveness analysis in coverage decisions does not mean that there will be no interest in costs or cost-effectiveness analysis, however. Several aspects of the health reform law will encourage hospitals, physicians, and other health care providers to bear more financial risk and to become more parsimonious in their use of resources, while at the same time improving the quality of care. Physicians, hospitals, and other health care providers, who will be more motivated to improve the efficiency of the care they deliver, will seek tools that can help them produce better health outcomes at lower cost. Since this is the challenge faced by virtually every health system, and the reason that other nations have adopted cost-effectiveness analysis as a tool to aid in health care resource allocation decisions, providers are likely to explore CEA and similar analytic tools.

In the United States, cost-effectiveness analysis can also support so-called value-based insurance design (Chernew et al., 2007), in which, for example, drugs that are highly cost effective are dispensed at little or with no cost to patients, while higher out-of-pocket payments accompany drugs with high cost-effectiveness ratios. In fact, independent of value-based design, cost-effectiveness analysis may also find a receptive audience among patients and their families, since even well-insured Americans often bear large out-of-pocket costs for health care.

Indeed, in nations that use economic evaluation to decide which technologies will be approved or adopted, there are broader uses for the method as well. As discussed above, in the UK there is a great deal of interest in adopting "value-based pricing," an approach that would essentially serve to facilitate negotiation until a new drug reaches an acceptable cost-effectiveness ratio. This contrasts with what has been the customary approach for NICE, which is to take the price of the drug as a given and to determine whether its cost-effectiveness ratio is acceptable. In principle, there may be little to distinguish between the past approach and value-based pricing, since in both cases NICE would be expected to issue a positive decision about any drug that has an acceptable cost-effectiveness ratio. But if the manufacturer sets the price without knowing how the drug will fare in a NICE appraisal—perhaps because the manufacturer cannot anticipate the modeling assumptions or data used in the appraisal—there is a chance that the price that seemed acceptable in the company's calculations will be too high to receive a positive NICE decision. Value-based pricing will make it possible for NICE and the manufacturer to settle on a price that will (just) satisfy the cost-effectiveness threshold that NICE employs.

Another approach by which to incorporate cost-effectiveness analysis into health care allocation decisions is sometimes called payment for outcomes or payment by results (not to be confused with the NHS program for case-rate reimbursement for hospital care by the same name). Payment by results shifts risk onto the provider or manufacturer by withholding some or all of the payment for a medical service or product unless an agreed-upon outcome is met. In a well-publicized example of payment by results, Johnson and Johnson, the manufacturer, and the NHS reached an agreement under which payments for Velcade, a drug used to treat multiple myeloma, would be returned for those patients for whom the drug did not appear to be effective (as measured by a reduction in the M-protein level, a marker of disease activity) (Garber and McClellan, 2007). A number of other arrangements of this nature have been implemented internationally (Carlson et al., 2007). Perhaps the most important distinction between a payment by results approach and one that pays based on cost effectiveness averaged over all patients is that it shifts risk. That is, if outcomes are better than expected, the manufacturer or provider gains by getting greater reimbursement, whereas unexpected good results offer no particular gain to the manufacturer under value-based payment, unless and until payment is modified to reflect the better-than-expected performance.

A major challenge to the broader use of payment by results is the need for appropriate outcome measures—ones that are easily monitored and difficult to manipulate, and that either represent desired outcomes themselves or are tightly correlated with outcomes.

4.1. Beyond the Cost-effectiveness Ratio

The adoption of cost-effectiveness analysis around the world suggests that the method is viewed as a useful tool, if an imperfect one. As a structured, relatively straightforward mechanism for promoting greater efficiency in health care, it meets a pressing public and private need. Yet there is much that it does not do, or at least does not do gracefully. A large number of considerations do not fall neatly into the analytic framework. Often the problems stem from considerations, such as distributional consequences that might lead policy makers and others responsible for medical care decisions to reject the incremental cost-effectiveness ratio as the sole decision criterion, that are fundamentally complementary to the efficiency orientation of cost-effectiveness analysis. Although modifications to the basic cost-effectiveness analysis can make it possible to incorporate distributional consequences, for example by assigning different weights to different individuals or population groups, overly enthusiastic application of such modifications can easily obscure the meaning of the computed ICER and the assumptions that underlie the analysis. The recognition that CEA cannot readily accommodate every concern relevant to a clinical policy decision has led nearly every group that recommends use of CEA (such as the US Panel on Cost-Effectiveness in Health and Medicine) (Gold et al., 1996) or that uses it directly (Henry et al., 2005; Laupacis, 2005; Rawlins, 1999) also to recommend that decisions not be based solely on the ICER, but should take into account important factors that are not embedded within the analysis.

Governments need to bear in mind other considerations as well. Understandability and acceptability to the public depend not only on a fair set of procedures and an open and transparent process for health care decision making, but also effective representation of public interests. Most bodies that engage in such decisions include representation of the general public; in the case of NICE, Citizens Councils have been particularly successful in bringing public voices into deliberations, in part by providing substantial methodological training to the public representatives. Effective communication and dissemination of information are essential if any such endeavor is to retain public trust for very long.

One limitation of the strict application of cost-effectiveness analysis is that it is a tool for static efficiency, but this has raised questions about whether it is sufficient to ensure dynamic efficiency. Large fixed costs are necessary to develop medical technologies such as drugs and devices, so marginal cost pricing will lead to negative profits. A strict cost-effectiveness criterion can lead to static efficiency, but some have argued that, under some circumstances, it will under-reward companies bearing the fixed costs of R&D, thereby leading to suboptimal innovation, i.e. creating dynamic inefficiency. Others have argued that cost-effectiveness analysis (perhaps complemented by value-based pricing and potentially a public role in funding R&D) signals the system's demand curve and, together with appropriate patent protection, can ensure innovation is directed to areas with the highest social returns (Claxton, 2007; Claxton et al., 2008). A small but growing literature addresses pricing approaches that can lead to both static and dynamic efficiency (Garber et al., 2006; Lakdawalla and Sood, 2009; Jena and Philipson, 2008). These approaches include variants of two-part pricing; it may not be feasible to achieve both static and dynamic efficiency under realistic conditions, however, so sometimes second-best solutions are proposed, such as increasing the cost-effectiveness threshold to account for incentives for innovation. Such approaches, it has been argued, sacrifice static efficiency in an effort to achieve greater dynamic efficiency.

Although there are limits to the power of cost-effectiveness analysis to guide health care allocation decisions, and although there remain methodological controversies, the technique offers a structured approach to assembling and presenting a wide range of evidence about the costs and effectiveness of alternative approaches to care. The challenges that have led to its adoption are not diminishing, nor have compelling alternative techniques emerged. It is likely to remain an important tool for health care allocation decisions in years to come, so it will be of paramount importance to do such analyses well and continue to refine the methods.

REFERENCES

Baker, R., Bateman, I., & Donaldson, C. (2008). *Weighting and valuing quality adjusted life years: Preliminary results from the Social Value of a QALY Project.* London: National Institute for Health and Clinical Excellence.

Baltussen, R. & Niessen, L. (2006). Priority setting of health interventions: The need for multi-criteria decision analysis. Cost Effectiveness and Resource Allocation, 4. 10.1186/478-7547-4-14.

Briggs, A., Claxton, K., & Sculpher, M. (2006). *Decision modelling for health economic evaluation.* Oxford: Oxford University Press.

Brouwer, W. B. F. & Rutten, F. F. H. (2010). The efficiency frontier approach to economic evaluation: Will it help German policy making? *Health Economics, 19,* 1128–1131.

Brouwer, W. B. F., Culyer, A. J., van Exel, N., & Rutten, F. F. H. (2008). Welfarism vs. extra-welfarism. *Journal of Health Economics, 27*(2), 325–338.

Carlson, J. J., Sullivan, S. D., Garrison, L. P., Neumann, P. J., & Veenstra, D. L. (2010). Linking payment to health outcomes: A taxonomy and examination of performance-based reimbursement schemes between healthcare payers and manufacturers. *Health Policy, 96*(3), 179–190.

Caro, J., Nord, E., Siebert, U., McGuire, A., McGregor, M., Henry, D., et al. (2010). The efficiency frontier approach to economic evaluation of health-care interventions. *Health Economics,* doi:10.1002/hec.1629.

Chalkidou, K., Hoy, A., & Littlejohns, P. (2007). Making a decision to wait for more evidence: When the National Institute for Health and Clinical Excellence recommends a technology only in the context of research. *Journal of the Royal Society of Medicine, 100*(10), 453.

Chalkidou, K., Lord, J., Fischer, A. and Littlejohns, P. (2008). Evidence-based decision making: When should we wait for more information? *Health Affairs (Project Hope), 27*(6), 1642.

Chernew, M., Rosen, A., & Fendrick, A. (2007). Value-based insurance design. *Health Affairs, 26*(2), w195.

Claxton, K. (2007). OFT, VBP: QED? *Health Economics, 16*(6), 545–558.

Claxton, K. & Sculpher, M. J. (2006). Using value of information analysis to prioritise health research: Some lessons from recent UK experience. *PharmacoEconomics, 24,* 1055–1068.

Claxton, K., Briggs, A., Buxton, M. J., Culyer, A. J., McCabe, C., Walker, S., et al. (2008). Value based pricing for NHS drugs: An opportunity not to be missed? *British Medical Journal, 336*(7638), 251–254.

Claxton, K., Sculpher, M., & Carroll, S. (2011). *Value based pricing for pharmaceuticals: Its role, specification and prospects in a newly devolved NHS.* York: University of York.

Claxton, K., Sculpher, M., McCabe, C., Briggs, A., Akehurst, R., Buxton, M., et al. (2005). Probabilistic sensitivity analysis for NICE technology assessment: Not an optional extra. *Health Economics, 14,* 339–347.

Claxton, K., Sculpher, M. J., Culyer, A. J., McCabe, C., Briggs, A. H., Akehurst, R., et al. (2006). Discounting and cost-effectiveness in NICE—stepping back to sort out the confusion. *Health Economics, 15*, 1–4.

Culyer, A., McCabe, C., Briggs, A., Claxton, K., Buxton, M., Akehurst, R., et al. (2007). Searching for a threshold, not setting one: The role of the National Institute for Health and Clinical Excellence. *Journal of Health Services Research & Policy, 12*(1), 56.

Culyer, A. J. (2009). *Deliberative processes in decisions about health care technologies: Combining different types of evidence, values, algorithms and people.* London: Office of Health Economics.

Department of Health (2010). *A new value-based approach to the pricing of branded medicines.* London, UK: Department of Health. Availabale from: < http://www.dh.gov.uk/prod_consum_dh/groups/dh_digitalassets/@dh/@en/documents/digitalasset/dh_122793.pdf/ >.

De Pouvourville, G. (2009). Pricing and reimbursment for drugs in France. What is the role for cost-effectiveness analysis? ESSEC Business School Working Paper. Paris.

Devlin, N. & Parkin, D. (2004). Does NICE have a cost-effectiveness threshold and what other factors influence its decisions? A binary choice analysis. *Health Economics, 13*(5), 437–452.

Dolan, P. (1998). The measurement of individual utility and social welfare. *Journal of Health Economics, 17*, 39–52.

Dolan, P., Edlin, R., Tsuchiya, A., et al. *The relative societal value of health gains to different beneficiaries.* London: National Institute for Health and Clinical Excellence.

Dolan, P., Gudex, C., Kind, P., & Williams, A. (1996). Valuing health states: A comparison of methods. *Journal of Health Economics, 15*, 209–231.

Drummond, M., Sculpher, M., Torrance, G., O'Brien, B., & Stoddart, G. (2005). *Methods for the economic evaluation of health care programmes.* New York: Oxford University Press, USA.

Fishman, A., Martinez, F., Naunheim, K., Piantadosi, S., Wise, R., Ries, A., et al. (2003). A randomized trial comparing lung-volume-reduction surgery with medical therapy for severe emphysema. *New England Journal of Medicine, 348*(21), 2059.

Freemantle, N. & Hill, S. (2004). *Evaluating pharmaceuticals for health policy and reimbursement.* Oxford: Blackwell.

Gafni, A. & Birch, S. (1997). QALYs and HYEs (healthy years equivalent). Spotting the differences. *Journal of Health Economics, 16*(5), 601–608.

Garber, A., Jones, C., & Romer, P. (2006). Insurance and incentives for medical innovation. *Forum for Health Economics and Policy, 9*(2), 4.

Garber, A., Weinstein, M., Torrance, G., & Kamlet, M. (1996). Theoretical foundations of cost-effectiveness analysis. In M. Gold, J. Siegel, L. Russell, & M. Weinstein (Eds.), *Cost-effectiveness in health and medicine* (pp. 25–53). New York: Oxford University Press.

Garber, A. M. (2000). Advances in cost-effectiveness analysis of health interventions. In J. P. Newhouse & A. J. Culyer (Eds.), *Handbook of health economics* (pp. 181–221). Amsterdam: North-Holland.

Garber, A. M. (2001). Evidence-based coverage policy. *Health Affairs (Millwood), 20*(5), 62–82.

Garber, A. M. (2004). Cost-effectiveness and evidence evaluation as criteria for coverage policy. *Health Affairs (Millwood),* Suppl. Web Exclusives: W4-284-96.

Garber, A. M. & McClellan, M. B. (2007). Satisfaction guaranteed—"payment by results" for biologic agents. *New England Journal of Medicine, 357*(16), 1575–1577.

Garber, A. M. & Phelps, C. E. (1997). Economic foundations of cost-effectiveness analysis. *Journal of Health Economics, 16*(1), 1–31.

Garber, A. M. & Skinner, J. (2008). Is American health care uniquely inefficient? *Journal of Economic Perspectives, 22*(4), 27–50.

Garrison, L. P. (2009). On the benefits of modeling using QALYs for societal resource allocation: The model is the message. *Value in Health, 12*, S36–S37.

Glick, H. A., Doshi, J. A., Sonnad, S. S., & Polsky, D. (2007). *Economic evaluation in clinical trials.* Oxford: Oxford University Press.

Gold, M., Stevenson, D., & Fryback, D. (2002). HALY S and QALY S and DALY S, OHMY: Similarities and differences in summary measures of population health. *Annual Review of Public Health, 23*(1), 115–134.

Gold, M. R., Siegel, J. E., Russell, L. B., & Weinstein, M. C. (Eds.) (1996). *Cost-effectiveness in health and medicine* New York: Oxford University Press.

Hall, R. & Jones, C. (2007). The value of life and the rise in health spending. *Quarterly Journal of Economics, 122*(1), 39–72.

Hatziandreu, E., Koplan, J., Weinstein, M., Caspersen, C., & Warner, K. (1988). A cost-effectiveness analysis of exercise as a health promotion activity. *American Journal of Public Health, 78*(11), 1417.

Henry, D., Hill, S., & Harris, A. (2005). Drug prices and value for money: The Australian Pharmaceutical Benefits Scheme. *JAMA, 294*(20), 2630.

Jena, A. & Philipson, T. (2008). Cost-effectiveness analysis and innovation. *Journal of Health Economics, 27* (5), 1224–1236.

Johannesson, M. & Jönsson, B. (1991). Economic evaluation in health care: Is there a role for cost-benefit analysis? *Health Policy, 17*(1), 1–23.

Jonsson, B. (2008). IQWiG: An opportunity lost. *European Journal of Health Economics, 9*, 205–207.

Kristensen, F. B., Mäkelä, M., Neikter, S. A., Rehnqvist, N., Håheim, L. L., Mørland, B., et al. (2009). European network for Health Technology Assessment, EUnetHTA: Planning, development, and implementation of a sustainable European network for Health Technology Assessment. *International Journal of Technology Assessment in Health Care, 25*(Supplement S2), 107–116.

Lakdawalla, D. & Sood, N. (2009). Innovation and the welfare effects of public drug insurance. *Journal of Public Economics, 93*(3–4), 541–548.

Laupacis, A. (2005). Incorporating economic evaluations into decision-making: The Ontario experience. *Medical Care, 43*(7), II-15–II-19.

Levin, L., Goeree, R., Sikich, N., Jorgensen, B., Brouwers, M., Easty, T., et al. (2007). Establishing a comprehensive continuum from an evidentiary base to policy development for health technologies: The Ontario experience. *International Journal of Technology Assessment in Health Care, 23*(3), 299–309.

McCabe, C., Claxton, K., & Culyer, A. (2008). The NICE cost-effectiveness threshold: What it is and what that means. *PharmacoEconomics, 26*(9), 733–744.

Mehrez, A. & Gafni, A. (1989). Quality-adjusted life years, utility theory, and healthy-years equivalents. *Medical Decision Making, 9*, 142–149.

Mishan, E. J. (1988). *Cost-benefit analysis.* London: Unwin Hyman.

Murray, C. & Acharya, A. (1997). Understanding DALYs. *Journal of Health Economics, 16*(6), 703–730.

National Emphysema Treatment Trial Research Group (NETT) (1999). Rationale and design of the national emphysema treatment trial (NETT): A prospective randomized trial of lung volume reduction surgery. *Journal of Thoracic and Cardiovascular Surgery, 118*(3) 518–528.

National Institute for Health and Clinical Excellence (NICE) (2008). *Guide to the methods of technology appraisal.* London: NICE.

National Institute for Health and Clinical Excellence (UK) (2009). Appraising life-extending, end of life treatments [cited November 2, 2010]. Available from: <http://www.nice.org.uk/media/E4A/79/SupplementaryAdviceTACEoL.pdf/>

Naunheim, K., Wood, D., Mohsenifar, Z., Sternberg, A., Criner, G., DeCamp, M., et al. (2006). Long-term follow-up of patients receiving lung-volume-reduction surgery versus medical therapy for severe emphysema by the National Emphysema Treatment Trial Research Group. *Annals of Thoracic Surgery, 82*(2), 431–443.

O'Brien, B. J., Drummond, M. F., Labelle, R. J., & Willan, A. (1994). In search of power and significance: Issues in the design and analysis of stochastic cost-effectiveness studies in health care. *Medical Care, 32*(2), 150–163.

Office of Fair Trading (2007). *The pharmaceutical price regulation scheme. An OFT market study.* London: OFT.

O'Hagan, A. & Luce, B. (2003). *A primer on Bayesian statistics in health economics and outcomes research.* Bethesda, Maryland: Medtap International.

Phelps, C. E. & Mushlin, A. I. (1991). On the (near) equivalence of cost effectiveness and cost benefit analysis. *International Journal of Technology Assessment in Health Care, 7*(1), 12–21.

Rawlins, M. (1999). In pursuit of quality: The National Institute for Clinical Excellence. *The Lancet, 353* (9158), 1079–1082.

Sculpher, M. & Claxton, K. (2010). Sins of omission and obfuscation: IQWIG's guidelines on economic evaluation methods. *Health Economics, 19,* 1132–1136.

Sculpher, M. & Drummond, M. (2006). Analysis sans frontières: Can we ever make economic evaluations generalisable across jurisdictions? *PharmacoEconomics, 24*(11), 1087–1099.

Stinnett, A. A. & Mullahy, J. (1998). Net health benefits: A new framework for the analysis of uncertainty in cost-effectiveness analysis. *Medical Decision Making, 18*(2 Suppl.), S68–S80.

Tarn, T. Y. & Smith, M. D. (2004). Pharmacoeconomic guidelines around the world. *ISPOR Connections, 10*(4), 5.

Thaler, R. & Rosen, S. (1976). The value of saving a life: Evidence from the labor market. In N. E. Terleckyj (Ed.), *Household production and consumption* (pp. 265–298). New York: National Bureau of Economic Research, Inc..

Tunis, S. & Pearson, S. (2006). Coverage options for promising technologies: Medicare's coverage with evidence development. *Health Affairs, 25*(5), 1218.

Viscusi, W. (1993). The value of risks to life and health. *Journal of Economic Literature, 31*(4), 1912–1946.

Weinstein, M. C. & Stason, W. B. (1977). Foundations of cost-effectiveness analysis for health and medical practices. *New England Journal of Medicine, 296*(13), 716–721.

Wilensky, G. R. (2008). Cost-effectiveness information: Yes, it's important, but keep it separate, please! *Annals of Internal Medicine, 148*(12), 967–968.

CHAPTER NINE

Competition in Health Care Markets[1]

Martin Gaynor* and Robert J. Town**
*Carnegie Mellon University, USA and University of Bristol, NBER, UK
**University of Pennsylvania, NBER, USA

Contents

[1] We wish to thank participants at the *Handbook of Health Economics* meeting in Lisbon, Portugal, Pedro Pita Barros, Rein Halbersman, and Cory Capps for helpful comments and suggestions. Misja Mikkers, Rein Halbersma, and Ramsis Croes of the Netherlands Healthcare Authority graciously provided data on hospital and insurance market structure in the Netherlands. David Emmons kindly provided aggregates of the American Medical Association's calculations of health insurance market structure. Leemore Dafny was kind enough to share her measures of market concentration for the large employer segment of the US health insurance market. All opinions expressed here and any errors are the sole responsibility of the authors. No endorsement or approval by any other individuals or institutions is implied or should be inferred.

Abstract

This chapter reviews the literature devoted to studying markets for health care services and health insurance. There has been tremendous growth and progress in this field. A tremendous amount of new research has been done since the publication of the first volume of this Handbook. In addition, there has been increasing development and use of frontier industrial organization methods. We begin by examining research on the determinants of market structure, considering both static and dynamic models. We then model the strategic determination of prices between health insurers and providers where insurers market their products to consumers based, in part, on the quality and breadth of their provider network. We then review the large empirical literature on the strategic determination of hospital prices through the lens of this model. Variation in the quality of health care clearly can have large welfare consequences. We therefore also describe the theoretical and empirical literature on the impact of market structure on quality of health care. The chapter then moves on to consider competition in health insurance markets and physician services markets. We conclude by considering vertical restraints and monopsony power.

Keywords: health care; competition; markets; industrial organization; antitrust; competition policy; hospitals; health insurance; physicians

JEL Codes: I11; L13; L10; L40; I18; L30

1. INTRODUCTION

The incentives provided by the competitive interactions of health care providers are a central force that shapes their behavior, affecting the price, quantity and quality of health care services. This is particularly true in the US, where 56 percent of total health expenditures are privately financed (Martin et al., 2011), and hence prices, quantities, and qualities for those services are determined by market interactions of buyers and sellers. Even when prices are administratively set, as they are for most publicly financed care,[2] strategic interactions between providers affect quantity, quality and access to care. In this chapter our goal is to review the state of knowledge on competition in health care markets, focusing on the literature that has arisen since the first volume of the *Handbook of Health Economics* published in 2000.[3]

The organizing principle for this chapter is loosely based on the Structure–Conduct–Performance (SCP) paradigm originating with Joseph Bain and Edward Mason (see Schmalensee, 1989, for a review). From the 1950s to the 1970s this was the dominant framework through which industrial organization economists conducted their analyses. The rise of game theory and the new empirical industrial organization displaced the SCP approach (Bresnahan, 1989). Nevertheless, the SCP framework is a useful guide for structuring this chapter. First, in order to provide some context for our discussion, we present data on recent trends in provider market structure and some of the recent research on the underlying forces behind the trends. Section 2 then discusses the research on the determinants of health care provider market structure. This section examines the roles of entry, exit, mergers, and productivity. Section 3 turns to the analysis of the consequences of differential market structure, focusing on its impact on hospital prices. Section 4 examines the impacts of these forces on hospital quality of care. Section 5 examines evidence on competition in health insurance markets, while section 6 focuses on physician services markets. As will be seen, the majority of the empirical literature on competition in health care markets is on hospitals. This is due to the ready availability of hospital data, and the paucity of data on insurance and physician markets. We conclude in section 8.

1.1. Market Environment

In this section we consider the market environment in which health care firms operate. We document some facts about market structure, mainly for hospitals and mainly for the US, but also for insurance and physician markets in the US and for hospital

---

[2] This is true of the US Medicare program and most health systems outside the US.

[3] See the excellent chapters by Dranove and Satterthwaite (2000) and Gaynor and Vogt (2000) in that volume for reviews of the literature to that point and for initial sketches of modeling strategies that have guided many of the subsequent papers in the area.

Table 9.1 Hospital Market Concentration, US, 1987–2006[a]

Year	Mean HHI[b]	Change[c]
1987	2,340	—
1992	2,440	100
1997	2,983	543
2002	3,236	253
2006	3,261	25

[a]Source: American Hospital Association. Data are for US Metropolitan Statistical Areas with population < 3 million.
[b]Herfindahl–Hirschmann Index. Means weighted by MSA population.
[c]Total change from the previous year in the table.

markets in England and the Netherlands. We then proceed in section 2 to discuss models of market structure and empirical research evidence.

Hospital and physician services comprise a large component of US Gross Domestic Product (GDP). In 2009, hospital care alone accounted for 5.4 percent of GDP—roughly twice the size of automobile manufacturing, agriculture, or mining, and larger than all manufacturing sectors except food and beverage and tobacco products, which is approximately the same size. Physician services comprise 3.6 percent of GDP (Martin et al., 2011).[4] The share of the economy accounted for by these sectors has risen dramatically over the last 30 years. In 1980, hospitals and physicians accounted for 3.6 percent and 1.7 percent of US GDP, respectively (Martin et al., 2011).[5] The size of these industries and their long-run trends suggest that understanding their structure, conduct, and performance is not only important for the performance of the health care industry, it is also important for understanding the economy as a whole.

Not only are these sectors large, but they have been undergoing significant structural shifts over the last several decades. The 1990s saw dramatic changes in the structure of hospital markets in the US, and this increase will likely have long-term impacts on the behavior of hospitals. Table 9.1 presents numbers for the population-weighted, Herfindahl–Hirschmann Index (HHI) for selected years from 1987 to 2006.[6] Two things are clear from this table. US hospital markets are highly concentrated and have become even more concentrated over time. Figure 9.1 displays the trends in the hospital HHI, the number of within-market hospital mergers and acquisitions, and the percentage of the population enrolled in an HMO from 1990 to

---

[4] The net cost of health insurance—current year premiums minus current year medical benefits paid—was 1 percent of GDP in 2009.

[5] The net cost of health insurance in 1980 was 0.34 percent.

[6] The HHI is the sum of squared market shares in the market. It is the most commonly used measure of market structure. We present population weighted averages for Metropolitan Statistical Areas (MSAs) (based on admissions). We limit the sample of MSAs to those with a population less than 3 million in 1990. We do this because it is likely that in MSAs with more than 3 million, there are multiple hospital markets and the HHI of that MSA is likely mismeasured.

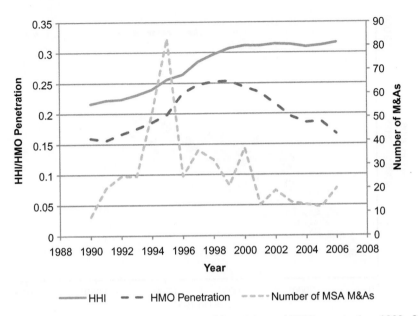

Figure 9.1 Trends in US hospital concentration, M&A activity and HMO penetration: 1990–2006.

2006. From the table and figure it is easily seen that hospital markets have become significantly more concentrated. In 1987, the mean HHI was 2,340 and by 2006 the HHI was 3,161—an increase of over 900 points.[7] In 1992, the mean hospital concentration levels (2,440) were (barely) below the recently updated Federal merger guidelines' (Federal Trade Commission and Department of Justice, 1992) cut-off point for classifying a market as "Highly Concentrated" (HHI ≥ 2,500), but by 2006 the mean concentration level (3,261) rose to well above this threshold. Town et al. (2006) note that mergers and acquisitions are the primary reason for the increase in hospital concentration over this period.

While hospital markets are highly concentrated on average, there is also wide variation in concentration. Figure 9.2 shows a scatterplot of the MSA level market concentration in 1990 and in 2006. This figure displays two phenomena. First, it shows the distribution of HHIs across MSAs. Most MSAs are "Highly Concentrated." In 2006, of the 332 MSAs in the US, 250 had HHIs greater than 2,500. Second, it is clear from Figure 9.2 that the increase in hospital concentration was a broad phenomenon—the vast majority of MSAs became more concentrated over this period. Particularly striking is the number of moderately concentrated MSAs in 1990 that by 2006 had become highly concentrated. By 2006, most health insurers now had to

---

[7] It is interesting that over roughly the same period of time the nursing home industry did not see significant increases in market concentration, even though it was also subject to a number of mergers and acquisitions.

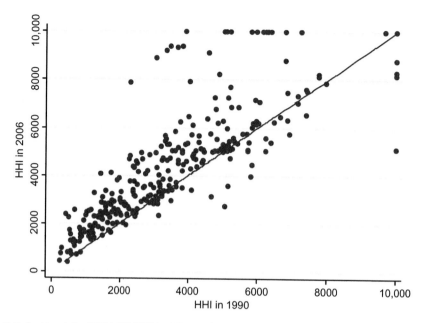

Figure 9.2 Scatterplot of US MSA HHI in 1990 and HHI in 2006.

negotiate with hospital systems in highly concentrated markets, which likely reduced their bargaining clout.[8]

An obvious question is why this wave of hospital consolidation occurred. Fuchs (2007) and others point to the rise of managed care as the principal factor driving this massive consolidation. A cursory glance at Figure 9.1 suggests this causal explanation. The idea is that the rise of HMOs introduced aggressive price negotiations between hospitals and health plans, thereby giving hospitals a strong incentive to acquire bargaining power through consolidation. The rise of HMOs during the 1990s is widely credited with significantly reducing health care cost growth, primarily through tough price negotiations (see, e.g., Cutler et al., 2000). Early suggestive evidence is provided by Chernew (1995), who finds that in the 1980s there is a relationship between HMO penetration and the number of hospitals operating in the market. Dranove et al. (2002) examine data from 1981 to 1994 and find a correlation between metropolitan area HMO penetration in 1994 and the change in market structure. However, Town et al. (2007) examine the change in hospital market structure and the change in HMO penetration and find little correlation, suggesting no direct causal link.

---

[8] Changes in Health Care Financing and Organization (http://www.hschange.com/index.cgi?func=pubs& what=5&order=date) present a number of market-by-market case studies that highlight the increase in hospital bargaining leverage over the last several decades.

These results present a puzzle. Anecdotal evidence suggests that HMOs were an important driver of the wave of hospital consolidation, yet the empirical evidence is mixed. Some have suggested that it was not the realization of the rise of managed care, but the anticipation (which in many cases was in error) that led hospitals to consolidate. Work in progress by Town and Park (2011) provides support for this hypothesis. They find that HMO exit, a measure of the exuberance of expectations regarding the demand for managed care in a location, is correlated with hospital consolidation.

The trend toward increasing concentration in hospital markets is not confined to the US. Tables 9.2 and 9.3 provide information on market structure levels and trends in England and the Netherlands. We see that the trends in these countries are very similar to the US—the total number of hospitals in both countries declined substantially over time. For England there are HHIs for local hospital markets for a number of years. Those reflect substantial concentration, although declining slightly over time. Figure 9.3 illustrates the change in the distribution of the HHI between 2003/04 and 2007/08 (fiscal years). It can be seen that there is a shift of the distribution from more concentrated to less concentrated markets. Most of the shift is in the middle of the distribution, as opposed to the tails. The decline in the hospital HHI in England documented here is most likely due to pro-competitive reforms of the English National Health Service that occurred in 2006 (see Gaynor et al., 2010).

Table 9.3 provides information on the total number of hospitals and independent outpatient treatment centers in the Netherlands by year. There is a clear downward

Table 9.2 Hospital Market Structure, England, National Health Service, 1997−2007

Year	# NHS Hospitals[a]	# Mergers	HHI	# Private Hospitals[b]
1997	227	26	—	—
1998	214	21	—	—
1999	202	17	—	—
2000	193	23	—	—
2001	188	25	—	—
2002	174	6	—	—
2003	171	0	5,573	—
2004	171	0	5,561	3
2005	171	3	5,513	21
2006	168	3	5,459	32
2007	167	0	5,461	—
Total	—	124	—	—

[a]Source: UK Department of Health. Hospitals with fewer than 5,000 consultant episodes per year are excluded.
[b]Independent Sector Treatment Centres. These are private hospitals with contracts with the NHS.

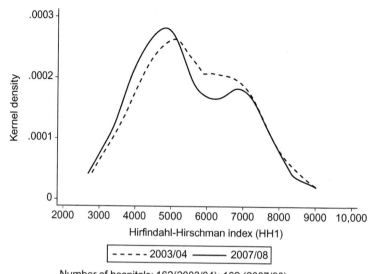

Number of hospitals: 162(2003/04); 162 (2007/08)
Market definition method: actual patient flows.

Figure 9.3 Kernel density estimates for the distribution of HHI (all elective services).

Table 9.3 Hospital Market Structure, The Netherlands, 1997–2010[a]

Year	# Hospitals[b]	Outpatient Treatment Centers[c]
1997	117	—
1998	117	—
1999	115	—
2000	111	—
2001	104	—
2002	102	—
2003	102	—
2004	101	—
2005	99	37
2006	98	57
2007	97	68
2008	97	89
2009	95	129
2010	94	184

[a]Source: Netherlands Healthcare Authority.
[b]Total number of hospitals, including general hospitals, specialty hospitals, and university medical centers. The vast majority are general hospitals.
[c]Independent Treatment Centers (ZBCs). These are freestanding outpatient treatment centers, not part of hospitals.

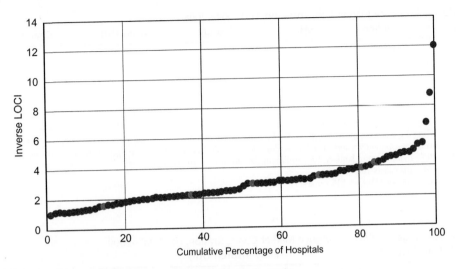

Figure 9.4 Cumulative distribution of LOCI, Netherlands, 2010.

trend in the number of hospitals—there were 23 fewer hospitals in 2010 than in 1997. More recently, there has been a large increase in the number of independent outpatient treatment centers. The number grew from 37 in 2005 to 184 by 2010.

Figure 9.4 shows the distribution of an alternative measure of market structure, LOCI (for Logit Competition Index),[9] for the Netherlands in 2010. LOCI is a measure of how much competition a firm faces in a differentiated products market. It varies between zero and one, where zero is pure monopoly and one is perfect competition. The graph shows the cumulative distribution of hospitals in the Netherlands by their values of the inverse of LOCI. As can be seen, approximately 20 percent of hospitals have values of inverse LOCI of 2 or below. A value of 2 implies the market is not very competitive—for example, a hospital in a duopoly that equally split the market with its rival would have a LOCI value of 1/2, i.e. an inverse LOCI of 2. One half of all hospitals have inverse LOCI values of 3 or less. This implies that half of Dutch hospitals operate in markets where they face competition from the equivalent of a triopoly or less.

Tables 9.4, 9.5, 9.6, and 9.7 provide information about health insurance market structures for the US and the Netherlands. The US information shows consistently high levels of concentration in health insurance markets. The levels of concentration in the Netherlands are substantially lower than in the US, but have grown substantially over time.

[9] This is a competition index for differentiated products Bertrand oligopoly with logit demand. See Akosa Antwi et al. (2006).

Table 9.4 Insurance Market Concentration, US, 2004–2008[a,b]

Year	Median	HHI	Change	Mean HHI	Change
2004	3,544	–	3,939	–	
2005	3,748	204	4,077	138	
2006	2,986	−762	3,440	−637	
2007	3,558	572	3,944	504	
2008	3,276	−282	3,727	−217	

[a]Source: These figures were graciously provided by David Emmons. See American Medical Association (2010) for more information on the data and calculations. American Medical Association (AMA) calculations for the combined HMO + PPO markets using January 1st enrollment data from HealthLeaders-InterStudy's (HLIS) Managed Market Surveyors HealthLeaders-Inter-Study.
[b]MSA-level HHIs for HMO + PPO markets.

Table 9.5 Large Employer Insurance Market Concentration, US, 1998–2009[a]

Year	Self + Fully Insured		Fully Insured Only	
	Mean HHI[b]	Change	Mean HHI[b]	Change
1998	2,172	–	2,984	–
1999	1,997	−175	2,835	
2000	2,175	178	3,092	
2001	2,093	−82	3,006	
2002	2,280	187	3,158	
2003	2,343	63	3,432	
2004	2,519	176	3,706	
2005	2,609	90	3,951	
2006	2,740	131	4,072	
2007	2,873	133	4,056	
2008	2,916	43	4,201	
2009	2,956	40	4,126	

[a]Source: These figures were graciously provided by Leemore Dafny. The data are for large multisite employers and do not represent the totality of the insurance market. For more information on the data source, see Dafny (2010).
[b]Weighted by number of enrollees.

The measures of HHI for HMO plus PPO markets in the US in Table 9.4 come from reports from the American Medical Association (AMA). They show high levels of concentration (although lower than for hospitals). The numbers show insurance market concentration declining somewhat over time (although not monotonically). However, there are some concerns about the accuracy of these numbers (see Capps, 2009; Dafny et al., 2011a).

Dafny (2010) and Dafny et al. (2011b), using data on the large employer segment of the insurance market, also show increasing concentration in health insurance markets. Dafny (2010, Figure 9.5) documents an increase in the percentage of

Table 9.6 Small Group Insurance Market Structure, US, 2000–2003[a]

Year	Median Market Share, Largest Carrier	# of States with 5 Firm Concentration Ratio ≥75 Percent
2002	33 percent	19 (of 34; 56 percent)
2005	43 percent	26 (of 34; 77 percent)
2008	47 percent	34 (of 39; 87 percent)

[a]Source: Government Accountability Office (2009).

Table 9.7 Insurance Market Structure, The Netherlands, 2005–2010[a]

Year	Mean HHI
2005	1,346
2006	1,625
2007	1,630
2008	2,124
2009	2,119
2010	2,111

[a]Source: Netherlands Healthcare Authority.

markets with 1–4, 5–6, or 7–9 insurance carriers in the US from 1998 to 2005, and a decrease in the percentage of markets with 9–10 or more than 10 carriers. Dafny et al. (2011b) state that the mean HHI in their sample increased from 2,286 to 2,984 from 1998 to 2006, the median four-firm concentration ratio increased from 79 to 90 percent, and the mean number of carriers per market fell from 18.9 to 9.6. They show (Figure 9.1 in their paper) that 78 percent of the markets they study had increases in the HHI of 100 points or more from 2002 to 2006, and 53 percent experienced increases of 500 points or more. Table 9.5 lists mean HHIs by year from the data used in those papers. These numbers indicate that the large employer segment of the health insurance market is concentrated and has grown more so over time. These numbers are roughly similar in magnitude to those calculated by the AMA. However, they show concentration increasing over time (by about 400 points from 2004 to 2008), while the AMA numbers exhibit a slight decrease over time.

A recent report by the US Government Accountability Office (Government Accountability Office, 2009) compiled information on the market structure of the small group health insurance market in the US. Table 9.6 reproduces numbers from that report. As can be seen, those markets appear to be fairly heavily concentrated, and increasing in concentration. A recent paper by Schneider et al. (2008a) utilizes a unique data source for California to construct HHIs for insurance plans at the county level for 2001. They find an average insurance HHI for California counties of 2,592.

They report that 21 percent of counties have HHIs below 1,800,[10] 55 percent had HHIs between 1,800 and 3,600, and 24 percent had HHIs above 3,600. The information from these various data sources seems broadly consistent.

Table 9.7 contains information on the structure of the health insurance market in the Netherlands. The mean HHI is not very high in 2005, but increased by nearly 800 points by 2010. The mean HHI in 2010 is slightly higher than the HHI for an equally divided five-firm market (2,000). While not trivial, this is below the recently revised *Horizontal Merger Guidelines* cut-off for considering a market highly concentrated (HHI = 2,500). What is most notable is the large increase in concentration over the period, which may be a cause for concern.

There have also been substantial changes in market structure in US physician markets. Liebhaber and Grossman (2007) report that the percentage of physicians in solo or two-person practices declined from 40.7 percent in 1996–97 to 32.5 percent in 2004–05. Further, the proportion in practices of 3–5 physicians fell over the same period. The proportion of physicians practicing in groups of 6 or more grew from 15.9 to 21.8 percent. The number of physicians in other practice settings (primarily employed by others) grew from 31.2 to 36.0 percent over this period. Since the number of physicians per 1,000 persons has not really changed (~2.5) since 1997 (National Center for Health Statistics, 2011), this represents an increase in concentration.

There is no good systematic information on the structure of local physician markets. Those markets, especially for specialized services, may be very concentrated, but there is no information generally available at the national level. Schneider et al. (2008a) constructed HHIs for physician organizations in California at the county level for 2001. They find the average county HHI for physician organizations was 4,430, implying a high degree of concentration on average. They found that 17 percent of California counties had a physician organization HHI below 1,800, 33 percent had an HHI between 1,800 and 3,600, and 50 percent had an HHI above 3,600.

In addition to information on market structure, there is some information on trends in prices and the contribution of health care prices to overall health care cost growth. Akosa Antwi et al. (2009) document a 100 percent increase in hospital prices in California from 1999 to 2006, although they do not find market concentration to be a contributor to the increase. Martin et al. (2011) decompose US health spending growth into growth due to prices versus growth due to non-price factors (e.g. population, intensity of care). They find that prices account for 60 percent of the increase in overall spending from 2008 to 2009. The proportion of health spending growth due to prices varies over time (see Exhibit 6 in Martin et al., 2011), but has been growing steadily since 2001.

---

[10] The old Federal merger guidelines cut-off for considering a market highly concentrated (Federal Trade Commission and Department of Justice, 1992).

Some recent reports from state governments document growth or variation in health care prices. A report from the Massachusetts Attorney General's office (Massachusetts Attorney General, 2010) finds that price increases caused most of the increases in health care spending in the state in recent years. The report also finds significant variation in prices and that the variation is uncorrelated with quality of care, but is correlated with market leverage. A report on Pennsylvania hospitals found substantial variation in prices for heart surgery, but no correlation of prices with quality (Pennsylvania Health Care Cost Containment Council, 2007).

Overall, the statistics presented here paint a picture of health care and health insurance markets that are concentrated and becoming more so over time. There is also some evidence that prices are rising faster than quantities, and that price variation is not related to quality but may be due to market power. These statistics are not a complete picture, however. In particular, they do not take account of the ease or difficulty of market entry, nor of conduct in these markets. We discuss economic models for thinking about these issues, and what we know at present from research, in what follows as the main body of this chapter.

2. ENTRY, EXIT, AND TECHNOLOGY INVESTMENTS BY PROVIDERS

Health care policies, either through intent or as an unintended consequence, often affect the incentives of health care providers to enter, exit, invest, merge, and innovate. That is, health policy may affect provider market structure and thus change outcomes influenced by market structure, such as price, quantity, or quality, that were outside of the intent of the policy. These incentives may differ by ownership status and thus policies may change the mix of not-for-profit (NFP), for-profit (FP), and public organizations.

For example, the Hill—Burton program in the US provided subsidies to NFP and public hospitals for construction and expansion. That policy affected the number of hospitals, productive capacity, and ownership mix, and therefore also likely affected market outcome such as price, quantity, and quality. Another example is public payments to providers. Hospitals and most physicians earn a large percentage of their revenue from providing care to publicly insured patients (in some countries all, or nearly all, of their revenues) and those reimbursements are administratively determined. Changes in those payments affect the returns to these providers to enter, exit, invest, merge, and innovate. Thus, to fully understand the impact of a given policy often requires an understanding of how the policy will affect market structure through its impact on the behavior of providers. In this section, we briefly discuss recent developments in our understanding of evolution of provider market structure.

Over the last decade significant methodological and theoretical advances have occurred in the analysis of (dynamic) oligopoly models in which firms are making entry, exit, and investment decisions. These decisions are dynamic in the sense that they require upfront expenditures in which the organization will earn a return over a span of time or the decisions are difficult to reverse. As long noted by economists, understanding the dynamic implications of these models often requires estimating policy invariant parameters and the natural (albeit often challenging) way to do that is to specify and estimate parameters from a model that captures the essential features of the industry relevant for the question of interest. In this section we outline a basic framework for examining entry, exit, and investment decisions as well as review the small but growing literature devoted to understanding dynamic behavior of firms. Space limitations prevent us from discussing the details on solving and estimating fully dynamic models. However, there are several excellent summaries of this literature and the interested reader is referred to Ackerberg et al. (2007), Doraszelski and Pakes (2007), and the citations therein for a more complete presentation of these issues.

We present the outline of a simple model that is loosely based on the work of Gowrisankaran and Town (1997), which in turn is heavily influenced by the work of Ericson and Pakes (1995) and Pakes and McGuire (1994). Static returns to the organization are modeled as depending on the current state of the (potential) market participants, the actions they take in the period, and unobservables.[11] More formally, we denote the profits in period t, $\pi(s_t, a_t, \xi_t)$, that hospitals earn from the vector of state variables, one for each market participant, $s_t \in S$, and actions, $a_t \in A$ (actions can be investments, entry, exit, mergers, etc.), that affect the evolution of s_t.[12] The probability that a given action is successful is affected by i.i.d. shocks, ξ_t. Each hospital's shock is private information to the hospital. In this framework, s_t may represent the bargaining leverage of the hospital, a_t technological investments made by the hospital, and ξ_t is a shock that affects the successful implementation of the investments. There are a number of approaches to modeling state transitions, but in general they allow the state to evolve according to a first-order Markov process, where the actions of hospitals in period t affect the distribution of the states in period $t+1$. That is, $s_{t+1} = f(s_t, a_t, \xi_t)$ where f is a pdf of a distribution function that captures the relevant process through which states are updated.

So far, this set-up is generic and is not specific to a given provider setting or to a research question. However, we can incorporate a number of the institutional features of the hospital (or other provider) setting into this framework. For example, to

---

[11] There are many models of static firm behavior that are consistent with this representation, including the bargaining model presented in section 3.1.

[12] We suppress individual firm subscripts for clarity in notation.

endogenously account for the presence of NFP hospitals, the NFP hospital utility function can be posited as a function of profits and its state and actions, S_t and a_t (Newhouse, 1970).[13] NFP utility can operationalized as $U_t(s_t, a_t, \xi_t) = \pi(s_t, a_t, \xi_t) + (1 - \gamma)q_t(s_t)$ where q_t is the number of patients treated and γ is the relative weight the hospital places on profits relative to the number of patients treated. In this framework it is also easy to allow FP hospitals to face income and property taxes (from which NFPs are exempt), which may differentially affect their investment decisions. The fact that most hospitals treat both private and public pay patients with variation in payment generosity can also be incorporated into this model.

The state evolves according to a Markov process that depends on the actions of the hospital and its competitors. Hospitals seek to maximize the present discounted value of utility. The equilibrium concept that is generally employed in these settings is Markov Perfect Equilibrium, which imposes that each hospital selects it actions in order to maximize the present value of utility given its rational beliefs of the strategies of the other hospitals and this simultaneously holds for all hospitals.

For each period, all hospitals solve:

$$\max_{a_t} E_t \left[\sum_t \beta^{t-1} U_t(s_t, a_t, \xi_t) \right] \qquad \text{s.t.} \quad s_{t+1} = f(s_t, a_t, \xi_t) \qquad (9.1)$$

where E_t is the expectations operator given the information set available to the hospital in period t. The solution to this problem is a mapping from each state and realization of a hospital's shock to an action.

Entry is incorporated by allowing for a set of potential entrants who receive a random entry cost shock, while exit is incorporated by assigning hospitals a scrap value they receive if they exit. Hospitals will enter if the expected present discounted value of market participation exceeds the cost of entry, while exit occurs if the expected presented discounted value of continuing to participate in the market is less than the scrap value. If the return function is smooth and concave and if the evolution of the state variables is also well behaved, usually at least one equilibrium exists. In general, there is no closed form solution for these types of models. However, given the parameters of the model, there are well-established algorithms for solving these models.[14]

The model's economic and policy implications will depend upon the parameters chosen by the researcher. Thus, selection of "reasonable" parameter values is critical in order for these models to provide policy guidance. A natural choice of parameter values are those that are consistent with the patterns in the data. The static parameters—those that relate the states to the single period returns—can be estimated by

---

[13] Clearly, other objective functions of the hospital are possible and the appropriate one will depend on the question under consideration.

[14] See, e.g., Pakes and McGuire (1994), Gowrisankaran (1995), and Doraszelski and Satterthwaite (2010).

specifying a demand and supply system and solving for the static equilibrium for every possible state. Given estimates of the single period returns, the remaining parameters to estimate are the dynamic ones. These parameters typically capture sunk costs of entry, scrap values from exit, fixed costs of production, and parameters of the investment process. An important literature has arisen that develops econometric methods to estimate these parameters.

Gowrisankaran and Town (1997) is the first attempt to estimate the structural parameters from a dynamic oligopoly model of entry, exit, and quality investments. The goal of their work is to examine the impact of different policy initiatives on the structure of the hospital industry and patient welfare. In their model there are three types of patients: privately insured, Medicare beneficiaries, and uninsured; and two types of hospitals: NFP and FP. NFP hospitals seek to maximize the present discounted value of utility, which depends on profits and the number of treated patients. FP hospitals pay property taxes on their capital stock. To estimate the parameters they use a method of moments estimator in which for every trial parameter value they solve for the fixed point of the dynamic game. At the estimated parameter values, they find that NFP hospitals are longer lived (FPs are both more likely to enter and to exit), and have higher quality. Decreasing Medicare payment levels reduces the number of hospitals—this occurs principally because FP hospitals exit the market, and lead to higher quality adjusted prices for private pay patients. FP hospitals are more likely to be the marginal hospital, whose market participation is more sensitive to shifts in demand or government policy.

Several applied theoretical papers examine the entry and exit of health care providers in simpler settings than the dynamic context described above, thus allowing for the derivation of analytic results. Lakdawalla and Philipson (2006) examine a simple, traditional, perfectly competitive equilibrium model familiar to most economists, and add the ability of not-for-profit firms to enter and compete with for-profit firms. In their framework, for-profit hospitals maximize profits, while not-for-profit hospitals maximize utility, which has profits and output (and potentially inputs) as arguments. Lakadawalla and Philipson show that when NFP hospitals place positive weight on output they will behave as if they are profit maximizers with lower marginal costs, and in equilibrium will always earn negative profits. In general, NFP firms crowd out FP organizations. However, if the number of potential not-for-profit firms is limited, then for-profit firms participate in the market. In this case the market environment is determined by the response of for-profit firms, since they are the marginal organizations.

Hansmann et al. (2003) highlight that for-profit hospitals are the most responsive to reductions in demand, followed, in turn, by public hospitals and religiously affiliated non-profits, while secular non-profits are distinctly the least responsive of the four ownership types. Glaeser (2002) notes that the governance structures on the managers of NFP institutions are generally weak. He constructs a model of the NFP sector that examines the implications that governing boards of NFPs are not responsible to anyone outside of the organization. He further notes that the behavior of hospitals displays patterns consistent with capture by management and physicians.

2.1. Structural Estimates of the Dynamic Behavior of Providers

Over the last two decades there have been significant advances in econometric approaches to estimating parameters from dynamic models of oligopoly. Early approaches (e.g. as previously mentioned, Gowrisankaran and Town, 1997) solved for the equilibrium of the model for each trial parameter value. Recently, two-step approaches have been developed. These two-step methods alleviate the need to solve the model in order to recover the parameters, and thus significantly reduce the computational burden of estimation. Bajari et al. (2007), Aguirregabiria and Mira (2007), and Pakes et al. (2007) all develop approaches to estimate parameters from dynamic oligopoly.[15]

Schmidt-Dengler (2006) studies the adoption of nuclear magnetic resonance imaging (MRI) by US hospitals. Specifically, he examines the strategic incentives that hospitals have to adopt the technology. Adopting the technology allows the hospital to "steal" volume from their competitors and it may also deter or delay entry into this service line by competing hospitals. He estimates the parameters of a structural model of the timing of technology adoption (solving for equilibrium for each trial parameter vector) in order to disentangle these two effects. His simulations show that business stealing is the primary profit impact of MRI adoption, and that preemption has a small but significant impact on hospital profits.

Beauchamp (2010) estimates a dynamic model of the entry, exit, and service provision of abortion providers using the two-step method of Arcidiacono and Miller (2010). The goal of this work is to examine the reasons underlying the increasing concentration of abortion providers. He finds that high fixed costs explain the growth of large clinics and that increased provider regulation raised fixed entry costs for small providers. Interestingly, his simulations show that removing all regulations leads to increased entry by small providers into incumbent markets, increasing competition and the number of abortions.

Nursing homes are an extremely large industry where the federal and state governments are the primary payers. Two million US residents reside in 18,000 nursing homes. Because nursing homes do not set prices for most of their patients, competition is primarily along quality dimensions. However, it is well documented that the quality of care in nursing homes in the US is low. Seventy-three percent of nursing homes were cited for quality of care violations during routine

---

[15] Also see Arcidiacono and Miller (2010) and Pesendorfer and Schmidt-Dengler (2008).

inspections.[16] In order to study the dynamic response of the nursing home industry to different policy experiments, Lin (2008) estimates the parameters of an Ericson and Pakes (1995) type model. In the most interesting of her three policy experiments, she increases government payments for providing high-quality care by 40 percent. This leads to dramatic increases in both the percentage of high-quality homes and the total number of homes.

The Rural Hospital Flexibility Program that was passed in the Balanced Budget Amendment of 1997 has as its overarching goal maintaining access to quality hospital care for rural residents. To achieve this objective, the program created a new class of hospitals, Critical Access Hospitals (CAH). Participating hospitals opt out of Medicare's standard prospective payment system (PPS) and instead receive relatively generous cost-based reimbursements from Medicare. In return, they must comply with a number of restrictions, principally limits on their capacity to 25 beds or less and patient length-of-stay to 96 hours or less. By 2006, 25 percent of all general acute care US hospitals had converted to CAH status. Gowrisankaran et al. (2011) estimate the structural parameters of a dynamic oligopoly capacity game in order to assess the impact of this program on rural hospital infrastructure. They extend recent work on estimating dynamic oligopoly games by constructing a one-step ahead estimator that significantly reduces the computational burden of estimation. Preliminary results suggest that the program only had a modest impact on the likelihood of exit, while it dramatically changed the size distribution of rural hospitals. The estimates suggest that the reduction in the size of rural hospitals had a detrimental impact on rural residents and outweighs the benefits they received from keeping open a few hospitals that would otherwise close.

Dunne et al. (2009) estimate a dynamic, structural model of entry and exit for dentists and chiropractors using the method of Pakes et al. (2007). Their goal is to understand the roles of entry, fixed costs, and toughness of competition in determining market structure. They find that all three factors are important in determining market structure. To understand the role of entry costs in affecting market structure they simulate the impact of reducing entry costs and find that increased price competition offsets the reduction in entry costs.

As noted by Brenahan and Reiss (1990, 1991) (BR), market structure is endogenous and the relationship between market structure (i.e. the number of firms) and market size (e.g. population) speaks to the nature of static price competition. The BR method uses a simple, general entry condition to model market structure. The intuition is that if the population (per-firm) required to support a given number of firms in a market grows with the number of firms then competition must be getting tougher. The tougher competition shrinks profit margins and therefore requires a larger

---

[16] Office of the Inspector General, "Trends in Nursing Home Deficiencies and Complaints," OEI-02-08-00140.

population to generate the variable profits necessary to cover entry costs. For example, if the size of the market needs to triple in order to add an additional entrant, that suggests that the addition of that firm dramatically reduces firm profits. Thus, the key data required for this method are both minimal and commonly available: market structure and population.

Abraham et al. (2007) specify a static entry model modified from Bresnahan and Reiss (1991) to better understand the nature of hospital competition. Abraham et al. augment the BR approach by incorporating the use of quantity data. Their method allows the separate identification of changes in the fixed costs of entry and changes in the toughness of competition. Their estimates imply that the threshold per-firm population required to support one hospital is approximately 7,000, increases to 12,600 to support two hospitals, is approximately 19,000 for three hospitals, and just under 20,000 for four or more hospitals. They also find that increases in the number of hospitals in the market dramatically increases the number of patients up until there are three hospitals—by 23 percent with the entry of the second hospital and 15 percent with the entry of the third hospital. This implies substantial increases in the toughness of competition with the entry of a second or third firm, but not afterwards. These results point to substantial effects on competition even from having only a second firm in the market. However, the magnitude of the effects (23 percent increase in quantity associated with moving from a monopoly to a duopoly) seem extremely large.

Schaumans and Verboven (2008) specify a static entry model of pharmacy and physician entry in which pharmacies and physicians may be complementary services. Their model is in the spirit of Bresnahan and Reiss (1991) and Mazzeo (2002). In Europe, pharmacies have frequently received high, regulated markups over wholesale costs, and have been protected from additional competition through geographic entry restrictions. These restrictions may affect more than the market structure for pharmacies but may also spill over and affect entry of other complementary services. They estimate the parameters of the model using data from Belgium. They find that the entry decisions of pharmacies and physicians are strategic complements. Furthermore, the entry restrictions have directly reduced the number of pharmacies by more than 50 percent, and indirectly reduced the number of physicians by about 7 percent. Their model is discussed in more detail in section 6 on markets for physician services.

2.2. Reduced Form Studies of Dynamic Behavior of Providers

Understanding the patterns of the evolution of health care provider market structure can yield important insights into the underlying roles of policy and other factors that shape market structure. Towards that end, several papers examine the entry, exit, investment, and technology adoption patterns of providers using reduced form techniques. Given clean identification, these approaches can provide important insight into underlying relationships that affect the dynamic behavior of providers. A limitation of these approaches is that it is difficult to use these estimates to perform counterfactual policy experiments.

The most important change in US health care policy over the last century was the introduction of Medicare and Medicaid in the mid-1960s. Large portions of the population that were in poor health became insured under this program. That is, the introduction of Medicare and Medicaid constituted a large, positive shock to the demand for hospital and physician services which, in turn, had the potential to affect the entry, exit, and investment decisions of providers. Finkelstein (2007) examines the impact of this program on hospital dynamic behavior. She uses a long panel of American Hospital Association data and employs a difference-in-difference identification strategy. This strategy relies on geographic variation in the rates of hospital insurance prior to the introduction of Medicare/Medicaid to identify the impact of these programs. The idea is that areas in which large percentages of the population had insurance prior to the introduction of Medicare and Medicaid were less exposed to the treatment (the demand shock associated with the introduction of these programs) than areas of the country with lower insurance coverage. She finds that the Medicare program significantly increases the size of hospitals, increased admissions, increased hospital entry rates, and there is some evidence that it increased the rate of adoption of new technologies.

Not only does the presence of insurance affect hospital incentives, but the nature of the insurance market may affect reimbursement rates and thus affect the incentives of firms to invest in technology. In particular, managed care organizations negotiate lower payments and restrict utilization, and thus may affect technology adoption. In a series of papers, Laurence Baker and co-authors find evidence that managed care penetration affects technology adoption. Baker and Wheeler (1998) find that high HMO market share is associated with low levels of MRI availability and utilization. This suggests that managed care may be able to reduce health care costs by influencing the adoption and use of new medical equipment and technologies. Baker and Brown (1999) find evidence that increases in HMO activity are associated with reductions in the number of mammography providers and with increases in the number of services produced by the remaining providers. They also find that increases in HMO market share are associated with reductions in costs for mammography and with increases in waiting times for appointments, but not with worse health outcomes. Baker and Phibbs (2002) find that managed care slowed the adoption of neonatal intensive care units (NICUs) by hospitals, primarily by slowing the adoption of mid-level NICUs rather than advanced high-level units. Slowing the adoption of mid-level units would likely have generated savings. Moreover, contrary to the frequent supposition that slowing technology growth is harmful to patients, in this case reduced adoption of mid-level units could have benefited patients, since health outcomes for seriously ill newborns are better in high-level NICUs and reductions in the availability of mid-level units appear to increase the chance of receiving care in a high-level center.

The entry behavior of providers can be used to uncover the relative generosity of different payers. Chernew et al. (2002) use this insight to measure the relative payment generosity for coronary artery bypass graft (CABG) surgery. They examine the behavior of hospitals in California from 1985 to 1994—a period in which CABG was diffusing and hospitals were actively making decisions whether to provide this procedure. Chernew et al. (2002) use geographic variation in the distribution of patients with differing insurance arrangements to identify returns to CABG entry as a function of the expected volumes by payer class. They first estimate a hospital choice model for CABG and then use the predicted volumes by insurer type in a simple entry regression. They find that fee-for-service (FFS) insurance provides a high return throughout. Medicare reimbursements were initially generous but declined throughout the study period. HMOs pay at approximately average variable costs, and, interestingly, the return varies inversely with competition.

Chakravarty et al. (2006) examine hospital entry and exit rates through the lens of the model of Lakdawalla and Philipson (2006). They analyze the entry and exit behavior of hospitals from 1984 to 2000 and find higher exit and entry rates for FP hospitals than for NFPs. In addition, FP hospitals are more sensitive to shifts in demand. These results are all consistent with theoretical predictions—FPs are the marginal firm. Ciliberto and Lindrooth (2007) derive a random effects estimator of hospital exit and find that increases in Medicare reimbursements and improvements in efficiency reduced the probability of exit. Deily et al. (2000) find that during the late 1980s increases in relative inefficiency increased the probability that FP and NFP hospitals would exit, but not public hospitals.

Public policy can directly or indirectly affect hospital closure. The direct impact can occur by closing public hospitals, forcing existing private hospitals to close, or by bailing out failing hospitals. For example, in New York state, the recent Berger Commission Report (Commission on Health Care Facilities in the 21st Century, 2006) requires the reconfiguration and/or closure of 59 hospitals, or 25 percent of all hospitals in the state. Changes in payment or regulatory policy can indirectly affect the financial viability of hospitals and thus their probability of exit. The welfare impact of such closures will depend upon relative costs of the closed hospital and the value patients place upon having access to that hospital.

Lindrooth et al. (2003) examine the impact of hospital closure on the average cost of hospital care in the community. They find that the hospitals that closed were less efficient and that costs per discharge declined by 2—4 percent for all patients and 6—8 percent for patients at the closed hospital due to patients shifting to more efficient hospitals. Capps et al. (2010b) compare the loss in consumer surplus to patients from closing a hospital to the potential cost savings from closing inefficient hospitals. They examine five hospital closures in Arizona and Florida and conclude that, for the closures they study, the cost savings from closures more than offset the reduction in patient welfare. In contrast, Buchmueller et al. (2006) find that hospital closures in California had negative health consequences on the surrounding population. Specifically, they find that increases in the distance to the closest hospital increases deaths from heart attacks and unintentional injuries. These health effects are not captured in the consumer surplus analysis of Capps, Dranove, and Lindrooth.

Entry can significantly shape market structure and can have significant impacts on incumbent firms in the market. If firms can deter entry or if there are frictions that prevent the entry of organizations that might otherwise become market participants, it can have a significant impact on providers and health care consumers. In addition to the work of Schmidt-Dengler (2006), two other papers have addressed issues of entry deterrence and entry frictions: Ho (2009a) and Dafny (2005).

Kaiser Permanente is a vertically integrated, staff-model Managed Care Organization (MCO) based in California that owns hospitals and directly employs physicians and other health care providers. In California and Hawaii, Kaiser is quite successful, with large market shares in many California markets. However, outside of the West Coast of the US, Kaiser is not a significant factor. Much of Kaiser's success is attributable to its ability to provide reasonably high-quality care at low cost. Kaiser members generally do not receive care outside of the Kaiser provider network and thus they have limited provider choices. Given their comparative advantages and California success, an interesting question is why Kaiser is unable to replicate its California business model and enter in other markets. Kaiser has attempted to enter seven different markets and only successfully gained a foothold in three of these markets. Using simulation methods based on her previous work (Ho, 2006), Ho (2009a) examines the underlying reasons for Kaiser's lack of success outside of the West Coast. She finds that the premium reductions that Kaiser would have offered because of their limited provider network are large and not likely offset by any cost advantages they may possess. In addition, even in locations in which incumbent plan quality is low, customer informational asymmetry over plan quality implies that it will take Kaiser a long time to achieve the necessary scale economies to be profitable. Finally, she notes that Certificate of Need laws also raise the cost of entry for Kaiser, affecting their likely success rate.

As we discuss later in this chapter (section 4.4.3), there are significant volume-outcome effects in the provision of many hospital services, i.e. patients that go to hospitals that do larger volumes of a procedure typically have better health outcomes. Hospitals therefore may have an incentive to invest in building volume in the hopes of leaving insufficient patients for any potential entrants to attract if they were in fact to enter.[17] Dafny (2005) tests for this type of preemption for electrophysiological studies, a procedure to identify and correct cardiac arrhythmias. Building on the ideas of Ellison and Ellison (2007), she notes that entry preemption will most likely occur in markets where the entry probability is intermediate. In markets in which entry probabilities are high, entry will likely occur even with incumbent strategic behavior. In low entry probability markets, entry deterrence is unnecessary, because entry is unlikely even without preemption. Using Medicare claims data she tests this proposition and finds that incumbent volume growth for electrophysiological studies is largest in markets in which there is only one potential entrant (an intermediate entry probability case) and that the greater the number of entrants, the lower the incumbent volume growth. Thus, the evidence suggests that hospitals do engage in entry deterrence in accordance with the theory.

The analysis of entry and exit by providers other than hospitals is quite limited. Orsini (2010) examines the impact of changes in Medicare home health reimbursement rates that were passed in the Balanced Budget Act of 1997 on home health agency exits. Orsini finds that a decline in reimbursement of one visit per user increases the hazard of exit of a home health care agency by 1.13 percent with no differential response in exit by ownership type. Bowblis (2010) studies closures in the nursing home industry and finds that FP homes are slightly more likely to close than NFP homes. Also, homes that care for more publicly insured patients and those with poor financial performance were more likely to close.

2.2.1. The Impact of the Introduction of New Classes of Providers

The basic structure, roles, and segmentation of health care providers has remained relatively constant over the last half of the century. Hospitals provide a variety of inpatient and outpatient services and, depending on their specialty, physicians provide care in either their office and/or the hospital. Cutler (2010) comments on the lack of entrepreneurial vigor addressing the inefficiencies in the provision of health care. He cites two reasons for these inefficiencies. First, fee-for-service reimbursement schemes give providers little incentive to reduce the cost of the care they provide. Second, information on the cost and quality of care is generally not transparent. Thus, the returns to developing new care modalities that result in higher-quality and/or lower-cost care are likely to be modest. Cebul et al. (2008) also consider organizational issues in health care. They point to sociological factors, legal barriers, and issues with information (the compatibility and deployment of information technology specifically) as the key reasons for the inefficient organization of this sector. While Cutler and Cebul

---

[17] This can form a barrier due to fixed costs of entry or due to a volume-outcome effect. Insufficient volume may result in such poor quality that entry will not occur.

et al. are right to note the organization problems and lack of large entrepreneurial advances in health care provision, there are some important exceptions.

More broadly, the literature outside of health care generally finds that the introduction of new products can have large positive impacts on consumer welfare (e.g. Petrin, 2002; Gentzkow, 2007). However, this need not be the case in the health care sector. The large role of public programs where prices are set administratively, the importance of private third-party payers, and the presence of asymmetric information imply that new organizational forms can plausibly reduce consumer well-being. That is, these organizations could be designed to exploit administrative pricing irregularities, the inability of insurers to curtail patient utilization, or knowledge gaps between patients and providers over the quality and necessity of the care they receive. There are at least three types of new organization types that have been introduced over the last several decades, and we discuss them below.

There is a long history of hospitals that are devoted to specific conditions or populations—women's, children's, psychiatric, and tuberculosis hospitals have existed for over a century. However, in the early 1990s a new type of "specialty" hospital was born. Specialty hospitals are inpatient facilities that treat a limited range of conditions (e.g. cardiac and orthopedic). These hospitals are principally for-profit organizations, with physicians owning a significant stake in the hospital. Specialty hospitals are controversial. Critics argue that specialty hospitals are a mechanism to exploit asymmetric information by providing kickbacks to physicians for referrals, and they restrict the ability of general hospitals to internally cross-subsidize unprofitable services by skimming off high-margin patients. Proponents contend that there are important gains from specialization. Specialty hospitals may offer greater economic efficiency, higher quality, more consumer-responsive products and services, and provide beneficial competition to general hospitals.[18] Barro et al. (2006) study the impact of specialty hospitals and find that markets experiencing entry by a cardiac specialty hospital have lower spending for cardiac care without significantly worse clinical outcomes. In markets with a specialty hospital, however, specialty hospitals tend to attract healthier patients and provide higher levels of intensive procedures than general hospitals. Carey et al. (2008) find that orthopedic and surgical specialty hospitals appear to have significantly higher levels of cost inefficiency. Cardiac hospitals, however, do not appear to be different from competitors in this respect.

Chakravarty (2010) employs a number of analyses to assess the impact of specialty hospitals on general hospitals. In one, he uses propensity score matching and difference-in-difference analysis on a national dataset to estimate the effect of specialty hospitals on the profits of general hospitals. He finds no statistically significant impacts of the entry of specialty hospitals on general hospital profits. In this analysis

---

[18] See Schneider et al. (2008b) for an overview of the economics of specialty hospitals.

he is unable to control for the extent to which specialty hospitals may select healthier patients. He employs a dataset from the state of Texas with detailed clinical information to conduct an analysis controlling for the possibility that specialty hospitals skim healthier patients. He finds that there is heterogeneity in the effects of specialty hospital entry on general hospital profits: entry lowers general hospital profits in counties where specialty hospitals have healthier patients than the median (county), but not in other counties. He also looks at the impacts of specialty hospital entry on general hospital exit and merger. He finds no evidence of an impact on exit, but some evidence that specialty hospital entry increases the probability of general hospital mergers.

Ambulatory Surgical Centers (ASCs) were introduced in the US in the 1970s as more and more surgical procedures shifted to an outpatient setting, and have grown to become an important type of health care provider. There are 4,500 freestanding ASCs performing more than 15 million procedures annually (Cullen et al., 2009). ASCs provide non-emergent, outpatient surgical services, generally focusing on specific sets of procedures (e.g. cataract surgery, orthopedics). ASCs compete with each other and with the outpatient departments of general acute care hospitals for the provision of these services. Weber (2010) examines the welfare benefits of ambulatory surgical centers. She does this by estimating the demand for ASCs as a function of distance and patient and facility characteristics, using data from the state of Florida. Her estimates show that consumers place relatively little value on having access to an ASC. If all ASCs were closed, potential consumers of ASC services would conservatively lose approximately $1.50 of surplus per episode for the least valued procedure and about $27 per episode for the most valued procedure. Approximately two-thirds of the welfare loss comes from the loss of ASCs and their unique attributes, while the remaining one-third stems from consumers facing smaller choice sets and greater travel times.

Retail clinics (or convenience clinics) are a relatively new type of health care provider that compete with physician clinics for the diagnosis and treatment of several common, low acuity conditions. The first retail clinic opened in a Cub grocery store in St. Paul, MN, in 2000. Retail clinic patients do not need an appointment, and care is provided by nurses with advanced training (usually nurse practitioners) who are overseen by a physician (often remotely). Currently, there are over 1,200 clinics operating in the US. The prices for each service are typically posted at the clinic as well as online, making the patient financial obligation transparent. These fees are much lower than most physician office visit charges, making retail clinics a more attractive option for the uninsured. The clinics also are usually located in a retail establishment (drug store, grocery store, big box retailer) and have extensive evening and weekend hours. Using a large, national database of private insurer claims, Parente and Town (2011) examine the impact of these clinics on the cost and quality of care. They find that the cost of care at these clinics is significantly lower relative to the care provided in a physician's office, with no obvious quality differences. As a consequence, these results suggest that the introduction of retail clinics resulted in significant consumer welfare gains. Some recent results by Ashwood et al. (2011), using data from a different large national insurer, find increased utilization and cost associated with retail clinics, however. Retail clinics are associated with reductions in utilization and costs for physician office visits and emergency room visits. However, the increase in retail clinic visits is larger than the reductions in other types of utilization.

3. HOSPITAL MARKET STRUCTURE, COMPETITION, AND PRICES

3.1. A Model of Hospital Insurer Negotiation

As mentioned in the introduction, the hospital industry is one of the largest industries in the US economy. Not only is the hospital industry large, but it operates in a very unique institutional setting. Over the last decade a series of papers have been written that model the price setting behavior of hospitals. These models recognize that institutional features of the hospital market in the United States are unique and these features have ramifications for the role of competition in affecting prices and the quality of care. There are at least four key distinguishing features of hospital markets that play an important role in affecting competitive interactions between hospitals.

First, privately insured patients primarily access hospital care through their health insurance, therefore the set of available hospitals will depend on the health plan's provider network structure. Health insurers often contract with a subset of hospitals in a given location. The effective hospital choice set for a patient when they need to be treated will therefore depend upon their health insurance plan (Ho, 2006). Second, patients do not pay directly for inpatient care. Most of the cost of an inpatient episode is covered under the patient's insurance and hence any price differential between hospitals is not generally reflected in the patient's out-of-pocket cost. Third, the health insurance choice of the patient is generally made prior to the need for inpatient treatment. In this sense, hospitals are an option demand market. Fourth, hospitals negotiate with private insurers over inclusion in their provider network and the reimbursement rates the hospital will receive from treating the insurer's enrollees. These negotiations also determine how hospital utilization will be monitored and controlled as well as details of the billing arrangements. Health insurers, in turn, compete with each other based on premiums (which are a function of the prices they pay hospitals) on the breadth and quality of their provider networks. Employers, through whom most private insurance is acquired, have preferences over hospitals which are an aggregation of their employees' preferences, and select the set of health plans they offer to their workers based on expected costs, benefit structure, and provider networks.[19]

Below, we outline a simple model of hospital—insurer bargaining. There are several goals we wish to accomplish with this model. First, we wish to understand the role of market power and its source in affecting the price of hospital care. Second, a related goal is to understand how hospital mergers affect the price of inpatient care and the impact on welfare. Third, we provide guidance to empirical modelers so that one can estimate parameters that can be linked, either directly or indirectly, to the underlying theory of hospital price determination. We also note that this model, while faithful to key institutional details specific to health care, is generic enough that it can be applied to other health care providers besides hospitals, most prominently physicians. It also could be expanded in the direction of encompassing a richer model of the insurer market, although one for pragmatic purposes one would then have to simplify the insurer-provider part of the model.

The model combines the insights of research on hospital competition by Gal-Or (1997), Town and Vistnes (2001), Capps et al. (2003), Gaynor and Vogt (2003), Ho (2009b), Haas-Wilson and Garmon (2011), and Lewis and Pflum (2011). The structure of this model is also similar to the bargaining models of Crawford and Yurukoglu (2010) and Grennan (2010), who study cable television distribution and the negotiations between hospital and medical device suppliers over the price of stents, respectively. Our formulation most closely follows the exposition in Brand et al. (2011) (BGGNT).

Hospitals differ from most products in that the vast majority of consumers obtain their hospital services through their health plan. In order for health insurers to offer products that are viable in the marketplace, insurers must construct networks of hospitals from which enrollees can receive health care services. The breadth and depth of the provider network is a large determinant of the desirability of the different health plans, as consumers value access to a variety of hospitals in the event of adverse illness shocks. At the same time, consumers value income and so health insurance plans with lower premiums are also more attractive. As will be seen, there is a trade-off between the inclusiveness of an insurer's network and insurer premiums. Health plans with more inclusive networks will *ceteris paribus* have less bargaining power with hospitals and thus pay higher prices, resulting in higher premiums.

We model hospital competition as taking part in three stages. First, health plans and hospitals bargain to determine both the set of hospitals to include in the plan networks and the payment from the health plan to the hospital for each admitted patient. Second, patients choose health plans. Finally, patients realize illness shocks, and choose a hospital based on their illness shock and the hospitals in their network. Hospitals

---

[19] Most large employers are self-insured and thus changes in negotiated prices between providers and health plans are directly passed on to the employer.

and health plans are assumed to have "passive beliefs," i.e. if a plan or hospital gets an alternative offer in the negotiating process, this will not change their beliefs about the offers made or received by its competitors. We describe each of the three stages of the game in turn, starting from the final stage.

There are H health plans and N hospitals operating in the market. A set of patients, denoted $i = 1, \ldots, I$, live in the market area and may enroll in a health insurance plan and, after they have enrolled, they may become ill enough to require inpatient treatment. In the final stage of the game, each patient takes her health plan h and associated set J_h of in-network hospitals as given. At the beginning of the third stage, each patient learns her illness shock. Denote these shocks $m = 1, \ldots, M$, where each m corresponds to a particular illness, or no illness, $m = 0$. Let $\rho_{i1}, \ldots, \rho_{iM}$ denote the *ex-ante* probability of each shock. Each diagnosis has an accompanying weight $w_1, \ldots, w_M$. The weights describe the relative importance of each diagnosis in both the cost and utility function, as we discuss below. In empirical implementations, the m values would generally correspond to Diagnosis Related Groups (DRGs) or some other disease classification system.

Given diagnosis m, patients choose a hospital at which to obtain treatment. Patients are assumed not to pay an out-of-pocket differential price based on which hospital they select, provided the hospital is in-network. The utility that patients receive depends on the characteristics of the hospital (e.g. the services offered and the perceived quality of care), characteristics of the patients (e.g. demographics and diagnosis), the travel time to the hospital, and an idiosyncratic error term.[20] We let the *ex-post* utility for patient i from hospital $j \in J_h$ with illness shock m_i be given by:

$$u_{ij,m} = w_m[f(x_j, z_i, d_{ij}, m_i; \theta) + e_{ij}] \tag{9.2}$$

where x_j is a vector of hospital characteristics including a hospital indicator, z_i is a vector of patient characteristics including age, sex, and race, d_{ij} is the distance to the hospital from the patient's home, m_i is diagnosis, θ is a parameter vector to be estimated, and e_{ij} is an i.i.d. error term that is a distributed Type I extreme value, which is revealed to the patient at the same time as her illness shock. In practice, u_{ij} is parameterized to be a linear function of a hospital fixed effect, travel time and interactions between hospital characteristics (such as bed size, ownership type, teaching status, service offerings), patient characteristics, diagnosis, diagnosis weight, and travel time.

---

[20] In our formulation of utility, we assume that patients do not face any price differential across hospitals. We make this assumption primarily for expositional ease. There is some evidence that hospital prices do in fact affect hospital choice (e.g. Gaynor and Vogt, 2003). This could be a consequence of patient cost-sharing arrangements, insurers negotiating on their enrollees' behalves, or because physicians are incentivized to use lower-cost hospitals (Ho and Pakes, 2011). The advantage of allowing prices to enter patient utility is that recovering the utility parameter on price allows for the monetization of the patient's surplus from a given hospital network.

In addition to the J_h hospitals, the patient can also choose the outside option 0, which corresponds to going to an out-of-network or out-of-area hospital or no hospital. We normalize the utility from the outside option to have zero base utility, so $u_{i0} = e_{i0}$. We assume that if the health shock $m = 0$ then the utility of hospital treatment is sufficiently low that the patient always chooses the outside option 0.

Given the logit assumption, the probability that an individual i with illness m will seek care at hospital j is

$$s_{ijm} = \frac{\exp(f(x_j, z_i, d_{ij}, m; \theta))}{1 + \sum_{k \in J_j} \exp(f(x_k, z_i, d_{ik}, m; \theta))}$$

In turn, the *ex-ante* expected utility that a patient receives from a given hospital choice set J_h is given by:[21]

$$W_i(J_h) = \sum_{m=1...m} \left(\rho_{im} w_m \ln \left(1 + \sum_{j \in J_j} \exp(f(x_j, z_i, d_{ij}, m; \theta)) \right) \right) \tag{9.3}$$

Conditional on illness severities and probabilities, the distribution of x_j and the geographic distribution of hospitals, the welfare a patient receives from a health plan's network is a function of the identities of the hospitals in the plan's network.

Turning now to the second stage, each enrollee (and potential patient) is faced with a set of health plans, $h = 1, \ldots, H$, from which they select. Each plan has a set of hospitals in its network, J_h, and each plan simultaneously chooses its premium for its customers.[22] Plan attributes are given by a set of characteristics, c_h. We posit that the expected utility for consumer i of plan h is given by:[23]

$$v_{ij} = W_i(J_h; \theta) + \gamma c_h + \xi_h + \alpha^P \ln(income_i - Prem_h) + \varepsilon_{ih}$$

where $Prem_h$ is the insurance premium for plan h, ξ_h captures differences in the unmeasured (by the econometrician) desirability of the plan, γ and α^P are parameters, and where ε_{ih} is distributed i.i.d. Type I extreme value.[24] Let $\tilde{v}_{ih}$ denote the unconditional expected value of v_{ih} and let W_i and $Prem$ denote the vectors of the plan values

---

[21] To ease the notational burden, we index $W_i(J_h)$ only by J_h but it is understood that it is a function of patient and hospital characteristics and θ.

[22] BGNGT model the health plan as a cooperative whose objective is to maximize enrollee surplus. The advantage of this approach is that it allows for an explicit solution to the hospital/insurer bargaining game without modeling health plan competition. In that approach, consumer surplus directly enters the bargaining solution.

[23] For expositional ease we treat health plan enrollees as homogeneous conditional on their z_i and e. However, in an empirical implementation it may be desirable to allow for random coefficients over the preference parameters, as in Berry et al. (1995).

[24] In this parameterization of utility the pre-tax benefit treatment of health insurance is captured, in a reduced form way, in α^P.

for these variables for all plans in the market. The probability that individual i enrolls in plan h is:

$$y_{ih}(J, \xi, Prem; \theta, \gamma, \alpha) = \frac{\exp(\tilde{v}_{ih})}{\sum_l \exp(\tilde{v}_{il})}$$

where J is an $H \times N$ matrix of ones and zeros which denote the hospital networks of all the H plans and ξ is the $H \times 1$ vector of ξ_h values. The market share for plan h is then the summation of the probabilities of selecting the plan across the population: $Y_h(J, \xi, Prem) = \sum_i y_{ih}(J_1, \ldots, J_H, Prem)$.[25] The profits the health plan earns from a given network are then:

$$\pi_h(J, \xi, Prem) = \left(Prem_h - ac_h - \sum_j p_{jh} q_{jh} \right) Y_h(J, \xi_h, Prem) - Fixed_h$$

where ac_h is the other variable costs incurred by the plan outside of hospital expenditures, e.g. administrative and marketing costs. We assume that the plan's cost structures are known to all the other plans. Health plans are assumed to select a single premium to maximize profit. That is, treating their own and the competitors' hospital networks as fixed, the first-order conditions are:

$$Y_h(J, \xi, Prem) + \left(Prem_h - ac_h - \sum_j p_{jh} q_{jh} \right) \frac{dY_h(J, \xi, Prem)}{dPrem_h} = 0 \qquad (9.4)$$

The equilibrium of the premium setting game is one in which all of the plans' premiums satisfy (9.4) simultaneously. Caplin and Nalebuff (1991) prove that there is a unique equilibrium in the premium setting game given the set of health plan hospital networks. The premiums and thus the profits of all the health plans will depend upon the structure of all the competing plans' hospital networks, their costs, and the distribution of patients across geography and incomes.

Finally, at the first stage of the game, we assume that hospitals and health plans bargain over the price of inpatient care. The outcome of this bargaining game determines which hospitals and health plans will agree to a contract and the prices health plans will pay hospitals for caring for their enrollees. Although the contract terms between hospitals and health plans are complex, we assume that health plans and hospitals are constrained to negotiate a base price for each patient. The actual price paid by the health plan to the hospital will be the base price multiplied by the disease weight, w_m. Since the weights are effectively meant to capture costs, one could implement this by using DRG weights, which have roughly the same purpose. With the interpretation of the w terms as DRG weights, we believe that this structure for a

---

[25] We ease the notational burden by subsuming the parameter index into Y_h.

contract between a health plan and hospital is a reasonable approximation of actual contracts.

We consider a model of bargaining and competition similar to Horn and Wolinsky (1988).[26] There are JH pairs of hospitals and health plans which are negotiating over a price (p_{jh}) the health plan pays to the hospital for each patient the hospital treats. The hospital's marginal cost of treating the patient is C_j.[27] Nature chooses a random ordering among each of these pairs and assigns an initial offerer to each pair. The parties then engage in a bargaining process over prices. Prior to the match, the health plan receives an i.i.d. synergistic cost term from the match, cm_{jh}, that is common knowledge to both firms and which will generate randomness to the *ex-ante* outcomes. A natural starting point for analyzing the bargaining game is to focus on the Nash bargaining solution.[28] This solution takes each insurer–hospital pair in isolation, holding the other hospital–insurer prices fixed. The Nash bargaining solution we consider ignores the strategic interactions that a given insurer–hospital price might have on other insurer–hospital prices. Importantly, this framework is an approximation to the game in which prices and the entire provider networks are determined.[29] Clearly, allowing a richer set of strategic interactions would be a welcome advance.

To calculate the Nash bargaining outcome we need to specify the agreement and disagreement values for the hospital and the insurer. The agreement value for the hospital is the net revenues they earn from the insurer's flow of patients to the hospital. Under the disagreement outcome the hospital is assumed to receive a fixed net revenue, r_h. For the insurer, the agreement value is the gross revenue they earn from having hospital network J_h in place less the expenditures on inpatient care at the hospital. Holding the other plans' hospital networks fixed, we denote the gross revenue as:

$$F_h(J_h) = Prem_h^*(J_h, J_{-h}) Y_h(J_h, J_{-h}, \xi, Prem_h^*) \tag{9.5}$$

where $Prem_h^*$ is the vector of premiums that solves (9.4), and we decompose the matrix of hospital networks into two components, plan h's network and the networks of the other plans, J_{-h}. Denote the hospital network that excludes hospital j as J_{h-j}. The gross revenue from the network that excludes hospital j is then:

$$F_h(J_{h-j}) = Prem_h^*(J_{h-j}, J_{-h}) Y_h(J_{h-j}, J_{-h}, \xi, Prem_h^*) \tag{9.6}$$

The insurer's disagreement value is then $F_h(J_{h-j}) - \sum_k p k_j q_{kh}^{J_h-j}$, where $q_{kh}^{J_h-j}$ is the flow of patients to network hospitals given network J_{h-j}. If the net surplus

---

[26] More recent analyses of bargaining games in supplier network contexts include Stole and Zwiebel (1996), Inderst and Wey (2003), and de Fontenay and Gans (2007).

[27] We assume costs do not vary by health plan.

[28] See Dranove et al. (2007) for an examination of the "levels" of rationality that hospitals possess in the bargaining game.

[29] Ho (2009b) and Pakes (2010) consider a game of hospital network formation which endogenizes the network structure.

from the hospital–insurer match is not greater than zero, then bargaining does not take place and the hospital is not in the insurer's network. That is, bargaining only takes place if $F_h(J_h) - F_h(J_{h-j}) - c_{jh}q_{jh} - \Sigma_{l\neq j}p_{lh}d_{jlh} - cm_{jh} > 0$, where $d_{jk} = (q_{kh}^{J-j} - q_{kh})$.

Summarizing the agreement and disagreement values we have:

$$H_{\text{agree}} = (p_{jh} - c_j)q_{jh}(J_h)$$

$$H_{\text{disagree}} = r_j$$

$$M_{\text{agree}} = F_h(J_h) - p_{jh}q_{jh}(J_h) - \sum_{l\neq j}p_{lh}q_{lh}(J_h) - cm_{jh}$$

$$M_{\text{disagree}} = F_h(J_{h-j}) - \sum_{l\neq j}p_{lh}q_{lh}(J_{h-j})$$

Under Nash bargaining each bilateral price maximizes the Nash product of hospital net profits and the net insurer surplus from agreement, taking the other prices as given, solving

$$\max_p [H_{\text{agree}} - H_{\text{disagree}}]^\beta [M_{\text{agree}} - M_{\text{disagree}}]^{1-\beta}$$

where $\beta \in [0,1]$ is the relative bargaining ability or non-modeled bargaining power of the hospital relative to the insurer. Differentiating and solving for p_{jh} yields:[30]

$$p_{jh} = (1-\beta)\left(c_j - \frac{r_j}{q_{jh}}\right) + \frac{\beta}{q_{jh}}(F_h(J_h) - F_h(J_{h-j}) - cm_{jh}) + \beta\sum_{l\neq j}p_{lh}d_{jlh} \qquad (9.7)$$

where we refine d as a share so $d_{jk} = (q_{kh}^{J-j} - q_{kh})/q_{jh}$ and q_{kh}^{J-j} is the number of patients that flow to hospital k if the network is J_{h-j}. That is, d_{jk} is the diversion share from hospital j to hospital k when hospital j is no longer available.

The Nash bargaining solution predicts that, quite intuitively, a hospital's price will be increasing in its costs, bargaining ability, the prices of other competing hospitals, and, importantly, the net value that the hospital brings to the insurer's network. In this framework, we have left the insurer few tools to affect their bargaining position. There are circumstances in which if the health plan can steer patients to lower priced hospitals it can significantly affect the bargaining outcome. This is true theoretically as well as empirically. Sorensen (2003) and Wu (2009) find that health plans which are better able to channel patients can extract greater discounts from hospitals.

Part of the goal of this analysis is to provide a framework for the analysis of hospital mergers. To start this analysis assume that the hospitals negotiate separately while under joint control but take into account the impact of disagreement on the

[30] Note that $\frac{\partial F(V_{Jh},p_{jh})}{\partial p_{jh}} = 0$ by the envelope theorem.

flow of patients to the other hospital in the system.[31] This changes the threat points and thus the Nash bargaining solution. The agreement and disagreement outcomes are now:

$$H_{\text{agree}}^{j+k} = (p_{jh} - c_j)q_{jh} + (p_{kh} - c_k)q_{kh}(J_h)$$

$$H_{\text{disagree}}^{j+k} = (p_{kh} - c_k)q_{kh}(J_{h-j}) + r_j$$

$$M_{\text{agree}}^{j+k} = F_h(J_h) - p_{jh}q_{jh} - \sum_{l\neq j,k} p_{kj}q_{lh}(J_h) - cm_{jh}$$

$$M_{\text{disagree}}^{j+k} = F_h(J_{h-j}) - \sum_{l\neq j} p_{kh}\tilde{q}_{lh}(J_{h-j})$$

Solving the first-order conditions for this bargaining game yields the following Nash bargaining solution:

$$p_{jh}^{j+k} = (1-\beta)\left(c_j + \frac{r_h + d_{jkh}p_{kh}}{q_{jh}}\right) + \frac{\beta}{q_{jh}}(F_h(J_h) - F_h(J_{h-j}) - cm_{jh}) + \beta\sum_{l\neq j} p_{lh}d_{jlh} \quad (9.8)$$

Assuming that hospital costs are not affected by the merger and holding β constant, the change in price caused by the merger is given by:

$$\Delta p_{jh}^{j+k} = (1-\beta)d_{jkh}p_{kh} - c_j \quad (9.9)$$

The impact of the merger on hospital k's price is symmetric. Intuitively, the increase in price is a function of the diversion share between j and k. If no patients view hospital k as the closest substitute for j when j is not available, then the merger will have no effect on price. The impact of the merger on hospital j's price is increasing in k's price and the bargaining leverage of hospitals.

Now let the hospitals negotiate jointly. Specifically, assume that the hospitals make an all-or-nothing offer. That is, the insurer can either have all of the hospitals in the system or none of the hospitals in the system in their network. Here we assume that hospitals j and k merge to form a system and they will commit to charging one price for both hospitals in the system. The post-merger agreement and disagreement values are now:

$$H_{\text{agree}}^{j+k} = (p_{jh} - c_{j+k})(q_{kh}(J_k) + q_{kh}(J_h))$$

$$H_{\text{disagree}}^{j+k} = r_j + r_k$$

$$M_{\text{agree}}^{j+k} = F_h((J_j) - p_{jk}(q_{jh}(J_h) + q_{kh}(J_h)) - \sum_{l\neq j,k} p_{lh}q_{lh}(J_h)$$

---

[31] Balan and Brand (2009) perform similar analysis in their simulation analysis of hospital merger simulations.

$$M_{\text{disagree}}^{j+k} = F_h(J_{h-j-k}) - \sum_{l \neq j,k} p_{lh} q_{lh}(J_{h-j-k})$$

where c_{j+k} is the volume weighted average cost of the newly merged system.

Solving as before yields the solution:

$$
\begin{aligned}
p_{jh} = (1-\beta)\left(c_{j+k} + \frac{r_{j+k}}{q_{jh} + q_{kh}} \right) \\
+ \frac{\beta(F_h(J_h) - F_h(J_{h-j-k}) - cm_{j+kh})}{q_{jh} + q_{kh}} + \beta \sum_{l \neq j} p_{lh} d_{(j+k)lh}
\end{aligned}
\tag{9.10}
$$

The diversion shares, $d_{(j+k)lh}$, are now relative to the merged entity and $d_{(j+k)kh} = 0$. The impact of a given hospital merger will depend on the changes in the relative threat points. However, if the hospitals are viewed as substitutes by potential patients, then post-merger prices will increase. To see this, let hospitals j and k be symmetric in the sense that they have the same pre-merger prices, average costs and volumes, and assume that the match value terms are unaffected by the merger.[32] Let $\Delta^{J_{h-j}} = \frac{1}{q_{jh}}(F_h(J_h) - F_h(J_{h-j}))$, which is the average loss in net revenue to the insurer per patient if no agreement is reached. The corresponding value for the merged hospital is $\Delta^{J-j-k} = \frac{1}{q_{jh} + q_{kh}}(F_h(J_h) - F_h(J_{h-j-k}))$. The change in the price of hospital j is then:

$$\Delta p_{jh} = \Delta^{J-j-k} - \Delta^{J-j} + \sum_{l \neq j,k} p_{lh}(d_{j+klh} - d_{jlh}) \tag{9.11}$$

The merger will increase price as long as the additional loss in per-patient welfare (relative to network J) from hospital network J_{h-j-k} is greater than the loss in welfare from hospital network J_{h-j}. This will be the case if and only if patients view hospitals j and k as substitutes. To see this, assume that hospitals j and k are not substitutes in the sense that $\frac{d_{jkh}}{q_{jk}} < a$ where a is a sufficiently small (say 0.05), so that $F_h(J_h) - F_h(J_{h-j-k}) \approx 2F_h(J_h) - F_k(J_{h-j}) - F_h(J_{h-k})$. Then $\Delta^{J-j-k} \approx \Delta^{J-j}$ and $\Delta p_{jh} \approx 0$.[33]

In order to assess the welfare impact of a change in hospital market structure, we need to trace out the pass-through from changes in hospital prices to changes in health insurance premiums. In this framework, hospitals are an input into the production of health insurance, thus any change in hospital prices will only affect consumer surplus if those changes are passed through to consumers. Given parameters on health plan utility and the appropriate data, it is possible to quantify the impact of the hospital merger on welfare. Suppose competing hospitals j and k successfully merge and in

---

[32] It is straightforward but notationally cumbersome to let prices differ by hospital for this exercise.

[33] In the random utility hospital choice model there will always be some non-zero substitution between hospitals in the choice set and thus there is no two-hospital pair for which $d_{jkh} = 0$.

their new negotiations with health insurers change hospital prices by Δp_{j+k}, where Δp_{j+k} is an $H \times 1$ vector. We assume the merger does not affect the structure of any health plan's hospital network or any other health plan attributes.[34]

To calculate the impact of the merger on premiums at the new hospital prices, resolve the health plan's first-order conditions (9.4) for the new post-merger premiums. Denote the post-merger premiums as $Prem^{j+k}$. Let $v_{ih}^*(Prem_j, W_i, c_h, \xi_h; \alpha^p, \gamma) = v_{ih} - \varepsilon_{ih}$. The consumer surplus from health insurance for individual i is:

$$CS_i(Prem, W_i, c_h, \xi_h; \alpha^p, \gamma) = \frac{1}{\alpha^p} \ln \left[1 + \sum_{h+1\ldots H} \exp(v_{ih}^*) \right] \qquad (9.12)$$

The impact of the hospital merger on consumer welfare through its impact on hospital prices is then:

$$\Delta CS_i = CS_i(Prem^{j+k}) - CS_i(Prem) \qquad (9.13)$$

The aggregate impact is then the summation of ΔCS_i across the affected population (e.g. those not enrolled in public health insurance).

3.2. Estimating the Impact of Hospital Market Power on Price

The most active area of research in the industrial organization of health care is the analysis of the impact of hospital concentration on hospital prices. There are several different approaches to estimating the role of bargaining leverage on hospital prices. The approaches differ in the nature of identification, data quality, the structure imposed on the data generating process, and complexity of the econometrics. Nevertheless, virtually all the approaches implicitly or explicitly rely on a version of the insurer−hospital bargaining framework. The basic strategy (with some important exceptions) is to estimate the parameters in equation (9.7) or, more commonly, to approximate the functional relationship in (9.7). With those parameter estimates in hand it is relatively straightforward to calculate merger counterfactuals by computing the predicted post-merger price using (9.11). We discuss three broad classes of empirical strategies used to estimate the impact of changes in market structure on prices: (1) reduced form; (2) merger case studies; and (3) structural and semi-structural approaches.

Examining the distribution of realized hospital prices alone is informative about the functioning of hospital markets. Ginsburg (2010) uses administrative claims data for eight geographic areas from four large insurers to construct inpatient hospital prices. He finds that there is significant variation both within and across regions in

---

[34] If they are quantifiable and measurable, it is straightforward to incorporate any other changes to health plan attributes into this analysis. For example, see Petrin (2002).

hospital prices. For example, San Francisco has the highest average hospital prices in 2008 with prices equal to 210 percent of the Medicare reimbursement rate. The lowest rate is Miami-South Florida with mean prices that are 147 percent of Medicare rates—the mean price in San Francisco is 43 percent higher than Miami. Within San Francisco, the interquartile range is 116 percent of the Medicare price. Of course, there are a number of possible reasons for this variation. Cost, quality, and demand differences will generally imply price differences. However, it seems unlikely that there is enough variation across those factors to generate such wide variation in price. It is important to note that in the bargaining framework outlined above, it is easy to generate large variations in price both across and within markets by simply varying the ownership structure of hospitals, suggesting to us that the variation in prices is likely related to variation in hospital bargaining leverage.

3.2.1. Reduced-form Estimates

Reduced-form approaches to estimating price concentration have a long history in the industrial organization and health economics literature. In this approach, researchers construct measures of market concentration, usually some form of the Herfindahl–Hirschmann Index (HHI),[35] and regress it on the variable of interest (e.g. prices) controlling for observable confounding variables. Reduced-form approaches allow researchers to be somewhat agnostic about the underlying theoretical model and thereby let the data speak directly to the relationships between the variables of interest.[36] While the broader industrial organization literature has largely moved away from employing reduced-form approaches, it nevertheless remains a popular research approach in the health economics and health services research literatures.

There are several reasons underlying the movement away from reduced-form strategies. First, in most applied settings it is difficult to square a strict functional relationship between price and the HHI with economic theory. Basic oligopoly theory posits a functional relationship between HHI and prices only with Cournot behavior—quantity setting with homogeneous products. Homogeneous product, quantity setting models are inconsistent with the institutional facts of hospital markets, as we have previously indicated.

Some alternative models generate pricing power as a function of market shares, and are thus related to the HHI. Akosa Antwi et al. (2006) develop a competition index for differentiated product oligopoly with logit demand and Bertrand pricing.

---

[35] The HHI is the sum of squared market shares.

[36] See Gaynor and Vogt (2000) and Dranove and Satterthwaite (2000) for summaries of early portions of this literature.

They call the index "LOCI" for Logit Competition Index. LOCI takes the following form:

$$\Lambda_j = \sum_{t=1}^{T} \frac{N_t \bar{q}_t s_{tj}}{\sum_{t=1}^{T} N_t \bar{q}_t s_{tj}} (1 - s_{tj}) \qquad (9.14)$$

where Λ_j is LOCI, hospitals are indexed by j, consumers are of differing types indexed by t, N_t is the number of type t consumers, $\bar{q}_t$ is the average quantity consumed by type t, and s_{tj} is the proportion of type t consumers going to hospital j. The pricing equation for this model is:

$$p_j = c_j + \frac{1}{\alpha} \frac{1}{\Lambda_j} \qquad (9.15)$$

where c_j are hospital marginal costs and α is the marginal utility of income from the underlying utility function. This is a coherent economic model that generates an equation with price as a function of market shares.

In another approach, which also utilizes logit demand, Capps et al. (2003) show that

$$W_i(J_h) - W_i(J_h - j) = \ln\left(\frac{1}{1 - s_{ij}}\right) \qquad (9.16)$$

and thus a hospital system's bargaining leverage is an aggregation of a non-linear function of the individual hospital choice probabilities. A common approach to calculating the HHIs is to construct an HHI at the zip code level and then aggregate up to the hospital level. That gives the following measure of concentration: $HHI_j = \sum_z \bar{s}_z^j \sum_k s_{zk}^2$, where $\bar{s}_z^j$ is the hospital's share of its patients it culls from zip code z. This formulation of the HHI is functionally related to WTP below and thus will be imperfectly correlated with the WTP. One might more broadly think of the HHI as a proxy for the expected toughness of competition based on market structure. The HHI is not explicitly derived from an underlying theoretical framework, but is intended to capture the potential for competition. This has some appeal, but it is important to realize that while the HHI can be constructed to imperfectly capture geographic and product differentiation, nonetheless it likely contains meaningful measurement error. Many analysts who have estimated equations using the HHI have been sensitive to this and have attempted to deal with the problem, usually through the use of instrumental variables. As always, the resulting estimates will be as good as the instruments.

The second concern regarding the reduced-form approaches is that market structure is endogenous.[37] There likely are unobservables, such as the quality of the services

---

[37] The problem of endogenous market structure is not unique to reduced-form methods. Structural approaches generally simply assume fixed market structure, and so they also face the challenge of estimating models when market structure is endogenous.

provided, or unobserved cost differences, that will be correlated with price and market structure. For example, if price is not appropriately adjusted for quality, then standard regression analysis of concentration on hospital price will yield biased coefficients. Some of this concern can be mitigated by estimating a multinomial model of hospital choice and using the estimates to construct hospital-specific measures of market concentration. Kessler and McClellan (2000) and Gowrisankaran and Town (2003) develop such an approach to construct measures of market concentration and much of the recent literature has moved to constructing hospital-specific versions of the HHI. These HHI measures are generally the weighted (by hospital patient shares) zip code HHIs. More generally, instrumental variable approaches can be employed to deal with the endogeneity problem, including the approach just described.

The third issue is that hospitals sell differentiated products, and traditional approaches to calculating the HHI do not account for this differentiation. The hospital-specific measures described above constitute an ad hoc approach to dealing with this problem. The LOCI measure described above is a competition index explicitly derived for differentiated products oligopoly.

Fourth, reduced-form approaches generally require specifying a geographic market. This often relies on geopolitical boundaries (e.g. counties or Primary Metropolitan Statistical Areas (PMSAs)) to define the market. Geopolitical boundaries are unlikely to correspond to market definitions, and thus this approach will generate measurement error. As mentioned above, many recent SCP approaches construct a hospital-specific measure of the HHI by measuring the HHI at the zip code level and taking a share weighted average across zip codes to construct the hospital's HHI. This approach to calculating the HHI mitigates, at least to some degree, the third and fourth criticisms listed above.

The principal challenge in estimating models of hospital price competition is constructing an accurate measure of hospital price. Hospital contracts with insurers are generally complicated and have numerous prices for different services. In general, there are three classes of contracts: DRG-based, per-diem, and percent of charges. It is common for hospital contracts to contain combinations of these approaches. For example, a hospital/insurer contract might have a DRG structure for general medical/surgical services and "carve-out" obstetrics using a per-diem formulation. These contracts give hospitals different incentives for resource use. Anecdotally, bargaining leverage appears to play a significant role in the determination of the contract form, with hospitals preferring contracts with lower-powered incentives and insurers preferring higher-powered contracts.

There is little work that considers the role of competition in determining insurer—hospital contract structure.[38] In their analysis of insurer contracts for transplant

---

[38] Town et al. (2011) examine the degree of physician risk-bearing in their contracts with health insurers. They find that physicians facing less competition are more likely to have fee-for-service contracts.

services, Bajari et al. (2010) find that the majority of hospital contracts rely on a non-linear, percent of charges structure. Because of the complexity of insurer–hospital contracts, in most circumstances actual administrative claims data used to adjudicate payments between hospitals and insurers will provide the best measure of price. Constructing price using administrative claims requires adjusting for differential severity and types of services. Unfortunately, administrative claims data from payers and hospitals are not widely available. Researchers more commonly use measures of price constructed from state mandated hospital financial reports. Capps and Dranove (2004), Tenn (2011), Haas-Wilson and Garmon (2011), Thompson (2011), Ginsburg (2010), and Brand et al. (2011) are a subset of the papers that use insurer claims data to construct prices in this way.

Table 9.8 presents a summary of the reduced form papers published since 2000. This literature has moved away from primarily using data from California which, because of data availability issues, was the primary data source for prior work. All but one of the papers listed in this table finds a positive relationship between hospital concentration and price. Not surprisingly, this relationship appears to be a function of the structure of the health plan. Specifically, during the rise of MCOs during the 1990s, this relationship strengthened and the growth in the correlation appears to wane during the managed care backlash. In addition, the correlation is stronger in markets with high MCO penetration or in areas with a large number of managed care organizations. The relationship between price and measures of market structure also holds in other countries. Halbersma et al. (2010) find hospital–insurer prices are positively correlated with hospital concentration and negatively correlated with insurer concentration after the introduction of market-based health care reforms in the Netherlands in 2004.

3.2.2. Estimates of the Impact of Consummated Mergers on Price

The second popular approach to the analysis of the impact of hospital mergers is to study the impact of consummated mergers. The analysis of actual mergers has obvious appeal. The variation in market structure is driven by the phenomenon of primary interest. Understanding the outcomes of past hospital mergers speaks directly to the role of competition and the impact of consolidation on hospital prices, and ultimately downstream health care consumers. Studying consummated mergers also suggests a natural estimation strategy. Most of the papers in this literature rely on a difference-in-difference research design in which the merging hospitals (or sometimes their close rivals) are the treatment group and researchers locate other hospitals to use as controls. In an effort to better understand the appropriate merger enforcement strategy, the Federal Trade Commission has embarked on a program to retrospectively study consummated mergers. The results of these studies are published in a recent issue of *International Journal of the Business of Economics*.

Table 9.8 Summary of Hospital Price-Concentration Literature

Study	Primary Data Source, Services, Location and Time Period	Measures of Market Structure/Price	Empirical Approach	Results
Akosa Antwi et al. (2009)	OSHPD; Inpatient; CA; 1999–20025	County-level HHI; average net revenue per discharge	Graphical analysis of price growth trends	Prices increased 2-fold over period and growth is highest in monopoly markets; however, changes in market structure are not associated with differential price growth
Burgess et al. (2005)	AHA, OSHPD, inpatient; CA; 1994–1998	Average net private revenue per private discharge; hospital system HHI is weighted average zip code HHI	Estimate GEE to account for within-hospital correlations	Hospital system HHI is positively correlated with price
Dranove et al. (2008)	OSHPD, Florida State Center for Health Statistics; AHA; inpatient; CA and FL; 1990–2003	Hospital system HHI based on actual and predicted patient flows	OLS and IV regression of price on concentration and measure of MC intensity	The association between concentration and price increased during the 1990s and leveled off during the 2000s
Melnick and Keeler (2007)	OSHPD, AHA; inpatient; CA; 1999–2003	Average net private revenue per private discharge; hospital system HHI is weighted average zip code HHI	Linear regression of log price on concentration indexes and system indicators	System HHI is positively associated with price growth; hospitals in large systems experienced higher price growth
Moriya et al. (2010)	MedStat insurance claims, AHA data; all inpatient; US; 2001–2003	HHI calculated using AHA data, DRG-adjusted prices from claims data	Estimate the relationship between insurer/hospital concentration and price using OLS w/market FE	Insurer concentration is negatively associated with hospital prices; hospital

(Continued)

Table 9.8 (Continued)

Study	Primary Data Source, Services, Location and Time Period	Measures of Market Structure/Price	Empirical Approach	Results
				price/concentration relationship is insignificant
Wu (2008)	Medicare cost reports, AHA; inpatient; MA; 1990–2002	Outcome of interest is change in private payments per admission	Examines impact of hospital closures on prices using DDD approach	Hospitals in which a rival closed experienced a price increase relative to controls
Zwanziger et al. (2000)	OSHPD; inpatient; CA; 1980–1997	Outcome of interest is hospital revenue and expenditures, HHI is weighted average zip code HHI	Estimate the impact of hospital concentration allowing for the impact to vary by year; estimate with hospital FE	The association between market concentration and hospital revenue is monotonically increasing from 1983 to 1997
Zwanziger and Mooney (2005)	HMO annual reports, SPARCS, NY cost reports; inpatient; NY; 1995–1999	Price is HMO payments/risk-adjusted discharges; hospital/system HHI is weighted average zip code HHI	Estimate the relationship between hospital concentration and price leveraging NY deregulation of hospital pricing in 1997 w/hospital FE	The relationship between system HHI and prices became large and significant after reform

Note: Lists only those studies published after 2000.

Despite its appeal, there are a number of challenges to implementing merger case study analysis. Principal among these challenges is defining a sensible set of control group hospitals. Over the last decade hospital inflation has been significant and persistent—the producer price index for hospitals increased on average 3.8 percent per year. Thus, simply examining pre-post-hospital prices may lead to misleading inferences regarding the underlying change in the competitive environment induced by the merger. In addition, a merger may change the quality or the set of services provided by the merging hospitals, which may also affect inference. The set of control hospitals should have cost and demand shocks that mimic what would have happened to the merging hospitals under the counterfactual that the merger did not take place.

In their study of the impact of the Evanston Northwestern Healthcare and Highland Park Hospital merger and the St. Therese Medical Center and Victory Memorial Hospital, Haas-Wilson and Garmon (2011) used the non-federal general acute-care hospitals in the Chicago Primary Metropolitan Statistical Area that were not involved in mergers over the relevant time period. However, as is clear from the pricing equation (9.7) from our bargaining model, hospital mergers will affect the prices of competitors. That is, a hospital merger that leads to increased bargaining power will also spill over and increase the prices of competing hospitals that are not party to the merger. Using a set of control group hospitals that are geographically proximate to the merging hospital will control for local demand and cost shocks, but risks inducing a downward bias in the estimated impact due to the spillover effect. Using hospitals that are not proximate as a control group reduces the bias from spillovers, but increases the likelihood that demand and costs shocks will not be adequately controlled.

Table 9.9 provides a summary of the papers examining the impact of consummated mergers on estimated prices. There are several patterns worth noting. Because of the size of this literature, we do not have the space to discuss in detail all of the papers, and therefore highlight the patterns and the papers that are particularly noteworthy. First, the large number of hospital mergers in concentrated markets provides many opportunities for the examination of price effects of mergers. This is reflected in the numbers of papers (nine in total) that estimate merger price effects. In the broad industrial organization literature, the number of papers devoted to examining pricing behavior post-merger is rather limited.[39] Second, on average, the impact of consolidation on prices is positive and large. Third, while the average impact is large, there does seem to be heterogeneity across health plans in the change in the post-merger negotiated price. The model presented above can account for this heterogeneity in a limited way through changes in the bargaining leverage parameters that occur

---

[39] This literature has focused primarily on mergers in the airline and banking industries.

Table 9.9 Summary of Hospital Merger Literature

Study	Primary Data Source and Time Period	Location/Merger	Services	Price Measure	Empirical Approach	Results
Capps and Dranove (2004)	Insurer claims 1997–2001	Analysis of 12 inpatient hospitals involved in mergers	Inpatient	Inpatient prices from claims	Difference-in-difference (DID)	Nine of the 12 hospitals had price increases exceeding the median
Dafny (2009)	AHA, Medicare reports 1989–1996	Analyzes 97 hospital mergers US	Inpatient	CMI-adjusted inpatient revenue per discharge	Instrumental variables	Merging hospitals had 40 percent higher prices than non-merging hospitals
Haas-Wilson and Garmon (2011)	Insurer claims 1997–2003	Evanston, mergers of Evanston NW and Highland Park and St. Therese and Victory Memorial	Inpatient	Inpatient prices from claims	DID	Post-merger, Evanston-NW hospital had 20 percent higher prices than control group; no price effect at St. Therese–Victory
Krishnan (2001)	Ohio Dept. of Health and OSHPD 1994–1995	OH and CA analysis of 37 different hospital mergers	Inpatient	DRG prices based on charge to revenue information	DID	Merging hospitals increased price 16.5 and 11.8 percent in OH and CA, respectively
Spang et al. (2001)	AHA, Medicare cost reports 1989–1997	Analyzes 204 hospital mergers across US	Inpatient	Adjusted inpatient revenue per admission	OLS	Merging hospitals experienced a 5 percentage point lower price growth relative to rivals

(Continued)

Table 9.9 (Continued)

Study	Primary Data Source and Time Period	Location/Merger	Services	Price Measure	Empirical Approach	Results
Tenn (2011)	Insurer claims 1997–2002	SF Bay Area, CA Sutter/Summit merger	Inpatient	Risk-adjusted inpatient price from claims	DID	Summit prices increased 28.4 to 44.2 percent compared to control group
Thompson (2011)	Insurer claims 1997–98 and 2001–02	Wilmington, NC New Hanover-Cape Fear 1998 merger	Inpatient	Risk-adjusted inpatient price from claims	DID	Three of 4 insurers experienced a large price increase; one insurer experience a decrease in prices
Town et al. (2006)	CPS, AHA and InterStudy, 1991–2003	Entire US	Not applicable	Rate of uninsurance	DID	Aggregate merger activity increased the uninsured rate by 0.3 percentage points
Sacher and Vita (2001)	OSHPD data, 1986–1996	Santa Cruz, CA merger of Dominican and Watsonville hospitals	Inpatient	Average net revenue received per inpatient acute-care admission	DID	Average net revenue from private payers Dominican hospital prices were 22 percent higher after the merger relative to controls

Note: Lists only those studies published after 2000.

post-merger. Nevertheless, it is a puzzle why the post-merger price effects are not more homogeneous across markets and across insurers within markets.

All but one of the studies find that, for the majority of the mergers they analyzed, prices increased (or increased faster relative to trend) for hospitals that consolidated relative to the control group hospitals.[40] These studies can be classified into two categories: those that use aggregated measures of price (usually from reported accounting data) and those that use insurer claims data to construct prices. The pricing information constructed from claims likely contains significantly less measurement error. Focusing on those studies, for 17 of the 23 hospital merger/MCO combinations, hospital prices increased significantly relative to the control group.[41] The typical increase in price is often quite large. For example, Tenn (2011) finds that the prices at Sutter hospital increased between 28 and 44 percent after its merger with Alta-Bates hospital, relative to the control group.[42]

The pattern that mergers between competing hospitals in concentrated markets often leads to significant price increases also holds in international settings. While most non-US OECD countries rely on administered prices, the health reforms implemented in 2004 in the Netherlands allow insurers and hospitals to negotiate over prices. Two hospital mergers between competing hospitals were consummated just prior to the reforms. Kemp and Severijnen (2010) estimate the impacts of the mergers on the price of hip surgery and find that the hospitals involved in the most controversial merger experienced a significant increase in price relative to the control hospitals.

One concern in studies that use a difference-in-difference approach is that the merger is endogenous. That is, there are unobservables (to the econometrician) that affect the returns to merger and the prices that would have occurred absent the merger. For example, a hospital that is in decline might be more likely to merge, and it is likely that its future prices are likely to be lower than one would expect given observables.[43] In this case, the estimating merger effect would be biased towards zero. Dafny (2009) addresses the endogeneity issue by constructing an indicator of whether hospitals are co-located (located within 0.3 miles of one another) as an instrument. The underlying idea is if distance is predictive of mergers (which it should be as the gains from merger are a function of the distance between hospitals), but is

---

[40] The one study that did not find a price increase at merging hospitals, Spang et al. (2001), is the oldest paper in the review and uses relatively poor measures of price and costs and the study design is not well suited to identify hospital merger effects.

[41] We exclude St. Therese—Victory hospital merger from this calculation.

[42] Since the price increase at Alta-Bates was comparable to the control group, this suggests that the hospital system used their bargaining leverage after the merger only for higher rates at Sutter hospital.

[43] The are other possible sources of bias. For example, a hospital that is a poor negotiator with MCOs may be more likely to be acquired or the hospital may change its post-merger characteristics (e.g. quality), which may affect its post-merger price. See discussion by Gowrisankaran (2011) and Leonard and Olley (2011) regarding the potential biases of difference-in-difference estimates of merger price effects.

uncorrelated with these unobservables, then it should correct for the selection into merger. She then examines the impact of a hospital's rivals merging on that hospital's price using this IV strategy and finds that OLS analyses lead to lower estimated merger effects relative to IV, consistent with the idea that hospitals select into merger. Her analysis crucially relies on the linear separability of the unobservable. That is, in order for the instrument to be valid, the unobservable's impact on profits cannot be a function of the distance between rivals.

Finally, while the literature clearly shows that mergers between rivals in concentrated settings is likely to increase prices for insurers, it is unclear how those increased prices affect consumers. In the framework outlined above, as is clear from equations (9.12) and (9.13), the welfare impact of a hospital merger depends on the pass-through from increased hospital prices to insurance premiums. Two companion papers examine this pass-through, albeit in an indirect way. Town et al. (2006) examine how changes in hospital market structure affect rates of uninsurance. If increases in hospital prices are not passed on to consumers, then there should be little association between hospital mergers and insurance take-up. They find that, in fact, hospital mergers lead to declines in the rates of insurance and the more competitive the insurance market (measured by the number of HMOs), the larger the impact of hospital mergers. There is little work on the equity and access consequences of provider consolidation. Town et al. (2007) find that the declines in health insurance take-up caused by hospital consolidation were most pronounced for low-income and minority populations.

In sum, there is a clear message from this literature. Mergers between rival hospitals are likely to raise the price of inpatient care in concentrated markets. While the direction of the impact of hospital mergers is clear, the estimated magnitudes are heterogeneous and differ across market settings, hospitals, and insurers. The difference-in-difference approach does not lend itself to uncovering the reasons for the wide range of price responses. Employing methodological approaches that address the limitations of difference-in-difference analysis and forming a better understanding of the diversity of price responses to hospital mergers are areas that deserve future research attention.

3.2.3. Results from Structural and Semi-structural Approaches

More recently, researchers have placed greater emphasis on estimating the price impact of hospital mergers using structural and semi-structural techniques. The advantages of structural approaches are clear. Structural approaches estimate the primitives of a specific economic model and thus can predict counterfactual outcomes in an internally consistent manner. However, there are also important disadvantages to structural estimation. It requires the specification of a specific economic model that is unlikely to perfectly correspond to the actual data generating process. Thus, there is likely to be some bias from model misspecification, and the importance of that bias is difficult to quantify.

Semi-structural estimation approaches also have advantages and disadvantages. They have a foundation in economic theory and estimate some of the primitives of an economic model but do not impose a specific economic model on the estimation. However, this flexibility has consequences, as the estimated parameters may not be invariant to changes in costs, demand, or market structure and thus might lead to inaccurate counterfactual predictions. It should be noted that reduced-form methods also impose a specific data generating process: however, that data generating process is often ad hoc and might not be consistent with any economic model. As the reduced-form approaches do not estimate economic primitives, the coefficients may be functions of factors that might be affected by changes in the market environment. Thus, reduced-form approaches may also lead to poor counterfactual predictions.

The inherent limitations of any empirical approach should not deter researchers from applying these methods—empirical nihilism is not an attractive option. In particular, policy makers will continue to make policies that affect the outcomes of provider markets and it is important for economists to produce the best evidence they can on the likely impact of these policies. That will require economists to use the best empirical tools to make inferences from the available data, understanding and probing the limitations of their chosen empirical strategy.

Town and Vistnes (2001) and Capps et al. (2003) (CDS) are papers that first developed semi-structural approaches consistent with the institutional framework in which hospitals compete to estimate the price effects of hospital mergers. Let

$$V_h(J_h) = \sum_{i \in I_h} W_i(J_h) \tag{9.17}$$

where $W_i(J_h)$ is defined in (9.3) and I_h is the relevant health plan population to aggregate over. Equation (9.17) is the gross value to health plan enrollees of having access to hospital network J_h. The basic idea is to structurally estimate what CDS call the willingness-to-pay (WTP) for each hospital, $WTP_j = V(J_h) - V(J_{h-j})$, using patient discharge data. From (9.7), hospital prices are a function of $F_h(J_h) - F_h(J_{h-j})$, divided by the expected number of patients from that payer.[44] The key assumption is that the WTP measure well approximates $F_h(J_h) - F_h(J_{h-j})$ or rather the functional relationship between price and $F_h(J_h) - F_h(J_{h-j})$ is well approximated by the functional relationship between price (or profits) and the WTP.

With the WTP measure in hand the researcher can then regress WTP on prices or hospital profits. This is done by first estimating a multinomial logit hospital choice

---

[44] If price is the dependent variable then the appropriate measure of WTP will be normalized by the expected volume of patients. The dependent variable in CDS is profits and thus their WTP measure is based on the aggregate gross value of the network.

model using patient discharge data. These data contain information on the hospital where the patient was admitted, home zip code, diagnosis, and patient demographics, which allow the estimation of θ in equation (9.2). With an estimate of θ and illness severity weights, it is straightforward to calculate WTP using (9.3). Given the estimates from this model, the values of $W_i(J_h) - W_i(J_{h-j})$ are calculated and then the WTP is calculated by integrating over the probability of each illness for each individual, using the empirical distribution of illnesses in the data. The fundamental assumption is that the hospital system threatens to pull all of the hospitals from the insurer's system if an agreement is not reached at any of its hospitals.

To calculate the price impact of a merger between hospitals j and k one can simply compute the new value of $WTP_{j+k} = V(J_h) - V(J_{h-(j+k)})$ and use the regression estimates to compute the post-merger price increase. Let θ be the coefficient on WTP. The impact of the merger is determined by the net increase in bargaining leverage: $\theta(\Sigma_i V(J_{h-j}) + V(J_{h-k}) - V(J_{h-(j+k)}))$. Compared to pure reduced form approaches, the primary advantage of this approach is that it is more closely grounded in the underlying theory.

While the semi-structural approach is better grounded in the theory, and can be thought of as a reduced-form approximation to a number of different bargaining games, the estimation is nevertheless not tied to a specific theory that predicts this particular functional relationship. Thus, the residuals from the regression have no structural interpretation. The residuals capture all factors that affect price but are not included in the observables, which could include bargaining ability, unobserved costs, or complementary organizational assets (e.g. the ownership of physician groups, or health plans).

In calculating the expected post-merger price increase of a merger between hospitals j and k, one needs to make assumptions regarding the appropriate treatment of the residuals. One possible approach is to calculate the change in the fitted prices and use that change as the predicted price change from the merger. Another approach would be to take the average of j and k's residuals and apply them to the newly formed hospital. Finally, if there are important asymmetries between hospitals j and k (e.g. one hospital is part of an existing large system and one hospital is a stand-alone community hospital), one might reasonably apply the residual from the large system to all hospitals in calculating the price increase. Here the price increase would then account for both increases in the bargaining leverage due to the merger, as well as the impact of organizational-specific attributes that affect price (e.g. better bargaining skill, the ownership of complementary assets). In addition, another important limitation to this approach is that it assumes that there is no spillover effect of the merger on the pricing behavior of other hospitals in the market (i.e. it only allows for unilateral effects).

Town and Vistnes (2001) acquired data on negotiated price between two MCOs and hospitals in Southern California to estimate the relationship between the net value that a hospital brings to the network and price. One of the challenges in estimating bargaining models is specifying the counterfactual outcome that would occur if the hospital and MCO fail to reach an agreement. In the bargaining framework outlined above, the disagreement outcomes are quite simple and only consider the possibility that the hospital is dropped from the network without replacement. However, there are other possible counterfactual networks that could arise under a disagreement.

Town and Vistnes consider two counterfactual disagreement outcomes to estimate the parameters. The first counterfactual is that absent an agreement, the MCO will simply exclude the hospital from the network. The second counterfactual they consider is that MCOs will contract with the closest hospital not currently in the network. They then estimate a switching regression model in which one of these two counterfactuals determines the bargaining leverage of the hospital, and hence will determine the negotiated price. They find that hospitals with higher bargaining power (as measured by these two counterfactuals) negotiate higher prices. They also run merger counterfactuals, and their results indicate that mergers between neighboring hospitals can lead to significant increases in hospital prices, even in an urban environment with many other competing hospitals.

CDS use data from San Diego, CA, to estimate the relationship between WTP and hospital bargaining leverage. They calculate WTP as described above and regress it against hospital profits. Rearranging (9.7) and aggregating over MCOs, hospital profits will be a complicated function of the WTP. They find a strong positive correlation between WTP and hospital profits—a one unit increase in WTP increases hospital profits by \$2,233. This implies that hospitals that are more attractive to consumers have greater bargaining power, and hence earn substantially higher profits. Lewis and Pflum (2011) expand upon the CDS framework. They estimate a hospital cost function and specify a simple bargaining model and find that WTP is correlated with market power. They also find that systems operating in multiple markets have higher bargaining power, indicating that focusing only on local markets in evaluating the potential effect of a merger may be insufficient. A hospital's physician arrangements and other characteristics can also have a significant effect on its bargaining power.

Several papers take a significantly more structural approach to examining hospital competition. Gaynor and Vogt (2003) take a different approach to structurally estimating the impact of hospital mergers. They adapt the structural models of Berry et al. (1995) (BLP), who developed an estimation framework for differentiated products consumer goods to the hospital industry. In both cases the products are differentiated, but individuals pay directly for consumer goods, without the intermediate step of health plans. The Gaynor and Vogt (2003) approach modifies the utility model in equation (9.2) so that total price paid by the insurer is an argument in the utility function, and thus affects hospital choices. The interpretation is that this is a reduced-form choice function incorporating the objectives of consumers and insurers.[45] They specify a supply side, allowing for differences between NFP and FP hospitals.

Gaynor and Vogt use data from hospital discharge and financial data from California. They use the discharge data to estimate a multinomial logit model of hospital choice, and use data on hospital revenues to construct a measure of prices. They estimate the average elasticity of demand faced by a hospital to be -4.85, and find that hospitals are highly spatially differentiated—cross-price elasticities fall sharply with the distance between two hospitals. NFP hospitals set lower prices than FPs, but mark up prices over marginal costs by the same amount. They then go on to simulate the impact of a hospital merger in San Luis Obispo, California, and predict that hospital prices would increase by up to 53 percent, with no significant difference in merger effects if the merging hospitals are NFP or FP. The advantage of using this approach is that it allows for a rich model of consumer demand, direct information on hospital costs is not necessary, and given the data and the parameter estimates, it is straightforward and transparent to calculate the impact of a merger of prices.

This posted price BLP model is fairly different from a bargaining model. BLP-style models have been widely applied to examine mergers for many other industries.[46] There are two issues with adapting BLP-style estimation to the hospital industry. First, using a BLP approach requires obtaining an accurate estimate of the price elasticity of demand from the choices of consumers. Yet consumers rarely pay different out-of-pocket prices for different hospitals in-network so it is not entirely clear how the variation in hospital prices affects consumer choice. Second, in general, BLP models assume a Bertrand price equilibrium. However, as noted by Grennan (2010), the Bertrand price equilibrium is a special case of the Nash bargaining equilibrium with $\beta = 1$ and no price discrimination. If $\beta < 1$, imposing a Bertrand equilibrium will lead to misspecification. Of course, all models are simplifications and thus are necessarily misspecified, so it is unclear how important this misspecification is for merger analysis. Given that bargaining models can be complicated and also subject to misspecification, one way to think about the posted price model is that it is a reduced-form way of capturing a complicated underlying bargaining relationship.

Ho (2009b) represents a significant breakthrough in the modeling of hospital competition. The key insight she develops is that given consumer preferences over MCO characteristics (including the structure of its hospital network), and the realized hospital network, one can estimate the parameters of the hospital profit function. She

---

[45] Gaynor and Vogt prove that, under fairly general conditions, insurers, in effect, act on behalf of consumers. In this case the demand function they estimate recovers consumer preferences. Consumers may not pay differential prices at the point of choosing a hospital, but they do pay higher premiums if hospital prices are higher. Insurers' objectives are not affected by hospital characteristics, but they must attract consumers who do care about these factors.

[46] For example, see Nevo (2000).

estimates a hospital choice model and uses those parameter estimates to construct V (J_m) (where the m subscripts insurers) for each hospital and each insurer for the large metropolitan areas in the US. She also uses the parameters to construct counterfactual $V(K_m)$, where $J_m \neq K_m$: the values associated with alternative hospital networks. With the measures of $V(J_m)$ in hand, she then posits that insurers compete in static Nash equilibrium in prices and estimates the utility parameters of insurer choice using the approach of BLP, where $V(J_m)$ is included as an argument in the consumer's utility function.

In Ho's model, all hospitals make simultaneous take-it-or-leave-it offers to all plans in the market. Then, all plans simultaneously respond. MCOs select the hospital network that maximizes profits relative to counterfactual network configurations. That is, $E(\pi_m(V(J_m))) \geq E(\pi_m(V(K_m)))$ $\forall K_m \neq J_m$ where π denotes the profits for MCO m. These profits are the revenues the MCO earns, given its hospital network, less the payments made to the hospitals in its network.

This observation suggests the use of an inequality method of moments estimator developed by Ho and co-authors (Pakes et al., 2006). While the underlying econometric theory is non-trivial, the basic idea behind this estimator is straightforward. Given a set of instruments which help address measurement error, the estimator finds the set of parameters that result in the observed network producing the highest expected profits relative to other counterfactual hospital networks.[47] The challenge is to construct profit functions for counterfactual networks that are consistent with the underlying bargaining model. Ho assumes "passive beliefs"—the hospital believes that the MCO will not change its beliefs about the offers the hospital makes to other MCOs were it to receive the counterfactual offer. Instead of positing a structural approach to hospital profits, she specifies a reduced-form hospital profit function where a hospital's profits are a function of the number of expected admissions, market and hospital characteristics. Ho does not have access to hospital pricing information, which limits the ability to directly estimate the bargaining model.

Ho finds that hospitals in systems take a larger fraction of the surplus and also penalize plans that do not contract with all members. Hospitals that are attractive to consumers also capture high markups, and hospitals with higher costs per patient receive lower markups per patient than other providers. The limitation of Ho's approach is that it is not directly applicable to analyzing the impact of hospital mergers or other changes in hospital market structure. For example, in her framework, two hospital systems that merge would not affect the equilibrium surplus division, and thus would not have an impact on prices. In related work, Ho (2006) notes that the realized equilibrium selective network may be inefficient. Under selective contracting,

---

[47] The parameters are only set identified.

hospitals contract with a subset of the hospitals in the market, thus limiting the choice set of the patient when they select an MCO.

Brand et al. (2011) use both semi-structural and structural approaches to estimate the impact of a proposed hospital merger in Northern Virginia between the large 1,800-bed INOVA hospital system and Prince William Hospital, a 170-bed facility in Manassas, VA. The FTC challenged this merger in 2006 and the parties abandoned the transaction. In their structural work, Brand et al. (2011) manipulate an equation similar to (9.7) to recover bargaining and cost parameters and then use pricing relationships similar to those in equations (9.8) and (9.10) to calculate the impact of the merger.

Pakes (2010) furthers the ideas in Ho (2009b) and Pakes et al. (2006) by examining the MCO/hospital network formation decision, allowing for richer error structures. Again, the underlying idea is that the revealed choice of the insurer network can be used to infer deeper parameters of the hospital profit function. While the focus of Pakes's work is methods development, the estimation and simulation results reveal interesting patterns. In the simulation results he computes the full in formation Nash equilibrium for the game in which hospitals make take-it-or-leave-it offers to insurers and insurers decide whether to accept or reject the offers. The equilibrium margins for hospitals are decreasing in the excess capacity and costs relative to the other hospitals in the market. The hospital's margins are increasing in the insurer's margins.

The structural analysis of buyer—seller networks is a young and quickly evolving literature. While this literature is relatively new, the underlying policy implications of these papers is similar to the other strands of the literature. Hospitals (particularly those in systems) can acquire and exercise market power. The availability of high-quality data sets combined with recent theoretic and econometric advances point to this line of work leading to important findings in the near future.

3.2.4. Not-for-profit Firm Behavior

The hospital sector is characterized by the fact that there is a mixture of firms with different ownership types. Not-for-profits are the most common, but there are substantial numbers of for-profit hospitals and public hospitals. Interesting questions arise in this context about differences in behavior between for-profit and not-for-profit firms (and publics), and the impact of the mixture of different types of firms in a market on firm conduct.

Some of the studies we have already reviewed (e.g. Capps et al., 2003; Gaynor and Vogt, 2003) have addressed the issue of not-for-profit/for-profit differences in competitive conduct. Those studies do not find any significant differences in pricing behavior. A recent study by Capps et al. (2010a) examines whether not-for-profit hospitals are more likely than for-profit hospitals to offer more charity care or unprofitable services in response to an increase in market power. The implication is that, if there were such a difference, not-for-profits would be spending their profits from market power on socially beneficial activities. Capps et al. examine seven years of data on California hospitals and find no evidence of any such differences—not-for-profits do not engage in any more socially beneficial activities than do for-profits when they possess market power.

Dafny (2005) asks whether hospitals engage in "upcoding," choosing more profitable diagnosis codes for patients when the profitability of doing so increases. She uses a 1988 policy reform that generated large price increases for many, but not all, Medicare admissions and finds evidence of substantial upcoding by hospitals. This is much more pronounced among for-profit hospitals than among not-for-profits.

Duggan (2000) uses an increase in government reimbursements for treating indigent patients to test for differences in behavior between for-profit, not-for-profit, and public hospitals. He finds that both for-profit and not-for-profit hospitals responded strongly to the financial incentives in the policy. Both types of private hospitals treated the most profitable indigent patients and avoided unprofitable ones. Public hospitals' behavior did not change. In addition, both for-profit and not-for-profit hospitals used the revenues from the indigent care program to increase financial assets, as opposed to improve medical care for the poor.

Duggan (2002) uses the same government policy as in his previous paper to identify behavior. In this paper he is concerned with the mix of hospital ownership types and impacts on behavior. He finds that not-for-profit hospitals located in areas with many for-profit hospitals were substantially more responsive to the changed financial incentives than not-for-profit hospitals located in areas with few for-profits. A fruitful area for future research may be to further examine the determinants of the mix of ownership types and impacts on other types of conduct.

3.2.5. Impact of Hospital Mergers on Costs

It is clear that mergers can result in efficiencies because of economies of scale, increased purchasing power, the ability to consolidate services, or the transfer of managerial techniques and skill to the acquired hospital. Williamson (1968) noted that mergers that result in significant market power but also lead to meaningful reductions in marginal costs can be welfare improving. However, mergers also have the potential to increase costs. Larger systems imply larger bureaucracies. In addition, hospital costs are not necessarily exogenous to market structure. Hospitals that are able to bargain for higher prices may have the incentive to use the resulting profits for the benefit of physicians and hospital executives (e.g., through capital expenditures that benefit physicians or increases in executive compensation or perks). This is particularly likely if there is no residual claimant (as is the case for not-for-profit organizations) or monitoring by the residual claimant is costly. Thus, the analysis of the cost impacts is central to understanding the impact of hospital mergers. The evidence presented above suggests that, on average, hospital mergers result in increases in price. Consequently if there are significant cost reductions associated with mergers they are not passed onto the purchasers of hospital services in the form of lower prices.

The analysis of the impact of hospital mergers and acquisitions on cost faces a notable challenge in finding accurate and reliable measures of costs. Medicare Cost Reports and state financial data are the primary source of cost data, but these data generally lump inpatient and outpatient expenditures into one category, are not easily adjusted for changes in patient severity, and are subject to the vagaries of accounting methodologies. Dranove and Lindrooth (2003) is the most convincing analysis. Using data on mergers of previously independent hospitals that consolidate financial reporting and operate under a single license post-merger, they find that, on average, these hospitals experience post-merger cost decreases of 14 percent. System mergers in which the hospitals were not as fully integrated (as measured by the use of multiple licenses) did not realize cost savings. These findings suggest that integration of merging hospitals is necessary to achieve meaningful efficiencies. Harrison (2010) uses AHA data to examine differences in expected hospital costs, and finds that immediately following a merger costs declined, but eventually rose to pre-merger levels. This finding is difficult to reconcile with the view that mergers require significant upfront costs but have benefits that accrue in later years. In sum, the evidence discussed above suggests that mergers between competitors in concentrated markets lead to hospital price increases. That is, on average hospital mergers in these circumstances do not appear to generate enough efficiencies to offset the gains in market power. The circumstances in which mergers are most likely to result in meaningful cost decreases are those in which the merging facilities operate as a more fully integrated entity.

3.3. Recent Developments in Antitrust Enforcement and Competition Policy in Health Care

3.3.1. Antitrust Developments in the US

Traditionally, the hospital sector has been one of the most active areas of antitrust enforcement.[48] However, the decade of the 2000s saw a significant slowdown in the number of US antitrust cases in the health care sector. While there were not as many significant cases as the previous decades, there nonetheless were at least two cases that went to trial that were important.

In a separate development, the DOJ and FTC recently revised the *Horizontal Merger Guidelines* (Federal Trade Commission and Department of Justice, 1992) to

---

[48] In this segment we review the recent case developments and refer the reader to Whinston (2007) for a more complete discussion of recent developments in the economics of antitrust. The Department of Justice (DOJ) and Federal Trade Commission's (FTC) report *Improving Health Care: A Dose of Competition* (2004) also provides an excellent overview of the competition policy issues in health care markets.

more accurately reflect the agencies' approach to mergers. Relative to the previously issued versions, the revised *Merger Guidelines* take a more conservative and more flexible approach to merger analysis, increasing the HHI cut-off for defining "Highly Concentrated" markets to 2,500. The *Merger Guidelines* also make clear that the agencies use econometric and economic theory-based approaches to merger analysis, in addition to using the traditional methodologies.

In this section we discuss these two significant antitrust developments since the 1990s as well as discussing other cases that affect the current implementation of competition policy. The 1990s saw a string of losses by the US federal antitrust agencies. As discussed in Gaynor and Vogt (2000), the federal antitrust agencies lost these cases for two broad reasons. First, the courts sometimes have viewed the not-for-profit status of hospitals as mitigating the anticompetitive impact of increased market power that might accrue to hospitals because of the merger.[49] Second, the courts have tended to side with plaintiffs in accepting broad geographic market definitions or viewing the presence of other possible competitors as sufficient to constrain the exercise of market power.[50]

While each case brings a different set of facts, the courts' decisions on both of these issues run counter to the general findings from the health economics literature. The evidence consistently shows that not-for-profit status does not affect static hospital behavior in significant ways—not-for-profit hospitals are just as willing as for-profits to exercise market power should they possess it. Second, hospitals are differentiated products, where patient distance plays a major role in differentiating hospitals. Hospital competition occurs locally, and thus mergers involving two closely located competitors in a large urban area may result in the ability of the merged hospitals to negotiate substantially higher prices.

The most important case in the 2000s for merger enforcement towards health care providers is *FTC v. Evanston Northwestern Healthcare Corp.*[51] In 2000, Evanston Northwestern Healthcare Corporation merged with Highland Park Hospital. Both hospitals are located in Evanston, IL, an affluent suburb of Chicago. The case was initiated as part of the FTC's post-merger retrospective, in which they reviewed a number of hospital mergers that occurred in the late 1990s to the early 2000s. The FTC filed suit in 2004, alleging that the merger violated Section 7 of the Clayton Act. The Administrative Law Judge (ALJ) issued an Initial Decision finding that, "[FTC] proved that the Challenged merger has substantially lessened competition in the product market of general acute inpatient services [sold to managed care organizations] and in the geographic market of the seven hospitals described above."

---

[49] *FTC v. Butterworth Health Corp.*, 946 F. Supp. 1285, 1300–1301 (W.D. Mich. 1996).

[50] For example, see *United States v. Mercy Health Services*, 902 F. Supp. 968 (N.D. Iowa 1995).

[51] Evanston Northwestern Healthcare Corp., FTC Docket No. 9315, Initial Decision (Oct. 20, 2005), available at http://www.ftc.gov/os/adjpro/d9315/051021idtextversion.pdf.

The initial relief of Evanston Northwestern was to divest Highland Park hospital and essentially re-create the market structure that existed prior to the merger. The parties appealed the case (which is referred to the Commissioners under the FTC administrative law process) and the Commissioners upheld the ALJ's initial ruling but significantly altered the relief. The Commissioners feared that the hospitals were already too integrated to effectively de-merge and thus ruled that hospitals could remain as a merged entity but had to maintain separate negotiating functions that would independently negotiate with MCOs.

This case is notable for a number of reasons. First, the merger was already consummated and the hospital operations had been integrated prior to the FTC's challenge. Because many of the functions (including insurer negotiations) had been integrated, the impact of the merger on prices could be directly analyzed, as pre- and post-merger insurer claims data were available to analyze. In most merger investigations, post-merger price increases must be inferred and predicted from the available evidence. In this case, the post-merger prices were available to study. Both testifying economic experts found there was a significant post-acquisition price increase (with the hospital's expert finding a post-merger increase of approximately 10 percent for inpatient services and the FTC expert finding significantly higher post-merger price increases).

Second, the ALJ found that the merger increased Evanston Northwestern's market power in a suburban market with a number of other competing hospitals.[52] Previously, the federal antitrust enforcement agencies have lost cases where, under very plausible geographic market definitions, the merger was a two-to-one consolidation. Thus, the implication is that mergers in hospital markets with several competitors can lead to significant increases in price. Of course, this is consistent with the framework outlined above, but the courts have traditionally been hesitant to embrace the basic premise that market power can be exercised in settings with more than one competitor. Finally, the ALJ and the Commissioners outlined an approach to analyzing hospital mergers that explicitly accounts for the institutional features of the industry—specifically, that hospitals and insurers engage in negotiations that determine prices, and that an increase in market power from a given merger will be determined by the increase in bargaining leverage.

Since the Evanston Northwestern case, the FTC has been more aggressive in challenging hospital mergers in urban and suburban settings. In 2008, the FTC challenged INOVA's acquisition of Prince William hospital. INOVA is a large, five-hospital system in Northern Virginia and they sought to acquire the community hospital in Mannasas, VA. The FTC sued to enjoin the transaction and the parties abandoned the

---

[52] The ALJ determined the pre-merger HHI as 2,739 with an increase of 384 (assuming the shares are unchanged, post-merger).

merger soon after the FTC filed its case. In 2009, Scott and White merged with King's Daughter hospital—both hospitals are located in Temple, TX. The FTC staff viewed the merger as anticompetitive; however, King's Daughter hospital was in very poor financial shape and would likely close soon without a merger with another hospital. The FTC did not challenge the merger, as they determined that there was not another, less anticompetitive purchaser for King's Daughter. More recently, the FTC has sued to stop ProMedica's acquisition of St. Luke's hospital. ProMedica is a large hospital system with three hospitals in and around Toledo, OH, and St. Luke's hospital is located in the adjacent suburb of Maumee, OH. At this writing that case is still being adjudicated; however, at the initial preliminary injunction hearing in the Federal District Court the judge ruled in the FTC's favor.[53] In analyzing the competitive impact of hospital mergers, the FTC has looked to the recent literature on hospital competition and is incorporating the recent approaches in its analysis.

There has been very limited enforcement regarding consolidation in outpatient and physician services. While some of these transactions may well result in increases in bargaining leverage and thus increases in prices, most of these transactions likely fall below the Hart–Scott–Rodino thresholds which specify the value of the transaction that is necessary for the parties to notify the federal antitrust agencies. However, in 2008, the FTC issued an administrative complaint challenging Carilion Clinic's 2008 acquisition of two outpatient clinics in the Roanoke, VA, area.[54] Carilion is a large integrated health system and they had acquired an outpatient surgery center and an imaging center. The FTC secured a consent decree from Carilion which divested the two clinics.

Market power need not only be exercised by selling a product but can also be used to gain lower prices on the purchase of inputs. In health care markets this can occur when insurers have significant upstream market share and use this leverage to secure lower provider prices. Hospitals may also be able to leverage their market power in the labor market by offering nurses lower wages.[55] In the consent decree in *United States v. UnitedHealth Group Incorporated and PacifiCare Health Systems, Inc.* the US Department of Justice clearly states that they will prosecute cases in which the merger leads to increases in monopsony power. In this case, United Health Group acquired PacifiCare, a large health insurer on the West Coast of the US. One of the relevant product markets where the DOJ alleged competitive harm was the purchase of physician services. The DOJ required divesture in order to preserve competition in this market. *United States and the State of Arizona v. Arizona Hospital and Healthcare Association and AzHHA Service Corporation* is a case regarding the

---

[53] *FTC v. ProMedica Health System*, Docket No. 215, Case No. 3:11 CV 47, Findings and Conclusions available at http://www.ftc.gov/os/caselist/1010167/110329promedicafindings.pdf.

[54] See http://www.ftc.gov/os/adjpro/d9338/index.shtm.

[55] Unlike on the selling side of the market, the welfare impact of lower input prices is less clear.

exercise of monopsony power in the nurses market.[56] AzHHA Registry Program is a hospital group purchasing organization which contracts with nursing agencies to provide temporary nursing services for most Arizona hospitals. The DOJ defined the relevant market as the "hospitals' purchases of per diem nursing services in the Phoenix and Tucson metropolitan areas" and claimed that the hospitals participating in AzHHA were able to obtain rates for temporary nursing services below competitive levels. The consent decree prevented AzHHA from jointly negotiating nurses' wages for its member hospitals.

Hospitals and other integrated providers offer a number of different services and, importantly, the services they offer (e.g. primary, secondary, and tertiary care) may differ from their competitors.[57] The fact that hospitals offer a variety of services implies that they may have an incentive to bundle those services for exclusionary purposes when they negotiate with insurers. In *Cascade Health Solutions v. Peace Health* the plaintiffs argued that Peace Health, a three-hospital system in Lane County, OR, with a large hospital, Sacred Heart, that offers primary, secondary, and tertiary care, bundled and tied their products in an attempt to monopolize primary and secondary services. Cascade Health Solutions is a 114-bed hospital that does not offer tertiary services. Specifically, Peace Health offered insurers substantial discounts on their entire range of services if they did not contract with Cascade Health Solutions. The Ninth Circuit Court of Appeals ruled that when the party has monopoly power, bundling is legal unless the discounts result in prices that are below an appropriate measure of costs.[58] This standard is in conflict with the Third Circuit standard of anticompetitive harm which does not consider the relationship between price and the appropriate measure of costs.[59]

The second antitrust case of importance that occurred during the 2000s is *In the Matter of North Texas Specialty Physicians (NTSP)*.[60] NTSP is an organization of independent physicians and physician groups that was formed, managed, and operated by physicians. Many of the physicians in NTSP directly compete with one another. NTSP's main functions are to negotiate and review contract proposals for member services that are submitted by payers, including insurance companies and health plans; to review payment issues; and to act as a lobbyist for its members' interests.

---

[56] See http://www.justice.gov/atr/cases/azhha.htm.

[57] "Tertiary" refers to complex services like invasive cardiovascular surgery and intensive neonatal care, whereas "primary" and "secondary" acute hospital services are more common medical services like bone-setting and tonsillectomies.

[58] The parties later settled the case once it was remanded back to the District Court.

[59] See *LePages, Inc. v. 3M.* "Bundled price discounts may be anti-competitive if they are offered by a monopolist and substantially foreclose portions of the market to a competitor who does not provide an equally diverse group of services and who therefore cannot make a comparable offer."

[60] *In the Matter of North Texas Specialty Physicians*, Docket No. 9312. The initial decision can be found at http://www.ftc.gov/os/adjpro/d9312/041116initialdecision.pdf.

The fundamental issue in this case was whether NTSP served as a price fixing agent for its member physicians or if the facilitation of setting premiums was an ancillary activity and their primary function was to enable the setting of risk contracts between it and its member physicians. Previously, the courts have found that physician organizations that set rates for the group can be illegal under a rule of reason analysis.[61] Organizations like NTSP can serve as a conduit for establishing risk contracts that can allow the implementation of high-powered incentives for physicians and these high-powered incentives can induce more efficient behavior than standard, fee-for-service reimbursement. However, the use of risk-bearing contracts by insurers has declined since the 1990s, and thus the purpose of organizations like NTSP for such purposes is unclear.

NTSP negotiates both risk-sharing contracts and non-risk-sharing contracts for its members; however, the vast majority of the contracts were non-risk-sharing contracts. NTSP's physicians enter into an agreement with NTSP that grants NTSP the right to receive all payer offers and imposes on the physicians a duty to forward payer offers to NTSP promptly. The physicians agree that they will not individually pursue a payer offer unless and until they are notified by NTSP that it has permanently discontinued negotiations with the payer. NTSP surveys members, uses the information to calculate the mean, median, and mode of the minimum acceptable fees identified by its physicians, and then uses these measures to establish its minimum contract prices.

The ALJ ruled (and the Commission later affirmed) that the activities of NTSP were "inherently suspect" and, taken as a whole, amounted to horizontal price fixing which is unrelated to any pro-competitive efficiencies. NTSP's conduct could be characterized as *per se* unlawful under the antitrust laws. The broad lessons from this ruling are: (1) activities by physician organizations that look inherently suspect and are likely price fixing will be treated under a *per se* standard; (2) if a physician organization intends to argue that efficiencies justify collection and dissemination of reimbursement rates, the organization needs to be ready to explain why those efficiencies could not be achieved without price fixing. Going forward, as physicians form accountable care organizations (ACOs) under the recently passed health reform legislation, those activities should be limited to the implementation of the ACO and behavior among those physicians that resembles collective negotiations of MCO contracts will be examined closely. Unless those activities can be viewed as necessary to the implementation of the ACO, they will likely be treated harshly by the federal antitrust enforcement agencies.[62]

---

[61] See *Arizona v. Maricopa Co. Med. Soc'y*, 457 US 332, 356–357 (1982).

[62] In contrast to the NTSP case, the FTC's review of "TriState Health Partners" lays out an example of where joint contracting by a collection of physicians is subordinate to the efficiencies the organization may yield. See http://www.ftc.gov/os/closings/staff/090413tristateaoletter.pdf.

As of this writing there is at least one antitrust case that was recently initiated and has yet to be resolved that may significantly affect competition policy once decided. In *United States and State of Michigan v. Blue Cross Blue Shield of Michigan* the DOJ alleges that BCBS used its monopsony power to secure most-favored nation contracts with hospitals in which the hospitals were contractually obligated to charge competing MCOs 25 percent higher rates. The apparent purpose of such contracts is to increase BCBS's rivals' marginal costs as well as increasing entry costs. In a differentiated products setting higher rival costs allow a firm to charge higher prices and earn higher profits.

While the decade of the 2000s was a relatively quiet one for health care provider antitrust policy, it seems likely that the courts will have to address important issues in the near future. In particular, providers are becoming more integrated—hospitals are acquiring more physician groups and other outpatient services (e.g. imaging, rehabilitation, outpatient surgery). As these "integrated" organizations become more common the likelihood is that they will attempt to use bargaining leverage in some services to other services (or that their behavior will be interpreted as attempting to leverage market power) through the use of tying, bundling or other means. The recently passed health care reform provides incentives for increased provider integration and will likely only increase the number of integrated organizations. Thus, it seems likely that it is only a matter of time before the courts will have to examine the legality of such behavior by integrated hospital systems.

3.3.2. Competition Policy towards Health Care in OECD Countries

There has not been nearly as much antitrust activity towards health care outside of the US. This is mostly due to health care systems in other countries being more centrally controlled and heavily regulated. However, a number of countries have pursued decentralization and competition in reforms of their health systems. The Netherlands, Germany, and the United Kingdom (England in particular) are notable in this regard. Varkevisser and Schut (2009) review antitrust policy towards hospital mergers in the Netherlands, Germany, and the US.

The Netherlands has a competition agency, the Netherlands Competition Authority (NMa), for general competition policy. They oversee cartel, dominance abuse, and merger cases including health care. They closely cooperate with the Netherlands Healthcare Authority (NZa) for oversight of the functioning of health insurance and health care markets. The NZa has become the primary government agency entrusted with regulation and dominance abuse in health care markets, although they do work closely with the NMa.[63] The Netherlands has had a few antitrust matters arise over the past few years. They have had concerns about hospital mergers, as in the US, and also have

---

[63] The NZa plays an advisory role to the NMa in hospital merger cases, for example.

had concerns about vertical restraints, including vertical integration, between insurers, hospitals, and doctors. As Canoy and Sauter (2009) note, there was an uptick in merger activity following market liberalization, and a consequent need for greater merger control. The NMa has reviewed nine hospital mergers. All were approved, although some were subject to extensive review. A notable development has been the adoption of a market definition methodology for hospitals based on a structural model (the model of Gaynor and Vogt, 2003, estimated for the Netherlands).

Competition policy enforcement in Germany is under the control of the Federal Cartel Office (Bundeskartellamt, BKA). Most of the concern in health care has been with the acquisition of public hospitals by private hospital systems. With many local and regional governments facing large budget deficits, there has been a wave of take-overs of public hospitals by private chains. The BKA has examined over 100 hospital mergers and acquisitions. Relatively few of these have been challenged, but some have been blocked, and there was one merger which was allowed subject to divesti-ture. At this point economic and econometric modeling have not played a large role in these decisions.

In 2009 the UK established an agency charged with oversight of competition in the NHS, following their reforms (in England) in 2006 designed to promote competi-tion. The establishment of a new agency was necessary, because the conduct of NHS entities was exempt by fiat from oversight by the UK's competition authority (the Office of Fair Trading). The Cooperation and Competition Panel (CCP) is the agency that has been established for the oversight of competition in health care and has fairly broad authority to regulate mergers and general conduct. Since beginning operations in 2009, the CCP has reviewed over 50 merger cases and a number of conduct cases.

4. HOSPITAL COMPETITION AND QUALITY

Thus far (in section 3) we have focused on hospital competition over prices. The product is differentiated, but product characteristics are not subject to choice by hospitals. As we have seen, this is an extremely useful framework for analyzing hospital price competition. Nonetheless, quality[64] is subject to hospital control, and can be an important instrument for competition. In what follows, we first lay out approaches to

---

[64] At this point we use quality in a very generic sense. In particular, this encompasses both horizontal and vertical differentiation. To be clear, horizontal differentiation is sometimes alternatively referred to as "product variety," while vertical differentiation is alternatively referred to as "product quality." Our use of the term quality should be understood to encompass both of these except where we specifically indicate otherwise.

modeling quality competition, then review the relevant literature.[65] The models differ substantially depending on whether price is set administratively (e.g. by a regulator) or if it is a strategic variable. As a consequence, we cover these as separate cases, beginning first with administratively set prices and then progressing to market determined prices.

4.1. Hospital Choice of Quality

In what follows, we write down models in which hospitals directly choose the quality of service they provide. This is convenient for writing down a parsimonious model. There are some potentially important ways, however, in which this model may not conform precisely to empirical phenomena. One reason is that hospitals may not directly choose the quality of care they provide. Hospitals may not explicitly choose a quality level that maximizes profits (or some other objective). Hospitals may instead choose overall effort, or slack, based on the incentives they face. Quality of care for a given patient(s) may then be determined (in part, perhaps stochastically) by effort. This distinction is immaterial for the purposes of modeling. A model where quality is chosen directly is isomorphic to one where it is determined indirectly by effort.

In empirical modeling, the most commonly used measure of quality is patient mortality. It is important to note that mortality is not a measure of quality of service *per se*, but an outcome determined (in part) by quality of service. Hospitals are thus not choosing mortality, but choosing a quality of service level that has an impact on mortality. Patients are heterogeneous in their responsiveness to treatment. The most common reason for this is severity of illness. Severely ill patients are more likely to die, *ceteris paribus*, than healthier ones.[66] In addition, the relationship between quality of service and mortality is stochastic. A patient's outcome cannot be predicted with certainty based on a certain quality of care, even given patient and hospital observables. Nonetheless, a given service level generates an expected level of mortality. As a consequence, it is immaterial whether a model is written down in which hospitals choose service quality or expected mortality.

Last, consider the fact that hospitals do not compete for all kinds of cases. In particular, patients in urgent situations do not usually choose their hospital. A prominent example of this which has been extensively studied in the empirical literature is AMI (acute myocardial infarction, or "heart attack"). Heart attack patients do not choose the hospital they are taken to, yet empirical studies (Kessler and McClellan, 2000) find that heart attack mortality is lower in less concentrated (and presumably

---

[65] For prior reviews of hospital quality competition see Gaynor (2006b), Pauly (2004), or Vogt and Town (2006).

[66] See Gowrisankaran and Town (1999) and Geweke et al. (2003) for an econometric approach to correcting measured mortality for this problem, and others.

more competitive) hospital markets. How can hospitals be competing for patients who do not choose where they go?[67] The story is that hospitals choose a general level of effort for the hospital as a whole, which affects quality of service, and thus mortality, as described above. Hospitals that are subject to tougher competition in general choose greater effort, thus increasing the chances of survival of heart attack patients, even though they are not competing for heart attack patients. Again, this can be described using a model in which hospitals choose quality directly. Here, however, hospitals choose quality of service for the entire hospital based on a sector where choice is possible. This hospital-wide level of quality then determines patient outcomes, including those for services where there is not competition, like AMI.

4.2. Administratively Set Prices

In many situations, prices are set administratively, rather than being market determined. This is true of entire health systems (e.g. the British National Health Service), or sectors of health systems (e.g. the Medicare program in the US). In this situation, when competition among firms occurs it will be via non-price means. We call any non-price output characteristic(s) quality. In what follows, we will treat this as vertical differentiation,[68] i.e. we will treat quality as uni-dimensional. This is for ease of exposition. The basic intuition that follows from such a treatment carries over to a horizontally differentiated world, although this is not truly general. We refer to literature which models horizontal differentiation where relevant.

The model we present here follows Gaynor (2006b). Let quality have only a vertical dimension, i.e. "more is better." For simplicity in exposition, assume that the demand that any firm j faces is separable in its market share, s_j, and the level of market demand, D. Firm j thus faces a demand of:

$$q_j = s_j(z_j, \mathbf{z}_{-j})D(\bar{p}, z_j, \mathbf{z}_{-j}) \tag{9.18}$$

where s_j is firm j's market share, z_j is firm j's quality, $\mathbf{z}_{-j}$ is a vector of all other firms' qualities, D is market demand, and $\bar{p}$ is the regulated price.[69] Assume that j's market share is increasing in own quality, decreasing in the number of firms, and that the responsiveness of market share to own quality is also increasing in the number of firms.

---

[67] Even if patients do not choose where they go, emergency crews may choose among hospitals based on quality, especially in urban areas with a number of hospitals within a short distance of each other.

[68] Alternatively referred to as product quality.

[69] Note that for consumers insulated from the cost of consumption, as in health care, the price they face will be less than the price received by the firm. We ignore this in order to keep this sketch of a model simple. It would not affect the conclusions in any event.

Assume that firms all use the same technology and face the same input prices. Then they each have costs described by:

$$c_j = c(q_j, z_j) + F \tag{9.19}$$

where $c(\cdot)$ is variable cost and F is a fixed cost of entry.

Further assume that there is free entry and exit, so that all firms earn zero profits in equilibrium. Then, assuming Nash behavior, equilibrium is described by the solutions to the following across all firms j:[70]

$$\frac{\partial \pi_j}{\partial z_j} = \left[\bar{p} - \frac{\partial c_j}{\partial q_j} \right] \left\{ \frac{\partial s_j}{\partial z_j} D(\cdot) + s_j \frac{\partial D(\cdot)}{\partial z_j} \right\}$$
$$- \frac{\partial c_j}{\partial z_j} = 0 \tag{9.20}$$

and

$$\pi_j = \bar{p} \cdot q_j - c_j = 0 \tag{9.21}$$

Inspection of (9.20) yields some immediate insights. First, compare equilibrium quality under monopoly to that with multiple firms. Notice that, since a monopolist faces market demand, the first term in curly brackets in 9.20 vanishes and $s_j = 1$. Since $\frac{\partial s_j}{\partial z_j}$ is positive by assumption, the term in curly brackets will be larger in most cases with multiple firms than with a monopolist, so equilibrium quality is higher with competition. This is definitely the case if competition is only over market share, which is ofter the case in health in health care markets

In markets for normal consumer goods, whether welfare is higher depends on the relative magnitudes of $\frac{\partial s_j}{\partial z_j}$ and $\frac{\partial D}{\partial z_j}$. In particular, if $\frac{\partial D}{\partial z_j}$ equals zero, then increases in quality do not shift market demand, and quality competition is simply over market share, and hence wasteful. In health care markets that is not likely to be the case. Consumers who are ill may not respond to changes in quality by changing the aggregate quantity consumed. Nonetheless, increased quality may result in substantial gains in welfare if it results in improved health.

Since $\frac{\partial s_j}{\partial z_j}$ increases with the number of firms (i.e. the firm's demand becomes more elastic with respect to own quality the more alternatives there are for consumers), quality competition will be more intense with entry and equilibrium quality will increase with the number of firms in the market. This benefits consumers, but may not increase social welfare. In particular, the increase in consumer surplus from increased quality may be outweighed by the increased costs (recall that there is a fixed cost of entry for every firm in the market), particularly if there is diminishing marginal utility from quality and diminishing returns in quality production. As indicated previously, this may result in excessive quality levels. In the case of health care it is

[70] We assume here that firms maximize profits. We relax that assumption below. See section 4.2.2.

most likely that quality will be excessive if it has little effect on health. Quality that substantially improves a patient's chance of survival will be very valuable, and such benefits are more likely to outweigh costs. We can do a simple back of the envelope calculation to illustrate this. For example, the typical estimate of the value of one life-year is $100,000. If an increase in quality leads to one additional life-year for every sick person and there are 1,000 sick people in the market, then costs would have to increase by more $100 million for the increase in quality to be inefficient.

The positive predictions of this model are clear. Quality is increasing in the number of firms in the market, i.e. competition leads to more quality. Further, quality is increasing in the regulated price. One may write down a firm's equilibrium quality function as the (implicit) solution to equations (9.20) and (9.21),

$$z^e = z(\bar{p}, c_q, c_z, s_j, D) \tag{9.22}$$

where c_q and c_z denote first derivatives. The firm's level of quality depends on the level of the regulated price, the marginal cost of quantity, the marginal cost of quality, the level of demand, market share, and the quality elasticities of market share and market demand. This can be seen informally by manipulating (9.20) to obtain the following expression:

$$z = \frac{(\bar{p} - c_q)[\eta_z^s + \eta_z^D](s_j \cdot D)}{c_z} \tag{9.23}$$

where η_z^s and η_z^D are the quality elasticities of market share and market demand, respectively. Quality is increasing in price, the elasticity of demand with respect to quality, and the firm's total demand. Quality is decreasing in the marginal costs of quantity or quality.

This has implications for econometric specifications for empirical analysis. The equation to be estimated is (9.22). However, measures of marginal cost, market share, and demand are likely to be endogenous in an econometric equation. One would employ exogenous determinants of these factors, such as cost shifters (W), demand shifters (X_D), and the number of firms (N). A reduced form econometric specification would thus look something like the following:

$$z^e = Z(\bar{p}, W, X_D, N, \varepsilon) \tag{9.24}$$

where ε is a random error term.

The normative implications of the model are somewhat less clear than the positive ones. Depending on how valuable quality is (specifically how responsive health is to quality), competition may lead to excessive quality provision. Since every firm pays a fixed cost of entry, but does not consider the effects of demand stealing, there can be too many firms in a free entry competitive equilibrium. Similarly, a higher regulated price may reduce welfare by leading to excessive quality. This is less likely to be the case where quality leads to highly effective treatment, and that treatment has a large impact on consumer well-being. It is important to note, however, that consumers are never made worse off by competition. If competition leads only to demand stealing they are no better off as a result, but if it leads to any increase in market demand then consumers are unequivocally better off.

4.2.1. Spillovers

Now let health outcomes, H, be determined by the following equation:

$$H_{itj} = h_t(z_j, \xi_{it}) \tag{9.25}$$

where H_{itj} is the health outcome of patient i of type t treated in hospital j, h_t is the health production function for type t, z_j is quality of service in hospital j, and ξ_{it} is a vector of unobservable patient-type specific factors, with a known distribution.[71]

Let there be patients of two types, $t = 1,2$. Type 1 patients choose their hospital based on the expected health outcome at that hospital, $\overline{H}_j = E_{it}[H_{itj}]$. Type 2 patients simply arrive at the hospital. For example, type 1s may be maternity or orthopedic patients, and type 2s heart attack patients. To start, assume, without loss of generality, that there is one (fixed) price the hospital receives for treating either patient type, and that costs do not depend on patient type.[72] In this case, the hospital's profits are as follows:

$$\pi_j = \overline{p} \cdot [s_{j1}(\overline{H}_j, \overline{H}_{-j}) D_1(\overline{p}, \overline{H}_j, \overline{H}_{-j})] + \overline{p} \cdot [s_{j2} D_2(\overline{p})] - c(s_{j1} D_1 + s_{j2} D_2, z_j) - F \tag{9.26}$$

Equilibrium here is the solution to the following first-order conditions across all firms:

$$\frac{\partial \pi_j}{\partial z_j} = \left[\overline{p} - \frac{\partial c_j}{\partial q_{1j}} \right] \left\{ \frac{\partial s_{1j}}{\partial \overline{H}_j} \frac{\partial \overline{H}_j}{\partial z_j} D_1(\cdot) + s_{1j} \frac{\partial D_1(\cdot)}{\partial \overline{H}_j} \frac{\partial \overline{H}_j}{\partial z_j} \right\}$$

$$- \frac{\partial c_j}{\partial z_j} = 0 \tag{9.27}$$

and

$$\pi_j = 0 \tag{9.28}$$

Notice that the first-order condition for the choice of quality is unaffected by type 2s. They simply show up at the hospital, regardless of the level of service quality, so they have no impact on the hospital's choice of quality. Quality is chosen to maximize

---

[71] We could make some of the patient-type specific factors observable, but we omit that detail to avoid additional notation.

[72] The only assumption that matters here is that there is one quality level for both patient types.

profits from type 1s. This then determines expected health outcomes for type 1s and type 2s.

The comparative statics of this model are the same as the previous model (with a single type). Quality is increasing in the number of firms. As competition gets tougher, firms choose higher quality in order to attract more type 1 patients. Since quality is hospital-wide, this spills over into higher quality for type 2s. Thus competition leads to higher quality for type 2s, even though there is no direct competition for type 2 patients. This is also true with regard to the regulated price. In the model above, there is a single regulated price for both type 1s and type 2s. If we relax this assumption so there are different prices for each type, then quality will be increasing in the price for type 1s, but not for type 2s.[73]

4.2.2. Non-profit Maximizing Behavior

The model outlined above is not specific to health care. In particular, the majority of firms in the hospital industry are not-for-profit or public. Let us now write down a simple model that captures this aspect of the health care industry. There have been many models of not-for-profit hospitals (Pauly and Redisch, 1973; Newhouse, 1970; Lee, 1971; Lakdawalla and Philipson, 1998; Capps et al., 2010a) While there is no agreement on a general model, most models posit an objective function which includes profits and some other argument, such as quantity or quality. Therefore, let us assume that not-for-profit hospitals have an objective function which includes quality and profits (as a shorthand for everything else they care about). Further, for simplicity, let this function be additively separable in quality and profits and linear in profits:

$$U_j = u(z_j, \pi_j) = v(z_j) + \pi_j \tag{9.29}$$

We can now revisit the first-order conditions for quality choice (9.20), modified to take account of this objective function:

$$\frac{\partial U_j}{\partial z_j} = \left[\bar{p} - \frac{\partial c_j}{\partial q_j} \right] \left\{ \frac{\partial s_j}{\partial z_j} D(\cdot) + s_j \frac{\partial D(\cdot)}{\partial z_j} \right\}$$
$$- \frac{\partial c_j}{\partial z_j} + \frac{\partial v}{\partial z_j} = 0 \tag{9.30}$$

Notice that the only difference with the first-order conditions for an industry of profit maximizing firms is the presence of the last term, $\frac{\partial u}{\partial z_j}$. Since this term is positive, the value that not-for-profit firms put on quality acts like a reduction in the marginal cost of producing quality, i.e. not-for-profit firms will act like for-profit firms

---

[73] This is a testable hypothesis.

with a lower marginal cost of quality.[74] This implies that quality will be higher in equilibrium. The comparative statics, however, are identical with an industry of profit maximizing firms. Quality is increasing in the number of firms and the regulated price, as before.

In the case of the spillover model with two patient types, we might imagine that a not-for-profit or public hospital may care directly about the health outcomes of each patient type. In that case, the hospital's first-order condition looks like this:

$$
\begin{aligned}
\frac{\partial \pi_j}{\partial z_j} &= \left[\overline{p} - \frac{\partial c_j}{\partial q_{1j}} \right] \left\{ \frac{\partial s_{1j}}{\partial \overline{H}_j} \frac{\partial \overline{H}_j}{\partial z_j} D_1(\cdot) + s_{1j} \frac{\partial D_1(\cdot)}{\partial \overline{H}_j} \frac{\partial \overline{H}_j}{\partial z_j} \right\} \\
&\quad - \frac{\partial c_j}{\partial z_j} + \frac{\partial v}{\partial \overline{H}_{1j}} \frac{\partial \overline{H}_{1j}}{\partial z_j} + \frac{\partial v}{\partial \overline{H}_{2j}} \frac{\partial \overline{H}_{2j}}{\partial z_j} = 0
\end{aligned}
\tag{9.31}
$$

As before, this implies that quality will be higher for non-profit maximizers than for profit maximizers, but that the comparative statics are unchanged.

4.3. Market Determined Prices

We now turn to examining quality determination in an environment where prices are market determined. We expand the model of a bargaining game in prices among hospitals previously described in section 3.1 to allow for hospital choice of quality. In that game hospitals are differentiated, but that differentiation is not a strategic choice. Here we relax that assumption to allow hospitals to choose quality. As before, we treat quality as vertically differentiated. Hospitals choose their qualities in a (new) first stage, then the price bargaining game in section 3.1 ensues, treating qualities as fixed. The other two stages in the model, patient choice of health plan and patient choice of hospital, then ensue, as before. This expanded model now has four stages, with the quality game among hospitals being the first stage.

Let demand be determined by underlying utility functions, as in the model of the price bargaining game in section 3.1. These aggregate up to demand functions facing each hospital.

Let each hospital j choose quality z_j to maximize utility, as follows:

$$
\max_{z_j} \ U_j = p_j(z_j) \cdot D_j(p_j(z_j), z_j, X_{ij}) - c(D_j(p_j(z_j), z_j, X_{ij}), z_j, W_j) + v(z_j)
\tag{9.32}
$$

X_{ij} is a vector of firm and consumer characteristics. W_j is a vector of input prices. Both are regarded as fixed by the firm. The price p_j is determined in the bargaining game in the next stage. In this stage hospitals take account of the effects of their quality choices on price through the pricing equation from the next stage, equation (9.7):

---

[74] This is the same specification and result as for not-for-profit firms that care about quantity, as opposed to quality. See Lakdawalla and Philipson (1998); Gaynor and Vogt (2003).

$$p_{jh} = (1-\beta)\left(c_j(z_j) + \frac{r_h}{q_{jh}}\right) + \frac{\beta}{q_{jh}}(F(V_{J_h}(z_j, \mathbf{z}_{-j}, p_{jh}) - F(V_{J_h - j}(\mathbf{z}_{-j}) - cm_{jh}) + \beta\sum_{l\neq j} p_{lh}d_{jlh}$$

$$(9.7)$$

Our goal here is to understand the effect of competition on quality (in this stage) and subsequently on price, in the continuation game. We can obtain the basic intuition about impacts on price by employing the equation derived in the previous section that describes the effect of a merger of two hospitals on price:

$$\Delta p_{jh}^{j+k} = (1-\beta)d_{jkh} \cdot p_{kh} - c_j$$

The impact on price is determined by the diversion ratio (holding β and hospital k's price constant). The diversion ratio is larger the more that consumers view hospitals j and k as substitutes. If hospital j's quality is higher than hospital k's, then consumers will view them as less close substitutes than if they had the same levels of quality. As a consequence, a merger would not have a large impact on prices. If, however, hospitals are symmetric, so j and k choose the same quality levels, then there is (at least to a first approximation) no impact of quality on the change in prices due to merger.

We now turn to the impact of competition on quality. Treating the pricing equation (9.7) as a function of quality and differentiating the objective function with respect to z_j we get the first-order condition for hospital j:

$$p \cdot \frac{\partial D}{\partial z} + D(\cdot)\frac{\partial p_j}{\partial z_j} + p_j \cdot \frac{\partial D_j}{\partial p_j}\frac{\partial p_j}{\partial z_j} - \frac{\partial c}{\partial D} \cdot \frac{\partial D}{\partial z} - \frac{\partial c}{\partial D} \cdot \frac{\partial D}{\partial p}\frac{\partial p_j}{\partial z_j} - \frac{\partial c}{\partial z} + \frac{\partial v}{\partial z_j} = 0 \quad (9.33)$$

Now consider the impact of competition. Assume that competition increases the quality responsiveness of demand since there are closer substitutes for hospital j (e.g. a hospital enters nearby). We assume that competition has no impact on costs or the hospital's marginal utility from quality $\left(\frac{\partial u}{\partial z_j}\right)$. With regard to the first-order condition for price, competition will increase the terms $\frac{\partial D}{\partial z}$ and $\frac{\partial D_j}{\partial p_j}$. The effect on $\frac{\partial p_j}{\partial z_j}$ is indeterminate in general. If, however, we focus only on the effects on price through the net value a hospital brings to an insurer's network (the terms $F_h(J_h) - F_h(J_h - j)$), then the effect of quality on price is positive.[75]

The overall effect is as follows (where n represents the number of firms):

$$\left(p_j - \frac{\partial c}{\partial D}\right) \cdot \frac{\partial^2 D}{\partial z \partial n} + D(\cdot)\frac{\partial^2 p_j}{\partial z_j \partial n} + \left(p_j - \frac{\partial c}{\partial D}\right) \cdot \frac{\partial^2 D_j}{\partial p_j \partial n}\frac{\partial p_j}{\partial z_j}$$

$$+ \left(p_j - \frac{\partial c}{\partial D}\right) \cdot \frac{\partial D_j}{\partial p_j}\frac{\partial^2 p_j}{\partial z_j \partial n}$$

$$(9.34)$$

[75] The impact on an insurer's revenue of having a higher-quality hospital in its network is higher when there is more hospital competition. With more competition a hospital's demand is more responsive to quantity, so a higher-quality hospital will garner more patients.

In general, this derivative cannot be signed. Assuming price is greater than marginal cost, the first two terms are positive, while the second two terms are negative.[76] If we assume, however, that demand is not responsive to price (which can be reasonable for hospital care where consumers are largely insulated from prices by the presence of health insurance) then the derivative is positive, i.e. competition will lead hospitals to optimally increase their quality. Assuming symmetry and Nash behavior, all hospitals will increase their qualities.

In equilibrium this may not actually lead to increased prices. It may be that hospitals increase quality, but do not change their relative attractiveness to insurers. In that case, hospitals' bargaining positions haven't changed, so in equilibrium there is no effect on price. It may be, however, that this is not the case. Suppose that hospitals have different costs of producing quality. In this situation, some hospitals will choose higher quality than others and their relative values to an insurer's network will change. This will lead to some hospitals (those with lower marginal costs of quality) having more bargaining power with insurers and commanding higher prices.

4.4. Econometric Studies of Hospital Competition and Quality

There is a rapidly growing empirical literature on competition and quality in health care. At present the evidence from this literature is entirely on hospital markets. In what follows we review this literature. We first review the results from econometric studies of markets with administered prices, and then market determined prices.[77]

The studies reviewed here employ a variety of econometric approaches. The modal approach is what we call a "Structure–Conduct–Performance" (SCP) specification. These econometric models are derived from a conceptual model that hypothesizes a causal link from market structure to firm conduct and then to industry performance.[78] Most SCP models applied to health care focus on the link between market structure and firm conduct, and omit industry performance. The typical conduct measure in the general industrial organization literature is price or price–cost margin. The typical measure of market structure is the Herfindahl–Hirschmann Index (HHI), which is the sum of the squares of all firms' market shares.[79] The equation usually estimated has roughly the following appearance:

$$p = \beta_0 + \beta_{1q} + \beta_2 X_D + \beta_3 W + \beta_4 \text{HHI} + \varepsilon \qquad (9.35)$$

---

[76] $\frac{\partial D_i}{\partial p_i}$ and $\frac{\partial^2 D_i}{\partial p_j \partial n}$ are negative—demand slopes down and even more so in the presence of more firms.

[77] We focus on work that occurred after the publication of the first volume of the *Handbook of Health Economics* in 2000. Most of the empirical literature on quality is relatively recent, and so occurs after that date.

[78] See Carlton and Perloff (2005).

[79] That is, $\text{HHI} = \sum_{i=1}^{N} s_i^2$, where s_i is firm i's market share, and there are N firms in the market.

where X_D represents demand shifters and W captures cost shifters. The SCP studies of quality simply employ a measure of quality as the dependent variable in this equation, rather than price.

The SCP approach has a number of well-recognized problems when price is the dependent variable (see Bresnahan, 1989; Schmalensee, 1989, on these issues). These problems also apply when quality is the dependent variable, and there are some additional issues. First, the use of the HHI in a pricing equation can be explicitly derived only from a homogeneous goods Cournot model of conduct.[80] Obviously an SCP regression with quality as the dependent variable does not derive from this framework. In the case of administered prices, theory does point to an econometric model with a measure of market structure on the right-hand side (see equation (9.24)). Even in this case, or even if one thinks of a quality SCP regression as deriving from a broad conceptual framework as opposed to a specific theoretical model, a number of issues remain. The HHI (or any market structure measure) is usually regarded as endogenous. Unmeasured variation in demand and cost factors affect both quality and market structure. For example, a firm with low costs is likely to have both a high market share (leading to a high HHI) and choose high-quality.

Two additional specification issues arise in regard to SCP studies of markets with administered prices. When firms set prices it is clear that price and quality are determined simultaneously, so an SCP model might either include price and treat it as endogenous, or simply include exogenous determinants of price. Typically price is not included in the studies reviewed here, although it is not clear whether the authors were explicitly trying to include exogenous determinants of price. When price is regulated, however, price (or the price–cost margin) should appear as an exogenous determinant of quality (again, see equation (9.24)). In some studies price is omitted based on the argument that, since price is regulated, price does not affect demand (e.g. for Medicare beneficiaries). The regulated price should be included, however, because it is a determinant of supply, not demand. In addition, it is possible that the regulated price may be correlated both with quality and concentration. For example, firms in unconcentrated markets may produce higher quality due to tougher competition. They may also have higher costs due to producing higher quality, and therefore receive higher regulated prices. Therefore, omitting price may lead one to overestimate the effect of concentration on quality.

There is another complication due to the nature of hospitals. The major purchasers of hospital services in the US are Medicare and private health insurers. Medicare sets regulated prices. Prices from private health insurers are determined in the market. Since hospitals generally sell in both markets, one must either account for this or

---

[80] In that case, the coefficient on the HHI in an SCP regression captures the elasticity of demand, not firm conduct (which is already assumed to be Cournot).

presume that there are no complementarities between the two (e.g. demand and cost
are completely separable in Medicare and private output). Many of the studies that
focus on Medicare seemingly make the implicit assumption of separability. This is not
generally an issue in other countries, where there is essentially a single payer for health
care services.[81]

While the majority of the studies we review here employ an SCP framework,
some employ different approaches. Some studies evaluate the impact of mergers, some
evaluate the impact of regulatory changes (e.g. price deregulation), and a number
estimate the relationship between hospital volume of a surgical procedure and patient
health outcomes. In addition, there are a small number of studies that take a structural
approach: there are some that estimate demand, and some that examine the determi-
nants/impacts of the number of firms. Each of these approaches has its advantages and
disadvantages. We discuss these in the context of evaluating the various studies.

Before proceeding, however, we want to note that the results of the majority of
these studies provide evidence only on positive questions, e.g. "Does competition
increase quality?" Few of these studies allow for normative analysis. This first wave of
studies consists for the most part of policy evaluation and reduced-form studies.[82] It is
not generally possible to evaluate effects on welfare with these kinds of studies. This
should not be taken as a criticism of these studies, but simply a recognition of what
sorts of inferences can be drawn from them.

4.4.1. Studies with Administered Prices

There are a number of studies of the impact of competition on hospital quality under
an administered price regime. These derive from the US Medicare program and from
the English NHS, which made a transition to administered prices in a reform in 2006.
The amount a Medicare beneficiary pays is the same, regardless of where she obtains
care (again, in a given area at a given point in time). As a consequence, price is not a
strategic variable for hospitals serving Medicare patients. Patients in the NHS pay
nothing, so price plays no strategic role in that system either. Table 9.10 presents a
summary of these studies and their findings. The entry in the column labeled "Effect
of competition on quality" indicates the direction of the relationship between the
competition measure and the quality measure. For example, in the first row, the entry
"Increase" in that column indicates that the quality is higher in more competitive
markets. For the study cited in the first row (Kessler and McClellan, 2000), quality is
measured by mortality and competition is measured by the HHI. Quality is inversely
related to mortality—lower mortality is higher quality. Competition is inversely

[81] Most countries do have some private insurers, but they are generally so small that their roles can be safely ignored.
[82] By policy evaluation studies, we mean econometric specifications that evaluate the impact of some policy or
(economic) environmental factor, but are not derived from an explicit economic model. By reduced form, we
mean an econometric specification that is the reduced form of a specific economic model.

Table 9.10 Health Care Quality and Competition Empirical Studies: Regulated Prices

Study	Time Period	Geographic Area	Medical Condition	Payers	Quality Measure	Competition Measure	Effect of Competition on Quality
Kessler and McClellan (2000)	1985, 1988, 1991, 1994	US	Heart attack	Medicare	Mortality	HHI	Increase (*mortality* ↓)
Gowrisankaran and Town (2003)	1991–1993 (Heart attack), 1989–1992 (pneumonia)	Los Angeles	Heart attack, pnemonia	Medicare	Mortality	HHI	Decrease (*mortality* ↑)
Kessler and Geppert (2005)	1985–1996	US (non-rural)	Heart attack	Medicare	Readmission, mortality	HHI	Increase (*mortality* ↓, *readmissions* ↓)
Mukamel et al. (2001)	1990	US (134 MSAs)	All	Medicare	Mortality	HHI	No effect
Shen (2003)	1985–1990, 1990–1994	US (non-rural)	AMI	Medicare	Mortality	# of hospitals interacted with Medicare payment, HMO penetration	Interacted with Medicare payment: 1985–90—no effect, 1990–94—increase (*mortality* ↓); interacted with HMO penetration: 1985–90—decrease (*mortality* ↑), 1990–94—no Effect
Tay (2003)	1994	California, Oregon, Washington	Heart attack	Medicare	Mortality	Demand elasticity	Increase (*mortality* ↓)
Gaynor et al. 2010	2003/04, 2007/08	England	Heart attack, all conditions	NHS	Mortality	HHI	Increase (*mortality* ↓)

(Continued)

Table 9.10 (Continued)

Study	Time Period	Geographic Area	Medical Condition	Payers	Quality Measure	Competition Measure	Effect of Competition on Quality
Cooper et al. (2011)	2003/04, 2007/08	England	Heart attack	NHS	Mortality	HHI	Increase (*mortality* ↓)
Bloom et al. (2010)	2006	England	Heart attack, emergency surgery	NHS	Mortality	# of hospitals	Increase (*management* ↑ → *mortality* ↓)
Gaynor et al. 2011	2003/04, 2007/08	England	Coronary artery bypass graft	NHS	Mortality	Demand elasticity	Increase (*mortality* ↓)

related to the HHI—the HHI is lower in more competitive markets. So, the finding that competition increases quality is based on a positive empirical relationship between mortality and the HHI—mortality is higher in less competitive markets.

Kessler and McClellan (2000) is one of the first studies attempting to make inferences about a causal effect of competition on quality for hospitals. This is a study of the impact of hospital market concentration on risk-adjusted one-year mortality from acute myocardial infarction (AMI, i.e. a heart attack) for Medicare patients. Expenditures on these patients are also studied. The study included data on all non-rural Medicare beneficiaries with AMI during selected years from 1985 to 1994. Kessler and McClellan use the SCP framework discussed above, with some modifications. They instrument for the HHI with hospital market shares predicted from a model of patient choice of hospital, where patient choice is largely determined by distance from the hospital. They also employ zip code fixed effects. As a consequence, the effects of hospital market concentration are identified by changes in the predicted HHI. The specification they employ, however, omits the regulated Medicare price. A number of hospital and area characteristics are included, HMO enrollment among them. It is unclear whether they are considered demand or cost shifters.

The results from this study are striking. Kessler and McClellan find that risk-adjusted one-year mortality for Medicare AMI patients is significantly higher in more concentrated markets. In particular, patients in the most concentrated markets had mortality probabilities 1.46 points higher than those in the least concentrated markets (this constitutes a 4.4 percent difference) as of 1991. This is an extremely large difference—it amounts to over 2,000 fewer (statistical) deaths in the least concentrated vs. most concentrated markets. The results with regard to expenditures have a somewhat different pattern. Prior to 1991, expenditures were higher in less concentrated markets, while the reverse is true as of 1991.

The positive inferences from this study are clear. Mortality from heart attacks for Medicare patients is lower in less concentrated markets. The effects of concentration are stronger beginning in 1991 and are reinforced by HMO enrollment. The omission of the regulated price is unfortunate, although for this omission to lead to biased estimates the changes in the omitted price would have to be correlated with the within zip code changes in the predicted HHI. It is unclear whether the inclusion of market and hospital characteristics is intended to control for possible hospital complementarities between Medicare and private output. So long as it is unlikely there are important omitted factors there should be no problem with bias. While it is clear that concentration affects hospital quality, the mechanism by which this works is not.

It seems unlikely that hospitals deliberately choose lower quality in the form of an increased probability of death. What may be happening is that hospitals in more concentrated markets take some of their excess profits by exerting lower effort. Low effort in the hospital may have the unintended consequence of higher mortality. Another issue with regard to this application is whether hospitals compete for heart attack patients. Tay (2003) states that one-half of heart attack patients arrive at the hospital via ambulance. It seems unlikely that these patients have any choice of hospital, hence hospitals cannot compete for these patients. We think the most likely story is that heart attack patients are the "canary in the mine shaft." Hospitals in more competitive environments are pressured to be better across the board, and that manifests itself clearly in a very sensitive area—heart attack patient mortality.

While the basic positive results from this study are clear, we do not believe that there are clear normative inferences. The results show that both expenditures and mortality are lower in less concentrated markets, implying gains in benefits with a reduction in costs. Kessler and McClellan state that this implies there is a welfare gain from competition. This may be so, but the inference is not entirely clear. The measure of Medicare expenditures they use is not a measure of economic cost. Therefore, the finding that quality is higher in less concentrated markets tells us that consumers are likely better off, but does not tell us if social welfare has necessarily been improved.

Gowrisankaran and Town (2003) estimate the effects of hospital market concentration on risk-adjusted mortality rates for AMI and pneumonia, for both Medicare and HMO patients. We discuss their findings with regard to Medicare patients here, since the price is regulated for them, and discuss the findings with respect to HMO patients in the next section. Gowrisankaran and Town use data from Los Angeles county from 1991 to 1993 for AMI and 1989 to 1992 for pneumonia. Their approach is similar to that of Kessler and McClellan. They use an SCP framework, instrumenting for the HHI with hospital market shares predicted from a patient choice equation, where distance is the main determinant of hospital choice. An innovation is that they construct separate, hospital-specific, HHIs based on (predicted) hospital market shares for Medicare, HMO, Medicaid, indigent and self-pay patients, and indemnity patients.

Gowrisankaran and Town find, in contrast to Kessler and McClellan, that mortality is worse for Medicare patients treated in hospitals with lower Medicare HHIs. The implication is that competition reduces quality for Medicare patients. Gowrisankaran and Town hypothesize that Medicare margins are small or negative, or that hospitals may deviate from profit-maximizing behavior. If Medicare margins are indeed negative (i.e. $p < MC$), then the results are consistent with theory. It seems unlikely, however, that this is true for AMI. Heart treatments for Medicare patients are widely thought to be profitable. Indeed, there is substantial entry of hospitals specializing only in the treatment of heart disease. Since Medicare patients are a substantial portion of heart patients, it seems as if Medicare margins must be significant in order to generate the observed entry. Small or negative Medicare margins for pneumonia, however, do seem plausible. We do not observe the entry of hospitals specializing in pneumonia, or pulmonary disorders generally.

This study also omits Medicare price. Since Gowrisankaran and Town only examine Los Angeles county there may be little or no variation in Medicare price across hospitals for a given year. Although there should be temporal variation, they have only a short time period. As a consequence, there may not be enough variation in their sample to estimate a parameter for Medicare price. It includes some hospital characteristics, although it is unclear if these characteristics are considered demand or cost shifters.

It is hard to know why the results of this study contrast so markedly with the previous one. It may be that the Medicare price is below marginal cost (on average) for the hospitals in Gowrisankaran and Town's study, while the opposite is true for the hospitals in Kessler and McClellan's study. Since neither study included Medicare price it is impossible to evaluate this hypothesis. It is also possible that the estimated relationship between the HHI and mortality is sensitive to the choice of instruments. Gowrisankaran and Town and Kessler and McClellan use similar, but not identical, instrumenting strategies. Obviously identification is driven by the instruments, so it is possible that the differences in instruments are driving the differences between the studies. This is only speculation, however. The opposite results from the two studies suggest caution in drawing strong conclusions about the impact of market structure on hospital mortality.

Kessler and Geppert (2005) extend the framework employed by Kessler and McClellan to consider the impact of concentration on differences in quality between patients. Their work is inspired by the theoretical result that oligopolists will find it optimal to engage in product differentiation in order to relax price competition (see Tirole, 1988, section 7.5.1). These theory papers are not directly relevant for Kessler and Geppert's empirical exercise, since the theory examines quality dispersion when firms set prices. Kessler and Geppert examine Medicare patients, for whom price is set via regulation. Clearly any incentive to engage in product differentation is not related to a desire to relax price competition for Medicare patients. It is possible that hospitals may be attempting to relax price competition for private patients, and are unable to quality discriminate between Medicare and private patients, perhaps for legal or ethical reasons. It seems like it should be a straightforward result from models where firms choose both product variety and product quality that oligopolists operating in a market with a regulated price have an incentive to differentiate themselves with regard to product variety in order to avoid the kind of quality competition described previously.[83]

Kessler and Geppert examine outcomes (readmissions, mortality) and expense (expenditures, various measures of utilization) for Medicare heart attack patients, as in

[83] If one takes the kind of model used in Lyon (1999) or Kamien and Vincent (1991), where firms locate on a line, it seems evident that firms will have an incentive to locate as far apart from each other as possible (at the ends of the line), rather than nearby (in the middle). If they locate in the middle, the firms are identical, so the one that produces the highest product quality will take the entire market. Thus firms will engage in fierce product quality competition, up until the point that profits are dissipated. If firms are located at the ends of the line, then each firm will be considerably more attractive to consumers located very close to it. This will dampen quality competition.

Kessler and McClellan. They contrast outcomes and expenditures for high-risk and low-risk patients in highly concentrated vs. unconcentrated markets. High-risk patients are those who were hospitalized with a heart attack in the previous year, whereas low-risk patients had no such hospitalization. They find that low-risk patients receive more intensive treatment in highly concentrated markets, but have no statistically significant difference in outcomes. High-risk patients, on the other hand, receive less intensive treatment in highly concentrated markets, and have significantly worse outcomes. They conclude that competition leads to increased variation in patient expenditures, and that it is welfare enhancing, since [on net] outcomes are better and expenditures are lower. Medicare price is omitted, as in previous studies.

This chapter adds to the evidence that concentration is significantly correlated with readily observable measures of quality for hospitals. The statistical relationship between quality dispersion and concentration is surprising and interesting. So far as we know, this is the only paper to examine quality dispersion. What economic behavior generated these patterns in the data is an intriguing puzzle.

Mukamel et al. (2001) examine risk-adjusted hospital mortality for Medicare patients in 134 Metropolitan Statistical Areas (MSAs) in 1990. They focus on the impact of HMOs, but also examine hospital market concentration. Mukamel et al. (2001) find that HMO penetration (the percentage of the MSA population enrolled in an HMO) has a negative impact on excess hospital mortality (the difference between observed mortality and predicted risk-adjusted mortality), i.e. HMO penetration is associated with better quality. Hospital market concentration (measured by the HHI) has no statistically significant impact on mortality. HMO market concentration is also included as an explanatory variable, although it is not significant. Medicare price is omitted. It is unclear what to make of these results. First, Mukamel et al.'s specification includes inpatient expenditures, which are certainly endogenous, as well as hospital HHI, HMO HHI, and HMO penetration, which may very well be endogenous, so it is unclear that the resulting estimates are consistent. It is possible that hospital concentration does truly have an impact on mortality, but that it is not consistently estimated in this study. Second, it is not clear how enrollment in private HMO plans affects the mortality of Medicare patients. Presumably there has to be some spillover effect, but the nature of the mechanism is unclear, as Mukamel et al. acknowledge.

A study that is notable for taking account of Medicare price effects is Shen (2003). Shen examines the impact of financial pressure from reduced Medicare payments and HMO penetration on mortality from AMI, controlling for the hospital's competitive environment.[84] She examines data from 1985 to 1990 and 1990 to 1994 for most

---

[84] There have been a number of studies assessing the impact of the change in Medicare hospital payment from cost-plus to fixed price (the Medicare Prospective Payment system). See, for example, Kahn et al. (1990); Cutler (1995).

non-rural hospitals in the US. Shen's measure of market structure is an indicator of whether there are five or more other hospitals within a 15-mile radius of a hospital. This is interacted with a measure of the change in the Medicare price and the change in HMO penetration. There are direct effects of Medicare price and HMO penetration, but not market structure.

Shen finds a negative and significant relationship between the change in Medicare price and mortality. The interaction between the market structure and Medicare price variable is negative and significant for 1990–1994, but has no significant impact on mortality for 1985–1990. These results are consistent with standard theory. Hospitals respond to an increase in the regulated price by increasing quality. This response is amplified when hospitals face more competitors.

The effects of HMO penetration also appear to be roughly consistent with theory. Shen finds that HMO penetration leads to higher mortality, and that hospitals in markets with more competitors appeared to respond to HMO penetration with quality reductions in 1985–1990, although not thereafter. HMOs are hypothesized to increase the price elasticity of demand facing hospitals. If so, then the increased price elasticity will likely lead to a quality reduction. This should be amplified in markets with more competitors, since that should also increase the price elasticity. Shen also does a simple normative analysis of the effects of financial pressure, but not the effects of competition.

A paper by Tay (2003) takes a more structural approach. Tay specifies and estimates a structural econometric model of hospital choice by Medicare enrollees with AMI.[85] Tay uses data on urban enrollees in conventional Medicare, located in California, Oregon, and Washington in 1994. She examines the effect of a number of aspects of quality and distance on the probability a patient is admitted to a particular hospital. The quality measures include two clinical outcomes (the mortality rate and the complication rate); a measure of input intensity (nurses per bed); and whether the hospital can perform two high-tech cardiac services (catheterization or revascularization). All measures of quality are treated as exogenous.

Tay finds that hospital demand is negatively affected by patient distance and positively affected by quality. She then simulates the effects of changes in the various aspects of a hospital's quality, holding the total number of heart attack patients fixed, the locations of patients and hospitals fixed, and the qualities of all other hospitals fixed. Adopting a catheterization lab is predicted to increase demand by 65 percent, while adding revascularization in addition to catheterization increases demand by

[85] A number of papers have previously examined whether choice of hospital is affected by quality (Luft et al., 1990; Burns and Wholey, 1992; Chernew et al., 1998). These studies find that clinical quality, as measured by deviation between expected and actual mortality rates, has a significant impact on hospital choice—hospitals with lower mortality are more likely to be chosen. The responsiveness found in these studies indicates the potential for quality competition among hospitals, although how much is not clear, since the studies were not designed to assess this.

76 percent. If the number of nurses per bed is increased by 1 percent, then demand is predicted to increase by 24 percent.

Tay shows that hospital demand is significantly affected by quality and distance, thus there are potentially high payoffs to hospitals increasing quality. While this represents an advance over the previous literature by using more detailed modeling, there are nonetheless some limitations to the inferences that can be drawn from this study.

As with the previous studies, the Medicare price is omitted. It is possible that this omission is inconsequential, but we see no way to tell. Tay assumes that hospitals set the same level of quality for Medicare and non-Medicare patients. This is also an untested assumption, although it is at least explicit.

More fundamentally, the supply side of the market is not modeled. As a consequence, competition itself is not modeled and cannot be examined explicitly. There is no structure in place for dealing with the potential endogeneity of the quality variables. There is the usual reason to be concerned about endogeneity, since quality is chosen by the firm. In addition, it has been observed for a number of hospital procedures that hospital volume causes patient outcomes (see section 4.4.3 below for a review of some studies). This suggests endogeneity of the mortality and complication rates.

Further, the simulation is an out-of-equilibrium prediction. Tay's predicted effects of adding a catheterization lab or other services on demand are likely too large, since they hold rivals' responses fixed. If rivals respond by also adopting catherization labs or other services, then the equilibrium effects should be smaller, potentially even zero. It is also unclear whether firms would actually make the predicted choices. If rivals respond strongly to a firm's adoption of services, the responses may make adoption unprofitable. As a consequence it is hard to assess the magnitude of quality effects. Last, as Tay acknowledges, without a supply side no welfare analysis can be performed.

Two recent studies (Cooper et al., 2011; Gaynor et al., 2010) examine the impact of competition on hospital quality using a recent reform in the English National Health Service (NHS). The NHS introduced a reform in 2006 intended to promote competition among hospitals. Prices were administratively determined based on patient diagnoses, via a method very similar to that employed by the US Medicare system. As a consequence, hospitals were to compete solely on non-price dimensions. Although they differ in the precise methods employed, both Cooper et al. (2010) and Gaynor et al. (2010) find that, following the reform, risk-adjusted mortality from AMI fell more at hospitals in less concentrated markets than at hospitals in more concentrated markets.

Gaynor et al. (2010) also look at mortality from all causes and mortality from all causes, excluding AMI, and find the same qualitative results as for AMI, although the estimated effects are smaller in magnitude. They also examine measures of utilization and expenditure, and find that length of stay rose in less concentrated markets relative to more concentrated markets after the reform, but there were no impacts on expenditures. Quantitatively, Gaynor et al. (2010) find that the reform reduced heart attack mortality by 0.2 percent.[86] Since the reform saved lives without increasing costs, they conclude it was welfare improving. The measure of costs is hospital expenditures. As noted before, this may not accurately capture economic costs, so welfare inferences are not necessarily clear. Gaynor et al. also control for the impact of the NHS administered prices on outcomes. They estimate a positive, but statistically insignificant, effect.

Gaynor et al. (2011) estimate a structural model of demand for heart bypass surgery (CABG) in England to evaluate the effect of the reform studied by Cooper et al. and Gaynor et al. (2010). In particular, one part of the reform required referring physicians to give patients five choices of hospitals (previously they had been required to give none). Gaynor et al. (2011) use individual data on patient treatment to estimate a multinomial logit model of demand faced by individual hospitals for CABG surgery. They find that the demand elasticity with respect to a hospital's (risk-adjusted) mortality rate is greater after the reform than before. Post-reform the elasticity with respect to the adjusted mortality rate is roughly equal to 0.3. In the case of the mortality rate, an increase of one standard deviation (about a 20 percent increase) implies a drop in the choice probability of about 6 percent. This elasticity is significantly larger than the pre-reform mortality rate elasticity. They also find substantial geographic differentiation—cross-elasticities between hospitals with respect to their mortality rates fall dramatically with distance. This indicates that close-by hospitals compete with each other over quality, but not with hospitals far away. There is considerable individual heterogeneity in patient responsiveness. More seriously ill patients (as measured by a higher co-morbidity count) are more sensitive to the hospital mortality rate than the average patient. With the introduction of the reform their preference for quality, relative to the average patient, increases even more. They also find larger effects of the reform on low-income patients. This study takes a structural approach toward studying the effect of competition on quality. The English reform was intended to increase competition, and apparently did increase demand responsiveness.

Some insight into the mechanisms underlying the relationship between market structure and quality identified in Cooper et al. and Gaynor et al. (2010) is provided by Bloom et al. (2010). Bloom et al. use data for the English NHS and employ a

---

[86] Both the Cooper et al. (2011) and Gaynor et al. (2010) estimates of the impact of competition post-reform are quantitatively similar. Cooper et al. (2011) calculate that a one standard deviation increase of their measure of competition would lead to a reduction in the heart attack mortality rate of 0.3 percent per year. Gaynor et al. (2010)'s estimates imply that a one standard deviation decrease in concentration reduces heart attack mortality by 0.33 percent per year.

measure of management quality developed by Bloom and Van Reenen (2007) to examine the impact of market structure on management quality and, ultimately, on hospital quality (AMI mortality, emergency surgery mortality, and other measures). They find that having more close-by competitors has a strong and significant impact on management quality and hence on clinical quality of care. Their estimates imply that adding a rival hospital close by increases the measure of management quality by one-third of a standard deviation and thereby reduces heart attack mortality by 10.7 percent. This study employs only cross-sectional data (2006), so the methods differ from those in Cooper et al. and Gaynor et al. (2010). Identification of the effect of market structure is achieved by using political marginality of a hospital's geographic area. Because hospital openings, mergers, and closures are determined by a government agency (Department of Health), they are subject to political influence.

4.4.2. Studies with Market Determined Prices

We now turn to econometric studies of competition and quality where prices are determined in the market.[87] Most of these employ the SCP model, while some examine the impacts of mergers or price deregulation. A smaller number are structural (or related) and estimate entry behavior.

The results are summarized in Table 9.11. In the table the entry in the column labeled "Effect of competition on quality" indicates the direction of the relationship between the competition measure and the quality measure. The measure of quality used in the study is listed under the column heading "Quality measure," and the measure of competition is listed in the column labeled "Competition measure."

There have been a number of recent studies of competition and quality in hospital markets. These all cover time periods from the 1990s or later, when it is generally agreed that price competition had emerged in hospital markets. We first discuss SCP studies, then cover merger studies, then finally move to studies of price deregulation. In considering these studies we need to refer back to economic theory for guidance. Unlike the case of regulated prices, economic theory on competition and quality is less clear (see Gaynor, 2006b). Nonetheless, theory does provide a guide to what to look for, and what economic factors might be underlying an estimated relationship.

Some insights into the determinants of quality levels can be gained from the model of Dorfman and Steiner (1954). Their model is nominally about choice of price and advertising, but can also be interpreted as about price and quality (although in a somewhat restrictive way).[88]

---

[87] We omit older studies of the "Medical Arms Race." For a review that includes these studies see Gaynor (2006b).

[88] Dorfman and Steiner model a monopolist's behavior. We can consider this an approximation to the behavior of a monopolistically competitive firm if we think of the demand function as a reduced-form demand, e.g. an oligopolist's residual demand curve (see, e.g., Dranove and Satterthwaite, 2000).

Table 9.11 Health Care Quality and Competition Empirical Studies: Market Determined Prices

Study	Time Period	Geographic Area	Medical Condition	Payers	Quality Measure	Competition Measure	Effect of Competition on Quality
Gowrisankaran and Town (2003)	Heart attack, 1991–1993; pneumonia, 1989–1992	Los Angeles	Heart attack, pneumonia	HMO	Mortality	HHI	Increase (*mortality* ↓)
Sohn and Rathouz (2003)	1995	California	PTCA	All	Mortality	Competition coefficient	Increase (*mortality* ↓)
Mukamel et al. (2002)	1982, 1989	California	All, AMI, CHF, pneumonia, stroke	All	Mortality	HHI	Decrease (*mortality* ↑)
Encinosa and Bernard (2005)	1996–2000	Florida	All, nursing surgery	All	Patient safety event	Low hospital operating margin	Decrease (*patient safety events* ↑)
Propper et al. (2004)	1995–1998	UK	Heart attack	NHS	Mortality	Number of competitors	Decrease (*mortality* ↑)
Sari (2002)	1991–1997	16 states	All	All	Quality indicators	HHI	Increase (*quality indicators* ↑)
Ho and Hamilton (2000)	1992–1995	California	Heat attack, stroke	All	Mortality readmission	Merger	No effect; mortality increase: readmission (↓)
Capps (2005)	1995–2000	New York	All	All	Quality indicators	Merger	No effect: 13 inpatient and patient safety indicators Decrease: 1 year post-merger in-hospital mortality for AMI, heart failure (*mortality* ↑)

(*Continued*)

Table 9.11 (Continued)

Study	Time Period	Geographic Area	Medical Condition	Payers	Quality Measure	Competition Measure	Effect of Competition on Quality
Volpp et al. (2003)	1990–1995	New Jersey	Heart attack	All	Mortality	Price deregulation	Decrease (*mortality* ↑)
Burgess et al. (2008)	1991–1999	UK	Heart attack	NHS	Mortality	Deregulation, number of competitors	Decrease (*mortality* ↑)
Howard (2005)	2000–2002	US	Kidney transplant	All	Graft failure	Demand elasticity	Increase (small) (*elasticity* ↑)
Abraham et al. (2007)	1990	US	All	All	Quantity consumed	# of hospitals	Increase (*quantity* ↑)
Cutler et al. (2010)	1994, 1995, 2000, 2002, 2003	Pennsylvania	CABG	All	Mortality	Entrants' market share	Increase (*market share of high-quality (low mortality) physicians* ↑)
Escarce et al. (2006)	1994–1999	California, New York, Wisconsin	Heart attack, hip fracture, stroke, gastrointestinal hemorrhage, congestive heart failure, diabetes	All	Mortality	HHI	Increase—CA, NY; no effect—WI (*mortality* ↓, 0)
Rogowski et al. (2007)	1994–1999	California	Heart attack, hip fracture, stroke, gastrointestinal hemorrhage, congestive heart failure, diabetes	All	Mortality	1-HHI, 1–3 firm concentration ration, # of competitors	Increase (3–5 conditions), no effect (*mortality* ↓, 0)

Study							
Mutter et al. (2008)	1997	US	All	All	Inpatient quality indicators, patient safety indicators	Various (HHI, # of competitors, …)	Increase, no effect, decrease (*quality indicators* ↑, 0, ↓)
Romano and Balan (2011)	1998–99, 2001–03	Chicago PMSA	All	All	Inpatient quality indicators, patient safety indicators	Merger	No effect, increase (*quality indicators* 0, ↑)
Mutter et al. (2011)	1997–2001, 1998–2002	16 US states	All	All	25 inpatient quality indicators, patient safety indicators	42 Mergers	Increase, no effect, decrease (*quality indicators* ↑ 0, ↓)

Using this model, we can obtain the following formula, known as the Dorfman–Steiner condition (see Gaynor, 2006b, for the derivation):

$$\frac{z}{p} = \frac{1}{d} \cdot \frac{\varepsilon_z}{\varepsilon_p} \tag{9.36}$$

where d is the average cost of quality per unit of quantity, i.e. $\text{cost} = c \cdot q + d \cdot z \cdot q$ where q is quantity.

This says that the ratio of quality to price should go up if the quality elasticity of demand increases or the price elasticity of demand declines, and vice versa. An increase in the quality elasticity increases the payoff to increased quality. A decrease in the price elasticity increases the price–cost margin, which also increases the payoff.

Some other papers provide a similar intuition, although the models are quite different from Dorfman and Steiner. Dranove and Satterthwaite (1992) consider the effects of information on price and quality when consumers are imperfectly informed about both. They find that if consumers have better information about price than about quality, then this can lead to an equilibrium with suboptimal quality. Intuitively this is similar to what happens in the Dorfman–Steiner framework with an increase in the price elasticity of demand, and no increase in the quality elasticity. The price–cost margin will fall, leading to a decreased payoff to quality, and a decrease in the quality–price ratio.

Allard et al. (2009) explicitly consider competition in the physician services market. They consider a repeated game between physicians and patients. The patient's health is determined by observable medical care and physician effort. Physician effort is anything physicians do that affects patient health. It can be thought of as quality. The patient observes his health *ex post*, so physician effort is observable, but is non-contractible. In the static game physicians will supply suboptimal effort. However, in the repeated game there is an equilibrium in which physicians supply optimal effort. This equilibrium obtains under certain conditions, in particular if patient switching costs are not too high and there is an excess supply of physicians. If switching costs are high then effort will be suboptimal, but competition will result in effort levels above the minimum.[89] Again, there are parallels to the Dorfman and Steiner intuition. In the Allard et al. model optimal effort occurs when patient switching costs are not too high. This is similar to the quality elasticity of demand being sufficiently high in the Dorfman and Steiner model. Suboptimal effort occurs when switching costs are high, analogous to a low-quality elasticity of demand.

While there are no determinate conclusions from this framework, it does offer some useful guidance for thinking about issues of competition in health care markets.

---

[89] In addition, if there is uncertainty in the relationship between patient health and physician actions, then physicians face some risk of patients switching even if they have supplied optimal effort. In this case their physicians will supply supra-optimal effort.

For example, the advent of managed care in the 1990s is commonly thought to have increased the price elasticity of demand facing health care firms (hospitals in particular). This should have led to decreased prices, and indeed seems to have done so. If there was no sufficiently countervailing increase in the quality elasticity, then quality should have fallen.

Another change in health care markets is the recent emphasis on medical errors and quality improvement. If that leads to the quality elasticity of demand increasing, then quality will increase. If the price elasticity remains unchanged this will increase price (since increased quality raises marginal cost), but price−cost margins will remain unchanged.

A study by Gowrisankaran and Town (2003) examined the relationship between market structure and AMI and pneumonia mortality in Los Angeles county in the early 1990s for both Medicare and HMO patients. We discussed the findings for Medicare patients in the previous section. We now turn to HMO patients. Gowrisankaran and Town find that risk-adjusted mortality is significantly lower in less concentrated parts of Los Angeles county. This implies that competition in quality is increasing for HMO patients. With a standard model of price and quality competition (see Gaynor, 2006b) this could occur if the quality elasticity of demand is higher in less concentrated markets, or if the price elasticity is lower. Since we generally think that elasticities are higher with more competitors, the former seems plausible (and the latter does not).

Sohn and Rathouz (2003) study the impact of competition on risk-adjusted mortality for patients receiving percutaneous transluminal coronary angioplasty (PTCA) in 116 hospitals in California in 1995. They construct a "competition coefficient" that varies between zero and one depending on the degree of overlap in the patient pools of a pair of hospitals. Sohn and Rathouz find that mortality is lower for patients in hospitals facing more competition. This effect is stronger in lower volume hospitals. Again, this result seems to imply that the quality elasticity is higher in more competitive markets.

Mukamel et al. (2002) examine the impact of competition on risk-adjusted mortality for California patients in 1982 and 1989. The two years cover the period before and after the introduction of insurer-selective contracting in California. They hypothesize that the introduction of selective contracting increased price competition and that hospitals responded by shifting resources from clinical activities, which are hard to observe, to hotel activities, which are more easily observed. Mukamel et al. estimate the effects of the level of hospital concentration (measured as the HHI) in the base year and the change in hospital concentration on the change in inpatient clinical expenditures, and then the impact of the change in expenditures and the level of the hospital HHI in 1989 on the level of risk-adjusted mortality in 1989. They find that the change in the HHI had a negative and significant impact on both clinical and hotel expenditures for not-for-profit hospitals, but no significant impact on for-profit hospitals. The estimated relationship between clinical expenditures and mortality is negative. Mukamel et al. find that together these two results imply that increased competition from 1982 to1989 led to increased mortality, operating via competition reducing clinical expenditures on patients. The introduction of selective contracting is likely to have increased the price elasticity of demand facing hospitals, without increasing the quality elasticity by a similar proportion. In this case, the Dorfman and Steiner model predicts that quality will fall.

Encinosa and Bernard (2005) use data on all inpatient discharges from Florida hospitals from 1996 to 2000 to examine the impacts of financial pressure on patient safety. Encinosa and Bernard employ a newly available set of quality indicators developed by the Agency for Health Care Research and Quality (AHRQ). These indicators measure a variety of factors reflecting clinical quality, including mortality, obstetric complications, adverse or iatrogenic complications, wound infections, surgery complications, cesarean section, and inappropriate surgery.[90] Encinosa and Bernard estimate the impact of within-hospital changes in lagged operating profit margins[91] on the probabilities of adverse patient safety events. They find that patients at hospitals in the lowest quartile of operating profit margins have significantly higher probabilities of adverse safety events than those in any of the higher quartiles. There are no significant differences in the probability of adverse events between patients in the highest, second-highest, or third-highest quartiles.[92] Thus patients at hospitals that are doing poorly financially are at greater risk of suffering from a patient safety problem than those who are at hospitals that are doing better financially. There seems to be no impact of doing better financially above a threshold (bottom quartile of operating margin).

This finding is roughly consistent with theory. We expect that quality will be positively related to marginal profits, so the empirical finding that quality is lower at hospitals with low profits seems likely. Standard theory would predict a continuous effect of profits on quality, however, not a threshold. It is possible that this could be due to data limitations. Encinosa and Bernard have to rely on accounting data, so they are unable to measure economic profits or construct a measure of marginal profits.

There are also some issues with the econometrics. Encinosa and Bernard use hospital dummies to control for hospital-specific unobserved factors. The estimating equations are logits for the probabilities of adverse patient safety events. This is a nonlinear estimator, so unlike least squares, hospital-specific effects are not differenced away. As a consequence, it is not clear to what extent their estimates of the effects of

---

[90] Go to http://http://www.qualityindicators.ahrq.gov for more information.

[91] The ratio of net operating profit to net operating revenue.

[92] The first quartile covers patients at hospitals with margins below −0.5 percent. The second quartile covers margins between −0.5 percent and 4.4 percent, the third between 4.4 percent and 9.3 percent, and the fourth covers margins greater than 9.3 percent.

profits on safety are truly purged of potentially confounding hospital-specific effects. Another issue is that slope estimates from non-linear models with group fixed effects are only consistent when the number of observations per group goes to infinity. In this context, that means that the number of years each hospital is observed has to be large. Since the sample in this paper covers five years, it seems unlikely this condition is met, hence the estimates may not be consistent.

  While this study does not directly examine competition, it may have implications for the impact of competition on quality. To the extent that competition reduces hospital operating margins to low levels as in Encinosa and Bernard it may put patients at higher risk of adverse safety events.

  Propper et al. (2004) use an SCP approach to examine the effect of hospital competition in the United Kingdom following reforms to the National Health Service in the 1990s. These reforms encouraged payer-driven competition among hospitals. Propper et al. examine the impact of this payer-driven competition on mortality for AMI patients. They examine the impact of a measure of market structure (roughly, the number of competitors) on mortality over the period 1995–1998 and find that mortality increases with the number of competitors. This finding certainly contrasts with that of US SCP studies, but (for better or for worse) it is consistent with theory. The presence of more competitors can increase quality elasticity, price elasticity, or both. If the price elasticity increases more than the quality elasticity, then quality will fall. Whether this is the mechanism driving the result in this paper cannot be determined, although it provides some direction for future research. As previously, the welfare impacts of this finding are unclear. If increasing the number of competitors is associated with a decrease in market power, then a quality decrease may be welfare improving. Alternatively, it could be harmful.

  An interesting study is by Sari (2002). Sari uses the same quality indicators as Encinosa and Bernard. Sari is one of the first studies to employ these indicators rather than following the common practice of using risk-adjusted mortality as a quality measure. He employs data on hospitals in 16 states covering the period 1992–1997 and estimates the SCP model using fixed effects, random effects, and instrumental variables with fixed effects. Sari finds that quality is significantly lower in more concentrated markets—he estimates that a 10 percent increase in hospital market share leads to a 0.18 percent decrease in quality. He also finds evidence that managed care penetration increases quality for some of the quality indicators, although there is no statistically significant relationship for others.

  Ho and Hamilton (2000) and Capps (2005) are two papers that examine the impact of hospital mergers on quality of care. Ho and Hamilton (2000) study 130 hospital mergers of various types over the period 1992 to 1995. The quality measures they employ are inpatient mortality, readmission rates, and early discharge of newborns. They employ hospital-specific fixed effects to control for time invariant hospital characteristics that may be related to merger. Ho and Hamilton find no detectable impact of merger on mortality for either heart attack or stroke patients. They do find that some mergers increase readmission rates for heart attack patients and the early discharge of newborns. It is unclear whether Ho and Hamilton find no effect because there truly is no effect or because they are unable to identify the effect in the data. The effects of mergers are notoriously difficult to identify. First, there are not a large number of mergers, so there is not a lot of statistical power with which to detect an effect. Second, the identifying variation in this study comes from within-hospital variation over time. If that is not the primary source of variation in outcomes then the estimates of the parameters will be imprecise. Third, mergers are certainly endogenous. Mergers occur for reasons that are often related to the outcome variables of interest. If mergers occur for reasons related to hospitals' changing circumstances over time, then the hospital fixed effects will not control for endogeneity, so it will be difficult to obtain consistent estimates of a merger effect.

Capps (2005) uses the AHRQ quality indicators to examine the effect of hospital mergers on quality. He compares merging to non-merging hospitals in New York state during 1995–2000. There are 25 merging hospitals, and 246 total. Control groups are constructed in two ways. The first method is to select non-merging hospitals that are similar to merging hospitals in observable characteristics (e.g. teaching status, size, ownership, etc.). The second method is to use propensity scores to identify a control group. The control group for a merging hospital then consists of the ten non-merging hospitals that have predicted probabilities of merging that are closest to the predicted probability of the merging hospital.

Using the first method Capps finds no statistically significant effect of mergers on most of the quality indicators. There is no effect on four of six inpatient indicators for quality procedures, no effect for indicators for three other surgical procedures, and no effect for six patient safety indicators. Merger is found to have a negative effect on the inpatient quality indicators for two cardiac procedures: AMI and congestive heart failure (CHF). Merger is estimated to lead to an additional 12 deaths per 1,000 AMI or CHF admissions in the year following the merger, although there is no significant effect in the second year after the merger. There are no statistically significant effects of merger on any of the quality indicators when propensity scores are used to generate a control group. As with the Ho and Hamilton paper it is hard to know how to interpret the overall lack of statistical significance. Mergers may truly have had no impact on hospital quality in New York state over this period, or it may just be very difficult to precisely test the hypothesis.

Two very interesting recent papers use changes in regulation as a way to learn about the effect of hospital competition on quality. Volpp et al. (2003) study the effect of the deregulation of hospital prices in New Jersey to try to learn about the impact of the introduction of price competition on hospital quality. In 1992 New Jersey deregulated hospital prices. The neighboring state of New York had no change in its hospital regulatory regime. Volpp et al. use data on AMI hospital admissions in New Jersey and New York from 1990 to 1996 to learn about the effect of the deregulation. They look at the difference in risk-adjusted inpatient AMI mortality between New Jersey and New York before and after regulatory repeal. They find that mortality in New Jersey relative to New York increased after price deregulation. At first glance this result contrasts markedly with the SCP type studies previously discussed. However, consider the impact of price deregulation. The biggest impact should be to increase the price elasticity of demand, and decrease price.[93] The quality elasticity seems unlikely to be significantly affected. The prediction of a standard model is that quality will fall when the price elasticity of demand increases. It is impossible to say what the impact on welfare might be. If the regulated prices were set too high, then this quality decrease is welfare increasing, and vice versa.

A paper by Burgess et al. (2008) employs a similar approach to Volpp et al. In this paper Burgess et al. (2008) examine the impacts of competitive reforms in the NHS on mortality for AMI patients. Burgess et al. (2008) use a different strategy in this paper than in Propper et al. (2004). Here they use the change in regulation in the UK over the period 1991–1999, combined with geographic variation in the number of competitors.[94] Competition was introduced in 1991 and actively promoted up until 1995. It was downplayed after 1995 and actively discouraged from 1997 onwards. The impact of competition is identified by differences between hospitals facing competitors and those who are not between the time periods when competition was encouraged versus when it was discouraged.

Burgess et al. (2008) find that competition reduces quality. The differences in mortality for hospitals in areas with competitors versus those with no competitors was higher during the period when competition was promoted (1991–1995), than during the period when competition was discouraged (1996–1998). The estimated cumulative effect of competition over the entire period is to raise mortality rates by roughly the same amount as the cumulative effect of the secular downward trend in heart attack mortality (presumably due to technological change). This is a large impact. As with Volpp et al. (2003), these results can be interpreted as consistent with economic theory, although that is not testable within the framework employed in the paper. Also as before, the welfare inferences are unclear.

Howard (2005) is a paper that focuses on demand, as in the paper by Tay. Howard models the demand for kidney transplantation facilities, focusing on the effect of quality on consumer choice of facility. Howard examines the choices of all patients receiving transplants, including Medicare patients, Medicaid patients, and those with private insurance.

---

[93] Unfortunately Volpp et al. do not have any evidence on the effect of deregulation on prices.

[94] Only variation in the number of competitors is used in Propper et al. (2004).

Quality is measured as the difference between expected and actual one-year post-transplant graft failure rates at a center. Howard assumes that there are no price differences that affect choice between transplant centers, thus price is omitted. The explanatory variables are the quality measure, patients' distances from transplant centers, and patient characteristics. The average estimated choice elasticity with respect to quality is -0.12. The quality elasticity for privately insured patients is larger: -0.22.

These elasticity estimates are not particularly large. The low value of the average estimated quality elasticity implies that this does not give transplant centers a large incentive to compete on quality, as indicated by equation (9.23). Since Howard does not model the supply side, his model does not directly predict the impacts of competition (it is not intended to do so).

As with the Tay paper there are also some concerns about price and endogeneity. Howard assumes that price has no impact on where patients obtain their transplants. This may be true for Medicare, but it seems unlikely for patients who are privately insured. Privately insured patients face very large differences in out-of-pocket costs between providers that are in and out of their coverage networks. In addition, health insurance plans make decisions on which providers to include in their networks based on price. Thus it seems as if price should be included for those with private insurance. Further, if price is positively correlated with quality, then its omission could lead to a downward bias in the estimated effect of quality on demand. Patients may appear less responsive to quality differences than they really are if high-quality transplant centers are also high cost to them. Endogeneity of quality may also be an issue, for the same reasons as the Tay paper.

Abraham et al. (2007) has some welfare implications. Abraham et al. examine the determinants of the number of hospitals in isolated markets in the US for 1990. They do not examine price or quality explicitly. Instead, they infer whether competition is increasing by the population required to support another firm in the market. If the population required to support another firm is increasing, then average profits available post-entry must be decreasing, thus increasing the volume necessary to make entry profitable. They find that market size is the primary determinant of the number of hospitals, and that the quantity bought and sold in the market rises, and variable profits fall, as the number of hospitals in a local market increases. This implies that the market is getting more competitive as the number of hospitals increases. Further, it shows that entry is not simply demand-stealing—more hospitals increase demand. The reason is that quantity demanded can increase only if price is lower or quality is higher. Since that does happen, people are consuming more and must be better off.[95] As a

---

[95] As pointed out previously, increased aggregate demand is not necessary for increased quality to be welfare enhancing.

consequence, they conclude that competition increases with the number of hospitals, and that competition is welfare improving.

Cutler et al. (2010) is a recent very interesting study that, like Abraham et al., utilizes information on entry (in the coronary artery bypass graft surgery market, i.e. CABG) to make inferences about the impacts of competition. Cutler et al. use the repeal of entry restricting regulation (hospital certificate of need regulation, CON) in Pennsylvania to examine the effect of entry of hospitals into the CABG surgery market. They hypothesize that overall production is capacity constrained—cardiac surgeons are a scarce input and supply cannot be altered easily. As a consequence, entry will not lead to increased quantities of CABG surgery, but may lead to improved quality; in particular, they hypothesize that it will increase the market shares of high-quality surgeons. This hypothesis is confirmed in the empirical analysis. They find that in markets where entrants have 11—20 percent market shares of CABG surgeries, high-quality surgeons' market shares increased 2.1 percentage points more than for standard quality surgeons. Overall, they conclude that entry led to increased quality, but that there was no net effect of entry on social welfare. Their estimates of the gains from reduced mortality due to entry are approximately offset by the estimated fixed costs of entry. This is one of the few papers with welfare results.

Escarce et al. (2006) examine the relationship between hospital concentration and patient mortality for adults hospitalized for myocardial infarction, hip fracture, stroke, gastrointestinal hemorrhage, congestive heart failure, or diabetes in California, New York, and Wisconsin. They find that the probability of death is lower in less concentrated markets in California and New York, but not Wisconsin. This adds to the evidence that there can be substantial quality competition among hospitals, but also that there can be substantial heterogeneity, depending on market specifics. It is possible that in Wisconsin price competition dominates quality competition, although the study does not present evidence on that and of course there could be other reasons for the result.

A different study by Rogowski et al. (2007) examines the same six conditions in the state of California. In this study Rogowski et al. find that mortality is lower in less concentrated markets for three to five of the six conditions, depending on the measure of concentration employed. Interestingly, they find no statistically significant impact of market structure on heart attack mortality, in direct contrast to many other studies which find the opposite result.

Mutter et al. (2008) use national data on hospitals from the US Agency for Healthcare Research and Quality's Hospital Cost and Utilization Project state inpatient databases to examine the relationships between 38 different measures of inpatient quality and 12 different measures of hospital market structure. They find a variety of differing relationships: some quality measures positively related to measures of market structure, some negatively, and some not at all (insignificant). The use of national data is an improvement on prior studies which only use data from a single state. While the results seem somewhat murky, perhaps the variety of patterns they uncover in the data is not surprising. First, since there is both price and quality competition, anything can happen. Second, the use of multiple states, while laudable, does introduce additional heterogeneity, which can be hard to measure. Third, finding results in every direction is not terribly surprising with such a large number of different outcome measures.

Romano and Balan (2011) is an interesting recent study. Romano and Balan study the impact on quality of care of a consummated merger between two hospitals in the Chicago suburbs (Evanston Northwestern Hospital and Highland Park Hospital). This merger was the subject of an antitrust suit by the Federal Trade Commission, and the authors provided evidence on the case. This study uses the Inpatient Quality Indicators and Patient Safety Indicators used by Encinosa and Bernard and by Sari. The authors use a difference-in-differences methodology and compare the changes in quality measures at the two merged hospitals before and after the merger to the changes at control hospitals over the same time period. They find no significant impact of the merger on many quality measures, but there is a significant negative impact on some and a few with positive impacts. AMI, pneumonia, and stroke mortality went up at Evanston Northwestern Hospital post-merger compared to control hospitals, although there was no statistically significant impact at Highland Park. There was some improvement in quality for some nursing-sensitive quality measures: the incidence of decubitis ulcers (bedsores) fell at both merged entities, as did infections at Evanston Northwestern. Conversely, the incidence of hip fractures rose at Evanston Northwestern. Last, they found increases in some measures of obstetric outcomes (birth trauma to the newborn, obstetric trauma to the mother), and decreases in some other measures. They conclude that overall there is no reason to infer that the merger had salutary effects on quality.

Mutter et al. (2011) expand on other studies by examining the impacts of multiple mergers (42) in multiple (16) US states. The authors use difference-in-difference analysis to contrast changes in 25 different measures of quality (the AHRQ Inpatient Quality Indicators and Patient Safety Indicators) at merging hospitals against changes at control hospitals over the same time period. Mutter et al. find mixed results— mergers result in increased, decreased or no change in quality depending on the measure and the nature of the merger. For the majority of cases, mergers have no impact on quality. For a few measures there are statistically significant impacts of mergers on quality, although there are both positive and negative effects. Overall, the authors have a hard time finding statistically significant impacts of hospital mergers on quality, implying that on average there is no detectable effect. Their results do indicate, however, that mergers can have either negative or positive quality impacts, depending on the measure of quality and the specifics of the merger. The nature of these results has a lot in common with their previous study (Mutter et al., 2008), which focused on measures of market structure, rather than merger. As with that study, while the results seem somewhat murky, perhaps that is to be expected, given the large degree of heterogeneity in hospital mergers, and the large number of outcome measures employed.

4.4.3. Studies of the Volume–Outcome Relationship

There have been a very large number of studies of the "volume–outcome" relationship, the majority in the medical literature. These studies commonly find a significant correlation with the volume a hospital does of a procedure and the medical outcomes of patients receiving the procedure at that hospital. The obvious concern with studies of this kind is endogeneity. It may be that hospitals that do more of a procedure are better at it, whether from learning by doing or by making quality improving investments. It may also be true, however, that patients are attracted to hospitals with the best outcomes. The studies in the medical literature are unable to distinguish between these two alternatives.

This is important for assessing competition in the hospital sector and for antitrust enforcement. If volume causes quality, then there may be some efficiencies from improved patient outcomes in more concentrated markets. This could also affect hospital merger evaluation. We review three relatively recent studies below that present the strongest evidence to date on the volume–outcome effect: Ho (2002), Gowrisankaran et al. (2004), and Gaynor et al. (2005). The results of these studies are summarized in Table 9.12.

Ho (2002) examines the volume–outcome relationship for PTCA using data from California hospitals from 1984 to 1996. The outcomes she examines are mortality and emergency CABG. She estimates the effects of hospital cumulative and annual volume on outcomes, employing hospital and time fixed effects. Ho finds substantial improvements in outcomes over time, but a small effect of annual hospital volume on outcome. The effect of cumulative volume on outcomes is imprecisely estimated.

Gowrisankaran et al. (2004) attempt to recover the causal relationship between volume and outcome using instrumental variables. They study the volume–outcome relationship for three surgical procedures: the Whipple procedure (removing tumors from the pancreas); CABG; and repair of abdominal aortic aneurysm (this repairs weak spots in the abdominal artery). They use data on hospitals from Florida from 1988 to 1999 and California from 1993 to 1997. The instrumental variables approach is to use patient distance from the hospital to estimate patient choice of hospital and then construct predicted volume. Gowrisankaran et al. find that increasing volume causes better outcomes for all three procedures and find significant and large effects of hospital volume on patient mortality. This implies that volume–outcome effects can be important to consider when evaluating the impact of hospital competition. If competition leads to reduced volume then outcomes will decline. If competition leads to specialization then outcomes will improve.

Table 9.12 Health Care Quality and Competition Empirical Studies: Volume–Outcome

Study	Time Period	Geographic Area	Medical Condition	Payers	Quality Measure	Factor Affecting Quality	Effect on Quality
Ho (2002)	1984–1986	California	PTCA	All	Mortality, CABG	Surgical volume	Increase (small) (*volume* ↑ → *mortality* ↓)
Gowrisankaran et al. (2004)	1993–1997 (CA), 1988–1999 (FL)	California, Florida	Whipple procedure, CABG, abdominal aortic aneurysm	All	Mortality	Surgical volume	Increase (*volume* ↑ → *mortality* ↓)
Gaynor et al. (2005)	1983–1999	California	CABG	All	Mortality	Surgical volume	Increase (*volume* ↑ → *mortality* ↓)
Huckman and Pisano (2006)	1994–1995	Pennsylvania	CABG	All	Mortality	Surgical volume (physician)	Increase (*volume* ↑ → *mortality* ↓)
Ramanarayanan (2008)	1998–2006	Florida	CABG	All	Mortality	Surgical volume (physician)	Increase (*volume* ↑ → *mortality* ↓)
Huesch (2009)	1998–2006	Florida	CABG	All	Mortality	Surgical volume (new surgeons)	No effect (*volume* ↑ → *mortality*)

Gaynor et al. (2005), in a similar paper, use instrumental variables techniques to estimate the volume—outcome relationship for CABG. They use data from California for 1983—1999. Gaynor et al. find a causal, and substantial, effect of volume on outcome. For example, if CABGs could only be performed in hospitals with a volume of 200 or greater, the average mortality rate from CABG would fall from 2.5 to 2.05 percent, saving 118 (statistical) lives. In a related working paper by the same authors, Seider et al. (2000) simulate the effects of two mergers: a hypothetical "standard merger," in which two out of five firms with equal market shares merge; and the actual merger of Alta Bates Medical Center and Summit Medical Center in Oakland, California. They find that, for larger hospital mergers (hospital volumes >140), the value of saved lives from the standard merger outweighs the loss of consumer surplus from increased prices. For the Summit—Alta Bates merger, which does not, however, have a large effect on volume, the effect is a net loss of $2.8 to $4.4 million. The reason is that the increase in volume due to the merger is too small to have much effect on outcomes, while the price increase reduces welfare.

Huckman and Pisano (2006) examine the slightly different question of the relationship between volume and outcome for surgeons. Specifically, they ask whether it is a surgeon's volume at a particular hospital, or his/her overall volume that influences surgical outcomes. Examining cardiac bypass (CABG) cases in Pennsylvania in 1994 and 1995, they find that the mortality rate of a surgeon's patients at a specific hospital improves significantly with increases in his or her volume at that hospital but not with increases in his or her volume elsewhere. They do not specifically address the possibility of endogeneity of volume, although concerns over this may be allayed somewhat by the findings from Gowrisankaran et al. (2004) and Gaynor et al. (2005) that fail to reject exogeneity (although Ramanarayanan (2008), discussed below, rejects exogeneity in his study).

Ramanarayanan (2008) also attempts to identify physician specific volume—outcome effects for CABG surgery. Ramanarayanan's approach differs from Huckman and Pisano in that he uses an instrumental variables strategy for identification (Huckman and Pisano use lagged volume and lags of surgeon and hospital risk-adjusted mortality to try to address endogeneity concerns) and uses data from Florida for 1998—2006. The instrument is the departure of a surgeon—this departure has the impact of exogenously shifting volume to remaining physicians. Ramanarayanan finds that individual physician volume does have a significant impact on patient outcomes. Unlike Huckman and Pisano, he does find that surgeon experience is somewhat portable across hospitals. However, it is not fully portable—surgeon volume at the "home" hospital has a much bigger impact on outcomes than does volume at other hospitals. The results from these two papers (Ramanarayanan, 2008; Huckman and Pisano, 2006) provide a more nuanced view on the volume—outcome relationship. Physicians play an important role, but it is not simply the physician's volume that determines outcomes. There are hospital-specific aspects to the volume–outcome relationship, implying that concentrating procedures at a hospital can play a significant role in improved outcomes.

In a novel approach to try to identify learning effects, Huesch (2009) estimates the volume–outcome relationship for 57 "new cardiac surgeons" (physicians who had completed their residencies immediately before the beginning of the time period he examines). Huesch uses the same data covering the same time period as does Ramanarayanan. He finds no evidence of a volume–outcome relationship for these new cardiac surgeons. Indeed, allowing for forgetting, he finds that the effects of prior experience do not carry over from one quarter to the next. Huesch uses fixed effects and instrumental variables methods, although he does not reject exogeneity of volume for the new doctors he examines. This result stands in marked contrast to Huckman and Pisano and Ramanarayanan. One would expect that new physicians would be those doing the most learning. This is not supported by the results of this study. It is well known that learning by doing is difficult to identify empirically (see Thompson, 2010). Huesch and Sakakibara (2009) point out a number of possible mechanisms that could be driving observed empirical volume–outcome relationships, and suggest further thought on how to identify these specific mechanisms is in order.

4.5. Summary

The empirical literature on competition and quality in health care markets is for the most part fairly recent, and has grown very rapidly. The results from empirical research are not uniform. Most of the studies of Medicare patients show a positive impact of competition on quality. This is not surprising, since economic theory for markets with regulated prices predicts such a result. However, the results from studies of markets where prices are set by firms (e.g. privately insured patients) are much more variable. Some studies show increased competition leading to increased quality, and some show the opposite. While this may appear surprising, it is not. Economic theory predicts that quality may either increase or decrease with increased competition when firms are setting both quality and price.

This first generation of studies has provided a very valuable base of knowledge for further research. The base that has been constructed, while extremely useful, does not allow for normative analysis, for the most part. The results of these studies do not allow us to make inferences about whether their estimated results imply that competition increased or decreased social welfare.

These results also contain some useful lessons for research on competition and quality in other industries, specifically what can and cannot be learned via non-structural (SCP) econometric approaches, and what is required to obtain more refined results.

A major next step for research in this area is sorting out the factors that determine whether competition will lead to increased or decreased quality. Economic theory can be a helpful guide for these next generation studies. While theoretical models of price and quality determination are complex and usually yield indefinite predictions, there is also some simple intuition that can be gleaned from theory. Whether competition leads to increased or decreased quality will depend on its relative impacts on firms' price and quality elasticities of demand. Future research can focus on trying to recover estimates of these key elements. Additionally, studies of price regulated markets can refer back to theory to specify econometric models that include the regulated price and marginal cost (or its determinants). In general, the sorts of studies discussed above will allow for more precise positive analysis of the impact of competition on quality in health care, and provide opportunities for normative analysis as well.

We need more detailed models, however, in order to perform normative analysis. Thus, an important, although formidable, task for future work is to pursue the estimation of more complete econometric models of quality determination in health care markets. This means trying to recover preferences and costs (i.e. demand and supply). The benefit of this approach is the ability to make clearer inferences about welfare, since estimates of preference and cost parameters are in hand. The drawback is that such estimates are not easily obtained. In particular, they usually can only be obtained at the cost of making untestable assumptions. The quantity, and detail, of health care data may make some of the assumptions employed in settings with sparser data unnecessary, however. Augmenting modern bargaining models of price determination with quality choice may also be a fruitful approach to trying to identify the price and quality effects of competition where prices are market determined. In the previous section 4.3 we provided a preliminary sketch of what such a model might look like. Clearly more work remains to be done, but this may be a promising avenue for future research.

5. STUDIES OF HEALTH INSURANCE MARKETS

5.1. Introduction

While a great deal of effort in health economics has been devoted to studying health insurance, most research has been focused on consumer behavior, or on the implications of asymmetric information for selection and market outcomes (see Breyer et al., 2012, for coverage of these topics). Until recently there has been very little work on competition by health insurance firms. Part of the reason for this has been the paucity of sufficient data for given markets to construct measures of prices or market shares in the US and internationally. For the US, there are detailed household-level data (the Medical Expenditure Panel Survey, http://www.meps.ahrq.gov/mepsweb/) on health insurance decisions and prices, but these data are from surveys of approximately 4,000 households selected to be nationally representative. As a consequence, they do not fully describe the choices in a given market, or catalog the prices of alternatives, let alone the market shares of sellers. Other data (National Association of Insurance Commissioners, http://www.naic.org) do capture market shares, but at the level of a state. Since the vast majority of health insurance restricts enrollees' choices to a network of providers, most of whom are local, the geographic market for health insurance is local, and smaller than a state. In addition, there are no comprehensive data on health plans' networks of providers. The most comprehensive data on health insurance markets have been for private insurance associated with the Medicare program (Medigap coverage, Medicare + Choice/Medicare Advantage). Internationally, some countries have enacted reforms that have led to the creation or expansion of private health insurance markets (Germany, the Netherlands, Switzerland). Data from those markets have become available over the last few years.

Another reason has been the difficulty of specifying a coherent model of competition in this market due to its complexity. For the US, the majority of private health insurance is provided by employers to their workers as a (pre-tax) fringe benefit. Within this category, some employers self-insure, and contract with insurers only to administer their plans (including assembling a network of providers and negotiating terms with them). This is typical of large employers. Other employers do purchase the underwriting of risk from insurers, as well as administration. Of those that purchase actual insurance, small employers are faced with very different circumstances than large employers, mostly due to their smaller risk pool. Thinking about demand here is complicated. First, employers are faced with the task of somehow aggregating employees' preferences.[96] Employers want to retain and attract productive employees, and so have to offer competitive total compensation, including health insurance. Countries like Germany, the Netherlands, and Switzerland do not have this particular complicated institutional structure on the demand side, but have their own institutional idiosyncracies that also present a challenge to economic modeling. Second, the demand for a health insurance plan depends on its associated network of providers, as we noted previously (this tends to be true in every country). Competition among health plans is affected by their provider networks.

5.2. Empirical Studies

Empirical studies have taken a number of different forms. One group of studies have tried to study the impacts of competition on outcome variables. This includes

---

[96] Dafny et al. (2010) present evidence that employers' choices do not maximize employees' welfare, although they do not allow for effects of restricted choice on provider prices, and hence premiums. Also see Goldstein and Pauly (1976).

reduced-form studies, SCP studies, and studies of entry. Another set of studies have written down complete demand- and supply-side models of the health insurance market and proceeded with structural estimation. Yet another set of studies have estimated the elasticity of demand for an insurance plan (as opposed to aggregate demand for insurance). These studies are relevant to competition in insurance markets, since the elasticity faced by sellers plays a large role in competition. In what follows, we review these studies. We divide them into studies of competition and studies of demand elasticity.

5.2.1. Studies of the Impacts of Competition

Table 9.13 contains summaries of recent studies of health insurance market competition. This table is organized in a similar way to the previous tables summarizing empirical studies of hospital market competition.

Dafny (2010) is one of the first of some new studies on insurance market competition. Dafny uses data from a benefits consulting firm on the plans purchased and premiums paid by a large number (776) of large employers over the period 1998–2005. While these data are not necessarily complete by market or nationally representative, they do represent the most extensive and comprehensive data set with prices and quantities for the insurance market. Dafny's empirical approach is motivated by a bargaining model between insurers and employers.[97]

Her identification strategy is to examine the effect of shocks to employer profitability on the changes in the insurance premiums they pay. The idea is that if insurers possess no market power then the premiums they charge will not vary with employer profitability. Only if insurers have market power will they be able to price discriminate based on employer profitability.[98] Dafny finds strong evidence that premiums increase with the buyer's profitability. She also interacts profitability with the number of insurers in the market. As the number of firms increases, market power should decline. Her results are consistent with this hypothesis—the effect of employer profitability on insurance premiums falls with the number of firms in the market. This provides some evidence on competition in insurance markets where previously there was none.

Of course, like any other study, it is possible that other factors could be driving the results. In particular, premiums are not an ideal measure of the price of insurance. Premiums consist of expected medical expenses, plus the insurer's administrative costs, plus any markup due to market power. In essence, the premium is a measure of

---

[97] This is analogous to the bargaining model between insurers and hospitals that we presented in section 3.1. We did not specify a bargaining model between insurers and hospitals, although bargaining between these agents surely occurs. This emphasizes the complexity of the institutional structure of insurance markets and the difficult modeling choices researchers must confront.

[98] Dafny is thinking in terms of a bargaining, as opposed to posted price, model, but the basic intuition is the same.

Table 9.13 Insurance Market: Competition Empirical Studies

Study	Time Period	Geographic Area	Empirical Approach	Payers	Outcome Measure	Competition Measure	Effect of Competition
Dafny (2010)	1998–2005	US	Reduced form; insurer–employer bargaining	Private, large employers	Premiums	# of firms	Increase (↑)
Dafny et al. (2011b)	1998–2005	US	SCP	Private, large employers	Premium	HHI	Increase (↑)
Dranove et al. (2003)	1997	US	Entry model	Private HMOs	Population required to support another firm	# of HMOs	Increase (*population* ↑ ⇒ *profits* ↓)
Frank and Lamiraud (2009)	1997–2000	Switzerland	Health plan switching	Private health insurers	Effect of # of plans on probability of switching	# of plans	Decrease (# *of plans* ↑ ⇒ *switching* ↓)
Maestas et al. (2009)	2004	US	Price dispersion; consumer search	Medigap	Price dispersion; consumer search	NA	NA; ∃ price dispersion; substantial search costs
Bolhaar et al. (2010)	2005–2006	Netherlands	Price dispersion; search costs	Private health insurance	Price dispersion; search costs	NA	NA; ∃ price dispersion; education, youth, group contract (discount) → search ↑
Starc (2010)	2004–2008	US	Structural (demand, claims, costs: variable, fixed, sunk)	Medigap	Demand elasticity, welfare	Demand elasticity (−1.14), simulations	Increase welfare (*compensating variation net of profits* ↑ $230 per consumer)
Lustig (2010)	2000–2003	US	Structural (demand, fixed, MC of generosity)	M + C	Demand elasticity welfare	# of firms	Increase (# *of firms* → *welfare* gain from no adverse selection ↑)
Town and Liu (2003)	1993–2000	US	Structural (demand, pricing equation–marginal costs)	M + C	Consumer surplus	# of firms	Increase (# *of firms* → *consumer surplus* ↑)

quantity of health insurance as well as the price. Expected medical expenditures are the quantity—they will vary with the generosity of the health insurance plan, the characteristics of the enrollees (sickness and preferences for medical care)—and provider prices. The part of the premium not due to medical expenses, the "load" or "load factor," is the price of insurance.

As Dafny realizes, the issue here is that if employers who experience positive profit shocks share some of the rents with employees via more generous insurance coverage then the observed relationship between employer profitability and health insurance premiums may be quantity increases as opposed to price. One of her purposes in estimating the specification with interactions between employer profitability and insurance market structure is to test for this possibility. The fact that this effect is larger in markets with fewer insurers suggests that it is not primarily due to increased plan generosity.[99] Dafny also includes a control for plan design to try to control for generosity. Including this variable does not alter the results. It is notable that there are significant effects of employer profitability in insurance premiums even for markets with 9—10 insurers (the effect is insignificant for markets with 10 or more insurers). It seems surprising that insurers would possess market power in markets with 8—9 rivals (9—10 firms total). This empirical result does raise some doubts, but research by Dranove et al. (2003) found patterns in 1997 suggesting there may be market power in HMO markets with up to six firms. In any event, Dafny is a contribution that opens a line of empirical research on competition in health insurance markets.

Dafny et al. (2011b) take a more traditional SCP approach to examining health insurance market competition. They employ the same dataset as in Dafny (2010), but examine how the growth rate of an employer's health insurance premiums is affected by health insurance market concentration (HHI). They include variables intended to control for factors that could influence medical spending or administrative costs (as opposed to markup): a demographic factor, plan design factor, and the number of enrollees in a plan. Initial OLS regressions reveal no significant effect of insurer market concentration on premium growth. Of course, the HHI may be endogenous. In order to deal with that problem Dafny et al. instrument for the observed HHI with changes in local market concentration due to a large merger in 1999 between two national health insurers: Aetna and Prudential Healthcare. Using this instrumental variables approach, they find a significant impact of the predicted change in HHI due to the merger on the change in premiums. They find that the cumulative effect of insurer market consolidation on premiums is approximately 7 percent.

Dafny et al. also recognize that insurers may have bargaining power (market power in a posted price world) with regard to providers. They therefore examine the effect

---

[99] More precisely, what Dafny finds is that the effect of increased profitability for an employer is to increase premiums in markets with few insurers by more than in markets with a large number of insurers, for the *same* employer.

of insurer concentration on changes in earnings and employment for physicians and for nurses as a way of testing for the presence of insurer monopsony power. They find that the merger reduced physician earnings growth on average by 3 percent, while nurses' earnings rose by approximately six-tenths of 1 percent. There is no significant effect on physician employment, while nurse employment grows as a result of the merger-induced increase in concentration. It's not clear if this is evidence of monopsony power, but it is consistent with plan concentration leading to downward pressure on physician earnings and ultimately to substitution of nurses for physicians. Overall, while the estimation results depend crucially on the use of the Aetna–Prudential merger as an instrumental variable, they show evidence of a significant relationship between changes in insurer market concentration and changes in premiums, implying a link between market structure and the exercise of market power.

Dranove et al. (2003) employ a modification of the methodologies of Brenahan and Reiss (1991) devised by Mazzeo (2002) to examine competition among HMOs. They use data from 1997 on the number of HMOs in local markets, distinguishing between HMOs that are national and those that are not. They first estimate threshold ratios (the ratio of the population necessary to support $n + 1$ firms to that necessary to support n) for all HMOs together. They find somewhat puzzling results: the threshold ratio for two firms is 0.93 and for three firms is 1.58 (it declines thereafter). A threshold ratio of 1 indicates that it takes exactly the same population (demand) to support the second firm as to support the first. In the Brenahan and Reiss framework this implies that there is no change in profitability with the entry of the second firm, i.e. there's no increase in competition in duopoly HMO markets compared to monopoly. The threshold ratio above 1 for the third firm indicates that it takes substantially more population (per firm) to support three HMOs than two, implying that profit margins must be falling with the entry of the third firm (but not the second).

Dranove et al. speculate that this seemingly strange pattern in the threshold ratios may be due to product differentiation. If local HMOs do not compete strongly with national HMOs (national employers may strongly prefer to buy from national HMOs and local employers from local HMOs), then the estimates produced by pooling them together could be misleading. Dranove et al. then employ the framework of Mazzeo (2002), allowing for the possibility of any combination of any number of firms (up to five) of each type. The parameter estimates indicate that the profits of local HMOs are virtually unaffected by the number of national HMOs, and vice versa. By contrast, the presence of a second same-type HMO reduces profits by approximately one-half. The effects of subsequent same-type competitors on profits are negative, but declining in magnitude. These results indicate that there is substantial competition in HMO markets, but also substantial product differentiation. Dranove et al.'s results indicate that there is virtually no competition at all between national and local HMOs.

The studies by Dafny (2010), Dafny et al. (2011b), and Dranove et al. (2003) find evidence that market structure affects conduct—more firms in a market are associated with tougher competition. Some other studies call that relationship into question.

Frank and Lamiraud (2009) examine the functioning of health insurance markets in Switzerland. Switzerland requires all residents to have health insurance. Health insurance is privately supplied, but the market is heavily regulated. The government defines a standardized benefit for the required coverage, mandates guaranteed issue by insurers, adjusts the payments insurers receive to compensate them for risk,[100] and provides public information on prices. Frank and Lamiraud document a high degree of price dispersion in Swiss health insurance markets, with little evidence of convergence over time. The number of health insurers has declined over time, but the mean number of health plans per canton rose from 40 in 1997 to 56 in 2004. Switching rates across plans were low: 4.8 percent in 1997, 2.1 percent in 2000, then stabilizing at around 3 percent.

Frank and Lamiraud find this puzzling, given the rather large price differences across plans with identical benefits. They speculate that the presence of a large number of choices may lead to decision overload. They make use of survey data on individuals and publicly reported information on health insurance plans to estimate a model of individual health plan switching and attempt to test these hypotheses. They find that switching is significantly larger in areas with fewer plans, and that those who switched paid significantly less than those staying with the same plan (15.9 percent less; 33.18 CHF). These results do not seem consistent with price competition getting tougher with the number of firms. Now, to be clear, the studies by Dafny, Dafny et al., and Dranove et al. are on the large employer segment of the US private health insurance market. There, purchasing decisions are made by large corporations, so one would presume that these decisions are likely to be rational. The Frank and Lamiraud study examines the decisions of individual consumers in Switzerland. The most important difference is that individuals are making decisions, not large employers. Individuals are more likely to be affected by transactions costs or irrationality than are large corporations. Of course, the institutions in the Swiss individual health insurance market and the US large employer market are also quite different, but it seems to us that the most likely reason for the different patterns observed in these studies is due to the differences between decision making for individuals vs. that for large employers.

Similar patterns with regard to price dispersion have been documented in the US market for Medigap insurance and in the Netherlands health insurance market. Medigap is private insurance purchased by Medicare beneficiaries to cover the "gaps" in the Medicare coverage provided by the government. The insurance covers coinsurance

---

[100] Payments are adjusted up or down based on the expected medical expenses of the insurer's enrollee pool.

payments, deductibles, and those items or services that are excluded from the publicly provided coverage (most notably prescription drugs before the introduction of Medicare Part D).

Maestas et al. (2009) document substantial price variation in Medigap insurance markets, even though plans are standardized.[101] They apply the search model of Carlson and McAfee (1983) and find that insurers have substantial differences in costs, and hence loading fees, which contribute to the observed variation in prices. This price dispersion is an equilibrium due to substantial search costs—Maestas et al. estimate an average search cost for consumers in the market of $72 and a maximum of $144.

Bolhaar et al. (2010) also find substantial price dispersion in the Netherlands market for health insurance. This market is also subject to substantial regulation, including policy standardization and the dissemination of information to consumers, so the existence of price dispersion is somewhat surprising. They employ a unique dataset, the Dutch Health Care Consumer Panel, which contains information on actual consumer search behavior. They find that more educated consumers and younger consumers are more likely to search. In the Dutch system, there are also group contracts (e.g. an employment group). These are offered at a discount. They find a very strong correlation between an offer for a group contract and the probability of search.

Starc (2010) models the Medigap market, allowing for adverse selection and market power. She documents that the market is highly concentrated—the national four-firm concentration ratio is 83 percent (compared to 44 percent for private passenger automobile insurance or 34 percent for life insurance), and two firms (United Health, 46 percent; Mutual of Omaha, 24 percent) account for almost all of that. Starc documents substantial price dispersion for Medigap policies, confirming Maestas et al., and documents a positive relationship between premiums and market concentration, the same qualitative result as in Dafny et al. (2011b), albeit for a very different market. A 1 percent increase in the two-firm concentration ratio is associated with a 0.26 percent increase in premiums.

Starc estimates a structural model of insurance demand, claims, and seller costs (variable, fixed, sunk) using data from the National Association of Insurance Commissioners (NAIC) and the Medicare Current Beneficiary Survey for 2006–2008. She estimates the average price elasticity of demand to be −1.12. This is a very low elasticity for firm demand, especially given the standardization of the products sold in this market. It is possible this is due to aggregation—the NAIC data are at the level of the state and the true geographic market is likely much smaller than that. It is also possible that the instruments are weak and that is what is driving the seemingly low estimate. The

---

[101] Studies of quite a few other markets have found substantial price dispersion, even in what one might think are competitive markets (e.g. Pratt et al., 1979; Dahlby and West, 1986; Gaynor and Polachek, 1994; Sorensen, 2000).

estimate of the claim function (estimated jointly with demand) reveals that insurer claims increase with premiums—a $100 increase in premiums will lead to a $15 increase in claims. This indicates the presence of adverse selection—higher risk consumers are less price sensitive. In the case of adverse selection, claims are increasing in the premium charged by the insurer. As a consequence, insurers facing adverse selection will charge lower markups of premiums over marginal costs than they otherwise would. This is a classic case of the second best—two distortions are better than one. The monopoly power of insurers is actually reduced by the "additional" distortion of adverse selection.

Starc also recovers estimates of cost parameters. For variable costs this is done in the usual manner, via a pricing equation and an assumption about conduct, but with the following wrinkle to account for an institutional feature of health insurance markets. Health insurers are subject to minimum loss ratio regulations by the federal government—65 percent of premiums collected are required to be paid out to enrollees as reimbursements for covered services. Starc incorporates this into estimation as an inequality constraint on pricing (premium setting). She estimates that United Health's variable (administrative) costs are about 6 percent of premiums, while they are estimated to be 18 percent of premiums for Mutual of Omaha.

Estimates of bounds on fixed or sunk costs can be recovered from the data. This employs the following intuition. First, assume that Mutual of Omaha faces fixed costs of entering each local market (a state). United Health, by contrast, expends resources on promotion (e.g. obtaining AARP's endorsement) entering the national market. These are sunk costs. Second, we observe, for example, one firm employing Mutual of Omaha's strategy. This implies that Mutual of Omaha is profitable, and a second firm employing that strategy would not be profitable. Therefore the lower bound for Mutual's fixed costs are the expected variable profits for a second firm employing their strategy, and the upper bound is the expectation of variable profits. The same exercise is performed to identify the bounds on the sunk costs of entering the national market. The bounds on Mutual of Omaha's fixed costs of entering a state are estimated at approximately $445,000 and $796,000, implying fixed costs of entering all of the 50 state markets between $22 and $40 million. The bounds on United Health's sunk costs of entering the national market are approximately $99 million and $488 million. The standard errors on these estimates are very large.

With these estimates in hand, Starc proceeds to welfare analysis. First, the impact of adverse selection in insurers' pricing is computed by setting the derivative of claims with respect to price to zero and then finding optimal prices.[102] This increases premiums by 9 percent and reduces the size of the market (lowers insurance coverage) by

---

[102] Recall that adverse selection is manifested as a positive impact of premiums on claims. This positive relationship reduces the profit-maximizing price for insurers, since setting a higher price attracts enrollees who are higher risk and more expensive.

18 percent. Welfare falls by 7 percent. This is interesting, because in this situation where there is market power, welfare is improved by the presence of adverse selection. This is entirely the opposite of the impact of adverse selection in a competitive insurance market. Starc goes on to calculate the impact of setting premiums equal to average and to marginal claims. These lead to large reductions in prices—44 and 45 percent, respectively. The median compensating variation to consumers is $644 ($670), and falls to $230 ($230) net of reduced producer profits.

These results emphasize the substantial market power exercised in this market. It points out that insurance subsidies or mandates will mostly result in increased rents to sellers, with little impact on welfare. Starc interprets the low demand elasticity and associated high degree of market power as due to strong brand loyalty. The strong brand loyalty provides sellers with a strong incentive to engage in extensive marketing and promotion activities. Policies to reduce brand effects, such as providing better consumer information, or attracting entry, can substantially enhance welfare.

Another paper that models both adverse selection and market power in insurance markets is Lustig (2010). Lustig examines the market for Medicare + Choice plans in 2000−2003. Medicare + Choice are private managed care plans that Medicare beneficiaries may choose as an alternative to traditional Medicare (the current version of this program is called Medicare Advantage). Lustig has a clever idea to identify adverse selection. Consumers' preferences for plan generosity should increase plans' costs if there's adverse selection. He recovers preferences from demand estimation, then estimates plans' cost function to test for adverse selection. He finds that generosity preferences have a significant impact on plan fixed costs, but not the marginal cost of plan generosity. Further, consumers' health risk has no significant impact on insurers' costs. This is a very clever test, and the results are interesting, but they do not seem very supportive of adverse selection. It seems like generosity preferences should affect insurers' marginal costs of generosity, as should consumers' health risks. Lustig then goes on to do welfare analysis. In particular, he uses the model estimates to simulate welfare when adverse selection is eliminated, then compares this to welfare measured at the allocation observed in the data. This gain from eliminating adverse selection is simulated for markets with increasing numbers of insurers $(1,2,\ldots,6,>6)$ to generate effects of competition. Lustig finds that the gains to eliminating adverse selection increase monotonically in the number of insurance firms. For example, in one of his simulations Lustig finds that removing adverse selection eliminates 17 percent of the difference in welfare between the observed and socially optimal outcomes where there's a monopoly, while it eliminates 35 percent of the difference in a duopoly, and 50 percent where there are six or more firms. This implies that when there is market power most of the welfare loss is due to the exercise of market power as opposed to adverse selection.

An earlier paper by Town and Liu (2003) focuses on estimating the welfare associated with Medicare + Choice, and conducts an analysis of the impact of competition on welfare. Their model does not allow for adverse selection. They find that the creation of the M + C program resulted in approximately $15.6 billion in consumer surplus and $52 billion in profits from 1993 to 2000 (in 2000 dollars). They find evidence of competitive effects. Consumer surplus increases in the number of plans in a county, and most of the increase in welfare is due to increased premium competition. Comparing monopoly markets versus markets with four firms, they find that 81 percent of the difference in welfare (higher in quadropoly markets) is due to increased premium competition. Of the remainder, 3 percent is from increased product variety and 8 percent from prescription drug coverage.

As stated previously, most of the literature on health insurance markets has focused on market imperfections due to asymmetric information (Breyer et al., 2012). The smaller and newer literature on market power in health insurance markets, which we have just been describing, abstracts away from issues of asymmetric information. The papers by Starc and Lustig represent significant innovations by modeling a health insurance market with adverse selection and market power. While the models differ, and are applied to different markets (Medigap, Medicare Advantage), both sets of results point to market power as the major source of welfare loss in this market, as opposed to adverse selection. We should also note that the studies by Starc (2010) and Lustig (2010) are not necessarily inconsistent with the studies by Dafny (2010), Dafny et al. (2011b), and Dranove et al. (2003). Both sets of studies point to the existence of market power in health insurance, and market power decreasing in the number of firms. It is also worth noting that these structural studies of health insurance markets find much larger estimates of demand responsiveness than have studies that estimate demand using insurance choices by employees within a single firm. Those studies find evidence of substantial switching costs (Handel, 2010) or large (and persistent) plan preference heterogeneity (Carlin and Town, 2009) that are associated with low estimates of demand elasticity.

5.2.2. Studies of the Elasticity of Demand for Health Insurance

There have been many studies of the elasticity of demand for health insurance. We do not attempt a complete review here. Our purpose is instead to report a few estimates as a means of providing insight into the potential for competition in the health insurance market. If the elasticity of demand facing a firm is low, then there is not much potential for market power.[103] Most of the US evidence comes from studies of employee choice among plans within firms. The Carlin and Town and Handel studies

---

[103] A traditional measure of market power, the Lerner Index, which measures the ratio of the price—marginal cost markup to price, is equal to the absolute value of the inverse of the firm's own-price elasticity of demand.

are recent examples of that. Prior work estimating demand elasticities using employee choice among plans at a single employer found substantially larger demand responsiveness than the more recent studies (e.g. Cutler and Reber (1998), -0.3 to -0.6; Royalty and Solomon (1999), -1 to -3.5; Strombom et al. (2002), -0.84 to -6.59). Unfortunately these estimates are from choices within a firm. We do not really know how much they tell us about the market. If they are informative they indicate that firms do face demand for insurance products with some elasticity, but not much. Even an elasticity of -6.59 implies that 15 percent of the price is markup (Lerner Index $= 0.15$), which is a substantial amount of market power.

Table 9.14 summarizes some relevant studies. There are some older studies of insurance choice in markets. Dowd and Feldman (1994) examine the health plan choices of five employers located in Minneapolis–St. Paul. They estimate a firm demand elasticity of -7.9. Atherly et al. (2004) estimate the choices of Medicare beneficiaries among Medicare + Choice plans. They estimate a firm demand elasticity of -4.57. As we noted previously, even a firm demand elasticity of $(\sim)$ -8 implies a substantial markup (12.5 percent).

A number of recent studies estimate the elasticity of demand using choice among health insurance plans in the Netherlands and in Germany. The Netherlands mandates that all individuals purchase health insurance, which is sold by private firms. As in Switzerland, benefits are standardized (although there is supplemental coverage available) and there is guaranteed issue. Insurers set their own community-rated premiums. The specifics of the German system differ from that of the Netherlands, but the key factor is that individuals have choice across insurers (referred to as sickness funds), and the amount that they pay differs. Van Dijk et al. (2008) use administrative data from

Table 9.14 Insurance Market: Firm Demand Elasticity Empirical Studies

Study	Time Period	Geographic Area	Payers	Estimates
Dowd and Feldman (1994)	1988–1993	US (Minneapolis, St. Paul)	Private insurers	-7.9
Atherly et al. (2004)	1998	US	M + C	-4.57
van Dijk et al. (2008)	1993–2002	Netherlands	Private Insurers	-0.10 to -0.38
Schut et al. (2003)	1997–2000 (Germany), 1998–2000 (Netherlands)	Germany, Netherlands	Private insurers	-3.45 (Germany), -0.41 (Netherlands)
Tamm et al. (2007)	2001–2004	Germany	Private insurers	-0.45 (short run), -12 (long run)

the Netherlands, and estimate the price elasticity of residual demand facing an insurance firm as ranging from -0.10 (for women aged $55-64$) to -0.38 (for men aged $25-34$). These are very low firm elasticities, which seems to imply little potential for competition in the Dutch health insurance market. Since no profit-maximizing firm should operate in the inelastic portion of their demand curve, these numbers seem too low to represent actual residual demand elasticities. Unfortunately van Dijk et al. only have one year of actual data—they construct a synthetic panel from the actual data, given institutional facts about the market. This may have something to do with the low estimates of elasticities.

Schut et al. (2003) estimate demand elasticities for the Netherlands and for Germany. They estimate the firm elasticity of demand for Germany to be -3.45 (in $1997-2000$). The Dutch elasticity is estimated at most to be -0.41 ($1998-2000$). Again, this seems implausible as a firm elasticity of demand. Tamm et al. (2007) use panel data from Germany over the period $2001-2004$ and find a short-run price elasticity of approximately -0.5. The long-run elasticity is approximately -12.

Overall, the results that find estimated firm demand elasticities below (minus) 1 are hard to understand. Those that are greater than 1 in absolute value are what one would expect. Nonetheless, those numbers, like the earlier estimates from the US, taken at face value, indicate the presence of substantial market power on the part of insurers in the German health insurance market.

5.3. Summary

There has not been much empirical research on competition in health insurance markets until very recently, as the dates of most of the studies reviewed in this section demonstrate. Most of the studies find evidence that competition leads to lower prices. In the US, the papers by Dafny and Starc present evidence that the markets for large employer insurance and for Medigap are highly concentrated, leading to higher prices. The studies by Frank and Lamiraud, Maestas et al., and Bolhaar et al. document substantial price dispersion and search costs. The Frank and Lamiraud study suggests that consumers may be subject to psychological biases that undermine the market mechanism. There are not many studies of the elasticity of demand faced by insurance firms for their products in the market. Those that exist for the US and Germany do find fairly substantial elasticities of demand, although it should be noted that even those estimates imply that insurers possess substantial market power. The demand elasticity estimates for the Netherlands are all below -1. Since firms should not be operating on the inelastic portions of their demand curves this presents a bit of a puzzle. Further work is required to understand what is driving these estimates. If it truly is consumer behavior, then more work has to be done understanding the demand side of this market.

Overall, the studies reviewed in this section represent substantial additions to knowledge. Further research is required on both the demand and supply sides of this market. The Netherlands insurance market and the market for private health insurance in the US present opportunities for employing careful economic modeling to advance our understanding of this complicated market. In addition, at present there are no studies of competition in the US (private) markets for small group or individual insurance (we presume due to data limitations). Those are the markets most frequently referred to as functioning poorly. Understanding how well these markets function, and the role played by competition, is an important task for economic research.

6. STUDIES OF PHYSICIAN SERVICES MARKETS

6.1. Introduction

Over the years a great deal of attention has been paid by health economists to issues regarding physicians. The majority of that work has focused on the role of asymmetric information. A great deal of that has been about the impact of asymmetric information on the market relationships between patients and physicians, i.e. physician-induced demand. Another component has been focused on incentives and payment mechanisms for physicians. Relatively little, however, has focused on competition *per se.* One of the reasons for that, perhaps, is the fact that the majority of physician services markets have large numbers of sellers and entry into a (local) market is relatively easy. It seems reasonable to characterize most markets for physician services as monopolistically competitive, and a relatively mild form of monopolistic competition at that.

There are some reasons, however, to think that the monopolistic competition model may be an accurate depiction of these markets no longer. Insurers no longer allow their enrollees to see any physician they like. Physicians must be members of the insurer's network. This implies that entry into a market requires entry into an insurer's provider network (at least one). This may be a more substantial cost associated with entry than existed previously. Separately, the nature of competition also depends on the product markets. Markets for more specialized services have fewer sellers. The costs of entry into a specific local market may be higher due to the need for access to specialized labor and facilities. In any event, the extent of competition in the aggregate is limited by the total stock of physicians who can supply these specialized services. Given the limited entry of new physicians into the specialties that supply these services there is only so much competition possible.

In addition, geographic markets may be fairly limited. They are almost certainly smaller than an entire metropolitan area. As a consequence, buyers who wish to have physician practices in their network in locations convenient for their enrollees may be facing fewer sellers than it might appear. An additional factor is the possibility of monopsony power in physician services markets. Insurance companies are large relative to physician practices. It may appear that insurers may be able to exercise monopsony power as buyers. The monopolistic competition model does not admit that possibility and thus is not useful for considering this issue. A posted price model of monopsony (or more accurately oligopsony) is an alternative, but does not really capture the true nature of buyer and seller interchange in this market.

There is some recent theoretical work which considers the impact of competition among physicians in an asymmetric information setting. Allard et al. (2009) examine physicians' provision of care under information asymmetry in a dynamic game. Without repetition all physicians provide minimum effort. With repetition, competition can serve to discipline physicians—it is even possible the physicians will supply optimal effort. Introducing patient switching costs reduces the effect of competition, but it still serves to set a lower bound on physician effort. Competition serves a socially useful role in disciplining shirking by physicians in the face of asymmetric information.

Dulleck and Kerschbamer (2009) analyze the case where there is a competitive market with experts and discounters supplying consumers. Experts can diagnose and treat problems, while discounters can only offer a treatment (without performing diagnosis). They show that in a competitive market experts may refrain from diagnosis to prevent consumers from obtaining a lower price for treatment from a discounter. In this setting, competition does not enhance welfare.

The bargaining model we describe in section 3.1 could also be applied to physicians, although it does not include asymmetric information. It admits market power on either side of the market through the bargaining abilities and threat points of the buyers and sellers. However, at present data limitations (at least for the US) preclude the estimation of such a model. Indeed, the empirical literature on physician competition is quite sparse. This is undoubtedly mostly due to lack of data with which to test hypotheses about competition. It may also be that health economists' attention has been drawn elsewhere. There is no doubt that there are interesting and important issues to address in this area.

6.2. Empirical Studies of Physician Services Markets

In what follows, we review the empirical literature on competition in physician services markets. We focus mostly on research that has been published (or at least written) since the previous volume of this Handbook came out. The papers are divided into two areas: entry and market structure, and studies of pricing conduct. Table 9.15 contains summary information on these studies.

Table 9.15 Physician Services Market: Competition Empirical Studies

Study	Time Period	Geographic Area	Empirical Approach	Payers	Outcome Measure	Competition Measure	Effect of Competition
Newhouse et al. (1982)	1970, 1979	US; 23 states	Reduced form	All	Physician location	Total # of physicians	Increase # MDs($\uparrow$) → *Prob. MD in small community* $\uparrow$
Rosenthal et al. (2005)	1979, 1999	US; 23 states	Reduced form	All	Physician location	Total # of physicians	Increase # MDs($\uparrow$) → *Prob. MD in small community* $\uparrow$
Isabel and Paula (2010)	1996, 2007	Portugal	Reduced form	All	Physician location	Total # of physicians	Increase # MDs($\uparrow$) → *Prob. MD in small community* $\uparrow$
Brown (1993)	1990	Alberta, Canada	Reduced form	All	Physician location	Total # of physicians	Increase # MDs($\uparrow$) → *Prob. MD in small community* $\uparrow$
Dionne et al. (1987)	1977	Quebec, Canada	Reduced form	All	Physician location	Total # of physicians	Increase # MDs($\uparrow$) → *Prob. MD in small community* $\uparrow$
Schaumans and Verboven (2008)	2001	Belgium	Entry model; simulation	All	Population required to support another firm	# of physicians, pharmacies	Increase (simulation) *Pharmacy free entry → welfare* $\uparrow$
Gunning and Sickles (2007)	1998	US	Structural (demand, pricing equation, marginal costs, conduct parameter)	Private insurers	Price–cost margin	Conduct parameter	Reject perfect competition; do not reject Cournot

Wong (1996)	1991	US	Reduced form	Private insurers	Price–cost margin	Panzar–Rosse test statistic	Reject monopoly, perfect competition; do not reject monopolistic competition
Bradford and Martin (2000)	1986	US	Reduced form (demand, pricing, incentives, # of partners)	Private insurers	Price, incentives, # of partners	Physican density	Increase physician density → price ↓, incentives ↑, # of *partners* ↓
Schneider et al. (2008a)	2002	California	SCP	Private insurers	Price	Physician HHI, insurance HHI	Physician HHI: increase (↑); insurer HHI: no effect
Eisenberg (2011)	1996, 1998, 2000, 2004, 2008	US	Reduced form	Medicare	Physician participation	NA	Inelastic physician supply response to Medicare price ⇒ monopsony power

6.2.1. Studies of Entry and Market Structure

Location theory implies that there will be a minimum population necessary for a given area to support a physician of a particular specialty. The smaller the total number of physicians in a given specialty, the greater the critical value of population. If the total number of physicians expands, the minimum population necessary to support a physician will fall. This was first exposited and tested by Newhouse et al. (1982), who found that the size of a town affects the probability of having a physician located there. They also make use of the fact that the number of specialists in the US increased dramatically over the decade of the 1970s. The theory predicts that towns that did not previously have a specialist would gain them at a greater rate than those that did. They find that this is so.

Rosenthal et al. (2005) revisit this hypothesis using data from the 1980s and 1990s. They examine 23 states with low physician to population ratios. The total number of physicians in these states doubles from 1970 to 1999. They find that communities of all sizes gained physicians over this period, but that the impact was larger for smaller communities, as predicted by the theory.

A recent paper by Isabel and Paula (2010) examines some of these issues using data for Portugal from 1996 and 2007. The total number of physicians in Portugal grew by approximately 30 percent over that period and the number per capita grew by approximately 22 percent. They estimate a static model using 2007 data and find that population size has a large and significant impact on the number of physicians per capita located in an area. They also test a dynamic model and find that areas that had more physicians per capita in 1996 had lower growth in the number of physicians per capita. This is consistent with the hypothesis of Newhouse et al. Brown (1993) finds confirmation of the hypothesis for the Canadian province of Alberta, although the evidence is not overwhelming. A study by Dionne et al. (1987) also found this to be true for the province of Québec, Canada.[104] The results of these studies are consistent with competitive effects from entry.

A recent paper by Schaumans and Verboven (2008) examines the determinants of entry in physician services markets in Belgium. They consider the entry decisions of pharmacies as well. Pharmacies and physician practices provide complementary services—physicians prescribe drugs and pharmacists dispense them. As a consequence, each type of firm benefits from the presence of the other. Both prescription drug prices and physician services prices are heavily regulated in Belgium. Therefore, both pharmacies and physician practices only engage in non-price competition (convenience, quality of service, quality of care, etc.). The entry of physicians into local

---

[104] Dionne et al. have the innovation of controlling for the number of good restaurants in a community. They find this to influence physician location. It remains an open question if Québécois physicians are uniquely responsive to restaurant quality—alas, no such data have been employed by researchers in other countries (or other parts of Canada).

markets is free, but pharmacy entry is regulated—there is a maximum number of pharmacies allowed in an area based on the local population. Schaumans and Verboven adapt the models of Brenahan and Reiss (1991) and Mazzeo (2002) to allow for entry restrictions for pharmacies and that products sold by the two types of firms (pharmacies and physicians) may be strategic complements.[105] As in the Brenahan and Reiss and Mazzeo work, this is a static game and the outcomes in terms of market structure (numbers of firms of both types), as opposed to firm identities, is what is modeled. They find that the population necessary to support a given number of firms increases approximately proportionately with the number of firms. As in Brenahan and Reiss, this implies that entry does not lead to tougher competition. As mentioned previously, price competition is not feasible for physicians' practices or pharmacies in Belgium. These results imply that they do not engage in more intense price competition as more firms of their own type enter a market. They also find that the population necessary to support another physician practice falls with the number of pharmacies, and vice versa. This supports the hypothesis of strategic complementarities.

Schaumans and Verboven then use the parameter estimates from the model to simulate the impacts of policy reform toward pharmacies. They consider easing entry restrictions by increasing the maximum number of pharmacies allowed in an area, and reducing pharmacies' regulated markups. They find that simply allowing free entry (no change in markups) would increase the number of pharmacies by 173 percent. The complementarities between pharmacies and physician practices lead to a 7 percent increase in the number of physician practices as a result of the entry liberalization for pharmacies. If pharmacy markups are reduced to 50 percent of their original levels then with free entry the number of pharmacies increases by 44 percent and the number of physician practices increases by six-tenths of 1 percent. Not surprisingly, a drop in markups decreases the magnitude of entry, but it is still extensive. The results of Schaumans and Verboven do not indicate conduct changing with the number of firms, but this is a very heavily regulated environment, so it is unlikely the results are very general except for other countries with similar regulatory environments.

6.2.2. Studies of Pricing Conduct

Gunning and Sickles (2007) estimate a structural model of pricing conduct by physician practices. They employ the framework described in Bresnahan (1989) to estimate the conduct parameter θ in the following pricing equation (for quantity setters):[106]

---

[105] Brenahan and Reiss (1991) test whether conduct changes with the number of firms in the market for doctors, dentists, plumbers, and tire dealers located in isolated markets (mostly rural) in the US. They find evidence that competition among doctors gets tougher with the number of practices in a market, up until the third. After three practices there is no further increase in the toughness of competition.

[106] Bresnahan's framework covers quantity or price setting. He refers to equation (9.37) as a "supply relation."

$$p_j = \frac{\partial c}{\partial q_j} - q_j \left[\frac{\partial q_j}{\partial p_j}\right]^{-1} \theta \tag{9.37}$$

The conduct parameter, θ, is a parameter to be estimated, along with demand and costs. The value of θ provides information about the toughness of competition. A value of θ equal to zero implies perfect competition (no markup). The farther that θ is from zero, the farther is conduct from competitive. Gunning and Sickles use data from the 1998 American Medical Association Socioeconomic Monitoring Survey (AMASMS) to estimate this model. They estimate average firm price elasticities of -1.75 to -2.35. Taken alone, these imply substantial market power and substantial markups. Their overall estimate of the conduct parameter is -1.34.

They strongly reject the null hypothesis of perfect competition, but cannot reject the hypothesis of Cournot conduct ($\theta = 1$). For generalist physicians the estimate of θ is -1.87, and the hypotheses of perfect competition and Cournot conduct are both rejected. While this is a worthy exercise, the results are surprising. An estimate of a negative value of θ implies that physician practices are pricing *below* marginal cost. This seems implausible, especially if one takes the elasticity estimates as valid. Those estimates indicate that physician practices have substantial power to mark up price over marginal cost, but the conduct parameter indicates that they do the opposite.

Identification of the conduct parameter requires a "demand rotator" (Bresnahan, 1989). Suppose an exogenous variable rotates the demand curve around the equilibrium point. If the market is perfectly competitive, there is no change in price (or quantity). If the market is imperfectly competitive there will be a change. It is not clear what sort of exogenous variation Gunning and Sickles have to rotate the demand curve. In addition, they estimate the cost function as part of the model. This is an heroic attempt. It is not clear how to measure the most important cost of a physician practice—physician opportunity cost. Since θ is estimated from the pricing equation, bias in the estimation of cost will be transmitted to the estimate of θ if cost is estimated jointly with (9.37). As a consequence, it is possible that difficulties in consistently estimating the parameters of the cost function may be a source of bias for estimating the conduct parameter.

An older paper by Wong (1996) uses a test devised by Panzar and Rosse (1987) for testing hypotheses about market structure. The Panzar–Rosse test statistic is

$$\phi^* \equiv \sum_i \frac{w_i}{R^*} \left(\frac{\partial R^*}{\partial w_i}\right) \tag{9.38}$$

where w_i represents the price of factor i and R^* is the firm's reduced form revenue function, which is a function of exogenous demand and cost shifters. The test statistic, ϕ^*, is the elasticity of equilibrium firm revenue with regard to factor prices. In the case of monopoly, the test statistic must be negative. If all factor prices increase, then marginal costs increase. The firm will then optimally choose a lower quantity and a higher price. Since a monopolist always operates on the elastic portion of their demand curve, revenues will fall. If the market is perfectly competitive, Panzar and Rosse argue that the value of the test statistic is 1. If factor prices increase, then the long-run cost curves will increase, but the quantity at which long-run average cost reaches a minimum is unchanged. As a consequence, price will increase by 1 percent, but quantity will remain unchanged, hence the value taken by ϕ^* will be 1. The derivation of the test statistic under monopolistic competition implies that ϕ^* will be less than or equal to 1 if the market is monopolistically competitive.

Wong uses data from the AMASMS in 1991 to estimate the test statistic. He estimates values of ϕ^* of 0.83 for primary care, 0.76 for general and family practice, 0.94 for internal medicine, and 0.85 for surgery. All of these estimates are significantly different from zero. The test statistics for primary care, general and family practice, and surgery are all significantly different from 1. Therefore he rejects the hypotheses of monopoly and of perfect competition (except for internal medicine). The results are consistent with monopolistic competition.

Bradford and Martin (2000) specify and model physician partnerships, then derive and estimate the reduced forms. In their model the partnership's choice of internal incentive system (profit sharing) depends on whether the firm is demand constrained. When the partnership is demand constrained, it is optimal to employ strong incentives to motivate physicians to exert more effort which will bring in business. This means unequal profit sharing, i.e. profit shares based on individuals' productivities. When the firm is not demand constrained the opposite is true. This also applies to the number of physician partners in a practice. More partners leads to weaker incentives and free riding, so their theory predicts smaller partnerships in the presence of a demand constraint. They use data from the Physician Practice Cost and Income Survey for 1986 to test their hypotheses.

They do find evidence consistent with their theory. In addition, the firm chooses the number of partners and the price they charge for their services. They find that profit sharing, partnership size, and price all respond to the number of physicians per capita in the market. Physician partnerships are significantly less likely to choose equal profit sharing the more potential competition they face in a market due to more physicians per capita being present. These firms also choose smaller size in response to more physicians per capita. Physician practices in markets where there are more rivals (physicians per capita) also set lower prices. Bradford and Martin also estimate a practice demand curve. They find that demand is responsive to the amount of physician time per visit in the practice, which they interpret as quality. The parameter estimate implies that a physician spending 3 more minutes per visit (at 10 percent increase) will lead to 9.1 more weekly visits to the practice. They also find that price decreases quantity demanded from the firm, although the implied elasticity (-0.49) is less than 1. Overall, the results of this study are consistent with physician firms' conduct becoming more competitive in response to market structure.

Schneider et al. (2008a) estimate an SCP-type model similar to what Shen et al. (2010) and Moriya et al. (2010) do for the hospital industry. They examine the impact of HHIs for physician organizations and for insurers in California on physician prices. While these models are ad hoc, one can think of them as attempting to capture the impacts of relative bargaining power on price, using buyer and seller HHIs as proxies for bargaining power. They find that physician market concentration is associated with significantly higher prices. A 1 percent increase in the physician HHI leads to 1–4 percent higher physician prices. Conversely, the health insurer HHI has no statistically significant impact on physician prices.

These results stand in sharp contrast to the findings of Shen et al. and Moriya et al., who find significant impacts of insurer concentration on price (negative). Schneider et al. stands out—there are very few studies that look at price competition in physician markets. The results have to be interpreted with some caution, however. As noted elsewhere in this chapter, SCP studies are vulnerable to problems associated with endogeneity of the HHI. The usual practice is to find some means to address this, commonly through the use of instruments of fixed effects. This issue is not addressed by Schneider et al., so some caution must be applied before making causal inference from the results of this study.

Eisenberg (2011) is a recent paper that examines monopsony power in the physician services market. Eisenberg examines whether the US Medicare program has monopsony power. He uses nationally representative data on physicians in selected markets[107] for selected years from 1996 to 2008, along with data on Medicare physician reimbursement. The idea is that Medicare physician payment rates are set administratively and should be exogenous to physician decisions.[108] Therefore variation in payment rates should trace out the physician supply curve to Medicare. One difficulty is that physicians in the US sell both to Medicare and to private insurers. If unobserved variation in the private market is correlated with Medicare payments then it will not be possible to estimate an unbiased causal effect of Medicare payment on physician supply. Unfortunately private insurance prices are not observable in the data. Eisenberg takes two approaches to deal with this problem. First, he includes a number of characteristics of local markets that likely influence the level of private insurer payments, including a measure of the insurer HHI. As a supplementary strategy, he examines only physicians in contiguous counties that had different Medicare payment rates. The idea is to reduce heterogeneity, including the private market.

---

[107] The Community Tracking Survey of the Center for Studying Health System Change, http://www.hschange.com/index.cgi?data=04.

[108] Medicare payments are based to some degree on physician practice costs but it seems unlikely that the regulators are systematically capturing marginal costs in their payment rates.

Eisenberg estimates the impact of Medicare payment rates on the probabilities that physicians will accept all, some, or no new Medicare patients. He finds that a 1 percent increase in the Medicare payment rate increases the probability that a physician will accept all new Medicare patients by 0.39–0.77 percent, reduces the probability they will only see some new Medicare patients by 0.29–0.56 percent, and reduces the probability that they will see no new Medicare patients by 0.83–1.62 percent. Physicians' participation responses are inelastic, implying that Medicare possesses monopsony power with regard to physician participation in the program. This study does not answer the question of whether Medicare has monopsony power with regard to the supply of services, nor does it address whether Medicare exercises monopsony power (although this seems unlikely given political constraints and government bureaucracy).

6.3. Summary

Empirical research on competition in physician services markets is sparse. The main reason for this is lack of data. This is frustrating, since this is a very important market and evidence is limited and often dated. Researchers in industrial organization have developed sophisticated methods for the analysis of markets. Adapting these methods or inventing new ones that address the idiosyncrasies of physician services markets represents an exciting opportunity. However, researchers will have to be entrepreneurial and innovative in finding or collecting data to estimate models of physician services markets.

7. VERTICAL RESTRAINTS AND MONOPSONY

The previous sections have all dealt with issues of horizontal competition and market power—hospitals competing against hospitals, insurers against insurers, physicians against physicians. In this section we take on two different issues regarding market power—vertical restraints and monopsony.

7.1. Vertical Restraints

7.1.1. Vertical Restraints—Theory

There is a small, but important, literature on vertical restraints in health care.[109] As in the general case, vertical integration can serve to achieve efficiencies. It can eliminate

---

[109] In health care the focus has been on vertical integration and exclusive dealing. We therefore restrict our attention to these two forms of vertical restraint. We refer to vertical integration for the most part, but make clear when exclusivity is important.

double marginalization, hold–up problems, transaction costs, and information asymmetries (improved monitoring). In the case of hospitals and insurers, there are also important spillover effects which integration can internalize. Insurers and hospitals make decisions over many matters like pricing, information systems, etc. which affect each other. Integration can allow for efficient coordination on such choices.[110]

It is also worth pointing out some other sources of potential efficiencies beyond the usual ones. Insurers may be able to obtain lower prices from hospitals, leading to improved consumer welfare. Gal-Or (1997, 1999) shows that at an exclusionary equilibrium (all insurers and hospitals are exclusive pairs), insurers obtain lower prices from hospitals in exchange for guaranteed larger volume and consumers are better off (provided that there is not too much differentiation).

Another source of possible efficiencies is the elimination of inefficient substitution. If there are multiple hospitals, say, and one hospital has greater market power than the others, and thus higher markups, an insurer will inefficiently substitute away from the hospital with market power to the other hospitals. If hospitals are not perfect substitutes to patients then this will result in a loss of utility.

It is also possible that vertical integration can lead to reduced prices. Suppose that integration eliminates double marginalization and that the integrated firm is not exclusive, i.e. it buys and sells with other market participants. Then other hospitals have to set their prices at least as low as the marginal cost of the hospital in the integrated firm in order to sell to the insurer in the integrated firm. If the hospital in the integrated firm wants to sell to outside insurers, it has to set its price as low as the outside hospitals. So, it is possible (but not necessary) that integration could lower prices via this mechanism.

The traditional concern with vertical integration, however, is that it can serve to enhance or extend market power. An integrated insurer—hospital firm may find it profitable to exclude rival insurers from access to the hospital, or charge them prices higher than the internal transfer price of the integrated firm (raising rivals' costs) (see Ma, 1997).[111] The same could be true for excluding rival hospitals from access to the insurer in the integrated firm. There may also be a horizontal aspect to the vertical integration, if, say, there are multiple hospitals that join the integrated firm. This may

---

[110] Eggleston et al. (2004) study a model of vertical integration between hospitals and physicians and hospitals and insurers. They find that vertical integration does not necessarily increase net revenues.

[111] There have been some recent theoretical advances in this literature, using more general frameworks than in previous work. These newer papers tend to find anticompetitive effects of integration or exclusivity. Bijlsma et al. (2009) show that there can be foreclosure and anticompetitive effects if there are uninsured consumers. Douven et al. (2011) demonstrate foreclosure and anticompetitive effects using a more general bargaining framework due to de Fontenay and Gans (2007). They show that any exclusionary equilibrium is likely to be anticompetitive—a much stronger result than previous work. Halbersma and Katona (2011) find that vertical integration always harms consumers. The elimination of double marginalization results in a softening of price competition between the insurers.

have the standard anticompetitive effect of horizontal merger increasing market power. Another horizontal effect is that integration may facilitate collusion. If the insurer in the integrated firm buys from outside hospitals, it can communicate pricing information between the hospital in the integrated firm and its rivals, thereby facilitating collusion.

In an industry with uncertainty and with differentiated products, like health care, integration can be inefficient without being anticompetitive, simply by reducing choice. The key here is exclusivity, not integration *per se*. If a hospital—insurer pair are exclusive, then consumers' choices are restricted. When consumers choose an insurer they do not know what kind of illness they will have should they fall ill, and therefore they have an option demand for hospitals that can best treat any illness they might contract. Exclusivity restricts choice and therefore results in a loss of utility, even if there is no anticompetitive effect. Gaynor and Ma (1996) show a loss of consumer welfare from exclusive dealing in the absence of foreclosure in such a situation.

In health care there is also the possibility of another effect on consumers—risk segmentation. Consider the following situation. Let there be two differentiated upstream hospitals: H1 and H2. Let H1 offer specialized care for very ill patients, e.g. H1 is a tertiary care facility. Let H2 offer ordinary care, but nothing specialized, e.g. H2 is a primary care facility. H1 has higher costs than H2. Let there be two downstream homogeneous insurers: I1 and I2. There are two types of consumers: high risk and low risk. The high-risk consumers have a high probability of contracting a serious illness that will require treatment at a tertiary care facility. The low-risk consumers have a low probability of this happening. Suppose that I1 and H1 are integrated and exclusive (by implication I2 and H2 also are exclusive).[112]

We conjecture that there is an equilibrium with risk segmentation.[113] I2 will offer insurance at a lower premium, since H2 has lower costs. High-risk consumers will want insurance from I1 and low-risk consumers from I2. Since there is risk segmentation, there is an efficiency loss (in addition to any welfare effects due to pricing and restriction on choice, as discussed previously). This is a very informal argument—it may not be correct. But it points to a factor to examine in health care markets.

7.1.2. A Model of Vertical Integration and Hospital Prices

The framework we laid out in section 3.1 can be used to examine the impact of hospital—insurer integration on hospital prices paid by independent insurers.[114] In

---

[112] Enhancement of market power is not the effect of interest here.

[113] Baranes and Bardey (2004) have a formal model where exclusivity leads to risk segmentation. The setup of their model is quite different from what we have proposed here. They find that exclusivity reduces hospital differentiation and intensifies price competition. They conclude that exclusivity is welfare improving.

[114] Halbersma and Katona (2011) lay out a sketch of a potential empirical framework based on their model in Appendix B of their paper.

other industries, vertical integration has been linked to an increase in rivals costs, and that is the phenomenon we focus on here.[115] More concretely, assume that hospital j is now owned by insurer m and, for now, that the insurer does not contract with any other hospitals. The insurer's ownership of the hospital changes the bargaining game by changing the agreement and disagreement payoffs for the hospital.[116] As previously in section 3.1, the negotiations between the insurer and hospital j take the other prices as given. Let $\pi_m(p_j^h)$ be the profit the insurer m earns as a function of the price hospital j negotiates with insurer h holding all other prices constant.[117] Assume that if there is an agreement $\frac{\partial \pi_m}{\partial p_j^h} > 0$ for all l—increasing the price hospital h negotiates with other insurers raises their costs and therefore raises the profits of insurer m. Disagreement profits for the vertically integrated hospital are denoted $\pi_m(D)$. We assume that the insurer profits under a disagreement between hospital j and any other insurer are greater than the insurer's profits under agreement. That is, $\pi_m(D) \geq \pi_m(p_j^h)$, $\forall p_j^h < \infty$.

The hospital's agreement and disagreement outcomes are now:

$$H_{\text{agree}} = (p_{jh} - c_j)q_{jh}(J_h) + \pi_m(p_j^h)$$

$$H_{\text{disagree}} = r_j + \pi_m(D)$$

Because π_m is a function of p_h there is no simple closed-form relationship between hospital price and the other parameters of the model. However, it is straightforward to assess the impact of integration on prices. As long as $\beta > 0$, hospital prices are decreasing in the difference between the hospital's agreement and disagreement outcomes. The more important the agreement is to the hospital, the lower are prices. Here the difference is $(p_{jh} - c_j)q_{jh}(J_h) - r_j + (\pi_m(p_j^l) - \pi_m(D))$, which is smaller than in the non-integrated case. In addition, the marginal return from increasing prices is now $q_{jh}(J_h) + \frac{\partial \pi_m}{\partial p_j^l}$, which is greater than without integration. These two effects work to force prices higher.

Similar logic shows that insurer m it will be able to negotiate lower rates with the other hospitals in the market. If the insurer pays hospital j its marginal cost for providing care, then the difference in the agreement and disagreement values for insurer h when it is negotiating with hospital k is: $c_j d_{kh} + (F_h(J_h) - F_h(J_{h-k}) - cm_{kh}) + \beta\sum_{l \neq j,k} p_{lh} d_{jlh}$. The difference between the agreement and disagreement values if the insurer owns hospital j is $(p_{jh} - c_j)d_{kh} > 0$, where p_{jh} is the price the insurer and hospital j would have negotiated if they were not jointly owned.

The intuition is straightforward. A vertically integrated insurer pays its hospital marginal cost, which implies that under a disagreement with another hospital it will

---

[115] Hastings and Gilbert (2005) study the impact of vertical integration in the gasoline industry on rivals' prices.

[116] The structure of the payoffs for the insurer is unaffected by the integration; however, the functional relationships (e.g. $F_h(J_h)$ and $F_h(J_h - j - k)$) will almost surely change.

[117] We assume that the insurer pays the hospital a transfer price equal to the marginal cost of care.

have lower disagreement expenditures. To summarize, in this framework, vertical integration leads the vertically integrated hospital to negotiate higher prices with other payers and the vertically integrated insurer to negotiate lower prices with the other hospitals in the market.

7.1.3. Empirical Evidence on Vertical Restraints

There is very little evidence at present on the impact of vertical restraints on market power. In part, that is because vertical integration has not been that common in health care. It was quite rare until the mid-1990s, and then declined rapidly thereafter. Integration between hospitals and physician practices peaked in 1996 at approximately 40 percent of all hospitals, and declined thereafter (Burns and Pauly, 2002; Ciliberto, 2005). This pattern was repeated with vertical integration of hospitals into the insurance market, although the extent of vertical integration was never as great as between hospitals and physicians (Burns and Pauly, 2002). This growth coincided with the growth of managed care, and in particular with the perceived growth in managed care organizations' negotiating power with hospitals. Nonetheless, there are reports that vertical integration and exclusive deals are on the increase in health care, in part because of elements of the health reform law in the US. Burns et al. (2000) find that hospital–physician alliances increase with the number of HMOs in the market. They infer that providers may be integrating in order to achieve or enhance market power. More recently, Berenson et al. (2010) conducted 300 interviews with health care market participants, and report that increased bargaining power through joint negotiations listed as one of several reasons for hospital–physician alliances.

Certain types of vertical relations in health care have been the subject of significant antitrust scrutiny—exclusive dealing between physician practices and hospitals (usually for a specialized service, e.g. radiology, anesthesiology, or pathology), and most-favored-nations clauses between insurers and providers, which require the provider to give the insurer a rate as low as it gives to any buyer (see Gaynor and Haas-Wilson, 1998; Haas-Wilson, 2003, for reviews of vertical issues in health care).[118]

In spite of the interest in this topic, there is relatively little evidence on the effects of vertical restraints in health care. The evidence comes from reduced-form studies.

---

[118] Complaints about exclusive contracts between hospitals and physician practices are the most numerous type of antitrust case brought in health care. One of these cases was decided by the Supreme Court (*Jefferson Parish Hosp. Dist. No. 2 v. Hyde*, 466 US 2(1984)), and represents an important legal precedent on exclusive dealing and tying. There have also been a number of cases on most-favored-nations clauses, e.g. *Ocean State Physicians Health Plan v. Blue Cross & Blue Shield*, 883 F.2d 1101 (1st Cir. 1989), *cert. denied*, 494 US 1027 (1990) and *Blue Cross & Blue Shield v. Marshfield Clinic*, 65 F.3d 1406 (7th Cir. 1995), *cert. denied*, 116 S. Ct. 1288 (1996).

Ciliberto and Dranove (2005) and Cuellar and Gertler (2005) are the only two papers of which we are aware that examine the competitive impacts of vertical integration in health care. Both papers look at the effects of hospital—physician practice integration on hospital prices. The two studies find opposite results—Cuellar and Gertler find evidence consistent with anticompetitive effects of physician—hospital integration, while Ciliberto and Dranove find no such evidence. As Gaynor (2006a) points out, these seemingly contradictory results are fully consistent with economic theory—vertical integration can be anticompetitive and lead to higher prices or be efficiency enhancing and have the opposite result.

Research on efficiencies from integration is not very encouraging. Burns and Muller (2008) review the empirical evidence on hospital—physician relationships. They find little evidence of an impact of integration on costs, quality, access or clinical integration. Madison (2004) investigates the relationship between hospital—physician affiliations and patient treatments, expenditures, and outcomes using data on Medicare heart attack patients. She finds little evidence of any impacts of hospital—physician relationships.

If integration between various types of providers or providers and insurers grows, there may be continued interest (and more data) in these relationships. The model we sketched out above in section 7.1.2, or one like it, may provide a useful framework for future empirical investigation.

7.2. Health Care Providers and Monopsony Power

It is well known that market power in the purchase of health care inputs can (but does not necessarily) lead to welfare loss.[119] While the textbook depiction of monopsony results in a reduction in output below the competitive equilibrium, other models of monopsony can yield more ambiguous welfare results. Herndon (2002) shows that if sellers are forced into all-or-nothing decisions by a buyer with monopsony power that there is no reduction in output and no welfare loss. Consumers are better off, because the sellers' prices have been reduced with no decrease in output. She argues that this model applies to health care, where insurers are able to force such decisions on providers.

There is also a literature that examines why large purchasers (e.g. Walmart) are able to negotiate more favorable terms with their suppliers (e.g. Snyder, 1996). Insurer economies of scale may ultimately be based on their ability to exercise some monopsony power and negotiate lower provider payment rates. The issue of the role of monopsony extends beyond any individual antitrust case or the understanding of the provider price-setting mechanism, but is relevant for considering health system design. Health policy commenters have argued that the relative cost advantage of

---

[119] The analysis of monopsony power dates to Robinson (1933). Gaynor and Vogt (2000) provide a nice review of the theory of monopsony and vertical foreclosure.

single payer systems principally rests in their ability to exercise monopsony power over providers.[120]

Health care providers sell their services to insurers and purchase labor and other inputs in order to produce their services. Because of the role in the supply chain, health care providers can both exercise monopsony power in the purchase of inputs (namely labor) or can be subject to monopsony power by insurers. The framework outlined above in section 3.1 provides a lens through which one can examine the role of insurer bargaining power in affecting provider prices. A hospital negotiating with a monopsonist insurer will face a large discrepancy between its agreement and disagreement outcomes, which, in turn, implies that the negotiated price will be lower than if there were other insurers in the market. In this model, the mechanism through which this occurs is the increased volume of patients that a monopsonist insurer brings to the hospital under an agreement. Higher volumes imply a lower price.

The empirical literature examining monopsony generally examines the role of insurance market concentration on provider prices. Much of this literature naturally overlaps with the analysis of provider market concentration and provider prices. The typical analysis will include measures of both insurer and provider market concentration as right-hand-side variables. Shen et al. (2010) find that hospital revenue was significantly lower in markets with high levels of HMO penetration and low hospital concentration. Moriya et al. (2010) find that increases in insurance market concentration are significantly associated with decreases in hospital prices, whereas increases in hospital concentration are non-significantly associated with increases in prices, although the results are very sensitive to the inclusion of one or two states. A hypothetical merger between two of five equally sized insurers is estimated to decrease hospital prices by 6.7 percent. However, given the fragility of the results, this effect should be interpreted with caution. As mentioned previously, Schneider et al. (2008a) apply a model similar to Shen et al. and Moriya et al. to the physician services market. In contrast to the preceding papers, they find no significant impact of insurance market concentration on physician prices. However, they find that physician market concentration raises physician prices significantly.

A longstanding concern with hospital market power is that not only can they leverage it into higher prices from insurers but they may be able to reduce nurses' wages below competitive levels. Yett (1975) argued that the chronic shortage of nurses may result from monopsony equilibrium. However, the importance of monopsony in the nursing market is inversely related to the elasticity of labor supply. For a number of reasons, including the large number of non-hospital nursing jobs and the large numbers of nurses that move into and out of the labor force, that elasticity is likely to be high. Sullivan (1989) is one of the early papers that uses the methods of the new

---

[120] For example, see Reinhardt et al. (2004) and Anderson et al. (2003).

empirical industrial organization (Bresnahan, 1989). He estimates the inverse elasticity of nurse labor supply to hospitals as 0.79 over a one-year period and 0.26 over a three-year period. He interprets these estimates as evidence of substantial monopsony power on the part of hospitals.

More recently, the role of monopsony in the purchase of health care labor inputs has received significantly less attention. Staiger et al. (2010) rely on exogenous changes in Veterans Affairs hospitals to identify the extent of hospital monopsony power. They find very inelastic labor supply curves and conclude that their results are consistent with the presence of monopsony power. Hirsch and Schumacher (2005) critique the Staiger et al. (2010) approach and use variation in hospital market structure over time to estimate a reduced-form wage regression. They find no link between hospital market concentration and nurses' wages suggesting that hospitals do not exercise monopsony power.

Matsudaira (2010) uses the effects of a minimum staffing law in California to estimate the elasticity of labor supply in long-term care facilities. Only those facilities whose staffing was below the required level had to hire additional staff. Matsudaira finds that these facilities added staff with no corresponding increase in wages, implying a perfectly elastic labor supply curve, and no monopsony power.

As mentioned previously, the recent study by Eisenberg (2011) examines whether Medicare has monopsony power as a purchaser of physician services by estimating the impact of Medicare physician payment rates on physician willingness to participate in the program by taking on new Medicare patients. He finds that physician participation with regard to Medicare payment is positive, but inelastic, implying that Medicare has monopsony power (whether they exercise it is another question).

To summarize, it is clear that the bargaining leverage of insurers, which is determined by their size and the presence of alternative insurers, lowers provider prices. It is in that sense that monopsony clearly affects the costs of health care provision. However, evidence of monopsony in health care markets is quite limited.

8. SUMMARY AND CONCLUSIONS

In this chapter we have attempted to lay out a framework for thinking about competition in health care markets. In particular, we sketched out what a relatively simple model of bargaining between insurers and providers might look like. Many of the market relationships in health care can be captured with such a model. It provides an intuitive framework for thinking about the economics of these markets as well as a springboard for developing econometric models for estimation.

We also reviewed the recent literature on competition in health care markets. There has been an explosion of work in this area since the publication of the first volume of the *Handbook of Health Economics*. Four developments in particular are worth noting.

One is the increasing use of modern structural models of industrial organization, adapted to the specifics of health care markets. The chapters by Dranove and Satterthwaite (2000) and Gaynor and Vogt (2000) described structural models that might be estimated, but that had not yet been executed at the time of the Handbook's publication. The models described in those chapters, and more sophisticated models, were estimated only a few short years ago. In addition, there has been increasing (and productive) interchange between health economics and industrial organization scholars, leading to more sophisticated and informative modeling of health care markets.

Second is the volume of empirical work on hospital markets, particularly work on quality competition. At the time of the writing of the first volume of the Handbook there was a fair amount of non-structural work on hospital price competition, but virtually none on hospital quality competition. This has changed dramatically.

Third is the entry of work on competition in health care markets in countries other than the US, and by non-US scholars working in this area. This is largely due to health system reforms in countries like England, the Netherlands, and Switzerland designed to increase the use of markets. This has become an important area of work internationally and is no longer US-centric.

Fourth is the very recent work on health insurance markets. This development is so recent that most of the papers we cite in this chapter are yet to be published. This expansion of interest in this area is something that hopefully will continue.

It is disappointing that there is so little empirical research on competition in physician services markets. In the US this is largely due to data limitations. Hopefully scholars will find ways to surmount this problem and we will see the kinds of advances in knowledge about this market that we have seen for hospital markets.

There are tremendous research opportunities for ambitious scholars interested in the economics of health care markets. We expect to see further developments in thinking about the economics of these markets and in devising estimable models for analysis.

REFERENCES

Abraham, J. M., Gaynor, M., & Vogt, W. B. (2007). Entry and competition in local hospital markets. *Journal of Industrial Economics, LV, 2*, 265–288.

Ackerberg, D., Benkard, L., Berry, S., & Pakes, A. (2007). Econometric tools for analyzing market outcomes. In J. Heckman & E. Leamer (Eds.), *Handbook of econometrics* (Vol. 6). Amsterdam and London: Elsevier North-Holland.

Aguirregabiria, V. & Mira, P. (2007). Sequential estimation of dynamic discrete games. *Journal of Econometrics, 75*(1), 1–53.

Akosa Antwi, Y. O. D., Gaynor, M., & Vogt, W. B. (2006). *A competition index for differentiated products oligopoly with an application to hospital markets.* Carnegie Mellon University.

Akosa Antwi, Y. O. D., Gaynor, M., & Vogt, W. B. (2009). A bargain at twice the price? California hospital prices in the new millennium. *Forum for Health Economics and Policy, 12*(1), Article 3. < http://www.bepress.com/fhep/12/1/3/ >.

Allard, M., Léger, P., & Rochaix, L. (2009). Provider competition in a dynamic setting. *Journal of Economics & Management Strategy, 18*(2), 457–486.

American Medical Association (2010). Competition in health insurance: A comprehensive study of US markets. Technical report, American Medical Association, Chicago, IL, 2006–2010 editions.

Anderson, G., Reinhardt, U., Hussey, P., & Petrosyan, V. (2003). It's the prices, stupid: Why the United States is so different from other countries. *Health Affairs, 22*(3), 89–105.

Arcidiacono, P. & Miller, R. (2010). *CCP estimation of dynamic discrete choice models with unobserved heterogeneity.* Carnegie Mellon University, Duke University.

Ashwood, S. J., Reid, R. O., Setodji, C. M., Weber, E., Gaynor, M., & Mehotra, A. (2011). *What is the impact of retail clinics on overall utilization?* The Rand Corporation, Carnegie Mellon University.

Atherly, A., Dowd, B. E., & Feldman, R. (2004). The effect of benefits, premiums, and health risk on health plan choice in the Medicare program. *Health Services Research, 39*(4, Part 1), 847–864.

Bajari, P., Benkard, L., & Levin, J. (2007). Estimating dynamic models of impefect competition. *Econometrica, 75*(5), 1331–1370.

Bajari, P., Hong, H., Park, M., & Town, R. (2010). *Regression discontinuity designs with an endogenous forcing variable and an application to contracting in health care.* University of Minnesota.

Baker, L. & Brown, M. (1999). Managed care, consolidation among health care providers, and health care: Evidence from mammography. *RAND Journal of Economics, 30*(2), 351–374.

Baker, L. & Phibbs, C. (2002). Managed care, technology adoption, and health care: The adoption of neonatal intensive care. *RAND Journal of Economics, 33*(3), 524–548.

Baker, L. & Wheeler, S. (1998). Managed care and technology diffusion: The case of MRI. *Health Affairs, 17*(5), 195–207.

Balan, D. & Brand, K. (2009). *Simulating hospital merger simulations.* Federal Trade Commission.

Baranes, E. & Bardey, D. (2004). Competition in health care markets and vertical restraints. Cahiers de Recherche du LASER 013-03-04, Laboratoire de Sciences Économiques de Richter (LASER), Université de Montpellier, Montpellier, France. Available at < http://www.laser.univ-montp1.fr/Cahiers/cahier130404.pdf/ >.

Barro, J., Huckman, R., & Kessler, D. (2006). The effects of cardiac specialty hospitals on the cost and quality of medical care. *Journal of Health Economics, 25*(4), 702–721.

Beauchamp, A. (2010). *Regulation, imperfect competition, and the US abortion market.* Boston College.

Berenson, R., Ginsburg, P., & Kemper, N. (2010). Unchecked provider clout in California foreshadows challenges to health reform. *Health Affairs, 29*(4), 699.

Berry, S., Levinsohn, J., & Pakes, A. (1995). Automobile prices in market equilibrium. *Econometrica, 63*(4), 841–890.

Bijlsma, M., Boone, J., & Zwart, G. (2009). *Selective contracting and foreclosure in health care markets.* Tilburg University.

Bloom, N. & Van Reenen, J. (2007). Measuring and explaining management practices across firms and nations. *Quarterly Journal of Economics, 122*(4), 1351–1408.

Bloom, N., Propper, C., Seiler, S., & Van Reenen, J. (2010). *The impact of competition on management quality: Evidence from public hospitals.* Cambridge, MA: National Bureau of Economic Research.

Bolhaar, J., Lindeboom, M., & van der Klaauw, B. (2010). *Insurance search, switching behavior and the role of group contracts.* Vrije Universiteit Amsterdam.

Bowblis, J. (2010). Ownership conversion and closure in the nursing home industry. *Journal of Health Economics, 20*(6), 631–644.

Bradford, D. & Martin, R. (2000). Partnerships, profit sharing, and quality competition in the medical profession. *Review of Industrial Organization, 17*, 193–208.

Brand, K., Garmon, C., Gowrisankaran, G., Nevo, A., & Town, R. (2011). Estimating the price impact of hospital mergers: Inova's proposed acquisition of Prince William hospital. Unpublished manuscript, Federal Trade Commission, University of Arizona, Northwestern University, University of Minnesota.

Bresnahan, T. & Reiss, P. (1990). Entry in monopoly markets. *Review of Economic Studies, 57*(4), 531–553.

Bresnahan, T. & Reiss, P. (1991). Entry and competition in concentrated markets. *Journal of Political Economy, 99*(5), 977–1009.

Bresnahan, T. F. (1989). Empirical studies of industries with market power. In R. Schmalensee & R. Willig (Eds.), *Handbook of industrial organization* (Vol. 2, pp. 1011–1057). Amsterdam and New York: Elsevier Science, North-Holland Chapter 17.

Breyer, F., Bundorf, M. K., & Pauly, M. V. (2012). Health care spending risk, health insurance, and payment to health plans. In T. G. McGuire, M. V. Pauly, & P. Pita Barros (Eds.), *Handbook of health economics* (Vol. 2, chapter 11, pp. 691–763). Amsterdam and London: Elsevier North-Holland.

Brown, M. (1993). Do physicians locate as spatial competition models predict? Evidence from Alberta. *Canadian Medical Association Journal, 148*(8), 1301–1307.

Buchmueller, T., Jacobson, M., & Wold, C. (2006). The effect of hospital closures on access to care. *Journal of Health Economics, 25*, 740–761.

Burgess, J., Carey, K., & Young, G. (2005). The effect of network arrangements on hospital pricing behavior. *Journal of Health Economics, 24*(2), 391–405.

Burgess, S., Propper, C., & Gossage, D. (2008). Competition and quality: Evidence from the NHS internal market 1991 – 99. *Economic Journal, 118*, 138–170.

Burns, L. & Muller, R. (2008). Hospital–physician collaboration: Landscape of economic integration and impact on clinical integration. *Milbank Quarterly, 86*(3), 375–434.

Burns, L., Bazzoli, G., Dynan, L., & Wholey, D. (2000). Impact of HMO market structure physician–hospital strategic alliances. *Health Services Research, 35*(1), 101–132.

Burns, L. R. & Pauly, M. V. (2002). Integrated delivery networks: A detour on the road to integrated health care? *Health Affairs, 21*(4), 128–143.

Burns, L. R. & Wholey, D. R. (1992). The impact of physician characteristics in conditional choice models for hospital care. *Journal of Health Economics, 11*(1), 43–62.

Canoy, M. & Sauter, W. (2009). *Hospital mergers and the public interest: Recent developments in the Netherlands*. Tilburg University.

Caplin, A. & Nalebuff, B. (1991). Aggregation and imperfect competition: On the existence of equilibrium. *Econometrica, 59*(1), 25–59.

Capps, C. (2005). *The quality effects of hospital mergers*. Bates White LLC.

Capps, C. & Dranove, D. (2004). Hospital consolidation and negotiated PPO prices. *Health Affairs, 23* (2), 175–181.

Capps, C., Carlton, D., & David, G. (2010a). *Antitrust treatment of nonprofits: Should hospitals receive special care?* Bates White LLC, University of Chicago, University of Pennsylvania.

Capps, C., Dranove, D., & Lindrooth, R. (2010b). Hospital closure and economic efficiency. *Journal of Health Economics, 29*, 87–109.

Capps, C., Dranove, D., & Satterthwaite, M. (2003). Competition and market power in option demand markets. *RAND Journal of Economics, 34*(4), 737–763.

Capps, C. S. (2009). *Federal health plan merger enforcement is consistent and robust*. Bates White LLC.

Carey, K., Burgess, J., & Young, G. (2008). Specialty and full-service hospitals: A comparative cost analysis. *Health Services Research, 43*(5), 1869–1887.

Carlin, C. & Town, R. J. (2009). *Adverse selection, welfare, and optimal pricing of employer sponsored health plans*. University of Minnesota.

Carlson, J. A. & McAfee, R. P. (1983). Discrete equilibrium price dispersion. *Journal of Political Economy, 91*(3), 480–493.

Carlton, D. W. & Perloff, J. M. (2005). *Modern industrial organization*. Boston, MA: Addison-Wesley.

Cebul, R. D. Rebitzer, J. B., Taylor, L. J., & Votruba, M. E. (2008). Organizational fragmentation and care quality in the US healthcare system. *Journal of Economic Perspectives, 22*(4), 93–113.

Chakravarty, S. (2010). *Much ado about nothing? Entry and operations of physician owned specialty hospitals*. Rutgers University.

Chakravarty, S., Gaynor, M., Klepper, S., & Vogt, W. (2006). Does the profit motive make Jack nimble? Ownership form and the evolution of the US hospital industry. *Health Economics, 15*, 345–361.

Chernew, M. (1995). The impact of non-IPA HMOs on the number of hospitals and hospital capacity. *Inquiry, 32*(2), 143–154.

Chernew, M., Gowrisankaran, G., & Fendrick, A. (2002). Payer type and the returns to bypass surgery: Evidence from hospital entry behavior. *Journal of Health Economics, 21*, 451–474.

Chernew, M., Scanlon, D., & Hayward, R. (1998). Insurance type and choice of hospital for coronary artery bypass graft surgery. *Health Services Research, 33*(3), 447–466.

Ciliberto, F. (2005). *Does organizational form affect investment decisions?* University of Virginia.

Ciliberto, F. & Dranove, D. (2005). The effect of physician–hospital affiliations on hospital prices in California. *Journal of Health Economics, 25*(1), 29–38.

Ciliberto, F. & Lindrooth, R. (2007). Exit from the hospital industry. *Economic Inquiry, 45*(1), 71–81.

Commission on Health Care Facilities in the 21st Century (2006). A plan to stabilize and strengthen New York's health care system. Final report, Commission on Health Care Facilities in the 21st Century, New York, NY. June.

Cooper, Z., Gibbons, S., Jones, S., & McGuire, A. (2011). Does hospital competition save lives? Evidence from the NHS patient choice reforms. *Economic Journal, 121*(554), 228–260.

Crawford, G. & Yurukoglu, A. (2010). *The welfare effects of bundling in multichannel television markets.* University of Warwick, Stanford University.

Cuellar, A. E. & Gertler, P. J. (2005). Strategic integration of hospitals and physicians. *Journal of Health Economics, 25*(1), 1–28.

Cullen, K., Hall, M., & Golosinskiy, A. (2009). *Ambulatory surgery in the United States, 2006.* Center for Disease Control.

Cutler, D. (2010). *Where are the health care entrepreneurs? The failure of organizational innovation in health care.* National Bureau of Economic Research.

Cutler, D., McClellan, M., & Newhouse, J. (2000). How does managed care do it? *RAND Journal of Economics, 31*(3), 526–548.

Cutler, D. M. (1995). The incidence of adverse medical outcomes under prospective payment. *Econometrica, 63*(1), 29–50.

Cutler, D. M. & Reber, S. J. (1998). Paying for health insurance: The trade-off between competition and adverse selection. *Quarterly Journal of Economics, 113*(2), 433–466.

Cutler, D. M., Huckman, R. S., & Kolstad, J. T. (2010). Input constraints and the efficiency of entry: Lessons from cardiac surgery. *American Economic Journal: Economic Policy, 2*(1), 51–76.

Dafny, L. (2005). Games hospitals play: Entry deterrence in hospital procedure markets. *Journal of Economics and Management Strategy, 14*(5), 513–542.

Dafny, L. (2009). Estimation and identification of merger effects: An application to hospital mergers. *Journal of Law and Economics, 52*(3), 523–550.

Dafny, L. (2010). Are health insurance markets competitive? *American Economic Review, 100,* 1399–1431.

Dafny, L., Dranove, D., Limbrock, F., & Scott Morton, F. (2011a). *Data impediments to empirical work in health insurance markets.* Northwestern University, Yale University.

Dafny, L., Duggan, M., & Ramanarayanan, S. (2011b). Paying a premium on your premium? Consolidation in the US health insurance industry. *American Economic Review,* forthcoming.

Dafny, L., Ho, K., & Varela, M. (2010). An individual health plan exchange: Which employees would benefit and why? *American Economic Review, 100,* 485–489.

Dahlby, B. & West, D. S. (1986). Price dispersion in an automobile insurance market. *Journal of Political Economy, 94*(2), 418–438.

De Fontenay, C. & Gans, J. (2007). *Bilateral bargaining with externalities.* University of Melbourne.

Deily, M., McKay, N., & Dorner, F. (2000). Exit and inefficiency: The effects of ownership type. *Journal of Human Resources, 35*(4), 734–737.

Dionne, G., Langlois, A., & Lemire, N. (1987). More on the geographical distribution of physicians. *Journal of Health Economics, 6,* 365–374.

Doraszelski, U. & Pakes, A. (2007). A framework for applied dynamic analysis in IO. In M. Armstrong & R. Porter (Eds.), *Handbook of industrial organization* (Vol. 3). Amsterdam and London: Elsevier North-Holland.

Doraszelski, U., & Satterthwaite, M. (2010). Computable Markov-perfect industry dynamics. *RAND Journal of Economics, 41*(2), 215–243.

Dorfman, R. & Steiner, P. (1954). Optimal advertising and optimal quality. *American Economic Review, 44*(5), 826–836.

Douven, R., Halbersma, R., Katona, K., & Shestalova, V. (2011). *Vertical integration and exclusive vertical restraints between insurers and hospitals.* Tilburg University.

Dowd, B. E. & Feldman, R. (1994). Premium elasticities of health plan choice. *Inquiry, 31*(4), 438–444.

Dranove, D. & Lindrooth, R. (2003). Hospital consolidation and costs: Another look at the evidence. *Journal of Health Economics, 22*, 983–997.

Dranove, D., Gron, A., & Mazzeo, M. (2003). Differentiation and competition in HMO markets. *Journal of Industrial Economics, 51*(4), 433–454.

Dranove, D., Lindrooth, R., White, W., & Zwanziger, J. (2008). Is the impact of managed care on hospital prices decreasing? *Journal of Health Economics, 27*, 362–376.

Dranove, D., Satterthwaite, M., & Sfekas, A. (2007). *Boundedly rational bargaining in option demand markets: An empirical application.* Northwestern University.

Dranove, D., Simon, C., & White, W. (2002). Is managed care leading to consolidation in health-care markets? *Health Services Research, 37*(3), 573–594.

Dranove, D. D. & Satterthwaite, M. A. (1992). Monopolistic competition when price and quality are imperfectly observable. *RAND Journal of Economics, 23*(4), 518–534.

Dranove, D. D. & Satterthwaite, M. A. (2000). The industrial organization of health care markets. In A. Culyer & J. Newhouse (Eds.), *Handbook of health economics* (pp. 1094–1139). New York and Oxford: Elsevier Science, North-Holland, Chapter 20.

Duggan, M. (2000). Hospital ownership and public medical spending. *Quarterly Journal of Economics, 115*(4), 1343–1373.

Duggan, M. (2002). Hospital market structure and the behavior of not-for-profit hospitals. *RAND Journal of Economics, 33*(3), 433–446.

Dulleck, U. & Kerschbamer, R. (2009). Experts vs. discounters: Consumer free-riding and experts withholding advice in markets for credence goods. *International Journal of Industrial Organization, 27*(1), 15–23.

Dunne, T., Klimek, S., Roberts, M., & Xu, D. (2009). *Entry, exit, and the determinants of market structure.* National Bureau of Economic Research.

Eggleston, K., Pepall, L., & Normany, G. (2004). Pricing coordination failures and health care provider integration. *Contributions to Economic Analysis and Policy, 3*(1), 1–29.

Eisenberg, M. (2011). *Reimbursement rates and physician participation in Medicare.* Carnegie Mellon University.

Ellison, G. & Ellison, S. (2007). *Strategic entry deterrence and the behavior of pharmaceutical incumbents prior to patent expiration.* National Bureau of Economic Research.

Encinosa, W. E. & Bernard, D. M. (2005). Hospital finances and patient safety outcomes. *Inquiry, 42*(1), 60–72.

Ericson, R. & Pakes, A. (1995). Markov-perfect industry dynamics: A framework for empirical work. *Review of Economic Studies, 62*(1), 53–82.

Escarce, J. J., Jain, A. K., & Rogowski, J. (2006). Hospital competition, managed care, and mortality after hospitalization for medical conditions: Evidence from three states. *Medical Care Research and Review, 63*(6 Suppl.), 112S–140S.

Federal Trade Commission and Department of Justice (1992). Horizontal merger guidelines. Issued April 2, 1992, Revised September, 2010.

Finkelstein, A. (2007). The aggregate effects of health insurance: Evidence from the introduction of Medicare. *Quarterly Journal of Economics, 122*(1), 1–37.

Frank, R. & Lamiraud, K. (2009). Choice, price competition and complexity in markets for health insurance. *Journal of Economic Behavior and Organization, 71*, 550–562.

Fuchs, V. (2007). Managed care and merger mania. *Journal of the American Medical Association, 277*(11), 920–921.

Gal-Or, E. (1997). Exclusionary equilibria in health-care markets. *Journal of Economics and Management Strategy, 6*(1), 5–43.

Gal-Or, E. (1999). Mergers and exclusionary practices in health care markets. *Journal of Economics and Management Strategy, 8*(3), 315–350.

Gaynor, M. (2006a). Is vertical integration anticompetitive? Definitely maybe (but that's not final). *Journal of Health Economics, 25*(1), 175.

Gaynor, M. (2006b). What do we know about competition and quality in health care markets? *Foundations and Trends in Microeconomics, 2*(6) < http://www.nowpublishers.com/product.aspx?product = MIC&doi = 0700000024/ >

Gaynor, M. & Haas-Wilson, D. (1998). Vertical relations in health care markets. In M. A. Morrisey (Ed.), *Managed care and changing health care markets* (pp. 140−163). Washington, DC: AEI Presschapter 7.

Gaynor, M. & Ma, C.-t. A. (1996). *Insurance, vertical restraints, and competition.* Carnegie Mellon University.

Gaynor, M. & Polachek, S. W. (1994). Measuring information in the market: An application to physician services. *Southern Economic Journal, 60*(4), 815−831.

Gaynor, M. & Vogt, W. B. (2000). Antitrust and competition in health care markets. In A. Culyer & J. Newhouse (Eds.), *Handbook of health economics* (pp. 1405−1487). New York and Oxford: Elsevier Science, North-Holland, Chapter 27.

Gaynor, M. & Vogt, W. B. (2003). Competition among hospitals. *RAND Journal of Economics, 34*(4), 764−785.

Gaynor, M., Moreno-Serra, R., & Propper, C. (2010). *Death by market power: Reform, competition and patient outcomes in the British National Health Service.* Carnegie Mellon University, Imperial College.

Gaynor, M., Propper, C., & Seiler, S. (2011). *Free to choose: Reform and demand response in the British National Health Service.* Carnegie Mellon University, Imperial College London, London School of Economics.

Gaynor, M., Seider, H., & Vogt, W. B. (2005). Is there a volume-outcome effect and does it matter? Yes, and yes. *American Economic Review, Papers and Proceedings, 95*(2), 243−247.

Gentzkow, M. (2007). Valuing new goods in a model with complementarity: Online newspapers. *American Economic Review* 713−745.

Geweke, J., Gowrisankaran, G., & Town, R. J. (2003). Bayesian inference for hospital quality in a selection model. *Econometrica, 71,* 1215−1238.

Ginsburg, P. (2010). *Wide variation in hospital and physician payment rates evidence of provider market power.* Center for Studying Health System Change.

Glaeser, E. (2002). *The governance of not-for-profit firms.* National Bureau of Economic Research.

Goldstein, G. S. & Pauly, M. V. (1976). Group health insurance as a local public good. In R. N. Rosett (Ed.), *The role of health insurance in the health services sector* (pp. 73−114). Cambridge, MA: National Bureau of Economic Research, Chapter 3.

Government Accountability Office (2009). State small group health insurance markets. Technical report, US Government Accountability Office, Washington, DC. GAO-09-363R.

Gowrisankaran, G. (1995). *A dynamic analysis of mergers.* Yale University.

Gowrisankaran, G. (2011). Estimating the impact of a hospital merger using the difference-in-differences of prices. *International Journal of the Economics of Business, 18*(1), 83−89.

Gowrisankaran, G. & Town, R. (1997). Dynamic equilibrium in the hospital industry. *Journal of Economics and Management Strategy, 6*(1), 45−74.

Gowrisankaran, G. & Town, R. (2003). Competition, payers, and hospital quality. *Health Services Research, 38,* 1403−1422.

Gowrisankaran, G. & Town, R. J. (1999). Estimating the quality of care in hospitals using instrumental variables. *Journal of Health Economics, 18,* 747−767.

Gowrisankaran, G., Ho, V., & Town, R. (2004). *Causality and the volume−outcome relationship in surgery.* University of Minnesota.

Gowrisankaran, G., Lucarelli, C., Schmidt-Dengler, P., & Town, R. (2011). *Government policy and the dynamics of market structure: Evidence from critical access hospitals.* University of Arizona, Cornell University, London School of Economics, University of Minnesota.

Grennan, M. (2010). *Price discrimination and bargaining: Empirical evidence from medical devices.* University of Toronto.

Gunning, T. S. & Sickles, R. C. (2007). *Competition and market power in physician private practices.* Rice University.

Haas-Wilson, D. (2003). *Managed care and monopoly power: The antitrust challenge.* Cambridge, MA: Harvard University Press.

Haas-Wilson, D. & Garmon, C. (2011). Hospital mergers and competitive effects: Two retrospective analyses. *International Journal of the Economics of Business, 18*(1), 17−32.

Halbersma, R. & Katona, K. (2011). *Vertical restraints in health care markets.* Tilburg University.

Halbersma, R., Mikkers, M., Motchenkova, E., & Seinen, I. (2010). Market structure and hospital–insurer bargaining in the Netherlands. *European Journal of Health Economics,* Online Paper, <http://www.springerlink.com/content/477hx26326t61467/>.

Handel, B. (2010). *Adverse selection and switching costs in health insurance markets: When nudging hurts.* Berkeley: University of California.

Hansmann, H., Kessler, D., & McClellan, M. B. (2003). Ownership form and trapped capital in the hospital industry. In E. L. Glaeser (Ed.), *The governance of not-for-profit organizations* (pp. 45–70). National Bureau of Economic Research.

Hastings, J. & Gilbert, R. (2005). Market power, vertical integration and the wholesale price of gasoline. *Journal of Industrial Economics, 53*(4), 469–492.

Herndon, J. (2002). Health insurer monopsony power: The all-or-none model. *Journal of Health Economics, 21,* 197–206.

Hirsch, B. & Schumacher, E. (2005). Classic or new monopsony? Searching for evidence in nursing labor markets. *Journal of Health Economics, 24,* 969–989.

Ho, K. (2006). The welfare effects of restricted hospital choice in the US medical care market. *Journal of Applied Econometrics, 21*(7), 1039–1079.

Ho, K. (2009a). Barriers to entry of a vertically integrated health insurer: An analysis of welfare and entry costs. *Journal of Economics and Management Strategy, 18*(2), 487–545.

Ho, K. (2009b). Insurer-provider networks in the medical care market. *American Economic Review, 99*(1), 393–430.

Ho, K. & Pakes, A. (2011). Physician responses to financial incentives: Evidence from hospital discharge records. Unpublished Manuscript.

Ho, V. (2002). Learning and the evolution of medical technologies: The diffusion of coronary angioplasty. *Journal of Health Economics, 21*(5), 873–885.

Ho, V. & Hamilton, B. H. (2000). Hospital mergers and acquisitions: Does market consolidation harm patients? *Journal of Health Economics, 19*(5), 767–791.

Horn, H. & Wolinsky, A. (1988). Bilateral monopolies and incentives for merger. *RAND Journal of Economics, 19,* 408–419.

Howard, D. H. (2005). Quality and consumer choice in healthcare: Evidence from kidney transplantation. *Topics in Economic Analysis and Policy, 5*(1), Article 24, 1–20. <http://www.bepress.com/bejeap/topics/vol5/iss1/art24/>.

Huckman, R. S. & Pisano, G. P. (2006). The firm specificity of individual performance: Evidence from cardiac surgery. *Management Science, 52*(4), 473–488.

Huesch, M. D. (2009). Learning by doing, scale effects, or neither? Cardiac surgeons after residency. *Health Services Research, 44*(6), 1960–1982.

Huesch, M. D. & Sakakibara, M. (2009). Forgetting the learning curve for a moment: How much performance is unrelated to own experience? *Health Economics, 18,* 855.

Inderst, R. & Wey, C. (2003). Bargaining, mergers, and technology choice in bilaterally oligopolistic industries. *RAND Journal of Economics, 34,* 19–41.

Isabel, C. & Paula, V. (2010). Geographic distribution of physicians in Portugal. *European Journal of Health Economics, 11,* 383–393.

Kahn, K. L., Keeler, E. B., Sherwood, M. J., Rogers, W. H., Draper, D., Bentow, S. S., Reinisch, E. J., Rubenstein, L. V., Kosecoff, J., & Brook, R. H. (1990). Comparing outcomes of care before and after implementation of the DRG-based prospective payment system. *Journal of the American Medical Association, 264*(15), 1984–1988.

Kamien, M. I. & Vincent, D. R. (1991). *Price regulation and the quality of service.* Center for Mathematical Studies in Economics and Management Science, Northwestern University.

Kemp, R. & Severijnen, A. (2010). *Price effects of Dutch hospital mergers: An ex post assesment of hip surgery.* Netherlands Competition Authority (NMa).

Kessler, D. & McClellan, M. (2000). Is hospital competition socially wasteful? *Quarterly Journal of Economics, 115*(2), 577–615.

Kessler, D. P. & Geppert, J. J. (2005). The effects of competition on variation in the quality and cost of medical care. *Journal of Economics and Management Strategy, 14*(3), 575–589.

Krishnan, R. (2001). Market restructuring and pricing in the hospital industry. *Journal of Health Economics*, *20*, 213–237.

Lakdawalla, D. & Philipson, T. (1998). *Nonprofit production and competition*. National Bureau of Economic Research.

Lakdawalla, D. & Philipson, T. (2006). The nonprofit sector and industry performance. *Journal of Public Economics*, *90*, 1681–1698.

Lee, M. (1971). A conspicuous production theory of hospital production. *Southern Economic Journal*, *38*(1), 48–58.

Leonard, G. & Olley, G. S. (2011). What can be learned about the competitive effects of mergers from natural experiments? *International Journal of the Economics of Business*, *18*(1), 103–107.

Lewis, M. & Pflum, K. (2011). *Diagnosing hospital system bargaining power in managed care networks*. Ohio State University.

Liebhaber, A. Grossman, J. M. (2007). Physicians moving to mid-sized, single-specialty practices. Technical report, Center for Studying Health System Change, Washington, DC. Tracking Report No. 18.

Lindrooth, R., Lo Sasso, A., & Bazzoli, G. (2003). The effect of urban hospital closure on markets. *Journal of Health Economics*, *22*, 691–712.

Luft, H. S., Garnick, D. W., Mark, D. H., Peltzman, D. J., Phibbs, C. S., Lichtenberg, E., & McPhee, S. J. (1990). Does quality influence choice of hospital? *JAMA*, *263*(21), 2899–2906.

Lustig, J. (2010). *Measuring welfare losses from adverse selection and imperfect competition in privatized Medicare*. Boston University.

Lyon, T. P. (1999). Quality competition, insurance, and consumer choice in health care markets. *Journal of Economics and Management Strategy*, *8*(4), 545–580.

Ma, C.-t. A. (1997). Option contracts and vertical foreclosure. *Journal of Economics and Management Strategy*, *6*(4), 725–753.

Madison, K. (2004). Hospital–physician affiliations and patient treatments, expenditures, and outcomes. *Health Services Research*, *39*(2), 257–278.

Maestas, N., Schroeder, M., & Goldman, D. (2009). *Price variation in markets with homogeneous goods: The case of Medigap*. National Bureau of Economic Research.

Martin, A., Lassman, D., Whittle, L., & Catlin, A. (2011). Recession contributes to slowest annual rate of increase in health spending in five decades. *Health Affairs*, *30*, 111–122.

Massachusetts Attorney General (2010). Investigation of health care cost trends and cost drivers, pursuant to G.L. c.118G, § 6 1/2(b). Preliminary report, Office of Attorney General Martha Coakley, Boston, MA, January 29.

Matsudaira, J. D. (2010). *Monopsony in the low-wage labor market? Evidence from minimum nurse staffing regulations*. Cornell University.

Mazzeo, M. (2002). Product choice and oligopoly market structure. *RAND Journal of Economics*, *33*(2), 221–242.

Melnick, G. & Keeler, E. (2007). The effects of multi-hospital systems on hospital prices. *Journal of Health Economics*, *26*(2), 400–413.

Moriya, A. S., Vogt, W. B., & Gaynor, M. (2010). Hospital prices and market structure in the hospital and insurance industries. *Health Economics, Policy and Law*, *5*, 459–479.

Mukamel, D., Zwanziger, J., & Bamezai, A. (2002). Hospital competition, resource allocation and quality of care. *BMC Health Services Research*, *2*(1), 10–18.

Mukamel, D., Zwanziger, J., & Tomaszewski, K. J. (2001). HMO penetration, competition and risk-adjusted hospital mortality. *Health Services Research*, *36*(6), 1019–1035.

Mutter, R. L., Romano, P. S., & Wong, H. S. (2011). The effects of US hospital consolidations on hospital quality. *International Journal of the Economics of Business*, *18*(1), 109.

Mutter, R. L., Wong, H. S., & Goldfarb, M. G. (2008). The effects of hospital competition on inpatient quality of care. *Inquiry*, *45*(3), 263–279.

National Center for Health Statistics (2011). *Health, United States, 2010*. Hyattsville, MD: National Center for Health Statistics, Center for Disease Control.

Nevo, A. (2000). Mergers with differentiated products: The case of the ready-to-eat cereal industry. *RAND Journal of Economics*, *31*(3), 395–421.

Newhouse, J. (1970). Toward a theory of nonprofit institutions: An economic model of a hospital. *American Economic Review, 60*(1), 64–74.

Newhouse, J. P., Williams, A. P., Bennett, B. W., & Schwartz, W. B. (1982). Does the geographical distribution of physicians reflect market failure? *Bell Journal of Economics, 13*(2), 493–505.

Orsini, C. (2010). *Ownership and exit behavior in home health care: Responses to government financing in a health care market with low entry and exit barriers.* University of Aarhus.

Pakes, A. (2010). Alternative models for moment inequalities. *Econometrica, 78*(6), 1783–1822.

Pakes, A. & McGuire, P. (1994). Computing Markov-perfect Nash equilibria: Numerical implications of a dynamic differentiated product model. *RAND Journal of Economics, 25*(4), 555–589.

Pakes, A., Ostrovsky, M., & Berry, S. (2007). Simple estimators for the parameters of discrete dynamic games (with entry/exit examples). *RAND Journal of Economics, 38*(2), 373–399.

Pakes, A., Porter, J., Ho, K., & Ishii, J. (2006). *Moment inequalities and their application.* Harvard University.

Panzar, J. C. & Rosse, J. (1987). Testing for "monopoly" equilibrium. *Journal of Industrial Economics, 35*(4), 443–456.

Parente, S. & Town, R. (2011). *The impact of retail clinics on cost, utilization and welfare.* University of Minnesota.

Pauly, M. & Redisch, M. (1973). The not-for-profit hospital as a physicians' cooperative. *American Economic Review, 63*(1), 87–99.

Pauly, M. V. (2004). Competition in medical services and the quality of care: Concepts and history. *International Journal of Health Care Finance and Economics, 4*, 113–130.

Pennsylvania Health Care Cost Containment Council (2007). Cardiac surgery in Pennsylvania 2005. Report, Pennsylvania Health Care Cost Containment Council, Harrisburg, PA. June.

Pesendorfer, M. & Schmidt-Dengler, P. (2008). Asymptotic least squares estimators for dynamic games. *Review of Economic Studies, 75*, 901–928.

Petrin, A. (2002). Quantifying the benefits of new products: The case of the minivan. *Journal of Political Economy, 110*(4), 705–729.

Pratt, J. W., Wise, D. A., & Zeckhauser, R. (1979). Price differences in almost competitive markets. *Quarterly Journal of Economics, 93*(2), 189–211.

Propper, C., Burgess, S., & Green, K. (2004). Does competition between hospitals improve the quality of care? Hospital death rates and the NHS internal market. *Journal of Public Economics, 88*(7–8), 1247–1272.

Ramanarayanan, S. (2008). *Does practice make perfect: An empirical analysis of learning-by-doing in cardiac surgery.* Anderson School of Management, UCLA.

Reinhardt, U., Hussey, P., & Anderson, G. (2004). US health care spending in an international context. *Health Affairs, 23*(3), 10–25.

Rogowski, J., Jain, A. K., & Escarce, J. J. (2007). Hospital competition, managed care, and mortality after hospitalization for medical conditions in California. *Health Services Research, 42*(2), 682–705.

Romano, P. & Balan, D. (2011). A retrospective analysis of the clinical quality effects of the acquisition of Highland Park hospital by Evanston Northwestern healthcare. *International Journal of the Economics of Business, 18*(1), 45–64.

Rosenthal, M. B., Zaslavsky, A., & Newhouse, J. P. (2005). The geographic distribution of physicians revisited. *Health Services Research, 40*(6, Part 1), 1931–1952.

Royalty, A. B. & Solomon, N. (1999). Health plan choice: Price elasticities in a managed competition setting. *Journal of Human Resources, 34*(1), 1–41 pp.

Sacher, S. & Vita, M. (2001). The competitive effects of a not-for-profit hospital merger: A case study. *Journal of Industrial Economics, 49*(1), 63–84.

Sari, N. (2002). Do competition and managed care improve quality? *Health Economics, 11*, 571–584.

Schaumans, C. & Verboven, F. (2008). Entry and regulation: Evidence from health care professions. *RAND Journal of Economics, 39*, 949972.

Schmalensee, R. (1989). Inter-industry studies of structure and performance. In R. Schmalensee & R. Willig (Eds.), *Handbook of industrial organization* (Vol. 2, pp. 951–1009). Amsterdam and New York: Elsevier Science, North-Holland, Chapter 16.

Schmidt-Dengler, P. (2006). *The timing of new technology adoption: The case of MRI.* London School of Economics.

Schneider, J., Li, P., Klepser, D., Peterson, N., Brown, T., & Scheffler, R. (2008a). The effect of physician and health plan market concentration on prices in commercial health insurance markets. *International Journal of Health Care Finance and Economics*, 8, 13–26.

Schneider, J., Miller, T., Ohsfeldt, R., Morrisey, M., Zellner, B., & Li, P. (2008b). The economics of specialty hospitals. *Medical Care Research and Review Journal*, 65(5), 531–553.

Schut, F., Greß, S., & Wasem, J. (2003). Consumer price sensitivity and social health insurer choice in Germany and the Netherlands. *International Journal of Health Care Finance and Economics*, 3, 117–138.

Seider, H., Gaynor, M., & Vogt, W. B. (2000). *Volume–outcome and antitrust in US health care markets*. Universität Augsburg, Carnegie Mellon University.

Shen, Y., Wu, V., & Melnick, G. (2010). Trends in hospital cost and revenue, 1994–2005: How are they related to HMO penetration, concentration, and for-profit ownership? *Health Services Research*, 45(1), 42–61.

Shen, Y.-S. (2003). The effect of financial pressure on the quality of care in hospitals. *Journal of Health Economics*, 22(2), 243–269.

Snyder, C. (1996). A dynamic theory of countervailing power. *RAND Journal of Economics*, 27(4), 747–769.

Sohn, M.-W. & Rathouz, P. J. (2003). *Competition among hospitals and quality of care: Hospital-level analysis*. University of Chicago.

Sorensen, A. T. (2000). Equilibrium price dispersion in retail markets for prescription drugs. *Journal of Political Economy*, 108(4), 833–850 pp.

Sorensen, A. T. (2003). Insurer–hospital bargaining: Negotiated discounts in post-deregulation Connecticut. *Journal of Industrial Economics*, 51(4), 469–490.

Spang, H., Bazzoli, G., & Arnould, R. (2001). Hospital mergers and savings for consumers: Exploring new evidence. *Health Affairs*, 20(4), 150–158.

Staiger, D., Spetz, J., & Phibbs, C. (2010). Is there monopsony in the labor market? Evidence from a natural experiment. *Journal of Labor Economics*, 28, 211–236.

Starc, A. (2010). *Insurer pricing and consumer welfare: Evidence from Medigap*. Harvard University.

Stole, L. & Zwiebel, J. (1996). Bargaining, mergers, and technology choice in bilaterally oligopolistic industries. *Review of Economic Studies*, 63, 375–410.

Strombom, B. A., Buchmueller, T. C., & Feldstein, P. J. (2002). Switching costs, price sensitivity and health plan choice. *Journal of Health Economics*, 21(1), 89–116.

Sullivan, D. (1989). Monopsony power in the market for nurses. *Journal of Law and Economics*, 32(2), S135–S178.

Tamm, M., Tauchmann, H., Wasem, J., & Greß, S. (2007). Elasticities of market shares and social health insurance choice in Germany: A dynamic panel data approach. *Health Economics*, 16, 243–256.

Tay, A. (2003). Assessing competition in hospital care markets: The importance of accounting for quality differentiation. *RAND Journal of Economics*, 34(4), 786–814.

Tenn, S. (2011). The price effects of hospital mergers: A case study of the sutter-summit transaction. *International Journal of the Economics of Business*, 18(1), 65–82.

Thompson, E. (2011). The effect of hospital mergers on inpatient prices: A case study of the New Hanover-Cape Fear transaction. *International Journal of the Economics of Business*, 18(1), 91–101.

Thompson, P. D. (2010). Learning by doing. In B. Hall & N. Rosenberg (Eds.), *Handbook of economics of technical change* (pp. 429–476). North-Holland, New York and Oxford: Elsevier Science, Chapter 10.

Tirole, J. (1988). *The Theory of Industrial Organization*. Cambridge, MA: MIT Press.

Town, R. J. & Liu, S. (2003). The welfare impact of Medicare HMOs. *RAND Journal of Economics*, 34, 719–736.

Town, R. J. & Park, M. (2011). *Market structure beliefs and hospital merger waves*. University of Minnesota.

Town, R. & Vistnes, G. (2001). Hospital competition in HMO networks. *Journal of Health Economics*, 20(5), 733–752.

Town, R., Feldman, R., & Kralewski, J. (2011). Market power and contract form: Evidence from physician group practices. *International Journal of Health Care Finance and Economics*, forthcoming.

Town, R., Wholey, D., Feldman, R., & Burns, L. (2006). *The welfare consequences of hospital mergers*. National Bureau of Economic Research.

Town, R., Wholey, D., Feldman, R., & Burns, L. (2007). Revisiting the relationship between managed care and hospital consolidation. *Health Services Research, 42*(1), 219–238.

Van Dijk, M., Pomp, M., Douven, R., Laske-Aldershof, T., Schut, E., de Boer, W., & do Boo, A. (2008). Consumer price sensitivity in Dutch health insurance. *International Journal of Health Care Finance and Economics, 8*, 225–244.

Varkevisser, M. & Schut, F. (2009). *Hospital merger control: An international comparison.* Erasmus University, Rotterdam.

Vogt, W. B. & Town, R. J. (2006). *How has hospital consolidation affected the price and quality of hospital care?* Princeton, NJ: Robert Wood Johnson Foundation.

Volpp, K. G., Williams, S. V., Waldfogel, J., Silber, J. H., Schwartz, J. S., & Pauly, M. V. (2003). Market reform in New Jersey and the effect on mortality from acute myocardial infarction. *Health Services Research, 38*(2), 515–533.

Weber, E. (2010). *Measuring welfare from ambulatory surgery centers: A spatial analysis of demand for healthcare facilities.* Carnegie Mellon University.

Wong, H. (1996). Market structure and the role of consumer information in the physician services industry: An empirical test. *Journal of Health Economics, 15*, 139–160.

Wu, V. (2008). The price effect of hospital closures. *Inquiry, 45*, 280–292.

Wu, V. (2009). Managed care's price bargaining with hospitals. *Journal of Health Economics, 28*, 350–360.

Yett, D. (1975). *An economic analysis of the nurse shortage.* Lexington, MA: Lexington Books.

Zwanziger, J. & Mooney, C. (2005). Has price competition changed hospital revenues and expenses in New York? *Inquiry, 42*, 183–192.

Zwanziger, J., Melnick, G., & Bamezai, A. (2000). The effect of selective contracting on hospital costs and revenues. *Health Services Research, 35*(4), 849–867.

CHAPTER TEN

Health Care Markets, Regulators, and Certifiers

David Dranove
Northwestern University, Chicago, USA

Contents

Handbook of Health Economics, Volume 2
ISSN: 1574-0064, DOI: 10.1016/B978-0-444-53592-4.00010-4

639

1. INTRODUCTION

Firms transact in a variety of ways. Many firms unilaterally choose product attributes and prices in response to market demand. Others negotiate contracts with buyers that specify output, quality, and compensation. Sometimes the buyer dictates the terms of the contract; this is often the case when the buyer is a government regulator. Economists have devoted considerable attention to the question of whether market transactions, contracts, and/or regulation can generate efficient outcomes. In this chapter, we explore how economists have answered this question for health care services markets.

Section 2 begins where many health economics papers begin, with a discussion of Arrow's (1963) analysis of whether health care markets are "different" from textbook markets. Arrow argues that the conditions facilitating an "optimal state" are often missing in health care. This section examines these conditions and pays particular attention to asymmetric information about quality. Section 3 reviews the empirical evidence on the performance of competitive health care markets. At one time the conventional wisdom was that competition led to higher prices, an idea captured by the theory of the Medical Arms Race. With the growth of selective contracting between providers and payers, competition is now associated with lower prices. Empirical methods for studying competition, once steeped in the traditional structure—conduct—performance paradigm, have been replaced by structural models that are well suited for antitrust analysis.

Section 4 considers regulatory approaches to containing prices. Theory suggests that a mixed payment scheme combining a fixed "prepayment" with partial cost sharing should outperform either pure prepayment or pure cost-based payment. Empirical evidence does not directly test the theory, but does confirm that payments affect costs and quality in expected ways. Section 5 considers yet another quality assurance mechanism—third party certification embodied by health care report cards. Despite widely cited unanticipated and undesirable consequences, report cards for health insurers and providers seem to offer several benefits: they move market share away from the worst sellers, encourage all sellers to improve quality, and facilitate matching between severely ill patients and the best providers. Section 5 also explores pay for performance schemes, which combine elements of incentive contracts and quality certification. Section 6 concludes.

If the question is: "Do markets, contracts, or regulation generate first-best outcomes?" then the answer is no. Even though the first-best is unachievable, research does provide insight into how efficiency can be enhanced. This chapter highlights papers that improve our understanding of how this can be done.

2. HEALTH CARE MARKET FAILURE

In discussing the implications of his first and second theorems of welfare economics, Arrow (1963) states that competitive markets, if they exist, facilitate an "optimal state" in which total surplus is maximized. In this "optimal state," all goods and services are produced at minimum average cost, and the marginal benefits of consumption always equal or exceed the marginal costs of production. Any government intervention to reallocate goods and services is justifiable solely on distributional grounds. The requirements for competitive markets are well known, though rarely observed in practice: all valued goods and services must be transacted; there must be many buyers and sellers with costless entry and exit; and all buyers and sellers have symmetric and complete information about all terms of transactions.

There is a large literature devoted to identifying the myriad ways in which markets fail to satisfy the necessary Arrow conditions, either because they are not competitive or because they are incomplete due to defective property rights or imperfect information. In this section we explore these conditions and discuss how they apply to health care markets.

2.1. Non-competitive Markets

Many markets ranging from airframes to cardiovascular drugs to cola products have only a handful of sellers. The oligopolistic structure of these markets may be traced to high fixed costs in production or endogenous sunk costs from R&D and branding (Sutton, 1991). Most theories of oligopoly predict that prices are positively related to market concentration and that oligopoly pricing exceeds optimal levels. However, the theory of contestable markets posits that if entry involves no sunk costs and is immediately reversible, even monopolists are constrained to mimic competitive outcomes (Baumol et al., 1982).

The empirical literature on price and market concentration generally confirms that prices are higher in more concentrated markets (Weiss, 1989). As we discuss below, empirical research on US health care provider markets has not always reached the same conclusion.[1] Simple correlations between price and concentration may be of limited usefulness for three reasons. First, they may suffer from endogeneity bias; in particular, concentration may be correlated with unobservable characteristics that predict prices. Second, simple correlations usually involve ad hoc market definitions that may be problematic for antitrust analysis. Finally, considerations of price and concentration correlations cannot be divorced from considerations of quality and concentration, making it

---

[1] See Gaynor and Town (2011, this Handbook) for extended discussion of the theoretical and empirical literature on competition and health care.

difficult to establish welfare results about competition. Advances in empirical industrial organization, including structural modeling of pricing and entry, have allowed economists to solve the first two problems. Consistency among research studies allows for some unambiguous welfare statements.

Low entry and exit costs, combined with production that displays little to no returns to scale, serve to limit market concentration. Learning economies, branding economies, and network externalities can create increasing returns and entry barriers in markets as diverse as professional services, consumer products, and electronics and information technology (Sutton, 1991). Although there are high fixed costs for hospitals (Friedman and Pauly, 1981), the benefits of scale seem to be limited as evidenced by the fact that most hospitals in the United States have fewer than 300 beds and average bed size fell during the 1990s, when, as we describe below, the hospital market was most competitive. As a result there are many hospitals in most metropolitan areas, even though mergers have reduced the number of competitors to just a handful in some places (Capps, 2009). Economies of scale for physician services appear to be minimal for all but the smallest practices (Pope and Burge, 1996). Nor do larger general practices seem to produce higher quality (Doran et al., 2006).

There are many situations in which multiple sellers offer differentiated goods, entry barriers are minimal, and market demand is high relative to minimum efficient scale. In these monopolistically competitive situations, each firm faces downward sloping demand and enjoys some degree of market power. Examples include many professional services (e.g. hair salons) and retailing (e.g. restaurants). Physician markets are a quintessential example. Market equilibrium under monopolistic competition does not yield welfare maximizing quality and price except under strong conditions on cost functions and preferences which are implausible in many health care markets (Gravelle, 1999).

Location is a key source of differentiation in health care. Consider that patients are an input in the production of health care in that much of health care requires that the patient and provider are in the same place at the same time. Since patients are spatially dispersed, demand for care at any provider will depend, *inter alia*, on the distance between patient and provider. Geographically dispersed providers will therefore inevitably have market power in that they can raise prices or lower quality, relative to other producers, without losing all their patients (Morrisey, 1998).

2.2. Health Insurance and Moral Hazard

The onset of illness is uncertain and the expense to restore health can be considerable. Hence, individuals wish to be insured against that expense. Uncertainty is not a source of market failure *per se*, even in the market for health care. A complete set of competitive markets for the delivery of goods and services contingent on the state of the world yields a Pareto efficient allocation. This can include complete state contingent income markets (i.e. insurance markets), provided that individuals have perfect foresight about the prices ruling in each state (Arrow, 1963).

Pareto efficiency may be unachievable if patients have private information about their *ex-ante* health state, leading to adverse selection in insurance markets, or if it is costly to implement a price schedule in which patients face full marginal costs for the last unit of health services they consume. Considering the remarkable range of health states (there are over 12,000 diagnoses in the ICD-10 and a continuous range of severities within each ICD), it would be prohibitively costly to design such a schedule. In fact, cost–sharing parameters for insured patients are largely invariant to health state, with patients paying only a small fraction of marginal costs. The result is *ex-post* moral hazard. Patients may also exhibit *ex-ante* moral hazard because insurance discourages efficient investments in health capital.

2.3. Information Asymmetry: Consumers and Producers

Markets may also break down due to asymmetric information. The concepts of experience and credence goods are used to describe situations where consumers lack important information about product attributes.[2] With experience goods, consumers may not be able to evaluate their utility until after consuming the good. With credence goods, utility may still be difficult to evaluate after consumption. Providers may have limited incentives to increase quality of experience and credence goods and the resulting quality may be inefficiently low.

Patients regularly purchase some health care services (e.g. dental care) and can easily evaluate the outcomes of others (e.g. acne treatment). For these services, low-quality providers may have to reduce price or be driven from the market. Patients who receive complex treatments like heart surgery or joint replacement may find it much more difficult to evaluate quality. And there are some services for which patients may never know for sure whether their provider did a good job. Prevention and mental health may be good examples. When patients cannot easily evaluate quality, it may be necessary for third parties to certify quality by aggregating outcomes across many patients.

2.4. Intrinsic Motivation and Altruism

Many economists have suggested that health care providers do not possess the venal motives that normally lead profit-maximizing sellers of experience and credence goods to shirk on quality. Arrow (1963) argues that physicians are socialized to act as perfect agents for their patients, stating: "The social obligation for best practice is part

---

[2] The theories apply symmetrically when sellers are inadequately informed. An important example is health insurance, where sellers may not know the health risks of buyers.

of the commodity the physician sells, even though it is a part that is not subject to thorough inspection by the buyer." Theoretical models in which physician utility includes both income and patient well-being suggest, unsurprisingly, that concern for patient well-being tends to increase quality (McGuire, 2000). However, unless there is perfect agency in the sense that providers and patients have identical marginal valuation for quality, quality will be inefficiently low.

Hansman (1980) and Weisbrod (1991) suggest that the ban on inurement in non-profit organizations (i.e. compensation of non-profit managers cannot be tied to financial returns) limits their incentives to underprovide hard-to-measure attributes. There is some evidence that non-profit hospitals attract managers with altruistic motives (Roomkin and Weisbrod, 1999). Gregg et al. (2008) find that workers in the non-profit sector are more likely to donate labor as unpaid overtime, than those in the for-profit sector. We consider the implications of altruistic motivation for the design of financial incentives in section 4.2.

2.5. Quality Assurance Mechanisms

Consumers of credence and experience goods rely on a variety of mechanisms to ascertain quality. Table 10.1 lists some quality assurance mechanisms and examples from health care and other markets.

Experience is a common quality assurance mechanism but it is rarely sufficient. One limitation is that consumers may find it difficult to link *ex-post* product failure with a product defect; think of an automobile owner establishing the reason for unexpected acceleration. Experience also has limited value when products are infrequently purchased, such as executive education or a hip replacement.

Branding, another common quality assurance mechanism, is usually initiated and maintained through the seller's marketing efforts. It is unclear whether branding acts as a "bond" in which the seller sinks an investment in branding to signal its high quality or whether branding makes it easier for consumers to recall their positive experiences when making repeat purchases.[3] Consumers may find third party disclosure more trustworthy than brands and information sources such as *Consumer Reports* and Edmunds.com have flourished. These certifiers may not always have adequate information to perform their jobs and the motives of certifiers can sometimes lead to biased reporting (Hubbard, 1998).

Sellers may offer warranties if the value of the product is large relative to the cost to consumers of exercising the warranty. Thus, we see warranties for automobiles and televisions, but not for diapers or light bulbs. Warranties are also uncommon for professional services because consumers have difficulty gauging service quality even after consumption.

---

[3] See Bagwell (2007) for a summary of advertising literature.

Table 10.1 Quality Assurance Mechanism in Health Care and Other Markets

Mechanism	How It Works	Examples: Other Markets	Health Care
Personal experience	Consumers predict future quality based on past experience	Most consumer goods. Professional services	Family physicians. Dentists
Brand	Firms invest in establishing brand which consumers interpret as imprimatur of quality	Consumer electronics	Provision of dental and optical services by Boots. Kaiser hospitals and health plans
Voluntary disclosure by firms	Firms publicly report product quality without independent verification	Cellular networks reporting speed and coverage	
Regulation	Government requires firms to achieve minimum quality standard	Food safety; automobile safety	Prescription drugs
Government certification/licensing	Government agency evaluates and certifies quality data	Licensing of professionals	National and state medical licensing
Third party certification agency	Third party evaluates quality data and certifies that quality exceeds threshold	Underwriter's laboratory certifying product safety	Leapfrog Group (US)
Third party ratings	Third party evaluates and reports quality data	*Consumer Reports*	healthgrades.com
Warrantees	Contract makes firm financially responsible for quality defect	Hyundai's ten-year warranty	
Litigation	Tort law makes firm financially liable for poor quality	Litigation against Toyota for unexpected acceleration	Medical malpractice suits

3. MARKET STRUCTURE AND PROVIDER PERFORMANCE

The United States has long served as a crucible for testing the effects of competition in health care markets. Unlike other nations where health care spending is largely government controlled, approximately half of all US health expenditures are private and providers either post their prices for private patients or negotiate fees with private insurers. Most US metropolitan areas have at least two independent hospitals or hospital systems and many physicians. Mergers are frequent. Researchers have exploited variation in market structure in the cross-section and over time to test for the effects of competition on costs, prices, and quality. The prevailing wisdom about the benefits of competition has evolved, matching important changes in the role of insurers as pricing intermediaries. Antitrust policy to assure market competition has lagged, although recent structural approaches to studying competition have led courts to adopt a tougher stance on hospital mergers.

3.1. Theoretical Effects of Health Care Competition: The Structure, Conduct, and Performance Paradigm

Early empirical research on competition followed the structure—conduct—performance (SCP) paradigm, which has its theoretical underpinnings in oligopoly theory. Simple models of Cournot and differentiated Bertrand competition predict a direct relationship between market structure, firm conduct, and market performance (measured by prices and/or profits). In a nutshell, more concentrated markets facilitate cooperative behavior that leads to higher prices and profits. The SCP paradigm has been confirmed for a wide range of markets and the relative simplicity of the approach has made it popular for studying health markets.[4] However, the paradigm did not square with casual observation about health care markets, where prices seemed to be higher in markets with more providers, an observation that led to the demand inducement hypothesis (McGuire, 2000).

In an effort to explain the positive correlation between prices and the extent of competition, Satterthwaite (1979) suggests that it may be more appropriate to study health care competition among physicians through the lens of Chamberlin's model of monopolistic competition. In this model, the willingness of consumers to switch from one seller to another is a key determinant of price. Satterthwaite argues that increasing the number of physicians could reduce the ability of patients to confidently find a new physician, thereby reducing switching and allowing physicians to raise prices. In Satterthwaite's model, consumers know the quality of their own physician. Consumers who wish to switch providers seek out information about the quality of other

---

[4] See Weiss (1989) for a review of SCP studies across dozens of markets.

physicians by speaking with other consumers. In order to obtain precise information about any given physician, consumers must speak with *several* of that physician's patients. As the physician/population ratio increases, this becomes increasingly difficult, so consumers are less likely to switch. This enhances each physician market power, leading to a positive correlation between prices and the physician/population ratio.

In the 1980s, health economists introduced the theory of the medical arms race (MAR) to help explain why competition might cause hospital costs to increase. The key assumption underpinning the MAR is that physicians choose hospitals on behalf of their patients. As described by Robinson and Luft (1985), the MAR is a form of quality competition in which hospitals compete for physicians (and thus their patients) by offering high tech services, high levels of staffing, and other perks. Such competition drives costs higher than competitive levels in at least three ways. First, there will be an excess supply of high fixed cost medical technologies such as diagnostic equipment and surgical suites. Second, there will be excessive staffing of allied medical personnel. Third, with many hospitals dividing up the market, each may fail to move down the learning curve. This may not only drive up costs, it may drive down quality. Such a problem is suggested by Phibbs et al. (2007), who find that the proliferation of Neonatal Intensive Care units has resulted in a large number of units experiencing low volumes. Very low birth weight infants born in low volume NICUs tend to have higher mortality.

The effects of market structure on quality choice can be complex. In general, quality choice depends on three factors:

1. Consumer price sensitivity to quality.
2. Price/marginal cost margins.
3. The marginal cost of increasing quality.

Increasing the number of providers might increase consumer (i.e. physician) sensitivity to quality. For example, in a spatially differentiated market, increasing seller density might make it less costly for consumers to switch when a nearby seller improves quality. But increasing the number of providers presumably reduces price/marginal cost margins through the usual competitive impact on price. Thus, the predicted impact of increasing the number of providers on quality is ambiguous.

In the past few years, researchers have questioned the relevance of the traditional SCP approach to studying health care markets. Cournot and Bertrand models assume that sellers set capacity, quantity or price and sell directly to consumers. The MAR adapts this framework to the situation where hospitals sell directly to physicians acting on behalf of patients. Neither the standard Cournot/Bertrand model nor the MAR considers the role of the insurer, which acts as a financial intermediary in the transaction. It may have been acceptable to ignore the insurer prior to the 1980s. At that time, most Americans had indemnity insurance that paid whatever providers charged and required enrollees to pay modest coinsurance.

Beginning in the 1980s, however, insurers known as Preferred Provider Organizations, or PPOs, began engaging in a process known as "selective contracting." Through selective contracting, insurers directly negotiate fees with providers. Providers who offer attractive rates are included in insurer "networks" and insurers give enrollees financial incentives to choose in-network providers. There were two elements to the financial incentive. First, enrollees who choose an in-network provider pay a very modest copayment—perhaps 10 percent versus 30 percent for out-of-network use. Second, enrollees who go out-of-network could be responsible for 100 percent of the difference between the provider's charges and the price that is deemed "reasonable" by the insurer. For example, suppose an in-network provider negotiates a price of $1,000 for a diagnostic service, which the insurer deems to be reasonable, and the out-of-network provider charges $2,000. Then a patient who chooses the in-network provider would be responsible for $100 in copayments; the patient who goes out-of-network could be responsible for as much as $1,300. By the 1990s, nearly all Americans under age 65 were enrolled in an insurance plan that engaged in selective contracting. This remains true today.

Dranove et al. (1992b) describe the evolution of selective contracting as a shift from "patient-driven" to "payer-driven" competition. Prior to selective contracting, patients were fully insured or nearly so and did not care about price. They chose their providers based on other attributes and largely delegated the choice of hospital to their physicians. As a result, the price elasticity of demand facing providers was low and providers had little incentive to reduce prices, even in markets with many other providers.[5] Selectively contracting insurers keep any discounts they negotiate with providers, or use the discounts to lower premiums and increase market share. This gives them a strong incentive to shop for the lowest prices. This effectively increases the price elasticity of demand facing providers, encouraging providers to reduce prices. The more easily insurers could substitute from one provider to another, the higher the elasticity and the lower the price.

Town and Vistnes (2001) and Capps et al. (2003) argue that under selective contracting, competition takes place in two stages. In the first stage, hospitals and insurers negotiate and insurers form their networks. When forming networks, insurers worry about both price and non-price dimensions. For example, insurers may wish to contract with prestigious teaching hospitals in order to make their networks more attractive to enrollees. At the same time, they may be concerned that the high costs of care in a teaching hospital would price their insurance policy out of the market. In the second stage, patients choose among hospitals in their insurer network. Because there is likely to be little price variation within network,

---

[5] Many years ago, noted antitrust economist Dennis Carlton once asked me (Dranove) why prices weren't infinity. I did not have a good answer!

and because copayments are very small, this competition occurs almost exclusively on non-price dimensions and resembles patient-driven competition. It is during the first stage that hospitals compete on price.

Capps et al. (2003) capture the essentials of selective contracting. They directly model the value that a hospital brings to a network. They observe that consumers usually choose their insurer, and therefore choose their network, during their employer's annual "open enrollment" period. They then assume that when consumers choose their insurer, they are uncertain about their future health needs. Thus, they must consider which illnesses they are likely to contract and the providers they would wish to visit. Consumers will highly value a network that gives them the option to choose those providers who will best meet their future needs as they arrive. Capps et al. call this "option demand." For example, a consumer with a history of heart problems will value a network that includes the best heart hospital in town. Another consumer contemplating starting a family will value a network that includes a nearby hospital with a maternity ward.

Capps et al. (2003) model option demand using a logit demand framework and show that the value that a hospital brings to a network depends on its shares in "micromarkets," which are defined by data availability but roughly correspond to unique combinations of locations, illness types, and demography. A hospital that dominates several important micromarkets will have high option demand from many patients and the insurer will have a high willingness-to-pay to include that hospital in its network.

3.2. Empirical Studies of the Effects of Competition on Costs and Prices

Many empirical studies ask whether prices, costs, and quality are higher in more competitive markets. Pauly and Satterthwaite (1981) test Satterthwaite's (1979) search model. They regress physician prices on a set of predictors that are plausibly related to the ability of patients to gather information about physicians, including the physician/population ratio as well as the use of public transportation and the transience of the local population. Their findings suggest that prices are lower when consumers can more easily learn about physicians from other consumers.

With the exception of an older demand inducement literature reviewed by McGuire (2000), most of the subsequent empirical studies of provider competition examine hospitals. They typically focus on US markets and use patient-level discharge data from Medicare and state databases, often augmented by hospital-level data from the American Hospital Association. Costs are derived from standardized reporting forms in which as much as half of reported costs are allocated fixed costs, which can result in very noisy measures. Prices are estimated from "charges" (the maximum charge collected from a full-paying patient or insurer) and "discounts" (the discount

given to government payers that set prices by fiat and to private insurers who negotiate prices through selective contracting). Discounts are often aggregated across all
payers for both inpatient and outpatient services, so that the resulting net prices are
often rough estimates, at best, of actual inpatient transaction prices.

An important group of studies draws its theoretical inspiration from the theory of
the Medical Arms Race.[6] James Robinson and co-authors estimate hospital-level SCP
models. The key predictor is the number of other hospitals within a 15-mile radius.
They find that hospitals with more competitors tended to have higher costs per
patient (Robinson and Luft, 1985), more employees per patient (Robinson, 1988),
and offered more high-tech services such as coronary bypass surgery and mammography services (Robinson et al., 1987; Luft et al., 1986). Noether (1988) examines competition and pricing. She measures competition using the Herfindahl index (sum of
squared market shares) at the level of the metropolitan area. She finds that hospital
costs are higher in less concentrated markets. She also finds that prices (measured as
full charges) are uncorrelated with the degree of competition, suggesting that consumers might not bear the burden of the MAR. Overall, these empirical studies fed the
conventional wisdom that health care competition was harmful.

The growth of selective contracting led economists to challenge the conventional
wisdom. To test whether the effects of competition had changed, Zwanziger and
Melnick (1988a) estimate separate Robinson-style SCP regressions for consecutive
years of data in California in the 1980s, a period of rapid PPO growth. Their underlying empirical model takes the form:

$$C_{it} = B_0 + B_{1t}H_{it} + B_2X_{it} + \varepsilon_{it}$$

where C_{it} represents per patient costs at hospital i in period t, H_{it} is a measure of market structure, X_{it} are control variables, and ε_{it} is the error term. The key parameter in
the model is B_{1t}, which is hypothesized to change over time. Zwanziger and Melnick
confirm that costs and concentration are negatively correlated at the beginning of
their sample period. By the last years, the relationship is gone. Zwanziger and
Melnick (1988b) show that the rate of growth of costs in California during this time
is much smaller in more competitive markets.

Dranove et al. (1992b) examine prices and price/cost margins in California over a
similar time period using a similar empirical framework. They control for possible
changes in service intensity by estimating prices for a standard "market basket" of services including a set number of patient days, tests, therapy services, drugs, and medical
supplies. They find that price/cost margins were falling during their sample period of

[6] Studies of competition among physicians were usually framed as studies of supplier-induced demand and apparently
show that utilization and spending are higher in markets that have more physicians per capita. Note that these
inducement papers tend to ignore the Satterthwaite search explanation for any observed positive correlation between
price and physician supply.

1983–1988. This presumably reflected the pricing pressure brought about by selective contracting. More importantly, margins were unrelated to the market Herfindahl in 1983, but are significantly positively related in 1988. Using national data through the early 1990s, Connor et al. (1998) also find a reversal of the cost/concentration relationship. The overall conclusion is that the growth of selective contracting eliminated or even reversed the perverse relationship between market performance and market concentration.

Capps et al. (2010) use similar methods to show that the beneficial effect of market forces on hospital pricing diminished after 2000. They suggest that growing patient preferences for inclusive hospital networks gave hospitals the upper hand in selective contracting negotiations and made it difficult for insurers to negotiate discounts even in markets with many hospitals.

Lynk (1995) presents empirical evidence suggesting that competition led to lower prices for for-profit hospitals, but that the relationship was reversed for non-profits. Lynk computes average prices for ten high-volume DRGs and performs traditional SCP regressions of market concentration on price, estimating separate equations for non-profits and for-profits. Dranove and Ludwick (1999) test the robustness of Lynk's methods, finding that the results hinged on several critical and questionable assumptions. Keeler et al. (1999) point out that Lynk relied on a single cross-section. When the SCP relationship is examined over a longer time series, the results resemble those in previous studies; prices are negatively correlated with concentration in early years and positively correlated in later years, even for non-profits.

In the early SCP studies, concentration is usually measured as the number of hospitals within a specified geographic area, by applying a concentration measure such as the Herfindahl.[7] In the former case, two hospitals that are direct competitors may be assigned different measures of market concentration, depending on how many other hospitals are in their respective radii. Although the Herfindahl is usually computed for an entire geographic area such as an MSA, and each hospital within that area is assigned the same value for the Herfindahl, some researchers have computed a hospital-specific Herfindahl. For example, one might compute each hospital i's market share in each zip code that it serves: s_{iz}. Hospital i's Herfindahl would equal $\sum_z \lambda_z (\sum_j (s_j^2))$, where λ_z is the share of hospital i's patients who come from zip code z, and $\sum_j (s_j^2)$ represents the Herfindahl index (i.e. the sum of squared market shares for all hospitals j) for zip code z.

One interesting sidebar to this SCP research agenda is the wide variety of measures of market concentration. The use of hospital-specific measures conflicts with conventional oligopoly theory in which all sellers compete in a single market. Market-level measures must adopt arbitrary boundaries defined by the census for some purpose

---

[7] Escarce et al. (2006) also use geographic radii in a traditional SCP framework.

other than characterizing health care competition. Despite the different approaches and concerns, the measures are usually highly correlated, with most of the variation derived from differences across urban areas of different sizes and between urban and rural areas.

A general problem with the SCP approach is that market concentration, no matter how it is measured, may be correlated with unobserved demand and strategic factors, creating endogeneity bias. Zwanziger and Melnick (1988a), Dranove et al. (1992b), and Connor et al. (1998) avoid endogeneity bias to some extent by estimating the cross-section SCP model over successive time periods. The coefficient B_{1t} may be biased in each cross-section regression; nonetheless, comparisons of B_1 across successive time periods reveal the evolving role of competition. Kessler and McClellan (2000) offer an innovative measure of market structure that limits endogeneity bias in cross-section analysis. They estimate multinomial choice models to predict patient choices of hospitals based on hospital location and a limited set of characteristics such as teaching status. They compute hospital-specific Herfindahls using predicted rather than actual patient choices. Kessler and McClellan's identification strategy still assumes that hospital locations and teaching status, and the resulting measures of competitiveness, are uncorrelated with unobservable patient characteristics.

Dranove et al. (1992a) show that ignoring the locations of hospitals, particularly the geographic relationships among different hospital markets, can lead to biased results. They posit that the locations of small town and rural hospitals, as well as the "high-tech" services they offer, depend critically on the locations of hospitals in nearby cities. For example, a hospital in a small town that is located a short distance from a metropolitan area may be less likely to offer a service such as neonatology than a hospital located in a similar sized community that is situated far from an urban center. By the same token, hospitals in a city that is surrounded by many smaller communities will be more likely to offer high-tech services than hospitals in a similar sized city that has few surrounding communities. They test these assertions by estimating ordered probit regressions of hospital service offerings, such as open heart surgery, neonatology, and MRI. They find that a small city's distance to larger markets positively predicts service offerings of hospitals in those small cities. The population of communities surrounding larger markets positively predicts service offerings of hospitals in the larger markets. While the market-level Herfindahl is a strong positive predictor of service offerings when these location issues are ignored—this is the MAR result—the importance of the Herfindahl is greatly diminished when location issues are included. Dranove et al. conclude that failure to properly account for the relative locations of hospitals and markets leads to biased estimates in SCP modeling.

The propensity of patients to travel creates a related bias associated with unobservable hospital quality. Suppose that quality and illness severity are complements in production; that is, the returns to quality are highest for the most severely ill patients. If travel is costly, then relatively healthy patients will disproportionately visit their local hospital, regardless of quality, while relatively sick patients will travel further to high-quality hospitals. Geweke et al. (2003) confirm this hypothesis using Monte Carlo methods to show that patients with high unobserved illness severity are, in fact, disproportionately admitted to high-quality hospitals. The implication for empirical research is alarming—observable hospital characteristics, including location and service offerings—are likely to be correlated with unobservable patient characteristics. For example, suppose (reasonably) that hospitals in the central city tend to be of higher quality, perhaps because they are associated with academic medical centers. These hospitals will have higher costs because they attract sicker patients. They may also appear to face more competition, particularly if one uses a hospital-specific measure of competition. This will induce a spurious negative relationship between concentration and costs. Despite this, nearly all studies of hospital competition rely on cross-section evidence rather than longitudinal, fixed-effects methods and assume that at least some hospital characteristics are exogenous. An alternative approach would be to rely on fixed effects methods that take advantage of time-series variation in market structure. Unfortunately, the extent of competition is likely to show little exogenous variation over time, with the possible exception of mergers, a topic taken up later in this chapter.

Following trends in industrial organization economics, health economists have recently developed structural models of hospital pricing. These are described in much greater detail in Gaynor and Town (2011, this Handbook) and I will only briefly summarize them here. Gaynor and Vogt (2003) develop a model of competition in a differentiated goods market and derive estimates of cross-price elasticities of demand. They use these estimates to simulate merger effects, a crucial step in antitrust analysis that we describe below. Town and Vistnes (2001) use a logit demand framework to measure a hospital's bargaining power with insurers. Capps, Dranove, and Satterwaite (2003) (hereinafter CDS) build off Town and Vistnes to derive a formula for a managed care payer's willingness to pay to include a hospital in its network. In all three papers, the key formula describing a hospital's pricing power contains information about market shares in micromarkets. CDS report that WTP is a powerful predictor of hospital profits and use the model to predict merger effects. Gaynor and Vogt also use their model to predict merger effects. Both studies find that mergers can lead to substantial price increases.

Ho (2009) observes that many hospitals do not contract with insurers, which is inconsistent with the CDS model. To explain this phenomenon, she develops a model in which insurers compete by assembling attractive networks and hospitals compete to be included in those networks. Ho argues that some hospitals may find it more profitable to admit patients out-of-network at full charges rather than offer discounts necessary to be in-network providers. In some cases these are hospitals that are operating near capacity. But Ho also identifies what she calls "star" hospitals which will attract sufficient out-of-network patients that it is not worth their while to offer the discounts necessary to be included in a network. Ho identifies several characteristics of the typical star hospital, including market share and service offerings.

Town/Vistnes, CDS, and Ho all model the first stage of the two-stage competition process described earlier. In the second stage in Town/Vistnes and CDS, patients choose among hospitals in the network. Ho allows patients to go out of network if they will pay the full price of care. Some insurers have introduced tiered networks, with a complex copayment structure. A survey among government employees conducted by Sinaiko and Rosenthal (2010) found that only about half of all respondents are aware of their physician's tier and only some of them would base their choice of provider on the tier. To date, there have been no theoretical or systematic empirical studies of competition in tiered networks.

Structural models offer several advantages over the traditional SCP framework. First, they are often tailored to the institutional environment and therefore have the potential for much greater predictive power. Second, they do not require the researchers to make necessarily arbitrary decisions about market definition. Third, they reveal underlying demand and cost parameters, which facilitate policy simulations. Structural models continue to take provider locations and provider attributes as given, however, and are therefore susceptible to endogeneity bias, although there are no studies to date that explore the potential extent of such bias.

3.3. Studies of Competition and Quality

Although early discussions of the MAR studies were couched in the language of costs and efficiency, they were implicitly about quality competition. Many other studies use the SCP framework to directly study the relationship between competition and outcomes. Nearly all examine outcomes for heart attack patients, largely for reasons of data availability. Heart attacks are frequent, the patients show up in publicly available hospital discharge data, and the outcome of interest, mortality, is not too rare. Using the instrumental variables approach to measuring concentration described above, Kessler and McClellan (2000) find that risk-adjusted mortality for heart attack patients is significantly higher in more concentrated markets. Kessler and Geppart (2005) refine these methods to show that the harmful effect of concentration is strongest for the most severely ill patients, who receive less intensive treatment but also have higher mortality. Gowrisankaran and Town (2003) refine Kessler and McClellan by estimating separate HHIs by insurance type and find that concentration increases mortality for Medicare patients.

Other studies of competition and quality yield mixed results. Propper et al. (2004) examine heart attack mortality in the United Kingdom following reforms to the

National Health Service. In 1991 the UK government introduced competition among providers by a set of publicly funded regional health authorities (RHAs) that were free to purchase health care for their populations from both public and private sector suppliers. The RHAs purchased services from hospitals through block contracts and the marginal financial effects of varying volume from the negotiated level was small. Competition was promoted until a change in government in 1996. Propper et al. examine how this change in policy affected death rates from heart attacks. They find that death rates fall across the board over time, probably due to technological advancement. However, the fall in mortality is largest in areas of the UK where there is minimal hospital competition. In areas with the most competition, mortality is nearly unchanged. After 1996, mortality declines somewhat in competitive markets. Propper et al. (2008) confirm these findings but add that waiting times were reduced in competitive markets. It is difficult to translate these results into a free market context because it is difficult to know what parameters were considered by the RHAs when evaluating hospitals for contracting, and the financial returns from attracting more than the contracted number of patients were minimal.

In 2006, the British government reintroduced competition, this time allowing all patients to choose their hospital and directly tying hospital revenue to volume. Prices were fixed using a prospective payment system along the lines described in the next section. Using Kessler/McClellan-style measures of competition in a DID framework, Gaynor et al. (2010) and Cooper et al. (2010) find that death rates for heart attack patients fell more rapidly in more competitive markets. Gaynor et al. also find that changes in hospital spending were independent of the level of competition.

Sari (2002) studies hospital quality in 16 states over the period 1992–1997. He measures quality using indicators developed by the Agency for Healthcare Research and Quality (AHRQ). She finds that quality is lower in more concentrated markets and that mergers are associated with reductions in quality. She also finds that higher managed care penetration is associated with higher quality on some but not all AHRQ measures. Mutter et al. (2008) study hospital quality using a single cross-section of US hospitals in 1997. They examine 36 different AHRQ measures and consider 12 different concentration measures. They obtain mixed results across quality measures.

Mukamel et al. (2002) use difference-in-differences (DID) methods to examine how changes in HHIs affect quality. They combine evidence that increased clinical spending is associated with lower mortality for a range of high mortality diagnoses, including heart attack, with evidence that increasing HHI is associated with lower spending and conclude that increasing HHI causes higher mortality. An important limitation is that changes in HHI may be endogenous to changes in quality.

Table 10.2 summarizes the empirical literature on the effects of competition on costs, prices, and quality. There are some consistent themes. The shift to payer-driven

Table 10.2 Summary of Empirical Studies of Competition

Authors	Dependent Variable	Methodology	Findings
Pauly and Satterthwaite (1981)	Physician prices	SCP	Prices higher when search is more difficult
Robinson and co-authors (1985, 1987)	Hospital costs and services	SCP	Costs lower in more concentrated markets
Noether (1988)	Hospital prices and costs	SCP	Costs lower in more concentrated markets. No relationship between prices and competition
Zwanziger and Melnick (1988a)	Hospital costs	SCP in repeated cross-sections	Negative relationship between cost and concentration disappears over time
Dranove et al. (1992b)	Hospital prices and costs	SCP in repeated cross-sections	Negative relationship between price/cost margins and concentration disappears over time
Connor et al. (1998)	Hospital prices	SCP in repeated cross-sections	Negative relationship between prices and concentration disappears over time
Capps et al. (2010)	Hospital prices	SCP in repeated cross-sections	Trend in which concentration leads to higher prices diminishes after 2000
Dranove et al. (1992a)	Hospital services	SCP	Failure to account for hospital location leads to biased coefficients on concentration
Lynk (1995)	Hospital prices	SCP	Negative relationship for non-profits but not for for-profits
Dranove and Ludwick (1999)	Hospital prices	SCP	Lynk results not robust to changes in key assumptions
Keeler et al. (1999)	Hospital prices	SCP in repeated cross-sections	Negative relationship for non-profits disappears over time
Gaynor and Vogt (2003)	Hospital prices	Structural	Competition leads to lower prices
Town and Vistnes (2001)	Hospital prices	Structural	Competition leads to lower prices
Capps, Dranove, and	Hospital prices	Structural	Competition leads to lower prices

(*Continued*)

Table 10.2 (Continued)

Authors	Dependent Variable	Methodology	Findings
Satterthwaite (2003) Ho (2009)	Hospital prices	Structural	"Star" hospitals and hospitals near capacity may charge high prices and end up "out of network"
Kessler and McClellan (2000)	Mortality of heart attack patients	SCP	Innovative measure of market structure; mortality is higher in more concentrated markets
Kessler and Geppart (2005)	Mortality of heart attack patients	SCP	Harmful effect of concentration greater among most severely ill patients
Gowrisankaran and Town (2003)	Mortality of heart attack patients	SCP	Harmful effect of concentration greater for Medicare patients
Propper et al. (2004)	Mortality of heart attack patients	DID	Mortality is lower in more concentrated markets after UK reforms encouraging competition
Propper et al. (2008)	Mortality and waiting times for heart attack patients	DID	Mortality is lower and waiting times higher in more concentrated markets after 1990s UK reforms encouraging competition
Gaynor et al. (2010)	Mortality for heart attack patients	DID	Mortality is higher in more concentrated markets after 2006 UK reforms encouraging competition
Cooper et al. (2010)	Mortality for heart attack patients	DID	Mortality is higher in more concentrated markets after 2006 UK reforms encouraging competition
Sari (2002)	AHRQ quality indicators	SCP	Quality is lower in more concentrated markets
Mukamel et al. (2002)	Mortality for high-risk diagnoses	DID	Mortality is higher in more concentrated markets
Mutter et al. (2008)	AHRQ quality indicators	SCP	Mixed results using a range of measures of concentration

competition in the United States caused a fundamental shift in the SCP relationship; health care markets now resemble traditional markets. Recalling that much of the variation in market structure comes from urban/rural differences, the cross-section SCP regressions confirm basic intuitions about urban markets: they are less concentrated, but also offer a higher intensity of services, at a higher cost, and likely with better outcomes. Indeed, it would be difficult to reconcile real world travel patterns (patients often travel from rural homes to urban hospitals, but not vice versa) with any other set of results. Unobservable differences in patient severity make it difficult to draw any firm conclusions about differences in costs across markets with different levels of concentration. Most studies suggest that competition either improves quality or is neutral; a possible exception is the Propper et al. (2004) study of competition in the UK during the 1990s. More recent competitive reforms in the UK seem to have improved quality without increasing costs. Note that it is inappropriate to draw conclusions about US-style competition from UK results and vice versa. While prices are set by the market in the US, prices in the UK continue to be regulated by the central government.

3.4. Competition and Antitrust

The research literature on prices, costs, and quality is largely favorable towards competition. This section describes how antitrust enforcement is necessary to reinforce the effectiveness of competition. See Gaynor and Town (2011, this Handbook) for more detail.

In the United States, hospital market power is held in check by several antitrust laws. Part I of the Sherman Act prohibits combinations in restraint of trade and applies to mergers. Part II prohibits illegal monopolization and applies to situations where a provider uses existing market power to extend its dominance. An example of the latter may be when a dominant hospital demands exclusive rights to sell outpatient services as part of a contract to sell inpatient services. The Clayton Act directly prohibits anticompetitive mergers.

In the wake of the growth of selective contracting, the United States witnessed a rash of provider mergers. During the period 1997–2006, the HHI increased by at least 1,000 points in 39 metropolitan areas.[8] Table 10.3 lists 12 MSAs where the HHI increased by at least 2,000 during this period.[9] To get some perspective, according to guidelines issued by the US antitrust agencies—the Department of Justice and the Federal Trade Commission—every market in which the HHI increased by 1,000 points or more would be classified as highly concentrated (US Department of Justice and Federal Trade Commission, 2010). Table 10.4 lists the mergers that were

[8] The HHI equals the Herfindahl $\times$ 10,000.
[9] Source: Capps (2009).

Table 10.3 MSAs with Large Increases in Concentration, 1997–2006

MSA	State	Increase in HHI
Merced	CA	5,338
Fort Myers	FL	5,199
Cumberland	MD	4,787
Vineland	NJ	4,376
Pocatello	ID	4,314
Johnstown	PA	4,039
Altoona	PA	3,277
Fayetteville	NC	2,700
Worcester	MA	2,579
Florence	AL	2,316
Glens Falls	NY	2,188
Punta Gorda	FL	2,092

Table 10.4 Litigated Merger Cases

Year	Merging Party	Location	Merger Blocked?
1989	Rockford Memorial Hospital	Rockford, IL	Yes
1994	Ukiah Adventist Hospital	Ukiah, CA	No
1995	Freeman Hospital	Joplin, MO	No
1995	Mercy Health Services	Dubuque, IA	No
1996	Butterworth Health Corp.	Grand Rapids, MI	No
1997	Long Island Jewish Medical Center	New Hyde Park, NY	No
1998	Tenet Healthcare Corp.	Poplar Bluff, MO	No
2000	Sutter Health System	Oakland, CA	No
2004	Evanston Northwestern Healthcare	Evanston, IL	Judge ruled that consummated merger was anticompetitive
2008	Inova Health System	Manassas, VA	Yes
2011	Promedica	Toledo, OH	Yes (pending trial)

challenged by the Department of Justice or Federal Trade Commission, beginning in 1989.[10] Not only did the agencies challenge a very small percentage of the mergers, they lost nearly every challenge, including a streak of seven straight in the 1990s. The tide turned in the 2000s, as the FTC and DoJ have presented to the courts new economic theories and empirical evidence.

American courts generally accept the salutary benefits of hospital competition. Even so, when US antitrust agencies challenged mergers, they were hampered by the

---

[10] Source: Capps (2009) and the author's addition.

absence of direct evidence of anticompetitive effects. Responding to challenges by the antitrust agencies, hospitals cited the conventional wisdom that competition did more harm than good. With economics experts presenting evidence on both sides of the issue, antitrust challenges turned on two other critical issues. Most cases were decided by market definition, with the courts usually accepting large geographic markets in which the merging hospitals had small market shares. In one case, the court held that competition was not essential to constrain pricing by non-profit hospitals and permitted the merger of the two largest hospitals in a four-hospital market.

In the wake of these merger cases, economists have sought answers to three questions that are critical to merger analysis:

1. Is there direct evidence of merger effects?
2. How should markets be defined so as to best measure the extent of competition?
3. Does competition enhance performance of non-profit hospitals?

Several studies document the effects of mergers on prices. Mukamel et al.'s (2002) study, described earlier, estimates a differences-in-differences model with market fixed effects. Changes in the HHI result from mergers and fluctuations in patient flows. They find that increased concentration is associated with higher spending. Capps and Dranove (2004) also use a DID approach, this time with hospital fixed effects. The unique features of this paper are that the authors obtain actual transactions prices from insurance companies and they focus their attention on a handful of markets in which there were prominent hospital mergers. Using patient flows to measure hospital-specific HHIs and focusing on HHI increases that result from mergers, they find a large and statistically significant relationship between increases in the HHI and increases in prices.

Dafny (2009) observes that prior studies take mergers as exogenous, but that mergers may be endogenous to changes in unobservable shocks to supply and demand. To avoid endogeneity bias she instruments for mergers using co-location, which is defined as two or more hospitals located very close to one another. (Dafny tries a range of distances to test for robustness.) Dafny examines the effects of co-location on the prices of *other hospitals* in the same market, the logic being that these hospitals are more likely to be in a market in which a merger has occurred, and that mergers should allow all hospitals in the market to raise prices. She finds that instrumented mergers of co-located hospitals are strong significant predictors of higher prices at other hospitals.

There have also been several case studies of hospital mergers. A major advantage of these case studies is that the researchers are able to obtain actual transactions prices. Most of the case studies compare price changes at the merging hospitals with price changes at other hospitals in the same market. Krishnan (2001) studies two mergers in Ohio and California and finds that prices at the merging hospitals increased more for those procedures in which the hospitals had the most market power. Vita and Sacher (2001) find that prices increased subsequent to a merger of two hospitals in a concentrated market. Economists working for or at the Federal Trade Commission recently produced studies that examined price changes in the aftermath of three mergers that were not litigated (Haas-Wilson and Garmon, 2011; Thompson, 2011; Tenn, 2011). Prices unambiguously increased after two of the three mergers. Price changes after the third merger were mixed. The Netherlands recently moved from regulated to market-based prices for hospital services. Kemp and Severijnen (2011) study the effects of two subsequent mergers on the price of hip replacement surgery and find a significant increase after one merger but not the other.

There are also a few studies of the effects of mergers on quality. Using DID methods, Ho and Hamilton (2000) (measuring mortality for heart attacks, strokes, and newborns) and Capps (2005) (using AHRQ quality measures) find little to no effect of hospital mergers on quality. In a case study, the Federal Trade Commission found that the Evanston/Northwestern merger (which it litigated retrospectively) had no impact on quality (Romano and Balan, 2011). Finally, Gaynor et al. (2011b) examine the impact of mergers in the United Kingdom. During the period 1997–2006, the UK government forced about half of the hospitals to merge, claiming that this would boost quality. Gaynor et al. match merged and non-merged hospitals using propensity scores and measure quality using the standardized mortality rate of the hospital's catchment area. They find no difference in quality between merged and non-merged hospitals.

Table 10.5 summarizes the literature on hospital mergers. Consistent with the empirical studies of competition under selective contracting, mergers seem to increase prices with little effect on quality. Thus, on balance it appears that mergers are welfare reducing. (Bear in mind that all of the mergers in the case studies caused appreciable increases in market concentration.)

The fact that mergers mostly appear to increase prices stands in contrast with the outcomes of litigated merger cases. As noted in Table 10.4, antitrust agencies lost a string of merger challenges in the 1990s. Antitrust merger analysis is essentially an exercise in prediction: the courts use available theory and evidence to predict whether a proposed merger will cause prices to increase. These predictions have historically been derived by first defining a market and then computing the market HHI. If the HHI is small and/or the merger has a small impact on the HHI, then prices are not predicted to increase and the merger is normally approved. Thus, the outcome of a merger challenge usually hinges on market definition.

In most of the 1990s merger cases, courts accepted market definitions derived from patient flow analysis. This method, first suggested in a pair of studies of the coal market by Elzinga/Hogarty (henceforth EH), examines the extent to which goods and services are exported and imported into a proposed geographic market. If either outflows or inflows (of goods or customers) exceed a pre-specified threshold, it is concluded that firms outside of the proposed market are competitors and therefore the boundaries of the market must be expanded. EH recommended a threshold of 10 percent, although there is no theoretical foundation for either the examination of

Table 10.5 Studies of Hospital Mergers

Authors	Dependent Variable	Methodology	Results
Mukamel et al. (2002)	Costs	Difference in differences	Increases in concentration associated with higher costs
Capps and Dranove (2004)	Actual transactions prices	DID	Increases in concentration associated with higher prices
Dafny (2009)	Prices	Instrumental variables	Instrumented mergers associated with higher prices for other hospitals in market
Krishnan (2001)	Prices	Case study	Price increases at merged hospitals positively correlated with concentration increases
Vita and Sacher (2001)	Prices	Case study	Merged hospitals raised prices
Haas–Wilson and Garmon (2011)	Prices	Case study	Merged hospitals raised prices
Thompson (2011)	Prices	Case study	Mixed results
Tenn (2011)	Prices	Case study	Merged hospitals raised prices
Ho and Hamilton (2000)	Mortality for three diagnoses	DID	Mergers have little effect
Capps (2005)	AHRQ quality measures	DID	Mergers have little effect
Romano and Balan (2011)	Clinical quality measures	Case study	Merger had little effect
Gaynor et al. (2011b)	Regulator's measure of hospital quality	DID with propensity score matching	Hospitals forced to merge by UK government and independent hospitals had similar quality

flows or the threshold (Werden, 1992). Capps and Dranove (2004) and the FTC economists showed that using EH methods, none of their merging hospitals possessed market power. This does not square with the observed substantial price increases. If EH does not reliably predict merger effects, it cannot be used for market definition.

This raises the question of what method, if any, should replace EH? FTC/DoJ Merger Guidelines offer some guidance. They recommend implementing the "hypothetical monopolist" or "SSNIP" (small, sustainable, non-transitory increase in price) test.[11] In a nutshell, a market is well defined if a hypothetical merger of all sellers in

---

[11] See US Department of Justice and Federal Trade Commission (2010).

the proposed market would cause prices to increase by 5—10% or more for a period of one year or more. This kind of simulation is easily accommodated by structural models such as those developed by Capps et al. (2003) and Gaynor and Vogt (2003), and Gaynor et al. (2011a) show how to use their earlier model to implement the SSNIP. The underlying theory of pricing under selective contracting presented by CDS was central to the FTC's winning case against Evanston Northwestern Healthcare and the FTC used a modified version of the Capps et al. (2003) model in a recent challenge to a merger in Virginia; the hospitals withdrew their merger application before going to trial.

4. REGULATING PRICES

Section 3 examined whether competitive markets are efficient and whether there are potential gains from regulation of market structure through antitrust enforcement. This section considers more direct regulation of provider prices.

Historically, hospitals were treated like natural monopolies and their prices were regulated accordingly. Either annual budgets or prices for specific services were based on prior costs. Cost-based reimbursement was blamed for health care cost inflation and the Medical Arms Race. Beginning in the 1970s, several US states began setting hospital prices prospectively. The best example was New York which set fixed prices per diem. Overall, rate setting seemed to reduce the rate of cost inflation (Biles et al., 1980).

In 1983, Medicare introduced the Prospective Payment System (PPS), which paid hospitals a fixed fee per admission. Payments in the PPS are adjusted by diagnosis and procedure, or Diagnosis Related Group (DRG). Medicare and many private insurers continue to use the DRG system, although there have been proposals to pay a fixed fee for an episode of illness. Most other developed nations use similar prospective payment systems, which are often referred to as Activity Based Funding.

4.1. Optimal Price Regulation

Shleifer (1985) provides a theoretical foundation for prospective payment. Shleifer describes "yardstick competition" in which prices are set by diagnostic category and the price within each category is set equal to the previous year's average cost. Providers may invest in efforts to reduce their costs. Shleifer shows that yardstick competition leads to first-best efforts, so that average costs equal those that would be realized in a competitive market.

Shleifer makes two critical assumptions. First, he assumes that quality is either unimportant or perfectly observable (so that the regulator can set a quality-adjusted price). Second, he assumes that there is no variation in the efficient treatment cost within each diagnostic category. That is, all patients within a given DRG have the same medical needs. If we relax the first assumption, then providers receiving a fixed payment may have incentives to shirk on quality; this point is detailed below. If we relax the second assumption, providers may be reluctant to treat patients who have above average medical needs, because the prospective payment may not cover their costs. Dranove (1987) shows this can cause hospitals to dump patients on less efficient safety net hospitals and argues for increasing the number of DRGs so as to reduce within-DRG patient heterogeneity.

Chalkey and Malcomson (2002) estimate the efficiency gain from reducing within-DRG heterogeneity. They consider a model where hospitals can make effort to improve efficiency, patients have varying medical needs that are not adequately controlled by DRG classification, and the social planner wishes to minimize provider payments while assuring that all patients receive treatment. If the fee is not high enough, patients are dumped at a cost to the social planner. By assuming specific functional forms for hospital utility and the returns to cost-reducing effort, and calibrating these functional forms to the data, Chalkey and Malcomson simulate how costs would change as model parameters changed. They estimate that eliminating variation of patient medical need within DRGs could reduce costs by 17–70 percent. In 2007, Medicare refined the DRG system, nearly doubling the number of categories and reducing within-category heterogeneity.

4.2. Regulated Prices and Quality

Introducing quality into the model of yardstick competition has problematic welfare implications. Unless quality is observable and prices are perfectly quality adjusted, prospective payment may not lead to the first-best level of quality (Spence, 1975). If quality is poorly observed, one would expect it to be underprovided relative to the first best. Following Arrow (1963), researchers have resolved these difficulties by assuming that providers are partially altruistic. Altruism can be direct (providers value patient utility) or indirect (providers value quality.)

Ellis and McGuire (1986) show that when there is a single payer, a single altruistic provider (valuing quality), and patients are risk neutral, then it is optimal for the insurer to pay the provider a mixed payment regime of the form $P_i = \lambda R + \alpha C_i$, where P_i is the fee for treating patient i, R is a fee that is the same for all patients, C_i is the cost of treating patient i (to be computed from accounting or billing records) and λ, $\alpha < 1$. Ellis and McGuire (1988) obtain a similar result when efficient costs vary by patient medical need. Ma and McGuire (1993) relax the assumption that there is only a single payer and consider a situation in which a public payer can directly reimburse for "joint costs" that are shared across all payers, while private payers either do not or cannot pay for joint costs. They show that it is optimal for the public payer to partially reimburse for joint costs even though private payers free ride, in order to limit the underprovision of joint costs. Jack (2005) further extends this work by assuming that the degree of altruism is unknown and varies by physician. He shows that under the right conditions, it is optimal to offer providers a menu of Ellis/McGuire-style linear mixed payment regimes. More altruistic physicians self-select into contracts with higher fixed fees and lower cost sharing.

With the assumption of altruism, Ellis and McGuire (1986) provide a convenient way to give providers some utility from increasing quality. Another way to introduce a return to quality is to allow patients to choose their provider based on quality. Basic economic theory suggests that when demand becomes more elastic, quality improves and the cost-sharing parameter α can be reduced. Mougeot and Naegelen (2005) consider hospitals that compete for patients but receive expenditure caps from the government. This is analogous to yardstick competition at an annual (rather than per patient) level. They show that in a Cournot model, quality improves as the number of competitors increases, as do investments to reduce costs, though neither quality nor investments are at first-best levels.

Analogous issues arise when providers choose quantity instead of or in addition to quality. When prices are set by the social planner, they may not be high enough to clear the market. Ellis and McGuire (1990) consider a situation in which patients and providers may bargain over quantity when the fee schedule is not market clearing. They show that when the first best is feasible, it involves full insurance for patients and a mixed payment scheme for providers.

Nearly all theoretical studies conclude that some form of mixed reimbursement is optimal. Yet mixed reimbursement is rarely observed in practice, except for DRG adjustments which do not exactly fit the requirements of the theory. Researchers offer no compelling explanations for the divide between theory and practice. In spite of its theoretical appeal, a mixed reimbursement system has been infrequently observed in practice. Hospital payment by DRGs embodies some features of a "mix." Payment to the new Accountable Care Organizations (ACOs) created by health care reform in the US will lead to "shared risk" in losses and possibly gains, in effect, then, paying these organizations with a mixed system.

4.3. Empirical Evidence on Regulated Prices

The introduction of Medicare's DRG-based Prospective Payment System in 1983 generated a cottage industry in regulatory studies. In an early study that examined aggregate trends without control variables, Sloan et al. (1988) find that admissions and lengths of stay fell slightly after the implementation of the PPS and that the rate of increase of costs per admission fell by half. Friedman and Coffey (1993) control for state rate-setting programs and HMO penetration and also find a strong moderating effect of PPS on cost inflation. Interestingly, state rate setting becomes ineffective after PPS is introduced. Biorn et al. (2003) study the introduction of Activity Based Funding in Norway, finding that technical efficiency, measured as the output for a given set of inputs, improves after implementation, but that overall costs do not fall (perhaps because wages increased).

Cutler (1995) explores the effect of the PPS on outcomes. He notes that the PPS led to relative changes in profitability across DRGs. Using a differences-in-differences (DID) framework, he finds that declining reimbursements in some DRGs were associated with higher mortality. Shen (2003) defines "financial pressure" as the profitability of a specific DRG and measures pressure from both Medicare and private insurers. He finds that financial pressure from Medicare and HMOs is associated with higher short-term mortality but that there is no relationship between financial pressure and long-term mortality. Seshamani et al. (2006) use a similar measure of pressure and show that cutbacks in Medicare funding caused a small but significant increase in mortality in high-impact hospitals, while Encinosa and Bernard (2005) find that financial pressure leads to more adverse patient safety events. Using first differences of lagged dependent variables as instruments, Bazzoli et al. (2008) also show that quality suffers when overall financial performance deteriorates, although the effect is small. Volpp et al. (2005), on the other hand, find little evidence that Medicare payment reductions affected either care processes or outcomes for patients with heart attacks.

Several studies examine prospective payment for services other than hospitals. In 1998, Medicare introduced a per diem payment for skilled nursing while simultaneously slashing total payments for skilled nursing. Using DID methods, Konetzka et al. (2004) find that, after the cutbacks, staffing levels fell in those facilities that housed the highest percentage of skilled nursing patients. The British National Health Service introduced prospective payment for some surgery services in 1991, at the same time that it allowed regional health authorities to selectively contract with providers. Hamilton and Bramley-Harker (1999) find that the reforms led to reduced wait times for hip replacement surgery but that patients were more likely to be discharged to other providers rather than to their homes. The impact on outcomes was minimal. Israel introduced prospective payment for selected procedures in 1990. Shmueli et al. (2002) examine prospective payment in Israel, finding that lengths of stay fell, readmission rates increased, and mortality remained unchanged.

Prospective payment has had some unintended consequences. Morrisey et al. (1988) find that after the implementation of PPS, patients were discharged earlier, were slightly sicker at discharge, and were more likely to be discharged to another facility. This practice came to be known as discharging "quicker but sicker." Carter et al. (2002) find that some of the apparent increase in severity of Medicare hospital patients after the implementation of PPS was due to a change in diagnostic coding. This practice, sometimes derisively called "upcoding," helped hospitals maximize reimbursements. Dafny (2005) exploits a regulatory change to show that for-profits are more likely to upcode. In 1988, Medicare redefined how hospitals should classify patients undergoing specific medical procedures. This affected how hospitals classified patients as having "complications" and thereby affected the level of reimbursement. Dafny shows that for-profit hospitals coded patients more aggressively after the change. (So did non-profits, but to a lesser extent.) By examining trends, she rules out that the observed coding reflected changes in the patient populations and instead must indicate upcoding.

Table 10.6 summarizes the empirical studies of price regulation described above. The findings nearly universally confirm simple economic theories. Higher

Table 10.6 Empirical Research on Regulated Prices

Author	Setting	Findings
Sloan et al. (1988)	Medicare PPS: Hospitals	Admissions and length of stay decline after PPS is implemented. Cost inflation moderates
Friedman and Coffey (1993)	Medicare PPS: Hospitals	Cost inflation moderates after PPS is implemented. State rate setting no longer effective
Cutler (1995)	Medicare PPS: Hospitals	Declining reimbursements associated with increases in short-run mortality
Shen (2003)	Medicare PPS: Hospitals	Financial pressure from Medicare and HMOs associated with higher short-term mortality; no effect on long-term mortality
Seshamani et al. (2006)	Medicare PPS: Hospitals	Cutbacks in Medicare funding associated with higher mortality
Encinosa and Bernard (2005)	Medicare PPS: Hospitals	Financial pressure associated with adverse patient safety events
Bazzoli et al. (2008)	Medicare PPS: Hospitals	Poor financial performance causes a small decline in quality
Volpp et al. (2005)	Medicare PPS: Hospitals	No relationship between Medicare cutbacks and quality
Konetzka et al. (2004)	Medicare PPS: Long-term care	Cutbacks cause decline in staffing
Hamilton and Bramley-Harker (1999)	British NHS adopts PPS and contracting	Reforms lead to reduced wait times but minimal impact on outcomes
Shmueli et al. (2002)	Israel adopts PPS	Lengths of stay fall, readmission rates increase, mortality unchanged after PPS adopted
Morrisey et al. (1988)	Medicare PPS: Hospitals	Patients discharged "quicker but sicker"
Carter et al. (2002)	Medicare PPS: Hospitals	Evidence of more complete coding (sometimes called "upcoding")
Dafny (2005)	Medicare PPS: Hospitals	For-profit hospitals more likely to "upcode" in response to rule change

reimbursements lead to higher quality, but the specific way in which prospective payment is implemented encourages hospitals to shorten lengths of stay, reduce staffing, and take steps to maximize reimbursements. It is possible to draw limited welfare conclusions from these studies. It appears that a revenue neutral shift from cost-based reimbursement to prospective payment produces unambiguous savings with no obvious quality reductions. However, revenue reductions do lead to lower quality; unfortunately, we do not know the direction of the local gradient and therefore cannot determine whether fee reductions are harmful to welfare, let alone determine the optimal fee. And while the observed responses to reimbursement changes are consistent with the assumptions underlying theories of optimal reimbursement, the existing empirical results are entirely inadequate for calibrating these theories for the purposes of real world implementation.

The theory of determination of the optimal supply-side cost sharing can be contrasted to the theory of optimal demand-side cost sharing in this respect. The optimal demand-side cost sharing can be derived as a function of risk aversion and demand response, though other factors such as cross-elasticities also come into play (McGuire, 2011, this Handbook). Determining the optimal supply-side cost sharing depends on the degree of provider altruism, difficult to measure or even observe. Thus, while it may be unambiguously welfare enhancing to adopt limited mixed reimbursement (i.e. small α), it is much more difficult to determine the optimal α. And if the optimal α turns out to be small, the cost of gathering the information necessary to implement a mixed reimbursements scheme may exceed the welfare gains.

5. THIRD PARTY INFORMATION DISCLOSURE

Section 1 described how patients may have limited information about provider quality and how traditional market mechanisms for quality assurance, such as social networks, branding, and warrantees, are often inadequate. Theoretical models of price regulation and competition suggest that the result can be an inefficient underprovision of quality. Indeed, a theoretical model by Dranove and Satterthwaite (1992) shows that when price competition intensifies in the absence of easily observable quality, the result can be a race to the bottom on quality, with catastrophic welfare consequences. These theoretical findings are supported by much of the empirical work described in sections 3 and 4, although the hypothesized race to the bottom seems not to have emerged.

When traditional quality assurance mechanisms fail, third party certifiers often fill the breach. Third party certification is widespread in many industries—*Consumer Reports* reviews of automobiles come to mind. The US Healthcare Financing

Administration (now the Center for Medicare and Medicaid Services) introduced the first widely disseminated hospital report card in 1984. The report card included mortality rates, by DRG, for thousands of hospitals. The first report card received a lot of criticism because it failed to include risk adjustment. As a result, many highly regarded hospitals, which also happened to treat very severely ill patients, had high reported mortality and providers who received low rankings invoked the "holy writ" of provider report cards: "My patients are sicker." Although HCFA added risk adjusters the next year, interest in report cards waned and HCFA stopped them in the late 1980s.

In the past decade, certification of health care providers through health care report cards, and the closely related use of pay for performance (P4P) contracts, has become widespread. Report cards for health care payers have also proliferated. Some of the best known provider report cards in the United States include healthgrades.com (a for-profit venture that relies on Medicare utilization data), leapfrog.org (the product of a consortium of purchasers and employers that relies on Medicare data and information provided by hospitals) and Medicare, which reports on quality of hospitals and nursing homes. Figures 10.1 and 10.2 are screenshots from the Medicare Hospital Compare report card. Report cards are appearing in other nations as well. The Simon Frasier Institute recently released mortality rankings for hospitals in British Columbia and Ontario while the University of Manitoba has done the same for that province. DrFosterHealth.co.uk is the British counterpart to healthgrades.com while the Australian Medical Association's Hospital Report Card mainly focuses on waiting times for emergency room care and elective surgeries. Pay for performance programs are also rapidly proliferating. The United Kingdom has an ambitious P4P program targeting primary care. Results from preliminary studies of the UK program are summarized at the end of this section.

This section discusses the development, use, and responses to report cards and P4P.

5.1. Defining and Reporting Quality

The first step in designing a provider report card is choosing what to measure. Sociologist Avedis Donabedian is credited with developing a taxonomy of possible metrics:

Outcomes: This is what consumers ultimately care about. Examples include mortality rates, surgical complication rates, and patient satisfaction. Figure 10.1 shows outcome measures from Medicare Hospital Compare.

Process: Does the provider use accepted practices? Examples include vaccination rates, mammography rates, and dispensing of appropriate medications. Figure 10.2 shows process measures from Medicare Hospital Compare.

Inputs: Numbers and training of labor; access to the latest technologies? Examples include nurse staffing ratios and ratios of registered nurses to nurses' aides, and

Hospital Death (Mortality) Rates Outcome of Care Measures

"30-Day Mortality" is when patients die within 30 days of their admission to a hospital. Below, the death rates for each hospital are compared to the U.S. National Rate. The rates take into account how sick patients were before they were admitted to the hospital. **Read more information about hospital mortality measures.**

	View Graphs »	View Tables »

	NORTHWESTERN MEMORIAL HOSPITAL	LOUIS A WEISS MEMORIAL HOSPITAL	EVANSTON HOSPITAL
	251 E HURON ST CHICAGO,IL 60611 (312) 926-2000	4646 N MARINE DRIVE CHICAGO,IL 60640 (773) 878-8700	2650 RIDGE AVE EVANSTON,IL 60201 (847) 432-8000
	Acute Care Hospitals 14.1 miles	Acute Care Hospitals 7.7 miles	Acute Care Hospitals 1.2 miles
	Map & Directions Add To My Favorites	Map & Directions Add To My Favorites	Map & Directions Add To My Favorites
Death Rate for Heart Attack Patients	No Different than U.S. National Rate	No Different than U.S. National Rate	Better than U.S. National Rate

Hospital Readmission Rates Outcome of Care Measures

"30-Day Readmission" is when patients who have had a recent hospital stay need to go back into a hospital again within 30 days of their discharge. Below, the rates of readmission for each hospital are compared to the U.S. National Rate. The rates take into account how sick patients were before they were admitted to the hospital. **Read more information about Hospital Readmission Measures.**

	View Graphs »	View Tables »

	NORTHWESTERN MEMORIAL HOSPITAL	LOUIS A WEISS MEMORIAL HOSPITAL	EVANSTON HOSPITAL
	251 E HURON ST CHICAGO,IL 60611 (312) 926-2000	4646 N MARINE DRIVE CHICAGO,IL 60640 (773) 878-8700	2650 RIDGE AVE EVANSTON,IL 60201 (847) 432-8000
	Acute Care Hospitals 14.1 miles	Acute Care Hospitals 7.7 miles	Acute Care Hospitals 1.2 miles
	Map & Directions Add To My Favorites	Map & Directions Add To My Favorites	Map & Directions Add To My Favorites
Rate of Readmission for Heart Attack Patients	No Different than U.S. National Rate	No Different than U.S. National Rate	No Different than U.S. National Rate

Figure 10.1 Medicare hospital compare report card example: outcome measures.

	NORTHWESTERN MEMORIAL HOSPITAL	LOUIS A WEISS MEMORIAL HOSPITAL	EVANSTON HOSPITAL
	251 E HURON ST CHICAGO,IL 60611 (312) 926-2000	4646 N MARINE DRIVE CHICAGO,IL 60640 (773) 878-8700	2650 RIDGE AVE EVANSTON,IL 60201 (847) 432-8000
	Acute Care Hospitals 14.1 miles	Acute Care Hospitals 7.7 miles	Acute Care Hospitals 1.2 miles
	Map & Directions	Map & Directions	Map & Directions
	Add To My Favorites	Add To My Favorites	Add To My Favorites
Surgery patients who were taking heart drugs called beta blockers before coming to the hospital, who were kept on the beta blockers during the period just before and after their surgery	86%[2]	92%[2]	100%[2]
Surgery patients who were given an antibiotic at the right time (within one hour before surgery) to help prevent infection	97%[2]	97%[2]	99%[2]
Surgery patients who were given the right kind of antibiotic to help prevent infection	99%[2]	98%[2]	98%[2]
Surgery patients whose preventive antibiotics were stopped at the right time (within 24 hours after surgery)	94%[2]	96%[2]	99%[2]
Heart surgery patients whose blood sugar (blood glucose) is kept under good control in the days right after surgery	96%[2]	83%[1,2]	99%[2]
Surgery patients needing hair removed from the surgical area before surgery, who had hair removed using a safer method (electric clippers or hair removal cream – not a razor)	100%[2]	100%[2]	100%[2]
NEW Surgery patients whose urinary catheters were removed on the first or second day after surgery.	84%[2]	97%[2]	98%[2]
Surgery patients whose doctors ordered treatments to prevent blood clots after certain types of surgeries	98%[2]	98%[2]	99%[2]
Patients who got treatment at the right time (within 24 hours before or after their surgery) to help prevent blood clots after certain types of surgery	94%[2]	96%[2]	99%[2]

[1] The number of cases is too small to be sure how well a hospital is performing.

[2] The hospital indicated that the data submitted for this measure were based on a sample of cases.

Figure 10.2 Medicare hospital compare report card example: process measures.

availability of open versus closed MRI. Input measures are not usually included in report cards.

There is general agreement that outcomes are the gold standard for report cards; good processes and the proper inputs are merely means to good outcomes. Even so, process and input measures are acceptable if outcome data are unavailable, if the outcome of interest is a rare event that limits the power of statistical comparisons, or simply as a complement to outcomes.

Differences in outcomes may reflect differences in provider ability or differences in patient severity. Controlling for the latter is called *case-mix* adjustment. Although the specific implementation of case-mix adjustment varies across report cards, all case-mix adjustments follow the same basic steps. For example, consider the construction of a simple mortality report card. Let i denote the patient and j denote the provider. $Death_{ij}$ is a dummy variable that equals 0 if the patient lives and 1 if the patient dies. S_i is a vector of risk adjusters that may include demographic and/or diagnostic information about patient i. Finally, let N_j represent the number of patients treated by provider j. The observed mortality rate (OMR) for provider j is given by OMR $= \sum(death_{ij})/N_j$. The expected mortality rate (EMR) is recovered from the regression $death_{ij}=B_0+B_1 S_i+\varepsilon_i$, where the regression coefficients are used to predict probability of each person dying, $pdeath_i$, and $EMR_j=\sum(pdeath_i)/N_j$, where $pdeath_i$ is summed over all patients who visit doctor j. A comparison of OMR and EMR provides the basis for the risk-adjusted report card. For example, some report cards show the risk-adjusted mortality rate $RAMR_j = OMR_{average} \cdot (OMR_j/EMR_j)$, where $OMR_{average}$ is the average population mortality rate.

Certifiers often ignore the various problems associated with report cards. For example, report cards and P4P schemes for pediatricians often include the raw percentage of each pediatrician's patients who have received the appropriate childhood vaccinations. But vaccination rates are known to vary with patient income and education, so that pediatricians who treat lower income, less educated patients receive lower scores through no fault of their own. Nor is risk adjustment a panacea given the limited availability of informative risk adjusters. Many report cards rely on administrative claims data, such as Medicare data, which contains only a few demographic variables plus a restricted set of diagnostic and procedure codes. Iezzoni (1997) shows that report card rankings may vary profoundly according to the chosen risk adjusters. Moreover, the predictive power of mortality regressions remains low because important risk adjusters are unavailable, inflating the confidence intervals around RAMR and other report card scores. Medicare Hospital Compare identifies only a small percentage of hospitals as having mortality rates significantly above or below the mean. Iezzoni's results also suggest that rankings may be very sensitive to the choice of risk adjusters.

5.2. Do Health Care Organizations Fully Disclose Quality?

The well-known theory of unraveling suggests that under some conditions, there will be no need for certification because providers will voluntarily disclose quality (Grossman, 1981). To illustrate the theory, consider ten hospitals that have each measured their own cardiac surgery mortality rates. Heart surgery patients will prefer hospitals with lower mortality rates but may be unaware that there are any differences among hospitals. When no hospitals disclose, they share patients equally among them. The hospital with the lowest mortality rate will wish to disclose in order to boost its share. Once it has done so, the patients who do not go to the best hospital will divide themselves equally among the remaining nine. The second best hospital will therefore also wish to disclose, and so forth, until the ninth hospital discloses, which simultaneously identifies the worst hospital.

The theory of unraveling requires several strong assumptions. Providers must be able to cheaply and accurately assess everyone's quality. Otherwise the best may not set the unraveling in motion. The theory also assumes that patients have reasonable beliefs about the distribution of quality. Otherwise, the best provider may be reluctant to disclose its quality. For example, suppose that a hospital determines that its mortality rate for heart surgery is 1 percent—a very good rate. If patients believe that hospital mortality rates are usually much lower, then this hospital will be reluctant to disclose what ought to be considered good quality. Providers may also be reluctant to disclose if they have not been vigorously competing on quality. Calling attention to quality differences may increase consumer sensitivity to quality so that each seller ends up investing to improve its rankings. Unless sellers can pass these costs along through higher prices, they may earn lower profits than they did when consumers were unaware of quality differences.

Health care providers do disclose some quality information. Physicians must be licensed to practice and often display their certification. Most hospitals belong to the Joint Committee for the Accreditation of Healthcare Organizations, which bases accreditation on a number of input and process measures, as well as outcomes such as harmful "sentinel events." These mechanisms fall far short of full disclosure, however, and patients seeking a specialist or hospital must often rely on the recommendations of their (potentially self-interested) referring physicians.

Health plans have also failed to fully disclose quality. Formed in 1980, the National Committee on Quality Assurance (NCQA) represents foundations, employers, and payers. Its HEDIS report discloses a wide variety of measures of health plan quality. Jin (2005) explores why only half of all health maintenance organizations (HMOs) voluntarily disclose HEDIS scores. Disclosure costs cannot explain the failure to disclose, as some reporting HMOs explicitly instruct NCQA to withhold information already collected. Jin finds early disclosers are more likely to operate in highly competitive markets, a finding consistent with product differentiation. She also finds that the average disclosure rate tends to be lower in competitive markets, however. The counter-intuitive relationship between competition and disclosure is not necessarily surprising; theorists have argued that zero-cost disclosure should unravel in a monopoly market (Grossman, 1981) but may not unravel in a differentiated duopoly (Board, 2009). Jin and Sorensen (2006) further show that the distribution of quality among reporting HMOs that authorize NCQA to disclose quality overlaps the distribution of quality among HMOs that do not authorize public disclosure, although the former do report better quality on average.

5.3. Does Disclosure Improve Consumer Choice?

One of the purported benefits of disclosure is that it facilitates better matches between consumers and products. Consumers may migrate towards higher-quality providers ("vertical sorting") or to sellers whose product characteristics best meet their idiosyncratic needs ("horizontal sorting"). Both types of sorting could substantially increase welfare even if product attributes remain unchanged.

Several studies examine vertical sorting among health insurers. Wedig and Tai-Seale (2002) examine health plan choices when plan report cards were introduced to federal employees in 1996. They estimate a nested multinomial logit model of health plan choice where the nests represent different types of plans (IPA or HMO) and report card scores are key predictors. They estimate separate models for 1995 and 1996, comparing the coefficients on quality in the two years. (This is analogous to the Zwanziger/Melnick approach to estimating SCP models of hospital pricing.) They find that health plan quality is negatively correlated with plan choice in 1995, when quality has not yet been reported, and suggest that this might reflect higher marketing expenses by low-quality plans. In 1996, the effect of quality is positive and significant, with an especially strong effect for new employees.

Scanlon et al. (2002) study how General Motors employees responded to the dissemination of health plan ratings in 1997. An important feature of the GM report card is that it provided simple "diamond"-based ratings (plans could score 1, 2, or 3 diamonds) in just six categories, such as "Preventive Care" and "Women's Health." Scanlon et al. estimate a fixed-plan effects model that exploits the introduction of the report card, and changes in report card scores and prices over time. They find that plans lose market share for each "1 diamond" rating they receive, but that plans do not gain market share for "3 diamond" ratings. Chernew et al. (2008) examine the same GM health plan report card using a structural learning model embedded within a nested logit demand framework, where the nests represent different types of health plans (PPO, HMO or indemnity). GM employees have beliefs about plan quality prior to the release of the report cards, where the precision of these beliefs is a parameter of the model. Beliefs about quality are updated with the report card release. Chernew et al. find that report cards lead to only a modest updating of beliefs about plan quality, so that only 3.9 percent of employees switch plans as a result of the report cards.

Beaulieu (2002) studies plan choices among Harvard employees. Harvard's report card, which was introduced in 1996 for enrollment in 1997, gave plans one to five stars in 12 categories. Beaulieu estimates both a simple switching model as well as a conditional logit demand model. She finds that the enrollees were more likely to switch plans after the release of the report card and the odds of choosing a particular plan increases by approximately 10% for every unit increase in the plan's quality rating. Unlike Scanlon et al. (2002), quality ratings mattered more to employees with longer tenure than for new employees.

Jin and Sorensen (2006) examine how enrollees in the Federal Employees Health Benefits Plan (FEHBP) respond to publicized health plan ratings provided by the National Committee for Quality Assurance (NCQA). FEHBP issued minimal health plan quality information throughout the 1990s. In 1998, *US News and World Reports* published health plan quality information compiled by the NCQA. A novel aspect of this study is that NCQA tabulated quality scores for prior years. Thus, Jin and Sorensen can control for prior quality, therefore isolating the effect of disclosure. They find that NCQA scores have a modest positive correlation with enrollment prior to 1998, and a much larger positive impact after 1998, when they are publicly disclosed. A one standard deviation increase in the publicly disclosed score is associated with a 2.63 percent higher probability of plan choice.

Dafny and Dranove (2008) focus on Medicare enrollees' choices of Medicare managed care plans subsequent to the publication of *Medicare & You* quality rankings in 1999. Enrollments in Medicare managed care grew steadily throughout the 1990s, which Dafny and Dranove treat as a period of "market learning" about quality. Estimating nested logit demand models (the nests are traditional Medicare and Medicare managed care), they find that plans that received high report card scores were gaining market share prior to 1999, but that the publication of the report card scores further boosted their share. The effects of market learning and the report cards were comparable in magnitude.

There is also strong evidence of vertical sorting among providers. Bundorf et al. (2009) find that fertility clinics with high birth rates gain market share after the US Center for Disease Control and Prevention began publishing success rates in 1997. Schneider and Epstein (1998) and Romano and Zhou (2004) fail to find any movement towards higher ranked providers after publication of hospital report cards. Cutler et al. (2004), however, find that lower ranking hospitals in New York lost market share, especially among less severely ill patients. This result is similar to Scanlon et al.'s (2002) findings about asymmetric responses to health plan quality. Dranove and Sfekas (2008) argue that disclosure may fail to affect demand if ratings confirm what consumers already know about quality. They estimate a structural learning model. Prior beliefs are estimated from a multinomial hospital choice model in the pre-report card period. The model includes hospital fixed effects that are converted to z-scores and interpreted as quality rankings. Report card rankings are also converted to z-scores and a second multinomial choice model is estimated for the post-period. They find that report card rankings are positively correlated with prior beliefs but that "news" in rankings—differences between the ranking z-score and the fixed effect z-score—positively predicts hospital demand. Again, the effect is asymmetric—bad news hurts but good news does not help. In a similar vein, Wang et al. (2011) used a fixed effects framework to show that surgeons who received poor ratings on Pennsylvania CABG report cards experienced a decrease in volume.

Many of the aforementioned studies find heterogeneous consumer responses to quality information. For example, health plan ratings are more likely to affect individuals choosing a plan for the first time (Wedig and Tai-Seale, 2002; Jin and Sorensen, 2006), ratings are more effective in the areas where consumers had less information prior to the publication of quality measures (Dafny and Dranove, 2008; Dranove and Sfekas, 2008), and quality reporting for fertility clinics has a greater effect in the states that mandate insurance coverage for the reported fertility treatment (Bundorf et al., 2009).

Consumer response is sensitive to the reported measures of quality. Scanlon et al. (2002) find that GM employees respond to overall quality indices but not to specific quality measures. Similarly, Dafny and Dranove (2008) find that the effect of health plan report cards on Medicare beneficiaries is driven by responses to consumer satisfaction scores, while other more objective quality measures did not affect enrollment decisions. Pope (2006) finds that changes in *US News and World Reports* discrete hospital rankings affected patient choice, even after controlling for continuous quality. This array of findings suggests that consumers focus on measures that are easier to understand. As a counter example, Bundorf et al. (2009) find that consumers show considerable sophistication when selecting a fertility clinic. Patients do not necessarily frequent clinics with high raw birth rates, which may reflect patient mix, but instead favor clinics with strong report card scores, which adjust for patient mix.

Several studies described above monetize the value of disclosure to consumers and providers. Jin and Sorensen (2006) find that the publication of plan ratings motivates 0.7 percent of federal annuitants to change their health plan choices, due to the enormous inertia in individual plan choice. For those individuals whose decisions are materially affected by the ratings, the value of the information is estimated to be $160 per person per year. Averaged over all individuals in the sample, the value of the published scores is only $1.11 per person. Chernew et al. (2008) estimate that GM employees were willing to pay about $330 per year (about 5 percent of premiums) to avoid one subpar performance rating, and the average value of the report card was about $20 per employee per year. Finally, Dranove and Sfekas (2008) find that hospitals whose mortality report card scores are two standard deviations above the expected score stood to gain $1.4 million dollars in revenues annually. This is much smaller than the dollar value of the lives saved by high-quality hospitals (based on conservative estimates of the value of a life).

5.4. Does Disclosure Improve Quality?

The value of a report card is not limited to the demand response, however. Consumers can reap potentially bigger benefits if sellers respond by raising quality. Two studies in the area of public health find favorable responses to disclosure. Jin and Leslie (2003) find that after Los Angeles County posted restaurant hygiene grade cards in 1998, hospitalizations from food-borne diseases declined by 20 percent, largely because restaurants improved hygiene. Bennear and Olmstead (2009) examined the 1996 Amendments to the Safe Drinking Water Act, which mandated disclosure of contaminant levels. They find that utilities reduced total violations by 30−44 percent and reduced more severe health violations by 40−57 percent.

Only a handful of studies systematically examine the effect of report cards on health care provider quality. In 1990−1992, New York and Pennsylvania adopted a hospital and surgeon report card based on cardiovascular mortality rates. Chassin (2002) reports that risk-adjusted inpatient surgical mortality in New York fell dramatically after the publication of the report cards. As discussed below, this optimistic finding may be premature because Chassin cannot rule out that hospitals refused to treat patients who had risk factors not included in the risk adjustment algorithm.[12] A study of hospitals in Ontario that received report card results at staggered intervals found that those in the early feedback group were quicker to implement process changes, such as allowing emergency room physicians to administer beta blockers, than the hospitals in the late feedback group (Tu et al., 2009). Chen (2008) studies Medicare's Nursing Home Quality Initiative (NHQI). Medicare introduced NHQI in 2002, when it began publishing nursing home quality ratings at the Nursing Home Compare link at the Medicare.gov website. The NCQI contains dozens of quality indicators that are summarized by four composite scores, including an overall rating. Chen builds off of a theoretical model of vertical quality differentiation and finds that all nursing homes raised quality but that lower-quality nursing homes improved relative to high-quality homes. The most striking changes occur in more competitive markets, suggesting that the NHQI helped limit information asymmetries that allowed low-quality nursing homes to compete head to head against higher-quality homes.

Kolstad (2010) provides a novel empirical test of whether report cards motivate providers for "extrinsic" reasons (i.e. they want to attract more patients) or "intrinsic" reasons (they want to offer high quality regardless of the financial implications, a la

---

[12] Nor can Chassin rule out the possibility that hospitals inflated patient risk factors.

Ellis and McGuire (1986)). Kolstad examines outcomes for heart bypass surgery before and after the release of surgeon report cards in Pennsylvania in 1998. His identifying assumption (supported by the data) is that patients do not use risk adjustment information when responding to report cards, but that physicians do use this information when assessing their own performance. Thus, market share may move in response to unadjusted report card rankings, and physicians may improve quality as a result (extrinsic rewards). Or physicians may improve quality in response to news in adjusted report card rankings (intrinsic rewards). Kolstad finds that extrinsic rewards due to quality reporting lead to a 0.09 percentage point decline in mortality (off a base of 3.42 percent), while intrinsic rewards lead to 0.30 percentage point decline.

Disclosure may harm consumers if quality is multidimensional and only some dimensions are disclosed, as firms may boost reported quality but shirk on unreported quality. This is related to multitasking, which is discussed below in the context of pay for performance. Werner et al. (2009) and Lu (2008) both find evidence that this occurred with the Nursing Home Quality Initiative. NHQI collects data on a wide variety of quality dimensions but only reports a subset of this data. Both studies find that reported quality increased after the introduction of the NHQI, but that quality deteriorated along different dimensions of unreported quality. Wu (2011) studies the fertility clinic report cards described earlier. In the first round of public reporting, the report cards highlighted the birth rate but buried the multiple gestation rate (a generally unwanted outcome) well down on a list of other less important metrics. In the second round, the multiple gestation rate was highlighted near the top. Wu found that after the first round, clinics boosted overall fertility but at the same time they increased the multiple gestation rate, apparently by implanting more embryos per round of treatment. In the second round, the multiple gestation rate returned to pre-report card levels.

Sellers may respond to report cards by taking steps that superficially boost scores without any tangible improvement in quality. For example, when reported quality depends on the characteristics of the consumer as well as the performance of the seller, sellers can improve performance by strategically selling to the "right" consumers. Hospital report cards provide an excellent example, as illustrated by the New York and Pennsylvania report cards. These report cards use extensive risk adjusters obtained from clinical records. Even so, the risk adjustment is necessarily imperfect, giving hospitals incentive to refuse to operate on severely ill patients. Using national data on Medicare patients at risk for cardiac surgery, Dranove et al. (2003) find that cardiac surgery report cards in New York and Pennsylvania led to selection by providers. Dranove et al. focus on heart attack patients, as all or nearly all will appear in hospital utilization data. They measure severity using prior year hospitalization and prior year hospital expenditures; both are positively correlated with mortality and neither is used as a risk adjuster by New York or Pennsylvania. They control for trends in hospitalization by comparing New York and Pennsylvania with the rest of the

nation and with other eastern states. They find that after the report cards are introduced, relatively healthy heart attack victims were more likely to undergo surgery in
the report card states and relatively sicker heart attack victims were less likely to have
surgery. Only the former result is significant. They also find that heart attack patients
in report card states experience delays in receiving ancillary services including catheterization and angioplasty. The result is that costs are higher for all patients and outcomes are worse for all patients, especially relatively sick patients.

Werner et al. (2005) note that race can be an important predictor of mortality but
is not used as a risk adjuster. They find that the incidence of cardiac surgery for
minority heart attack patients relative to white heart attack patients declined in New
York subsequent to the introduction of report cards. The effect is startling. Prior to
the publication of report cards, the discrepancy in CABG surgery rates was 2.7 percentage points for white versus black patients and 0.7 percentage points for white
versus Hispanic patients. After the report cards, the discrepancy increased to 5.0 and
3.2 percentage points, respectively.

Despite these concerns, there has been little theoretical analysis of how to design
optimal report cards when providers can "game" the system. An exception is Fong
(2009). She considers a principal agent setup where a noisy measure of surgeon performance is available to the social planner; it is helpful to think of surgical mortality.
The surgeon has a fixed ability, privately observed, but can engage in activities that
boost performance without necessarily improving patient outcomes. The social planner wishes to maximize patient outcomes but can only observe the surgeon's performance—that is, the surgeon performing surgeries and the patients either living or
dying. Fong introduces novel continuous-time contracting techniques to solve for the
optimal contract. She shows that the optimal scoring rule is typically characterized by
four distinct regions. If prior performance is very low, the surgeon is fired. If prior
performance is very high, the surgeon receives "tenure" and can never be fired. For
surgeons with in-between performance, there are two distinct regions that differ by
the sensitivity of the score to performance. If prior performance is low, the surgeon
remains in a hot seat and the score is highly sensitive to performance. Conversely, if
prior performance is high, the surgeon is given the benefit of the doubt and the score
is much less sensitive to performance.

5.5. Matching

Report cards may also benefit consumers by allowing for better matching of patients
to providers. It seems likely that provider quality and patient severity are complements, so that the sickest patients enjoy the largest returns from seeing the best providers. Very few studies to date examine such matching. Epstein et al. (2010) provide
evidence that matching occurs within obstetrics groups—high-risk maternity patients

are more likely to be treated by more experienced, higher skilled obstetricians. Such matching is less common for patients visiting independent physicians. Curiously, matching is not associated with statistically superior outcomes. Zhang (2011) shows that the introduction of hospital-level cardiovascular surgery report cards in New York in 1990 led to an increase in severity matching. However, the release of physician-level report cards in 1992 reversed this trend. Apparently, the best physicians accepted tougher cases when doing so would help their hospital's ranking, but stopped doing so when it risked their own ranking.

Table 10.7 summarizes the empirical literature on quality report cards.

5.6. Pay for Performance

A central question in the theoretical research on optimal payment design is how to balance the goals of cost containment and quality assurance. Pure prepayment will generally lead to underprovision of quality unless consumers are well informed about quality and switching costs are low. Optimal mixed payment models may generate second best solutions but payers have been slow to adopt mixed payments. Quality disclosure can increase the elasticity of demand for quality facing each seller, but the empirical evidence suggests that consumer responses to disclosure are modest and that disclosure can have unintended negative consequences.

Agency theory suggests an alternative to mixed payment models and disclosure—direct contracting for quality, or pay for performance (P4P). Research on P4P in health care is motivated by two simple theoretical propositions:

- If a principal pays an agent on a "fee for X" basis, then as the fee increases, the agent's production of X will increase. This is a *standard incentive* story.
- Suppose an agent can produce X and Y, where the two are substitutes in production. (That is, producing more of one raises the marginal cost of producing the other.) Then if a principal pays an agent on a "fee for X" basis, then as the fee increases, the agent's production of Y will decrease. This is known as *multitasking*.

The theory of multitasking is developed by Holmstrom and Milgrom (1991). In addition to introducing the basic concept of multitasking, Holmstrom and Milgrom describe how to optimally design a multitasking contract, the scope of activities to assign to the agent, the grouping of tasks, and the allocation of tasks across agents. To date, the empirical studies of P4P in health care focus on the basic question of whether multitasking occurs and do not address the more advanced subtle issues raised by Holmstrom and Milgrom.

Empirical research on P4P programs began to proliferate in the early 2000s and over 100 studies have been published to date (Van Herck et al., 2010). The studies are of varying quality; many have inadequate controls or involve simultaneous treatments

Table 10.7 Empirical Studies of Quality Report Cards

Author	Subject	Results
Jin (2005)	Health plans	Plans do not fully disclose quality
Jin and Sorensen (2006)	Health plans	Higher quality plans more likely to disclose; disclosure moves market shares[a]
Wedig and Tai-Seale (2002)	Health plans	Report cards move market shares
Scanlon et al. (2002)	Health plans	Report cards move market shares; effect strongest for low-quality plans and for new employees
Chernew et al. (2008)	Health plans	Report cards lead to a modest updating of beliefs about plan quality
Beaulieu (2002)	Health plans	Report cards move market share effect stronger for employees with longer tenure
Dafny and Dranove (2008)	Medicare managed care	Report cards move market share; "market learning" was occurring prior to report card release
Bundorf et al. (2009)	Fertility clinics	Report cards move market shares; patients are sophisticated when interpreting report card scores
Schneider and Epstein (1998)	Hospitals	Report cards do not move market share
Romano and Zhou (2004)	Hospitals	Report cards do not move market share
Cutler et al. (2004)	Hospitals	Lower ranking hospitals lose market share
Dranove and Sfekas (2008)	Hospitals	"News" in report cards moves market share away from lower ranking hospitals
Pope (2006)	Hospitals	Report cards move market share, even when controlling for continuous quality scores
Jin and Leslie (2003)	Restaurant hygiene	Disclosure leads to improvements in hygiene
Bennear and Olmstead (2009)	Drinking water	Disclosure leads to reduction in contaminants
Chen (2008)	Nursing homes	Report cards lead to quality improvements, especially in competitive markets
Kolstad (2010)	Surgeons	Report cards lead to quality improvements; most of the improvement comes from intrinsic motivation
Werner et al. (2009)	Nursing homes	Disclosed dimensions of quality improve; undisclosed dimensions get worse
Lu (2008)	Nursing homes	Disclosed dimensions of quality improve; undisclosed dimensions get worse

(Continued)

Table 10.7 (Continued)

Author	Subject	Results
Wu (2011)	Fertility clinics	Disclosed dimensions of quality improve; undisclosed dimensions get worse
Dranove et al. (2003)	Hospitals	Hospitals avoid sicker patients
Werner et al. (2005)	Hospitals	Hospitals avoid minorities
Zhang (2011)	Hospitals	Report cards facilitate matching of toughest cases to the best physicians; physician report cards undo matching

[a]Unless otherwise stated, market share moves away from lower ranked plans towards higher ranked plans.

that make it difficult to isolate the effects of P4P (Christianson et al., 2008). Van Herck et al. report that, on average, P4P programs generate small improvements in the targeted processes and outcomes. P4P is especially effective for immunizations and for diabetes care and is generally more effective for process measures than for outcomes. Only a few studies show that performance declined for non–incentivized measures (multitasking).

Mullen et al. (2010) provide a good example of a P4P evaluation. Beginning in 2002, California insurer Pacificare paid bonuses to medical groups that performed at or above the 75th percentile of the previous year's scores on several quality measures. One year later, five other California health plans joined in. The bonuses were potentially substantial—a small medical group could receive up to $30,000 annually in bonus pay. Mullen et al. compare trends in quality measures before and after P4P is implemented using a DID methodology; medical groups in the Pacific Northwest form the comparison group. They find that the effects of P4P are modest at best; only one P4P measure, cervical cancer screening, showed a statistically significant increase relative to trend. Another measure, appropriate asthma medication, showed a significant decrease. Appropriate antibiotic usage, which was not part of the P4P program, also declined. Overall, Mullen et al. fail to find evidence that the P4P program either altered care delivery or improved quality.

The United Kingdom Quality and Outcomes Framework (QOF), introduced in 2004, is the most extensive ongoing P4P program. QOF specifies 80 P4P targets concentrated in three diseases: asthma, diabetes, and heart disease. QOF applies to all primary care practitioners and bonus pay can amount to as much as 30 percent of practice income. In 2009 the UK implemented a parallel program for hospitals, home care, and mental health providers—the Commissioning for Quality and Innovation

(CQUIN) payment program. To date, CQUIN payments can add up to 2 percent to hospital reimbursements.

Several studies, including Campbell et al. (2007), McDonald and Roland (2009), and Campbell et al. (2009), report early results of the QOF. They find that the rate of improvement in the quality of care increased for asthma and diabetes immediately after the implementation of QOF, but the rate of improvement subsequently slowed. There was no improvement in care quality for heart disease. The QOF requires physicians to enter data into an electronic medical record and physicians report that the structure of their office visits is often dictated by the requirements of the QOF program. It is therefore not surprising that quality of care on dimensions not included in the QOF declined for asthma and heart disease (multitasking).

P4P programs are likely to proliferate. For example, Medicare proposes using 65 quality metrics in a new P4P program for managed care organizations. Research on P4P is likely to proliferate as well. Studies to date have confirmed both the standard incentive story and multitasking. There have been no strong welfare conclusions. Nor have researchers used results to improve P4P design by implementing concepts in Holmstrom and Milgrom. This may require a more structural approach that allows researchers to identify the underlying utility and cost parameters essential to optimal contract design.

5.7. Conclusion

Health care consumers lack the information necessary to make fully informed purchases. Because providers have failed to fully disclose quality, report cards may play a vital role in improving purchase decisions. To date, the available evidence suggests that report cards are not realizing their potential.

Health care consumers do not seem to be highly moved by quality disclosure, though the best studies do suggest that consumers respond when rankings differ from preconceptions. The nature of the response depends on whether the disclosed information is easy to access and understand, and whether consumers pay attention to disclosure. In any event, responses are modest and the dollar value of report cards—both to consumers and to high-quality sellers—appears to be rather low.

Report cards are also struggling to generate uniformly salutary seller responses. On balance there is some evidence that disclosure motivates sellers to improve quality. However, there is also considerable evidence that sellers have attempted to game the system at the expense of consumers, especially if the measured quality does not cover all dimensions of quality or does not adjust for characteristics of consumers that can affect the rankings.

The literature on health care report cards is central to a larger economics literature on third party quality certification. A question that is often addressed in the broader literature but has been ignored to date by health economists is the incentives for certifiers. As Dranove and Jin (2010) observe, there are many studies showing that certifiers in fields ranging from finance to auto emissions testing produce biased quality evaluations. Studying the motivations of health quality certifiers, and the implications for their certifications, is potentially fertile ground for future research.

6. CONCLUDING REMARKS

Nearly five decades ago, Arrow (1963) explained how uncertainty and asymmetric information confound health care markets. Individuals are uncertain about the onset and expense of illness so they purchase insurance. When illness strikes, patients have poor information about what services they need and where to obtain them, so they delegate nearly all important medical decisions to their physician. These choices solve some problems but create others. Insurance leads to moral hazard. Delegation creates potential conflicts of interest and does not guarantee that patients are directed to the highest quality providers. Since Arrow's seminal work, economists have clarified these problems and examined a range of regulatory and market mechanisms that might improve market performance.

Early studies presented a theory of harmful competition that was the direct result of moral hazard and delegation—the Medical Arms Race. Empirical research steeped in the tradition of the structure—conduct—performance paradigm showed that health care costs did seem to be higher in more competitive markets, although these studies never fully addressed concerns about endogeneity bias inherent in SCP regressions. As US markets transitioned to selective contracting, and the locus of purchasing power shifted from the individual patient to the insurer, evidence showed that prices were higher in more concentrated markets and that mergers also led to higher prices. In the past decade, empirical research has become more structural; these models confirm the adverse consequences of provider market power and are integral to antitrust analyses of mergers.

Payers in both competitive and regulated markets must design compensation rules that address the potential conflict of interest that arises from physician agency. A large theoretical literature studies the problem of how to compensate providers when quality is unobservable. Pure fee-for-service payment leads to excessive costs and quality; pure prepayment does the opposite. These studies usually conclude that a mixed payment mechanism is optimal under a variety of assumptions about provider motives and market structure. Even so, payers have been slow to adopt mixed payments.

In the past decade, public policy has shifted focus from concerns about costs to concerns about quality. The prevailing view is that without intervention by third party certifiers, markets generate suboptimal quality. As a result, report cards and pay for performance compensation rules have proliferated. The weight of the research evidence suggests that report cards and P4P have improved quality, although the effects seem small. Multitasking remains a problem and theorists have made little to no headway towards designing optimal report cards and P4P programs.

Some analysts interpret Arrow (1963) as evidence that health care is different and defies economic analysis.[13] This is a fundamental misunderstanding of Arrow's work. Economics provides a powerful lens for studying health care, provided one is sensitive to the importance of institutional features such as insurance and physician agency. And it turns out that the basic principles of oligopoly theory and agency theory apply about as well in health care as they do in most other markets. Health care is different, but perhaps only in the sense that all industries are different. Even so, many questions remain unanswered:

- In a competitive health care system, prices are lower in competitive markets while quality is comparable or higher. But are these outcomes superior to what can be achieved in a regulated health care system?
- Mixed payment methods appear to best balance conflicting incentives to reduce costs while maintaining quality. How can one use real world data to construct an optimal compensation system?
- Third party certification affects both the demand for high-quality sellers and the incentives to improve quality. But it has many unintended consequences. What are the elements of an optimal report card and/or pay for performance contract? How can one use real world data to construct an optimal report card/P4P contract?
- Most health economics research on markets, regulators, and certifiers answers the question "did an intervention have an effect?" rather than "how do we design an optimal intervention?" The latter requires a general equilibrium approach; welfare matters. It remains to be seen whether this involves careful consideration of existing theories, such as Holmstrom and Milgrom (1991), or the development of new theories, such as Fong (2009). Likewise it is unclear whether empirical implementation of theory will involve reduced-form analyses with careful identification, or more structural approaches, with equally careful identification.

REFERENCES

Arrow, K. (1963). Agency and the welfare economics of medical care. *American Economic Review, 53*(5), 941−973.
Bagwell, K. (2007). The economic analysis of advertising. In M. Armstrong & R. Rob Porter (Eds.), *Handbook of industrial organization* (Vol. 3, pp. 1701−1844). Amsterdam: North-Holland.
Baumol, W., Panzar, J., & Willig, R. (1982). *Contestable markets and the theory of industry structure*. New York: Harcourt Brace Jovanovich.

[13] For example, see Krugman (2011).

Bazzoli, G., Chen, H., Zhao, M., & Lindrooth, R. (2008). Hospital financial condition and the quality of patient care. *Health Economics*, *17*, 977–995.

Beaulieu, N. (2002). Quality information and consumer health plan choices. *Journal of Health Economics*, *21*(1), 43–63.

Bennear, L. S. & Olmstead, S. M. (2009). The impacts of the "right to know": Information disclosure and the violation of drinking water standards. *Journal of Environmental Economics and Management*, (Forthcoming).

Biles, B., Schramm, C., & Atkinson, J. (1980). Hospital cost inflation under state rate-setting programs. *New England Journal of Medicine*, *303*, 658–665.

Biorn, B., Hagen, T., Iversen, T., & Magnussen, J. (2003). The effect of activity-based financing on hospital efficiency: A panel data analysis of DEA efficiency scores 1992–2000. *Health Care Management Science*, *6*(4), 271–283.

Board, O. (2009). Competition and disclosure. *Journal of Industrial Economics*, *57*, 197–213.

Bundorf, M., Chun, N., Goda, G., & Kessler, D. (2009). Do markets respond to quality information? The case of fertility clinics. *Journal of Health Economics*, 718–727.

Campbell, S., Reeves, D., Kontopantelis, E., Middleton, E., Sibbald, B., & Roland, M. (2007). Quality of primary care in England with the introduction of pay for performance. *New England Journal of Medicine*, *357*(2), 181–190.

Campbell, S., Reeves, D., Kontopantelis, E., Sibbald, B., & Roland, M. (2009). Effects of pay for performance on the quality of primary care in England. *New England Journal of Medicine*, *361*(4), 368–378.

Capps, C. (2005). *The quality effects of hospital mergers.* Paper 05-6. Department of Justice, Economic Analysis Group Discussion.

Capps, C. (2009). *The extent of hospital consolidation and its effects on national health expenditures.* Working Paper.

Capps, C. & Dranove, D. (2004). Hospital consolidation and negotiated PPO prices. *Health Affairs*, *23*(2), 175–181.

Capps, C., Dranove, D. & Lindrooth, R. (2010). Hospital closure and economic efficiency. *Journal of Health Economics*, *29*(1), 87–109.

Capps, C., Dranove, D., & Satterthwaite, M. (2003). Competition and market power in option demand markets. *RAND Journal of Economics*, *34*(4), 737–763.

Carter, G., Newhouse, J., & Relles, D. (2002). How much change in the case mix is DRG creep? *Journal of Health Economics*, *9*(4), 411–428.

Chalkey, M. & Malcomson, J. (2002). Cost sharing in health service provision: An empirical assessment of cost savings. *Journal of Public Economics*, *84*, 219–249.

Chassin, M. (2002). Achieving and sustaining improved quality: Lessons from New York state and cardiac surgery. *Health Affairs*, *21*(4), 40–51.

Chen, M. (2008). *Minimum quality standards and strategic vertical differentiation: An empirical study of nursing homes.* PhD dissertation, Northwestern University.

Chernew, M., Gowrisankaran, G., & Scanlon, D. (2008). Learning and the Value of Information: The case of health plan report cards. *Journal of Econometrics*, *144*, 156–174.

Christianson, J., Leatherman, S. & Sutherland, K. (2008). Lessons from evaluations of purchaser pay-for-performance programs. *Medical Care Research and Review, 65*(6, Suppl.), 5S–35S.

Connor, R. A., Feldman, R., & Dowd, B. E. (1998). The effects of market concentration and horizontal mergers on hospital costs and prices. *International Journal of the Economics of Business*, *5*(2), 159–180.

Cooper, Z., Gibbons, S., Jones, S., & McGuire, A. (2010). *Does hospital competition save lives? Evidence from the English NHS patient choice reforms.* Working Paper 16/2010. London School of Economics.

Cutler, D. (1995). The incidence of adverse medical outcomes under prospective payment. *Econometrica*, *63*(1), 29–50.

Cutler, D., Huckman, R., & Landrum, M. B. (2004). The role of information in medical markets: An analysis of publicly reported outcomes in cardiac surgery. *American Economic Review, 94*(2), 342–346.

Dafny, L. (2005). How do hospitals respond to price changes? *American Economic Review, 95*(5), 1525–1547.

Dafny, L. (2009). Estimation and identification of merger effects: An application to hospital mergers. *Journal of Law and Economics*, *52*(3), 523–550.

Dafny, L. & Dranove, D. (2008). Do report cards tell consumers anything they don't already know? The case of Medicare HMOs. *RAND Journal of Economics*, *39*(3), 790–821.

Doran, T., Fullwood, C., Gravelle, H., Reeves, D., Kontopantelis, E., Hiroeh, U., et al. (2006). Pay-for-performance programs in family practices in the United Kingdom. *New England Journal of Medicine*, *355*(4), 375–384.

Dranove, D. (1987). Rate-setting by diagnosis related groups and hospital specialization. *RAND Journal of Economics*, *18*(3), 417–427.

Dranove, D. & Jin, G. Z. (2010). Quality disclosure and certification: Theory and practice. *Journal of Economic Literature*, *48*(4), 935–963.

Dranove, D. & Ludwick, R. (1999). Competition and pricing by nonprofit hospitals: A reassessment of Lynk's analysis. *Journal of Health Economics*, *18*(1), 87–98.

Dranove, D. & Satterthwaite, M. (1992). Monopolistic competition when price and quality are not perfectly observable. *RAND Journal of Economics*, *23*(4), 518–534.

Dranove, D. & Sfekas, A. (2008). Start spreading the news: A structural estimate of the effects of New York hospital report cards. *Journal of Health Economics*, *27*(5), 1201–1207.

Dranove, D., Kessler, D., McClellan, M., & Satterthwaite, M. (2003). Is more information better? The effects of report cards on healthcare providers. *Journal of Political Economy*, *111*(3), 555–588.

Dranove, D., Shanley, M. & Simon, C. (1992a). Is hospital competition wasteful? *RAND Journal of Economics*, *23*(2), 247–262.

Dranove, D., Shanley, M., & White, W. (1992b). Price and concentration in hospital markets. *Journal of Law and Economics*, *32*(1), 143–162.

Ellis, R. & McGuire, T. (1986). Provider behavior under prospective reimbursement: Cost sharing and supply. *Journal of Health Economics*, *5*(2), 129–151.

Ellis, R. & McGuire, T. (1988). Insurance principles and the design of prospective payment systems. *Journal of Health Economics*, *7*(3), 215–237.

Ellis, R. & McGuire, T. (1990). Optimal payment systems for health services. *Journal of Health Economics*, *9*(4), 375–396.

Encinosa, W. & Bernard, D. (2005). Hospital finances and patient safety outcomes. *Inquiry*, *42*(1), 60–72.

Epstein, A., Ketchum, J., & Nicholson, S. (2010). Specialization and matching in professional services firms. *RAND Journal of Economics*, *41*(4), 811–834.

Escarce, J., Jain, A., & Rogowski, J. (2006). *Hospital competition, managed care, and mortality after hospitalization for medical conditions: Evidence from three states*. Working Paper 12335. NBER.

Fong, K. (2009). *Evaluating skilled experts: Optimal scoring rules for surgeons*. Working Paper. Stanford University.

Friedman, B. & Coffey, R. (1993). *Effectiveness of state regulation of hospital revenue in the 1980s*. Washington, DC: AEI Press.

Friedman, B. & Pauly, M. (1981). Cost functions for a service firm with variable quality and stochastic demand: The case of hospitals. *Review of Economics and Statistics*, *63*(4), 620–624.

Gaynor, M. & Vogt, W. (2003). Competition among hospitals. *RAND Journal of Economics*, *34*(4), 764–785.

Gaynor, M., Kleiner, S., & Vogt, W. (2011a). A structural approach to market definition with an application to the hospital industry. *Journal of Industrial Economics* (forthcoming).

Gaynor, M., Ludicella, M., & Propper, C. (2011b). *Can governments do it better? Merger mania and hospital outcomes in the English NHS*. Working Paper. Carnegie Mellon University.

Gaynor, M., Moreno-Serra, R., & Propper, C. (2010). *Death by market power: Reform, competition, and patient outcomes in the National Health Service*. Working Paper 16164. NBER.

Geweke, J., Gowrisankaran, G., & Town, R. (2003). Bayesian inference for hospital quality in a selection model. *Econometrica*, *71*(4), 1215–1238.

Gowrisankaran, G. & Town, R. (2003). Competition, payers, and hospital quality. *Health Services Research*, *38*(6), 1403–1422.

Gravelle, H. (1999). Capitation contracts: Access and quality. *Journal of Health Economics*, *18*(3), 315–340.

Gregg, P., Grout, P., Ratcliffe, A., Smith, S., & Windmeijer, F. (2008). *How important is pro-social behaviour in the delivery of public services? Centre for markets and public organisation*. Working Paper 08/197, University of Bristol.

Grossman, S. (1981). The informational role of warranties and private disclosure about product quality. *Journal of Law and Economics, 24*, 461–489.

Haas-Wilson, D. & Garmon, C. (2011). Two hospital mergers on Chicago's north shore: A retrospective study. *International Journal of the Economics of Business* (forthcoming).

Hamilton, B. & Bramley-Harker, R. (1999). The impact of the NHS reforms on queues and surgical outcomes in England: Evidence from hip fracture patients. *Economic Journal, 109*, 437–462.

Hansman, H. (1980). The role of non-profit enterprise. *Yale Law Journal, 89*(5), 835–901.

Ho, K. (2009). Insurer-provider networks in the medical care market. *American Economic Review, 99*(1), 393–430.

Ho, V. & Hamilton, B. (2000). Hospital mergers and acquisitions: Does market consolidation harm patients? *Journal of Health Economics, 19*(5), 767–791.

Holmstrom, B. & Milgrom, P. (1991). Multitask principal–agent analyses: Incentive contracts, asset ownership, and job design. *Journal of Law, Economics and Organization, 7*, 24–52.

Hubbard, T. (1998). An empirical examination of moral hazard in the vehicle inspection market. *RAND Journal of Economics, 29*(2), 406–426.

Iezzoni, L. (1997). The risks of risk adjustment. *Journal of the American Medical Association, 278*(19), 1600–1607.

Jack, W. (2005). Purchasing health care services from providers with unknown altruism. *Journal of Health Economics, 24*(1), 73–93.

Jin, G. (2005). Competition and disclosure incentives: An empirical study of HMOs. *RAND Journal of Economics, 36*(1), 93–112.

Jin, G. & Leslie, P. (2003). The effects of information on product quality: Evidence from restaurant hygiene grade cards. *Quarterly Journal of Economics, 118*(2), 409–451.

Jin, G. & Sorensen, A. (2006). Information and consumer choice: The value of publicized health plan ratings. *Journal of Health Economics, 26*(2), 248–275.

Keeler, E., Melnick, G. & Zwanziger, J. (1999). The changing effects of competition on non-profit and for-profit hospital pricing behavior. *Journal of Health Economics, 18*(1), 69–86.

Kemp, R. & Severijnen, A. (2011). *Price effects of Dutch hospital mergers: An ex post assessment of hip surgery.* Working Paper. Netherlands Competition Authority.

Kessler, D. & Geppart, J. (2005). *The effects of competition on variation in the quality and cost of medical care.* Working Paper 11226. NBER.

Kessler, D. & McClellan, M. (2000). Is hospital competition socially wasteful? *Quarterly Journal of Economics, 115*(2), 577–615.

Kolstad, J. (2010). *Information and quality when motivation is intrinsic: Evidence from surgeon report cards.* Working Paper. University of Pennsylvania.

Konetzka, R., Yi, D., Norton, E., & Kilpatrick, K. (2004). Effects of Medicare payment changes on nursing home staffing and deficiencies. *Health Services Research, 39*(3), 463–488.

Krishnan, R. (2001). Market restructuring and pricing in the hospital industry. *Journal of Health Economics, 20*(2), 213–237.

Krugman, P. (2011). Kenneth Arrow was here. *New York Times Opinion Pages* 6/9/2011 < http://krugman.blogs.nytimes.com/2011/06/09/kenneth-arrow-was-here/. Searched 6/28/2011.

Lu, F. (2008). Information disclosure, competition and the behavior of firms: Evidence from nursing homes. University of Rochester, Simon School of Business.

Luft, H., Robinson, J., Garnick, D., Maerki, S., & McPhee, S. (1986). The role of specialized clinical services in competition among hospitals. *Inquiry, 23*, 83–94.

Lynk, W. (1995). Nonprofit hospital mergers and the exercise of market power. *Journal of Law and Economics, 38*(2), 437–461.

Ma, A. & McGuire, T. (1993). Paying for joint costs in health care. *Journal of Economics and Management Strategy, 2*(1), 71–95.

McDonald, R. & Roland, M. (2009). Pay for performance in primary care in England and California: Comparison of unintended consequences. *Annals of Family Medicine, 7*(2), 121–127.

McGuire, T. (2000). Physician agency. In Culyer & Newhouse (Eds.), *Handbook of health economics* (Vol. I). Elsevier.

Morrisey, M. (1998). Are patients travelling further? *International Journal of the Economics of Business*, *5*(2), 203–221.

Morrisey, M., Sloan, F., & Valvona, J. (1988). Shifting Medicare patients out of the hospital. *Health Affairs*, *7*(5), 52–64.

Mougeot, M. & Naegelen, F. (2005). Hospital price regulation and expenditure cap policy. *Journal of Health Economics*, *24*(1), 55–72.

Mukamel, D., Zwanziger, J., & Bamezai, A. (2002). Hospital competition, resource allocation and quality of care. *BMC Health Services Research*, *2*, 10.

Mullen, K., Frank, R., & Rosenthal, M. (2010). Can you get what you pay for? Pay-for-performance and the quality of healthcare providers. *RAND Journal of Economics*, *41*(1), 64–91.

Mutter, R., Wong, H., & Goldfarb, M. G. (2008). The effects of hospital competition on inpatient quality of care. *Inquiry*, *45*(3), 263–279.

Noether, M. (1988). Competition among hospitals. *Journal of Health Economics*, 7, 259–284.

Pauly, M. & Satterthwaite, M. (1981). The pricing of primary care physician's services: A test of the role of consumer information. *Bell Journal of Economics*, *12*, 488–506.

Phibbs, C., Baker, L., Caughey, A., Danielsen, B., Schmitt, S., & Phibbs, R. (2007). Level and volume of neonatal intensive care and mortality in very-low-birth-weight infants. *New England Journal of Medicine*, *356*(221), 2165–2174.

Pope, D. (2006). *Reacting to rankings: Evidence from "America's best hospitals and colleges"*. PhD dissertation, University of California, Berkeley.

Pope, G. & Burge, R. (1996). Economies of scale in physician practice. *Medical Care Research and Review*, *53*(4), 417–440.

Propper, C., Burgess, S., & Green, K. (2004). Does competition between hospitals improve the quality of care? Hospital death rates and the NHS internal market. *Journal of Public Economics*, *88*, 1247–1272.

Propper, C., Burgess, S., & Gossage, D. (2008). Competition and quality: Evidence from the NHS internal market 1991–9. *Economic Journal*, *118*, 138–170.

Robinson, J. (1988). Market structure, employment, and skill mix in the hospital industry. *Southern Economic Journal*, *55*(2), 315–325.

Robinson, J. & Luft, H. (1985). The impact of hospital market structure on patient volume, the average length of stay, and cost of care. *Journal of Health Economics*, *4*, 333–356.

Robinson, J. C., Garnick, D. W., & McPhee, S. J. (1987). Market and regulatory influences on the availability of coronary angioplasty and bypass surgery in US hospitals. *New England Journal of Medicine*, *317*(2), 85–90.

Romano, P. & Balan, D. (2011). A retrospective analysis of the clinical quality effects of the acquisition of Highland Park Hospital by Evanston Northwestern Healthcare. *International Journal of the Economics of Business* (forthcoming).

Romano, P. & Zhou, H. (2004). Do well-publicized risk-adjusted outcomes reports affect hospital volume? *Medical Care*, *42*(4), 367–377.

Roomkin & Weisbrod (1999). Managerial compensation and incentives in for-profit and nonprofit hospitals. *Journal of Law, Economics, and Organization*, *15*(3), 750–781.

Sari, N. (2002). Do competition and managed care improve quality? *Health Economics*, *11*(7), 571–584.

Satterthwaite, M. (1979). Consumer information, equilibrium industry price, and the number of sellers. *Bell Journal of Economics*, *10*, 483–502.

Scanlon, D., McLaughlin, G., & Solon, G. (2002). The impact of health plan report cards on managed care enrollment. *Journal of Health Economics*, *21*(1), 19–41.

Schneider, E. & Epstein, A. (1998). Use of public performance reports: A survey of patients undergoing cardiac surgery. *Journal of the American Medical Association*, *279*(20), 1638–1642.

Seshamani, M., Zhu, J., & Volpp, K. (2006). Did postoperative mortality increase after the implementation of the Medicare Balanced Budget Act? *Medical Care*, *44*(6), 527–533.

Shen, Y. (2003). The effect of financial pressure on the quality of care in hospitals. *Journal of Health Economics*, *22*(2), 243–269.

Shleifer, A. (1985). A theory of yardstick competition. *RAND Journal of Economics*, *16*(3), 319–327.

Shmueli, A., Intrator, O., & Israeli, A. (2002). The effects of introducing prospective payment on length of stay, quality of care and hospitals incomes: The early experience of Israel. *Social Science and Medicine*, *55*(6), 981−989.

Sinaiko, A. & Rosenthal, M. (2010). Consumer experience with a tiered physician network: Early evidence. *American Journal of Managed Care*, *16*(2), 123−130.

Sloan, F., Morrisey, M., & Valvona, J. (1988). Effects of the Medicare payment system on hospital cost containment: An early appraisal. *Milbank Memorial Fund*, *66*(2), 191−220.

Spence, M. (1975). Monopoly, quality and regulation. *Bell Journal of Economics*, *6*(2), 417−429.

Sutton, J. (1991). *Sunk costs and market structure*. Cambridge: MIT Press.

Tenn, S. (2011). The price effects of hospital mergers: A case study of the Sutter-Summit Transaction. *International Journal of the Economics of Business*, *18*(1), 65−82.

Thompson, A. (2011). The effect of hospital mergers on inpatient prices: A case study of the New Hanover-Cape Fear Transaction. *International Journal of the Economics of Business*, *18*(1), 91−101.

Town, R. & Vistnes, G. (2001). Hospital competition in HMO networks. *Journal of Health Economics, 20,* 733−753.

Tu, J., Donovan, L., Lee, D., Wang, J., Austin, P., Alter, D., et al. (2009). Effectiveness of public report cards for improving the quality of cardiac care. The EFFECT study: A randomized trial. *Journal of the American Medical Association*, *302*(21), E1−E8.

US Department of Justice and Federal Trade Commission (2010). *Horizontal merger guidelines*. Issued August 19, 2010. < http://www.justice.gov/atr/public/guidelines/hmg-2010.html > (searched 11/29/2010).

Van Herck, P., De Smedt, D., Annemans, L., Remmen, R., Rosenthal, M., & Sermeus, W. (2010). Systematic review: Effects, design choices, and context of pay-for-performance in health care. *BMC Health Services Research*, *20*, 247−259.

Vita, M. G. & Sacher, S. (2001). The competitive effects of not-for-profit hospital mergers: A case study. *Journal of Industrial Economics*, *49*(1), 63−84.

Volpp, K., Konetzka, T., Zhu, J., Parsons, L., & Peterson, E. (2005). Effect of cuts in Medicare reimbursements on process and outcome of care for acute myocardial infarction patients. *Circulation*, *112*, 2268−2275.

Wang, J., Hockenberry, J., Chou, S., & Yang, M. (2011). Do bad report cards have consequences? Impacts of publicly reported provider quality information on the CABG market in Pennsylvania. *Journal of Health Economics* (forthcoming).

Wedig, G. & Tai-Seale, M. (2002). The effect of report cards on consumer choice in the health insurance market. *Journal of Health Economics*, *21*(6), 1031−1048.

Weisbrod, B. (1991). The health care quadrilemma: An essay on technological change, insurance, quality of care, and cost containment. *Journal of Economic Literature*, *29*(2), 523−552.

Weiss, L. (1989). *Concentration and price*. Cambridge: MIT Press.

Werden, G. (1992). Four suggestions on market delineation. *Antitrust Bulletin*, *37*(1), 107−121.

Werner, R., Asch, D., & Polsky, D. (2005). The unintended consequences of coronary artery bypass surgery graft report cards. *Circulation*, *111*, 1257−1263.

Werner, R., Konetzka, R., & Kruse, G. (2009). Impact of public reporting on unreported quality of care. *Health Services Research*, *44*(2 Pt 1), 379−398.

Wu, B. (2011). *Information presentation, consumer choice and provider multitasking—evidence from fertility clinic report cards*. Working Paper. Northwestern University.

Zhang, Y. (2011). *Are two report cards better than one? The case of CABG surgery and patient sorting*. Working Paper. Northwestern University.

Zwanziger, J. & Melnick, G. (1988a). The effects of hospital competition and the Medicare PPS program on hospital cost behavior in California. *Journal of Health Economics, 8,* 457−464.

Zwanziger, J. & Melnick, G. (1988b). Hospital behavior under competition and cost containment policies. The California experience. *JAMA: Journal of the American Medical Association*, *260*(18), 2669−2675.

CHAPTER ELEVEN

Health Care Spending Risk, Health Insurance, and Payment to Health Plans

Friedrich Breyer, M. Kate Bundorf and Mark V. Pauly

Contents

Handbook of Health Economics, Volume 2
ISSN: 1574-0064, DOI: 10.1016/B978-0-444-53592-4.00011-6

Abstract

This chapter will deal with the actual and efficient functioning of health insurance in settings where risk (expected value) of medical spending or insurance benefits varies across individuals at a given point in time or over time for a given individual. It will deal with equilibrium in insurance markets with risk variation and will also deal with various configurations of information, the impacts on such markets of regulation motivated by risk variation, and the actual and optimal impact of governmental policies to deal with risk variation in national insurance systems.

Keywords: health care spending; health care markets; insurance; public policy; risk variation

JEL Code: I1

1. VARIATION IN HEALTH CARE SPENDING BETWEEN PERSONS AND OVER TIME

Annual spending on health care varies significantly across individuals. The top 5 percent of spenders account for approximately half of US health care expenditures in a given year (Zuvekas and Cohen, 2007). That statistic is, however, misleading as a measure of the extent of risk variation because risk, when defined as expected value, represents the predictable component of spending or claims, and not all or even most of actual spending variation across people or over time is predictable. Table 11.1, taken from Pauly and Herring (1999), compares actual and predicted variation in spending on insured medical expenses for non-elderly individuals without public insurance in the US in 1987. There is substantial variation in both actual spending and in risk, but the two are not the same, with much less of the distribution of risk concentrated on people with close to zero or very high actual spending.

The extent to which and for whom risk variation is predictable has important implications for health insurance markets. While the unpredictable component of variation in expenditures generates demand for insurance, and, indeed, is the reason for

Table 11.1 Key Statistics on Actual and Predicted Insurable Expenses*

A: Key Statistics on Actual Insurable Expenses

Coefficient of variation = 377.80

Mean	$797
99th percentile	$12,811
95th percentile	$3,220
90th percentile	$1,549
75th percentile	$450
50th percentile	$137
25th percentile	$22
10th percentile	$0

B: Key Statistics on Predicted Individual Insurable Expenses: Linear Prediction Model, Using 1986 Conditions

Coefficient of variation = 85.61

Mean	$822
99th percentile	$3,710
95th percentile	$2,263
90th percentile	$1,592
75th percentile	$991
50th percentile	$647
25th percentile	$402
10th percentile	$223

Note: Number of observations = 8,010. All amounts are in 1987 dollars. Only insured individuals under age 65 with no public assistance are included.
*Pauly and Herring (1999), p. 31 (Table 3-1).
Source: NMES data.

insurance to exist, the predictable component influences the functioning of insurance markets. At one extreme, if almost none of the variation is predictable by anyone, premiums will be uniform for any nominal level of coverage and competitive markets with voluntary insurance purchase will work well, so that those persons unlucky enough to have high spending will have their financial risk cushioned and their consumption smoothed. At the other extreme, if each person's spending is exactly predictable by everyone, there would be no utility gains from voluntary insurance but there may be policy pressure to improve equity by redistributing premium costs from low risks to high risks.

When the power to predict risk is between these two extremes, there are two concerns that motivate potential public intervention to improve welfare. The standard concern in theoretical models of competitive insurance markets of all types is that, if consumers have and use more information about their expected loss than insurers do, adverse selection may limit efficiency. In markets where insurers can predict risk at least as well as consumers can, there are policy concerns about fairness in health insurance premiums, and about mitigation of lifetime risk of the variation of premiums imposed in single period settings, the so-called "reclassification risk" (Hirshleifer, 1971). Here the issue is whether unregulated insurance markets develop mechanisms to protect against such risk, and there is considerable evidence that they do.

Regulators need as much risk information as insurers have to play a proper role both in setting payments to plans and in regulating enrollee premiums. If insurers know more than regulators but premiums are not varied with risk, insurers may engage in cream skimming. Thus, the relative predictability of health expenditures from the perspectives of insurers, regulators, and consumers is a potentially important determinant of the functioning of health insurance markets and of health insurance regulation.

While risk variation thus is the motivation for a great deal of research and policy advice in this area, it is important to note at the outset that the contexts for this research and advice differ widely. Both in terms of global prevalence and certainly in terms of research weight, the empirical evidence on the effects of risk variation in insurance markets is nearly always based on a situation in which regulation or some other policy is already present that limits or forbids insurers from tailoring current-period premiums paid by consumers specifically to risk. Often as well there are substantial subsidies to the insurance purchased by almost everyone in the market. Other work, almost all conceptual and much smaller in quantity, deals with potential inefficiencies in private health insurance markets without regulation or other policy constraints, compared to what public policy could or should do as a way of improving matters. In what follows we will attempt to be clear which situation is furnishing the context for the research being summarized and discussed.

1.1. Cross-sectional Variation across Individuals

Most empirical studies of the predictability of health expenditures have been conducted from the perspective of regulators who wish to risk adjust payments to health plans whose explicit premiums (if any) are required to be uniform across buyers (community rated). We begin with analysis of US data from the perspective of regulation of its Medicare program. In the early 1980s, the Medicare program for the aged and disabled began offering beneficiaries the opportunity to replace their traditional publicly managed insurance benefits with coverage from a private plan, and the introduction of the program led to one of the first attempts to implement a system of risk adjustment.

In response to the concern that the initial methods used by government regulators to risk adjust payments to private plans were inadequate, early studies sought to calculate the maximum amount of variation in annual health expenditures which was potentially explainable in order to provide a benchmark of how well a system of external risk adjustment could in theory perform (Newhouse et al., 1989; van Vliet, 1992). The perspective is primarily that of a regulator that wishes to adjust payments received by insurers based on the risk of those they insure. Using panel data from the Rand Health Insurance Experiment, Newhouse et al. (1989) decomposed the variation in observed expenditures into the within- and between-person components, and identified the between-person variance as potentially explainable. Recognizing, however, that an enrollee may be able to anticipate at least some changes over time in health care expenditures (a classic example is pregnancy, although it is not very relevant to Medicare), they considered the between-person component to be a lower bound estimate of the maximum variation either insurers or beneficiaries could explain or predict. Studies adopting methods to model autocorrelation in individual spending (including regression to the mean) found that, while such autocorrelation existed, the additional explanatory power of these models was not substantially higher (Welch, 1985; Newhouse et al., 1989; van Vliet, 1992). Taken together, these studies suggested that the maximum explainable between-person variation was between 15 and 20 percent of total health expenditures, and that explainable variation was higher for outpatient care and pharmaceuticals than for inpatient spending. They also demonstrated that the types of risk adjusters initially used by the Medicare program (age, sex, Medicaid status, institutional status, and employment status) explained only about 1 percent of variation in expenditures. Thus, by providing a benchmark against which Medicare's then-limited risk adjustment scheme could be compared, this research demonstrated that regulated payments likely reflected only a subset of the information available to insurers and potentially to regulators.

1.1.1. Observable Individual Characteristics which Explain Expenditure Variation

Studies consistently demonstrate that, while health expenditures are highly correlated with the demographic characteristics of age and sex, demographic variables alone explain a very small portion—about 1 to 5 percent—of variation in health spending across individuals or households (Newhouse et al., 1989; Ellis and McGuire, 2007; Prinsze and van Vliet, 2007; Lamers, 2001). Indicators of chronic conditions (direct measures of the presence of conditions or indicators of prior-period spending on treatments for them) substantially increase the explanatory power of models of health expenditures (Newhouse et al., 1989; Shen and Ellis, 2002; Luft and Dudley, 2003; Ellis and McGuire, 2007), but still leave much unexplained. For example, Ellis and McGuire (2007) estimate that adding diagnostic indicators to a model with initial information only on age and sex increases the R-squared from 0.01 to 0.11. However, many studies find that measures of prior use make an independent contribution to the explanatory power of models, even after controlling for the presence of chronic conditions (Newhouse et al., 1989; Lamers, 2001; Shen and Ellis, 2002; Hsu et al., 2009). An exception is Ellis and McGuire (2007), who find that including prior year use has little effect on the explanatory power of their models. Rather they find that models estimated separately by service type, using diagnostic measures, have greater explanatory power than those estimated including prior spending related to total expenditures.

Relatively few studies have examined the correlation of spending with other (non-medical) individual characteristics such as socioeconomic status and medical care preferences, particularly after controlling for measures of health status. This is probably because many studies use insurance claims data which generally include relatively few socioeconomic or preference measures. However, if spending varies positively with income at any level of coinsurance, then expected expenses will be higher for people with higher incomes. If people at different income levels buy the same nominal insurance policy at a uniform premium, higher income people, expecting higher benefit payments, will for this reason alone be more likely to seek insurance coverage. There will be adverse selection if premiums do not vary with income, even though there is no variation in health risk. We will discuss this point further below.

While Newhouse et al. (1989) find that a limited set of subjective (self-assessed) measures of health have relatively little incremental explanatory power after controlling for measures of health status generated from claims data, there are many other characteristics of individuals not so easily observable in claims data that are potentially important determinants of expected expenditures. For example, Cohen et al. (2006) find that individual characteristics such as family income and marital status predict the likelihood of high spending in a given year, even after controlling for prior year health expenditures. Cutler et al. (2008) document a correlation between measures of risk tolerance and medical expenditures and use of medical care. Thus, while these types of individual characteristics are correlated with health expenditures, little evidence exists on their quantitative importance in predicting expenditures, particularly after controlling for health status.

1.1.2. How Much Variation is Predictable by Consumers?

Relatively little is known about how well consumers are able to predict their future health expenditures. On the one hand, the consumer potentially has the most complete set of information about next-period spending. Not only do consumers know their prior utilization, which the literature indicates is correlated with future expenditures, but they also have private information on how their utilization is likely to change in the next time period. Potential examples include health measures like pregnancy, elective surgery, or genetic risk, and preference measures like whether the person is a hypochondriac or alternatively prefers to avoid hospitals at all costs. On the other hand, consumers may be the least sophisticated users of some types of information. For example, consumers may be uninformed about the relationship between age and expected expenditure and thus may not accurately incorporate aging into their forecast.

What is relevant to the possibility of adverse selection and market equilibrium is not whether consumers can predict their future expenses accurately overall, or more precisely than insurers can, but rather whether they know or know more accurately important indicators of risk that insurers do not, and how they interpret and use this information, even if imperfectly, to judge their likely claims under different insurance policies. Competition among insurers would cause premiums to reflect everything insurers know about risk even if consumers were totally ignorant, but adverse selection could still arise if consumers had better information on other important variables that predict future spending, such as their conditions or preferences. On the other hand, if consumers estimate their risk levels differently than insurers do (perhaps because they do not know how to convert current period characteristics into future expected expenses), they may decline coverage offered at accurately risk-rated premiums and modest administrative expenses, or may seek overly generous coverage at high administrative expense levels. Still, as risk adjustment becomes more sophisticated, it is entirely possible that the regulator or the insurer may know more and more accurate information than any information the consumer might use. For example, an insurer or regulator who has population-level information on the relationship between the presence of chronic disease and health expenditures may more accurately forecast the impact of a newly developed chronic condition on future spending than could the consumer. (Consumers may still know their preferences and symptoms, however.) Yet we are unaware of any direct evidence on what types of information consumers use when forecasting health expenditures. Of course, if consumers believe that insurers always set their premiums close to expected benefits, then those faced with a high premium will modify any subjective judgment and assume that they must be high risk.

A fundamental question then is whether health insurance buyers in some markets actually do know useful information about risk that insurers do not. If insurers are forbidden to charge premiums based on risk variables they know, there can still be inefficient adverse selection. And the inefficiency associated with mispricing would depend on how responsive demand is to that mispricing. Conversely, for various reasons to be discussed, consumers may sort by risk but this is not necessarily inefficient, especially if there was no information asymmetry that motivated the sorting (Chiappori and Salanié, 2000; Einav et al., 2007). The gold standard would then be direct measurement of relative information about risk predictors, but this is rarely available. Instead, the best that can be done is to look at selection controlling for information supposedly observed by the insurer—to see if there is selection based on information not available to the insurer (Chiappori and Salanié, 2000).

1.1.3. How Much Variation is Predictable by Insurers and Regulators?

At the time of enrollment, insurers and regulators in theory have access to similar types of information about an individual's expected benefits. In practice, when insurers face relatively few regulatory restrictions on the use of information in underwriting, they ask applicants relatively detailed questions about their and their family's medical history and pre-existing medical conditions. In some cases, they have applicants undergo a medical examination or provide a physician contact. For example, an application from a US commercial insurer selling coverage in the individual market asks whether the applicant has received care for or had symptoms of 24 different conditions over the last 20 years. The applicant must provide detailed information on the treatment of those conditions, including the contact information of health care providers. The application also includes questions about tobacco use, alcohol consumption, prescription drug use over the last 12 months, and whether the applicant has ever had any application for either health or life insurance restricted in any way. In many countries, insurers have the right to cancel individually purchased insurance if they find that the applicant provided incomplete or inaccurate information. Requirements for information and aggressiveness of cancellations (rescissions) vary across insurers. Usually, however, insurers who collect less information charge higher premiums.

Little formal evidence exists, however, on how insurers use this information. Insurers may use the information to decide whom to offer coverage, what services to cover, and what premium to charge. Some German health insurers provide lists of percentage surcharges for certain conditions (e.g. gallstones 40 percent, gout 40 percent, cervical spine syndrome 40 percent, thyroid hyperfunction 30 percent, hay fever 20 percent) and for denial of coverage (e.g. epilepsy, mental illness, Crohn's disease, cancer within seven years). However, because underwriting practices are an integral part of an insurer's business strategy, most treat them as a confidential business practice, and whether and how insurers use different types of information likely varies across carriers. Anecdotal information from insurers suggests that many companies use the information they collect from applicants to develop a risk adjustment factor, which indicates an applicant's expected expenses relative to the average premium. For applicants with a risk adjustment factor above a particular threshold (in Germany, 500 percent of baseline), an insurer is likely to decline making an offer of coverage. For others, insurers may customize the terms of coverage. Some insiders indicate that, in the absence of strict regulations governing how they use information, insurers use the detailed information they gather in a relatively nuanced way. For example, an applicant whose diabetes is well controlled would be treated differently from one whose is not. Thus, underwriting in the US is based in part on objective data but in part on the judgment the underwriter makes after viewing all available information; premium adjustments are usually tied in a predetermined way to objective data (like the presence of a chronic condition) but an underwriter can turn down an application entirely based on judgment.

In the US market, the level of detail in the information insurers collect and use when setting coverage terms varies based on the size of the group. While small group insurance was risk rated at the level of the group before regulations in most states limited it, there was less attention to risk than in the case of individual insurance. In individual insurance markets without regulation, after adjusting for age and sex, insurers will typically rate new applicants as "standard" or "non-standard" based on health information, and increase premiums for the latter group by up to 200 percent of standard before declining to insure entirely (Pauly and Herring, 1999).

Another possibility is that insurers or insureds may have information on genetic risk from genetic tests. Of course, insurers have traditionally collected as part of the underwriting process information that included the answers to questions about causes of death for parents and siblings, which of course is genetic information. But the advent of genetic tests has raised questions about substantial improvements in the ability to predict future medical costs. Up to this point, however, genetic tests have not been a major factor in underwriting, largely because they are not much better than is family history at predicting costs in the next time period (but before the person goes on Medicare), which is what the insurer wants to know. At best they predict what illnesses the person eventually may have, but not precisely when. There are some exceptions for tests for relatively rare breast cancer and cystic fibrosis, but in general insurers professed to be not interested in using such tests themselves—although paradoxically they were concerned when the insurance purchaser had test results (Subramanian et al., 1999). Nevertheless, laws often now do greatly limit insurers' ability to ask for and use such information.

Subsequent to enrollment, however, an insurer can accumulate extensive information regarding an individual's risk because the insurer observes the person's claims.

Studies suggest that, subsequent to enrollment, the risk adjustment systems used by regulators represent a subset of the information available to insurers. Shen and Ellis (2002) simulate potential insurer profitability associated with effective insurer selection under differing assumptions about the information sets available to insurers and regulators. They find that even when regulators use fairly sophisticated risk adjustment, insurers can still identify individuals who can generate costs in excess of the risk-adjusted payments. Although this study does not provide evidence on what plans actually do, the results indicate that they face relatively strong incentives to seek to induce some individuals to disenroll. In contrast, as will be discussed in more detail below, the bulk of individual insurance in the United States is written under a contract provision in which the insurer promises not to use any such information to single out insureds for premium changes or refusals to renew coverage.

1.2. Persistence in Health Expenditures

Estimates of the maximum explainable variation are based in part on the degree of persistence (serial correlation) in individual spending. Both van Vliet (1992) and Newhouse et al. (1989) present evidence that expenditures are somewhat, but not particularly highly, correlated over time. For example, van Vliet (1992) calculated a correlation coefficient of approximately 0.25 for year one and year two spending and approximately 0.10 for year one and years three through five spending. While subsequent literature uses different methods to quantify the degree of persistence, they confirm this general finding of some, but limited correlation in, year-to-year expenditures. For example, using claims data from a sample of large, self-insured firms, Eichner et al. (1997) find that average expenditures for enrollees in the top decile of spending in a given year were $11,249, or eight times the sample average. Expenditures of the highest spending group in the initial year remained higher than, but moved substantially closer to, the average in subsequent years. In the following two years, they were approximately 5 and 3 times average spending. Similarly, average expenditures for those with the lowest expenditures in the initial year—zero spending for the three lowest deciles—increased to about the sample average in subsequent years. Using two years of data from the nationally representative US Medical Expenditure Panel Survey, Monheit (2003) finds that, of the top 5 percent of spenders in 1996, 30 percent were in the top 5 percent of spenders in 1997. These studies also find that the persistence of health care spending increases with age (Eichner et al., 1997; Monheit, 2003; Pauly and Zeng, 2004), but that the degree of persistence among older adults is limited by mortality, which generates a sharp increase in spending in the last year of life (Garber et al., 1998). Spending persistence also varies significantly across types of services. For example, spending on prescription drugs is much more persistent than total spending or hospital spending (Pauly and Zeng, 2004).

To date, empirical analyses of persistence are based on longitudinal data spanning time periods from two to eight years. Yet evidence from a longer time period, even a lifetime perspective, is important for evaluating the efficiency and distributional implications of different forms of health insurance. Using data from a three-year panel to simulate health expenditures over a working lifetime, Eichner et al. (1997) find that concentration declines significantly over time. Based on their simulations, the percentage of the population accounting for 80 percent of spending increases from 10 to 29 percent and to 48 percent over one, five, and 35 years, respectively.

1.3. Implications

Overall, these studies of predictability and persistence in health care spending indicate that a significant portion of the cross-sectional variation in annual health care spending is unpredictable to consumers and insurers, suggesting that insurance does provide an important benefit in the form of a reduction in the uncertainty of spending on medical care. (In the case of independent events, insurers can profit without knowing which individuals will turn out to be high cost by charging a premium that more than covers average or expected expense.) While the degree of unexplained variation supports the desirability of insurance, evidence of the existence of differences across consumers in the extent to which spending is predictable suggests that, in theory, asymmetric information could threaten the functioning of competitive insurance markets. In addition, because some people are unlucky enough to contract chronic conditions which persist over years and are associated with high spending, they could suffer from high premiums for a long period of time. In practice, however, because studies provide little information on the extent to which information is asymmetric between health insurance consumers and insurers, this literature offers little insight on the degree to which adverse selection is likely to occur. An exception is the above-mentioned study by Pauly and Zeng (2004), which demonstrates that, because spending on prescription drugs is highly persistent, unsubsidized stand-alone insurance is unlikely to be feasible due to adverse selection. Either bundling prescription drug coverage with insurance for other types of medical care or high subsidies are necessary to provide such coverage. This literature provides stronger evidence of a potential gap between insurers and regulators in the predictability of spending. When neither insurers nor regulators have information on prior spending, they in theory have access to similar information when an individual initially enrolls. Subsequent to enrollment, however, the literature identifying the importance of prior spending in explaining future spending suggests that an individual's claims history will provide an insurer with more information on likely expenditures than has been incorporated in most risk adjustment systems. While one way to address this would be to introduce measures of prior utilization into a system of risk adjustment, a problem is that some predictors of higher spending may themselves be manipulated by beneficiaries or insurers. For example, to the extent that an insurer can gain from increasing prior year spending or utilization that is used in a risk adjustment system, that system will cause inefficiency in health care delivery as it attempts to reduce inefficiency due to risk selection. (The ultimate cause of the risk selection was a decision to limit the extent to which premiums vary with risk.) Thus, the extent to which systems of risk adjustment can be refined to address this gap is an important area of research (see section 4.3.5 below).

It also important to acknowledge that estimates of both maximum explainable variation and spending persistence are specific to both the population and the time period studied. The degree to which health expenditures are predictable likely depends both on the prevalence of chronic relative to acute disease within a population and on the availability and use of technology. For example, in the context of the US Medicaid program, Kronick and Dreyfus (1996) demonstrate that health care expenditures are more predictable for a disabled than for an average population. The reduction in relative prevalence of infectious compared to chronic disease on a population basis has likely made medical care expenditures more predictable—by regulators, insurers, and consumers—and the greater prevalence of chronic diseases in older populations likewise potentially makes their spending more predictable. The future effects of technological change on predictability and persistence, however, are more difficult to predict a priori because different types of technological change would have different implications for expenditure persistence. For example, the development of treatments which reduce mortality from chronic conditions without affecting symptoms can make health care spending to alleviate those symptoms more persistent, while those which prevent or completely cure formerly chronic conditions will make spending less persistent. And technological change may even have different impacts on spending persistence and predictability. Empirical evidence is lacking, however, on the extent to which the predictability of health expenditures has changed over time, the causes of any changes or the implications for the extent and form of insurance coverage.

2. INSURANCE MARKET EQUILIBRIUM WITH RISK VARIATION AND RATING VARIATION: MARKET EQUILIBRIUM BENCHMARKS

Health insurance markets throughout the world are heavily regulated. In order to understand the effects of regulation, it is useful to consider the market equilibrium in both unregulated, competitive markets and regulated markets as benchmarks. The model which is typically used to study the insurance market is based on the following assumptions (see, e.g., Dionne and Doherty, 1992):

1. The risk of illness can be described by a probability distribution of the possible health state-associated loss for each individual. In the simplest case, there are only two future states of the world, and the individual can become sick and will then incur a purely financial loss (cost of medical care) of M, with probability π, otherwise he or she stays healthy with health care costs of zero.

2. Individuals can differ in their risk of illness π (but not in the size of the possible loss M). In the simplest case, there are only two risk types, $i = H, L$, with $\pi_H > \pi_L$.

3. The individual is risk-averse and will always buy full coverage if this is available at the fair premium, $\pi_i \cdot M$.

4. Initially individuals do not differ in risk aversion, demand for medical care conditional on illness, or preferences for other aspects of insurance (such as extent and form of managed care limitations, provision of information about disease management, or rapid and convenient claims payment).

5. There are a large number of insurance companies who can select what policy or coverage to offer but which, for a given level of coverage, then charge premiums which yield zero economic profits.

We first characterize the market equilibrium within this simple framework to establish a benchmark. We then consider the implications of a series of deviations from this simple model including the effects of costly information on risk, consumer heterogeneity in characteristics other than risk that influence demand for coverage, and asymmetric information between insurers and consumers.

2.1. Equilibrium with Single-period Insurance and with No Regulation and No Information Asymmetry: Underwriting and Risk Rating

2.1.1. Costless Risk Information

In the simplest case, the insurer can observe the probability of illness π_i over a particular time period for each individual i and can therefore calculate the expected loss (or fair premium level) $\pi_i \cdot M$. In the absence of administrative costs (i.e. costs of the underwriting process, selling costs and commissions, costs of billing and of claims processing), competition will drive down premiums for prospective new buyers in that time period towards the fair premium, and the consumer will thus buy full coverage. If buyers differ in risk and insurers can costlessly determine each buyer's risk level, premiums will vary in proportion to risk. For new buyers of single-period insurance coverage, a competitive equilibrium will exist and will be Pareto optimal.

2.1.2. Costly Information

Acquisition and processing of information is costly, and thus interesting questions are how much risk discrimination is efficient and how much is chosen by insurance companies that need to cover these costs. To answer the first question, it is useful to consider two extremes. If insurance companies do not try to acquire any information on the different risk levels, but applicants know their individual π_i values, then we are in a typical "asymmetric information" situation leading to adverse selection, which will be analyzed below (in section 2.2.1) and in which the efficiency or even existence of market equilibrium is doubtful. If, on the other hand, insurers invest as many resources as needed to perfectly measure the individual $\pi_i s$ (given the information available to the consumers), then this likely results in an inefficient allocation as well since the last unit of information costs primarily serves to discriminate risks, may have little marginal value in doing that, but has even less value in inhibiting adverse selection. Thus there must be some interior private and social optima (not necessarily the same) for the amount of information acquired by the insurers. That is, insurers will not bother to seek information on risk if the risk variation is small or if the information is costly—but they may carry the search for information further than is socially optimal. That is, while they clearly have an incentive to seek information that prevents inefficient adverse selection, they may seek costly information even if adverse selection might be small (for example, because consumers are not aware of risk differences) (Crocker and Snow, 1985). The inefficiency is the use of resources to engage in risk discrimination, not the risk discrimination *per se*. Paradoxically, if insurance buyers are not very price responsive so there will be little inefficiency from adverse selection, there may be offsetting inefficiency as insurers seek excessive information to assist in cream skimming. If there is some information which buyers cannot or will not get that discriminates among risks, insurers will choose to acquire too much of such information, since such information only serves to redistribute (discriminate) among risks.

Often insurers are limited by law, regulation, or custom in using information that predicts risk that they do have or can obtain at low cost. This will lead to an adverse selection outcome even if there is no information asymmetry. The efficient outcome described in the first case will not occur because of regulation.

2.1.3. Impact of Other Insurance and Medical Care Demand Determinants

Insurance demand is determined by more than just the relationship of premiums to expected benefits. The degree to which these other influences are correlated with risk will influence the correlation between risk and coverage in the market, potentially creating a correlation between risk and coverage even in the absence of asymmetric information (see section 2.2). One possibility is that individuals may vary in risk aversion, and that more risk-averse people may be lower risks. Finkelstein and McGarry (2006) find evidence of this type of relationship in the market for long-term care insurance. Fang et al. (2008) find a similar effect in the market for Medicare supplemental insurance, but they attribute it to differences in cognition rather than to differences in risk aversion. People with poor cognition have poorer health, but their poor cognition also means that they do not recognize the high net value of community-rated insurance to them, so cognition is positively correlated with demand for coverage but negatively correlated with expected utilization.

2.2. Equilibrium with Information Asymmetry: The Benchmark Adverse Selection Model and its Relevance to Health Insurance

2.2.1. Rothschild–Stiglitz Models with Managed Care and Cost Sharing

Various equilibrium concepts have been proposed for the typical adverse-selection situation in which applicants know their risk type but insurers can observe only the share of high risks in the applicant population, μ, but not the risk type of any given individual. An equilibrium à la Rothschild and Stiglitz (1976) is a set of contracts offered by insurance companies with the following properties:

1. Each contract yields a non-negative expected profit to the insurer;
2. There is no potential contract outside this set which would yield a non-negative expected profit to the insurer;
3. Each individual picks the contract which maximizes his expected utility among those offered.

In such an equilibrium with only two risk levels, two contracts are offered: one with full coverage and premium equal to $\pi_H \cdot M$, which is purchased by all high-risk applicants and thus just breaks even, and one with partial coverage M' ($M' < M$) and premium $\pi_L \cdot M'$, which is bought by all low-risk types and also breaks even. The crucial precondition for the self-selection mechanism of the risk types is that M' must be sufficiently lower than M to make it unattractive to high risks (compared to the full coverage, higher-priced alternative). A problem with this equilibrium is that its existence requires the share of high risks, μ, to be sufficiently large. If this condition is violated, the model is without equilibrium and so is silent about what will actually happen at any point in time.

2.2.2. Wilson–Spence–Miyazaki Equilibrium

The equilibrium concept introduced by Rothschild and Stiglitz (1976) has been criticized on several accounts. First, it requires that insurance companies make non-negative profits with each contract they offer. This assumption is not very realistic because it ignores the ability of firms to cross-subsidize among their contracts. Second, it ignores the ability of firms to anticipate the reaction of their competitors to a market entry. Taking both points into account, Wilson (1977), Spence (1978), and Miyazaki (1977) have proposed an alternative equilibrium concept, which is based upon the following assumptions:

1. Each insurer offers a bundle of contracts which, as a whole, yields a non-negative expected profit;

2. No potential bundle of contracts outside the set defined in (1) would yield a positive expected profit if those bundles of contracts which would become unprofitable in response to this offer were taken from the market;

3. Each individual chooses among all contracts offered the one which maximizes his expected utility.

The crucial point which distinguishes this concept from the one by Rothschild and Stiglitz (1976) is that insurance firms contemplating market entry do anticipate the reaction of the incumbent firms. Furthermore, low risks can cross-subsidize high risks. Both features can be interpreted as steps towards more realism in markets with relatively small numbers of foresighted insurers.

Unlike the Rothschild–Stiglitz equilibrium, a Wilson–Spence–Miyazaki equilibrium always exists. It is also a separating equilibrium in which high risks get full coverage but pay a premium lower than $\pi_H \cdot M$, thus they are subsidized by the low risks. In effect, this payment is a bribe from low risks to high risks to keep the latter from further distorting the market for low risks.

Thus the implications of the two equilibrium concepts differ sharply. Unfortunately, the question of whether any of these models describe well the market for health insurance, even an unregulated individual insurance market, is hard to resolve. The possibility of cross-subsidization seems plausible as insurers can use this as a means to increase expected profits. However, the assumption that insurers anticipate the withdrawal of competing contracts in response to their own contract offer remains controversial. Hellwig (1987) has analyzed this issue in a game-theoretic framework which explicitly allows for withdrawals. He finds that the order in which firms move is crucial. However, it is not clear that such an order can be observed in the market for health insurance; indeed, it may not exist at all. Newhouse (1996, pp. 1242ff.) invokes positive costs of writing separate contracts with the low-risk group to generate a pooling equilibrium in which the low risks get their optimal coverage and the high risks get their best feasible coverage.

2.2.3. Equilibrium with Managed Care Plans

The ability of managed care plans to adjust dimensions of insurance other than coverage of a predetermined loss means that there can be a different kind of equilibrium in health insurance. Glazer and McGuire (2000) extend the Rothschild and Stiglitz model to a managed care setting by modeling a health plan as a contract which offers a predefined level of two different types of care, acute and chronic, contingent upon the health status of an enrollee. Consumers are defined by their probability of contracting either an acute or chronic illness, and high risks are those with a higher probability of contracting the chronic condition. In their model, a separating equilibrium exists under the usual conditions with managed care plans underproviding chronic care to low risks. Chernew and Frick (1999) consider the effect of managed care on the existence and form of equilibria by introducing contracts characterized by two attributes, patient cost sharing and the degree of "managedness," into the R&S framework. "Managedness" refers to a set of non-financial (with respect to patients) restrictions on utilization which could take the form of, for example, utilization review, constraints on physician choice, and provider payment methods. They find that, while the introduction of this second dimension improves the ability of low risks to distinguish themselves from high risks, this ability has ambiguous effects on the existence of equilibria. In some cases, an equilibrium exists when it would not when insurers were limited to a single mechanism. In other cases, it allows an insurer to generate a pooling policy which could break a separating equilibrium, leading to non-existence of equilibrium. Thus, the ultimate effect of managed care on the existence of equilibria in unregulated insurance markets is indeterminate.

2.2.4. Asymmetric Information on Total Coverage

In both equilibrium types described above, a differentiation of the premium per unit of coverage is possible because the insurers are assumed to observe total coverage of each applicant. In other words, they have the power to "ration" health insurance by offering "price-quantity contracts." As a consequence, the price schedule is not linear, but convex: greater coverage implies a higher per-unit price. If total coverage were unobservable, high-risk applicants desiring to fully insure could buy two or more contracts with partial coverage from different insurance companies and thus avoid the steep part of the price schedule. Hence, only linear price schedules would be enforceable, which would render the equilibria described above unattainable.

In that case, only one price could prevail in the market, and two types of equilibria are possible: either

1. the price per unit of coverage equals the loss probability of high risks, π_H, high risks buy full insurance and low risks do not insure at all; or

2. the price lies between π_L and π_H, so that high risks are subsidized and buy more than 100% coverage, whereas low risks buy less than full insurance. Of course, regulation could enforce a limit of 100 percent on total coverage, which would prevent greater than full coverage among high risks.

In practice, health insurance companies try to determine total coverage by asking insureds about other coverage—but they cannot do so with perfect accuracy. Electronic methods for payments of claims to medical providers prevent duplicate benefits. However, there are insurers in the US that offer insurance that pays cash, based on the fact of a hospitalization or the onset of a disease like cancer, regardless of what other insurers pay for care. In practice, the ability to observe total coverage may be less relevant for preventing adverse selection than it is for controlling moral hazard for which incomplete coverage (i.e. co-payments) is crucial.

2.2.5. Equilibrium when Other Insurance Demand Determinants or Competition Varies

Insurance demand depends on more than risk; it also depends on risk aversion, price (premium or loading), and extent of moral hazard. Does the market equilibrium and attendant possibility of adverse selection vary in theory with any of these factors?

The general message is that as long as the market is competitive and any such other factors are distributed independently of risk, their variation does not matter. Chiappori et al. (2006) show rigorously that the positive correlation property (risk correlated with amount of coverage) holds under a wide variety of assumptions as long as insurers are free to offer any coverage they like and competition constrains economic profits. Even if insurers have knowledge of these other demand determinants (e.g. know who is more risk-averse and therefore more willing to pay for insurance), competition prevents them from taking advantage of any such information. The only examples of adverse selection in competitive health insurance markets are in markets where coverage is relatively unimportant, such as private insurance in the UK (Vera-Hernández, 2003).

Things potentially change if insurers have market power. Then they will be expected to discriminate in price if they have information on demand determinants. Even if they do not, they will know that people with stronger risk aversion will demand more insurance at a given price and so will mark up premiums more for more generous coverage.

If the zero profit constraint continues to hold but not all levels of coverage are available (either because of marketing costs or regulation) that could limit the scope of adverse selection but is unlikely to matter significantly as long as offered options roughly span the set of choices.

In contrast, if other demand determinants are correlated with risk—for example, if either risk aversion or cognitive ability is higher for lower risks—then competitive equilibrium might display either no relationship between risk and coverage or even favorable selection, as noted earlier.

2.3. Variation in Lifetime Risk versus Single Year Risk: Implications for Insurance Design and Market Equilibria

2.3.1. Reclassification Risk

Health insurance is typically obtained over multiple time periods, and for any individual the risk level may change over time. Arrow (1963) has advised us that in such settings the ideal is "insurance with a longer time perspective," but what form might such insurance take?

Consider a simple but realistic model where a population begins as a set of homogeneous low risks but expects the onset of chronic conditions to convert some proportion each time period to higher risk status. If insurance is priced for finite short time periods (e.g. a year) and is priced based on the risk level at the beginning of each period, those people who become high risks will find their future premiums higher as they are reclassified into higher risk classes at the beginning of the next policy period. Other things being equal, risk-averse people would prefer to protect themselves against unpredictable fluctuations in future premiums. Are there ways markets can and do provide such protection?

2.3.2. Insurance Features to Deal with Reclassification Risk: Guaranteed Renewability

The simplest solution would be to sell insurance with a single lifetime premium, paid in an initial period when most people will still be of equal risk. These premiums would be high enough to cover the expected present discounted value of lifetime medical costs, given expectations about the onset and medical (and non-medical) costs of uncertain shocks to health status. In principle, a binding contract obligating buyers to pay the premium in installments would also be possible. Of course, uncertainty about future medical prices and technology would make offering such insurance a challenge, and the possibility of insuring future cost levels (even for constant medical risk) is limited.

Such a long-term insurance contract might be limited both by capital market imperfections (cost of raising the upfront lifetime premium) and the difficulty of enforcing future behavior (by buyers or sellers). So is there an alternative market arrangement in which premiums are paid at shorter time intervals, but still without the need for binding contracts for buyers?[1] The answer is affirmative. Consider a simple three-period model in which a given proportion of low risks (with constant low loss probability) convert to high risks in each period, and then remain high risks until the end. (We use a three-period model to illustrate the time–age path of premiums.) Suppose an insurer offers a premium schedule for the three periods in which the last period premium is the low-risk premium, the second last period premium is the low-risk premium plus the difference between the high- and low-risk premiums for the proportion of the initial population who convert to high risk in that period, and the initial period premium is the second period premium plus the difference between the low- and high-risk premium times the proportion of the population who convert to high risk in the first period. (Note that the proportion of the initial population

---

[1] This raises the more fundamental issue of the relevant time period for insurance demand and evaluation. With perfect capital markets and perfect foresight the right perspective would be the lifetime perspective, but it is clear that even well-off consumers do not want to finance a high medical cost in the current period by spreading it over time (even if they could do so). On the other hand, no one would want to plan insurance based on the risk of a high expense relative to income in a single day. Ehrlich and Becker (1972) distinguish self insurance (financing by borrowing or drawing down savings) and market insurance as two alternatives. How these fit together when risk varies over periods shorter than lifetime is unknown.

converting to high risk is lower in the second period than in the first because some people have already converted to high risk.)

It is easy to see that this schedule will be attractive to everyone, regardless of risk level, in all periods, since it guarantees premiums and since no subset of risk can do better by dropping out in any period. This "original guaranteed renewable" (OGR) premium concept was developed independently by Cochrane (1995) and Pauly et al. (1995). In effect, it is an arrangement in which the total premium in each period but the last has two parts, one part to cover the unexpected medical spending that may occur in that period, and the other part to cover the (present discounted value of) the increment in future premiums due to the risk of becoming a high risk in that period. It is incentive compatible and avoids both the risk of reclassification and (if it might have occurred) adverse selection. The premium still rises with overall health care costs.

Some features of this model are deserving of comment. If the low-risk premium is constant over time, the OGR premium schedule will be one in which premiums eventually decline over time as the extent of "frontloading" to protect those who become high risks diminishes. Empirically, because expected costs of a given benefit package even for low risks increase with age, the actual time path of GR insurance will be one in which premiums rise with age—but less steeply than if there were single period risk rating.

While low risks should rationally remain with the initial seller, it does not matter if they switch sellers, since the prepayments needed to assure low and stable premiums for those who have become high risks have already been collected. In this sense, this arrangement is not vulnerable to turnover of low risks. But if high risks expect to leave this firm for something more attractive (a public program or labor-related benefits), this diminishes the appeal of the GR arrangement.

One potential problem with this arrangement concerns the possibility that the insurer may not discharge the full contract for the high risks; it might compromise in some way on quality or service (however that might be defined) because the high risks have no attractive outside alternative (van de Ven and van Vliet, 1992), or it might try, despite the contract provision, to charge a selectively higher premium to the high risks, or just charge higher premiums to everyone. Usually the insurance contract is not explicit about the method of determining future premiums or the guarantees of all dimensions of future quality or service. Or the insurer might raise premiums for the class while at the same time offering a low premium to those who remain low risks if they leave the class. Reputation effects should inhibit such behavior (if I am still a low risk, but worried about the future, why would I sign up for coverage in a new class from a firm that has just increased its premiums to high risks?), but may not prevent it. It is in principle possible to design a more complex contract that gives those who have become high risks and who wish to change insurers the right to claim the frontloading to which they would be entitled if they remained with the original seller. Cochrane (1995) imagines that high risks could demand a "dividend" which would be enough to cover high-risk premiums at other sellers, thus diminishing the original insurer's incentive to skimp. (Note that if this provision is in place then there should be little reason for insureds to actually leave; with proper incentives for quality, they should be willing (if not happy) to stay "married to their insurer.")

The other potential problem concerns the time path of premiums. If capital markets were perfect, consumers could pay a lifetime premium and there would be no need for guaranteed renewability. But while OGR reduces the capital burden for insurance early in life, the high frontloading in principle might still be a problem. If it were, a potential solution would be to deviate from the OGR model in which all risks pay the same premium in any time period, and instead allow some modest risk rating with attendant modest reclassification risk as a way of reducing the amount of premium that is frontloaded. However, as we shall see, for health insurance the frontloading burden may not be so large because the low-risk premium will increase with age and with medical progress.

2.3.3. Empirical Evidence on Guaranteed Renewability in Individual Insurance Markets and in Mixed Markets

2.3.3.1. United States

The most surprising empirical fact here is historical. Individual health insurance in the United States typically included a GR provision even before it was required by law in 1998. That is, in response to market demand, individual insurers usually promised not to re-underwrite (except for specifically designated temporary insurance), so that a person would not be singled out for a premium increase because of claims experience. In this way it was following on similar provisions in disability insurance and term life insurance. While information is imperfect, it appears that, although this provision was not universal and was sometimes violated in practice (often by reviewing the person's initial application and "rescinding" a low-risk classification if there was error or a possibility of error), individual insurance did display two characteristics consistent with GR frontloading, premium to claims ratio higher in the early years of coverage and relative insensitivity of premiums to risk (Pauly and Herring, 1999).

More recent work (Herring and Pauly, 2006) showed that the actual time path for OGR coverage, given the relationship between age and risk in the United States, is one in which the premium is actually lower at younger ages than at older ones, though not as low as under single period risk rating. "Risk" is defined as expected expenses (and so is correlated with but is not identical to measures of health or health status, whether physiological or subjective). Compared to the age profile based on average risk at each age, OGR is somewhat higher at younger ages but lower at older ages. The amount of "excess" frontloading is 34 percent of the (modest) healthy young person premium, high enough to matter but not so high as to present a high barrier to financing. Moreover, they found that the actual age profile of premiums for individual health insurance in the US seems close to the OGR profile, especially after adjusting for (involuntary) turnover, further evidence that the market actually does what it promises.

Despite some cases in which insurers avoided or shed high risks under GR, the protection provided by GR is substantial. Compared to small group health insurance (where there is no protection against re-underwriting at the individual level), high risks were much less likely to lose coverage, other things equal. Thus it is far from obvious that group insurance for a person who might leave a job provides better protection against changes over time in health insurance risk than does individual insurance.

2.3.3.2. Germany

Germany is the OECD country outside the US with the largest private health insurance market. Private insurance in Germany primarily serves the self-employed, civil servants, and upper-income employees who choose private insurance over social insurance. By law, private insurance premiums must be calculated by the principle that they stay constant during the whole lifetime of the customer as long as the overall level of medical technology and prices does not change. This means that the customer is insured not only: (1) against health expenditures in the current period; but also (2) against changes of his individual risk assessment (reclassification risk); and (3) against rising health expenditures with age, whereas he is not insured against the (systemic) risks of medical progress and health care cost inflation. Premiums thus only depend on gender and age of entry into the contract (and, possibly, supplements for excess risk at entry). As a counterpart, the insurance company must display so-called "aging provisions" in its balance sheet, which account for the gap between expected future health care expenditures of and future premium revenues from its present set of customers. The whole arrangement is a combination of GR and a savings process which helps finance the predictable increase of health expenditures with age, in the absence of reclassification.

The main problem with this arrangement is that it may be possible to distinguish the premium which covers type (1) of risk from the accrual to the aging provision, but it is very difficult to disentangle the premium for the coverage of reclassification risk (2) from the "pure savings" part of the premium (3). Hence, when the insured wants to cancel his insurance contract and switch to another insurer, it is not clear which part of the aging provision should be transferable (Baumann et al., 2008). In fact, German law stipulated until 2008 that aging provision could not be transferred at all, and thus there was practically no competition between private health insurers except for first-time customers. The law was changed in 2009 so that now part of the aging provisions has to be transferred to the new insurer in case of a move from one company to another, but the method of calculation is simply dividing the total amount of aging provisions in a demographic group (defined by age, sex, and age of entry) by the number of heads in that group. Instead, the correct procedure would be to calculate and transfer "individualized prospective aging provisions" by the method described above (expected future health care expenditures minus expected future premium revenue; see Cochrane, 1995).

3. GROUP INSURANCE

Employment-based group insurance is the predominant form of private health insurance in the United States, and it is also present in many other countries. In some countries, such as the US, employer-sponsored coverage is explicitly promoted through tax subsidies. While subsidization promotes employment-based coverage, it is "neither necessary nor sufficient" to explain the prominence and durability of voluntary group coverage more generally (Glied, 2005). In the US, employers often provided health insurance prior to the implementation of policies favoring employer-sponsored coverage over individual purchase. In addition, voluntary employment-based coverage exists in many other countries, even when tax subsidies are not available (i.e. UK supplemental market). Thus, employment-based group coverage may emerge even in the absence of policies promoting its existence, perhaps as a response to inefficiency in individual markets. Because policy often promotes employment-based group purchasing, however, it is difficult to disentangle the extent to which group purchasing represents the emergence of an alternative institutional arrangement for purchasing coverage in response to inefficiency in the individual market from an apparent normative preference of policy makers in promoting this institutional arrangement.

Despite the prominence of group purchasing, its economics, particularly with respect to the implications of group purchase for the performance of insurance markets in response to risk variation, has received relatively little formal attention among health economists.

3.1. Group Insurance Model and Theory

Several characteristics define group insurance:

1. Eligibility determined by worker status (usually as employee although there are some guilds of workers (often self-employed) who obtain insurance in a group, such as the Screen Actors Guild or the carpenters' or teamsters' unions);
2. Choice of number and types of insurance policies determined by the employer or group leadership;

3. Group membership and whether to enroll in the coverage offered by the group are both voluntary.

Group purchasing has two advantages over individual purchasing. First, groups experience less stringent underwriting than individuals. Usually a large share of the premium is covered as part of compensation, with only at most a minority of the premium paid by the insured. These provisions mean that the great bulk of workers take insurance through the job, and the premium is tied to the claims experience of the group; as a result, outside insurers usually do not find it worthwhile to risk underwrite or screen applicants to group insurance. Moreover, the set of workers can change over the period of coverage without affecting the premium charged. This means that, as long as the worker stays employed at the firm, changes in risk level associated with chronic conditions will not lead to changes in premiums the worker pays: there is protection against risk reclassification. (Of course, this protection is lost should the worker lose or change jobs.) Second, group coverage has lower administrative costs than individual insurance, largely because it is not necessary to persuade individual workers to take coverage; the effective subsidy to each individual's decision about coverage greatly reduces administrative costs in its own right.

In this type of group purchasing, risk variation may affect worker behavior in two ways. First, individual risk may influence the choice of employment and corresponding employer-provided benefit packages. Individual risk may also influence the choice of whether and in which plan to enroll within a firm. In other words, there can be risk selection both across and within firms.

3.2. Group Insurance and Current-period Risk

Two features of group insurance make it similar in theory to a local public good—the ability of workers to move across firms and the role of the employer (or group leader) in choosing a single or subset of potential health insurance plans of offer to workers. Analyzing group coverage from this perspective, Goldstein and Pauly (1976) demonstrate that, when employees vary in their preferences for health insurance, but are similar along other dimensions including their risk, labor market competition will lead to perfect sorting of workers across firms, with each firm offering a single plan which represents the most preferred plan for a particular subgroup of workers. This model highlights two important mechanisms which influence the functioning of group markets. First, cost-minimizing employers have strong incentives to offer workers efficient levels of coverage, where efficient is defined as the trade-off between health insurance and cash wages the worker would have chosen in the absence of group coverage. Second, labor market mobility tends to limit the degree to which outcomes in the employer-sponsored market in any one firm can deviate from those at other firms or in individual markets. Using the Goldstein and Pauly framework as a starting point, we consider the impact of risk variation on worker sorting across and within firms in a single period model.

3.2.1. Worker Sorting and Wage Incidence

Generally the incidence of insurance costs nominally "contributed" by the employer will be on money wages. In the Goldstein and Pauly model above, workers were homogeneous with respect to risk, and wage offsets varied across but not within firms based on plan generosity. When the labor force consists of workers with heterogeneous risks, the extent to which wage offsets vary with individual risk will affect the stability of group markets. If we consider the simple case in which the entire premium is taken from compensation, and if we assume that money wages are reduced uniformly for all workers in a firm regardless of risk level, there could be substantial adverse selection as high-risk workers avoid firms not offering benefits and select employment at firms offering more generous benefits. While low-risk workers would have incentives to separate into homogeneous firms with lower than average premiums and correspondingly higher wages, high-risk workers would seek to join low-risk firms for the same reasons, creating dynamics similar to those in the standard Rothschild and Stiglitz model. If we instead assume that wage offsets vary with individual current-period risk, then, maintaining the assumption of perfect labor mobility, we return to the local public good equilibrium: workers sort among firms based on their preferences for health insurance. In this situation, in contrast, worker wages reflect individual risk due to differential wage offsets for health insurance. In short, movements away from risk-based individual incidence within employment-based groups create greater pressure for risk selection at the group level.

There is evidence that some dimensions of risk do affect the incidence of premiums on wages, so that higher-risk workers' wages are reduced more than lower-risk workers' wages when both are in the same insurance plan. For this reason, the apparently uniform explicit premiums in group insurance do not necessarily mean there is no risk of discrimination. Obesity, older age, and child-bearing status (which increase risk, other things being equal) have been shown to affect wages with group insurance (and to a greater extent than any effect on wages in a firm not offering insurance coverage) (Bhattacharya and Bundorf, 2009; Pauly and Herring, 1999; Gruber, 1994). But there are many other characteristics which are likely not reflected in wage offsets. As in standard models of insurance equilibrium in the presence of asymmetric information, this unpriced risk variation may cause adverse selection. In employment-based group markets, however, the adverse selection problem from the health insurance market "spills over" into the labor market (Bhattacharya and Vogt, 2006).

Some qualifications to these simple observations are as follows: given the small fraction of the premium explicitly charged for the lowest premium option, there will ordinarily not be adverse selection between individual and group insurance, because even a risk-rated, low-risk premium in individual insurance will usually be *greater* than the explicit worker premium in group insurance. So even low-risk workers with group insurance will not move to individual insurance. Workers may sort among firms based on risk, though we have little evidence or theory for this case. For there to be adverse selection between individual and group insurance, low-risk workers would need to be able to recover both their contribution and the employer contribution if they opted for risk-rated individual coverage, and usually there is no mechanism by which the employer share can be captured by individual workers who decide not to take group coverage.

Despite the likely absence of perfect individual risk rating through wage offsets, employment-based group purchasing appears to provide a relatively stable solution in many settings. What factors account for this apparent stability? Labor market friction likely plays a role. Workers come together in firms for purposes other than obtaining insurance, and this alternative basis for grouping (and the search and switching costs associated with different jobs) is a barrier against frictionless adverse selection. Consistent with this explanation, Bhattacharya and Vogt (2006) find that industries in which jobs typically require greater job-specific human capital have higher rates of insurance coverage. In addition, selection effects may be limited by the need for employers to design compensation packages which attract adequate numbers of average-risk workers. It is hard to think of a model in which benefits attract the average-risk worker enough to matter (in lowering employer total compensation cost) but do not differentially appeal to higher-risk workers. In the US, the extent to which risk-based selection is problematic in group markets is also likely tempered by the existence of public programs, including Medicaid and Medicare, which serve disproportionately high-risk populations (Cogan et al., 2010), and the tax subsidy to employment-based insurance which encourages low-risk workers to remain within the group market by restricting subsidies to this setting (Selden, 1999). Finally, some adverse selection may exist in the employer-sponsored market due to the absence of individual risk rating of premiums. Bundorf et al. (2010) document that, among people potentially eligible for employer-sponsored coverage based on family employment status, rates of insurance coverage increase with risk, particularly for people with low to medium incomes.

3.2.2. Premium Differentials, Efficiency, and Firm Objectives

Risk variation may also affect employee behavior within firms. Many employers offer multiple plans potentially leading to risk selection across plans if higher-risk workers choose more generous coverage. Risk selection may even occur in firms offering a single plan if the plan requires an explicit premium contribution and low-risk employees are more likely to opt out of coverage in response to that contribution.

The potential for risk selection within the firm raises questions of why firms offer multiple plans and require employee premium contributions. Theoretical research has focused primarily on heterogeneity in employee preferences for coverage as an explanation for choice and less on the implications of heterogeneity in risk. Goldstein and Pauly introduce the potential for firms composed of employees with heterogeneous preferences for coverage into the local public good model by relaxing the assumption that workers are perfectly substitutable and instead assume that firms require workers of differing types for production purposes and that preferences for health insurance vary across worker types. They show that, for an employer offering a single plan, the cost-minimizing plan reflects a weighted average of the preferences of different types of workers. Firms may instead offer multiple plans in response to heterogeneous preferences of employees, balancing the trade-off between the greater administrative costs associated with managing multiple plans and the savings associated with greater customization with respect to employee preferences (Bundorf, 2002). While offering multiple plans may alternatively be a strategy by employers to promote greater within-firm competition among plans for enrollees (Enthoven and Kronick, 1989), Bundorf (2010) demonstrates that patterns of premiums and coverage are more consistent with choice as a response to diverse employee preferences than an explicit strategy to promote greater within-firm competition.

Offering more than one plan, however, creates the possibility for risk-based selection across plans. While employers often require different contributions for different plans, they rarely vary the contribution for a particular plan by individual characteristics related to risk. The widespread exception is family size—contributions often vary by the number of people covered under a policy—and sometimes contributions vary by employee wage. Although federal regulation currently prohibits varying contributions by age or health status, even when it was not forbidden by law, employee premiums almost never varied with employee risk. Thus, the potential for adverse selection is significant given that the prices faced by enrollees do not vary by easily observable characteristics related to risk. Cutler and Reber (1998) document a situation in which offering multiple plans and requiring employees to pay the full marginal premium for more expensive coverage led to significant adverse selection into more generous plans. If fostering/permitting adverse selection is viewed as (or is) a cost to employer profits, then there is a trade-off, as usual, between offering policies to fit differences in individual preferences that are unrelated to risk levels and causing adverse selection. The employer, however, can determine the size of the differential premium for one plan over another, and even when both plans are bought from outside insurers (rather than being self-insured), there is no necessity that the differential reflect the actual difference in average premiums.

Given the constraint on explicit discrimination across workers, there has been a large amount of work specifying what premium differentials should be (for second-best efficiency) and some work examining what those differentials are in reality. The model developed by Cutler and Reber (1998), Pauly and Herring (1999), and Cutler and Zeckhauser (2000) imagines that the goal of the group insurance plan is second-best optimality in employee choice of plan. Assuming that different plan designs yield higher benefits to workers at different risk levels, and that the high-risk plan is more costly than the low-risk plan, the problem is to incentivize workers to choose the appropriate matching plan. A strategy which sets a fixed dollar employer contribution and then sets the premium differential equal to the difference in average expenses of workers who choose each plan type will not be efficient, because the premium differential will reflect both the "true" incremental cost of the more generous plan for the high risks and the difference in risk levels. This will cause a death spiral for the more generous plan. If there are only two risk levels, setting the premium differential at the incremental cost for high risks will cause an efficient allocation of risks to plans, but if the distribution of risks is continuous the actual difference will reflect the average incremental cost, not the optimal incremental cost for the risk level at the margin of indifference between the two plans. Rather than asking what is optimal for the set of workers, Miller (2005) asks what contribution policy an employer minimizing total compensation costs would choose in a similar setting. He finds, not surprisingly, that such an employer will choose to set the monopoly price for some of the plans. He does not consider possible effects of employer premium-pricing policy on the distribution of workers across employers.

These models rely on two important assumptions: (1) that more generous coverage is efficient for high risks but not for low risks because they have stronger preferences for more generous plans; and (2) that preferences for coverage are perfectly correlated with risk type (Bundorf et al., 2008). More generally, a single uniform contribution in the presence of heterogeneous risks will achieve a first-best allocation if and only if the single crossing property holds—the value that consumers place on the more generous plan increases more quickly with risk than the incremental cost. In this situation, the key challenge for setting the socially efficient contribution is identifying which risk type is marginal. But it is entirely possible that the single crossing property does not hold. Perhaps less generous plans generate greater cost savings for high than low risks. In this case, preferences for more generous coverage may increase less quickly with risk than incremental costs and no single uniform contribution can generate an efficient allocation. More generally, preferences for different types of plans may be either uncorrelated or imperfectly correlated with risk. In this case, a uniform contribution will represent a second-best solution and the second-best contribution will depend upon the distribution of risk types and preferences for coverage in the population. A first-best allocation would require risk-rated contributions.

Important gaps remain in research in this area. One is that each of these studies treats the composition of the group as fixed. A more realistic treatment would allow the mix of workers to depend on the plans offered and their premium differentials. Moreover, in reality employers usually do not charge as explicit premiums either the welfare maximizing configuration or the labor cost minimizing configuration for a given set of workers. Surprisingly little is known about what employers actually do. Either their objectives differ from these goals, or they have imperfect information on how to do so. Nevertheless, the conclusion is that it is hard to describe the positive empirical benchmark for what happens (in the absence of regulation) and therefore even harder to describe how things would change if external circumstances or incentives changed.

3.3. Group Insurance and Risk Variation Over Time

While things therefore are far from perfect, are there nevertheless ways in which group insurance improves how consumers are treated when it comes to risk? The most obvious reason for a positive answer is that the insensitivity of explicit premiums and money wages to risk constitutes a kind of informal mechanism for protecting people against the reclassification risk they might find in simple (if unrealistic) models of individual health insurance markets. In some settings, this may be a reason for the existence of group insurance, as an alternative and perhaps less costly arrangement than individual insurance with guaranteed renewability. That is, as long as the worker continues group coverage, the explicit premium he pays does not change even if risk changes for the worker or dependents. Bhattacharya and Vogt (2006) demonstrate that this type of risk pooling over time is dependent upon the degree to which employment transitions are costly and the extent to which health transitions are persistent. In contrast to the GR approach, there is no need to frontload the premiums to offset growth in risk should a firm's workforce age, because the explicit employee premium will almost always be less than the premium charged by any individual insurer. (There is a possibility of adverse selection from another employer who offered less generous coverage and higher money wages in order to skim off the healthy workers.)

But the protection provided by group insurance extends only as far as the individual firm employment contract. Let the high-risk worker change or lose her job, and she may be confronted with substantial increases in premiums or reductions in wages. This type of concern is consistent with the job lock literature which finds that people with employment-based health insurance, particularly those who are high risk, are less likely to transition jobs than those in jobs without such coverage (see Gruber, 2000, for a review). Indeed, Pauly and Lieberthal (2008) find that, among those in poor health, the likelihood of losing health insurance is greater for those with coverage from a small firm than for those with individual coverage.

4. PUBLIC POLICY TOWARD RISK VARIATION

A striking feature of the health care systems of all developed countries is the prominence of policies governing the degree of variation in premiums in health insurance markets. In countries with single payer systems, risk variation in premiums is essentially eliminated by the absence of premium payments. In systems in which people make payments for health insurance, the degree to which they are related to individual risk is nearly always influenced by regulation.

Both efficiency and equity rationales for the pervasiveness of government intervention along this dimension exist. As discussed earlier, in theory health insurance markets may operate inefficiently due to information asymmetries between consumers and insurers, and government intervention is a potential response to this inefficiency. Most of the literature on the rationale for government intervention in insurance markets due to adverse selection, however, takes as its starting point a single-period model of individual purchase of coverage. Yet we have shown that the way in which unregulated private markets deal with risk is, because of guaranteed renewability and group insurance, a far cry from simple single-period risk rating. That is, the alternative to insurance markets with public intervention is not necessarily or even usually individual insurance markets of the Rothschild–Stiglitz type subject to adverse selection. Thus we face a serious dilemma at the outset. If regulation is already present and we are trying to see if it is justified, we really do not know what would happen if regulations and tax subsidies were removed, but we do know that it is unlikely to fit any of the theoretical models well. To evaluate the welfare effects of regulation, we need more complete knowledge of the nature of the market or markets that do exist in the absence of regulation.

There are some powerful reasons why we would not expect unregulated markets to fit the Rothschild–Stiglitz model. Arrow (1963) noted that the medical care sector as a whole as well as the health insurance sector display properties inconsistent with the description implied by simple models of competitive equilibrium because of a variety of differences between risky medical care and standard commodities. Some of those differences surely come from regulation that is universal (like physician licensure), but some also come from differences from the simple model apparently generated by the market itself to deal with what would otherwise be uninsured risk: the most prominent of these are guaranteed renewability and group insurance. That is, when we take the fetters off health insurance to generate an unfettered free market, we do not get the simple Rothschild–Stiglitz model. While both guaranteed renewability and group insurance historically were in the US accompanied by and doubtless fostered by favorable tax and regulatory treatment, it remains true that it is difficult if not impossible to find an empirical counterpart to the simple single-period risk rating insurer market equilibrium even in a setting where regulation of individual coverage is minimal and tax subsidies small. Both public and private sectors, probably to avoid market failure, have set up markets different from the simple model. It seems plausible, as Arrow argued, that citizens will develop multiple ways, some public and some private, to deal with the peculiarities and inefficiency of the health insurance system. But then one will logically be unable to find the simple but inefficient model in practice. There still may be some variation (driven by heterogeneity in individual behavior in response to insurance market inefficiencies) and some inefficiency in the real world since individual responses will represent a second-best solution.

While there is a possible if unproven efficiency argument based on reclassification risk against a market with single-period risk-based premiums, the strongest arguments among policy makers (in contrast to economists) for regulation to inhibit risk-based pricing are based either on equity or some other postulated social norms. Presumably the reason for policies which limit the degree of risk-based premium variation is the expectation that, in their absence, premiums would vary with risk in undesired ways. On equity grounds, charging high risks more may be said to be unjust, although a full treatment of equity should probably account for income as well as risk variation. Or sometimes it is simply asserted that "society" has decided to "pool risks." Insurance with risk rating in a single-period setting attains the optimal amount of risk pooling; presumably this is a statement calling for risk averaging rather than the pooling of risk of any event that is yet to happen within the term of insurance coverage. These arguments can be addressed against risk-based pricing of a high-risk insured new to a given insurer even when that person had or could have had premium protection through guaranteed renewability in an earlier time period before becoming a high risk.

Policies which limit premium variation to achieve equity objectives, however, generate economic inefficiency. From this perspective, the key economic question is how to achieve the normatively optimal distribution as potential policy interventions generate different trade-offs between efficiency and equity. Once again, however, the lack of a positive, second-best benchmark restricts our ability to evaluate these trade-offs.

Despite reasons to be less concerned about the way unregulated markets handle risk, the possibilities of inequity and inefficiency have motivated regulation. We therefore explore what impact such regulation might have. In the following sections, we discuss the types of policy instruments that have been analyzed in theory to address each rationale. We think it is worth analyzing these policies even while retaining substantial skepticism about the relevance of the rationale.

4.1. Regulation for Efficiency in Markets with Risk Variation

4.1.1. Policies to Address Inefficiency due to Anticipated Asymmetric Information and Associated Adverse Selection

One of the efficiency justifications of public intervention in health insurance markets is based on the theoretical result that a Rothschild—Stiglitz equilibrium is not Pareto efficient if the share of high risks is moderately large. (The welfare evaluation of cases in which no equilibrium exists is less clear, though one can certainly assert in such cases that no efficient equilibrium exists.) In this case a combination of mandatory partial insurance with community rating and voluntary supplementary insurance can make both risk types better off (Eckstein et al., 1985). Even this is only a second-best optimum because in a first-best world—and in the absence of moral hazard—every risk-averse individual would want to buy full coverage at a fair premium. In contrast, in the equilibrium of the mixed public—private insurance market, low risks are still underinsured and pay a total price that exceeds the fair premium.

This simple efficiency justification of mandatory public insurance breaks down because unregulated markets for health insurance are better described by alternative models. For example, if the assumptions of the Wilson—Spence—Miyazaki model hold, mandatory public insurance no longer increases efficiency relative to the market equilibrium because the corresponding equilibrium in that model is always Pareto optimal given the informational constraints (Crocker and Snow, 1985). Perhaps more realistically, as discussed earlier, it breaks down even further if insurance is offered in a group setting or is offered as individual coverage with guaranteed renewability to a population with homogeneous risks (that change differentially over time).

4.1.2. Administrative Costs Associated with Risk Variation and Methods of Reducing Them

Underwriting costs must be incurred if risks vary and premiums depend on risk. Explicit underwriting costs do not seem to be large, perhaps at most 1 percent of premiums, but they are not negligible. And some of the selling expense may be attributable to underwriting if insurers pay brokers to avoid or at least identify higher risks. How much underwriting expense an insurer will choose to incur depends on the extent to which risk actually varies in its population of potential insured. In a simple model where risks are either "high" or "low," the expense of distinguishing between these two risks will depend on their proportion in the population and the difference in expected damages between the two classes. The obvious point is that if risk does not vary much it may not pay an insurer to incur much expense to discriminate among risks. It also will not pay to incur high costs of risk discrimination if either type of risk is a small fraction of applicants for the insurer. If there are few high risks it will not pay to find them, and if there are few low risks they will not pay to have this found out. The fact that underwriting does occur, however, suggests that the benefits to health insurers of discriminating among risk types, at least to some degree, exceed the costs.

Regulations requiring community rating will reduce explicit underwriting costs. Community rating, however, introduces the need for a third party to implement a system and transfers across insurers based on enrollee risk in order to prevent insurers from competing on risk selection. Thus, a reduction in the cost of underwriting on the part of insurers is offset by the introduction of resources devoted to risk adjustment. Community rating has additional efficiency implications which we consider in sections 4.3.4 and 4.3.5.

4.2. Regulation for Equity in Insurance Markets with Risk Variation

Private markets may function efficiently but the market outcome may deviate from society's normative preferences for distribution, based on either health status or income, and government intervention may be an attempt to achieve this desired redistribution. In a private market for health insurance, the buyer seeking coverage from a new insurer would pay a premium which—given the amount of coverage—reflects the expected value of future health care costs. Those with a higher risk of illness would thus have to pay higher premiums than those with a lower risk. Many consider this market solution unjust—that those unlucky enough to be in poor health must pay more for access to health care, particularly when poor health is due to inequality in health endowments (e.g. congenital diseases or handicaps) rather than differences in the person's health-related behavior (lung cancer caused by smoking). Risk rating of the former is often considered less acceptable from a normative perspective than risk rating of the latter.

It is also important conceptually to distinguish between the single period and lifetime models when considering the rationale for policies to reduce risk variation in premiums. In particular, the single-period model introduces the risk of risk reclassification, which may be viewed as undesirable for either equity or efficiency reasons. As discussed earlier, insurance policies with guaranteed renewability can be an appropriate remedy for reclassification risk. Even long-term insurance contracts with guaranteed renewability, however, do not eliminate risk-based premium variation if differences in risk are present at the initiation of the contract. In this case, transfers from low to high risks can be justified using the concept of the veil of ignorance introduced by Harsanyi (1955) and Rawls (1971). People behind the veil of ignorance do not know whether they will be born as high or low risks. On top of their health risk as such, they face a lottery concerning their expected health care costs and thus their health insurance premiums. Given risk aversion behind the veil of ignorance, they would be willing to insure against this premium risk. Hence, if the hypothetical veil of ignorance is accepted as the basis of a fair decision, not guided by particular interests, equalization of health insurance premiums between high and low risks may be desirable.

Given the present state of scientific knowledge, the proportion of the population who are high risks at birth is small, perhaps 1 to 4 percent. Specific public programs for the disabled as part of social insurance are able to address much of this type of concern. Provisions in unregulated insurance markets in the United States also provide substantial protection. If prospective parents have family insurance coverage, premiums for that coverage are generally not altered when a baby is added and, even if premiums are changed, the adjustment only takes account of the number of children put on the policy, not their health state. Thus, at least up until the child goes off the parents' coverage (now age 26), the family can be protected against the costs associated with a high-risk child.

While it is possible that genetic testing will eventually provide information on differences in lifetime total medical spending, at present low-cost genetic tests are sufficiently accurate for only a few rare conditions such as cystic fibrosis and Huntington's disease. If genetic tests become cheaper and more accurate over time, individuals should be advised by public authorities to purchase their desired amount of (life and health) insurance coverage before they undergo such a test to preserve their ignorance at the point of insurance purchasing. This would be a much milder public intervention than the one proposed by Tabarrok (1994), who proposes that genetic tests may only be sold to persons who can prove that they have already purchased "adequate" insurance coverage. Alternatively, the use of genetic test results for underwriting can be prohibited by law, which is done in many countries, but this regulation is not welfare enhancing because it creates adverse selection (Strohmenger and Wambach, 2000) as buyers of insurance use their genetic test information to decide on insurance coverage.

4.3. Government Intervention in Practice

The set of policies in place which influence the degree of premium variation vary significantly both across and within country. In theory, policy makers could achieve a desired final distribution of insurance, medical care, and income through a variety of mechanisms. For example, ignoring administrative costs, a system of community rating of insurance premiums combined with an individual mandate and income-based subsidies could achieve a similar outcome as a system of single-period risk rating combined with risk and income-based transfers. Yet the implications for efficiency of the different choices may differ substantially depending on the degree of price responsiveness among consumers, the distribution of risks within the population, and the efficiency of the tax system. Thus, differences in policies may be driven by either the administrative or the efficiency costs of different mechanisms or the desired final distribution across countries. In practice, however, it is difficult to reconcile observed policies with economic criteria of either efficiency or equity. As discussed earlier, in the case of efficiency, the lack of understanding of the competitive benchmark hinders our ability to determine whether regulation is welfare improving. And in the case of an equity rationale, the normative criterion which policy makers are trying to achieve is rarely clearly expressed, making it difficult to determine whether observed policies are meeting distributional objectives and to evaluate the efficiency trade-off necessary to achieve that standard. Perhaps the most than can be said is that policy makers seem to have a strong normative preference against single-period risk-based pricing which appears to motivate substantial government intervention in health insurance markets.

In the next sections, we identify the different types of actual and proposed policies which influence risk variation in premiums and discuss some of the equity and efficiency implications.

4.3.1. Single Payer System

This solution has been chosen by countries such as the United Kingdom and Italy. By eliminating competition among insurers, a single payer necessarily eliminates the possibility of inefficiency due to adverse selection, and tax-based financing eliminates the explicit link between a person's health status and his or her contribution for health insurance. The efficiency costs, however, may be substantial. The elimination of competitive insurance markets eliminates any benefits from insurer competition in the form of cost, quality, and customization of insured medical care. Tax-based financing, the magnitude of which is substantial in a single payer system, also creates economic distortions.

4.3.2. Person-specific Transfers to High Risks

An alternative is to allow insurers to charge risk-based premiums and to delegate the task of subsidizing high risks to the tax-transfer system. For example, Pauly et al. (1992) propose introducing refundable tax credits which reflect a household's risk category and are inversely related to household income. Citizens with little or no tax liability would receive a transfer payment.[2] Calculating risk-based subsidies, however, may represent a challenge to a regulator who does not directly observe the health status of any given individual. In practice, only a few diseases which are easily diagnosed would probably be used to determine the transfers.

One approach would be to use the premium charged by a risk-rating insurer as an indicator of risk. Zweifel and Breuer (2006) propose to subsidize risk-based premiums

---

[2] See also van de Ven and Ellis (2000) for a discussion of this approach.

based on the extent to which they exceed a certain percentage of household income. In this way, they aim to target subsidies to individuals who are both high risk and low income, arguing that high risks with high incomes need not be subsidized. Zweifel and Breuer claim that in the presence of moral hazard, efficiency requires tailor-made individual insurance contracts in which individual parameters such as price elasticities play a role and that risk-based premium reductions for cost sharing require risk-based premiums to begin with. In their view, risk adjustment, in contrast, must always be imperfect and can never completely remove incentives for risk selection.

However, premium subsidies as envisaged by Zweifel and Breuer create a number of problems. First, they create an incentive for both the insurer and the insured to include additional services in the contract in order to increase the transfer. This can only be avoided by defining a detailed (minimum) benefit package. Then, however, an important advantage of competition in the health insurance market—diversity of insurance contracts—would be limited. Alternatively, the subsidy could be scaled not to the individual premium but to an average defined over a broadly defined risk class.

The second problem is that recipients of the transfer lose all their incentives to shop around for an inexpensive insurer because effectively their contribution is limited by a certain percentage of their income (van de Ven, 2006).

Kifmann and Roeder (2010) have analyzed under what conditions risk-based premiums accompanied by premium subsidies for low-income households are more "equitable" than community rating, where equity is measured by a Rawlsian social welfare function. They show that this is more likely the case the more negative is the correlation between health and productivity (earnings potential). In light of the vast literature on the association between income and health (Wagstaff and van Doorslaer, 2000), a negative correlation must be considered an exception rather than a rule. But even in this unlikely case, a combination of community rating and premium subsidies for low-income households would dominate the Zweifel—Breuer solution.

4.3.3. Person-specific Insurance Programs for High Risks

Another way to limit the degree of risk-based variation in insurance markets is to develop public programs targeted to high risks. These programs can take the form of public insurance with eligibility restricted to high risks or private insurance offered through subsidized high-risk pools at a price higher than that available to medium or low risks but lower than that available to high risks in the unsubsidized market. These pools accept people who have been deemed high risks by insurers; they charge premiums somewhat higher than standard and offer rather limited coverage in order to discourage people from being eager to enter the high-risk pool to claim high subsidies. And they only limit the coverage sought by those who want to use the pools; people who buy their insurance in the risk-rated open market may obtain whatever coverage they wish from competitive insurers. Even within the pool insurers can compete on the basis of premiums since the per-person subsidy is usually specified as a predetermined amount or subject to a predetermined cap. The main problem such pools have had arises from limitations on financing by the state governments who, until health reform, organized and financed them; there were often waiting lists for the pools. A second problem with the state-run pools is that they were largely financed with assessments on other insurance purchases, thus increasing incentives for adverse selection there. The recently passed legislation reforming the US health care system establishes high-risk pools as a temporary measure to provide coverage to high risks until more extensive reform is implemented. The version in health reform is, however, funded by general revenue taxation (but with a relatively modest total budget).

In addition to reducing premiums for high risks who are made eligible for the coverage, these types of programs may make private coverage in regular markets more accessible for those high risks who are not eligible for the programs. Newhouse (1996) demonstrates how costly contracting can increase the likelihood of a pooling equilibrium in which insurers offer the more limited contract preferred by low risks. An implication of the Newhouse model is that a decrease in the size of the high-risk population increases the likelihood of a pooling equilibrium and increases the generosity of the coverage offered. In other words, when competitive markets are characterized by the assumptions of the Newhouse model, programs which remove a portion of the high risks from the competitive market may correct some of the distortions generated by asymmetric information. Cogan et al. (2010) demonstrate that the extension of Medicare coverage to the disabled in the 1970s had these types of effects.

4.3.4. Insurance Market Regulation

Many countries rely on private insurance but regulate the degree to which premiums may vary with risk. The concern, of course, is that, taken in isolation, this type of regulation may actually cause adverse selection. A number of studies have examined the effect of rate regulation on adverse selection in individual markets for both primary and supplemental health insurance. These studies compare rates of insurance coverage in states with laws restricting the extent to which insurers are allowed to vary premiums based on individual characteristics to rates in states without these types of rating restrictions. Most studies find that, while these laws have a relatively small effect on overall rates of coverage, the lack of an overall effect represents the combination of an increase in coverage among high risks and a reduction in coverage among low risks. For example, Davidoff et al. (2005) find that reforms in the small group market which restricted rating variance increased rates of coverage among high risks by 4.5 percentage points and reduced rates of coverage by 1.7 percentage points among low risks. This finding is remarkably consistent across settings, including the market for individual primary coverage (Herring and Pauly, 2007; Lo Sasso and Lurie, 2009) and private supplemental coverage (Bundorf and Simon, 2006). Researchers have also documented a similar effect in the US small group market (Buchmueller and DiNardo, 2002; Monheit and Steinberg Schone, 2004; Simon, 2005; Davidoff et al., 2005). Buchmueller and DiNardo (2002) suggest that the lack of an overall effect on rates of coverage in the small group market was generated by a shift from indemnity to HMO coverage among low risks, and Lo Sasso and Lurie (2009) find a similar shift in response to rate regulation in the individual market. Thus, at best, restrictions in insurer rating practices generate a transfer between low and high risks. And in settings in which consumers are price responsive, rating restrictions could generate significant welfare loss due to adverse selection.

There is an idealized version of regulation that would deal optimally (in both efficiency and equity terms) with risk variation, but its requirements are very demanding. We outline this model primarily to show what compromises more realistic regulatory structures would have to make to achieve a second-best optimum. In particular, if the optimal insurance coverage for every person (taking into account variation in risk aversion, administrative loading, and income effects on the demand for medical care) has been determined, if insurers can be assumed to operate with maximum efficiency, if it is possible to adjust premiums for the ideal insurance for each person based on income and risk, and if purchase of the optimal insurance can be made mandatory with an effective mandate, then the outcome can be called ideal. Thus, in practice, using community rating to achieve a more equitable distribution of insurance requires mandatory purchase of coverage to keep low risks in the market and a system of risk adjustment combined with regulation of the benefit package to prevent insurers from distorting coverage for the purpose of risk selection. We discuss the challenges of risk adjustment in greater detail in section 4.3.5. This seems to be the conceptualization of regulation underlying the Dutch and to some extent the Swiss system, but it is hard to achieve in practice even there. It will be doubly hard to achieve in a more heterogeneous setting such as the United States.

4.3.5. Risk Adjustment

Risk adjustment, the process of administratively adjusting the premiums paid to health plans based on enrollee risk, is one piece of a regulatory response to the potential inefficiency generated by community rating requirements. Requiring insurers to accept any individual at a uniform premium leads to expected losses for high risks and expected profits for low risks, creating incentives for insurers to enroll low risks (*cream-skimming*) while avoiding high risks (*dumping*). Under competitive pressure, even not-for-profit insurers will have incentives to risk select since they will need a sufficient number of low risks to break even.

Risk selection can take two forms. On the one hand, health insurers can perform *direct risk selection* by influencing who signs a contract. Regulations requiring insurers to accept all applicants, known as guaranteed issue or open enrollment requirements, are intended to address this type of behavior. Health plans, however, may use more subtle mechanisms than outright rejection to achieve favorable selection. For example, insurers may "lose" the application submitted by a person who is considered expensive and may encourage people who are expected to use little health care to enroll by offering them supplementary services at a discount or, in the extreme case, outright payments. Although there is little evidence of this type of direct risk selection in regulated markets in the US, an audit study found that German insurers who were unable to vary premiums based on geographical differences in expected expense were more likely to respond to applicants from low-cost than to those from high-cost areas (Bauhoff, 2010).

Indirect risk selection, on the other hand, refers to designing insurance products in order to induce consumers to self-select into different plans based on their risk. For example, plans with high cost sharing are more attractive to low risks who expect to use less care. Community rating is also generally accompanied by regulations specifying a minimum benefit package to limit the ability of insurers to risk select through benefit design. But even if the basic benefit package is fixed by the regulator, insurers can still engage in indirect risk selection. In markets in which private insurance supplements the public system, insurers may offer supplementary benefits to low risks at a discount, while charging high risks a mark-up if payments for the basic package are not properly risk adjusted (Kifmann, 2006). Competition among insurers translates this mark-up into a lower price for the basic benefit. As a consequence, cross-subsidies from low-risk to high-risk types are reduced, effectively undoing the cross-subsidization of community rating.

Managed care plans, however, may represent a greater challenge to a regulator concerned about indirect risk selection. Relative to traditional insurance coverage, managed care plans make greater use of supply-side cost sharing in order to create incentives for providers to deliver care more efficiently. Supply-side cost sharing, however, also creates incentives for risk selection on the part of providers, and thus generates a trade-off between efficiency in production and risk selection at the point of service (Newhouse, 1996). When health plans face strong incentives for risk selection, they may choose to design contracts with providers in ways which facilitate favorable selection at the expense of efficiency in care delivery. Because the techniques of managed care are not easily observable to a regulator, limiting inefficient behavior on the part of plans through regulation is difficult (Newhouse, 1996).

Theoretical studies have examined different ways in which managed care plans may distort coverage to achieve favorable selection including their choice of supply and demand size utilization controls (Eggleston, 2000), differential rationing across different types of services (Frank et al., 2000) and service-level carve-outs (Biglaiser and Ma, 2003). Testing the empirical predictions of the Frank et al. (2000) model using data from the US Medicare program, Cao and McGuire (2003) find evidence consistent with HMOs choosing service levels to achieve favorable selection. Based on the same model, Ellis and McGuire (2007) develop an empirical index to identify which services are likely to be distorted by HMOs in order to achieve favorable selection. In their analysis, they introduce the distinction between predictability and predictiveness in health care spending. The utilization of a certain health care service is called *predictable* if a large part of the interpersonal variation in spending for this service can be predicted by using observable characteristics of the insured. The service is *predictive* if its utilization is highly correlated (positively or negatively) with the overall use of health care services by a particular patient. The authors then argue that services which are both predictable and predictive are candidates for rationing by managed care plans for the purpose of risk selection and construct an index which measures the potential for under- or overprovision. They propose that regulators could specify minimum levels of intensity for the services with particularly high values of the respective index in order to reduce the degree to which managed care plans distort services in response to incentives to risk select.

4.3.5.1. Defining Risk Adjustment

Risk adjustment is a regulatory response to the inefficiency created by restrictions in insurer rating practices which create incentives on the part of plans for risk selection. In this section, we define risk adjustment as the process of administratively setting premium payments to health plans based on the risk of enrollees. When regulation prevents health plans from charging consumers risk-rated premiums directly, risk adjustment essentially reintroduces risk-based variation in the payment a plan receives for enrolling a particular consumer.

Implementing risk adjustment requires a sponsor or an intermediary to collect revenues, either in the form of taxes or enrollee premium contributions, and to redistribute these revenues in the form of risk-based premium payments to health plans. To highlight the role of the intermediary, Figure 11.1 contrasts a competitive market with a regulated system relying on risk adjustment. In panel A, consumers purchase insurance directly from health plans and the premium the consumer pays is the premium which the plan receives for covering the consumer's medical expenditures. In panel B, in contrast, the payment made by a consumer differs from the premium received by the plan. In this section, we refer to the payment made by the consumer as the "enrollee contribution." As shown in panel B, enrollee contributions are often supplemented by tax-based revenue. We refer to the payment made by the intermediary to the health plan for providing covered services as the "premium payment." The key distinction between panels A and B for the purpose of risk adjustment is that the payment received by the plan is determined in the market in panel A and is determined administratively by the sponsor in panel B.

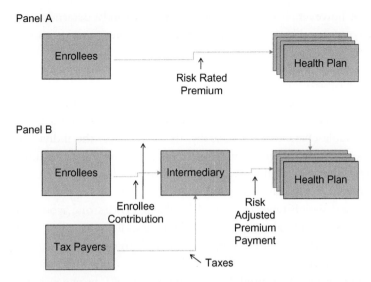

Figure 11.1 Competitive Market versus Regulated Market with Risk Adjustment.

We note that our definition of risk adjustment does not encompass administratively adjusting any component of the enrollee contribution. Keenan et al. (2001), for example, refer to the process of adjusting employee premium contributions to reflect differences in plan cost but not differences in enrollee risk as "risk adjustment of employee premium contributions." In other words, we define risk adjustment as a supply-side regulatory strategy. Other studies have referred to risk adjustment, as we have defined it here, as "risk equalization" (e.g. Armstrong et al., 2010).

Risk adjustment is used in a variety of settings, and, in practice, the simple model outlined above can be implemented in different ways. Van de Ven and Ellis (2000) differentiate between mandatory enrollee contributions which are not linked to plan choice and those which are. They refer to the former, which are often linked to income, as "solidarity contributions" and the latter as "premium contributions." Solidarity contributions are intended to reflect the redistributive objectives of the financing system, and the payment linked to plan choice is intended to create incentives for consumers to make efficient coverage choices.

Van de Ven and Ellis (2000) also describe two different modalities for the flow of funds for risk adjustment. In one, consumers make both a solidarity contribution to a sponsor and a premium contribution directly to a plan. In the other, consumers make a single contribution, including both solidarity and direct premium components, to health plans and then the sponsor administers a system of transfers across plans. The advantage of the latter model is that it reduces the extent of funds transfer across organizations and the associated administrative cost. The key feature which is common across settings, however, is that an intermediary ultimately determines the degree to which the payment a plan receives for a particular enrollee varies with risk.

4.3.5.2. Risk Adjustment Methods

In practice, risk adjustment involves setting the premium payment to a plan proportional to the expected cost of a particular enrollee by weighting a base payment for different observable characteristics. Usually, the weights on the individual characteristics are developed from a regression estimating health care costs as a function of those characteristics. Research on the development of risk adjustment methods has focused primarily on how to maximize the explanatory power of the model used to derive these weights and which types of individual characteristics one would include in the model. Van de Ven and Ellis (2000) provide an excellent overview of the technical issues in estimating these models. Here we identify some of the issues in the debate over which characteristics one would include in a risk adjustment model. The simple risk adjustment model presented by Newhouse (1996) provides a framework for discussion:

$$Y_{i,t} = \alpha + X_{i,t}\beta + \mu_i + \varepsilon_{i,t}$$

where $Y_{i,t}$ is person i's medical care consumption in time period t, α is a constant, β is a coefficient, $X_{i,t}$ is a vector of risk adjusters, μ_i is a time-invariant, person-specific effect with a mean of zero, and $\varepsilon_{i,t}$ is a random error term with an expected value of zero.

Newhouse et al. (1989) raise the concern that a predictable component of person-specific variance, μ_i, exists even after controlling for observable characteristics in X such as age, health status and indicators of chronic conditions, suggesting that even detailed systems of risk adjustment may leave incentives for plans to risk select. They propose that adding a measure of prior health utilization can address this by increasing the predictive power of the model. Consistent with this concern, Hsu et al. (2009) demonstrate that measures of prior use significantly increase the predictive power of the relatively detailed risk adjustment formula used for the US Medicare Part D Prescription Drug Benefit and that premium payments based on this richer model reduce plan incentives for risk selection. Prior use, however, is also a measure of plan efficiency and conditioning payment on prior use dilutes plan incentives to produce efficiently. Thus, risk adjustment which conditions on prior use creates a trade-off between risk selection and efficiency in production of medical care (Newhouse, 1996). Alternative "risk-sharing" schemes exist and many are discussed by van de Ven and Ellis (2000). What they have in common is that the plan is reimbursed for some component of actual rather than predicted utilization, as a way of dealing with the likelihood that things may not always turn out as predicted.

Lamers et al. (2003) argue that a regulator would want to exclude some of the exogenous determinants of health care costs as risk adjusters based on equity criteria.[3] They view the risk-adjusted premium payment as a subsidy and the choice of which factors to include in X as a choice over which factors the regulator views as important to solidarity. For example, most systems of risk adjustment would include characteristics such as age, sex, and the presence of chronic conditions. But if income were strongly correlated with health care costs, would a regulator include income as a risk adjuster? Van de Ven and Ellis (2000) frame this largely as an equity issue and propose that a regulator would have to differentiate between the types of characteristics society would and would not like to subsidize. Yet if people with low incomes use more services, holding other measured factors such as health status constant, then risk adjustment which did not condition on income would create incentives for insurers to avoid people with low income. Hsu et al. (2010) provide an example of income-based selection in the form of competing plans avoiding high-cost, low-income beneficiaries due to the inability of the risk adjustment system used in the context of US Medicare Part D prescription drug coverage to account for differences in expected utilization by income.

Breyer et al. (2003) discovered three variables that added to measured R-squared in a regression explaining expenditures of a German sickness fund in 1993: income, being single, and being in the last year of life. Due to the income-related contributions to the German social health insurance system, sickness funds can observe their members' incomes. First, the authors found an income elasticity of health care expenditures of roughly -0.5. Second, among members above 60 years, those that appeared to live alone (i.e. who had neither a spouse nor a dependent child in the fund), spent 14 percent more than the mean of all pensioners. Finally, a dummy for members that appear to have died in the respective year (because they were no longer in the data set in the following year) was highly significant with a coefficient of roughly 12,000 DM for members under 60 and 6,000 DM for members over 60. Altogether, these three variables raise adjusted R-squared from 0.0527 to 0.0709. Although it may be difficult to base risk adjustment payments on the percentage of singles among fund members, income is more easily observable, and a retrospective lump-sum payment for every deceased plan member, which was first proposed by Beck and Zweifel (1998), is also feasible. This would greatly reduce insurers' incentives to attract high-income persons and to fend off applicants with an elevated risk of dying.

A related issue is whether geographic variation in health care spending should be incorporated into a system of risk adjustment. If it is included, then people living in underserved areas implicitly subsidize those living in well- or overserviced areas,

---

[3] See the chapter "Equity in Health and Health Care" by Fleurbaey and Schokkaert in this volume for a broader discussion of equity issues in health care.

which can be considered unfair. There are adjustments to subsidies in US Medicare for high-medical-cost areas relative to low-cost areas, but the community rating for the under 65 population envisioned under US health reform will allow substantial geographic variation in premiums that reflects geographic variation in medical costs. One of the problems here is that we do not know whether and to what extent those who suffer from higher local costs might also be getting care that is better or more technologically sophisticated.

Finally, some of the characteristics a regulator would want to include in X are subject to plan manipulation, particularly because the data for risk adjustment is usually based on insurance claims provided by the plan. When payment is based on diagnostic coding of insurance claims, plans have strong incentives to code more aggressively. Song et al. (2010) examine how the risk scores of Medicare beneficiaries change when they move to a new geographic location based on the intensity of medical care delivery in both their original and their new location. They find that moving from a low-intensity to a high-intensity practice-style area was associated with a substantial increase in the number of diagnoses coded. This suggests that not only are current methods of calculating risk scores possibly ineffective in disentangling exogenous health status from plan efficiency, but that risk scores may be relatively easily manipulated through treatment decisions and coding practices.

4.3.5.3. The Regulator's Perspective

Relatively little work has explicitly considered the objective of the regulator in risk adjustment. In the methodological literature, the objective when developing a system of risk adjustment is usually to maximize the predictive power of the underlying model of health care costs, which Glazer and McGuire (2000) refer to as the "statistical approach" to risk adjustment. These authors, in contrast, examine how the regulator can set payments to induce plans to behave in the way that the regulator desires. Using this principal—agent approach, they analyze whether a regulator with imperfect information on consumer risk can improve on the market outcome in a situation in which asymmetric information exists between consumers and health plans. They modify the Rothschild and Stiglitz setting to consider the case of managed care by allowing plans to manipulate levels of care across different types of health care services. In their model, consumers know their risk type but regulators and insurers receive only (the same) noisy signal regarding an individual's risk type. Modeling a regulated market in which the regulator requires community rating of enrollee premium contributions to achieve equity objectives and uses risk adjustment to minimize the inefficiency in coverage levels chosen by competing plans, they show that "conventional risk adjustment"—setting payments to plans equal to the expected cost of enrollees conditional on the noisy signal—improves outcomes relative to no risk adjustment. While in both cases high risks enroll in a contract which provides less care, both acute and chronic, than is socially optimal, and low risks enroll in a plan providing more acute care and less chronic care than is socially optimal, the deviations from the socially optimal level of rationing are smaller in magnitude with conventional risk adjustment than with no risk adjustment.

The authors demonstrate, however, that the regulator can come closer to the socially optimal allocation by setting the payment rates for high risks higher than the expected cost and conversely setting the payment rates for low risks lower than the expected cost. The key contribution of this analysis is that, when a regulator has only a noisy signal of risk, which is often the case in practice, he or she can improve upon current methods of risk adjustment by adjusting payment rates to counteract selection incentives. Using a different modeling approach, Jack (2006) makes a similar point. Building on this work, Glazer and McGuire (2002) define the set of weights a regulator should choose for a given set of risk adjusters to achieve particular objectives regarding access and efficiency and provide an empirical example.

4.3.5.4. Risk Adjustment and Efficiency

Risk adjustment is a regulatory tool intended to reduce the inefficiency associated with community rating of health insurance premiums. Can a system of risk adjustment achieve a first-best efficiency when premiums are community rated? Work by Glazer and McGuire (2002) suggests that, even if a regulator has imperfect information on individual risk, he can improve on expected cost-based models by designing payments which counteract the residual incentives for risk selection. In other words, even if the regulator cannot perfectly observe relative costs, the possibility exists of designing payment systems which would eliminate the incentives on the part of plans to distort their services for the purpose of risk selection.

However, two problems remain for administered pricing on the supply side. The first, relating to productive efficiency, is whether the data available to the regulator will allow him to estimate relative costs in ways which promote efficient utilization. All systems of risk adjustment are implemented using claims data from a particular setting in which health care delivery is unlikely to be efficient. In this case, the estimates of relative costs across different risk types would reflect the inefficiency of the system upon which they are based. The second issue is whether administered pricing can achieve allocative efficiency. Premiums set in competitive markets provide a signal of the value of spending on health care relative to other goods and services and administered pricing schemes eliminate that signal. The US Medicare program, which has struggled in setting the average premium to induce the correct/efficient level of entry on the part of health plans, provides a good example of this challenge.[4] Glazer and McGuire (2002) identify this weakness when they note that their system of risk

---

[4] See McGuire et al. (2011) for a detailed discussion.

adjustment will induce first-best levels of rationing only when the regulator sets the budget at the appropriate level. Otherwise, the outcome is second best with overall levels of care either over- or underprovided depending on the budget set by the regulator. Systems which require enrollees to pay a contribution linked to the cost of a particular plan address this issue in part.

An additional challenge to efficiency faced by systems of community rating comes from the demand side. In most studies of adverse selection in health insurance markets and risk adjustment, demand is determined entirely by risk. Variation in preferences for health plans or style of health care delivery within a given risk type, however, introduces an intractable problem for community rating. When preferences vary within a risk type, risk-based pricing on the demand side is necessary to induce consumers to make efficient choices across different plans. Bundorf et al. (2008) show that the welfare loss due to inefficient matching of consumers to health plans in the absence of risk-rated premium contributions is quantitatively important in the context of US employer-sponsored coverage. Yet risk rating of enrollee contributions compromises the distributional objectives which motivated the regulation in the first place. Glazer and McGuire (2009) identify possible alternatives. They show that when taste can be used as the basis of taxation, as in the case of income, a simple tax can achieve the efficient allocation and preserve the equity criteria of uniform premiums by risk. But when taste is not observable and, thus, cannot be used as the basis for taxation, efficiency and equity, as defined as equal premium contributions for a given plan for differing risk types, cannot be achieved simultaneously. They propose a weaker version of equity, which they refer to as weak solidarity, and show how it can be achieved.

4.3.5.5. Recent Developments in the Practice of Risk Adjustment

A number of countries have implemented and refined systems of risk adjustment since the early 1990s. In this section we provide a brief overview of developments in the practice of risk adjustment in Europe (the Netherlands, Switzerland, and Germany) and the United States.

Germany, the Netherlands, and Switzerland introduced greater competition among sickness funds in the 1990s in an attempt to control rapidly rising health care expenditures and achieve a more efficient allocation of resources in the health care sector. To protect the desired extent of redistribution between risk classes, the competitive framework was accompanied by community rating and open enrollment. Moreover, all three countries introduced risk adjustment systems (RAS) (van de Ven et al., 2003).

In the US, the Medicare program has used a system of risk adjustment when paying private plans, which serve as a voluntary replacement for the traditional benefit, since the program was established during the early 1980s. The system, however, has been widely documented as inadequate in the sense that, due to favorable risk selection, the average Medicare payment to private plans exceeded the amount Medicare would have paid for the beneficiary under traditional coverage.[5] As a result, a revised risk adjustment system which makes greater use of diagnostic information was phased in between 2000 and 2007. The recently implemented prescription drug benefit for Medicare beneficiaries, which relies on competing private plans to deliver publicly subsidized insurance coverage, also relies on a system of risk adjustment. And under the reforms specified by the Patient Protection and Affordable Care Act passed in 2010, risk adjustment will be applied both to private plans participating in newly established health insurance exchanges as well as plans operating outside the exchange.

4.3.5.5.1. Switzerland In Switzerland, the RAS was introduced in 1993 and the competitive framework in 1996. The RAS, using only the parameters of age and sex, was performed using the cell approach. For each age and sex cell, average expenditures were calculated for each of the 26 cantons separately and used as a basis for equalizing payments between sickness funds. It was expected that risk compositions of competing funds would assimilate over time so that the RAS could be removed after ten years (Beck et al., 2003).

The competitive framework is characterized by a basic insurance package, which is mandatory for all residents, and voluntary supplementary insurance packages. Basic insurance was provided by 86 private insurance companies in 2008, down from 118 ten years earlier. The four largest companies had a joint market share of almost 50 percent. Supplementary insurance, which is frequently offered by subsidiary companies, is provided at risk-based premiums, and applicants can be refused by an insurer. As more than 70 percent of the population has taken out supplementary insurance and often with the same insurer, the insurer possesses additional information on their client's health.

The premium for the basic insurance is uniform for all clients of a company and is calculated separately for three age groups (under 18, 18–25, and over 25 years) so as to guarantee zero profits. Discounts can be granted if the client accepts a higher deductible or participates in a managed care plan. Clients can change their insurer every six months. Citizens with low income can apply at their canton for a "premium subsidy" which covers the part of the premium that exceeds a certain percentage (usually 4 to 12) of their total income so that for this clientele the premium is essentially income dependent. Fifty percent of the costs of public hospitals are borne directly by the canton so that insurance companies only reimburse the other half.

4.3.5.5.2. Germany The German RAS was introduced in 1994 in the wake of a more competitive framework of the social health insurance (SHI) system. The main

---

[5] See McGuire et al. (2011) for a discussion of this literature.

target of the RAS was to reduce the wide spread of earnings-related contribution rates of sickness funds (which ranged from 8 to 16 percent) and thus to create a level playing field. Historically, many sickness funds catered only to particular industries or occupational groups so that their risk and earnings compositions differed widely. While before 1996 most blue-collar workers could not choose their sickness fund, free choice was introduced in 1996, mainly to remove the privileges of white-collar employees, not primarily to enhance efficiency through more competition (Buchner and Wasem, 2003).

The first RAS used the parameters age, sex, and disability status to group the insured in 360 cells, within each of which the average expenditures were calculated to determine the "contribution needs" of each sickness fund. As contributions are levied as a share of earnings up to some limit, the RAS also had to take into account the "financial power" of each fund, which is simply the sum of the contributable earnings of all fund members multiplied by an average contribution rate across funds. The difference between contribution needs and financial power was refunded by a central pool.

Since its introduction, the German RAS has been reformed several times. In 2002, insured persons who suffered from one of seven chronic conditions and who voluntarily enrolled in one of seven "disease management programs" were put into extra cells for which average expenditures were calculated separately. Moreover, in 2002 a high-cost pool was introduced which covered 60 percent of expenditures exceeding 20,450 euros in a given year. Finally, in 2009 a direct morbidity component was introduced (see below).

The German health care system is a two-tier system which consists of a social and a private tier. Since 2009 there has been mandatory insurance for every resident. Employees with earnings below a certain threshold (currently around 50,000 euros per year) are members of SHI whereas high earners, civil servants, and the self-employed can opt out of SHI and take out private insurance. While in the private tier premiums are risk rated, the SHI tier is characterized by a legally determined benefit package, free enrollment and earnings-related contributions at a uniform contribution rate, which is fixed by government, but sickness funds are allowed to levy an additional contribution, allowing for a small element of price competition. Moreover, since 2007 sickness funds are allowed to offer rebates for contracts with higher co-payments or restricted physician access. The number of sickness funds has fallen dramatically since the introduction of free choice of funds in 1996, from 642 to less than 200 in 2010. Earnings-related contributions and government subsidies (presently almost 10 percent of total SHI expenditures) go to a central fund, which distributes the money to the sickness funds according to their risk profile.

The latter is measured using the traditional risk adjusters of age, sex, and disability status, but each sickness fund receives a supplement for every client who suffers one of 80 specific chronic diseases. Patients are identified using "diagnostic information" and drug prescriptions and allocated to one of 152 risk groups for which expected costs for the following year are determined using a linear regression.

4.3.5.5.3. Netherlands

The introduction of the RAS in the Netherlands in 1991 was an important part of market-oriented health care reform which was proposed 1987 by the Dekker Committee (Helderman et al., 2005) and inspired by Enthoven (1988). Its guiding principle was that of regulated competition among health insurers and health care providers and more cost responsibility for insurers. Many of these ideas surfaced again in the health care reform of 1996. At first, the RAS used only age and sex as risk adjusters and was accompanied by a large cost reimbursement scheme containing a high-cost pool (Lamers et al., 2003; van de Ven and Schut, 2008). In 1995 the additional risk adjusters "urbanization" and "income" were included, but in 2000 "previous expenditures" were used again, turning the RAS into a partial cost reimbursement system. In 2002 "previous expenditures" were replaced by "pharmaceutical cost groups" and in 2004 "diagnostic cost group" and "employment status" (Douven, 2007).

Since the health care reform of 2006, there has been a mandatory basic insurance in the Netherlands, which is provided by five large private insurance companies in a strictly regulated environment with annual free enrollment, a regulated benefit package and community rating. Insurers are allowed to selectively contract with health care providers and to run their own pharmacies (van de Ven and Schut, 2008). Fifty percent of the revenues of basic insurance plans are financed through income-related contributions, which flow into a central RAS fund (Douven, 2007). The remaining 50 percent are financed through a per-capita premium which is levied directly by the insurance company from all insured persons above 18 years of age. The premium is not risk related but differs between insurers. Insurers may give a rebate of up to 10 percent for group insurance contracts (57 percent of all insureds) and further deductions for co-payments exceeding 150 euros per year (van de Ven and Schut, 2008). About two-thirds of the population receive a premium subsidy from the government, which depends on the average premium so that incentives to choose a cheap contract remain intact.

The revenues from the income-related part flow from the central fund to the insurers in the form of risk-related allocations (Douven, 2007). The procedure consists of several steps (van de Ven and Schut, 2008). In the first step, the expenditures of the coming year are estimated to determine the required contribution rate to finance one-half of total expenditures. In the second step, individual expenditures are estimated, which determine individual risk-related transfer payments. Finally, switches between insurers are estimated to calculate allocations to insurers (Douven, 2007). Individual health expenditures are estimated on the basis of age, sex, urbanization, pharmaceutical cost group (20 groups), and diagnostic cost group. Since 2008, "socio-economic status" has been used as an additional risk adjuster to equalize previously unexplained differences between insured persons who were previously members of social as opposed to private health insurers. Income was not suited to explain this difference (Douven, 2007). Although the Dutch RAS has many risk adjusters, calculated budgets and true expenditures can differ widely, and at the end of each year this difference is partly covered in an attempt to further reduce incentives for risk selection. This is achieved via retrospective partial cost reimbursement and a mandatory high-cost pool which covers 90 percent of all costs exceeding 20,000 euros (van de Ven and Schut, 2008).

4.3.5.5.4. The United States The US Medicare program provides publicly funded health insurance for aged and disabled populations. Since the early 1980s, Medicare beneficiaries have had the option of replacing this traditional coverage with insurance from a private plan.[6] Participating plans sign an annual contract with the Centers for Medicaid and Medicare Services (CMS) agreeing to provide benefits to beneficiaries. Plans must provide a minimum level of benefits equivalent to that of traditional Medicare, may, and often do, provide additional benefits, such as lower cost-sharing or additional covered services, and may charge beneficiaries a premium for enrolling. The beneficiary premium must be community rated within a given service area and plans must accept all beneficiaries who would like to enroll. Plans are allowed to use managed care techniques to coordinate care.

For beneficiaries who choose to enroll in a private plan, the Medicare program makes a risk-adjusted capitated payment to the health plan on the beneficiary's behalf.[7] Historically, CMS linked plan payments to the level of Medicare spending among FFS enrollees in a geographic area and adjusted the payment for demographic characteristics of enrollees. Payments were set at 95 percent of the adjusted average per capita cost (AAPCC) in the county, calculated separately for aged and disabled populations, and the individual characteristics used for risk adjustment were age, sex, Medicaid enrollment, institutional status (nursing home resident), and working status. This "demographic model," however, explained only 1 percent of the variation in Medicare spending, creating considerable opportunity for favorable risk selection into private plans. Correspondingly, several studies found that, due to favorable selection, the Medicare program paid private plans more for enrollees than it would have cost if they had remained in the traditional program.[8]

---

[6] Traditional Medicare coverage is composed of Parts A and B, which correspond roughly to inpatient and outpatient services, respectively. A private plan, technically Medicare Part C, replaces both Part A and Part B coverage. Part D, Medicare coverage for prescription drugs, was enacted in 2003 and first became available in 2006. Prior to the enactment of Part D, Medicare did not cover outpatient prescription drugs.

[7] See Pope et al. (2004) for a detailed description of the development of this system.

[8] See McGuire et al. (2011) for a discussion of the effect of Medicare Part C payment methods on program costs.

In response to these concerns, the Balanced Budget Act of 1997 mandated the eventual risk adjustment of plan payments based on enrollee health status.[9] In 2000, CMS began risk adjusting payments using information on inpatient diagnoses. Initially, the system was limited to inpatient diagnoses due to the lack of reliably coded data from the outpatient setting, and only 10 percent of the weight was based on the modified risk adjustment system due to the concern that it created incentives for plans to hospitalize patients in order to increase payments. Subsequent legislation mandated that, by 2004, CMS base its risk adjustment on data from both inpatient and ambulatory settings, and, in 2004, CMS introduced a more comprehensive system of risk adjustment based on hierarchical condition categories (HCCs) derived from both inpatient and outpatient data. Risk-adjusted payments represented 30, 50, and 75 percent of a blended rate in 2004, 2005, and 2006, respectively. Starting in 2007, risk adjustment was based entirely on the HCC model.

The new model, which added indicators of diagnoses to the existing demographic model, uses diagnoses from a base year to predict utilization in a subsequent year. Indicators of diagnoses were developed by mapping over 15,000 ICD-9 codes to approximately 180 condition categories, from which only a subset, selected based on their predictive power and other criteria, was ultimately used in the model. Among the clinically similar condition categories included in the model, a hierarchy is imposed so that only the most severe condition within a group is coded. Individuals may be coded with multiple conditions when the conditions are not clinically similar. Ultimately the model included 70 diagnostic categories, six diagnostic category interactions, and five interactions of diagnostic categories with indicators of entitlement by disability. The new model, which was calibrated using 1999—2000 Medicare claims data, has greater predictive power than the demographic model, explaining about 10 percent of variation in costs among beneficiaries enrolled in traditional coverage.

Risk adjustment is also a key component of the Medicare Part D Prescription Drug Benefit. The Medicare program extended outpatient prescription drug coverage to beneficiaries beginning in 2006, and the new benefit relies exclusively on competing private insurance plans to deliver publicly subsidized coverage.[10] Private insurance plans contract with Medicare to provide coverage in specific regions. While the program has defined a standard benefit, plans may deviate from that standard in designing coverage providing they meet certain standards with respect to actuarial equivalence, and beneficiaries must pay the full incremental cost for a particular plan relative to a standard plan when they choose to enroll in a particular plan. Thus, plans compete for enrollees based on benefit design, price, and service. Overall Medicare subsidizes

---

[9] The BBA of 1997 also marked the beginning of a series of payment reforms which increased the level of payments to private plans irrespective of risk and these changes also significantly increased Medicare spending. See McGuire et al. (2011) for a comprehensive discussion of these changes.

[10] See Duggan et al. (2008) for a detailed description of this program.

the premium by about 75 percent and provides additional subsidies for low–income beneficiaries.

Medicare's payments to plans and enrollee contributions are determined through a competitive bidding process. Each year participating plans submit bids to the Medicare program for covering a beneficiary of average health. The enrollee premium for a plan is the difference between the plan bid and 74.5 percent of the national average bid, and the enrollee premium does not vary by individual risk.[11] The base payment to the plan, which is the difference between the plan bid and the enrollee contribution, is adjusted for enrollee risk.

The general approach to risk adjustment is similar between the Part C and Part D benefits.[12] The system is based on a model which uses individual diagnoses derived from insurance claims in one year to predict utilization in a subsequent year. Because data on prescription drug utilization for Medicare beneficiaries were not available prior to the implementation of the program, the model is based on prescription drug expenditure data from Federal retirees and Medicaid beneficiaries which were then linked to Medicare inpatient and outpatient utilization data. As in the case of risk adjustment for private managed care plans, indicators of diagnoses were generated by mapping ICD-9 codes into clinical conditions and then determining which clinical conditions were most predictive of subsequent year utilization. Both the aggregation of ICD-9 codes into clinical conditions and the relationship between clinical conditions and utilization differed between the two settings. The final prescription drug spending model used for risk adjustment includes indicators of age and sex, an indicator of disability status, 84 RX-HCCs (disease indicators), and the interaction of disabled status with three different disease indicators. As in the case of the HCC model, coding for indicators for a subset of clinically similar conditions is hierarchical based on disease severity while the remainder of condition indicators are additive. The risk-adjusted payment is adjusted by a scaling factor for beneficiaries receiving low-income subsidies and those who are institutionalized, reflecting the higher expected spending for these groups.

Brown et al. (2011), analyzing the transition from the demographic to the HCC risk adjustment system, provide the first evidence of the effects of risk adjustment in the US Medicare program. They find that risk selection along the dimensions measured in the HCC model declined as risk adjustment was phased in, suggesting that more detailed risk adjustment did create incentives for plans to enroll higher–risk beneficiaries for whom they received greater compensation. However, plans also responded to incentives for greater risk selection along the unmeasured dimensions. In other words, plans increased the degree of risk selection conditional upon the risk scores. Their analysis suggests that these responses ultimately increased the cost to the

---

[11] An adjustment also exists for individual reinsurance subsidies received by the plan.

[12] See Robst et al. (2007) for a detailed description of the development of the system of risk adjustment for Medicare Part D.

government of the Medicare program, by increasing the difference between the amount Medicare paid private plans for enrollees and the amount they would have paid for these beneficiaries in the traditional program.

5. EMPIRICAL EVIDENCE ON INSURANCE MARKET PERFORMANCE

5.1. Risk Variation and the Demand for Insurance

How should the demand for insurance vary with the person's risk or perception of risk? This simple question actually has a complex answer. One's intuition is that insurance is more valuable to a person with larger expected benefits from that insurance, and so higher risks should be both more likely to demand a given policy (compared to none) and more likely to demand more generous coverage than lower risks. But in competitive insurance markets new high-risk buyers will face higher premiums (both in total and for increments in coverage) than low-risk buyers. Which should win out?

The most transparent answer, given by Ehrlich and Becker (1972), is that, absent income effects on the demand for insurance, there should be a tie, so that the demand for insurance is independent of risk levels in fully informed competitive markets. They conclude that demand should depend only on the loading factor, and not on the probability or amount of loss.

As with all comparative statics results in consumer choice, these statements about demand can be changed if there are large income effects. Compared to being a low risk, someone who is a high risk will pay a high premium (or without insurance face higher expected expense) which reduces real income. That reduction in real income may then affect the demand for insurance if risk aversion (absolute or relative) varies with income or wealth. That is, whether higher risk affects the demand for insurance depends on how risk aversion varies with (expected) real income. The demand for insurance could then either rise or fall as risk and premiums change: if high insurance premiums take a larger bite out of my income because I am a high risk, I might increase demand because I am poorer and more vulnerable to losses or reduce my demand because insurance loading and services are luxuries I can no longer afford.

What about the common concern that risk rating will make health insurance "unaffordable" for low-to-moderate income high risks? This can happen if income positively affects the demand for medical care but insurance pricing does not take income into account. If I am a low-income low-risk person but am faced with premiums that vary only with risk and not income, I will be paying a premium that largely depends on the choices of higher-income people—a premium I may regard as excessive relative to the (smaller) expected out-of-pocket payment I would face without insurance. If income effects on the demand for care are large, insurance markets will need to be segmented by income to function properly. Bundorf et al. (2010) find empirical evidence consistent with these types of income effects in the employment-based large group market in the US. Rather than observing low rates of coverage among low-income high risks, however, they observe relatively low rates of coverage among low-income low risks, which they attribute to the effect of pooled premiums on the affordability of coverage among low risks. In other words, among low risks, pooled premiums represent a larger barrier to coverage among those with low rather than those with high incomes.

The effect of risk on demand for coverage may also be affected by the extent to which preferences for coverage, due to factors such as risk aversion, are correlated with risk. For example, if high risks are also more risk averse, then they will have stronger demand for coverage, even when the load does not vary by risk type.

5.2. Empirical Evidence on the Functioning of Insurance Markets

Little evidence exists on the extent to which adverse selection affects the operation of unregulated, voluntary individual health insurance markets. Because health insurance markets are highly regulated in nearly all countries and the purchase of coverage is compulsory in most, few opportunities exist to observe consumer and insurer behavior in a truly competitive market. Even when public programs do not explicitly replace private markets for the majority of the population, institutions have evolved which differentiate the market from the textbook single-period risk-rating model. While the purchase of coverage is voluntary in the US, employer-sponsored health insurance is highly subsidized through the exclusion of premiums from taxable compensation and the bulk of the population obtains group insurance through employers. Because employers control most aspects of benefit design, including insurer entry and enrollee premium contributions, the performance of the employer-sponsored market likely differs from that of a competitive individual market. In addition, both federal and state regulation influences the employer-sponsored market in a variety of ways. Although insurance markets in the US are generally regulated at the state level, employers who self-insure are exempt from state regulation and regulated instead by a series of federal regulations such as (but not limited to) non-discrimination requirements, restrictions on the types of factors that may be considered in setting employee premium contributions, and limitations on the exclusion of pre-existing conditions. State regulation, which applies primarily to the individual and small group markets in the US, affects many aspects of insurer behavior including mandated benefit requirements and restrictions on insurer rating practices. States have adopted very different regulatory models.

The US individual health insurance market, particularly in states with relatively weak regulatory environments, is likely the context which most closely resembles an unregulated market. Yet few studies in this context exist. The individual market is relatively small and self-selected in the US—most people with private health insurance obtain it through an employer, and even more surely could if they were willing to take a job at a firm that offered coverage (such as Starbucks)—and obtaining data on both consumer and insurer behavior in this context is challenging. In addition, the existence of the tax-favored employer-sponsored market likely influences the functioning of the individual market, making it virtually impossible to disentangle the two. As a result, most studies of adverse selection in insurance markets are based on either highly regulated markets for individual primary or supplemental coverage or on employment-based group markets (often with tax subsidies but with relatively low explicit regulation).

While many other countries rely on private health insurance to varying degrees, the markets vary substantially across as well as within countries. In the Netherlands, for example, the vast majority of the population purchases primary coverage from private insurers who compete in a highly regulated, "managed competition" setting. In Germany, in contrast, the bulk of the population purchases primary coverage through a regulated social insurance system, but civil servants and high-income individuals are allowed to opt out and purchase coverage in a private insurance market.

The degree of heterogeneity in the institutional environments in which studies of risk selection take place suggests caution in generalizing the results from a particular study to an alternative setting. In effect, any empirical setting to be examined involves an imperfectly understood mix of employer, insurer, and regulatory features that affect risk variation, and so cannot be extended to some other setting involving equally mixed policies.

5.3. Empirical Methods Used to Examine Risk Selection

The key empirical challenge in identifying risk selection in markets for health insurance, no matter what the institutional arrangement, is separating the effect of risk on the purchase of coverage from the effect of insurance on the utilization of medical care. Economic theory predicts both that high risks will purchase greater quantities of insurance than low risks at a given premium (adverse selection) and that, holding *ex-ante* risk constant, insurance coverage will increase the probability and/or size of a loss (moral hazard) (Pauly, 1968; Rothschild and Stiglitz, 1976). Because both theories predict that *ex-post* expenditures are positively correlated with the amount of insurance, it is difficult to disentangle empirically adverse selection from moral hazard when comparing medical care expenditures among people with differing levels of insurance coverage (Chiappori, 2000).

Researchers have used a variety of approaches to address this issue. "Switcher studies" compare, among people enrolled in a particular type of coverage in a given year, the utilization of people who changed their coverage with those who did not in the subsequent year. The advantage of this type of study is that, by limiting the study sample to people enrolled in the same type of coverage in the initial year, comparisons of expenditures are not biased by differences in the effects of plan characteristics on the utilization of health care. The primary weakness is that utilization one period prior to enrollment may not necessarily be representative of longer-term differences between the two groups. If pre-enrollment differences in utilization represent transitory shocks, rather than permanent differences in health status and medical care utilization, the average difference between enrollees with different types of coverage will be smaller than the marginal difference (Hellinger, 1987; Brown et al., 1993). If, as seems to be the case, prior period spending is one thing that motivates changing insurance, the identification problem is even worse.

Other studies compare indicators of health status, rather than measures of expenditures, between two groups. By examining all enrollees, not just those who switch plans, these studies provide estimates of the difference in health status of the average, rather than the marginal enrollee. However, in order to avoid bias created by the effect of plan characteristics on utilization, rather than examine medical care expenditures or utilization, researchers usually examine measures of health that are less likely to be influenced by plan characteristics, such as indicators of health conditions and self-reported health status. Most studies examine multiple measures and find evidence of favorable selection along some, but not others, and few translate the findings into differences in expenditures, making it difficult to determine whether the observed differences in health represent substantive differences in health expenditures. The potential endogeneity of measures of health represents an additional concern. To the extent that insurance coverage increases the rate of diagnosis of conditions (in the case of indicators of chronic conditions) or the effectiveness of treatment (in the case of self-reported health status), these studies will overestimate the extent of risk-based selection.

As will be shown, studies using these methods have been concerned primarily with documenting simply whether coverage varies with risk—whether higher-risk people are more likely to have health insurance or to have more generous coverage than lower-risk people. Fewer studies provide evidence on whether risk-based selection is indeed due to asymmetric information between insurers and consumers. More precisely, to attribute risk selection to asymmetric information, it is necessary to demonstrate that those who have insurance and have more generous insurance are higher risk conditional on the information available to and used by insurers. As mentioned earlier, potential alternative explanations for a positive relationship between risk and coverage include moral hazard, income effects, and a correlation between risk and preferences for insurance. Finkelstein and McGarry (2006) provide an example of the role of preferences in the market for long-term care insurance. In this case, however, the absence of a difference in claims rates between those with and without coverage is due to a negative correlation between risk and preferences for coverage. Thus, documenting a positive correlation between risk and coverage is neither necessary nor sufficient to demonstrate the existence of risk-based selection due to asymmetric information.

This observation that, in many markets, insurers are either prevented by regulation or voluntarily forego using information that is correlated with claims motivates the "unused observables" test for adverse selection proposed by Finkelstein et al. (2006). A correlation between these unpriced observable risk factors and the purchase of health insurance, conditioning on the factors used in pricing, demonstrates the existence of adverse selection. In the case of health insurance markets, regulation often prevents insurers from using easily available information, such as age, sex or the presence of health conditions, in pricing coverage. Thus, this approach implicitly underlies analyses of the effects of these types of regulations on rates of coverage which tend to find that rating restrictions increase rates of coverage among high risks and reduce rates of coverage among low risks (Buchmueller and DiNardo, 2002; Monheit and Steinberg Schone, 2004; Simon, 2005; Davidoff et al., 2005; Bundorf and Simon, 2006; Pauly and Herring, 2007; Lo Sasso and Lurie, 2009).

Perhaps due to the availability of richer data sets and the development of more sophisticated empirical methods, a growing literature is examining risk selection due to asymmetric information in health insurance markets using structural models (Cardon and Hendel, 2001; Bundorf et al., 2008; Carlin and Town, 2010; Bajari et al., 2010). A study by Cardon and Hendel (2001), based on nationally representative survey data, was the first in this line of research. Cardon and Hendel use variation across workers in the set of plans offered by their employer to identify the effect of plan type on health care utilization (moral hazard) among similar consumers (based on observable characteristics).[13] They then test whether *ex-post* differences in expenditures are related to insurance choice after accounting for observable characteristics. This approach not only distinguishes between moral hazard and adverse selection in accounting for utilization differences among people enrolled in different types of coverage, but also allows for private information about risk type to influence choice. The authors find little evidence of selection on unobservables, suggesting that adverse selection may not be an important factor in unregulated group health insurance markets because the individual characteristics which affect choice could easily be incorporated into price. Its findings are not necessarily consistent with the absence of adverse selection in the market for employer-sponsored coverage. This is because selection on observables may represent adverse selection if the observable characteristics are not used in pricing. In other words, if neither employee premium contributions nor wage

---

[13] The assumption that choice sets are exogenous with respect to worker demand for health insurance is controversial. Empirical evidence suggests that the choice sets offered by employers are related to employee preferences for health insurance (Moran et al., 2001; Bundorf, 2002).

offsets vary with observable characteristics of consumers that influence plan choice, then selection on these characteristics represents selection on unpriced risk factors. This distinction demonstrates the importance of carefully considering the institutional features of a particular market when interpreting evidence on the extent of risk-based selection from a particular setting. Einav et al. (2007) propose an alternative method for identifying adverse selection in health insurance markets. Their method requires a situation in which the premium for insurance varies exogenously and the analyst has information on consumer demand as well as insurer costs. They demonstrate how, under these conditions, the expected benefits cost curve of the insurer will respond endogenously to price in the presence of risk selection. When adverse selection is present, insurer cost increases with price, and when advantageous selection is present, insurer cost declines with price. The intuition is that at high premiums only high risks will purchase, and will then incur high benefits costs, whereas at lower premiums lower risks will buy. Of course, the firm will only be able to operate at those points on this "cost" curve at which demand is adequate to cover these costs. Pauly (1974) and Pauly and Zeng (2004) provide simple examples of these kinds of models.

A key advantage of these more structural approaches to analyzing risk selection in health insurance markets is that, by estimating models of both demand and costs, the analyst can evaluate the welfare impact of adverse selection (Einav et al., 2010b). It is necessary, however, to identify the relevant benchmark when interpreting these estimates. For example, Carlin and Town (2010), analyzing the employer-sponsored market, compare the observed and potential alternative uniform contribution policies relative to the most efficient uniform contribution. In other words, this study takes as its benchmark an environment with limited individual variation in premiums and identifies the welfare loss of alternative policies relative to this second-best, effectively measuring the degree of welfare loss associated with the policies the employer did adopt relative to what the employer could have adopted within the existing institutional constraints. Bundorf et al. (2008), in contrast, calculate the welfare costs of different pricing policies relative to an alternative benchmark—an individual's single-period risk-rated premium. While use of this benchmark allows them to consider how existing institutional arrangements influence the efficiency of health insurance markets, the benchmark does not represent first-best. In this case, however, risk-rated premiums expose consumers to dynamic reclassification risk, and for the purpose of policy analysis, one would also want to consider this source of inefficiency. Finally, estimates from Einav et al. (2010a), using data from the employer-sponsored market, compare a hypothetical competitive uniform contribution relative to the most efficient (second-best) uniform contribution, providing little insight into the extent of welfare loss in the current employer-sponsored market. This work is related to the problem of optimal premium differentials in group insurance discussed in section 3.2.2.

More generally, the absence of a benchmark unregulated insurance model is an important limitation of these types of calculations. Interestingly, "out-of-equilibrium" pricing enables researchers to make welfare calculations by allowing them to observe how different types of consumers behave when facing different prices, which are unrelated to demand. However, the fact that "out-of-equilibrium" is widespread in health insurance markets indicates that it is virtually impossible to know what the relevant competitive market outcome would look like.

5.4. Empirical Evidence on Risk Selection

In this section, we organize evidence on risk selection by whether the coverage is primary or supplementary and whether the study examines the consumer's decision to purchase any health insurance or what type of coverage.

5.4.1. Primary Coverage
5.4.1.1. Risk Selection into Coverage
Only a few studies have examined the role of risk in whether people purchase health insurance in the individual market in the US. While Pauly and Herring (1999) did not find a statistically significant relationship between risk (measured by expected medical expenses) and insurance coverage in the individual market, in more recent work, they find that high-risk people, based on the presence of chronic conditions, are *less* likely than lower risks to purchase coverage, particularly in states without regulations restricting the rating practices of insurers (Pauly and Herring, 2007), which could be driven by income constraints.

Studies comparing measures of health status of uninsured and insured people in the employer-sponsored market often find that the insured are more likely to report having a chronic condition but also are less likely to report poor health (Monheit and Vistnes, 1994; Bernard and Selden, 2002). Studies examining people offered health insurance from an employer have found that those who decline coverage and are uninsured are healthier than those who enroll on some physical health measures but less healthy on others (Blumberg et al., 2001). Similarly, those who decline coverage are more likely to report poor health, yet less likely to have a high-cost chronic condition than those who enroll (Bernard and Selden, 2002).

Pauly and Herring (1999) did not find a statistically significant relationship between risk (measured by expected medical expenses) and insurance coverage in the large group market, although they did find that high-risk, lower-income people working for small firms were less likely to obtain insurance than otherwise similar low-risk people. Bundorf et al. (2010), in contrast, find a positive correlation between health risk, as measured by expected expenditures based on a more detailed list of self-reported health conditions, and coverage in the employer-sponsored market. The existence of a positive relationship between risk and coverage suggests that the

premiums consumers face for coverage in this setting, in the form of employee contributions and potential wage offsets, incorporate less information about individual risk
than consumers use when deciding whether to obtain coverage. In the large group
market, the positive relationship between health risk and coverage is stronger for people with low than for people with high incomes. The finding of a moderate degree of
adverse selection into employer-sponsored coverage is consistent with evidence from
Bhattacharya and Vogt (2006) that greater job-specific capital among workers is associated with higher rates of employment-based coverage and that this effect is strongest
among low-risk workers. The results from Bundorf et al. (2010) are consistent with
this type of separation, particularly among low- and medium-income workers.
Switching costs may be adequately high in large firms, particularly for high-income
workers, to promote pooling among this group.

5.4.1.2. Risk Selection among Health Plans

A relatively large literature examines risk selection among health plans. Van Vliet
(2006) analyzed data from the Dutch sickness fund system in the first eight years after
the introduction of free plan choice (1994–2002). Of a total of 10 million sickness
fund members, 130,000 switched plans. Those who switched plans incurred expenditures that were some 40 percent lower than the average insured so that a uniform capitation payment from the central fund to the insurer in the year 2002 would overpay
for switchers (of the years 2000 and 2001) by 50.2 percent. However, switchers were
on average younger and thus, when adjusted for age and sex composition, this over-
payment drops to 9.3 percent. Adding region and social entitlement brings this number down to 5.7 percent and finally, adding the medical parameters, to an insignificant
1.4 percent. The author concludes that although switchers are on average better risks,
the Dutch RAS is able to eliminate the difference, in particular since the addition of
medical information in the risk adjustment formula.

In the US, literature examining risk selection among plans has focused primarily
on the decision to enrol in an HMO or other type of managed care plan rather than
other less restrictive forms of coverage.

In the case of the US Medicare program, beneficiaries are able to replace their traditional publicly managed benefit with a private alternative, and a large literature
examines the relationship between beneficiary risk and enrollment in private plan
alternatives, with most studies indicating that private plans experience favorable selection (Hellinger, 1995; Hellinger and Wong, 2000; and Mello et al., 2003 provide
reviews).

Studies have also examined risk selection among different types of plans in the US
employer-sponsored group market. While early studies generally found evidence of
favorable selection into HMOs relative to indemnity plans (Hellinger, 1995), studies
from the 1990s and later of the extent to which managed care plans (generally

HMOs) experience favorable selection relative to less managed plans (generally PPOs or indemnity plans) produce mixed evidence (Hellinger and Wong, 2000). In general, switcher studies provide the strongest evidence of favorable selection into HMOs relative to less tightly managed plans. Nicholson et al. (2004) find evidence of favorable selection into HMOs based on both demographics and other measures of health status such as the existence of chronic conditions. One switcher study provides evidence of favorable selection based on demographic characteristics into HMOs relative to an indemnity plan (but not relative to a PPO) (Altman et al., 1998). Another finds evidence of unfavorable selection for HMOs in switching behavior for maternity admission but favorable selection for non-maternity admissions (Robinson et al., 1993).

Studies examining differences in the average characteristics of enrollees in different types of plans in the US employer-sponsored market generally do not find evidence of large differences in risk. Some studies find little to no evidence of differential selection based on either demographics or health status (Fama et al., 1995; Goldman, 1995; Schaefer and Reschovsky, 2002; Polsky and Nicholson, 2004). Others examine only age and find no evidence of favorable selection (Florence and Thorpe, 2003). Other studies of settings in which multiple managed care plans are offered show that some experience favorable selection and others do not (Robinson and Gardner, 1995; Shewry et al., 1996). A series of studies conducted in a large employer group find evidence of favorable selection into an HMO relative to an indemnity plan based on average demographic and health characteristics of enrollees but suggest that the characteristics of PPO enrollees are more similar to those of HMO enrollees (Cutler and Zeckhauser, 1998; Altman et al., 2003). In a setting in which employers offer both tightly managed HMO products and more loosely managed PPOs, Bundorf et al. (2008) find that, while no single plan consistently experiences unfavorable selection, different plans experience unfavorable selection along differing components of risk. Similarly, while Carlin and Town (2010) find that an HMO experiences favorable selection along measures of both demographic characteristics and health status relative to a high-deductible plan, a different managed care plan experiences favorable selection based on age but unfavorable selection based on health status. Bajari et al. (2010) find evidence of adverse selection into a firm's PPO plans relative to its HMO.

Bundorf et al. (2008) suggest that the absence of systematic risk selection by plan type in more recent years may be due to the evolution of the types of insurance products in the market. In particular, over the last 20 years, the market for health insurance has witnessed a dramatic shift from traditional insurance products which differed primarily based on their cost sharing to managed care products which adopt a combination of supply- and demand-side utilization controls. Because people are likely to vary in their preferences for different types of utilization controls, this shift from vertical to horizontal product differentiation may have increased the relative importance of sorting based on preferences relative to sorting based on risk. Similarly, others have proposed that individual characteristics such as income (Schaefer and Reschovsky, 2002) or existing relationships with providers are more important determinants of plan choice (Goldman, 1995). Finally, employers may either intentionally or unintentionally set premium contributions in ways that reduce the extent of risk selection by generally subsidizing more expensive plans (Pauly and Herring, 2001).

Most studies in the emerging literature quantifying the welfare impact of adverse selection are based on the employer-sponsored market. Carlin and Town (2010) analyze the welfare implications of alternative employee contribution policies relative to an employer's observed policy, restricting their analysis to those that vary across plans but not across workers. They estimate that observed contributions lower welfare by about $13 per employee per year relative to the optimal uniform contribution. Although employee contributions under the optimal uniform contribution policy differ dramatically from observed contributions for many of the plans, the resulting welfare loss is relatively small because employees' demand is extremely price inelastic. Thus, a change in plan premiums due to a change in the risk composition of enrollees has little effect on choice behavior. Consistent with these findings, Handel (2010) finds that, while switching costs prevent consumers from adapting their decisions appropriately when the market environment changes, switching costs also reduce the degree of welfare loss due to adverse selection. Bundorf et al. (2008) also find relatively little welfare loss associated with a firm's actual choice of a uniform contribution relative to the most efficient uniform contribution. However, they estimate that individualized pricing—varying contributions based on individual risk—generates a larger increase in welfare.

5.4.2. Private Insurance Supplementing Public Coverage

Many studies of the interaction between private insurance and publicly funded programs examine the experience of the US Medicare program for the aged and disabled. US Medicare beneficiaries may choose to supplement their public coverage with a private plan purchased in a highly regulated market. For example, beginning in 1992, federal regulation restricted the sale of insurance supplementing Medicare to a set of ten predefined plans and required guaranteed issue and prohibited the use of health information in rate setting for 65-year-olds newly entering the program. These regulations have been adjusted over time to accommodate changes in the market such as the diffusion of PPO products and the implementation of the Medicare prescription drug benefit. In addition, particular states have alternative forms of benefits standardization and rating restrictions which supersede the federal requirements.

Studies examining the correlation between beneficiary characteristics and the likelihood of purchasing supplemental insurance produce mixed evidence on the direction and importance of the effect of health. Some studies find that better health is positively associated with the purchase of supplemental health insurance (Del Bene and Vaughan, 1992; Short and Vistnes, 1992; Vistnes and Banthin, 1997—1998), others find no relationship (Browne and Doerpinghaus, 1994–1995), and others find evidence of unfavorable selection into these plans (Wolfe and Goddeeris, 1991). Studies that examine the effects of chronic conditions often find that some conditions, but not others, affect rates of coverage (Ettner, 1997; Vistnes and Banthin, 1997–1998). One study finds that the effect of health status on the likelihood of purchasing Medigap coverage depends on beneficiary knowledge about Medicare benefits (Davidson et al., 1992).

More recent work finds that, while those with higher expected medical expenditures due to the existence of health conditions are more likely to purchase supplemental coverage, this effect is offset by the effects of other characteristics, such as income and cognitive ability, that are both positively correlated with the purchase of supplemental coverage and negatively correlated with medical care spending (Fang et al., 2008). The net effect is advantageous selection into supplemental plans. Not only does this potentially provide insight into the conflicting findings of earlier work, but it also has interesting implications for the form of the welfare loss due to risk selection in this market. If premiums do not vary with individual risk, advantageous selection will tend to lead to overinsurance among high risks in this market. Empirical evidence on adverse selection in markets for private supplemental insurance is less ambiguous in the case of prescription drug insurance. National legislation implemented in 1992 restricted the sale of private insurance supplementing US Medicare to a set of ten predefined plans, with prescription drug benefits available in only three of those plans. Anecdotal evidence pointed to severe problems of adverse selection for the prescription drug coverage. Medigap policies that provided drug coverage typically imposed an upper limit on benefits—usually $1,000 to $1,200 per year, but the difference in premiums between Medigap plans with drug coverage and those without found that the premium differential was almost as large as the coverage limit, surely evidence of severe adverse selection. Relatively few beneficiaries enrolled in these plans (US GAO, 2002) and the incremental premium for these benefits relative to the average actuarial value of the benefits was relatively high (Robst, 2006).

In 2006, highly subsidized prescription drug coverage was added to the US Medicare benefit. The new benefit is provided exclusively by private insurers who compete in a highly regulated setting. Beneficiary premiums are community rated and payments to plans are risk adjusted. While insurers are required to offer coverage at least as generous as a specified minimum, they are allowed to deviate from the standard benefit in two ways. First, they are allowed to offer modified plans that are actuarially equivalent to the standard benefit. Second, they may offer coverage that is more generous than the standard benefit. The costs of enhanced benefits, however, are not subsidized by the government and are not subject to risk equalization. Because the program is relatively new, few studies have examined the extent of risk selection in this market.

A smaller literature exists on risk selection in countries other than the US, focusing primarily on supplemental coverage. Doiron et al. (2008) find for Australia that persons with chronic health conditions are more likely to purchase supplemental private health insurance, which provides access to private hospitals, which would support the adverse selection hypothesis. They propose that the well-documented positive relationship between self-reported health status and coverage is driven by a positive correlation between self-reported health status and other characteristics, such as income and risk aversion, associated with greater demand for health insurance. Shmueli (2001) finds for supplemental coverage in Israel that sicker individuals are more likely to apply for private health insurance, but are also more likely to be rejected.

6. INTERACTIONS BETWEEN RISK VARIATION AND OTHER TOPICS IN HEALTH ECONOMICS

6.1. Risk Variation and Insurance Pricing to Consumers: Bonus-Malus Systems, Discounts for Good Health Practices

Well-insured people will have higher levels of health spending, other things being equal, than less well-insured or uninsured people either under moral hazard or adverse selection. Indeed, one of the main empirical challenges in measuring one influence is to separate out the other. But is there additional interaction between risk variation and moral hazard? There might be correlation. Adverse selection occurs in the standard Rothschild–Stiglitz model by offering insurance with higher levels (in health insurance terminology) of cost sharing, but that cost sharing in turn affects expected expense if moral hazard is present. If two services had the same distribution of risk in the no-insurance world but different degrees of moral hazard, the one with the higher moral hazard would optimally have a higher level of coinsurance—but then the equilibrium in an adverse selection situation would be different. Whether these considerations are important for health insurance in general is not known, but it is possible that the market for insurance for outpatient mental health care—which is known to display high-demand elasticity—is more troubled by adverse selection (at least under premium regulation) for this reason.

A more serious possible interaction arises when insurance premium changes are tied to the experience of the insured, as under bonus-malus schemes. Then, as noted by Chiappori et al. (2006), there can be interaction between risk levels and moral hazard. The potential change in next year's premium if I use more care acts to control moral hazard. But, depending on how experience rating works, if I make no claims because I did not get sick that period (and not because I was a low risk), the resulting low premium may encourage moral hazard (by encouraging more generous coverage in the next period). The key issue here is whether the "bonus" is calibrated properly to risk, or just to spending levels.

A third interaction between risk variation and other aspects of the health care system arises when providers are paid on some basis other than fee for service. Higher than average risk then means lower profits to a provider paid capitation or bundled payment, and lower utility to a provider paid a salary. Providers may react by trying to attract lower risks, necessitating risk adjustment if it is feasible and raising the possibility of either cream skimming or underservice of higher risks if it is not.

In effect, paying providers on some bundled or predetermined basis without adequate risk adjustment adds distorted incentives for those providers to any incentives for insurers to "cream skim." Indeed, even if premiums for competitive insurers were fully risk adjusted, high risks could still suffer provider supply restrictions if they were paid on such a basis *and* their payment was not fully risk adjusted. The possibility of inefficient underservice for high risks and overservice for low risks is a defect of bundled payments (whatever their desirable incentives for cost minimization). Presumably risk adjustment for insurers reduces their incentive to use bundled provider payment (as one of a number of ways of attracting low risks to the insurer) and increases their incentive to use risk adjustment for provider payments if they do use bundled payment (Ma and McGuire, 1997).

7. CONCLUSION

7.1. Risk Variation in a Model of Public Choice: Will the Healthy People Outvote the Sick?

Above, three different types of financing health insurance systems were distinguished:
1. Risk-rated premiums;
2. Community rating with fixed per-capita premiums;
3. Income-related premiums, e.g. a payroll tax.

It was further argued that in a competitive health insurance system, options (2) and (3) require risk adjustment schemes to prevent excessive risk selection. However, it is not clear a priori whether such a system can be politically sustained in a democracy provided that citizen-voters know their risk type and their income-generating capacity. Kifmann (2005) analyzes this question in a model with two-stage voting: in stage 1, the constitutional stage, a public health insurance system of type (2) or (3) is elected if there is unanimous agreement in its favor, and in stage 2, the size of the benefit package is determined by majority rule. The model is based on a number of restrictive assumptions. In particular, premium risk cannot be insured in the private market and at the constitutional stage voters know their income but not their risk type. There are only two income levels and two risk types and thus four different types of voters.

At the constitutional stage, the poor always prefer the payroll-tax financed system (3) because it redistributes in their favor and eliminates premium risk. For the rich, the second (positive) effect has to be balanced against the first (negative) effect. They may also accept system (3) if their share in total population is larger than the share of high-risk types in the population, if they are sufficiently risk averse, if risk types are sufficiently different and therefore future premiums sufficiently uncertain, and if income inequality as measured by the income ratio is high enough to induce poor and healthy individuals to be in favor of public health insurance but low enough to avoid excessive transfers to the poor.

7.2. Whither Risk Policy?

As we have noted, almost all countries have constructed elaborate mechanisms to control how insurance premiums vary with risks. Those mechanisms in turn affect what insurance plans people choose, and by extension what risk protection they have and what medical expenses they experience. We now know much more about how people respond to such mechanisms, but there is as yet no generally accepted or generally satisfactory method for dealing with the conflicting social goals associated with risk variation.

REFERENCES

Altman, D., Cutler, D., & Zeckhauser, R. (2003). Enrollee mix, treatment intensity, and cost in competing indemnity and HMO plans. *Journal of Health Economics, 22,* 23–45.

Altman, D., Cutler, D. M., & Zeckhauser, R. J. (1998). Adverse selection and adverse retention. *American Economic Review, 88,* 122–126.

Armstrong, J., Paolucci, F., McLeod, H., & Van de Ven, W. P. (2010). Risk equalization in voluntary health insurance markets: A three country comparison. *Health Policy, 98,* 39–49.

Arrow, K. J. (1963). Uncertainty and the welfare economics of medical care. *American Economic Review, 53,* 941–973.

Bajari, P., Hong, H., Khwaja, A., & Marsh, C. (2010). *Moral hazard, adverse selection, and health expenditures: A semiparametric analysis.* Working Paper.

Bauhoff, S. (2010). *Do health plans risk-select? An audit study on Germany's social health insurance.* Working Paper. Harvard University, Cambridge, MA.

Baumann, F., Meier, V., & Werding, M. (2008). Transferable aging provisions in individual health insurance contracts. *German Economic Review, 9,* 287–311.

Beck, K. & Zweifel, P. (1998). Cream-skimming in deregulated social health insurance: Evidence from Switzerland. In P. Zweifel (Ed.), *Health, the medical profession and regulation* (pp. 211–227). Dordrecht, The Netherlands: Kluwer.

Beck, K., Spycher, S., Holly, A., & Gardiol, L. (2003). Risk adjustment in Switzerland. *Health Policy, 65,* 63–74.

Bernard, D. & Selden, T. M. (2002). Employer offers, private coverage, and the tax subsidy for health insurance: 1987 and 1996. *International Journal of Health Care Finance and Economics, 2,* 297–318.

Bhattacharya, J. & Bundorf, M. K. (2009). The incidence of the healthcare costs of obesity. *Journal of Health Economics, 28,* 649–658.

Bhattacharya, J. & Vogt, W. B. (2006). *Employment and adverse selection in health insurance.* NBER Working Paper 12430. National Bureau of Economic Research, Cambridge, MA.

Biglaiser, G. & Ma, C.-T. A. (2003). Price and quality competition under adverse selection: Market organization and efficiency. *RAND Journal of Economics, 34,* 266–286.

Blumberg, L. J., Nichols, L. M., & Banthin, J. S. (2001). Worker decisions to purchase health insurance. *International Journal of Health Care Finance and Economics, 1,* 305–325.

Breyer, F., Heineck, M., & Lorenz, N. (2003). Determinants of health care utilization by German sickness fund members—with application to risk adjustment. *Health Economics, 12*(5), 367–376.

Brown, J., Duggan, M., Kuziemko, I., & Woolston, W. (2011). *How does risk selection respond to risk adjustment? Evidence from the Medicare Advantage Program.* NBER Working Paper No. 16977. National Bureau of Economic Research, Cambridge, MA.

Brown, R. S., Clement, D. G., Hill, J. W., Retchin, S. M., & Bergeron, J. W. (1993). Do health maintenance organizations work for Medicare? *Health Care Financing Review, 15,* 7–23.

Browne, M. J. & Doerpinghaus, H. I. (1994–1995). Asymmetric information and the demand for Medigap insurance. *Inquiry, 31,* 445–450.

Buchmueller, T. & DiNardo, J. (2002). Did community rating induce an adverse selection death spiral? Evidence from New York, Pennsylvania, and Connecticut. *American Economic Review, 92,* 280–294.

Buchner, F. & Wasem, J. (2003). Needs for further improvement: Risk adjustment in the German health insurance system. *Health Policy, 65,* 21–35.

Bundorf, M. K. (2002). Employee demand for health insurance and employer health plan choices. *Journal of Health Economics, 21,* 65–88.

Bundorf, M. K. (2010). The effects of offering health plan choice within employment-based purchasing groups. *Journal of Risk and Insurance, 77,* 105–129.

Bundorf, M. K. & Simon, K. (2006). The impact of rate regulation on access to supplemental health insurance. *American Economic Review Papers and Proceedings, 96,* 67–71.

Bundorf, M. K., Herring, B. J., & Pauly, M. V. (2010). Health risk, income, and employment-based health insurance. *Forum for Health Economics & Policy, 13,* Article 13.

Bundorf, M. K., Levin, J. D., & Mahoney, N. (2008). *Pricing and welfare in health plan choice.* NBER Working Paper No. 14153. National Bureau of Economic Research, Cambridge, MA.

Cao, Z. & McGuire, T. G. (2003). Service-level selection by HMOs in Medicare. *Journal of Health Economics, 22,* 915–931.

Cardon, J. H. & Hendel, I. (2001). Asymmetric information in health insurance: Evidence from the national Medicare expenditure survey. *RAND Journal of Economics, 32,* 408–427.

Carlin, C. & Town, R. (2010). *Adverse selection, welfare and optimal pricing of employer-sponsored health plans.* Working Paper, University of Minnesota, Minneapolis.

Chernew, M. E. & Frick, K. D. (1999). The impact of managed care on the existence of equilibrium in health insurance markets. *Journal of Health Economics, 18,* 573–592.

Chiappori, P. A. (2000). Econometric models of insurance under asymmetric information. In G. Dionne (Ed.), *Handbook of insurance* (pp. 363–392). Norwell, MA: Kluwer Academic Publishers.

Chiappori, P.-A. & Salanié, B. (2000). Testing for asymmetric information in insurance markets. *Journal of Political Economy, 108,* 56–78.

Chiappori, P.-A., Jullien, B., Salanié, B., & Salanié, F. (2006). Asymmetric information in insurance: General testable implications. *RAND Journal of Economics, 37,* 783–798.

Cochrane, J. (1995). Time-consistent health insurance. *Journal of Political Economy, 103,* 445–473.

Cogan, J. F., Hubbard, R. G., & Kessler, D. P. (2010). The effect of Medicare coverage for the disabled on the market for private insurance. *Journal of Health Economics, 29,* 418–425.

Cohen, S. B., Ezzati-Rice, T., & Yu, W. (2006). The utility of extended longitudinal profiles in predicting future health care expenditures. *Medical Care, 44,* 145–I53.

Crocker, K. J. & Snow, A. (1985). The efficiency of competitive equilibria in insurance markets with asymmetric information. *Journal of Public Economics, 26,* 207–219.

Cutler, D. M. & Reber, S. J. (1998). Paying for health insurance: The tradeoff between competition and adverse selection. *Quarterly Journal of Economics, 113,* 433–466.

Cutler, D. M. & Zeckhauser, R. J. (1998). Adverse selection in health insurance. *Forum for Health Economics & Policy, 1.* (Frontiers in health policy research), Article 2.

Cutler, D. M. & Zeckhauser, R. J. (2000). The anatomy of health insurance. In A. J. Culyer & J. P. Newhouse (Eds.), *Handbook of health economics* (Vol. 1, pp. 563–643). Amsterdam: Elsevier.

Cutler, D. M., Finkelstein, A., & McGarry, K. (2008). Preference heterogeneity and insurance markets: Explaining a puzzle of insurance. *American Economic Review, Papers & Proceedings, 98,* 157–162.

Davidoff, A., Blumberg, L., & Nichols, L. (2005). State health insurance market reforms and access to insurance for high-risk employees. *Journal of Health Economics, 24,* 725–750.

Davidson, B. N., Sofaer, S., & Gertler, P. (1992). Consumer information and biased selection in the demand for coverage supplementing Medicare. *Social Science and Medicine, 34,* 1023–1034.

Del Bene, L. & Vaughan, D. R. (1992). Income, assets, and health insurance: Economic resources for meeting acute health needs of the aged. *Social Security Bulletin, 55,* 3–25.

Dionne, G. Doherty, N. (1992). Adverse selection in insurance markets: A selective survey. In G. Dionne (Ed.), *Contributions to insurance economics* (pp. 97–140). Boston: Kluwer.

Doiron, D., Jones, G., & Savage, E. (2008). Healthy, wealthy and insured? The role of self-assessed health in the demand for private health insurance. *Health Economics, 17,* 317–334.

Douven, R. (2007). Morbidity-based risk adjustment in the Netherlands. In E. Wille, V. Ulrich, & U. Schneider (Eds.), *Wettbewerb und Risikostrukturausgleich im internationalen Vergleich* (pp. 161–202). Baden-Baden: Nomos.

Duggan, M., Healy, P., & Morton, F. S. (2008). Providing prescription drug coverage to the elderly: America's experiment with Medicare Part D. *Journal of Economic Perspectives, 22,* 69–92.

Eckstein, Z., Eichenbaum, M., & Peled, D. (1985). Uncertain lifetimes and the welfare enhancing properties of annuity markets and social security. *Journal of Public Economics, 26,* 303–320.

Eggleston, K. (2000). Risk selection and optimal health insurance-provider payment systems. *Journal of Risk and Insurance, 67,* 173–196.

Ehrlich, I. & Becker, G. S. (1972). Market insurance, self-insurance, and self-protection. *Journal of Political Economy, 80,* 623–648.

Eichner, M. J., McClellan, M. B., & Wise, D. (1997). Health expenditure, persistence, and the feasibility of medical savings accounts. *Tax Policy and the Economy, 11,* 91–128.

Einav, L., Finkelstein, A., & Cullen, M. R. (2010a). Estimating welfare in insurance markets using variation in prices. *Quarterly Journal of Economics, 125,* 877–921.

Einav, L., Finkelstein, A., & Levin, J. (2010b). Beyond testing: Empirical models of insurance markets. *Annual Review of Economics, 2,* 311–336.

Einav, L., Finkelstein, A., & Schrimpf, P. (2007). *The welfare cost of asymmetric information: Evidence from the U.K. annuity market.* NBER Working Paper 13228. National Bureau of Economic Research, Cambridge, MA.

Ellis, R. P. & McGuire, T. G. (2007). Predictability and predictiveness in health care spending. *Journal of Health Economics, 26,* 25–48.

Enthoven, A. (1988). *Theory and practice of managed competition in health care finance.* Amsterdam: North-Holland.

Enthoven, A. & Kronick, R. (1989). A consumer-choice health plan for the 1990s. *New England Journal of Medicine, 320,* 29–37.

Ettner, S. L. (1997). Adverse selection and the purchase of Medigap insurance by the elderly. *Journal of Health Economics, 116,* 543–562.

Fama, T., Fox, P. D., & White, L. A. (1995). HMOs care for the chronically ill? *Health Affairs, 14,* 234–243.

Fang, H., Keane, M. P., & Silverman, D. (2008). Sources of advantageous selection: Evidence from the Medigap insurance market. *Journal of Political Economy, 116,* 303–350.

Finkelstein, A. & McGarry, K. (2006). Multiple dimensions of private information: Evidence from the long-term care insurance market. *American Economic Review, 96,* 938–958.

Finkelstein, A., Poterba, J., & Rothschild, C. (2006). *Redistribution by insurance market regulation: Analyzing a ban on gender-based retirement annuities.* NBER Working Paper 12205. National Bureau of Economic Research, Cambridge, MA.

Florence, C. S. & Thorpe, K. E. (2003). How does the employer contribution for the federal employees' health benefits program influence plan selection? *Health Affairs, 22*, 211–218.

Frank, R. G., Glazer, J., & McGuire, T. G. (2000). Measuring adverse selection in managed health care. *Journal of Health Economics, 19*, 829–854.

Garber, A. M., MaCurdy, T. E., & McClellan, M. B. (1998). Persistence of medical expenditures among elderly beneficiaries. *Frontiers in Health Policy Research, 1*, 153–180.

Glazer, J. & McGuire, T. G. (2000). Optimal risk adjustment in markets with adverse selection: An application to managed care. *American Economic Review, 90*, 1055–1071.

Glazer, J. & McGuire, T. G. (2002). Setting health plan premiums to ensure efficient quality in health care: Minimum variance, optimal risk adjustment. *Journal of Public Economics, 84*, 153–175.

Glazer, J. & McGuire, T. G. (2009). *Gold and silver health plans: Accommodating demand heterogeneity in managed competition.* Working Paper, Boston, MA.

Glied, S. A. (2005). *The employer-based health insurance system: Mistake or cornerstone? Policy challenges in modern health care.* Rutgers University Press. Available at: < http://www.rwjf.org/pr/product.jsp?id=14805/ > .

Goldman, D. (1995). Managed care as a public cost containment mechanism. *RAND Journal of Economics, 26*, 277–295.

Goldstein, G. S. & Pauly, M. V. (1976). Group health insurance as a local public good. In R. N. Rosett (Ed.), *The role of health insurance in the health services sector* (pp. 73–114). New York: National Bureau of Economic Research.

Gruber, J. (1994). The incidence of mandated maternity benefits. *American Economic Review, 84*, 622–641.

Gruber, J. (2000). Health insurance and the labor market. In A. J. Culyer & J. P. Newhouse (Eds.), *Handbook of health economics* (Vol. 1, pp. 645–706). Amsterdam: Elsevier.

Handel, B. R. (2010). Essays in consumer behavior and market outcomes in health insurance. Dissertation, Department of Economics, University of California at Berkeley.

Harsanyi, J. (1955). Cardinal welfare, individualistic ethics, and interpersonal comparisons of utility. *Journal of Political Economy, 63*, 309–321.

Helderman, J., Schut, F., Van der Grinten, T., & Van de Ven, W. (2005). Market-oriented health care reforms and policy learning in the Netherlands. *Journal of Health Politics, Policy and Law, 30*, 189–209.

Hellinger, F. J. (1987). Selection bias in health maintenance organizations: Analysis of recent evidence. *Health Care Financial Review, 9*, 55–63.

Hellinger, F. J. (1995). Selection bias in HMOs and PPOs: A review of the evidence. *Inquiry, 32*, 135–142.

Hellinger, F. J. & Wong, H. S. (2000). Selection bias in HMOs: A review of the evidence. *Medical Care Research and Review, 57*, 405–439.

Hellwig, M. (1987). Some recent developments in the theory of competition in markets with adverse selection. *European Economic Review, 31*, 319–325.

Herring, B. & Pauly, M. V. (2006). Incentive-compatible guaranteed renewable health insurance. *Journal of Health Economics, 25*, 395–417.

Herring, B. J. & Pauly, M. V. (2007). The demand for health insurance in the group setting: Can you always get what you want? *Journal of Risk and Insurance, 74*, 115–140.

Hirshleifer, J. (1971). The private and social value of information and the reward to inventive activity. *American Economic Review, 61*, 561–574.

Hsu, J., Fung, V., Huang, J., Price, M., Brand, R., Hui, R., et al. (2010). Fixing flaws in Medicare drug coverage that prompt insurers to avoid low-income patients. *Health Affairs, 29*, 2335–2343.

Hsu, J., Huang, J., Fung, V., Price, M., Brand, R., Hui, R., et al. (2009). Distributing $800 billion: An early assessment of Medicare Part D risk adjustment. *Health Affairs, 28*, 215–225.

Jack, W. (2006). Optimal risk adjustment with adverse selection and spatial competition. *Journal of Health Economics, 25*, 908–926.

Keenan, P. S., Buntin, M. J., McGuire, T. G., & Newhouse, J. P. (2001). The prevalence of formal risk adjustment in health plan purchasing. *Inquiry, 38*, 245–259.

Kifmann, M. (2005). Health insurance in a democracy: Why is it public and why are premiums income related? *Public Choice, 124*, 283–308.

Kifmann, M. (2006). Risk selection and complementary health insurance: The Swiss approach. *International Journal of Health Care Finance and Economics, 6*, 151−170.

Kifmann, M. & Roeder, K. (2010). *Can risk-based premiums be more equitable than social insurance?* Working Paper, University of Augsburg.

Kronick, R. & Dreyfus, T. (1996). Diagnostic risk adjustment for Medicaid: The disability payment system. *Health Care Financing Review, 17*, 7−33.

Lamers, L. M. (2001). Health-based risk adjustment: Is inpatient and outpatient diagnostic information sufficient? *Inquiry, 38*, 423−431.

Lamers, L. M., Van Vliet, R., & Van de Ven, W. (2003). Risk adjusted premium subsidies and risk sharing: Key elements of the competitive sickness fund market in the Netherlands. *Health Policy, 65*, 49−62.

Lo Sasso, A. T. & Lurie, I. Z. (2009). Community rating and the market for private non-group health insurance. *Journal of Public Economics, 93*, 264−279.

Luft, H. S. & Dudley, R. A. (2003). Measuring quality in modern managed care. *Health Services Research, 38*, 1373−1379.

Ma, C.-T. A. & McGuire, T. M. (1997). Optimal health insurance and provider payment. *American Economic Review, 87*, 685−704.

McGuire, T. G., Newhouse, J. P., & Sinaiko, A. D. (2011). An economic history of Medicare Part C. *Milbank Quarterly, 89*, 289−332.

Mello, M. M., Stearns, S. C., Norton, E. C., & Ricketts, T. C., III (2003). Understanding biased selection in Medicare HMOs. *Health Services Research, 38*, 961−992.

Miller, N. H. (2005). Pricing health benefits: A cost minimization approach. *Journal of Health Economics, 24*, 931−949.

Miyazaki, H. (1977). The rat race and internal labor markets. *Bell Journal of Economics, 8*, 394−418.

Monheit, A. C. (2003). Persistence in health expenditures in the short run: Prevalence and consequences. *Medical Care, 41*, III53−III64.

Monheit, A. C. & Steinberg Schone, B. (2004). How has small group reform affected employee health insurance coverage? *Journal of Public Economics, 88*, 237−254.

Monheit, A. C. & Vistnes, J. P. (1994). Implicit pooling of workers from large and small firms. *Health Affairs, 13*, 301−314.

Moran, J. R., Chernew, M. E., & Hirth, R. A. (2001). Preference diversity and the breadth of employee health insurance options. *Health Services Research, 36*, 911−934.

Newhouse, J. P. (1996). Reimbursing health plans and health providers: Efficiency in production versus selection. *Journal of Economic Literature, 34*, 1236−1263.

Newhouse, J. P., Manning, W. G., Keeler, E. B., & Sloss, E. M. (1989). Adjusting capitation rates using objective health measures and prior utilization. *Health Care Financing Review, 10*, 41−54.

Nicholson, S., Bundorf, M. K., Stein, R. M., & Polsky, D. (2004). The magnitude and nature of risk selection in employer-sponsored health plans. *Health Services Research, 39*, 1817−1838.

Pauly, M. & Herring, B. (1999). *Pooling health insurance risks.* Washington, DC: AEI Press.

Pauly, M. V. (1968). The economics of moral hazard. *American Economic Review, 58*, 531−537.

Pauly, M. V. (1974). Overinsurance and public provision of insurance: The roles of moral hazard and adverse selection. *Quarterly Journal of Economics, 88*, 44−62.

Pauly, M. V. & Herring, B. (2001). Expanding insurance coverage through tax credits: Tradeoffs and options. *Health Affairs, 20*, 1−18.

Pauly, M. V. & Herring, B. (2007). Risk pooling and regulation: Policy and reality in today's individual health insurance market. *Health Affairs, 26(3)*, 770−779.

Pauly, M. V. & Lieberthal, R. (2008). How risky is individual health insurance? *Health Affairs, 27*, w242−w249 (published online May 6, 2008; 10.1377/hlthaff.27.3.w242).

Pauly, M. V. & Zeng, Y. (2004). Adverse selection and the challenges to stand-alone prescription drug insurance. In D. M. Cutler & A. M. Garber (Eds.), *Frontiers in health policy research* (Vol. 7, pp. 55−74). Cambridge, MA: National Bureau of Economic Research and the Massachusetts Institute of Technology.

Pauly, M. V., Danzon, P., Feldstein, P., & Hoff, J. (1992). *Responsible national health insurance.* Washington, DC: AEI Press.

Pauly, M. V., Kunreuther, H., & Hirth, R. (1995). Guaranteed renewability in insurance. *Journal of Risk and Uncertainty, 10*, 143−156.

Polsky, D. & Nicholson, S. (2004). Why are managed care plans less expensive? Risk selection, utilization, or reimbursement? *Journal of Risk and Insurance, 71*, 21−40.

Pope, G. C., Kautter, J., Ellis, R. P., Ash, A. S., Ayanian, J. Z., Iezzoni, L. I., et al. (2004). Risk adjustment of Medicare capitation payments using the CMS-HCC model. *Health Care Financing Review, 25*, 119−141.

Prinsze, F. J. & Van Vliet, R. C. (2007). Health-based risk adjustment: Improving the pharmacy-based cost group model by adding diagnostic cost groups. *Inquiry, 44*, 469−480.

Rawls, J. (1971). *A theory of justice*. Cambridge, MA: Harvard University Press.

Robinson, J. C. & Gardner, L. B. (1995). Adverse selection among multiple competing health maintenance organizations. *Medical Care, 33*, 1161−1175.

Robinson, J. C., Gardner, L. B., & Luft, H. S. (1993). Health plan switching in anticipation of increased medical care utilization. *Medical Care, 31*, 43−51.

Robst, J. (2006). Estimation of a hedonic pricing model for Medigap insurance. *Health Services Research, 41*, 2097−2113.

Robst, J., Levy, J. M., & Ingber, M. J. (2007). Diagnosis-based risk adjustment for Medicare prescription drug plan payments. *Health Care Financing Review, 28*, 15−30.

Rothschild, M. & Stiglitz, J. (1976). Equilibrium in competitive insurance markets: An essay on the economics of imperfect information. *Quarterly Journal of Economics, 90*, 629−650.

Schaefer, E. & Reschovsky, J. D. (2002). Are HMO enrollees healthier than others? Results from the community tracking study. *Health Affairs, 21*, 249−258.

Selden, T. M. (1999). Premium subsidies for health insurance: Excessive coverage vs. adverse selection. *Journal of Health Economics, 18*, 709−725.

Shen, Y. & Ellis, R. P. (2002). Cost-minimizing risk adjustment. *Journal of Health Economics, 21*, 515−530.

Shewry, S., Hunt, S., Ramey, J., & Bertko, J. (1996). Risk adjustment: The missing piece of market competition. *Health Affairs, 15*, 171−181.

Shmueli, A. (2001). The effect of health on acute care supplemental insurance ownership: An empirical analysis. *Health Economics, 10*, 341−350.

Short, P. F. & Vistnes, J. P. (1992). Multiple sources of Medicare supplementary insurance. *Inquiry, 29*, 33−43.

Simon, K. I. (2005). Adverse selection in health insurance markets? Evidence from state small-group health insurance reforms. *Journal of Public Economics, 89*, 1865−1877.

Song, Y., Skinner, J., Bynum, J., Sutherland, J., Wennberg, J. E., & Fisher, E. S. (2010). Regional variations in diagnostic practices. *New England Journal of Medicine, 363*, 45−53.

Spence, A. M. (1978). Product differentiation and performance in insurance markets. *Journal of Public Economics, 10*, 427−447.

Strohmenger, R. & Wambach, A. (2000). Adverse selection and categorical discrimination in the health insurance markets: The effects of genetic tests. *Journal of Health Economics, 19*, 197−218.

Subramanian, K., Lemaire, J., Hershey, J. C., Pauly, M. V., Armstrong, K., & Asch, D. A. (1999). Estimating adverse selection costs from genetic testing for breast and ovarian cancer: The case of life insurance. *Journal of Risk and Insurance, 66*, 531−550.

Tabarrok, A. (1994). Genetic testing: An economic and contractarian analysis. *Journal of Health Economics, 13*, 75−91.

US General Accounting Office (GAO) (2002). *MEDIGAP: Current policies contain coverage gaps, undermine cost control incentives*. GAO-02-533T, Washington, DC.

Van de Ven, W. (2006). Response: The case for risk-based subsidies in public health insurance. *Health Economics, Policy and Law, 1*, 195−199.

Van de Ven, W. & Ellis, R. (2000). Risk adjustment in competitive health plan markets. In A. J. Culyer & J. P. Newhouse (Eds.), *Handbook of health economics* (Vol. 1, pp. 755−845). Amsterdam: Elsevier.

Van de Ven, W. & Schut, F. (2008). Universal mandatory health insurance in the Netherlands: A model for the United States? *Health Affairs, 27*, 771−781.

Van de Ven, W. & Van Vliet, R. (1992). How can we prevent cream skimming in a competitive health insurance market? In P. Zweifel & H. Frech, III (Eds.), *Health economics worldwide* (pp. 23–46). Dordrecht: Kluwer.

Van de Ven, W., Beck, K., Buchner, F., Chernichovsky, D., Gardiol, L., Holly, A., et al. (2003). Risk adjustment and risk selection on the sickness fund insurance market in five European countries. *Health Policy, 65,* 75–98.

Van Vliet, R. (1992). Predictability of individual health care expenditures. *Journal of Risk and Insurance, 59,* 443–460.

Van Vliet, R. (2006). Free choice of health plan combined with risk-adjusted capitation payments: Are switchers and new enrolees good risks? *Health Economics, 15,* 763–774.

Vera-Hernández, M. (2003). Structural estimation of a principal–agent model: Moral hazard in medical insurance. *RAND Journal of Economics, 34,* 670–693.

Vistnes, J. P. & Banthin, J. S. (1997–1998). The demand for Medicare supplemental insurance benefits: The role of attitudes toward medical care and risk. *Inquiry, 34,* 311–324.

Wagstaff, A. & Van Doorslaer, E. (2000). Equity in health care finance and delivery. In A. J. Culyer & J. P. Newhouse (Eds.), *Handbook of health economics* (Vol. 1, pp. 1803–1862). Amsterdam: Elsevier.

Welch, W. P. (1985). Medicare capitation payments to HMOs in light of regression toward the mean in health care costs. *Advances in Health Economics and Health Services Research, 6,* 75–100.

Wilson, C. (1977). A model of insurance markets with incomplete information. *Journal of Economic Theory, 16,* 167–207.

Wolfe, J. R. & Goddeeris, J. H. (1991). Adverse selection, moral hazard, and wealth effects in the Medigap insurance market. *Journal of Health Economics, 10,* 433–459.

Zuvekas, S. H. & Cohen, J. W. (2007). Prescription drugs and the changing concentration of health care expenditures. *Health Affairs, 26,* 249–257.

Zweifel, P. & Breuer, M. (2006). The case for risk-based premiums in public health insurance. *Health Economics, Policy and Law, 1,* 171–188.

CHAPTER TWELVE

Markets for Pharmaceutical Products[1]

Fiona Scott Morton[*] and Margaret Kyle[**]

[*]Yale School of Management and NBER, USA
[**]Toulouse School of Economics and CEPR, France

Contents

[1] The authors thank Tom McGuire for editorial advice and improvements and participants at the Handbook conference for helpful suggestions.

Handbook of Health Economics, Volume 2
ISSN: 1574-0064, DOI: 10.1016/B978-0-444-53592-4.00012-8

Abstract

This chapter describes the market for pharmaceuticals, which exceeded $500 million in sales in 2010. The industry is also characterized by extensive regulation of almost every activity, from product development through manufacturing and marketing, which we summarize. We next describe the industry's market structure. Large, fully integrated, multinational firms that develop and market new drugs have historically dominated the industry, but the emergence of smaller firms focused on the application of biotechnology to drug development as well as firms that specialize in low-cost production of off-patent "generic" drugs has had an important impact on the market structure of the industry. The last two decades have seen a shift towards vertical specialization as well as many horizontal mergers. We discuss trends in the productivity of pharmaceutical research and incentives for innovation. We then summarize the pricing and marketing of drugs in the US and several other countries.

Keywords: pharmaceuticals; market structure; regulation; innovation; productivity; competition

JEL Codes: L65; I11; L22; I18; D12; D43

1. INTRODUCTION

The pharmaceutical industry generated more than $500 billion in sales in 2010, and sustained its position as one of the most research-intensive industries. Studies of the contribution of new pharmaceutical treatments to social welfare generally find that society has derived large benefits from these innovative efforts. However, the industry now faces concerns about access to new treatments and a potential decline in innovation.

The industry is also characterized by extensive regulation of almost every activity, from product development through manufacturing and marketing. Some of these regulations have unintended consequences as a result of strategic responses by firms. Increased globalization of research, development, and manufacturing poses new challenges to regulators, as the cost of monitoring compliance in facilities around the world is considerable, and regulations may have implications beyond the borders of the country for which they were adopted. In addition, changes in technology may necessitate adjustments to regulatory structures created to address market conditions several decades ago.

There is considerable heterogeneity across firms, both in size as well as business strategy. Large, fully integrated multinational firms that develop and market new drugs have historically dominated the industry, but the emergence of smaller firms focused on the application of biotechnology to drug development as well as firms that specialize in low-cost production of off-patent "generic" drugs has had an important impact on the market structure of the industry. The last two decades have seen a shift towards vertical specialization as well as many horizontal mergers.

This chapter describes the market for pharmaceuticals. We begin with a general summary of important regulatory features, and then present some statistics on pharmaceutical expenditures in major markets. We next describe the industry's market structure, including market definitions, the costs of drug development and marketing, the evolving vertical chain, and incentives for innovation. We then summarize the pricing and marketing of drugs in the US and several other countries. We conclude with a discussion of current regulatory challenges in the industry.

2. OVERVIEW OF REGULATION

2.1. Safety and Efficacy

Pharmaceuticals may be considered "experience" or "credence" goods, for which the consumer has less information about quality than the producer. A patient is usually unable to determine whether a pill is safe and effective just from examining it, and sometimes even after consuming it. As is well known in economics, this information asymmetry can lead to the "lemons problem" described by Akerlof (1970), wherein the quality of the product falls to inefficiently low levels. One solution to this market failure is the provision of information about a product's quality from a trusted third party, or, in the case of pharmaceuticals, a government agency's regulatory approval process.

In all developed countries, firms must receive regulatory approval to market a pharmaceutical product. The approval process generally involves demonstrating the safety and efficacy of a product. In the United States, this function is the responsibility of the Food and Drug Administration (FDA). The equivalent of the FDA in the European Union is the European Medicines Agency (EMA), though individual member states have their own authorities as well; in Japan, it is the Ministry of Health and Welfare (MHW). Over the last several decades, these agencies and their counterparts in other countries have harmonized their rules and regulations to some extent. For example, the EMA and FDA do work together on some issues such as Good Manufacturing Practices, post-marketing surveillance, and scientific advice, among others.[2] However, they do not always agree. The tolerance for Type I (approving a harmful drug) vs. Type II error (rejecting a beneficial drug) varies across agencies, and arguably over time within the same agency. Importantly, trade is generally prohibited between two countries even when both have approved the same pharmaceutical. Arbitrage of price differences across countries, or "parallel trade," is prohibited by

---

[2] http://www.ema.europa.eu/ema/index.jsp?curl=pages/news_and_events/news/2010/09/news_detail_001112. jsp&murl=menus/news_and_events/news_and_events.jsp&mid=WC0b01ac058004d5c1

intellectual property law or regulatory safety concerns, with the exception of trade between EU member states. Each country may therefore be considered a separate market.

For the sake of brevity, we focus on the FDA approval process here rather than attempt a comprehensive description of all countries; as noted above, efforts at international harmonization mean that the process is not very different elsewhere. Firms that wish to market a chemical or biological product that has not previously been sold in the US must file a New Drug Application (NDA) or a Biologics License Application (BLA) with the FDA. The dossier includes information about the applicant, manufacturing, preclinical and clinical trial data, and labeling information. Clinical trials to demonstrate safety and efficacy are the most expensive component of the application, and we describe this process in greater detail in section 4. The review process can be quite long, and in response to industry concerns about regulatory delays, the US adopted the Prescription Drug User Fee Act (PDUFA) in 1992, which mandated performance goals for the FDA while allowing the FDA to charge fees to applicants. Berndt et al. (2005) find that PDUFA contributed significantly to the decline in review times (from an average of 24.2 to 14.2 months) observed since the early 1990s. However, Olson (2008) finds that faster reviews are accompanied by an increase in reported adverse events following the marketing of a new drug.

The process is different for so-called "generic" drugs that are no longer under patent protection.[3] Prior to the passage of the Hatch-Waxman Act in 1984, all firms wishing to market a prescription pharmaceutical product were required to submit NDAs, even if the chemical had been previously approved for a different firm. Thus, even for off-patent drugs, winning regulatory approval required the full dossier of clinical trials. To encourage competition in off-patent (generic) drugs, the Hatch-Waxman Act established the Abbreviated New Drug Application (ANDA), which requires proof that the applicant's product is bioequivalent to the original product approved as an NDA but does not require clinical trials to demonstrate safety and efficacy. In order to provide an incentive for generics to challenge weak brand patents, the Hatch-Waxman Act offers 180 days of exclusivity to the first generic to file an ANDA claiming that one of the brand's patents is either not infringed by the generic or is invalid, which is referred to as a "Paragraph IV" challenge. Thus, the Hatch-Waxman Act sets up a race among generics to be the first firm to file and win the six-month "duopoly prize."

Pharmaceutical companies that wish to enter the European Union market can choose to apply for marketing authorization for a new drug in two ways. The first, which is required for applications with a biologic component or that uses

---

[3] The term generic refers to the practice of using the International Nonproprietary Name (INN) for the chemical, in contrast to a "branded" drug that is marketed with a shorter, trademarked name. For example, atorvastatin is the INN corresponding to Pfizer's Lipitor.

recombinant DNA technology but optional for others, is a single application to the EMA for approval in all EU member states. The EMA has 210 days to evaluate the evidence and makes a decision to recommend approval or not to the European Commission.[4] The second approach to market entry, known as the mutual recognition procedure, involves an application to the local authority in a member state. If a drug is authorized by that state's marketing authority, other member states should also grant authorization at the firm's request, unless they can justify an objection on scientific grounds. Indeed, one of the EMA's functions is to help arbitrate among states whose regulatory standards do not match up.[5]

Post-market surveillance of safety in both the United States and Europe is a key component of drug regulation. Given that clinical trials are only able to assess a drug's impact on a small subset of the population at large, many of a drug's side effects are not known until it is released into the market. The FDA and EMA both have a set of detailed post-marketing reporting requirements pharmaceutical companies must comply with. There is, however, an important distinction drawn by both agencies between, to use the FDA's terms, post-market requirements (PMRs) and post-market commitments (PMCs). The EMA uses the term "Specific Obligations" to describe PMRs and "Follow-up Measures" for PMCs. Post-marketing *requirements*, as their name suggests, are directives issued by the FDA that must be followed within the designated timeframe in order for a drug-sponsor to continue to be able to market and sell its drug. In contrast, marketing authorization does not require the completion of PMCs; unsurprisingly, some of the most recent criticism of FDA post-market surveillance is that so many PMCs go unfulfilled. A study by the Tufts Center for Drug Study and Development found that the average drug in the US has almost nine post-market study commitments attached to it, while the average European drug has almost 11, and the average Japanese drug almost two.[6]

Post-market surveillance is arguably most concerned with the safety of the approved drug, given that it is being used by a population much larger than that used in pre-approval clinical trials. The FDA requires all drug sponsors to support reporting systems where physicians or other providers can report adverse drug reactions and other reportable events. A survey of drug manufacturers found that mean spending on post-marketing safety per company was $56 million (0.3% of sales) in 2003. The innovator must submit a report to the FDA within 15 days of a report of an adverse reaction to a drug. The FDA also maintains Medwatch, a website that allows consumers to submit complaints about the safety of drugs currently on the market. FDA officials investigate the claims and take action against drug sponsors accordingly. Criticism of post-marketing surveillance in the US has focused on the FDA's lack of

---

[4] Details about the agency can be found at www.ema.europa.eu.

[5] http://www.euro.who.int/document/e83015_5.pdf

[6] http://www.medicalnewstoday.com/articles/114749.php

sufficient authority to ensure compliance with post-marketing requirements as well as the general underreporting of adverse effects. There are few economic studies in this interesting area. One paper by David et al. (2010) models and finds evidence for increased adverse drug reactions accompanying increased (less appropriate) promotion of a drug.

2.2. Pricing and Reimbursement

Outside the United States, there is a second regulatory hurdle to clear in developed markets and some developing countries. In order for a new drug to be eligible for reimbursement by national insurance programs, the firm must negotiate a price with the national government agency. This often requires presenting economic evidence on cost effectiveness or negotiating over price. We discuss several examples in more detail in section 5.

It is important to note that pricing and reimbursement policies vary much more across countries than do the standards required for marketing approval. There has been far less effort to harmonize regulatory approaches. In the EU, for instance, the EMA can approve a new drug for all member states, but a firm must still negotiate pricing and reimbursement with each individual country. This has a number of important consequences, to which we return later.

2.3. Restrictions on Marketing, Prescribing, and Dispensing

Demand for pharmaceuticals is complex for many reasons, not least of which is the involvement of multiple decision makers: physicians, pharmacists, insurers, and patients. Pharmaceutical firms, like firms in many other industries, engage in marketing efforts to persuade decision makers. Regulatory agencies recognize that an innovator firm is unlikely to be an unbiased source of information about its products and their merits compared to the competition. The FDA and its counterparts in other countries therefore strictly regulate what a firm can claim about a drug in its marketing efforts to ensure that the marketing is not false or misleading.[7] The NDA for a new drug is approved with a label that contains the claims about efficacy that the FDA has approved, as well as side effects and warnings. A large component of promotional expenditure goes on "detailing," short visits to physician offices by representatives of the firm who discuss a new or existing drug with the doctor. For a widely used drug, there would typically be hundreds of detailing representatives visiting thousands of physicians across the country. Each detailing representative is typically paid on a steep incentive scheme, whereby financial compensation is linked to increased sales

---

[7] http://www.fda.gov/AboutFDA/CentersOffices/CDER/ucm090142.htm is the link to the Division of Drug Marketing, Advertising, and Communications (DDMAC) at the FDA.

in a geographic territory or among a set of physicians. In the US, promotional visits to the physician may not focus on the price of the drug because of concerns that this encourages inappropriate prescribing. In other countries, regulations limit the amount of time detailing representatives may spend with physicians. The combination of the incentives, the impossibility of direct monitoring, and the enormous amount of non-FDA approved information available on new drugs means that achieving perfect compliance with the FDA's regulations on detailing is a challenge. Direct-to-consumer advertising (DTCA) of pharmaceuticals is not permitted in developed countries with the exception of New Zealand and the US.

Most countries separate prescribing and dispensing to address potential agency problems. That is, dispensing is the responsibility of a pharmacist, so that the physician's choice between pharmaceutical treatments is not influenced by a profit motive. There are exceptions: US physicians who administer drugs in their offices are reimbursed, and in many Asian markets there is a tradition of physicians who dispense the drugs they prescribe. Separation of these practices does mean that physicians are often unaware of the prices of drugs they prescribe, so while they may have less incentive to prescribe treatments than would be the case if they profited directly from doing so, physicians do not necessarily have incentive to prescribe relatively inexpensive or cost-effective treatments.

Pharmacists must dispense the chemical, dosage form and strength specified in a physician's prescription. For drugs with generic competition, the pharmacist has some discretion. In order to encourage the use of generic drugs, many US states and some (not all) developed countries require the pharmacist to fill a prescription with a generic version if one is available; other jurisdictions may encourage but not require generic substitution. A pharmacist's incentive to supply the generic version with the lowest cost depends on additional country-specific regulations and practices. In many European countries, pharmacists are subject to profit controls. Some countries (for example, Germany and the Netherlands) use a system of awarding the entire national market for a drug to a single generic supplier that tenders the lowest bid, leaving the individual pharmacist no choice.

3. BASIC FACTS ON PHARMACEUTICAL EXPENDITURES AND PRICES

In the United States in the 1980s, pharmaceutical expenditure as a percentage of total health spending was about 5—6%. However, the proportion increased significantly during the 1990s and early 2000s. From 2004 onwards, pharmaceutical expenditure as a percentage of total health care spending in the United States has been approximately 11 to 12 percent,[8] five to six percentage points below the OECD member-nation average of 17 percent. In some countries such as Korea, Hungary, and Poland, however, pharmaceutical expenditure accounts for a far greater portion of total health spending. The modest share for the US is driven by a large denominator, not a low absolute expenditure on pharmaceuticals. If we examine a related measure, per capita expenditure on pharmaceuticals, the US in 2005 ranked the highest among OECD countries, spending USD PPP 792 per capita. Canada, the next highest ranking country, spent USD 589 per capita. Two years later, in 2007, the Commonwealth Fund reported that US prescription drug spending per capita had increased to USD 878. The high growth rates of biologic prices and usage will likely cause total US expenditure to continue growing. Table 12.1 shows per capita pharmaceutical expenditures for OECD countries from 1990 to 2008.

The US is the largest market for pharmaceuticals, accounting for about half of global sales for most of the previous three decades. Historically, Japan has been the second, followed by Germany, France, and the United Kingdom; China now holds the number two position. Pharmaceutical industry sales growth averaged around 12−13 percent between 1987 and 1999 (Berndt, 2002). Since 2000, IMS Health reports that sales in the US, Japan, and Europe have been rather flat (less than 4 percent per year), though Latin America, China, and other emerging markets show much higher sales growth. There has been some work attempting to determine whether price increases, quantity increases, introduction of new products, or some other force has driven that growth. Berndt (2002) has shown that from 1994 to 2000, "...price growth accounted for only about one-fifth of revenue growth (2.7 percentage points out of 12.9%), with the remaining four-fifths reflecting volume/mix changes in utilization rates for incumbent drugs, as well as expenditures on new pharmaceuticals. Hence, in recent years, price increases have been relatively less important, and instead, quantity growth—greater utilization of incumbent and new products—has been the primary driver of increased spending" (p. 48). Berndt argues that increased quantity growth is a function of "increased drug insurance benefit coverage and enhanced marketing efforts." Expenditures on new products may reflect the changing nature of medicine and science, which now allows many more diseases to be treated with pharmaceutical products. Indeed, the impetus for including prescription drug coverage in the Medicare Program (Part D) was financial risk to the elderly. When Medicare began in 1965, drugs were a small part of health care spending: 10.7 percent in 1960 and 8.2 percent in 1970, according to Berndt (2002). In the years since, expenditures on pharmaceuticals became a

---

[8] http://www.cbo.gov/ftpdocs/106xx/doc10681/DrugR&D.shtml, http://www.commonwealthfund.org/Content/Charts/Chartbook/Multinational-Comparisons-of-Health-Systems-Data–2008/P/Percentage-of-Total-Health-Care-Spending-on-Pharmaceuticals–1996-and-2006.aspx

Table 12.1 Pharmaceutical Expenditures as Percent of Health Expenditures in OECD Countries

	1995	1996	1997	1998	1999	2000	2001	2002	2003	2004	2005	2006	2007	2008
Australia	12.2	12.4	12.7	13.3	13.8	14.8	15.1	14.5	15.0	14.8	14.3	14.3	14.3	
Austria	9.4	9.7	10.9	11.4	12.0	12.3	12.5	12.8	13.3	13.0	13.0	13.1	13.3	13.3
Belgium	16.2	15.5	15.8			15.9	16.2	16.6	16.0	16.4	15.9	16.5	15.0	15.1
Canada	13.9	14.1	14.8	15.3	15.6					17.3	17.2	17.3	17.2	17.2
Czech Republic	25.1	25.0	24.9	22.9	23.0	23.4	24.0	23.9	24.2	24.8	24.8	22.8	21.5	20.4
Denmark	9.1	8.9	9.0	9.0	8.7	8.8	9.2	9.8	9.1	8.7	8.6	8.5	8.6	
Estonia					19.5	22.3	25.2	26.5	24.0	25.4	23.9	23.5	21.4	20.7
Finland	12.7	13.2	13.6	14.0	14.8	14.7	15.0	15.2	15.3	15.5	15.5	14.3	14.1	14.4
France	15.0	14.8	15.0	15.5	16.0	16.5	16.9	16.8	16.7	16.8	16.7	16.5	16.5	16.4
Germany	12.8	13.0	13.1	13.5	13.5	13.6	14.2	14.4	14.4	13.9	15.1	14.8	15.1	15.1
Greece	15.7	16.1	16.2	13.9	14.4	18.9	18.0	18.8	20.4	22.0	21.5	22.7	24.8	
Hungary	25.0	26.0	25.9				28.5	27.6	27.5	28.8	31.1	31.7	31.1	31.6
Iceland	13.4	14.0	15.1	14.1	13.6	14.5	14.1	14.0	15.2	15.4	14.4	14.2	13.5	13.9
Ireland	11.4	12.1	11.9	12.4	13.2	14.1	14.3	14.5	14.9	15.6	16.5	17.4	17.7	17.3
Italy	20.7	21.1	21.2	21.5	22.1	22.0	22.5	22.5	21.8	21.2	20.2	19.8	19.3	18.4
Japan	22.3	21.6	20.6	18.9	18.4	18.7	18.8	18.4	19.2	19.0	19.8	19.6	20.1	
Korea	26.1	25.9	25.8	24.6	24.5	25.9	25.2	25.8	25.8	26.0	25.5	25.4	24.5	23.9
Luxembourg	12.0	11.5	12.6	12.3	11.9	9.1	10.0	9.3	10.1	9.5	9.2	8.8	9.1	9.1
Mexico					18.6	19.4	19.5	21.2	25.2	26.1	25.4	26.3	28.2	28.3
Netherlands	11.0	11.0	11.0	11.2	11.4	11.7	11.7	11.5						
New Zealand	14.8	14.5	14.4					9.4	9.2	10.4	10.4	11.0	10.2	9.6
Norway	9.0	9.1	9.1	8.9	8.9	9.5	9.3	9.4		9.4	9.1	8.7	8.0	7.6
Poland								28.4	30.3	29.6	28.0	27.2	24.5	22.6
Portugal	23.6	23.8	23.8	23.4		22.4	23.0	23.3	21.4	21.8	21.6	21.8		
Slovak Republic					34.0	34.0	34.0	37.3	38.5	31.4	31.9	29.7	27.9	27.6
Slovenia								20.9	20.5	20.7	20.6	20.5	19.8	18.7
Spain	19.2	19.8	20.8	21.0	21.5	21.3	21.1	21.8	23.2	22.7	22.3	21.6	21.0	20.5
Sweden	12.3	13.6	12.4	13.6	13.9	13.8	13.9	14.0	13.8	13.9	13.7	13.7	13.4	13.2
Switzerland	10.1	10.2	10.5	10.4	10.6	10.8	10.7	10.4	10.6	10.5	10.6	10.4	10.3	
Turkey					26.2	26.6								
United Kingdom	15.3	15.6	15.9			14.1	13.9	13.5	13.5	13.2	12.8	12.3	12.2	11.8
United States	8.7	9.0	9.5	10.0	10.8	11.3	11.7	12.0	12.1	12.2	12.0	12.2	12.0	11.9

significant burden on the elderly, as we see in the current 12 percent pharmaceutical expenditure share.

4. MARKET STRUCTURE

4.1. Supply Side

4.1.1. Drug Development and Production

The process of developing a new drug is long and expensive. New drugs do not result from R&D spending in a predictable way. Rather, innovation is stochastic. In addition, the productivity of R&D changes over time due to advances in basic science and research techniques. Thus, the enterprise of inventing innovative biopharmaceuticals is inherently risky. Its cost structure—large fixed and sunk costs of drug discovery and development and relatively low marginal costs of production, the details of which we describe below—is another important feature of the pharmaceutical industry. Imitation costs are also quite low: once a product is known to be safe and effective, it can be backward-engineered with little difficulty. If competition from imitators drives price down to marginal cost, as standard industrial organization models would predict, then firms would be unable to recoup the fixed and sunk costs of development and thus would not engage in risky innovative activities. Of course, many other industries share these features, such as movie production, book publishing, and software. A key difference between the pharmaceutical industry and these others is that the social cost of a bad drug brought to market is considerably higher than the cost of a bad movie, which is a justification for its extensive regulation. The cost structure and ease of imitation *ex post* also explain why patent protection is considered more important in the pharmaceutical industry than in any other (Cohen et al., 2000). We address alternative mechanisms for inducing innovation later in this chapter.

Over recent decades, drug discovery has evolved from random screening of chemicals to "rational drug design," which is based on the understanding of a biological process. Drug candidates, once almost exclusively small molecules, now include large, complex molecules usually referred to as biologics. Once a drug candidate has been identified, preclinical work begins in animal subjects, followed by an Investigational New Drug (IND) filing with regulatory authorities if preclinical results are sufficiently promising (see Figure 12.1 for a diagram). The drug candidate is then tested in three phases of human clinical trials, with costs increasing at each phase. Phase I clinical trials involve a small number of healthy patients to establish safety and toxicity. If successful, Phase II trials are initiated. These involve a larger number of participants for the purpose of establishing efficacy, in addition to safety. Phase III trials are randomized controlled trials, often conducted in multiple centers or locations. The

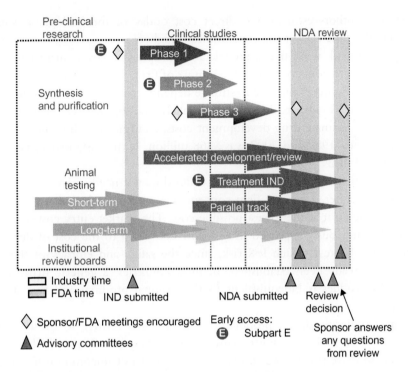

Figure 12.1 Drug development process. *Source: CDER handbook.*

length and cost of these trials varies by disease, since more time is required to assess the effectiveness of a cancer treatment than an antibiotic, for example. For each phase, clinical endpoints that are acceptable to regulatory authorities must be established *ex ante*, and this is not always straightforward. For example, should a cancer treatment be judged based on tumor shrinkage or survival? Failure is common: Pammolli et al. (2011) report that the average probability of reaching the market for a project at the preclinical stage is less than 5 percent for most disease areas. The results of these tests are submitted as part of the NDA to the FDA as proof of safety and efficacy.

Estimating the economic cost of inventing a few successfully marketed drugs is challenging. One must include the cost of examining all the drugs that failed, including the costs of the capital to carry out all the research, and the cost of development and approval—not just the actual expenditures on clinical testing. A 2003 study by DiMasi, Hansen, and Grabowski using a sample of drugs that were first tested on humans between 1983 and 1994 estimated the average cost of drug development to be $802 million per successful molecule. DiMasi and Grabowski (2007) later update their estimate of the cost of invention of a new molecular entity to $1.2 billion using the most recent part of the sample. That paper concludes that the fixed development cost for a biologic product is similar in total to that of a traditional chemical product.

However, the authors estimate the direct cost outlay of the biologic is somewhat lower, while the time cost of the expenditure is higher.

The DiMasi et al. work uses a proprietary database that covers primarily large US firms. In addition to concerns about the sample of firms used and the reliability of the self-reported expenditure data, their estimate depends critically on the assumed cost of capital. Adams and Brantner (2006) use a publicly available dataset on drug development projects to estimate drug development costs, and find that the cost to produce a new drug between 1989 and 2002 was $868 million, with substantial variation across disease areas and firms.

Note that a firm that produces generic drugs does not need to engage in discovery of new drugs. Rather, a generic firm concentrates on accurately imitating an existing drug and producing it at the lowest possible cost. The market entry cost for a generic imitation of a previously approved drug is low compared to the cost of developing a new molecule. There is much less risk, since the safety and efficacy of the original molecule has already been established. In most countries, a generic firm need only show that its product is bioequivalent to the original product, and that it is safely manufactured.

For small-molecule drugs, production costs are low relative to the cost of drug development. For molecules with many generic competitors, in which we expect competition to drive price close to marginal cost, it is not uncommon to see generic prices less than 25 percent that of the branded version. For biologic drugs, manufacturing costs are a larger percentage of total cost, but the same general relation between fixed/sunk and marginal cost applies. While specific manufacturing costs are closely guarded, recent 10-K filings from biologic manufacturers list aggregate "product sales" and "cost of sales" in the range of 15–28 percent. As this number is generated for accounting purposes, it is probably an upper bound on marginal costs. Thus, even for biologics, most of the cost of producing an innovative pharmaceutical product is fixed and sunk.

4.1.2. Organizational Forms

Historically, the pharmaceutical industry has been divided into innovator firms that develop new treatments (also referred to as "brand name" or "ethical" firms) and imitator firms that produce generic copies of off-patent treatments. Prominent generic drug firms include Israel-based Teva, US-based Mylan Labororatories, and Indian-based Dr. Reddy's. A small number of firms engage in both activities. For example, the Sandoz division of Novartis specializes in generic drugs. The generic sector in India has been of particular importance in recent years because of its role in producing HIV treatments for developing countries (Waning et al., 2010).

The organizational form of firms conducting biopharmaceutical discovery, development, and manufacture has been slowly changing over the last few decades.

Table 12.2 US Biotech Industry Statistics

Year	2010	2009	2008	2007	2006	2005	2004	2003
Sales (bn US$)	52.6	48.1	$57.00	$52.70	47.7	42.1	33.3	28.4
Revenues	61.6	56.2	70.1	64.9	58.8	51.8	46	39.2
R&D expense	17.6	17.1	30.4	26.1	27.1	20.8	19.8	17.9
Net loss	4.9	3.7	−3.7	−4.2	−5.6	−3.6	−6.4	−5.4
Public firms	315	314	371	395	336	331	330	313
Total firms	1,726	1,703	1,754	1,758	1,452	1,475	1,346	1,444

Figures are billions of USD.
Source: Ernst & Young annual reports on biotech industry.

Table 12.3 EU Biotech Industry Statistics

Year	2010	2009	2008	2007	2006	2005	2004	2003
Revenues	13	11.6	15.3	13.6	13.3	11.8	11.3	11.3
R&D expense	3.4	3.2	6.8	6.6	5.7	5.3	6.2	6.4
Net loss	−0.5	−0.5	−2	−3.1	−2.5	−3.3	−2.1	−1.9
Public firms	172	167	178	185	156	122	98	96
Total firms	1,834	1,842	1,836	1,869	1,621	1,613	1,815	1,861

Figures are billions of euros.
2009−2010 figures are for public companies only.
Source: Ernst & Young annual reports on biotech industry.

Traditionally, "big pharma" firms were highly vertically integrated, with activities spanning basic research, development, clinical trials, the regulatory approval process, manufacturing, promotion, and post-marketing activities. Such firms still exist, but there has been a shift towards vertical specialization in each of these stages of production and increased use of "markets for technology" (Arora, 2001).

Perhaps the most well-known change in the organization of the pharmaceutical industry is the movement of innovative activity outside large vertically integrated pharmaceutical firms whose researchers have stronger incentives or greater expertise in new scientific areas: in more concrete terms, the "biotech industry." (See Tables 12.2 and 12.3 for a profile of the biotech industry in the US and Europe.) If there are diseconomies of scope or poor incentives for discovery of new drugs inside a large firm, then it may be efficient for the large firm to contract with smaller firms who will be more productive on average. Smaller biotech firms often lack the capacity to manage large-scale clinical trials to manufacture and navigate the regulatory approval process. Typically the biotech firm will start with venture capital and then when it has some success will contract with a larger firm. The contract can take many forms: payments in stages as the innovation clears particular scientific hurdles,

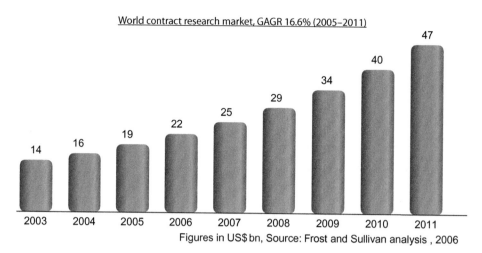

<u>World contract research market, GAGR 16.6% (2005–2011)</u>

Figures in US$ bn, Source: Frost and Sullivan analysis , 2006

Figure 12.2 Growth of contract research.

licensing of the intellectual property on certain terms, purchase of the firm in stages as particular benchmarks are reached, or purchase of the small firm outright.

Clinical trials are another area where a firm may have capacity that is costly to increase or decrease, and where specialized firms known as contract research organizations (CROs) have emerged (see Figure 12.2). While CROs can create high-powered incentives to achieve specific goals, such as a time deadline or an enrollment number, they are not as good at capturing "softer" knowledge and retaining it in the firm. Clinical trials are increasingly conducted in emerging markets like India and Eastern Europe, where the cost of running trials in emerging markets is relatively low (Thiers et al., 2008). Azoulay (2004) shows that there are costs to outsourcing of clinical trials.

Outsourcing of functions further along the vertical chain has also increased (see Figure 12.3). There now exists a number of firms, particularly in emerging markets such as India, that specialize in contract manufacturing, and some "traditional" firms (such as Boerhinger Ingelheim and Abbott) that contract out their excess manufacturing capacity. A firm may also outsource its marketing to the sales force of another. This will occur when the second firm has spare capacity and the first does not have the right type or quantity of sales force of its own. For example, if a firm has invented a product that is outside its traditional therapeutic areas, its own sales people may not be trained in the therapeutic area and may not have connections with the appropriate set of specialist physicians. Rather than spend the fixed costs to develop a sales force for one drug, it may instead contract for an appropriate sales force.

All of these organizational changes make particular sense given the stochastic nature of the innovative process in pharmaceuticals, which implies that a firm will often find its capacity for manufacturing, testing, or promoting to be too high or too

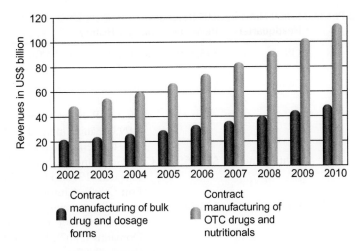

Figure 12.3 Growth in contract manufacturing.

low for its current portfolio of drugs. Sharing that capacity, or renting to other firms in the industry, is an efficient choice, particularly when the lessee is not a direct competitor on the product market. Technology and the frontier of science change rapidly and we should therefore not expect a single organizational form to be optimal across time and projects.

In addition to changes in vertical structure, the pharmaceutical industry has seen considerable (mostly horizontal) merger activity. Table 12.4 shows the top firms ranked by 2009 revenues with examples of their recent mergers and acquisitions. Grabowski and Kyle (2008) report that the top ten firms' share of revenues increased from 28.3 percent in 1989 to 48.3 percent in 2004. Mergers may also be an attempt to bolster weak drug development pipelines (Higgins and Rodriguez, 2006), although the use of licensing could achieve the same purpose. Another motive for merger activity may be achieving sufficient size to realize economies of scale in activities for which outsourcing is not observed (such as managing the regulatory approval process or the development and protection of intellectual property). In the following section, we summarize the evidence on R&D productivity and its relationship with size, organizational type, and other characteristics.

4.1.3. R&D Productivity

In recent years, the productivity crisis in the pharmaceutical industry has been the topic of much discussion; see, for example, Cockburn (2007) and Pammolli et al. (2011). Certainly, the number of new drugs approved has fallen in recent years, as illustrated in Figure 12.4. There are a number of hypotheses for this decline. One

Table 12.4 Top Pharmaceutical Firms by 2009 Revenues

Firm	Headquarters	Revenues	Merger History
Pfizer	US	$45,448	Warner-Lambert (2000), Pharmacia (2002), Wyeth (2009), King (2011)
Sanofi-Aventis	France	$40,871	Sanofi merged with Synthelabo (1999), Rhone-Poulenc merged with Hoescht Marion Roussel to form Aventis (1999), Sanofi merged with Aventis (2004), Genzyme (2011)
Novartis	Switzerland	$38,455	Ciba-Geigy merged with Sandoz to form Novartis (1996), Hexal (2005), Eon (2005), Chiron (2006)
GlaxoSmithKline	UK	$36,746	GlaxoWellcome merged with SmithKline Beecham (2000), Block Drug (2001), Domantis (2007), Reliant (2007), Praesis (2007)
Roche	Switzerland	$36,017	Boehringer Mannheim (1998), BioVeris (2007), NimbleGen (2007), 454 Life Sciences (2007), Genentech (2009)
AstraZeneca	UK	$31,905	Astra merged with Zeneca (1999), MedImmune (2007)
Merck & Co.	US	$26,929	Schering (2009)
Johnson & Johnson	US	$22,520	Centocor (1999), Alza (2001), Tibotec (2002), Crucell (2011)
Eli Lilly & Co.	US	$20,629	ICOS (2007), Imclone (2009)
Bristol-Myers Squibb	US	$18,808	Medarex (2009), ZymoGenetics (2010)
Abbott Laboratories	US	$16,486	Knoll (2001), Solvay (2010)
Amgen	US	$14,642	Kinetex (2000), Immunex (2001), Abgenix (2006), BioVex (2011)
Takeda Chem Ind.	Japan	$14,204	Syrrx (2005), Millennium (2008), IDM (2009), Nycomed (2011)
Boehringer-Ingelheim	Germany	$14,027	microParts (2004)
Teva Pharma	Israel	$13,814	Novopharm (2000), Sicor (2004), IVAX (2006), Barr (2008)
Bayer Schering	Germany	$13,344	Bayer acquired Schering (2006)
Astellas	Japan	$10,509	Yamanouchi Pharmaceutical and Fujisawa Pharmaceutical merged to form Astellas (2005), Agensys (2008)
Daiichi-Sankyo	Japan	$9,757	Sankyo Co. and Daiichi Pharmaceutical Co. merged (2005)
Novo Nordisk	Denmark	$9,566	
Eisai	Japan	$8,441	Morphotek (2007), MGI Pharma (2008)
Otsuka	Japan	$7,717	Taiho Pharmaceutical (2007)

(Continued)

Table 12.4 (Continued)

Firm	Headquarters	Revenues	Merger History
Merck Serono	Switzerland	$7,454	Merck KGaA acquired Serono (2007)
Gilead Sciences	US	$6,469	Nexstar (1999), Triangle (2003), Myogen (2006), CV Therapeutics (2009)
Baxter BioScience	US	$5,573	Immuno International (1997), North American Vaccine (2000), Cook Pharmaceutical Solutions (2001)
Mylan	US	$5,015	Generics division of Merck KGaA (2007)
Biogen Idec	US	$4,247	Biogen merged with Idec (2003), Conforma (2006), Syntonix (2007)
Genzyme	US	$3,562	Acquired by Sanofi-Aventis (2011)
CSL Ltd.	Australia	$3,211	Aventis Behring (2004), Zenyth Therapeutics (2006)
Allergan	US	$1,310	Inamed (2006)

Source: Contract Pharma. Figures are millions of USD.

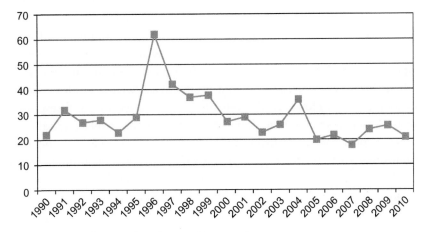

Figure 12.4 New drugs approved in the US, 1990–2010.

possibility is that discovery of new treatments is simply more difficult because the "low hanging fruit" has already been picked. Some blame increased costs of clinical trials and regulatory compliance. The decline in R&D productivity has coincided with the trends discussed in the previous section, suggesting that consolidation or outsourcing may have failed to yield efficiency gains.

Because of advances in science, we would expect productivity of R&D to change over time, thus making it difficult to predict current probabilities using old data. Moreover, success probabilities depend on which innovations are pursued, which are endogenous choices of the firm. However, the long time lag in research and development does not allow analysis of outcomes until long after the initial discovery. A 1993 report by Office of Technology Assessment summarized two earlier studies that placed the probability of ultimate approval at 13 and 23 percent. DiMasi (2001) finds that about 21 percent of the drugs whose INDs were first filed between 1981 and 1992 had been approved for marketing in the United States by 1999. According to DiMasi et al. (2003), the cost of pharmaceutical drug development increased at 7.4 percent per year above inflation between 1984 and 1997. Their evidence suggests that the clinical component (human trials in particular) rather than the preclinical (bench science) is responsible for the marked increase in costs, and that increasing complexity of trials is driving this trend (p. 178). DiMasi et al. argue that trials may have become more expensive because of stronger FDA requirements, an increase in drugs being tested, and need for lengthier trials due to many drugs treating chronic conditions.

More recent work by Pammolli et al. (2011) estimates the probability of success from the preclinical stage (earlier than that in the DiMasi work) to market approval at less than 5 percent for most disease areas, based on data from 1990 to 2004. They find that much of the decline in productivity is the result of investing in more challenging disease areas, where the risk of failure is higher but where unmet need is greatest. This is not necessarily inconsistent with the DiMasi et al. results, but it does have different implications. If firms are rationally directing their research where social value is highest, then that is less worrisome than a productivity decline resulting from excessive regulatory burdens. However, this remains an open question for future research.

There is considerable academic literature on factors that explain variation in productivity across pharmaceutical firms. One factor is size: Henderson and Cockburn (1996) found that large pharmaceutical firms exhibited both economies of scale and scope in pharmaceutical research during the 1980s. This result suggests that the increased outsourcing (or licensing in) of R&D to smaller biotech firms is somewhat puzzling. One possibility is that the optimal organizational form has changed since the period of their study. As discussed earlier, economies of scale could also exist in later stages of drug development. Grabowski and Kyle (2008) provide some evidence consistent with the theory that large firms have an efficiency advantage in the management of large clinical trials. They find that the fraction of drug development projects that advance from Phase III to marketing approval is increasing in the number of projects a firm is managing.

Subsequent work by Cockburn and Henderson (1998) on the organization of research inside large pharmaceutical firms focused on the organizational culture and incentives that attract and stimulate good researchers, such as the ability to co-author externally and publish research findings. Such incentives may be easier to provide inside smaller firms, giving them an efficiency advantage over large firms in early-stage research and creating opportunities for licensing. But Guedj and Scharfstein (2004) suggest that agency problems may contribute to differences in productivity across large and small firms. Because small firms have everything riding on a small number of projects, the decision to stop pursuing development of a drug candidate has far more serious consequences for firm survival than would be the case for a large firm with several hundred projects. For a marginal project, managers in small firms may therefore be more likely to continue development than managers in large firms. Using data on drug candidates for cancer, they show that small firms were more likely to have projects that advanced from Phase I to Phase II than larger firms, but had a higher failure rate from Phase II to Phase III.

Realizing the gains from vertical specialization requires that markets for technology work efficiently. There are a number of potential frictions in such markets, including search costs in finding a firm to transact with, uncertain intellectual property rights, and asymmetric information on the idea or drug candidate at issue. Lerner and Merges (1998), among others, have examined the structure of licensing contracts in biotechnology, but few papers address whether contracting costs and other frictions overwhelm the efficiency gains that are theoretically possible. Using a theoretical model supported by empirical evidence, Allain et al. (2011) focus on how information asymmetries can lead biotechnology firms to delay the stage at which they license their products. Such delays reduce the efficiency gains of vertical specialization.

Finally, another stream of research has focused on the relationship between location and R&D productivity. Research efforts often generate knowledge externalities. The desire to benefit from spillovers from other firms is one explanation for geographic clustering; the New Jersey—Pennsylvania—Maryland corridor and Basel, Switzerland, are examples of historical clusters of pharmaceutical activity. Furman et al. (2005) examine how geographic proximity to academic science and to other pharmaceutical labs affects R&D productivity. They find that productivity within a disease area, as measured by patent applications, is positively associated with proximity to universities, especially universities whose faculty publish many papers related to that disease. However, proximity to other pharmaceutical labs does not enhance productivity. Their results are consistent with relocation of pharmaceutical research to places like Cambridge, Massachusetts, and the San Francisco Bay area that has occurred in the years following the end of their data. Fabrizio and Thomas (2011) find that local demand, not just local technological spillovers, influences R&D performance. Firms located in countries with high demand for particular therapies are more likely to create new treatments for those therapies, and their innovative efforts are less sensitive to global demand than local demand.

4.1.4. Incentives for Innovation

The innovation we observe occurs in response to policy choices—both government spending on basic research and on drug development, and policies that affect the financial rewards to innovation, whether that is a price level in the private sector or a financial prize from a non-profit. The financial inducement to innovate in the pharmaceutical industry is significant. Global annual sales of pharmaceuticals were $837 billion in 2009[9] while sales of biologics were $112 billion.[10] Additionally, there are significant sources of public and non-profit investment in research and development. For example, the National Institutes of Health in the US spend over $30 billion annually on medical research.

Naturally, if societies rely on the for-profit motive to generate innovation, firms will invent therapies that have market demand. In some cases, this may not maximize social welfare. For example, where consumption of a treatment produces externalities, individuals will not account for the potential benefits to others and market demand will be too low. Vaccines are the most obvious case of this issue. Kremer and Snyder (2003) present a model of vaccine R&D, and explain why market forces will cause private firms to invest in drugs rather than vaccines. If individuals have high discount rates and thus place a lower value on the benefits of long-term prevention of a disease, or if insurers are reluctant to pay for disease prevention on policyholders who are not enrolled for a long time, then willingness-to-pay for treatment will be higher than for prevention. In addition, the presence of other market failures—the lack of health insurance markets, or an inability to finance treatments—can lead to situations where market demand is low despite high social need. Such market failures are especially prevalent in developing countries.

To date, the for-profit motive has resulted in therapies affecting large populations in the US, EU, and Japan, and therapies that treat rather than prevent illness. In addition to vaccines, there are two categories of disease that offer low profits to the private sector: orphan diseases, which affect a small population, and neglected diseases, which affect mostly poor people. The same WHO report referenced above finds that less than 5 percent of the R&D in 1992 was spent on diseases suffered by citizens of developing countries. Glennerster, Kremer, and Williams report that 1,233 drugs were licensed worldwide between 1975 and 1997. Of this group, only 13 treat tropical diseases.

As China, India, Brazil, Africa, and the rest of the developing world grow and become both richer and adopt greater protection of intellectual property, the needs of the citizens of these countries will create financial incentives for innovation also. The adoption of patent protection for pharmaceuticals is required for members of the World Trade Organization (WTO) under its TRIPS Agreement. Kyle and McGahan (2011)

---

[9] http://uk.reuters.com/article/idUKTRE63J0Y520100420

[10] Brill 3 (he got these figures from an FTC report: "Emerging Health Care Issues: follow-on biologic drug competition"; the $112 billion figure is described as the "total global value of the biologics industry" and Figure 1.1 shows that top-selling biologic products in 2008 had sales <$100 billion, so the $112 billion figure might not be a bad approximation of 2009 sales).

examine whether the introduction of patent protection in developing countries is associated with an increase in drug development efforts targeting diseases that are most prevalent in poorer countries. They find that R&D responds to patent protection in rich countries, but even with patent protection, the profit potential in poor countries is too low to induce R&D. They argue that IP protection and income are both necessary to generate R&D tailored to local needs, and that alternatives to patents may be more appropriate.

An expansion of intellectual property rights through additional years of patent protection or market exclusivity can effectively increase the market size of a drug. To spur for-profit innovation for diseases suffered by small populations, the US Congress passed the Orphan Drug Act (ODA) in 1983. The Act gives innovators seven years of exclusivity (regardless of patent status) for approved orphan drugs, which are those that treat diseases affecting fewer than 200,000 people. Additional years of market protection can be offered by the regulator in exchange for services that benefit the public, such as clinical trials in children. In the US, an innovator may earn an additional six months of exclusivity if it performs pediatric studies. Lichtenberg and Waldfogel (2003) find an increase in treatments developed for orphan diseases following the ODA, but Yin (2009) shows that some of this increase reflects the efforts by firms to redefine diseases as narrowly as possible, so that their treatments qualify for the ODA's benefits.

An important policy question is how innovative effort responds to market size. Estimation of this responsiveness presents a number of challenges. First, disaggregate R&D expenditures data are difficult to find, so the empirical literature does not usually consider the cost of inputs. Researchers have variously used data on patents, published papers, early stage trials, and drug launches as measures of innovative output. Similarly, measuring potential market size for treatments that do not exist is difficult, so market size is measured as revenues, mortality, or disability-adjusted life years (DALYs).[11] A second challenge is that innovative efforts are likely to respond to global market size. Isolating the impact of a policy change in a single country is therefore quite difficult. Many researchers focus on the large US market for this reason, but generally ignore changes in other markets that might also influence R&D investment choices. Fortunately, researchers are able to use variation over time and across disease areas or therapeutic classes, which facilitates identification.

Dubois et al. (2011) exploit the changing market size of a therapeutic class as the demographics and wealth in different countries change. These changes alter the financial returns to innovation in those therapeutic classes and this should alter the number of New Chemical Entities (NCEs) launched in the therapeutic classes.

---

[11] Examples of such papers include Blume-Kohout and Sood (2008), Maloney and Civan (2006, 2009), and Lichtenberg (2005).

The identification of the response of innovation to market size addresses the endogeneity of market size and innovation. Market size could call forth innovation, which is the relationship of interest, but a great innovation could generate a lot of revenue and therefore create market size, which is the reverse causality. Using instrumental variables, Dubois et al. (2011) find the estimated elasticity of new molecular entities to market size is 0.25; the estimate implies that a 1 percent increase in market size increases the number of new molecules launched by about 0.25 percent. On average, this means a market has to grow by about $1.8 billion to induce entry of a new molecule. Kyle and McGahan (2011) also use variation across diseases and time, but across a larger number of countries. They employ a different dependent variable (new clinical trials) and measure of market size (mortality). They estimate a similar elasticity of innovation to patent-protected market size in relatively rich countries. These recent results are much smaller than the estimate in earlier work by Acemoglu and Linn (2004), who used data only on the US market. However, the order of magnitude of the more recent estimates is consistent with the DiMasi findings on the cost of innovation combined with marginal production and distribution costs on the order of 50 percent.

Alternatives to the traditional approach of using market exclusivity (patents) to provide incentives for innovation are an important area of academic research and policy experiments. As noted above, the patent system has neglected many high-burden diseases that affect poorer countries. Donors can help solve this problem by contractually creating a market for drugs needed in developing countries; these contracts are known as Advanced Market Commitments. Michael Kremer has written extensively about AMCs; examples include Kremer et al. (2006, 2011). A Gates Foundation press release succinctly describes the purpose of an AMC:

> Normally pharmaceutical companies have little interest in investing in research, development and manufacturing of vaccines for the developing world because countries usually cannot afford them. Through an AMC, donors commit money to guarantee the price of vaccines once they have been developed and manufactured, thus creating the potential for a viable future market. In turn, companies that participate in the AMC will make legally binding commitments to supply the vaccines at lower and sustainable prices after the donor funds are spent.[12]

This mechanism has the advantage of solving the access problem: rather than relying on high prices to recover their R&D costs, firms receive a lump sum payment and the products can be sold at cost. Another policy intervention focused on incentives for neglected diseases is the Priority Review Voucher (PRV) described by Ridley et al. (2006b). A PRV allows a firm that wins approval on a new treatment for

---

[12] "Ministers of finance and global health leaders fulfill promise to combat world's greatest vaccine-preventable killer of children," Gates Foundation Press Release, June 12, 2009.

a neglected disease to receive priority review of another NDA under review by the FDA, or to sell the voucher to another firm. The first PRV was awarded in 2009 to Novartis, for its malaria treatment Coartem. Public—private partnerships such as DNDi and the Institute for Oneworld Health are another example of creative efforts to solve the neglected disease problem.

Analysis of alternative market designs to spur particular kinds of innovation is a promising area of research. Another area of research interest is the problem of eliciting information from private parties on the performance of drugs. For example, many drugs are used "off-label." A physician may prescribe a drug for a use unapproved by the FDA (assuming the drug has been approved for a different use), which happens when the physician has a reason to think that the drug may be efficacious despite the lack of FDA approval. For example, relatively few drugs have been tested in children, so a great many pediatric prescriptions are off-label; obstetrics is also a specialty with a lot of off-label prescribing. Without a financial incentive, the innovator will not bear the expense of an additional clinical trial in order to prove the new indication is valid. This may occur if the new use is discovered when the patent has too few years remaining on it to allow for significant sales after time is allocated for trials and FDA approval. However, if the innovator lacks FDA approval for its new indication, it may not legally market the drug for that use. So the innovator faces a trade-off between the cost of the trial and the incremental gain from marketing the new use to physicians. The nature and amount of existing research evidence for the new use may also affect the trade-off.

When the innovator chooses not to carry out the trial, social welfare can be harmed because physicians either may not want to prescribe the drug absent guidance, or do prescribe the drug, but without the knowledge of efficacy, dosing, and side effects that would be gained from a large randomized clinical trial. In the US there are currently limited regulatory mechanisms to get around this problem. A new indication can be patented—and the indication can even have orphan drug designation—so that other versions of the molecule may not list that indication on their labels. However, that does not stop physicians from prescribing a generic for the patented indication and depriving the innovator of rents, because off-label prescribing is legal. In addition, an additional 20 years of patent protection for a new indication may be inappropriate, since the original product represents a more significant inventive step.

Subgroups of the population may benefit more or less from an approved drug. As with off-label use, there is no incentive for the innovator to conduct a trial to find those subgroups. This is because the firm is likely to lose sales from other subgroups when it determines which group of patients gains most from the drug. This is also an issue in the development of diagnostic tests to identify subpopulations. There is little academic work on the incentives in this system, and little on the design of regulatory mechanisms that might raise social welfare, either in a single-payer system or a market-based system like the US. Yet these are important topics.

4.2. Demand Side

4.2.1. Market Definitions

One reason the pharmaceutical industry has been extensively studied by industrial organization economists is the ease in defining a market. A narrow definition is the molecule itself, with competition between the originator product and generic imitators and between the generic imitators themselves. A broader definition is a disease area or therapeutic class, in which several different chemicals or biologics may compete for patients with the same or similar diseases. For example, metformin is a drug used to treat Type 2 diabetes. The narrow market considers competition between the branded version, called Glucophage, and bioequivalent generic versions. The broader definition includes other drugs that treat Type 2 diabetes, such as glimepiride (brand name Amaryl) and rosiglitazone (brand name Avandia). The broader market definition is often the most relevant to the physician's or insurer's choice, and the narrow market definition is often appropriate for decisions of the pharmacist.

Antitrust authorities have applied both of these market definitions in various cases. For example, the US Federal Trade Commission (FTC) used the molecule as the relevant market in complaints against Abbott Laboratories, Hoescht Marion Roussel, and Schering-Plough, and in merger challenges involving Baxter International-Wyeth, Glaxo Wellcome-SmithKline Beecham, and Pfizer-Pharmacia. But the FTC has also recognized the broader market definition when considering mergers between firms with different chemicals treating the same disease, and required divestitures in some of these cases (such as Pfizer-Warner Lambert, for which Warner Lambert divested its Alzheimer's treatment Cognex because of Pfizer's competing treatment Aricept).

As noted earlier, regulatory structures and the application of intellectual property laws limit pharmaceutical markets to country borders, with the exception of EU member states. In other words, a US physician cannot prescribe a drug approved in Mexico but not in the US. If the drug is marketed in both countries, wholesalers and pharmacists cannot purchase the product in Mexico and resell it in the US. In principle, therefore, the US and Mexican markets are separate and prices in Mexico should not affect US prices. (We return to this issue later in this chapter, in our discussion of international pricing.) The European Union's promotion of free movement of goods between member states has changed links between country markets there. While prices are regulated at the level of the member states, firms cannot prevent arbitrageurs from purchasing their products in countries with low prices and reselling them in higher-priced markets, a practice known as parallel trade. Treating countries as entirely independent markets within the EU is therefore inappropriate.

Most diseases have multiple chemically distinct treatments available. The newest treatments usually have patent protection, and are marketed under brand names. Usually, these markets are characterized as differentiated oligopolies, since it is rare to observe more than 10 treatments still on patent at the disease level. Competition between versions of the same molecule tends to be more intense because there is less scope for differentiation. These versions may include the branded or originator's product, generic drugs, and parallel import versions in EU countries (which may have different packaging than the non-parallel import version of the originator). Arguably, the branded or originator version of a molecule could be perceived as having higher quality, or enjoy brand loyalty. Economists typically consider generic versions of the same molecule to be homogeneous goods. There are many studies that estimate demand for therapies within a disease market and the cross-price elasticities between treatments (branded and generic), which we discuss in the next section. We discuss competitive responses and antitrust considerations in section 5.

4.2.2. Estimates of Pharmaceutical Demand

As previously noted, pharmaceutical demand is rather more complicated than in most other settings due to the participation of multiple parties in the pricing and consumption decision. Large buyers, whether government agencies or insurance companies, negotiate a price for each treatment and in turn set a reimbursement rate or copayment for which the patient is responsible. A physician chooses among competing treatments to prescribe, but price is not necessarily part of his or her objective function. Pharmacists may select a particular manufacturer's product when there are multiple sources available. The patient, therefore, does not usually face the full price of a treatment (at least in developed countries), and does not really have the opportunity to choose between existing treatments without investing in learning about the alternatives and discussing them with the physician. Empirical work on estimating demand in pharmaceutical markets rarely models all these components explicitly. That is, the "consumer" at the heart of demand systems is a mix of physicians, insurers, pharmacists, and patients.

A typical approach is that used by Ellison et al. (1997). Using market-level data, they model the retail demand for a class of antibiotics as a two-stage budgeting problem using a representative consumer approach. In the first stage, the physician chooses between competing molecules, and in the second stage, the pharmacist (perhaps influenced by the patient and insurers, and constrained by laws on substitution) chooses between the brand and generic versions of that molecule. The top-level estimating equations are the log of each molecule's quantity as a function of total revenue in the class of drugs and weighted prices of each drug in the class. The estimating equation for the bottom level regresses the share of a molecule on the relative prices of the brand and generic versions and the dependent variable from the top-level equation. As with all demand estimation, the endogeneity of price is a concern, and the authors use changes in the number of firms in the market as an instrumental variable that is expected to trace out the demand curve as well as prices in the hospital market. As expected, cross-price elasticities are higher between competing versions of the same molecule than between molecules, which are more differentiated. In addition, own-price elasticities are more negative for generic versions than for branded versions, suggesting that consumers of generic products are more sensitive to price.

The use of a representative consumer model precludes consideration of how insurance and patient heterogeneity affect patient demand for pharmaceuticals. Since patients with insurance coverage do not face the full price of the treatment, there is a potential moral hazard problem. The resulting increase in pharmaceutical consumption has obvious implications for pharmaceutical expenditures overall. Almost all prescription drugs in the US are now purchased using private or public insurance: between 1980 and 1999, the proportion of prescription costs paid out of pocket (OOP) by the consumer fell from nearly 70 percent to only 8 percent in 2010 (Danzon and Pauly, 2002; Berndt and Aitken, 2010). Using a demand response assumption of a -0.3 own-price elasticity, Danzon and Pauly (2002) conclude that demand response or moral hazard "...may account for one-fourth to one-half of growth in drug spending." Clearly, accounting for insurance coverage is important in estimating demand.

Cleanthous (2002) was among the first to estimate the effect of insurance coverage on pharmaceutical consumption in a paper estimating demand for antidepressants. He specifies a discrete choice model of demand in which each consumer's utility is a function of drug characteristics and prices, with individual heterogeneity. That is, different consumers can place different weight on each characteristic. Using aggregate market data on prices, market shares and drug characteristics combined with demographic data on insurance and income, Cleanthous estimates a random coefficient logit model using the approach of Berry et al. (1995). He finds a preference for branded versions over generic versions, and that consumers generally dislike characteristics such as side effects. But more importantly, incorporating information on insurance reduces the price sensitivity of patients to -1.1 from a range of -1.6 to -2.6 in models without this inclusion. He concludes that the moral hazard of insurance coverage in demand for antidepressants is indeed economically significant. Calculating the welfare gains of innovation in pharmaceuticals should therefore distinguish between private and social willingness-to-pay.

Moral hazard may differ across disease areas or be changing over time, however. Like Cleanthous (2002), Dunn (2010) uses a discrete choice model of demand for anti-cholesterol treatments, but exploits the information on individual patients available in the MEPS data. Patient characteristics matter: those with heart disease prefer Zocor, while younger patients prefer Lipitor and Crestor. Patients with health insurance and with pharmaceutical coverage have higher preferences for drugs overall. However, he finds that even patients with insurance coverage are sensitive to price, with an estimated elasticity of -1.81.

The Dunn (2010) paper can only address how the existence of insurance coverage affects pharmaceutical demand, but not the specifics of that insurance such as reimbursement rates and co-payments, which can vary considerably across plans. While there are numerous papers in the literature that examine co-payment elasticities for medical care, they do not generally consider competition and the co-payments of alternative therapies. One exception is Ridley (2011), who examines pharmaceutical demand in two disease areas using data at the level of drug−insurance−group−month that includes co-payments. He estimates a log-linear demand system where total quantity of a drug demanded by an insurance group each month is a function of the co-payment and advertising for that drug in addition to the co-payments and advertising levels of competing drugs (he also allows for unobserved drug, patient, and insurance group characteristics). Instruments for co-payments and advertising include mean hourly earnings for pharmaceutical workers and advertising workers, a manufacturer's sales in other disease areas, a manufacturer's new product launches, and other firm-specific variables. Ridley (2011) finds that a drug's sales are more sensitive to an increase in co-payment when the co-payments of substitute therapies are constant or falling, as would occur when the insurer moves the drug to a different tier on the formulary. When co-payments for all competitors move together (the co-payment for a formulary tier changes but the treatments remain in the same tiers), demand appears relatively insensitive to price. Limbrock (2011) finds that being the "most preferred drug" on the formulary, or the drug with the lowest out-of-pocket cost in the therapeutic class, has a positive incremental effect on market share even when controlling for absolute price levels.

The physician's role in pharmaceutical demand, and in particular whether physicians consider price, has been addressed in a few papers. As discussed earlier, physicians in most countries do not have a financial incentive to prescribe one treatment over another. This is deliberate in many cases, in the hope that a physician's choice reflects an objective assessment of each drug's (clinical) suitability for a patient. However, a physician might be acting as a good agent by considering the economic circumstances of a patient when prescribing. Alternatively, the physician may perceive that he or she should act as an agent for an insurance company rather than a patient, and in fact regulators in some European countries have introduced incentives for physicians to consider price in their decisions in an effort to control expenditures. Hellerstein (1998) found that physicians were more likely to prescribe the generic version of a drug to patients who were members of HMOs, which suggests that HMOs were somewhat successful in increasing awareness of less expensive alternatives. The physician's use of trade names or generic names is less important today, as pharmacists have greater freedom (or the obligation) to dispense generic versions even if the prescription is written using the trade name and insurers have become more aggressive in promoting generic substitution.

Little work exists on how the relative prices of competing molecules affect prescribing, and it usually involves cases in which physicians do have a financial incentive. Since chemotherapy drugs are administered in the physician's office, physicians are reimbursed by Medicare for providing such treatment. Jacobson et al. (2006) examined how Medicare reimbursement to physicians affected their chemotherapy choices, and found that physicians were more likely to administer chemotherapy regimens with more generous reimbursement. Chou et al. (2003) studied the Taiwanese market, which experimented with separating the prescribing and dispensing functions in the late 1990s. They found that post-separation, the probability of prescribing and total drug expenditure was lower at clinics without an on-site pharmacy (i.e. with no financial interest in prescribing) relative to control sites. In a study of the Japanese market, another in which physicians may sell the drugs they prescribe, Iizuka (2007) found that prescriptions were influenced by the (regulated) markup physicians could charge. However, he found that physicians were nonetheless sensitive to the potential out-of-pocket charges faced by their patients. Additional work on agency problems in pharmaceutical markets would be valuable in light of efforts to change physician behavior.

There is an important caveat that applies to data on pharmaceutical prices, especially in the US. Invoice prices to drugstores and wholesalers do not reflect performance rebates paid by the manufacturer to a PBM months later for purchases spread across different drugstores. Information about rebates is proprietary and is never disclosed publicly, since manufacturers use the confidentiality of prices to price discriminate among buyers. Rebates are believed to have increased in prevalence and magnitude over time, particularly in classes with close therapeutic substitutes. The most interesting prices in the industry are not available to researchers and therefore there is little evidence on the change in elasticities of demand over time. Datasets that do not include rebates (such as that of IMS Health, the most commonly used by economists) likely have significant measurement error in the price variable for at least some drugs.

4.2.3. Buyer Power

Going back a number of decades, insurance coverage for prescription drugs was relatively rare (Berndt, 2002) and most consumers paid the full price of a drug out of pocket. With insurance that subsidizes pharmaceutical purchases, consumers do not face the full price of pharmaceutical treatments and may therefore overconsume. In the case of a cash-paying consumer, this moral hazard problem is minimized, and a pharmaceutical firm with market power sets price in the standard way.[13] As Berndt

---

[13] Although there are interesting questions about externalities on other people through use or non-use of prescription drugs, and the impact of price on compliance of "behavioral" consumers, such as when the drug produces a benefit that is delayed or not observable to the patient.

shows clearly, once a patient has insurance, the optimal price for a firm with market power increases dramatically.

The insurer can take an active role in negotiating for the pharmaceuticals it subsidizes, however, and exploit countervailing buyer power. Large buyers have a number of advantages over individuals. Typically, a patient is uninformed about the efficacy of the drug and, in particular, the relative efficacy of the drug. The physician has little knowledge of drug prices, and may suffer from an agency or information problem that prevents him or her from fully internalizing the cost to the patient (Hellerstein, 1998). An informed buyer, like an insurer, can trade off the merits of competing treatments versus their prices. It is critical that some competition between treatments exists, and a large buyer can foster such competition by creating a formulary, or list of covered drugs, that may exclude cost-ineffective drugs. Elasticities in response to co-payments have been shown to be substantial, as noted in the previous section, so the formulary can create financial incentives for the patient to consume cost-effective products, such as generics. Empirically, countervailing power can be important for ex-manufacturer prices as well as consumption patterns. Ellison and Snydor (2010) showed that hospitals in the US are able to negotiate for larger discounts than drugstores because the former can impose restrictive formularies.

In countries with national health insurance, the buyer is the government. In the US, this role is played by private insurers, hospitals, and drugstores as well as the various government agencies that provide health insurance to subpopulations (Medicare, Medicaid, and the Veterans' Administration (VA)). In many cases, these buyers are monopsonists with respect to their covered populations. For example, the VA is a monopsonist when it comes to buying for VA patients and can use its power to extract price concessions from a monopolist. Because drug development costs are sunk, pharmaceutical firms are exposed to *ex post* expropriation by buyers. That is, conditional on having invested R&D, a pharmaceutical firm should be willing to supply a product at any price that covers its marginal costs. In the long run, of course, the firm cannot cover its fixed costs with such pricing. This threat of expropriation is particularly severe in the case of government buyers, who in the extreme have the option of invalidating patents and issuing compulsory licenses.[14] For example, in 2006 the government of Thailand announced it would institute compulsory licensing of Kaletra (efavirenz), an HIV drug, and several other products of Abbott Laboratories. In 2001, after the anthrax attacks in the United States, there was discussion of overriding the Bayer patent on its anthrax drug in order to quickly and cheaply obtain large amounts of ciproflaxin. A further difficulty in this context is the public good nature of R&D. Each country or private insurance firm prefers to shift the burden of paying for R&D to others, i.e. that other countries or insurers pay prices high enough to

---

[14] Compulsory licensing is permitted under the TRIPS Agreement in the case of public health emergencies.

compensate firms for their innovative efforts but to pay close to marginal cost themselves. This is especially true for small countries, whose individual populations are too
small to have significant impact on R&D investment choices.

The extent to which buyers anticipate the long-term consequences of their purchasing strategies has not been studied extensively. Critics have blamed the downturn
in the vaccines industry on the US government's exploitation of its power as a large
purchaser. Similar concerns have been raised about the move towards "pooled procurement" of treatments for developing countries, an arrangement in which a single
buyer such as the Global Fund to Fight AIDS, Tuberculosis and Malaria negotiates on
behalf of many low-income countries. Danzon and Pereira (2011) found that the
increased volume of vaccine sales associated with government purchasing largely offset
the price reductions extracted. This remains a vital area for future work.

5. COMPETITION

5.1. Generic Entry

5.1.1. US

The 1984 Hatch-Waxman Act encouraged a great deal of generic entry in the late
1980s and 1990s. Many blockbuster drugs experienced dozens of generic entrants and
the ensuing price competition was fierce. Frank and Salkever (1997) and Reiffen and
Ward (2005) demonstrated that markets with more generic firms have lower generic
prices relative to the branded price.[15] In the Frank and Salkever dataset, which contains drugs experiencing generic entry in the 1980s, generic price is 70 percent of the
brand's price at launch, declines to 50 percent with four entrants, 30 percent with 12
or more, and falls to around 10 percent with 18–23 entrants. Price competition
appears to be confined to the generic segment, with little price response by brands
(Regan, 2008). A recent paper by Berndt and Aitken (2010) calculates average generic
prices relative to the brand price at the time of initial generic launch using data from
2005 to 2009.[16] They find that after six months, the index is at 78 (its initial value at
the time of generic launch is 100), falling to 50 at one year post-generic entry, 23 at
two years, and then less than 10 more than two years after generic entry.[17]
Figures 12.5 and 12.6 illustrate the intensity of generic competition in the US.

In addition to declining with entry, generic prices move with supply and demand.
For example, events such as closure of a factory due to fire, flood, or violation of

[15] Richard Frank and David Salkever (1997) Generic entry and the pricing of pharmaceuticals. *Journal of Economics and Management Strategy*, 6(1): 75–90.

[16] Ernst Berndt and Murray Aitken (2010) Brand loyalty, generic entry, and price competition in pharmaceuticals in the quarter century after the 1984 Waxman-Hatch legislation. NBER Working Paper.

[17] In this dataset, at two years after entry there are on average 12 generic entrants.

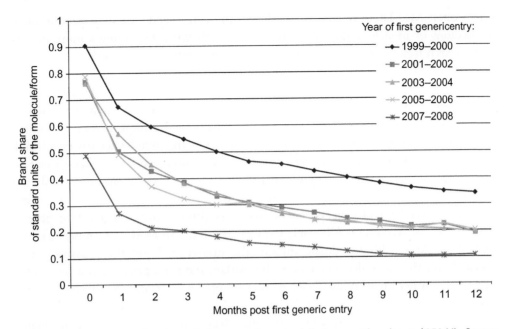

Figure 12.5 Brand share for drugs facing generic entry (all drugs with sales >$250 M). *Source: Grabowski et al. (2011).*

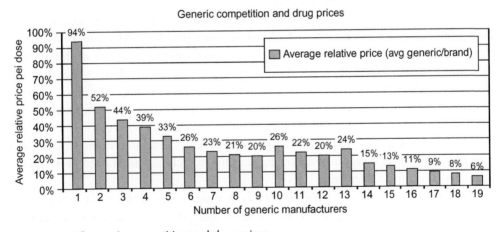

Figure 12.6 US generic competition and drug prices.

current Good Manufacturing Practices will drive up prices, at least temporarily, because of the supply shortage. As the molecule declines in popularity—perhaps due to new treatments becoming available—generic manufacturers tend to leave the market. When there are sufficiently few manufacturers and therefore less competition, prices often rise. There is little research into the nature and extent of generic price fluctuations or models of their determinants, though this is becoming a more important research topic as the share of prescriptions filled with generics grows.

Pharmacies search across generic firms in order to buy from the one with the lowest contract price. Payments for generic drugs to pharmacies from insurers are often at a fixed price, implying that the pharmacist has a profit incentive to find the lowest price source. Small pharmacies band together into buying groups or join a wholesaler's "sourcing program" to obtain access to the prices that wholesaler has negotiated. The constant change in the generic marketplace—entry, exit, price movements—means that insurers trying to pay pharmacies for a generic drug cannot typically use industry list prices to approximate market prices, as they often do with brands. Instead, insurers and pharmacy benefit managers (PBMs) invest in creating generic price lists called Maximum Allowable Cost (MAC) lists. An MAC list simply has on it each drug along with the dollar amount the insurer will pay the pharmacy. It is updated over time to reflect changes in the market, and is proprietary, as it reflects the PBM's investment in learning about market supply and demand. Most generic drug payments in the US today are paid based on an MAC price. This stands in contrast to payments for branded drugs, which are often based on the list price of the brand, wholesale acquisition cost (WAC), or average wholesale price (AWP). When insurers do not want to create an MAC list, they can use a list price formula, such as AWP-60%, to pay pharmacies for generic drugs.

Because the entry game in the US generic industry is simultaneous, generic firms have a difficult problem choosing which markets to enter. Scott Morton (1999) shows that generic firms tend to enter where they have prior expertise either in distribution or manufacturing. When there are more (fewer) entrants *ex post* than expected in the market, the firm can adjust its output down (up)—including down to zero—if desired. Exit is distinct from zero production, as exit requires a withdrawal of the ANDA by either the firm or the FDA. A useful way to think about the firm's problem is to consider the generic firm as having a filing cabinet containing many ANDAs and a factory containing many manufacturing machines; each month it optimizes what it produces according to demand.

The brand and its generics are sufficiently homogeneous so that price competition in these markets is intense. Low marginal costs and price competition result in very low prices—as discussed above. Such low prices attracted the attention of insurers and policy makers, who began to encourage consumption of generics instead of brands in the late 1980s. Consumers took time to get used to the idea that a generic was as high quality as its reference brand. Additionally, the process of institutional change to favor generics took time. For example, state laws that allow a pharmacist to substitute a generic in place of a brand were not universal in 1984, and financial incentives for patients to consume generics have become more sophisticated over time. The US generic fill rate, or what Berndt and Aitken (2010) term the "efficiency rate," increased from 84 percent in 2003 to 92 percent in 2009.

However, even if 100 percent of prescriptions that could be filled with generics were filled with generics, the generic share is limited by sales of brands under patent protection. Because of relatively unproductive or unlucky pharmaceutical R&D in the last decade, there have been fewer blockbuster new molecules approved by the FDA. Hence, while medications have lost patent protection steadily during the decade, new brands are not fully filling that space. The share of prescriptions "accessible to generic substitution" has increased from 64 percent in 2003 to 81 percent in 2009 (Berndt and Aitken, 2010). In addition, aggressive formulary management has tended to move prescriptions away from brands and towards molecules with a generic option. Continuing with the statin example above, suppose one of the four brands were going to lose patent protection before the others. A PBM would use its tools to start patients on the early-expiring brand and to switch patients from other brands to the early-expiring brand. Then, upon generic entry, the PBM would automatically convert all its patients on the expiring brand to a generic. Aitken, Berndt, and Cutler (2008) describe this pattern when generic versions of Zocor (simvastatin) and Pravachol took prescriptions away from branded Lipitor in 2007. Simvastatin prescriptions rose by 75 percent while prescriptions of Lipitor fell by 12 percent.

The net result in the US today is that the proportion of prescriptions filled with a generic has risen to 74.5 percent from only 19 percent in 1984 (Berndt and Aitken, 2010). The extensive use of generics in the US creates a massive and continuing social welfare gain, as these products will be available at close to marginal cost if demand is sustained and the generic markets remain competitive. PBMs' aggressive promotion of generics, as well as other contributing factors such as mandatory substitution laws, means that the branded product typically loses 75 percent or more of its market share very quickly—often in the first year after generic entry. This cliff-like pattern of revenue may be creating strong incentives for innovation by the former monopolist as suggested originally by Arrow (1962).

5.1.2. Other Countries

Generic entry rates in other countries are typically much less impressive than those in the US market. Smaller economies may have less competition because their markets cannot sustain as many generic firms. However, more importantly, many other nations do not have a system that generates strong price competition among generic producers. For example, regulation of pharmacy profit margins at fixed levels is common in Europe, meaning the pharmacist has no incentive to purchase from the least expensive supplier. This may be one reason why generic drugs are much more expensive, on average, outside the US and why they achieve lower market penetration (Danzon and

Table 12.5 Generic Shares Across Selected Countries
EXHIBIT 5

Originator Versus Generic Market Shares for Drugs, 2005

Country	Share of Unit Volume				Share of Sales			
	Originator		Generic		Originator		Generic	
	Single-source	Multi-source	Branded Generic	Unbranded Generic	Single-source	Multi-source	Branded Generic	Unbranded Generic
US	20.2%	8.5%	18.2%	53.1%	70.2%	10.4%	9.6%	9.8%
Canada	16.2	8.4	45.1	30.3	55.5	12.5	24.3	7.8
France	23.0	16.3	44.7	16.0	56.4	14.7	21.1	7.9
Germany	10.0	15.4	43.8	30.8	42.6	14.5	29.3	13.6
Italy	23.7	26.0	39.7	10.5	49.6	20.9	24.9	4.6
Spain	20.6	27.3	35.4	16.7	48.0	23.1	21.4	7.4
UK	11.8	19.5	21.3	47.4	47.3	16.0	13.3	23.4
Japan	19.3	25.6	42.3	12.7	50.0	27.1	18.8	4.1
Australia	20.1	20.2	49.5	10.2	55.0	18.0	24.2	2.8
Brazil	4.9	24.6	46.3	24.2	18.4	25.2	37.3	19.2
Chile	1.9	7.5	37.7	52.9	9.2	20.3	49.1	21.3
Mexico	7.5	25.5	51.4	15.6	25.9	38.8	31.4	3.9

Source: Authors' calculations based on data from IMS Health MIDAS database, 2005. Source: Danzon, P. M. Furukawa, M. F. (2008). International prices and availability of pharmaceuticals in 2005. *Health Affairs*, 27(1), 221–233.

Furukawa, 2008). Table 12.5 provides a summary of how generic shares compare across major markets.

Payment policies also likely inhibit competition. For example, Canadian provinces fix prices for generic drugs at a percentage (such as 45 or 50 percent, but formerly much higher) of the branded price (Bell et al., 2010). More than half the market is supplied by two generic drug firms. In Quebec and some other provinces, the government payment to the pharmacist for any generic version is the lower of the percentage described above or the lowest price paid by any other province, which weakens a manufacturer's incentive to reduce price and tends to create a price floor across the nation. British Columbia pays the actual acquisition cost to the pharmacy of the lowest priced generic in the province. This rule means that the generic firm that may have cut its price in order to sell to a pharmacy will find that it has in fact created no advantage for itself, since every rival product will cost the pharmacy the same lower amount. And, due to the most-favored-nation (MFN) rule in other provinces, the low price will set a new national floor. Generic manufacturers do not have an incentive to compete on price in such an environment.

While some generic firms such as Teva (the largest generic manufacturer) sell in many countries, many generic firms operate in one country or region. Often, these are relics of industrial policies that favored domestic producers: prior to 1987, for example, Canada used compulsory licensing to bolster its local producers. The fact that generic manufacturers are the "local" firms in most countries outside the US, and both they and the local pharmacies benefit from less vigorous price competition in that country, may partly explain the durability of some of the regulations limiting price competition among generics outside the United States.

5.2. Biologic Drugs and Biosimilars

Biologic drugs represent about a quarter of total US spending on pharmaceuticals and are forecast to be close to 40 percent by 2020. Biosimilars are still a relatively new technology, and because their regulations have not been established and there are no entrants, existing academic work is largely speculative. Such work would be very valuable and is likely to be a frontier area in health economics in the coming decades.

Biologics differ considerably from small-molecule drugs (SMDs) in off-patent competition. Biologics, some of which have been on the market since the 1980s, face very little direct competition from imitators producing an identical molecule. There is some dispute over whether such imitation would ever result in a biosimilar that is as close to the original version as a generic copy of a small-molecule drug is to its original version. Indeed, biologics produced by the same firm in different plants can demonstrate different characteristics, due to small differences in the manufacturing process. This debate underlies the 2010 Patient Protection and Affordable Care Act, which proposed two regulatory pathways for an imitative biologic. One is a biosimilar pathway, where the product is demonstrated to be very close to the reference product. The second pathway is for products seeking an exchangeable designation from the FDA, which means the products are identical and could be exchanged at the pharmacy level. Many observers feel that this second standard is not achievable with current technology. The FDA must create regulations delineating these pathways, accept an application into a pathway, and then approve the product before a biosimilar would be permitted to enter the US market.

Biosimilars are successfully competing in Europe, where they have been approved since 2006. To date the EMA has approved biosimilars in three areas: granulocyte colony-stimulating factor (stimulates production of white blood cells), erythropoietin (stimulates production of red blood cells), and somatropin (human growth hormone). In May 2010, the National Institute for Clinical Excellence (NICE) in the UK issued a report evaluating Sandoz's biosimilar Somatropin and concluded that the biosimilar had the same safety and efficacy as the brand. NICE encouraged providers to choose the least expensive product among those that are therapeutically appropriate. There is no empirical work currently examining the impact of biosimilars on branded prices in Europe, but some facts have recently emerged. In both France and Germany, biosimilars entered the market at a discount and the price of the original version fell also.[18] However, some of this reduction is due to price regulations in these countries (discussed in section 6).

The critical aspect of regulations on biosimilars in the US is the extent to which they create a barrier to entry that reduces competition in the sector. The FDA could require tests that are only slightly less extensive than those required of the brand, which would mean entry costs for the biosimilar would be nearly as high as the brand's, or even potentially higher (Grabowski et al., 2007). Since each entrant must expect to cover its high fixed entry cost, few biosimilars would want to enter the market via the pathway and prices would not fall as dramatically as we have observed in SMDs. This would be true particularly for drugs with small patient populations. Alternatively, entry costs could be relatively low which would attract many entrants and drive prices lower. The extent to which entrant biosimilars would be able to put price pressure on brands is an open question. A pharmacist will not be able to substitute a biosimilar for the reference product without consulting a physician because the drugs are not identical. The extent of perceived heterogeneity will affect price competition. Consumers may not want to consume the biosimilar if they think it is different from the brand. Because of the differentiation among products and their complexity, biosimilar competitors may advertise in a way that we do not see in SMDs. The biosimilar's impact on prices may also be affected by whether a drug is taken chronically (the patient has switching costs) or for a short period of time. All of these issues are fertile areas for economic research in biologics.

FDA regulations are also important because they affect the nature and extent of technical progress in manufacturing, as Cockburn et al. (2006) describe. For example, if the biosimilar must carry out every aspect of production exactly as the brand described in the brand's original application, then the biosimilar entrant cannot use the latest manufacturing techniques or equipment. Since it could be 20 years or more since the brand's manufacturing process was designed, this may have significant productivity consequences. In particular, process innovation would likely reduce variable costs, which in turn is likely to affect equilibrium prices.

5.3. Parallel Trade

Parallel trade allows competition from the originator's product sold in another country. Parallel trade constitutes the resale of goods first purchased outside the country and without the authorization of the firm that owns the intellectual property rights pertaining to the goods. Typically, the originator (the innovator or patentholder) blocks competition from a third party engaged in resale of its products by invoking IP laws. If national IP laws consider the IP to be "exhausted" once the product has been

---

[18] http://www.gabionline.net/Biosimilars/General/The-hurdles-to-biosimilars-in-Europe.

put on the market in another country, then the originator cannot prevent resale and parallel trade can occur. While not currently permitted in the US, relaxing rules on imports of pharmaceutical products from Canada and Europe, where prices are often lower, has been suggested as an effort to contain US prices. Australia, New Zealand, and Switzerland have considered similar adjustments. In the European Union, parallel trade in pharmaceuticals is permitted and is economically important in some countries.

Because parallel trade is effectively arbitrage of price differences, countries with relatively low prices (typically Greece, Portugal, and Spain) tend to be sources of parallel exports, which are then resold in countries where prices are high (such as the UK and Scandinavian markets). Maskus and Ganslandt (2004) examine parallel trade for best-selling drugs in Sweden, and find that entry by parallel traders resulted in price reductions by originators. However, as documented in Kanavos and Costa-Font (2005) and Kyle et al. (2008), competition from parallel imports has not resulted in significantly lower prices overall or in price convergence across countries. Kanavos and Costa-Font (2005) and Kyle (2011) explain that this outcome is due to a combination of regulations that dampen incentives for pharmacists and patients to switch to lower-priced parallel imports and strategic responses by firms.

5.4. Strategic Responses by Originators

Innovative (as opposed to generic) pharmaceutical firms have large gross margins and strong incentives to protect those margins from generic competition, price regulation, and threats to intellectual property protection. The low marginal costs of pharmaceutical firms and their long experience in global regulatory environments means their responses to laws and regulations are often strategic and very sophisticated. The pharmaceutical industry is an excellent place to carry out research on firm behavior and the unintended consequences of well-meaning regulation.

The responses of innovator companies to generic entry are particularly interesting. Brands often file multiple patents for attributes of the same drug, for example on the basic molecule, the process, the release mechanism, and even the shape of the pill. Waiting for all these patents to expire would create a long period of monopoly pricing. A feature of the Hatch–Waxman Act that seems to have been unanticipated was the ability of the generic to settle "Paragraph IV" patent litigation in a manner that arguably harms consumers. If there are, for example, a number of years left to run on the challenged patent at the time of litigation, and the generic wins, the brand will lose monopoly profit for that entire remaining time period. By contrast, the generic will only gain six months of duopoly profit as an exclusive generic and thereafter the market will become competitive with additional generic entry. The lost profit for the remaining years (less six months) accrues to consumers in the form of lower prices.

Given this situation, the generic is clearly better off by settling for a share of the monopoly rents of the brand and agreeing not to enter: a standard contract of this type would have the brand paying the generic to settle the patent litigation, and a condition of the settlement is that the generic does not enter the market.[19] This strategy (sometimes called "pay for delay") is generally profitable for both firms, but deprives consumers of early generic entry in cases where the brand patent is weak.

The FTC began taking these agreements, known as "reverse payments," to court on the grounds that they violated the antitrust laws, but a series of judges since 2005 found in favor of the firms.[20] This issue is still one of active policy debate, as despite the adverse legal rulings, the FTC continues to sue in cases of reverse payments. An agency study found that agreements with compensation to the generic results in 17 additional months of patent protection relative to agreements with no generic compensation.[21] The FTC currently considers a settlement negotiation over the entry date of the generic without a financial transfer to be pro-competitive. In such a settlement, each side's assessment of the strength of the patent determines how far into the remaining patent term the generic is permitted to enter. Consumers then get the benefit of competition at a date that reflects the strength of the patent. Having settled (or won) in patent litigation, the generic may use its 180 days of exclusivity during which time no additional generic may enter the market.[22]

A second strategic response to generic competition by innovators is the use of so-called "authorized generics." Prior to patent expiration, innovators using this strategy choose to launch their own generic version or to sell a license allowing another firm to do so. This authorized generic version reaches the market earlier than would otherwise be the case, and thus has the potential to increase consumer welfare. However, this early entrant may deter subsequent competitors. Appelt (2010) examines the consequences of authorized generics in Germany. She found that the primary motive for the introduction of authorized generics appears to be earning generic profits without affecting the number of entrants or price, rather than entry deterrence.

Brands employ other strategies to retain their monopoly position by investing in incremental innovation, such as developing extended release formulations or over-the-counter (OTC) versions. Berndt et al. (2003) describe the effects of this practice for antiulcer treatments. Critics describe this as "evergreening," though of course there may well be patients who benefit from this type of new product. The answer to whether the innovation is socially useful is often clearer when the product line

---

[19] Sometimes the payments take the form of compensation for unrelated transactions such as marketing or manufacturing assistance provided by the generic (which may be a way to make reverse payments less transparent).

[20] Pay-for-delay: how drug company pay-offs cost consumers billions (January 2010) FTC Staff Study.

[21] Pay-for-delay: how drug company pay-offs cost consumers billions (January 2010) FTC Staff Study.

[22] For further analysis, see Scott Hemphill and Mark Lemley (2011) Earning exclusivity: generic drug incentives and the Hatch-Waxman Act. *Antitrust Law Journal*, forthcoming.

extension is put to a market test. If the new product is not sufficiently better than the old one, conditional on price, it may not be given good formulary placement by PBMs. OTC versions, because they do not require a visit to a doctor in order to obtain a prescription, may increase use of pharmaceuticals by the uninsured population. For example, OTC versions of smoking cessation products could reach a much larger population than the prescription versions. Naturally, the risk of inappropriate use (or abuse) is a first-order consideration to regulators considering whether to approve OTC versions. The application to market Plan B, the so-called "morning after pill," was a high-profile example of this concern.

However, sometimes the introduction of new versions has more to do with regulatory features that reward product proliferation, albeit unintentionally. Duggan and Scott Morton (2006) show that launch prices are higher when the buyer (Medicaid enrollees) is inelastic. The same paper shows that when the government rebate grows over time the firm has an incentive to introduce new products in order to "reset" the inflationary component of the rebate. In Japan, launch prices are unconstrained but the government mandates steep price reductions each year. As a result, manufacturers in Japan introduce new products much more frequently than do firms in other jurisdictions (Thomas, 2001). Kyle (2011) shows that firms select packaging and dosage type in order to make parallel trade more costly in Europe.

Scott Morton (1999) provides evidence that when the federal government wanted to lower the cost of drugs in the Medicaid program, it did so in a way that benefited manufacturers, mandating Most Favored Nation protection for Medicaid purchases. Manufacturers and many industry observers forecast the likely effects of the MFN clause, and anticipated the dampening effect it would have on large price discounts which had been extracted by some buyers before the law. The year after the MFN took effect, the average price of branded drugs with high sales to Medicaid rose.

6. PRICING AND MARKETING

6.1. International Prices

While policy interest primarily focuses on prices, there is a surprising amount of variability in the portfolio of drugs sold across different countries also. Kyle (2011) documents a number of relevant facts, such as that only one-third of prescription drugs sold in one of the seven largest national markets in the world (US, Japan, Germany, France, Italy, UK, Canada) are also sold in the other six markets. Since marginal costs are low and fixed costs are high, innovators have a strong incentive to sell as much of their product as possible. Moreover, presumably governments would like their citizens to have access to as many effective treatments as possible. Lack of entry under these conditions suggests that approval costs may be limiting competition in many markets. An interesting issue for further study is whether lowering entry costs might stimulate competition among additional products and lower drug expenditures.

There is a large literature examining the differences in the price of pharmaceuticals across countries. For example, Danzon and Furukawa (2008) present a comparison between rich countries (summarized in Table 12.6), and Yadav (2010) focuses on prices in developing countries. The consumption patterns of drugs vary considerably across nations. Danzon and Chao (2000) show that it makes a large difference to the calculation of relative price levels whether one weights with US quantities or own country quantities. Differences in the product mix and consumption patterns mean that direct price comparisons can be misleading, but there are two important stylized facts that have emerged from the literature. First, large price differences exist, even across high-income countries. Second, these price differences may not be large enough: on a purchasing-power parity basis, low-income countries pay relatively high prices and hence have lower access.

From the standpoint of economic theory, when a seller can price discriminate across markets, we expect to see higher prices in markets with lower demand elasticity. International data do not allow easy comparison across countries in terms of demand elasticity. We do, however, see a pattern of richer countries paying more, which may have to do with not just higher income, but with the insurance/reimbursement and regulatory structures in those countries. Most economists would argue that price discrimination favoring lower income countries should be encouraged in this context. Theory shows that price discrimination raises social welfare if it expands quantity consumed (Varian, 1985). Drugs sold at high prices in rich countries, but also sold at low prices to citizens of poor countries, seem very likely to be satisfying this condition and raising welfare. By contrast, if drugs were sold at a uniform price across all countries, that price would likely reduce access for lower-income people around the world.

Danzon and Towse (2003) argue that something close to optimal Ramsey prices could be achieved by basing prices on national income. The policy implication is that governments around the world should accept differential prices as welfare enhancing instead of engaging in reference pricing, or benchmarking their prices to those in other countries. Charging low prices to very poor countries like Sudan or Malawi is not controversial. Everyone appreciates that these consumers cannot pay for drugs and yet need them. Middle-income countries, particularly those that have been growing fast (e.g. Brazil, Turkey), may begin to object to differential pricing. These countries are used to paying low prices for pharmaceuticals but their incomes now justify higher prices; the policy response to international price discrimination as innovation and incomes change is an interesting area for future research.

Table 12.6 Comparison of Pharmaceutical Prices Across Selected Countries
EXHIBIT 6

Pharmaceutical Price Indexes, Relative to US Prices (US = 100), 2005

Country	Comprehensive Indexes[a]				Originator versus Generic[b,c,d]			Rx versus OTC[b,c,d]	
					Originator		Generic		
	Manuf.[d] at Exch. Rates[c]	Public[e] at Exch. Rates[c]	Public[e] at GDP PPPs[f]	Manuf.[d] Normalized by Income[g]	Single-source[c]	Multi-source	Branded and Unbranded	Rx	OTC
US	100	100	100	100	100	100	100	100	100
Canada	81	81	79	103	74	60	133	79	189
France	74	91	78	100	64	37	108	69	262
Germany	75	90	95	106	74	65	151	77	192
Italy	67	87	82	94	55	68	150	63	527
Spain	59	69	71	93	62	40	109	57	377
UK	72	81	68	93	76	61	131	77	202
Japan	111	99	50	151	81	99	211	101	362
Australia	69	70	66	90	63	62	138	70	195
Brazil	69	80	68	336	62	109	128	64	186
Chile	56	65	119	206	56	55	138	58	312
Mexico	102	107	157	414	90	87	216	110	218

Note: ATC3 is Anatomical Therapeutic Classification.
[a]Bilateral matching with US by molecule-atc3.
[b]Bilateral matching with US by molecule-atc3-form-strength.
[c]Price converted to US dollars at exchange rates.
[d]Manufacturer prices.
[e]Public prices.
[f]Prices converted to US dollars at gross domestic product (GDP) purchasing power parities (PPPs).
[g]Price index normalized by GDP per capita.
Source: World Development Indicators, 2005; and authors calculations based on data from IMS Health MIDAS database, 2005. Source: Danzon, P. M. & Furukawa, M. F. (2008). International prices and availability of pharmaceuticals in 2005. *Health Affairs*, 27(1), 221–233.

Differential pricing can be difficult to sustain for a number of reasons. Firms sell to monopsonist purchasers in most rich countries, and these large buyers have counter-vailing power (particularly relative to low-income countries, where government health coverage and purchasing may not exist). In addition, these large buyers either explicitly or implicitly reference prices used in other countries. As discussed earlier, parallel trade between countries undermines the ability of firms to price discriminate. While parallel trade is currently limited to the EU, the use of "international reference pricing" has the same effect of linking prices across countries and is widespread. For example, in France, government policy is to pay a price that is "similar" to that accepted by the manufacturer of an innovative product in a group of reference countries: Spain, Italy, UK, and Germany. Greek policy is to pay no more than the lowest price within Europe. Of course, the choice of which countries—high price or low price—are in the reference basket will have a large impact on the final negotiated price.

From the manufacturer's point of view, the revenue earned from a country with reference pricing depends strongly on the prices the manufacturer sets or negotiates with peer countries. Therefore a manufacturer should want to negotiate over prices and launch new products in high-price countries first, so as to positively affect any reference price used by later countries. Danzon et al. (2005) show that countries with lower price levels experience longer launch delays (or fewer products launched), con-trolling for per capita income. Kyle (2011) finds that markets with regulated prices have less entry overall, and more entry delay when entry does occur. As predicted by economic theory, markets with lower prices tend to be harmed by policies that encourage uniform pricing. Interestingly, a product that has been launched earlier in a low-price market (or belongs to a domestic firm in that market) is less likely to be launched in additional markets compared to a drug that is marketed in high-price countries. This may arise because of implicit or explicit reference pricing by other countries that condition their prices on existing prices for the product, and therefore determine the profitability of additional entry.

Even without formal international reference pricing, low prices charged to others often create political pressure on branded pharmaceutical prices in richer countries. Politicians in the US have responded to high branded prices by proposing bills to allow importation of cheaper branded drugs from Canada. The likely result of any such policy would be to cause manufacturers to set higher prices in Canada, manufac-turers to limit sales in Canada, the government to disallow exports to the US, or all three. In response to growth in cross-border trade enabled by internet pharmacies, in 2004 GlaxoSmithKline began to ration sales to Canadian pharmacies suspected of exporting products to the US. Several other large pharma firms followed suit. Economic theory demonstrates that well-intentioned efforts to increase transparency of drug prices in different countries, such as those spearheaded by Medicins Sans Frontières, have the potential to harm the populations they are meant to help.

The process of setting prices across different countries is difficult to describe concisely because the institutions vary across countries, there are many countries with significant pharmaceutical sales, and policies are always changing. Useful resources are PPRI, an information network providing Pharmaceutical Pricing and Reimbursement Information for EU countries and EU applicant countries (e.g. Turkey),[23] and Annex K to a 2007 report "International survey of pharmaceutical pricing and reimbursement schemes" from the Office of Fair Trading in the UK.[24] Another non-profit site that explains pricing and approval processes across various countries is the International Society for Pharmacoeconomics and Outcomes Research.[25] Kyle (2011) provides a one-page summary of different types of regulation across 25 markets, which MacGarvie and Koenig (2011) supplement .[26] Rather than provide an exhaustive summary of the information contained in these sources for many countries, we focus on several examples that illustrate general types of approaches: Germany for a strong reference price system, Australia for incremental cost effectiveness, France for strong state regulation of prices, and the UK for its clinical effectiveness institute. We also touch briefly on the Japanese market, the second largest in the world, which has a number of important differences from Western regulatory structures. There are many reports by agencies, consulting firms, and non-profits that examine these national schemes. A fruitful area of research going forward may be to model different national schemes and explicitly contrast their welfare consequences.

Launch prices are unregulated in Germany. When the EMA or the local German authority approves a new product, it is almost always covered by social insurance in Germany (those deemed insufficiently innovative are placed on the negative list). However, the reimbursement level is regulated by G-BA (Gemeinsamer Bundesausschuss). The Institut für Qualität und Wirtschaftlichkeit im Gesundheitswesen (IQWiG), or the agency for "medical efficiency, quality, and effectiveness," evaluates the drug and provides a recommendation to G-BA. G-BA devises reference drug categories and sets reimbursement levels. Usually, a reference group includes therapeutic substitutes as well as generic versions, if available. If the drug can be placed in an existing reference group, then its reimbursement is determined in the following way. The reference price is at the 33rd percentile of the price distribution of the group; it must also be a price at which 20 percent or more of the prescription (and volume) of the group can be purchased. The patient is responsible for the difference between the reference price and the price of the drug he or she consumes.

---

[23] http://ppri.oebig.at/index.aspx?Navigation=r|0|2-
[24] http://www.oft.gov.uk/shared_oft/reports/comp_policy/oft885k.pdf
[25] http://www.ispor.org/Default.asp
[26] http://www.cmj.hr/2002/43/4/12187524.pdf

Germany has recently adopted a more formal cost-effectiveness approach, which is explained clearly by the International Society for Pharmacoeconomics and Outcomes Research (www.ispor.org) on their Germany page:

> In January 2008 (updated to version 2.0 in March 2009), the IQWiG published their first draft of the "Methods for Assessment of the Relation of Benefits to Costs in the German Statutory Health Care System". In contrast to other HTA agencies…IQWiG did not use the incremental-cost-effectiveness-ratio (ICER) approach, but they introduce a different methodological instrument, the efficiency frontier. Within the efficiency frontier, all available compounds/agents have to be compared using their total benefit in relation to their total costs. This results in an efficiency frontier. New agents have to show comparable efficiency, compared to (a) the cost–benefit ratio of the alternative with the best available maximum benefit, or (b) compared to the mean cost–benefit ratio within the specific indication.

The German system and the US system are similar in the sense that a truly innovative new product does not face a regulated price. However, drugs that provide smaller benefits are lumped into a reference price group, which essentially treats them as undifferentiated. Drugs in a group can, in theory, charge consumers a premium. However, many manufacturers set their products' prices at the reference price benchmark. Pavcnik (2002) considered how manufacturers respond to the introduction of reference pricing in Germany, and found that the increase in out-of-pocket expenditures created by this system induced firms to cut their prices, with the decline in brand-name prices being especially steep. McGuire and Bauhoff (2011) showed that the German reference price system was very effective in inducing substitution for Lipitor. Brekke et al. (2011) examined the reference price system in Norway, and found that its use significantly lowered prices of both brand-name and generic products as well as increased generic uptake.

In Australia, approval and pricing of new drugs either follows a "cost-minimization" track or a "cost-effectiveness" track. The former track is used by all generics and any brand that does not think it has a significant clinical advantage over other products in the therapeutic category. The Pharmaceutical Benefits Advisory Council (PBAC) identifies a reference group comprised of therapeutic substitutes; the lowest price (per dose) of the drugs in this group sets the benchmark price. All products are reimbursed at the benchmark, but a brand can add a premium to its price that the consumer must pay, provided there is another product in the therapeutic group that is available at the benchmark price. Innovative products that are improvements over the status quo follow the cost-effectiveness track and must present evidence of their clinical merits to PBAC in order to obtain the designation of cost effective. Then the Pharmaceutical Benefits Pricing Authority (PBPA) sets the reimbursement price, which depends on clinical effectiveness and other factors. A significant fraction of cost-effectiveness applicants are rejected, in the sense that the agency does not find their product a significant improvement and they have to accept the benchmark price if they want to enter the market.

Australia also uses risk-sharing agreements to address total expenditure by the government. If a product is successful and sales are higher than a negotiated cap, the manufacturer must rebate some of its revenues. This technique preserves the list price for international reference pricing purposes, while still offering the Australian government a discount. In addition, it renders the contract similar to a lump sum payment by the government with small marginal payments for additional quantities, which is efficient (given low marginal costs). Lastly, some of the caps are for a therapeutic class rather than an individual drug, with rebates paid according to market share in the class. This gives manufacturers incentive to compete in price, because pure business-stealing will not trigger a rebate.

In France, there is no therapeutic reference price group and initially no cost effectiveness. First, the Haute Autorité de Santé (HAS) evaluates a new drug for its clinical attributes and the seriousness of the underlying condition, and assigns it a score relative to therapeutic substitutes. The Comité Economique des Produits de Santé (CEPS), a separate committee, is responsible for pharmaceutical prices. Low-scoring products must negotiate a price. High-scoring products may, in theory, freely choose a price, but this price may not exceed the average list price in Germany, Italy, Spain, and the UK (this is an example of explicit international reference pricing).

Risk sharing in France is similar to that in Australia in that firms must pay rebates if government spending in a category gets too high, growth rates exceed targets, or volume exceeds targets. However, rebates are also payable if volume of an individual, innovative, but expensive drug rises above a cap. Importantly, the government negotiates for special rebates for high-scoring, and therefore "unregulated," drugs when it thinks the European average price is too high. Thus, high-scoring innovative products may have restricted pricing, despite the apparent pricing freedom provided in the launch regulation. The existence of the rebate means that net price is not easily observed, but will clearly be lower than the published price.

These measures have not controlled expenditures very effectively: France's per capita spending on pharmaceuticals is one of the highest in Europe, despite its relatively low prices. Its regulatory system does not produce high rates of use of generics. According to the OFT report, generic prescriptions are 7 percent of French pharmaceutical spending. In addition, French consumers face very low co-payments and consequently tend to be quite insensitive to price.

In the UK, pharmaceutical prices are determined through a voluntary contract called the Pharmaceutical Price Regulation Scheme (PPRS), which is renewed periodically for a set number of years. Approved new products may be priced at the discretion of the manufacturer. Instead of directly regulating prices, the PPRS limits the profitability, or rate of return on capital, of the firms in the industry (21 percent in 2009). Price increases are not allowed unless the firm can demonstrate its forecast of its return on capital is below 40 percent of the allowed rate. If the introduction of a popular new product raises, or is forecast to raise, the firm's return on capital above the limit, it must negotiate price reductions to bring firm-wide profitability down. Clearly, a firm's portfolio of products—some more successful than others—will affect its average return on capital. Products may be sold to other pharmaceutical firms, but their prices may not increase for three months after the sale. In this situation one would expect detailed rules for the method of calculating return on capital, and these are provided. The PPRS terms may call for an across-the-board price cut, an overall expenditure reduction requirement (which can be met with any combination of price reductions across products), mandatory generic substitution, or other terms that reduce price.

The UK's NICE reviews medications (new or existing) and issues opinions on whether local health authorities should purchase and administer those treatments. NICE does not publicly set prices, nor does it negotiate prices. It determines the value of medications—primarily through measurement of Quality Adjusted Life Years (QALYs), though it is permitted to account for other factors—and compares the drug's value to the price chosen by the firm. If the treatment is cost effective, NICE will issue a favorable recommendation. Originally, such a conclusion meant that all health authorities in the country had to offer that treatment, but recent (2010) changes by the government make the NICE decision non-binding on providers. If the price per QALY is too high, NICE will recommend against providing the treatment. Local health trusts may still make their own decisions about the treatment, but they are not obligated to offer it. While NICE does not publish a formal limit, observers note that treatments with costs above 30,000 GBP per QALY are less likely to be approved. The lack of price negotiation means that the manufacturer is playing a one-shot game that is high risk. A higher price raises profit conditional on acceptance; but a higher price lowers the probability of acceptance. The firm must choose a submission price balancing these forces and taking into account its expectations of NICE's own data, analytical process, and likely conclusion; see Jena and Philipson (2007) for a discussion.

A useful feature of PPRS 2009 is that the regulation allows the one-shot game to have a second stage in some cases. A manufacturer may adjust the price of a medication up (by as much as 30 percent) or down when new evidence on efficacy or additional indications becomes available. Another interesting feature to the scheme is that an additional indication may be priced above existing indications if it is more valuable than the original indications. This type of regulation addresses the problem of lack of incentives for additional knowledge gathering that were raised earlier in this chapter. A second innovation adopted by the PPRS is the option for performance-based contracts (known as "Patient Access Schemes"). This includes the conventional rebate, triggered by expenditure or usage, that we have seen in other countries. More exciting provisions include agreements that the manufacturer may seek a price increase if subsequent studies (agreed to by NICE upon initial approval) produce evidence of higher quality. Analogously, a price may be accepted initially, but NICE may commit to revising it subject to data from further studies. In this case the manufacturer will forfeit funds if the treatment does not perform as expected. The implications of NICE policies for firm pricing strategies are a very interesting area for future research.

Lastly, and most interestingly, are sophisticated and novel risk-sharing contracts that bring down average costs and sharpen incentives for manufacturers. These are agreements where UK patient health outcomes determine the price of the treatment. For example, an agreement might specify that all appropriate patients receive a cancer drug, as would be the case in the US. However, only those patients whose tumors shrink will trigger payment from the NHS to the manufacturer. Such an arrangement allows the manufacturer and the government to hold different views on the efficacy of the drug, and for both to be satisfied with the contract. In particular, such a contract protects the government from paying for expensive medicines that do not perform as expected. Risk sharing is especially useful when considering expensive drugs that have heterogeneous effects in the population. The heterogeneity results in a small average effect and means that these products are likely to fail NICE's threshold test. In the example above, if some fraction of patients responds to the drug (e.g. 25 percent) while others do not, and the price of a dose is high, average price per QALY is high. When only 25 percent of doses are purchased, price per QALY falls to 25 percent of its former size and the NICE threshold may be passed. Because of the prevalence of international reference pricing, the fact that the list price remains constant is another advantage of the contract to the manufacturer.

The Japanese pharmaceutical market has a number of features that distinguish it from other markets in high-income countries. Some of these are not directly related to its pricing, but have implications for competition. There is also a tradition of protectionist policies. Clinical trials conducted on non-Japanese participants were not always accepted in applications for new drug approvals, and foreign firms had difficulty penetrating the market. Japan has the smallest shared set of drugs marketed in comparison with the six other largest markets (Kyle, 2011). We noted previously that there is a tradition in Asian markets that physicians both prescribe and dispense drugs. The system of approving and paying for pharmaceuticals in Japan has an important interaction with this practice. Because physicians earn a margin on each drug they prescribe, they have an incentive to write many prescriptions for each patient (Thomas, 2001) and to prescribe those for which they earn the highest margins (Iizuka, 2007). Further, the government does not limit introductory prices but does require frequent price reductions. The result is that many new products are introduced over time, but these are not generally new chemical entities. Instead, they are mainly versions of existing drugs because releasing a new version allows the firm to set the launch price again.

6.2. US

With 45 percent of global pharmaceutical spending, the US is both the largest market and the least regulated in terms of price. However, between Medicare Part D, Medicaid, and other programs, the government buys more than 50 percent of drugs in the US directly or indirectly.[27] This means that the manufacturers face significant political pressure to keep prices down in the US, even in the absence of explicit price controls. Ellison and Wolfram (2006), examining the behavior of pharmaceutical firms when health care reform was considered in the early 1990s, found that these firms took steps to forestall price regulation such as limiting price increases.

6.2.1. Private Sector

The "free market" in the US means that buyers must negotiate to secure lower drug prices for their members. The use of buyer power in pharmaceutical markets was discussed in section 4.2.3. In the private sector, PBMs are the most important buyers: PBMs manage more than 70 percent of the prescriptions dispensed in the US. Though US prices are not regulated, the emergence of the PBM and the formulary has made demand more elastic. HMOs like Kaiser and the Yale Health Plan receive low prices from manufacturers because they are willing to drop a drug from their formulary unless the manufacturer's price is low. In response to small price changes, these buyers switch large volumes among competing products (Limbrock, 2011). They create price competition among branded therapeutic substitutes by means of formulary tiers. Tier 1 drugs, usually generic drugs and perhaps a few inexpensive brands, have the lowest co-pay. Preferred brands are on the next tier, with perhaps a $20 co-pay, and non-preferred brands are on tier 3 with a higher co-pay. Insurers also sometime have a fourth tier for "specialty pharmaceuticals" that are often expensive biologics. This tier typically has co-insurance rates of 30 percent or something similar. The PBM can also restrict consumption of particular brands to certain clinical subgroups to limit usage.

The process of identifying "preferred brands" is where the formulary is most useful in creating bargaining power for the insurer. This dynamic is nicely summarized in Berndt et al. (2011). Suppose there are four branded cholesterol-lowering drugs, none of which faces generic competition, and the insurer has decided they are very similar. An insurer can offer to prefer the manufacturer's product with its group of customers in exchange for a lower contract price—or a higher rebate. "Preferring" the product means the insurer will increase its market share by using tools such as its formulary

---

[27] Other government purchasers include the Department of Defense, the Veterans' Administration, and the Bureau of Indian Affairs.

and financial incentives. The manufacturer decides how much of a discount it is willing to offer for the business of the group which, because it represents lots of volume and is elastic across therapeutic substitutes, has more bargaining power than any individual consumer. The insurer holds what one can think of as an auction for access to its customers, and comes away with a preferred brand and a low price. Naturally, the more differentiated are the brands, the more difficult it is for the insurer to threaten to put all but one on a high tier and discourage their use. An insurer can have a preferred brand in a category, but allow a second brand to be on the first tier for particular patients or indications. For example, Mevacor might be a preferred brand for patients needing a statin for cholesterol, while Lipitor might be preferred only for patients with cholesterol levels above a certain cutoff. Sometimes the contract between the insurer and the preferred brand, call it Brand A, includes a performance requirement, and sometimes the discounts are geared to the level of performance by the insurer. For example, suppose Brand A had a 20 percent share nationally. The insurer might get a 5 percent discount regardless of usage, an additional 10 percent discount if the market share of Brand A—among all drugs in the therapeutic class—reached 30 percent, and a further 5 percent discount if the market share of Brand A was as high as 50 percent. Thus to obtain the lowest prices on branded drugs in the US, a buyer should be both large and able to effectively "move market share" across brands.

It is not as easy to move patients from one brand to a similar brand as it is to effect generic substitution. As described in section 2, pharmacists can or must substitute generics for brands without informing or obtaining permission from the doctor. However, changing the drug dispensed to a therapeutic substitute requires a different prescription from the physician. Insurers or PBMs must work with physicians, pharmacists, and patients using information, social norms, and financial incentives in order to shift prescribing behavior. A PBM can mail a letter describing the formulary to the physician, but since a physician typically has hundreds of patients belonging to dozens of insurance plans, each with a formulary that changes over time, this is often not very effective. Using a large dataset of statin (anticholesterol) purchases, Limbrock (2011) demonstrates that "preferred" status is associated with a much higher incremental market share gain for an HMO than for a standard indemnity insurer. However, he does not observe exactly what techniques the plan uses, outside of prices, to achieve this result. For example, location of physicians, concentration of insurers in the patient population, and structure of information are all plausible drivers of insurer performance. These issues form an important area for research in the intersection of health economics and organizational economics.

6.2.2. Public Sector

Because the US state and federal governments purchase a large share of pharmaceuticals, prices for government purchases are not totally unregulated. The various agencies that administer drug benefits have considerable buyer power, and have implemented a variety of purchasing policies.

6.2.2.1. Medicaid

There are mandatory rebates for drugs sold to state Medicaid programs (approximately 17 percent of the pharmaceutical market). The federal government administers the rebate program; it requires each manufacturer to calculate and submit two summary pricing measures: AMP and best price. AMP stands for Average Manufacturer Price and is the average in a calendar quarter of sales to the retail class of trade, including discounts.[28] "Best price" is the lowest per unit price at which the firm has sold in the previous quarter to any non-public buyer—essentially a minimum price. Using these inputs, the Centers for Medicare and Medicaid Services (CMS) calculate a unit rebate amount. For brands, this has two parts. First, the greater of 23.1 percent (HR 3590 Sec. 2501 Patient Protection and Affordable Care Act) or the difference between AMP and best price. In this way, the rebate rule ensures that Medicaid receives the minimum price offered by the manufacturer if that generates a lower net price than the fixed percentage discount. This rebate rule is easy to recognize as a most-favored nation (MFN) provision. Scott Morton (1999) shows that, upon imposition, these rules raised minimum (and average) prices for pharmaceutical products in markets where Medicaid market share was high. In addition, the rebate has an inflation component, which has grown to be of significant magnitude. If a manufacturer increases prices faster than the rate of inflation (CPI-U), the additional increase must be returned to the state Medicaid programs as part of the rebate. Since drug prices have grown faster than general prices over the last 20 years, many drugs have significant inflation components. Duggan and Scott Morton (2006) find suggestive evidence that for high-Medicaid-share products the inflation component creates an incentive for manufacturers to launch new versions (pill versus capsule) of their drugs in order to obtain a new launch price (and reset the inflation calculation). The sum of the inflationary component plus the greater of the basic rebate or best price forms the rebate percentage. The head of the Congressional Budget Office testified in 2005 that the total rebate for branded drugs averaged 31.4 percent.[29] The rebate for generics is smaller because the basic rebate is lower for generics (11 percent, increasing to 13 percent in 2011) and the inflationary component is less significant since nominal prices tend to fall over time.

---

[28] The calculation of AMP is somewhat complex; the discounts and customers that are included or excluded from AMP calculations are provided in federal regulation.

[29] See Mr. Holtz-Eakin's testimony for a summary of the Medicaid rebate and pharmaceutical pricing. http://www.cbo.gov/doc.cfm?index=6564&type=0

6.2.2.2. Medicare

Two components of Medicare now cover pharmaceutical purchases. Prior to the introduction of Part D, Medicare Part B (physician services) only reimbursed drugs delivered in a physician's office.[30] Physician-administered drugs are drugs that are not taken at home by the patient, but are administered—usually injected or infused—in a physician's office. Prior to 2006, Medicare paid the physician a percentage of a branded drug's list price and many private payers did the same. For example, a list price of $100 would first be marked up by 25 percent (to create AWP), and then be reimbursed at 95 percent of $125, or $119. The patient is responsible for a 20 percent co-payment on the drug, or $24 in this example. This system yielded a positive margin on the drug if the physician could collect the co-payment from the patient and purchased the drug near list price.[31] However, in situations where there was therapeutic competition among physician-administered products, purchase prices of these drugs sometimes fell significantly below list prices. Because many of these products are expensive, the margin the physician earned for dispensing the drug grew large in dollar terms in these situations. In 2006, the Medicare Modernization Act (MMA) altered the Medicare payment for physician-administered drugs to 106 percent of the average sales price (ASP) of the product in the previous quarter, including all discounts and rebates. ASP is calculated by the manufacturer for each of its drugs and reported to CMS each quarter. ASP data became public beginning in 2005 through CMS. Many private payers changed their reimbursement procedures to match Medicare, so the ASP methodology is now very prevalent. The profit margin for the physician on the drug is proportional to the cost of the drug, which is appropriate if some of the physician's costs are inventory, for example. Furthermore, the physician has an incentive to search for low-cost sources of the drug, since he is reimbursed at a fixed price. If buyers create price competition that drives down market price, or price changes for any other reason, the next quarter's ASP will reflect those changes.

Payments to hospitals are made using fixed payments for diagnoses. Medicare pays hospitals a set rate for a patient with a particular condition (DRG, or diagnosis-related group). This leaves the hospital as residual claimant and so it has an incentive to minimize costs. Physician-administered drugs given in a hospital are therefore not reimbursed directly (using ASP or any other methodology) but the hospital must pay for them out of the bundled DRG payment. The hospital, however, has influence over

---

[30] This is also largely true in private sector health plans—the physician-administered drugs are included under the medical benefit rather than the pharmacy benefit. Interestingly, the management services of the PBM have not been used extensively in the medical benefit compared to their penetration in the pharmacy benefit. Rather than creating a formulary and establishing financial incentives to use particular products, as would be done by a PBM, payers often reimburse the physician for physician-administered drugs using a fixed-price contract.

[31] Patients with supplemental insurance, such as Medigap, use that coverage to pay their co-payments. In a simple example like this, a physician can break even on drug costs even if a large fraction of his patients do not pay their drug co-payments.

the pharmaceutical treatments physicians can prescribe to patients in the hospital. The hospital can therefore bargain in the same manner as a PBM. It negotiates for the lowest price possible, and can threaten to use a therapeutic substitute if its price and quality are superior.

The share of pharmaceutical expenditure that is physician administered is growing because the biologic market is growing and many of these drugs are injectables. The problem of developing cost-effective procurement techniques for biologics and physician-administered drugs is unresolved and will be an interesting area for future research. For example, one physician likely sees patients from many different insurance plans, and those plans may contract with different competing physician-administered drugs. If there were several biosimilars on the market, it is hard to know how the physician would stock them all, handle the logistics, keep track of expiration dates, and afford the inventory cost. While the institutions that have grown to create competition among generic drugs and drive down prices do not generally exist for biologics, Medicare's significant share of the market implies that the regulations by which Medicare purchases or reimburses physicians for biologics will greatly affect incentives for price competition and entry.

The introduction of Medicare Part D expanded coverage of pharmaceuticals. Part D does not, at present, require rebates, though beneficiaries only pay about 25 percent of the cost of the basic Part D benefit, with federal subsidies making up the balance. Instead, private insurance companies negotiate over prices as usual with manufacturers. Critics thought this would result in high prices being paid by Part D and indirectly by taxpayers. In fact, Duggan and Scott Morton (2010, 2011) show that prices in Part D, at least for the first two years of the program, were lower than cash prices paid by seniors who were uninsured before the inception of the program. The analysis exploits variation across drugs in the share of patients eligible for Medicare in 2002/03, before the program was passed or begun. The drugs with higher sales to Medicare-eligible patients experience a drop in price (IMS revenue divided by IMS quantity) in 2006 relative to other drugs. Further, the drop moves with the drug's share of "uninsured in 2003, but Medicare eligible" patients. Lastly, the drop does not occur for drugs with market power due to their position on the CMS formulary. This suggests that insurer bargaining was ineffective in lower prices for drugs that had no therapeutic substitutes.

6.2.2.3. Other

Other government entities, such as the Veterans' Administration and the Department of Defense, also purchase drugs, and achieve some of the lowest transaction prices. These agencies purchase drugs off the Federal Supply Schedule and have some of the most aggressive and restrictive formularies in the country, especially the VA. This results in the Veterans' Administration purchasing at what are widely regarded as the lowest prices in the US. Many comparisons are made to VA prices without adequate recognition that the VA restricts access by beneficiaries to many therapies that it considers cost ineffective. The VA and DoD are also helped in their negotiations by being exempt from the "best price" provision in the Medicaid rebate rules so that discounts made to them do not trigger an increase in a manufacturer's rebates. Clearly, a buyer that has the ability to negotiate for a low price would prefer to be exempt from the Medicaid MFN so that the seller is not weighing the fact that all his Medicaid sales will also occur at the negotiated price. Many buyers would therefore like to be exempt from the best price rule. Since 1991, Congress has passed additional regulations that exempt progressively more buyers. The regulations are subject to interpretation, but many observers conclude that rebates to a PBM that does not take delivery of the product should be exempted from the best price calculation—and PBMs collectively serve a large share of the market. By contrast, a manufacturer's price to a traditional HMO that runs its own pharmacies (e.g. Kaiser) does get included in the best price calculation. We see here an example of how the government's price regulation favors certain organizational forms in the delivery of health care and penalizes others.

A recent clever pricing innovation from manufacturers that makes an interesting topic for future research is the impact of brand coupon cards. These are cards issued by a manufacturer that pay the difference between a patient's generic co-payment and branded co-payment. That charge is borne by the manufacturer, which directly pays the pharmacy. By absorbing the difference between the products, the manufacturer removes the patient's financial incentive to buy the generic. As explained above, this financial incentive is created purposefully by the PBM to drive consumption to more cost-effective products. Because the difference in the co-payment is typically much smaller than the difference in price of the two products, the insurer's costs are higher when the consumer chooses the brand. The problem for the insurer is that typically it cannot tell that the consumer has used the coupon card because the data from the pharmacist only shows that the branded co-pay was paid—not how it was paid. This nicely demonstrates the strategic interaction between the PBM, who is trying to drive demand to low-cost products, and the branded manufacturer, who is trying to negate those incentives.

7. MARKETING OF PHARMACEUTICALS IN THE UNITED STATES

Because pharmaceutical firms spend as much on promoting their products as they do on research and development (Gagnon and Lexchin, 2008), drug advertising is a contentious issue in policy debates. Few products sell for the markups of price over marginal cost that characterize drugs. High margins also imply what a manufacturer will spend on marketing to increase demand (Dorfman and Steiner, 1954). The net revenue return on marketing depends on the elasticity of quantity with respect to marketing and the margin of price over cost. Particularly for new products, marketing can introduce awareness and thereby increase quantity. However, marketing efforts that provide financial or non-pecuniary benefits to physicians may be less benign. Competition also drives advertising: if a rival invests in promotional efforts, a firm's best response is to increase its own marketing.

A significant fraction of all pharmaceutical firm promotional expenditure is spent on "detailing." Promotion of prescription pharmaceutical products directly to physicians appears to be effective in selling those drugs, though it is important to know whether the increase in sales is a result of information provision or the physician acting as an imperfect agent for patients. In a perfect world, physicians might choose which drugs to prescribe by reading professional journals where academic studies or new advances in the field were presented impartially, perhaps by experts in the area. Instead, a significant source of physician information about new pharmaceutical treatments is the manufacturers of the products themselves (Podolsky et al., 2008). While physicians may believe that their judgment is not affected by detailing, academic work on the use of generics suggests otherwise. In the few months before a brand loses patent protection, its manufacturer typically stops detailing it because the manufacturer anticipates much of the resulting sales will accrue to the generic drug. When the patent expires and the generic enters, the effective price of the molecule falls. However, Huckfeldt and Knittel (2010) show that on average, the total number of units of the drug consumed, both brand and generic, *also* falls noticeably around patent expiration, which is not what an ordinary model of demand would predict. They estimate a 20 percent drop in quantity prescribed on average from six months before patent expiration to six months after. The authors conclude that the reduction in detailing best explains the decline in the quantity sold of the molecule. The drug itself is unaltered and, indeed, has become cheaper. The effect of drop in marketing must on average outweigh any positive incentives due to the price fall.[32]

This is only one example of imperfect agency; as physicians are people subject to the behavioral biases, one might expect there are other instances of the impact of promotion on prescribing. Empirically identifying the effect of promotion on prescribing is very difficult because almost all promotion of pharmaceuticals is accompanied by some scientific information, though one would expect for a drug promoted for 10 years or more during its patent life that the "new information" content would be minimal after its introduction. Determining the causal impact of the two separately is therefore very hard. A recent article finds that Japanese physicians surveyed "believed

[32] The exception to this pattern is the entry of the first generic in a large therapeutic class with close substitutes, as in the example of Zocor and Lipitor above.

that they were unlikely to be influenced by promotional activities, but that their colleagues were more susceptible to such influence than themselves." This asymmetry of beliefs is a recurring theme in this literature (Saito et al., 2010). The authors conclude that Japanese doctors are "at risk" from pharmaceutical promotions. The impact of promotion on prescribing behavior is an important area for more, and better, academic research. Another interesting area for future research is the optimal regulation of pharmaceutical promotion under different assumptions about physician behavior.

Another fertile area for both empirical work and economic modeling is the nexus between off-label prescribing and promotion. Dresser and Frader (2009) point out that a problematic interaction between off-label prescribing and detailing could easily arise. The detailing force has an incentive to promote the off-label use, as this will boost sales with low effort. (Additionally, off-label sales do not generate liability for the manufacturer, as it is the physician's decision to prescribe off-label.) Further, detailing representatives are permitted to distribute academic literature that reports on off-label uses. Kirsch (2009) argues that the subset of clinical trial results that are published in the academic literature are chosen by the firm to be favorable to the product and therefore useful in marketing efforts. Osborn (2010) provides a legal treatment of regulations in off-label area and areas of potential improvement.

Promotion of pharmaceuticals is currently an active area for litigation and for new regulation. It is also an active area for self-regulation by both the medical profession and pharmaceutical firms. Many medical schools (and many HMOs) have recently significantly limited interactions with detailing representatives.[33] Medical schools and journals are also requiring more disclosure about financial ties a physician may have with a pharmaceutical firm.

Arguably, much of the impact of promotional tactics by pharmaceutical firms is likely to be business stealing and therefore zero sum. To the extent that firms are not expanding the market for the treatment but shifting shares among themselves, they may be in a prisoner's dilemma. Each firm would like to detail less, but only if the others detail less. In 2009, the industry trade association PhRMA introduced a voluntary Code on Interactions with Healthcare Professionals. This code limits informational presentations to the workplace or similar settings, limits entertainment to "modest meals," and prohibits trips to resorts, sponsored recreation, and gifts to the physicians, including little trinkets such as pens and pads with drug names on them. The Code requires the independence of continuing medical education (CME) content and the content of sponsored conferences. Companies may pay physicians to be speakers as long as the speakers are trained and their financial ties are disclosed. Manufacturers cannot agree among themselves to limit marketing without violating US antitrust laws. Nonetheless, the 2009 voluntary PhRMA code may be advantageous

---

[33] http://www.amsascorecard.org/ is an interesting website containing medical school policies.

for the industry in several ways: it lessens the possibility of regulation and restricts promotional competition among firms. It also arguably improves the quality of information received by medical professionals. The impact of these changes on the design of clinical trials, marketing choices by firms, utilization, and prices is an important area for future research.

There is a burgeoning literature on the effects of Direct-to-Consumer (DTC) advertising on drug consumption and cross-price elasticities of demand. DTC is often used to expand the market. Many of the therapeutic categories in which there is a lot of DTC are underdiagnosed or undertreated therapeutic areas, such as depression or seasonal. A person who sees an ad on TV may not have realized that there was a treatment for her problem and seek the advice of a doctor; Iizuka and Jin (2005) found that every $28 of spending on DTC advertising led to an additional doctor's visit within 12 months. A second category of DTC advertising focuses on long-term treatments for which patients have poor compliance. The length of time for which a person newly diagnosed with a chronic disease takes his medication is approximately three years on average. Wosinska (2005) shows that seeing advertisements on TV will help the patient remember that the drug is doing him good and improve his compliance. Despite its visibility, DTC is a relatively small component of total pharmaceutical promotional expenditures.

The marketing of prescription drugs in the United States is an area of active regulation and active private sector policy change. For this reason, research in areas of optimal regulation of marketing, organizational and incentive design in physician groups, and strategy and incentives of firms would make significant contributions to the economics literature and to policy.

8. CONCLUSION

Past trends are likely to be an imperfect guide to the near future with respect to trends in drug pricing and costs. Although the underlying technology of drug treatments changes slowly, regulatory chance and patent-related events can have significant effects on market conditions. There are currently a number of blockbuster small-molecule products that have just lost, or are about to lose, patent protection (Berndt and Aitken, 2010), including the world's largest selling drug by sales, Pfizer's Lipitor. The prices of these medicines will fall as generic entry occurs and (with inelastic demand) overall expenditure on small-molecule drugs will also fall, at least for the drugs with generic competitors.

Biologics may have sufficient price and quantity growth to cause overall pharmaceutical spending to continue to rise smartly. For example, one consulting report forecasts that biologic revenues will grow at a CAGR of 10 percent over the next 15 years.[34] Another sends the same message: "Big Pharma companies forecast about 60% of revenue growth to come from biologic products. The forecast revenue growth rate to 2010 for biologics is 13%, compared to 0.9% for small molecule products."[35] As noted above, what remains unclear is the extent to which competition from biosimilars will check this forecast growth.

The US and most other countries face a serious problem with rising health care costs and will have to find some method to restrict expenditure growth. A system of paying for any treatment a physician determines is necessary, at any price the innovator chooses, is unsustainable. Research into the effectiveness of solutions used in various countries will be necessary and informative to the policy debates taking place in developed countries as well as emerging markets.

In particular, current pricing patterns and mechanisms to induce innovation will continue to be challenged. As countries like India, China, and Brazil achieve higher levels of development, they will have greater ability to contribute to the cost of providing incentives for new product development. But declining R&D productivity and concerns about the shortcomings of the patent system may require rethinking the model of drug development and marketing.

REFERENCES

Acemoglu, D. & Linn, J. (2004). Market size in innovation: Theory and evidence from the pharmaceutical industry. *Quarterly Journal of Economics*, *119*(3), 1049−1090.

Adams, C. P. & Van Brantner, V. (2006). Estimating the cost of new drug development: Is it really $802 million? *Health Affairs*, *25*(2), 420−428.

Akerlof, G. A. (1970). The market for "lemons": Quality uncertainty and the market mechanism. *Quarterly Journal of Economics*, *84*(3), 488−500.

Allain, M.-L., Henry, E., & Kyle, M. (2011). *Inefficiencies in technology transfer: Theory and empirics*. CEPR Working Paper 8206.

Appelt, S. (2010). *Authorized generic entry prior to patent expiry: Reassessing incentives for independent generic entry*. SFB/TR 15 Discussion Paper 357.

Arora, A., Fosfuri, A., & Gambardella, A. (2001). *Markets for technology: The Economics of innovation and corporate strategy*. MIT Press.

Arrow, K. (1962). Economic welfare and the allocation of resources for invention. In *The rate and direction of inventive activity: Economic and social factors* (pp. 609−626). National Bureau of Economic Research, Inc.

Azoulay, P. (2004). Capturing knowledge within and across firm boundaries: Evidence from clinical development. *American Economic Review*, *94*(5), 1591−1612.

Bell, C., Griller, D., Lawson, J., & Lovren, D. (2010). *Generic drug pricing and access in Canada: What are the implications?* Toronto: Health Council of Canada.

Berndt, E. (2002). Pharmaceuticals in U.S. health care: Determinants of quantity and price. *Journal of Economic Perspectives*, *16*(4), 45−66.

Berndt, E. & Aitken, M. (2010). *Brand loyalty, generic entry and price competition in pharmaceuticals in the quarter century after the 1984 Waxman-Hatch legislation*, NBER Working Paper 16431.

[34] Biosimilars and follow-on biologics: the global outlook 2009−2024 (2010), visiongain LTD, London, England.

[35] http://www.pharmameddevice.com/app/homepage.cfm?appname=100485&linkid=23294&moduleid=3162

Berndt, E., McGuire, T., & Newhouse, J. (2011). *A primer on the economics of prescription pharmaceutical pricing in health insurance markets*. NBER Working Paper 16879.

Berndt, E. R., Gottschalk, A. H. B., Philipson, T., & Strobeck, M. W. (2005). Assessing the impacts of the Prescription Drug User Fee Acts (PDUFA) on the FDA Approval Process. *Forum for Health Economics & Policy*, Vol. 8 (Frontiers in Health Policy Research), Article 2.

Berndt, E. R., Ling, D., & Kyle, M. (2003). The long shadow of patent expiration: Do Rx to OTC switches provide an afterlife? In R. Feenstra & M. Matthew Shapiro (Eds.), *Scanner data and price indexes* (pp. 229–267). Chicago: University of Chicago Press.

Berry, S. T., Levinsohn, J., & Pakes, A. (1995). Automobile prices in market equilibrium. *Econometrica*, *63*(4), 841–890.

Blume-Kohout, M. E. & Sood, N. (2008). *The impact of Medicare Part D on pharmaceutical research and development*. NBER Working Paper 13857.

Brekke, K. R., Holmas, T. H., & Straume, O. R. (2011). Reference pricing, competition, and pharmaceutical expenditures: Theory and evidence from a natural experiment. *Journal of Public Economics*, *95* (7–8), 624–638.

Chou, Y. J., Yip, W. C., Lee, C.-H., Huang, N., Sun, Y.-P., & Chang, H.-J. (2003). Impact of separating drug prescribing and dispensing on provider behaviour: Taiwan's experience. *Health Policy and Planning*, *18*(3), 316–329.

Cockburn, I. & Henderson, R. (1998). Absorptive capacity, coauthoring behavior, and the organization of research in drug discovery. *Journal of Industrial Economics*, *46*(2), 157–182.

Cockburn, I., Grabowski, H., & Long, G. (2006). The market for follow-on biologics: How will it evolve? *Health Affairs*, *25*(5), 1291–1301.

Cockburn, I. M. (2007). Is the pharmaceutical industry in a productivity crisis? In A. B. Jaffe, J. Lerner, & S. Stern (Eds.), *Innovation policy and the economy* (Vol. 7, pp. 1–32). The MIT Press (Chapter 1).

Cohen, W. M., Nelson, R. R., & Walsh, J. P. (2000). *Protecting their intellectual assets: Appropriability conditions and why U.S. manufacturing firms patent (or not)*. NBER Working Paper No. 7552.

Danzon, P. & Chao, L.-W. (2000). Cross-national price differences for pharmaceuticals: How large and why? *Journal of Health Economics*, *19*, 159–195.

Danzon, P. & Furukawa, M. (2003). Prices and availability of pharmaceuticals: Evidence from nine countries. *Health Affairs, Jul.-Dec.*(Web Exclusives), W3-521–W3-536.

Danzon, P. & Furukawa, M. (2006). Prices and availability of biopharmaceuticals: An international comparison. *Health Affairs*, *25*(5), 1353–1362.

Danzon, P. M. & Furukawa, M. F. (2008). International prices and availability of pharmaceuticals in 2005. *Health Affairs*, *27*(1), 221–233.

Danzon, P. & Pauly, M. (2002). Health insurance and the growth in pharmaceutical expenditures. *Journal of Law and Economics*, *45*, 587–613.

Danzon, P. & Pereira, N. (2011). Exits from vaccine markets in the US: The role of competition vs. regulation. Forthcoming in *International Journal of the Economics of Business*.

Danzon, P. & Towse, A. (2003). Differential pricing for pharmaceuticals: Reconciling access, R&D, and patents. *International Journal of Health Care Finance and Economics*, *3*, 183–205.

Danzon, P., Wang, Y. R., & Wang, L. (2005). The impact of price regulation on the launch delay of new drugs—evidence from twenty-five major markets in the 1990s. *Health Economics*, *14*(3), 269–292.

David, G., Markowitz, S., & Richards, S. (2010). The effects of pharmaceutical marketing and promotion on adverse drug events and regulation. *American Economic Journal: Economic Policy*, *2*(4), 1–25.

DiMasi, J. A. (2001). Risks in new drug development: Approval success rates for investigational drugs. *Clinical Pharmacology & Therapeutics*, *69*, 297–307.

DiMasi, J. A. & Grabowski, H. G. (2007). The cost of biopharmaceutical R&D: Is biotech different? *Managerial & Decision Economics*, *28*, 469–479.

DiMasi, J. A., Hansen, R. W., & Grabowski, H. G. (2003). The price of innovation: New estimates of drug development costs. *Journal of Health Economics*, *22*(2), 151–185.

Dorfman, R. & Steiner, P. O. (1954). Optimal advertising and optimal quality. *American Economic Review*, *44*, 826–836.

Dresser, R. & Frader, J. (2009). Off-label prescribing: A call for heightened professional and government oversight. *Journal of Law, Medicine & Ethics, 37*(3), 476−486.

Dubois, P., De Mouzon, O., Scott Morton, F., & Seabright, P. (2011). *Market size and pharmaceutical innovation*. CEPR Discussion Paper 8367.

Duggan, M. & Scott Morton, F. (2006). The distortionary effects of government procurement: Evidence from Medicaid prescription drug purchasing. *Quarterly Journal of Economics, 121*(1), 1−30.

Duggan, M. & Scott Morton, F. (2010). The effect of the Medicare drug benefit on pharmaceutical prices and utilization. *American Economic Review, 100*(1), 590−607.

Duggan, M. & Scott Morton, F. (forthcoming 2011). The medium-term impact of Medicare Part D on pharmaceutical prices. *American Economic Review Papers and Proceedings*.

Dunn, A. (2010). *Drug innovations and welfare measures computed from market demand: The case of anti-cholesterol drugs*. Bureau of Economic Analysis Working Paper.

Ellison, S. F. & Snydor, C. (2010). Countervailing power in wholesale pharmaceuticals. *Journal of Industrial Economics, 58*, 32−53.

Ellison, S. F. & Wolfram, C. (2006). Coordinating on lower prices: Pharmaceutical pricing under political pressure. *RAND Journal of Economics, 37*, 2.

Ellison, S. F., Cockburn, I., Griliches, Z., & Hausman, J. (1997). Characteristics of demand for pharmaceutical products: An exploration of four cephalosporins. *RAND Journal of Economics, 28*(3), 426−446.

Fabrizio, K. & Thomas, L. G. (2011). The impact of local demand on product innovation in a global industry. *Strategic Management Journal* (forthcoming).

Frank, R. G. & Salkever, D. S. (1997). Generic entry and the pricing of pharmaceuticals. *Journal of Economics and Management Strategy, 6*, 75−90.

Furman, J., Kyle, M., Cockburn, I., & Henderson, R. (2005). Public & private spillovers, location, and the productivity of pharmaceutical research. *Annales d'Economie et Statistique, 79/80*, 165−188.

Gagnon, M.-A. & Lexchin, J. (2008). The cost of pushing pills: A new estimate of pharmaceutical promotion expenditures in the United States. *PLoS Medicine, 5*(1), e1 (doi:10.1371).

Grabowski, H. & Kyle, M. (2008). Mergers and alliances in pharmaceuticals: Effects on innovation and R&D productivity. In K. P. Gugler & B. B. Yurtoglu (Eds.), *The Economics of corporate governance and mergers*. Cheltenham, UK: Edward Elgar Publishing.

Grabowski, H., Kyle, M., Mortimer, R., Long, G., & Kirson, N. (2011). Evolution of market exclusivity. Paragraph IV Challenges and Generic Penetration.

Grabowski, H., Ridley, D. B., & Schulman, K. A. (2007). Entry and competition in generic biologics. *Managerial and Decision Economics, 28*, 439−451.

Guedj, I. & Scharfstein, D. S. (2004). *Organizational scope and investment: Evidence from the drug development strategies and performance of biopharmaceutical firms*. NBER Working Paper Series 10933.

Hellerstein, J. (1998). The importance of the physician in the generic versus trade-name prescription decision. *RAND Journal of Economics, 29*(1), 108−136.

Hemphill, S. & Lemley, M. (2011). Earning exclusivity: Generic drug incentives and the Hatch-Waxman Act. *Antitrust Law Journal* (forthcoming).

Henderson, R. & Cockburn, I. (1996). Scale, scope, and spillovers: The determinants of research productivity in drug discovery. *RAND Journal of Economics, 27*(1), 32−59.

Higgins, M. J. & Rodriguez, D. (2006). The outsourcing of R&D through acquisitions in the pharmaceutical industry. *Journal of Financial Economics, 80*(2), 351−383.

Huckfeldt, P. & Knittel, C. (2010). *Pharmaceutical use following generic entry: Paying and buying less*. University of California at Davis Working Paper.

Iizuka, T. (2007). Experts' agency problems: Evidence from the prescription drug market in Japan. *RAND Journal of Economics, 38*, 844−862.

Iizuka, T. & Jin, G. (2005). The effects of prescription drug advertising on doctor visits. *Journal of Economics & Management Strategy, 14*(3), 701−727.

Jacobson, M., O'Malley, J., Earle, C. C., Gaccione, P., Pakes, J., & Newhouse, J. P. (2006). Does reimbursement influence chemotherapy treatment for cancer patients. *Health Affairs, 25*(2), 437−443.

Jena, A. & Philipson, T. (2007). Cost-effectiveness as price controls. *Health Affairs, 26*(3), 696−705.

Kanavos, P. G. & Costa-Font, J. (2005). Pharmaceutical parallel trade in Europe: Stakeholder and competition effects. *Economic Policy, 20*(44), 751–798.

Kirsch, I. (2009). *The emperor's new drugs: Exploding the antidepressant myth.* London: The Bodley Head.

Kremer, M. & Snyder, C. M. (2003). *Why are drugs more profitable than vaccines?* NBER Working Paper No. 9833.

Kremer, M., Berndt, E., Glennerster, R., Lee, J., Levine, R., Weizsäcker, G., et al. (2011). Advance market commitments for vaccines against neglected diseases: Estimating costs and effectiveness. Forthcoming in *Health Economics.*

Kremer, M., Glennerster, R., & Williams, H. (2005). The price of life. *Foreign Policy, May/June*(2005), 26–27.

Kremer, M., Glennerster, R., & Williams, H. (2006). Creating markets for vaccines. *Innovations, 1*(1), 67–79.

Kyle, M. (2011). Strategic responses to parallel trade. *B.E. Journal of Economic Analysis and Policy: Advances, 11*(2), Article 2.

Kyle, M. & McGahan, A. (2011). Investments in pharmaceuticals before and after TRIPS. Forthcoming in *Review of Economics and Statistics.*

Kyle, M., Allsbrook, J., & Schulman, K. (2008). Does re-importation reduce price differences for prescription drugs? Lessons from the European Union. *Health Services Research, 43*(4), 1308–1324.

Lerner, J. & Merges, R. P. (1998). The control of technology alliances: An empirical analysis of the biotechnology industry. *Journal of Industrial Economics, 46*(2), 125–156.

Lichtenberg, F. (2005). Pharmaceutical innovation and the burden of disease in developing countries. *Journal of Medicine and Philosophy, 30,* 663–690.

Lichtenberg, F. R. & Waldfogel, J. (2003). *Does misery love company? Evidence from pharmaceutical markets before and after the Orphan Drug Act.* NBER Working Paper No. 9750.

Limbrock, F. (2011). Pecuniary and non-pecuniary incentives in prescription pharmaceuticals: The case of statins. *B.E. Journal of Economic Analysis & Policy (Advances), 11*(2), Article 1.

MacGarvie, M. & Koenig, P. (2011). *Regulatory policy and the location of bio-pharmaceutical FDI in Europe.* Boston University Working Paper.

Maloney, M. & Civan, A. (2006). The determinants of pharmaceutical research and development investments, with Abdulkadir Civan. *B.E. Journal of Economic Analysis & Policy: Contributions, 5*(1), Article 28.

Maloney, M. & Civan, A. (2009). The effect of price on pharmaceutical R&D. *B.E. Journal of Economic Analysis & Policy: Contributions, 9*(1), Article 15.

Maskus, K. & Ganslandt, M. (2004). The price impact of parallel imports in pharmaceuticals: Evidence from the European Union. *Journal of Health Economics, 23*(5), 1035–1057.

McGuire, T. & Bauhoff, S. (2011). Adoption of a cost-saving innovation: Germany, UK and simvastatin. In N. Klusen, F. Verheyen, & C. Wagner (Eds.), *England and Germany in Europe—what lessons can we learn from each other?* (pp. 11–26). Baden-Baden, Germany: Nomos Verlag.

Olson, M. K. (2008). The risk we bear: The effects of review speed and industry user fees on new drug safety. *Journal of Health Economics, 27*(2), 175–200.

Osborn, J. (2010). Can I tell you the truth? A comparative perspective on regulating off-label scientific and medical information. *Yale Journal of Health Policy, Law & Ethics, 10,* 299.

Pammolli, F., Magazzini, L., & Riccaboni, M. (2011). The productivity crisis in pharmaceutical R&D. *Nature Reviews Drug Discovery, 10,* 428–438.

Pavcnik, N. (2002). Do pharmaceutical prices respond to patient out-of-pocket expenses? *RAND Journal of Economics, 33*(3), 469–487.

Podolsky, S. H. & Greene, J. A. (2008). A historical perspective of pharmaceutical promotion and physician education. *JAMA: The Journal of the American Medical Association, 300*(7), 831–833.

Regan, T. (2008). Generic entry, price competition, and market segmentation in the prescription drug market. *International Journal of Industrial Organization, 26,* 930–948.

Reiffen, D. & Ward, M. R. (2005). Generic drug industry dynamics. *Review of Economics and Statistics, 87*(1), 37–49.

Ridley, D. (2011). *Payments, promotion and the purple pill.* Duke University Working Paper.

Ridley, D. B., Grabowski, H. G., & Moe, J. L. (2006b). Developing drugs for developing countries. *Health Affairs, 25*(2), 313–324.

Ridley, D. B., Kramer, J. M., Tilson, H. H., Grabowski, H. G., & Schulman, K. A. (2006a). Spending on postapproval drug safety. *Health Affairs, 25*(2), 420–428.

Saito, S., Mukohara, K., & Bito, S. (2010). Japanese practicing physicians' relationships with pharmaceutical representatives: A national survey. *PLoS ONE, 5*(8), e12193.

Scott Morton, F. M. (1999). Entry decisions in the generic pharmaceutical industry. *RAND Journal of Economics, 30*(3), 421–440.

Thiers, F. A., Sinskey, A. J., & Berndt, E. R. (2008). Trends in the globalization of clinical trials. *Nature Reviews Drug Discovery, 7*, 13–14.

Thomas, L. G. (2001). *The Japanese pharmaceutical industry: The new drug lag and the failure of industrial policy.* Cheltenham, UK: Edward Elgar.

US Congress Office of Technology Assessment (1993). Pharmaceutical R&D: cost, risks, and rewards. Pub. no. OTA-H-522. Washington: US Government Printing Office.

Varian, H. (1985). Price discrimination and social welfare. *American Economic Review, 75*(4), 870–875.

Waning, B., Diedrichsen, E., & Moon, S. (2010). A lifeline to treatment: The role of Indian generic manufacturers in supplying antiretroviral medicines to developing countries. *Journal of the International AIDS Society, 13*, 35.

Wosinska, M. (2005). Direct-to-consumer advertising and drug therapy compliance. *Journal of Marketing Research, 42*(3), 323–332.

Yadav, P. (2010). Differential pricing for pharmaceuticals: Review of current knowledge, new findings and ideas for action. Department for International Development (DFID) Report.

Yin, W. (2009). R&D policy, agency costs and innovation in personalized medicine. *Journal of Health Economics, 28*(5), 950–962.

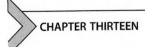

CHAPTER THIRTEEN

Intellectual Property, Information Technology, Biomedical Research, and Marketing of Patented Products

Dana Goldman and Darius Lakdawalla

Contents

Handbook of Health Economics, Volume 2
ISSN: 1574-0064, DOI: 10.1016/B978-0-444-53592-4.00013-X

Abstract

Intellectual property rights are viewed as essential to medical innovation, but very often involve social costs due to patent monopolies and other inefficiencies. We review the positive theory of innovation in health care, as it relates to the determination of innovation demand and supply. The positive theory is related to a host of competing normative models of intellectual property, including patent races, cumulative or sequential innovation, and the implications of health insurance. We also discuss how intellectual property can be used to solve a variety of production externalities that afflict health care, including network externalities, underprovision of marketing, and inefficient provision of diagnostic information. Finally, we discuss novel approaches to protecting intellectual property, including rewards, innovation subsidies, and publicly provided health insurance.

Keywords: innovation; patents; pharmaceuticals; medical devices

JEL Codes: O3; I12; I18

1. INTRODUCTION

Controversies over the appropriate scope of intellectual property (IP) rights are commonplace in today's economies, where the production and sale of knowledge has become increasingly important. Health care is no stranger to these debates, due to the important role played by costly new therapies and procedures. Similar issues arise in markets for information technology, the media, finance, and a variety of other areas that involve the production and exchange of ideas.

The primary purpose of IP rights is to provide incentives for innovators to bring their ideas to market. In many cases, the absence of IP rights would stifle new discoveries, because innovators would have no legal ability to prevent free-riding by other firms wishing to exploit their new idea. The basic principle is obvious and compelling, but the implementation is less clear. IP rights define the nature and scope of an innovator's claim over his ideas, yet a number of questions arise concerning optimal IP policy. How long should an innovator's claim over his idea last? How broad should be the innovator's ability to lay claim to related but slightly dissimilar ideas? Economists have proposed a number of different, and sometimes conflicting, answers to these questions.

The fundamental challenge posed by these and related questions traces back to the intangible nature of the ideas being protected. They are sometimes hard to define, and almost always difficult to explicitly trade in a market. As a result, the traditional approach to IP has been to protect both the idea *and* all the goods and services embodying the idea. This is the purpose of granting a patent monopoly to an innovator that protects his ability to produce goods and services over and above the idea itself.

While this patent monopoly approach is easy to implement, the drawback is clear: ideas are expensive to produce, but the resulting goods and services are often cheap. Yet IP protection of goods erases this distinction and causes both to be sold at relatively high prices. The result is an environment where, for example, prescription drugs are often very cheap to produce but sold at five to six times their marginal cost. In a purely theoretical sense, there exists a clear solution to this tension. Innovators could simply be paid for their new idea, rather than being granted property rights over all goods derived from it. This is usually very difficult to implement directly, but innovative approaches to IP are often based upon the more general principle of decoupling the innovator's reward from the prices consumers pay for goods and services resulting from the discovery.

On the other hand, granting an innovator IP over both goods and ideas may have some desirable properties as well. It allows the innovator to internalize a number of externalities that may be present in competitive markets, including: spillovers from marketing activity, network externalities from the adoption of information technology, and complementarity between diagnostic and therapeutic technology.

We survey the complex effects of traditional IP arrangements, as well as explore more recent and novel approaches to IP protection. Section 2 begins by describing forms of IP protection, both legal and *de facto*. Section 3 then theoretically and empirically describes the functioning of IP in its core role of promoting innovation. Following this positive analysis, section 4 presents a normative analysis of IP arrangements, with particular attention to the problem of ensuring dynamically efficient incentives to innovate, and statically efficient pricing of newly discovered products. Section 5 considers some of the benefits of IP for static efficiency, in terms of internalizing production externalities that competitive markets might experience. Finally, section 6 considers several alternative approaches to protecting IP.

2. FORMS OF INTELLECTUAL PROPERTY PROTECTION

We begin by describing the most common forms of IP protection in use today. These can be separated into legal exclusivity, regulatory exclusivity, and corporate secrecy.

2.1. Legal Exclusivity

The canonical approach to IP protection is the award of a patent, which grants the holder a monopoly right to produce and market the goods and services covered under the patent, typically for 20 years from the time of the application (Menell and Scotchmer, 2007). Patents are often referred to as claims of "legal exclusivity." There are two features distinguishing patent exclusivity from the two other forms we discuss. First, patents require disclosure of the underlying idea. A patent application becomes a matter of public record; this is an important distinction between a patented invention and, for instance, a corporate secret. Second, patents are legal claims that can be challenged in court. A competitor could sue to invalidate a patent by arguing that the underlying idea is not sufficiently novel to have been patented, or even that it infringes on an earlier patent that remains in force. This contingent nature of patents distinguishes them from "regulatory exclusivity," which is not subject to legal challenge.

The typical way of thinking about patents is as a means of encouraging innovation, but at the expense of competitive and efficient pricing of the newly discovered good (2010). This is the consequence of bundling the idea with the resulting goods and services. More subtly, patents offer market exclusivity in exchange for the innovator disclosing the idea. The patent allows the innovator to prevent the entry of imitators. At the same time, however, the disclosure requirement encourages other firms to incorporate the new knowledge into future innovations, and encourages the development of improvements (Menell and Scotchmer, 2007).

On balance, some innovators choose patents, in spite of the costs of disclosure, because of the promise of a lengthy monopoly on production, much longer than that afforded by regulatory exclusivity, and safer than corporate secrecy. The value of a patent can be measured by the incremental value added to an invention at the time the patent is secured. Significantly, the patent premium is positive and significant in only a few industries, but in some industries the premium is quite high. In fact, patent premiums are the highest for medical instrument, biotechnology, and pharmaceutical companies (Arora et al., 2008). The health care industry may be uniquely immune to the emerging criticism that patents are not necessary inducements for innovation (Boldrin and Levine, 2004, 2008).

The terms of patents vary and are impacted by several cross-cutting laws. Under current law, most patents hold for 20 years, apart from so-called "design patents," which persist for 14. However, the Drug Price Competition and Patent Term Restoration Act

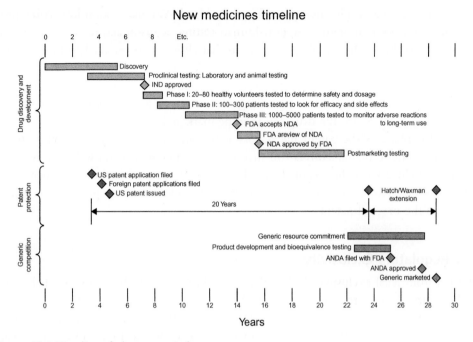

Figure 13.1 Timeline of pharmaceutical patent process.

of 1984 (Public Law 98-417), often referred to as the "Hatch-Waxman Act," recognized that part of a drug's patent life occurs prior to the date of FDA approval. Therefore, the innovator cannot recover profits for at least part of the patent term. As a result, the Hatch-Waxman Act extended the term of pharmaceutical patents by five years.

The Hatch-Waxman Act also establishes the process by which generic manufacturers can seek approval from the US Food and Drug Administration (FDA) for generic small molecule drugs. The Act allows generic manufacturers to file an Abbreviated New Drug Application (ANDA), which obviates the need to conduct new clinical trials for a generic molecule, and allows the generic applicant to rely on the data generated by the original innovator. Moreover, the Hatch-Waxman Act also provides incentives for generic manufacturers to challenge patents in court, under its "Paragraph IV." Patent challenges entail a free-riding problem similar to that of innovation itself: it is costly to invalidate a patent in court, yet a whole host of firms could benefit from a successful challenge. The result is that no firm has adequate incentive to challenge a patent. Paragraph IV of the Hatch-Waxman Act provides generic manufacturers with six months of generic exclusivity in the event that they successfully challenge the patent of a branded manufacturer. During this period, only two firms can produce the molecule (Mossinghoff, 1999; Sanjuan, 2006).

Figure 13.1, taken from Mossinghoff (1999), provides a timeline of the pharmaceutical patent process. After new drug discovery, a patent is filed. The initial term of the patent is 20 years, plus five years from the Hatch-Waxman extension. After pre-clinical testing in a laboratory or non-human setting, a manufacturer can receive an Investigational New Drug (IND) application that allows it to proceed to human testing. This occurs in three phases, with progressively larger study populations. If the molecule successfully passes all three phases of testing, the innovator can submit a New Drug Application (NDA), including the results of all phases of testing. If the FDA approves this NDA, the drug can then be marketed.

The last phase of the patent life occurs as the product nears patent expiration. At this point, generic manufacturers can invest in tests designed to show bioequivalence of their product with the original branded drug. If successful, they can receive an ANDA, which allows them to market the generic product at the expiration (or invalidation) of the original patent.

2.2. Regulatory Exclusivity

Distinct from legal exclusivity is "regulatory exclusivity," which cannot be challenged in the courts. There are several channels through which regulatory exclusivity may be granted. One is through the Orphan Drug Act, which grants an innovator an exclusive license to market an eligible orphan drug for a specific indication, for 7 years (Thamer et al., 1998). An "orphan drug" is a treatment for a rare or orphan disease, as defined by the Orphan Drug Act (ODA). Passed in 1983, the US ODA defined an orphan drug as one that treats a disorder affecting fewer than 200,000 people in the US. Orphan drug exclusivity is the strongest form of regulatory exclusivity. It cannot be challenged in court, and no competitor can gain approval for a drug treating the relevant orphan indication.

A more common channel of regulatory exclusivity is known as "data exclusivity." Specifically, data exclusivity in the pharmaceutical industry refers to the period of time after approval of a new chemical entity before a generic manufacturer can use the proprietary safety and efficacy data that were submitted during the original approval process in seeking marketing approval (Goldman et al., 2011). Given the high cost of conducting clinical trials, data exclusivity makes it costly for competitors to enter, even though they technically can choose to conduct their own clinical trials and seek approval on the basis of their own studies. In practical terms, this is often a prohibitively costly barrier to entry. Apart from the patent provisions described above, the Hatch-Waxman Act provides originators of new chemical entities with five initial years of data exclusivity, plus an additional three years for supplemental applications. In addition, the Food and Drug Administration Modernization Act of 1997 provides a six-month extension for pediatric applications. For comparison, the duration of data exclusivity in Europe is 10 years plus an additional year if a new indication is added that provides significant clinical benefits over existing therapies. The National Academies of Science and Engineering have called for the US to "adopt the European [data exclusivity] period" of 10 years and recommended that research be undertaken to determine whether even that duration is adequate, "given the complexity and length of drug development today."

Data exclusivity affords intellectual property protection that is distinct from the protection provided by patents. In the US, patents begin at the date of patent filing—generally before clinical trials begin—whereas data exclusivity begins on the date a drug is approved for marketing by the FDA. Patents can and often are challenged in courts, thus creating uncertainty for the patent-holder. Data exclusivity, by contrast, cannot be legally challenged. So data exclusivity protection not only provides extended periods of protection even after patents expire, but also provides insurance to patent-holders while patents are in effect, since there is a risk that the patents will be invalidated. Once a small-molecule drug enjoys neither patent protection nor data exclusivity, generic companies can apply for the right to market a generic version of the original drug on the basis of bioequivalence tests rather than new clinical trials. Since data exclusivity protects the trial data submitted and used by the FDA in its approval determination, its scope depends in part on the preferences and rules of regulatory bodies. Agencies that impose greater evidentiary burdens on applicants end up granting broader protection through data exclusivity, and vice versa.

Regulatory exclusivity in all its forms differs from patent protection in its immunity from legal challenge, and in the absence of a disclosure requirement. Indeed, data exclusivity is founded on the innovator's right not to disclose data. Prior to the adoption of the Hatch-Waxman Act mentioned above, pharmaceutical test data was protected as a trade secret (Sanjuan, 2006).

2.3. Corporate Secrecy

A final form of IP protection is corporate secrecy. This is not used in the pharmaceutical industry for approved drugs, because the FDA approval process requires disclosure. However, it may be relevant for other forms of health care innovation, such as information technology or medical devices. In addition, failed preclinical research efforts may be protected by secrecy rather than patent applications. Similarly, before a new drug enters the FDA review process, a constellation of facts surrounding it may also be kept secret. Moreover, manufacturing and research processes may also be protected by secrecy, even in the pharmaceutical industry. In general, regulatory constraints impinge upon firms' ability to keep secret information about drugs that enter the clinical testing phase. However, drugs, processes, and other discoveries that never enter testing are not subject to these constraints, and may be protected by secrecy.

In general, the trade-off between secrecy and other forms of IP protection turns on the costs of delay, disclosure, and the risks of information leak. An innovator with a time-sensitive idea might wish to avoid the time cost of a patent application. Conversely, an innovator with a long-lived idea might wish for protection that is longer than 20—25 years (Menell and Scotchmer, 2007). Indeed, outside the pharmaceutical industry, patents tend to be the least emphasized form of IP protection (Cohen et al., 2000).

Corporate secrecy is not entirely *de facto*, but is also assisted by trade secret law. Once an idea is released, it is not protected by trade secret law. However, if an inventor takes "reasonable" steps to secure an idea, it can take remedial legal action against any firm or individual that appropriates the idea for their own use. In this way, trade secret law lowers the cost of protecting sensitive information by suggesting a "reasonable" threshold up to which an inventor must protect the idea (Menell and Scotchmer, 2007).

A recent phenomenon that falls outside the rubric of the secrecy—IP trade-off is that of "open-source" technology development. Open-source development is the free and public exchange of information without any secrecy or intellectual property restrictions. Most often observed in the software industry, the open-source movement may seem hard to explain in the context of traditional economic theory. Lerner and Tirole (2009) acknowledge this poor fit, but also point out a number of simple economic explanations that predict open-source. Developers who wish to signal their own skill might like to disclose their inventions, in the hopes of securing better jobs and investment capital in the future. Such "career concerns" are more directly related to the incentives of the individual developers, and farther removed from a firm that might employ them. While they do not make explicit comparisons to health care, their explanation does suggest why we do not often see open-source pharmaceuticals, for instance. Software can be developed by an individual or a small group of individuals, with relatively modest capitalization requirements. The primary incentive may thus be the developers' personal career goals. More expensive research projects will tend to draw in investors and firms with stronger interests in safeguarding their intellectual property, either through secrecy or patent protection. That said, the open-source software movement has not yet been fully analyzed by economists.

3. MARKET EXCLUSIVITY AND THE INCENTIVES TO INNOVATE

There are a number of alternative theories of innovation (Menell and Scotchmer, 2007). The "evolutionary model" asserts that R&D investment occurs whenever profit drops below a threshold level (Nelson and Winter, 1982). The "induced technical change" model argues that changes in relative factor prices spur invention to economize on the scarcer factor of production (Hicks, 1932). The "ideas" model of innovation, on the other hand, stresses that the idea itself is the scarce factor driving new discoveries (O'Donoghue et al., 1998). The distribution of ideas across firms and entrepreneurs thus plays a critical role.

3.1. The Simple Theory of Innovation

As a vehicle for organizing our discussion, we take the last and perhaps "canonical" theory of innovation, due to Nordhaus (1969), who argues that investments into the discovery of innovation rise with the profits expected from successful discovery.

This point can be made most simply in the context of a model with two periods—one for investments into discovery, and one in which the outcome of this investment is realized. A critical assumption of the model is the monotonic relationship between innovative investments and the probability of successful discovery. Define I as the total level of investment into innovative activity, and $p(I)$ as the probability of a successful discovery, where $p'(I) > 0$ and $p''(I) < 0$. Next, define D as the state of the world in which a discovery occurs, and N as the state in which no discovery occurs. $E(\pi|D)$ is the innovator's expected profit, conditional on discovery, and similarly for $E(\pi|N)$. Innovation investments will be undertaken if and only if $E(\pi|D) > E(\pi|N)$. To allow for the possibility that the firm may not have to bear all the cost of innovation—e.g. if some portion of research is publicly funded—define $\phi(I) \le I$ as the firm's investment outlay. Finally, define r as the cost of capital.

The resources that the firm expects to have in the event of discovery are equal to $E(\pi|D) - (1+r)\phi(I)$, and in the event of no discovery, $E(\pi|N) - (1+r)\phi(I)$. Therefore, the privately optimal level of innovation is given by the solution to:

$$\max_I p(I)E(\pi|D) + (1 - p(I))E(\pi|N) - (1 + r)\phi(I)$$

This has the first-order condition:

$$p'(I)[E(\pi|D) - E(\pi|N)] = (1 + r)\phi'(I)$$

This condition implies that the marginal private cost of capital (right-hand side) is set equal to the marginal private return of innovation investment (left-hand side). This simple and intuitive condition has a number of important implications. First, all else being equal, innovation investment will rise with the expected gain from discovery, which is the term in square brackets. Second, investment will also rise with increases in the marginal productivity of investment, $p'(I)$. Third, increases in the marginal cost of capital will depress innovation investments.

3.2. Empirical Evidence on the Simple Theory

Pharmaceutical innovation is costly. Estimates suggest that the average capitalized cost of bringing a new biopharmaceutical to market is $1.2 billion in total (DiMasi and

Grabowski, 2007). This suggests the importance of innovation incentives in determining the level of innovation. Since this is an equilibrium number averaged over all observed drugs, it also suggests the high willingness of buyers to pay for new products that are more expensive to develop, and presumably more innovative.

In an early study, Mansfield argues that 65 percent of pharmaceuticals would not have been introduced and 60 percent would not have been developed without patents. For the next highest industry, chemicals, the percentages are 30 and 38 percent, respectively (Mansfield, 1986a). The contribution of intellectual property protection, and patents in particular, has remained an active area of empirical research. Consensus has emerged that patent protection stimulates innovation, but the magnitude remains open to debate.

3.2.1. Demand for Innovation Investment

The primary rationale for patents and other "pull" mechanisms for encouraging innovation is that innovative investment and activity will increase with the expected gain from discovery: patents create monopolies for newly discovered or invented products and therefore increase expected gains from investments in innovative activity. Thus, the way innovators respond to increases in profit opportunities plays a key role in the policy debate over the optimal design of patents. This knowledge is also paramount in understanding the potential dynamic welfare implications of public policies—like price regulation, national health insurance, and the like—that affect the expected gains from discovery of new products. Such public policies are especially common in pharmaceutical markets where several OECD countries have a range of regulations in place for curtailing revenues and profits of pharmaceutical firms (Sood et al., 2009).

Despite the importance of this parameter, especially for pharmaceutical markets, only a few studies credibly estimate innovator responsiveness to changes in expected gain from discovery. Here, we summarize existing studies and highlight some of the empirical challenges in estimating this parameter.

3.2.1.1. Price Regulation and Innovation

There are two strands of studies in this literature. The first establishes the extent to which price regulations reduce prices and revenues in pharmaceutical markets, and whether innovative products are disproportionately affected by such regulations. The second examines the extent to which price regulations affects innovative activity and R&D investments.

Several papers find that price regulations reduce pharmaceutical revenues and prices, and some studies find that new and innovative drugs are hit harder by such regulations. Some of these papers compare pharmaceutical prices or spending in regulated and unregulated markets (Comanor, 1986; Ekelund and Persson, 2003;

Martikainen et al., 2005). For example, a recent study by the US Department of Commerce reviewed pricing in 11 OECD countries and found that, for patented drugs that were best sellers in the United States, the prices in other OECD countries were between 18 and 67 percent less than US prices, depending on the country. They conclude that price deregulation in these countries would increase pharmaceutical revenues from 25 to 38 percent (US Department of Commerce, 2004). Similarly, Ekelund and Persson (2003) find that in contrast to the unregulated market in the US, prices of new drugs in all classes fall faster in the regulated market of Sweden. Another study, Martikainen et al. (2005), finds that wholesale prices for newly launched reimbursable pharmaceuticals were highest in countries where manufacturers are free to set their own prices. Finally, Danzon and Chao (2000) find a negative relation between strict price regulation and the price of widely approved molecules. In general, these studies are limited by their reliance on cross-sectional variation in revenues or prices, and their resulting vulnerability to heterogeneity across countries in type of regulation and other price determinants.

There are some studies that address the heterogeneity problem by analyzing longitudinal data and comparing pharmaceutical expenditure before and after policies take effect (Pavcnik, 2002; Pekurinen and Hakkinen, 2005). For example, Pavcnik estimated a 10 to 26 percent decrease in drug prices as a result of a reference pricing policy introduced in Germany after 1989. Similarly, Brekke et al. (2009) estimated that introduction of reference pricing in Norway reduced both brand name and generic prices within the reference group, with the effect being stronger for brand names. Pekurinen and Hakkinen (2005) suggested that voluntary generic substitution and prescribing policies had no effect on expenditures in Finland, but that compulsory generic substitution decreased prices and led to cost savings in the first year after introduction. Sood et al. (2009) exploit variation in a variety of pharmaceutical regulations in 19 OECD countries over the period 1992 to 2004. They find that most regulations reduce pharmaceutical revenues significantly and that the cost-reducing effects of price controls accumulate with time since implementation. However, these estimates might underestimate the true effects of regulations if countries implement regulations in response to rising pharmaceutical spending.

Although the evidence on the effects of price regulation on pharmaceutical revenues is fairly substantial and convincing, the evidence on the effects of price regulation on pharmaceutical innovations is not as well developed. Vernon (2005) examines whether firms with a larger proportion of sales in the US market invest more in pharmaceutical R&D. The argument is that firms with larger US sales share are less exposed to price regulation, as most other major pharmaceutical markets have some sort of price regulation in place. The empirical evidence is consistent with the hypothesis that price regulation reduces pharmaceutical R&D. However, it is also possible that firms that are not focused on innovation tend to operate in non-US markets.

Other studies in this literature estimate the relationship between (current or lagged) revenues and R&D investments (or innovation) and use these results to simulate the expected effects of price controls. Most of these studies do not explicitly address the problem that sales or revenue in turn might be affected by the level of innovation. However, some recent papers have used discrete policy changes or instrumental variables to estimate the causal relationship between expected revenues and innovation. The next section describes these papers in detail.

3.2.1.2. Market Size, Public Policies, and Innovation

Acemoglu and Linn (2004) is one of the few papers to estimate a direct causal link between expected market size and innovation in the pharmaceutical industry. They exploit plausibly exogenous variation in market size for different drug classes driven by demographic trends in the US population. They find that innovation is fairly responsive to expected market size. In particular, they find that a 1 percent increase in expected market size is associated with a 4 to 6 percent increase in the number of new molecular entities entering the market. These results are robust to controls for a variety of supply-side factors such as public R&D funding and drug class-specific time trends. However, they may overstate the true causal parameter, if increased innovation in one drug class comes at the expense of reduced innovation in other drug classes. Suppose, for example, that the future demand for oncology products rises, but that the demand for childhood vaccines remains constant. If innovators face imperfect capital markets, they may finance the increase in oncology innovation by cutting spending on childhood vaccines. Specifically, this type of outcome requires that innovators face lower costs of internal capital compared to external funding from lenders and investors; while this is difficult to prove conclusively, we discuss the evidence below. In any event, Acemoglu and Linn assume away this type of negative spillover, which would bias their estimate upward.

Other papers in this strand of literature use variation in market size induced by discrete policy changes to estimate the responsiveness of innovation. In a recent paper, Blume-Kohout and Sood (2009) assess the impact of Medicare Part D on pharmaceutical research and development (R&D), using time-series data on: (a) the number of drugs in clinical development by therapeutic class, and (b) R&D expenditures by firm. They demonstrate that the passage of Medicare Part D was associated with significantly higher pharmaceutical R&D for drug classes with higher Medicare market share, and for firms specializing in higher Medicare-share drugs. The magnitude of their estimates appears to be consistent with Acemoglu and Linn. For example, Duggan and Scott Morton (2010) predict that Medicare Part D increased pharmaceutical revenues by roughly 33 percent for drugs with Medicare market share of 100 percent. For a drug class with the average Medicare market share in their sample (42 percent), Duggan and

Scott Morton's result translates to a 14 percent change in pharmaceutical revenues following Medicare Part D. Combining these results with the innovation elasticity estimates from Acemoglu and Linn, one would expect an increase of between 49 and 83 percent in new drug development for the average drug class. The Blume-Kohout and Sood estimates are generally within this range, if toward the more conservative end in many cases.

Another important paper in this literature is Finkelstein (2004), who studies R&D investments in vaccine markets. Finkelstein finds that the Centers for Disease Control and Prevention (CDC) recommendation that all infants be vaccinated against Hepatitis B, the decision by Medicare to cover the costs of flu vaccinations for Medicare beneficiaries, and the introduction of a policy that reduced liability costs for vaccine manufacturers led to an approximately 2.5-fold increase in new clinical trials for vaccines for affected diseases. These estimates are difficult to compare to the prior literature as they apply only to the market for vaccines, and because the paper does not report the elasticity of innovation with respect to market size.

3.2.1.3. Health Insurance and the Demand for Innovation

Health insurance is frequently thought of as both a cause and effect of the demand for innovation investment. On the one hand, insurance expands demand for newer, more expensive technologies. On the other, increases in health care cost raise the demand for insurance products themselves (Weisbrod, 1991).

A useful example of this mutual causation is the case of prescription drug insurance (Danzon and Pauly, 2001). Advances in information technology allowed for the near-immediate adjudication of claims at pharmacies. This development stimulated the spread of insurance for prescription drugs. In turn, the increase in insurance stimulated more prescription drug purchases, which then led to a further expansion in the demand for coverage. This example illustrates the role of supply-side breakthroughs in the insurance market on the demand for innovation investment. Effectively, insurance innovations lead to health care innovation, which then stimulates demand for a greater quantity of insurance. More generally, insurance technology and medical technology should be seen as co-evolving variables.

3.2.2. Supply of Innovation Investment

In this section, we review the empirical evidence on the effectiveness of "push" or supply-side mechanisms for encouraging innovation. All such mechanisms promote R&D investment by lowering the cost of innovation. We focus on two strands of literature. The first estimates pharmaceutical industry response to policy changes that reduced the cost of innovation. The second estimates the relationship between R&D spending and cash flow or current period revenues.

3.2.2.1. Supply-side Public Policies and Pharmaceutical R&D

Studies in this literature estimate the effects of a variety of public policies aimed at reducing the costs of R&D. Most of these studies find that pharmaceutical firms significantly increase R&D expenditures and innovation in response to such policies.

McCutchen (1993) studies the impact of R&D tax credits on pharmaceutical R&D expenditures. The evidence indicates a positive and statistically significant change occurred in pharmaceutical R&D spending patterns after the tax credit went into effect. The industry increased R&D expenditures by 29.3 cents for each $1 of tax credit. Mansfield (1986b) finds that tax deductions in the US, Sweden, and Canada increased R&D by about 1–2 percent in these countries. The ratio of tax-induced R&D to foregone government revenue ranged between 30 and 40 percent.

Lichtenberg and Waldfogel (2003) analyze the effects of the Orphan Drug Act (ODA) on pharmaceutical innovation and find that it significantly increased new drug introductions. The ODA provided incentives for research through both push and pull mechanisms. The push mechanisms include a 50 percent tax credit on clinical trials for orphan drugs, clinical research grants, and FDA advice and counseling. The ODA also included a guaranteed seven-year market exclusivity period. The FDA has characterized this pull mechanism as the most sought-after incentive. Lichtenberg and Waldfogel find that in the period (1979 to 1983) before the implementation of the ODA in 1983, the number of orphan drugs increased at about the same rate as the number of other drugs. By 1998, there were more than five times as many orphan drugs as there had been in 1979, and fewer than twice as many non-orphan drugs.

In a subsequent study, Yin (2008) also finds that the ODA had a significant impact on rare disease drug development, both in terms of new clinical trials for established rare diseases, and by the recasting of existing drugs as treatments for rare diseases. He also finds that the effects of ODA were larger for more prevalent diseases. This suggests that push and pull incentives are complements, and policies that increase market size are likely to improve the effectiveness of supply-side policies that reduce the costs of R&D. A related policy is the "priority review" system, under which pharmaceutical firms developing orphan drugs are rewarded with a voucher allowing a fast-track FDA review for another (presumably more profitable) drug. A priority review appears to be worth more than $300 m for a blockbuster drug (Ridley et al., 2006).

Berndt et al. (2004) study the impact of the Prescription Drug User Fee Acts (PDUFA) of 1992 and 1997. They show that these acts reduced the cost of bringing a drug to market by reducing the time required for FDA approval. They find that implementation of PDUFA led to substantial incremental reductions in approval times beyond what would have been observed without these acts (6–7 percent annual declines during PDUFA I and 3–4 percent during PDUFA II). However, they also find that the cumulative number of new molecular entities following the passage of

PDUFA remained largely unchanged. Thus, their findings suggest that the reduction in approval times had little effect on R&D investments. One limitation of this study is the reliance on a treatment effect that is uniform across the drugs studied. As a result, they rely solely on time-series variation and lacked a contemporaneous control group. This makes it impossible to separate the effects of PDUFA from other secular trends in innovation.

Public expenditures on basic research and training of a scientific workforce might also reduce the costs of developing new drugs. Toole (2007) estimates that a link exists between public expenditures on basic and clinical research and pharmaceutical R&D expenditures. Using panel data on expenditures for seven medical classes, he finds that pharmaceutical R&D expenditures increase with public investments in basic and clinical research. The estimates indicate that a $1.00 increase in expenditures on basic and clinical research increases pharmaceutical R&D expenditures by $8.38 and $2.35, respectively. In a recent paper, Blume-Kohout (2009) finds that public expenditures on basic research increase the number of clinical trials initiated by the pharmaceutical industry. Earlier research by Ward and Dranove estimates that a 1 percent increase in government-funded basic research in a particular therapeutic category causes a 0.76 percent increase in pharmaceutical industry R&D within that category (Ward and Dranove, 1995).

3.2.2.2. Current Period Revenues and the Supply of Innovation Investments

Perhaps the most empirically important private determinant of R&D spending is cash flow. Grabowski (1968) and Grabowski and Vernon (2000) study the determinants of R&D expenditures of major pharmaceuticals firms during the period 1958 to 2004. They consistently find that cash flows are important predictors of firm-level R&D to sales ratios. Specifically, they find that pharmaceutical profit expectations and cash flows are the two biggest determinants of R&D expenditures, with cash flows as the larger contributor. This relates to the more general point, echoed by others, that the source of financing will affect investment behavior in the existence of capital market imperfections (Hubbard, 1998). Consistent with this more general literature, they hypothesize that this is the case because the internal cost of capital associated with these pharmaceutical companies is lower than the external cost of capital new debt or equity financing.

Similarly, Scherer (2001) finds that deviations from trends in gross profit margins and R&D expenditures are highly correlated. Under the canonical model, there would be no link between these variables, since short-run fluctuations in profitability should not impact the investment behavior of a forward-looking firm. However, if internal capital is cheaper, the short-run availability of profits may influence R&D expenditures.

The effects of cash flow suggest a possible role for differential costs of capital by source of funds. Define I^0 and I^1 as an investment from two different sources of capital, with costs r^0 and r^1, respectively, and $r^0 < r^1$. We can then write:

$$\max_{I^0, I^1} p(I^0 + I^1)E(\pi|D) + (1 - p(I^0 + I^1))E(\pi|N) - (1 + r^0)\phi(I^0) - (1 + r^1)\phi(I^1)$$
$$s.t. \ I^0 \leq I$$
$$I^1 \geq 0$$

Associating the multipliers λ^0 and λ^1 with these constraints, respectively, this has the first-order conditions:

$$p'(I)[E(\pi|D) - E(\pi|N)] = (1 + r^0)\phi'(I^0) + \lambda^0$$
$$p'(I)[E(\pi|D) - E(\pi|N)] = (1 + r^1)\phi'(I^1) - \lambda^1$$

The following implications emerge from this extension of the model. First, the firm will exhaust the cheaper (internal) source of funds first before relying on external financing. Second, it will only seek external funds if the marginal return on investment at the investment level $\bar{I}$ exceeds the cost of external capital. Third, the marginal return on investment will vary with $\bar{I}$. Specifically, increases in the availability of internal funds may decrease the marginal return demanded on capital investment as these funds are cheaper. Short-run bursts in profitability may temporarily lower the rate of return on investment within the firm. Note that this feature can be used to distinguish capital constraints models from expectations-based explanations. If, for example, firms use temporary bursts in profitability to infer long-run increases in profitability, then short-term increases in profits will be associated with higher return on investment. The capital constraints model, however, implies the opposite result.

Several empirical studies have found that current period cash flow predicts R&D. For instance, Bhagat and Welch find a negative relationship between prior year debt ratio and tax payments, and current R&D expenditures, along with a positive relationship between two-year lagged stock returns and current R&D (Bhagat and Welch, 1995). In addition, Giaccotto et al. (2005) find that R&D spending increases with real drug prices, with an elasticity of around 0.6.

The literature has so far not clearly distinguished between a "capital constraints" explanation and an explanation emphasizing the use of current profits as a proxy for future profits. However, there is some evidence that transient deviations from trend profits predict R&D expenditures (Scherer, 2001). The latter finding suggests the presence of capital constraints, but does not rule out the role of current-period profits in expectation formation.

A comprehensive review of the issues surrounding financing and R&D is presented by Hall and Lerner (2011). Overall, they conclude that capital market imperfections are most compelling for small and new firms. The evidence for larger firms is mixed, although they do note the revealed preference of many large firms for using internal funds. In sum, the link between cash flow and R&D is well substantiated in a number of areas, although some doubts might arise for firms with seemingly high-quality access to capital markets.

3.3. IP Design and Incentives to Innovate

A key determinant of innovation effort is the design of the patent awarded to innovators. Patents vary along at least four dimensions: length, breadth, and the variability of each of these. Patent length is the amount of time for which an innovator receives market exclusivity. Patent breadth governs the scope of market exclusivity, and the scope of product variations across which competitors cannot infringe. Both patent length and scope are subject to legal challenges and interpretation, which create uncertainty.

3.3.1. Patent Length

Technically, we are concerned more with the length of market exclusivity than with the length of patent protection *per se*. Market exclusivity combines both patent length and the length of data exclusivity (along with secrecy, for inventions without disclosure requirements). As mentioned earlier, patents can and often are challenged in courts, thus creating uncertainty for the patent-holder. Data exclusivity, by contrast, cannot be legally challenged. Therefore, the variability of market exclusivity depends on the length of patents, the length of data exclusivity, and the potential for patent challenges. Once a (small-molecule) drug loses either patent protection or data exclusivity, generic companies can apply for the right to market a generic version of the original drug on the basis of bioequivalence tests rather than new clinical trials.

Even without any capital market imperfections, firms will prefer a certain patent length to an uncertain one, if the marginal value of patent length is falling. Analytically, the marginal value of patent length extension is equal to per period profits earned. It thus follows that, if per period profits fall over the lifecycle of a patent, the firm will be averse to uncertainty in patent length. This implies that increased uncertainty about patent protection—holding mean patent length constant—will tend to depress innovation. Naturally, increases in the risk of patent challenges or poor patent enforcement will also reduce mean patent length, but risk aversion implies that the firm will contract innovation investments by more than the reduction in expected value alone would suggest.

3.3.2. Patent Breadth

In the economics literature, a patent is often viewed as a guarantee of monopoly power for the inventor, but the legal reality is more complicated. Patents can be fully invalidated, posing a significant risk to patent length. But, on the other hand, they can also be restricted or expanded in scope. At least two legal doctrines govern these decisions: the "doctrine of equivalents" and its companion, "the reverse doctrine of equivalents."

Practically speaking, competitors could make minor changes to a protected product and thus make an end-run around patent protection. To guard against this, courts have developed the doctrine of equivalents, which grants an inventor protection against products that are "insubstantially different" from the protected product. Clearly, however, complex issues arise when a court attempts to decide whether or not a new product is in fact "insubstantially different" from an old one. Courts may decide to exclude new inventions under the doctrine of equivalents, or allow them and thereby restrict the scope of the original patent. On the other hand, the "reverse doctrine of equivalents" holds that new products that perform essentially the same function as a patented product, but that do so in a much-improved way, do not infringe upon the original patent. These two doctrines make concrete the considerable uncertainty surrounding the enforcement of a patent.

In the pharmaceutical context, the doctrine of equivalents revolves around whether a biochemical modification constitutes an "insubstantial" change or not. Substantiality is often judged according to the "triple identity test," which identifies patents' similarity by whether they perform the same function to a varying degree, perform that function in basically the same way, and yield the same or similar results (Albainy-Jenei, 2006).

From an economic point of view, uncertainty in patent scope, as opposed to length, creates uncertainty in the level of per period monopoly profits. In the canonical model, the net present value of expected profits is linear in per period profits, implying risk neutrality in patent scope. The situation may become more complicated if internal funds are cheaper than external funds, and if this increases the value of smooth cash flow over time.

Another subtle and relevant point is raised by Gans et al. (2008), who note that an imperfectly efficient market for technology transfer can be impacted by the degree of uncertainty surrounding patent protection. For example, asymmetric information about patent scope and value can cause the trade of ideas to break down. In this context, the resolution of uncertainty along either of these dimensions may favor one party over the other. If an inventor knows he has an unusually valuable technology, it may be worth his while to wait before attempting to sell it. In the presence of these frictions, uncertainty over patent scope or value can affect the timing of licensing decisions and can cause delays in the efficient trade of ideas. The issue of uncertainty in patent rights more generally is discussed in detail by Lemley and Shapiro (2005).

The profits earned by an innovator are a function of both patent length and breadth, and therefore several papers have explored the trade-off between patent length and breadth. That is, should patents be "long and narrow" or "short and broad?" Gilbert and Shapiro (1990) argue that long and narrow patents are preferred, because the deadweight loss from monopoly pricing increases more than proportionally with patent breadth and proportionally with patent length. However, this result is mitigated if one considers the costs of developing substitute products. Gallini (1992) argues for short and broad patents as they avoid socially wasteful costs of developing substitutes or "me-too" products. In the context of sequential innovation, a larger patent breadth effectively implies a longer patent length as larger breadth implies more time is required to introduce a patentable product. In this case, if the underlying pace of innovation is high, short and broad patents provide higher incentives for innovation (O'Donoghue et al., 1998). Finally, Klemperer argues that wider patents reduce distortion of choice between patented products and their cheaper, unpatented competitor products, but increase deadweight cost; the trade-off between deadweight costs from imperfect substitution and standard deadweight loss thus governs the relationship (Klemperer, 1990).

Finally, Encaoua et al. (2006) note that the breadth–length trade-off depends on a number of properties, such as the rate at which new innovations arrive (and thus get excluded by broader patents), and the level of technological opportunities; on balance, they conclude that the optimal patent length is 15–19 years.

3.3.3. Patent Challenges

3.3.3.1. Hatch-Waxman Challenges

As discussed above, the Hatch-Waxman Act was passed in 1984. The intended goal was to increase the availability of generic drugs,[1] although it also contained several mitigating provisions designed to extend market exclusivity for innovators. On the generic side, Hatch-Waxman streamlined the process of generic drug approval and provided rewards—six months of generic exclusivity—to generic manufacturers for successfully challenging a pharmaceutical patent. On the branded side, Hatch-Waxman provided five years of data exclusivity to innovators, beginning at the date of approval, and extended patent life by an additional five years. On balance, the passage of Hatch-Waxman appeared to increase generic drug utilization. The Congressional Budget Office estimated that the increased competition from generic drugs saved consumers \$8–10 bn in costs, but reduced after-tax returns from pharmaceutical R&D by 12 percent (Congressional Budget Office, 1998).

Paragraph IV of the Hatch-Waxman Act provides both a means and an end for generic manufacturers to challenge branded drug patents. Generic drug makers can sue to invalidate a patent on the grounds that it infringes on an existing one, or that the patent itself was not warranted. Patent challenges imply that the effective duration

---

[1] Hatch-Waxman applies primarily to "small-molecule" drugs, rather than "large-molecule" biotechnology products (Grabowski, 2008).

of market exclusivity is less than the theoretical patent life of 20 plus five, minus the length of the approval period. Less than half of patents survive to the Hatch-Waxman extension period: between 1990 and 1995, the average effective life of a pharmaceutical was 11.7 years with an average Hatch-Waxman extension of 2.33 years (Grabowski, 2002).

Patent challenges lower the expected length of market exclusivity and also create risk. In principle, pharmaceutical firms should be risk-neutral if this duration is completely random and unrelated to any of their decision variables. Therefore, increases in patent challenges function just like a reduction in patent length for pharmaceuticals. In this way, they resemble policies like price regulation, which depress the rewards for innovation. On the other hand, successful patent challenges also reduce static deadweight loss, which must be weighed against the depressive effects on innovation.

3.3.3.2. Data Exclusivity

As an additional IP protection from the Hatch-Waxman Act, regulators allow a data exclusivity period in which generic companies may not use the innovator's data on safety and efficacy. During the exclusivity period, a generic competitor seeking approval would have to conduct its own costly clinical trials. While this serves to strengthen market exclusivity, it is distinct from a patent, which grants IP over the chemical structure of a drug, rather than data about the drug. Since data exclusivity is immune to legal challenges, it establishes a "floor" on patent length (Grabowski, 2008).

Interestingly, data exclusivity protections are stronger in Europe, which ordinarily provides weaker rewards to innovators. The European Union provides 10 years of data exclusivity for new molecular entities. It also adds an extra year for drugs that get a "significant new indication" approved within their first eight years on the market (Grabowski, 2008).

The duration of the period of data exclusivity entails a trade-off between current and future generations. A longer period of data exclusivity delays entry of generic competitors, effectively extending the originator company's market exclusivity. The prospect of higher profits gives pharmaceutical companies a stronger incentive to innovate—both to create new drugs and to find new indications for existing products. At the same time, however, a delay in generic competition imposes a greater spending burden on current consumers.

3.3.4. Critiques of the Patent Mechanism

The role of patents in contributing to innovation is somewhat controversial. On the one hand, the near-universal acceptance of patents speaks to several of their key advantages (Encaoua et al., 2006; Menell and Scotchmer, 2007). First, patents create a natural scheme for Pareto-improving innovation. Innovators sell their inventions to consumers only if the consumer's willingness-to-pay exceeds the price. Second, patents decentralize the innovation process, and avoid the agency or moral hazard costs associated with direct control of research or indirect control through subsidies. Decentralization also allows well-informed inventors to make decisions about how to allocate research dollars.

The traditional model of stand-alone innovation outlined earlier implies that patents encourage innovation by increasing the rate of return on innovation. However, if one views innovation as a cumulative process where new inventions rely critically on prior knowledge, the effects of patents on innovation become less clear (Boldrin and Levine, 2002; Encaoua et al., 2006). Boldrin and Levine argue that innovators can enjoy competitive rents from innovation even in the absence of patents and these rents might be enough to promote innovation. The intuition is that imitating or copying new technologies is difficult and innovators can use their first mover advantage and complementary products to protect their invention from imitators. They argue that patents might limit innovation as they restrict the use of new technologies for follow-on products and applications. As a result, patents may fragment property rights for prior inventions among several innovators. This may introduce substantial transaction costs for "follow-on" innovators who would then have to negotiate license agreements with several prior innovators. A concrete pharmaceutical example of this problem is offered by Heller and Eisenberg. To learn as much as possible about the therapeutic effects and side-effects of potential products at the preclinical stage, firms want to screen products against all known members of relevant receptor families. But if these receptors are patented and controlled by different owners, gathering the necessary licenses may be difficult or impossible (Heller and Eisenberg, 1998). On the other side, patents may encourage rent-seeking behavior by firms who undertake just enough additional investment to create a patentable invention, even if that investment does not generate real social value. This is sometimes referred to as the phenomenon of "me-too" pharmaceuticals, although there is a substantial amount of debate over the quantitative importance of this inefficiency (Jayadev and Stiglitz, 2008; Jena et al., 2009).

Recent empirical evidence from the context of genomic sequencing provides evidence for the follow-on costs of patents conjectured by Boldrin and Levine. Williams (2010) studies the impact of patents granted to the private firm Celera for gene sequencing data. Celera obtained IP over data from a gene that it sequenced, but lost it if the publicly funded Human Genome project resequenced that gene. While Celera held IP rights over a gene's data, it received royalties from all users of the data. As a result, sequencing data discovered first by Celera were costly to access, while all sequencing data from the Human Genome project were free. Williams finds that the IP protected genes exhibited 30 percent less follow-on innovation than genes that were sequenced but not protected.

Pauly (2009) makes a distinct but concordant point about the welfare effects of pharmaceutical patents. Even those patented innovations that reduce real resource costs might not reduce spending, as the "cost-offset" will be partially or completely captured by the innovator. More generally, the "purely distributive" consequences of patents might have efficiency consequences in a world where health care spending is financed through the public sector, with its attendant deadweight loss.

Of course, a full empirical analysis of the Boldrin and Levine argument would require a comparison of these costs with the consumer surplus generated by the additional inventions of pioneer private firms, an issue less relevant in the human genome context, where public funding was a viable alternative to private R&D. Moreover, aside from their direct effect as a stimulant, patents might also benefit society by decreasing secrecy. If patent protection is not available, innovators might resort to secrecy to protect others from using their inventions. Such secrecy might impede the diffusion of knowledge and hinder follow-on innovations. One advantage of patents is that they require public disclosure of the invention, which may in itself spur follow-on discoveries. A related point is the disclosure inherent in the FDA approval process. The structure of marketed pharmaceuticals becomes a matter of public record, unlike, say, a mobile telephone. This facilitates imitation and makes it harder for inventors to protect their ideas absent patents.

In summary, whether patents encourage or discourage innovation depends on several factors, including: (1) whether the innovation process is stand-alone or cumulative, (2) the extent of transaction costs of licensing rights to prior innovation, and (3) the incentive effects of disclosure. Both these conditions might vary across industries and across markets within industries. The empirical literature suggests that the pharmaceutical industry tilts more towards the side of patents rather than secrecy or other means of IP protection. For example, Arora et al. (2003) finds that the return to patenting inventions varies across industries but is always advancing in drugs, biotech, and medical instrument industries. Similarly, Mansfield (1986a) surveyed US manufacturing firms and estimates the proportion of its inventions developed in 1981−83 would not have been developed without patent protection. He finds this proportion to be highest (60 percent) in the pharmaceutical industry. These findings are consistent with earlier evidence on the importance of patents for pharmaceutical innovation (Mansfield et al., 1981). Naturally, this evidence is merely suggestive, as it speaks to the relative suitability of patents in pharmaceuticals, rather than to an absolute measure of net benefit.

Direct evaluation of changes in patent protection on pharmaceutical innovation is difficult as most pharmaceutical products are marketed globally and thus a change in patent protection in one country will only have a small effect on the incentives to innovate. However, the adoption of the TRIPS (Trade-Related Aspects of Intellectual Property Rights) agreement by members of the WTO provides a useful case study.

Recent evidence shows that the introduction of patent protection for pharmaceutical products in developing countries did little to spur innovation for developing country diseases (Kyle and McGahan, 2009). However, this does not imply that patents do not encourage innovation or that R&D does not respond to market size. Rather, it is more likely that pharmaceutical firms have lower expectations for the enforcement of patents in developing countries, and their substantially smaller market sizes. The authors note that patent protection is associated with greater R&D investment in diseases that affect high income countries, and the treatments developed as a result may benefit people in poorer countries as well.

3.4. Cost Effectiveness and Innovation

Public provision of health care and its attendant regulations have a substantial impact on incentives to innovate. Earlier, we discussed the impact of direct price regulation on innovation, but there are a number of indirect approaches that have more complex yet important effects.

An important example is a regulatory regime based on cost-effectiveness thresholds, such as in the United Kingdom. The UK's National Institute for Health and Clinical Excellence (NICE) provides guidance to the National Health Service (NHS) on the launch of new pharmaceutical therapies. NICE typically requires that every new drug approved produce at least one additional quality-adjusted life-year for every £30,000 that it costs. Cost-effectiveness thresholds function as a type of price regulation, where price is tied to the efficacy demonstrated in clinical trials (Jena and Philipson, 2007).

Under the canonical model, the efficient price is equal to consumer surplus, and thus every marketed innovation should be just on the margin between cost effectiveness and ineffectiveness. Therefore, mandatory cost-effectiveness thresholds distort pricing decisions and depress profits below their efficient level (Jena and Philipson, 2008). The result is a decrease in innovation, as well as a decrease in the static efficiency of pricing. The normative consequences of this depend in large part on whether one thinks innovation is inadequate or excessive, but the positive implications are clear.

The counterfactual in the Jena and Philipson analysis is a hypothetical unregulated market in which innovators hold all the market power associated with their invention. The positive and normative implications are less clear in the presence of health insurance, however. First, manufacturer pricing may not affect consumer utilization, but may instead affect only rent sharing between payers and manufacturers (Lakdawalla and Sood, 2006). In this case, there would be no static efficiency consequences of publicly mandated cost-effectiveness thresholds. From a dynamic perspective, cost-effectiveness thresholds might be more or less favorable to innovators than an unregulated market, depending on the market power of health insurers. If insurers have substantial negotiating leverage against innovators, they will extract price concessions that translate into reduced profits for innovators (Lakdawalla and Yin, 2009). These could be equal to or even greater than the price restrictions imposed by cost-effectiveness thresholds.

A less conventional point arises when one considers the strategic behavior of manufacturers facing cost-effectiveness thresholds. In cases where CE thresholds are not binding, they may actually function as price floors, rather than price ceilings, as manufacturers shift their prices upward to meet the threshold (Jena and Philipson, 2009). Regulators may counter by observing prices set in countries without such thresholds, but it is clear that the price distortions introduced by such thresholds could move in either direction. In this case, CE thresholds differ fundamentally from factors related to the market power of buyers.

An emerging trend in this area is the movement towards value-based pricing, for example in the United Kingdom (Claxton et al., 2008; Goldman et al., 2010). Conceptually, value-based pricing seeks to tie the reimbursement for a therapy to its social value. It is hard to argue with this goal, but the implementation is challenging, and it is as yet unclear what form it will take. Economic theory suggests the use of patient willingness-to-pay as a benchmark for value, but this is generally unknown for a drug prior to launch, which is when pricing policies must be set. Effectively, value-based pricing in this context is much like a central planning problem, where inferences about value must be made in the absence of market-based data on revealed preference.

4. THE NORMATIVE THEORY OF MARKET EXCLUSIVITY

The normative theory of IP protection, and market exclusivity in particular, analyzes the trade-off between incentives for dynamic efficiency, and static costs associated with some forms of IP protection. Patents are the usual focus of this literature, which then weighs incentives to innovate against the deadweight costs of patent monopoly.

4.1. The Simple Normative Theory of Market Exclusivity and Innovation

Define $E(CS|D)$ as expected consumer surplus in the discovery state and $E(CS|N)$ as expected consumer surplus in the no-discovery state. The canonical model then implies the following social planner's problem:

$$\max_I p(I)E(CS|D) + (1 - p(I))E(CS|N) - (1 + r)I$$

The planner's problem has the following first-order condition:

$$p'(I)[E(CS|D) - E(CS|N)] = (1 + r)$$

Private incentives will be perfectly aligned with public incentives, so long as:

$$\phi(I) = I$$

$$E(\pi|D) - E(\pi|N) = E(CS|D) - E(CS|N)$$

Efficiency in the canonical model requires that the innovator bear the full cost of the innovation outlay, and be able to appropriate the entire marginal social value of his invention. The latter is equal to the total increment in consumer surplus generated by the new discovery.

Developing the normative implications further requires clarity around the "*ex post*" period in which profits are earned. The most common circumstance is one in which the innovator (or her licensee) enjoys a monopoly on the sale of all goods connected with the new invention. In the no-discovery state, we can think of the firm as a standard competitor, in which profits are equal to zero. A monopolist with access only to a linear pricing instrument will never be able to appropriate the full measure of consumer surplus.

This problem is made even more acute in the case of goods sold to healthy people, such as vaccines (Kremer and Snyder, 2006). Vaccines are sold before consumers know their ultimate illness status and while there is still private information about infection risk. Drugs to treat illness, on the other hand, are sold to sick people exclusively, when there is no longer private information about disease risk. The existence of private information creates heterogeneity in willingness-to-pay: individuals who face higher risk of infection are willing to pay more, and vice versa. This heterogeneity makes it harder to extract the full measure of consumer surplus. In the extreme case of homogeneous willingness-to-pay, for example, a manufacturer with monopoly power could extract all available consumer surpluses in the form of a uniform, linear price. Notably, this type of reasoning would apply, albeit in weakened form, to drugs that treat illness, but also serve as secondary prevention. For example, treatments for diabetes also prevent ophthalmologic complications, amputation, and other sequelae of the disease. Individuals may have private information about their predisposition to any or all of these potential complications; this can affect their willingness-to-pay in a similar manner.

The argument above should not be taken to imply that perfect price discrimination is always possible for a treatment. Indeed, individuals vary in their severity of illness and willingness-to-pay for treatment. However, the important point is that vaccines are sold to markets with an additional dimension of heterogeneity, making it correspondingly more difficult to extract the full measure of consumer surplus.

In sum, it will be true that

$$E(\pi|D) - E(\pi|N) < E(CS|D) - E(CS|N)$$

This leads to the underprovision of innovation. Moreover, monopoly power in the event of discovery leads to underprovision of the good that embodies the new idea. The canonical model thus predicts the existence of too little innovation investments, too few new discoveries, and too little dissemination of the new goods discovered.

These two problems are complementary, in the sense that one cannot hope for first-best innovation in the presence of second-best provision. For example, suppose one were to aim for efficient innovation investment by subsidizing investment. It would appear that the optimal policy would be to construct a subsidy such that:

$$\phi'(I) < 1$$

$$\frac{E(\pi|D) - E(\pi|N)}{\phi'(I)} = E(CS|D) - E(CS|N)$$

However, note that the presence of monopoly provision of the good lowers the consumer surplus that is actually achieved by that good. Therefore, at best, we can achieve a second-best level of innovation that is optimal, relative to the new, lower level of consumer surplus. Policy approaches that tackle both problems simultaneously are thus preferable.

The argument for underprovision of innovation relies on the inability of the innovator to capture the full value of social surplus. Several papers in the literature have empirically examined the rate at which innovators appropriate total social surplus. Nordhaus (2004) examines a range of innovations—not just in the pharmaceutical industry—from 1948 to 2001. He concludes that innovators capture 2.2 percent of total present value to society of their inventions. Nordhaus bases his approach on a calibrated model of demand, consumer surplus, and profit. A key assumption is the linear pricing of inventions, and the "appropriability ratio," or the extent to which innovators can harvest consumer surplus given the type of demand curve they face.

An appropriability estimate specific to the pharmaceutical literature is that of Philipson and Jena (2006). They consider the case of HIV treatments, where they estimate that approximately 5 percent of the social surplus is appropriated by innovators. They calculate social surplus using estimates of survival increase implied by the new treatments, and then valuing these using an economic framework for the willingness-to-pay for survival gains. They also recognize, however, that the case of HIV treatment is unique, in the magnitude of social value generated. As a result, they take a broader view, using a database reporting cost-effectiveness ratios for more than 200 drugs. This database allows them to estimate survival gains for all these drugs, and value these using an economic framework. The rate of appropriation is lower for HIV drugs, but they argue that the general rate of appropriation in the pharmaceutical industry remains low—around 10 percent of total social value generated.

4.2. Critiques of the Simple Theory and Their Implications

The canonical model implies that innovators should receive the full measure of what consumers are willing to pay. A number of criticisms have been lodged against this implication. In particular, the canonical model conceives of a single innovator creating an innovation that stands on its own, and selling it to consumers in a purely private market. Any or all of these assumptions can be questioned in the health care context.

4.2.1. Patent Races

The canonical model predicts fewer entries into the innovation industry, because profits are less than consumer surplus. However, if multiple firms can enter into a race to produce a given innovation, the predictions change. Each new entrant reduces the probability that any given incumbent firm will "win" the race to invent.[2] This negative externality, which is not internalized by the entrant, leads to excessive entry. This needs to be weighed against the incomplete extraction of consumer surplus, which leads to insufficient entry (Menell and Scotchmer, 2007).

Due to the negative externality, it is efficient for innovators to receive strictly less than the social surplus created by their invention. However, it is unclear in general whether there are too many or too few firms entering into patent races. This depends on the relative magnitudes of the positive and negative externalities. In turn, these depend on the costs and benefits of duplicating research effort. For instance, if all firms succeed or fail together, there is no incremental social benefit to the entry of a new firm; if successes and failures are highly uncorrelated, however, the opposite is true (Loury, 1979; Lee and Wilde, 1980).

A number of more subtle issues may also arise in the analysis of patent races. Inefficiencies can be created by asymmetric information, whether this is about cost efficiency, the value of innovation, or the state of technical progress (Scotchmer and Green, 1990; Bhattacharya et al., 1992).

4.2.2. Cumulative Innovation

The canonical model conceives of a firm producing a single innovation, which exists independently of other past or present discoveries. In reality, new discoveries depend on previous inventions and unlock the door to future inventions. This poses a number of incentive problems. On the one hand, inventors may lack the incentive to stimulate follow-on research by competing firms. In this sense, cumulative innovation

---

[2] Another type of patent race is one where one firm *loses something* if a competing firm discovers the idea first. In such a race, rival firms prefer no discovery to the case in which a competing firm discovers the idea first (Harris and Vickers, 1985).

exacerbates the problem of underinvestment in innovation. On the other hand, "follow-on" inventors may be motivated by the prospect of "capturing" the market held by an incumbent. This creates excessive incentive to innovate, since the new entrants are capturing value that the incumbent has already created.

One solution to the "capture" problem is to strengthen the patent rights of the incumbent and make it harder for follow-on inventors to enter the market. Yet this solution depresses the rate of discovery and may lead to excessively low levels of investment. Intellectual property (IP) licensing can help solve this problem, as the incumbent can receive a payment for providing the original idea, which is then enhanced by the efforts of the follow-on firm. More generally, profit-sharing arrangements between the initial and subsequent innovators can increase the profits of both sides without inhibiting future innovation, but the original innovator cannot monopolize all profits from later improvements. Moreover, since profit sharing has a depressing effect on each firm's incentives, optimal patent length goes up, when cumulative research is undertaken by multiple firms (Green and Scotchmer, 1995).

Equilibrium licensing arrangements will generally depend on the "strength" of the incumbent's underlying patent rights. If intellectual property law strongly proscribes the use of an original idea, it will be more costly to develop a follow-on product without licensing the original idea. This in turn will lead to higher license fees, and vice versa. The question of patent strength is thus quite similar to the questions of patent length and breadth. In addition, it has often been noted that licensing suffers from transaction costs that could impede the efficiency of this solution to follow-on invention (Menell and Scotchmer, 2007).

From a judicial perspective, courts should seek to protect broadly those inventions with very large stand-alone relative to follow-on value. Less obvious, however, is the point that courts should also strive to protect patents with very little stand-alone value relative to the value of the follow-on improvements it may stimulate. Major breakthroughs are worth protecting even if their sole value lies in the inventions that are to come (Chang, 1995). This point is particularly salient in the case of pharmaceuticals, where new molecules may inspire safer and more effective, but similar, products. For example, the first statin to lower cholesterol, lovastatin, proved to be inferior to later statins, but nonetheless paved the way for its heirs (Davidson et al., 1997).

4.2.3. Implications of Health Insurance

A complication of innovation in the health care context is the existence of a third-party payer. In an unregulated equilibrium with well-functioning insurance markets, there are few impacts, as consumers will pay premiums that reflect their *ex ante* willingness-to-pay for health care products (Lakdawalla and Sood, 2006). However, a variety of regulations and imperfections complicate this prediction. Subsidies for health insurance, whether through direct public provision of insurance or through tax-exempt premium expenditures, create a wedge between private willingness-to-pay for products and the willingness-to-pay for an insurance contract. A perfectly price-discriminating innovator could capture consumer surplus from his invention *plus* the value of all subsidies for health insurance. This incentive leads toward excessive innovation and counteracts the problem of imperfect consumer surplus appropriation by firms (Garber et al., 2006).

4.3. Political Economic Analysis

Our discussion has cleanly separated normative from positive implications. Political economy considerations link the two. Patent policy is set at a national level, in a global innovation marketplace where new discoveries in one country benefit the entire world. In theory, there are internationally agreed terms of patent protection, but these might be violated directly or—more likely—weakened by implicit or explicit price controls that serve the same purpose as patent limitations. Therefore, any one country fails to internalize the global benefits of innovation that take place or are used within its borders. The result is a "race to the bottom" in which each country has an incentive to free-ride off others. This incentive is particularly acute for small countries, whose innovation policies have negligible impact on the global pace of innovation. At its most extreme, this free-riding problem may result in the absence of all patent protection, which may constitute a Nash equilibrium.

In practice, free-riding incentives are checked by the presence of a few very large markets, whose decisions have material impacts on global innovation rates. For instance, the US represents about half the global pharmaceutical market and thus internalizes a substantial fraction of global innovation's benefits. Large markets may coordinate among themselves to protect intellectual property and then bring pressure to bear on smaller markets to cooperate.

However, free-riding may manifest in ways other than direct protection of intellectual property. Countries can strictly regulate the prices paid for new inventions; this has the same positive effect as a shorter or weaker patent, since it lowers the expected payoff to the inventor. The normative effect depends on whether price remains above or below the consumer surplus associated with the invention. Direct or indirect pricing regulations are prevalent in the pharmaceutical market (Sood et al., 2009). In this context, small countries have incentives to pay lower prices, given the knowledge that their policies will have very small impacts on global innovation rates.

To prevent free-riding in the case of pharmaceuticals, the World Trade Organization (WTO) agreement on Trade-Related Aspects of Intellectual Property (TRIPS) requires all but the least-developed member countries to issue 20-year patents in all fields of technology. However, this works only imperfectly. Many bilateral trade agreements contain limitations on these provisions (Hubbard and Love,

2004). The behavior of pharmaceutical firms also suggests the limited impact of the TRIPS agreement, which has not stimulated innovation among pharmaceutical firms (Kyle and McGahan, 2009).

4.4. Unique Considerations for Medical Devices

The bulk of the economic literature on health care innovation focuses on the pharmaceutical industry. As a result, much of the discussion so far has centered on this industry in particular. However, medical innovation includes other kinds of goods, like medical devices and procedures. In general, many of the same considerations apply to devices and procedures. Specifically, the positive theory of innovation is similar for these sectors as well; innovators of all stripes respond to costs and incentives in similar ways, although the institutional constraints clearly vary. However, the normative implications may differ by more. In this section, we discuss some of the unique considerations that distinguish devices and procedures from their more widely studied peers in the pharmaceutical industry.

Medical device innovation exhibits at least three key differences, compared to pharmaceutical innovation:
1. Length, cost, and nature of the innovation process;
2. Scope of patent protection;
3. Safety regulation.

4.4.1. The Innovation Process for Medical Devices

The innovation process for medical devices is typically much shorter than for pharmaceuticals, and the identity of the innovator different. While sometimes developed by firms, devices are also created by their end-users—e.g. surgeons—in academic settings, rather than in the context of a firm conducting long-term research projects (Roberts, 2003). An innovator then typically licenses the invention to a larger firm that engages in production and marketing activity.

In some respects, this is not radically different from small pharmaceutical firms engaging in research with the hope of being acquired by, or licensing discoveries to, a larger company that undertakes marketing and distribution. However, as Roberts (2003) notes, individual device innovators are often less sophisticated than firms of any size, and may have a variety of non-pecuniary incentives that affect their willingness to license an invention. For example, they may wish to avoid the time and effort of negotiation, or may wish not to commercialize their discovery. To the extent that these characteristics hold true, the positive effects of expected profitability on device innovation may be muted.

From a normative perspective, the length of the innovation process is relevant. With lower capital requirements, there is less risk of underinnovation due to capital market imperfections. With shorter time from inception to discovery, there is also mechanically less time for competing innovators to enter "patent races." The latter implies there is less risk of overinnovation. However, in the absence of perfect price discrimination, there continues to be a push towards underinnovation, if it is first-best for innovators to receive the full social surplus generated by their inventions.

4.4.2. Scope of Patent Protection for Medical Devices

The 2007 Supreme Court decision in *KSR International Co. v. Teleflex Inc.* had significant implications for the patentability of medical devices in particular. Patent protection is granted if the applicant can demonstrate: novelty, usefulness, and "non-obviousness." The decision in KSR impacted applicants' ability to show non-obviousness in the case of medical devices. The KSR decision concerned the patentability of an automotive device developed by Teleflex—an adjustable vehicle control pedal's connection to an electronic throttle control. KSR argued that this patent was in fact obvious, because it was the combination of two previously known elements. Since the recombination of existing technologies—valves, gears, etc.—often underlies the development of new medical devices, this ruling was interpreted as having possible implications for the patentability of such devices (Lee, 2008).

Specifically, the KSR decision raises the burden of proof required for the demonstration of non-obviousness by applicants for medical device patents. Since the patent application process is uncertain, this higher standard lowers the expected probability of patent protection and thus the expected return to innovation investment. Naturally, this decision lowers the rate of innovation, but the normative implications are less clear. These depend on how one views the legal logic of the decision itself. If in fact combinations of existing products are obvious to all potential manufacturers and innovators, eliminating patent protection will have no effect on consumer surplus, as it should be free to "discover" such devices. However, if "combination" is interpreted more broadly and ends up precluding patent protection for new devices that were costly to discover, the result is suboptimally narrow patent protection that precludes the development of marginal, but still valuable, inventions that combine existing elements.

4.4.3. Safety Regulation in the Medical Device Context

The FDA has a fixed process for the review of drug safety and efficacy, but its review of devices varies according to the type of device. In particular, the FDA groups medical devices into three classes (Gutman, 2004):

- Class I devices present minimal potential harm to the user, as long as general standards of care are followed, as in the case of tongue depressors and arm slings, for instance.
- Class II devices require special standards of care to ensure patient safety. A Class II device manufacturer must provide the FDA with guidance documents,

performance standards, and post-market surveillance. In this case, the manufacturer must provide pre-market notification. Examples of Class II devices include instruments for measuring glucose or hemoglobin.

- Class III devices require special controls in order to ensure safety and efficacy, and also pose substantial risks to patient health. Class III devices support or sustain human life, are substantially important in safeguarding health, or present serious risks of illness or injury. Such devices require pre-market approval by the FDA to ensure safety and efficacy. Examples include tests for cancer diagnoses or serious infectious diseases, as well as replacement heart valves and silicone breast implants.

Class III devices undergo an approval and review process that is closer to the process for pharmaceuticals, but Class I and II devices endure much less scrutiny. This reinforces the earlier observation that the process of discovery and development is shorter for devices, as less safety and efficacy evidence is required, outside the Class III context.

Devices face a range of pre-marketing costs, from high to low. Devices with limited pre-marketing expenses correspondingly face limited capital constraints. Moreover, if less investment is required for product launch, the innovation impact of a given change in spending might be higher. Of course, these issues relate to the magnitude of the relationships governing device innovation, rather than their direction. The existence of a pre-marketing development period, and a post-marketing period during which profits are recouped, make devices, procedures, and indeed all innovative goods fundamentally similar.

5. THE ROLE OF IP IN SOLVING PRODUCTION EXTERNALITIES

The inefficiencies associated with IP are often emphasized, but there are a number of important ways in which IP solves specific kinds of productive inefficiencies in the marketplace. Two prominent examples are spillover externalities in pharmaceutical advertising, and network externalities in the adoption of health care information technology.

5.1. Pharmaceutical Marketing

Marketing and intellectual property are intimately linked in a number of ways. First, to the extent that marketing raises profits, it also feeds directly into the rewards of innovators and thus the incentive to innovate. Second, in a competitive market, marketing creates spillovers across firms selling similar products; consumers may choose to buy from a competitor after seeing an effective advertisement. Therefore, market exclusivity tends to boost marketing investments over and above a competitive market. A final and related point is that the extent and nature of marketing influences consumer utilization, and the level of deadweight loss from a patent monopoly. If market exclusivity raises prices and marketing activity, it is not immediately clear that it restricts utilization, relative to a competitive market. At issue are the relative sizes of the demand elasticities with respect to pricing and to advertising. This has normative implications for market exclusivity. As a side note, even so-called "persuasive" marketing that overstates value will tend to improve efficiency, if it moves equilibrium quantity towards its competitive level (Lakdawalla and Philipson, forthcoming). The content of marketing is less important than its implications for quantity.

5.1.1. Types of Pharmaceutical Marketing

The pharmaceutical industry exhibits relatively high marketing to sales ratios, compared to other industries, with marketing expenditures at approximately 15–20 percent of sales (Berndt et al., 1995). One explanation for this is the "experience-good" nature of medicines. Consumers must try products before they know they will work. As a result, there are substantial returns to inducing consumers, as well as substantial costs of initiating a new therapy (Berndt, 2002). Both of these tend to increase marketing expenditures.

The largest component of marketing has typically been "detailing" to physicians. This involves the pharmaceutical company dispatching sales representatives to visit doctors and promote their products. Visits typically last three to ten minutes, and the content is regulated by the FDA. Over the course of a detailing visit, sales representatives typically leave behind product samples, which is another significant source of marketing expenditures (Berndt et al., 1995). Less significant are ads placed in medical journals, as well as direct-to-consumer advertising, although the latter is important for a few highly selected and high-revenue drugs (Iizuka and Jin, 2005, 2007).

Direct-to-consumer marketing has increased substantially since the FDA relaxed regulation of this in 1997 (Berndt, 2002). Specifically, annual spending on direct-to-consumer advertising tripled from 1996 to 2000, when it reached nearly $2.5bn. Even so, this still accounts for no more than 15 percent of total pharmaceutical advertising, and remains concentrated among a relatively small number of products. For instance, over the same period of time, spending on detailing and samples rose by $5bn (Rosenthal et al., 2002).

5.1.2. Alternative Theories of Marketing

The nature of marketing is not obvious, yet the normative and positive implications for IP depend on it. Marketing in the health care context may provide valuable information about safety and efficacy that would not otherwise be incorporated into patients' and physicians' decision problems. It could also persuade physicians and consumers to use a product, holding their information sets constant. In the latter case, persuasive advertising may move consumers towards or away from appropriate treatments. In the background, the incentives to innovate and the efficiency of goods provision depend on marketing.

5.1.2.1. Informative Advertising

The simplest and perhaps oldest approach to modeling advertising is as information provided to the consumer and her agents, such as health care providers (Telser, 1964). Under this view, marketing activity better informs consumption decisions and shifts the demand curve towards its ideal, fully informed level. This view of advertising has some support in the empirical literature on pharmaceuticals, where it has been observed that most direct-to-consumer advertising is done by newer drugs that are market leaders, targeted at a broad patient base. As a result, the ads are easily understood and present a "fair balance" of risks and benefits (Roth, 1996).

Under this view of advertising, branded pharmaceuticals are underutilized for two reasons: the monopoly power of the patent-holder and the lack of consumer information. Interestingly, patent monopoly stimulates informative advertising about a molecule's safety and efficacy, as the monopolist does not have to worry about its advertising creating spillover benefits for competitors producing the identical drug. Therefore, relative to a competitive market, patents lower utilization by means of monopoly pricing, but raise utilization by stimulating advertising activity (Lakdawalla and Philipson, forthcoming). We analyze this issue in more detail below.

5.1.2.2. Persuasive Advertising

There seems little doubt that some types of pharmaceutical marketing disseminate information about the safety and efficacy of products. However, it remains possible that some types of marketing expenditures serve a different purpose, such as enhancing the "image" of a product in the minds of physicians or consumers, holding fixed its actual characteristics (Leffler, 1981). Advertising that is "persuasive," rather than informative, raises demand, but in this case there is no notion of a theoretically ideal or fully informed level of demand. Persuasive advertising may move consumers towards their true marginal value products of use, but it is also possible that it moves consumers past this efficient level. A more sinister version of this model would imply that advertising produces "misinformation" that deceives consumers or health care providers about a drug's value, in spite of legal prohibitions against it.

Interestingly, the implications of persuasive advertising may have less to do with the intention of the advertiser, and more to do with the initial efficiency of the market. Denote by Q^* the point of static utilization efficiency in the market, and denote by Q the actual level of utilization under a patent monopoly, but without any advertising. It is generically true that $Q < Q^*$. Now suppose that persuasive advertising raises demand either through effective "image" management, or through outright deception. The result is the new level of utilization, Q^A. In either case, persuasive advertising is welfare improving if $Q^A \leq Q^*$, and potentially welfare reducing if $Q^A > Q^*$. We say "potentially," because the degree of inefficiency from overutilization may or may not be greater than the inefficiency associated with the monopoly utilization level. Growth in demand is welfare improving until utilization overshoots its efficient level; the source of this growth is not strictly relevant (Lakdawalla and Philipson, forthcoming).

These simple conclusions may be reversed if one entertained a more complicated model of persuasive advertising that did not just shift demand, but also changed the ordering of consumers along the demand curve. To take one example, suppose persuasive advertising targets the elderly, even for products the elderly place zero value on. In this case, advertising could raise demand by triggering utilization among a group of patients that is far outside the margin and ends up using an inappropriate type of therapy. In this case, advertising does more than shift or rotate demand; it also changes the underlying shape of the demand curve, and changes the identity of the consumers at or near the margin.

5.1.3. Empirical Studies of Marketing and Pharmaceutical Demand

Pharmaceutical marketing has been found to boost demand and utilization from a positive point of view. In the anti-ulcer market, for example, Berndt et al. find the sales elasticity highest for detailing (0.553), followed by medical journal advertising (0.198), and lowest for direct-to-consumer advertising (0.008), although it is notable that this study was conducted on data prior to major relaxation of rules governing direct-to-consumer pharmaceutical marketing (Berndt et al., 1995). More recent studies of direct-to-consumer marketing find larger effects (Rosenthal et al., 2003). Indeed, in more recent work, Berndt and co-authors argue it is likely that direct-to-consumer elasticities have risen relative to direct-to-physician elasticities. They point to increases in the prevalence of prescription drug insurance, which increases the base of consumers in the marketplace, as well as insurance benefit design that is attempting to steer patients to preferred drugs (Berndt et al., 2002).

A key distinction is often drawn between direct-to-physician and direct-to-consumer advertising. In a series of papers, Iizuka and Jin argue that direct-to-physician advertising affects the choice of medication, while direct-to-consumer advertising affects initiation (Iizuka and Jin, 2005, 2007). Put another way, direct-to-consumer advertising leads patients to seek treatment from their physicians, while direct-to-physician advertising influences physicians' patterns of prescribing for the patients who come into their office.

5.1.4. Marketing and Intellectual Property

Competitive markets may underprovide marketing activity when competitor firms benefit from these. This will be the case if providing information, or even persuasion, about a molecule benefits all producers of that molecule. In this way, intellectual property stimulates marketing activity and moves it towards its efficient level, as discussed above. The reverse is also true. Growth in marketing possibilities or the efficiency of marketing technology stimulates profits and in this way boosts the rewards for innovation. Marketing and innovation are sometimes viewed as substitutes in the popular debate over prescription drugs, but they are in fact complements. Restricting one is likely to have negative effects on the other (Lakdawalla and Philipson, forthcoming).

The relationship between marketing and IP also has dynamic consequences, as explored by Bhattacharya and Vogt. Since drugs are experience goods, public knowledge about them is valuable to their producers. Above, we discussed how marketing can produce such knowledge, but in reality both price and marketing can be used in this manner. Price reductions stimulate use and build experiential knowledge, while marketing builds communicated knowledge. Since knowledge about a molecule benefits all firms producing the molecule, including generic competitors, the value of knowledge will decrease over the lifecycle of a patent. Therefore, the prediction is for rising prices and falling marketing over the patent lifecycle, both of which seem to fit empirical patterns in the pharmaceutical industry (Bhattacharya and Vogt, 2003). The empirical findings are echoed by Ellison and Ellison, who find that advertising decreases just prior to patent expiration, and particularly for the drugs where generic entry was the most likely (Ellison and Ellison, 2007).

An alternative mechanism for this pattern is suggested by Caves et al. They study the case in which advertising is aimed at the subpopulation of patient with the best available substitutes. Therefore, to the extent that reductions in advertising release these patients to a competitor, the optimal price might rise due to a corresponding reduction in the price responsiveness of demand (Caves et al., 1991).

5.2. Network Externalities and the Development of Health Care IT

Analogous but somewhat different problems of spillovers and appropriation present themselves in the context of health care IT as well. This is due to the familiar problem of network externalities. "Interoperability" is defined as the capacity of IT systems at different firms to interact with each other. For example, interoperable systems across two hospitals might permit the sharing of medical records, while interoperable systems across a hospital and a payer might permit more efficient billing and reimbursement. However, in a decentralized marketplace, it is difficult to harvest the gains from interoperability. A firm adopting a highly interoperable system provides benefits to all future adopters, but it cannot capture these benefits.

An obvious solution to this problem is to grant IP over the technology itself to its originator. A firm marketing a technology that is highly interoperable with other platforms would thus expect greater rewards. Unfortunately, this solution is highly imperfect, because interoperability of this kind also provides benefits to all the firm's current competitors, who can now boast of one more "compatible" product in the marketplace. Therefore, in a marketplace of competing patent-holders, IP alone is not sufficient to align the incentives of firms and society.

An alternative solution would be a broader scope for IP protection in this context. Suppose, for example, that a single patent were granted for health care information technology. The resulting monopolist would internalize all the spillovers associated with network externalities, but market equilibrium would also suffer from the usual problems associated with the lack of competition, including high prices and inefficiently low utilization.

Other market failures exist on the demand side of health care IT. The complex and decentralized nature of most health systems make it logistically challenging to adopt uniform health care IT standards, as the interoperability problem hinders coordination among the many units of a single, complex system (Shortliffe, 2005).

5.3. Personalized Medicine and the Development of Diagnostic Testing

Information of a different sort also plays an important role in the pharmaceutical industry, as evidenced by the relationship between diagnosis and treatment. The value of therapies depends in part on the quality of information about which patients are most likely to benefit from them. Such information can be as simple as an X-ray, or as complex as a genetic biomarker test in the treatment of cancer. Since diagnostic information provides benefits that accrue to the providers of treatments, separating the two functions can lead to underprovision of both diagnosis and treatment. In principle, pharmaceutical innovators would already have incentives to house both these functions under one roof, if the complementarities were strong enough to overwhelm offsetting inefficiencies, such as the additional complexity of two different research enterprises.

However, this solution is not without its perils. If drug manufacturers coordinate the development of drugs with diagnostics, they will consider the potentially negative impact of improved tests in informing some patients that they should *not* use the drug. This mitigates, at least partially, the increased value derived by patients who learn that they should be using the drug. Some authors have also emphasized the difficulty of rewarding the development of diagnostic tests that reveal the inappropriateness of therapy (Meurer, 2003). Of course, patients value this information and are willing to pay for it, at least as much as they pay for the therapy itself. While a test that leads primarily to less treatment might not be a worthwhile development for a company manufacturing the therapy in question, a different firm may be quite willing to extract this information value from consumers.

Historically, IP for diagnostic products has focused on platform (e.g. machines and instruments) and not content (e.g. information). This arrangement made sense when the information itself is fairly obvious—e.g. a knee injury clearly calls for diagnostic investigation of the knee. However, recent advances in personalized medicine have destabilized this distinction. Unlike determining the obviously appropriate site of an X-ray or MRI, it may be quite difficult and costly to determine where and how to find a genetic biomarker that influences a patient's susceptibility to a particular type of chemotherapy. Current IP law allows a firm to protect new techniques it may have developed for finding this biomarker, but not the biomarker itself (Garrison and Austin, 2006). This creates a potentially distortionary incentive for diagnostic firms to link new patentable techniques to the discovery of particular biomarkers, even when established techniques would have sufficed.

That said, allowing IP rights over genetic and other information poses difficult questions for efficiency. IP over genetic information may restrict the use of genetic information and the flow of follow-on innovation. Indeed, Williams argues that this seems to be true in the case of the Human Genome Project, and its private competitors (Williams, 2010).

6. ALTERNATIVE APPROACHES TO STIMULATING DISCOVERY

Decoupling innovator's rewards from consumer prices allows policy to separate and thereby address the optimal reward for innovation and the efficient price of innovative goods. In terms of the previous discussion, it allows for the optimal manipulation of $E(\pi|D)$, without constraining the consumer price of the good that is eventually sold.

Patents create a trade-off between dynamic incentives to innovate and static inefficiency. Longer patent life leads to greater incentives for innovation but also greater static deadweight loss. A number of policies have been proposed to escape this trade-off. All rely on decoupling the inventor's rewards from the *ex post* price paid by consumers.

6.1. Rewards for Inventors

Kremer (1998, 2000a and b) proposed patent buyouts, or rewards, as a mechanism for ensuring innovation with minimal deadweight loss. He presents as a motivating example the case of the Daguerreotype, an early type of photographic process developed by Louis Daguerre and collaborators. In 1839, the French government awarded Daguerre a lifetime pension, in lieu of patent protection. That same year, the French government announced the invention as a gift "Free to the World." Under the buyout mechanism proposed by Kremer, governments would use an auction to estimate the private value of patents and then offer to buy out patents at this private value, with an added fixed markup. The markup would depend on the ratio of the social and private value of typical inventions. In most instances the government would buy the patents and place these patents in the public domain, but in a few instances the patent will be sold to the highest bidder in order to induce the bidder to reveal their true valuation.

While conventional patents reward inventors with monopoly power, Daguerre was rewarded with a cash transfer in lieu of monopoly power. In principle, this provides incentives to innovate without any of the static distortions caused by monopoly. The principal challenge for patent buyouts, however, is setting the appropriate price of the buyout. For rewards, it is difficult to forecast the value of the invention at the time of discovery. Patent monopolies have the virtue of tying innovator rewards, however imperfectly, to revealed willingness-to-pay.

Kremer proposes a clever auction mechanism for revealing private willingness-to-pay, although this mechanism relies more heavily on accurate forecasts of value than do patents. Moreover, even this mechanism fails to address the wedge between private and social willingness-to-pay; to address it, Kremer proposes to apply a uniform multiplier that captures the ratio of private to social valuations.

6.2. Subsidies for Inventors

Another mechanism for decoupling the returns to innovation from the price of innovative goods is the direct or indirect provision of innovation by the public sector. This could involve the direct conduct of research, as done by the National Institutes of Health (Blume-Kohout et al., 2009), or it could involve subsidies paid to research firms. The key characteristic of research subsidies, as opposed to rewards, is that payment is not contingent on the success of the research program.

Subsidies for research have been shown to stimulate private R&D spending, while subsidies for "development" do the opposite (Clausen, 2009). Clausen argues this supports the argument that private markets underprovide research spending, due to substantial positive externalities, but more effectively allocate funding for development activities, where returns are more readily appropriated.

Compared to rewards for innovation, the advantage is the potential for decoupling the innovation process from the sale of the innovative good. This eliminates the need for monopoly power over innovative goods. However, it also imposes a variety of agency costs, particularly if the research is conducted entirely in the public sector.

This raises a particular problem of gauging the optimal level of research, since public research agencies do not face direct incentives that tie their decisions to consumer surplus or demand. Theoretically, basic research with a pure public goods aspect is best conducted by the public sector, but the distinction between basic and "applied" or translational research may not be clear. The optimal policy approach should recognize the difficulty of this distinction, and that publicly conducted research should "stop" when it approaches a translational stage that is tied more directly to the development of a particular product.

A more subtle advantage concerns the state of the world in which the transfer is made. Unlike rewards or patents, research subsidies are paid to the inventor regardless of whether a discovery is made. Therefore, some resources are transferred from the state of the world in which no discovery takes place. This may be an improvement in efficiency if innovations raise the marginal utility of wealth, as this would then involve transfers from a low marginal utility of wealth state to a higher marginal utility of wealth state (Lakdawalla and Sood, 2004).

6.3. Health Insurance and Two-part Pricing

Health insurance represents another means for decoupling consumer prices from the returns to innovation. Insurance literally decouples the price paid by consumers from the price received by manufacturers. Consumers are liable for a co-payment or coinsurance, payable to the insurer. Manufacturers receive a reimbursement from the insurer (at least indirectly).

If an insurance scheme is publicly designed, policy makers have the freedom to configure co-payments and reimbursement rates in a socially optimal fashion. In particular, the government can set fixed co-payment levels in order to drive consumer prices toward socially efficient marginal cost pricing, even as manufacturers receive monopoly reimbursement levels from the insurance scheme. The result is an improvement in static efficiency without compromising dynamic incentives to innovate. The difference between consumer prices and manufacturer reimbursements is covered by premium payments, government spending, or some combination of the two. Provided that the innovator does not get overcompensated for his efforts as a result, it is welfare improving to configure insurance in this manner (Lakdawalla and Sood, 2009).

Subsidies for privately provided prescription drug insurance are also welfare improving by the same argument. One caveat here concerns the potential impact of insurance benefit design features. If insurers design benefits around a percentage coinsurance, rather than a flat co-payment, innovators could potentially mitigate or even offset the effects of insurance by raising their own price. As a result, consumers might not enjoy price reductions, and the manufacturer would capture all the rents from the public insurance subsidy without any improvement in efficiency. The government can avoid this by regulating the cost-sharing schedule offered to manufacturers. Drug insurance will improve static efficiency if, at the monopolist's margin, increases in the manufacturer price impose greater out-of-pocket costs on consumers. Intuitively, price *increases* should be less well insured. In practice, such arrangements are widespread in private health insurance markets, and these regulations are unlikely to bind (Lakdawalla and Sood, 2009).

Finally, guaranteeing a well-functioning but purely private health insurance market also confers welfare benefits. Due to the presence of asymmetric information, health insurance contracts typically take the form of an *ex ante* premium payment, coupled with an *ex post* unit price for the consumer. In form, this resembles the standard "two-part pricing" contract used by monopolists to extract maximum profit without constraining quantity (Oi, 1971); specifically, the monopolist has incentives to charge an efficient unit price, so as to maximize the amount of consumer surplus available for extraction through the *ex ante* "entry fee." In equilibrium, this form of the health insurance contract also matches its function. Firms with market power will exploit the presence of two-part health insurance contracts, even when such contracts are offered downstream by vertically non-integrated health insurers. Theoretically, the presence of health insurance reduces deadweight losses from monopolies of all kinds, including patent monopolies. Empirically, there is evidence that better insured drugs exhibit smaller deadweight costs of patent monopolies (Lakdawalla and Sood, 2006).

This logic bears on the longstanding issue of how health insurance relates to static efficiency in the health care marketplace. For decades, many health economists developed and then relied upon the intuition that health care competition reduces welfare. According to this argument, monopoly restrictions on output improve welfare, because moral hazard creates socially excessive utilization under competitive circumstances (Crew, 1969; Frech, 1996; Folland et al., 2001). Monopoly was thought to be a second-best improvement to a market afflicted by moral hazard.

Gaynor et al. (2000) exposed the flaw in this reasoning: if private insurers could make their customers better off by raising co-payments, they would surely do so. The early literature abstracted from this response of insurance contract design to medical care prices. Incorporating this response reverses the implications of market power for welfare.

Taken together, the literature on insurance and static efficiency reaches several conclusions that bear on the normative analysis of patents and innovation incentives. First, health care market power (including patent-protected power) does not *benefit* consumers (Gaynor et al., 2000), although it may not be as socially costly as in other industries (Lakdawalla and Sood, 2006). Second, the presence of overutilization does not play the central role in the welfare analysis of market power; it merely facilitates the two-part contractual structures that do play this role. In particular, health insurance allows health care providers to price discriminate, and it allows health insurers to extract surplus from consumers more efficiently than a single, uniform, linear price would allow. When a patent monopolist must name a single (linear) price for the entire market, the standard deadweight losses from monopoly accrue.

6.4. Patent Menus

Optimal patent length and breadth varies by the characteristics of the innovative process and the markets in which new goods are sold. In principle patent length and breadth should vary by industry and in markets within industry; however, the administrative hassles of running such a system are enormous. A new line of research has proposed patent length or breadth menus to circumvent this problem. Under one such system, the patentee could choose from a menu of patent fee and corresponding lengths, where fees are a non-decreasing function of patent length (Scotchmer, 1999). Under an alternate system for follow-on inventions, Llobet et al. (2000) propose a menu of mandatory buyout prices and corresponding patent fees, with fees increasing with buyout price. The buyout price is the price at which the innovator agrees to sell his invention to any new innovator improving upon his invention. Thus, in this scheme the innovator essentially chooses patent breadth and avoids the uncertainty of defending patents in courts.

In the pharmaceutical context, prescription drug user fees are analogous to patent menus, albeit in a very limited sense. Innovators have the option to pay for expedited review, which shaves about three months off the average review period (Berndt et al., 2004). While limited in scope, the advantage of the PDUFA mechanism is that extensions in the marketing period actually increase net consumer surplus, even in a static sense. In other words, holding the patent length fixed, increases in the marketing period lead to more surplus for producers and consumers. However, by nature, the gains to this mechanism are limited by the length of the approval period.

6.5. The Case For and Against Government Buyers

A direct way of rewarding innovation is for governments to guarantee the purchase of a good in the event of its discovery. This policy is often advocated in the context of vaccines against known diseases, like HIV or malaria. It is also often suggested in the context of health care IT, where a large government buyer could coordinate its efforts and help mitigate externalities due to interoperability.

6.5.1. Vaccines

Vaccines for communicable diseases present a well-known externality in consumption: increases in vaccination rates provide protection to the remaining unvaccinated patients, because they face less risk of exposure. The predictable result is underconsumption of vaccines, which is often addressed through mandatory vaccina-tion programs (i.e. unfunded mandates), or through public provision of vaccines. However, a number of subtler failures emerge from both private and mixed public/private models of vaccine provision.

Private markets will generally not be able to eradicate disease, because incentives to vaccinate fall rapidly with the prevalence of the disease. Subsidies and even manda-tory vaccines do not erase this underlying incentive problem; they merely mitigate it. In short, government provision is "rolling the ball uphill" against these incentives, in spite of oft-repeated goals of disease eradication (Geoffard and Philipson, 1997).

Other supply-side problems emerge. One is a problem of time consistency. Once a successful vaccine is developed, and if public purchasers hold a great deal of leverage, the government may have incentives to compel the innovator to sell at below-monop-oly prices (Philipson and Mechoulan, 2003). This could lead to less investment in innovation. Compounding this is another problem of surplus appropriation that plagues vaccine development. By nature, vaccines are sold to both healthy and sick patients, or, alternatively, both high-risk and low-risk populations. Therefore, the marginal vaccine consumer may have a very low demand for the product. This is in contrast to the marginal drug consumer, who is sick with a disease. This dampens the ability of the innovator to charge higher prices to the highest-risk patients, at least if the goal of universal or near-universal vaccination is to be achieved (Kremer and Snyder, 2006).

The market failures present for vaccines cut across a simple consumption external-ity that could be addressed through Pigovian subsidies or public purchasing. Deeper incentive problems on both the demand and supply side pose challenges that public purchasers need to consider.

6.5.2. Health Care IT

Analogous externalities plague the adoption of health care IT as well. Regardless of who holds the IP over health care IT, providers would pay for upgrades, yet it is esti-mated that payers would harvest 90 percent of the associated gains, leaving providers with only 10 percent (Middleton, 2005). This would result in underadoption of health care IT, relative to its efficient level.

A natural solution would be for payers to bear some of the costs associated with health care IT upgrades. However, private payers may be quite reluctant to do so, as providers' IT remains outside their direct control, and it would be problematic for payers to maintain an ownership stake in providers' IT systems. Public payers may be an exceptional case, due to their market size and power, and their willingness to subsidize adoption of technologies they do not directly own (Rosenfeld et al., 2005).

REFERENCES

Acemoglu, D. & Linn, J. (2004). Market size in innovation: Theory and evidence from the pharmaceutical industry. *Quarterly Journal of Economics, 119*(3), 1049–1090.

Albainy-Jenei, S. (2006). Claim construction and the doctrine of equivalents in Amgen v Transkaryotic Therapies, Inc. *Journal of Intellectual Property Law Practice, 1*(13), 819–821.

Arora, A., Ceccagnoli, M., & Cohen, W. M. (2008). R&D and the patent premium. *International Journal of Industrial Organization, 26*(5), 1153–1179.

Berndt, E., et al. (2004). Did the Prescription Drug Use Fee Act affect the FDA approval process? In *Frontiers in Health Policy Research*. Chicago: University of Chicago Press.

Berndt, E. R. (2002). Pharmaceuticals in U.S. health care: Determinants of quantity and price. *Journal of Economic Perspectives, 16*(4), 45–66.

Berndt, E. R., et al. (1995). Information, marketing, and pricing in the U.S. antiulcer drug market. *American Economic Review, 85*(2), 100–105.

Berndt, E. R., et al. (2002). An analysis of the diffusion of new antidepressants: Variety, quality, and marketing efforts. *Journal of Mental Health Policy and Economics, 5*(1), 3–19.

Bhagat, S. & Welch, I. (1995). Corporate research & development investments: international comparisons. *Journal of Accounting and Economics, 19*(2–3), 443–470.

Bhattacharya, J. & Vogt, W. B. (2003). A simple model of pharmaceutical price dynamics. *Journal of Law and Economics, 46*(2), 599–626.

Bhattacharya, S., Glazer, J., & Sappington, D. E. M. (1992). Licensing and the sharing of knowledge in research joint ventures. *Journal of Economic Theory, 56*(1), 43–69.

Blume-Kohout, M. (2009). *Drug development and public research funding: Evidence of lagged effects*, RAND.

Blume-Kohout, M. & Sood, N. (2009). *Medicare Part D and pharmaceutical R&D*. Santa Monica, CA: RAND Corporation.

Blume-Kohout, M. E., Kumar, K. B., & Sood, N. (2009). *Federal life sciences funding and university R&D*. Cambridge, MA: National Bureau of Economic Research.

Boldrin, M. & Levine, D. K. (2004). 2003 Lawrence R. Klein Lecture: The case against intellectual monopoly. *International Economic Review, 45*(2), 327–350.

Boldrin, M. & Levine, D. K. (2008). *Against intellectual monopoly*. Cambridge and New York: Cambridge University Press.

Brekke, K. R., Grasdal, A. L., & Holmas, T. H. (2009). Regulation and pricing of pharmaceuticals: Reference pricing or price cap regulation? *European Economic Review, 53*(2), 170–185.

Caves, R. E., Whinston, M. D., & Hurwitz, M. A. (1991). Patent expiration, entry, and competition in the US pharmaceutical industry. *Brookings Papers on Economic Activity*, 1–48.

Chang, H. F. (1995). Patent scope, antitrust policy, and cumulative innovation. *RAND Journal of Economics, 26*(1), 34–57.

Clausen, T. H. (2009). Do subsidies have positive impacts on R&D and innovation activities at the firm level? *Structural Change and Economic Dynamics, 20*(4), 239–253.

Claxton, K., et al. (2008). Value based pricing for NHS drugs: An opportunity not to be missed? *BMJ, 336*(7638), 251–254.

Cohen, W. M., Nelson, R. R., & Walsh, J. P. (2000). Protecting their intellectual assets: appropriability conditions and why U.S. manufacturing firms patent (or not). National Bureau of Economic Research Working Paper Series No. 7552.

Comanor, W. S. (1986). The political economy of the pharmaceutical industry. *Journal of Economic Literature, 24*, 1178–1217.

Congressional Budget Office (1998). *How increased competition from generic drugs has affected prices and returns in the pharmaceutical industry*. Washington, DC: Congressional Budget Office.

Crew, M. A. (1969). Coinsurance and the welfare economics of medical care. *American Economic Review, 59*(5), 906–908.

Danzon, P. M. & Chao, L. (2000). Does regulation drive out competition in pharmaceutical markets? *Journal of Law and Economics, 43*(2), 311–357.

Danzon, P. M. & Pauly, M. V. (2001). Insurance and new technology: From hospital to drugstore. *Health Affairs, 20*(5), 86–100.

Davidson, M., et al. (1997). Comparison of one-year efficacy and safety of atorvastatin versus lovastatin in primary hypercholesterolemia. Atorvastatin Study Group I. *American Journal of Cardiology, 79*(11), 1475–1481.

DiMasi, J. A. & Grabowski, H. G. (2007). The cost of biopharmaceutical R&D: Is biotech different? *Managerial and Decision Economics, 28*(4–5), 469–479.

Duggan, M. & Scott Morton, F. (2010). The effect of Medicare Part D on pharmaceutical prices and utilization. *American Economic Review, 100*(1), 590–607.

Ekelund, M. & Persson, B. (2003). Pharmaceutical pricing in a regulated market. *Review of Economics and Statistics, 85*(2), 298–306.

Ellison, G. & Ellison, S. F. (2007). Strategic entry deterrence and the behavior of pharmaceutical incumbents prior to patent expiration. National Bureau of Economic Research Working Paper Series No. 13069.

Encaoua, D., Guellec, D., & Martinez, C. (2006). Patent systems for encouraging innovation: Lessons from economic analysis. *Research Policy, 35*(9), 1423–1440.

Finkelstein, A. (2004). Static and dynamic effects of health policy: Evidence from the vaccine industry. *Quarterly Journal of Economics, 119*(2), 527–564.

Folland, S., Goodman, A. C., & Stano, M. (2001). *The economics of health and health care* (3rd ed.). Upper Saddle River, NJ: Prentice Hall.

Frech, H. E. (1996). *Competition and monopoly in medical care.* Washington: AEI Press.

Gallini, N. (1992). Patent policy and costly imitation. *RAND Journal of Economics, 23*, 52–63.

Gans, J. S., Hsu, D. H., & Stern, S. (2008). The impact of uncertain intellectual property rights on the market for ideas: Evidence from patent grant delays. *Management Science, 54*(5), 982–997.

Garber, A., Jones, C., & Romer, P. (2006). Insurance and incentives for medical innovation. *Forum for Health Economics and Policy, 9*(2) (Article 4).

Garrison, L. P. & Austin, M. J. F. (2006). Linking pharmacogenetics-based diagnostics and drugs for personalized medicine. *Health Affairs, 25*(5), 1281–1290.

Gaynor, M., Haas-Wilson, D., & Vogt, W. B. (2000). Are invisible hands good hands? Moral hazard, competition, and the second-best in health care markets. *Journal of Political Economy, 108*(5), 992–1005.

Geoffard, P.-Y. & Philipson, T. (1997). Disease eradication: Private versus public vaccination. *American Economic Review, 87*(1), 222–230.

Giaccotto, C., Santerre, R. E., & Vernon, J. A. (2005). Drug prices and research and development investment behavior in the pharmaceutical industry. *Journal of Law and Economics, 48*(1), 195–214.

Gilbert, R. & Shapiro, C. (1990). Optimal patent length and breadth. *RAND Journal of Economics, 21*, 106–112.

Goldman, D., et al. (2010). Valuing health technologies at NICE: Recommendations for improved incorporation of treatment value in HTA. *Health Economics, 19*(10), 1109–1116.

Goldman, D. P., et al. (2011). The benefits from giving makers of conventional "small molecule" drugs longer exclusivity over clinical trial data. *Health Affairs, 30*(1), 84–90.

Grabowski, H. (1968). The determinants of industrial research and development: A study of the chemical, drug and petroleum industries. *Journal of Political Economy, 7*(6), 292–306.

Grabowski, H. (2002). Patents and new product development in the pharmaceutical and biotechnology industries. *Science and Cents: Exploring the Economics of Biotechnology Conference.*

Grabowski, H. (2008). Follow-on biologics: Data exclusivity and the balance between innovation and competition. *Nature Reviews Drug Discovery, 7*(6), 479–488.

Grabowski, H. & Vernon, J. (2000). The determinants of pharmaceutical research and development expenditures. *Journal of Evolutionary Economics, 10*(1–2), 201–215.

Green, J. R. & Scotchmer, S. (1995). On the division of profit in sequential innovation. *RAND Journal of Economics, 26*(1), 20–33.

Gutman, S. (2004). Regulation of medical devices. Accessed: December 30, 2010.

Hall, B. H. & Lerner, J. (Eds.) (2011). *Handbook of the economics of innovation.* Amsterdam: Elsevier-North Holland.

Harris, C. & Vickers, J. (1985). Patent races and the persistence of monopoly. *Journal of Industrial Economics, 33*(4), 461–481.

Hicks, J. (1932). *The theory of wages.* London: Macmillan.

Hubbard, R. G. (1998). Capital-market imperfections and investment. *Journal of Economic Literature, 36*(1), 193–225.

Hubbard, T. & Love, J. (2004). A new trade framework for global healthcare R&D. *PLoS Biology, 2*(2).

Iizuka, T. & Jin, G. Z. (2005). The effect of prescription drug advertising on doctor visits. *Journal of Economics and Management Strategy, 14*(3), 701–727.

Iizuka, T. & Jin, G. Z. (2007). Direct to consumer advertising and prescription choice. *Journal of Industrial Economics, 55*(4), 771.

Jayadev, A. & Stiglitz, J. (2008). Two ideas to increase innovation and reduce pharmaceutical costs and prices. *Health Affairs.*

Jena, A. & Philipson, T. (2009). Endogenous cost-effectiveness analysis in health care technology adoption. National Bureau of Economic Research Working Paper Series No. 15032.

Jena, A. B. & Philipson, T. (2007). Cost-effectiveness as a price control. *Health Affairs (Millwood), 26*(3), 696–703.

Jena, A. B. & Philipson, T. J. (2008). Cost-effectiveness analysis and innovation. *Journal of Health Economics, 27*(5), 1224–1236.

Jena, A. B., et al. (2009). Me-too innovation in pharmaceutical markets. *Forum for Health Economics and Policy, 12*(1).

Klemperer, P. (1990). How broad should the scope of patent protection be? *RAND Journal of Economics, 21*, 113–130.

Kremer, M. (1998). Patent buyouts: A mechanism for encouraging innovation. *Quarterly Journal of Economics, 113*(4), 1137–1167.

Kremer, M. (2000a). Creating markets for new vaccines. Part I: Rationale. National Bureau of Economic Research, Inc., NBER Working Papers.

Kremer, M. (2000b). Creating markets for new vaccines. Part II: Design issues. National Bureau of Economic Research, Inc., NBER Working Papers.

Kremer, M. & Snyder, C. (2006). *Why is there no AIDS vaccine?* Cambridge, MA: Harvard University.

Kremer, M. & Williams, H. (2010). Incentivizing innovation: Adding to the tool kit. *Innovation Policy and the Economy, 10*(1), 1–17.

Kyle, M. & McGahan, A. (2009). *Investments in pharmaceuticals before and after TRIPS.* Cambridge, MA: National Bureau of Economic Research.

Lakdawalla, D. & Sood, N. (2006). *Health insurance as a two-part pricing contract.* Cambridge, MA: National Bureau of Economic Research.

Lakdawalla, D. & Yin, W. (2009). Insurer bargaining and negotiated drug prices in Medicare Part D. National Bureau of Economic Research, Inc., NBER Working Papers: 15330.

Lakdawalla, D. N. & Philipson, T. J. (forthcoming). Intellectual property and marketing in the pharmaceutical industry. *Journal of Law and Economics.*

Lakdawalla, D. N. & Sood, N. (2004). Social insurance and the design of innovation incentives. *Economics Letters, 85*(1), 57–61.

Lakdawalla, D. N. & Sood, N. (2009). Innovation and the welfare effects of public drug insurance. *Journal of Public Economics, 93*, 541–548.

Lee, J. (2008). How KSR broadens (without lowering) the evidentiary standard of nonobviousness. *Berkeley Technology Law Journal, 23*(1), 15–46.

Lee, T. & Wilde, L. L. (1980). Market structure and innovation: A reformulation. *Quarterly Journal of Economics, 94*(2), 429–436.

Leffler, K. B. (1981). Persuasion or information? The economics of prescription drug advertising. *Journal of Law and Economics, 24*(1), 45–74.

Lemley, M. A. & Shapiro, C. (2005). Probabilistic patents. *Journal of Economic Perspectives, 19*(2), 75–98.

Lerner, J. & Tirole, J. (2009). *Some simple economics of open source*: Elgar Reference Collection. International Library of Critical Writings in Economics, vol. 241. Cheltenham, UK and Northampton, MA: Elgar.

Lichtenberg, F. R. & Waldfogel, J. (2003). *Does misery love company? Evidence from pharmaceutical markets before and after the Orphan Drug Act.* Cambridge, MA: National Bureau of Economic Research.

Llobet, G., Hopenhayn, H., & Mitchell, M. (2000). *Rewarding sequential innovators: Prizes, patents and buyouts.* Minneapolis, MN: Federal Reserve Bank of Minneapolis.

Loury, G. C. (1979). Market structure and innovation. *Quarterly Journal of Economics, 93*(3), 395–410.

Mansfield, E. (1986a). Patents and innovation: An empirical study. *Management Science, 32*(2), 173–181.

Mansfield, E. (1986b). The R&D tax credit and other technology policy issues. *American Economic Review, 76*(2), 190–194.

Martikainen, J., Kivi, I., & Linnosmaa, I. (2005). European prices of newly launched reimbursable pharmaceuticals—a pilot study. *Health Policy, 75*(3), 235–246.

McCutchen, W. W. (1993). Estimating the impact of the R&D tax credit on strategic groups in the pharmaceutical industry. *Research Policy, 22*(4), 337–351.

Menell, P. S. & Scotchmer, S. (2007). Intellectual property law. In A. M. Polinsky & S. Shavell (Eds.), *Handbook of law and economics* (vol. 2, pp. 1473–1570). New York: Elsevier.

Meurer, M. J. (2003). Pharmacogenomics, genetic tests, and patent-based incentives. *Advances in Genetics, 50*: 399–426; discussion 507–510, 399–426; discussion 507–510.

Middleton, B. (2005). Achieving U.S. health information technology adoption: The need for a third hand. *Health Affairs, 24*(5), 1269–1272.

Mossinghoff, G. J. (1999). Overview of the Hatch-Waxman Act and its impact on the drug development process. *Food & Drug LJ, 54*, 187.

Nelson, R. R. & Winter, S. G. (1982). *An evolutionary theory of economic change.* Cambridge, MA: Belknap Press of Harvard University Press.

Nordhaus, W. D. (1969). An economic theory of technological change. *American Economic Review, 59*(2), 18–28.

Nordhaus, W. D. (2004). *Schumpeterian profits in the American economy: Theory and measurement.* Cambridge, MA: National Bureau of Economic Research.

O'Donoghue, T., Scotchmer, S., & Thisse, J.-F. (1998). Patent breadth, patent life, and the pace of technological progress. *Journal of Economics and Management Strategy, 7*(1), 1–32.

Oi, W. Y. (1971). A Disneyland dilemma: Two-part tariffs for a Mickey Mouse monopoly. *Quarterly Journal of Economics, 85*, 77–96.

Pauly, M. V. (2009). Is it time to reexamine the patent system's role in spending growth? *Health Affairs, 28*(5), 1466–1474.

Pavcnik, N. (2002). Do pharmaceutical prices respond to potentional out-of-pocket expenses? *RAND Journal of Economics, 33*(3), 469–487.

Pekurinen, M. & Hakkinen, U. (2005). *Regulating pharmaceutical markets in Finland.* STAKES. Julkaisut.

Philipson, T. & Mechoulan, S. (2003). Intellectual property & external consumption effects: generalizations from pharmaceutical markets. National Bureau of Economic Research Working Paper Series No. 9598.

Philipson, T. J. & Jena, A. B. (2006). *Surplus appropriation from R&D and health care technology assessment procedures.* Cambridge, MA: National Bureau of Economic Research.

Ridley, D. B., Grabowski, H. G., & Moe, J. L. (2006). Developing drugs for developing countries. *Health Affairs, 25*(2), 313–324.

Roberts, E. B. (2003). *Technological innovation and medical devices.* Cambridge, MA: Massachusetts Institute of Technology (MIT), Sloan School of Management.

Rosenfeld, S., Bernasek, C., & Mendelson, D. (2005). Medicare's next voyage: Encouraging physicians to adopt health information technology. *Health Affairs, 24*(5), 1138–1146.

Rosenthal, M. B., et al. (2002). Promotion of prescription drugs to consumers. *New England Journal of Medicine, 346*(7), 498–505.

Rosenthal, M. B., et al. (2003). Demand effects of recent changes in prescription drug promotion. *Frontiers in Health Policy Research, 6*, 1–26.

Roth, M. S. (1996). Patterns in direct-to-consumer prescription drug print advertising and their public policy implications. *Journal of Public Policy & Marketing, 15*(1), 63–75.

Sanjuan, J. (2006). *U.S. and E.U. protection of pharmaceutical test data. Consumer project on technology.* Washington, DC: Consumer Project on Technology.

Scherer, F. M. (2001). The link between gross profitability and pharmaceutical R&D spending. *Health Affairs, 20*(5), 216–220.

Scotchmer, S. (1999). On the optimality of the patent renewal system. *RAND Journal of Economics, 30*(2), 181—196.

Scotchmer, S. & Green, J. (1990). Novelty and disclosure in patent law. *RAND Journal of Economics, 21*(1), 131—146.

Shortliffe, E. H. (2005). Strategic action in health information technology: Why the obvious has taken so long. *Health Affairs, 24*(5), 1222—1233.

Sood, N., et al. (2009). The effect of regulation on pharmaceutical revenues: Experience in nineteen countries. *Health Affairs (Millwood), 28*(1), w125—w137.

Telser, L. G. (1964). Advertising and competition. *Journal of Political Economy, 72*(6), 537—562.

Thamer, M., Brennan, N., & Semansky, R. (1998). A cross-national comparison of orphan drug policies: Implications for the U.S. Orphan Drug Act. *Journal of Health Politics, Policy and Law, 23*(2), 265—290.

Toole, A. A. (2007). Does public scientific research complement private investment in research and development in the pharmaceutical industry? *Journal of Law and Economics, 50*(1), 81—104.

US Department of Commerce (2004). *Pharmaceutical price controls in OECD Countries: Implications for U.S. consumers, pricing, research and development, and innovation.* Washington, DC: ITA US Department of Commerce.

Vernon, J. A. (2005). Examining the link between price regulation and pharmaceutical R&D investment. *Health Economics, 14*(1), 1—16.

Ward, M. R. & Dranove, D. (1995). The vertical chain of research and development in the pharmaceutical industry. *Economic Inquiry, 33*(1), 70—87.

Weisbrod, B. A. (1991). The health care quadrilemma: An essay on technological change, insurance, quality of care, and cost containment. *Journal of Economic Literature, 29*(2), 523—552.

Williams, H. (2010). *Intellectual property rights and innovation: Evidence from the Human Genome.* Cambridge, MA: Dissertation, Harvard University, Department of Economics.

Yin, W. (2008). Market incentives and pharmaceutical innovation. *Journal of Health Economics, 27*(4), 1060—1077.

CHAPTER FOURTEEN

Medical Workforce

Sean Nicholson[*] and Carol Propper[**]

[*]Cornell University and NBER, USA
[**]University of Bristol and Imperial College London, UK

Contents

Abstract

The medical workforce is important based merely on its size and takes on even greater importance given the influence physicians, nurses, dentists, and pharmacists have on patient treatment. On the supply side, most governments regulate health professions to assure that the inputs into the health production function are of sufficiently high quality. But such regulation can also cause harm. This

Handbook of Health Economics, Volume 2
ISSN: 1574-0064, DOI: 10.1016/B978-0-444-53592-4.00014-1

873

chapter examines the supply and demand for medical labor and the effects of the market failure and government intervention. We begin by examining the supply side, describing a medical labor market with no market failures. We enumerate the various market failures that justify government regulation and discuss the implications of regulation on medical labor and consumers. We then examine several possible explanations for the persistent variation in medical labor productivity across markets and organization forms, including government regulation, differences in reimbursement incentives, politics, the effect of incentives to manage people within organizations, human resources management, and motivated agents. We end by suggesting some potential areas for future research.

Keywords: medical labor force; demand and supply; government regulation; labor restrictions; wage regulation

JEL Codes: I11; I18; J20; J45; J38

1. INTRODUCTION

The medical workforce is important based merely on its size. Almost 14 million people were employed in the US health care delivery sector in 2010, for example, which represents 10.6 percent of the country's total employment (Altarum Institute, 2010).[1] Health professions take on even greater importance when one considers the influence physicians, nurses, dentists, and pharmacists have on treatment decisions in their roles as patients' agents.

Health professions are regulated in most countries, either directly by the government or by a sanctioned non-government organization. The principal reason for regulation is that because of asymmetric information consumers may not be able to determine the quality of services provided by the medical workforce (Arrow, 1963). The objective is to assure consumers that the inputs into the health production function are of sufficiently high quality. Regulation typically consists of some combination of required licensing, certification, accreditation for universities providing the degrees, and subsidized medical education. In the United States and United Kingdom, for example, about 81 percent and 73 percent, respectively, of the workforce in the health care delivery sector are legally required to have a license before working.

Regulating health professions can also cause harm by placing constraints on the health production function, reducing product variety and increasing wages due to restricted entry. Many governments allow professional organizations to define and control the nature of the regulation and, in some cases, to explicitly determine the

---

[1] This is an underestimate of the size of the medical workforce because it omits labor in sectors other than health care delivery (e.g. scientists at pharmaceutical firms, managers at health insurance companies), but also an overestimate because some non-health-related labor is included (e.g. janitors).

number of people allowed to enter the profession or a specialty within the profession. This creates the appearance that the medical workforce is restricting entry to create and sustain rents.

The productivity of the medical workforce appears to vary substantially between providers within the same market. These differences in labor productivity are persistent, which suggests that the market does not induce firms to all configure production in the most efficient way. This raises the question of whether certain labor demand factors may explain these persistent productivity differences.

This chapter is organized as follows. In section 2 we describe a medical labor market with no market failures, using physicians as an example. We enumerate the market failures that justify government regulation in section 3, and then discuss the implications of regulation on medical labor and consumers. In section 4 we examine several possible explanations for the persistent variation in medical labor productivity across markets and organization forms, including government regulation, differences in reimbursement incentives, politics, the effect of incentives to manage people within organizations, human resources management, and motivated agents. We suggest some potential areas for future research in section 5.

2. PERFECTLY FUNCTIONING MEDICAL LABOR MARKETS

Most governments regulate medical labor markets by licensing occupations, subsidizing medical education, encouraging labor to locate in underserved areas, and sometimes explicitly restricting entry.[2] In order to understand the rationale for government regulation we begin by describing how a medical labor market with no market failures would function, using physicians as an example. We then describe the market failures that justify government regulation, and the implications of regulation on labor and, to a lesser extent, consumers.

2.1. Supply of Labor

The total number of hours of work physicians are willing to provide in a geographic market in a year depends on how many people chose to enter the profession in the past, how many decided to practice in a particular geographic market, and how many hours per year each physician decides to work. The following model of occupational choice is adapted from Rosen (1986).[3] Assume, for simplicity, that there are only two occupations available to college graduates, medicine and law, and the same amount of

---

[2] In some cases they also set wages directly. We discuss this in section 4.2 below.
[3] Nicholson (2008) presents a more detailed version of the model.

graduate education is required for each occupation. People derive utility from consumption and the non-monetary attributes of a specialty, W. Examples of non-monetary attributes include prestige, the intellectual content of an occupation, the types of consumers and colleagues one interacts with, and the flexibility of the work schedule. The expected lifetime difference in earnings between medicine (M) and law (L) is defined as $\Delta Y = (Y_M - Y_L)$, and the equalizing difference is defined as Z. Z, which could be positive or negative, is the additional earnings an individual must receive in medicine in order to be exactly indifferent between entering the two occupations.

If the earnings difference between medicine and law (ΔY) exceeds a person's given equalizing difference (Z), she will select medicine; otherwise she will select law. In equilibrium, all those selecting medicine will have a ΔY that exceeds their Z, and all those selecting law will have a ΔY that falls short of their Z. How many more students would choose to become physicians if the expected lifetime earnings in medicine increased due, for example, to an increase in the demand for physicians' services? It will depend on how many students have an equalizing difference close to ΔY. The distribution of equalizing differences could have any shape; there is no reason, for example, to believe it will be normally distributed around ΔY. If there are a lot of students with a value of Z close to ΔY, then many more students will choose medicine over law when the expected earnings in the former occupation rise; the aggregate labor supply curve will be elastic. We review empirical estimates of the labor supply elasticity of physicians and nurses in section 3.

The model above is also relevant for examining whether a graduating medical student decides to enter a primary care versus a non-primary care specialty, how a new physician chooses a market in which to practice, and how a physician chooses a practice mode (e.g. solo practice versus group practice). In these cases Z represents the equalizing difference between practicing in one specialty versus another, the value of amenities in one area versus another, or the equalizing difference between practice modes. We review empirical estimates of the importance of expected earnings on physicians' specialty choice and geographic location decisions in section 3.

Short-run aggregate labor supply (S^{SR}), depicted in Figure 14.1, will be steeper than long-run aggregate labor supply (S^{LR}) due to the length of required medical training and costs associated with moving between geographic markets (or between specialties when examining the supply of specialty-specific hours). If the physician wage increases, more hours will be supplied in the short run as physicians who are already trained and practicing in a market decide to work longer hours.[4] The long-run increase in hours will be greater as college graduates increasingly choose medicine

---

[4] In section 3.10 we review the literature on whether physician labor supply is, in fact, backward-bending. For now we adopt a traditional upward-sloping labor supply curve.

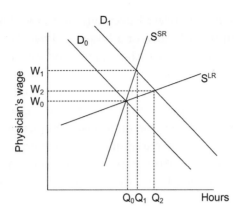

Figure 14.1

over other professions and experienced physicians relocate to high-wage markets. The size and specialty mix of the physician workforce changes slowly over time because the flow of newly trained physicians from residency training is small relative to the stock of physicians (for example, 3 percent in the USA).[5] In practice long-run supply may be dictated by the availability of medical school positions rather than student choices but we defer this discussion until section 3 because it is one implication of government regulation.

2.2. The Demand for Labor

In the Grossman (1972) model health has an investment and consumption value for consumers. Health cannot be purchased; it must be produced using medical care and a patient's time as inputs. Medical care in turn consists of labor, medical devices, pharmaceutical products, and other technology. Consumers' demand for medical care is thus derived from their demand for health (Grossman, 1972).

As Phelps (2010) points out, it is important to distinguish "...physicians as inputs into a productive process; physicians as entrepreneurs; and the final product of physician services, the actual event that involves patients." A solo practicing physician is an entrepreneur who manages capital inputs, nursing and other labor inputs, and her own labor input. Physicians in group practices have the added challenge of designing incentives to manage many physicians' inputs. We refer to the product provided by a solo physician or group practice as "physician services," but clearly this consists of a

---

[5] Across specialties in the United States the flow of newly trained physicians ranges from 3 to 5 percent of the stock of physicians practicing in that specialty.

combination of diagnostic tests, referral decisions, and procedures that may occur in the office, a separate outpatient facility, or a hospital.[6] Physician services are produced with physician time, nurse time, other labor inputs, and capital. A group practice will hire physicians until the marginal revenue product equals the wage, w. The aggregate labor-demand curve depicted in Figure 14.1 (D_0) is the summation of the firm-level marginal revenue products. Although we focus here on a group practice, the market wage represents the opportunity cost for a physician considering operating on her own in a solo practice or the amount offered by another group practice in the same city.[7]

Consider a simple physician services production function with the only inputs being physicians and capital (K). Using the terminology in Hamermesh (1993), the price elasticity of labor demand, η_{LL}, is:

$$\eta_{LL} = -[1-s]\sigma - s\eta \qquad (14.1)$$

where s is the share of labor in total revenue (or costs), σ is the elasticity of substitution between labor and capital, and η is the product demand elasticity (i.e. the price elasticity for physician services in our example).[8] Labor demand is relatively inelastic when labor's share is high, it is difficult to substitute capital for labor, and demand for the final product is inelastic. The cross-elasticity of demand for labor in response to a change in the price of capital (or a different labor input in a more realistic production function), η_{LK}, is:

$$\eta_{LK} = [1-s][\sigma - \eta] \qquad (14.2)$$

2.3. Equilibrium

Now consider a shift outward in the demand for physician services as a result of increased consumer income. Initially the quantity of services demanded will increase at the original prices; if supply is not perfectly elastic, as is assumed in Figure 14.1, prices will increase. A physician's marginal revenue product increases as a result of the higher price of physician services in the output market, so the demand for physicians shifts from D_0 to D_1.[9] Wages and the quantity of hours will rise in the short run to W_1 and Q_1, respectively. More college graduates will enter medicine now that ΔY has increased. If students have static or "cobweb" income expectations, they will expect the wage to remain permanently at W_1. In this case supply will increase

---

[6] Some of these services may not even be billed by the physician; for example a hospital may send a separate bill for the use of the operating room while the surgeon bills only for "surgeon services." Nevertheless, consumers would not demand surgeon services and operating room time separately.

[7] We discuss the organizational form of physician-firms in section 4.3.

[8] See Hamermesh (1986, 1993) for a more detailed treatment of labor demand.

[9] Alternatively, labor demand could shift directly due to a technological shock to the health production function.

substantially in the long run, thereby creating a surplus of physicians, a subsequent reduction of the flow of students into medicine as the wage falls, and endless cycles of surpluses and shortages (e.g. Freeman, 1976). There is considerable empirical evidence, however, that the income expectations of prospective engineers, lawyers, and teachers are forward looking; they correctly anticipate that cohorts will arbitrage away temporary rents, and correctly expect the new long-run wage to be W_2 (Ryoo and Rosen, 2004; Zarkin, 1985; Siow, 1984). In fact, Nicholson and Souleles (2001) find that medical students in the US anticipate future earnings changes when forming their own income expectations during the fourth year of medical school.

Labor surpluses and shortages will be self-correcting in efficient labor markets. If physicians are willing to supply more hours than firms are willing to hire at the prevailing wage, wages and physician incomes should fall. As the occupation becomes less attractive and fewer college graduates enter medicine, the reduced flow of newly trained physicians will increase wages and expected earnings until the financial return to medical education is once again commensurate with the return in other professions (adjusted by the equalizing differences). Conversely, if there is a shortage such that patients must wait months to schedule an appointment with a physician, consumers and/or health insurers will bid up physician fees, such that wages and physician earnings rise. Higher earnings will encourage a greater number of students to enter medicine until long-run supply again equals demand.

3. LABOR SUPPLY TOPICS

3.1. Rationale for Government Intervention in Medical Labor Markets

In practice, medical markets have not been allowed to operate as described above, so we have no knowledge of whether they would in fact do so. Most medical labor markets are heavily regulated because policy makers do not believe the unaided market will produce the optimal number, quality, specialty mix, and/or geographic location of health professionals. The principal concern is that because of asymmetric information consumers will not be able to determine the quality of services provided by medical labor (Arrow, 1963). One response is to try to assure consumers that the inputs into the health production function exceed a minimum acceptable quality level.[10] The policies consist of some combination of: (1) requiring workers to be licensed before they may legally practice; (2) certifying workers who pass an exam to

---

[10] Arrow's implicit assumption is that high-quality labor will produce high-quality services, whereas they could produce a greater quantity of average-quality services.

distinguish them from lower-quality labor; and (3) accrediting schools and programs to ensure that graduates face a rigorous curriculum. In the United States, for example, physicians must graduate from an accredited medical school and complete at least one year of residency training at an accredited program before being eligible for a medical license. In Japan, an aspiring physician must graduate from an accredited medical school, complete a two-year internship, and pass a national licensing exam before being allowed to treat patients.

Another way to increase the quality of the medical workforce is to subsidize medical education, which creates rents for successful applicants and produces an excess of applicants relative to available positions. High-ability students are more likely to be admitted when medical school positions are rationed. Rationed entry is likely to make licensing irrelevant for physician services; medical schools will reject applicants at the lower part of the quality or ability distribution (Arrow, 1963). Licensing can still play an important quality assurance role for non-physician personnel whose education is not subsidized and rationed, and for graduates of international medical schools who may not have been subject to as rigorous an admission screen as domestically trained physicians (Cooper and Aiken, 2001).

There are costs associated with medical licensing generally and restrictions on entering medical school. Licensing places constraints on the health production function by making it illegal to substitute between certain types of labor inputs for certain tasks. Licensing fees and the education requirements necessary to receive a license increase the cost of entering a profession and reduce labor supply at all wages, and the rationing of medical school slots truncates the supply of physician services. This will increase costs in output markets (e.g. physician services), increase the wages of licensed professions, and restrict product variety available to consumers. As Arrow (1963) pointed out almost 50 years ago, "Both the licensing laws and the standards of medical-school training have limited the possibilities of alternative qualities of medical care. The declining ratio of physicians to total employees in the medical care industry shows that the substitution of less trained personnel, technicians, and the like, is not prevented completely, but the central role of the highly trained physician is not affected at all" (Arrow, 1963, p. 953).

The regulation of medical labor markets creates rents, which in turn creates incentives for providers to organize to capture (and expand) these rents. In fact, governments often allow medical professions to define and control the nature of the regulation by allowing professional associations to define the requirements for obtaining a license, to administer licenses, or, in some cases, to explicitly determine the number of people allowed to enter the profession or a specialty within the profession. This creates the appearance that medical professions are restricting entry to create rents, and is supported by theoretical predictions that a professional group allowed to define the minimum quality threshold will set a standard that exceeds the socially optimal benchmark (Leland, 1979).

In the United States the Liaison Committee on Medical Education, which is formed by the Association of American Medical Colleges (AAMC) and the American Medical Association (AMA), accredits US medical schools. Because it is difficult for a student who attends a non-accredited medical school to practice medicine in the US, the number of US medical schools is essentially determined by physician organizations. As described in section 3.5, specialty associations in the US determine how many residents can train in each specialty, and therefore determine the flow of new entrants.

Self-regulation by non-governmental medical labor organizations is common in many other countries. For example, the Medical Council of India, the Korean Institute of Medical Education, the General Medical Council (UK), the Netherlands-Flemish Accreditation Organization, and the Japan University Accreditation Organization approve curricula and accredit medical schools in their respective countries.

3.2. Licensing, Certification, and Accreditation: Objectives and Implications

In this section we examine theoretical arguments for how the government can address the asymmetric information problem, the extent of occupational regulation that actually occurs in practice, and the implications of occupational regulation on output quality, the quantity of licensed and unlicensed labor, prices, and the earnings of regulated professions.

If producing information is costless, the ideal solution is to eliminate information asymmetries directly by providing consumers with information about the attributes and quality of medical services (Leland, 1979). Consumers are primarily interested in the expected health outcomes that result from a production process, not the quality of inputs that enter into the production process. That is, they want information on the efficacy of bypass operations performed by a particular physician at a particular hospital, not information on the quantity and type of education and training received by the physician, nurses, operating room technicians, pharmacists, and therapists who work at that hospital.

Dranove and Jin (2010) define quality disclosure "as an effort by a certification agency to systematically measure and report product quality for a nontrivial percentage of products in a market." Such disclosure could be self-reported voluntarily by sellers, or disclosed by a third party. The US health care market is moving in this direction, particularly with third-party reports by organizations such as *US News & World Report*, Medicare, the Leapfrog group, and New York and Pennsylvania for Cardiovascular Care. Although most empirical studies find that highly ranked providers benefit after the dissemination of information, the effects tend to be small (Dranove and Jin, 2010). Two possible explanations are that it is difficult to measure a provider's value added given the difficulty of measuring a patient's health, both before and after treatment, and consumers and referring providers already knew the information in the report cards.

A second way to address information asymmetry would be to make sellers liable for poor quality (Leland, 1979), as is currently done with medical malpractice. If quality problems are easy to detect and providers bear the cost of poor quality, malpractice might be an effective policy. Unfortunately there is little evidence that the medical malpractice system deters negligent behavior because few of the patients who experience malpractice actually sue, these patients are as likely to win a lawsuit or settlement as patients who did not in fact experience negligence, and physicians' malpractice premiums are not experience rated (Danzon, 2000).

A third alternative is to have health insurers, acting as consumers' agents, write quality-contingent reimbursement contracts with providers (Shapiro, 1986). If health insurers can observe the quality of medical services or the patient's health outcome, high-ability providers and providers who invest in quality-enhancing skills will be rewarded. As with provider report cards, this is the direction in which the market is headed. Primary care physicians in the United Kingdom, for example, received average incremental payments of about $40,000 per year (32 percent of their income) for providing services deemed to be high quality. In most countries, however, pay-for-performance payments constitute a small percentage of a provider's income or profits. A US physician who received the maximum pay-for-performance payments, for example, would have received an estimated 5 percent of her base income as a bonus, and a hospital only an estimated 2 percent of their profit (Nicholson, 2008).

A potentially less expensive alternative to the above quality assurance approaches is to regulate certain inputs into the health production function and thereby assure consumers indirectly about output quality. This indirect approach is not ideal, but it may be the most feasible approach, particularly because licensing enforcement is done one time only when a professional is trained, rather than perpetually in the case of output regulation (Shapiro, 1986).[11] Kleiner and Krueger (2009) highlight three different types of occupational regulation. Registration, the least restrictive form, requires individuals to provide their name, address, and qualifications to a government agency before practicing. Certification allows any person to provide a service, but the government or a private, non-profit agency distinguishes providers who have passed an exam. Under licensing, the strictest form of occupational regulation, it is illegal for a

---

[11] Some health insurers in the US require providers to get re-certified, which makes the indirect approach more expensive than it otherwise would be (but perhaps more accurate, too).

person to work in an occupation for compensation without first meeting the state or federal licensing standard. A licensing board typically examines a candidate's credentials, determines whether the schools and degrees satisfy the minimum training standards, and then sets the pass rate of the licensing exam (Kleiner, 2006).

According to a 2008 survey, an estimated 29 percent of all US workers indicated that they were required to have a government-issued license to perform their job (Kleiner and Krueger, 2009). In the United Kingdom, by contrast, about 13.5 percent of the general workforce required a license in 2008. Licensing is much more common in health-related occupations. Among non-physician US health care workers, about 76 percent require a license (Humphris et al., 2011), and all physicians are required to be licensed.[12] In the UK, an estimated 73 percent of the medical workforce (including physicians) requires a license.[13]

There are two prominent theoretical models describing the motivation for and likely impact of occupational licensing. Leland (1979) focuses on how licensing can ameliorate the adverse selection problem stemming from information asymmetries. As in Akerlof's (1970) model of used cars, if physicians know their own abilities but consumers do not, physician fees will not vary by quality, and prospective physicians of relatively high ability will decide not to enter the profession. This withdrawal reduces the average quality of physician services, reduces prices, and results in a profession of quacks only.[14] Social welfare can be increased if a licensing authority establishes a minimum quality level, but if a professional group is allowed to define the quality threshold necessary for a license, the minimum quality level will exceed the socially optimal level. Licensing will be most beneficial in markets where: (1) consumers value quality highly; (2) demand is inelastic; and (3) the marginal cost of providing quality services is relatively low. Although the second criterion is likely to be true for most medical services and probably the first as well, the marginal cost of providing quality services is likely to be high.

In Figure 14.1, licensure increases the cost of entering an occupation and shifts upward the supply of labor. Entry costs will increase if workers have to pay license fees or, more importantly, if the licensing authority requires substantial education/training or a long residency requirement. If consumers believe that licensing improves output quality, demand for medical services and the prices of those services may rise,

---

[12] This is consistent with a separate analysis of US employment data, which finds that about 81 percent of the 9.6 million workers in the two main health-related SOC codes (including physicians) require a license to provide services in a particular occupation. The SOC categories are Healthcare Practitioner and Technical Occupations (29-0000) and Healthcare Support Occupations (31-0000). These categories contain most of the workers who provide medical services, but not all employees in the health care industry (e.g. scientists at pharmaceutical firms).

[13] Results of the licensing analysis for the US and UK are available from the authors by request.

[14] Leland (1979) does not incorporate into his model the situation, common in most countries, where an accrediting body restricts the number of medical school slots. The subsequent rationing of slots should screen out quacks and could make licensing irrelevant (Arrow, 1963).

thereby increasing the licensed profession's marginal revenue product and shifting out labor demand.[15] Both of these phenomena would cause the wage of the licensed occupation to rise.

The impact of licensing on health outcomes is unclear theoretically. Licensing screens out low-quality providers, restricts supply, creates rents, and increases the expected returns to quality-enhancing training. This will increase the quality of labor inputs and thus the quality of medical services provided. However, the higher licensed wage will encourage firms to substitute capital and non-licensed labor for licensed labor where possible.[16] Licensure may also place restrictions on the health production function, such as forbidding nurse assistants from administering drugs or requiring that certified registered nurse anesthetists be supervised by an anesthesiologist. These constraints, along with higher wages for licensed labor, will increase output costs, output prices, and reduce the quantity consumed. If licensed labor represents a large share of the production costs, the marginal rate of technical substitution between licensed labor and other inputs is small, and output demand is inelastic, which all would appear to be true empirically for medical services in general, then production costs and prices may increase substantially as a result of licensing. Higher prices will reduce the amount of medical services received. Therefore the quality of medical services actually provided should increase due to licensing, but the amount of services provided should decrease; the net effect on population health is ambiguous (Kleiner and Kudrle, 2000).

In the Leland model, quality is innate and licensing prevents low-quality workers from entering an occupation, truncates the ability/quality distribution, and thereby improves average worker (and output) quality. Shapiro (1986), on the other hand, argues that quality derives in part from endogenous human capital investment. In Shapiro's model all providers receive the same price for services rendered during an initial "introductory" period. Once consumers observe reputations, however, providers who invested substantially in human capital receive a higher price than providers who accumulated less human capital. Licensing requires workers to receive a minimum level of human capital. This constraint increases the price of low-quality services (to encourage entry) but *reduces* the price of high-quality services based on the critical assumption that an increase in training reduces the marginal cost of quality.

In Shapiro's model licensing benefits consumers who value quality highly (due to the lower price of high-quality services) but harms consumers who do not (due to the higher price of low-quality services). The social cost of licensing is the excessive training received by low-quality service providers—training that is not appreciated by consumers who do not value quality highly. Although it is difficult to determine

---

[15] Licensing could actually decrease the demand for medical care if the higher-quality workers are more productive.

[16] Individuals who are discouraged from entering a licensed occupation may enter unlicensed occupations, thereby increasing labor supply and driving down the unlicensed wage (Kleiner, 2000).

whether the benefits of enhanced quality outweigh the excess training costs, Shapiro highlights that strict licensing is likely to reduce welfare when: (1) consumers and/or referring physicians can observe a provider's reputation very soon after the training period; (2) when the marginal cost of quality is large; and (3) when few consumers value quality highly.

Are provider reputations likely to provide sufficiently strong incentives for workers to invest in human capital to the point of rendering licensing irrelevant? Recent empirical work on bypass surgery would indicate that the answer is "no." Johnson (2010) finds that relatively low-quality cardiovascular surgeons are 10 percent more likely to stop performing surgeries or to relocate relative to higher-quality surgeons. She finds no evidence, however, that high-quality cardiovascular surgeons perform more procedures or generate more charges than low-quality surgeons. This weak relationship between provider quality and earnings could be due, in part, to poor information. Kolstad (2009) presents evidence that when Pennsylvania publicly reported the quality of cardiac surgeons, health outcomes improved substantially due to physician's intrinsic motivation. That is, once a physician realized where she stood in the quality distribution, she invested in additional human capital for reasons other than increasing her earnings.

The existing empirical studies generally provide a pessimistic assessment on the welfare effects of licensing in medical labor markets. These studies conclude that licensing is associated with restricted labor supply, an increased wage of the licensed occupation, rents, increased output prices, and no measurable effect on output quality. Kleiner (2006) summarizes the literature on the effect of licensing on earnings as follows: "For the higher-education and higher-income occupations working mainly in the quasi-private sector, like physicians, dentists, and lawyers, licensing appears to have large effects (on earnings) through either limiting entry or restricting movement to the state." For other medical occupations the results generally show no effect on wages, such as for nurses (White, 1980), or a small effect on wages, such as for radiologic technicians (Timmons and Thornton, 2008) and clinical laboratory personnel (White, 1978). Kleiner (2006) concludes that occupations that work independently and interact directly with customers, such as physicians and dentists, receive larger benefits from licensing than paraprofessionals who are supervised by others, such as nurses.

However, no study has yet examined the effect of licensing on the demand for physician services and the health outcomes produced by physician services, which is arguably the most important licensing policy question given the central role played by physicians. This gap in the literature exists not for lack of interest in the result, but for lack of a research design that produces causal effect of licensing. The non-licensing counterfactual is difficult to predict when physicians in all developed countries are licensed. Furthermore, rationing of medical school slots may screen out low-ability physicians such that the licensing requirements are not binding. Arrow (1963), among others, believes that there are likely to be substantial positive welfare gains associated with at least some degree of physician licensing.

The simplest way to estimate the wage effect of licensing is to compare the wages of licensed occupations to unlicensed occupations that have similar skill and education requirements. More sophisticated studies also control for individual-level human capital and demographic control variables that might have independent wage effects. Using the latter method and data from the 1990 and 2000 US censuses, Kleiner (2006) finds that physicians and dentists earn 50 percent and 90 percent more, respectively, than biological and life scientists (an unlicensed occupation), controlling for other individual characteristics.

Other studies exploit differences across states in whether licensing is required, or the degree of licensing (e.g. the percent of applicants who pass a dental licensing exam, or whether a state accepts a dental license from another state) when licensing is required in all states. Anderson et al. (2000) find that US physicians who practice in states with strict regulations on the practice of alternative medicine earn higher incomes. Kleiner and Kudrle (2000) find that US dentists practicing in states with the strictest licensing requirements earn 12 percent more than those practicing in less regulated states, and White (1978) finds that clinical laboratory personnel in licensed states earn 17 percent more than those in unlicensed states.

The above results are at odds with the studies reviewed later in section 3.4, which find that dentists and physicians earn similar (or lower) rates of return relative to "similar" occupations. The studies in the previous paragraph assume that selection on unobservables is unimportant within an occupation between states (e.g. productive dentists do not locate disproportionately in states with strict licensing requirements); the rate of return studies assume that selection on unobservables is unimportant between occupations (e.g. productive college graduates do not choose an MBA degree disproportionately versus a medical degree). Although one of these selection effects is likely to be more important than the other, it is difficult to determine which one.

Two studies use instrumental variables or a regression discontinuity design to estimate the effect of licensing on wages while accounting for the possibility that individuals with relatively high or low unobserved ability may select into licensed occupations (or states requiring a license within the occupation). Kugler and Sauer (2005) find that physicians emigrating to Israel from the Soviet Union who had slightly more than 20 years of prior experience, and thus were granted a license to practice in Israel, earned more than three times as much as physicians with slightly less than 20 years of experience, who faced a more onerous re-licensing process.[17] Interestingly, the OLS estimate is 50 percent smaller, indicating that immigrant

---

[17] It should be noted that this substantial effect of licensing is unlikely to generalize to other countries and situations because a majority of the Soviet Union physicians who did not receive a license in Israel switched professions entirely, and they may not have emigrated for economic reasons only.

physicians who acquired a license had lower earnings potential than those who did not. That is, relatively low-ability workers may seek the economic protection provided by licensing. Timmons and Thornton (2008) find similar negative selection for radiologic technicians. The estimated effect of licensing on wages using instrumental variables (7 percent) is twice as large as the OLS estimate.[18]

Licensing also appears to increase wages in the European Union. In the United Kingdom, wages in the licensed occupations of medical practitioners, pharmacists, pharmacologists, and dental practitioners are an estimated 6 to 65 percent higher than otherwise similar workers in unlicensed occupations (Kleiner, 2006).[19] Physicians and dentists in France earn an estimated 8 to 21 percent more than their unlicensed colleagues, whereas workers in those professions in Germany have similar wages relative to unlicensed occupations.

Empirical studies confirm that licensing increases wages by restricting labor supply. Kleiner (2006) finds that the supply of respiratory therapists and dieticians grew faster in US states that did not require a license for these occupations versus states that did. Kleiner and Kudrle (2000) find that the number of dentists per capita grew more slowly between 1980 and 1990 in US states with stricter dental licensing regulations. Finally, Wanchek (2009) finds that the supply of dental hygienists per capita is higher in US states with fewer entry restrictions.

Although there are many studies documenting a link between licensing and rents to the regulated occupation, there are no known studies identifying a positive effect of licensing on the quality of medical services or patients' health outcomes—the rationale for licensing. Kleiner and Kudrle (2000) surveyed new enlistees in the Air Force to collect information on where they grew up, whether their family had dental insurance, and the other household characteristics. They combined this information with data on the strictness of dental licensing requirements in each US state, and a comprehensive dental exam performed at the time of enlistment. They find that strict dental licensing is not associated with better dental care, fewer complaints to a state licensing board, or lower dental malpractice premiums. Strict licensing is associated, however, with higher dental prices, suggesting that the reduced demand associated with licensing could offset any improvement in input quality (although they do not detect differences in input quality in this study). Wanchek (2009) reaches a similar conclusion with regards to dental hygienist licensing: higher wages for dental hygienists due to strict licensing rules are associated with a lower demand for dental care. It is worth repeating, though, the empirical difficulty of measuring the benefits of physician licensing, as mentioned above.

---

[18] Timmons and Thornton (2008) use the number of members on the licensing board to instrument for the strictness of the licensing requirements in a state.

[19] This analysis is based on data from 1993 to 1997. The unlicensed occupations include chemists, biological scientists, and biochemists.

One policy recommendation is for the government to certify rather than license medical labor. Under this scheme, a government agency administers an exam and certifies individuals who pass, while still allowing individuals who do not pass to legally practice the profession. This would allow consumers (and/or health insurers) to decide whether to pay higher wages for workers deemed to be high quality without barring low-quality workers altogether (Kleiner, 2000). This policy, which would still provide incentives for human capital investment, would seek to eliminate or reduce excessive training received by low-quality service providers—the source of the social costs of licensing in Shapiro's (1986) model. Shapiro points out, however, that certification can still lead to overinvestment by high-quality workers in an attempt to signal their quality.

Humphris et al. (2011) examine the welfare effects if the US federal government no longer paid a wage premium on non-physician licensed labor.[20] They estimate that such a policy would shift $102 billion (in 2008) from medical labor to consumers, thereby reducing medical spending by about 5 percent.

Given the negative empirical findings, why is licensing so prevalent in the medical labor market? One option would be to license professionals who interact directly with consumers, such as physicians and dentists, and allow the quality of paraprofessionals (e.g. nurses, technologists) who work under the supervision of professionals to be monitored by the professionals. White and Marmor (1982) consider such a structure, where professionals have an incentive to use paraprofessionals as long as the productivity gains exceed the costs. They argue, however, that medical professionals in the US have avoided this monitoring role because they lack administrative training and the opportunity cost of their time is high. Another explanation might be that in a fee-for-service system such as the US, no single professional is responsible for a consumer's health. When many providers work independently (e.g. home care nurse or physical therapist), there is a greater need to license paraprofessionals. This raises the possibility that in countries or health systems that rely more heavily on capitation or explicitly place physicians in charge (e.g. UK), licensing may be less valuable. Cooper and Aiken (2001) argue that the main impact of the proliferation of paraprofessional (or non-physician clinician) licensing is to empower chiropractors, optometrists, psychologists, physician assistants, nurse practitioners, and nurse anesthetists to provide services that substitute for physician services. Under this interpretation paraprofessional licensing increases the marginal rate of technical substitution between physicians and non-physician clinicians, and reduces physician rents associated with licensing and entry barriers generally.

---

[20] The government could implement this by reducing the prices they pay for medical services. The Humphris et al. (2011) calculation assumes implicitly that private health insurers would reduce provider prices by an equivalent amount.

3.3. Subsidizing Medical Education

In 1906 the Council on Medical Education of the American Medical Association (AMA) inspected the 160 medical schools that were operating in the United States and fully approved only 82.[21] In 1910 the Carnegie Foundation issued the Flexner Report, which recommended fewer medical schools and controls to assure a quality educational curriculum. The number of medical schools fell to 85 in 1920, 73 in 1930, and 69 in 1944, before rising to its current level of 126 (Kessel, 1958). Early economic studies concluded that the AMA controlled the number of medical school positions and set the number to generate rents (Friedman and Kuznets, 1945; Kessel, 1958). Kessel likened the AMA's position to "giving the American Iron and Steel Institute the power to determine the output of steel" (Kessel, 1958, p. 29).

The ratio of applicants to medical (and dental) school positions seems to support the hypothesis that a cartel restricts entry to generate rents. There are about ten times as many applicants as available positions in the UK and China, two to three times as many in the US and the Netherlands, and about twice as many dental school applications as positions in the UK (Jetha, 2002). As McGuire (2000) points out, if medical school tuition were set equal to cost, the surplus of applicants would indeed constitute strong evidence for the cartel theory.

But medical school is heavily subsidized, so of course the demand for slots will be higher than if tuition was set equal to cost. The complexity of medical school finances makes it difficult to measure the percentage of a medical school education actually paid by students. In 2006 tuition and student fees accounted for only 3.4 percent of US medical schools' revenues. The largest funding sources were medical services provided to patients (38.0 percent), federal research grants and contracts (20.0 percent), transfers from universities and teaching hospitals (20.0 percent), federal, state, and local government appropriations (6.1 percent), and gifts and endowment income (4.5 percent).[22] Although this probably overstates the magnitude of the subsidy, government transfers relax medical schools' budget constraints and allow them to set tuition below the cost of education. That said, medical schools choose to subsidize tuition, possibly to satisfy donors' preferences; they are not mandated to do so. An older study that collected detailed spending data concluded that in 1993 US medical school tuition covered only 16 percent of instruction costs in 1993 (Ganem et al., 1995).[23]

There are several implications of subsidized medical education. First, medical schools have great control over the medical workforce; their decisions regarding how

[21] The Council deemed 32 schools to be completely unacceptable.
[22] LCME Part I-A Annual Financial Questionnaire, February 2009.
[23] Jones and Korn (1997) review a number of studies and conclude that the cost of educating a medical student ranged from $40,000 to $50,000 in 1996 dollars. Median tuition in 1996 was $23,700 at private medical schools and $8,800 at public medical schools for in-state students. This would imply slightly smaller subsidies than in Ganem et al. (1995).

many students to accept determine the flow of domestically trained physicians. Second, determining whether medical schools are restricting entry to create physician rents rather than fulfilling other more noble objectives requires a model of non–profit behavior, which several authors have articulated (Hall and Lindsay, 1980; Eckstein et al., 1988).[24] Third, the rationing of medical school positions may make licensing irrelevant or less important because schools will weed out (some) low-quality applicants (Arrow, 1963). Fourth, it is unclear whether there would be fewer or more physicians trained if medical schools set tuition equal to cost (McGuire, 2000). Fewer students would demand a position once the subsidy is removed, but positions would now be determined by supply and demand rather than by fiat.

3.4. Rates of Return to Medical Training and Specialization

Entry barriers can create rents. Above we reviewed the literature on the effect of licensing on wages, but licensing is only one possible entry barrier. In this section we review the literature on the rate of return to medical training and to specialization within medicine, which should capture the complete effects of all entry barriers. Persistently high rates of return provide evidence for the existence of entry barriers. Calculating rates of return requires data on expected lifetime earnings in a medical profession and an alternative profession, the costs of education, and the length of training. Ideally the alternative profession accounts for any possible selection on unobserved characteristics.

Nicholson (2008) summarizes eight studies that estimate the rate of return to a medical school education in the United States between 1929 and 1990. The general conclusion is that the financial returns from entering medicine are generally in line with the returns experienced by similar occupations. Using earnings data from 1990, Weeks et al. (1994) estimate that physicians can expect a 16 percent return on their investment relative to high school graduates. The same study reported that dentists (21 percent), lawyers (25 percent), and MBAs (28 percent) could expect greater rates of return than US physicians. Weeks and Wallace (2002) updated their analysis using 1997 rather than 1990 income data, and estimated similar rates of return. Using cross-section earnings data from 2008 and assuming a 3 percent real discount rate, Vaughn et al. (2010) report that the average primary care physician could expect to earn $2.5 million over his lifetime, net of education costs, versus $1.7 million for an MBA

[24] Hall and Lindsay (1980) present evidence that medical school enrollments rise in response to both donors' (e.g. government, patients, health insurers, philanthropists, alumni, and industry) demand for trained physicians and the number of applications. Eckstein et al. (1988) develop a dynamic model to explore how a university decides on the quality and quantity of engineers it should accept. In response to an increase in applicants, a university will increase both the quantity and quality of accepted students, which reduces the marginal cost of training current and future students, but also reduces the future number of applicants by increasing the stock of engineers and reducing their expected future wages.

graduate and $340,000 for the average college graduate. This study does not report rates of return that account for different training lengths.

The three studies above assume that the current earnings—experience profile will remain the same in the future and they do not allow occupation-specific earnings to depend on a person's observed or unobserved abilities. The Weeks et al. (1994) 16 percent rate of return estimate is likely to be too high because physicians could certainly expect to earn more than the average high school graduate if they decided to forego medicine. Using earnings data between 1979 and 2004 from the 1979 National Longitudinal Survey of Youth (NLSY), Glied et al. (2009) model the earnings physicians would receive if they decided not to attend medical school based on their observed ability (e.g. grade point average, AFQT test score). They estimate a relatively low 7 to 9 percent rate of return for US primary care physicians.

Few rate of return studies have been performed for other health professions in the US, or for other countries. Using 1996 earnings data, Stark (2007) finds that physicians, dentists, optometrists, and veterinarians in Canada experience rates of returns similar to professions such as engineering, business, and college graduates generally. Morris and McGuire (2002) estimate that nurses in the United Kingdom experience rates of return of 8 to 13 percent in the early 1990s, and Mott et al. (1995) present evidence that pharmacists in the US in the 1980s and early 1990s had rates of return similar to high school graduates. Taken as a whole, the literature generally does not find excessive rates of return to a health education.

By contrast, most studies find that physicians who specialize in non-primary care earn substantial returns relative to general practitioners or family practitioners. Nicholson (2008) summarizes four studies that estimate the returns to medical specialization in the US between 1951 and 1998. The results of these studies show that the returns to specializing in a particular area within medicine (e.g. surgery, radiology, obstetrics/gynecology) are high and have increased sharply over time. Between 1987 and 1998, for example, the rate of return in radiology (relative to family practice) has ranged from 47 to 105 percent. The persistence of these high rates of return, combined with an excess of applicants relative to available positions, indicates that there are entry barriers. In the next section we discuss whether specialty associations functioning as cartels create these barriers, or whether they are due to more benign factors. Cordes et al. (2002) also find large rates of return to specializing within dentistry in the United States: 16.6 percent for orthodontics and 26.8 percent for oral and maxillofacial surgeons. Finally, Vaughn et al. (2010) estimate that a cardiologist could expect to earn twice as much as a primary care physician ($5.2 million versus $2.5 million) in 2008 dollars, net of income taxes, living expenses, and education expenses.[25]

---

[25] If physicians as a whole experience rates of return to their training that are comparable to non-medical professions but specialists earn much higher returns than primary care physicians, it raises the possibility that primary care physicians experience below-market returns.

3.5. Economics of Professional and Specialty Associations

In this section we explore why there are persistent high rates of return to physician specialization. Medical school graduates must receive at least one year of residency training at an accredited residency program in order to practice medicine in the United States. Therefore, the market for residents functions as an intermediate market that largely determines the number and specialty distribution of physicians in the United States. In 2008, a total of 22,000 first-year residency positions were offered by over 1,200 hospitals in 26 different specialties. Sixty-nine percent of these positions were filled by students who graduated from US medical schools, with most of the remainder filled by international medical graduates (IMGs). Because there is routinely an excess supply of residents, any increase in the number of US medical school positions (as is currently occurring) without a concomitant increase in the demand by hospitals for residents is likely to crowd out IMGs without affecting the flow of newly licensed physicians.

In the United States a computer algorithm allocates prospective residents to residency programs each spring in the National Resident Matching Program, or the "Match."[26] Highly desirable specialties, usually those with high rates of return, tend to have an excess supply of residents. Between 1991 and 2009, for example, the ratio of the supply of residents (i.e. the number of applicants ranking a specialty as their first choice) to the demand for residents (i.e. the number of available first-year residency positions) exceeded 1.40 in orthopedic surgery in all but one year, and between 1997 and 2009 the ratio exceeded 1.60 in dermatology in all but one year.[27]

In a well-functioning labor market, the excess supply of residents should reduce the residents' wage in oversubscribed specialties, encourage hospitals to open more positions in those specialties, eventually increase the number of licensed physicians entering the market, and equalize rates of return across specialties. The fact that this does not happen confirms that there are barriers restricting entry to certain non-primary care specialties. These barriers exist in other countries as well. It is common for medical school graduates in Greece to wait several years for a non-primary care residency position opening (Mariolis et al., 2007), and only 3 percent of Greek medical school graduates enter the relatively low-paying family practice specialty.

The high rates of return to specialization and the entry barriers have created a tournament of sorts among US medical students. The four most difficult specialties to enter in the US in Match in recent years have been plastic surgery, dermatology, orthopedic surgery, and otolaryngology (i.e. ear, nose, and throat surgery). Not surprisingly, these specialties have high mean incomes and/or desirable work schedules.

---

[26] The Match is a computer algorithm that assigns prospective residents to residency programs based on explicit preferences. Students agree to attend the program to which they are assigned.

[27] 1997 was the first year dermatology positions were allocated in the Match.

Between 18 and 45 percent of US medical school graduates who ranked one of these four specialties as their first choice in the 2007 Match were not able to secure a first-year residency position in that specialty. Students need to perform well in medical school if they want to obtain a residency position in one of these competitive specialties. After the second year of medical school, all US medical students take the National Board of Medical Examiners Step 1 exam. The mean Step 1 score for US medical students who successfully entered these four specialties ranged from 236 (orthopedics) to 246 (plastic surgery), well above the overall mean score of 220.[28]

There also appears to be a tournament in Japan for entrance into certain specialties. The Japanese government keeps its health care costs relatively low by setting prices. But prices are not regulated in services that are excluded from national health insurance, such as cosmetic surgery. Ramseyer (2008) finds that cosmetic surgeons in Japan earn more than other specialists, are more talented, have superior training, and are more likely to have attended a prestigious medical school.

The entry barriers at the specialty level do not appear to be justified on the basis of asymmetric information between providers and consumers regarding the quality of medical services. All physicians must be licensed, regardless of specialty, and all prospective residents have already run the medical school gauntlet that screens out low-ability students. Nicholson (2003) explores four possible explanations for the persistently large rates of return to specialization in the US: cartel behavior by professional associations, a shortage of teaching material, wage rigidity, and entry barriers to deter supply-induced demand. Physicians exert great control over specialty entry, so the question is not whether physicians restrict entry, but whether their motives are purely self-serving.

One possible explanation is that Residency Review Committees (RRCs), private organizations in the US that consist primarily of physicians from a particular specialty, restrict the flow of new physicians to that specialty to create rents. The Accreditation Council of Graduate Medical Education (ACGME), a private organization responsible for overseeing residency training, is sponsored by five provider organizations (Accreditation Council of Graduate Medical Education, 1996).[29] The ACGME sets overall policies and allows a separate RRC to review and accredit residency programs in each of the 26 specialties. Each of the five sponsoring organizations appoints four representatives to an RRC and the government appoints one non-voting representative.

---

[28] Medical students who are unable to enter high-paying specialties do have the option to train as a primary care physician but market themselves to patients and referring physicians as a specialist. This path may become more common, especially if patients and referring physicians are not well informed and/or formal specialized training is not perceived to be important.

[29] The five organizations are the American Medical Association, the American Board of Medical Specialties (e.g. American Board of Dermatology), the Association of American Medical Colleges, the American Hospital Association, and the Council of Medical Specialty Societies (e.g. American Academy of Dermatology).

A teaching hospital that wants to open a new residency program or increase the number of residents in an existing program must apply to the relevant RRC.[30] Therefore an RRC essentially has complete control over the flow of physicians into a specialty because medical students who attend residency programs that are not certified by the ACGME are not eligible to take the licensing exam, and thus are not able to practice in the United States. Entry into specialties in the Netherlands is also strongly influenced by the physicians themselves: "medical school graduates can only register as general practitioners or medical specialists after completing specific training programs. The capacity of the training programs and the criteria for registration are determined largely by professional associations" (Schut, 1995, p. 644).

An RRC has the same power as a labor union that is the sole source of a certain type of labor and negotiates collectively with a firm or set of firms (Nicholson, 2003). Economists have modeled labor unions as maximizing a utility function whose arguments are the quantity of union members employed and either the workers' rents or the total wage bill, subject to the firms' labor demand (Pencavel, 1984; MaCurdy and Pencavel, 1986). The union chooses the wage and firms respond by hiring a quantity of union workers such that the marginal product equals the wage.

The relevant constraint for an RRC is consumers' aggregate demand for physician services. Whereas a union chooses the wage and allows a firm to choose the profit-maximizing quantity of labor conditional on that wage, an RRC chooses the flow of residents that will in the long run produce the desired, utility-maximizing quantity of physician services (and therefore the quantity of physicians) and the price of those services (and therefore the rents).[31] One problem with this argument is that it fails to explain why RRCs appear to differ in their ability or desire to generate rents, with non-primary care RRCs apparently more effective at erecting barriers to entry than primary care RRCs. A simple, but difficult to prove, explanation is that preferences for rents versus the quantity of physicians in the specialty may differ across RRCs. Or perhaps smaller specialties (e.g. non-primary care specialties) are better able to restrict entry across a relatively small number of residency programs than more populous specialties (e.g. primary care). That said, Bhattacharya (2005) does conclude that entry barriers differ between specialties in the US, as will be discussed below.

A second possible explanation for persistently high rates of return to various non-primary care specialties is that there may be a shortage of patients in certain specialties that constrains the number of residents who can develop competencies. An RRC considers a number of factors when deciding whether to approve a program and how

---

[30] The RRCs also periodically review established programs to ensure they are in compliance with the standards.

[31] Noether (1986) models the supply of physicians as a combination of the level that would result with no entry barriers and the level that maximizes physician income. This is consistent with the RRCs focusing solely on rent generation. She finds that the US physician stock moved from the cartel extreme toward the perfect competition extreme between 1965 and 1982.

many residents may be trained at each program: "Those numbers (of residents who may be trained by a program) will be based primarily on the number, qualifications, and commitment of the faculty; the volume and variety of the patient population available for educational purposes; the quality of the educational offering; and the totality of the institutional resources" (Accreditation Council of Graduate Medical Education, 1996).[32]

A third possible explanation is that teaching hospitals may not be willing, due to equity concerns, or able to adjust resident wages to allow the market to clear (Nicholson, 2003). The ACGME used to require teaching hospitals to pay all residents the same wage, regardless of specialty. Although they changed that policy, they still require that residents be paid an undefined minimum wage, which presumably is positive. This restriction might prevent the wage from adjusting to clear the excess supply of residents to certain non-primary care specialties.

A fourth possible explanation is that RRCs may restrict entry not to create rents for that specialty but to control medical spending by deterring physician-induced demand behavior (Cooper and Aiken, 2001). According to this line of argument, if the dermatology RRC allowed programs to expand, practicing dermatologists would respond by exploiting their information advantage to promote low-value medical services to patients.[33]

3.6. How Elastic Is Medical Workforce Labor Supply?

We now turn to the question of whether money exerts a strong influence on six different decisions made by the medical workforce: occupational choice by prospective physicians, specialty choice by physicians, geographic location by physicians, labor force participation by nurses, and hours of labor supplied by nurses and physicians. If money is important for these decisions and wages/prices are determined by market forces, then labor shortages and surpluses will be short-lived: labor will relocate, enter/leave occupations, shift between specialties, and respond to higher wages by working more.

3.7. Physician Specialty Choice

Studies on physician specialty choice can be categorized according to whether they account for barriers to entering certain specialties; whether they allow specialty choice to be endogenous when forecasting a medical student's expected earnings in each specialty; and the source of the variation in expected earnings between specialties that identifies the occupational choice expected earnings elasticity. Three studies (Sloan,

---

[32] One way to increase a resident's experience would be to increase the length of a residency program, although this never happens in practice.

[33] See McGuire (2000) for an extensive review of the role of physicians as agents, and their ability to induce demand for their services.

1970; Bazzoli, 1985; Gagne and Leger, 2005) examine multiple cohorts of graduating medical students and identify an elasticity based on changes over time in specialty-specific expected earnings or, in one case, changes over time in province-specific fees. The two key assumptions in these studies are that changes in specialty-specific non-monetary attributes (e.g. prestige, work schedule, psychological costs associated with malpractice suits) are uncorrelated with changes in specialty-specific expected earnings, and all students graduating in the same year expect to earn the same amount over their lifetime in the same specialties (i.e. unobserved ability does not affect expected earnings, or specialty choice is assumed to be exogenous when forecasting expected earnings).

Sloan (1970) reports specialty-specific elasticity estimates (the percentage change in residents associated with a 1 percent increase in the net present value (NPV) of expected earnings in that specialty) that range from zero to 0.28. Bazzoli (1985) finds that medical students are more likely to choose primary care when the expected earnings are relatively large, but this effect is small. Specifically, a $10,000 increase in the expected earnings of primary versus non-primary care (about a 20 percent increase in the mean value) is associated with a 1.4 percentage point increase in the probability of choosing primary care. Gagne and Leger (2005) predict that a 10 percent increase in the fee-per-consultation for a specialist in Quebec, for example, would lead to a 0.4 percent reduction in the proportion of medical students entering general practice and a 2.5 percent increase in the proportion entering surgical specialties. Thus all three of these studies conclude that although expected earnings do influence a medical student's specialty choice, the effect is rather small; medical students place great importance on non-monetary attributes when selecting a specialty.[34]

The papers reviewed above assume that medical students can enter whatever specialty they like. That is, these studies do not account for the possibility that some medical students who want to enter a specialty will be unsuccessful. As discussed earlier, residency positions in high-income specialties are rationed and many medical students fail to enter their preferred specialty. Nicholson's (2002) main contribution is to examine how differences in expected earnings affect the number of students who *desire* to enter a specialty rather than the number who actually *enter* a specialty. He finds that medical students' specialty choices are quite responsive to expected earnings: the average income elasticity across seven specialties is 1.42. Medical students appear to be willing to incur the risk of not receiving any residency position (by ranking a competitive specialty as their first choice) in order to secure large rents in certain non-primary care specialties.

---

[34] The recent increase in the pay of family physicians in several countries relative to hospital-based physicians (for example, in the UK) would make an interesting avenue for future research on the impact of pay on specialty choice.

Bhattacharya (2005) is the only study that has jointly modeled specialty choice and expected earnings and allowed unobserved factors to affect both. He presents some evidence that is consistent with the first three studies discussed above—money is not the most important determinant of specialty choice. Bhattacharya predicts, for example, that physicians who decided to become family practitioners would actually earn more than surgeons had they decided (and been able) to enter surgery. His results also provide some justification for the typical assumption that all medical students in a cohort could expect to earn the same amount in the same specialty. In 17 of 20 comparisons, a physician's predicted lifetime earnings if he entered a specialty other than the one he actually entered would be within 4 percent of the observed earnings in that specialty. Bhattacharya finds that only half of the earnings difference between primary and non-primary care physicians can be explained by differences in work effort, the required training period, and observed and unobserved ability. He concludes that differences between specialties in entry barriers are the most likely explanation for the residual earnings difference.

3.8. Physicians' Geographic Location Decisions

A number of papers in the 1970s and early 1980s recognized that in the US the physician-to-population ratio is urban areas was much higher than in rural areas, and the difference was growing over time. The conventional explanation was that physicians preferred living in cities and could continue locating there in spite of the high existing supply by inducing demand for their services (Newhouse et al., 1982). A number of policies were enacted to encourage physicians to locate in rural areas, such as the National Health Services Corps program that would pay off a medical school debt for physicians willing to practice in underserved areas.

Newhouse et al. (1982) criticized these studies for failing to apply standard economic location theory to the physician market. They argued that areas above a critical size would be able to attract and support a physician within a particular specialty, whereas areas below this threshold would not. Furthermore, the specialty-specific growth over time would depend on whether or not an area initially had a physician in that specialty.[35] As predicted, Newhouse et al. (1982) find that general/family practitioners locate disproportionately in counties with small populations, and the number of general practitioners decreased more rapidly in small versus large towns between 1970 and 1979 whereas the reverse pattern occurred for specialists. Frank (1985) concludes that the fee a psychiatrist can expect to receive in a market is not a particularly important determinant of location decisions. He also finds that the stock of psychiatrists adjusts slowly in response to a change in the fee: between 20 and 40 percent of the gap between the current and long-run equilibrium number of psychiatrists is filled

---

[35] This is similar to the model later developed by Bresnahan and Reiss (1991).

each year. This is consistent with substantial transactions costs of moving a practice for experienced physicians and the fact that the flow of newly trained physicians is small relative to the stock.

Polsky et al. (2000) also conclude that changes in market conditions have a minor effect on the location decisions of practicing physicians, which is consistent with amenities being important relative to income and with large transactions costs. An increase in the HMO penetration rate in a market did not affect the probability that primary care physicians, hospital-based specialists, or late-career medical/surgical specialists would stop providing patient care in that market, and the effect on early-career medical/surgical specialists was minor. Expected income appears to be more important, however, among new physicians when transactions costs are the same across markets. Physicians in all specialties who completed residency training in 1994 were less likely to locate in markets with high HMO penetration, presumably because expected earnings were relatively low in these markets (Escarce et al., 1998).

3.9. Nurses' Labor Supply

The early literature on nurse labor supply is summarized nicely by Shields (2004): "With respect to the likely impact of increasing the RN (registered nurse) wage rate, although there are considerable differences and inconsistencies across the studies reviewed, the main conclusion is that the wage elasticity is unresponsive (or inelastic) and that very large increases in wages would be needed to induce even moderate increases in nurse labor supply" (p. F493). Shields (2004) also concludes that nurse wages have a stronger effect on labor force participation than the number of hours worked conditional on working. It should be noted, however, that the wage elasticities from the early nursing literature, which average about 0.30, are in fact consistent with the general (medical and non-medical professions) literature on female workers (Borjas, 2000).

Many of the older studies do not address in a convincing way the key empirical challenges inherent in estimating labor supply: identifying plausibly exogenous variation in wages across workers and/or across time; measuring wages and hours accurately; accounting for self-selection into the workforce; and controlling for individual unobserved heterogeneity that should affect wages, such as differences in motivation, ability, and job characteristics (e.g. shift work).

Several recent studies use natural experiments, panel data, comprehensive administrative data sets, and/or more sophisticated econometric methods. Holmås (2002) follows 5,300 Norwegian nurses over a five-year period. He finds that a 1 percent increase in the nurse wage is associated with a 4.9 percent decrease in the hazard of exiting the labor force. This implies that a permanent 10 percent increase in the nurse wage would reduce the exit rate by approximately 1 percentage point per year for five years, from baseline exit rate of about 2 percent per year. When Holmås omits an indicator for whether a nurse is required to work off-hour shifts, the wage estimate is 50 percent smaller, which highlights the importance of modeling individual heterogeneity. Frijters et al. (2007) follow 28,000 nurses in the United Kingdom over a one-year period. They instrument for a nurse's wage with her pre-nurse educational qualifications, and find that a 10 percent increase in a nurse's wage would reduce the annual exit rate by 0.7 percent, a much smaller effect than in the Holmås (2002) study.

Askildsen et al. (2003) use the same Norwegian panel data as Holmås (2002). After instrumenting for the wage using the financial status of the local municipality, the lagged wage of auxiliary nurses working in the same municipality as a particular nurse, and a nurse's work experience, they estimate an uncompensated wage elasticity of 0.21. As above, this low elasticity indicates that it would be expensive to eliminate nurse vacancies by increasing the wage. Specifically, they estimate that the wage would have to rise by 43 percent to eliminate 4,000 nurse vacancies in Norway, and thereby increase overall health expenditures by about 4 percent. Staiger et al. (1999) exploit a 1991 policy that changed nurse wages in the Veterans Affairs (VA) hospitals exogenously by a different amount across different US markets. They estimate a wage elasticity ranging from zero to 0.2, consistent with the Askildsen et al. (2003) study.

In 2004, 66 percent of registered nurses in the United States were married (Buerhaus et al., 2007). Most nurse labor supply studies conclude that an increase in the wage of a nurse's spouse and an increase in non-labor income reduces her hours worked (Antonazzo et al., 2003; Buerhaus et al., 2007; Holmås, 2002). Furthermore, these effects are stronger for the labor force participation decision than on hours worked among nurses who are already working. As we discuss in the next section, these effects are likely to aggravate the tendency for the medical labor market to oscillate between situations of shortages and surpluses. Wages and non-labor income tend to increase when the economy is strong. The demand for medical labor is pro-cyclical due to a positive income elasticity of the demand for health, whereas the supply of nurse labor may be counter-cyclical due to the strong effects of spouse-wage and non-labor income.

3.10. Physicians' Labor Supply

Staiger et al. (2010) report that mean hours worked per week by physicians practicing in the US decreased by 7 percent between 1996 and 2008. Between 1981 and 2001, Canadian physicians worked an average of five fewer hours per week (Crossley et al., 2006). These trends are causing concern among policy makers who believe developed countries have, or will soon have, a shortage of physicians (Cooper et al., 2002). The most likely explanation for this decreasing work effort is that in many countries physician fees have been falling and/or preferences for leisure have changed. Between 1995 and 2006 in the United States, for example, physician fees decreased by 25 percent in real terms (Staiger et al., 2010). In this section we review the empirical literature regarding the magnitude of the income and substitution effects of a change in the physician wage, and whether the physician labor supply curve is in fact backward bending. As with nurses, most empirical studies conclude that physicians' labor supply is not more responsive to the wage than other professions. Furthermore, recent studies using micro data also conclude that changes in income do not have a strong effect on physician work effort—the income effect is small.

Most early studies used aggregate time series data on physician services and fees to infer the shape of the physician labor supply curve. Almost all of these studies concluded that physicians' labor supply functions were backward bending—the negative uncompensated wage elasticity implied that the income effect of a wage increase was stronger than the substitution effect (Feldstein, 1970; Vahovich, 1977; Brown and Lapan, 1979; Hu and Yang, 1988; Brown, 1989). The one exception is Sloan (1975), who found that physicians' hours worked were not responsive to wages or non-labor income. A backward-bending labor supply curve could hamper a policy that tries to control medical expenditures by constraining physician fees. If physicians' marginal utility of income is large, they may respond to fee cuts by inducing demand for their own services, such that expenditures may not fall (McGuire and Pauly, 1991). However, studies using aggregate data were not able to separately measure the income and substitution effects, and early studies that looked strictly at income effects generally found the income elasticity to be zero or small (McGuire and Pauly, 1991).

The results of more recent studies, which use micro data to estimate traditional labor supply equations, generally find small positive uncompensated wage elasticities and no or small income effects. Using US data from the mid-1980s, Thornton (1998) first estimates a production function for physician services and then derives the physicians' marginal shadow wage. He then estimates an uncompensated wage elasticity of 0.06 and an income elasticity of −0.09, both consistent with Sloan's (1975) conclusion that physicians are not particularly responsive to wage and non-labor income. Rizzo and Blumenthal (1994) use experience to instrument for a physician's wage. Their key assumption is that experience affects labor supply only through its effect on a physician's wage, which seems reasonable given that they examine physicians under the age of 40 rather than those close to retirement. They find that the substitution effect exceeds the income effect. Specifically, they estimate an uncompensated wage elasticity of 0.27, an income elasticity of −0.17, and a compensated wage elasticity estimate of 0.44.[36] Rizzo and Blumenthal also find that the labor supply decisions of female physicians are more responsive than those of male physicians.[37]

---

[36] Rizzo and Blumenthal (1994) use two non-practice income variables: medical school debt and a spouse's income.

[37] The uncompensated wage elasticity for female physicians is 0.49, twice as high as for male physicians (0.23).

Thornton and Eakin (1997) use market-level demand variables such as per capita income and degree of urbanization to instrument for a physician's wage. They estimate a small negative uncompensated wage elasticity (-0.02, and not significantly different from zero) and a small negative income elasticity (-0.03) for solo practicing physicians. Although they conclude that the labor supply curve is backward bending, it is nearly vertical and consistent with the results in Sloan (1975) and Thornton (1998).

Showalter and Thurston (1997) examine how US physicians' labor supply behavior in the mid-1980s was affected by variation between states in the maximum marginal tax rate. They estimate an uncompensated (net of the tax) wage elasticity of 0.30 for self-employed physicians but find that employee physicians are not responsive to differences in the wage. Baltagi et al. (2005) estimate a dynamic labor supply model using panel data on Norwegian physicians. The wage effect is identified in part by a wage settlement in 1996 that increased physician wages differently across markets. They report short- and long-run uncompensated wage elasticity estimates of 0.30 and 0.55, respectively, and no income effect. Finally, Sæther (2005) uses data on Norwegian physicians to estimate a static labor supply model that allows a wage change in one sector of a physician's practice (e.g. hospital, private office) to affect labor supply in the other sector. He reports an uncompensated wage elasticity estimate of 0.18 across both sectors, with a greater response in the office than the hospital setting.[38]

To summarize, the six studies discussed above that use micro data report uncompensated wage elasticity estimates ranging from zero to 0.30, with four of the estimates between 0.18 and 0.30. The four studies that examine income effects report elasticity estimates ranging from zero to -0.17. Given the different methods, data sources, and countries studied, there appears to be general agreement that as with most occupations, physicians are not particularly responsive to wage changes. And income elasticities are small.

3.11. Shortages and Surpluses of Medical Labor: Cyclicality and Persistence

In this section we examine why medical labor markets in many countries cycle between surpluses and shortages, and why shortages/surpluses often persist for many years. In Canada, for example, "the speed with which the shortage has arisen is even more surprising (than the unprecedented shortage of family practitioners in relatively large cities): in less than a decade, the supply of physicians in Canada reversed from a

---

[38] Although they do not estimate a wage elasticity, Whalley et al. (2008) report that mean hours worked among general practitioners in the United Kingdom fell by 8 percent following the institution of a generous pay-for-performance program, which was associated with an increase in mean income of 26 percent. Hours worked were trending down prior to the reimbursement change, however.

perceived surplus of physicians to a perceived shortage" (Crossley et al., 2006, p. 1). In 1991 the Barer–Stoddart report, which was commissioned by the Canadian Ministry of Health, recommended reducing medical school enrollment by about 10 percent and reducing Canada's dependence on internationally trained physicians in order to maintain the physician-to-population ratio into the future (Barer and Stoddart, 1991). The Canadian government accepted these recommendations the following year (Tyrell and Dauphinee, 1999), and the policy worked; after peaking in 1993 at 2.2 physicians per 1,000 people, the ratio has stabilized at 2.1 since then. The Canadian government has now reversed course. Since 1998, the number of medical school positions has increased by 39 percent (Esmail, 2005).

Japan also reversed its physician workforce policy over a short time period. Japan reduced the number of medical school positions by 8 percent between 1986 and 2006 based on a perceived impending surplus (Toyabe, 2009).[39] The education ministry recently reversed its policy and decided to consider accrediting new medical schools to expand the flow of physicians.[40] Medical school positions in 2010 are now at an all-time high.[41] In the US a shortage of registered nurses began in 1998 and lasted for 10 years, well beyond what would be predicted by standard economic models. At the peak in 2001, 13 percent of hospital RN positions were vacant (Buerhaus et al., 2009). Norway, the United Kingdom, Canada, Australia, and South Africa all experienced nurse shortages during the 2000s (Shields, 2004).

How would one know there is in fact a shortage or surplus of a particular type of medical labor? In most markets a shortage would generate rising wages, rising earnings, an increase in the flow of new entrants, longer patient waiting times for an appointment (in the case of physicians/dentists), shorter appointments with a provider, and an increased use of substitute labor to the extent the production function allows it. With administered prices, several of these mechanisms might not be triggered unless public and private insurers respond as the market would. Furthermore, entry barriers may delay or prevent the supply response. These challenges make it difficult to determine whether a shortage or surplus exists. Since 2000 there have been many studies concluding that the US has or soon will have a physician shortage—18 reports from states, medical societies, and hospital associations, and 19 reports from medical organizations since 2000 (Iglehart, 2008). However, these studies usually reach that conclusion by applying demographic projections to current treatment levels rather than documenting market evidence of a shortage.

---

[39] Italy reduced its medical school positions by 30 percent between 1985 and 1995, and France by 50 percent during that time period.

[40] *Japan Times*, June 22, 2010.

[41] The Netherlands also implemented an aggressive physician manpower policy recently by doubling medical school enrollment between 1993 and 2003.

Long et al. (2008) argue that one should not base a nursing shortage on vacancy rates because hospitals increasingly use temporary or agency nurses as a strategic response to volatile demand conditions; costs can be minimized by hiring fewer full-time nurses and using part-time nurses to respond to demand shocks.[42] Governments may also relax immigration policy to respond to physician shortages. Most developed countries are relying increasingly on physicians trained abroad. For example, internationally trained physicians account for a larger proportion of the physician workforce in 2007 than in 2000 in the following countries: Ireland (33 percent of physicians in 2007 were trained abroad), New Zealand (31 percent), US (25 percent), and Switzerland (21 percent) (OECD Health Data, 2009).

We provide several explanations for the persistence and cyclical nature of medical labor surpluses and shortages. First, the demand for health is reasonably income elastic. Using changes in oil prices interacted with oil reserves in a locality to measure the causal effect of income on hospital spending, Acemoglu et al. 2009 estimate an income elasticity of 0.72. This indicates that as a country's income rises and falls, the demand for health by its citizens will likewise rise and fall, although not to such an extent that health care is a luxury good. Because the demand for medical labor is derived from the demand for health, the demand for labor will be pro-cyclical. Labor supply, however, will respond slowly to the income-induced demand changes for several reasons: training periods are often long, the flow of newly trained labor is usually small relative to the stock of labor, and administered prices may prevent the market signals from reaching eligible labor.

Another explanation for the cyclicality of shortages and surpluses is that governments are not particularly good at forecasting future supply and demand and are heavy-handed when they act. Nicholson (2009) describes the US government's long history of trying to forecast the future supply of and demand for physician services, beginning in the early 1900s. Government physician manpower policy responds to, and perhaps accentuates, the oscillation from a perceived (and perhaps real) surplus to perceived shortage of physicians. The Canadian and Japanese experiences described at the beginning of this section are similar to the US experience. Perhaps there is a political explanation why attitudes about the adequacy of professional occupations are cyclical.

A final explanation for the persistence of physician shortages (real or perceived) is that policy makers and academics have different normative perspectives regarding the role of physicians in the health care system. Nicholson (2009) presents a simplified argument where people can be divided into two camps depending on how they answer two questions: (1) are policy makers willing and able to reform the health care

---

[42] Another reason not to put too much stock in vacancy rates is that hospitals may not expect vacancies to be filled at the prevailing wage, such that "vacancies" become an administrative data entry.

system and improve its efficiency?; and (2) if more physicians begin practicing, will the value of their incremental services exceed their cost? People such as Cooper et al. (2002) who are skeptical that policy makers (or the market) can reform the health care system to improve physician productivity, and who believe that physicians cannot or do not induce demand for their own services, are likely to support expanding the physician workforce in anticipation of growth in demand for physician services due to the growth and aging of the population and rising real income. People such as Goodman and Fisher (2008), who are optimistic that policy makers (or the market) can reform payment systems to improve physician productivity, who believe that adding physicians will take pressure off policy makers and make reform less likely, and who believe incremental physician services would be low value, are likely to favor constraining the growth of the physician workforce. Policies enacted by one camp will trigger cries of "surplus" or "shortage" by the other camp.

As Blumenthal (2004) points out, "The physician-supply debate is therefore now enmeshed in and inseparable from a larger discussion about the value of the services physicians provide and the future of the health care system—how big it should be, how to organize it, and whether its trajectory can be controlled. Proponents of the deficit theory (i.e., U.S. has a physician shortage) argue that ignoring or resisting inevitable increases in the demand for physicians' services will only lead to 'public discontent' and invite other health care professionals to take over the roles traditionally played by physicians. Proponents of the surplus theory (i.e., no physician shortage) seem to believe that constraining the supply of physicians is one way to begin restructuring our health care system in order to improve its rationality and efficiency."

4. LABOR DEMAND TOPICS

The productivity of the medical workforce appears to vary substantially between individual providers and between organizational forms. Several studies have shown that productivity varies across physicians within markets in the US (Epstein et al., 2010; Phelps, 2000; Welch et al., 1994), Canada (Roos et al., 1986), and Norway (Grytten and Sorensen, 2003). Furthermore, physicians in group practices appear to be more productive than solo practitioners (Reinhardt, 1972; Brown, 1988), although small groups are more productive than large groups (Gaynor and Gertler, 1990; Gaynor and Pauly, 1990).

These differences in labor productivity are persistent, which indicates that rents for labor do not get arbitraged away as they would in a perfectly competitive market. This raises the question of what labor demand factors may explain these persistent productivity differences. After first reviewing traditional empirical studies of factor demand, this section explores a number of possible explanations for the variation in labor productivity, including government regulation, differences in reimbursement incentives, politics, the effect of incentives to manage people within an organization, human resources management and motivated agents.

4.1. Factor Demand: Own- and Cross-price Elasticity Estimates

In this section we review empirical estimates of own- and cross-price elasticities in various health care production settings. These estimates shed light on the nature and flexibility of the production function, how wages in many occupations are likely to respond to shifts in labor supply, and the likely impact of shortages and surpluses. As an example, consider the recent growth in non-physician clinicians (NPCs). There were 70,000 physician assistants in the US in 2007 and 140,000 nurse practitioners in 2004, versus essentially zero of each in 1970 (Wilson, 2008). A recent report on the physician workforce predicts that the number of NPCs will grow by 60 percent in the US between 2005 and 2020, and each NPC will provide 40 percent of the work currently provided by a physician (Health Resources and Services Administration, 2006). The implicit assumptions that NPCs and physicians are substitutes and NPCs face few entry barriers reduce the projected shortage of physicians that would otherwise occur.

Early studies of US physician practices agreed that physicians were not using non-physician staff efficiently, but disagreed regarding whether they were using too few (Reinhardt, 1972, 1975) or too many (Brown, 1988).[43] Reinhardt (1972) estimates a production function using survey data that contain three output measures for a physician practice (number of office visits; total visits, including hospital and home visits; and annual billings) and factor inputs, including a physician's hours worked. He concludes that if physicians doubled their use of registered nurses, technicians, and office aides (grouped together as "physician aides"), they could have boosted output by 25 percent. Brown (1988) also estimated a production function using more recent data than that used by Reinhardt. Acknowledging that physician's choose their hours worked, Brown used a physician's age, an indicator for an urban practice, and an indicator for having a capitated practice to instrument for physician hours worked. By comparing the marginal product-to-wage ratio between physicians and other inputs, Brown concludes that physicians are overutilizing aides but underutilizing licensed practical nurses (LPNs).

Other authors used cost regressions to examine labor demand in physician practices (Gillis et al., 1991; Pope and Burge, 1995; Escarce, 1996). Escarce and Pauly (1998) comment that the (important) opportunity cost of physician's time had been

---

[43] There is considerable research on economies of scale and scope in physician practices and hospitals, and productivity differences between solo practices and groups (see, for example, Pope and Burge (1992) for a review of the findings for physician practices). We do not review this literature in this chapter, focusing instead on labor demand.

omitted from these regressions. US physicians usually own their practices and hire inputs to maximize their income (or some other objective function), so researchers do not observe a physician's wage. They develop a model where physicians jointly choose their labor supply and other inputs to maximize a utility function consisting of leisure and net income. Escarce and Pauly find that physicians are substitutes with all other inputs combined, and that as their output grows they use non-physician inputs disproportionately relative to their own labor.

Thornton and Eakin (1997) developed the same insight regarding the interdependence of physicians' labor supply and production decisions. In the first stage physicians choose non-physician labor inputs for every possible value of their own labor input; in the second stage physicians choose the quantity of their own hours that maximizes utility.[44] They find that the demands for assistants (i.e. all non-physician employees) and medical supplies are inelastic, with own-price elasticities of −0.26 and −0.05, respectively. Using a similar approach with 1998 US data, Gunning and Sickles (2011) also find input demand to be inelastic. Specifically, the own-price elasticity estimates for non-physician staff and capital are −0.22 and −0.24, respectively. These results are consistent with a low marginal rate of substitution; the physician services production function is fairly rigid.

There are several empirical challenges when estimating hospital cost functions. First, hospitals produce many different outputs (e.g. emergency room visits, clinic visits, surgical admissions, medical admissions) that cannot be accurately captured by a single variable. Second, patient severity, and therefore cost, is likely to differ substantially between hospitals. Third, although physicians are an important input in hospital production, often there is no observed physician wage (especially in the US where most physicians are paid by health insurers rather than hospitals). Fourth, the quality of labor inputs may differ across hospitals within the broad categories used in regressions, such as nurses or technicians. Vita (1990) estimates a hospital cost function using a flexible functional form (the translog function). He allows for five unique outputs, observes input prices for five inputs, and includes a case mix variable to control for differing patient severity. The demand for nurses (estimated own-price elasticity of −0.34), medical supplies (−0.17), and non-physician medical practitioners and technicians (−0.75) is inelastic, while the demand for managers and supervisors (−1.94) and auxiliary staff (−1.27) is elastic. Not surprisingly, non-clinical personnel appear to be more discretionary than clinical personnel.

Gaynor et al. 2011 develop a new output index model to estimate a cost function for 320 California hospitals in 2003. Unlike earlier studies that included counts of five (or so) types of outputs as regressors, Gaynor et al. include detailed data on the diagnoses and services received by 3.5 million patients in their cost function estimation.

---

[44] They instrument for a physician's hours worked with age and gender.

The factor inputs with the lowest own-price elasticities (in absolute value) are registered nurses (−0.17), medical supplies and equipment (−0.35), and clerical staff (−0.42). As with Vita (1990), they find that management is the most price elastic input (−1.06).

Other studies provide insights into the flexibility of the health production function. As discussed above, Gunning and Sickles (2011) incorporate a physician's labor supply choice with their factor input decisions to estimate a multi-product cost function. They estimate a cross-price elasticity between non-physician staff and capital (measured by office rent) of 0.45, indicating that these two inputs are substitutes. Doyle et al. (2010) exploit a situation where patients were randomly assigned to clinical teams at hospitals with different quality rankings. Although patient outcomes were not significantly different between the two hospitals, patients at the lower-ranked institution stayed in the hospital longer, experienced more expensive stays, and received more diagnostic tests. This is consistent with the substitution of time (and hospital labor generally, such as nursing time) and diagnostic tests for skill/judgment. Wanchek (2009) finds that dental hygienists are substitutes for dentists and dental assistants, and Anderson et al. (2000) find that homeopaths (i.e. "alternative medicine" providers) and physicians are substitutes. Although various inputs are substitutes, the conclusion remains that the health production function does not respond substantially to differences/changes in input prices. However, grouping different quality inputs into broad categories would attenuate regression coefficients toward zero, so that the true elasticities may be larger in absolute value.

4.2. Reimbursement, Politics, and Government Regulation

In traditional labor demand analyses, firms are assumed to choose labor inputs to either maximize profits or minimize costs conditional on chosen output level. In many countries hospitals are run by the state, either at local or national level, and physicians are employed by the state. If hospitals and physicians deviate from standard profit-maximizing behavior in these less competitive settings, this may provide one explanation for the variation in labor productivity and population health across geographical areas. Furthermore, the way a provider is reimbursed may affect their labor demand. Fee-for-service reimbursement pays practices according to the services they provide to patients. However, services are sometimes defined according to what labor inputs are used. An office visit with a primary care physician, for example, may be reimbursed at a higher rate than a visit with a nurse practitioner even if both have the same effect on the patient's health, or a visit that involves capital (e.g. MRI exam) may trigger a higher payment than one that does not. Reimbursement can subsidize or tax certain labor inputs unless the rates are set to generate equal profit margins across all possible services. In this section we examine four factors that may affect the demand for labor by hospitals and physician practices: reimbursement methods, the degree of competition, government wage regulation, and politics.

4.2.1. Reimbursement Methods

Schoen et al. (2009) surveyed primary care physicians in 11 countries and asked them, among other things, about the health production function they use. Only 2 and 6 percent of physicians in Sweden and the United States, respectively, indicated that they could benefit financially from hiring additional non-physician clinicians to their practice. In Italy and the Netherlands, by contrast, 44 and 60 percent of physicians responded that they could benefit financially from such hiring. In France, which has a fee-for-service physician reimbursement system, only 11 percent of respondents indicated that they use non-physician staff to manage chronic care, versus 98 percent in the UK where there are strong pay-for-performance incentives. Jacobson et al. (1998) conducted interviews at nine health maintenance organizations and multi-specialty clinics in the US. They found that organizations with a relatively large managed care population, and presumably a large percentage of revenue being generated via capitation, gave nurse practitioners and physician assistants a considerable amount of clinic autonomy. These two studies show that physician practices in countries or organizations where capitation is important have relatively strong incentives to hire physician substitutes and define their responsibilities broadly.

Two economic studies formally examine how reimbursement affects factor demand. Acemoglu and Finkelstein (2008) study the effect of a 1983 Medicare hospital reimbursement rule (the prospective payment, or DRG, system) in the US that increased the price of labor relative to capital. As expected, they find that the capital-to-labor ratio subsequently increased as the policy spurred the adoption of (expensive) medical technologies. Moreover, hospitals responded by increasing their nurse skill mix, presumably because skilled labor is a complement of capital/technology. The same payment policy also provided teaching hospitals with an extra $70,000 for each medical resident they hired. Because the reimbursement formula is based on a hospital's resident-to-bed ratio, this subsidizes residents and taxes beds. Nicholson and Song (2001) find that hospitals responded to these incentives by hiring more residents, but did not close beds. In fact, the subsidy can explain about 40 percent of the increase in residents between 1984 and 1991.

The studies above indicate that the prevailing reimbursement system has a strong influence on providers' factor demand. Two studies comparing Canadian and US hospitals, however, come to an opposite conclusion. Hospitals in Quebec are highly regulated: their budgets are determined by prior experiences and political decisions rather than from market forces, and they do not compete directly with other hospitals. US hospitals, by contrast, are less regulated and face more competition. However, Bilodeau et al. (2000) find that Canadian and US hospitals have similar cost functions—both consistent with short-run cost minimizing behavior. This result is consistent with earlier analysis by Haber et al. (1992). They found that labor shares in US and Canadian hospitals in 1985 were very similar despite different environments and incentives. For example, registered nurses represented 45.6 percent of hospital labor in both countries.

4.2.2. Input Wage Regulation

In many sectors of the economy wages are mandated to be very similar across different geographic labor markets. In this case, if the competitive outside wage is higher than the regulated wage, the wage regulation essentially acts as a wage ceiling for medical labor. There are many studies of labor quantity restrictions (e.g. firing costs) and labor price floors (e.g. minimum wages), but this type of wage regulation has been much less studied in economics. Yet it is likely to be important in the health care sector because of the large role for the public sector as a direct employer of labor. Within Europe, such centralized wage regulation occurs in the UK, France, and Spain.

Propper and Van Reenen (2010) advance a simple two-sector, two-region equilibrium model of an occupational labor market to capture the salient features of pay regulation in the nursing labor market and use this to explore how this affects productivity. Their set-up is the following. They consider an economy with two sectors, $j = \{1, 2\}$, where sector 1 is the "skill-sensitive sector," which they assume to be the public sector provider of health care. Sector 2 is less sensitive to skill (they propose the nursing home sector, which is much more low-tech than the hospital sector but employs some individuals who are trained as nurses). There are two regions, $r = \{L, H\}$, where L is the low-price region and H is the high-price region. Prices are P_r and $P_H > P_L$ (e.g. because of ground rental prices due to land scarcity). Region H (L) is the "high (low) outside wage" region because nominal wages are higher in the unregulated sector 2. There are two skill types, $s = \{S, U\}$, where S is skilled and U is unskilled, and with nominal wages W_{js}.

They assume that consumers in region r need to be serviced by hospitals located in region r and that producer prices and consumption prices are equal within a region. Unskilled workers' wages are fixed in the world market and there is an infinitely elastic supply of such workers. The basic premise is that nurses will respond to the wages they are offered and are geographically mobile though there may be some fixed costs of moving which add frictions. Three predictions emerge from this model.

First, if the pay regulation causes wages to fall, nurses are likely to geographically migrate to where wages are relatively higher. The hospitals in areas to which they migrate will benefit in performance through having access to higher-quality human capital. The regulated wage will make the high-price region less attractive to nurses relative to the low-price region. Consequently, some skilled nurses move to the low-price region, and relative productivity in the high-price region deteriorates. Second, even if they remain in the same region, nurses can move into sectors where their pay is not regulated. This will tend to cause productivity to rise in the unregulated sector as skilled workers switch toward this sector. A third result is that for some plausible values of the regulated wage, we may observe "convexity" in the sense that the deterioration in the quality of public health care in the high outside wage region is greater than the (possible) increase in quality in the low outside wage region. Thus the regulation can decrease aggregate productivity in the public health care system.

They test the predictions of this model using data from the English NHS where wages are regulated centrally. As a measure of hospital quality, they use deaths following emergency admissions for heart attacks (acute myocardial infarction, AMI). The unskilled sector is taken to be the nursing home sector. They find all three predictions of the model are supported. The quality of care in hospitals located in high outside wage areas is lower, the quality of care in nursing homes in high wage areas is higher and, finally, there is non-convexity in the quality effect. The negative effect of regulation on hospital quality is much stronger in the high-cost areas (where regulated wages are much lower than the outside wage) than the positive effect in the low-cost areas (where regulated wages are higher than the outside wage). Thus, the aggregate effect of the pay regulation is to increase aggregate death rates and to strongly reduce social welfare. Essentially any gains from wage regulation in terms of keeping down the wage bill in high-cost areas are more than offset by the extra deaths which arise from low quality.

Nurse shortages are a perennial problem of many nursing labor markets, as discussed in section 3.11. Propper and Van Reenen (2010) do not directly explore the implications of their model for nurse shortages, although a wage shock in the high outside wage region of their model will lead nurses to move to the low-wage region and/or into the unskilled sector, so leaving hospitals in the high-wage region with a nurse shortage. They may fill these with less skilled temporary nurses and this may be one explanation of decreased productivity in high-wage areas. Some evidence to support this is presented in Hall et al. (2008).

Elliott et al. (2007) explicitly focus on this issue and examine the vacancy rate for nurses in the UK NHS in areas of different outside wages. Their analysis uses a large number of small areas but is cross-sectional in nature. They find that a reduction in the wage gap in a local area results in an increase in the long-term vacancy rate for National Health Service (NHS) nurses. The competitiveness of nursing pay has a strong effect on the ability of the NHS to attract and retain nurses. While they do not undertake a full cost–benefit analysis, they, like Propper and Van Reenen (2010), conclude that changing relative pay between qualified nurses in different areas of Britain is a mechanism for affecting health authority vacancy rates, and that measures to introduce a greater responsiveness of nurses' pay to local labor market conditions are required. As discussed in section 3, nurse wage elasticities are consistent with estimates from the general female labor supply literature.

4.2.3. Politics

Clarke and Milicent (2008) also explore the interface between government actions and labor demand in an analysis of employment in French hospitals. French public hospitals are funded and run by local government. Clarke and Milicent argue that left wing local administrations, who are committed to keeping down unemployment, will use hospital employment as a way of dealing with local unemployment, thereby increasing their chances of remaining in office. They test this on a sample of French hospitals and find that hospital employment is consistently higher in public hospitals than not-for-profits or private hospitals. Public hospital employment is positively correlated with the local unemployment rate, whereas no relationship is found in non-public hospitals. This is consistent with public hospitals providing employment in depressed areas. They find the relationship between public hospital employment and local unemployment is stronger the more left wing the local municipality. This latter result holds especially when electoral races are tight, consistent with a concern for re-election.

4.3. The Organizational Form of Firms: Why Do Physicians Form Groups?

There are large documented differences in the productivity of physician firms. Physicians in group practices appear to be more productive than solo practitioners (Reinhardt, 1972; Brown, 1988), and small groups are more productive than large groups (Gaynor and Gertler, 1990; Gaynor and Pauly, 1990). There have also been changes in the organization of physician firms. For example, in the US in 1980 the majority of physicians were solo practitioners whereas in 2006 only 32 percent of primary care physicians practiced alone (DeFelice and Bradford, 1997; Bodenheimer and Pham, 2010).

To date, much of the research on partnerships in health care has been motivated by theoretical work in industrial organization and the theory of the firm, which examined the issue of production in teams and the associated potential for moral hazard. It therefore adopts the "design" perspective stresses that different organizational forms are the optimal response to external or internal constraints, so that single and group practices will be optimal in different circumstances.

A significant barrier to well-functioning principal–agent relationships between the firm and its constituent members is the difficulty associated with monitoring effort. Holmstrom (1982) showed that where effort is difficult to monitor and output is rewarded at the team level, the larger the team the greater the potential for free riding and shirking by any individual member. This work points to the importance of firm size and homogeneity for efficiency. Groups that are relatively homogeneous will have constituent members whose objective functions do not vary significantly from the "average" member's objective function. If the group's welfare function is a simple amalgam of its members' objectives, then each member's goals will stand in less serious contrast to those of the firm, which will mitigate (although not completely alleviate) the problems associated with shirking. On the other hand, more heterogeneous firms will have members whose objective function is significantly different from the firm's; members will then have greater incentive to take actions that are in their interest and not the group's as a whole.

If shirking is a problem, then firm size may be important. While on one hand economies of scale may encourage larger firms, it is also likely that as the firm grows monitoring of effort by workers becomes more difficult. Smaller groups may have an easier time monitoring and may be able to do so without an explicit and expensive contract (or at least use contracts which are less comprehensive and rely more upon social or peer pressure). In larger groups, it is more likely that shirking problems would require more complete contracts as well as formal monitoring and punishment schemes. In the limit, in a solo practice there is by definition no distinction between the objective function of the physician and the firm—they are one and the same and shirking is not a relevant concept.

Physician firms, because of their relatively small size and the availability of financial and labor input information, have been used to test these ideas (see also the reviews in Scott (2000) and DeFelice and Bradford (1997)). Gaynor and Gertler (1995), for example, examine the relationship between the degree of risk sharing, compensation, and effort among primary care physicians in the US in medical group practice. They specify a model where demand is uncertain, and where physicians choose effort to maximize utility in response to the incentives in the firm's compensation structure. The utility maximizing level of effort is where the marginal revenue product of effort is equal to its marginal disutility. They derive comparative static results of the effect of changes in internal compensation on the number of patients seen (defined as effort). They also examine the effect of risk aversion on choice of compensation structure. The empirical results found that a stronger link between compensation and productivity leads to more office visits per week (effort), and that the greater the risk aversion of physicians the less strongly the compensation structure is related to productivity.

Encinosa et al. (2007) explore why compensation may not always be linked to productivity in medical groups, using the sociological concept of "group norms" incorporated into an economic framework of risk sharing and multi-tasking. Group norms are defined as the social interactions resulting from comparisons of effort and pay within groups. They demonstrate that group income and effort norms make small groups more likely to adopt equal sharing rules than large groups, and that risk aversion and multi-tasking make equal sharing more likely in large groups. They find evidence that group norms do influence choice of compensation method, in addition to the usual factors analyzed in principal—agent models (risk aversion and multi-tasking).

In the same contracting theme, Gaynor (1989) raises the issue of intra-firm competition, i.e. competition between members of the practice. In Gaynor's model, physicians' revenue depends in part on their individual productivity. Physicians who produce more visits receive a larger share of the firm's net revenue. Physicians may attract patients from two sources: they may bring them in from outside the firm or they may attract them away from other partners within the firm. So the incentives of the individual partner may be incompatible with the interests of the group.

Under the design perspective, each firm will choose whatever organizational form is optimal. The question is therefore not whether partnerships or solo practices are more or less efficient, but under what conditions is one form preferable to another. This also has the implication that testing which form in general is more efficient makes little sense because there will be some conditions under which one form is optimal and another set of conditions under which another form is optimal. On the other hand, empirical analyses that relate organizational form to the extent of risk sharing or risk to optimal size of a partnership do have value.

A more recent literature has emphasized the matching of patients, physicians, and firms as a reason for the existence of firms. Theoretical work in industrial organization and organizational economics has established that one reason firms exist is to promote specialization by matching opportunities, consumers in the case of professional services, to workers who have a particular comparative advantage (Garicano and Santos, 2004; Garicano and Hubbard, 2007, 2009). This matching encourages workers to specialize because the returns to specialization are greater when workers have more opportunities to use their specialized skills.

Matching by firms may be particularly important in economic sectors with human-capital intensive production. In professional services markets such as law, medicine, automobile repair, consulting and financial advising, asymmetric information is likely to inhibit the amount of matching in the market. Professionals in these fields acquire considerable human capital. Without this training, consumers may not know the specific nature of their problems nor, once obtaining a diagnosis, are they able to identify the most appropriate professional to address that problem. Likewise, adverse selection due to asymmetric information between professionals also inhibits matching. Professionals who diagnose problems have incentives to refer only the least profitable consumers to their peers, which in turn deters other professionals from accepting these referrals (Garicano and Santos, 2004).

Epstein et al. (2010) test this idea in the context of medical firms. They examine how one type of professional services firm, obstetrics practices, coordinates workers and matches them with consumers. They test two hypotheses from the models of firms as coordinators of human capital. First, do firms overcome asymmetric information and institutional barriers to achieve higher levels of specialization and coordination than occur in the market? Second, does firm specialization improve productivity, especially in ways that benefit consumers?

In their first set of analyses they examine the extent to which physicians specialize in certain medical problems, and whether the amount of specialization differs between solo physicians and those in groups. In the second set of analyses they consider the implications of specialization on aspects of productivity that benefit consumers. To do the latter they exploit the random pairing of workers and jobs that results from obstetricians' weekend call schedules to overcome endogeneity in the matching of worker and consumer and use this random pairing to develop unbiased measures of each physician's skills in performing Cesarean section deliveries and vaginal deliveries. They consider whether firm coordination increases productivity by matching patients to workers based on workers' absolute and comparative advantages.

Their results provide support for both hypotheses. Relative to solo physicians, physicians in group practices are more likely to specialize in treating patients with high-risk health conditions. Furthermore, those in groups who treat such patients treat substantially more of them than solo physicians. They find this despite also observing very similar total caseloads and frequencies of high-risk conditions among group and solo physicians overall. As a result, high-risk patients in group practices are more likely to match with an appropriate specialist than are patients of solo practitioners. On balance, this suggests that obstetrics markets themselves provide some coordination, but firms are able to improve on this.

Huckman and Pisano (2006) also examine matching of firms and workers. In their case, they examine freelancers and ask the question of whether they are more productive when matched with a particular firm. In many settings, firms rely on independent contractors, or freelancers, for the provision of certain services. The benefits of such relationships for both firms and workers are often understood in terms of increased flexibility. Less understood is the impact of freelancing on individual performance. While it is often presumed that the performance of freelancers is largely portable across organizations, it is also possible that a given worker's performance may vary across organizations if he or she develops firm-specific skills and knowledge over time. They examine this issue empirically by considering the performance of cardiac surgeons, many of whom perform operations at multiple hospitals within narrow periods of time. Using patient mortality as an outcome measure, they find that the quality of a surgeon's performance at a given hospital improves significantly with increases in his or her recent procedure volume at *that* hospital, but does not significantly improve with increases in his or her volume at *other* hospitals. These findings suggest that surgeon performance is not fully portable across hospitals (i.e. some portion of performance is firm specific).

The fastest growing physician specialty in the US is hospitalists, who provide general medical care in the hospital setting only, rather than splitting time between the outpatient clinic/office and the hospital. Meltzer (2001) and Meltzer and Chung (2010) present theories to explain this trend. They argue that the benefits of having a single physician who provides coordinated care in both the clinic and hospital settings used to dominate a model where some physicians would specialize in each sector, and there would be coordination costs when "handing off" a patient between sectors. However, as the transportation costs of switching from one sector to the other increased (e.g. driving across town), the model of specialized human capital became preferred. Using a similar argument, Cebul et al. (2008) suggest that the hospitalist movement may be a method to lower the cost of coordination in an increasingly fragmented health care system. All three of these papers provide support for the use of firms versus solo practitioners.

Other ideas as to why group practices arise include smoothing production and reputation. Physicians supply services that clearly are not amenable to inventory storage. For some specialties, most notably obstetrics and gynecology, production is a lumpy process, with deliveries occurring throughout the day. It may be easier to share such duties within a firm than to write contracts between independent contractors (DeFelice and Bradford, 1997). Getzen (1984) examines the role of reputation. Reputation is an important component of the market for physician services; simultaneously, information used to form reputations may be very costly for consumers to obtain. Getzen argues that larger firms, by concentrating physicians, may be able to take advantage of "reputational economies of scale," and so support higher fees within consumer search models. In summary, there is no single message from the literature as to the optimal form of organization for physicians. In general, the literature on physician organization has been dominated by a focus on the organizational form as a response to risk sharing and the need to induce effort when it is not fully contractible. This fits more generally with a focus in health economics on responses to financial incentives and the design of optimal contracts, as discussed in Chapter 5 of this Handbook. But there has been considerably less work focused on why changes in the organizational form of physician firms have come about and on the role of market-level factors, for example competition. In addition, issues in the organization of physicians and their related productivity may benefit from the "technology" perspective on firm organization. This is discussed in more detail in section 4.4 below, but briefly, this perspective does not stress the optimality of any single organizational form, but stresses that frictions and the impact of regulation may leave certain forms existing while they are not the most efficient. For example, thinking of the organization as a form of technology may allow a diffusion perspective, which might help explain why large differences in productivity between different physician firms persist over time and why solo practices continue to exist in many markets where group practices have been shown to have advantages. In addition, the stress in the technology perspective on responses to changes in external factors, for example product market competition or regulation, provides another perspective to explore in order to explain why some forms of organization of medical labor are more productive than others.

In the final two sections, we highlight two areas in labor economics which are receiving increasing attention outside health economics. Both seem to us to be promising areas for research in the economics of labor in health care. The first is human resource management, the second motivated agents.

4.4. Human Resource Management in Health Care

Traditionally, labor economics has focused on the labor market rather than looking inside the "black box" of firms. This has changed dramatically in the last two decades and Human Resource Management (HRM) is a growing field in labor economics. The hallmark of this work is to use standard economic tools applied to the special circumstances of managing employees within companies. HRM covers a wide range of activities. Bloom and Van Reenen (2007) include remuneration systems (e.g. individuals or group incentive/contingent pay), the system of appraisal, promotion, and career advancement, the distribution of decision rights (autonomy/decentralization) between managers and workers, job design (e.g. flexibility of working, job rotation), teamwork (e.g. who works with whom), and information provision. Several of these topics as they arise in the health care field are covered in this volume, although not necessarily labeled as HRM. Since we see this as a promising avenue for future research in health care, we sketch here recent economic approaches to HRM and discuss applications to date in health economics.

Bloom and Van Reenen (2007) argue that, in thinking about the reasons for variations in HRM and productivity, a contrast can be drawn between two possible approaches. The first, which is the now classic approach of Personnel Economics, they label the "design" approach. The view here is that the HRM practices we observe are chosen by a profit-maximizing firm; they are explicit strategic choices of the firm, and variations in HRM reflect variations in the firm's environment. This perspective is situated within the broader fields of the economics of contracts (see Bolton and Dewatripont, 2005, for an overview) and the economics of organizations (see Gibbons and Roberts, 2008).[45] The key feature of the design approach is that the HRM practices we observe are chosen by firms to maximize profits in an environment that departs from perfectly competitive spot markets. This approach puts the reason for heterogeneity in the adoption of different practices as mainly due to the different environments firms face rather than inefficiencies at the firm level. For example, the technology of an industry will determine why certain labor remuneration practices are adopted and others not. So, for example, changes in technology that allow better monitoring of employee output will allow the introduction of

---

[45] This perspective assumes firms and workers are rational maximizing agents (profits and utility, respectively), that labor and product markets must reach some sort of price−quantity equilibrium and the stress is very much on private efficiency with an emphasis on why some employment practices, which may look to be perplexing and inefficient on the surface (e.g. mandatory retirement and huge pay disparities for CEOs), may actually be (at least privately) optimal (see Lazear and Oyer, 2009).

performance-related pay where previously it was not possible. With this perspective, the growth of pay-for-performance (P4P) in health care can be seen as a response to widespread development of better health care performance measurement systems (for a review of recent development in performance measurement in health care see Smith et al. (2009)) and one that should improve productivity in health care.

Bloom and Van Reenen (2007) identify a second approach as "managerial technology." In this view some aspects of HRM could be considered as a technology or "best practice." Management is partially like a technology, so there are distinctly good (and bad) practices that would raise (or lower) productivity. This view sees a large role for inefficiencies: firms can persist in their adoption of "bad" technology for some time. While low-productivity firms are selected out over time, there will be some stochastic element to this, so in the steady state there will always be some dispersion of productivity. This managerial technology approach raises the question of why differences in managerial quality persist. Bloom and Van Reenen (2007) put forward several reasons. One is that all technologies have some diffusion curve whereby not all firms immediately adopt them. A second is that there is imperfect competition. With imperfect competition firms can have differential efficiency and still survive in equilibrium. With perfect competition inefficient firms should be rapidly driven out of the market as the more efficient firms undercut them on price. A corollary is that an increase in competition should lead to better management practices and, as a consequence, an increase in productivity. A third is "frictions." Costs of adjustment are ubiquitous in capital investment and have usually been found for labor, especially skilled labor (see Bond and Van Reenen, 2008, for a survey). Thus, firms facing asymmetric shocks will adjust differentially to their new conditions only slowly over time even if they all have identical adjustment cost technologies. In such an environment, low total factor productivity (TFP) firms will not immediately vanish, as there is an option value to remaining active in the sector.

Within the economics of health care, there has been little interest in managerial practices or the quality of management, although there is a large literature on the response to incentive pay and on the optimal design of incentives in hospitals and physician firms, as discussed in Chapters 9–11 of this Handbook. However, in a recent paper, Bloom et al. (2010) use the methodology developed by Bloom and Van Reenen (2007) to measure management quality in UK hospitals. They find that management quality is positively associated with a range of performance measures used to assess hospital quality, including death rates, financial performance, and staff satisfaction. In addition, they investigate whether managerial quality in the health care system is a function of competition. Exploiting the fact that hospitals in marginal political seats are rarely closed in the UK, they derive an instrument for competition defined by numbers of hospitals located in an area. They find that competition appears to improve managerial quality in UK hospitals. This result accords with findings for firms in the rest of the economy (Bloom and Van Reenen, 2007).

4.5. Motivated Agents

The use of models in which agents display some type of other-regarding preferences is only recently becoming common in the economics literature (e.g. Fehr and Schmidt, 2006). Health economics is probably one exception to this. The role of doctor as an agent has been a recurring theme in health economics and is discussed in McGuire (2000). Here we do not discuss the agency role *per se*, but focus on recently emerging literature in economics on pro-social behavior and motivated agents. This literature has implications for the design of optimal incentives, the selection of motivated agents and its interaction with monetary rewards, and the optimal organizational form required to exploit such motivations.

In a recent review, Francois and Vlassopoulos (2008) distinguish between extrinsic motivation which stems from the standard pecuniary or other material rewards that an individual may receive from outside and intrinsic motivation which is where an individual pursues actions not because of external rewards but because the activity is valuable in its own right. Two conceptualizations of intrinsic motivation have been used in the economics literature—Impure or Action-oriented Altruism in which the individual receives a "warm glow" from the actual act of contributing to a public good and Pure or Output-oriented Altruism where the individual cares about the overall value of the public good to which he contributes but does not receive a benefit from the direct provision of the good.

Besley and Ghatak (2005) examine impure altruism and its implications for the optimal incentive contract in a moral hazard setting. Their paper studies the provision of optimal incentives in a principal—agent model when some agents are driven by pro-social motivations while others have conventional pecuniary motivations. Agents are matched with principals who have "missions." Missions can be seen as attributes of a project over and above the financial payoff that the project has. The effect of impure altruism is to lower the need for "power" in incentives. The essence of the idea is that when agents match to principals who hold similar missions to them, the agent's identification with a firm or principal's "mission" lowers the cost of agent effort and so they require less monetary compensation. This is akin to a compensating differential where the greater the agent's motivation the less high powered incentive pay needs to be. One corollary is that when agents are motivated, effort will be negatively correlated with incentive pay. This is in stark contrast to the usual setting for incentive pay where incentive pay is used to increase effort. This impure altruism approach suggests that services such as health care may be cheaper to deliver when people have pro-social motivations.

Francois (2000, 2007) uses pure altruism to explain why not-for-profit firms are widespread in the provision of public services. The punch line of his model is that a government bureaucracy or non-profit firms, because they do not have a residual claimant, can obtain labor donations due to the service motivation of their employees when a private firm could not. This suggests that such organizations will produce public services more cheaply. This theory may be one explanation for the widespread presence of not-for-profits firms in health care provision, though it does not explain why for-profits have not been completely driven out of the hospital market.

Few models of altruism have been tested within a health care setting.[46] However, they add to the arguments that in health care worker motivation may outweigh the need for high-powered incentives and that not-for-profits may be an optimal way of organizing medical practice.

5. AREAS FOR FUTURE RESEARCH

We conclude by highlighting a few areas where future research would be valuable. Most of the existing literature on the medical workforce focuses on the US market, and this is particularly true with respect to estimates of labor supply elasticities. Given the importance of institutions and incentives on labor supply and demand, studies that examine non-US markets with differently structured health care systems would help confirm whether the existing findings can be generalized.

One of the most vexing policy challenges is how to improve the value of health care spending. One strategy is to encourage providers to modify the health production function in order to produce greater health at current spending levels, or to spend less without reducing health. To address this challenge policy makers and providers need to understand the health care production function, including how easily inputs can be substituted for one another, how inputs respond to changes in input prices, and how inputs respond to changes in how output is reimbursed. The existing literature on the health care production function is pretty basic and hampered by concerns regarding how to properly measure input and output quality. Finally, new ideas from labor economics on the management of human resources and the motivation of agents could be fruitfully applied to labor supply and demand in health care.

REFERENCES

Accreditation Council of Graduate Medical Education (1996). Graduate medical education Directory, 1996–1997.

Acemoglu, D. & Finkelstein, A. (2008). Input and technology choices in regulated industries: Evidence from the health care sector. *Journal of Political Economy, 116*(5), 837–880.

Acemoglu, D., Finkelstein, A., & Notowidigdo, M. J. (2009). *Income and health spending: Evidence from oil price shocks.* National Bureau of Economic Research Working Paper 14744.

---

[46] Gregg et al. (2008) examine the donated labor across different settings (caring and non-caring and for-profit and not-for-profit), where the caring sector is defined as including the health care sector. They find that donated labor is higher in the not-for-profit and the caring sectors.

Akerlof, G. A. (1970). The market for 'lemons': Quality uncertainty and the market mechanism. *Quarterly Journal of Economics, 84*, 488–500.

Altarum Institute (2010). Labor Brief #10-09, October 15. < www.altarum.org/>.

Anderson, G. M., Halcoussis, D., Johnson, L., & Lowenberg, A. D. (2000). Regulatory barriers to entry in the healthcare industry: The case of alternative medicine. *Quarterly Review of Economics and Finance, 40*, 485–502.

Antonazzo, E., Scott, A., Skatun, D., & Elliott, R. F. (2003). The labour market for nursing: A review of the labour supply literature. *Health Economics, 12*, 465–478.

Arrow, K. J. (1963). Uncertainty and the welfare economics of medical care. *American Economic Review, 53*(5), 941–973.

Askildsen, J. E., Baltagi, B. H., & Holmas, T. H. (2003). Wage policy in the health care sector: A panel data analysis of nurses' labor supply. *Health Economics, 12*, 705–719.

Baltagi, B., Bratberg, E., & Holmås, T. H. (2005). A panel data study of physicians' labor supply: The case of Norway. *Health Economics, 14*, 1035–1045.

Barer, M. L. & Stoddart, G. L. (1991). *Toward integrated medical resource policies for Canada*. Report prepared for the Federal/Provincial and Territorial Conference of Deputy Ministers of Health.

Bazzoli, G. J. (1985). Does educational indebtedness affect physician specialty choice? *Journal of Health Economics, 4*, 1–19.

Besley, T. & Ghatak, M. (2005). Competition and incentives with motivated agents. *American Economic Review, 95*(3), 616–636.

Bhattacharya, J. (2005). Specialty selection and lifetime returns to specialization within medicine. *Journal of Human Resources, 40*(1), 115–143.

Bilodeau, D., Cremieux, P. -Y., & Ouellette, P. (2000). Hospital cost function in a non market healthcare system. *Review of Economics and Statistics, 82*(3), 489–498.

Bloom, N. & Van Reenen, J. (2007). Measuring and explaining management practices across firms and countries. *Quarterly Journal of Economics, 122*(4), 1341–1408.

Bloom, N., Propper, C., Seiler, S., & Van Reenen, J. (2010). The impact of competition on management quality: Evidence from public hospitals. NBER Working Paper No. 16032.

Blumenthal, D. (2004). New steam from an old cauldron—the physician-supply debate. *New England Journal of Medicine, 350*(17), 1780–1787.

Bodenheimer, T. & Pham, H. H. (2010). Primary care: Current problems and proposed solutions. *Health Affairs, 29*(5), 799–805.

Bolton, P. & Dewatripont, M. (2005). *Contract theory*. Cambridge: MIT Press.

Bresnahan, T. F. & Reiss, P. C. (1991). Entry and competition in concentrated markets. *Journal of Political Economy, 99*(5), 977–1009.

Bond, S. & Van Reenen, J. (2008). Micro-econometric models of investment and employment. In J. Heckman, & E. Leamer (Eds.), *Handbook of econometrics* (Vol. 6A, pp. 4417–4498).

Borjas, G. (2000). *Labor economics*. Boston, MA: Irwin/McGraw-Hill.

Brown, D. M. (1988). Do physicians underutilize aides. *Journal of Human Resources, 23*, 342–355.

Brown, D. M. & Lapan, H. E. (1979). The supply of physicians' services. *Economic Inquiry, 17*, 269–279.

Brown, M. C. (1989). Empirical determinants of physician incomes – evidence from Canadian data. *Empirical Economics, 14*(4), 273–289.

Buerhaus, P. I., Auerbach, D. I., & Staiger, D. O. (2009). The recent surge in nurse employment: Causes and implications. *Health Affairs-Web Exclusive* 657–668.

Buerhaus, P. I., Staiger, D. O., & Auerbach, D. I. (2007). *The future of the nursing workforce in the United States: data, trends, and implications*. Sudbury, MA: Jones and Bartlett Publishing.

Cebul, R. D., Rebitzer, J. B., Taylor, L. J., & Votruba, M. (2008). Organizational fragmentation and care quality in the U.S. health care system. *Journal of Economic Perspectives, 22*(4), 93–113.

Clark, A., & Milcent, C. (2008). Public employment and political pressure: The case of French hospitals. Paris School of Economics, Discussion Paper No. 2008-18.

Cooper, R. A. & Aiken, L. A. (2001). Human inputs: The health care workforce and medical markets. *Journal of Health Politics, Policy and Law, 26*(5), 925–937.

Cooper, R. A., Getzen, T. E., McKee, H. J., & Laud, P. (2002). Economic and demographic trends signal an impending physician shortage. *Health Affairs, 21*(January/February), 140–154.

Cordes, D. W., Doherty, N., & Lopez, R. (2002). Assessing the economic return of specializing in orthodontics or oral and maxillofacial surgery. *Journal of the American Dental Association, 132*, 1679–1684.

Crossley, T. F., Hurley, J., & Jeon, S.-H. (2006). Physician labour supply in Canada: A cohort analysis. Social and Economic Dimensions of an Aging Population, SEDAP Research Paper No. 162.

Danzon, P. M. (2000). Liability for medical practice. In A. J. Culyer, & J. P Newhouse (Eds.), *Handbook of health economics* (Vol. 1). Amsterdam: Elsevier.

DeFelice, L. C. & Bradford, D. W. (1997). Relative inefficiencies in production between solo and group practice physicians. *Health Economics, 6*, 455–465.

Doyle, J. J., Ewer, S. M., & Wagner, T. H. (2010). Returns to physician human capital: Evidence from patients randomized to physician teams. *Journal of Health Economics, 29*, 866–882.

Dranove, D. & Jin, G. Z. (2010). Quality disclosure and certification: Theory and practice. NBER Working Paper 15644.

Eckstein, Z., Weiss, Y., & Fleising, A. (1988). University policies under varying market conditions: The training of electrical engineers. *Economics of Education Review, 7*(4), 393–403.

Elliott, R. F., Ma, A. H. Y., Scott, A., Bell, D., & Roberts, E. (2007). Geographically differentiated pay in the labour market for nurses. *Journal of Health Economics, 26*, 190–212.

Encinosa, W. E., Gaynor, M., & Rebitzer, J. B. (2007). The sociology of groups and the economics of incentives; theory and evidence on compensation systems. *Journal of Economic Behavior & Organization, 62*, 187–214.

Epstein, A., Ketcham, J., & Nicholson, S. (2010). *RAND Journal of Economics, 41*(4), 811–834.

Escarce, J. (1996). Using physician practice cost functions in payment policy: The problem of endogeneity bias. *Inquiry, 33*, 66–78.

Escarce, J., Polsky, D., Wozniak, G., Pauly, M., & Kletke, P. (1998). Health maintenance organization penetration and the practice location choices of new physicians. *Medical Care, 36*, 1555–1566.

Escarce, J. J. & Pauly, M. V. (1998). Physician opportunity costs in physician practice cost functions. *Journal of Health Economics, 17*, 129–151.

Esmail, N. (2005). Canada's physician shortage: Problem solved, or disaster in the making? *Fraser Forum, May*, 15–20.

Fehr, E. & Schmidt, K. M. (2006). The economics of fairness, reciprocity and altruism: Experimental evidence. In S. Kolm & J. M. Ythier (Eds.), *Handbook of the economics of giving, altruism and reciprocity* (Vol. 1). New York: North Holland.

Feldstein, M. S. (1970). The rising price of physician's services. *Review of Economics and Statistics, 52*(2), 121–133.

Francois, P. (2000). "Public service motivation" as an argument for government provision. *Journal of Public Economics, 78*(3), 275–299.

Francois, P. & Vlassopoulos, M. (2008). Pro-social of social services motivation and delivery. *CESifo Economic Studies, 54*(1), 22–54.

Frank, R. G. (1985). Pricing and location of physician services in mental health. *Inquiry, 38*, 115–133.

Freeman, R. B. (1976). A cobweb model of the supply and starting salary of new engineers. *Industrial Labor Relations Review, 29*(2), 236–248.

Friedman, M. & Kuznets, S. (1945). *Income from independent professional practice*. New York: National Bureau of Economic Research.

Frijters, P., Shields, M. A., & Wheatley Price, S. (2007). Investigating the quitting decision of nurses: Panel data evidence from the British National Health Services. *Health Economics, 16*, 57–73.

Gagne, R. & Leger, P. T. (2005). Determinants of physicians' decisions to specialize. *Health Economics, 14*, 721–735.

Ganem, J. L., Beran, R. L., & Krakower, J. K. (1995). Review of US medical school finances, 1993 – 1994. *JAMA, 274*(9), 723–730.

Garicano, L. & Hubbard, T. N. (2007). Managerial leverage is limited by the extent of the market: Hierarchies, specialization, and the utilization of lawyers' human capital. *Journal of Law and Economics, 50*, 1–43.

Garicano, L. & Hubbard, T. N. (2009). Specialization, firms and markets: The division of labor within and between law firms. *Journal of Law, Economics, and Organizations, 25*, 339 −371.

Garicano, L. & Santos, T. (2004). Referrals. *American Economic Review, 94*(3), 500−525.

Gaynor, M. (1989). Competition within the firm: Theory plus some evidence from medical group practice. *RAND Journal of Economics, 20*, 59−76.

Gaynor, M. & Gertler, P. (1995). Moral hazard and risk spreading in medical partnerships. *RAND Journal of Economics, 26*, 591−613.

Gaynor, M. & Pauly, M. V. (1990). Compensation and productive efficiency in partnerships: Evidence from medical group practice. *Journal of Political Economy, 98*(3), 544−573.

Gaynor, M., Kleiner, S., & Vogt, W. B. (2011). Analysis of hospital production: An output index approach. Mimeo.

Getzen, T. E. (1984). A "brand name firm" theory of medical group practice. *Journal of Industrial Economics, 33*, 199−215.

Gibbons, R. & Roberts, J. (2008). *The handbook of organizational economics*. Princeton: Princeton University Press.

Gillis, K. D., Lee, D. W., Mandy, D. M., & Willke, R. J. (1991). The technical structure of physician practice costs: Estimation results and implications for Medicare payment. Paper presented at the APHA Meetings, Atlanta, GA, November.

Glied, S., Prabhu, A. G., & Edelman, N. (2009). The cost of primary care doctors. *Forum for Health Economics & Policy, 12*(1), 1−23.

Goodman, D. C. & Fisher, E. S. (2008). Physician workforce crisis? Wrong diagnosis, wrong prescription. *New England Journal of Medicine, 358*(16), 1658−1661.

Gregg, P., Grout, P., Ratcliffe, A., Smith, S., & Windmeijer, F. (2008). how important is pro-social behaviour in the delivery of public services. CMPO, University of Bristol, Working Paper 08/197.

Grossman, M. (1972). On the concept of health capital and the demand for health. *Journal of Political Economy, 80*, 223−255.

Grytten, J. & Sorensen, R. (2003). Practice variation and physician-specific effects. *Journal of Health Economics, 22*(3), 403−418.

Gunning, T. S. & Sickles, R. C. (2011). A multi-product cost function for physician private practices. *Journal of Productivity Analysis, 35*(2), 119−128.

Haber, S. G., Zwanziger, J., Thorpe, K. E., & Newhouse, J. P. (1992). Hospital expenditures in the United States and Canada: Do hospital worker wages explain the differences? *Journal of Health Economics, 11*, 453−465.

Hall, E., Propper, C., & Van Reenen, J. (2008). Can pay regulation kill? Panel data evidence on the effect of labor markets on hospital performance. NBER Working Paper 13776.

Hall, T. D. & Lindsay, C. M. (1980). Medical schools: Producers of what? Sellers to whom? *Journal of Law and Economics, 23*(1), 55−80.

Hamermesh, D. S. (1986). The demand for labor in the long run. In O. Ashenfelter, & R. Layard (Eds.), *Handbook of labor economics*. Amsterdam: North-Holland.

Hamermesh, D. S. (1993). *Labor demand*. Princeton, NJ: Princeton University Press.

Health Resources and Services Administration (2006). *Physician supply and demand: Projections to 2020*. US Department of Health and Human Services, Bureau of Health Professions.

Holmås, T. H. (2002). Keeping nurses at work: A duration analysis. *Health Economics, 11*(6), 493−503.

Holmstrom, B. (1982). Moral hazard in teams. *The Bell Journal of Economics, 13*, 324−340.

Hu, T. & Yang, B. M. (1988). The demand for and supply of supply of physician services in the US: A disequilibrium analysis. *Applied Economics, 20*, 995−1006.

Huckman, R. & Pisano, G. (2006). The firm specificity of individual performance: Evidence from cardiac surgery. *Management Science, 52*, 473−488.

Humphris, A., Kleiner, M. M., & Koumenta, M. (2011). How does government regulate occupations in the UK and US? Issues and policy implications. In *Labour Market Policy for the 21st Century*. Oxford University Press.

Iglehart, J. K. (2008). Grassroots activism and the pursuit of an expanded physician supply. *New England Journal of Medicine, 358*(16), 1741−1749.

Jacobson, P. D., Parker, L. E., & Coulter, I. D. (1998). Nurse practitioners and physician assistants as primary care providers in institutional settings. *Inquiry*, *35*(4), 432–446.

Jetha, S. A. (2002). *The economics of occupational licensing and dental practitioners*. London School of Economics. Masters Thesis.

Johnson, E. (2010). Ability, learning and the career path of cardiac specialists. Working Paper.

Jones, R. F. & Korn, D. (1997). On the cost of educating a medical student. *Academic Medicine*, *72*(3), 200–210.

Kessel, R. A. (1958). Price discrimination in medicine. *Journal of Law and Economics*, *1*, 20–53.

Kleiner, M. M. (2000). Occupational licensing. *Journal of Economic Perspectives*, *14*(4), 189–202.

Kleiner, M. M. (2006). *Licensing occupations: Ensuring quality or restricting competition?* Kalamazoo, MI: W. E. Upjohn Institute for Employment Research.

Kleiner, M. M. & Krueger, A. B. (2009). Analyzing the extent and influence of occupational licensing on the labor market. NBER Working Paper 14979.

Kleiner, M. M. & Kudrle, R. T. (2000). Does regulation affect economic outcomes? The case of dentistry. *Journal of Law and Economics*, *43*, 547–582.

Kolstad, J. (2009). Information and quality when motivation is intrinsic: Evidence from surgeon report cards. Mimeo.

Kugler, A. D. & Sauer, R. M. (2005). Doctors without borders? Relicensing requirements and negative selection in the market for physicians. *Journal of Labor Economics*, *23*(3), 437–465.

Lazear, E. & Oyer, P. (2009). Personnel economics. In E. Gibbons & D. J. Roberts (Eds.), *Handbook of organizational economics*. Princeton: Princeton University Press.

Leland, H. E. (1979). Quacks, lemons, and licensing: A theory of minimum quality standards. *Journal of Political Economy*, *87*(6), 1328–1346.

Long, M. C., Goldfarb, M. G., & Goldfarb, R. S. (2008). Explanations for persistent nursing shortages. *Forum for Health Economics & Policy*, *11*(2), 1–35.

MaCurdy, T. E. & Pencavel, J. H. (1986). Testing between competing models of wage and employment determination in unionized markets. *Journal of Political Economy*, *94*(3), S3–S39.

Mariolis, A., et al. (2007). General practice as a career choice among undergraduate medical students in Greece. *BMC medical education*, < http://www.biomedcentral.com/1472-6920/7/15/> .

McGuire, T. G. (2000). Physician agency. In A. J. Cuyler & J. P. Newhouse (Eds.), *Handbook of health economics* (Vol. 1A). Amsterdam: Elsevier.

McGuire, T. G. & Pauly, M. V. (1991). Physician response to fee changes with multiple payers. *Journal of Health Economics*, *10*, 385–410.

Meltzer, D. & Chung, J. W. (2010). Coordination, switching costs and the division of labor in general medicine: An economic explanation for the emergence of hospitalists in the United States." NBER Working Paper 16040.

Meltzer, D. O. (2001). Hospitalists and the doctor–patient relationship. *Journal of Legal Studies*, *30*, 589–606.

Morris, S. & McGuire, A. (2002). The private net present value and private internal rate of return to becoming a nurse in Great Britain. *Applied Economics*, *34*(17), 2189–2200.

Mott, D. A., Kreling, D. H., & Cain, G. G. (1995). The relationship between internal rates of return, pharmacist supply and applications and admissions: A case study in Wisconsin. *American Journal of Pharmaceutical Education*, *59*, 59–66.

Newhouse, J. P., et al. (1982). Does the geographical distribution of physicians reflect market failure? *Bell Journal of Economics*, *13*, 493–505.

Nicholson, S. (2002). Physician specialty choice under uncertainty. *Journal of Labor Economics*, *20*(4), 816–847.

Nicholson, S. (2003). Barriers to entering medical specialties. NBER Working Paper 9649.

Nicholson, S. (2008). Medical career choices and rates of return. In F. A. Sloan & H. Kasper (Eds.), *Incentives and choice in health and health care*. Cambridge, MA: MIT Press.

Nicholson, S. (2009). Will the United States have a shortage of physicians in 10 years? Changes in Health Care Financing & Organization report: <www.hcfo.org/> .

Nicholson, S. & Song, D. (2001). The incentive effects of the Medicare indirect medical education policy. *Journal of Health Economics*, *20*(6), 909–933.

Nicholson, S. & Souleles, N. (2001). Physician income expectations and specialty choice. NBER Working Paper 8536.

Noether, M. (1986). The growing supply of physicians: Has the market become more competitive? *Journal of Labor Economics*, *4*(4), 503–537.

Organization for Economic Cooperation and Development (OECD) Health Data (2009). < www.oecd. org/>, Accessed October 2010.

Pencavel, J. (1984). The tradeoff between wages and employment in trade union objectives. *Quarterly Journal of Economics*, *99*(2), 215–231.

Phelps, C. E. (2000). Information diffusion and best practice adoption. In A. J. Cuyler & J. P. Newhouse (Eds.), *Handbook of health economics*. Amsterdam: Elsevier Science.

Phelps, C. E. (2010). *Health economics* (4th ed.). New York: Addison-Wesley.

Polsky, D., Kletke, P. R., Wozniak, G. D., & Escarce, J. J. (2000). HMO penetration and the geographic mobility of practicing physicians. *Journal of Health Economics*, *19*(5), 793–809.

Pope, G. C. & Burge, R. T. (1992). Inefficiencies in physician practices. *Advances in Health Economics and Health Services Research*, *13*, 129–164.

Pope, G. C. & Burge, R. T. (1995). The marginal practice cost of physicians' services. *Journal of Socioeconomic Planning Science*, *29*, 1–16.

Propper, C. & Van Reenen, J. (2010). Can pay regulation kill? Panel data evidence on the effects of labor markets on hospital performance. *Journal of Political Economy*, *118*(2), 222–273.

Ramseyer, J. M. (2008). Talent and expertise under universal health insurance: The case of cosmetic surgery in Japan. American Law & Economics Association Annual Meetings, Paper 44

Reinhardt, U. (1975). *Physician productivity and demand for health manpower*. Cambridge, MA: Ballinger Publishing Company.

Reinhardt, U. E. (1972). A production function for physician services. *Review of Economics and Statistics*, *54*(1), 55–66.

Rizzo, J. & Blumenthal, D. (1994). Physician labor supply: Do income effects matter? *Journal of Health Economics*, *13*, 433–453.

Roos, N. P., Flowerdew, G., Wajda, A., & Tate, R. B. (1986). Variations in physicians' hospitalization practices: A population-based study in Manitoba, Canada. *American Journal of Public Health*, *76*(1), 45–51.

Rosen, S. (1986). The theory of equalizing differences. In O. Ashenfelter & R. Layard (Eds.), *Handbook of labor economics* (Vol. 1, pp. 641–692). Elsevier Science Publishers BV.

Ryoo, J. & Rosen, S. (2004). The engineering labor market. *Journal of Political Economy*, *112*(1), S110–S140.

Sæther, E. M. (2005). Physicians' labor supply: The wage impact on hours and practice combinations. *Labour*, *19*(4), 673–703.

Schoen, C., Osborn, R., Doty, M. M., Squires, D., Peugh, J., & Applebaum, S. (2009). A survey of primary care physicians in eleven countries, 2009: Perspectives on care, costs, and experiences. *Health Affairs*, w1171–w1183.

Schut, F. T. (1995). Health care reform in the Netherlands: Balancing corporatism, statism, and market mechanisms. *Journal of Health Politics, Policy and Law*, *20*(3), 615–652.

Shapiro (1986). Investment, moral hazard, and occupational licensing. *Review of Economic Studies*, *53*, 843–862.

Shields, M. A. (2004). Addressing nurse shortages: What can policy makers learn from the econometric evidence on nurse labour supply? *Economic Journal*, *114*, F464–F498.

Showalter, M. H. & Thurston, M. (1997). Taxes and labor supply of high-income physicians. *Journal of Public Economics*, *66*, 73–97.

Siow, A. (1984). Occupational choice under uncertainty. *Econometrica*, *52*, 631–645.

Sloan, F. A. (1970). Lifetime earnings and physicians' choice of specialty. *Industrial and Labor Relations Review*, *24*, 47–56.

Sloan, F. (1975). Physician labor supply behaviour in the short run. *Industrial and Labor Relations Review*, *28*(2), 549–569.

Smith, P. C., Mossialos, E., Papanicolas, I., & Leatherman, S. (Eds.) (2009). *Performance measurement for health system improvement: Experiences, challenges and prospects.* Cambridge, UK: Cambridge University Press.

Staiger, D. O., Auerbach, D. I., & Buerhaus, P. I. (2010). Trends in the work hours of physicians in the United States. *JAMA, 303*(8), 747–753.

Staiger, D., Spetz, J., & Phibbs, C. (1999). Is there monopsony in the labor market? Evidence from a natural experiment. NBER Working Paper Series, Working Paper 7258, <http//www.nber.org/papers/w7258/>.

Stark, A. (2007). Which fields pay, which fields don't? An examination of the returns to university education in Canada by detailed field of study. Department of Finance, Canada, mimeo.

Thornton, J. (1998). The labour supply behaviour of self-employed solo practice physicians. *Applied Economics, 30*(1), 85–94.

Thornton, J. & Eakin, K. B. (1997). The utility-maximizing self-employed physician. *Journal of Human Resources, 32*(1), 98–128.

Timmons, E. J. & Thornton, R. J. (2008). The effects of licensing on the wages of radiologic technologists. *Journal of Labor Research, 29*(4), 333–346.

Toyabe, S. (2009). Trend in geographic distribution of physicians in Japan. *International Journal for Equity in Health, 8*(5), 1–8.

Tyrell, L. & Dauphinee, D. (1999). Task force on physician supply in Canada. Report prepared for the Canadian Medical Forum Talk Force

Vahovich, S. (1977). Physicians' supply decisions by specialty: TSLS model. *Journal of Health Economics, 13*, 433–453.

Vaughn, B. T., DeVrieze, S. R., Reed, S. D., & Schulman, K. A. (2010). Can we close the income and wealth gap between specialists and primary care physicians? *Health Affairs, 29*(5), 933–940.

Vita, M. (1990). Exploring hospital production relationship with flexible functional forms. *Journal of Health Economics, 9*, 1–21.

Wanchek, T. (2009). Dental hygiene regulation and access to oral health care: Assessing the variation across the U.S. States. Working Paper.

Weeks, W. B. & Wallace, A. E. (2002). The more things change: Revisiting a comparison of educational costs and incomes of physicians and other professionals. *Academic Medicine, 77*, 312–319.

Weeks, W. B., Wallace, A. E., Wallace, M. M., & Welch, H. G. (1994). A comparison of the educational costs and incomes of physicians and other professionals. *New England Journal of Medicine, 330*(18), 1280–1286.

Welch, H. G., Miller, M. E., & Welch, W. P. (1994). Physician profiling: An analysis of inpatient practice patterns in Florida and Oregon. *New England Journal of Medicine, 330*(9), 607–612.

Whalley, D., Gravelle, H., & Sibbald, B. (2008). Effect of the new contract on GPs' working lives and perceptions of quality of care. *British Journal of General Practice,* January, 8–14.

White, W. D. (1978). The impact of occupational licensure of clinical laboratory personnel. *Journal of Human Resources, 13*(1), 91–102.

White, W. D. (1980). Mandatory licensure of registered nurses: Introduction and impact. In S. Rottenberg (Ed.), *Occupational licensure and regulation.* Washington, DC: American Enterprise Institute.

White, W. D. & Marmor, T. R. (1982). New occupations, old demands. *Journal of Policy Analysis and Management, 1*(2), 243–256.

Wilson, J. F. (2008). Primary care delivery changes as nonphysician clinicians gain independence. *Annals of Internal Medicine, 149*(8), 597–600.

Zarkin, G. (1985). Occupational choice: An application to the market for public school teachers. *Quarterly Journal of Economics, 100*, 409–446.

CHAPTER FIFTEEN

Public and Private Sector Interface

Pedro Pita Barros[*] and Luigi Siciliani[**]
[*]Nova School of Business and Economics, Campus de Campolide, Lisboa, Portugal
[**]Department of Economics and Related Studies, and Centre for Health Economics, University of York, UK

Contents

Handbook of Health Economics, Volume 2
ISSN: 1574-0064, DOI: 10.1016/B978-0-444-53592-4.00015-3

Abstract

A major feature of the health sector is the existence of health insurance, either public or private. Often both coexist in the same country. Public health insurance is often accompanied by public provision of health care. We consider two main areas of public–private interface: in funding of health care expenditures and in provision of health care. Within each area, both positive and normative views are explored. On funding issues, the role of three main sources of funds— public health insurance, private health insurance, and out-of-pocket payments—and their interactions are addressed. Topics covered in provision of health care include interaction of public and private providers, dual practice, and public–private partnerships. Empirical evidence is also reviewed.

Keywords: public–private interface; funding of health expenditures; interaction of public and private providers

JEL Codes: I18; H42; H44

1. INTRODUCTION

In the United States, government funding of health expenditures reaches 46.6 percent of the total health spending. Private health insurance accounts for 38.3 percent. The United Kingdom has 82.6 percent of public funding of health expenditures, and commercial private health insurance is 1.4 percent. Out-of-pocket payments are roughly similar in both countries: 12.1 percent of total funding for health in the United States and 11.1 percent in the United Kingdom. They are two different countries: one has more reliance in the private sector than the other; the government plays an important role in both countries, but is much more extensive in the United Kingdom. What underlies these differences? What are the implications? The interaction of private and public activities in the health sector is present in many countries and with considerable diversity.

A major feature of the health sector is the existence of health insurance, either public or private. Often both coexist in the same country. Different types of health insurance may involve distinct ways to organize provision of health care. The insurance arrangement determines the origin of funds to pay for health care, but it may also determine how health care is delivered to the population.

Several countries have chosen to have a National Health Service, meaning both public funding and direct government provision of health care. Others take an approach relying on the private health insurance market, coupled with regulation, and mainly private provision of health services and goods. Still, no pure system exists. In countries with a National Health Service, it is common to observe (supplementary) private health insurance. The fundamental defining characteristic of a National Health

Service is to be tax based on the funding side, and having direct public provision of care. In countries with strong private health insurance we find important government-sponsored programs which are no less than a form of public health insurance. Another common form of funding health insurance is the so-called social insurance. Its defining characteristics are the compulsory nature (covering most, if not all, of the population) and being based on income-related contributions. Sometimes, these funds are topped up with government transfers (introducing therefore elements of tax-based funding). Private health insurance has contributions (payments) based on risk of the population that take the contracts offered. The countries relying more on private health insurance follow either a model of employer-based insurance or compulsory health insurance, where premiums may blend community-rated components with risk-related premiums.

In many circumstances, the health insurance arrangement does require patients to make co-payments. Patients may go to health care providers they freely choose if they are willing to pay at the moment of consumption. Co-payments may differ according to existing agreement between the providers and the payers (health insurance companies). The out-of-pocket payments constitute another source of funds. Part of it is due to pure demand decisions by patients while the other results from health insurance schemes. Tax systems often have special treatment of health expenditures, leading to a different way of providing public health insurance, be it through exclusion of the income tax base of health care expenditures or of private health insurance premiums.

Following Paris et al. (2010), a classification of four different systems for health funding can be identified in modern economies: National Health Service, decentralized (local) health services, single payer systems, and multiple insurer systems, with a further distinction in the latter of employer-based health insurance in several countries. Countries with a National Health Service include Australia, Hungary, Ireland, Iceland, Italy, New Zealand, Portugal, Sweden, and the United Kingdom. Countries with local health services include Canada, Denmark, Finland, Norway, and Spain. Under the single payer system, we find Belgium, Korea, Luxembourg, Poland, and Turkey. Multiple payer and employed-based health insurance is present in Austria, France, Greece, Japan, Mexico, and the United States. Finally, there are countries with multiple health insurers but no direct attachment with employment or other defining characteristics. This set of countries includes the Czech Republic, Germany, the Netherlands, Slovak Republic, and Switzerland.

The interface between public and private sectors occurs both in health insurance and in health care provision. This leads to a simple 2×2 matrix of funding $\times$ provision that helps to organize our views on the public—private interface in the health sector. Of course, there is no pure system, and in all countries all four cells of this matrix are non-negative (see Table 15.1).

Table 15.1 Public and Private Mix in Health Care

	Public Funding	Private Funding
Public provision	National Health Service	
Private provision	Social insurance	(Regulated) private insurance

Note: Under public funding we include mandatory income-related contributions to sickness funds, whether public or private institutions, as well as tax-based contributions.

In private funding, we have both out-of-pocket payments and health insurance, which have very different properties. We depict this in the matrix, where each of the major types of organization in health care lies. The classification just uses the most important source of health expenditures' funding and mode of delivery. Each combination leads to a different set of questions.

We have two main areas of public–private interface in health: in funding of health care expenditures and in provision of health care. Within each area, both positive and normative views can be explored.

The funding side corresponds to the origin of funds. The main issues relate to observed ways the population makes available funds to pay for health care, voluntarily or under government rule. The normative view of how the different sources of funds should be combined to achieve objectives of efficiency and equity also rank high on the agenda.

The second area of interface is provision of care, as providers can be public or private, for-profit or not profit oriented.

Naturally, funding and provision are interdependent in several ways. A less (technologically) efficient provision system will demand a larger amount of funds. Economic inefficiency in the sense of underprovision of care dictates fewer funding requirements. Funding arrangements also influence provision efficiency (technological, allocative or economic efficiency). The most celebrated example is a system based on funding whatever care is demanded by providers (like the old pure retrospective reimbursement health insurance model). It leads to too much health care being provided at a too high price.

There is another important distinction between these two broad areas of public–private interface. Funding issues mostly relate to decisions taken prior to realization of uncertainty, regarding the need of health care. Provision is mainly related to what happens after the "sick" state of Nature has been realized. Thus, uncertainty regarding sickness is a dividing line between the two types of public–private interface.

The important role of the government in purchasing health care services was already described in Chalkley and Malcomson (2000). The main issue addressed in their review was how the different contractual arrangements influence the results under information asymmetries (the leading example being unverifiable quality of care). We focus here on the distinct issue of how public and private health insurance and/or provision coexist in a health system.

1.1. What do the Data tell Us?

The OECD Health Data (2010) was used to obtain a cross-country comparison of main features of public and private interfaces. Tables 15.2 and 15.3 describe the basic characteristics of OECD countries.

To assess the role of public and private sector interface in the health care sector, a good starting point is provided by three indicators: the ratio of health expenditures to GDP, public health care expenditures per capita, and the share of public health care expenditure on the total spending in health.

Public funding has remained fairly stable over the last decade, and it accounts for more than 50 percent (the US being the exception), and for many countries more than 75 percent, of total funding. For several countries, overall health expenditure has reached 10 percent of GDP. The US is again an outlier at a ratio of total health expenditure over GDP of about 16 percent.

Out-of-pocket payments, including both co-payments imposed by the health insurance coverage (be it public or private) and pure private consumption by families deciding to take outside insurance coverage (for example, visits to specialists in the private sector or self-medication), have in general been in the range of 10–20 percent for most OECD countries, though they have slightly increased over the last 20 years.

1.2. Plan of the Chapter

The chapter is organized as follows. Section 2 focuses on theory. Section 2.1 provides a simple framework, which describes the choice faced by patients in opting for public or private care. We then separate the analysis by discussing issues related to public–private *funding* interface in section 2.2 and issues on public–private *provision* in section 2.3. Section 2.2.1 takes a political-economy approach: it reviews the theoretical literature which explains why public and private funding is likely to coexist in the health sector. Section 2.2.2 turns to normative issues: it investigates whether a mix of public and private funding is optimal from a welfare perspective. Section 2.2.3 investigates how an expansion of public insurance coverage affects private insurance coverage (i.e. whether there is crowding out or crowding in). Section 2.2.4 investigates the role of co-payments (i.e. private expenditure for consumers) within publicly funded health care systems.

Section 2.3 covers four different issues related to provision: (1) how rationing rules in the public sector affect private provision (section 2.3.1); (2) the rationale for having doctors working simultaneously in both the public and private sectors (also known as dual practice or moonlighting) (section 2.3.2); (3) sources of differential behavior between public and private (profit and non-profit) providers (section 2.3.3); and (4) public–private partnerships (section 2.2.4).

Table 15.2 Main Sources of Funding in OECD Countries

	Public Funding (%)		Out-of-pocket (%)		Private Health Insurance (%)	
	2000	2009	2000	2009	2000	2009
Australia	66.8	67.5	19.8	18.0	13.3	14.4
Austria	76.9	76.9	15.3	15.1	7.8	8.0
Belgium	68.3	66.7	19.0	20.5	4.9	4.8
Canada	70.4	70.3	15.9	14.8	13.7	15.0
Czech Republic	90.9	82.6	9.7	15.7	0.2	1.8
Denmark	82.4	80.2	16.0	13.8	1.7	1.7
Estonia	77.1	77.8	19.9	19.7	2.9	2.5
Finland	71.1	74.2	22.3	19.4	6.6	6.3
France	79.4	77.7	7.1	7.4	13.5	14.8
Germany	79.8	76.7	11.1	13.0	9.1	10.3
Greece	60.0	60.3				
Hungary	70.7	71.0	26.3	23.9	4.4	5.1
Iceland	81.1	82.0	18.9	16.6	1.4	1.4
Ireland	75.3	76.9	15.2	14.4	9.4	8.6
Israel	57.5	53.0	24.1	29.7	8.6	11.9
Italy	72.5	77.3	24.5	19.4	3.0	3.2
Japan	81.2	79.4	16.9	14.6	1.8	3.5
Korea	45.5	55.4	45.2	35.0	9.2	9.8
Luxembourg	85.1	84.0	11.8	11.6	3.2	4.3
Mexico	46.6	47.5	50.9	48.8	2.5	3.6
Netherlands	63.1	75.3	9.0	5.7	26.9	10.8
New Zealand	78.0	80.5	15.4	13.9	6.7	5.7
Norway	82.5	84.1	16.7	15.1	0.8	0.7
Poland	70.1	72.2	30.0	22.4	4.1	5.4
Portugal	72.5	71.5	22.2	22.9	6.0	5.5
Slovak Republic	89.4	67.8	10.6	25.2	0.0	7.0
Slovenia	71.9	72.2	11.9	12.8	16.2	14.9
Spain	71.7	72.5	23.6	20.7	5.2	6.8
Sweden	84.9	81.9	15.9	15.6	2.3	2.5
Switzerland	55.5	59.6	33.0	30.3	11.6	10.1
Turkey	62.9	67.8	27.6	21.8	9.4	10.4
United Kingdom	79.3	82.6	13.4	11.1	7.0	5.2
United States	43.2	46.6	14.5	12.1	42.4	41.4

Notes: (i) 2009 or nearest year value; some series are incomplete or based on estimates; (ii) private health insurance includes commercial private health insurance, corporation plans, and non-profit organization health plans.
Source: OECD Health Data (2010).

Section 3 turns to empirical evidence. Again we distinguish between issues related to funding (section 3.1) and provision (section 3.2). On *funding* we review the empirical evidence which investigates how the quality of public care affects private health insurance coverage (section 3.1.1) and how public health insurance coverage affects

Table 15.3 Expenditures in Health Care

	Health Exp./GDP		Exp. Per Capita		Public Exp. Per Capita	
	2000	2009	2000	2009	2000	2009
Australia	8.0	8.5	2,266	2,776	1,514	1,874
Austria	9.9	10.5	2,862	3,431	2,199	2,638
Belgium	9.0	11.1	2,481	3,460		
Canada	8.8	10.4	2,519	3,292	1,772	2,311
Chile	6.6	6.9	613	812	319	483
Czech Republic	6.5	7.1	982	1,490	887	1,230
Denmark	8.3	9.7	2,383	3,074	1,964	2,597
Estonia	5.3	6.1	522	1028	403	800
Finland	7.2	8.4	1,855	2,650	1,318	1,967
France	10.1	11.2	2,553	3,048	2,027	2,371
Germany	10.3	10.5	2,669	3,021	2,130	2,319
Greece	7.9	9.7	1,451	2,316	871	1,398
Hungary	7.0	7.3	853	1,167	603	829
Iceland	9.5	9.6	2,740	3,157	2,221	2,649
Ireland	6.1	8.7	1,763	3,170	1,328	2,438
Israel	7.5	7.8	1,766	2,010	1,097	1,145
Italy	8.1	9.5	2,064	2,384	1,497	1,843
Japan	7.7	8.1	1,969	2,301	1,600	1,883
Korea	4.8	6.5	824	1,527	375	845
Luxembourg	7.5	7.8	3,269	3,214	2,781	2,702
Mexico	5.1	5.9	508	657	237	308
Netherlands	8.0	9.9	2,340	3,288	1,476	
New Zealand	7.7	9.9	1,607	2,329	1,254	1,873
Norway	8.4	8.5	3,043	3469	2,510	2,921
Poland	5.5	7.0	583	1031	409	745
Portugal	8.8	9.9	1,511	1736	1,097	1,242
Slovak Republic	5.5	8.0	604	1418	540	961
Slovenia	8.3	8.3	1,453	2013	1,076	1,455
Spain	7.2	9.0	1,538	2,217	1,101	1,608
Sweden	8.2	9.4	2,286	3,038	1,941	2,487
Switzerland	10.2	10.7	3,221	3,729	1,785	2,205
Turkey	4.9	6.2	433	684	272	487
United Kingdom	7.0	8.7	1,837	2,637	1,456	2,178
United States	13.4	16.0	4,703	6,160	2,032	2,866

Notes: 2009 or nearest year value; expenditures per capita in US$ 2000 PPP.
Source: OECD Health Data (2010).

private health insurance coverage, taking first the evidence on crowding out (section 3.1.2) and then on crowding in (section 3.1.3).

On *provision* we review the empirical literature which investigates how quality in the public sector affects the choice of opting for private care as opposed to the choice of buying private insurance (section 3.2.1) and how access to care (as proxied by individuals holding private health insurance, which effectively reduces the price of private care at the moment of use) affects the choice between public and private care (section 3.2.2). Differences in quality and efficiency between public and private providers are reviewed in section 3.2.3. Section 3.3 discusses directions for future empirical work on the public–private interface. Section 4 concludes.

2. THEORY

2.1. A Tale of Two Margins

In this section we provide a simple framework of individuals making choices between public and private provision. These choices relate to two different margins. We illustrate them with the public–private interface in provision, though the same principles are applicable to funding.

The first margin relates to choices of individuals when care is provided both publicly and privately but the quality and price differ between the two sectors. The care provided by the private sector is duplicative, or alternatively public and private care are economic substitutes.

The second margin relates to care which is not covered by public care but can potentially be covered by private care. Public and private sector still interface because what is covered by the public sector potentially crowds out the private one: private care therefore complements public care.

More formally, in many countries with public health insurance and public provision (for example, a National Health Service), individuals who fall sick are faced with a choice: either going to the public sector at zero (or negligible) price, or going to the private sector and paying a price p (if the individual holds a private health insurance, p can be interpreted as a co-payment which can be equal to zero as a special case). Define q as the clinical quality received in the public hospital, b the benefit from health care, a the level of amenities, w the waiting time, y individual (or household) net income (net of taxes or insurance premiums), and p the price charged by the private sector.[1] Define $u(b, q, a, w, y)$ as the utility function of a patient. We assume such function to be increasing in benefit, clinical quality, amenities, and income (or a composite good) but decreasing in waiting time. Moreover, we assume utility to be concave in income ($u_{yy} < 0$).

Public health care systems have limited budgets. They aim at providing health care which has the highest benefit (or highest benefit–cost ratio) compatible with the

---

[1] See Martin and Smith (1999) for a similar model. We expand their model by also including quality and amenities. See also Lindsay and Feigenbaum (1984), Goddard et al. (1995), and Gravelle and Siciliani (2008).

budget that is allocated to them through the political process. We capture this idea by assuming that the public sector provides care when $b \geq b^{pu}$, where b^{pu} is the benefit level that leads to provision by the public sector.[2] Superscripts pu and pr stand for public sector and private sector, respectively.

2.1.1. The First Margin

Suppose that a treatment has $b \geq b^{pu}$ and is therefore covered by the public sector. If an individual with benefit b and income y goes to the public sector then her utility is $u(b, q^{pu}, a^{pu}, w^{pu}, y)$. If she goes to the private sector her utility is $u(b, q^{pr}, a^{pr}, 0, y - p)$. We therefore assume that waiting time in the private sector is zero (this is a simplification but it is likely to be low, or lower compared to the public sector). In general, clinical quality in the public and private sectors will be different (but *a priori* no ordering needs to be assumed). Amenities are likely to be higher in the private sector ($a^{pr} > a^{pu}$).

Individuals go to the private sector for treatment if $u(b, q^{pr}, a^{pr}, 0, y - p) > u(b, q^{pu}, a^{pu}, w^{pu}, y)$. If the utility function is separable in each argument: $u(b, q, a, w, y) = b - g(w) + V(a) + v(q) + U(y)$, the condition becomes:

$$V(a^{pr}) - V(a^{pu}) + g(w) + v(q^{pr}) - v(q^{pu}) > U(y) - U(y - p)$$

Intuitively, the individual chooses the private sector only if the utility gain from amenities and lower waiting times plus, eventually, clinical quality is larger than the loss of utility from paying a positive price. The assumption that amenities are higher and waiting times lower in the private sector is intuitive. The existence of the private sector relies on their ability to attract patients: high-income patients are more likely to afford amenities than poorer ones.

Whether quality is higher in the public or the private sector is less straightforward. If we consider a visit to a physician, it may be argued that the individual, by being able to choose the specialist in the private sector (by reputation or word of mouth), may receive a more accurate diagnosis than going to a general practitioner (GP) in the public sector. In terms of actual treatment, for example from a surgical operation, private hospitals may be small and have limited emergency facilities. Public hospitals may benefit from economies of scope. If the volume of patients treated is higher in public than in private hospitals, then public provision may display better outcomes. Note that even if quality is higher in the public sector, some patients may still opt for the private sector if they value highly lower waiting times and better amenities.

---

[2] To focus on the choice of individuals across providers, we do not specify the details of health insurance. Public provision is usually associated with public health insurance. Private provision can occur under private health insurance or when the patient pays out of pocket. Private provision may occur also under public insurance if the private sector is contracted to provide treatment for publicly funded patients.

Some individuals have private health insurance provided by their employer. Assuming that the choice of a job does not depend on insurance coverage (which is plausible to a large extent in many countries), those individuals should prefer private to public treatment unless they face a significant co-payment in the care provided by the private sector or their perceived quality of the public sector is higher. In countries with a small private sector, private hospitals tend not to be uniformly distributed over the territory. Therefore, a private option may not always be available. If the distance cost to the closest available private hospital is sufficiently high, individuals may prefer their local public hospital even if they are insured and the quality in the private sector is higher.[3]

Suppose that benefit from health care b and income y are distributed according to the joint density function $f(b, y)$ over a rectangular support. Define $y^*(b)$ as the level of income such that individuals with income $y > y^*(b)$ go private (for a given b). If utility is separable (as assumed above) then the income threshold $y^*(b) = y^*$ does not depend on benefit. Intuitively this suggests that it is the well-off who choose to go private (in particular, when marginal utility of income is smaller than 1). This is represented in Figure 15.1.

This provides what we call the "first margin." Both public and private care are provided, but some patients opt for private care because they are attracted by the lower waiting times and higher amenities and are not deterred by the price they have to pay.

On some occasions, waiting times for patients with high benefit from treatment can be zero or low in the public sector (for example, cancer treatment or emergency care). In such cases, the only motive to go private is differences in amenities. The choice is weakened even further if quality is higher in the public sector. In such circumstances we expect the proportion of patients going private to be low or non-existent, as the choice will be mainly driven by clinical quality.

In several countries, waiting times tend to be significant for some elective treatments (for example, cataract and hip replacements). For such procedures it is likely that patients with higher income or high private benefit will opt for the private sector.

2.1.2. The Second Margin

For certain types of care, the public sector may not provide coverage. This may be the case for basic types of dental care or eye treatment. They are simply not covered by the public sector, and the only option is the private sector. We therefore assume

---

[3] Distance costs can be introduced in the above framework by putting more structure to the model and adding a geographical dimension (making the utility a function of distance to the closest public and private hospital). In the theoretical literature this is normally done within a Hoteling or Salop framework (Brekke et al., 2006). The empirical evidence also suggests that distance is the main predictor of hospital patient's choice (Tay, 2003).

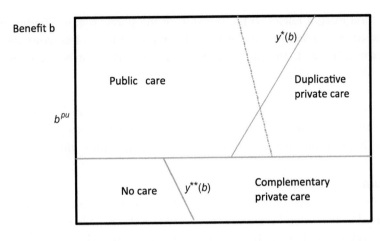

Figure 15.1 Choice between public and private care.

that $b < b^{pu}$. All patients with $b < b^{pu}$ face the choice between private treatment and no treatment. In this case individuals will choose private care if $u(b, q^{pr}, a^{pr}, 0, y - p) > u(0, 0, 0, 0, y)$. We can identify $y^{**}(b)$ as the income threshold over which individuals demand private treatment. Under separable utility the individual demands private care if $V(a^{pr}) + b + v(q^{pr}) > U(y) - U(y - p)$. See again Figure 15.1.

Importantly, when the public sector varies the threshold b^{pu} what is covered by the private sector varies. Whenever the public sector relaxes the threshold, many or all patients will switch from the private to the public sector. This is what we refer to as the "second margin."

To summarize, if the public sector provides care with no waiting and at a reasonable quality (e.g. cancer treatment) there is no scope for a private sector (except for a small group who might value amenities): the public sector provision crowds out the private one. If the public sector has significant waiting times (e.g. elective surgery), the care provided by the private sector is duplicative: it is similar to the care provided in the public sector (but at a shorter wait and with more amenities). If the public sector does not provide care (e.g. dental care) there is greater scope for a private sector; in this case the private sector is complementary to the public one: it provides care not covered by the public sector.

We have identified two main margins through which the public and private sectors interface. The first relates to care provided by both public and private sectors but where waiting times, amenities, and prices differ between the two. More broadly, the same health needs can be satisfied by each sector, but choice is left to the individual.

The second margin relates to the decision of the public sector whether to cover a certain type of care. The more inclusive is the public care, the less scope there is for a private sector to exist. If the public sector does not offer the relevant services then patients' health needs will be satisfied by the private sector.

The theoretical literature reviewed below includes both types of margin: they assume the public and the private sector interface on the "first" margin or on the "second" (very rarely on both). It is therefore important to keep this distinction in mind as the implications that arise from the modeling are quite different.

2.1.3. Insurance

The framework presented above can be extended to an insurance set-up. It can also be interpreted as the second stage of a model where the patient has already fallen sick and has to decide whether to choose public or private provision. The framework can be extended by allowing for a first stage where the patient has to choose whether to buy private health insurance or not. Public health insurance is normally mandatory and in most countries (though not in all of them) individuals cannot opt out.

Suppose that the cover offered by private health insurance (PHI) is duplicative (i.e. it covers the same care provided by the public sector, like elective surgery). We assume that the individual is sick with probability π and healthy with probability $(1 - \pi)$. If the patient is sick and treated in the public sector, her utility is $u^s(b, q^{pu}, a^{pu}, w^{pu}, y(1 - t))$ where y is gross income, b is the benefit from treatment, q is quality, a is amenities, w is waiting time, and t is a proportional income tax. If the patient is treated in the private sector her utility is $u^s(b, q^{pr}, a^{pr}, 0, y(1 - t) - P)$ where P is the premium charged by the private insurer. If the premium is actuarially fair then it will be set at $P = \pi p$ where p is the price of private care in the event of illness, otherwise $P > \pi p$. We are assuming full insurance coverage. If the patient is healthy her utility is $u^h(y(1 - t))$ with no private health insurance and $u^h(y(1 - t) - P)$ with private health insurance.

When deciding whether to buy PHI the individual compares her expected utility with no PHI which is equal to $EU^{pu} = \pi u^s(b, q^{pu}, a^{pu}, w^{pu}, y(1 - t)) + (1 - \pi)u^h(y(1 - t))$, to the one with PHI which is equal to $EU^{pr} = \pi u^s(b, q^{pr}, a^{pr}, 0, y(1 - t) - P) + (1 - \pi)u^h(y(1 - t) - P)$. The individual chooses to buy private health insurance if $EU^{pr} > EU^{pu}$.

Assuming that the utility is separable, as above, the condition is:

$$\pi[V(a^{pr}) - V(a^{pu}) + g(w) + v(q^{pr}) - v(q^{pu})] > u^h(y(1 - t)) - u^h(y(1 - t) - P)$$

Intuitively, individuals buy PHI if their expected benefit in the event of illness in terms of higher amenities, lower waiting (and quality) is higher than the loss of utility from paying the insurance premium. Whether individuals buy PHI also depends on their perceived probability of illness: some individuals may be "optimistic" and underestimate the probability of falling sick. Also, individuals need to value significantly waiting times and amenities for this condition to be satisfied. Some individuals may find the premium charged excessive if this is set at non-competitive rates or there is a loading factor to account for administrative costs of insurance.

Note that the model assumes PHI to be duplicative as it covers care already covered by the public sector. The condition would be simpler for insurance which offers complementary or supplementary care: $EU^{pr} > 0$. This condition should always be satisfied if the individual is risk averse and the premium is actuarially fair. Again, this condition may or may not be satisfied depending on the perceived probability of illness and the premium charged by the private insurance. Another reason why individuals may not buy PHI is that they may self-insure themselves through personal (precautionary) savings: the individual can set aside every period some amount of money in anticipation of a negative health shock in the future.

Another form of PHI is the one that applies to expenses incurred when asking for treatment in the "public sector." For example, in the French health system there are substantial co-payments (for secondary care) on medical expenses incurred. Again, the standard insurance theory set-up can be applied. Individuals will buy coverage to protect against high co-payment costs in case of illness.[4]

2.2. Funding

We can identify three main sources of funding: public insurance, private insurance, and out-of-pocket payments (see Table 15.2). Each of these funding sources has variants. The public health insurance has as its distinctive feature the mandatory nature of contributions, using the coercive power of the government. Contributions are usually related to wage or income. This heading includes both NHS-type health insurance, where funding results mainly from general taxation, and social insurance, in which contributions are directed to sickness funds or specialized not-for-profit agencies/companies.

Private insurance relies on contracts offered by insurance companies, which set premiums based on risk, either individual risk or group risk depending on the type of insurance policy. Taking private insurance can be either voluntary or mandatory. In the latter, the mandate for the population to acquire health insurance is accompanied

---

[4] Colombo and Tapay (2004) distinguish between three different roles for private health insurance. Private health insurance is duplicative when it is contracted to provide a private alternative to the public coverage, allowing access additional to the one provided by the public health care system. Private health insurance is complementary when it ensures coverage of services and goods not included in the primary health insurance coverage. It is supplementary when private health insurance is used to cover fees charged by providers of health care and not covered by the primary health insurance coverage.

by heavy regulation or insurance contract offers, to prevent abuse of market position by health insurers.

Finally, out-of-pocket payments include both payments resulting from insurance co-payments, private and public, and decisions to consume health care not covered by insurance arrangements.

Any funding arrangement for the health system will imply a division of origin of funds across these three broad sources. Each country has a different way to combine them. Understanding the economic forces behind the public—private mix in funding is a first key issue.

2.2.1. Political Economy

A main question is how to explain the existence at the same time of both private and public provision of health care. This section discusses the public funding of health care when the amount of public care is decided under a majority voting rule. It therefore takes a positive approach and relies on democratic frameworks to define the level of government involvement in provision of goods and services. The main result is that governments tend to underprovide publicly funded care in the presence of a private sector. For most of this section, and unless otherwise specified, public funding is identified with public provision of health care and private health care is funded by out-of-pocket payments.

Epple and Romano (1996a and b) investigate the mix of public and private funding using a median-voter approach. They assume that: (1) individuals differ in income; (2) the public sector provides a uniform quantity of health care; and (3) the private sector provides heterogeneous quantities. In a system with no private sector, the prediction of the model is straightforward: the optimal amount of heath care is determined such that it maximizes the preferences of the individual with median income. As long as the median income is below the mean income, this result also implies a quantity below the one decided by a utilitarian government if health care is a normal good (Atkinson and Stiglitz, 1980).

In the presence of a private sector, individuals who opt for the private sector (the rich ones) have a preference for zero public health care: they pay taxes but do not receive public care. Since such a group forms a "coalition" with low-income individuals, who want a low level of provision of health care to avoid large contributions, the preferences of the median voter now differ from the median income: the median voter has an income below the median ("ends against the middle"). Intuitively, this might explain low support for public systems (or explain down-sized public systems).

The model assumes that the public sector is financed with a proportional tax rate. In many countries poor individuals are completely exempted from contributing or receive income support. Introducing this assumption modifies the median voter. Since the very poor do not contribute to the system they favor higher quantities of health care together with the upper-middle income individuals. Instead, the lower-middle income ones and the very rich favor less public care. The median voter is such that the two groups are equalized (see footnote 11 of Epple and Romano, 1996b). We conjecture that this implies that the median voter has now higher income compared to the case where the marginal tax rate is positive for the poor, which in turn implies higher support for public care.

The key result of "ends against the middle" is common to Epple and Romano (1996a and b). One key difference between the two studies is that the first assumes that an individual can consume either the public good or the private good, but not both (the "first margin" we refer to above in section 2.1). This is the case where private health care is duplicative, for example elective surgery: a patient can receive a hip replacement either in the public or the private sector (public and private care are substitutes) but the quality or amenities offered by the private sector are higher. The second study instead assumes that the individual can consume simultaneously both the public and private good (say, visits to different physicians about the same problem, lab or imaging tests). Private health care is supplementary to the public one: public health care and private health care complement each other (the "second margin" described in section 2.1).

The intuition for the main result (median voter has income below the median income) is that very rich individuals are paying such a high marginal tax rate at the margin that they favor a reduction in the provision of the public good. If private care is duplicative, rich individuals have a zero marginal benefit from an increase in public goods, as they only consume the private one. If care is supplementary, rich individuals are willing to substitute public care with the private one because it can be bought at the cheaper price set by a competitive private market.

An additional result from Epple and Romano (1996b), where private care supplements public, is the following: under the median-voter equilibrium a regime with dual provision, i.e. with both public and private consumption, is preferred by the majority to a regime where either only the public good is provided or only the private one is provided. Since voters could choose zero public care but they do not, the equilibrium with dual (public and private) positive provision of public care defeats the one with zero public care (i.e. private care only). Moreover, since for a given combination of taxation and public care, the dual provision Pareto dominates the private provision only by revealed preferences (i.e. the rich are better off if they go private), the dual provision will be preferred by the majority (see Epple and Romano, 1996b, p. 67). It is also shown that overall expenditure (public plus private) is higher under a mixed regime than under a public-only or private-only one.

Gouveia (1997) derives, at the same time, a similar result in a more general setting where individuals differ in income and health (as measured by the probability of illness), and where individuals can buy supplementary private health insurance

(Epple and Romano assume that private care can be bought out of pocket, but there is no insurance market). He shows that a majority would oppose the elimination of a private alternative. Gouveia (1997) does not consider moral hazard and there is no variation in the consumption of health care across the population.

The prediction that a public—private insurance system arises under a majority voting rule holds when expected utility theory is used to model individuals' behavior. Hindriks and De Donder (2003) show that under a non-expected utility framework (i.e. Yaari's dual theory of choice under uncertainty which adopts risk aversion without diminishing marginal utility), this result no longer holds. A compulsory social insurance regime, optimally designed, leads to either full coverage under the social insurance scheme or no coverage at all. They also show that the presence of adverse selection in private insurance markets also weakens the case of a mixed system.[5] The related paper by Hindriks (2001) also shows that within the above-mentioned non-expected utility framework a mixed system may be optimal only if public insurance is distortionary and the deadweight loss increases sufficiently rapidly with the level of public insurance.

One limitation of the analyses presented above is the assumption that the public provision is uniform in the public sector and therefore inefficient (as individuals are heterogeneous). This seems at odds with allocation rules within the public sector where care is provided on the basis of need (or health status) and is therefore not uniform (though it is true that provision in the public sector does not depend on income). However, this would make the policy multidimensional, which raises issues about the existence and uniqueness of the equilibrium. Moreno-Ternero and Roemer (2007) address the question of public funding decided by voting in a multidimensional policy space. Health care is funded by only two sources: general taxation (public health insurance) or co-payment (out-of-pocket payment). Electoral competition takes place over two variables: the tax rate that funds public health expenditures, and the co-payment. They consider a population heterogeneous on income level, but homogeneous in health risks. Their main concern is the role of technology progress in originating growth of public health expenditures in equilibrium, within the context of a voting model. Electoral competition leads parties to propose adoption of the latest and more expensive technology. The political process promotes growth of expenditures based on new technologies.

2.2.1.1. A Simple Model of the Political Economy Choice of Public—Private Mix

This model is adapted from Epple and Romano (1996a and b). Suppose individuals are in need of a non-emergency (elective) treatment, like a hip replacement or a cataract. There is no uncertainty, and therefore there is no role for health insurance in the

---

[5] An older qualitative survey is contained in Besley and Gouveia (1994).

model. Individuals differ in income y which is distributed according to density function $f(y)$ and cumulative density function $F(y)$. Individuals have utility $b + q^{pu} + u(y(1 - t))$ if they receive treatment in the public sector, where b is the benefit from treatment, q^{pu} is quality of health care in the public sector, y is income, and t is a proportional income tax. If the individual goes private she has utility $b + q^{pr} + u(y(1 - t) - p)$, where q^{pr} is the quality in the private sector and p is the price to receive treatment.[6] We assume that q^{pr} and p are exogenous and determined in a competitive private market. Instead, the quality in the public sector q^{pu} is determined through a majority voting system. We assume that higher quality of services is costly and is financed through the proportional income tax. The cost of quality in the public sector is $c(q^{pu})$.

Define $\hat{y}$ as the income threshold level such that the individual is indifferent between public and private treatment: $b + q^{pu} + u(\hat{y}(1 - t)) = b + q^{pr} + u(\hat{y}(1 - t) - p)$. Since utility is concave, then rich individuals with income $y > \hat{y}$ go private and poorer individuals with income $y < \hat{y}$ go public. The quality in the public sector has to satisfy the following budget constraint $c(q^{pu})F(\hat{y}) = tY$, where $Y = \int yf(y)dy$ is total income.

For people opting for the public sector, do richer individuals prefer higher or lower public health care quality? Their preferences can be illustrated in the following way. Recall the utility from going public is $b + q^{pu} + u(y(1 - t))$. The indifference curves in the (q^{pu}, t) space are such that:

$$M(y, t, q^{pu}) \equiv \frac{dt}{dq^{pu}} = \frac{1}{yu'} > 0$$

The function $M(y, t, q^{pu})$ can be interpreted as the marginal rate of substitution between public health care quality and taxation. Intuitively, the individual is indifferent only if higher taxation is combined with higher quality. If M increases (decreases) with income then richer individuals have a higher (lower) preference for higher quality. Differentiating with respect to income we obtain: $\frac{dM(y, t, q^{pu})}{dy} = + \frac{(1 - t)u''}{y(u')^2} - \frac{1}{y^2 u'}$, which is in general indeterminate. There are two effects going in opposite directions. The first effect is an "income" effect: since income is higher, the individual can afford more quality. The second effect is a "substitution" effect: since income is higher, the marginal tax rate (i.e. the effective price paid by that individual) is higher, and preference for quality may be lower.

It seems plausible to assume that the income effect dominates over the substitution one and richer people have a higher preference for quality in the public sector $\left(\frac{dM(y, t, q^{pu})}{dy} > 0\right)$. For a given quality in the public sector, individuals with income above $\hat{y}$ opt for the private sector and therefore have a preference for the lowest possible quality in the public sector: they contribute to the public system through income taxation but they do not benefit from public services.

---

[6] The results would be similar if private health insurance was explictly modeled. See Gouveia (1997) on this.

Under such a setting, the level of quality in the public sector chosen under a majority voting rule is not the one preferred by the median-income voter: since individuals with income above the threshold $\hat{y}$ vote for zero quality, this shifts the income of the median voter downwards. The decisive median voter is therefore below the median income. Formally, the median voter has income y^* which is determined such that $\int_{y^*}^{\hat{y}} f(y) dy = 0.5$.

Intuitively, there are two groups who would like less quality in the public sector: (1) the very poor and (2) the very rich. The very poor (with income below y^*) would like positive levels of public quality but less than the one desired by the median voter as they value other consumption more (being poor). The very rich (with income above $\hat{y}$) go private and need no public services. The median voter is such that the number of people who would like less public care (the very poor and the very rich) is equal to the number of individuals who would like more public care (those with middle income).

2.2.2. Normative Analyses

In contrast to the previous section, this section takes a normative approach to the optimal interface between public and private care. Most studies reviewed below assume that the government maximizes a utilitarian welfare function.

The existing literature can be split between studies that focus on the "first margin" and on the "second margin" (see section 2.1). They either assume that: (1) free public care exists but the government decides the level of quality provided by the public sector and also cannot control quantity directly (if quality in the public sector is as high as in the private sector, the private sector is completely crowded out); or (2) the government can choose how much public care to provide and any additional unit of care provided crowds out private care: private care has a supplemental role (quality is implicitly the same under public and private care). The literature under (2) is framed within an insurance set-up where individuals decide optimal private health insurance coverage, while the literature under (1) often assumes that patients pay out of pocket if they opt for the private sector.

Under the first set of assumptions individuals can choose between public care at zero price but inferior quality, and private care at a positive price and superior quality. Here, quality has the simple meaning of any attribute the private sector is able to offer and the public sector is not that positively valued by the patient. The question then is whether it is worth distorting quality in the public sector to shift patients from the public to the private sector. The main result is that distorting quality and therefore having a public–private mix is optimal only when governments have constraints on taxes they can collect and/or on the allocation rule which they can implement.

Under the second set of assumptions the question is whether public care should be zero leaving health care to private markets, or 100 percent with public care completely crowding out private care, or somewhere in between where what is not provided by public insurance is supplemented by a private one. The main result is that public coverage should be higher when the correlation between ability to earn income and illness is negative and large, when adverse selection is present and lower (under some circumstances) in the presence of moral hazard.

2.2.2.1. Funding and Redistribution: Quality and Waiting Times

Besley and Coate (1991) investigate the potential redistributive role of public provision of private goods (like health care) when (1) there are two income levels (rich and poor); (2) every individual is taxed through a lump-sum transfer, which is identical across the two income groups and finances public health care: this is a key assumption as it implies that the tax system is regressive (both rich and poor pay the same amount of taxes); (3) the government cannot redistribute through lump-sum transfers from rich to poor; (4) every individual can consume only one unit of care (say a surgical treatment, like hip replacement) which can be received either in the public or in the private sector, but not both (the care provided in the private sector is therefore duplicative); and (5) the government provides a common level of quality in the public sector while quality can be bought at varying levels in the private sector (private care is charged at a competitive rate, and no insurance markets are assumed).

They show that it may be optimal for a utilitarian government to distort quality downwards in the public sector to induce rich individuals to prefer to demand health care in the private sector. Rich individuals will therefore pay for their private care but also subsidize the public care of poor individuals through general taxation: a redistribution from rich to poor.

Such types of redistribution are in general suboptimal: if the government could implement lump-sum transfers which differ across individuals by directly taxing the rich and redistributing income to the poor, there would be no need to distort the quality in the public sector.

The above results have been extended to a scenario where the government can use any non-linear tax system (and are endogenous as opposed to exogenous), but individuals differ in ability. Ability is private information so that there are limits to the amount of redistribution (a set-up a la Mirrlees, 1971).[7]

One important dimension of quality in the health sector is waiting times, i.e. the time the patient has to wait before treatment is received. Waiting can be interpreted as a negative form of quality. Hoel and Saether (2003) investigate the optimality of a public–private mix when there is rationing by waiting times.[8]

---

[7] See Boadway and Marchand (1995) who assume that care is "supplemental" as opposed to duplicative, which may hold only for some types of care. More interestingly, Blomquist and Christiansen (1995) assume that care is "duplicative."

[8] Earlier work by Iversen (1997) shows that the introduction of a private sector may increase or reduce waiting times.

In contrast to the above papers, they assume that individuals differ in their marginal cost of waiting rather than income (though the differing marginal costs could be related to income but not necessarily so). Public health care is financed through a proportional income tax, which is more realistic than a uniform lump-sum tax. The government maximizes a welfare function that gives (weakly) a lower weight to individuals with higher marginal cost of waiting (perhaps the richer, i.e. those who go private). They show that increasing waiting times and therefore the size of the private sector increases welfare only if individuals with lower cost of waiting (the poor) are given a higher weight in the welfare function.[9] Therefore, in contrast to Besley and Coate (1991), a utilitarian welfare function would not set a positive waiting time.

An extension of the analysis of Hoel and Saether (2003) is done by Marchand and Schroyen (2005) assuming that labor supply is endogenous. Overall, they find that in this more general second-best set-up, welfare gains from increasing the private sector through longer waiting times are positive but small.

As for section 2.2.1, these results hold for a rationing rule of the government that is suboptimal. If the government treats patients only when benefits are higher than the cost, then there would be little scope for a private sector: most (or all) patients with low benefit would find the price set by the private sector too high, so that no one would choose the private sector.[10]

The above results assume that patients pay out of pocket for private care. The results are likely to hold also if patients buy private health insurance to cover private expenditure: when quality is low (or waiting times are high) individuals anticipate that they will have private expenditure and will rationally choose to buy private health insurance.

The crucial point is that funding of health care cannot be seen independently from redistributive properties, with quality and waiting times being used as indirect tools to redistribution. The redistribution is performed by letting richer people pay out of pocket when going to the private sector but also contribute to the public sector financing through income taxation. The absence of uncertainty abstracts from the design and take-up of private health insurance, which is taken up in the next subsection.

2.2.2.2. A Simple Model of Funding of Health Care with Indirect Tools for Income Redistribution

The key points mentioned above can be illustrated with a simple model. Suppose there are two types of individuals with equal size and risk characteristics but different income levels (population in each income group is normalized to 1) $y^i = y^H$, y^L (high

---

[9] See also Bucovetsky (1984) for a model with two types of individuals and commodity linear tax.

[10] The interaction between public allocation and private sector is discussed (to some extent) in Hoel (2007).

and low) with $y^H > y^L$. The utility from going to the public sector for treatment is $b - dw + u(y^i - T)$, where b is the benefit from treatment, w is waiting time, d is the disutility per unit of waiting time, and T is a regressive tax which finances the public sector health expenses (note that the tax function T does not vary with income). The utility from going private is $b + u(y^i - p - T)$, where p is the price charged by the private sector. The cost of health care is c, regardless of the sector. The private sector is competitive and therefore charges price $p = c$.

If there is no waiting time, both patients go to the public sector and the tax paid by rich and poor is the same and equal to $T = \frac{2c}{2} = c$. Their utility is equal to $b + u$ $(y^i - c)$. There is no redistribution since both types pay the same. Total welfare is, in a utilitarian framework: $2b + u(y^L - c) + u(y^H - c)$.

Suppose now that a positive waiting time is introduced in the public sector such that all rich people go to the private sector. In such a case the rich who choose to be treated in the private sector still have to pay taxes which finance the public sector expenditure, i.e. $T = c/2$, on top of the private care paid at $p = c$. If they go private their utility is $b + u\left(y^H - \frac{3}{2}c\right)$. When they prefer treatment in the public sector (i.e. if all rich individuals go to the public sector) then they pay $T = c$, in which case the utility is $b + u(y^H - c)$. The minimum waiting time which ensures that rich individuals prefer the private sector is such that

$$d\hat{w} = u(y^H - c) - u\left(y^H - \frac{3}{2}c\right)$$

The utility of the poor is now

$$b + u\left(y^L - \frac{1}{2}c\right) - d\hat{w} = b + u\left(y^L - \frac{1}{2}c\right) - \left[u(y^H - c) - u\left(y^H - \frac{3}{2}c\right)\right],$$

and for the rich individual is

$$b + u\left(y^H - \frac{3}{2}c\right)$$

Total welfare is:

$$2b + u\left(y^L - \frac{1}{2}c\right) + u\left(y^H - \frac{3}{2}c\right) - \left[u(y^H - c) - u\left(y^H - \frac{3}{2}c\right)\right]$$

Can welfare be higher when a positive waiting time is set? Welfare is higher under a positive waiting time when:

$$u\left(y^L - \frac{1}{2}c\right) - u(y^L - c) - \left[u(y^H - c) - u\left(y^H - \frac{3}{2}c\right)\right] > u(y^H - c) - u\left(y^H - \frac{3}{2}c\right)$$

i.e. when the utility gain from the poor individuals from paying only half of health expenses, minus the disutility from waiting, is higher than the utility loss from the rich individuals from paying one-and-a-half times the cost of medical expense. The condition reduces to:

$$u\left(y^L - \frac{1}{2}c\right) - u(y^L - c) > 2\left[u(y^H - c) - u\left(y^H - \frac{3}{2}c\right)\right]$$

which is always satisfied if the utility function is sufficiently concave in income. The case for redistribution is weakened if the tax system is proportional. Thus, waiting time (and quality of care or amenities, more generally) work as a substitute for a more progressive tax system.

Clearly, a government that can set transfers differentially across income groups can pursue redistributive goals without introducing waiting time. Indeed, welfare is maximized when waiting time is zero and income is redistributed so that all individuals have the same level of consumption $(y^H + y^L)/2$, so that welfare is equal to $2b + u\left(\frac{y^L + y^H}{2} - c\right)$.

In practice, governments do have constraints on the amount of redistribution they can pursue (for example, due to incentive constraints on the labor market). As long as redistribution is not perfect, there is a scope for waiting times and quality in the public sector to pursue such redistributive goals, though this role decreases with the degree of progressivity in income and other forms of taxation.

2.2.2.3. Optimal Public Health Insurance—the Role of Correlation between Income and Morbidity

An extensive literature investigates the mix between (mandatory) public insurance and private (voluntary) insurance when public care is funded through income taxation (either linear or non-linear) and private insurance markets are competitive and set prices according to risk types (premiums are actuarially fair). Under what conditions would a utilitarian government set public insurance to zero leaving health care to private markets, or 100 percent with public care crowding out completely private care, or somewhere in between where what is not provided by the public insurance is supplemented by a private one?

The contribution of Rochet (1991) highlights the role played by the correlation between income and morbidity. He assumes that individuals differ in the ability to generate income (productivity) and the probability of being sick (morbidity). Both moral hazard and adverse selection are ruled out. The fundamental aspect is the correlation between morbidity and productivity. Under a private health insurance market that sets insurance prices according to risk, a negative correlation implies that insurance prices will be larger for lower incomes. He shows that if the correlation between morbidity and productivity is negative, a utilitarian government would always benefit from a marginal increase in public provision so that social insurance is complete (under weak regularity conditions) and private markets are completely crowded out.

The intuition is the following. A negative correlation entails a redistribution effect that is regressive. If traditional instruments of government redistribution (taxes and transfers) do not achieve all the income redistribution desired by the government, public health care allows (imperfect) targeting of poorer citizens, who have a higher marginal utility from income, and pursues redistributive goals. The assumption that the correlation is negative is plausible (Wagstaff and van Dorslaer et al., 2000). The work of Cremer and Pestieau (1996) extends Rochet's analysis by allowing for non-quasi-linear preferences. They show that again full public insurance may be desirable.[11]

Boadway et al. (2006) introduce both adverse selection and moral hazard. In their model (1) individuals are taxed according to proportional tax; (2) private markets are characterized by both adverse selection on morbidity (probability of illness is private information); in contrast, productivity is observable to the private sector; (3) the government covers a proportion (between zero and one) of health expenditure regardless of their probability of illness and ability/productivity; and (4) sick individuals choose how much health care to consume, which generates *ex-post* moral hazard: when the proportion of public health care reimbursed is higher patients consume more health care.

A major difference between a public and a private health insurance system at a country level lies in the way heterogeneous preferences are accommodated across the population, either resulting from income disparities or other reasons. Under public health insurance, typically only one health plan exists, fully determined by the government (in the case of an NHS). In contrast, private health insurance markets can tailor the price of each contract to the risk profile of each member of the population. Thus, even if redistribution of income is not an objective *per se* in the design of the public health insurance coverage, the imposition of a single premium or payment rule, common to all people in the population, results in redistribution across risks. Under a single insurance contract, based on the population average, the members of the population with a preference for lower coverage—lower contribution will be implicitly subsidizing the members of the population with preference for high coverage—high contribution. Since the payment is not tailored to individual risk characteristics, not all members of the population will look for full insurance coverage.

2.2.2.4. Adverse Selection as a Driver for Public Health Insurance

The case for public intervention is reinforced in the presence of adverse selection. In the absence of government intervention, low-risk individuals have only partial coverage while they desire full coverage (i.e. the standard Rothschild and Stiglitz (1976) result). The increase in public health care reduces the welfare loss from the low-risk

[11] See also Henriet and Rochet (2006) and Petretto (1999).

individuals, and makes public intervention even more desirable for a utilitarian government.

A different way of looking at the case for government intervention was laid out in Pauly (1974). The approach used here is whether Pareto improvements can be obtained by interfering with private insurance markets (as opposed to an intervention which maximizes a utilitarian welfare function that may entail the reduction of utility for some individuals). In the presence of adverse selection, compulsory public insurance may lead to a Pareto improvement because the gain from low risks from full coverage is higher than the loss from subsidizing the high risk. However, this result holds only if the proportion of high-risk individuals is relatively small. Feldman et al. (1998) show that compulsory partial coverage insurance may be superior to a system where only private markets work, or public insurance is complete. Hansen and Keiding (2002) derive a similar result but public insurance is determined by a majority voting rule.

2.2.2.5. A Simple Model: Adverse Selection and the Role of Public Health Insurance

Define π^H and π^L as the probability of illness of high-risk and low-risk types, with $\pi^H > \pi^L$. We also assume that individuals differ in their ability to generate income. There are two types of ability (high and low) which allow individuals to gain respectively high and low income y^H and y^L with $y^H > y^L$. The two groups are of equal size. We distinguish two cases: (1) ability is perfectly correlated with risk of illness so that rich individuals also have a lower probability of illness and (2) ability is not correlated with risk of illness: rich individuals have the same probability of illness as the poor.

Standard insurance theory predicts that risk-averse individuals will buy full coverage against illness in perfectly competitive private insurance markets. We treat first the case of perfect negative correlation of risk and income. To keep the presentation simple we assume that utility does not depend on the health status and is equal to $u(y)$, and also rule out moral hazard. If the loss from incurring medical expenses is D, then under private insurance markets, the rich and low-risk individuals have an expected utility equal to $u(y^H - \pi^L D)$, and poor and high-risk individuals have an expected utility equal to $u(y^L - \pi^H D)$. Note that poor individuals are penalized twice: they have lower income and are charged a higher premium.

We assume that under "social insurance" everyone pays the same premium in return for covering medical expenses D in the event of illness: $\pi^M = (\pi^L + \pi^H)/2$, so that utility is $u(y^H - \pi^M D)$ for the rich and $u(y^L - \pi^M D)$ for the poor. For a utilitarian government which maximizes the utility of all individuals, welfare is always higher under social insurance. Since the marginal utility from consumption is decreasing by assumption, social insurance entails redistribution from rich to poor which is welfare increasing since $u\left(y^H - \frac{\pi^L + \pi^H}{2}D\right) + u\left(y^L - \frac{\pi^L + \pi^H}{2}D\right) > u(y^H - \pi^L D) + u(y^L - \pi^H D)$.

Suppose now that the probability from illness is the same for rich and poor, i.e. $\pi^H = \pi^L = \pi^M$, so that the correlation is zero. In a private insurance market and under social insurance the utility for the rich and the poor is the same and respectively equal to $u(y^H - \pi^M D)$ and $u(y^L - \pi^M D)$. Since the private insurance market charges the same premium to rich and poor, there is no redistributive role arising from social insurance (which also charges the same premium). Note that if instead it is the rich who have the highest probability of illness, then social insurance would entail redistribution from poor to rich which would be welfare reducing.

Assuming that income is not observable, the role of social insurance survives and is probably reinforced in the presence of adverse selection on the probability of illness. In line with Rothschild–Stiglitz predictions, we assume that under a private insurance market, the high risk has full coverage. We focus on the special case where low-risk and rich individuals have no coverage at all. The expected utility for high-risk and poor individuals is now $u(y^L - \pi^H D)$ and for the low-risk and rich individuals is $\pi^L u(y^H - D) + (1 - \pi^L) u(y^H)$. Under social insurance, the utility for the high-risk and poor individuals is now $u(y^L - \pi^M D)$ and for the low-risk and rich individuals is $u(y^H - \pi^M D)$. Therefore, under social insurance poor individuals gain thanks to the lower premium. The rich individuals may also gain if they are sufficiently risk averse. If both benefit, public health insurance constitutes a Pareto improvement. Clearly, the assumption of perfect correlation between risk and income is extreme. Note that under imperfect (but still positive) correlation the argument would be similar: richer individuals are more likely to get no coverage and are keener on social insurance.

Suppose now that it is the rich who have the higher probability of illness. In this case the poor (low risk) have no coverage under private insurance and rich (high-risk) individuals have full coverage. Under social insurance poor individuals would gain full coverage but at the price of subsiding the premium for the rich. Rich individuals gain from the subsidized premium. There may still be scope for social insurance but it is weakened.

2.2.2.6. Moral Hazard and Private Health Insurance
In contrast, the case for public intervention is weakened by the presence of moral hazard: high levels of public coverage encourage excessive consumption.[12] The latter point is made clearly by Barigozzi (2006) and, under a median-voter model, by Jacob and Lundin (2005). Barigozzi (2006) assumes that: (1) the correlation between ability and probability of being sick is zero, (2) she rules out adverse selection, and (3) only allows for *ex-post* moral hazard. She shows that if moral hazard is sufficiently pronounced, then it is the case that under private insurance only, rich individuals buy

[12] Boadway et al. (2003) show the argument survives the introduction of *ex-ante* moral hazard (i.e. when preventive effort affects the probability of illness).

more private coverage than poor individuals, and critically they overconsume more than the poor. Under such circumstances, the introduction of public insurance would exacerbate moral hazard (i.e. overconsumption) and simultaneously would not help in terms of redistribution because the rich consume more than the poor (therefore to some extent the poor subsidize the overconsumption of the rich if moral hazard is sufficiently pronounced). A marginal increase in public coverage does not increase a utilitarian welfare function and is therefore not welfare improving.[13] A crucial assumption is the sequence of the decisions, the public sector moving first and the private sector second: the public sector anticipates the private market equilibrium and adjusts public coverage accordingly. The striking result of this simple set-up is that a rational public insurer would select zero public coverage.

The work of Jacob and Lundin (2005) addresses the voluntary acquisition of private health insurance on top of a public health insurance system. The existence of supplementary (voluntary) private health insurance creates an (asymmetric) adjustment margin for people in the population with preferences different from those of the median voter. The members of the population that want more insurance coverage than the one resulting from the political equilibrium have the opportunity to buy it in the private health insurance market. Quite distinctly, those in the population that would prefer a lower level of insurance coverage have no adjustment margin. An interesting issue then is how the public co-payment value changes when the voluntary private health insurance exists. The presence of further insurance coverage aggravates the moral hazard problem, imposing an externality upon the public sector. To better control it, the co-payment required by the public health insurance system increases. Under sequential decision making, as in Barigozzi (2006), this brings the extreme result of zero public health insurance if the private market coverage is able to achieve the second-best allocation.

It is worth detailing the intuition behind this result. Suppose first a "naïf" public health insurer. It disregards the role of supplemental private health insurance, and sets a coverage level with some co-payment (usually modeled as co-insurance) by the patient (the consumer), to exert some control over the *ex-post* moral hazard problem in the demand for health care. Then, starting from this second-best allocation, private health insurance (under perfect competition) offers actuarially fair contracts from their perspective. However, the competitive pricing of the private health insurance coverage does not take into account that extra coverage imposes more expenditure in the public health insurance component. This happens as the extra private health insurance coverage aggravates the moral hazard problem common to both public and private

---

[13] See Blomqvist and Johansson (1997) for a similar result within a model with moral hazard only.

health insurance. Therefore, too much health insurance coverage is offered by private health insurers and taken by consumers.

2.2.2.7. A Simple Model of Welfare Reduction Due to Private Health Insurance under Moral Hazard

Let X be the health care demanded by a representative patient. The level of care is selected after the patient is sick. Let $u(\cdot)$ be the utility from consumption (or income) and $H(X)$ be the health benefit from consumption of health care X. Both functions have positive but decreasing marginal valuations. The health loss of sickness is $\overline{H}$, with $\overline{H} > H(X)$, $\forall X$, i.e. the individual does not recover full health even after medical care. We assume consumption utility and health utility to be separable (to simplify exposition). Income is denoted by y, net of taxes. The private health insurance premium paid in a previous stage is P, while c denotes the fraction of health care costs paid by the public insurer and s denotes the fraction of health care costs paid by the private health insurance policy.

The choice of health care X is determined after sickness emerges, and given by the solution to the following problem:

$$\max_{\{X\}} u(y - P - X + cX + sX) - (\overline{H} - H(X))$$

The first-order condition for utility maximization is:

$$H'(X) = u'(y - P - X = cX + sX)(1 - c - s)$$

and a straightforward comparative statics exercise yields:

$$X = X(c + s), \quad X_c = X_s > 0,$$

where X_i denotes first derivative. Higher coverage (public or private) encourages consumption. Take now the previous stage of choice of private insurance coverage. Let π be the probability of sickness. Private health insurance can be bought at fair prices. The problem of choosing the optimal level of private health insurance coverage is:

$$\max_{\{s\}} \pi u(y - \pi X(c + s)s - X(c + s) + sX(c + s)cX(c + s)) + (1 - \pi)u(y - \pi X(c + s)s)$$

The associated first-order condition renders $s < 1$ in equilibrium as standard in this class of models. The expected health expenditures by the public health insurer are $c\pi X(c + s)$. An increase in s increases this public expenditure. If, in a previous step, the value of c, the coverage level by the public health insurer, was naively set to its (second-best) optimal value in the absence of private health insurance, then an increase in s from zero will be (second-best) suboptimal by definition. The reason why the individual buys the private health insurance is the price of additional insurance coverage. This price is too low from a social point of view as it fails to account for the increase in the public health insurer expenditures.

Under the public health insurer contract only, contributions collected are equal to expected health expenditures: $T(y^G) = \pi c X(c + 0)$, where $T(y^G)$ denotes income-related contributions to fund payments by the public health insurer and y^G is gross income. In the presence of private health insurance, the overall constraint is:

$$T(y^G) + P = (c + s)\pi X(c + s).$$

Under the previous rule for the public health insurer contributions, the private health insurance premium that ensures that overall payments cover all expenditures is:

$$P^+ = (c + s)\pi X(c + s) - c\pi X(c + 0) = s\pi X(c + s) + \pi c(X(c + s) - X(c + 0))$$

However, in a private health insurance market under competition, the fair insurance prices do not include the last term.

It is also straightforward to check that once c has been selected optimally to maximize expected utility of individuals, under the assumption of $s = 0$, then when the private health insurance premium is P^+, expected utility has zero marginal value at $s = 0$ and negative marginal value for $s > 0$. No private health insurance would be demanded if the external expected cost $\pi c(X(c + s) - X(c + 0))$ were to be included in the insurance price.

A public insurer rationally anticipates that extra private insurance coverage will decrease public coverage. Such adjustment may lead to total disappearance of public health insurance. Since at the heart of this effect lies an externality from private health insurance upon the public health system, it suggests that supplemental private health insurance should not be allowed (in the simplest setting) or be subject to a tax, intended to internalize the moral hazard externality across health insurance arrangements.[14]

2.2.2.8. The Samaritan's Dilemma

Another relevant choice is between in-kind or cash support to health insurance. In current societies, it is not credible that uninsured sick people will not be treated, at least for some types of treatment. In-cash transfers allow consumers to take other decisions than buying health insurance. Public provision of insurance may also be justified, on normative grounds, by the existence of altruism and dynamic inconsistency about support policies (Coate, 1995). Providing in-cash support to poor people relaxes their budget constraint. If sufficiently large, the in-cash transfer allows a poor individual to

---

[14] Chetty and Saez (2010) develop a model of optimal public insurance when a private insurance is also available. They also find that in the presence of moral hazard public insurance should be zero, when private health insurance is set optimally (second best). Their contribution is to report a formula for a relatively easy computation of the welfare effect of expanding public health insurance programs, in the context of a private health insurance market.

buy health insurance. The question is whether the poor individual will do it or prefers to use the cash received in some other way. The answer depends crucially on the commitment of the rich individuals in the population not to treat the poor if sick and without health insurance. Whenever such commitment exists, the in-cash transfer is a sufficient instrument to enlarge health insurance coverage (as long as the health insurance contract becomes affordable).

The opposite occurs when society does not accept leaving someone in need of medical treatment going untreated. In this case, the best course of action for the poor individual is to use the cash in other consumption, and when sick ask for help from the richer people of the population. The presence of altruism will ensure that further resources are committed by the rich to treat the sick poor. The rich individuals then pay twice for the care of the poor ones. Providing the health insurance contract directly avoids this problem, as it guarantees the initial funds made available are used in the intended way.

2.2.3. Crowding Out and Crowding In

The mix of public and private health insurance has been discussed earlier. We are now interested in a related, but different, problem: the strategic interaction between the two types of insurance.

Since the decision to offer public health insurance is not taken by the regular operation of the market, the more relevant effects of crowding out (or eventually crowding in) are associated with the impact of expansion (or creation) of public health insurance upon the private health insurance market.

We do not repeat here the motives for existence of public health insurance, as this theme was already treated above. Still, it is worth noting that according to theory, public health insurance can completely crowd out the private health insurance market. A comprehensive and universal public health insurance funded by compulsory contributions leaves little room for private health insurance.

Also, when the design of public health insurance anticipates the development of private health markets, it will reduce its coverage (in some conditions, to zero public health insurance).

Nonetheless, when public health insurance programs are not universal or comprehensive, then a private health insurance market may be present. The private health insurance market can be smaller or larger, depending on the particular features of the public health insurance program.

When public insurance is introduced within a private market, a main issue is the possibility of crowding out, which takes the form of some people dropping their private coverage to take up the public one. Thus, for crowding out to exist, eligibility criteria for public health insurance must include people that currently choose to have a private health insurance contract. The issue of crowding out is mainly an issue for targeted health insurance programs. The prime examples are the US Medicaid and US Medicare programs.

The existence of crowding out can be highly dependent on the specific institutional setting. The US Medicaid program provides a good example. Its particular features regarding long-term care expenditures may cause a strong crowding-out effect. The theoretical motive has been laid out by Pauly (1990). The argument put forward by Pauly (1990) relies on the specific feature of Medicaid—public health insurance—as second payer: it takes first any private insurance coverage payment, and only after that has been exhausted does Medicaid pay. These characteristics imply that any private health insurance that transfers income from the good state of Nature to the bad one (sickness) implies a one-to-one reduction in the public insurance payment. The payment of a premium does not lead to increased net wealth in sickness unless all private health insurance has been used up. Absence of insurance saves the premium, at no cost to the utility when sick, and consequently no insurance will exist. Also, since private health insurance compensates individuals in the "sick" state of Nature, it also decreases the likelihood that eligibility criteria for Medicaid (income and wealth thresholds) are met. The specific rules of Medicaid as public health insurance have implications for the budget constraint, and it crowds out the private health insurance market. The duplication of benefits at zero cost to the individual under Medicaid is sufficiently important to deter growth of the private health insurance market. According to the simulation exercise by Brown and Finkelstein (2008), two-thirds of people would not take up private health insurance due to existence of Medicaid. Moreover, Medicaid only offers adequate long-term care coverage to the lower tail of the income distribution. Thus, a limited coverage by a public insurance system may induce a significant crowding-out effect in the private health insurance market.

The crowding-out effect relies on the duplication of benefits. A richer set of possibilities occurs when, upon introduction of public health insurance, the private insurance market adjusts both price and quality of care covered. The work of Encinosa (2003) addresses the adjustment in both prices and quantities that follow the introduction of a public health insurance program in a market with private health insurance. The adjustment in private health insurance contracts creates further possibilities on top of the expected simple crowding-out effect. In particular, if the private health insurance market reacts by lowering prices and quality, some previously uninsured consumers may now buy it (a crowding-in effect). On the other hand, if the reaction of private insurers leads to higher quality of care and higher insurance prices, then a push-out effect occurs (in the terminology of Encinosa, 2003) by which further people stop contracting health insurance in the private market. The push-out effect is particularly negative, as it may increase the number of uninsured people, while the crowding-in effect would be an additional positive effect from introduction of public programs.

The model by Encinosa (2003) builds on Cutler and Gruber (1996), having unobservable types of consumers (differing in their willingness to pay for health care) and income heterogeneity (though distribution of types and distribution of income are independent). The heterogeneity in income provides a cut-off below which people cannot afford and do not buy health insurance in the private market.

The introduction of the public health insurance creates, at first impact, a crowding-out effect: some people drop the private health insurance contract and these are more likely to be individuals with a high intensity of preference for health care. The mix of individuals under private insurance changes toward a composition of people who have on average a smaller valuation for quality. The adjustment of the private sector to this mix change is to lower quality and insurance prices. This is one effect.

The other effect results from the need for a lower quality of care (and insurance price) to attract more people to the private health insurance. With a public insurance program, the relevance of these consumers with low valuation for quality decreases considerably. Concentrating on the population groups with a higher preference for quality, the adjustment by private insurers may involve higher quality and higher prices. The two effects run in opposite directions and *a priori* there is no reason to believe one to be stronger than the other.

"Crowding in" results from public health insurance working as a device to induce market segmentation of consumers.

A different channel by which crowding-in and crowding-out effects may occur is through the tax system, as it may change the relative price–benefit comparison of the two types of insurance. Gruber (2001) looks at the tax subsidization to private health insurance in the US and its impact on decisions of insurance. The health insurance premium is excluded from the income tax base. The resulting fiscal benefit depends on the marginal tax rate. Taxes are an important element in the decision of firms to offer health insurance to their workers. It also affects the decision to hold exclusively public health insurance coverage.

2.2.4. Co-payments

Co-payments are a small component of private health expenditure. Here, we discuss the role of co-payment (private expenditure) mainly within publicly funded health systems. Co-payments are a standard prescription from insurance theory under either *ex-ante* moral hazard—prevention—or *ex-post* moral hazard—excessive demand for health care. The role of co-payments is usually to discipline demand and provide better incentives for consumption of health care.

Co-payments introduce risk of medical expenditures to families. Co-payments in health care usually take the form of co-insurance or deductible. Co-insurance means that a fraction of the cost has to be paid by the patient at the point of consumption.

A deductible is a fixed amount to be paid by the patient, above which full insurance coverage is provided. A combination of deductible and co-insurance above the threshold level of the deductible can also be used.

Co-payments are a particular form of public—private interface, as it is a private contribution determined by the public health insurer.

Much of our knowledge on co-payment effects comes from the RAND health insurance experiment (see Newhouse and the Insurance Experiment Group, 1993, for a summary). This social experiment took place in the United States during the early 1970s. It followed thousands of families for five years under randomized health plans, which had different degrees of co-payments. The results clearly pointed out that co-payments (co-insurance, more precisely) do matter for demand for health care, and for a wide range of medical services.

Within publicly funded health systems co-payments tend to be zero or negligible for inpatient care (e.g. surgery) but are sometimes more significant for drugs or dental care (for example, in the UK a prescription charge is paid for every prescription issued by the family doctor, though some more vulnerable groups are exempted). One way to rationalize these different co-payments is to relate them to elasticity of demand. Arguably, the demand for major surgeries is inelastic, as going through surgery is rather unpleasant, while for pharmaceuticals or dental care it is more elastic and moral hazard is a more significant issue. A co-payment may discourage excessive consumption.

Co-payments are one instrument to address moral hazard but others are available. There is therefore an issue whether co-payments are better than other instruments to contain moral hazard. One specific alternative is to have waiting times. Gravelle and Siciliani (2008) investigate whether a policy maker who has at her disposal both instruments (co-payments and waiting times) would use both instruments, waiting times only (setting co-payments to zero) or co-payments only (setting waiting time to zero). They suggest that a policy maker would always choose to use co-payments and set waiting time to zero. The intuition behind this result is that both co-payments and waiting times can curb moral hazard. However, waiting times generate a loss to patients which is not recovered by anyone else. In contrast, co-payments raise revenues which contribute to health care finance, even if they are not a major source of funds.

The role played by out-of-pocket payments in developed countries and in developing countries is quite different. In developing countries, especially the poorer ones, out-of-pocket is the main source of funding other than public insurance. Moreover, public insurance in these countries tends to have a small scope. One of the reasons is the incipient tax system, not allowing enough public funds to be raised to have a complete network of providers and a broad range of services effectively provided. Governments in poorer countries are usually unable to provide access to health care to the population in an effective way (Banerjee and Duflo, 2006; Xu et al., 2003).

In developing countries, out-of-pocket spending in health services may often be "catastrophic" (broadly speaking, forcing people into poverty). The weaker the public insurance available, the more likely that health expenditures out of pocket become catastrophic (Xu et al., 2007). The role of the public (health insurance) and private interface in reducing exposure to the financial side of adverse health shocks in developing countries also implied expansion of government-sponsored health insurance (see Sepehri et al. (2006) for analysis of the Vietnamese experience). The creation of a voluntary public health insurance system in Vietnam decreased out-of-pocket payments significantly, and more so for the poor (Jowett et al., 2003).

An active role of aid donors is often present. Developing countries, and the poorer ones in particular, face a different set of problems in the public–private interface. The out-of-pocket expenditure dominates as the main source of funding, and health insurance still has to make its way.

2.3. Provision

This section investigates four different types of interface between public and private provision. The first relates to the interface between the public sector and the private one when the first treats exclusively publicly funded patients and the latter one treats exclusively privately funded ones. The second interface relates to systems where doctors are allowed to work in both the public and the private sectors. The third one investigates differences in behavior between public and private providers. The fourth interface investigates whether some activities of publicly funded hospitals can be transferred, under a long-term contract, to a private party (for example, construction, building maintenance, and management of non-clinical activities).

2.3.1. Interaction between Public and Private Provision

In this section we investigate the interaction between the public and private provision of health care. In contrast to the following section 2.3.2 on dual practice, we assume throughout that doctors working in the private sector treat only privately funded patients (who pay out of pocket or are privately insured), and doctors working in the public sector treat only publicly funded patients.

2.3.1.1. Price and Waiting Time as Rationing Devices

In the traditional demand–supply model in economics, price is the balancing factor, providing signals to both production and consumption: a higher price rations demand and stimulates supply so that in equilibrium balance is achieved. In health care, waiting time is another variable that may balance demand and supply and act as a non-monetary price. This is especially true in countries where public provision of care and public health insurance remove monetary price to the consumer as the usual guide for decisions. Since price continues to be present in private supply and in the demand for private services, there will be two "rationing" variables—price and waiting time (the non-monetary price)—which are used differently by the private and public sectors. The public sector relies more on waiting time (though small monetary prices, like co-payments, may also be present), and the private sector relies more on price (though short waiting times may also be present).

The interface between public and private providers can then lead to different market allocations according to the particular instruments available to each sector. The first question that can be asked is the impact of a private sector on top of a public sector (a positive analysis).

The analysis of Iversen (1997) investigates the effect of introducing a private sector (which treats privately funded patients) alongside a free public sector. He shows that if the demand for a public health care is sufficiently elastic to waiting times, the introduction of a private sector may be associated with a longer waiting time for patients treated in the public sector. This arises because by increasing waiting times, the public sector can obtain a large reduction in public expenditure.

A similar result is obtained by Olivella (2003). The incentives of the public sector to reduce waiting times are weakened in the presence of a private sector. Such incentives are even weaker if fees charged by the private sector are regulated, since this increases the elasticity of demand with respect to waiting time and increases the optimal waiting time set by the public purchaser. The degree of competition in the private sector therefore influences the decisions in the public sector.

2.3.1.2. A Simple Model of the Role of Waiting Times

Individuals differ in income y, characterized by distribution function $F(y)$. Individuals have utility $bg(w) + u(y)$ if they receive treatment in the public sector, where b is the benefit from treatment, w is waiting time, and $g(w) < 1$ is the discount function to account for the disutility of waiting. If the individual goes private she has utility $b + u(y - p)$, where p is the price to receive treatment. Define $\hat{y}$ as the income threshold level such that the individual is indifferent between public and private treatment: $bg(w) + u(\hat{y}) = b + u(\hat{y} - p)$. Demand for public care is $F(\hat{y})$. The government chooses waiting time to maximize $B(w) - C(w, F(\hat{y}))$, where $B(w)$ is the disutility from having waiting times (for example, in terms of higher patient dissatisfaction and health status, political costs from lower probability of winning the elections, or in terms of government popularity), and $C(w, F(\hat{y}))$ is the cost of providing care: we assume that the cost is increasing in the number of patients treated, $F(\hat{y})$, and decreasing in waiting time w. The latter assumption is justified in terms of lower probability of idle capacity (i.e. the probability that doctors do not have any patient to visit/treat) when waiting times are larger. If there is no private sector, the waiting time is set to maximize: $B(w) - C(w, 1)$, so that the marginal benefit from lower cost is equal to the marginal disutility from waiting: $\frac{dB(w)}{dw} - \frac{dC(w,1)}{dw} = 0$. In the presence of a private sector, the optimal waiting time is such that:

$$\frac{dB(w)}{dw} - \frac{dC(w, F(\hat{y}))}{dw} - \frac{dC(w, F(\hat{y}))}{dF} f(\hat{y}) \frac{d\hat{y}}{dw} = 0$$

The last term is positive: an increase in waiting times reduces demand and saves costs. Therefore, the optimal waiting time is higher in the presence of a private sector.

2.3.1.3. Prioritization, Cream Skimming, and Rationing Rules

Suppose that individuals with higher benefit have more to lose from waiting. This is plausible as one main effect of waiting is to postpone benefits. For example, if the benefit from treatment when the patient has to wait is $bg(w)$ with $0 < g(w) < 1$ then, using the same model provided in section 2.1, individuals will go private if $V(a^{pr}) - V(a^{pu}\}) + b[1 - g(w)] + v(q^{pr}) - v(q^{pu}) > U(y) - U(y - p)$. In this case, $\partial y^*(b)/\partial b < 0$: the income threshold is higher when the benefit from treatment is higher. That is, when benefit is higher more patients go private.

This seems a counter-intuitive result as one of the underlying principles behind several publicly funded systems is that patients with higher benefit should have some form of priority in having access to public sector treatment. Therefore, if patients with high benefit tend to go private, that would be deemed to be a failure of public systems.

The above model relies on the assumption that waiting time is fixed and does not vary across patients with different benefit. In practice public systems prioritize patients, and patients with high benefit wait less.

Formally, if waiting time is $w(b)$ with $\partial w/\partial b < 0$, then if the prioritization is sufficiently steep, we can have $(\partial y^*(b))/\partial b > 0)$: when benefit is higher, there are fewer (more) patients treated in the private (public) sector (see Figure 15.1). There may be other channels through which $\partial y^*(b)/\partial b \neq 0$. If price p is a function of benefit with $\partial p/\partial b > 0$ (either because of higher costs or more extraction of consumer surplus) we can again have $\partial y^*(b)/\partial b > 0$: patients with higher benefit are more likely to go public.

Barros and Olivella (2005) investigate the incentives for doctors to cream skim when patients have to pay out of pocket if they opt for a private provider. They show how the incentive for doctors to cream skim depends on the rationing rule implemented by the public purchaser. If the threshold severity level over which patients are eligible for public care is at intermediate level, the incentive to cream skim will be highest. Cream skimming may be on patients with middle severity rather than lowest severity as patients with lowest severity may not be eligible for public treatment and may not want to pay the price charged by the private sector (if health benefits are proportional to severity).

Cuff et al. (2011) look at the role of rationing rules in public and private sector interaction. The main point is to show that the rationing rule decided by the public sector has implications for the demand and behavior of the private sector (including the price charged). They assume that the public sector has a capacity constraint, and focus on two rationing rules: (1) needs based and (2) random rationing. They show that the private market is smaller when the public sector rations according to need than when allocation is random. This is because random rationing makes private care more desirable. As a result the price charged by the private sector is also higher.

A similar message arises in Gravelle and Siciliani (2008), who investigate public and private allocation under rationing by waiting. The rationing rule in the public sector influences the choice of going private. Prioritization increases the number of low-benefit patients who go private and increases the number of high-benefit patients who go public.

The study of Grassi and Ma (2011) investigates the pricing behavior of the private sector in the presence of two alternative rationing rules in the public sector: (1) the public sector rations on the basis of wealth (like an income-tested access to care: only poor patients have access to public care, like in Medicaid) and (2) the public sector rations on the basis of wealth and costs (or cost effectiveness).

Under the first scenario, the price charged increases with the budget allocated to the public sector. The intuition is that a higher budget implies a lower number of individuals in the private sector who have a lower willingness to pay and value health care less. The private sector can then charge them more. The normative side of this rationing is, however, hard to accept. Taken literally it implies that a public sector should dump poor patients in the private sector so that rich patients may benefit from lower prices (as providers face a less favorable mix of patients). Under the second scenario, the price is independent of the budget allocated to the public sector. Patients are better off under the second rationing rule.

2.3.1.4. Incentives to Contain Costs

The interaction between the public and private sectors under different rationing rules and its impact on incentives to contain health care costs is an important issue. The work of Ma (2003) addresses the issue in a model where individuals are located on a Hoteling line with a (representative) public and private hospital located at the extremes of the unit line. Individuals' heterogeneity may be due to several factors, including income. The private sector is modeled as a contestable market (price equal to average cost, but the representative firm sets the price in a profit-maximizer fashion).

The quality (which is fixed) and marginal cost of treatment are positive in the private sector and are normalized to zero in the public sector. Moreover, the private sector can exert cost-containment effort. The main result of the study is that if the public sector does not ration, then cost-containment effort and the number of patients treated will be too low in the private sector.

Since the private sector charges a price equal to the average cost (due to contestability) which is higher than the marginal cost, then the number of patients treated in the private sector is too low (the number would be optimal if the price was set at the marginal cost). The lower number of patients treated brings cost-containment effort down as the marginal benefit from cost containment is proportional to activity.

The first-best levels of quantity and effort could be recovered by a public rationing rule enforcing the optimal number of patients treated (for example, by offering the public service to poor patients and not to rich ones). By enforcing the optimal activity, it increases the incentives to provide effort at the optimal level. In most countries, such type of rationing is not observed as everyone is entitled to the public services. Under the alternative rationing rule of random rationing where every patient along the line is treated with a certain probability, welfare can still be improved compared to "no rationing" but it is less efficient than rationing on the basis of the observable characteristics.

2.3.1.5. Public Leadership in Mixed Markets

One interface of public and private provision occurs in the marketplace when a public provider competes with a private provider (in the sense of the "first margin" described initially). That is, in health care it is not uncommon to see mixed markets. A particular feature extends the scope of mixed markets in health care. Even when the funding institution is private (say, a sickness fund or an insurance company), it is often the case that it defines sets of preferential providers. Not all providers in the market are equal to the payer. Special relationships between the funding institution and the health care provider started in the context of managed care, and have become widespread (even in countries with a National Health Service).

As the public payer (operating directly as a health care provider) tends to be large relative to the market and has the coercive power of the government behind it, the assumption of leadership by the public agency regarding decisions is a natural one. In the context of both quality and price decisions Barros and Martinez-Giralt (2002) look at two different situations. In the first one, all decisions of the public provider are taken first. In the other one, the public provider chooses its quality level, which is also observed by the private provider, who then decides on its own quality. Next, both providers decide on prices. Providers are not perfect substitutes in the patients' eyes. Both vertical and horizontal differentiation of health services provided are present. Market equilibria are characterized under alternative assumptions on patients' co-payments and timing of decisions. The role of the public provider as a Stackelberg leader (can commit to capacity decisions) is explicitly addressed. The alternative co-payment system is imposed by the public insurer (who also runs the public provider) when patients opt to go to the private provider.

The main result is that under (Stackelberg) leadership by the public provider and sequential decisions regarding quality, the first-best choice of qualities is achieved under two co-payment systems (either no payment if the private provider is selected or the public health insurer pays the same whatever provider is chosen, and equal to the payment received by the public provider). Otherwise, the public provider will overinvest in quality to gain a strategic edge, and the private provider will follow, due to strategic complementarity, resulting in too high qualities in equilibrium. Higher qualities (than optimal ones) also imply higher costs in the delivery of health care. The first-mover advantage and the adequate co-payment rules are sufficient instruments to achieve the first-best choice of qualities.[15]

The second way in which the public provider can exert leadership has sequential choices in quality, followed by simultaneous price decisions by both providers. Under this timing of decisions, the optimal choices by the public provider will always have too much quality from a social point of view, and also the private provider will offer too much quality. The higher quality of the public provider also implies a higher price by the public provider.

The main point of Barros and Martinez-Giralt (2002) is the importance of reimbursement systems and leadership for efficiency in mixed markets. These two aspects influence in a crucial way the public–private interface in provision of care delivered through the market.

2.3.2. Dual Practice

In many countries, doctors working for publicly funded health systems (of the NHS type) are also allowed to work privately. This is the case, for example, in France, Italy, Portugal, Spain, and the Scandinavian countries. Such an institutional feature is known as "dual practice" (doctors working in a dual public/private system) or "moonlighting" (doctors working in the evening after compulsory hours in public hospitals, or during the weekend).

It is common for doctors to be salaried in the public sector, and paid fee-for-service in the private sector. This setting may raise some incentive issues. For example, doctors may have an incentive: to work less in the public sector (shirk), where they are salaried; to divert effort into the private sector, where the marginal revenue is positive and high; to "inflate" the waiting lists in order to induce patients to go private (Yates, 1995); and to cream skim patients from the waiting list.

[15] Since total demand was fixed in the Barros and Martinez-Giralt (2002) set-up, prices just share surplus.

On the other hand, the purchaser can potentially pay less to doctors who also work in private practice. Dual practice may also enhance quality in the public sector if doctors need to establish a reputation for their private practice; private practice may reduce pressure on the public sector if patients are instead treated and financed privately. Also, if dual practice is forbidden, the public sector may have problems recruiting a doctor if the overall doctor capacity is limited (see Socha and Bech, 2011; Eggleston and Bir, 2006; Garcia-Prado and Gonzalez, 2007, 2011, for recent reviews of the literature; the latter also provides a typology of dual practice arrangements across a range of countries).

Health care systems differ in the way dual practice is regulated (Garcia-Prado and Gonzalez, 2007). In some countries dual practice is forbidden (for example, in Canada). In others it is allowed but with restrictions on the income gained in the private practice (France and the United Kingdom) or the number of hours or quantity provided in the private practice (Austria and Italy). Some countries offer higher salaries to doctors who work exclusively for the public sector (Portugal and Spain). Finally, dual practice may be practiced outside the public hospital or within the public hospital (*intra moenia* or *intra mura*).

Some recent papers discuss formally whether dual practice is welfare improving. In contrast to the section above we now assume that it is the same doctors who work for both public and private sectors. The studies mentioned above are silent about this aspect: patients who go private pay a positive price but it is not explicit which doctors provide the treatment.

One advantage of dual practice is that it may induce doctors to provide more diagnostic effort in the public sector: doctors need to establish a good reputation to attract patients in their private practice. This idea is described formally in Gonzalez (2004), which provides a model where the demand is inelastic and doctors can exert different levels of diagnostic effort that can make that diagnosis more or less accurate. Allowing dual practice may induce doctors to provide more diagnostic effort in the public sector as this will help them to establish a good reputation and attract patients in their private practice. Therefore this effect increases welfare for public patients. However, if this effect is too strong, overtreatment may arise. Depending on whether the purchaser gives more weight to patient's benefit as opposed to cost containment, then welfare may increase or decrease when dual practice is forbidden.

One disadvantage of dual practice is that it may generate "crowding out," i.e. a reduction of effort in the public sector. This idea is formally discussed by Brekke and Sørgard (2007), who investigate the role of dual practice when doctors split their labor supply between public and private sectors (i.e. they decide how many hours they spend in each sector), and the number of doctors is fixed (i.e. there are no doctors working in the private sector only, at least in equilibrium). They suggest (perhaps in contrast to Gonzalez, 2004) that dual practice may generate "crowding out": allowing dual practice for salaried doctors will reduce their effort in the public sector. Paying doctors more eliminates (or reduces) such crowding out. However, banning dual practice may be a more efficient policy but only if: (1) the number of doctors is low (so that competition among doctors is less fierce); (2) public and private care are sufficiently substituted (clearly, if they are not there is no crowding out); and (3) the weight given to patients as opposed to doctors' profit is high.

The study by Brekke and Sørgard (2007) explicitly does not include waiting times. The idea that dual practice may lead to higher waiting times has been formalized by Iversen (1997). He shows that waiting times are longer when dual practice is allowed and doctors work in both the public and private sectors, as opposed to the case where doctors work exclusively in the public or the private sector (but not both). Morga and Xavier (2001) provide a similar insight and show that expanding dual practice (and the revenues which arise from it) is associated with fewer patients treated (i.e. crowding out) in the public sector, which is then associated with longer waiting times.

Dual practice may also have the advantage of attracting doctors to the public sector which would otherwise exclusively work in the private sector. Bir and Eggleston (2003) make this point formally. They show that with dual practice doctors divert attention and effort to their private practice and patients in public hospitals have longer waiting times and lower quality of care. However, this effect can be offset if the dual practice attracts more qualified and talented doctors who provide higher quality in the public sector, and who would otherwise not work in the public sector without dual practice.

Dual practice may also encourage doctors to cream skim patients by diverting the "easier" cases from the public to the private practice. Gonzalez (2005) describes this effect in a model where publicly funded patients can be treated both by a public and private provider (therefore importantly patients pay zero price in both the public and private sectors). Allowing dual practice exacerbates the cream skimming operated by the private provider, which in turn increases the average severity in the public sector. Since the marginal cost of treating the patient is now higher in the public sector, the purchaser may have an even stronger incentive to contract patients to the private sector.

The adverse effects from dual practice (or crowding out) may be attenuated if cost sharing is used and set at the appropriate level. Rickman and McGuire (1999) investigate optimal incentive schemes for doctors when they can work both in the public and private sectors. The model is an extension of Ellis and McGuire (1986), which finds that an optimal payment scheme for (semi-) altruistic providers involves a fixed payment (lump-sum transfer) combined with some degree of cost sharing. This result also holds when doctors work both in the public and private sectors, though the result needs to be qualified to take into account the degree of substitution or complementarity between public and private health care. If they are substitutes the optimal degree of cost sharing is higher: doctors tend to provide too little public care and need to be incentivized through a reduction in the marginal cost (through a reduction in cost sharing). Conversely, if they are complements the optimal cost sharing is lower: doctors tend to provide too much care. If the degree of cost sharing is zero by assumption, and the provider is paid a fixed payment (say a DRG tariff), then the amount of public care is even more suboptimal in the presence of a private sector when public and private care are substitutes: by reducing public care the provider can shift more care into the private sector.

In a model where doctors differ in their ability, Gonzalez and Macho-Stadler (2011) compare three forms of regulation: (1) banning dual practice, (2) providing rewards to doctors working exclusively in the public sector, and (3) limiting dual practice, either as a limit to earnings or limits to involvement in private activities. They show that if limiting dual practice is optimal, then limiting earnings is always worse than limiting involvement. This arises because limiting involvement in private activities acts directly on the intensity of dual practice. Banning dual practice is never optimal since the benefits from the lower salary needed to retain doctors working in public hospitals is always smaller than the cost which arises from the distortions associated with dual practice. Offering exclusive contracts to doctors who voluntarily choose to work exclusively in the public sector is optimal only if the there are limits in enforcing policies which limit dual practice.

Biglaiser and Ma (2007) study the effect of dual practice (moonlighting) on the quality of care provided and welfare in a model where doctors differ in their degree of motivation (some doctors are dedicated while others are not). They show that a policy limiting moonlighting through price ceilings can reduce the adverse effects in the public sector and increase quality. They overall suggest that moonlighting can generally improve welfare, though in some cases the impact is ambiguous.

In their analysis, there are two types of physicians, dedicated physicians and moonlighters, and two types of patients: poor patients, who can only afford the public system, and rich patients, who can opt for the private sector by paying a price. A key assumption is that monitoring physicians' decisions (regarding quality) in the public sector is not as effective as in the private sector.

Patients are matched to physicians. Dedicated physicians choose the quality level they provide to each patient. Moonlighters may either treat the patient in the public sector or refer the patient to their private practice. When matched to a patient, a physician learns the benefit value from treatment for that patient. The price in the private sector is determined by a Nash bargaining procedure between patients and physicians.

Under a ban on moonlighting, the moonlighter physician sets quality to the lowest possible if quality is not monitored and the payment is unrelated to quality, while dedicated doctors set it at some strictly positive level. If the public sector has some auditing mechanism in place, then moonlighting doctors will provide more than the lowest possible level of quality.

When moonlighting is allowed, it now matters whether a rich or a poor patient is matched with a moonlighting doctor. If a poor patient is paired with a moonlighting doctor, the lowest quality level is provided, as the patient cannot benefit from an offer to be treated in the private sector. The difference to no moonlighting lies in what happens when a rich patient is matched to a moonlighting doctor. Since they enter a bargaining process in which none has all the bargaining power, the disagreement payoff is the one corresponding to the equilibrium without moonlighting. Thus, allowing moonlighting means it only occurs when it is mutually beneficial to rich patients and doctors. Quality provided by the moonlighter will exceed that which they choose in the public sector. Total welfare will be larger under moonlighting, due to this effect (all other patients and doctors are unaffected by moonlighting).

Biglaiser and Ma (2007) show this argument holds true in the presence of an auditing game in which the moonlighters in the public sector report a quality level and are audited about it. The gain from moonlighting still arises because quality can be checked in the private sector, and a price corresponding to a high-quality level can be used to achieve an efficient level of quality. Since quality choices are patient specific and no externality exists across patients, the argument also survives the introduction of asymmetric information (irrespective of who holds better information about benefits, the patient or the doctor).

To find a negative effect upon the public sector from the possibility of moonlighting it is sufficient to have a common resource constraint (say, effort time). Whenever the resource constraint is binding to the physician in the public sector without moonlighting, allowing moonlighting diverts scarce resources to the private sector and a reduction in effort time in the public sector will be necessary so that the physician can make an effort in the private sector.

Another sort of externality from moonlighting is the way it affects dedicated doctors, who in the basic version of the model are unaffected by moonlighting. If dedicated doctors are dissatisfied with their relative position to moonlighters, and decide to become moonlighters as well, quality provided by them in the public sector drops. Overall, this may be a strong enough effect to make moonlighting welfare decrease (though rich patients opting for the private market are better off anyway). This externality also creates a role for price regulation in the private market, as a price ceiling will discourage dedicated doctors from becoming moonlighters (despite introducing some distortion in quality levels in the private sector).

Delfgaauw (2007) investigates the allocation of physicians between the public and private sectors when doctors differ in the degree of altruism. He shows that the introduction of a mixed market with public providers treating patients for free and private providers charging patients at average cost can benefit all patients (compared to a public-only system). Since the more altruistic doctors self-select into the public sector, public (poor) patients will receive higher quality because they have a higher chance of being treated by an altruistic doctor, and private patients will receive a higher quality in the private sector which is subject to competition.

2.3.2.1. A Simple Model of Waiting Time Distortion in the Presence of Dual Practice

We provide a simple model which illustrates why waiting times may be higher when dual practice is allowed. Suppose that individuals differ in income y, characterized by distribution function $F(y)$. Individuals have utility $bg(w) + u(y)$ if they receive treatment in the public sector, where b is the benefit from treatment, w is waiting time, and $g(w) < 1$ is the discount function to account for the disutility of waiting. If the individual goes private she has utility $b + u(y - p)$, where p is the price to receive treatment. Define $\hat{y}$ as the income threshold level such that the individual is indifferent between public and private treatment: $bg(w) + u(\hat{y}) = b + u(\hat{y} - p)$.

Demand for public care is $F(\hat{y})$. The provider (a hospital) chooses waiting time to maximize her surplus $p^{drg}F(\hat{y}) - C(F(\hat{y}))$, where p^{drg} is a DRG type of payment from the government to the hospital for every patient treated, and $C(F(\hat{y}))$ is the cost of providing care: we assume that the cost is increasing in the number of patients treated, $C'(\cdot) > 0$, at an increasing rate, $C''(\cdot) > 0$. The latter assumption can be thought as a smooth capacity constraint (for a given number of beds it becomes increasingly difficult to treat an additional patient). The waiting time is chosen such that $\left(p^{drg} - \frac{dC(\cdot)}{dF} \right) \frac{dF}{dw} = 0$ so that the marginal benefit is equal to the marginal cost.

Suppose now that patients in the private sector are treated by the same doctors working in the public sector (dual practice). Suppose that they receive a fee s for every patient treated (this could be, for example, $s = p - c$, i.e. the difference between the price paid by the patient in the private sector p and the cost to treat the patient in the private sector c). The utility function of the provider is now $p^{drg}F\hat{y} - C(F(\hat{y})) + s[1 - F(\hat{y})]$ and the optimal waiting time is such that:

$$\left(p^{drg} - \frac{dC(\cdot)}{dF} - s \right) \frac{dF}{dw} = 0$$

Dual practice reduces the marginal benefit from reducing waiting times: lower waiting times imply a lower number of patients choosing to opt for the private practice with a subsequent loss of income for the doctors. Waiting times are higher with dual practice.

2.3.2.2. A Simple Model of Quality Provision in the Presence of Dual Practice

The following is adapted from Biglaiser and Ma (2007). It illustrates the main mechanism through which dual practice increases consumers' welfare. There are two types of doctor and two types of patient. All doctors work in the public sector. If dual practice is allowed then they can treat some of the patients in their private practice.

Suppose that individuals differ in income y, and there two types of income y^R and y^P with $y^R > y^P$. Individuals have utility $b + q^{pu} + u(y^i)$ if they receive treatment in the public sector, where $b + q^{pu}$ is the benefit from treatment and q^{pu} is the quality provided in the public sector. If the individual goes private she has utility $b + q^{pr} + u(y - p)$, where p is the price charged to receive treatment and q^{pr} is the quality provided in the private practice.

Half of the doctors are dedicated (or altruistic) and half are selfish. The utility of a selfish doctor from treating a patient in the public sector is $T - c(q^{pu})$, where T is the salary of the doctor and $c(q)$ is the cost of providing quality q. The selfish doctor always provides zero quality (which can be interpreted as the lowest possible contractible quality). If the doctor is dedicated, her utility is $T + (b + q^{pu}) - c(q)$. A dedicated doctor provides positive levels of quality such that the marginal benefit equals its cost: $1 = c'(q^*)$.

If the allocation of rich and poor people is random then the total utility is:

$$\left[b + \frac{q^*}{2} + u(y^R) \right] + \left[b + \frac{q^*}{2} + u(y^P) \right]$$

Half of the patients receive zero quality and half of the patients receive positive quality.

Suppose now that dual practice is allowed. Suppose again that the allocation of patients is random. For each doctor half of the patients are rich and half are poor. Since the dedicated doctor always provides the optimal quality, the patients of the dedicated doctor always opt for public care (they receive optimal quality without paying a positive price).

The selfish doctor provides zero quality in the public sector but is willing to provide positive (optimal) quality q^* in their private practice at price p. The patient is better off under private care if $q^* > u(y^i) - u(y^i - p)$, where p is the price charged in the private practice, which is strictly higher than the cost of first-best quality $c(q^*)$ (otherwise the selfish doctor would be indifferent between treating the patient in the private practice or not; this assumption is realistic if the doctor has some bargaining power). We assume that rich patients can afford to pay for such quality while poor cannot.

Patients are better off under dual practice. Too see this, note that patients of dedicated doctors always get the same welfare $b + q^{pu} + u(y^i)$. Patients of selfish doctors get $b + u(y^P)$ if they are poor, and $b + q + u(y^* - p)$ if they are rich. By revealed preferences, the latter group is better off under dual practice (otherwise they would not choose to receive care in the private practice).

2.3.3. *Public versus Private Providers*

In countries with universal coverage like England, France, Italy, and Spain, publicly funded patients can be treated either by public or private hospitals. Normally, public hospitals treat only publicly funded patients. In contrast, private hospitals often treat both publicly funded patients and privately funded ones.[16]

In some countries, publicly funded patients treated by a private provider are a small proportion of the total (like in the UK), while in other countries this proportion is much more significant. The institutional setting is different in the US (and other countries with no compulsory public insurance) where individuals who are below 65 years old (who do not fall within Medicare) or are not poor (and do not fall within Medicaid) rely on voluntary private health insurance. In such a setting also privately funded patients can access both public and private providers. In general, private hospitals have two possible types of ownership: they can be for-profit or non-profit organizations. The latter group typically has constraints on the use of any residual surplus but may benefit from a more favorable tax regime.

The composition of public and private hospitals varies significantly across countries. For example, in Italy in 2001, about 39 percent were for-profit hospitals, 38 percent were public, and 22 percent were non-profit; public hospitals are much larger, employing 79 percent of total personnel, while non-profit and for-profit ones employ respectively 11 and 10 percent (Barbetta et al., 2007). In Germany in 2003, the share of public, private, and non-profit hospitals was respectively equal to 36, 25, and 39 percent (Herr, 2009). In the US in 1998 it was respectively equal to 26, 60, and 14 percent, non-profit hospitals therefore being the majority (Lakdawalla and Philipson; 2006; Shen, 2002).

Public and private hospitals can potentially differ in several dimensions. First, the payment system may be different. Private hospitals are often paid fee-for-service. Doctors working for private hospitals are also commonly paid fee-for-service. This is in contrast with public hospitals, where doctors are typically salaried. Similarly, public hospitals have been paid in the past on the basis of a fixed-budget rule in several European countries, though since the early 1990s DRG payments have been employed, which pay a tariff for every patient treated. However, such systems are often combined with volume restrictions: the tariff drops after a certain volume has been reached. Overall, public hospitals have more constraints on volume than private ones.

Second, public and private providers can differ in the use they can make of profits: for-profit hospitals can distribute profits to their shareholders; public and non-profit hospitals cannot (the surplus has, for example, to be reinvested).

---

[16] Some non-profit hospitals treat publicly funded patients only, and some for-profit hospitals treat privately funded patients only.

Third, there may be differences in their objective functions arising, in addition to the different constraints on profit distribution, from different degree of motivation or altruism: this may be caused, for example, by more altruistic (greedy) doctors selecting to work in public (private) hospitals (Lakdawalla and Philipson, 2006).

Fourth, there may be differences in the "softness" of the budget, with public hospitals having softer budgets than private ones (Duggan, 2000), as well as differences in tax regime, pension system, and legal institutional setting (Street et al., 2010).

Finally, in some countries private providers do not provide emergency services while public providers do. In the case of severe complications patients may be transferred from private to public providers.

It must be emphasized that differences in behavior between public and private providers may be due to any of the above and it may therefore be difficult to attribute differences in behavior to a specific determinant. Suppose, for example, that we find mortality rates to be lower in public hospitals: this may be due to the profit motive, the payment system, or the different degree of altruism. In some institutional settings the payment system is the same across public and private providers (for example, if DRG payment is used for both public and private providers) in which case differences due to differential payment can be ruled out.

The existing theoretical literature is far from unanimous in modeling behavior of health care providers and their objective functions (even for a given payment system). Some studies assume that public hospitals, like private ones, maximize profits.[17] They argue that although this assumption may on the surface seem unrealistic since public hospitals have constraints on the distribution of profits, public hospitals can still be modeled as profit maximizers as they can add to their reserves the financial surplus obtained. Moreover, hospital managers may spend the surplus to pursue other objectives such as increasing physician staff, expanding the range of services, or even increasing managerial perks.

In contrast, other studies argue that health care providers (possibly regardless of their public or private status) are to some extent altruistic or motivated and maximize a weighted sum of patients' benefit (or output) and profits.[18] It may then be that: (1) both public and private providers are profit maximizers; (2) both public and private providers are altruistic or motivated (to the same extent); and (3) public providers are more altruistic/motivated than private ones.

Lakdawalla and Philipson (2006) suggest that if entry is free, altruistic providers are more likely to enter the hospital market than for-profit ones. Moreover, under some conditions, they are also more likely to choose a non-profit status as opposed to

---

[17] See Dranove and White (1994), Ma (1994), Chalkley and Malcomson (1998b), De Fraja (2000), Bos and De Fraja (2002), Mougeot and Naegelen (2005).

[18] See Newhouse (1970), Ellis and McGuire (1986), Chalkley and Malcomson, (1998a), Rickman and McGuire (1999), and Eggleston (2005).

a for-profit one. The intuition for the first result is that non-profit hospitals work at a negative profit margin, which gives them a competitive advantage. The intuition for the second result is that since profits are negative there are no gains from being able to distribute profits (i.e. to choose for-profit status). Instead, tax advantages available to non-profit hospitals reduce the negative profit increasing the scope for higher output. Moreover, the non-profit status makes them eligible for donations, which can be used to cover part of the negative profit. They also suggest that non-profit hospitals' behavior is analogous to for-profit ones, but crucially as if they had a lower marginal cost of treatment.

Glaeser and Shleifer (2001) show that non-profit hospitals provide higher quality when quality is costly for the provider, not verifiable for patients, and hospitals have reputational concerns or care about quality. Since the non-profit hospital does enjoy perquisites as much as cash which arise from a surplus, the non-profit hospital is more willing to provide quality. Pursuing a similar line of research, Brekke et al. (2011) also investigate whether non-profit hospitals provide higher or lower quality than for-profit hospitals, and assume that providers are semi-altruistic (and altruism is uniform across providers) and hospitals compete on quality (within a Hoteling set-up). The comparison is in general indeterminate and depends on different forces at play. On the one hand, constraints on profits reduce the incentive to compete on quality for non-profit hospitals as the additional revenues and profits from higher demand can be appropriated less easily. On the other hand, they increase the relative weight given to patients as opposed to profits inducing non-profit hospitals to provide higher quality. When altruism is sufficiently high (low), the second (first) effect dominates and non-profit hospitals provide higher (lower) quality.

Francois (2003) provides another argument for providers with profit constraints being more willing to provide high effort (better services) when providers are altruistic. For-profit providers have an incentive to reduce other inputs when the altruistic provider increases effort: but since the provider can anticipate this, she will provide less effort to start with under a for-profit management. Profit constraints ensure that the higher effort exerted by workers will not be expropriated by the management to lower costs or raise profits, and therefore increases the willingness of workers to provide higher effort.

In terms of cost containment, we may expect private providers to have a stronger incentive to exert cost-containment effort as they can appropriate any residual surplus. This incentive will be weaker for non-profit hospitals as the returns cannot be appropriated as easily. Public and private providers may also differ in their incentive to "upcode" with private providers having stronger incentives to upcode again driven by the easier appropriability of the financial surplus.

Driven by lower altruism or a stronger profit motive, private providers may also engage in (stronger) cream-skimming practices by selecting patients with low severity, also known as "cherry picking," and by discouraging or refusing to treat high-severity patients, also known as "skimping" and "dumping" respectively.[19] These effects are likely to be reinforced when public and private hospitals operate in the same market and public hospitals have an obligation to treat all patients while private ones have discretion over the patients they treat.

Finally, if prices are not fixed (like in the US for non-Medicare patients), non-profit and for-profit providers may charge different prices, with for-profit charging a higher price (Gaynor and Vogt, 2003). This holds for a given level of cost-containment effort. As mentioned above, non-profit hospitals may have a weaker incentive to contain costs which in turn tends to increase price (Brekke et al., 2011).

In countries with universal public health insurance, governments can choose through legislation whether to confer hospitals a non-profit or a for-profit status. They can alternatively introduce more restrictions on the use of profits or instead facilitate it. In England, for example, before 2003 all publicly funded hospitals had severe restrictions on how to spend surpluses, but by 2014 they will all be obliged to have a new status known as Foundation Trusts, which implies greater financial flexibility. Between 2003 and now this status has been assigned on a voluntary basis, subject to the hospital satisfying a number of performance indicators (Marini et al., 2008).

The normative question is whether publicly funded hospitals should be restricted or facilitated in the use of surpluses. The analysis above suggests that restrictions will increase quality in the presence of sufficiently high altruism or reputational concerns, but will reduce incentives towards cost containment. The net welfare effect then depends on whether the benefits from higher quality overcome the costs from lower cost-containment effort.

The empirical literature investigating differences between public and private providers is reviewed in section 3.2.2.

2.3.4. Public—Private Partnerships

The last 20 years have witnessed a change in the way governments fund new health care infrastructures, especially when a National Health Service exists. Starting in the early 1990s in the UK, under the term Private Finance Initiative (or PFI), the use of public—private partnerships (PPPs for short) has become widespread. The most important partnerships in the health sector are related to the construction, and sometimes operation, of hospitals. PPPs are intended to replace standard procurement arrangements where the government pays a private contractor to build a hospital which is then owned by the government or another public body. The PPP takes a project traditionally executed by the public sector and transfers parts of it for

---

[19] Hospital incentives to cream skim and dumping were investigated by Ellis (1998) though there is no comparison between for-profit and non-profit hospitals.

execution to a private party. The transfer is regulated by a contract (or set of contracts). Since a project contains several phases (designing the facilities, building the facilities, raising the financial funds to execute the project, operate the facilities, etc.), it comes as no surprise that distinct models have emerged around the world, according to which phases are included in the PPP contract.

A couple of examples illustrate this diversity. In Britain, the PFI approach implied that the private party builds and maintains the hospital (operates non-clinical activities only). In Spain, in Valencia, the private party builds and fully operates the hospital, including clinical activities. The contract gives responsibility for comprehensive care provision to the private party. Italy, Sweden, and Portugal have seen a model of PPP without construction but with management awarded to a private entity. The public sector contracts private management for public facilities. The use of public–private partnerships has extended beyond developed economies' health sectors, and is also adopted in other countries.[20]

A public–private partnership has been defined in several ways, though two main features stand out: it is a long-term contract (often 30 years or more) and a risk transfer to the private contractor higher than under traditional public procurement.

An early account of PFI in Britain is due to Grout (1997) and Dawson (2001). Though not specific to the health sector, Grout already addresses potential benefits and costs which arise from PFI. He argues that the main benefit for the government is the lower public-sector borrowing required to invest in public hospitals. Note that this does not necessarily imply lower overall hospital expenditure: under a PFI initiative the public sector still has to pay for the services which will in turn cover the expenses for building the hospital. He also argues that the risk associated with building a hospital is weakly higher under a PFI initiative: a government that increases public borrowing would also have to pay interests like a large private investor but the government may be able to spread the risk more than the private sector. Grout (1997) also suggests that one problem with PFI is that it opens up the potential for renegotiation possibly to a greater extent than under a standard procurement contract (which is shorter in duration).

The economic treatment of the public–private partnerships in the health sector has been developed mainly within an incomplete contracts theoretical framework[21] and, more rarely, within an optimal contract theory one (like Martimort and Pouyet, 2008).[22]

---

[20] See Venkat-Raman and Bjorkman (2009), for example, on India. For the US, see Rosenau (2000), where a chapter is devoted to health care PPPs.

[21] The incomplete contracts approach is traced back to the works of Williamson (1975), Grossman and Hart (1986), Hart and Moore (1990), and Hart (1995).

[22] The basic economics of optimal contract theory can be found in the books by Laffont and Tirole (1993), Laffont and Martimort (2001), and by Bolton and Dewatripont (2005), among others.

The incomplete contracts approach is addressed by Hart (2003) and Bennett and Iossa (2006). Though they do not take into account explicitly the characteristics of the health sector, the arguments can be readily adapted to the hospital sector. A key assumption is that the contract cannot be complete with respect to all features relevant to the design and build of a new hospital, and therefore PPP as opposed to traditional procurement gives different incentives, which in turn have an impact on welfare.

The model of Hart (2003) assumes that the private contractor/party can choose two types of investment (i.e. has two key choice variables) regarding the design and the building of the hospital and these are not verifiable. The first type of investment, which we can interpret as a quality variable, relates to the design/architecture of the hospital: it increases patients' benefits and reduces costs. Such investments are clearly beneficial from a welfare perspective (they are called "productive" ones). The second type of investment, which we can interpret as a cost-containment effort variable, reduces costs though this comes at the expense of lower patients' benefits: Hart (2003) assumes that such investments reduce patients' benefits so much that they are undesirable, i.e. they reduce welfare despite the reduction in costs and should therefore be optimally set to zero from a welfare perspective (for this reason these investments are called "unproductive").

In the traditional procurement approach, the government hires a contractor to build the hospital and then directly operates it. Under a PPP arrangement, the private party has to construct and maintain the facilities, and provide the service (i.e. clinical activities). In the infrastructure-only model, the private party manages only construction and maintenance (i.e. excluding clinical activities).

Under traditional procurement, the private party sets both investments equal to zero. As investments are decided after the signing of the contract and they are costly, the private party has no incentive to invest. The contractor may therefore severely underinvest in the "productive" investment (i.e. the design/architecture investment). The contractor also underinvests in the "unproductive" one but since the cost-containment effort is socially wasteful (as well as being wasteful for the private party) then the unproductive investment is set at the optimal value.

Does a PPP improve welfare compared to traditional procurement? On the one hand, under PPP the private party now has an incentive to exert the "productive" investment in design/architecture, which increases welfare. On the other hand, it also has an incentive to increase the "unproductive" one, which reduces costs, which reduces welfare. The implication that follows is simple. PPPs increase welfare compared to traditional procurement when: (1) the design/architecture investment is relatively more important because it affects patients' benefits; (2) it is difficult to specify in the contract; and (3) the cost-reducing investment can be easily monitored (i.e. specified in the contract).

Most discussions on PPPs in health care derive from the general results of the theme. There are, however, particular features in health care PPPs that deserve special attention.

In the case of hospitals, clinical activities are a complex task and not easy to describe and/or monitor. Since we observe PPPs both with and without clinical activities management included, it is important to discuss under what conditions one or the other is preferred. That is, should a PPP for a new hospital involve only the construction of the building and its maintenance over the lifetime of the contract, or should the management of clinical activities to take place in the new hospital also be included in the scope of the contract of the public—private partnership? A careful appraisal of benefits and costs of each type of investment must be done. According to the above principles, a hospital involving medical research and advanced teaching and training probably has outcomes more sensitive to quality investment than a low-differentiation hospital. The latter can be more easily subject to a PPP, including the operation of clinical activities, than the former.

Let us interpret the design/architecture investment above as investment in improving the clinical activities management and associate the investment in effort with the construction and maintenance of the hospital physical infrastructure.

Under a PPP that excludes clinical activities the private party decides only construction-related investment, and the government decides the clinical activities investment, while in an integrated model for the PPP, both investments are decided by the private entity. The benefit of externality from investment in construction is never internalized and too much of it is done. Given the independence of effects of both investments, the only investment that differs across the two regimes is the clinical activities investment. Since the internalized component is different under each regime there is no possibility of establishing which of the two yields higher investment. It is only possible to say that it always falls short of the socially optimal level.

Bennett and Iossa (2006) extend the framework provided by Hart (2003) by allowing for possible renegotiation (after the contract has been signed) between the private party and the government under both traditional procurement and PPP. This assumption is realistic, as renegotiations are common over long periods of time: Guasch (2004), for example, suggests 41 percent of renegotiation cases, mostly government initiated, with an average of 2 to 3.5 years before it starts (for a sample of Latin American and Caribbean countries). Therefore, in contrast to Hart (2003), investment is verifiable but only *ex post*. Whenever renegotiations occur, it is assumed that the parties bargain over investment levels (a symmetric Nash bargaining process is used).

Like Hart (2003), Bennett and Iossa (2006) assume that there are two types of investment. They assume that one of the investments is decided in the stage of building the facility (the first period) while the other is decided at the management stage (the second period). In contrast to Hart (2003) they allow the "productive" investment (for example, clinical activities) to be one of two types: (1) the investment increases benefit and reduces costs (like in Hart, 2003) or (2) the investment increases benefits but *increases* costs: this case may also be plausible for a more beneficial and expensive technology at the building stage which also has a higher maintenance cost at the management stage. Moreover, unlike Hart (2003) they assume that there is a cost-containment effort in the management stage, which is also productive (i.e. it is optimal for the agent to exert positive levels of effort). Finally, they also allow the productive investment to have a residual value at the end of the contract, which seems plausible in the case of hospitals (for example, an investment in MRI technology today may lead to a higher hospital value in 25 years' time).

Similarly to Hart (2003), Bennett and Iossa (2006) suggest that under PPP the incentives to provide the productive investment are stronger than under traditional procurement, especially when it is a cost-reducing one. If the productive investment increases the cost at the management stage (for example, maintenance costs), then the case for PPP is weakened since the private party has a lower incentive to invest in such technology. They also show that since the residual value depends on investment of clinical activities, the PPP is more likely to dominate when the sensitivity of residual value to investment is large.

The results of Bennett and Iossa (2006) cannot be directly translated into the hospital sector, as their description of public ownership differs from the one commonly observed in the hospital sector. Instead of having the government bargaining with the firms on investment levels, we observe direct operation by government of clinical activities in the infrastructure-only model. Similarly, the integrated model for PPP implies that investments are decided by the private party, which again is in contrast to direct government operation. The benefits to patients from those investments are not appropriated by the private party, and consequently are not incorporated into the decision of how much to invest. The case of a PPP that covers only the infrastructure is also not explicitly addressed in Bennett and Iossa (2006), where the government decides the investment in construction and maintenance during the management of clinical activities.

The analysis of Iossa and Martimort (2008) extends previous work by Bennett and Iossa (2006) by introducing risk and uncertainty into the analysis. They assume that costs have a random component (high-, low-cost shock) and that the private contractor is risk averse, so that risk transfer is an issue (the government is assumed to be risk neutral). Their analysis contains both elements of the incomplete and complete contract theory literature: on the one hand, they allow operating costs to be verifiable and address the need to share the operating risk between the public and private party. On the other hand, they investigate incentives under different ownership set-ups, which is consistent with the property rights literature. The key insights in terms of "bundling," i.e. allowing the private party to build and also manage and maintain the facilities, are in line with Hart (2003) and Bennett and Iossa (2006). An additional result is that when bundling is optimal, more risk is transferred to the contractor, which implies a higher risk premium under PPP. They therefore conclude that bundling under PPP goes hand in hand with high-power incentives.

One key message from the above papers is that the creation of PPP may allow the internalization of externalities. By assigning the ownership to the party that decides over different investment levels, the party will have stronger incentives to exert such investments, which in turn will raise welfare compared to standard procurement. In summary, ownership follows the party that exerts the beneficial investment. Besley and Ghatak (2001) show that this result does not hold in general. Within a framework which allows for renegotiations, they suggest that if the value created by the investments constitutes a public good, then the party with the highest valuation should be the owner of the PPP, which may not coincide with the party which has a relative advantage in producing the investment. A key assumption is that both parties value the benefits from investment, which is in contrast to the assumption of Hart (2003) and Bennett and Iossa (2006) that instead assume that the private party maximizes profits.

The model presented in Martimort and Pouyet (2008) uses a complete-contract theory approach where investments are imperfectly contractible (for example, through a noisy indicator). Although the approach is different, the key insights are in line with those of Bennett and Iossa (2006). If quality investments also reduce costs, then bundling is optimal, while if they increase costs there may be a case for unbundling. The results hold under a range of different scenarios (benevolent government, non-benevolent government).

2.3.4.1. A Simple Model of PPP and Specific Investments

To emphasize the role of positive and negative externalities between construction and management (or maintenance) after the building stage, we provide a simple model. Similarly to Hart (2003) we assume that investments are not verifiable, as opposed to Bennett and Iossa (2006) where they are not contractible but verifiable *ex post* (which allows for renegotiation).

Define q as a measure of quality investment in the building stage. The benefit from such investment for the patients is $B(q)$ and its cost is $C(q)$.

Define e as a measure of effort at the management (or maintenance) stage. The cost of managing (or maintaining) the hospital is $[c(e) + k(q)]$, where $c'(e) < 0$: higher effort reduces costs. We assume that $k'(q)$ can be positive or negative. If $k'(q) < 0$ then quality investment exhibits a positive externality on management costs: for example, a more expensive technology is cheaper at the management stage. If $k'(q) > 0$ then quality exhibits a negative externality on management costs: a more expensive technology makes management and maintenance more expensive. The disutility from exerting effort is $g(e)$ with $g'(e) > 0$ and $g''(e) > 0$. We also assume that effort does not affect consumers' benefits.

The first best is such that maximizes the difference between all benefits and costs: $B(q) - C(q) - [c(e) + k(q)] - g(e)$, which gives the optimality conditions:

$$B'(q) - k'(q) = C'(q), \; -c'(e) = g'(e),$$

where it is recalled that $k'(q)$ can be positive or negative. Therefore, the optimal quality is higher in the case of a positive externality ($k'(q) < 0$) and is lower in the case of a negative one ($k'(q) > 0$).

Under traditional procurement, building and management are carried out by two separate firms. Suppose that such firms are profit maximizers and they receive a lump-sum transfer for carrying out the project respectively equal to T and F for building and management. The firm in charge of the building will choose quality to maximize $T - C(q)$, and will therefore choose zero quality. The management firm will choose effort to maximize $F - [c(e) + k(q)] - g(e)$, and therefore choose the optimal effort.

Under bundling or PPP both building and management are carried out by the same firm (which gets the sum of both transfers). The firm maximizes now,

$$U = T + F - C(q) - [c(e) + k(q)] - g(e),$$

and therefore effort is optimally chosen. Regarding quality, if there is a negative externality ($k' > 0$), quality is still zero since

$$\frac{dU}{dq} = -C'(q) - k'(q) < 0.$$

Higher quality always reduces profits. This is not the case in the presence of a positive externality ($k' < 0$), in which case the optimal quality is chosen such that $-k'(q) = C'(q)$. Note that quality is still not as high as under the first best because the firm does not take into account the benefit for consumers. Nevertheless, quality and welfare are higher under bundling or PPP.

The existing literature still leaves out an important renegotiation driver for PPPs in the health sector: the discovery of a new technology, which can be adopted, or not, by the PPP service provider. The price of that technology cannot be established beforehand (the technology itself may be completely unanticipated).

Overall, the choice of the optimal PPP format is not obvious. On top of the externalities' effects noted already in the literature, the impact of the future price of the new technology also needs to be accounted for. The effects are, however, ambiguous. A higher clinical-activities-specific investment today results in both higher benefits and lower costs for current treatments. This changes the threat point of the future negotiation to both sides. Whenever the value to the government increases more than the value to the private party, the future price of the new technology tends to decrease and investment incentive on the side of the firm is smaller. Thus, the incomplete contracts approach to the definition of a PPP model in health care does not render a single prediction. Depending on the effects not accounted for in each agent's decision-making process, a different solution is given by the analysis.

3. EMPIRICAL EVIDENCE
3.1. Funding

The empirical evidence we report below tests some of the theories presented in section 2 or some of their underlying assumptions. Since some of these theories are normative, they cannot be tested except for marginal departures from a given institutional setting.

Taking the National Health Service model first, the relevant empirical literature relates to the determinants of supplementary private insurance and to the interaction in provision of care between the public and private sectors.

In turn, looking at health systems rooted in private health insurance, the interest lies in evidence related to introduction and/or expansion of public health insurance (irrespective of involving public delivery of care, or not).

3.1.1. Determinants of Supplementary Private Health Insurance

The theoretical prediction is simple. Take a National Health Service providing both insurance protection and direct health care provision. Larger quality differences between public and private health care provision lead to higher private health insurance coverage.

The empirical evidence supports this prediction. Private health insurance is taken up as a way to have access to higher quality in the private sector. Quality of care has often been measured using waiting time.

Existing evidence suggests quality and waiting times affect the choice of buying supplementary private health insurance across a range of countries. Using geographical data from England, Besley et al. (1999) find that areas characterized by longer waiting lists are also characterized by higher private health insurance coverage. They match survey data with administrative data at health authority level in England, where 12 percent of households held private health insurance in the mid-1990s. An increase in the number of patients on the list waiting more than 12 months by one person per thousand increases the probability of buying private health insurance by 2 percent. Individuals with higher income, who are middle-aged and support the Conservative party, are also more likely to buy private health insurance. In their companion paper

(Besley et al., 1998) the authors focus on the opposite relationship: how private health insurance coverage affects waiting lists. They show that higher private health insurance coverage is positively associated with waiting lists even after instrumenting for the endogenous private health insurance-coverage variable. The instruments include mortality rates (which are correlated with resource allocation) and the proportion of population working in different public or private sectors (which are correlated with private health insurance). They explain this result by arguing that policy makers have an incentive to allocate fewer resources to regions with higher private health insurance coverage. The lower resources translate into a lower supply of public care leading to a higher excess demand and a longer waiting list.

In contrast to Besley et al. (1999), Propper et al. (2001) find that in England waiting lists do not play much of a role in explaining private health insurance. Instead, it is the number of private hospitals and senior doctors which are the largest determinants of private health insurance (together with age). The authors use survey data matched with administrative ones measured at regional level between the period 1978 and 1996. Quality in the public sector is measured through health expenditure per capita, waiting lists, and the number of public beds. In the private sector quality is proxied through the number of private hospitals and the number of doctors working part time in public hospitals.

There is evidence that waiting times affect private health insurance coverage also in Australia, Norway, and Spain. Johar et al. (2011) match survey and administrative data in New South Wales (one of the largest states in Australia). Their findings are mixed: average waiting time has no or a negative effect on private health insurance but the proportion of patients waiting more than 12 months increases private health insurance coverage. Aarbu (2010) finds that higher waiting times (as measured at county level) increase private health insurance coverage. Similarly, Jofre-Bonet (2000) finds that an increase of 15 days in the public hospitals' waiting times in Spain (as measured at province level) increases private health insurance coverage by 0.36 percentage points.

There is evidence from Spain which suggests that lower *perceived* quality in the public sector increases private health insurance coverage. Costa and Garcia (2003) employ survey data from Catalonia (Spain), where about 20–22 percent of individuals hold private health insurance, and investigate the role of perceived quality on private health insurance. Unlike previous studies, perceived quality is measured at individual level and measures an overall judgment of private and public health care on a one-to-ten scale, which varies from "very bad" to "excellent." They find, consistently with the theory, that the gap in perceived quality in provision between public (lower) and private sector (higher) increases the demand of private health insurance. An increase in the quality of private care by 10 percent increases private health insurance by 8.4 percent, keeping the quality of public care constant. They also find that individuals who are richer, older, more educated, and living in Barcelona (the capital city) have a higher probability of buying private health insurance. Higher insurance premiums reduce private health insurance coverage.[23]

In Ireland, individuals holding a "medical card" who are entitled to more generous public coverage have a lower probability of buying private health insurance (Harmon and Nolan, 2001).

Thus, overall quality of care provided by health insurance coverage does matter. In particular, barriers to access health care under public health insurance do trigger demand for health care.

3.1.2. Crowding Out

In many OECD countries, public insurance is universal and covers 100 percent of the population. Private insurance has a role only if the perceived quality of care is higher in the private sector or if it covers gaps in public sector coverage. Individuals who buy private health insurance do so on top of the mandatory public insurance, as they cannot opt out of the latter.

In contrast, in other countries, like the US, public insurance is not universal and covers targeted groups like the old (as under Medicare for the over-65s) and the poor (as under Medicaid). Those who do not fall under these targeted groups have a choice between no insurance or private health insurance. A significant proportion of individuals decide not to have any insurance. In such a setting, if policy makers expand public insurance coverage some uninsured individuals will become publicly insured but some privately insured individuals will drop their private insurance because they can benefit from the public one. In addition, there is also complementary private health insurance; that is, health insurance covering gaps left by the public health insurance. The gaps can be in the scope of coverage (say, taking up certain types of care not included in public health insurance), or in the financial coverage provided. In the latter case, the prime example is the Medigap health insurance in the US.

Therefore, public insurance may "crowd out" private insurance (Cutler and Gruber, 1996). If crowding out is perfect, an increase in public coverage will leave the total number of insured unchanged. If there is no crowding out, an increase of public coverage will increase total health insurance coverage by the same amount.

In the US, above 15 percent of individuals have no insurance. Several empirical studies have investigated the effect of increasing Medicaid public insurance coverage. The US Medicaid program has provided a test for empirical measurement of crowding out of private health insurance by public health insurance programs. The two

---

[23] López and Vera-Hernández (2008) use survey data to estimate the effect of premiums on private health insurance in Spain. They find that although higher premiums reduce private health insurance coverage, the demand for private health insurance is inelastic. One implication is that a reduction in tax credits for private health insurance expenses will not deter to a great extent individuals from buying private health insurance.

main issues addressed in empirical literature were the expansion of coverage of the State Children's Health Insurance Program and the long-term care insurance. The seminal study by Cutler and Gruber (1996) investigated the effect of public insurance expansion in the late 1980s and early 1990s. It suggested that the number of uninsured fell by only 50 percent compared to the increase in the number of publicly insured. Several empirical studies have contributed to this research and found smaller effects depending on the approach used. Most of the initial analysis of the Medicaid crowding-out was concentrated on the expansion of the US State Children's Health Insurance Program.

An effect smaller than that of Cutler and Gruber (1996) was found by Card and Shore-Sheppard (2004). They adopt a different research strategy to identify the crowding-out effect, as well as a different data set, making use of two expansions in coverage of Medicaid, and defining a control and a treatment according to who was affected by the coverage expansion.

The expansions of Medicaid—public health insurance—during the 1980s and the first half of the 1990s seem to have small crowding-out effects, while more recent years (mid–1990s to early 2000s) seem associated with somewhat larger effects.

Using a more detailed approach regarding the role of income, Gruber and Simon (2008) detected strong effects associated with crowding out of private health insurance by expansion of coverage in public health insurance. They review the period 1996—2002, and a maximum crowding out of 60 percent, though estimates are sensitive to the approach chosen. LoSasso and Buchmueller (2004) obtain estimates in the 50 percent range, roughly the same order of magnitude as the previous works.[24]

The reassessment of crowding-out estimates by Shore-Sheppard (2008) points out that other reasons for reduction in private health insurance coverage need to be identified. The early significant results of Cutler and Gruber (1996) were due to a particular assumption in their empirical strategy: age-invariant trend in coverage. Once this assumption is relaxed, crowding-out effects drop to zero or close to it.

A different stream of literature on crowding out uses data from the elderly population, rather than children, to estimate a large crowding-out effect associated with Medicaid. The focus is on the private long-term care insurance, which has a low rate of private health insurance coverage. The analysis of Brown et al. (2007) finds important effects on private health insurance from the public program Medicaid. They argue that data in previous studies may have under-reported, bringing uncertainty to the accuracy of earlier findings. Their empirical analysis is complemented by the simulation results of Brown and Finkelstein (2008). They look at the empirical counterpart of the Pauly (1990) argument for health insurance crowding out. The main result is that even large

---

[24] Other works detecting crowding-out effects from Medicaid are due to Sloan and Norton (1997) and Gruber (2003).

changes in Medicaid rules are unlikely to lead to significant increase in long-term care insurance by the elderly population. Thus, the thin private health insurance market is not the result of a crowding-out effect.[25] The existence of high margins in insurance prices for long-term care insurance is also discarded as a potential explanation. Even under fair pricing of insurance, the market would be small (Brown and Finkelstein, 2008).

A relevant issue in the assessment of existing estimates of crowding out is whether it looks at marginal effects, resulting from expansion of public health insurance programs, or deals with discrete effects of creating public health insurance programs when none existed.

The evidence discussed so far addresses only crowding-out effects at the margin. The discrete effect of a public health insurance program is addressed in Kim (2010). She uses the Health and Retirement Survey, as in Brown et al. (2007), and finds a small effect. The counterfactual simulations, allowing for savings decisions (which affect Medicaid eligibility), suggest that elimination of Medicaid would increase long-term care insurance by a small 5.3 percent.[26] The main adjustment to Medicaid hypothetical removal is by asset accumulation and not acquisition of health insurance.

Despite the relatively large literature on crowding out by the Medicaid program, one of the empirical challenges regarding empirical measurement of crowding out of the private health insurance market is the slow diffusion of public health insurance. This makes it harder to detect any significant statistical effect (as the approaches do not identify slow changes in trends).

3.1.3. Crowding In

A "crowding-in" effect of public health insurance occurs when the expansion of public health insurance also brings an expansion of private health insurance. In countries with a universal NHS or with mandatory universal health insurance, crowding in would correspond only to duplication of insurance coverage.

The United States provides the main ground for the analysis of this effect, as changes in the federal programs provide the necessary policy variation to detect crowding-in effects. Lakdawalla and Yin (2010) take advantage of the role of Medicare Part D expansion in extending insurance to previously uninsured elderly to look for this sort of effect. The expansion takes a particular form: it delegates management of coverage to private health insurers that compete for the Medicare Part D contracts. Existing insurers took up the expansion of Medicare Part D with virtually

---

[25] The role of tax incentives in the long-term care insurance market are treated in Courtemanche and He (2009) and Goda (2010). Subsidies to private long-term care insurance are unlikely to lead to a significant take-up of private insurance associated with a reduction of Medicaid expenditures. The effects of tax subsidies in inducing more long-term care insurance are concentrated in high-income groups, unlikely to fall under the Medicaid eligibility criteria.

[26] Kim (2010) uses a stochastic dynamic set-up to model the decision to buy long-term care insurance.

no entry of new players. Thus, private health insurers have an increase in their size, and therefore enhanced bargaining power vis-à-vis providers of health care. Lower prices are extended to all insurance policy holders. The exercise of this increased bargaining power benefits all contracts of the health insurer, not only the Medicare Part D ones. This creates a positive externality from expansion of public health insurance to private health insurance, as better contracts can be offered to the population not covered by Medicare Part D, and thus increase private health insurance coverage. Lakdawalla and Yin (2010) find evidence of this effect in price reductions for generic drugs and branded drugs facing therapeutic competition. The analysis of Duggan and Scott-Morton (2010) corroborates the potential channel of the crowding-in effect proposed by Lakdawalla and Yin. We do not find studies, in the literature, on the crowding-in effects theoretically pointed out by Encinosa (2003).

3.2. Provision

3.2.1. Waiting Times and Choice of Provider

The evidence reviewed in section 3.1.1 suggests that quality and waiting times in the public sector affect the choice of buying supplementary private health insurance. Once an individual falls sick, quality and waiting times may also affect the choice between public and private provision. If the individual holds private health insurance she will have strong incentives to go private. Even if she does not hold private health insurance she could still choose to go private if the benefits from lower waiting times and potentially additional quality and amenities in the private sector overcome the price charged by the private sector.

If the individual holds private health insurance she may substitute public care for private care, as well as consuming private care not covered by the public sector, leading to a higher total consumption. The empirical evidence reviewed below is broadly in line with such predictions.

Whatever the health insurance arrangement, in the event of sickness, the individual has to look for health care (or go untreated). Relative prices to be paid at that moment and (perceived) qualities and speed of access to treatment in each sector (public or private) determine the choice. Insurance arrangements influence directly the price paid by individuals and indirectly the remaining variables.

Using survey data Hanson et al. (2004) show that quality and waiting times affect the choice between the public and private sectors. Quality is measured through a range of questions which ask each individual to assess quality in both the public and private sectors. Quality measures are created through a range of categorical variables (from one to ten). Quality is differentiated between technical quality (ability of doctor to give correct diagnosis and treatment; outcome of treatment), interpersonal quality (amount of time doctor spends with patient; doctor's explanations, tests, procedures; courtesy and helpfulness of doctor), and system quality (cleanliness and comfort of waiting area and consultation area; ability to choose doctor). Waiting time is also measured by asking each individual how long they would expect to wait in each of the two sectors. The study shows that differences in perceived quality and waiting times are significant in explaining the probability of choosing the private versus the public sector.

The evidence for England is mixed. Martin and Smith (1999, 2003) develop respectively cross-sectional and panel-data analyses using small-area data in England. They find that higher waiting times reduce the demand for public health care (as measured by total number of admissions to hospital, and controlling for an index of private sector size for each small area). They also find that higher private bed availability reduces demand for public care. The demand for public care is inelastic to waiting times and is estimated at −0.1: a 10 percent increase in waiting times reduces demand by 1 percent.[27] One of the channels through which higher waiting times reduces demand for public care is that some patients opt for private care. However, Propper (2000) finds no direct evidence that waiting times in the public sector increase private care. She uses the British Household Panel Survey (BHPS) to investigate the choice between public, private, and no care. Using a multinomial logit model, she finds that it is income, being employed, and political attitude (if the individual is a Conservative supporter) which are significant predictors of going to a private care facility. Quality as measured by waiting lists is not. She also finds that past consumption is a significant predictor of current consumption, and past public (private) consumption increases current private (public) consumption, so that private and public care appear to be complements.

An older study by McAvinchey and Yannopoulos (1993) uses annual time-series data over the period 1955−1987 in England and estimates the effect of waiting list (non-monetary price of public care) and price of private insurance on the share of public and private health care consumption. They find as expected that waiting time reduces public consumption and higher insurance increases private consumption. They also find that public and private care can be complements in the short-run but not in the long-run equilibrium.

Mixed evidence is also provided by Fabbri and Monfardini (2009) for Italy. They use survey data from Italy and investigate the role of waiting times and charges on the consumption of public and private specialist visits (as well as family doctors' visits). Although they find that waiting times and charges respectively reduce the demand for public and private specialist care, the cross-elasticities are not statistically significant: a higher waiting time does not increase consumption of private visits, and higher charges do not increase consumption of public visits. They conclude that there is overall no substitution effect between the demand for public and private specialists.

---

[27] See also Gravelle et al. (2003) for a similar result.

Charges only act as a deterrent to consumption in the private sector which is not substituted for more public care. Similarly, waiting times act as a deterrent to consumption of public care which is not substituted with more private care. These results may be due to individuals seeking different types of care to the public and the private sector (i.e. care in the private sector complementing care in the public sector), as the study only observes the number of specialist visits.

The results in Atella and Deb (2008) instead suggest that public and private care are substitutes in Italy. They test the extent to which visits provided by public and private specialists are substitutes or complements using survey data. Intuitively, we would expect them to be substitutes. Atella and Deb point out that with no adequate care to control for endogeneity, regression results may lead to spurious regression. For example, a regression of public specialist visits on private ones is likely to give a positive coefficient, suggesting that public and private visits are complements. They suggest this may be due mainly to unobserved heterogeneity: for example, individuals who visit public specialists also tend to visit private ones. Once such endogeneity is taken into account by a simultaneous equation model, a higher number of public visits does crowd out private ones: public and private visits are substitutes.

3.2.2. Access Effects Due to Private Health Insurance

The choice of public versus private health care by patients is affected by health insurance in several ways. The first important point to note is that public provision is also accompanied, in the majority of cases, by public health insurance. The choice of going to private health care needs to weigh co-payments and quality characteristics in the public sector against price and quality characteristics in the private sector. The price paid in the private sector at the moment of choice of provider is determined by the existence of voluntary private health insurance. In our discussion of empirical results regarding choice of public versus private provider, the role of (supplementary) private health insurance is mainly a proxy for lower price faced by the private provider.

The presence of private health insurance triggers two different effects: an expansion effect—the individual may look for more care, given the lower price; and a diversion effect—private health insurance lowers the relative price of health care and some demand is diverted from public to private health care.

Evidence from Spain suggests that individuals who hold private health insurance are more likely to opt for private as opposed to public care, as well as demanding more total care. López and Vera-Hernández (2008) use survey data and find that individuals who have private health insurance have a higher probability (+ 6.3 percent) of visiting a private doctor (a family doctor or specialist) and a lower probability of being an inpatient in a public hospital (−5.3 percent). Vera-Hernandez (1999) investigates the effect of private health insurance on total number of specialist visits (public and private) using survey data from Spain. By estimating jointly both the determinants of visits and private health insurance, he controls for unobserved heterogeneity which might affect simultaneously both the choice of going private and to buy private health insurance (for example, unobserved health). He shows that holding private health insurance increases total specialist visits by 27 percent. The result that individuals who hold private health insurance consume more health care (public plus private) holds also for Ireland, Italy, Portugal, and the United Kingdom (Jones et al., 2006) and France (Buchmueller et al., 2004).

The role of additional health insurance coverage is addressed in Barros et al. (2008) and in Moreira and Barros (2010), taking advantage of a mandatory double coverage health insurance. The quantile regression approach in Moreira and Barros (2010) allows the impact on use of health care (visits to a physician) of supplementary insurance to vary along the conditional distribution. The identification strategy relied on the exogeneity of employer-provided health insurance. A prominent role is played by the additional health insurance offered in Portugal to civil servants and run by government department (separate from the Ministry of Health). This additional coverage is on top of the National Health Service, which is offered to all residents and with direct provision of care by the Ministry of Health. The results show that additional health insurance does have different impact at distinct points of the distribution of use of care. The effect is larger for infrequent users of health care. Average effects hide important differences, and supplemental health insurance has more bearing on the low users. The effects are stronger when the employer is from the current private sector (the mandatory double coverage only exists in large ex-state-owned companies, privatized more than a decade ago). These results extend the evidence of Barros et al. (2008), who used the same identification strategy, with a matching estimator approach, to detect extra use of health care due to the supplementary coverage.

3.2.3. Behavior Differences

In most countries patients can be treated by public and private providers. Typically public hospitals treat mostly publicly funded patients,[28] while private providers can have either a dedicated contract with a public purchaser, treat patients who pay out of pocket or are privately insured, or both. There is an extensive literature which tests whether public and private (profit or non-profit) hospitals differ in their behavior. Providers can potentially differ in quality, costs efficiency, patients' selection and incentive to upcode (coding episodes in a way to elicit a higher payment from the third-party payer). Most of the literature on differences between hospitals based on ownership status is from the US, with increasing contributions from other countries.

---

[28] In countries with a National Health Service, private provision competing directly with public provision tends to be small and private health insurance may be bought from public providers.

The literature for the US is reviewed in Sloan (2000). We therefore focus on contributions post-2000.

3.2.3.1. Quality

A recent meta-analysis suggests that differences in quality between public and private providers in the US give mixed evidence (Eggleston et al., 2008). They find that whether for-profit hospitals provide lower or higher quality depends on the context (region, data source, and period of analysis). Quality is measured through mortality and adverse events (surgical complications and medical errors). For most studies they find that differences across hospital ownership in mortality rates or adverse events are not statistically significant. Moreover, government hospitals have either higher or similar mortality rates and adverse events as private not-for-profits. They conclude "studies representative of the US as a whole tend to find lower quality among for-profits than private nonprofits." The review by Shen et al. (2007) and older review by Devereaux et al. (2002) suggest that private for-profit hospitals have higher mortality rates. The concern of patients' selection leads to the use of "adjusted" mortality rates.

Most of the studies covered by Eggleston et al. (2008) are cross-sectional. An interesting study is provided by Picone et al. (2002). Rather than relying on cross-sectional evidence, they investigate whether the change in status from non-profit to for-profit in the US had an impact on unobservable quality. The panel approach allows for better control for unobserved heterogeneity across hospitals (disentangling what is due to ownership as opposed to other time-invariant characteristics, like location, catchment areas, etc.). They show that mortality rates (measured by death at 30 days, six months, and one year) increased within two years of the change. In contrast, for-profit hospitals that changed from for-profit to government or to non-profit status had similar levels of quality before and after the change. A similar approach is followed by Shen (2002), who finds that the incidence of adverse outcomes (as measured by mortality rates for AMI) increases by 8–9 percent after a non-profit hospital converts to a for-profit one. The result that quality is lower in for-profit hospitals is consistent with theories which emphasize that non-profit status implicitly increases the weight given to patients as to monetary surplus, therefore making the provider more willing to provide higher quality.

When comparing mortality rates between public and private hospitals, it is critical to take the different patients' case mix into account. Milcent (2005) investigates differences in quality (as measured by AMI mortality rates) between public and private (for-profit and not-for-profit) hospitals in France. Public hospitals and private not-for-profit hospitals are subject to a global budget. Private for-profit ones are paid fee-for-service. Moreover, private hospitals can select patients and have more flexibility in recruiting staff. Basic descriptive statistics suggest that the mortality rate is twice as high in local public hospitals than in for-profit ones (15 versus 7 percent), and private non-profit hospitals have intermediate values (about 10 percent). Using duration analysis with multiple destinations and after controlling for differences in severity (as measured by age, gender, case mix, diagnoses, and other controls) the study finds that public hospitals and private non-profit ones have similar outcomes. Private for-profit hospitals have lower mortality rates than non-profit ones (though the difference is not significant when controlling for size and the number of innovative procedures, i.e. PTCA). The main message of the study is that differences in mortality rates (which are often used as a proxy of quality) are much smaller and perhaps not significantly different once appropriate control variables are taken into account.

A similar point is raised by Lien et al. (2008). Patients may choose the type of hospital (public versus private, profit versus non-profit) based on how severe they are, which may generate endogeneity (expected health outcome influencing the type of hospital). Using an instrumental-variable approach the authors find that in Taiwan patients treated by non-profit hospitals receive better quality care (as measured by one- or 12-month mortality rates for stroke and cardiac treatment) than for-profit ones: mortality rates are 2–3 percent lower for non-profit compared to for-profit hospitals. When endogeneity is not taken into account, OLS significantly underestimates the effect of non-profit on quality of care (the coefficient is about half the IV one). Jensen et al. (2009) control for possible selection by including in their sample of Australian hospitals only patients who were affected by their *first* AMI: they find that private hospitals have lower (unplanned) readmission and mortality rates associated with acute myocardial infarction.

3.2.3.2. Cost Efficiency

Non-profit and for-profit hospitals may also differ in terms costs, technical and allocative efficiency, cost-containment effort, revenues, and obviously profits. Moreover, such differences may be dampened or amplified depending on the degree of competition in the market, and the payment system (for example, DRG, fixed budget, or cost reimbursement).

In line with Eggleston et al. (2008), Shen et al. (2007) conduct a meta-analysis which compares in the US the financial performance of for-profit, non-profit, and government hospitals. The authors focus on four dimensions: costs, revenues, the profit margin (defined as revenues minus profits divided by revenues), and efficiency. The focus is on the hospital as a whole. The basic empirical approach is to regress total cost, revenues, and profit margins against a dummy variable for hospital ownership (and other control variables). Studies on efficiency involve a two-step procedure where, first, efficiency is measured (either through parametric—often stochastic frontiers techniques—or non-parametric ones—like Data Envelopment Analysis or Free Disposal Hull). They then conduct a meta-analysis to explore variations in results.

Overall, the study finds little difference in cost among types of hospital. For-profit hospitals have more revenue and profits than not-for-profit ones but the difference is modest in economic terms. Government and not-for-profit hospitals do not differ significantly in terms of profits and revenues. For-profit hospitals tend to be more efficient than non-profit ones. Rosko (2001) employs a sample of 1,631 hospitals in the US during the period 1990–1996 and finds that for-profit hospitals are more inefficient.

Several recent studies test for differences in efficiency between public and private hospitals in different European countries. The results are mixed. Barbetta et al. (2007) use a sample of 500 Italian hospitals. They employ both Data Envelopment Analysis and (econometric) stochastic frontiers techniques to compare how public and private non-profit hospitals responded to the introduction of a DRG-based payment system in the Italian NHS. They focus on technical efficiency, the output being measured in terms of number of patients treated and inpatient days, and the input in terms of personnel and number of beds (as a proxy of capital). They find that generally non-profit hospitals were more efficient than public ones before the introduction of the DRG system (when they differed in the payment system), and that mean efficiency converged after the introduction of the DRG system. Herr (2008) uses a large sample of 1,500 German hospitals to test for differences in cost and allocative efficiency. Technical efficiency is measured through a production frontier (as in Barbetta et al., 2007). Cost efficiency is measured regressing total hospital costs on output and input prices. The study employs stochastic-frontier analysis. Since the data set is a panel, weaker distributional assumptions on the error terms are required to estimate the degree of efficiency. It finds that private and non-profit hospitals are less costly and more technically efficient than public hospitals. Farsi and Filippini (2008) also use stochastic frontier methods to test for differences in cost efficiency between public, for-profit, and non-profit hospitals in Switzerland employing stochastic frontier techniques and find no significant differences by ownership. Marini et al. (2008) investigate the change of hospital status in England from "public hospital" to "Foundation Trust," a status which confers more financial independence in the management of eventual surpluses, and less monitoring and control. Since the introduction of Foundation Trusts was phased, they use difference-in-difference methods taking into account potential endogeneity due to the voluntary decision of becoming a Foundation Trust. The study finds that the new status had limited impact.

In most countries entry of public and private hospitals is highly regulated. Chakravarty et al. (2006) provide evidence that in the US for-profit hospitals are more likely to enter/exit the market in response to demand shocks compared to non-profit ones.

Gaynor and Vogt (2003) estimate a structural model in the Californian hospital industry and find that non-profit hospitals tend to have less elastic demand (to price) and lower prices. They suggest that non-profit hospitals behave in a similar fashion to for-profit ones, but crucially as if they had a lower marginal cost.

3.2.3.3. Patients' Selection

There is evidence that private hospitals may have a stronger incentive to select less severe patients. Duggan (2000) investigates whether public, private for-profit, and private non-profit responded differently to an exogenous policy change which made the reimbursement for treatment of poor (the Disproportionate Share Programme) patients much more generous in California. He finds that private hospitals, regardless of the for-profit or non-profit status, responded by cream skimming the patients who were profitable under the new scheme, and leaving the unprofitable ones to the public sector. In contrast, public hospitals were rather unresponsive. He also provides evidence that public hospitals have soft budget constraints, and that private for-profit and non-profit hospitals do not differ in their degree of altruism.

Some evidence of selection is also available from England. Street et al. (2010) investigate whether public hospitals have a different case mix compared to treatment centers (including private and public ones, the latter known as NHS treatment centers) which are dedicated to non-emergency (elective) treatment only. They find that patients treated in public hospitals were more likely to come from more deprived areas, to have more diagnoses, and to undergo significantly more procedures than patients seen by treatment centers, suggesting that public hospitals are treating more complex cases. The analysis therefore suggests that when private providers (as well as public dedicated ones, like the NHS treatment center) are used to treat publicly funded patients they may have a "lighter" case mix. Note that these results are derived within an institutional context where only a small proportion of elective care is contracted out to the private sector.

3.2.3.4. Incentives to Upcode

US private hospitals seem to have a stronger incentive to upcode than public ones. Dafny (2005) exploits an exogenous shock on hospital prices generated by a DRG refinement in the US (which eliminates some DRG with complications) and finds that the US public hospitals have a lower incentive to upcode than private ones (with private non-profit upcoding less than for-profit ones). The results are consistent with Silverman and Skinner (2004), who find that between 1989 and 1996 the amount of upcoding for DRG payments related to pneumonia and respiratory infections was higher among for-profit hospitals (by 23 percent) than non-profit ones (by 10 percent). Upcoding was also higher for hospitals converting from non-profit to for-profit status (37 percent). Interestingly, upcoding from non-profit hospitals was higher in markets where there was a larger proportion of for-profit hospitals. For-profit hospitals generate a negative externality on non-profit ones.

3.3. Directions for Future Empirical Work on Public—Private Interface

Other areas of the public—private interface have yet to produce a systematic body of empirical work. Political-economy models of public and private health insurance and/or provision are a potential area of future research. The empirical significance of the Samaritan's problem is still an open issue.

Dual practice has seen mainly descriptive or theoretical pieces. Socha and Bech (2011) provide a recent review of the literature, including the few empirical works. These rely on surveys to physicians. They address the motives but not the implications of dual practice. In particular, there is not a detailed treatment of verification of conditions for dual practice to be welfare improving.

Public—private partnerships for building health care infrastructures (and operating them, in several cases) are less prone to current empirical measurement, as they are ruled by long-term contracts (often spanning over 30 years). Empirical knowledge is probably built up through analysis of case studies and identification of their regularities.

4. CONCLUSIONS

This chapter aimed to present in a systematic way the public—private interface in the health sector. The chapter was organized along a $2 \times 2 \times 2$ framework: two sectors (public and private), two different layers (funding and provision), and two views (theory and empirical evidence).

We do not have a general theory of the public—private combination in funding. Countries have opted for distinct models. There is currently no theory or empirical work that provides an integrated comparison of the several ways to organize the public—private interface in funding of health care expenditures.

Our review clearly shows that institutional details matter for the identification and analysis of the more relevant public—private interface in a health system. Depending on the particular organization of the health system, different issues related to public—private interface arise.

In countries relying more on private health insurance as a primary funding source, the main concern has been how the existence and expansion of public health insurance impacts on the private health insurance market. There is a need for theoretical work on the optimal design of rules for public intervention in health insurance programs, to address the concerns of crowding out.

The focus is in the public—private interface in funding. The discussion of health insurance crowding out has remained, to a large extent, a US issue in the existing literature.

In countries with a health system based on a National Health Service, the main attention is focused on waiting lists and how they affect the choice of public versus private provider and the willingness to hold private health insurance to achieve faster access to care.

The literature comparing public and private economic agents in health care (covering almost exclusively the hospital market) emphasizes quality (measured most of the time by mortality rates) and cost efficiency. The link between this line of empirical research and the economic theory regarding the public—private interactions (either in funding or in provision) is often weak.

There is an extensive literature on difference in quality and efficiency between public and private providers. The results are often mixed and there are too many competing explanations for such differences. Future work needs to identify and decompose the source of such differences.

Whenever government (the public sector) is involved in the direct provision of health care, the question of dual practice by physicians arises. Several theoretical arguments in favor of and against it have been presented, but no systematic empirical evidence is currently available.

New forms of public—private interface in provision are also emerging, especially in countries with extensive public sector delivery of care: the public—private partnerships. These should be evaluated and assessed in the future.

We did not review two important areas of the public—private interface in health care: R&D efforts leading to technological innovation (in a broad sense) and the pharmaceutical market. Both have extensive government involvement and private agents. The issues in those areas are of a quite different nature. Moreover, technological innovation and intellectual property in health and health care and the pharmaceutical market have their own chapters in the current Handbook.

Overall, there is scope for further theory and for more empirical analysis on the public—private interface, whether in funding (health care insurance) or in provision of health care.

REFERENCES

Aarbu, K. O. (2010). Demand patterns for treatment insurance in Norway. Cesifo Working Paper.

Atella, V. & Deb, P. (2008). Are primary care physicians, public and private sector specialists substitutes or complements? Evidence from a simultaneous equations model for count data. *Journal of Health Economics*, 27(3), 770—785.

Atkinson, T. & Stiglitz, J. (1980). *Lectures in public economics*. New York: McGraw Hill.

Banerjee, A. & Duflo, E. (2006). The economic lives of the poor. *Journal of Economic Perspectives*, 21(1), 141—167.

Barbetta, G. P., Turati, G., & Zago, A. M. (2007). Behavioral differences between public and private not-for-profit hospitals in the Italian national health service. *Health Economics*, 16(1), 75—96.

Barigozzi, F. (2006). Supplementary health insurance with ex-post moral hazard: Efficiency and redistribution. *Annales d'Economie et Statistique*, *83–84*, 295–325.

Barros, P. P. & Martinez-Giralt, X. (2002). Public and private provision of health care. *Journal of Economics and Management Strategy*, *11*, 109–133.

Barros, P. P. & Olivella, P. (2005). Waiting lists and patient selection. *Journal of Economics and Management Strategy*, *14*, 623–646.

Barros, P. P., Machado, M., & Sanz de Galdeano, A. (2008). Moral hazard and the demand for health services: A matching estimator approach. *Journal of Health Economics*, *27*(4), 1006–1025.

Bennett, J. & Iossa, E. (2006). Building and managing facilities for public services. *Journal of Public Economics*, *90*(10–11), 2143–2160.

Besley, T. & Coate, S. (1991). Public provision of private goods and the redistribution of income. *American Economic Review*, *81*, 979–984.

Besley, T. & Ghatak, M. (2001). Government versus private ownership of public goods. *Quarterly Journal of Economics*, *116*(4), 1343–1372.

Besley, T. & Gouveia, M. (1994). Alternative systems of health care provision. *Economic Policy*, *19*, 199–258.

Besley, T., Hall, J., & Preston, I. (1998). Private and public health insurance in the UK. *European Economic Review*, *42*, 491–497.

Besley, T., Hall, J., & Preston, I. (1999). The demand for private health insurance: do waiting lists matter? *Journal of Public Economics*, *72*(2), 155–181.

Biglaiser, G. & Ma, C. T. (2007). Moonlighting: Public service and private practice. *RAND Journal of Economics*, Winter, 1113–1133.

Bir, A. & Eggleston, K. (2003). Physician dual practice: Access enhancement or demand inducement? *Discussion Papers Series*, Department of Economics, Tufts University.

Blomquist, S. & Christiansen, V. (1995). Public provision of private goods as a redistributive device in an optimum income tax model. *Scandinavian Journal of Economics*, *97*(4), 547–567.

Blomqvist, A. & Johansson, P.-O. (1997). Economic efficiency and mixed public/private insurance. *Journal of Public Economics*, *66*(3), 505–516.

Boadway, R. & Marchand, M. (1995). The use of public expenditures for redistributive purposes. *Oxford Economic Papers*, *47*(1), 45–59.

Boadway, R., Leite-Monteiro, M., Marchand, M., & Pestieau, P. (2003). Social insurance and redistribution. In S. Cnossen & H.-W. Sinn (Eds.), *Public finance and public policy in the new century* (pp. 333–358). Cambridge, MA: MIT Press.

Boadway, R., Leite-Monteiro, M., Marchand, M., & Pestieau, P. (2006). Social insurance and redistribution with moral hazard and adverse selection. *Scandinavian Journal of Economics*, *108*(2), 279–298.

Bolton, P. & Dewatripont, M. (2005). *Contract theory*. Cambridge, MA: The MIT Press.

Bos, D. & De Fraja, G. (2002). Quality and outside capacity in the provision of health services. *Journal of Public Economics*, *84*(2), 199–218.

Brekke, K. & Sørgard, L. (2007). Public vs. private health care in a National Health Service. *Health Economics*, *16*(6), 579–601.

Brekke, K., Siciliani, L., & Straume, O.-R. (2011). Quality competition with profit constraints: Do non-profit firms provide higher quality than for-profit firms? CEPR Discussion Paper No. 8284.

Brekke, K. R., Nuscheler, R., & Straume, O. R. (2006). Quality and location choices under price regulation. *Journal of Economics and Management Strategy*, *15*, 207–227.

Brown, J. & Finkelstein, A. (2007). Why is the market for long term care insurance so small. *Journal of Public Economics*, *91*(10), 1967–1991.

Brown, J. & Finkelstein, A. (2008). The interaction of public and private insurance: Medicaid and the long-term insurance market. *American Economic Review*, *98*(3), 1083–1102.

Brown, J., Coe, N., & Finkelstein, A. (2007). Medicaid crowd-out of private long-term care insurance demand: Evidence from the Health and Retirement Survey. *Tax Policy and the Economy*, *21*, 1–34.

Buchmueller, T. C., Couffinhal, A., Grignon, M., & Perronnin, M. (2004). Access to physician services: Does supplemental insurance matter? Evidence from France. *Health Economics*, *13*(7), 669–687.

Bucovetsky, S. (1984). On the use of distributional waits. *Canadian Journal of Economics*, *17*(4), 699–717.

Card, D. & Shore-Sheppard, L. (2004). Using discontinuous eligibility rules to identify the effects of Federal Medicaid expansions on low income children. *Review of Economics and Statistics, 86*(3), 752–766.

Chakravarty, S., Gaynor, M., Klepper, S., & Vogt, W. B. (2006). Does the profit motive make Jack nimble? Ownership form and the evolution of the US hospital industry. *Health Economics, 15*(4), 345–361.

Chalkley, M. & Malcomson, J. (1998a). Contracting for health services with unmonitored quality. *Economic Journal, 108*(449), 1093–1110.

Chalkley, M. & Malcomson, J. (1998b). Contracting for health services when patient demand does not reflect quality. *Journal of Health Economics, 17*(1), 1–19.

Chalkley, M. & Malcomson, J. (2000). Government purchasing of health services. In A. J. Culyer & J. P. Newhouse (Eds.), *Handbook of health economics* (Vol. 1). Amsterdam, The Netherlands: Elsevier Science.

Chetty, R. & Saez, E. (2010). Optimal taxation and social insurance with endogenous private insurance. *American Economic Journal: Economic Policy, 2*(1), 85–114.

Coate, S. (1995). Altruism, the Samaritan's dilemma and government transfer policy. *American Economic Review, 85*(1), 46–57.

Colombo, F. & Tapay, N. (2004). Private health insurance in OECD countries: The benefits and costs for individuals and health systems. OECD Health Working Papers no. 15.

Costa, J. & Garcia, J. (2003). Demand for private health insurance: How important is the quality gap? *Health Economics, 12*, 587–599.

Courtemanche, C. & He, D. (2009). Tax incentives and the decision to purchase long-term care insurance. *Journal of Public Economics, 93*(1), 296–310.

Cremer, H. & Pestieau, P. (1996). Redistribution taxation and social insurance. *International Tax and Public Finance, 3*, 281–298.

Cuff, K., Hurley, J., Mestelman, S., Muller, A., & Nuscheler, R. (2011). Public and private health-care financing with alternate public rationing rules. *Health Economics* (forthcoming).

Cutler, D. & Gruber, J. (1996). Does public insurance crowd out private insurance? *Quarterly Journal of Economics, 111*(2), 391–430.

Dafny, L. (2005). How do hospitals respond to price changes? *American Economic Review, 95*(5), 1525–1547.

Dawson, D. (2001). The private finance initiative: A public finance illusion? *Health Economics, 10*(6), 479–486.

De Fraja, G. (2000). Contracts for health care and asymmetric information. *Journal of Health Economics, 19*(5), 663–677.

Delfgaauw, J. (2007). Dedicated doctors: Public and private provision of health care with altruistic physicians. Tinbergen Institute DP 07–010.

Devereaux, P. J., Choi, P. T., Lacchetti, C., Weaver, B., Schunemann, H. J., Haines, T., et al. (2002). A systematic review and meta-analysis of studies comparing mortality rates of private for-profit and private not for-profit hospitals. *Canadian Medical Association Journal, 166*, 1399–1406.

Dranove, D. & White, W. D. (1994). Recent theory and evidence on competition in hospital markets. *Journal of Economics and Management Strategy, 3*(1), 169–209.

Duggan, M. (2000). Hospital ownership and public medical spending. *Quarterly Journal of Economics, 115*(4), 1343–1373.

Duggan, M. & Scott-Morton, F. (2010). The effect of Medicare Part D on pharmaceutical prices and utilization. *American Economic Review, 100*(1), 590–607.

Eggleston, K. (2005). Multitasking and mixed systems for provider payment. *Journal of Health Economics, 24*, 211–223.

Eggleston, K. & Bir, A. (2006). Physician dual practice. *Health Policy, 78*, 157–166.

Eggleston, K., Shen, Y.-C., Lau, J., Schmid, C. H., & Chan, J. (2008). Hospital ownership and quality of care: What explains the different results in the literature? *Health Economics, 17*(12), 1345–1362.

Ellis, R. P. (1998). Creaming, skimping, and dumping: Provider competition on the intensive and extensive margins. *Journal of Health Economics, 17*(5), 537–555.

Ellis, R. P. & McGuire, T. (1986). Provider behavior under prospective reimbursement: Cost sharing and supply. *Journal of Health Economics*, *5*(2), 129–152.

Encinosa, W. (2003). The economics of crowd-out under mixed public/private health insurance. *Portuguese Economic Journal*, *2*(2), 71 –86.

Epple, D. & Romano, R. (1996a). Public provision of private goods. *Journal of Political Economy*, *104*, 57–84.

Epple, D. & Romano, R. (1996b). Ends against the middle: Determining public service provision when there are private alternatives. *Journal of Public Economics*, *62*(3), 297–325.

Fabbri, D. & Monfardini, C. (2009). Rationing the public provision of healthcare in the presence of private supplements: Evidence from the Italian NHS. *Journal of Health Economics*, *28*(2), 290–304.

Farsi, M. & Filippini, M. (2008). Effects of ownership, subsidization and teaching activities on hospital costs in Switzerland. *Health Economics*, *17*(3), 335–350.

Feldman, R., Escribano, C., & Pellisé, L. (1998). The role of government in health insurance markets with adverse selection. *Health Economics*, *7*(8), 659–670.

Francois, P. (2003). Not-for-profit provision of public services. *Economic Journal*, *113*(486), C53–C61 (March).

García-Prado, A. & González, P. (2007). Policy and regulatory responses to dual practice in the health sector. *Health Policy*, *84*, 142–152.

Garcia-Prado, A. & González, P. (2011). Who do physicians work for? An analysis of dual practice in the health sector. *Journal of Health Politics, Policy and Law*, *36*(2), 265–294.

Gaynor, M. & Vogt, W. B. (2003). Competition among hospitals. *RAND Journal of Economics*, *34*, 764–785.

Glaeser, E. L. & Shleifer, A. (2001). Not-for-profits entrepreneurs. *Journal of Public Economics*, *81*, 99–115.

Goda, G. S. (2010). The impact of state tax subsidies for private long-term care insurance on coverage and Medicaid expenditures. *Journal of Public Economics*, *95*(7–8), 744–757.

Goddard, J. A., Malek, M., & Tavakoli, M. (1995). An economic model of the market for hospital treatment for non-urgent conditions. *Health Economics*, *4*, 41–55.

Gonzalez, P. (2004). Should physicians' dual practice be limited? An incentive approach. *Health Economics*, *13*, 505–524.

Gonzalez, P. (2005). On a policy of transferring public patients to private practice. *Health Economics*, *14*, 513–527.

Gonzalez, P. & Macho-Stadler, I. (2011). A theoretical approach to dual practice regulations in the health sector. University of Pablo Olavide, Department of Economics, Working Paper 11.01.

Gouveia, M. (1997). Majority rule and the public provision of a private good. *Public Choice*, *93*, 221–244.

Grassi, S. & Ma, C.-T. A. (2011). Public sector rationing and private sector selection. *Journal of Public Economic Theory* (forthcoming).

Gravelle, H. & Siciliani, L. (2008). Optimal quality, waits and charges in health insurance. *Journal of Health Economics*, *27*, 663–674.

Gravelle, H., Smith, P., & Xavier, A. (2003). Performance signals in the public sector: The case of health care. *Oxford Economic Papers*, *55*(1), 81–103.

Grossman, S. & Hart, O. (1986). The costs and benefits of ownership: A theory of vertical and lateral integration. *Journal of Political Economy*, *94*, 691–719.

Grout, P. (1997). The economics of the private finance initiative. *Oxford Review of Economic Policy*, *13*, 53–66.

Gruber, J. (2001). The impact of the tax system on health insurance coverage. *International Journal of Health Care Finance and Economics*, *1*(3/4), 293–304.

Gruber, J. (2003). Medicaid. In R. Moffit (Ed.), *Means tested transfer programs in the United States* (pp. 15–27). University of Chicago Press.

Gruber, J. & Simon, K. (2008). Crowd-out 10 years later: Have recent public insurance expansions crowded out private health insurance? *Journal of Health Economics*, *27*, 201–217.

Guasch, J. L. (2004). *Granting and renegotiating infra-structure concessions—doing it right*. Washington, DC: WBI Development Studies, World Bank Institute.

Hansen, B. O. & Keiding, H. (2002). Alternative health insurance schemes: a welfare comparison. *Journal of Health Economics, 21*, 739−756.

Hanson, K., Yip, W. C., & Hsiao, W. (2004). The impact of quality on the demand for outpatient services in Cyprus. *Health Economics, 13*(12), 1167−1180.

Harmon, C. & Nolan, B. (2001). Health insurance and health services utilization in Ireland. *Health Economics, 10*(2), 135−145.

Hart, H. (1995). *Firms, Contracts and Financial*. Oxford: Structure, Oxford University Press, UK.

Hart, O. (2003). Incomplete contracts and public ownership: Remarks, and an application to public−private partnerships. *Economic Journal, 113*(486), C69−C76.

Hart, O. & Moore, J. (1990). Property rights and the nature of the firm. *Journal of Political Economy, 98*, 1119−1158.

Henriet, D. & Rochet, J.-C. (2006). Is public health insurance and appropriate instrument for redistribution? *Annales d'Economie et de Statistique, 83/84*, 61−88.

Herr, A. (2008). Cost and technical efficiency of German hospitals: Does ownership matter? *Health Economics, 17*(9), 1057−1071.

Hindriks, J. & De Donder, P. (2003). The politics of redistributive social insurance. *Journal of Public Economics, 87*, 2639−2660.

Hindriks, J. (2001). Public versus private insurance with dual theory: A political economy argument. *Geneva Papers on Risk and Insurance Theory, 26*, 225−241.

Hoel, M. (2007). What should (public) health insurance cover? *Journal of Health Economics, 26*(2), 251−262.

Hoel, M. & Saether, E. M. (2003). Public health care with waiting time: the role of supplementary private health care. *Journal of Health Economics, 22*, 599−616.

Iossa, E. & Martimort, D. (2008). *The simple micro-economics of public−private partnerships*. The Centre for Market and Public Organisation 08/199, Department of Economics: University of Bristol, UK.

Iversen, T. (1997). The effect of a private sector on the waiting time in a national health service. *Journal of Health Economics, 16*, 381−396.

Jacob, J. & Lundin, D. (2005). A median voter model of health insurance with ex-post moral hazard. *Journal of Health Economics, 24*(2), 407−426.

Jensen, P. H., Webster, E., & Witt, J. (2009). Hospital type and patient outcomes: an empirical examination using AMI readmission and mortality records. *Health Economics, 18*(2), 1440−1460.

Jofre-Bonet, M. (2000). Public health care and private insurance demand: the waiting time as a link. *Health Care Management Science, 3*, 51−71.

Johar, M., Jones, G., Keane, M., Savage, E., & Stavrunova, O. (2011). Waiting times for elective surgery and the decision to buy private health insurance. *Health Economics* (forthcoming). DOI: 10.1002/hec.1707.

Jones, A., Koolman, X., & Van Doorslaer, E. (2006). The impact of supplementary private health insurance on the use of specialists in selected European countries. *Annales d'Economie et de Statistiques, 83*, 251−275.

Jowett, M., Contoyannis, P., & Vihn, N. D. (2003). The impact of public voluntary health insurance on private health expenditures in Vietnam. *Social Science and Medicine, 56*(2), 333−345.

Kim, G. (2010). *Medicaid crowdout of long-term care insurance with endogenous Medicaid enrolment*. University of Pennsylvania.

Laffont, J. -J. & Martimort, D. (2001). *The theory of incentives—the principal agent model*. Princeton University Press.

Laffont, J.-J. & Tirole, J. (1993). *A theory of incentives in procurement and regulation*. Cambridge, MA: MIT Press.

Lakdawalla, D. & Philipson, T. (2006). The nonprofit sector and industry performance. *Journal of Public Economics, 90*, 1681−1698.

Lakdawalla, D. & Yin, W. (2010). Insurers' negotiations, leverage and the external effects of Medicare Part D. NBER Working Paper Series 16251, August.

Lien, H.-M., Chou, S.-Y., & Liu, J.-T. (2008). Hospital ownership and performance: Evidence from stroke and cardiac treatment in Taiwan. *Journal of Health Economics, 27*(5), 1208–1223.

Lindsay, C. M. & Feigenbaum, B. (1984). Rationing by waiting lists. *American Economic Review, 74*(3), 404–417.

López, N. A. & Vera-Hernández, M. (2008). Are tax subsidies for private medical insurance self-financing? Evidence from a microsimulation model. *Journal of Health Economics, 27*(5), 1285–1298.

LoSasso, A. & Buchmueller, T. (2004). The effect of the State Children's Health Insurance Program on health insurance coverage. *Journal of Health Economics, 23*, 1059–1082.

Ma, C.-T. A. (1994). Health care payment systems: cost and quality incentives. *Journal of Economics and Management Strategy, 3*(1), 93–112.

Ma, C. -T. A. (2003). Public rationing and private cost incentives. *Journal of Public Economics, 88*, 333–352.

Marchand, M. & Schroyen, F. (2005). Can a mixed health care system be desirable on equity grounds? *Scandinavian Journal of Economics, 107*(1), 1–23.

Marini, G., Miraldo, M., Jacobs, R., & Goddard, M. (2008). Giving greater financial independence to hospitals—does it make a difference? The case of English NHS Trusts. *Health Economics, 17*(6), 751–775.

Martimort, D. & Pouyet, J. (2008). To build or not to build: Normative and positive theories of public–private partnerships. *International Journal of Industrial Organization, 26*(2), 393 –411.

Martin, S. & Smith, P. C. (1999). Rationing by waiting lists: An empirical investigation. *Journal of Public Economics, 71*, 141–164.

Martin, S. & Smith, P. C. (2003). Using panel methods to model waiting times for National Health Service surgery. *Journal of the Royal Statistical Society, Series A, 166*(3), 369–387.

McAvinchey, I. D. & Yannopoulos, A. (1993). Elasticity estimates from a dynamic model of interrelated demands for private and public acute health care. *Journal of Health Economics, 12*(2), 171–186.

Milcent, C. (2005). Hospital ownership, reimbursement systems and mortality rates. *Health Economics, 14*(11), 1050–1099.

Mirrlees, J. (1971). An exploration in the theory of optimum income taxation. *Review of Economic Studies, 38*(2), 175–208.

Moreira, S. & Barros, P. P. (2010). Double coverage and demand for health care: evidence from quantile regression. *Health Economics, 19*(9), 1075–1092.

Moreno-Ternero, J. & Roemer, J. E. (2007). The political economy of health care finance. CORE Discussion Paper.

Morga, A. & Xavier, A. (2001). Hospital specialists' private practice and its impact on the number of NHS patients treated and on the delay for elective surgery. The University of York, Discussion Papers in Economics 2001/01.

Mougeot, M. & Naegelen, F. (2005). Hospital price regulation and expenditure cap policy. *Journal of Health Economics, 24*(1), 55–72.

Newhouse, J. P. (1970). Toward a theory of nonprofit institutions: an economic model of a hospital. *American Economic Review, 60*, 64–74.

Newhouse, J. P. & the Insurance Experiment Group (1993). *Free for all? Lessons from the RAND health insurance experiment.* Cambridge, MA: Harvard University Press.

Olivella, P. (2003). Shifting public-health-sector waiting lists to the private sector. *European Journal of Political Economy, 19*, 103–132.

Paris, V., Devaux, M., & Wei, L. (2010). Health systems institutional characteristics: A survey of 29 OECD countries. OECD Health Working Papers No. 50.

Pauly, M. (1974). Overinsurance and public provision of insurance: The roles of moral hazard and adverse selection. *Quarterly Journal of Economics, 88*, 44–54.

Pauly, M. (1990). The rational non-purchase of long-term-care insurance. *Journal of Political Economy, 98*(1), 153–168.

Petretto, A. (1999). Optimal social health insurance with supplementary private insurance. *Journal of Health Economics, 18*(6), 727–745.

Picone, G., Shin-Yi, C., & Sloan, F. (2002). Are for-profit hospital conversions harmful to patients and to Medicare? *RAND Journal of Economics, 33*(3), 507−523.

Propper, C. (2000). The demand for private health care in the UK. *Journal of Health Economics, 19*(6), 855−876.

Propper, C., Rees, H., & Green, K. (2001). The demand for private medical insurance in the UK: A cohort analysis. *Economic Journal, 111*(471), C180−C200.

Rickman, N. & McGuire, A. (1999). Regulating providers' reimbursement in a mixed market for health care. *Scottish Journal of Political Economy, 46*, 53−71.

Rochet, J.-C. (1991). Incentives, redistribution, and social insurance. *Geneva Papers on Risk and Insurance Theory, 16*(2), 143−165.

Rosenau, P. V. (Ed.) (2000). *Public−private policy partnerships.* Cambridge, MA: MIT Press.

Rosko, M. D. (2001). Cost efficiency of US hospitals: A stochastic frontier approach. *Health Economics, 10*(6), 539−551.

Rothschild, M. & Stiglitz, J. E. (1976). Equilibrium in competitive insurance markets: An essay on the economics of imperfect information. *Quarterly Journal of Economics, 90*, 629−649.

Sepehri, A., Sarma, S., & Simpson, W. (2006). Does non-profit health insurance reduce financial burden? Evidence from the Vietnam living standards survey panel. *Health Economics, 15*, 603−616.

Shen, Y.-C. (2002). The effect of hospital ownership choice on patient outcomes after treatment for acute myocardial infarction. *Journal of Health Economics, 21*, 901−922.

Shen, Y.-C., Eggleston, K., Lau, J., & Schmid, C. H. (2007). Hospital ownership and financial performance: What explains the different empirical literature findings? *Inquiry, 44*, 41−68.

Shore-Sheppard, L. (2008). Stemming the tide? The effect of expanding Medicaid eligibility on health insurance coverage. *B.E. Journal of Economic Analysis and Policy, 8*(2)(Advances), Article 6.

Silverman, E. & Skinner, J. (2004). Medicare upcoding and hospital ownership. *Journal of Health Economics, 23*(2), 369−389.

Sloan, F. (2000). Not-for-profit ownership and hospital behaviour, chapter 21. In A. J. Culyer & J. P. Newhouse (Eds.), *Handbook of Health Economics* (pp. 1141−1174). Amsterdam: North-Holland.

Sloan, F. & Norton, E. (1997). Adverse selection, bequests, crowding-out, and private demand for insurance: evidence from the long-term care insurance market. *Journal of Risk and Uncertainty, 15*(3), 201−219.

Socha, K. Z. & Bech, M. (2011). Physician dual practice: A review of literature. *Health Policy, 102*(1), 1−7.

Street, A., Sivey, P., Mason, A., Miraldo, M., & Siciliani, L. (2010). Are English treatment centres treating less complex patients? *Health Policy, 94*(2), 150−157.

Tay, A. (2003). Assessing competition in hospital care markets: The importance of accounting for quality differentiation. *RAND Journal of Economics, 34*, 786−814.

Venkat-Raman, A. & Bjorkman, J. N. (2009). *Public−private partnerships in health care in india: Lessons for developing countries.* London: Routledge.

Vera-Hernandez, M. (1999). Duplicate coverage and demand for health care—the case of Catalonia. *Health Economics, 8*(7), 579−598.

Wagstaff, A. & van Doorslaer, E. (2000). Equity in health care finance and delivery, Chapter 34. In A. J. Culyer & J. P. Newhouse (Eds.), *Handbook of health economics* (Vol. 1, pp. 1803−1862). Elsevier.

Williamson, O. (1975). *Markets and hierarchies.* New York: Free Press.

Xu, K., Evans, D. B., Carrin, G., Aguilar-Rivera, A. M., Musgrove, P., & Evans, T. (2007). Protecting households from catastrophic health spending. *Health Affairs, 26*, 972−983.

Xu, K., Evans, D. B., Kawabata, K., Zeramdini, R., Klavus, J., & Murray, C. J. (2003). Household catastrophic health expenditure: a multicountry analysis. *The Lancet, 362*, 111−117.

Yates, J. (1995). *Private eye, heart and hip.* London: Churchill Livingstone.

CHAPTER SIXTEEN

Equity in Health and Health Care[1]

Marc Fleurbaey* and Erik Schokkaert**

*Princeton University, USA
**Department of Economics, K.U. Leuven and CORE (Université catholique de Louvain), Belgium

Contents

[1] This chapter was written when Marc Fleurbaey was research associate at CORE. We thank Chiara Canta, Tom McGuire, Tom van Ourti and Fred Schrogen for their useful comments.

Abstract

We discuss the conceptual foundations of measuring (in)equity in health and health care. After an overview of the recent developments in the measurement of socioeconomic inequalities and in racial disparities, we show how these partial approaches can be seen as special cases of the more general social choice approach to fair allocation and equality of opportunity. We suggest that this latter framework offers many new analytical possibilities and is sufficiently rich to accommodate various ethical views. We emphasize that horizontal and vertical equity are intricately linked to each other. We then argue that a focus on overall well-being is necessary to put the partial results on health (care) inequity into a broader perspective, and we discuss the pros and cons of various methods to evaluate the joint distribution of health and income: multidimensional inequality indices, dominance approaches, the use of happiness measures, and finally the concept of equivalent income. Throughout the chapter the theoretical analysis is complemented with an overview of recent empirical results.

Keywords: equity; racial disparities; equality of opportunity; equivalent income; dominance

JEL Codes: D630 Equity; Justice; Inequality, and Other Normative Criteria and Measurement; I140 Health and inequality; J150 Economics of Minorities and Races; Non-labor Discrimination

1. INTRODUCTION

The economic literature on equity in health and health care has grown considerably since Wagstaff and van Doorslaer (2000b) published their survey chapter in Volume 1 of the *Handbook of Health Economics*. First, there has been an explosion of the number of empirical applications. Second, the different measures of inequity, including the popular concentration index, have come under theoretical scrutiny and there has been a lively debate on their normative implications. In this chapter we start from where Wagstaff and van Doorslaer (2000b) ended. We do not aim at giving a comprehensive survey of the empirical work and will mainly focus on the methodological and theoretical questions that are raised by the recent literature. However, as the ultimate aim of our approach is to define measures of inequity that can be brought to the data, we will assess how the different theoretical proposals can be implemented.

The first generation literature on socioeconomic inequality (as reviewed in Wagstaff and van Doorslaer 2000b) drew its inspiration mainly from the economic approach to the measurement of income inequality. However, this framework is not sufficiently rich to analyse all the relevant questions that have been raised in the recent literature. Why should we be concerned about health (care) inequalities? More specifically, when are such inequalities a cause of concern and when are they ethically legitimate? And what implications do the answers on these questions have for the measurement of inequity? How to integrate different dimensions of inequity? And what is the place of health (care) in a broader concept of well-being? We will try to push these ongoing developments a bit further by exploring the potential contribution to health economics of modern social choice theory. Our approach is an attempt to integrate broader philosophical questions, measurement issues, and data considerations.

There are obvious limitations to this chapter. We will focus on inequity in health and in health care and only briefly refer to the literature on equity in finance. This is not only for reasons of space, but also because we believe that the issue of equity in finance can only be analyzed in a meaningful way within a broader welfare framework. We argue this in greater detail in section 5. Moreover, we are focusing on conceptual and measurement issues regarding equity (or justice). We are not treating incentive issues and we will therefore not discuss the equity—efficiency trade-off. Finally, we can only touch the voluminous literature outside economics (e.g. in public health). This is not to suggest that economists necessarily should have the last word in the debate. The approaches from different disciplines are complementary, but we want to describe what could be the specific contribution of economics to this joint venture. In our view, a crucial advantage of the economic approach is the development of a strong formal framework of analysis. Presenting such a formal framework is our main purpose.

Merely describing and explaining differences in health and in health care is a positive question, but measuring and evaluating what is inequitable in the given situation is a normative topic. Indeed, the evaluation of a given state of affairs requires value judgments as well as analysis of empirical data. Some might claim that answering such normative questions is not part of economic science. Yet, if economists refuse to address these crucial questions, who will do it for them? In his seminal monograph "Collective choice and social welfare," Sen (1970) introduced a distinction between two sorts of value judgments. Basic value judgments are purely philosophical statements. Kant's categorical imperative is an example. Yet, when evaluating economic situations such as the degree of inequity in health (care), what is involved are non-basic value judgments. These are contingent on empirical facts (or, at least, on a given interpretation of observable reality). Indeed, they crucially depend on the definition of relevant empirical concepts. We believe that the social sciences can and should make a contribution to the elaboration of such non-basic value judgments.

We will illustrate in the next section the intricate relationship between data and normative statements on equity in health and health care with a specific example. This will give us the opportunity to introduce some of the issues that will be discussed later in this chapter.

2. AN EXAMPLE

Health and health care obviously are unequally distributed over the population. Some older papers focused on health inequality as such (Le Grand, 1987), but one can doubt whether all health inequalities are *per se* inequitable. Some determinants of health (such as age) cannot be influenced by policy—if the health inequalities in two countries differ because of differences in the age composition of their population, few would see this as an indication of inequity. Moreover, a similar question may be asked if the inequalities in health reflect only differences in the lifestyle choices of populations. It seems therefore that not all health inequalities are inequitable. This is even more obvious for inequalities in health care use. Almost everybody agrees that differences in use of care which reflect differences in health status may be justified. Surely, therefore, a correction for needs is necessary before we can talk about inequity. The crucial question is how this correction should be performed. All this suggests that evaluating inequity in health and health care requires two steps. First, one has to see which factors explain the observed inequality in health (care). Second, one has to take a normative position on whether differences due to each of these factors can be ethically justified.

Let us illustrate the issue by looking in some detail at an example of a (very detailed) empirical study. Morris et al. (2005) investigate the inequity in the use of health care in the English NHS. The first step in their analysis is to estimate the empirical relationship between access to health care on the one hand and individual characteristics on the other hand. They pool data (1998, 1999, 2000) from the Health Survey for England for a total sample size of 50,977 individuals. These data contain all the usual demographic and socioeconomic information, but, more importantly, also exceptionally rich health information at the individual level (not only subjectively assessed health, but in addition information about types of longstanding illnesses and even GHQ-12 scores). They analyze the effects of all these characteristics on four use variables: a first variable indicating whether individuals had a GP consultation in the last two weeks, and three other indicators for having had an outpatient visit, day case treatment or an inpatient stay in the previous 12 months. After some statistical testing, they opt for a linear probability model in the first two cases, and for a probit model in the last two. Everything taken together, the estimated model contains over 200 explanatory variables. In Table 16.1 we summarize the significant effects for groups of variables, where significance is defined as $p \leq 0.0001$.[2] If no comment is added to the table, the effect of the variables goes in the expected direction (e.g. healthier people consuming less care).

The many significant coefficients clearly indicate that there is inequality in the use of health care, in that different individuals consume different amounts of care. But what about inequity? As mentioned before, we surely have to control for differences in health status. Indeed, the most common interpretation of *horizontal inequity* in this

---

[2] This strict criterion is chosen because of the very large sample size.

Table 16.1 Explaining Health Service Utilization (Morris et al., 2005)

	GP Consultations	Outpatient Visits	Day Case Treatment	Inpatient Stays
Age and sex	significant[a]	significant[a]	significant[a]	significant[a]
Self-reported general health	significant	significant	significant	significant
Acute ill health	significant			
Ward-level health variables	significant[b]	ns	ns	ns
Type of longstanding illness	significant	significant	significant	significant
Number of longstanding illnesses	ns	significant	significant	ns
GHQ-12 score	significant	significant	significant	significant
Income	ns	significant[d]	ns	ns
Social class	ns	ns	ns	ns
Economic activity[c]	significant[e]	significant[f]	significant	significant[f]
Education	ns	ns	ns	ns
Ethnic group	ns	significant[g]	ns	ns
Supply effects	ns	ns	significant[h]	ns

Notes: [a]Curvilinear relationship with age, depending on gender and on type of health care.
[b]Individuals living in a "healthier" environment have fewer GP consultations.
[c](Overall) significant effects of going to school, permanent long-term sickness, retired, temporary sickness: suggest that health variables are not sufficient.
[d]High-income people have a larger probability of outpatient visits.
[e]Individuals looking for paid work have fewer GP consultations.
[f]Individuals looking after the home have fewer outpatient visits and more inpatient stays.
[g]Fewer outpatient visits for Pakistani, Bangladeshi, Chinese ethnic groups.
[h]More day case treatment when more GPs per 1,000 patients.

context is that two individuals with the *same morbidity* receive different amounts of care. In this interpretation, the message of Table 16.1 seems clear. Since, after controlling for a large set of health variables, socioeconomic and ethnic variables still influence health care use, there was horizontal inequity in the NHS in the period 1998–2000. This is further corroborated by the significant supply effect in the regression for day care treatment. Yet some tricky questions remain. Socioeconomic and ethnic variables may capture to some extent differences in preferences. Are differences in use inequitable if they simply reflect choices by the patients? Is it possible to identify with real-world data differences in preferences versus differences in needs?

Suppose we have reached agreement about these questions and accept that the significant effects found for many non-need variables indicate that there is horizontal inequity in the system. There then still remains the methodological question of deriving a measure that would allow us to rank different situations with respect to the *degree* of horizontal inequity. What weight should be given to the different components of inequity? As the example shows, there are two different issues here. First, the pattern of inequity is different for different health care items. How to aggregate these? Can the fact that people of Pakistani origin go more often to the GP compensate for the fact that they have a smaller probability of outpatient visits? Simply taking total health care expenditures may be a very rough indicator. Second, how to bring together different forms of inequity, e.g. socioeconomic inequality, ethnic disparities and regional (supply-side) differences? Focusing on one of these forms leads to partial indicators, which may be very useful in their own right, but also raises new questions. Suppose we want to measure socioeconomic inequity in health care use. Should we derive our measure from a regression including all other variables as controls? Assume (realistically) that there is a positive relationship between supply and socioeconomic status (SES) of individuals, in that lower SES individuals live in regions with more limited supply. Would it then still be acceptable to control for supply-side differences? Or should we include them in our measure of socioeconomic inequity? If yes, how?

Until now we focused on horizontal inequity. Another issue is the one of *vertical equity*, which would be attained when "individuals with different levels of need consume appropriately different amounts of health care" (Morris et al., 2005, p. 1251). It is clear that estimation results such as the ones summarized in Table 16.1 only show the *observed* relationship between health status and health care use, and that there is no guarantee at all that this observed relationship is equitable. The problem of vertical equity is underexplored in the empirical literature, mainly because it requires answering the vexing question of what are "appropriate different amounts of health care" (but see Sutton, 2002). This may seem an almost unsolvable medical question, but things are even worse: giving an appropriate answer requires going beyond the health setting in the narrow sense, as it unavoidably raises the issue of the optimal trade-off between health and other dimensions of well-being. Surely, in a world with scarce resources, defining appropriate amounts of health care at different levels of need cannot boil down to giving everybody the best care that is technically possible.

The Morris et al. (2005) example focused on inequity and inequality in the use of health care, but it should be clear that analogous questions arise with respect to inequality and inequity in health. We mentioned already that health inequalities are also influenced by a host of different factors, some of which may be seen as perfectly legitimate. Moreover, health can also be measured on different dimensions. In fact, measuring health is more difficult than measuring health care use and we will see that this may complicate the evaluation of the degree of inequity. Finally, a broader perspective on health inequity certainly forces us to look at the broader picture of overall well-being.

All the questions that we have introduced here have cropped up in the recent literature on inequity in health and health care. This will become clear in section 3, in which we give an overview of the most popular "partial" approaches, focusing on socioeconomic inequities and on racial disparities. We will then introduce in section 4 the social choice approach to fair allocation and equality of opportunity and show how it may offer a theoretically integrated framework to answer these various questions in a coherent way. Section 5 focuses on the broader relationship between health care, health and well-being, and about its implications for measuring inequity. Section 6 concludes.

3. SOCIOECONOMIC INEQUITY AND RACIAL DISPARITIES IN HEALTH AND HEALTH CARE

The example in the previous section suggests that inequity in health (care) is inherently a multidimensional phenomenon. However, up to now, the literature has focused on partial indicators which are specifically meant to measure the influence of a certain individual or group characteristic (income, socioeconomic status, race, gender) on some variable of interest (health, health care). Such a partial approach requires less information than a complete multidimensional approach. More importantly, it can also be justified with the argument that policy makers and citizens seem to be strongly interested in these more specific questions. Two topics have been particularly salient. In subsection 3.1 we discuss the booming literature on "socioeconomic" inequities in health (care), which has been dominated by the concept of the concentration index. In subsection 3.2 we introduce the issue of racial (or gender) disparities. Since race and gender are discrete variables, the concentration curve approach cannot be applied and other methods have been proposed and implemented.

3.1. Socioeconomic Inequalities in Health and Health Care: The Concentration Curve and Index

The concentration curve and the concentration index have become the workhorses for a large and rapidly growing empirical literature on socioeconomic inequalities in health and health care. Papers measuring concentration dominated the chapter by Wagstaff and van Doorslaer (2000b) and more recent developments are the topic of the recent survey by van Doorslaer and Van Ourti (2011). The World Bank has published a practical guide, covering the most important theoretical issues related to the approach with a focus on implementation (O'Donnell et al., 2008). We will not duplicate these comprehensive surveys and rather cover the main methodological developments and questions. This will pave the way for the introduction of the equality of opportunity approach in section 4. We first give in subsection 3.1.1 a brief overview of the main normative presuppositions behind the concentration index. We will then comment (subsection 3.1.2) on the measurement issues that are related to the specific nature of the health variables. Finally we will argue in subsection 3.1.3 that the decomposition of the overall effect, which has become rather popular in recent applications, confronts us directly with the questions previewed in the previous section.

3.1.1. Principles

Let us briefly recall the basic rationale for the concentration index as a measure of socioeconomic inequality in health and health care. In the light of the ideas from the previous section, this is a partial approach aiming at measuring only the inequity resulting from inequalities between different socioeconomic groups. The measure can be applied to any indicator of socioeconomic status, provided it is possible to rank the individuals unambiguously from low to high SES. In fact, different indicators may give different results and the choice between them is an open issue that we will leave aside in this chapter. For convenience, we focus on income I. Let us denote the relevant outcome by y (we will use h when we refer exclusively to health and hc when we refer exclusively to health care). As an example, Figure 16.1 (taken from Wagstaff and van Doorslaer, 2000a) shows a concentration curve for medical care $L_M(R)$, plotting the cumulative proportion of medical care against the cumulative proportion of population ranked by socioeconomic status (here I). If the concentration curve coincides with the diagonal, there is no socioeconomic inequality. If the curve lies below (above) the diagonal there is inequity in favor of the better-off (worse-off). Inequity in favor of the rich means that the rich have relatively better outcomes than the poor.

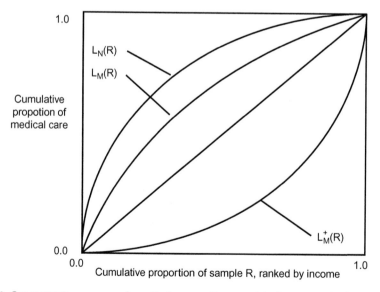

Figure 16.1 Concentration curves of medical care—direct and indirect standardization (Wagstaff and van Doorslaer, 2000a).

It is clear that the distance between the concentration curve and the diagonal gives us an idea about the degree of inequity. This intuition is captured by the concentration index (CI), which is defined as twice the area between the concentration curve and the diagonal, or

$$CI(y) = 1 - 2 \int_0^1 L_y(r) dr. \tag{1}$$

With a discrete number of individuals n, this can be shown to be equal to:

$$CI(y) = \frac{1}{n\mu(y)} \sum_{i=1}^{n} \left[y_i \left(2r_i^I - \frac{n+1}{n} \right) \right], \tag{2}$$

where $\mu(y)$ is the average value of y_i and r_i^I is the fractional rank of individual i in the distribution of I. The concentration index $CI(y)$ lies between -1 and $+1$. It takes positive (negative) values when the concentration curve lies below (above) the diagonal. This means that a positive (negative) value corresponds to inequalities favoring the rich (poor). Note that the concentration curve can cross the diagonal. Therefore $CI(y)$ can be 0, even if there are socioeconomic inequalities, provided inequalities in different parts of the distribution go in different directions and exactly compensate each other.

As (2) shows, the concentration index depends mainly on the covariance between y_i and r_i.[3] It is therefore proportional to the coefficient of the linear regression of y_i on r_i^I. More precisely, regressing the function

$$\frac{2\sigma_r^2}{\mu(y)} y_i = \alpha + \beta r_i^I + \varepsilon_i, \tag{3}$$

where σ_r^2 is the variance of r_i^I, one obtains an estimated $\hat{\beta}$ which is by construction equal to the concentration index (Kakwani et al., 1997). This is a convenient way to calculate the concentration index and to check its statistical properties.

This approach can be used immediately to measure socioeconomic inequalities in health (h), and the concentration index will then measure inequity if one accepts that all such socioeconomic health inequalities are illegitimate. We will return to this assumption later on, but let us for the moment assume that they are.[4] As argued before, however, for medical care hardly anybody thinks that it should be equal for all citizens. Consider again the concentration curve for medical care $L_M(R)$ in Figure 16.1. The curve shows that the poor consume relatively more health care, but this is not

---

[3] Inspired by Milanovic (1997), Koolman and van Doorslaer (2004) show that the concentration index depends on the coefficient of variation of y and on the correlation between y and the fractional rank.

[4] Note that socioeconomic inequality in health (as measured by the concentration index) does not coincide with inequality in health. See, e.g., Wagstaff and van Doorslaer (2004).

necessarily inequitable if they are more needy. Two approaches have been proposed in the literature to implement a correction for differences in health status (Wagstaff and van Doorslaer, 2000a). Let us assume for simplicity that we can write health care as a function of needs N and socioeconomic status SES, i.e. $hc_i = f(N_i, SES_i)$, neglecting all other variables. The first method is direct standardization, by which one calculates for each individual how much medical care she would have received if she had been in the same degree of need as the sample as a whole, i.e. $hc_i^+ = f(\overline{N}, SES_i)$, where $\overline{N}$ is average need in the sample. These recalculated health care levels hc^+ then can be used to construct the concentration curve $L_M^+(R)$ in Figure 16.1 and to calculate the corresponding concentration index $C^{DIR}(hc) = C(hc^+)$. The second method is indirect standardization. This considers the hypothetical situation indicating for each individual the amount of medical care she would have received if she had been treated like others with the same need characteristics, i.e. $f(N_i, \overline{SES})$, where $\overline{SES}$ is average SES in the sample. The "inequity" suffered by individual i can then be measured as $f(N_i, SES_i) - f(N_i, \overline{SES})$. In terms of the concentration curves, the overall evaluation will be based on a comparison of $L_M(R)$ with the needs concentration curve $L_N(R)$, where the latter is the concentration curve of $f(N_i, \overline{SES})$, i.e. of indirectly standardized medical care. The relevant concentration index $C^{IND}(hc)$ is twice the area between $L_N(R)$ and $L_M(R)$ and all the formulae can be adjusted in a straightforward way.

The CI approach is a convenient way to measure socioeconomic inequity in health and health care. Of course, it is only intended to be a partial approach, neglecting other relevant inequities in society. Taking this limitation for granted, what are its main normative presuppositions? First, defining inequity as twice the area between the concentration curve and the diagonal implies a specific weighting pattern. As (2) shows, $CI(y)$ is a weighted sum of shares with weights equal to $2r_i^I - \frac{n+1}{n}$. Although these weights are also those of the popular Gini index of income inequality, they remain arbitrary. Therefore, Wagstaff (2002) proposed a natural generalization of $CI(y)$, which is analogous to the extended Gini index:

$$ECI(y) = \frac{1}{n\mu(y)} \sum_{i=1}^{n} \left\{ y_i[1 - v(1 - r_i^I)^{v-1}] \right\}, \tag{4}$$

where the parameter v captures inequality aversion. If $v = 1$, there is no inequality aversion and $ECI(y) = 0$. For $v = 2$, we recover the standard concentration index in the case of large n. This extension has not been frequently used in the applied literature.

Second, deeper doubts with respect to both the concentration index and its generalizations have been brought to the fore by Fleurbaey (2006) and Bleichrodt and van Doorslaer (2006). Focusing on socioeconomic inequality in health (rather than in health care), Bleichrodt and van Doorslaer (2006) show that the social welfare function underlying the generalized concentration index is characterized by a set of conditions, including anonymity and what they call the principle of income-related health transfers.[5] *Anonymity* implies that the only characteristics that are allowed to influence social welfare judgments are the individual's health and her rank in terms of SES. This reflects the partial nature of the approach, but in this explicit formulation it is obviously very restrictive. The *principle of income-related health transfers* states that transferring health from someone who is better off in terms of SES to someone who is worse off in terms of SES does not lead to a reduction in social welfare. As Bleichrodt and van Doorslaer (2006, p. 955) emphasize, this principle is not very plausible. "It does not seem desirable to transfer health from a person with high living standards to a person with lower living standards when the person with high living standards is in poor health and differences in living standards are small." In fact, both conditions throw a sharp light on the limitations of the CI approach. These issues will be taken up again in sections 4 and 5. For the moment, we will remain within the CI framework.

3.1.2. Measurement Issues

As mentioned before, the original work on the CI took its inspiration mainly from the literature on measuring income inequality. Income is an unbounded variable that is measured at the ratio level. The same is true for health care expenditures and the whole apparatus of income inequality measurement can therefore be applied to health care without much of a problem. However, the measurement of health is less clear and recently there has been some debate on how to take account of the measurement characteristics of the health variable within the framework of the CI approach.[6]

The CI approach should only be used with variables measured on a ratio scale, i.e. when there is a natural zero. Take the case of SAH (subjectively assessed health), which has been a popular health indicator in applied work. Since this is a categorical measure, authors have tried in the past to map a cardinal scale on the categories. A good example is the paper by van Doorslaer and Jones (2003). They estimate an ordered probit model with SAH as the dependent variable and specify the underlying latent variable y_i^* as a function of a vector of socioeconomic characteristics, i.e. $y_i^* = x_i\beta + \varepsilon_i$ with $\varepsilon_i \sim N(0, 1)$. They then use as a measure of individual

[5] Other less disputable conditions used in the characterization are (1) *monotonicity* (if everybody's health increases, social welfare increases), (2) *the existence for each health profile of an equally distributed equivalent level of health*, and (3) *additivity* (take three ordered health vectors *h*, *h'* and *h"*. Then *h* is socially preferred to *h'* if and only if *h + h"* is socially preferred to *h' + h"*.) To characterize the CI (rather than the ECI) the principle of income-related health transfers has to be strengthened further to get at the specific weighting structure embodied in (2).

[6] Note that for application of the CI, it is sufficient to *rank* all individuals according to SES, i.e. for the SES variable an ordinal measurement is sufficient.

health the predictions of the linear index $x_i\beta$ after rescaling. However, as emphasized by Erreygers and Van Ourti (2010), this rescaling procedure is not innocuous, because the calculated CI will depend on the chosen zero point. If there is a natural zero point, health can be measured on a ratio scale and there is no problem. If there is no natural zero point, one should check the robustness of one's conclusions, e.g. for some comparison of distributions, with respect to the choice of zero. If the conclusions remain the same for all plausible values of the zero, there is no need to worry. Otherwise, it is necessary to specify exactly the range for which they hold.

Things get more complicated if the range of the health variable is bounded, i.e. if $h^{\min} \leq h_i \leq h^{\max}$ where both $h^{\min}$ and $h^{\max}$ are finite. Wagstaff (2005) noted that for binary health indicators (e.g. surviving yes or no), the theoretical bounds of the CI depend on the bounds of the health variable (in the example 0 and 1) and on the mean. This complicates the comparison of the results for different populations. Clarke et al. (2002) pointed to another issue. For any bounded health variable it is natural to define a corresponding ill-health variable as the shortfall

$$s_i = h^{\max} - h_i. \tag{5}$$

Take as an example chronic malnutrition of children as measured by stunting. We then can define either an individual 0-1 health variable taking the value 1 if the child is not stunted, or a 0-1 ill-health variable taking the value 1 if the child does suffer from chronic malnutrition. The choice between the two is essentially arbitrary, and it seems desirable that the evaluation of socioeconomic inequality would be consistent whether working with health or with ill-health. However, the results with the CI will be sensitive to this choice.

These problems were taken up and analyzed in an integrated approach by Erreygers (2009a and b) and Erreygers and Van Ourti (2010). They focus exclusively on the family of rank-dependent measures for bounded variables, represented by

$$I(y) = f(y^{\min}, y^{\max}, \mu(y), n) \sum_{i=1}^{n} z_i y_i, \tag{6}$$

where $z_i = n\left(r_i^I - \frac{n+1}{2n}\right)$, $y = h, s$ and $f(\cdot)$ is a continuous function. If y is unbounded, $f(\cdot)$ reduces to $f(\mu(y), n)$. It is easy to see that $CI(h)\left(= [2/(n^2\mu(h))]\sum_{i=1}^{n} z_i h_i\right)$ is a special case of (6). Erreygers and Van Ourti (2010) argue that an attractive rank-dependent index of socioeconomic inequality in health $I(y)$ should satisfy at least two conditions. The first is *scale invariance*: the index should be invariant to positive affine (linear) transformations of the distribution of health, if the latter is measured on a cardinal (ratio) scale. The second one is the *mirror* condition. If h is a given health distribution and s its associated ill-health distribution, then applying the index should yield consistent results in both cases, i.e., $I(h) = -I(s)$.[7] It is then shown that the following parametric subclass of the rank-dependent indices (6) satisfies both conditions:

$$I^\theta(h) = \frac{8}{n^2[4\mu(h^*)(1 - \mu(h^*))]^\theta} \sum_{i=1}^{n} z_i h_i^*, \tag{7}$$

where $h_i^* = (h_i - h^{min})/(h^{max} - h^{min})$. Note that the CI and the ECI are not included in the family (7). Indeed, the CI satisfies neither scale invariance nor mirror; the ECI is not scale invariant. The family does include a generalization of the proposal made by Wagstaff (2005) for $\theta = 1$. It also includes the index proposed by Erreygers (2009a and b) himself for $\theta = 0$.

The interpretation of the parameter θ is essential. Erreygers (2009b) and Erreygers and Van Ourti (2010) show that a scale-invariant rank-dependent index cannot satisfy at the same time the mirror property and measure only relative inequality, i.e. satisfy the condition that $I(y) = I(ry)$ when $0 < r < 1$. They then suggest that it is desirable for a rank-dependent index to give some weight to absolute inequality, i.e. to satisfy the condition that, for $0 < r < 1$: (1) if $I(y) > 0$, then $0 < I(ry) < I(y)$; (2) if $I(y) < 0$, then $I(y) < I(ry) < 0$; and (3) if $I(y) = 0$, then $I(ry) = I(y)$. For the parametric class of indices (7), absolute inequality will matter if $0 \leq \theta \leq 1$. The Wagstaff and Erreygers measures therefore are at the two extremes. For both a reasonable interpretation can be given.

Erreygers (2009b) and Erreygers and Van Ourti (2010) propose to impose a *convergence* property stating that $\lim_{r \to 0} I(rh) = 0$ (for h being a given distribution). For the parametric class in (7), this property will only hold if $\theta < 1$, i.e. it does not hold for the Wagstaff index. Moreover, if one imposes also a *linearity* condition ($I(ry) = rI(y)$ for $0 \leq r < 1$), θ has to be equal to 0, i.e. one ends up with the Erreygers index. The normative justification for this linearity condition is not very clear, however. Moreover, one can also wonder whether the convergence property is necessarily appealing. Is there really a problem with a discontinuity at $r = 0$? Wagstaff (2009) argues in favor of his own normalization on the basis of the following hypothetical example. Suppose for convenience that maximal health involves a health score of 1 and minimal health a score of 0. Suppose that in the initial situation the mean is 0.1 and that there are 100 individuals involved. The most pro-rich distribution possible is one where the richest 10 people have a health score of 1 and all the others have a health score of 0.

---

[7] The distinction between "achievement" and "shortfall" inequality is also relevant in the context of pure (rather than socioeconomic) health inequality. In this context, Erreygers (2009c) derives two inequality indices—variations of the absolute Gini coefficient and the coefficient of variation—that satisfy his "mirror" condition that inequality of attainments and inequality of shortfalls are cardinally identical, i.e. $I(h) = -I(s)$. This mirror condition is very strong and a more natural "consistency" requirement would be that the ranking of distributions of h should be the same as the ranking of distributions of s. However, Lambert and Zheng (2011) show that (for a much larger class of inequality indices) all indices satisfying this weaker consistency condition also satisfy Erreygers's strong mirror condition.

Table 16.2 Socioeconomic Inequalities in Stunting, Calculated with Different Measures

Country	$\mu(s)$	$-C(s)$	$C(h)$	$W(h)$	$E(h)$
Malawi 2000	0.4902	0.0756	0.0727	0.1483	0.1482
Ethiopia 2000	0.4730	0.0390	0.0350	0.0740	0.0738
Cameroon 2004	0.3165	0.1698	0.0786	0.2484	0.2150
Guinea 1999	0.2607	0.1067	0.0376	0.1443	0.1113
Haiti 2000	0.0797	0.2154	0.0187	0.2341	0.0687
Paraguay 1990	0.0394	0.3216	0.0132	0.3348	0.0507
Colombia 2005	0.0215	0.2699	0.0059	0.2758	0.0232

Countries are ranked in decreasing order of the prevalence of stunting ($\mu(s)$ being the mean). Stunting is a dummy variable. The different columns correspond respectively to minus the concentration index of stunting ($-C(s)$), the concentration index of non-stunting ($C(h)$), the Wagstaff index for non-stunting ($W(h)$), and the Erreygers index for non-stunting ($E(h)$).
Source: Erreygers (2009a).

Now suppose that mean health increases to 0.2. Then the most pro-rich health distribution would be one where the richest 20 people have health 1 and everyone else has zero health. Since in both these distributions maximum inequality is reached, it seems natural to say that they are just as unequal from a pro-rich perspective and should therefore give the same value to the index. The Wagstaff index ($\theta = 1$) satisfies this intuition, the Erreygers index ($\theta = 0$) does not.

Ultimately (and not surprisingly) the choice between the different indices boils down to an ethical choice between different normative ideas. That the choice does matter, however, is illustrated in Table 16.2 (which is a selection taken from Table 16.1 in Erreygers, 2009a). The table gives the results for socioeconomic inequality in stunting as calculated with different indices for various countries and time periods. If the prevalence of stunting is close to the middle of $h^{\min}$ and $h^{\max}$, $C(h)$ and $-C(s)$ are close to each other, and the same is true for the Wagstaff index $W(h)$ and the Erreygers index $E(h)$. However, for countries with a low prevalence of stunting the Wagstaff index gives much larger values than the Erreygers index (and is in effect close to $-C(s)$). This is of course the empirical illustration of the convergence properties that have been described before. Choosing a specific member of the family of rank-dependent indices (6) is not without consequences.

3.1.3. Developments in the Empirical Literature

As the measurement issues raised in the previous section have only appeared in the literature recently, they have not yet had much influence on applied work. This applied literature is rapidly growing. As van Doorslaer and Van Ourti (2011) have given a comprehensive overview of empirical results and of policy implications, we will only focus on what seem to be three important developments.

First, while the empirical applications of the CI approach initially focused on European and North American countries, there is now also an extensive coverage of developing countries (see, among others, Cisse et al., 2007; Lu et al., 2007; O'Donnell et al., 2008; Schneider and Hanson, 2006; Van de Poel et al., 2007; Wagstaff, 2000). The specific features of these countries have led to a growing interest in the link between health care and poverty. We will return to this link in section 5.

Second, from a methodological perspective, it is worth pointing to the growing popularity of decomposition methods. Wagstaff et al. (2003) have shown that, if the relevant outcome y can be written as a linear function of a set of characteristics x, i.e.

$$y_i = \beta_0 + \sum_{j=1}^{K} \beta_j x_{ij} + \varepsilon_i, \tag{8}$$

then the concentration index $CI(y)$ can be decomposed as

$$CI(y) = \sum_{j=1}^{K} \eta_j CI(x_j) + \frac{2 \, \text{cov}(\varepsilon_i, r_i^I)}{\mu(y)}, \tag{9}$$

where $\eta_j = \beta_j \mu(x_j)/\mu(y)$. Equation (9) shows that the effect of any variable x_j on $CI(y)$ will depend both on its own concentration index (or, if x_j is the SES indicator itself, its Gini coefficient) and on the "elasticity" η_j of y with respect to x_j.

This decomposition approach has been used to interpret differences in the concentration index between different countries or changes over time.[8] Indeed, the linear structure of (9) makes it possible to decompose changes and differences in the concentration index as in Oaxaca (1973) and Blinder (1973). Neglecting for convenience the last term in (9), the difference between two situations 1 and 2 can be written as

$$CI^1(y) - CI^2(y) = \sum_{j=1}^{K} \eta_j^1 [CI^1(x_j) - CI^2(x_j)] + \sum_{j=1}^{K} CI^2(x_j)[\eta_j^1 - \eta_j^2]. \tag{10}$$

Good examples for health and health care respectively are van Doorslaer and Koolman (2004) and van Doorslaer et al. (2004), both making use of data from the European Community Household Panel. In the case of socioeconomic inequalities in health, van Doorslaer and Koolman (2004) show that these are particularly high in Portugal, the UK, and Denmark. Demographic variables are part of the "explanation," but other important factors are income, education, labor force status, and region. The somewhat surprising result for Denmark is ascribed to the fact that the early retired in Denmark have much worse health and are strongly concentrated among the low-income groups. As to income-related inequalities in doctor utilization, van Doorslaer et al. (2004) point out that there is substantial pro-rich inequity in virtually every country

---

[8] Jones and Lopez-Nicolas (2004) have used a similar approach to decompose long-run socioeconomic inequality as a weighted sum of short-run concentration indices (and a term capturing mobility). See Allanson et al. (2010) for a further development along this line.

with respect to the probability of seeing a medical specialist. Income, education, and region are important contributing factors. While these decomposition results give interesting insights into the pattern of socioeconomic inequalities, they should be interpreted cautiously. More specifically, the titles of both papers suggest that the decompositions give an "explanation" of the socioeconomic differences. This is misleading, however, as it mistakenly suggests that one can give a causal interpretation to (8).

The decomposition approach has also been used to tackle the standardization problem. As mentioned before, socioeconomic inequalities in health care as such are not worrying, if they reflect differences in needs. Therefore a needs correction is needed. In a similar spirit, it is common practice to standardize the health data for demographic factors before measuring socioeconomic inequalities in health, under the supposition that health differences due to age and gender do not raise an equity issue. The decomposition approach makes it possible to calculate "partial concentration indices" by putting some of the components on the RHS of (9) equal to zero (Gravelle, 2003). Let us illustrate for socioeconomic inequalities in health care. Suppose that we can partition the vector x_i between needs (or standardizing) variables n_i and non-needs variables z_i, so that we can rewrite (8) as

$$hc_i = \beta_0 + \sum_{j=1}^{L} \beta_j^n n_{ij} + \sum_{j=1}^{M} \beta_j^z z_{ij} + \varepsilon_i \qquad (11)$$

As described before, the direct standardization method puts the needs factors in (11) at a fixed value, which yields

$$hc_i^+ = \beta_0 + \sum_{j=1}^{L} \beta_j^n \overline{n}_j + \sum_{j=1}^{M} \beta_j^z z_{ij} + \varepsilon_i$$

and, therefore,

$$CI^{DIR}(hc) = CI(hc^+) = \sum_{j=1}^{M} \eta_j^z CI(z_j) + \frac{2 \, \text{cov}(\varepsilon_i, r_i^I)}{\mu(hc)}$$

In the case of indirect standardization, one first calculates a "corrected" value for health care by putting the non-needs variables in (11) at a fixed value and one then focuses on the differences between actual health care levels and these "corrected" health care levels.[9] In terms of the concentration index this yields

---

[9] Gravelle (2003) argued that the traditional method of indirect standardization suffers from omitted variables bias, since it only includes the standardizing variables in (8). This problem is easily solved, however, by including all the explanatory variables and following the procedure described in the text (see also Schokkaert and Van de Voorde, 2004, 2009, and Fleurbaey and Schokkaert, 2009). This procedure is also followed in recent applied work on socioeconomic inequalities in health and health care.

$$CI^{IND}(hc) = CI(hc) - \sum_{j=1}^{L} \eta_j^n CI(n_j) = \sum_{j=1}^{M} \eta_j^z CI(z_j) + \frac{2\,\text{cov}(\varepsilon_i, r_i^I)}{\mu(hc)}$$

It turns out that the direct and indirect standardization methods in this case coincide. This is due to the additive separability between the variables n_i and z_i, that is implied by the linearity assumption in (11). Direct and indirect standardization will give different results if there are what Gravelle (2003) calls essential non-linearities, i.e. if the marginal effect on health care of the z variables depends on the values taken by the needs variables (Gravelle, 2003). The easy decomposition approach, however, crucially hinges on the linearity assumption.

Third, on the econometric side, panel data have been used to capture unobserved heterogeneity. There has been a move towards the estimation of complex non-linear models that are better able to capture the specific nature of the dependent variables (e.g. a random effects count data model in Van Ourti, 2004, or a latent class hurdle model in Bago d'Uva et al., 2009). The simple linear decomposition methods can then no longer be applied. Approximation methods have been proposed, but these are (by definition) only approximations and considerably complicate the interpretation of the error term (van Doorslaer et al., 2004).

In the literature on the CI, these issues have sometimes been seen as statistical problems. However, as we have argued in the example from the previous section, distinguishing needs and non-needs variables in (8) ultimately boils down to the normative judgment that differences in health care, due to differences in needs, are ethically legitimate. In the same way demographic standardization in the health case implies that socioeconomic differences in health due to differences in demographics are not inequitable. This suggests that one should broaden the approach and ask for each factor in (8) whether it leads to legitimate or illegitimate differences. As a matter of fact, this immediately raises the question why we should then keep focusing on socioeconomic inequalities only. We will continue that discussion in the next section, where we will propose to start from recent developments in the social choice theory on fair allocation and equality of opportunity. We will then also return to some of the empirical applications that have been mentioned in this subsection.

3.2. Racial Disparities in Health Care

While the literature on socioeconomic inequalities is dominated by European authors, in the US there has been much interest in the measurement of racial disparities (inequities) in health care. This is again a partial approach, focusing only on one possible dimension of inequity. The concentration index method is obviously not applicable, since race is a categorical variable without a natural order. Still, as we will see, the questions that have to be answered when measuring racial disparities are related to the issues raised in the previous section. We will first discuss the principles and then briefly describe some empirical applications.

As the literature on racial disparities focuses on health care, we will do the same in this section. A similar approach could be developed to measure disparities in health, however. Moreover, the methods described in this section can also be applied for measuring other disparities linked to a discrete variable, e.g. gender.

3.2.1. Principles

For simplicity, focus on the case of two groups, Black and White. An immediate indicator of inequality in the use of health care would be $\mu^W(hc) - \mu^B(hc)$, which is simply the difference in mean health care expenditures for Whites and Blacks. However, for the reasons described before, this difference does not necessarily point to any inequity, e.g. if there are differences in needs between Whites and Blacks. Obviously, a needs correction is necessary before we can talk about an inequitable "disparity." Yet, as illustrated by Table 16.1, health service utilization is determined by many other variables apart from race and needs. The partial nature of the approach raises the question of how these other variables have to be treated.

Let us distinguish four sets of variables: race (R_i, a dummy variable taking the value 1 for Whites), health care needs (hn_i), socioeconomic status (SES_i), and preferences (P_i). The latter three can be vectors of indicators. Socioeconomic status variables may include income, education, region, and so on. Health care needs can be approximated by direct measures of health and by demographic variables such as age and sex. The basic issue of how to measure inequitable disparity can then be most easily illustrated for the case in which an additively separable function describes the link between these sets of variables:[10]

$$hc_i = \alpha + \beta R_i + \gamma \psi(SES_i) + \delta \chi(hn_i) + \theta v(P_i) + \varepsilon_i, \qquad (12)$$

where ε_i is a disturbance term.

A natural measure of racial disparity in health care seems to be the estimated parameter $\hat{\beta}$, i.e. the average difference in health care between Whites and Blacks after having corrected for *all* the variables in (12). However, restricting ourselves to $\hat{\beta}$ means that we not only correct for the differences in needs hn_i, but also for the differences in socioeconomic status. This is a debatable approach. Suppose (realistically) that Blacks are overrepresented in lower SES groups and that SES also leads to differences in health care (even after correcting for needs): should this

---

[10] This is a slight extension of the linear equations (8) and (11) that were introduced in our discussion of the CI approach. In this case also, equation (12) is to be interpreted as a reduced form.

indirect effect through SES not be taken into account in measuring overall racial disparity?

The US Institute of Medicine (IOM) defines disparities in health care as "...racial or ethnic differences in the quality of health care that are not due to access-related factors or clinical needs, preferences and appropriateness of intervention" (Institute of Medicine, 2002, p. 32). This definition gives an explicit list of "legitimate" reasons for differences (needs and preferences), implying that the contribution of other factors (such as SES) to health care differences is illegitimate and should be included when measuring disparity. Implementing this definition requires constructing a counterfactual situation in which Blacks and Whites have the same health status (and preferences) but differ in SES. This yields two possible measures of disparity. The first takes the Black consumption of health care as reference and computes

$$dis = E(hc_i | R = 1, SES = W, hn = B, P = B) - E(hc_i | B), \tag{13}$$

where $E(hc_i | R = 1, SES = W, hn = B, P = B)$ is a shorthand expression for average health care in the counterfactual situation of White race, the White distribution of SES, the Black distribution of health care needs, and the Black distribution of preferences. The expression $E(hc_i | B)$ stands for average health care for the Black. The second measure, taking the White consumption as the reference, yields

$$dis^* = E(hc_i | W) - E(hc_i | R = 0, SES = B, hn = W, P = W). \tag{14}$$

There are no obvious theoretical reasons to choose between these two definitions, although one might claim that the former is perhaps a bit more politically relevant as it shows the difference between the Black health care consumption and their hypothetical consumption if there were no inequity. The distinction does not matter in the additively separable case, for which the two definitions coincide. In this case, racial disparity can be computed easily as it only requires information about the means of the distributions of the explanatory variables:

$$dis = dis^* = \hat{\beta} + \hat{\gamma} \, (E(\psi(SES_i) | W) - E(\psi(SES_i) | B)). \tag{15}$$

The interpretation is straightforward. Racial disparity is the sum of the "direct" effect of race $\hat{\beta}$ and the indirect effect that works through the difference in average SES (multiplied by the effect $\hat{\gamma}$ of SES on health care). This approach can easily be extended to the more general case where the coefficients in (12) are different for Blacks and Whites:

$$hc_i = \alpha + \beta R_i + (\gamma + \mu R_i) \, \psi \, (SES_i) + (\delta + \eta R_i) \, \chi \, (N_i) + (\theta + \tau R_i) v(P_i) + \varepsilon_i, \tag{16}$$

for which we get (applying as in (10) the Blinder–Oaxaca decomposition)

$$dis = \hat{\beta} + \hat{\gamma}(E(\psi(SES_i)|W) - E(\psi(SES_i)|B))$$
$$+ \hat{\mu}E\,(\psi(SES_i)|W) + \hat{\eta}E\,(\chi(N_i)|B) + \hat{\tau}E(\nu(P_i)|B).$$

The additional terms capture the fact that socioeconomic status, needs, and preferences may have a different effect on health care for the White and for the Black.

The calculation of racial disparities becomes much more tricky, however, as soon as the function linking health care to race, socioeconomic status, needs, and preferences is not additively separable. Information about the means of the distributions is then no longer sufficient to compute the relevant counterfactual situation. In fact, there are different possibilities to set up the counterfactual. Moreover, the two approaches (leading to *dis* and *dis**) are no longer equivalent. Cook et al. (2009) have proposed two interesting measures for this case. For ease of exposition, we neglect the effect of preferences and we assume that *SES* and *hn* are unidimensional (i.e. real numbers). The measure *dis** in (14)[11] can then be written as

$$E(hc_i|W) - \int\int hc(B, SES, hn) f^*(SES, hn)\, dSESdhn, \qquad (17)$$

with a fictitious distribution f^* that has the same marginal for *SES* as the Black and the same marginal for *hn* as the White. Different methods of calculating disparities boil down to different specifications of f^*.

One method, the *rank and replace* method, adjusts health status (needs) by ranking both the sample of Blacks and that of Whites by the values of *hn* and then replacing the value of *hn* of each Black individual with that of the correspondingly ranked White individual. Formally this means that one formulates *hn* as a function of race and percentile, $\eta(R_i, \pi_i)$, where π_i is the percentile of the individual in the distribution of *hn* for his racial group. In order to calculate *dis** one then replaces hn_i for every Black by $\eta(W, \pi_i)$. Disparity can then be computed as

$$E(hc_i|W) - \int\int hc(B, SES, \eta(W,\pi)) f(SES, \pi|B)\, dSESd\pi, \qquad (18)$$

which is equivalent to (17) with

$$f^*(SES, hn) = f(SES, F(hn|W)|B) f(hn|W),$$

where $F\,(hn|W)$ is the conditional CDF of *hn,* i.e. is the solution π to the equation $\eta(W, \pi) = hn$.

---

[11] Cook et al. (2009) focus on the other case with Black consumption as the reference. We have swapped the role of *B* and *W* here, for convenience.

The other method proposed in Cook et al. (2009) combines a rank and replace method with a correction by *propensity scores*. The first step is the construction with propensity scores of the following artificial distribution:

$$f(SES, hn|W)\frac{f(SES|B)}{f(SES|W)} = f(hn|SES, W)f(SES|B),$$

which automatically gives the marginal distribution of the Black for *SES*. However, this first correction is not sufficient as it does not yield the White marginal distribution of *hn*. Therefore, in a second step the rank and replace method is applied, and one then computes disparity as

$$E(hc_i|W) - \int hc\,(B, SES, \eta(W, F_0(hn)))f(hn|SES, W)f(SES|B)\,dSESdhn,$$

where $F_0(hn) = \int F(hn|SES, W)\,f(SES|B)\,dSES$.

It is not obvious how to choose between these two approaches. We will see in the next subsection that they may give similar results when applied to empirical data but this is no more than a convenient answer. We discuss some deeper normative questions in the following section.

At a more general level, the partial approach to measuring racial disparities raises similar questions as the ones we formulated already with respect to the use of the concentration index. First, why only focus on racial disparities? If racial differences mediated by socioeconomic differences are ethically illegitimate, then surely the same must be true for socioeconomic differences in health care use themselves, again of course after correcting for differences in needs. In this respect, Kawachi et al. (2005) argue that "race" and "class" should be seen as separate constructs and that an adequate measurement of inequity should explicitly analyze their independent and interactive effects. They emphasize that making race a highly visible feature of economic policy has the consequence (in their political analysis even the goal) of hiding or disguising class differences. As will become clear later on, we agree that one should take a broad view of (in)equity, integrating different dimensions. Even in such a broad approach, however, it can make sense to focus on the specific effects of one indicator, e.g. to focus on racial disparities. The question then remains how to integrate such a partial indicator in the overall picture. *A priori*, it is not impossible that policy measures lowering racial disparities lead to an increase of the overall inequity of the system.

Second, and related to the first question: Why concentrate on the differences in the means? If one is exclusively interested in the overall health care disparity between two well-defined groups such a focus on the difference in the means seems natural. However, in a broader perspective, it can hide substantial differences in the degree of inequitable treatment within each of the groups. The same average difference can follow from an almost uniform difference between Blacks and Whites in all regions of a country and across socioeconomic positions, but it may also be the case that some groups of Blacks are treated reasonably well, while for other groups the situation is extremely bad. It seems worthwhile to develop a richer approach that is able to accommodate such within-group inequalities.

3.2.2. Empirical Applications

The overall message of the extensive literature on racial and other health disparities in the US is clear. A detailed overview of the results, including an extensive list of references, can be found in the yearly National Healthcare Disparities Report (see, e.g., Agency for Healthcare Research and Quality, 2010). Racial disparities do exist and they are to the disadvantage of minority groups such as the Blacks and the Latinos. Rather than giving a necessarily incomplete overview of that literature, we will focus as before on some important methodological developments and questions.

First, it is essential to see if the different methods presented in the previous subsection indeed lead to different results. Some representative results from Cook et al. (2009) for Black–White disparities in total medical expenditures (2003–2004) and from Cook et al. (2010) for Black–White disparities in mental health care (2002–2006) are summarized in Table 16.3. It is clear that the measured disparity does not simply equal the unadjusted difference and that the adjustment method does matter. Comparing the results for the first two rows shows that the unadjusted difference in total medical expenditures is larger than the coefficient of race in a linear model: this is because there is a negative correlation between SES and total medical expenditures. The opposite is true for mental health expenditures. Including the indirect effect of SES through either the rank and replace method or the refined propensity score method has a strong effect on measured disparities. In all cases racial disparities as defined before, i.e. including the indirect effect of SES, are larger than the unadjusted difference.

Second, the empirical results show how important it is to go beyond simple linear models for the explanation of health care expenditures. This not only has an effect on the measured disparity (compare the two last rows in Table 16.3 with the other rows),

Table 16.3 Black–White Disparities in Health Care and Mental Health Care

	Total Medical Expenditures (2003–2004)	Mental Health Expenditures (2002–2006)
Unadjusted difference	$1082	$57
Full adjustment (coefficient in linear model)	$489	$96
Oaxaca–Blinder decomposition	$913	**na**
Rank and replace	$1407	$83
Propensity score with rank and replace	$1454	$111

Source: Cook et al. (2009, 2010).

it also gives a richer picture of reality and makes it possible to derive more convincing policy conclusions. As an example, Cook et al. (2010) use a two-part generalized linear model to explain mental health expenditures and find that there are important Black—White disparities in reaching the first mental health visit and filling the first prescription, while there are no Black—White disparities among those using mental health care services.[12] This points out that discrimination is probably less important than barriers to entry—and suggests that policy measures should focus on the latter. Such differentiated conclusions can only be obtained when one estimates a rich explanatory model, which also means of course that one needs disparity measures that can be used with such a non-linear model. Remember that for exactly the same reason we have been critical in section 3.1.3 about the use of linear decompositions in the concentration index approach.

Third, as soon as we want to adjust differences in health care expenditures for differences in needs and preferences and we want to include at the same time the indirect effect of socioeconomic status, it is evident that the results will depend on the quality of the information on needs, preferences, and socioeconomic status. Cook et al. (2009) have a rich dataset with detailed information on medical conditions and on different dimensions of socioeconomic status (including education, income, region, the fact of being insured) and they test how robust their conclusions are when some of this information is not used. Perhaps not surprisingly, it turns out that the omission of the medical conditions has a strong (negative) effect on the calculation of racial disparities, while the use of imperfect information on socioeconomic status is less harmful. Demographic variables (such as age and gender) and self-reported health are definitely not sufficient for an adequate needs correction. Note, moreover, that using demographic variables like age and gender as needs indicators makes it difficult to analyze gender or age disparities. If a given gender or age group is discriminated against by the health care system, it will be impossible to identify this effect in a reduced model, as both this potential discrimination and the needs differences will be captured by the same coefficients.

Fourth, the missing variable in almost all of the empirical work is preferences. As mentioned before, in the definition of health care disparities by the US Institute of Medicine, preferences are explicitly mentioned as a legitimate reason for health care differences. In empirical work, however, such preference differences are impossible to identify if one does not have direct preference indicators. In general the effect of the variable "race" will therefore not only represent direct illegitimate health care disparities, but will at the same time also capture preference differences. How important are these? Ayanian et al. (1999) conducted personal interviews to collect direct information on preferences with respect to renal transplantation. They report that Black patients

---

[12] The results for the Latinos are different—see Cook et al. (2010).

were less likely than White patients to want a transplant. However, these preference differences explain only a small fraction of the racial differences in access to transplantation. Other authors have raised a series of critical questions with respect to the interpretation of what might look like preference differences (Ashton et al., 2003; Armstrong et al., 2006). They point out that different attitudes can also reflect differences in communication skills and a possible lack of concordance of the communication style of the provider with the expectations of the patients; they can reflect differences in trust in the system or the lack of adaptation of supply-side characteristics to cultural differences—some cultural preferences (those of the White middle class) are better accommodated than others, because there is a greater willingness to accommodate them. In all these cases, what seem to be preference differences are ultimately shaped by the practices of the health care system itself. The treatment of preferences raises tricky issues, which are also important from a philosophical point of view. We will discuss them further in section 4.2.

4. A MORE GENERAL APPROACH? EQUALITY OF OPPORTUNITY IN HEALTH AND HEALTH CARE

In the previous section we have reviewed partial measures of inequity focusing on the influence of one specific individual or group characteristic (income, socioeconomic status, race) on health or on health care. We have raised the point that it is important—but not straightforward—to integrate these partial approaches in a broader view on the measurement of inequity. This could also help to strengthen the links between the philosophical debate on equity and the formal approaches in the applied health economic literature. In this section we propose to relate these issues to similar considerations that have recently emerged in the subfield of normative economics that deals with the concept of equal opportunities. The connection is quite direct because the theory of equal opportunities also revolves around the goal of compensating (or neutralizing) the influence of certain characteristics (such as social background or innate talent) on a relevant outcome, while disregarding the inequalities generated by other variables (such as effort or preferences). The core of the theory is about the structure of this partial compensation problem and can be applied to many different contexts, depending on how the boundary is drawn between the variables to be compensated and the other variables. The insights obtained in this field may therefore be helpful for the study of inequalities in health and health care (see, e.g., the editorial of Rosa Dias and Jones, 2007). Indeed, the number of empirical applications of the framework is now rapidly growing, both inside and outside the health context.

We first introduce the theory of equal opportunities and examine its application to health and health care, making connections with the partial approaches described in the previous section. In the second subsection we discuss the problem of where to draw the line between "legitimate" and "illegitimate" reasons for differences in health and health care, i.e. between variables for which no compensation is needed and variables for which compensation is necessary. We illustrate this somewhat philosophical discussion for the specific case of lifestyle differences, which will confront us again with the problem of how to interpret preferences. Finally, we give an overview of the most important empirical applications of the approach in the domain of health and health care.

4.1. Equality of Opportunity and Fairness in Health and Health Care

In normative economics, the idea of equalizing opportunities has generated a literature on how to deal with the distinction between legitimate and illegitimate inequalities.[13] Assume that among the different factors leading to inequalities among individuals, some do not lead to illegitimate inequalities, while the others do. The usual motivation for such a partitioning of factors, in the context of equalizing opportunities, relates to personal responsibility. For instance, the individual's social background will typically be considered a source of illegitimate inequality, while the individual's effort may be considered a source of legitimate inequality. Throughout this subsection we will ignore the philosophical debate about the partition, however, and we will focus on the formal structure of the compensation problem. The broader debate will be taken up in the second subsection.

It is useful to set the stage with the description of the approach proposed by Roemer (1993, 1998, 2002), the most popular in applied work in health economics. Suppose that a certain variable of individual success or advantage, denoted y_i, is determined by a vector of illegitimate factors of inequality called "circumstances" and denoted c_i and a vector of legitimate factors called "effort" and denoted e_i, via some function y. This function not only incorporates the technology of production of y_i but also the prevailing institutions that organize redistribution across individuals with different characteristics:

$$y_i = y(c_i, e_i). \tag{19}$$

In Roemer's terminology, individuals with the same circumstances are defined as being of the same *type*. Roemer then claims that equality of opportunity requires that individuals at the same level of effort should attain the same level of advantage. Other things being equal, at any given effort level $\tilde{e}$, the social objective could then be to

---

[13] A survey of the literature has been made by Fleurbaey and Maniquet (2011), and comprehensive monographs have been written by Roemer (1998) and by Fleurbaey (2008).

maximize the advantage of the individual that is worst off, i.e. that has the lowest level of advantage:[14]

$$\max_{c} \min \; y(c,\tilde{e}).$$

This criterion is not complete, as one still has to aggregate over the different effort levels. Given that differences due to effort are not illegitimate from an ethical point of view, Roemer suggests that a natural aggregation method is to take simply the sum (or the mean) over the outcomes at different effort levels.

This yields the following social objective:

$$\max \int_{e} \min_{c} \; y(c,e)f(e)de, \tag{20}$$

where $f(e)$ is the density function of effort in society.

Until now we assumed that "effort" can be measured and compared between types unambiguously. This is not always evident, however. Already in an early stage of the development of his theory, Roemer (1993) used a health example to illustrate the problem. Suppose the outcome is health, there are two types (blue- and white-collar workers) and effort is given by the number of cigarettes smoked. If blue-collar workers as a group smoke more on average, it is debatable to hold individual blue-collar workers responsible for their higher level of smoking, which is ultimately a characteristic of their type. Roemer therefore proposes to define effort directly as the rank (or percentile) of individual i in the distribution of cigarettes smoked for his own type. If there is a monotonic relationship between health and number of cigarettes smoked, the rank of individual i in the distribution for his type of cigarettes smoked will be the same as his rank in the distribution of health for his type. We can then rewrite (20) as

$$\max \int_{\pi} \min_{c} \; y(c,\pi)d\pi, \tag{21}$$

where π_i is the percentile of the individual i in the conditional distribution of outcome for his type $F(y|c)$.

While the Roemer approach has become popular in applied work, it is only one among several possible approaches. It makes specific assumptions that may not always be attractive, and the literature contains a number of interesting alternatives. We will therefore first introduce a more general formal framework for measuring the unfairness due to illegitimate inequalities. In this more general framework, the Roemer approach will be one special case. We will then show how the theory of selective (or responsibility-sensitive) egalitarianism can be applied to measuring inequity in health

---

[14] This maximin criterion is the natural extension of egalitarianism if one is also concerned about efficiency. Indeed, it implies that inequalities are only acceptable if they are to the advantage of the worst-off in society.

and health care. Finally we discuss how the concentration index and the measurement of racial disparities can be reinterpreted within this framework.

4.1.1. The Formal Framework of Selective Egalitarianism

In order to link our discussion more closely to the existing literature, let us briefly introduce the general concepts before examining how they can be applied to health.[15] A natural starting point is to depart from the measurement of inequalities in "total advantage" y_i and to construct a "partial" measure of the advantage of individual i in a way consistent with the idea that what is due to e_i does not matter for measuring inequalities and that only differences in c_i lead to illegitimate inequalities. An obvious solution consists of focusing on the expected value of the outcome given a certain value of c_i, i.e. $E(y|c_i)$. For individual i, the value of $E(y|c_i)$ can be considered as a measure of the part of his personal advantage y_i that is linked to c_i. One can then apply any suitable inequality index to the distribution of $E(y|c_i)$ over the population. Let us call this the "inequality of means" approach.[16]

This natural solution has a substantial shortcoming, however. Remember that the basic social objective in this approach is the elimination of illegitimate inequalities in individual advantage y_i, as determined by (19), where illegitimate inequalities are those linked to c_i. The goal of eliminating such inequalities is captured by the *compensation principle*, according to which *between individuals with identical e_i, priority should be given to the worse-off*.[17] Equality of $E(y|c_i)$ across individuals (or, equivalently, across types formed by different values of c_i) is compatible with arbitrarily large inequalities between individuals having the same e characteristics. The "inequality of means" approach therefore does not satisfy the compensation principle. There is an easy graphical way to see this. When all individuals have equal access to the same range of values of e_i, and if c_i is a fixed characteristic of individual i, one may consider that the whole graph of $y(c_i, \cdot)$ represents the opportunities offered to individual i. Equalizing $E(y|c_i)$ then corresponds to equalizing the areas below the graphs $y(c_i, \cdot)$, as in Figure 16.2a, while the full elimination of illegitimate inequalities would require that all the graphs of $y(c_i, \cdot)$ should be equal, as in Figure 16.2b.

A remedy to this problem is the following. For every individual i, consider the subpopulation of individuals having the same e_i as i, and compute the equally distributed equivalent of the distribution of y_i in every subgroup formed by individuals with

---

[15] In the paradigmatic case from the literature, y could refer to income (or welfare), c would be natural talent or socioeconomic status, e could stand for effort.

[16] Some authors (e.g. Lefranc et al., 2009) have proposed to analyze the degree of inequality of opportunity in terms of more general characteristics of the conditional distributions $F(y|c_i)$. We will return to this approach in our discussion of empirical applications (section 4.3). In this section we focus on the derivation of specific inequality measures.

[17] In Roemer's approach, absolute priority is given to the worst-off, but less extreme degrees of priority can be considered.

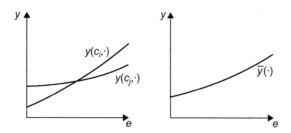

Figure 16.2 Equalizing opportunities.

the same e_i: $EDE(y|e_i)$.[18] The value of $EDE(y|e_i)$ does not measure the partial advantage that i gains from his own c_i, but it measures what y_i would be if the illegitimate inequalities in the subgroup sharing e_i were eliminated. Taking the average (or the sum) of these quantities for the different values of e_i yields a sensible social welfare objective. Let us call this the "average EDE" approach. The Roemer criterion, as defined in (20), is one member of this family with an inequality aversion equal to infinity, such that $EDE(y|e_i) = \min_c y(c, e_i)$.

Although this approach does not deliver an individual measure of partial advantage, an interesting index of illegitimate inequalities can be derived by computing the fraction (for a relative index) or the per capita amount (for an absolute index) of total y over the population that would be lost (or, stated alternatively, could be "saved") if every individual's y_i were replaced by $EDE(y|e_i)$. Such an index is equal to zero only if y_i is equal to $EDE(y|e_i)$ for every i, which is obtained only when y is equalized within every subpopulation sharing the same value of e, as requested by the compensation principle. There is a whole family of such measures, with each member of the family corresponding to a specific way of measuring $EDE(y|e_i)$, and in particular a specific degree of inequality aversion.[19]

The measures we have considered until now have one important, questionable feature in common. To see this, consider the special case in which there is only one value of c in the population, so that there is no illegitimate source of inequality. Everyone then shares the same $E(y|c_i)$, and $EDE(y|e_i)$ coincides with y_i for every i, so that the average value of $EDE(y|e_i)$ over the individuals is the same as $E(y|c_i)$. In other words, the two approaches introduced here (inequality of means and average EDE)

[18] Recall that the equally distributed equivalent is the value of individual outcome such that a perfectly equal distribution in which everyone enjoys this value of outcome is considered equally good from the point of view of social welfare as the contemplated distribution. Under strict inequality aversion, the equally distributed equivalent is strictly below the mean of the distribution whenever there are inequalities.

[19] It is also obviously possible to simply compute an inequality index for every subgroup sharing the same value of e, and then add up the indices over the whole population. Such an approach, however, is harder to relate to a sensible notion of social welfare.

merge and advocate focusing on $E(y|c_i)$. This means that in this particular context, social welfare boils down to the sum or the average of y_i over the whole population. At first sight this is not unreasonable. After all, maximizing the sum or average is tantamount to applying a social criterion with no aversion to inequality, which seems well in line with the idea that inequalities do not matter when they come from e. This was also the intuition behind Roemer's social objective function in (20). However, most theories of equality of opportunities advocate a different sort of policy for this special situation in which there is only one value of c in the population. They recommend a laisser-faire policy in which no particular transfers are made across individuals having different values of e. Indeed, what reason would there be to intervene if there is no illegitimate source of inequality? If maximizing the sum or average of y over the population required massive redistribution in favor of individuals whose value of e increases their marginal productivity of y with respect to resources, there would be a serious clash with this liberal recommendation of no transfer.

This discussion provides an important insight. The compensation principle is fully satisfied when the graphs of $y(c_i, \cdot)$ are equalized across individuals (or types), but is silent about the shape of the graph $y(c_i, \cdot)$. It is therefore possible to satisfy the compensation principle in the so-called "utilitarian" way that seeks to maximize the area below the graph of $y(c_i, \cdot)$, or in the "liberal" way that seeks to make $y(c_i, \cdot)$ correspond to the laisser-faire policy, or in many other ways. The theory of equality of opportunity is not complete until the compensation principle is supplemented by a *reward principle that tells how advantage should be apportioned to effort*, i.e. that specifies the desirable shape of the graph $y(c_i, \cdot)$. This also bears on the idea of measuring advantage in a partial way so as to focus on what is due to c_i. Such a measure necessarily reflects a particular reward principle, and one must therefore be careful to choose a measure that is consistent with the reward principle one believes in. As the reward principle underlying a particular measure is often implicit and hidden in the structure of the measure, it is a necessary and important preliminary step to check what it is before adopting a measure. This can be done, as in the previous paragraphs, by looking at what happens in the absence of inequalities in c.

Before turning to the measures that are in line with the liberal reward principle, let us introduce another important observation made by the theory of equal opportunity. The compensation principle and the reward principle, whatever the latter is, tend to clash in the sense that a measure that satisfies the compensation principle is typically less satisfactory with respect to the reward principle, and vice versa. This point can be illustrated with the two measures introduced before. When one measures inequalities in $E(y|c_i)$, one is totally indifferent to modifications of the distribution of y in a subgroup of individuals with the same c, provided that the sum of y remains unchanged in this subgroup. This very well reflects the *"utilitarian" reward principle stipulating that for individuals with the same c, one should have no inequality aversion and be interested only in the sum or the mean.* However, as emphasized before, this "inequality of means" approach does not satisfy the compensation principle. In contrast, the measure that is based on $EDE(y|e_i)$ can be affected by such redistributions of y within a subgroup of individuals with the same c, because the values of $EDE(y|e_i)$ for various values of e_i will then typically be altered. This second measure is indifferent to such redistributions only when all individuals share the same c. The "average EDE" measures, satisfying the compensation principle, are therefore less strict on the utilitarian reward principle.

This tension between compensation and reward can also be illustrated by measures that are based on the liberal variant of the reward principle. Such a "liberal" view about reward requires a richer framework in which the transfers to which individuals are submitted are explicitly distinguished in the outcome function. Letting t_i denote the transfer to which individual i is submitted, (19) is refined into:

$$y_i = y(t_i, c_i, e_i). \tag{22}$$

This new function y only reflects the technology of production of y_i, and no longer the transfer policy which is an explicit argument of it. The *liberal reward principle then stipulates that, among individuals with the same c_i, priority should be given to those with a lower t_i (independently of their e_i).* This implies that the transfers are ideally null in the hypothetical case in which there is only one value of c.

Again, in this new framework there is a natural solution, which consists of fixing a reference value for e_i, $\tilde{e}$, and considering that illegitimate inequalities are those that arise for the values of $y(t_i, c_i, \tilde{e})$. One can then simply focus on the distribution of these values instead of the distribution of y_i. Each individual i is treated as if $e_i = \tilde{e}$, ignoring the part of y_i that comes from a discrepancy between e_i and $\tilde{e}$. This approach is called "conditional equality" in the literature, in reference to the fact that it seeks equality conditionally on individuals adopting $\tilde{e}$. Note that equalizing the values of $y(t_i, c_i, \tilde{e})$ across individuals with identical c implies giving them equivalent t, as requested by the liberal principle of reward. But this approach fails the compensation principle whenever it may happen that there are two individuals i and j with identical e_i and such that $y_i < y_j$, while $y(t_i, c_i, \tilde{e}) > y(t_j, c_j, \tilde{e})$.[20] Compensation is guaranteed only for those with $e_i = \tilde{e}$.

The compensation principle is satisfied by the dual approach which fixes a reference value for c_i, $\tilde{c}$, and focuses on the inequalities in t_i^* across individuals, where t_i^* is the solution to the equation

$$y_i = y(t_i^*, \tilde{c}, e_i). \tag{23}$$

---

[20] Note that conditional equality does satisfy the compensation principle if the function $y(\cdot)$ takes a specific form, e.g. if it is separable such that $y_i = f(g(t_i, c_i), e_i)$. The worse-off in $f(g(t_i, c_i), \tilde{e})$ are the worse-off in $g(t_i, c_i)$, and therefore the worse-off in y_i for any given e_i.

Table 16.4 Variants of Responsibility-Sensitive Egalitarianism

	Utilitarian	Liberal
Compensation principle satisfied	Average EDE[†] $EDE(y\|e_i)$	Egalitarian-equivalence t_i^* s.t. $y_i = y(t^*, \tilde{c}, e_i)$
Reward principle satisfied	Inequality of means $E(y\|c_i)$	Conditional equality $y(t_i, c_i, \tilde{e})$

[†]In this family of measures, overall inequality is not simply the inequality in the values of $EDE(y\|e_i)$.

An intuitive understanding of this approach can be obtained by looking at what happens when equality of t_i^* across individuals is achieved. One then has a situation that is equivalent to a situation in which differences in y_i are only due to e_i, because $y_i = y(t^*, \tilde{c}, e_i)$ for a given t^*. These inequalities are thus legitimate. This approach is therefore called "egalitarian equivalence" because it seeks equivalence with an egalitarian situation. The cost of satisfying the compensation principle is that it may happen that inequalities in t_i^* may sometimes be the opposite of inequalities in t_i for some individuals with identical c_i, implying a failure of the liberal principle of reward for such individuals. Liberal reward is guaranteed only for those with $c_i = \tilde{c}$.[21]

In conclusion, within the literature on equality of opportunity a number of approaches have been put forward that aim at defining a partial measure of the advantage of individual i. "Illegitimate" inequalities can then be measured as inequality in these partial indicators. An overview is given in Table 16.4. Two insights have been highlighted. First, in addition to the compensation principle, each of the approaches also takes a stance with respect to the reward issue, i.e. the definition of acceptable inequalities. This cannot be ignored even if one only wants to measure *illegitimate* inequalities. Second, there is a tension between the compensation and reward principles. This tension and the multiplicity of possible reward principles create a variety of solutions. The four that have been introduced here (see Table 16.4) provide a good summary of the main insights. The choice between these different measures will necessarily depend on the attractiveness of the compensation principle and of the different reward principles in the specific case to be analyzed.

An important problem is created by configurations in which c and e are not independently distributed and c is suspected of causally influencing e, as in Roemer's (1993) smoking example described earlier. In such cases, it seems that for different c the individuals do not have the same access to various values of e and that the graph of $y(c_i, \cdot)$ no longer depicts individual i's opportunities. A simple theoretical solution to this difficulty is to assume that there is a latent variable of effort e^* that is

[21] Again, the liberal reward principle will be satisfied if $y_i = f(g(t_i, c_i), e_i)$. Equation (23) is then equivalent to $g(t_i, c_i) = g(t_i^*, \tilde{c})$ and for any given c_i inequalities in t_i are mimicked by inequalities in t_i^*.

independent of c and such that all individuals have equal access to it. The value of e is a function of c and of this latent variable e^*. One can thus write y_i as a function of c_i and e_i^* and proceed. In the special case in which y is increasing in e^*, for any given c, a rescaling of e^* can render the conditional distribution of e^* given any c uniform over the interval $[0, 1]$. After such rescaling, the graph of $y^*(c_i, \cdot)$ corresponds to the inverse of the cumulative distribution function of y given c. As we have seen, in a similar vein, Roemer (1993, 1998) proposes to measure effort e_i^* directly as the rank (or percentile) of i in the distribution of y given c. It follows from our discussion that such measurement convention is innocuous if y can be expected to be increasing in e^* and if the measure of inequality that is constructed on this basis is not sensitive to rescalings of e^*. The latter property holds for the four measures introduced here. The former property, however, is ultimately a statement about facts, which does not necessarily hold in all specific situations.

Note that the correlation between c and e does not necessarily imply that the inequalities due to e are partly illegitimate. For theories that ascribe responsibility for preferences, it is natural that preferences are linked to circumstances (bodily characteristics influence the taste for activities depending on such characteristics), but this fact does not detract from the value of respecting preferences and the choices such preferences motivate. It may also happen that e is coincidentally correlated with c without there being a causal impact of c on e.[22] In such a situation, the "inequality of means" approach is not appropriate because the value of $E(y|c_i)$ is influenced by the specific distribution of e conditionally on c_i. Standardizing the computation of the expected value by taking the same distribution of e for all values of c_i is the natural solution to this problem. The "average EDE" approach, in contrast, is not affected because the fact that the computation of $EDE(y|e_i)$ involves a different composition of c for different values of e_i does not matter, the c group to which an individual belongs being essentially an irrelevant piece of information for this approach. Conditional equality and egalitarian equivalence are also immune to the problem, the former because it ignores e_i (except insofar as t_i depends on it), the latter because it refers to a hypothetical situation in which everyone has the same $\tilde{c}$.

4.1.2. Application to Health and Health Care

The application to health and health care requires a careful reinterpretation of the general framework. Two issues are especially important. First, as was already clear from our discussion of the concentration index and of racial disparities, correlations between the different variables in e and c will be ubiquitous and their interpretation is

---

[22] The literature on equal opportunity often presumes causal influence whenever c and e are correlated. Of course, one may interpret a significant correlation between c and e as an indication that they are both linked to the same underlying variables. As we will see within the health context, the ethical implications of this situation may differ from case to case.

essential. When c and e are not independently distributed, one must decide whether one is interested in the inequalities generated by c only or in the inequalities generated by c directly and indirectly via its influence on (or correlation with) e. Second, a careful reconsideration of the reward principle is needed. Indeed, utilitarian and liberal reward principles are conceived for well-being. In the case of health or health care, there is a special ideal of a good relationship between health care and health needs which does not correspond to either principle and calls for a generalization that we explain below. It will turn out that the compensation principle is strongly linked to the concept of horizontal equity, while different reward principles capture different ideas about vertical equity.

We examine inequalities in health care and in health in turn. As a matter of fact, the intricate link between health care and health induces interesting connections between the two.

4.1.2.1. Health Care

The partial approaches to inequity in health care, which have been dominant in the literature until now, focus on the inequalities which are due to the specific influence of a particular socio-demographic characteristic such as gender, race, or socioeconomic status. From a more general perspective one may be interested in *all* inequalities in health care consumption that are not explained by differences in health needs. In this application the "effort" variables in e are those variables that do not lead to illegitimate inequalities in health care, while inequalities due to circumstances c are ethically objectionable. Therefore, in the partial approaches, the c variable measures the relevant socio-demographic characteristic (e.g. gender or race) and e captures all the rest. In the more general perspective, the e variable measures needs and c is all the rest. There has been a debate about whether differences in preferences and/or information trigger legitimate inequalities in health care, i.e. whether the variable of interest is health care use or access to health care. The various positions in this debate can be accommodated in the framework discussed here by moving the cut between c and e. Once a particular function of health care is written in the form $y(c, e)$, in principle it is possible to apply the different measures that are proposed in the theory. The correlation between c and e is an essential consideration in this context, however, because health needs, which belong to e here, can be expected to be influenced by c.

When one constructs a partial indicator (i.e. the inequity due to one c variable, e.g. race), one may be interested not just in the direct effects of that variable but also in the indirect effects via another variable (e.g. socioeconomic status). We have seen that this idea plays an essential role in the definition of racial disparities. In this case, one could in principle write down socioeconomic status as a function of race and other variables, and then distribute the influence of status in the y function between c (race) and e (the rest) accordingly. This decomposition of influences will often be impossible in practice due to data limitations or even deeper limitations in understanding the relevant causal mechanisms. But one can always write a function of statistical dependence, with $status = f(race, \pi)$, where π is the percentile of the individual in the conditional distribution of status given his race. If status is a discrete variable with few categories, there may remain some arbitrariness in the allocation of particular values of π to the different individuals.

To understand the different dimensions of the problem and make them more specific, it is useful to further develop the health care function (which corresponds to the advantage function (22) in this setting):

$$y(t_i, c_i, e_i) = hc_i = hc(hn(SES_i, d_i, P_i^1), SES_i, d_i, P_i^2). \tag{24}$$

Here hn stands as before for "health needs," determined by a vector SES of socioeconomic variables (including economic status, race, and region), a vector d of demographic variables (such as age and gender), and a vector P^1 of preference variables influencing lifestyle. Health care is also influenced by the vector P^2 capturing differences in treatment preferences. Equation (24) makes it possible to explicitly distinguish two effects: the indirect effect of SES and d on health care through their effect on health care needs, and the direct effect, pointing to differential treatment (or discrimination) if needs are identical.[23]

Suppose now that we follow the literature on socioeconomic inequalities and take $c = SES$ and $e = (d, P^1, P^2)$. In this interpretation, the compensation principle would impose that health care be equal for individuals with the same value of e, i.e. the same demographic and preference variables. This is not attractive, as it would mean that we disregard the effect of SES on health care needs. A better approach is to take $c = SES$ and $e = (hn, d, P^2)$. This obviously implies that e, and more specifically hn, and c are correlated and therefore rules out the "inequality of means" approach without proper standardization.[24] For the other measures the correlation does not raise any problem. Focusing on socioeconomic inequalities, i.e. taking $c = SES$, is only one possibility, however, and other ethical approaches can be accommodated by a different partitioning of the variables in (24) in c and e. One could take the position that differences in treatment are legitimate if they reflect differences in needs following from differences in lifestyle preferences P^1. This would mean that "legitimate" needs have to be redefined. Or one could also be concerned about discrimination in health care provision

---

[23] In this sense, equation (24) is a parsimonious way of writing a simple stylized structural model. Of course, in applied work, one will usually need a more elaborate specification (as in Fleurbaey and Schokkaert, 2009).

[24] Remember that this rejection of the simple "inequality of means" approach was the starting point for the formulation of more complex measures of racial disparity. We will return to this application in the next subsection, but here we will remain at a more general level.

related to d (e.g. age and gender), implying that $c = (SES, d)$ and $e = (hn, P^2)$. To focus our exposition, we will develop the analysis for the latter case. Our discussion can easily be adapted for the other ethical choices.

Some remarks can be made concerning the interpretation of (24). First, there may be correlation between c and the preference variables: whether this is seen as problematic or not will depend on the position taken with respect to the boundary between legitimate and illegitimate variables. Second, distinguishing between the direct effect of SES on health care and its indirect effect through health care needs imposes heavy requirements on the data. Things are even more difficult if we include the demographic variables in c, since most often we will need d in the empirical model as a proxy of health care needs.

With $e = (hn, P^2)$, the compensation principle implies that health care should be the same for individuals with the same health care needs and the same treatment preferences. It is immediately clear that this is a direct translation of the principle of *horizontal equity*. If one follows the dominant approach in the literature and focuses on horizontal inequity, measures that do not satisfy the compensation principle are therefore not very attractive in this setting. What about the reward principles? As described before, the best way of thinking about reward is to consider individuals within the same group of circumstances $c = (SES, d)$. These individuals may differ in health care needs and treatment preferences: allocating health care to such individuals is immediately related to *vertical equity*. It is obvious that vertical equity should play a role in evaluating different situations: indeed, horizontal equity would be achieved if all individuals received the same level of health care regardless of their health care needs (Sutton, 2002), and this is clearly not equitable. In fact, it has been emphasized in the literature that it is not possible to examine the extent to which the horizontal equity principle is violated without simultaneously specifying a vertical equity norm (see, e.g., O'Donnell et al., 2008). This is analogous to the insight from the literature on equality of opportunity that each measure of illegitimate inequality implies the specification of a reward principle. The reward principles from the equality of opportunity literature do not capture well the idea of vertical equity, however. Utilitarian reward focuses on the average amount of health care per group of circumstances $c = (SES, d)$. Taking a redistribution of health care within such a group as a matter of social indifference is almost like denying the relevance of vertical equity, i.e. of apportioning health care to health needs and preferences. The average amount of health care in a group of circumstances is a poor basis for the evaluation of unfairness at the individual level, even if it might be considered acceptable at the level of comparing circumstance groups themselves. Similarly, liberal reward is problematic because it requires identifying a "transfer" variable contributing to the outcome variable. Health care itself can be viewed as a transfer of resources, but it would make little sense to advocate that everyone should receive the same amount of health care within a group of circumstances. Again, health needs and preferences justify specific amounts of health care.

The fact that health care is itself a policy variable makes it difficult to derive an optimal form of the health care function on the basis of observable empirical evidence. The normatively ideal way in which health care should respond to health needs is linked to the available medical technology and the available resources. Let us posit that within a group of circumstances, there is a given ideal amount of health care, for every member of this group, which depends on health needs and treatment preferences:

$$hc^*(hn_i, P_i^2; SES_i, d_i).$$

It makes sense to consider that this ideal should not depend on socioeconomic status, but it may perhaps depend on demographic variables, e.g. if patients of different ages are legitimately given different degrees of priority (which does not prevent the analyst from seeking further differences due to discrimination). We will therefore write it $hc^*(hn_i, P_i^2; d_i)$ from now on. The advantage of individual i can then be defined as the gap between what i receives and the ideal amount:

$$\Delta_i = hc_i - hc^*(hn_i, P_i^2; d_i) \tag{25}$$

and illegitimate inequality can be measured as the inequality in these individual advantage measures.

The difficulty that remains is to define $hc^*(hn_i, P_i^2; d_i)$. Medical information about the best treatment for patients with different needs can be helpful to specify this function, but since $hc^*(\cdot)$ also has to capture the availability of resources, such medical information is not sufficient. Some useful approaches can be derived from observable data. Suppose first that d_i should actually play no role in the function $hc^*(hn_i, P_i^2; d_i)$. One can then hope that departures from the ideal even out over the population so that one can define the optimal amount of health care as the average quantity of health care received by individuals with the same needs and preferences $e = (hn_i, P_i^2)$. If one denotes this set of individuals by N_e and their number by n_e, one obtains:

$$hc^*(hn_i, P_i^2) = hc^{AV}(hn_i, P_i^2) \equiv \frac{1}{n_e} \sum_{i \in N_e} hc_i. \tag{26}$$

This is the assumption that is commonly made in the literature on socioeconomic inequity in health care delivery, formulated as: "On average, the system gets it right" (van Doorslaer et al., 2000—see also O'Donnell et al., 2008).[25] When d_i does play a role in $hc^*(hn_i, P_i^2; d_i)$, one cannot take the average amount of health care given to a

---

[25] A refinement to this approach has been proposed by Sutton (2002). We will discuss his approach in the next subsection.

group (hn_i, P_i^2, d_i) as a proxy for the ideal, because discrimination would also influence this average amount. There seems to be no simple statistical way to separate the normal influence of d_i on hc_i from an abnormal influence linked to discrimination.

Another possibility is to pick a reference value for c, $(\widetilde{SES}, \tilde{d})$, and consider that the optimal amount is what individuals with such characteristics receive:

$$hc^*(hn_i, P_i^2) = hc^{REF}(hn_i, P_i^2) \equiv hc(hn_i, \widetilde{SES}, \tilde{d}, P_i^2). \qquad (27)$$

This approach makes much sense if one believes that different socioeconomic groups are treated differently and that the treatment given to one specific group (e.g. the rich or the White) is close to the "optimal" treatment.

Fleurbaey and Schokkaert (2009) have proposed two measures that can be applied to health care as well as to health and are inspired by conditional equality and egalitarian equivalence (the two liberal criteria introduced in the previous subsection). The measure related to egalitarian equivalence is the *fairness gap*, which in the case of health care and under the assumptions retained here about the c, e classification is written as

$$hc_i - hc(hn_i, \widetilde{SES}, \tilde{d}, P_i^2), \qquad (28)$$

the general formula being $y_i - y(\tilde{c}, e_i)$. This formula corresponds to (25) with the "reference" specification (27). Note that the interpretation in terms of vertical equity suggests an interesting way to think about the choice of the reference values $(\widetilde{SES}, \tilde{d})$, a choice which is largely left open in the theory of selective egalitarianism.

The similarity with egalitarian equivalence comes from the presence of a reference $\tilde{c}$ in the formula, and equality of the expressions (28) across individuals implies that individuals with the same $e_i = (hn_i, P_i^2)$ necessarily have the same $y_i = hc_i$, in conformity with the compensation principle. Inequality in (28) is then an acceptable measure of horizontal inequity. As far as the implications of the reward principle are concerned, imagine a situation in which all individuals share the same c and this value is retained as the reference $\tilde{c}$. Then the fairness gap is null for all individuals, no matter what the y function is. However, if one looks at an ordinary situation with a variety of values of c in the population, and examines how to improve the situation of a particular group sharing the same c, one sees that this can be done in a specific way that is not neutral with respect to e. To illustrate this point, suppose that $y(c, e) = \alpha + \beta c + \gamma e + \delta ce$, in which all the symbols represent real numbers. One then has

$$y_i - y(\tilde{c}, e_i) = \beta(c_i - \tilde{c}) + \delta(c_i - \tilde{c}) e_i,$$

which implies that, in order to reduce inequalities, one should in priority help those with a high e_i in subgroups with $c_i < \tilde{c}$ (i.e. the unhealthy poor) and those with a low e_i in subgroups with $c_i > \tilde{c}$ (i.e. the healthy rich). This is easy to understand in the light of the interpretation of $y^*(\tilde{c}, e) = \alpha + \beta\tilde{c} + \gamma e + \delta\tilde{c}e$ as the "ideal" health care level corresponding to e (see (27)).

The alternative proposal, related to conditional equality, is simply to evaluate individual advantage as $y(c_i, \tilde{e})$, which in our example would be $hc(\widetilde{hn}, SES_i\, d_i, \widetilde{P^2})$. This measure, called *direct unfairness* by Fleurbaey and Schokkaert (2009), bears a striking similarity with conditional equality but is different because conditional equality is normally computed by retaining the transfer t_i fixed, not by computing what the transfer would be with reference $\tilde{e}$. Like conditional equality, it does not satisfy the compensation principle. It is therefore not attractive as a measure of horizontal inequity. In terms of reward, it has the property that the only individuals who are taken into account are those with $e_i = \tilde{e}$. Indeed, all the other individuals are in fact ignored because their situation is measured by what the individuals with similar c but reference e would obtain. One must therefore be cautious before using such a measure for normative purposes.

A final observation must be made because it will help connecting the measures described in this subsection with the measures of racial or gender disparity. When reference parameters such as c or e are introduced, one may also think of generalizing by taking a distribution of reference values rather than a single value. For instance, an immediate generalization of direct unfairness and the fairness gap can be obtained in this way by computing the expected value of the measures of individual advantage with respect to the distribution of reference parameters. For direct unfairness, if $f(\tilde{e})$ is the reference distribution for $\tilde{e}$, one can compute

$$\int y(c_i, \tilde{e}) f(\tilde{e}) d\tilde{e}. \tag{29}$$

For the fairness gap, with $g(\tilde{c})$ the reference PDF for $\tilde{c}$, one can compute

$$y_i - \int y(\tilde{c}, e_i)\, g(\tilde{c}) d\tilde{c}. \tag{30}$$

Note that when the reference distribution of $\tilde{e}$ corresponds to the actual distribution, and when e is independent of c, then $\int y(c_i, \tilde{e})\, f(\tilde{e})\, d\tilde{e} = E(y|c_i)$ and direct unfairness coincides with the inequality of means approach. When the reference distribution of $\tilde{c}$ corresponds to the actual distribution, and when e is independent of c, the expression $\int y(\tilde{c}, e_i)\, g(\tilde{c}) d\tilde{c}$ is the average outcome obtained by the group of individuals who have e_i. Obviously, these generalizations are not innocuous in terms of the implied reward principle.

4.1.2.2. Health Inequalities

In the case of health, we can develop the advantage function (22) further along the lines of (24):

$$y(c_i, e_i) = h_i = h(hc(hn(SES_i, d_i, P_i^1), SES_i, d_i, P_i^2), hn(SES_i, d_i, P_i^1)). \tag{31}$$

According to this function, health is determined by health needs and by health care.[26] As before, health care depends on health needs. Again, different views on responsibility will be reflected in different ways of allocating the variables on the RHS to either c or e. Almost everybody will agree that differences in socioeconomic variables should not lead to differences in health (after controlling for differences in preferences). The large bulk of the literature also takes it for granted that differences in health, caused by the demographic variables d, should *not* be seen as illegitimate, because they apparently cannot be influenced by policy. This position is not beyond criticism, however, as health differences due to demographic variables can be exacerbated or softened through policy (think about rationing decisions in health care)—and one may also take the position that in comparisons of inequity between countries and over time it is useful to include the effects of variables that (in the short run) cannot be influenced by policy. The most sensitive issues arise with respect to the interpretation of the preference variables. We will come back to that debate in the next section. In this section we will follow the dominant approach and focus on inequalities generated by socioeconomic status. As in the previous subsection, our discussion can easily be adapted for other ethical choices.

In this setting the compensation principle is compelling, and can be expressed by the requirement that "if a measure of unfair inequality is zero, there should be no illegitimate differences left, i.e. two individuals with the same value for the e variable (i.e. the same preferences and the same values for the demographic variables) should have the same health status, i.e. the same outcome y." As far as reward is concerned, once again the reward principles have to be reinterpreted carefully because health is not a global index of well-being.

Let us first consider the measures that are based on the utilitarian reward principle. The "inequality of means" approach, which would calculate the inequality in $E(h|SES_i)$, has been advocated by Bommier and Stecklov (2002) for the measurement of socioeconomic health inequalities. As we have seen, this approach is not satisfactory at the bar of compensation and also requires standardization in order to cope with the correlation between c (socioeconomic status) and e (demographic variables). On both counts, as explained above, the average EDE approach is preferable. Both measures rely on the utilitarian reward principle, stating that what matters is average (or total) health for each particular group of circumstances. Maximizing health is a time-honored principle and has become the dominant objective in the literature on cost-effectiveness analysis. Yet its ethical limitations are by now well understood. Socioeconomic inequalities could be improved, according to such measures, by enforcing health policies for the worst-off socioeconomic groups that give more

---

[26] At first sight there may be some confusion between "health" and "health needs." As is made clear by equation (31), we interpret final health as resulting from health care and (pre-health care) needs.

health care to those whose value of e makes health care more productive with them, thereby increasing average health in these groups. For instance, if the average health among the disadvantaged socioeconomic groups could be increased by sacrificing the severely ill patients and concentrating resources on curable diseases and prevention, this would be seen as improving the situation. These implications of health maximization are hard to swallow and are strongly rejected by the majority of the population (Gaertner and Schokkaert, 2011).

As was pointed out in the previous subsection on health care, the liberal reward principle is not very attractive either, as it seems strange to recommend equal health care for all individuals of the same circumstance group, regardless of their health needs. However, once an ideal health care function $hc^*(hn_i, P_i^2; d_i)$ has been defined, one can extend the theory in order to introduce this benchmark as a reward principle. Consider the following measure of individual advantage:

$$h\left(\Delta_i + hc^*(hn(SES_i, \tilde{d}, \tilde{P}^1), \tilde{P}^2; \tilde{d}), hn(SES_i, \tilde{d}, \tilde{P}^1)\right), \tag{32}$$

with Δ_i defined as in (25). This leads to a generalization of the conditional equality approach. Indeed, if the ideal $hc^*(hn_i, P_i^2; d_i)$ were constant (within a group of circumstances SES, but as it does not depend on this variable directly it would be constant overall), expression (32) would boil down to

$$h\left(hc_i, hn(SES_i, \tilde{d}, \widetilde{P^1})\right), \tag{33}$$

which is exactly the measure of individual advantage in the traditional conditional equality approach. The generalization (32) instead computes the level of health individual i would enjoy if the irrelevant ("responsibility") characteristics d_i, P_i^1, P_i^2 were at the reference level, and i's health care was at the corresponding ideal level plus the discrepancy Δ_i that i currently endures with respect to the ideal level i should receive (given i's actual characteristics). This discrepancy can be interpreted as a specific resource treatment that i is subject to. The idea of generalized conditional equality (32) is to assess how individuals would do if they had the reference irrelevant characteristics and kept Δ_i. Keeping Δ_i in the computation makes it possible to assess the consequences of the current unfairness in resources over the outcome (health) for a "reference" situation. When equality of (32) is achieved across individuals of the same SES, they must have the same Δ_i.

Alternatively, one can also generalize egalitarian equivalence. Solve in t_i^* the equation

$$h_i = h(t_i^* + hc^*(hn(\widetilde{SES}, d_i, P_i^1), P_i^2; d_i), hn(\widetilde{SES}, d_i, P_i^1)). \tag{34}$$

Illegitimate inequality can then be measured as inequality in the individual t_i^*. If one could equalize t_i^* across individuals, one would obtain a situation in which everyone would enjoy a level of health that would be the same as in a hypothetical situation in which health needs are no longer influenced by *SES*, and in which everyone would receive the ideal amount of health care, up to a uniform discrepancy.

As one can check, generalized egalitarian equivalence satisfies the compensation principle, whereas generalized conditional equality does not. When two individuals share the same irrelevant characteristics and differ only in their socioeconomic status, their t_i^* is equal only if their health level is equal. In contrast, if the irrelevant characteristics of these two individuals are not at the reference level, their individual advantages (32) may be equal even if their actual health levels are different. Since the compensation principle is natural in this context, generalized egalitarian equivalence (34) is a more attractive approach than generalized conditional equality.

However, both approaches make use of an "ideal" health care function $hc^*(hn_i, P_i^2; d_i)$. As discussed before, the specification of this function is an awkward problem, requiring additional assumptions and/or information that is not available in the observable data. As a shortcut, Fleurbaey and Schokkaert (2009) propose what sounds like a weak reward principle. It stipulates that differences in e_i (here demographic variables and preferences) across individuals should have as little impact on the measure of illegitimate inequalities as possible. This principle can be reinterpreted if one thinks that the ideal health care function $hc^*(hn_i, P_i^2; d_i)$, which typically depends on e_i, should be taken as a benchmark in order to measure unfairness at the individual level. As a matter of fact, there are circumstances under which "direct unfairness" and the "fairness gap" coincide with generalized conditional equality and generalized egalitarian equivalence respectively.

Applied to health, direct unfairness measures individual situations as

$$y(c_i, \tilde{e}) = h \left(hc(hn \left(SES_i, \tilde{d}_i, \widetilde{P^1} \right), SES_i, \tilde{d}, \widetilde{P^2} \right), hn \left(SES_i, \tilde{d}, \widetilde{P^1} \right)). \tag{35}$$

In contrast with the previous measure (32), this one is insensitive to the way in which health care reacts to different values of e characteristics. The direct unfairness measure for individual i then equals her individual advantage with generalized conditional equality if

$$\Delta_i \equiv hc_i - hc^*(hn_i, P_i^2; d_i) = hc(hn(SES_i, \tilde{d}, \widetilde{P^1}), SES_i, \tilde{d}, \widetilde{P^2}) - hc^*(hn(SES_i, \tilde{d}, \widetilde{P^1}), \widetilde{P^2}; \tilde{d}),$$

which basically means that the discrepancy between actual health care of individual i and the level of health care that is defined as optimal for her depends only on SES_i and not on the e characteristics, i.e. on the demographic and preference variables.

The fairness gap is, in this context, defined as the difference

$$y_i - y(\tilde{c}, e_i) = h_i - h(hc(hn \left(\widetilde{SES}, d_i, P_i^1 \right), \widetilde{SES}, d_i, P_i^2), hn \left(\widetilde{SES}, d_i, P_i^1 \right)).$$

Consider now a situation where the fairness gap equals zero for all individuals. For this situation without illegitimate inequality, (34) implies that

$$t_i^* + hc^*(hn\,(\widetilde{SES},\,d_i,\,P_i^1),\,P_i^2;\,d_i) = hc(hn(\widetilde{SES},\,d_i,\,P_i^1),\,\widetilde{SES},\,d_i,\,P_i^2).$$

If we now would like to have that generalized egalitarian equivalence also evaluates that same situation as one without illegitimate inequality, t_i^* has to be equal across individuals, i.e.

$$hc^*(hn\,(\widetilde{SES},\,d_i,\,P_i^1),\,P_i^2;\,d_i) = hc(hn(\widetilde{SES},\,d_i,\,P_i^1),\,\widetilde{SES},\,d_i,\,P_i^2) - t^*,$$

implying that for all values of the demographic and preference variables in the reference circumstance group, actual health care equals ideal health care up to a constant. This interpretation again may help in choosing the best reference values for an application of the fairness gap approach.

4.1.3. Comparison with the Concentration Index and with the Measurement of Racial Disparities

The main difference between the methodology described in the previous subsection and the more traditional approaches such as the concentration index or the measurement of racial disparities is that the latter are interested only in the summary measure of the impact of c on y, whereas the former (with the exception of the "average EDE" approach) starts with the computation of individual indices such that the unfair inequalities are precisely the inequalities in these specific indices. This makes it possible in particular to analyze the situation for subpopulations rather easily. Indeed, both the concentration index approach and the measurement of racial disparities are special cases of the more general methodology.

4.1.3.1. Concentration Index

The concentration index approach has been applied to situations in which y is health as well as to situations in which y is health care. In both cases c is interpreted as socioeconomic status and all the other variables are in e. As we have seen in section 3.1, the concentration index of y on c (socioeconomic status) is proportional to the coefficient of the linear regression of y_i on r_i^c, the rank of i in the distribution of c. Suppose that the following function, similar to (3),

$$\frac{2\sigma_r^2}{\mu(y)}y_i = \alpha + \beta r_i^c + \varepsilon_i,$$

describes how $y_i/\mu(y)$ is effectively produced, and that ε_i triggers only legitimate inequalities. Of course, the subtle ethical arguments that have been put forward in the previous subsection cannot be captured by this simple reduced-form approach. In addition, note that it is not applicable when c is multidimensional and cannot be unambiguously ordered, and that we have to assume that the y function is linear in r_i^c. Both assumptions are not needed in the more general approach of equality of opportunity.

However, if we accept the restrictive assumptions that c indeed can be ordered unambiguously and that the linear approximation is acceptable, the concentration index is closely related to the measures discussed in the previous subsection, as they all focus on $\hat{\beta}$. Indeed, $E(y_i/\mu(y)|c_i)$ is proportional to $\hat{\alpha} + \hat{\beta}r_i^c$, and the difference of these terms across individuals i and j is equal to $\hat{\beta}(r_i^c - r_j^c)$. The concentration index then directly reflects the degree of inequalities in $E(y_i/\mu(y)|c_i)$, implying a perfect concordance with the "inequality of means" approach on how to compare distributions. The linearity of the function moreover implies that the other approaches agree with the inequality of means on how to measure inequalities across individuals. The "average EDE" approach will evaluate the differences of expressions $\hat{\alpha} + \hat{\beta}r_i^c + \varepsilon_i$ for individuals with equal ε_i, obtaining the same formula $\hat{\beta}(r_i^c - r_j^c)$. Direct unfairness will similarly evaluate inequalities in expressions $\hat{\alpha} + \hat{\beta}r_i^c + \tilde{\varepsilon}$, and the fairness gap will be proportional to $\hat{\alpha} + \hat{\beta}r_i^c + \varepsilon_i - (\hat{\alpha} + \hat{\beta}\tilde{r}^c + \varepsilon_i) = \hat{\beta}(r_i^c - \tilde{r}^c)$, again yielding the same formula for inequalities across individuals.

Obviously, there may be a problem when some e variables are correlated with c but are nonetheless a source of legitimate inequalities (such as age when y is health, or health needs when y is health care). As explained in section 3, this is typically addressed by standardizing the relevant variables. The analysis in the previous section has shown that such standardization is not ethically innocuous, as it involves compensation and reward issues. Direct standardization substitutes $y(c_i, \bar{e})$, where $\bar{e}$ is the mean of e over the whole population, to y_i. If the function $y(c, e)$ is increasing in c (relative to the ordering of c that is used in the concentration index), the concentration index for $y(c_i, \bar{e})$ is the same as the Gini index. Computing the concentration index for $y(c_i, \bar{e})$ is then equivalent to computing the Gini index for direct unfairness $y(c_i, \tilde{e})$ with $\tilde{e} = \bar{e}$. Indirect standardization focuses on $y_i - y(\bar{c}, e_i)$, which is again strikingly similar to a concept of the previous subsection, namely the fairness gap. These similarities suggest two important insights. First, since direct unfairness does not satisfy the compensation principle, the same is true for measures based on direct standardization. This makes direct standardization particularly uninteresting for measuring horizontal inequity in health care delivery. Second, indirect standardization is equivalent to the fairness gap for $\tilde{c} = \bar{c}$. As described before, this imposes the assumption that "the system gets it right on average." While this assumption is not unreasonable (and is made explicitly in the literature), we have shown in the previous section that it is possible to generalize the approach for other, equally or more attractive, assumptions about the "ideal" health care function (see, e.g., (28)).

When the computation of the concentration index differs from the application of suitable inequality measures to direct unfairness or the fairness gap, for instance because the measure of individual advantage is not comonotonic with c, it appears better to rely on an inequality measure. As made clear by Bleichrodt and van Doorslaer (2006), the concentration approach gives absolute priority to individuals with a lower c, independently of their personal advantage, which is hard to defend (see section 3). It makes more sense to give priority to individuals who are worse off according to the relevant measure of advantage, given that this measure is tailored to highlight the benefit due to c. A natural solution is then to calculate the inequality in the measures of partial advantage as described in the previous subsection. Similar remarks can be made about the choice between the concentration curve applied to y (or its standardized variant) and the Lorenz curve applied to direct unfairness, the fairness gap, or similar measures of partial individual advantage.

4.1.3.2. Racial Disparities

Let us now turn to the analysis of racial disparity. Disregarding for simplicity differences in preferences, the approach described in section 3.2 can be translated in our more general setting by interpreting y_i as medical consumption and c_i as race (B or W). The special structure of the problem (with the IOM definition of racial disparities) requires some additional notation. We will say that the vector e has two components, socioeconomic status e_i^1, for which the correlation with c_i generates illegitimate inequalities, and health needs e_i^2 for which the correlation with c does *not* generate illegitimate inequalities. Note that in this approach correlation between c_i and e_i^1 is sufficient and that it is not necessary to impute causality.

Remember that the "inequality of means" approach, as usually applied, would simply compute the difference of average values of y between B and W. This is not acceptable because in this setting the correlation between c and e should be accounted for, i.e. differences in health care needs do not create illegitimate inequalities. It can be shown, however, that there is a close link between racial disparity and the concepts of conditional equality (direct unfairness) and egalitarian equivalence (fairness gap). Since racial disparity in the first place relates to horizontal inequity (remember the IOM definition), it is natural to focus on measures satisfying the compensation principle in the context of health care. We will therefore restrict ourselves to the latter. We will first consider the additively separable and then the more general case.

4.1.3.2.1. Additive Separability Under the assumption of additive separability, we start from (12), which we can rewrite in the present notation as

$$y_i = \alpha + \beta\varphi(c_i) + \gamma\psi(e_i^1) + \delta\chi(e_i^2) + \varepsilon_i,$$

where we let $\varphi(B) = 0$, $\varphi(W) = 1$. The measure of racial disparity then becomes (see (15)):

$$dis = \hat{\beta} + \hat{\gamma}\,(E(\psi(e_i^1)|W) - E(\psi(e_i^1)|B)).$$

To implement the IOM concept of racial disparity, in which socioeconomic status as such is a legitimate source of inequality and only its correlation with race is problematic, we use the method that was described in the previous subsection. Let us therefore define e_i^k, $k = 1, 2$, as a function of c_i and the fractional rank (percentile) of i in the distribution of e^k: $e_i^k = \eta^k(c_i, \pi_i^k)$, $k = 1, 2$. The y function then can be written as

$$y_i = \alpha + \beta\varphi(c_i) + \gamma\psi \circ \eta^1(c_i, \pi_i^1) + \delta\chi(e_i^2) + \varepsilon_i$$

and the fairness gap becomes

$$\hat{\beta}(\varphi(c_i) - \varphi(\tilde{c})) + \hat{\gamma}(\psi(e_i^1) - \psi \circ \eta^1(\tilde{c}, \pi_i^1)).$$

If we pick as the reference value $\tilde{c} = W$, this expression reads

$$\hat{\beta}(\varphi(c_i) - 1) + \hat{\gamma}(\psi(e_i^1) - \psi \circ \eta^1(W, \pi_i^1)). \qquad (36)$$

It is then immediately obvious that racial disparity is equal to minus the average fairness gap among the Black population. Note that all individual fairness gaps for White individuals are equal to zero by construction.

It is instructive to compare this result with what would be obtained when we consider both race and socioeconomic status to be illegitimate sources of inequality. This is in line with the approach in the previous subsections but not with the measurement of racial disparity in the IOM definition.[27] The fairness gap is then equal to

$$\hat{\beta}(\varphi(c_i) - \varphi(\tilde{c})) + \hat{\gamma}(\psi(e_i^1) - \psi(\tilde{e}^1)).$$

If $\tilde{c} = W$ and if the *distribution* of e^1 among the Whites is taken as the reference $\tilde{e}^1$, as in the expected form of the fairness gap defined in (30), the fairness gap becomes

$$\hat{\beta}(\varphi(c_i) - 1) + \hat{\gamma}(\psi(e_i^1) - E(\psi(e_i^1)|W)),$$

so that racial disparity is again equal to minus the average fairness gap among Blacks. Note that the assumptions about the reference values imply that the "ideal" level of health care is defined such that the system gets it right on average for the Whites. Indeed, the average fairness gap among the Whites is equal to zero. However, the individual fairness gap for a White individual will only be zero if $\psi(e_i^1) = E(\psi(e_i^1)|W)$.[28]

---

[27] It would probably be the favoured approach if one followed the Kawachi et al. (2005) criticism on measuring racial disparity.

[28] Analogous results are obtained if we take $\tilde{c} = B$ and the distribution of e^1 among the Blacks as the reference $\tilde{e}^1$. Racial disparity then equals the average fairness gap of the White. This close analogy only holds under the assumption of additive separability.

Of course, while disparity is minus the average fairness gap among the Blacks in both cases, the choices of the reference value and therefore the assumptions about what is the "ideal" reference level of health care do differ. In the first (IOM) case we assume that the ideal level of health care for any Black is that of a White with the same health care needs and occupying the same fractional rank in the (White) distribution of socio-economic status as the Black is occupying in the Black distribution. All individual fairness gaps for White individuals are then equal to zero by construction. In the second case we assume that the system gets it right on average for the Whites. Of course, since SES now is an illegitimate source of inequality, the individual fairness gap may be different from zero for White individuals also. These interpretations stand to reason.

In conclusion, for the additively separable case, racial disparity becomes a special case of the fairness gap and satisfies the compensation condition. Different choices of the reference values will lead to a family of different measures. The interpretations suggested in the previous subsection may be helpful in picking the most adequate measure out of this family. Moreover, with (36) one sees that the fairness gap provides an interesting distribution of individual indices which makes it possible to analyze in more detail the impact of race on health consumption that is mediated by socioeconomic status. For instance, it may happen that the average fairness gap (and therefore disparity) does not change but that the distribution of the fairness gap improves unambiguously when the impact of race on socioeconomic status becomes more uniform across the distribution. The availability of these individual indices (and their consistency with the measure of racial disparity) opens a lot of interesting new possibilities.

4.1.3.2.2. The Non-separable Case For the non-separable case we focus on the IOM definition of racial disparity and we will compare the different approaches that have been proposed for the non-separable case (see section 3.2) to the fairness gap measured as

$$y_i - \gamma(\tilde{c}, \eta^1(\tilde{c}, \pi_i^1), e_i^2).$$

The "rank and replace" method (see (18)) gives in the present notation

$$E(y_i|W) - \int\int \gamma(B, e^1, \eta^2(W, \pi^2))f(e^1, \pi^2|B)\, de^1\, d\pi^2 \tag{37}$$

and

$$f^*(e) = f(e^1, F(e^2|W)|B)f(e^2|W).$$

Consider the fairness gap for $\tilde{c} = B$ which gives

$$y_i - \gamma(B, \eta^1(B, \pi_i^1), e_i^2).$$

This implies that the fairness gap is zero for every Black. The average fairness gap among the Whites becomes

$$E(\gamma_i | W) - \int \int \gamma(B, \eta^1(B, \pi^1), e^2) f(\pi^1, e^2 | W) \, d\pi^1 \, de^2. \tag{38}$$

Equation (38) shows immediately that choosing $\tilde{c} = B$ boils down to transforming the distribution of e^1 for Whites imagining what would happen to them if they were treated like Blacks. The average fairness gap among the White population coincides with the measure of racial disparity (37). Indeed, the second term in (38) is equivalent to computing $\int \gamma (B, e^1, e^2) f^* (e) \, de$ with

$$f^*(e) = f(F (e^1 | B), e^2 | W) f (e^1 | B).$$

Moreover,

$$f(e^1, F(e^2 | W) | B) f(e^2 | W) = f(F(e^1 | B), e^2 | W) f(e^1 | B)$$

is equivalent to

$$f(F(e^2 | W) | e^1, B) = f(F(e^1 | B) | e^2, W),$$

which holds true because the distribution of percentiles is uniform. Therefore, under the rank and replace method, and under the reference parameters specified above, the measure of disparity coincides with the average difference between Whites and Blacks of the fairness gap. The possibility to take other reference parameters in the fairness gap approach may suggest interesting alternative measures of disparity.

The analogy between the concepts from the equality of opportunity approach and racial disparity is much less clear for the method of propensity scores with rank-and-replace correction.

4.1.4. Conclusion

In conclusion, the constructive contributions to the measurement of socioeconomic or demographic inequalities in health and health care that one can make by looking at the formally similar theory of equal opportunities are the following:
- It is possible to construct distributions of individual partial advantage which provide richer information than average magnitudes or concentration curves;
- It is easy to accommodate and compare different ethical approaches within a unifying framework; in fact, the most common approaches available in the literature until now (the concentration index and racial disparity) can be interpreted as special cases of this more general approach;

- There is no problem in handling situations with more than one source of illegitimate inequalities, or with a non-linear underlying structure;
- The compensation principle is not satisfied by all approaches and this may be a helpful criterion in the selection—in particular, standardization procedures are not just pure statistics and have ethical implications in this respect;
- The reward principle is also a possible selection criterion, and one can refine the measures in order to introduce ethical preferences about the distribution of health care;
- Inequality measures either coincide with, or are preferable to, concentration measures which require a specific ordering of socioeconomic conditions;
- Numerous variants of measures of inequality and disparity can be constructed from measures inspired by conditional equality and egalitarian equivalence (such as direct unfairness and the fairness gap). The "average EDE" approach is also another suggestion.

Finally, let us recall an important recommendation regarding methodology. The theory of equal opportunity makes a clear distinction between the function y, which is a matter of fact, and the normative evaluation of a particular situation. It is sound to separate the empirical, purely factual, step of estimating the equation $y(c, e)$ from the normative steps having to do with drawing the frontier between c and e, and with selecting a particular measure of inequality. Depending on the particular approach that is adopted, more or less information about the function y is needed. For instance, regressing y on c, omitting e, may be problematic if one needs an unbiased coefficient. Once one draws a clear distinction between the "estimation" and the "evaluation" stage, and one uses inequality measures that are able to accommodate a complicated non-linear structure of $y(c, e)$, it becomes possible to have complete freedom in the estimation stage. Given the essential importance of identifying causal relationships in order to interpret the correlation structure between c and e this seems to be a decisive advantage.

4.2. Substantive Debate: Where to Draw the Line between "Legitimate" and "Illegitimate" Inequalities?

The formal apparatus of the theory of equal opportunities can be applied to any partition between c and e, and in the previous subsection we have exploited the formal similarity between this theory and issues in socioeconomic health inequalities or racial disparities in health care. But the theory of equal opportunities also suggests that the boundary between c and e should be ethically relevant. For instance, focusing on racial disparities while neglecting the inequalities independently generated by socioeconomic status may give a very partial picture of the prevailing inequities. Focusing on socioeconomic inequalities while neglecting the impact of genetic endowments on inequalities in health may fail to track how unequal the individuals really are in their life prospects. Moreover, the considerations developed about the c, e partition in the normative literature resonate with important debates in health policy about personal responsibility for lifestyle and risk-taking. In this section we discuss some of these general normative issues. In the next section we will show how these philosophical considerations bear on the empirical work.

Our brief review will illustrate some interesting features of the formal framework of the equality of opportunity approach. First, it is sufficiently rich to make a link between different parts of the literature that have remained rather disparate until now. More specifically, it allows for the integration in the formal literature on inequality measurement of some of the philosophical literature on the one hand and of the empirical work on the causes of inequalities in health and health care on the other hand. Second, it is sufficiently flexible to accommodate different ethical and empirical approaches and to compare their implications for the measurement of inequity in health and health care. This is a decisive advantage in a domain where there are many, often conflicting, opinions.

In the first subsection we discuss the two broad approaches in the literature: one holding individuals responsible for their preferences, the other holding them responsible for their choices. We will illustrate the abstract arguments with specific examples taken from the literature on lifestyles and health.[29] In the second subsection we go more deeply into the treatment of risk and uncertainty. To avoid confusion, it is useful here to add a point of terminology. Mainly in the philosophical literature, what we have called responsibility-sensitive egalitarianism is often denoted as "luck egalitarianism," with "luck" referring to all circumstances that are beyond the control of the individual. This luck egalitarianism is therefore closely related to what we will call the "choice" approach. In this interpretation "luck" is broader than what most economists would call risk or uncertainty, although of course all circumstances can be seen as events resulting from a kind of natural or social lottery.

4.2.1. Preference and Choice Approaches

The philosophical debate about the "responsibility cut" has seen various positions being developed. The main distinction is that between what could be called the "preference" and the "choice" approaches. The former is already strongly present in the work of Rawls (1971, 1982), who argued that treating persons as autonomous moral agents necessarily implies that they should assume responsibility for their goals and their conception of the good life. His difference (or maximin) principle then states that the primary goods (such as income and wealth, and the social bases of self-respect) should be allocated so as to maximize the opportunities of the worst-off in

---

[29] An overview of the economic literature on health behavior is given by Cawley and Ruhm in Chapter 3 of this Handbook.

society. Dworkin (1981a and b, 2000) further elaborates on the idea that individuals should be held responsible for their preferences: in his view, an individual cannot sensibly endorse his own preferences about how to conduct his life and at the same time request special help from public institutions on the ground that his preferences are a sort of handicap. Only those who consider their preferences as burdens or cravings, with which they do not identify, can ask for additional resources.

The "preference approach" was attacked by authors such as Arneson (1989), Cohen (1989), and Roemer (1998). They claim that preferences are often the product of upbringing and social influences, for which individuals cannot be held responsible, and they instead advocate the "common-sense" view that individuals should be held responsible only for what they have genuinely chosen, as opposed to what they have inherited from circumstances. In their view one can only be held responsible if one has control.

A second distinction in the literature is somewhat orthogonal to that between the preference and choice approaches. It relates to the justification for introducing responsibility considerations into the evaluation of justice. One approach (implicitly followed by most of the authors mentioned before) accepts that the responsibility cut is primary data from which one derives the adequate division of labor between social agencies and individuals. In the alternative approach the responsibility cut is derived from other principles having to do with the value of freedom, the importance of political participation, and the like. In this line, Anderson (1999), Sen (1999), and Fleurbaey (2008) defend the view that individuals should be put in good conditions of autonomy and freedom so that they can be the master of their lives and participate fully in social interactions. Yet, when going beyond this general principle, the distinction between the preference and the choice approaches also crops up in this "freedom" approach. Overly simplifying, Sen (1999) interprets freedom as the ability to choose from capability sets (and is therefore to be situated rather in the choice-control approach), whereas Fleurbaey (2008) argues that respect for freedom implies respect for personal preferences.

Applied to health, the different approaches would suggest different partitions between factors of inequalities. We will focus on the distinction between the preference and the choice approach. However, the second distinction is also important. While the "freedom" approach is harder to link to a specific proposal in the context of health, one can imagine that it would consider undesirable all inequalities which cannot be traced to the exercise of certain valuable forms of autonomy and freedom. The difficulty would then be to identify what are valuable forms of autonomy, in connection with the population's preferences or with individual choices.

4.2.1.1. The Choice Approach
In the first approach individuals are held responsible for those characteristics which are under their own control. One can interpret this in a narrow sense and hold

individuals simply responsible for all their choices. Yet this is arguably not in line with the basic intuition of the approach, as choices are also determined by factors that are not under the control of individuals. Let us illustrate. At first sight, one could say that individuals are to a large extent responsible for their BMI, as this is related to their eating behavior and their level of physical activity. Careful empirical research has shown, however, that cues in the environment may have a great impact on these decisions. The construction of recreational amenities (fitness areas) in Indianapolis led to a significant decrease in the BMI of children visiting pediatric clinics (Sandy et al., 2009). Posting the calorie content of foods and beverages in New York City Starbucks led to a lower consumption of food calories—even extending to the behavior of commuters who later visited other Starbucks establishments in cities where there was no calorie posting (Bollinger et al., 2011). Surely, individual children (or their parents) are not responsible for the availability of fitness areas, nor can individual consumers be held responsible for the information on calorie content that is given in Starbucks. We also know that there is an education gradient in health behaviors, and that this gradient is explained to some extent by differences in cognitive abilities (Cutler and Lleras-Muney, 2010). Can it reasonably be stated that individuals control (or choose) their cognitive abilities?

It seems that "genuine control" requires that one corrects for interindividual differences in the environment and also for differences in the choice-making abilities of the individuals. This will be even more relevant if one reasons within the freedom approach to responsibility-sensitive egalitarianism. Yet this brings us on to a slippery slope. Is there any room left for genuine control in a deterministic world, if we better and better understand and explain behavior? In a world where the belief in determinism seems great, "it is difficult to expand equality of opportunity in ways that satisfactorily address the constraining effects of social circumstances, gender socialization, cultural convictions and so on, without undermining the idea of people as responsible agents" (Phillips, 2006, p. 19). The choice approach makes the responsibility cut depend on the theory of free will and therefore raises all sorts of thorny metaphysical issues that Rawls and Dworkin deliberately wanted to avoid.

The problem gets a special twist for economists working within the paradigm of rational choice. In this model, genuine choice is an elusive notion, as individual decisions result from a mechanical optimization exercise with a given objective (preferences) and a given set of options (determined by the budget set and possibly additional constraints). All endogenous variables are causally influenced by other variables of the model and therefore cannot embody free will (Fleurbaey, 2008, p. 87).

Authors within the choice approach have opted for a pragmatic way out of this deadlock. As we have seen, the most popular solution is that of Roemer (1998). He suggests that every society should be left to resolve the metaphysical debate for itself. "Types" (circumstance classes) are defined *a priori*, and, since effort is usually unobservable in practice, it is treated as a residual capturing all the differences that are not due to type. The proposed statistical device, which consists of defining that individuals exert the same effort when they lie at the same rank in the distribution of health for their type, makes it possible to take into account the effects of additional conditioning factors in an indirect way. Suppose that we define types on the basis of SES and education. If SES and education are correlated with features of the external environment or with cognitive abilities, the Roemer measure of effort will take into account these correlations. However, this approach is to some extent a black box and does not offer a really convincing answer to the basic philosophical criticism on the difficult delineation of what control is in a deterministic world. Moreover, even from a more mundane perspective, it will at best yield a lower bound of the true inequality of opportunity. Indeed, there will always be unobservable circumstances, such as genetic endowments, so that the *a priori* partition of the population into classes of circumstances is always coarser than one would like. Taking into account the correlation between types and these unobservable factors is not a satisfactory solution to this problem.

4.2.1.2. The Preference Approach

The "preference approach" holds individuals responsible for their preferences, i.e. their conceptions of a good life, even if these preferences are not chosen and are not under their control. This may lead to a very different evaluation of inequality of opportunity in actual applications. Take the case of two groups in the population with a different cultural background such that individuals belonging to the first group are working (too) hard without taking sufficient time to relax, while individuals from the second group opt for a more healthy lifestyle. In the choice approach one might consider the resulting health inequalities as inequitable, because they simply reflect parental influences during childhood for which individuals cannot be held responsible. In fact, in the Roemer approach differences in preferences that are linked to the type of the individuals will be corrected for when defining the level of "effort." In the preference approach, however, the differences in health and wealth between individuals from these two groups will not be seen as an indication of inequity, if the different lifestyles reflect genuinely different preferences concerning food consumption and physical activity or, more generally, concerning the trade-off between health and wealth.

Since preferences are one of the building blocks of all economic models, the preference approach may seem to fit the economic approach perfectly. Yet one should be careful about equating immediately "revealed" preferences with the *authentic* views of the good life that have to be respected. Even more care is needed if one relies on the freedom justification for responsibility-sensitive egalitarianism. The difficulty is then to separate cravings and involuntary addictions (which may be suspected in many unhealthy lifestyles) from genuine preferences. One could even claim that advertising and social pressure may lead to differences in preferences which cannot be seen as authentic.

Let us illustrate again with an example in the domain of health behavior. Chou et al. (2008) have shown that fast food restaurant advertising on television has a significant effect on obesity. According to their estimates, banning this advertising would reduce the number of overweight adolescents in the US by 12 percent. Our point is not to discuss the reliability of these estimates, nor the desirability of such a ban. What is relevant here is that these results raise the question whether preferences that are induced by television advertising for children (and that may last in their adult life) should be seen as genuine preferences that have to be respected, or rather as cravings caused by the social environment. This is a difficult question indeed, since we run again the risk of landing on a slippery slope. What is the criterion for determining what are authentic preferences? How to avoid ending in a paternalistic approach, in which the analyst ultimately imposes her own views of the good life on the individuals? Surely, such paternalism goes very much against respect for preferences. Empirical work on preference formation may be a valuable input in this kind of debate.

Some philosophers have proposed more general approaches establishing an explicit connection between theories of justice and applied issues in health. Segall (2010) focuses on one of the main challenges for luck egalitarianism (in the broader sense of the choice approach), which is the frightening prospect of denying health care to those who can be considered responsible for their health problems. Segall proposes to avoid this prospect by mixing luck egalitarian justice with a sufficientarian component guaranteeing that basic needs should be met for all, irrespective of their responsibility.

Another proposal for health policy evaluation has been developed by Daniels (1985, 2008). Daniels starts from the observation that Rawls made the simplifying assumption that the members of society are all healthy, and seeks how to extend Rawls' principles of justice in order to make room for the treatment of health inequalities. He rejects the simple solution of extending the list of primary goods governed by the difference principle and proposes to give health a special importance in view of its contribution to people's opportunities. Rawls' principle of "fair equality of opportunities" would, under this extension, require providing health care and managing the other determinants of health in order to guarantee to all, as much as possible, access to normal functioning as a precondition for an autonomous life. Daniels does not make a specific proposal about how to measure health inequalities, but argues that residual health inequalities would be just when all goods governed by the principle of fair equality of opportunities and by the difference principle would be fairly distributed. Obviously, even this does not specify how health priorities should be defined in ordinary health policy decisions. Regarding this issue, Daniels' proposal is procedural, not substantive: decisions should be made through a fair deliberative process. Although this procedural way out is a bit disappointing (after all, it is one of the tasks of philosophers to make a valuable substantive input into this deliberative process), Daniels conveys at least two interesting insights for our purpose. First, the thesis that health inequalities would be fair once all goods have been fairly distributed comes close to the idea that inequalities reflecting different goals in life may be acceptable for a Rawlsian approach. Yet according to Daniels inequity in health cannot be evaluated on its own, but has to be integrated in a broader view on inequity in overall life prospects. This insight will be the leitmotiv of section 5 of this chapter. Second, this broader view supports some skepticism about the possibility of assigning responsibility to individuals for their lifestyle and its health consequences. The priority is to guarantee normal functioning in view of promoting opportunities, and in this perspective the social hijacking made by those who develop risky lifestyles and become a burden for the health care system may be treated by preventive measures of education and incentives rather than by punitive ascriptions of responsibility and a denial of equality in care.

4.2.2. Luck and Risk

As we have seen, theories of justice that advocate neutralizing the differential impact over individual success of circumstances that can be considered a matter of sheer luck are branded as "luck egalitarian." However, most authors follow Dworkin (2000) in considering that not all kinds of luck should be submitted to the elimination of differential effects. Thinking of gamblers, Dworkin indeed drew the distinction between "option luck," the kind of luck gamblers deliberately submit themselves to, and "brute luck," the uninsurable luck that even reasonable and prudent people remain vulnerable to. This distinction obviously resonates with many issues in health, as one may think of making a distinction between those who deliberately take a risk by their unhealthy lifestyle and those who are simply the victims of unfortunate unforeseeable events.

However, this distinction has proved hard to specify more precisely. Dworkin himself acknowledged that the boundary between cases of option luck and cases of brute luck is fuzzy and a matter of proportion. In particular, when the risky option stochastically dominates the safe options, it is hard to hold individuals responsible for the unequal outcomes they obtain, as even the unlucky made the most prudent choice. Conversely, while it makes more sense to hold the unlucky responsible for submitting themselves to an unfavorable gamble when the risky option is dominated by the safe options, it is no longer clear that a good society should make such unfavorable gambles available when dominating safe options exist. However, even if usual casino gambles are indeed unfavorable (at least in terms of second-order stochastic dominance), the intuition that unlucky gamblers should be left to their fate appears to loom large in the literature on this topic and is motivated, as argued by Dworkin, by a certain respect for risky lifestyles.

More principled and radical attitudes have been defended. At one extreme, Vallentyne (2002) proposes to equalize initial prospects at the beginning of individuals' lives, and to compensate neither option nor brute luck effects, which eliminates the problem of specifying a distinction. One difficulty with this approach is that it is compatible with very large inequalities due to differential luck through life. Moreover, equality of prospects can be artificially organized by lotteries at the beginning of life (as imagined by Harsanyi, 1977, babies could be reallocated to families by lot), without apparently making the distribution of final situations more just. At the other extreme, one may argue that all kinds of luck are beyond individual responsibility (Le Grand, 1991) and that everyone deserves the expected outcome of his actions but not the differential gain or loss due to the random events that follow. Even if one accepts this view, one can still admit the existence of gambles in cases in which even the unlucky feel better off *ex post* than with the safer options, for instance because the thrill of risk is really what they enjoy (Lippert-Rasmussen, 2001).

As a follow-up to his distinction between option luck and brute luck, Dworkin proposes a particular way to evaluate health policies and to organize the health care system. The idea is simple. He considers that the ideal health care system would be one in which everyone would be perfectly informed about health risks and about the medical technology, and could take an insurance against adverse health events (including an unfavorable genetic endowment) on the basis of equal budget possibilities and in a perfect insurance market. Such an insurance system would transform all brute luck into option luck. This is obviously not possible but his proposal is to make the real health system mimic this ideal as much as possible, with taxes, public transfers, and subsidized provision of care replacing the movements of resources that would be implemented under the ideal (hypothetical) system.

This proposal has been criticized by Roemer (1985), who observed that when adverse health events decrease the marginal utility of income, individuals would *ex ante* refuse to take insurance (or would even want to counter-insure themselves and consume more when they are lucky and healthy). This is problematic even when individuals do have the opportunity to insure, because *ex post* the unlucky are in a bad situation. Their refusal to insure is based on their *ex ante* ignorance of their final situation. Had they known that they would be unlucky they would have opted for the insurance. *Ex ante* preferences are based on less information about the state of the world than *ex post* preferences and the latter should have precedence in social evaluation, as argued by Fleurbaey (2010). This reflects the classical divide in social choice between the *ex ante* approach that applies a standard social welfare criterion to individual expected utilities and the *ex post* approach that looks at the possible final distributions of welfare.

Dworkin's insurance device is even more questionable when applied to transfers across different individuals with unequal congenital endowments. It appears grossly unfair to assign lower resources to badly endowed individuals on the ground that if they had had a chance to be better endowed they would have preferred to concentrate their resources on the lucky state. In conclusion, Dworkin's hypothetical insurance proposal, which seems *prima facie* attractive if one thinks of ordinary insurance against losses which do not affect the utility function, may be unsuitable for an application to health care if adverse health events decrease the marginal utility of income.

What lessons can be drawn from these debates for the measurement of inequity in health and health care? We will discuss some specific methodological points in our overview of empirical applications in the next subsection. From a more general perspective, the most important insight is that measures focusing on racial or gender disparities, or on socioeconomic factors of inequality, should not be interpreted as measuring a comprehensive notion of unfairness. They only capture a part of what makes individuals unequally endowed in front of life. Insofar as public policies should be meant to improve the life chances of the worst-off and not just to remove certain specific factors of inequality, it might be a significant improvement for the literature on health inequalities to move the cut between relevant and irrelevant factors of inequality closer to the cut that theories of justice would suggest. More specifically, the impression that socioeconomic inequalities appear especially unjust because they are produced by human institutions should be resisted. The most problematic inequalities are those which are unfair and can most easily be eliminated. It is not necessarily the case that social institutions are more malleable than natural factors, or that their effects are more remediable than the effects of natural causes. If certain congenital handicaps can be easily cured this is a more urgent matter than hardwired inequalities due to early education.

4.3. Empirical Applications

Empirical applications of the idea of inequality of opportunity in health start from the estimation of some reduced-form outcome function $y = f(z)$, where y can refer to health or to health care, depending on the application. As emphasized before, it is important to distinguish clearly this estimation stage from the normative evaluation stage. The empirical analyst should be as free as possible to estimate the best possible explanatory model. The previous sections have suggested at least four important methodological issues that should be considered in going from the estimation stage to the evaluation stage.

The first essential step is the partitioning of the vector z in (c, e). This partitioning will be different depending on the ethical position that is taken. From an applied perspective, the distinction between the control and preference approaches seems the most relevant. While this distinction is clear in principle, there remain some hard nuts to crack for applied analysts. We have already given some examples in previous sections. Suppose one finds a significant effect of religion on the use of health care: Does this reflect differences in preferences (e.g. a genuinely different attitude towards physical suffering and death) or a bias due to indoctrination or a lack of correct information? If education has an effect on lifestyle and therefore on health, does this result from different cognitive capacities, from differences in the socioeconomic environment, or from deliberate choices? If there is a significant effect of region, does this capture differences in supply, in needs or in preferences? In fact, many observable variables will reflect a mixture of c and e considerations.

This brings us immediately to the second point. In most cases it is extremely useful to estimate the structural model underlying the reduced form $y = f(z)$. Many of the questions concerning the classification of the variables in c or e are ultimately identification questions, which could in principle be answered if a fully specified structural model could be estimated with a complete set of data. Statistical devices like the one proposed by Roemer would then no longer be needed—unless one takes the theoretical position that these statistical devices are not just approximations, but reflect a substantial and ethically attractive position.

Third, at the end of the estimation exercise there will remain some residual unexplained variation. In principle the vector z includes *all* variables including the error term, and the latter too, therefore, has to be allocated to either c or e. It is common practice to simply neglect the residuals and to focus on the deterministic part of the model. Yet this may be highly misleading in this setting—or, formulated more correctly, it implies a specific ethical position. The error term will to some extent capture purely random effects. Including it in c or not then relates to the philosophical discussion on brute versus option luck, or on *ex ante* versus *ex post*. However, in applied work the residual will also capture the effect of omitted variables and, in general, unobserved individual heterogeneity—which, in its turn, may be seen as c or e variables. There are no easy solutions, but careful and explicit consideration of the issue is definitely needed.

Finally, we have argued that measuring horizontal equity requires taking an explicit stance on vertical equity. The specification of the "ideal health care" function $hc^*(hn_i, P_i^2; SES_i, d_i)$ is crucial to understand the reward principles underlying the different measures of inequality of opportunity. If one is not happy with the pragmatic assumption that "on average, the system gets it right," one has to think about the additional question of how to specify $hc^*(\cdot)$.

Before turning to applications of the equality of opportunity approach proper, it should be mentioned that recent work within the traditional approaches (concentration

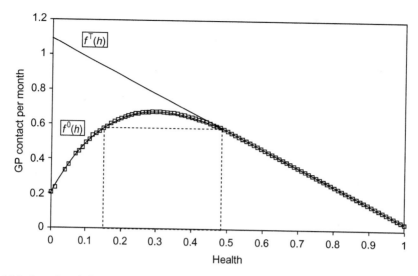

Figure 16.3 Actual and ideal health care function in Sutton (2002).

index or racial disparities) has explored some interesting possibilities that are highly relevant for measuring inequality of opportunity. One example, that has been mentioned already before, is the measurement of vertical equity by Sutton (2002). He starts from the following specification of the health care equation:

$$hc_i = f^0(h_i) + \gamma d_i + \delta SES_i + \varepsilon_i, \tag{39}$$

where $f^0(h_i)$ is a non-linear function, approximated in his empirical work by a polynomial. His empirical estimate of the relationship between health and general practitioner contacts in Scotland is shown in Figure 16.3. Sutton then claims that this empirical function does not necessarily capture the ideal "target" function $f^T(h_i)$ and interprets the difference as capturing "vertical inequity":

$$hc_i = [f^T(h_i) + f^{VI}(h_i)] + \gamma d_i + \delta SES_i + \varepsilon_i$$

To identify $f^T(h_i)$, he uses Arrow's (1971) insight that an optimal policy should be *input-progressive*, i.e. that df^T/dh should be negative if worse health is associated with a greater capacity to benefit from health care, which seems a natural assumption. He therefore draws the conclusion that the positively sloped segment in the estimated function $f^0(h)$ (for $h < 0.31$) cannot reflect "ideal" health care. He then reestimates (39) for the range of health values for which $df^0/dh < 0$—and interprets this estimated function as an approximation of $f^T(h_i)$. This function turns out to be nearly linear and is shown as the target function $f^T(h)$ in Figure 16.3. It is clear that Sutton needs strong and debatable assumptions to arrive at his results. Yet further work in this direction could help in getting a better insight in how to specify the (richer) function $hc^*(hn_i, P_i^2; SES_i, d_i)$, which plays an essential role in the measurement of vertical and horizontal equity.

A second interesting contribution is made by Bago d'Uva et al. (2009) in the context of measuring horizontal inequity with the concentration index (see also Van Ourti, 2004, and van Doorslaer et al., 2004). As we noted already, in recent years the awareness has grown that the correction for needs that is necessary for the measurement of horizontal inequity requires an explicit decision about what are the needs and non-needs variables. Recent applied work has implemented sophisticated non-linear models, for which the linear decomposition method does not work properly. Bago d'Uva et al. (2009) specify the unobserved individual heterogeneity with a latent class model and explain the probabilities of belonging to a given class with individual time-invariant characteristics. The latter can then be partitioned in needs and non-needs variables in the usual way. This allows for a richer interpretation of this individual heterogeneity in terms of the (c, e) partition. As for the remaining unexplained residual, Bago d'Uva et al. (2009) distinguish between what they call the "conventional" and the "conservative" approach. In the former all residual variation is assumed to be determined by non-needs factors; in the latter only the inequality that results from the observed systematic association between income and non-need factors is considered inequitable, i.e. the residual variation is seen as capturing needs. These two approaches can therefore be seen as the two extreme cases in which one interprets the residual in the health care equation as fully c or fully e respectively. The distinction turns out to be empirically relevant, with the conservative approach giving higher estimates of socioeconomic inequity. The treatment of the residuals does indeed matter.

Let us now turn to some explicit applications of the equality of opportunity approach in the health context. In these applications "circumstances" are usually defined to include the socioeconomic background and, more specifically, the childhood circumstances of the individuals. Lifestyle variables (such as smoking, eating behavior, physical activity) are seen as effort variables. The classification of other variables (e.g. educational level or region) is less clear. The literature does not relate explicitly to the philosophical approaches that we described in the previous section. It often implicitly accepts the choice approach and makes use of the Roemer statistical approximation.

A first set of empirical results gets its theoretical underpinning in the treatment of luck by Lefranc et al. (2009). These authors introduce luck explicitly as a third factor, in addition to effort and circumstances, claiming that "luck may appear as a fair source of inequality provided that it is decorrelated from circumstances, in short, even-handed" (p. 1190). Defining the distribution of outcome conditional on circumstances and effort as $F(y|c, e)$, they therefore claim that equality of opportunity is satisfied if: $\forall (c, c') \forall e, F(y|c, e) = F(y|c', e)$. In the terminology introduced before, this implies an *ex ante* approach in which individuals are not compensated for being unlucky. The

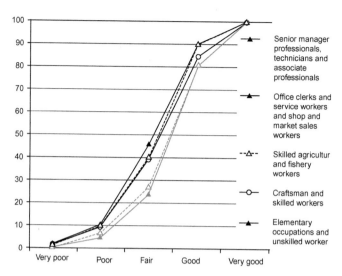

Figure 16.4 Cumulative distribution functions of self-assessed health according to socioeconomic status of mother (Trannoy et al., 2010).

condition can be simplified if one accepts the Roemer approach with effort defined as the rank of the individual in the outcome distribution of her own type, i.e. if effort is the residual after having taken circumstances into account. Under these conditions equality of opportunity is satisfied if $F(y|c) = F(y|c')$.[30] As we have emphasized before, in most empirical applications it is not possible to observe all relevant c variables and the definition of types will necessarily be coarse. However, it is easy to see that $F(y|c_1) = F(y|c_1')$ with c_1 a subvector of c is a necessary (but not sufficient) condition for equality of opportunity. This is still a very stringent condition. Therefore, the authors propose to work with stochastic dominance conditions. They claim that there is necessarily inequality of opportunity if $F(y|c_1)$ first-order dominates $F(y|c_1')$, i.e. if $F(y|c_1) \leq F(y|c_1')$ for all values of y, with the inequality being strict for some values of y.[31]

This approach is implemented by Trannoy et al. (2010) and by Rosa Dias (2010) with data for France and Great Britain respectively. In both cases circumstances are defined in terms of the characteristics of the parents. Figure 16.4 illustrates the French results with circumstances defined as the socioeconomic status of the mother. After

[30] Lefranc et al. (2009) emphasize that in this approach all random factors should be ascribed to effort. If not, the rank in the outcome distribution for a given type can no longer serve to retrieve effort. One may wonder why these authors introduce luck as a "third" factor, given that circumstances cover all variables for which individuals are not held responsible, and effort covers the rest. It is simpler to understand that they put all the variables that appear as random in the data in the effort category.

[31] Lefranc et al. (2009) also consider the case of second-order stochastic dominance. Health applications have focused on first-order dominance, however, mainly because of the ordinal nature of the health variables used.

formal testing, Trannoy et al. and Rosa Dias conclude that the health distributions for adults that had parents with a higher socioeconomic status dominate the health distributions for adults with parents of lower socioeconomic status. Trannoy et al. (2010) find similar results if circumstances are defined in terms of the health situation of the parents. The facts that types are defined here in a coarse way and the application of the extreme criterion of first-order stochastic dominance both strengthen the conclusion that there is inequality of opportunity with respect to health in France and in Great Britain.

Trannoy et al. (2010) and Rosa Dias (2010) realize that this approach in terms of stochastic dominance does not give a specific measure of the degree of inequality of opportunity. They therefore also show a second set of results in which they start from a parametric form of the outcome function $f(z)$. Following Roemer, Rosa Dias accepts that all correlation between effort and circumstance variables should ultimately be interpreted as part of the circumstances. He therefore (deliberately) omits all the e variables from $f(z)$ and estimates the equation

$$h_i = \alpha + \beta c_i + \varepsilon_i,$$

where ε_i is a residual and c_i is a vector of variables related to the childhood circumstances (such as smoking behavior, health and socioeconomic status of the parents). He then computes the pseudo-Gini[32] coefficient for $\hat{h}_i = \hat{\alpha} + \hat{\beta} c_i = h_i - \hat{\varepsilon}_i$. This is basically "direct unfairness" (conditional equality) as proposed by Fleurbaey and Schokkaert (2009) with the residual ε_i implicitly treated as the only effort variable, independent of circumstances c_i by construction, and put at its (mean) reference value zero. Rosa Dias (2009) finds that the pseudo-Gini applied to $\hat{h}_i$ is between 21 percent and 26 percent (varying over the waves) of the pseudo-Gini applied to h. Trannoy et al. (2010) interpret education (ED_i) and socioeconomic status as effort variables but clean them for the correlation with circumstances (socioeconomic situation and health of parents) by estimating the following model:

$$ED_i = \alpha_0^a + \alpha_1^a d_i + \beta^a c_i + u_i^a \tag{40}$$

$$SES_i = \alpha_0^b + \alpha_1^b d_i + \beta^b c_i + \eta^b \hat{u}_i^a + u_i^b \tag{41}$$

$$h_i = \alpha_0^c + \alpha_1^c d_i + \beta^c c_i + \eta^c \hat{u}_i^a + \theta^c \hat{u}_i^b + u_i^c, \tag{42}$$

where $\hat{u}_i^a$ and $\hat{u}_i^b$ are the generalized residuals from the binary probit models (40) and (41). They then compare the Gini and the Erreygers index for h_i and for the hypothetical situation where all individuals have the health situation h_i^* corresponding to the best possible circumstances. If all individuals had been fortunate enough to grow

---

[32] The use of the pseudo-Gini is necessary because h is measured by self-assessed health, measured on a discrete ordinal scale.

up with the best circumstances the Gini coefficient would decrease by 57 percent and the Erreygers index by 44 percent.[33]

These applications are based on Roemer's idea that effort should be purged of any contamination coming from circumstances. Jusot et al. (2010) compare the Roemer approach with what they call the Barry approach, named after the philosopher Brian Barry who claimed (as summarized by Roemer 1998) that "the fact that generally high levels of effort were due to familial pressure does not make their having expended high levels of effort less admirable and less deserving than it would have been absent such pressure." The Roemer and Barry approaches are obviously closely linked to the choice and preference views respectively. Jusot et al. (2010) use French data on subjectively assessed health (a binary variable, taking the value 1 for individuals reporting to be in good or very good health) and include childhood circumstances in c_i and lifestyle variables (smoking and eating behavior) in e_i. They then calculate predicted latent health status using a probit model. In Barry's context, predicted health status is calculated as

$$\hat{h}_i^B = \hat{\alpha}_0^B + \hat{\alpha}_1^B d_i + \hat{\beta}^B c_i + \hat{\eta}^B e_i. \tag{43}$$

In Roemer's context the approach is similar to that in Trannoy et al. (2010), with

$$\hat{h}_i^R = \hat{\alpha}_0^R + \hat{\alpha}_1^R d_i + \hat{\beta}^R c_i + \hat{\eta}^R \hat{u}_i, \tag{44}$$

where $\hat{u}_i$ stands for the generalized residuals from the probit model linking lifestyles to circumstances, i.e.

$$e_i = \lambda + \delta c_i + u_i.$$

They then use the variance decomposition (Shorrocks, 1982) to split the inequality in $\hat{h}_i^B$ and $\hat{h}_i^R$ into its different components. Note that their focus on predicted health means that they neglect the contribution of luck to total inequality. It turns out that the differences between the Roemer and Barry approaches are minimal. While the contribution of circumstances to total inequality is 46.4 percent in the former, it is still 45.7 percent in the latter.

Jusot et al. (2010) remain within a reduced-form approach. However, if there is sufficient information about effort and circumstances, it may be worthwhile to work with a fully specified structural model $y = f(c, e)$. Estimating such a full structural model makes it possible to interpret carefully the correlation between c and e variables. This may give useful insights into how to classify variables (such as

---

[33] Fixing a reference value for the circumstances is reminiscent of the fairness gap (Fleurbaey and Schokkaert, 2009). The latter, however, would compute the inequality in $(h_i - h_i^*)$. In general, this does not coincide with the difference between the inequality in h_i and that in h_i^*.

education or region) that obviously reflect a mixture of different underlying mechanisms. Moreover, a structural model is definitely needed if we want to link the measurement of inequity to the deeper philosophical debate on legitimate and illegitimate causes of inequality. For this purpose we need to be able to identify "genuine control" and "authentic preferences." In this regard, the treatment of unobserved heterogeneity is particularly relevant. As Deaton (2011) writes: "Facts and correlations, without an understanding of causation, are neither sufficient to guide policy nor to make ethical judgments ... It is possible that an inequality that might seem to be *prima facie* unjust might actually be the consequence of a deeper mechanism that is in part benevolent, or that is unjust in a different way."

Until now, the introduction of structural models in the literature on inequality of opportunity has been rare. One good example is Balia and Jones (2011). They specify a latent factor model for the initiation of smoking, cessation and mortality, and show that parental smoking plays an important role in the dynamics of smoking and indirectly affects mortality. As in Bago d'Uva et al. (2009), analysis of the latent factors makes it possible to get a better insight into the relative importance of unobserved differences in preferences. Balia and Jones (2011) analyze the predictions of two hypothetical scenarios: one in which everyone is given the best circumstances with respect to parental smoking and another one in which everyone is given the highest level of effort, i.e. nobody has started smoking. Average predicted median lifespan is 79.5 years in the actual data, and becomes 82.2 and 86.0 in the best circumstances and the best effort scenarios respectively. The inequality in predicted lifespans, as measured by the Gini, is 0.041 in the actual data, 0.039 in the best circumstances scenario, and 0.027 in the best efforts scenario. The contribution of circumstances to inequality is therefore relatively small. This is easy to explain: the level of "parental smoking" is only one (perhaps rather minor) aspect of circumstances.

If we want to exploit the full richness of the equality of opportunity framework in empirical work, the analysis of structural models is a promising way to go. This is all the more true as the literature on the causes of smoking and obesity is booming (see the chapter by Cawley and Ruhm in this volume). Moreover, the availability of richer datasets has recently led to a rapid growth in the literature on the effects of childhood circumstances on adult health and wealth (Case et al., 2002, 2005; Currie and Stabile, 2003; Currie, 2009; Rosa Dias, 2010; Van den Berg et al., 2006). This work makes it possible to analyze carefully the relative importance of the different pathways linking childhood circumstances to adult health (ranging from direct fetal influences to the indirect effect through educational performance and adult socioeconomic status). It seems very natural to integrate the empirical insights from this literature into the normative framework sketched in the previous section.

5. WHY CARE ABOUT EQUITY IN HEALTH? HEALTH AND WELL-BEING

In the previous sections we have followed the health economic literature and focused on inequity in health and in health care *per se*. One might wonder, however, why society should be interested in these partial inequities. Let us first consider inequity in health. If (as seems reasonable) individuals are mainly concerned about overall well-being and if different dimensions of well-being are to some extent substitutable, then "a state of affairs in which those who are otherwise worse off are healthier than those who are otherwise more fortunate is *more* just rather than less just than a state of affairs which is exactly the same except that health is equally distributed" (Hausman, 2007, p. 50). An exclusive focus on health (or, for that matter, any other dimension of well-being) could then lead to misleading conclusions about overall inequity. Rejecting the idea of substitutability leads us into specific egalitarianism (Tobin, 1970) with an ultimate requirement that equity should be achieved for all dimensions separately. Yet this requirement is extremely demanding and seems to neglect the fact that "people live differently and encounter different environments ... making egalitarianism into a monstrous fantasy of utter uniformity" (Hausman, 2007, p. 58). A focus on each dimension separately also goes strongly against the spirit of the theories of equality of opportunity which deliberately leave scope for choice and/or for differences in preferences.

All this does not imply that it is uninteresting to measure inequity in health. First, there is a (perhaps weak) pragmatic argument. The large stream of policy documents on the topic suggests that policy makers are concerned about health inequity, and surveys show that the same is true for the population at large. Second, in line with the ideas of Daniels (2008), one can take the position that health is perhaps not a dimension like the others but has a special importance in view of its contribution to people's overall opportunities—this, however, should be reflected in a suitable measure of overall well-being. Third, collecting information on inequity in health may correct the imbalance in a large part of the economic literature that reduces inequity in overall well-being to inequity in income or material welfare. As an example, adding information on socioeconomic inequity in health usually shows that overall inequity in well-being is larger than what one might suspect by looking at income only. It is probably this concern for cumulative deprivation, with the poorest being at the same time less healthy, that motivates the scientific literature and the policy interest in socioeconomic inequities in health. Of course, the information on inequities in health would be an equally valuable complement to the information on income inequality if the results went in the other direction. Yet in some cases evaluating the distribution of overall well-being (capturing both health and material welfare) is a more natural way of analyzing the issue of cumulative deprivation.

A somewhat different story can be told about inequity in health care. Nobody will argue that health care as such is a positive outcome that should appear in the list of desirable dimensions of individual well-being. Equity in health care should be seen in the first place as an instrumental objective—it is important insofar as it contributes to equity in health. One can extend this instrumental reasoning by considering the relevance of equity in health care for other relevant dimensions of individual well-being, such as the feeling of being treated in a fair way by society. Denying health care to people suffering from illness and pain may be seen as a particularly severe infringement on their human dignity, independent of the health effects. Of course, broadening the scope of relevant dimensions of well-being to include respect for human dignity brings us close to the view that society is concerned not only about outcomes, but also about the process through which these outcomes are reached. Equity in health care may obviously be taken up as an important element in such a process-sensitive view of justice (Sen, 2002).

While inequity in health and in health care remain interesting research topics, a focus on overall well-being is necessary to put the partial results on health inequity into a broader perspective. In this section we will therefore consider the relationship between equity in health (care) and equity in well-being. We first look briefly at the literature on equity in finance from this perspective. We then discuss the problem of evaluating the inequality in the bidimensional (income, health) vectors of different individuals.

5.1. Equity in Finance

In most societies there is a widespread conviction that health care is not a commodity like other commodities, because health care expenditures are largely imposed on individuals, rather than freely chosen. It follows that the financial burden should not disproportionately rest on those who suffer from illness, i.e. that it should be largely independent of the health risks. Many studies on equity in the financing of health care go even further and investigate whether health care financing is linked to ability to pay, partly because there seems to be a widespread commitment to this principle among policy makers (Wagstaff and van Doorslaer, 2000b). A financing structure is then called progressive if health care expenditures take a larger part of income for the rich than for the poor and regressive in the opposite case.

Comparative studies have investigated the degree of progressiveness of overall health care financing in different countries (van Doorslaer et al., 1999; Wagstaff and van Doorslaer 2000b; De Graeve and Van Ourti, 2003). The ethical relevance of this concept of "progressiveness" is not completely clear, however. Look at the simple example of Table 16.5. Countries A and B have the same pre-tax income distribution with the poor having an income of 50 and the rich having an income of 150. Total

Table 16.5 Health Care Financing—Hypothetical Example

	A (tax financed) Health Contributions	Tax	Total	B (social insurance) Health Contributions	Tax	Total
Poor (50)	2.5	10	12.5	5	7.5	12.5
Rich (150)	17.5	70	87.5	15	72.5	87.5
	20	80	100	20	80	100

health care expenditures are 20, and we assume that health care is free, i.e. that there are no out-of-pocket payments to be paid by the patients. Country A finances its health care expenditures with taxes—i.e. in a progressive way in line with the ability-to-pay principle. Country B has a system of proportional social insurance contributions and its health financing is therefore not progressive. However, in the example country B has a more progressive tax system (used to finance the other government expenditures) than country A. Overall, the total health care expenditures and the net income distribution are identical in countries A and B. In these circumstances it is hard to support the claim that the differences in the financing structure in the two countries have any direct social relevance. What ultimately matters is the overall well-being of the poor and the rich, and these are the same in countries A and B.

The problem with the example in Table 16.5 is directly linked to the fact that health care expenditures are financed out of the general budget and that the assignment of health care expenditures to different financing sources is in that case largely arbitrary. This issue does not arise when one focuses only on the effects of user charges or out-of-pocket payments of the patients. The empirical work shows that these out-of-pocket payments usually are a particularly regressive component of health care financing (Schokkaert and Van de Voorde, 2011). This is easy to understand. If the absolute level of health care expenditures were about the same for the poor and the rich (which seems a conservative assumption, given the available evidence on socioeconomic inequalities in health), then by construction these expenditures would take up a larger fraction of income for the poorer households. User charges can become "progressive," however, if the rich consume disproportionately more health care. The consequences of this are illustrated by the results for 13 Asian territories in O'Donnell et al. (2008). O'Donnell et al. find that out-of-pocket payments for health care are regressive only in Japan and Taiwan, that they are proportional to ability to pay in China, Hong Kong, Korea, Kyrgyzstan, and the Punjab, and that they are even progressive in Bangladesh, Indonesia, Nepal, the Philippines, Sri Lanka, and Thailand. However, this mainly reflects that the poor in these so-called "progressive" countries receive less health care since they simply cannot afford to pay and therefore forgo treatment. This suggests that looking at the financing side in isolation may be very misleading in a situation of underconsumption. It is necessary to consider simultaneously (equity in) provision and (equity in) financing.

We therefore agree with the conclusion that "rationalizing the widespread commitment to the ability-to-pay principle in health care financing appears to be harder than might at first be imagined" (Wagstaff and van Doorslaer, 2000b, p. 1818). From our perspective the findings suggest that one should indeed reason within a broader concept of well-being, including provision (health and health care) and net material consumption as two relevant dimensions. This conclusion remains valid when we drop the ability-to-pay principle and consider the less ambitious objective that individuals with health problems should not have to pay themselves for their treatment, i.e. that they should not be confronted with an income shock on top of the health shock. In applying this principle, the recent literature has mainly focused on the relationship between health care expenditures and poverty in developing countries.

Two approaches have been developed (Wagstaff and van Doorslaer, 2003; Wagstaff, 2008). The first is to look at so-called catastrophic payments, i.e. at situations in which out-of-pocket payments for health care take a (too) large share in the total household budget. Xu et al. (2003, 2007) define health care expenditures as catastrophic when they exceed 40 percent of household's non-subsistence spending, which is total spending minus the food spending of the household having the median food share in total household spending in the country. They estimate (based on surveys in 89 countries covering 89 percent of the world population) that 150 million people globally suffer financial catastrophe according to that definition. In their study for Asia, van Doorslaer et al. (2007) define catastrophic payments in terms of the share of out-of-pocket payments in total household expenditure and in non-food expenditure—and they show results for a range of "threshold" values. More than 5 percent of the households have a share of health care expenses larger than 10 percent of total household expenditures in Hong Kong, Kyrgyzstan Republic, Nepal, and Taiwan—and more than 10 percent of the households have catastrophic expenditures in Bangladesh, China, India, Korea, and Vietnam. A second approach defines households as having catastrophic health expenditures if they fall below the poverty line when health care expenditures are taken into account but would not be poor without them—the so-called "medical poverty trap." For 11 Asian countries, van Doorslaer et al. (2006) report that an additional 2.7 percent of the population under study (not less than 78 million people) ended up below the $1-a-day poverty line due to their health care expenditures.

These studies on the poverty consequences of health expenditures yield useful information on the issue of cumulative deprivation. Yet they suffer from similar limitations as the work on the ability-to-pay principle. First, most studies assume that health care expenditures are paid out of current income or out of current nonmedical expenditures. In reality households also resort to other coping strategies such as borrowing or selling a part of their stock of financial and physical assets. Taking these strategies into account changes the poverty picture seriously (Flores et al., 2008; Wagstaff, 2008). Therefore a complete evaluation would require the use of a full inter-temporal model that takes into account the long-run consequences of the depletion of assets. Second, in this context also a full description of an individual's well-being requires a combination of health and income (poverty) information. Individuals can avoid catastrophic health care payments or escape from the "medical poverty trap" either because they are rich enough or because the health care system delivers health care free of charge or, finally, because they are not consuming the health care they need. From a welfare point of view these three situations are very different. In fact, given that out-of-pocket payments have a negative price effect on the demand for health care, raising them could in principle lead to a decrease in the number of people ending in poverty, simply because the consumption of health care decreases. It would be weird to interpret this as a welfare improvement.

One can try to remedy the partial nature of these measures of "equity in finance" in two ways. The first is to complement them with other measures to yield a complete picture.[34] A study on the poverty effects of health care expenditures could then be complemented with information on equity in health care delivery and in health outcomes, or with measures of income inequality. Yet there is a danger that the overall picture remains a bit impressionistic, as it is not obvious how to integrate the different pieces of information in a coherent way. The second approach is more ambitious. It consists of evaluating (the inequality in) overall well-being, taking into account that this requires considering different dimensions, including health and income, in an integrated way. Let us now turn to this issue.

5.2. Health and Well-being

Individuals care about many things—about income or consumption, but also about health, job security, the environment in which they live, the fate of other people, etc. Well-being therefore seems inherently multidimensional. This is, for instance, explicitly recognized in the work of Sen (1993, 1999) on functionings and capabilities, which has already had some influence in health economics (Anand and Dolan, 2005). The question then arises whether it is needed and/or possible to aggregate these different dimensions in one index, and if so, how. The economic tradition with its strong utilitarian roots has a tendency to take the position that all these dimensions only matter insofar as they contribute to "utility," but there is a longstanding debate on the measurability of this concept of "utility" and on its interpersonal comparability.

In the first subsection we describe the intuitions behind the construction of so-called multidimensional inequality indices. We then show how the dominance

---

[34] This position is explicitly taken, for example, in Wagstaff and van Doorslaer (2003).

approach relaxes some of the stringent (and arbitrary) assumptions underlying the measurement of multidimensional inequality. Neither the multidimensional inequality measures nor the dominance approach respect the preferences of individuals concerning the trade-offs between the different dimensions. The recently booming happiness literature claims to do exactly that. However, in the third subsection we argue that, despite its interesting contribution, it suffers from some weaknesses. We finally discuss an alternative concept respecting individual preferences, the so-called equivalent income.

Throughout this section we restrict the analysis for simplicity to two dimensions. We assume that there is a population of n members and we represent the well-being of member i by a two-dimensional vector (y_i, h_i), where y_i stands for income or for material welfare and h_i stands for health. In some subsections it will be more convenient to switch to the notation (x_{i1}, x_{i2}). In that case x_{i1} stands for income and x_{i2} for health. The question is then how to evaluate inequality in these vectors (y_i, h_i) or (x_{i1}, x_{i2}). The largest part of the literature that is discussed in this section has not been published in traditional health economic journals. However, most authors take health as their prime example of a relevant dimension of well-being in addition to income or consumption.

5.2.1. Multidimensional Inequality Indices

The basic idea of the literature on multidimensional inequality measurement is to keep to the inherently multidimensional nature of well-being, i.e. to refrain from explicitly formulating a scalar index of well-being. This implies that the requirements of inequality measurement have to be formulated directly for the vectors $(x_{i1}, x_{i2})_{i=1,\ldots,n}$. In this respect, two important intuitions have been formalized in the literature (for an overview, see Weymark, 2006).

The first is an extension of the one-dimensional Pigou–Dalton principle, stating that an income transfer from an individual with a lower income to an individual with a higher income should increase inequality. To translate this idea into a multidimensional context, Kolm (1977) proposed the principle of *uniform majorization (UM)*. Consider the matrix X with the vectors (x_{i1}, x_{i2}) as rows. The condition *UM* states that there is at least as much inequality in X as in $X' = BX$, where B is a bistochastic matrix (i.e. a non-negative square matrix with all row and column sums equal to 1). The principle of uniform majorization captures the intuitive idea that a mean-preserving reduction in the dispersion yields lower inequality. Imposing *UM* together with different scaling and separability assumptions leads to natural generalizations of the best known one-dimensional inequality indices (Tsui, 1995, for the Atkinson and the Kolm–Pollak measures; Gajdos and Weymark, 2005, for the Gini).

A second consideration comes to the fore in the multidimensional context. As suggested already by the quotation from Hausman (2007) at the beginning of this section, we may also be interested in the correlation between the dimensions (Atkinson and Bourguignon, 1982). Tsui (1999) has formalized this as the principle of *correlation increasing majorization (CIM)*. Applied to our simplified setting with only two dimensions we say that X' is obtained from X by a correlation-increasing transfer if $x'_{i1} = \max(x_{i1}, x_{j1})$, $x'_{i2} = \max(x_{i2}, x_{j2})$, $x'_{j1} = \min(x_{i1}, x_{j1})$, $x'_{j2} = \min(x_{i2}, x_{j2})$ and $x_{kd} = x'_{kd}$ for $d = 1, 2$ and all $k \neq i, j$. The principle *CIM* then states that there is at least as much inequality in X' as in X. Tsui (1999) has shown that UM and CIM are independent principles. He also derived a family of multi-attribute generalized entropy indices that satisfy both.

It is striking that there are hardly any empirical applications of these multidimensional inequality indices in the health economic literature. Still, the work in this domain throws an interesting light on some of the issues that have been raised in the previous sections. Starting from the matrix X, one can distinguish two possible aggregation procedures to arrive at an overall judgment. One procedure is to first calculate indices of income inequality $I(x_1)$ and health inequality $I(x_2)$, where x_1 and x_2 are the first and the second column of X respectively, and then calculate overall inequality as a function $f(I(x_1), I(x_2))$. This reminds us of the idea that different "partial" measures of inequity (e.g. in health and in health financing) have to be brought together to get at an overall picture. The other procedure first defines an index of well-being $v_i = v(x_{i1}, x_{i2})$ for each individual and then calculates overall inequality in these individual indices. It has been shown that these two approaches only yield the same result under very restrictive conditions, basically boiling down to the assumption that the correlation between the dimensions does not matter (Dutta et al., 2003). This is easy to understand. A more constructive way of conveying the same message can be derived from the paper by Abul Naga and Geoffard (2006), who show that for the class of relative bidimensional inequality indices, overall inequality can be decomposed into two univariate Atkinson–Kolm–Sen inequality indices (one for income, one for health) and a third statistic which depends on the joint distribution of income and health. This last term drops out if the function $v(x_{i1}, x_{i2})$ is additively separable, i.e. can be written as $v^1(x_{i1}) + v^2(x_{i2})$. Since this is not a realistic assumption, one has to combine information on income and health at the individual level to obtain a coherent view on social inequalities.

Returning to the basic issue of the relationship between health and individual well-being, it should be emphasized that both principles UM and CIM are formulated on the matrix X without any reference to preferences. They therefore come into conflict with the ethical requirement that individual preferences should be respected (Fleurbaey and Trannoy, 2003). Moving from one dimension to more dimensions indeed changes the issue of measuring inequality in an essential way. In a one-dimensional context one aims at measuring inequality in an attribute (income or health) that can be considered to be desirable for everybody: all individuals agree that more income is better than less, and the same is true for health. Ordinal preferences are identical and different inequality measures then implement different ideas about how to measure inequality between individuals, i.e. how to evaluate the distribution of a universally desired attribute. In contrast, in a two-dimensional setting it becomes highly unrealistic to assume that all individuals share the same preferences over income-health bundles. Although it is claimed that multidimensional inequality measures respect the inherently multidimensional nature of well-being, they ultimately *impose* a specific rule for aggregating the different dimensions. Interpreted in terms of well-being, these measures not only assume (implicitly) that everyone has identical preferences, on top of that they pick (again implicitly) one specific formulation of these preferences, without any guarantee that this choice is representative of the population.

The issue of "responsibility" has not been tackled in this literature. In principle it would be possible, however, to substitute for h_i the individual measures of advantage that have been introduced in the previous section.

5.2.2. Dominance Approaches

The stochastic dominance approach bypasses the problem of arbitrary weighting of the different dimensions by focusing on the cases in which the comparison between two distributions is independent of the particular weighting system chosen. In such cases, the conclusions appear especially robust—the downside is that this can be achieved only for a limited subset of cases. The idea of seeking robust cases is simple, but its implementation is potentially complex, as one may have to make a huge number of calculations, considering many possible vectors of weights with a sufficiently fine grid. Even with computers, this implies a staggering amount of calculus when the applications bear on large samples of populations. The objective of the dominance literature has been to develop simple criteria which can be applied in a reasonable number of steps. The prime example of such a criterion is the Lorenz curve, which is constructed for unidimensional distributions. A remarkable result due to Hardy et al. (1952) establishes an equivalence, for the comparisons of two distributions (with the same mean) of a continuous variable in a finite population, between: (*HLP*1) a higher Lorenz curve; (*HLP*2) a greater social welfare for a wide class of social welfare functions; (*HLP*3) a finite number of permutations and progressive transfers.

The idea of extending this approach to multidimensional distributions was first explored by Atkinson and Bourguignon (1982, 1987).[35] The main focus has been

---

[35] There is a formally parallel analysis in the theory of risk (e.g. Richard, 1975; Levy and Paroush, 1974). An overview of the literature on multidimensional stochastic dominance can be found in Trannoy (2006).

on extending the equivalence ($HLP1$) ⇔ ($HLP2$) of the Hardy—Littlewood—Pólya theorem, the study of associated transfer principles (i.e. $HLP3$) appearing much more difficult than in the one-dimensional case (Trannoy, 2006; Gravel and Moyes, 2011). In line with our assumptions in this section, most of the literature is about the bidimensional case. Two situations can be distinguished: one in which both variables are continuous and a second one in which one variable is continuous and the other is discrete.[36] The two parts of the literature are relevant to our setting. Income is a continuous variable, while health can sometimes be treated as a continuous variable (QALYs) and sometimes as a discrete variable (e.g. self-assessed health with four or five categories).

Formally, social welfare is assumed to be defined as the sum of utilities:

$$\sum_{i=1}^{n} U(x_{i1}, x_{i2}), \tag{45}$$

where i is the individual index running over the population of n members. This apparently utilitarian form involves no more than separability and continuity, because there is no commitment to any particular measure of utility. Indeed, in this literature the function $U(\cdot)$ is not necessarily seen as a representation of individual preferences, it rather reflects the weighting scheme of the social planner. It can therefore easily be interpreted as a generalization of the specific functional forms that are embodied in the multidimensional inequality measures. While separability and continuity are both questionable assumptions, they are sufficiently popular in welfare economics to make the whole enterprise worthy of interest. Defining a class of social welfare functions under these two assumptions then boils down to defining a class of utility functions U.

The idea of stochastic dominance is to derive easily verifiable conditions on the joint distribution $F(x_1, x_2)$ (extensions of Lorenz-curve domination) that are equivalent to a higher social welfare for a whole class of utility functions U. Here we will not dwell on these particular criteria. They are easy to find in the quoted literature. What is more interesting for our purpose is to examine if the classes of utility functions appear sensible when the first variable is income and the second is health. These classes are characterized by properties of the derivatives of U. Let $U_t = \partial U / \partial x_{it}$, $t = 1,2$, $U_{st} = \partial U / \partial x_{is} \, \partial x_{it}$, s, $t = 1, 2$, and so on. When x_{i2} is a discrete variable taking the values $k = 1,\ldots, K$, one can understand the derivatives as $U_2 (x_{i1}, x_{i2}) = U (x_{i1}, x_{i2}) - U (x_{i1}, x_{i2} - 1)$, $U_{12} (x_{i1}, x_{i2}) = U_1 (x_{i1}, x_{i2}) - U_1 (x_{i1}, x_{i2} - 1)$, $U_{122} (x_{i1}, x_{i2}) = U_1 (x_{i1}, x_{i2}) - 2U_1 (x_{i1}, x_2 - 1) + U_1 (x_{i1}, x_{i2} - 2)$, and so on. Table 16.6

---

[36] The main application motivating the use of a discrete variable is when statistical units are households of different sizes. Household income and household size (or demographic composition, if a distinction is made between adults and children) then form the pair of variables.

Table 16.6 Dominance Approaches: Classes of Social Welfare Functions

Class	References
C1: $U_1, U_2 \geq 0, U_{11} U_{12} \leq 0, U_{112} \geq 0$	Moyes (1999)
C2: $U_1, U_2 \geq 0, U_{12}, U_{22} \leq 0, U_{112} \geq 0$	Moyes (1999)
C3: $U_1, U_2 \geq 0, U_{11}, U_{22}, U_{12} \leq 0,$ $U_{112}, U_{122} \geq 0, U_{1122} \leq 0$	Atkinson and Bourguignon (1982), Moyes (1999)
C4: $U_1, U_2 \geq 0, U_{11}, U_{22}, U_{12} \leq 0,$ $U_{112}, U_{122} \leq 0, U_{1122} \geq 0$	Atkinson and Bourguignon (1982)
C5: $U_1, U_2 \geq 0, U_{11}, U_{22}, U_{12} \leq 0,$ $U_{111}, U_{112} \geq 0$	Muller and Trannoy (2003)
C6: $U_1, U_2 \geq 0, U_{11}, U_{22}, U_{12} \leq 0,$ $U_{222}, U_{122} \geq 0$	Muller and Trannoy (2003)

summarizes the classes that have been studied and for which Lorenz-type criteria have been found.[37] The superscript d indicates that the second variable is discrete.

A class defined with more conditions is smaller and therefore corresponds to a dominance criterion which is more discriminating—but obviously, piling up conditions raises occasions for ethical objections. A simple way to get an intuitive grasp of the conditions on derivatives is to visualize what they imply for the evaluation of a change in the situation of one or more individuals (Moyes, 1999). Figure 16.5 shows changes (the initial position of an individual is represented by a circle, the final position by a star)[38] which are improvements if the corresponding condition on U is satisfied. Note that a condition on a derivative of order m requires a figure with 2^{m-1} individuals.

We are now in a position to examine these conditions and evaluate their relevance in the particular context in which dimension 1 is income (or consumption) and dimension 2 is health.

- $U_1, U_2 \geq 0$: It is very plausible to require utility to be increasing in both variables.
- $U_{11}, U_{22} \leq 0$: It is also plausible to have a decreasing marginal utility in both dimensions. This justifies transferring from the better-off to the worse-off in each dimension. (In the case of health, a "transfer" is just a symbolic expression describing a situation in which one distribution is less unequal than another.)

---

[37] We ignore the study of first-order stochastic dominance and focus on the extension of Lorenz dominance. Moreover, we do not include the cases in which the marginal distribution of variable 2 is kept fixed (Bourguignon, 1989), or in which $U_2 = 0$ for large x_{i1} (Jenkins and Lambert, 1993), because these are less relevant for our problem of evaluating allocations of income and health.

[38] An arrow illustrates the change for the first graph. Arrows are omitted for the other graphs because, except for the first graph, there are several possible ways to connect initial positions to final positions by arrows.

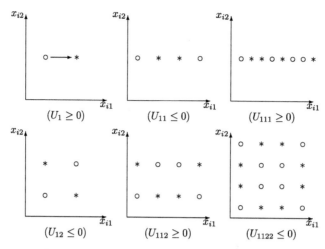

Figure 16.5 Illustration of the conditions on *U*.

- $U_{12} \leq 0$: This crucial condition means that less healthy individuals have greater priority in the distribution of income. As illustrated in the figure, a society in which the rich are sick and the poor are healthy is considered better than a society in which riches and health are concentrated in the same individuals. This reflects the intuition that was also captured by the principle *CIM* (correlation increasing majorization) in the literature on multidimensional inequality measurement. It goes against a certain utilitarian logic that would consider that healthier individuals are those who can benefit from income.
- $U_{112} \geq 0$: This condition means that the priority of the sick for the distribution of income decreases as they become richer. As illustrated in the figure, it means that it is more important to reduce the correlation between income and health among the poor than among the rich. It also means that the priority of the poor in the redistribution of income is less strong among healthier people. This condition therefore appears more plausible than the opposite condition $U_{112} \leq 0$.
- $U_{122} \geq 0$: This condition means that the priority of the sick in the distribution of income decreases among healthier people, and also that the priority of the sick in the distribution of health decreases among richer people. Again this condition does not seem unreasonable in the context of health, and is ethically more plausible than the opposite condition $U_{122} \leq 0$.
- U_{111}, $U_{222} \geq 0$: This rather plausible condition means that marginal utility decreases less steeply as income (resp. health) increases. Redistribution is less desirable among the well-off than among the badly-off.

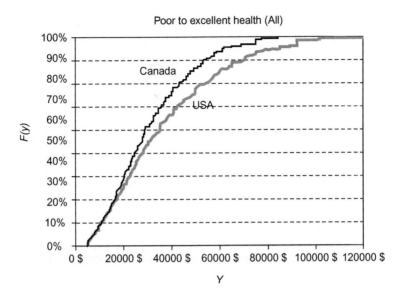

Figure 16.6 Cumulative income distributions in Canada and in the US (Duclos and Echevin, 2011).

- $U_{1122} \leq 0$: This is the hardest condition to intuitively understand and to assess. It means that the decrease in the priority of the sick as they become richer (healthier) is less steep for healthier (richer, respectively) individuals. As illustrated in the figure, this implies that decreasing the correlation between income and health is more important among the extremes (sick poor and healthy rich) than among the mixed positions (sick rich and healthy poor). Viewed in this way, it appears clearly more reasonable than the opposite condition $U_{1122} \geq 0$.

In conclusion, these comments suggest that most of the classes are worth considering in the context of income and health. One may, however, have doubts about class C4. Trannoy (2006) argues that C5 corresponds more to the case in which income is used as a tool for the compensation of sickness, while C6 considers using health as a compensation for poverty. Both perspectives seem to make sense, although the former is arguably more natural.

The power of the dominance approaches is illustrated in a recent paper by Duclos and Echevin (2011). They compare the situations of Canada and the US and also analyze the developments over time in both countries. By way of illustration we show in Figure 16.6 the cumulative income distributions in Canada and the US, showing that incomes are higher in the US than in Canada, and in Figure 16.7 the cumulative income distributions when one considers only the individuals in poor or in fair health. Duclos and Echevin (2011) test for the statistical differences between these curves (and similar ones for other health levels) and draw the conclusion that for all

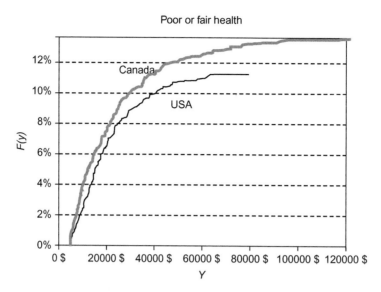

Figure 16.7 Cumulative income distribution functions in Canada and in the US (2003) for individuals in poor or fair health (Duclos and Echevin, 2011).

utility functions in the class C1 from Table 16.6, the social welfare is higher in Canada than in the US, *if* one focuses only on those with poor and fair health statuses. This is due to the fact that the worse income distribution in Canada is compensated by a better health distribution, by a lower correlation between health and income, and by lower income inequality in Canada than in the US. Using similar techniques, they also show that social welfare has not improved in the US during the decade 1996–2005, in spite of the overall increase in incomes. This is because the US health distribution has deteriorated over time and because this deterioration has not been offset by sufficient increases in incomes for the least healthy. For Canada, the normative evaluation of the change over time depends on which part of the joint health–income distribution is judged to be of greater normative importance.

Finally, let us mention two limitations of the dominance approach. First, dominance is not obtained in all comparisons, so that the ranking of distributions produced by such criteria is always incomplete. More restrictive classes yield less incomplete rankings, but never produce completeness. Second, the underlying social criterion involves a single utility function U, thereby ignoring the diversity of individual preferences. Even if a class of utility functions is always referred to in the dominance criteria, the unanimous judgment of a class of social welfare functions $\sum_{i=1}^{n} U(x_{i1}, x_{i2})$ for a variety of functions U is not the same as a judgment based on a function $\sum_{i=1}^{n} U_i(x_{i1}, x_{i2})$ in which different utility functions for different individuals are used at the same time. The diversity of subjective perspectives across individuals is the focus of the approaches presented in the next subsections.

5.2.3. Welfarism: Happiness and Health

Social choice theory is famous for Arrow's (1951) impossibility theorem, which has often been interpreted as implying that it is impossible to derive a welfare ordering of social states[39] on the basis of individual preferences, while at the same time respecting some ethical conditions (such as non-dictatorship). At first sight this impossibility theorem makes the quest for a preference-based evaluation of joint distributions of income and health meaningless. However, possibility results can be obtained by relaxing one or more of Arrow's conditions. In this respect, much research has focused on the axiom of Independence of Irrelevant Alternatives, which requires comparing two alternatives with information about individual preferences which is limited to whether any given individual prefers one alternative or the other. It has been shown that this axiom can be relaxed in two ways, both of which allow us to take into account more information about individual well-being. One way, initiated by Sen (1970), consists of introducing interpersonally comparable utility functions and allowing some information about utility levels or differences to play a role in the comparison of two alternatives. The other way, suggested by Hansson (1973) among others, consists of allowing information about indifference curves to be taken into account. In this section we consider the first way.

Within the economic tradition with its strong utilitarian roots, it would seem natural to take utility as an indicator of well-being, if the utility function $U_i(x_{i1}, x_{i2})$ were cardinally measurable and interpersonally comparable. For a long time, these assumptions of measurability and interpersonal comparability have been seen as unrealistic. Microeconomists have emphasized that choice behavior can only reveal ordinal preferences and that the utility function representing these individual preferences therefore is only defined up to a monotonic transformation. Recently, however, a growing number of economists have questioned the traditional skeptical attitude regarding *stated* preferences and accept that individual answers to survey questions are credible as direct measures of happiness or satisfaction with life. The formulations of these questions are different in different surveys, but a typical example would be: "All things considered, how satisfied are you with your life?" There is by now a wealth of evidence for different countries showing that the answers to these questions are reasonably coherent over time and that the measured level of subjective satisfaction is related in a meaningful way to observable characteristics of the situation of the respondents.

---

[39] In our simplified context a social state is a collection of income–health bundles for all individuals, i.e. $((y_1, h_1), \ldots, (y_n, h_n))$.

Some have argued that since we now finally are able to measure utility, we can start testing directly some predictions of economic theory (Frey and Stutzer, 2002). Others have drawn explicit normative conclusions from these findings in a utilitarian perspective (Layard, 2005).[40]

The typical approach in the literature has been the estimation of a so-called "happiness equation" $SWB_i = f(y_i, h_i, z_i, \varepsilon_i)$, where SWB stands for subjective well-being, z_i is a vector of observable individual characteristics (different from income and health), and ε_i is an error term. A common finding is that of a strong statistical relationship between health and happiness (Graham, 2008). Although causality runs in both directions, it is well documented that good health increases the level of happiness and that health shocks—such as serious diseases or permanent disabilities—have negative effects. The effect of health is even more robust than the effect of income. The estimation results make it possible to calculate the marginal rate of substitution between health and income $(\partial f/\partial h_i)/(\partial f/\partial y_i)$, which can also be interpreted as a willingness-to-pay for better health. This willingness-to-pay turns out to be large for chronic diseases. As an example, it is found that for West German workers hearing impediments are on average equivalent to an income reduction of about 20 percent, and heart or blood difficulties are equivalent to a 47 percent income reduction (Ferrer-i-Carbonell and Van Praag, 2002). For a 25-year-old Dutch male the monetary valuation of a heart disease ranges from \$114,000 to \$380,000 depending on the welfare level (Groot et al., 2004; Groot and Maassen van den Brink, 2006). Although care is needed because the results depend on the specification of the function $f(\cdot)$ and on the precise measure used for SWB, there is no doubt that the trade-off between income and health shows up clearly in these estimates.

All this suggests that it would be possible to use the individual values of SWB_i coming out of the surveys as a direct measure of individual well-being. One could then immediately calculate the inequality in these values and analyze how it relates to (inequity in) health or health care, to socioeconomic status and to the income consequences of having to pay for health care. Yet this would mean that we basically return to utilitarianism. In the social philosophical literature, utilitarianism has come under severe criticism, as exemplified by the extremely influential work of Rawls (1971). This criticism has also been taken up by a large fraction of social choice theorists (inspired among others by Sen, 1985). They doubt that subjective utility is really an ethically attractive indicator of well-being.

---

[40] The economic literature on happiness and on how to measure it has become so large that it is impossible to summarize it in a few pages. We therefore can only raise some general points, but we believe that our positive as well as our critical remarks are relevant for all the variants of happiness measurement. Moreover, note that we are only concerned here with measures of overall satisfaction with life, and *not* with subjective quality of life in the health economic tradition of QALY measurement nor with subjective health satisfaction or with self-assessed health. We focus in this section on finding an overall measure of well-being that would make it possible to formalize the trade-off between income and health.

Sen (1985) raises two sets of arguments. Both are taken up by Loewenstein and Ubel (2008) from a health perspective. First, Sen argues that utilitarianism suffers from "valuation neglect." Valuing a life is a reflective activity in a way that being happy or desiring need not be (Sen, 1985, p. 29). People not only live to feel happy, they care about the meaning that they derive from activities. Non-affective (i.e. cognitive) components of well-being are essential to most individuals. Or, in the words of Loewenstein and Ubel (2008, p. 1801), "experience utility fails to capture a wide range of dimensions of existence that people deeply and legitimately care about." As an example, people care a lot about dying a "good death." Second, serious issues are raised by the phenomenon of adaptation. Sen talks about "physical condition neglect." Loewenstein and Ubel (2008, p. 1799) state that numerous studies have found that people with chronic health conditions as severe as kidney failure or paraplegia report moods that are relatively close to those reported by healthy persons. However, although people may be able to emotionally adapt to a wide range of health conditions, that does not mean that they are indifferent between them. Quite the contrary, despite reporting levels of well-being that are similar to those of healthy persons, people in poor health conditions are willing to make large monetary or non-monetary sacrifices to become healthy again.

The last point brings us back to the distinction between preferences, represented by an ordinal utility function on the one hand, and cardinal happiness measures on the other hand. Take an individual i who prefers (y_i, h_i) to (y_i', h_i'). (We drop the variables z and ε for convenience.) If she answers the happiness question truthfully, then her preference will be reflected in her reported happiness values, i.e. $SWB_i = f(y_i, h_i) > SWB_i' = f(y_i', h_i')$. This means that the happiness measure corresponds to a cardinalization of the utility function that is representing her preferences. But let us now take two individuals that both prefer (y, h) to (y', h'). It will then still be true that $SWB_i > SWB_i'$ and that $SWB_j = f(y_j, h_j) > SWB_j' = f(y_j', h_j')$. However, it is very well possible that $SWB_j' \geq SWB_i$, if the aspiration levels of the two individuals differ, e.g. because individual j has adapted to the bad situation (y', h'). In other words, it is possible that individual j does not feel less happy in the income–health situation (y_j', h_j') than individual i in the situation (y_i, h_i), although they both prefer (y, h) to (y', h'). A similar phenomenon can occur if we consider one individual with changing aspirations over time. This reasoning shows a perhaps somewhat surprising result: evaluating individual well-being on the basis of subjective happiness measures does not necessarily respect preferences, because these happiness measures are contaminated by adaptation and differences in aspirations. If we want to respect individual preferences, we have to look for another approach. This brings us to the second escape route from Arrow's impossibility, which consists of using information about individual indifference curves.

5.2.4. Respecting Preferences: Equivalent Income

If using happiness measures does not respect preferences, what does? To get an intuition of what is at stake, consider a simple world in which individuals care only about one magnitude in their life, call it X. A life with more X is considered a better life by everyone. Respecting individual judgments about the quality of various lives therefore requires using X as the metric of success in life. Even in this simple unidimensional world, happiness measures do not respect preferences in general because one may have $X_i > X_j$ but $SWB_i(X_i) < SWB_j(X_j)$. There is a clear sense in which people care about X, not $SWB(X)$, and one should not mistake the evaluation ($SWB(X)$) for what is valued (X). Adopting the X metric, social preferences should then simply be defined as preferences over distributions of X.

What happens when life has several dimensions and individuals may have different preferences? Let us return to our setting with two dimensions, income y and health h. Intuitively, just as X was a suitable metric in the unidimensional case, something of the same nature as y or h should become the metric in this case. One attractive approach to do exactly this is that of the healthy-equivalent income (Fleurbaey, 2005).[41] It is measured in the same units as y, and is defined as the level of income y_i^* such that the individual is indifferent between his current situation and being healthy with income y_i^*, i.e. between (y_i, h_i) and (y_i^*, h^*), where h^* refers to perfect health. There are good reasons to take perfect health as the reference. More specifically, this choice implies that the healthy-equivalent income satisfies the property that individuals with good health can be compared directly in terms of incomes, independently of their preferences. Indeed, their equivalent incomes are then equal to their ordinary incomes, whatever their preferences may be. This is a rather nice property, as it is intuitive that, when healthy, an individual with more income than another enjoys a better situation, even if their preferences are different.

Figure 16.8 clarifies the concept. Suppose we want to compare the well-being of individual i in situation A with that of individual j in situation B. If we want to respect the preferences of individual i, we have to take situations A and A′ as equivalent, since they are on the same indifference curve. The same is true for situations B and B′ for individual j. Yet, given that A′ and B′ are situations with perfect health, it makes sense

---

[41] The notion of equivalent income and its interesting history in economics are explained in more detail in Fleurbaey (2009). The concept was first introduced, under the label "money-metric utility," by Samuelson (1974) and Samuelson and Swamy (1974) in the search for an index of quantities that would track individual preferences better than the usual Laspeyres, Paasche, and Fischer indexes. It was then used in the analysis of the distribution of household welfare by King (1983)—who coined the expression "equivalent income"—and features honorably in the classical monograph by Deaton and Muellbauer (1980). The fad quickly faded, however, when Blackorby and Donaldson (1988) observed that an additively separable social welfare function using money-metric utilities as the indices of individual well-being could not be quasi-concave with respect to quantities, therefore violating a basic requirement of inequality aversion. The recent theory of fair allocation provided fuel for a new interest in the notion. As Fleurbaey (2005) shows, it can be seen as a further elaboration of the idea of "egalitarian equivalence" introduced by Pazner and Schmeidler (1978) and already mentioned in this chapter.

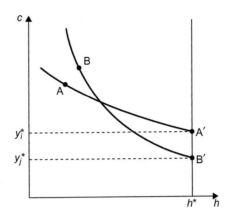

Figure 16.8 Healthy–equivalent income.

to compare them in terms of income—the healthy-equivalent incomes for the two individuals are then y_i^* and y_j^* respectively.

It is clear that the computation of equivalent incomes at any given allocation requires knowing people's indifference curves at this allocation, which corresponds exactly to the second solution to Arrow's impossibility that was introduced before. This approach respects preferences more than subjective welfarism. Indeed, offering an individual a situation that he himself prefers necessarily raises his equivalent income. Moreover, two individuals with the same preferences will necessarily rank their own situations in a way that is congruent with their equivalent incomes. The healthy-equivalent income is obviously not the only way to respect preferences in this manner. One could take health instead of income as the numeraire, or one could take a level other than good health as the reference in the computation of the equivalent income. Taking another health level as reference is not very interesting, however, as it would not imply the nice property that we can compare individuals with good health only on the basis of their incomes and that, in contrast, comparisons of individuals with less than perfect health require taking account of preferences. For a given level of bad health, indeed, an individual with more income than another is not necessarily in a better situation if his preferences care much more about health. Moreover, if a low level of health was taken as the reference, one might find individuals in good situations who would never accept trading their situation for worse health, even with an unlimited amount of income. In contrast, everyone considers good health to be at least as good as their current health, so that equivalent incomes are always lower than current incomes. One might theoretically imagine people whose situation is so bad that good health with a null income would be better than their current situation, but this is rather far-fetched, as a null income does not sustain life. Moreover, even if one finds people in such a situation, although they cannot be ranked in terms of equivalent incomes, at least they are clearly ranked as disadvantaged with respect to all people with a positive equivalent income.[42]

Once equivalent incomes are adopted as the measure of individual well-being, they can be used to compute inequality in well-being and, as for the happiness measures, this analysis can integrate the concerns for (inequity in) health or health care and for the income consequences of out-of-pocket payments for health care. Of course, the approach is rather demanding as far as data are concerned. Indeed, ideally it requires an estimation of the joint distribution of preferences and individual income—health situations. This is rather hard to obtain. Even specific surveys asking direct questions about preferences can hardly do more than estimating the average preferences for subgroups of the population. Note, however, that the difference between actual income y_i and equivalent income y_i^* is basically the willingness-to-pay of the individual to be in perfect health, i.e. $y_i^* = y_i - WTP_i$. Once we have observations for y_i and for this willingness-to-pay, we can approximate y_i^*.

Information about willingness-to-pay can be derived from different sources. First, one can use the estimates that are derived from the happiness equations, as described in the previous subsection. Graham et al. (2010) use this information to adjust the mean incomes of different countries for the cost of health problems. Note that in this approach one only needs the marginal rates of substitution between income and health $(\partial f/\partial h_i)/(\partial f/\partial y_i)$, which are invariant under monotonic transformations of $f(\cdot)$. These measures will therefore be much less sensitive to the adaptation issue, since it can be assumed that adaptation in the first place impacts on the measured *level* of happiness rather than on the orientation of preferences. Second, one can develop a contingent valuation approach to measure the willingness-to-pay for perfect health in a survey (see Fleurbaey et al., 2010). Third, one can calibrate meaningful willingness-to-pay measures using information from different sources, including observed choice behavior. This approach is followed by Becker et al. (2005) to compute for 96 countries equivalent growth rates incorporating the monetary equivalent of improved life expectancy and by Fleurbaey and Gaulier (2009) to compare the living standards of 24 OECD countries on the basis of a broad list of dimensions including life expectancy. Not only does this recent work show that the computation of equivalent incomes is feasible, it also confirms that health is an essential element of well-being and that explicitly taking it into account may have a strong impact on inequality measures. As an example, Becker et al. (2005) estimate for the period 1960—2000 an average yearly growth of equivalent income[43] of 4.1 percent for the poorest 50 percent of countries

---

[42] One might think of a dominance principle imposing that more income and better health always mean a better situation, independently of preferences (e.g. Sen, 1985). This would imply that in Figure 16.8 individual *j* in situation B is better off than individual *i* in situation A. However, this approach implies that preferences play no role in the evaluation of a situation and this goes against the basic motivation that is explored in this subsection.

[43] They use the terminology "full income."

in 1960, of which 1.7 percentage points are due to health, as opposed to a growth of 2.6 percent for the richest 50 percent of countries, of which only 0.4 percentage points are due to health.

It is interesting here to make a connection with the different views on equality of opportunity that have been introduced in the previous section. We there made the distinction between the so-called "choice" and "preference" approaches. It must now have become clear that the concept of equivalent income is very much in line with the preference approach. Respecting individual preference variation in the measurement of well-being is closely related to holding people responsible for their preferences. In theory it is not very difficult to enrich the approach by introducing preferences over lifestyles, in addition to income and health, in order to address the issues of personal responsibility for health that have been examined in the previous sections. This appears a promising alley for future research.

We conclude by mentioning an important challenge to the ideal of respecting individual preferences. The equivalent income approach assumes that it is possible to get reliable information about the genuine preferences of individuals on what is valuable in life and, even more basically, that these individual preferences are well defined. Now that behavioral studies have uncovered many ways in which individual preferences may deviate from this ideal, the equivalent income measure cannot be implemented without caution. One may even think that the underlying theory should be refined in order to accommodate the most common departures from rationality that have been revealed in the behavioral literature.

6. CONCLUSION

Distributional issues play an important role in all social discussions on health (care) policies. If economists want to give relevant advice, they need a coherent normative framework for policy evaluation. Such normative framework can also guide empirical research by suggesting what the important facts are and possibly what causal relationships should be analyzed. In this respect, the recent health economic literature has produced many interesting insights by focusing on specific issues, such as socioeconomic inequalities in health, inequities in health care delivery, racial disparities, and the income consequences of out-of-pocket payments. It would be useful, however, to integrate these partial insights into a broader framework.

First, concern about inequity in health and in health care should not be restricted to specific characteristics such as socioeconomic status or race. At a more fundamental level "horizontal equity" is only achieved when all individuals with the same needs and the same preferences get the same level of care—and all factors leading to deviations from this ideal should be considered together. Moreover, the issue of horizontal equity is intricately linked to that of vertical equity. In the same way, equity in health will only be achieved if the remaining health inequality can be fully ascribed to factors for which individuals can be held responsible. Of course, opinions differ about what these factors are exactly, e.g. to what extent individuals have to bear the health consequences of their choice of lifestyle.

Second, from the distributional point of view, we are ultimately interested in overall well-being. Despite the crucial importance of health, it is not the only relevant dimension. As the literature on equity in finance shows, it is at least necessary to be explicit about the trade-offs between health on the one hand and consumption on the other hand—but clearly, a sufficiently rich concept of well-being will have to include dimensions other than health and consumption too.

Recent developments in the welfare economic literature offer a promising framework to tackle both sets of questions. Inequity in health and in health care can be seen as a prime example of inequality of opportunity—and the theory of fair allocation now provides a host of interesting approaches to model that concept and gives clear insights into the normative implications of these different approaches. Much progress has also been made in the quest for an overall concept of well-being. Not only does it now seem possible to measure subjective well-being, we also understand better the ethical limitations of that notion and interesting alternatives (such as the equivalent income) have been developed. In this chapter we have tried to show how this literature relates to the specific issues that have been analyzed by health economists. It turns out that there is not really a conflict between them: quite the contrary, the typical health economic approaches can be seen as useful building blocks in the broader exercise. Moreover, further thinking along these lines will also make it possible to better see how the operational question of inequity measurement relates to deeper social philosophical questions on justice and individual responsibility, and it suggests why and where good econometrics is needed for the estimation of structural models. Building these bridges may enrich the theoretical content of the health economic applications and yield useful insights into the applicability of welfare economic theories.

REFERENCES

Abul Naga, R. & Geoffard, P.-Y. (2006). Decomposition of bivariate inequality indices by attributes. *Economics Letters, 90*(3), 362–367.
Agency for Healthcare Research and Quality (2010). *National healthcare disparities report 2009*. Rockville, MD: US Department of Health and Human Services, AHRQ Publication no. 10-0004.
Allanson, P., Gerdtham, U.-G., & Petrie, D. (2010). Longitudinal analysis of income-related health inequality. *Journal of Health Economics, 29*(1), 78–86.
Anand, P. & Dolan, P. (2005). Equity, capabilities and health. *Social Science and Medicine, 60*, 219–222.
Anderson, E. (1999). What is the point of equality? *Ethics, 109*, 287–337.

Armstrong, K., Hughes-Halbert, C., & Asch, D. (2006). Patient preferences can be misleading as explanations for racial disparities in health care. *Archives of Internal Medicine, 166*(8), 950–954.

Arneson, R. (1989). Equality and equal opportunity for welfare. *Philosophical Studies, 56,* 77–93.

Arrow, K. (1951). *Social choice and individual values.* New York: Wiley.

Arrow, K. (1971). A utilitarian approach to the concept of equality in public expenditures. *Quarterly Journal of Economics, 85,* 409–415.

Ashton, C., Haidet, P., Paterniti, D., Collins, T., Gordon, H., O'Malley, K., et al. (2003). Racial and ethnic disparities in the use of health services: Bias, preferences, or poor communication? *Journal of General Internal Medicine, 18*(2), 146–152.

Atkinson, A. & Bourguignon, F. (1982). The comparison of multi-dimensioned distributions of economic status. *Review of Economic Studies, 49,* 183–201.

Atkinson, A. & Bourguignon, F. (1987). Income distribution and differences in needs. In G. Feiwel (Ed.), *Arrow and the foundations of economic policy* (pp. 350–370). London: Macmillan.

Ayanian, J., Cleary, P., Weissman, J., & Epstein, A. (1999). The effect of patients' preferences on racial differences in access to renal transplantation. *New England Journal of Medicine, 341,* 1661–1669.

Bago d'Uva, T., Jones, A., & van Doorslaer, E. (2009). Measurement of horizontal inequity in health care utilisation using European panel data. *Journal of Health Economics, 28*(2), 280–289.

Balia, S. & Jones, A. (2011). Catching the habit: A study of inequality of opportunity in smoking-related mortality. *Journal of the Royal Statistical Society A, 174*(1), 175–194.

Becker, G., Philipson, T., & Soares, R. (2005). The quantity and quality of life and the evolution of world inequality. *American Economic Review, 95*(1), 277–291.

Blackorby, C. & Donaldson, D. (1988). Money metric utility: Harmless normalization? *Journal of Economic Theory, 46*(1), 120–129.

Bleichrodt, H. & van Doorslaer, E. (2006). A welfare economics foundation for health inequality measurement. *Journal of Health Economics, 25,* 945–957.

Blinder, A. (1973). Wage discrimination: Reduced form and structural estimates. *Journal of Human Resources, 8,* 436–455.

Bollinger, B., Leslie, P., & Sorensen, A. (2011). Calorie posting in chain restaurants. *American Economic Journal: Economic Policy, 3,* 91–128.

Bommier, A. & Stecklov, G. (2002). Defining health inequality: Why Rawls succeeds where social welfare theory fails. *Journal of Health Economics, 21,* 497–513.

Bourguignon, F. (1989). Family size and social utility: Income distribution dominance criteria. *Journal of Econometrics, 42,* 67–80.

Case, A., Fertig, A., & Paxson, C. (2005). The lasting impact of childhood health and circumstance. *Journal of Health Economics, 24,* 365–389.

Case, A., Lubotsky, D., & Paxson, C. (2002). Economic status and health in childhood: The origins of the gradient. *American Economic Review, 92*(5), 1308–1334.

Cawley, J. & Ruhm, C. J. (2011). The economics of risky health behaviors. In *Handbook of health economics* (Vol. 2, Chapter 3). Amsterdam: Elsevier.

Chou, S.-Y., Rashad, I., & Grossman, M. (2008). Fast-food restaurant advertising on television and its influence on childhood obesity. *Journal of Law and Economics, 51*(4), 599–618.

Cisse, B., Luchini, S., & Moatti, J. P. (2007). Progressivity and horizontal equity in health care finance and delivery: What about Africa? *Health Policy, 80*(1), 51–68.

Clarke, P., Gerdtham, U.-G., Johannesson, M., Bingefors, K., & Smith, L. (2002). On the measurement of relative and absolute income-related health inequality. *Social Science and Medicine, 55*(11), 1923–1928.

Cohen, G. (1989). On the currency of egalitarian justice. *Ethics, 99,* 906–944.

Cook, B., McGuire, T., Lock, K., & Zaslavsky, A. (2010). Comparing methods of racial and ethnic disparities measurement across different settings of mental health care. *Health Services Research, 45*(3), 825–847.

Cook, B., McGuire, T., Meara, E., & Zaslavsky, A. (2009). Adjusting for health status in non-linear models of health care disparities. *Health Services and Outcomes Research Methodology, 9,* 1–21.

Currie, J. (2009). Healthy, wealthy and wise: Socioeconomic status, poor health in childhood, and human capital development. *Journal of Economic Literature, 47*(1), 87–122.

Currie, J. & Stabile, M. (2003). Socioeconomic status and child health: Why is the relationship stronger for older children? *American Economic Review, 93*(5), 1813–1823.

Cutler, D. & Lleras-Muney, A. (2010). Understanding differences in health behaviors by education. *Journal of Health Economics* (forthcoming).

Daniels, N. (1985). *Just health care.* Cambridge: Cambridge University Press.

Daniels, N. (2008). *Just health. Meeting health needs fairly.* Cambridge: Cambridge University Press.

Deaton, A. (2011). *What does the empirical evidence tell us about the injustice of health inequalities?* Princeton University Mimeo.

Deaton, A. & Muellbauer, J. (1980). *Economics and consumer behavior.* Cambridge: Cambridge University Press.

De Graeve, D. & Van Ourti, T. (2003). The distributional impact of health financing in Europe: A review. *World Economy, 26,* 1459–1479.

Duclos, J. -Y. & Echevin, D. (2011). Health and income: A robust comparison of Canada and the US. *Journal of Health Economics, 30,* 293–302.

Dutta, I., Pattanaik, P., & Xu, Y. (2003). On measuring deprivation and the standard of living in a multi-dimensional framework on the basis of aggregate data. *Economica, 70,* 197–221.

Dworkin, R. (1981a). What is equality? Part 1: Equality of welfare. *Philosophy and Public Affairs, 10,* 185–246.

Dworkin, R. (1981b). What is equality? Part 2: Equality of resources. *Philosophy and Public Affairs, 10,* 283–345.

Dworkin, R. (2000). *Sovereign virtue.* Cambridge: Cambridge University Press.

Erreygers, G. (2009a). Correcting the concentration index. *Journal of Health Economics, 28,* 504–515.

Erreygers, G. (2009b). Correcting the concentration index: A reply to Wagstaff. *Journal of Health Economics, 28,* 521–524.

Erreygers, G. (2009c). Can a single indicator measure both attainment and shortfall inequality? *Journal of Health Economics, 28,* 885–893.

Erreygers, G. & Van Ourti, T. (2010). *Measuring socioeconomic inequality in health, health care and health financing by means of rank-dependent indices: A recipe for good practice.* Tinbergen Institute, Discussion Paper TI 2010-076/3.

Ferrer-i-Carbonell, A. & Van Praag, B. (2002). The subjective costs of health losses due to chronic diseases. An alternative model for monetary appraisal. *Health Economics, 11,* 709–722.

Fleurbaey, M. (2005). Health, wealth and fairness. *Journal of Public Economic Theory, 7*(2), 253–284.

Fleurbaey, M. (2006). Health, equity and social welfare. *Annales d'Economie et Statistique, 83-84,* 21–60.

Fleurbaey, M. (2008). *Fairness, responsibility and welfare.* Oxford: Oxford University Press.

Fleurbaey, M. (2009). Beyond GDP: The quest for a measure of social welfare. *Journal of Economic Literature, 47*(4), 1029–1075.

Fleurbaey, M. (2010). Assessing risky social decisions. *Journal of Political Economy, 118,* 649–680.

Fleurbaey, M. & Gaulier, G. (2009). International comparisons of living standards by equivalent incomes. *Scandinavian Journal of Economics, 111*(3), 597–624.

Fleurbaey, M. & Maniquet, F. (2011). *A theory of fairness and social welfare.* Cambridge: Cambridge University Press.

Fleurbaey, M. & Schokkaert, E. (2009). Unfair inequalities in health and health care. *Journal of Health Economics, 28*(1), 73–90.

Fleurbaey, M. & Trannoy, A. (2003). The impossibility of a Paretian egalitarian. *Social Choice and Welfare, 21*(2), 243–263.

Fleurbaey, M., Luchini, S., Muller, C., & Schokkaert, E. (2010). *Equivalent income and the economic evaluation of health care.* CORE-Discussion Paper 2010/6.

Flores, G., Krishnakumar, J., O'Donnell, O., & van Doorslaer, E. (2008). Coping with health-care costs: Implications for the measurement of catastrophic expenditures and poverty. *Health Economics, 17*(12), 1393–1412.

Frey, B. & Stutzer, A. (2002). What can economists learn from happiness research? *Journal of Economic Literature*, *40*(2), 402–435.

Gaertner, W. & Schokkaert, E. (2011). *Empirical social choice*. Cambridge: Cambridge University Press.

Gajdos, T. & Weymark, J. (2005). Multidimensional generalized Gini indices. *Economic Theory*, *26*, 471–496.

Graham, C. (2008). Happiness and health: Lessons—and questions—for policy. *Health Affairs*, *27*(1), 72–81.

Graham, C., Higuera, L., & Lora, E. (2010). Which health conditions cause the most unhappiness? *Health Economics* (forthcoming).

Gravel, N. & Moyes, P. (2011). Bidimensional inequalities with an ordinal variable. In M. Fleurbaey, M. Salles, & J. A. Weymark (Eds.), *Social ethics and normative economics*. Berlin: Springer.

Gravelle, H. (2003). Measuring income related inequality in health: Standardisation and the partial concentration index. *Health Economics*, *12*, 803–819.

Groot, W. & Maassen van den Brink, H. (2006). The compensating income variation of cardiovascular disease. *Health Economics*, *15*, 1143–1148.

Groot, W., Maassen van den Brink, H., & Plug, E. (2004). Money for health: The equivalent variation of cardiovascular disease. *Health Economics*, *13*, 859–872.

Hansson, B. (1973). The independence condition in the theory of social choice. *Theory and Decision*, *4*, 25–49.

Hardy, G., Littlewood, J., & Polya, G. (1952). *Inequalities*. Cambridge: Cambridge University Press.

Harsanyi, J. (1977). *Rational behavior and bargaining equilibrium in games and social situations*. Cambridge: Cambridge University Press.

Hausman, D. (2007). What's wrong with health inequalities? *Journal of Political Philosophy*, *15*(1), 46–66.

Institute of Medicine (2002). *Unequal treatment: Confronting racial and ethnic disparities in health care*. Washington, DC: National Academy Press.

Jenkins, S. & Lambert, P. (1993). Ranking income distributions when needs differ. *Review of Income and Wealth*, *39*, 337–356.

Jones, A. & Lopez Nicolas, A. (2004). Measurement and explanation of socioeconomic inequality in health with longitudinal data. *Health Economics*, *13*, 1015–1030.

Jusot, F., Tubeuf, S., & Trannoy, A. (2010). *Effort or circumstances: Does the correlation matter for inequality of opportunity in health?* IRDES, Paris, Working Paper DT 33.

Kakwani, N., Wagstaff, A., & van Doorslaer, E. (1997). Socioeconomic inequalities in health: Measurement, computation, and statistical inference. *Journal of Econometrics*, *77*, 87–103.

Kawachi, I., Daniels, N., & Robinson, D. (2005). Health disparities by race and class: Why both matter. *Health Affairs*, *24*(2), 343–352.

King, M. (1983). Welfare analysis of tax reforms using household data. *Journal of Public Economics*, *23*, 183–214.

Kolm, S.-C. (1977). Multidimensional egalitarianisms. *Quarterly Journal of Economics*, *91*(1), 1–13.

Koolman, X. & van Doorslaer, E. (2004). On the interpretation of a concentration index of inequality. *Health Economics*, *13*, 649–656.

Lambert, P. & Zheng, B. (2011). On the consistent measurement of achievement and shortfall inequality. *Journal of Health Economics*, *30*(1), 214–219.

Layard, R. (2005). *Happiness: Lessons from a new science*. London: Allan Lane.

Lefranc, A., Pistolesi, N., & Trannoy, A. (2009). Equality of opportunity and luck: Definitions and testable conditions, with an application to income in France. *Journal of Public Economics*, *93*, 1189–1207.

Le Grand, J. (1987). Inequalities in health: Some international comparisons. *European Economic Review*, *31* (1/2), 182–191.

Le Grand, J. (1991). *Equity and choice*. London: Harper Collins Academic.

Levy, H. & Paroush, J. (1974). Towards multivariate efficiency criteria. *Journal of Economic Theory*, *7*, 129–142.

Lippert-Rasmussen, K. (2001). Egalitarianism, option luck, and responsibility. *Ethics*, *111*, 548–579.

Loewenstein, G. & Ubel, P. (2008). Hedonic adaptation and the role of decision and experienced utility in public policy. *Journal of Public Economics*, *92*, 1795–1810.

Lu, R., Leung, G., Kwon, S., Tin, K., van Doorslaer, E., & O'Donnell, O. (2007). Horizontal equity in health care utilization—evidence from three high income Asian economies. *Social Science and Medicine, 64*, 199–212.

Milanovic, B. (1997). A simple way to calculate the Gini coefficient and some implications. *Economics Letters, 56*, 45–49.

Morris, S., Sutton, M., & Gravelle, H. (2005). Inequity and inequality in the use of health care in England: An empirical investigation. *Social Science and Medicine, 60*, 1251–1266.

Moyes, P. (1999). Comparison of heterogeneous distributions and dominance criteria. *Economie et Prévision, 138–139*, 125–146.

Muller, C. & Trannoy, A. (2003). *Multidimensional inequality comparisons: A compensation perspective.* Mimeo.

Oaxaca, R. (1973). Male–female wage differentials in urban labor markets. *International Economic Review, 14*(3), 693–709.

O'Donnell, O., van Doorslaer, E., Rannan-Eliya, R., Somanathan, A., Adhikari, S. R., Akkazieva, B. et al. (2008). Who pays for health care in Asia? *Journal of Health Economics, 27*, 460–475.

O'Donnell, O., van Doorslaer, E., Wagstaff, A., & Lindelow, M. (2008). *Analyzing health equity using household survey data.* Washington, DC: World Bank.

Pazner, E. & Schmeidler, D. (1978). Egalitarian equivalent allocations: A new concept of economic equity. *Quarterly Journal of Economics, 92*, 671–687.

Phillips, A. (2006). "Really" equal: Opportunities and autonomy. *Journal of Political Philosophy, 14*, 18–32.

Rawls, J. (1971). *A theory of justice.* Cambridge, MA: Harvard University Press.

Rawls, J. (1982). Social unity and primary goods. In A. Sen & B. Williams (Eds.), *Utilitarianism and beyond* (pp. 159–185). Cambridge: Cambridge University Press.

Richard, S. (1975). Multivariate risk aversion, utility independence and separable utility functions. *Management Science, 22*, 12–21.

Roemer, J. (1985). Equality of talent. *Economics and Philosophy, 1*, 151–187.

Roemer, J. (1993). A pragmatic theory of responsibility for the egalitarian planner. *Philosophy and Public Affairs, 22*, 146–166.

Roemer, J. (1998). *Equality of opportunity.* Cambridge, MA: Harvard University Press.

Roemer, J. (2002). Equality of opportunity: A progress report. *Social Choice and Welfare, 19*(2), 455–471.

Rosa Dias, P. (2009). Inequality of opportunity in health: Evidence from a UK cohort study. *Health Economics, 18*, 1057–1074.

Rosa Dias, P. (2010). Modelling opportunity in health under partial observability of circurmstances. *Health Economics, 19*, 252–264.

Rosa Dias, P. & Jones, A. (2007). Giving equality of opportunity a fair innings. *Health Economics, 16*, 109–112.

Samuelson, P. (1974). Complementarity: An essay on the 40th anniversary of the Hicks–Allen revolution in demand theory. *Journal of Economic Literature, 12*, 1255–1289.

Samuelson, P. & Swamy, S. (1974). Invariant economic index numbers and canonical duality: Survey and synthesis. *American Economic Review, 64*(4), 566–593.

Sandy, R., Liu, G., Ottensmann, J., Tchernis, R., Wilson, J., & Ford, O. 2009. *Studying the child obesity epidemic with natural experiments.* NBER Working Paper No. 14989.

Schneider, P. & Hanson, K. (2006). Horizontal equity in utilisation of care and fairness of health financing: A comparison of micro-health insurance and user fees in Rwanda. *Health Economics, 15*(1), 19–31.

Schokkaert, E. & Van de Voorde, C. (2004). Risk selection and the specification of the conventional risk adjustment formula. *Journal of Health Economics, 23*, 1237–1259.

Schokkaert, E. & Van de Voorde, C. (2009). Direct versus indirect standardization in risk adjustment. *Journal of Health Economics, 28*, 361–374.

Schokkaert, E. & Van de Voorde, C. (2011). User charges. In S. Glied & P. Smith (Eds.), *Oxford handbook on health economics* (pp. 329–353). Oxford: Oxford University Press.

Segall, S. (2010). *Health, luck and justice.* Princeton: Princeton University Press.

Sen, A. (1970). *Collective choice and social welfare.* San Francisco: Holden Day.

Sen, A. (1985). *Commodities and capabilities*. Amsterdam: North-Holland.

Sen, A. (1999). *Development as freedom*. New York: Knopf.

Sen, A. (2002). Why health equity? *Health Economics, 11,* 659–666.

Shorrocks, A. (1982). Inequality decomposition by factor components. *Econometrica, 50,* 193–211.

Sutton, M. (2002). Vertical and horizontal aspects of socio-economic inequity in general practitioner contacts in Scotland. *Health Economics, 11,* 537–549.

Tobin, J. (1970). On limiting the domain of inequality. *Journal of Law and Economics, 13,* 263–278.

Trannoy, A. (2006). Multidimensional egalitarianism and the dominance approach: A lost paradise? In F. Farina & E. Savaglio (Eds.), *Inequality and economic integration* (pp. 284–302). London: Routledge.

Trannoy, A., Tubeuf, S., Jusot, F., & Devaux, M. (2010). Inequality of opportunities in health in France: A first pass. *Health Economics, 19*(8), 921–938.

Tsui, K.-Y. (1995). Multidimensional generalizations of the relative and absolute inequality indices: The Atkinson–Kolm–Sen approach. *Journal of Economic Theory, 67,* 251–265.

Tsui, K.-Y. (1999). Multidimensional inequality and multidimensional generalized entropy measures: An axiomatic derivation. *Social Choice and Welfare, 16,* 145–157.

Vallentyne, P. (2002). Brute luck, option luck and equality of initial opportunities. *Ethics, 112,* 529–557.

van de Poel, E., O'Donnell, O., & van Doorslaer, E. (2007). Are urban children really healthier? Evidence from 47 developing countries. *Social Science and Medicine, 65,* 1986–2003.

van den Berg, G., Lindeboom, M., & Portrait, F. (2006). Economic conditions early in life and individual mortality. *American Economic Review, 96*(1), 290–302.

van Doorslaer, E. & Jones, A. (2003). Inequalities in self-reported health: Validation of a new approach to measurement. *Journal of Health Economics, 22,* 61–87.

van Doorslaer, E. & Koolman, X. (2004). Explaining the differences in income-related health inequalities across European countries. *Health Economics, 13,* 609–628.

van Doorslaer, E. & Van Ourti, T. (2011). Measuring inequality and inequity in health and health care. In S. Glied, & P. Smith (Eds.), *Oxford handbook on health economics* (pp. 837–869). Oxford: Oxford University Press.

van Doorslaer, E., Koolman, X., & Jones, A. (2004). Explaining income-related inequalities in doctor utilisation in Europe. *Health Economics, 13,* 629–647.

van Doorslaer, E., O'Donnell, O., Rannan-Eliya, R., Somanathan, A., Adhikari, S., Garg, C. et al. (2006). Effect of payments for health care on poverty estimates in 11 countries in Asia: An analysis of household survey data. *The Lancet, 368,* 1357–1364.

van Doorslaer, E., O'Donnell, O., Rannan-Eliya, R., Somanathan, A., Adhikari, S., Garg, C. et al. (2007). Catastrophic payments for health care in Asia. *Health Economics, 16,* 1159–1184.

van Doorslaer, E., Wagstaff, A., van der Burg, H., Christiansen, T., Citoni, G., Di Biase, R., et al. (1999). The redistributive effect of health care finance in twelve OECD countries. *Journal of Health Economics, 18,* 291–313.

van Doorslaer, E., Wagstaff, A., van der Burg, H., Christiansen, T., De Graeve, D., Duchesne, I., et al. (2000). Equity in the delivery of health care in Europe and the US. *Journal of Health Economics, 19,* 553–583.

van Ourti, T. (2004). Measuring horizontal inequity in Belgian health care using a Gaussian random effects two part count data model. *Health Economics, 13,* 705–724.

Wagstaff, A. (2000). Socioeconomic inequalities in child mortality: Comparisons across nine developing countries. *Bulletin of the World Health Organization, 78*(1), 19–29.

Wagstaff, A. (2002). Inequality aversion, health inequalities and health achievement. *Journal of Health Economics, 21,* 627–641.

Wagstaff, A. (2005). The bounds of the concentration index when the variable of interest is binary, with an application to immunization inequality. *Health Economics, 14,* 429–432.

Wagstaff, A. (2008). *Measuring financial protection in health*. World Bank: Policy Research Working Paper 4554.

Wagstaff, A. (2009). Correcting the concentration index: A comment. *Journal of Health Economics, 28,* 516–520.

Wagstaff, A. & van Doorslaer, E. (2000a). Measuring and testing for inequity in the delivery of health care. *Journal of Human Resources, 35*(4), 716−733.

Wagstaff, A. & van Doorslaer, E. (2000b). Equity in health care finance and delivery. In A. Culyer & J. Newhouse (Eds.), *Handbook of health economics* (Vol. 1B, pp. 1803−1862). Amsterdam: Elsevier (North-Holland).

Wagstaff, A. & van Doorslaer, E. (2003). Catastrophe and impoverishment in paying for health care: With applications to Vietnam 1993-1998. *Health Economics, 12*(11), 921−933.

Wagstaff, A. & van Doorslaer, E. (2004). Overall versus socioeconomic health inequality: A measurement framework and two empirical illustrations. *Health Economics, 13*, 297−301.

Wagstaff, A., van Doorslaer, E., & Watanabe, N. (2003). On decomposing the causes of health sector inequalities with an application to malnutrition inequalities in Vietnam. *Journal of Econometrics, 112*, 207−223.

Weymark, J. (2006). The normative approach to the measurement of multidimensional inequality. In F. Farina & E. Savaglio (Eds.), *Inequality and economic integration* (pp. 303−328). London: Routledge.

Xu, K., Evans, D., Carrin, G., Aguilar-Rivera, A., Musgrove, P., & Evans, T. (2007). Protecting households from catastrophic health spending. *Social Science and Medicine, 26*(4), 972−983.

Xu, K., Evans, D., Kawabata, K., Zeramdini, R., Klavus, J., & Murray, C. (2003). Household catastrophic health expenditure: A multicountry analysis. *The Lancet, 362*, 111−117.

INDEX

Printed and bound by CPI Group (UK) Ltd, Croydon, CR0 4YY

08/05/2025

01864976-0001